여러분 █████ KB086689 ██████ 원하는

해커스공무원의 특별 혜택

FREE 공무원 영어
동영상강의

해커스공무원(gosi.Hackers.com) 접속 후 로그인 ▶
상단의 [무료강좌] 클릭 ▶ 좌측의 [교재 무료특강] 클릭

[A] 공무원 보카 어플
이용권

QQU8NXI4ZV6GJG8X

구글 플레이스토어/애플 앱스토어에서
'해커스공무원 기출 보카 4800' 검색 ▶ 어플 설치 후 실행 ▶
'인증코드 입력하기' 클릭 ▶ 위 인증코드 입력

* 해당 자료는 [해커스공무원 기출 보카 4800] 교재 내용으로 제공되는 자료로,
공무원 시험 대비에 도움이 되는 유용한 자료입니다.
* 쿠폰 이용 기한: 등록 후 30일간 사용 가능(ID당 1회에 한해 등록 가능)

[A] 무료 핵심 기출
단어암기장[PDF]

무료
회독용 답안지[PDF]

해커스공무원(gosi.Hackers.com) 접속 후 로그인 ▶ 상단의 [교재·서점 → 무료 학습 자료] 클릭 ▶
본 교재의 [자료받기] 클릭

해커스공무원 온라인 단과강의
20% 할인쿠폰

D8A5AC964B296JL5

* 단과강의에만 적용 가능

해커스 회독증강 콘텐츠
5만원 할인쿠폰

2C73EE3AC6E436Q4

* 특별 할인상품 적용 불가
* 월간 학습지 회독증강 행정학/행정법총론 개별상품은 할인쿠폰 할인대상에서 제외

해커스공무원(gosi.Hackers.com) 접속 후 로그인 ▶ 상단의 [나의 강의실] 클릭 ▶
좌측의 [쿠폰등록] 클릭 ▶ 위 쿠폰번호 입력 후 이용

* 쿠폰 이용 기한: 등록 후 7일간 사용 가능(ID당 1회에 한해 등록 가능)

무료 모바일 자동 채점 + 성적 분석 서비스

교재 내 수록되어 있는 문제의 채점 및 성적 분석 서비스를 제공합니다.

* 세부적인 내용은 해커스공무원(gosi.Hackers.com)에서 확인 가능합니다.

바로 이용하기 ▶

쿠폰 이용 관련 문의 1588-4055

단기 합격을 위한
해커스 커리큘럼

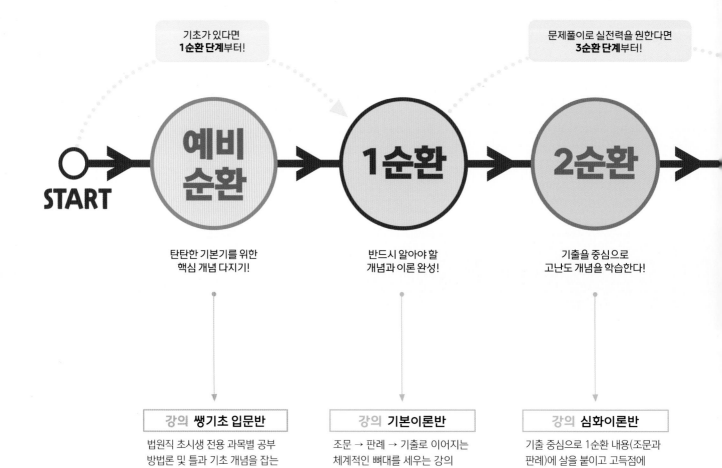

기초가 있다면
1순환 단계부터!

문제풀이로 실전력을 원한다면
3순환 단계부터!

START

예비순환
탄탄한 기본기를 위한
핵심 개념 다지기!

1순환
반드시 알아야 할
개념과 이론 완성!

2순환
기출을 중심으로
고난도 개념을 학습한다!

강의 쌩기초 입문반
법원직 초시생 전용 과목별 공부
방법론 및 틀과 기초 개념을 잡는
강의

강의 기본이론반
조문 → 판례 → 기출로 이어지는
체계적인 뼈대를 세우는 강의

강의 심화이론반
기출 중심으로 1순환 내용(조문과
판례)에 살을 붙이고 고득점에
필요한 구조화·체계화하는 강의

해커스법원직

최신판

15개년
기출문제집
영어

문제집

해커스공무원

해커스법원직

15개년
기출문제집
영어

문제집

해커스공무원

"기출문제" 그냥
풀어보기만 하면 될까?

—

합격자들이 모두 강조하니까 풀어봐야 할 것 같긴 한데
문제를 풀고 채점한 후 무엇을 더 해야 할지 모르겠어요.
틀린 문제를 다시 풀어보면 또 틀리기까지 해요...

기출문제, 그냥 풀어보기만 하면 되나요?

해커스는 자신 있게 대답합니다.

기출문제는 단순히 풀고 채점하는 것으로 끝나서는 안 됩니다. 기출문제 풀이를 통해 실제 시험의 문제 유형과 정답
및 오답의 출제 포인트를 이해하고, 자신이 취약한 부분을 파악 및 보완하여 실전에 대비할 수 있는 진짜 실력을 키
워야 합니다.

**『해커스법원직 15개년 기출문제집 영어』는
한 문제를 풀어도 완벽히 이해할 수 있도록 꼼꼼한 해설을 제공합니다.**

확실하게 실전에 대비하기 위해서는 기출문제의 출제 포인트와 정답 및 오답의 근거를 완벽히 이해할 수 있도록 해
야 합니다. 『해커스법원직 15개년 기출문제집 영어』는 한 문제를 풀어도 '출제 포인트 + 정답 해설 + 오답 분석 + 연
관 개념 정리'까지 포함하는 꼼꼼한 해설을 제공하여 확실한 실전 대비에 도움이 됩니다.

문제 유형에 맞는 풀이 비법을 익힐 수 있도록 기출로 보는 유형별 필승 비법을 제공합니다.

실제 시험장에서 정해진 시간 내에 모든 문제를 신속하고 정확하게 풀어내기 위해서는 각 문제 유형에 맞는 문제
풀이 전략을 알고 있어야 합니다. 『해커스법원직 15개년 기출문제집 영어』는 <기출로 보는 유형별 필승 비법>을
제공하여 기출 문제의 영역별 문제 유형들을 파악하고 각각의 유형에 맞는 문제풀이 비법을 익힐 수 있게 했습니다.

합격이 보이는 기출문제 풀이,
해커스가 여러분과 함께 합니다.

해커스공무원
gosi.Hackers.com

CONTENTS

해커스법원직 15개년 기출문제집
영어

법원직 9급 기출문제

회독을 통한 취약 부분 완벽 정복
다회독에 최적화된 **회독용 답안지** (PDF)
해커스공무원(gosi.Hackers.com) ▶
사이트 상단의 '교재 · 서점' ▶ 무료 학습 자료

기출문제집과 함께 공부하면 효과는 2배
어휘 잡는 **핵심 기출 단어암기장** (PDF)
해커스공무원(gosi.Hackers.com) ▶
사이트 상단의 '교재 · 서점' ▶ 무료 학습 자료

공무원 기출문제 무료 강의로 실전 대비
점수를 올려주는 **기출분석강의 (gosi.Hackers.com)**
해커스공무원(gosi.Hackers.com) ▶
무료강좌 ▶ 기출문제 해설특강

기출문제집도 해커스가 만들면 다릅니다!

01 꼼꼼한 해설로 기출문제에 대한 **완벽한 이해**가 가능합니다!

> '끊어읽기 해석 + 정답 해설 + 오답 분석 + 이것도 알면 합격'까지, 꼼꼼한 해설을 통해 문제를 완벽히 이해하여 자신의 실력을 향상시킬 수 있습니다.
> 해설집의 취약영역 분석표를 통해 약점을 진단하고 해당 영역을 집중 보완할 수 있습니다.

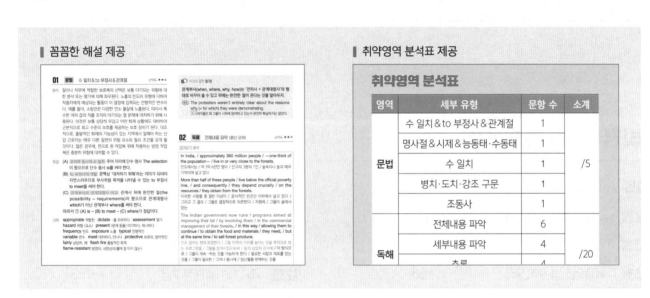

02 최신 출제 경향을 완벽하게 분석하여 **전략적 학습**이 가능합니다!

> 매년 달라지는 출제 경향을 영역별로 완벽하게 분석한 '최근 15개년 법원직 9급 영어 출제 경향'을 통해 최신 출제 경향을 파악할 수 있습니다.
> 출제 경향에 따라 영역별로 제시된 맞춤 학습방법을 통해 취약한 부분을 효율적으로 보완하고 전략적으로 시험에 대비할 수 있습니다.

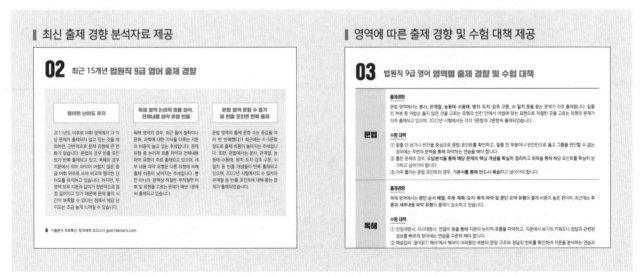

03 기출문제의 유형을 확실히 파악하여 **실전대비**가 가능합니다!

> 법원직 9급의 15개년 기출문제를 통해 풍부한 실전 경험을 쌓아 실전에 대비할 수 있습니다.
> 매 회차를 끝낸 직후 해당 시험의 정답을 모바일 페이지에서 입력하고 채점결과 및 성적 분석 서비스를 이용할 수 있도록, 각 회차마다 QR 코드를 삽입하였습니다.
> 유형별 필승 비법을 통해 각 문제의 유형을 파악하고 비법을 곧바로 적용하여 빠르고 정확하게 풀이할 수 있습니다.

| 15개년(2008-2022) 기출문제 수록

| 기출로 보는 유형별 필승 비법

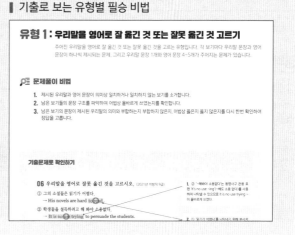

04 <어휘 잡는 핵심 기출 단어암기장>으로 **핵심 기출 어휘를 학습**할 수 있습니다!

> 시험에 나온 단어 중 가장 핵심 단어를 추린 <어휘 잡는 핵심 기출 단어암기장>으로 부족한 어휘를 반복해서 암기할 수 있습니다.
> 간단한 퀴즈를 통해 <어휘 잡는 핵심 기출 단어암기장>의 어휘와 표현을 확실히 암기했는지 확인할 수 있습니다.

| 핵심 기출 어휘 제공

| 어휘 Quiz 제공

법원직 9급 영어 이렇게 출제된다!

01 법원직 9급 영어 **시험 안내**

시험 개요

문제 유형	총 문항 수	2022년 경쟁률	2022년 합격선	시험 안내 사이트
4지선다형	25문항	16.2:1	78점	대한민국 법원 시험정보 (http://exam.scourt.go.kr)

영역별 출제 문항 수

법원직 9급 영어 시험은 총 25문항이며, 독해 영역이 약 90%를 차지하고 문법 영역이 약 10% 정도 출제됩니다. 어휘 영역은 2011년 이후로 더이상 출제되고 있지 않습니다. 공무원 영어 시험의 영역별 출제 문항 수는 변동이 적은 편이므로, 영역별 문항 수에 따라 풀이 시간을 적정하게 배분하는 연습을 할 수 있습니다.

법원직	4~5문항	20~21문항

■ 문법   ■ 독해

02 최근 15개년 **법원직 9급 영어 출제 경향**

평이한 난이도 유지

2011년도 이후로 어휘 영역에서 더 이상 문제가 출제되지 않고 있는 것을 제외하면, 전반적으로 문제 유형에 큰 변화가 없습니다. 문법의 경우 빈출 포인트가 반복 출제되고 있고, 독해의 경우 지문에서 의미 파악이 어렵지 않은 중급 어휘 위주로 쓰여 비교적 평이한 난이도를 유지하고 있습니다. 하지만, 두 영역 모두 지문의 길이가 전반적으로 점점 길어지고 있기 때문에 문제 풀이 시간이 부족할 수 있다는 점에서 체감 난이도는 조금 높게 느껴질 수 있습니다.

독해 영역 논리적 흐름 파악, 전체내용 파악 유형 빈출

독해 영역의 경우, 최근 들어 철학이나 문화, 과학에 대한 지식을 다루는 지문의 비중이 늘고 있는 추세입니다. 문제 유형 중 논리적 흐름 파악과 전체내용 파악 유형이 주로 출제되고 있으며, 세부 내용 파악 유형은 다른 유형에 비해 출제 비중이 낮아지는 추세입니다. 뿐만 아니라, 문맥상 적절한·부적절한 어휘 및 표현을 고르는 문제가 매년 1문제씩 출제되고 있습니다.

문법 영역 문항 수 증가 및 빈출 포인트 반복 출제

문법 영역의 출제 문항 수는 증감을 여러 번 반복했다가 최근에는 4~5문항 정도로 출제 비중이 높아지는 추세입니다. 또한, 문법에서는 분사, 관계절, 능동태·수동태, 병치·도치·강조 구문, 수일치 등 빈출 개념들이 반복 출제되고 있으며, 2022년 시험에서도 수 일치와 관계절 등 빈출 포인트에 대해 묻는 문제가 출제되었습니다.

03 법원직 9급 영어 **영역별 출제 경향 및 수험 대책**

문법

출제경향

문법 영역에서는 **분사, 관계절, 능동태·수동태, 병치·도치·강조 구문, 수 일치** 등을 묻는 문제가 자주 출제됩니다. 밑줄 친 부분 중 어법상 옳지 않은 것을 고르는 유형과 빈칸 안에서 어법에 맞는 표현으로 적절한 곳을 고르는 유형의 문제가 자주 출제되고 있으며, 2022년 시험에서는 각각 3문항과 2문항씩 출제되었습니다.

수험 대책

① 밑줄 친 보기나 빈칸을 중심으로 문법 포인트를 확인하고, 밑줄 친 부분이나 빈칸만으로 옳고 그름을 판단할 수 없는 경우에는 주변의 문맥을 통해 파악하는 연습을 해야 합니다.
② 틀린 문제의 경우, **오답분석을 통해** 해당 문제의 핵심 개념을 확실히 정리하고 회독을 통해 해당 포인트를 확실히 암기하고 넘어가야 합니다.
③ 자주 틀리는 문법 포인트의 경우, **기본서를 통해 반드시 복습**하고 넘어가야 합니다.

독해

출제경향

독해 영역에서는 **문단 순서 배열, 주제·제목·요지·목적 파악 및 문단 요약** 유형의 출제 비중이 높은 편이며, 최근에는 **추론과 세부내용 파악** 유형의 출제가 감소하고 있습니다.

수험 대책

① 인칭대명사, 지시대명사, 연결어 등을 통해 지문의 논리적 흐름을 파악하고, 지문에서 보기의 키워드나 정답과 관련된 정보를 빠르게 찾아내는 연습을 꾸준히 해야 합니다.
② 해설집의 '끊어읽기 해석'에서 해석이 어려웠던 부분의 문장 구조와 정답의 힌트를 확인하여 지문을 분석하는 연습과 시간 제한을 두고 문제를 푸는 연습을 하여 긴 독해 지문에 대비해야 합니다.
③ 틀린 문제의 경우, '기출로 보는 유형별 필승 비법'(12p)을 통해 세부 유형별 **문제풀이 비법**을 다시 한 번 확인한 후 비법을 적용해보며 **문제풀이 노하우**를 쌓아야 합니다.

어휘

출제경향

2011년 이후 어휘 영역에서는 문제가 출제되지 않고 있습니다. 대신 '문맥상 적절한/부적절한 어휘 및 표현 고르기' 유형으로 문맥을 통해 어휘의 의미를 파악하는 문제가 매년 출제되고 있습니다.

수험 대책

① 어휘를 암기할 때 유의어, 반의어 및 파생어를 폭넓게 학습하고, **형태는 비슷하지만 의미는 다른 표현들**을 정리하여 암기해야 합니다.
② 구동사 및 표현을 암기할 때는 **예문을 통해 의미를 익히고**, 표현에 전치사가 포함된 경우 **전치사에 유의하여 암기**해야 합니다.
③ 그동안 출제되었던 핵심 어휘와 표현을 모아 수록한 <어휘 잡는 핵심 기출 단어암기장>을 활용해 풍부한 어휘력을 키워야 합니다.

기출로 보는 유형별

필승 비법

유형 1 : 우리말을 영어로 잘 옮긴 것 또는 잘못 옮긴 것 고르기

주어진 우리말을 영어로 잘 옮긴 것 또는 잘못 옮긴 것을 고르는 유형입니다. 각 보기마다 우리말 문장과 영어 문장이 하나씩 제시되는 문제, 그리고 우리말 문장 1개와 영어 문장 4~5개가 주어지는 문제가 있습니다.

문제풀이 비법

1. 제시된 우리말과 영어 문장이 의미상 일치하거나 일치하지 않는 보기를 소거합니다.
2. 남은 보기들의 문장 구조를 파악하여 어법상 올바르게 쓰였는지를 확인합니다.
3. 남은 보기의 문장이 제시된 우리말의 의미와 부합하는지 부합하지 않은지, 어법상 옳은지 옳지 않은지를 다시 한번 확인하여 정답을 고릅니다.

기출문제로 확인하기

06 우리말을 영어로 잘못 옮긴 것을 고르시오. (2021년 지방직 9급)

① 그의 소설들은 읽기가 어렵다.
→ His novels are hard to read.

② 학생들을 설득하려고 해 봐야 소용없다.
→ It is no use trying to persuade the students.

③ 나의 집은 5년마다 페인트칠된다.
→ My house is painted every five years.

④ 내가 출근할 때 한 가족이 위층에 이사 오는 것을 보았다.
→ As I went out for work, I saw a family moved in upstairs.

1. ② '~해봐야 소용없다'는 동명사구 관용 표현 'It's no use -ing'(~해도 소용 없다)를 사용하여 나타낼 수 있으므로 It is no use trying ~이 올바르게 쓰였다.

2. ① '읽기가 어렵다'를 나타내기 위해 부사처럼 형용사(hard)를 꾸며줄 수 있는 to 부정사 to read가 올바르게 쓰였다.

③ every(모든)는 일반적으로 단수 가산 명사를 수식하지만, 특정한 숫자와 함께 오면 '~마다 한 번씩'의 뜻으로 쓰여 복수 명사 앞에 올 수 있으므로, every five years가 올바르게 쓰였다.

3. ④ 지각동사 see(saw)는 목적어와 목적격 보어가 능동 관계일 때 동사원형이나 현재분사를 목적격 보어로 취하는 5형식 동사인데, 주어진 문장에서 목적어(a family)와 목적격 보어가 '한 가족이 이사 오다'라는 의미의 능동 관계이므로 과거분사 moved를 동사원형 move나 현재분사 moving으로 고쳐야 한다.

유형 2 : 밑줄 친 부분 중 어법상 옳지 않은 것 또는 옳은 것 고르기

지문에서 밑줄 친 4~5개의 보기 중 어법상 옳지 않은 것 또는 옳은 것을 고르는 유형입니다.

🔍 문제풀이 비법

1. 밑줄 친 보기를 중심으로 보며, 수 일치, 형용사/부사, 동사의 종류, 자동사/타동사의 구분, 관용 표현 등에 유의하여 보기를 확인한 후, 정답이 될 수 없는 보기를 소거합니다.

2. 밑줄 친 보기만으로 어법상 옳은지 옳지 않은지를 확인할 수 없는 경우, 보기 주변의 문맥을 파악하며 보기가 올바르게 쓰였는지를 확인합니다. 이때, 관계절, 부사절, 병치/도치 구문 등에 유의합니다.

3. 남은 보기의 문장이 어법상 옳은지 옳지 않은지를 다시 한번 확인하여 정답을 고릅니다.

기출문제로 확인하기

07 밑줄 친 부분 중 어법상 옳지 않은 것은? (2020년 지방직 9급)

Elizabeth Taylor had an eye for beautiful jewels and over the years amassed some amazing pieces, once ① declaring "a girl can always have more diamonds." In 2011, her finest jewels were sold by Christie's at an evening auction ② that brought in $115.9 million. Among her most prized possessions sold during the evening sale ③ were a 1961 bejeweled timepiece by Bulgari. Designed as a serpent to coil around the wrist, with its head and tail ④ covered with diamonds and having two hypnotic emerald eyes, a discreet mechanism opens its fierce jaws to reveal a tiny quartz watch.

1. ① 주절의 주어(Elizabeth Taylor)와 분사구문이 '엘리자베스 테일러가 말했다'라는 의미의 능동 관계이므로 현재분사 declaring이 올바르게 쓰였다.

④ 동시에 일어나는 상황은 'with + 목적어(its head and tail) + 분사'의 형태로 나타낼 수 있는데 목적어 its head and tail과 분사가 '그것의 머리와 꼬리는 덮여있다'라는 의미의 수동 관계이므로 과거분사 covered가 올바르게 쓰였다.

2. ② 선행사 an evening auction이 사물이고, 관계절 내에서 동사 brought의 주어 역할을 하므로 주격 관계대명사 that이 올바르게 쓰였다.

3. ③ 장소를 나타내는 부사구(Among ~ sale)가 강조되어 문장 맨 앞에 나오면 주어와 동사가 도치되어 '동사 + 주어(a 1961 bejeweled timepiece)'의 어순이 되어야 한다. 주어 자리에 단수 명사 a 1961 bejeweled timepiece가 왔으므로 복수 be동사 were를 단수 be동사 was로 고쳐야 한다.

유형 3 : 어법상 옳은 문장 또는 옳지 않은 문장 고르기

주어진 4~5개의 영어 문장 중 어법상 옳은 문장 또는 옳지 않은 문장을 고르는 유형입니다.

🔍 문제풀이 비법

1. 주어진 보기들의 문장 구조를 파악한 후, 어법상 옳거나 옳지 않은 보기를 소거합니다. 이때, 주어와 동사의 수 일치, 형용사와 부사, 동사의 종류, 관계사의 쓰임 등 의미를 파악하지 않고도 한 눈에 알 수 있는 문법 요소들을 중심으로 확인합니다.

2. 어법상 옳거나 옳지 않은 것을 한 눈에 파악할 수 없는 보기의 경우, 문맥을 고려하여 문장이 어법상 올바르게 쓰였는지 확인합니다.

3. 남은 보기의 문장이 어법상 옳은지 옳지 않은지를 다시 한번 확인하여 정답을 고릅니다.

기출문제로 확인하기

06 어법상 옳은 것은? (2019년 지방직 9급)

① The paper charged her with ~~use~~ the company's money for her own purposes.

② The investigation had to be handled with the utmost care lest suspicion be aroused.

③ Another way to speed up the process would be ~~made~~ the shift to a new system.

④ Burning fossil fuels is one of the ~~lead~~ cause of climate change.

1. ① 전치사(with) 뒤에는 명사 역할을 하는 것이 와야 하므로 동사 use를 동명사 using으로 고쳐야 한다.

④ 명사를 수식하는 것은 형용사 역할을 하는 것이므로 명사 cause 앞의 동사 lead를 형용사 leading으로 고쳐야 한다.

2. ③ 동사 뒤에 목적어 the shift가 있고, 문맥상 주어와 동사가 '또 다른 방법은 ~ 전환하는 것이다'라는 의미의 능동 관계이므로 과거분사 made를 동명사 making 또는 to 부정사 to make로 고쳐야 한다.

3. ② 문맥상 '의혹을 불러일으키지 않도록'이라는 의미가 되어야 자연스러운데, '~하지 않도록'은 부사절 접속사 lest를 사용하여 나타낼 수 있고, 접속사 lest가 이끄는 절의 동사는 '(should) + 동사원형(be)'의 형태를 취하므로 lest suspicion be aroused가 올바르게 쓰였다.

유형 4 : 빈칸에 적절한 것 고르기

어법상 빈칸에 들어갈 가장 적절한 보기를 고르는 유형입니다. 빈칸이 하나인 문제가 가장 많이 출제되며, 빈칸이 2~4개인 문제가 출제되기도 합니다.

🔍 문제풀이 비법

1. 문장의 전체 구조를 파악한 후, 빈칸이 문장 내에서 하는 역할을 확인하여 정답 후보를 고릅니다.
2. 보기에 공통적으로 제시된 어휘나 표현이 있는지 확인하고, 그것이 문맥상 어떤 의미로 사용되어야 하는지 파악합니다.
3. 정답 후보들 간의 어법상 차이를 파악하고 문맥상 빈칸에 가장 적절한 보기를 정답으로 고릅니다.

기출문제로 확인하기

12 다음 밑줄 친 (A)와 (B)에 들어갈 가장 적절한 표현은?

(2020년 국회직 9급)

> If the police had asked for a safety licence for their new flying camera, it ____(A)____ a major crime-fighting success. Unfortunately they didn't, and as a result the young man they filmed stealing a car might go free. "As long as you have a licence, there is no problem using these machines," said a lawyer. ____(B)____ a properly licensed camera, it would have been fine."

	(A)	(B)
①	would have been	Had they used
②	will be	If they used
③	will have been	If they use
④	would be	Have they used
⑤	would have been	Had they been used

1. (A) 문맥상 '안전 면허를 요구했다면, ~ 성공이었을 것이다'라는 의미로 과거의 상황을 반대로 가정하고 있고, if절에 가정법 과거완료 'If + 주어 + had p.p.'(If the police had asked)가 왔으므로, 주절에도 가정법 과거완료 '주어 + would + have p.p.'의 형태를 만드는 would have been이 들어가야 적절하다.

2. (B) 문맥상 '만약 그들이 ~ 카메라를 썼다면, 괜찮았을 것이다'라는 의미로 과거의 상황을 반대로 가정하는 가정법 과거완료를 사용해 나타낼 수 있는데, 이때 if절에 if가 생략되면 주어와 동사 자리가 바뀌고, 주어(they)와 동사(use)가 '그들이 카메라를 쓰다'라는 의미의 능동 관계이므로 빈칸에는 Had they used가 들어가야 적절하다. 따라서 ① (A) would have been – (B) Had they used 이 정답이다.

유형 1 : 전체내용 파악하기 ① 주제, 제목, 요지, 목적 파악

지문의 중심 내용을 파악하여 지문의 주제, 제목, 요지, 목적을 고르는 유형입니다.

🔍 문제풀이 비법

1. 지문의 처음 또는 마지막에 중심 내용이 나오는 경우가 많으므로, 지문의 처음과 마지막을 먼저 읽고 대략적인 글의 중심 내용을 파악합니다.

2. 지문의 처음 또는 마지막에서 파악한 중심 내용과 맞지 않는 보기를 소거합니다.

3. 이후 남은 보기들 중 지문의 중심 내용을 가장 잘 표현한 보기를 정답으로 고릅니다. 이때, 보기의 내용이 지문과 관련된 내용이라 할지라도 지문의 중심 내용이 아닌 경우 정답이 될 수 없다는 점에 유의합니다.

기출문제로 확인하기

14 다음 글의 제목으로 가장 적절한 것은? (2020년 지방직 9급)

Louis XIV needed a palace worthy of his greatness, so he decided to build a huge new house at Versailles, **where a tiny hunting lodge stood. After almost fifty years of labor,** this tiny hunting lodge had been transformed into an enormous palace, a quarter of a mile long. Canals were dug to bring water from the river and to drain the marshland. Versailles was full of elaborate rooms like the famous Hall of Mirrors, where seventeen huge mirrors stood across from seventeen large windows, and the Salon of Apollo, where a solid silver throne stood. Hundreds of statues of Greek gods such as Apollo, Jupiter, and Neptune stood in the gardens; each god had Louis's face!

① True Face of Greek Gods

② The Hall of Mirrors, the Salon of Apollo

③ Did the Canal Bring More Than Just Water to Versailles?

④ Versailles: From a Humble Lodge to a Great Palace

1. 지문 처음을 통해 '루이 14세가 그의 위대함에 걸맞는 궁전이 필요해서, 베르사유의 작은 오두막이 거대한 궁전으로 변했다'는 것이 글의 중심 내용이라는 것을 파악할 수 있다.

2. 지문에서 파악한 중심 내용에 따르면 베르사유에 거대한 궁전이 지어졌다고 했으므로 운하에 대한 내용인 ③번은 정답이 될 수 없다.

3. ①번과 ②번은 베르사유에 있는 방과 조각상에 대한 내용으로, 지문의 중심 내용이 아니므로 정답이 될 수 없다.

따라서 글의 제목을 '베르사유: 초라한 오두막에서 거대한 궁전으로'라고 표현한 ④번이 정답이다.

유형 1 : 전체내용 파악하기 ② 문단 요약

전체 지문을 요약한 문장의 빈칸을 완성하는 유형입니다. 한 개의 빈칸을 채우는 문제와 두 개 이상의 빈칸을 채우는 문제가 있습니다.

문제풀이 비법

1. 전체 지문을 요약한 제시된 문장을 읽으며 핵심적인 키워드를 확인하면서 빈칸에 필요한 정보가 무엇인지 파악합니다.

2. 제시된 문장의 키워드가 지문에서 언급된 부분을 찾습니다. 키워드가 지문에 그대로 등장하는 경우도 있지만 다르게 바꾸어 표현되는 경우도 있으므로 이에 유의합니다.

3. 지문에서 키워드가 등장한 부분 및 그 앞뒤 문맥을 통해 지문의 내용을 파악하여 빈칸에 적절한 정답을 고릅니다.

기출문제로 확인하기

01 다음 글의 내용을 한 문장으로 요약하고자 한다. 빈칸 (A)와 (B)에 들어갈 말로 가장 적절한 것은? (2021년 법원직 9급)

Microorganisms are not calculating entities. They don't care what they do to you any more than you care what distress you cause when you slaughter them by the millions with a soapy shower. The only time a pathogen cares about you is when it kills you too well. If they eliminate you before they can move on, then they may well die out themselves. This in fact sometimes happens. History, Jared Diamond notes, is full of diseases that "once caused terrifying epidemics and then disappeared as mysteriously as they had come." He cites the robust but mercifully transient English sweating sickness, which raged from 1485 to 1552, killing tens of thousands as it went, before burning itself out. Too much efficiency is not a good thing for any infectious organism.

*pathogen 병원체

↓

The more ___(A)___ pathogens are, the faster it is likely be to ___(B)___.

(A)	(B)		(A)	(B)
① weaker	---- disappear		② weaker	---- spread
③ infectious	---- spread		④ infectious	---- disappear

1. 제시된 문장을 통해 빈칸 (A)에 병원체들이 더 어떨수록 그것들이 더 빨리 어떻게 될 가능성이 있는지에 대한 내용이 나와야 한다는 것을 알 수 있다.

2. 제시된 문장의 키워드인 pathogens(병원체)와 관련된 지문 주변의 내용을 확인한다.

3. 키워드와 관련된 지문 주변의 내용에서 병원체들은 그것들이 이동할 수 있게 되기 전에 인간을 없앤다면 스스로 소멸할 것이라고 한 뒤, 강력했지만 일시적이었던 영국 발한병을 예시로 들며 어떤 전염성 미생물에게도 과도한 효율은 좋은 것이 아니라고 설명하고 있으므로 (A)와 (B)에는 병원체들이 더 전염성(infectious)이 있을수록, 그것이 더 빨리 사라진다(disappear)는 내용이 와야 적절하다.

유형 1 : **전체내용 파악하기** ③ 글의 감상

전체적인 글의 흐름을 파악하여 글의 종류, 분위기, 전개방식, 또는 필자나 등장인물의 어조, 태도, 상황 등을 고르는 유형입니다.

🔍 문제풀이 비법

1. 문제와 보기를 먼저 확인하여 문제에서 묻는 것이 무엇인지를 정확히 파악합니다.

2. 문제에서 묻는 것에 대한 단서가 있는 부분을 찾아가며 지문을 읽습니다. 예를 들어, 문제에서 묻는 것이 등장인물의 상황이라면 특정한 상황을 나타나는 단서들에 유의하여 지문을 읽고, 정답을 고릅니다.

기출문제로 확인하기

20 다음 글에 나타난 Johnbull의 심경 으로 가장 적절한 것은?

(2021년 국가직 9급)

In the blazing midday sun, the yellow egg-shaped rock stood out from a pile of recently unearthed gravel. Out of curiosity, sixteen-year-old miner Komba Johnbull picked it up and fingered its flat, pyramidal planes. Johnbull had never seen a diamond before, but he knew enough to understand that even a big find would be no larger than his thumbnail. Still, the rock was unusual enough to merit a second opinion. Sheepishly, he brought it over to one of the more experienced miners working the muddy gash deep in the jungle. The pit boss's eyes widened when he saw the stone. "Put it in your pocket," he whispered. "Keep digging." The older miner warned that it could be dangerous if anyone thought they had found something big. So Johnbull kept shoveling gravel until nightfall, pausing occasionally to grip the heavy stone in his fist. Could it be?

① thrilled and excited
② painful and distressed
③ arrogant and convinced
④ detached and indifferent

1. 문제와 보기를 통해 trilled and excited(흥분하고 신이 난)와 같은 '화자의 심경'을 묻는 문제임을 알 수 있다.

2. 지문에서 필자는 어린 광부 Johnbull이 자갈들 사이에서 우연히 발견한 특이한 돌이 어쩌면 엄청나게 큰 다이아몬드일지도 모른다는 것을 알게 되는 일화를 소개하고 있다. 따라서 Johnbull의 심경을 '흥분하고 신이 난'이라고 표현한 ①번이 정답이다.

유형 2 : 세부내용 파악하기 ① 내용 일치·불일치 파악

지문의 세부내용을 파악하여 지문의 내용과 일치 혹은 일치하지 않는 보기를 고르는 유형입니다.

🔍 문제풀이 비법

1. 보기에 제시된 키워드가 지문에서 언급된 부분을 순서대로 찾아가며 각각의 보기가 정답이 될 수 있는지 확인합니다. 이때, 보기에서 쓰인 어휘 및 표현 등을 지문 내에서 다르게 표현할 수도 있으므로 이에 유의합니다.

2. 정답이 될 수 없는 보기들을 걸러내고 난 뒤, 남은 보기의 키워드가 지문에서 언급된 부분을 다시 한번 확인하며 정답을 고릅니다.

기출문제로 확인하기

10 다음 글의 내용과 일치하는 것은? (2017년 국가직 9급)

①Taste buds got their name from the nineteenth-century German scientists Georg Meissner and Rudolf Wagner, who discovered mounds made up of taste cells that overlap like petals. ②Taste buds wear out every week to ten days, and we replace them, although not as frequently over the age of forty-five: ③ our palates really do become jaded as we get older. It takes a more intense taste to produce the same level of sensation, and ③ children have the keenest sense of taste. A baby's mouth has many more taste buds than an adult's, with some even dotting the cheeks. Children adore sweets partly because ④ the tips of their tongues, more sensitive to sugar, haven't yet been blunted by trying to eat hot soup before it cools.

① Taste buds were invented in the nineteenth century.
② Replacement of taste buds does not slow down with age.
③ Children have more sensitive palates than adults.
④ The sense of taste declines by eating cold soup.

1. ① 미뢰가 19세기의 과학자인 George Meissner와 Rudolf Wagner에 의해서 '발견' 되었다고 했으므로, 미뢰가 19세기에 '발명'되었다는 것은 지문의 내용과 다르다.

② 미뢰는 일주일에서 10일마다 마모되어서 우리는 이것들을 교체하는데, 45세가 넘으면 이렇게 자주 교체하지는 않는다고 했으므로, 미뢰의 교체가 나이가 들면서 느려지지 않는다는 것은 지문의 내용과 반대이다.

④ 혀 끝은 뜨거운 스프가 식기도 전에 그것을 먹으려는 시도로 인해서 무뎌진다고 했으므로 미각이 차가운 스프를 먹음으로써 쇠퇴한다는 것은 지문의 내용과 다르다.

2. 우리의 미각은 나이가 들수록 감퇴하게 되며, 아이들은 가장 예민한 입맛을 가지고 있다는 내용이 있으므로, 아이들이 성인들보다 더욱 민감한 미각을 가지고 있다는 것을 알 수 있다. 따라서 ③번이 지문의 내용과 일치한다.

유형 2 : 세부내용 파악하기 ② 지칭 대상 파악

문제에서 묻는 특정한 정보를 지문에서 찾는 유형이며, 묻는 정보는 지문의 성격에 따라 다양하게 출제됩니다.

🔍 문제풀이 비법

1. 밑줄이 있는 문장을 읽고, 문제에서 묻는 것이 무엇인지 정확히 파악합니다.

2. 밑줄 친 부분이 가리키는 것을 찾고, 가장 적절한 보기를 정답으로 선택합니다. 이때 보기에서 쓰인 어휘 및 표현 등이 지문 내에서 다르게 표현될 수도 있으므로 이에 유의하며 정답을 고릅니다.

기출문제로 확인하기

18 밑줄 친 the issue가 가리키는 내용으로 가장 적절한 것은?
(2020년 법원직 9급)

Nine-year-old Ryan Kyote was eating breakfast at home in Napa, California, when he saw the news: an Indiana school had taken a 6-year-old's meal when her lunch account didn't have enough money. Kyote asked if that could happen to his friends. When his mom contacted the school district to find out, she learned that students at schools in their district had, all told, as much as $25,000 in lunch debt. Although the district says it never penalized students who owed, Kyote decided to use his saved allowance to pay off his grade's debt, about $74—becoming the face of a movement to end lunch-money debt. When California Governor Gavin Newsom signed a bill in October that banned "lunch shaming," or giving worse food to students with debt, he thanked Kyote for his "empathy and his courage" in raising awareness of the issue. "Heroes," Kyote points out, "come in all ages.

① The governor signed a bill to decline lunch items to students with lunch debt.

② Kyote's lunch was taken away because he ran out of money in his lunch account.

③ The school district with financial burden cut the budget failing to serve quality meals.

④ Many students in the district who could not afford lunch were burdened with lunch debt.

1. 밑줄이 있는 문장을 읽고, 지문에서 찾아야 하는 것이 캘리포니아 주지사가 Kyote에게 감사를 표한 이 문제임을 확인한다.

2. 지문을 읽으며 이 문제는 학생들이 점심 급식비를 빚고 있는 것임을 알 수 있으므로, 이를 '이 지역구의 점심값을 낼 형편이 되지 않는 많은 학생들은 점심값 빚을 지고 있었다(Many students in the district who could not afford lunch were burdened with lunch debt)'라고 바꾸어 표현한 ④번이 정답이다.

유형 3 : 추론하기 ① 빈칸 완성 – 단어·구·절

빈칸 앞뒤 지문의 흐름을 자연스럽게 연결하는 보기를 골라 빈칸을 완성하는 유형입니다.

🔍 문제풀이 비법

1. 빈칸이 있는 문장을 읽으며 빈칸 앞뒤에 제시되는 키워드를 통해 빈칸에 필요한 정보가 무엇인지 파악합니다.

2. 빈칸 주변이나 중심 내용을 위주로 지문을 읽고 문맥상 빈칸에 가장 적절한 정답을 고릅니다.

기출문제로 확인하기

20 밑줄 친 부분에 들어갈 말로 가장 적절한 것을 고르시오.

(2019년 지방직 9급)

Nobel Prize-winning psychologist Daniel Kahneman changed the way the world thinks about economics, upending the notion that human beings are rational decision-makers. Along the way, his discipline-crossing influence has altered the way physicians make medical decisions and investors evaluate risk on Wall Street. In a paper, Kahneman and his colleagues outline a process for making big strategic decisions. Their suggested approach, labeled as "Mediating Assessments Protocol," or MAP, has a simple goal: To put off gut-based decision-making until a choice can be informed by a number of separate factors. "One of the essential purposes of MAP is basically to _____ intuition," Kahneman said in a recent interview with *The Post*. The structured process calls for analyzing a decision based on six to seven previously chosen attributes, discussing each of them separately and assigning them a relative percentile score, and finally, using those scores to make a holistic judgment.

① improve
② delay
③ possess
④ facilitate

1. 빈칸에 MAP의 본질적인 목표 중 하나가 직관을 어떻게 하는 것인지에 대한 내용이 나와야 적절하다는 것을 알 수 있다.

2. 빈칸 앞 문장에 '조정을 통한 평가 프로토콜' 혹은 MAP라고 불리는 방식의 목표는 많은 독립된 요인들에 의해 선택의 범위가 통지될 수 있을 때까지 직감에 기반한 의사결정을 미루는 것이라고 했으므로, MAP의 본질적인 목표 중 하나는 기본적으로 직관을 '미루는' 것이라고 한 ②번이 정답이다.

유형 3 : 추론하기 ② 빈칸 완성 – 연결어

지문에 제시된 빈칸에 들어가기에 가장 적절한 연결어를 고르는 문제 유형입니다.

🔍 문제풀이 비법

1. 빈칸 앞뒤에 있는 문장을 읽고 두 문장 사이의 논리적 관계를 파악합니다.
2. 빈칸 앞뒤 문장 사이의 논리적 관계를 가장 잘 표현한 정답을 고릅니다. 보기로 자주 등장하는 연결어들을 파악해두면 쉽게 정답을 고를 수 있습니다.

기출문제로 확인하기

19 (A)와 (B)에 들어갈 말로 가장 적절한 것은? (2021년 지방직 9급)

Ancient philosophers and spiritual teachers understood the need to balance the positive with the negative, optimism with pessimism, a striving for success and security with an openness to failure and uncertainty. The Stoics recommended "the premeditation of evils," or deliberately visualizing the worst-case scenario. This tends to reduce anxiety about the future: when you soberly picture how badly things could go in reality, you usually conclude that you could cope. _____(A)_____, they noted, imagining that you might lose the relationships and possessions you currently enjoy increases your gratitude for having them now. Positive thinking, _____(B)_____, always leans into the future, ignoring present pleasures.

	(A)	(B)
①	Nevertheless	in addition
②	Furthermore	for example
③	Besides	by contrast
④	However	in conclusion

1. (A) 빈칸 앞 문장은 당신이 얼마나 나쁘게 상황이 흘러갈지 상상함으로써 미래에 대한 염려를 줄일 수 있다는 내용으로 '불행에 대한 계획'에 관해서 설명하는 내용이다. (A) 빈칸 뒤 문장은 현재 누리고 있는 것들을 잃을지도 모른다고 상상하는 것이 현재 갖고 있는 것에 대한 감사함을 증가시킨다는 내용으로 '불행에 대한 계획'에 관한 추가적인 설명이므로, (A)에는 Furthermore(게다가) 또는 Besides(게다가)가 나와야 적절하다.

2. (B) 빈칸 뒤 문장은 긍정적인 생각이 현재의 기쁨을 무시하고 미래에만 의지하게 하므로 부정적인 결과를 낳는다는 내용이고 (B) 빈칸 앞 문장은 가진 것들을 모두 잃는다는 부정적인 생각이 현재 갖고 있는 것들에 대한 감사함을 증가시킨다는 긍정적인 결과를 낳는다는 내용으로 앞 문장과 대조되므로, (B)에는 by contrast (대조적으로)가 나와야 적절하다.

유형 3 : 추론하기 ③ 내용 추론

지문을 통해 추론할 수 있는 보기를 고르는 유형입니다. 이때, 보기의 내용은 직접적으로 지문에 언급되지 않는 경우가 많습니다.

🔍 문제풀이 비법

1. 문제와 보기를 빠르게 읽으며 지문의 중심 내용과 지문에서 확인해야 할 정보가 무엇인지에 대해 미리 파악합니다.

2. 지문의 처음이나 마지막 부분을 통해 지문의 주제를 파악한 후, 앞서 파악한 보기의 내용을 기억하며 지문을 읽습니다. 보기의 키워드가 그대로 언급될 수도 있고, 같은 의미를 나타내는 다른 표현으로 언급될 수도 있으므로 이에 유의합니다.

3. 정답을 고를 때에는 반드시 지문에 기반하여 정답을 고릅니다. 보기의 내용이 상식적으로 옳거나 옳지 않다고 해도 지문을 통해서 추론할 수 없는 경우에는 정답이 될 수 없으니 이에 유의합니다.

기출문제로 확인하기

08 다음 글을 통해 IQ에 대하여 유추할 수 있는 것은?

(2016년 사회복지직 9급)

IQ is a lot like height in basketball. Does someone who is five foot six have a realistic chance of playing professional basketball? Not really. You need to be at least six foot or six one to play at that level, and, all things being equal, it's probably better to be six two than six one, and better to be six three than six two. But past a certain point, height stops mattering so much. A player who is six foot eight is not automatically better than someone two inches shorter. (Michael Jordan, the greatest player ever, was six six after all.) A basketball player only has to be tall enough—and the same is true of intelligence. Intelligence has a threshold.

① IQ is just a myth; it has nothing to do with how smart you are.

② Once your IQ is over a certain level, it may not really matter anymore in terms of intelligence.

③ The higher IQ you have, the more intelligent you must be.

④ The more you practice, the higher your IQ will get.

1. 문제와 보기를 빠르게 읽으며 지문의 중심 내용이 IQ(아이큐)라는 것을 파악하고, 그와 관련된 정보를 지문에서 확인해야 한다는 것을 파악한다.

2. 지문 마지막 부분을 통해 지문의 주제를 파악한다. 이후 앞서 파악한 보기의 내용을 기억하며 지문을 읽는다.

3. 지문 처음에서 아이큐는 농구에서의 키와 같다고 한 뒤, 지문 중간에서 어느 정도를 넘으면 키는 더 이상 중요하지 않다고 했다. 지문 마지막에서 농구선수는 충분히 키가 크기만 하면 되고 지능도 이와 마찬가지라고 했으므로, 일단 아이큐가 어느 정도를 넘어서면 지능 측면에서 그것은 더 이상 그다지 중요하지 않을 수 있다는 것을 추론할 수 있다. 따라서 ②번이 정답이다.

유형 4 : 논리적 흐름 파악하기 ① 문단 순서 배열

지문의 논리적 흐름을 파악하여 지문의 흐름이 자연스럽게 연결되도록 주어진 문단의 순서를 적절하게 배열하는 유형입니다.

🔍 문제풀이 비법

1. 첫 문장이 제시된 경우, 첫 문장을 통해 주제를 파악하고 앞으로 전개될 내용에 대해 예상합니다.

2. 제시된 문단들에서 연결어나 지시대명사 등을 통해 지문의 논리적 흐름을 파악하고, 그에 따라 문단의 순서를 배열합니다.

3. 배열된 순서대로 문단을 다시 읽으며 논리적 연결이 자연스러운지 확인하여 정답을 고릅니다.

기출문제로 확인하기

20 주어진 문장 다음에 이어질 글의 순서로 가장 적절한 것은?

(2019년 국가직 9급)

South Korea boasts of being the most wired nation on earth.

(A) This addiction has become a national issue in Korea in recent years, as users started dropping dead from exhaustion after playing online games for days on end. A growing number of students have skipped school to stay online, shockingly self-destructive behavior in this intensely competitive society.

(B) In fact, perhaps no other country has so fully embraced the Internet.

(C) But such ready access to the Web has come at a price as legions of obsessed users find that they cannot tear themselves away from their computer screens.

① (A) – (B) – (C)　　② (A) – (C) – (B)

③ (B) – (A) – (C)　　④ (B) – (C) – (A)

1. 제시된 문장을 통해 대한민국의 인터넷에 대한 내용이 전개될 것임을 예상할 수 있다.

2. 주어진 문장에서 대한민국은 인터넷에 가장 잘 연결된 국가인 것을 자랑한다고 하고, (B)에서 다른 어떤 국가도 인터넷을 그렇게 완전히 수용하지는 않았을 것이라고 하며, (C)에서 하지만 그러한 웹으로의 편리한 접근(such ready access to the Web)에는 중독된 사용자들이라는 대가가 따랐다고 한 후, 이어서 (A)에서 이러한 중독(This addiction)은 국가적인 사안이 되었다고 설명하고 있다. 따라서 ④ (B) – (C) – (A)가 정답이다.

3. 배열된 순서대로 문단을 다시 읽으며 논리적 연결이 자연스러운지 확인하여 정답을 고른다.

유형 4 : 논리적 흐름 파악하기 ② 문장 삽입

지문의 흐름이 자연스럽게 연결되도록 주어진 문장이 들어갈 적절한 위치를 고르는 유형입니다.

문제풀이 비법

1. 제시된 문장에 키워드가 있는지를 확인하여 글의 흐름상 제시된 문장 앞뒤에 나올 수 있는 정보가 무엇일지 예상합니다.
2. 지문을 읽으며 제시된 문장 앞뒤에 나올 것으로 예상했던 내용이 있는지 확인하고 제시된 문장이 들어갈 위치를 고릅니다.

기출문제로 확인하기

16 주어진 문장이 들어갈 위치로 가장 적절한 것은?

(2018년 국가직 9급)

Some **remain intensely proud of their original accent and dialect words, phrases and gestures, while** others **accommodate rapidly to a new environment by changing their speech habits,** so that they no longer "stand out in the crowd."

Our perceptions and production of speech change with time. (①) If we were to leave our native place for an extended period, our perception that the new accents around us were strange would only be temporary. (②) Gradually, we will lose the sense that others have an accent and we will begin to fit in—to accommodate our speech patterns to the new norm. (③) Not all people do this to the same degree. (④) Whether they do this consciously or not is open to debate and may differ from individual to individual, but like most processes that have to do with language, the change probably happens before we are aware of it and probably couldn't happen if we were.

1. 제시된 문장의 키워드를 통해 제시된 문장의 앞에 새로운 환경에서 사람마다 억양, 말투 등을 적응하는 방식이 다르다는 내용이 나올 것임을 예상할 수 있다.

2. ④번 앞 문장에 모든 사람들이 같은 정도로 이렇게 하는 것(새로운 억양에 적응하는 것)은 아니라는 내용이 있으므로, ④번 자리에 주어진 문장이 나와야 지문이 자연스럽게 연결된다. 따라서 ④번이 정답이다.

유형 4 : 논리적 흐름 파악하기 ③ 무관한 문장 삭제

보기로 제시된 문장들 중 지문의 흐름이 맞지 않는 것을 선택하는 문제 유형입니다.

문제풀이 비법

1. 첫 문장의 내용을 정확히 파악하여 이어질 지문의 내용이 무엇인지 예상합니다.
2. 지문을 읽으며 지문의 첫 문장이나 중심 내용과 관련이 없거나 흐름상 어색한 보기를 정답으로 고릅니다.

기출문제로 확인하기

10 다음 글의 흐름상 가장 어색한 문장은?   (2021년 국가직 9급)

The term burnout refers to a "wearing out" from the pressures of work. Burnout is a chronic condition that results as daily work stressors take their toll on employees. ① The most widely adopted conceptualization of burnout has been developed by Maslach and her colleagues in their studies of human service workers. Maslach sees burnout as consisting of three interrelated dimensions. The first dimension—emotional exhaustion—is really the core of the burnout phenomenon. ② Workers suffer from emotional exhaustion when they feel fatigued, frustrated, used up, or unable to face another day on the job. The second dimension of burnout is a lack of personal accomplishment. ③ This aspect of the burnout phenomenon refers to workers who see themselves as failures, incapable of effectively accomplishing job requirements. ④ Emotional labor workers enter their occupation highly motivated although they are physically exhausted. The third dimension of burnout is depersonalization. This dimension is relevant only to workers who must communicate interpersonally with others (e.g. clients, patients, students) as part of the job.

1. 지문의 처음 문장을 통해 번아웃의 특징에 대한 내용이 이 지문의 중심 내용이라는 것을 파악할 수 있다.

2. 지문 전반에 걸쳐 번아웃의 의미와 특징에 대해 설명하고 있으므로 모두 첫 문장과 관련이 있지만, ④번은 감정적인 노동자들은 신체적으로 지쳤는데도 의욕을 가지고 일을 한다는 내용으로 지문의 내용과 관련이 없다.

유형 4 : 논리적 흐름 파악하기 ④ 문맥상 적절한·부적절한 어휘 고르기

지문의 흐름을 파악하여 문맥상 적절한 혹은 적절하지 않은 것을 고르는 유형입니다.

🔍 문제풀이 비법

1. 지문의 처음 또는 마지막에 중심 내용이 나오는 경우가 많으므로, 지문의 처음과 마지막을 먼저 읽고 글의 중심 내용을 파악합니다.

2. 제시된 지문을 읽으며 문맥상 밑줄 친 보기에 들어가기 적절한 의미가 무엇일지 예상합니다.

3. 주어진 보기가 주변 문맥과 어울리는지 어울리지 않는지를 확인하고, 보기 어휘를 모를 경우에는 다른 오답 보기를 소거해 나가면서 정답을 고릅니다.

기출문제로 확인하기

10 다음 글의 밑줄 친 부분 중 문맥상 낱말의 쓰임이 가장 적절하지 않은 것은?

(2021년 법원직 9급)

Good walking shoes are important. Most major athletic brands offer shoes especially designed for walking. Fit and comfort are more important than style; your shoes should feel ① supportive but not tight or constricting. The uppers should be light, breathable, and flexible, the insole moisture-resistant, and the sole ② shock-absorbent. The heel wedge should be ③ lowered, so the sole at the back of the shoe is two times thicker than at the front. Finally, the toe box should be ④ spacious, even when you're wearing athletic socks.

① supportive   ② shock-absorbent
③ lowered   ④ spacious

1. 지문 처음 문장을 통해 '좋은 워킹화의 특징'이 이 글의 중심 내용이라는 것을 파악할 수 있다.

2. ③번 보기 뒷부분에서 '신발 뒤쪽의 밑창이 앞쪽보다 두 배 더 두껍도록' 해야 한다고 했으므로, ③번 보기에는 신발 뒤쪽 밑창인 굽의 쐐기가 '올라가야 한다'는 내용이 들어가야 한다.

3. 굽의 쐐기가 '낮춰져야 한다'는 것은 주변 문맥과 어울리지 않으므로 ③ lowered가 정답이다.

EVERYTHING COMES TO HIM
WHO HUSTLES WHILE HE WAITS.

THOMAS A. EDISON

성공은 열심히 노력하며 기다리는 사람에게 찾아온다.
토마스 *A*. 에디슨

법원직 9급
기출문제

제한시간 : 25분　시작 _____시 _____분 ~ 종료 _____시 _____분　나의 점수 _____　회독수 ☐☐☐

01 (A), (B), (C)의 각 네모 안에서 어법에 맞는 표현으로 가장 적절한 것은?

The selection of the appropriate protective clothing for any job or task (A) is / are usually dictated by an analysis or assessment of the hazards presented. The expected activities of the wearer as well as the frequency and types of exposure, are typical variables that input into this determination. For example, a firefighter is exposed to a variety of burning materials. Specialized multilayer fabric systems are thus used (B) to meet / meeting the *thermal challenges presented. This results in protective gear that is usually fairly heavy and essentially provides the highest levels of protection against any fire situation. In contrast, an industrial worker who has to work in areas (C) where / which the possibility of a flash fire exists would have a very different set of hazards and requirements. In many cases, a flame-resistant coverall worn over cotton work clothes adequately addresses the hazard.

* thermal : 열의

	(A)	(B)	(C)
①	is	to meet	where
②	is	meeting	which
③	are	meeting	where
④	are	to meet	which

02 다음 글의 내용을 한 문장으로 요약하고자 한다. 빈칸 (A), (B)에 들어갈 말로 가장 적절한 것은?

In India, approximately 360 million people—one-third of the population—live in or very close to the forests. More than half of these people live below the official poverty line, and consequently they depend crucially on the resources they obtain from the forests. The Indian government now runs programs aimed at improving their lot by involving them in the commercial management of their forests, in this way allowing them to continue to obtain the food and materials they need, but at the same time to sell forest produce. If the programs succeed, forest dwellers will be more prosperous, but they will be able to preserve their traditional way of life and culture, and the forest will be managed sustainably, so the wildlife is not depleted.

⇒ The Indian government is trying to ___(A)___ the lives of the poor who live near forests without ___(B)___ the forests.

	(A)	(B)
①	improve	ruining
②	control	preserving
③	improve	limiting
④	control	enlarging

03 다음 글의 내용을 한 문장으로 요약하고자 한다. 빈칸 (A), (B)에 들어갈 말로 가장 적절한 것은?

In the absence of facial cues or touch during pandemic, there is a greater need to focus on other aspects of conversation, including more emphasis on tone and inflection, slowing the speed, and increasing loudness without sounding annoying. Many *nuances of the spoken word are easily missed without facial expression, so eye contact will assume an even greater importance. Some hospital workers have developed innovative ways to try to solve this problem. One of nurse specialists was deeply concerned that her chronically sick young patients could not see her face, so she printed off a variety of face stickers to get children to point towards. Some hospitals now also provide their patients with 'face-sheets' that permit easier identification of staff members, and it is always useful to reintroduce yourself and colleagues to patients when wearing masks.

*nuance : 미묘한 차이, 뉘앙스

Some hospitals and workers are looking for ___(A)___ ways to ___(B)___ conversation with patients during pandemic.

(A)	(B)
① alternative	– complement
② bothering	– analyze
③ effective	– hinder
④ disturbing	– improve

04 주어진 글 다음에 이어질 글의 순서로 가장 적절한 것은?

Once they leave their mother, primates have to keep on making decisions about whether new foods they encounter are safe and worth collecting.

(A) By the same token, if the sampler feels fine, it will reenter the tree in a few days, eat a little more, then wait again, building up to a large dose slowly. Finally, if the monkey remains healthy, the other members figure this is OK, and they adopt the new food.

(B) If the plant harbors a particularly strong toxin, the sampler's system will try to break it down, usually making the monkey sick in the process. "I've seen this happen," says Glander. "The other members of the troop are watching with great interest—if the animal gets sick, no other animal will go into that tree. There's a cue being given—a social cue."

(C) Using themselves as experiment tools is one option, but social primates have found a better way. Kenneth Glander calls it "sampling." When howler monkeys move into a new habitat, one member of the troop will go to a tree, eat a few leaves, then wait a day.

① (A) – (B) – (C)	② (B) – (A) – (C)
③ (C) – (B) – (A)	④ (C) – (A) – (B)

05 다음 글의 Zainichi에 관한 내용으로 가장 일치하지 않는 것은?

Following Japan's defeat in World War II, the majority of ethnic Koreans (1–1.4 million) left Japan. By 1948, the population of ethnic Koreans settled around 600,000. These Koreans and their descendants are commonly referred to as Zainichi (literally "residing in Japan"), a term that appeared in the immediate postwar years. Ethnic Koreans who remained in Japan did so for diverse reasons. Koreans who had achieved successful careers in business, the imperial bureaucracy, and the military during the colonial period or who had taken advantage of economic opportunities that opened up immediately after the war—opted to maintain their relatively privileged status in Japanese society rather than risk returning to an impoverished and politically unstable post-liberation Korea. Some Koreans who *repatriated were so repulsed by the poor conditions they observed that they decided to return to Japan. Other Koreans living in Japan could not afford the train fare to one of the departure ports, and among them who had ethnic Japanese spouses and Japanese-born, Japanese-speaking children, it made more sense to stay in Japan rather than to navigate the cultural and linguistic challenges of a new environment.

* repatriate : 본국으로 송환하다

① 주로 제2차 세계대전 이후에 일본에 남은 한국인들과 후손을 일컫는다.
② 전쟁 후에 경제적인 이득을 취한 사람들도 있었다.
③ 어떤 사람들은 한국에 갔다가 다시 일본으로 돌아왔다.
④ 한국으로 돌아갈 교통비를 마련하지 못한 사람들은 일본인과 결혼했다.

06 다음 빈칸에 들어갈 말로 가장 적절한 것은?

There are a few jobs where people have had to _____. We see referees and umpires using their arms and hands to signal directions to the players—as in cricket, where a single finger upwards means that the batsman is out and has to leave the *wicket. Orchestra conductors control the musicians through their movements. People working at a distance from each other have to invent special signals if they want to communicate. So do people working in a noisy environment, such as in a factory where the machines are very loud, or lifeguards around a swimming pool full of school children.

* wicket : (크리켓에서) 삼주문

① support their parents and children
② adapt to an entirely new work style
③ fight in court for basic human rights
④ develop their signing a bit more fully

07 다음 글의 내용과 일치하지 않는 것은?

Opponents of the use of animals in research also oppose use of animals to test the safety of drugs or other compounds. Within the pharmaceutical industry, it was noted that out of 19 chemicals known to cause cancer in humans when taken, only seven caused cancer in mice and rats using standards set by the National Cancer Instituted(Barnard and Koufman, 1997). For example, and antidepressant, nomifensin, had minimal toxicity in rats, rabbits, dogs, and monkeys yet caused liver toxicity and *anemia in humans. In these and other cases, it has been shown that some compounds have serious adverse reactions in humans that were not predicted by animal testing resulting in conditions in the treated humans that could lead to disability, or even death. And researchers who are calling for an end to animal research state that they have better methods available such as human clinical trials, observation aided by laboratory of autopsy tests.

* anemia : 빈혈

① 한 기관의 실험 결과 동물과 달리 19개의 발암물질 중에 7개는 인간에게 영향을 미쳤다.
② 어떤 약물은 동물 실험 때와 달리 인간에게 간독성과 빈혈을 일으켰다.
③ 동물 실험에서 나타난 결과가 인간에게는 다르게 작용될 수 있다.
④ 동물 실험을 반대하는 연구자들은 대안적인 방법들을 제시하고 있다.

08 다음 중 문맥상 낱말의 쓰임이 가장 적절하지 않은 것은?

Cold showers are any showers with a water temperature below 70°F. They may have health benefits. For people with depression, cold showers can work as a kind of gentle electroshock therapy. The cold water sends many electrical impulses to your brain. They *jolt your system to ① increase alertness, clarity, and energy levels. Endorphins, which are sometimes called happiness hormones, are also released. This effect leads to feelings of well-being and ② optimism. For people that are obese, taking a cold shower 2 or 3 times per week may contribute to increased metabolism. It may help fight obesity over time. The research about how exactly cold showers help people lose weight is ③ clear. However, it does show that cold water can even out certain hormone levels and heal the **gastrointestinal system. These effects may add to the cold shower's ability to lead to weight loss. Furthermore, when taken regularly, cold showers can make our circulatory system more efficient. Some people also report that their skin looks better as a result of cold showers, probably because of better circulation. Athletes have known this benefit for years, even if we have only ④ recently seen data that supports cold water for healing after a sport injury.

* jolt : 갑자기 덜컥 움직이다 ** gastrointestinal : 위장의

09 다음 글의 내용을 한 문장으로 요약하고자 한다. 빈칸 (A), (B)에 들어갈 말로 가장 적절한 것은?

Researchers have been interested in the habitual ways a single individual copes with conflict when it occurs. They've called this approach conflict styles. There are several apparent conflict styles, and each has its pros and cons. The collaborating style tends to solve problems in ways that maximize the chances that the best result is provided for all involved. The pluses of a collaborating style include creating trust, maintaining positive relationship, and building commitment. However, it's time consuming and it takes a lot of energy to collaborate with another during conflict. The competing style may develop hostility in the person who doesn't achieve their goals. However, the competing style tends to resolve a conflict quickly.

The collaborating style might be used for someone who put a great value in _____(A)_____, while a person who prefers _____(B)_____ may choose the competing style.

	(A)	(B)
①	financial ability	interaction
②	saving time	peacefulness
③	mutual understanding	time efficiency
④	effectiveness	consistency

10 주어진 글 다음에 이어질 글의 순서로 가장 적절한 것은?

The historical evolution of Conflict Resolution gained momentum in the 1950s and 1960s, at the height of the Cold War, when the development of nuclear weapons and conflict between the superpowers seemed to threaten human survival.

(A) The combination of analysis and practice implicit in the new ideas was not easy to reconcile with traditional scholarly institutions or the traditions of practitioners such as diplomats and politicians.

(B) However, they were not taken seriously by some. The international relations profession had its own understanding of international conflict and did not see value in the new approaches as proposed.

(C) A group of pioneers from different disciplines saw the value of studying conflict as a general phenomenon, with similar properties, whether it occurs in international relations, domestic politics, industrial relations, communities, or between individuals.

① (B) – (A) – (C) ② (B) – (C) – (A)
③ (C) – (A) – (B) ④ (C) – (B) – (A)

11 (A), (B), (C)의 각 네모 안에서 어법에 맞는 표현으로 가장 적절한 것은?

The key to understanding economics is accepting (A) that / what there are always unintended consequences. Actions people take for their own good reasons have results they don't envision or intend. The same is true with *geopolitics. It is doubtful that the village of Rome, when it started its expansion in the seventh century BC, (B) had / have a master plan for conquering the Mediterranean world five hundred years later. But the first action its inhabitants took against neighboring villages set in motion a process that was both constrained by reality and (C) filled / filling with unintended consequences. Rome wasn't planned, and neither did it just happen.

* geopolitics : 지정학

	(A)	(B)	(C)
①	that	had	filled
②	what	had	filling
③	what	have	filled
④	that	have	filling

12 다음 빈칸에 들어갈 말로 가장 적절한 것을 고르시오.

Water and civilization go hand-in-hand. The idea of a "*hydraulic civilization" argues that water is the unifying context and justification for many large-scale civilizations throughout history. For example, the various multi-century Chinese empires survived as long as they did in part by controlling floods along the Yellow River. One interpretation of the hydraulic theory is that the justification for gathering populations into large cities is to manage water. Another interpretation suggests that large water projects enable the rise of big cities. The Romans understood the connections between water and power, as the Roman Empire built a vast network of **aqueducts throughout land they controlled, many of which remain intact. For example, Pont du Gard in southern France stands today as a testament to humanity's investment in its water infrastructure. Roman governors built roads, bridges, and water systems as a way of _____.

* hydraulic : 수력학의 ** aqueduct : 송수로

① focusing on educating young people
② prohibiting free trade in local markets
③ concentrating and strengthening their authority
④ giving up their properties to other countries

13 주어진 글 다음에 이어질 글의 순서로 가장 적절한 것은?

Ambiguity is so uncomfortable that it can even turn good news into bad. You go to your doctor with a persistent stomachache. Your doctor can't figure out what the reason is, so she sends you to the lab for tests.

(A) And what happens? Your immediate relief may be replaced by a weird sense of discomfort. You still don't know what the pain was! There's got to be an explanation somewhere.

(B) A week later you're called back to hear the results. When you finally get into her office, your doctor smiles and tells you the tests were all negative.

(C) Maybe it is cancer and they've just missed it. Maybe it's worse. Surely they should be able to find a cause. You feel frustrated by the lack of a definitive answer.

① (B) – (A) – (C)　　② (B) – (C) – (A)
③ (C) – (A) – (B)　　④ (C) – (B) – (A)

14 글의 흐름으로 보아, 주어진 문장이 들어가기에 가장 적절한 곳은?

The effect, however, was just the reverse.

How we dress for work has taken on a new element of choice, and with it, new anxieties. (①) The practice of having a "dress-down day" or "casual day," which began to emerge a decade or so ago, was intended to make life easier for employees, to enable them to save money and feel more relaxed at the office. (②) In addition to the normal workplace wardrobe, employees had to create a "workplace casual" *wardrobe. (③) It couldn't really be the sweats and T-shirts you wore around the house on the weekend. (④) It had to be a selection of clothing that sustained a certain image—relaxed, but also serious.

* wardrobe : 옷, 의류

15 다음 글의 밑줄 친 부분 중, 어법상 가장 틀린 것은?

You should choose the research method ① that best suits the outcome you want. You may run a survey online that enables you to question large numbers of people and ② provides full analysis in report format, or you may think asking questions one to one is a better way to get the answers you need from a smaller test selection of people. ③ Whichever way you choose, you will need to compare like for like. Ask people the same questions and compare answers. Look for both similarities and differences. Look for patterns and trends. Deciding on a way of recording and analysing the data ④ are important. A simple self created spreadsheet may well be enough to record some basic research data.

16 다음 글의 요지로 가장 적절한 것은?

Some criminal offenders may engage in illegal behavior because they love the excitement and thrills that crime can provide. In his highly influential work *Seductions of Crime*, sociologist Jack Katz argues that there are immediate benefits to criminality that "seduce" people into a life of crime. For some people, shoplifting and *vandalism are attractive because getting away with crime is a thrilling demonstration of personal competence. The need for excitement may counter fear of apprehension and punishment. In fact, some offenders will deliberately seek out especially risky situations because of the added "thrill". The need for excitement is a significant predictor of criminal choice.

* vandalism : 기물 파손

① 범죄를 줄이기 위해서 재소자를 상대로 한 교육이 필요하다.
② 범죄 행위에서 생기는 흥분과 쾌감이 범죄를 유발할 수 있다.
③ 엄격한 형벌 제도와 법 집행을 통해 강력 범죄를 줄일 수 있다.
④ 세밀하고 꼼꼼한 제도를 만들어 범죄 피해자를 도울 필요가 있다.

17 다음 빈칸에 들어갈 말로 가장 적절한 것은?

In one classic study showing the importance of attachment, Wisconsin University psychologists Harry and Margaret Harlow investigated the responses of young monkeys. The infants were separated from their biological mothers, and two *surrogate mothers were introduced to their cages. One, the wire mother, consisted of a round wooden head, a mesh of cold metal wires, and a bottle of milk from which the baby monkey could drink. The second mother was a foam-rubber form wrapped in a heated terry-cloth blanket. The infant monkeys went to the wire mother for food, but they overwhelmingly preferred and spent significantly more time with the warm terry-cloth mother. The warm terry-cloth mother provided no food, but did provide _____.

* surrogate : 대리의

① jobs
② drugs
③ comfort
④ education

18 다음 글의 밑줄 친 부분 중, 어법상 가장 틀린 것은?

I was released for adoption by my biological parents and ① spend the first decade of my life in orphanages. I spent many years thinking that something was wrong with me. If my own parents didn't want me, who could? I tried to figure out ② what I had done wrong and why so many people sent me away. I don't get close to anyone now because if I do they might leave me. I had to isolate ③ myself emotionally to survive when I was a child, and I still operate on the assumptions I had as a child. I am so fearful of being deserted ④ that I won't venture out and take even minimal risks. I am 40 years old now, but I still feel like a child.

19 다음 글의 밑줄 친 부분 중 어법상 가장 틀린 것은?

Music can have *psychotherapeutic effects that may transfer to everyday life. A number of scholars suggested people ① to use music as psychotherapeutic agent. Music therapy can be broadly defined as being 'the use of music as an adjunct to the treatment or rehabilitation of individuals to enhance their psychological, physical, cognitive or social ② functioning'. Positive emotional experiences from music may improve therapeutic process and thus ③ strengthen traditional cognitive/behavioral methods and their transfer to everyday goals. This may be partially because emotional experiences elicited by music and everyday behaviors ④ share overlapping neurological pathways responsible for positive emotions and motivations.

* psychotherapeutic : 심리 요법의

20 다음 빈칸에 들어갈 말로 가장 적절한 것은?

Cultural interpretations are usually made on the basis of _____ rather than measurable evidence. The arguments tend to be circular. People are poor because they are lazy. How do we "know" they are lazy? Because they are poor. Promoters of these interpretations rarely understand that low productivity results not from laziness and lack of effort but from lack of capital inputs to production. African farmers are not lazy, but they do lack soil nutrients, tractors, feeder roads, irrigated plots, storage facilities, and the like. Stereotypes that Africans work little and therefore are poor are put to rest immediately by spending a day in a village, where backbreaking labor by men and women is the norm.

① statistics
② prejudice
③ appearance
④ circumstances

21 글의 흐름으로 보아, 주어진 문장이 들어가기에 가장 적절한 곳은?

> But the demand for food isn't *elastic; people don't eat more just because food is cheap.

> The free market has never worked in agriculture and it never will. (①) The economics of a family farm are very different than a firm's: When prices fall, the firm can lay off people and idle factories. (②) Eventually the market finds a new balance between supply and demand. (③) And laying off farmers doesn't help to reduce supply. (④) You can fire me, but you can't fire my land, because some other farmer who needs more cash flow or thinks he's more efficient than I am will come in and farm it.
>
> * elastic : 탄력성 있는

22 다음 글의 주제로 가장 적절한 것은?

> Daily training creates special nutritional needs for an athlete, particularly the elite athlete whose training commitment is almost a fulltime job. But even recreational sport will create nutritional challenges. And whatever your level of involvement in sport, you must meet these challenges if you're to achieve the maximum return from training. Without sound eating, much of the purpose of your training might be lost. In the worst-case scenario, dietary problems and deficiencies may directly impair training performance. In other situations, you might improve, but at a rate that is below your potential or slower than your competitors. However, on the positive side, with the right everyday eating plan your commitment to training will be fully rewarded.

① how to improve body flexibility
② importance of eating well in exercise
③ health problems caused by excessive diet
④ improving skills through continuous training

23 다음 글의 주제로 가장 적절한 것은?

> A very well-respected art historian called Ernst Gombrich wrote about something called "the beholder's share". It was Gombrich's belief that a viewer "completed" the artwork, that part of an artwork's meaning came from the person viewing it. So you see—there really are no wrong answers as it is you, as the viewer who is completing the artwork. If you're looking at art in a gallery, read the wall text at the side of the artwork. If staff are present, ask questions. Ask your fellow visitors what they think. Asking questions is the key to understanding more—and that goes for anything in life—not just art. But above all, have confidence in front of an artwork. If you are contemplating an artwork, then you are the intended viewer and what you think matters. You are the only critic that counts.

① 미술작품의 가치는 일정 부분 정해져 있다.
② 미술 작품을 제작할 때 대중의 요구를 반영해야 한다.
③ 미술작품은 감상하는 사람으로 인하여 비로소 완성된다.
④ 미술 감상의 출발은 작가의 숨겨진 의도를 파악하는 것이다.

24 Argentina에 관한 다음 글의 내용과 가장 일치하지 않는 것은?

> Argentina is the world's eighth largest country, comprising almost the entire southern half of South America. Colonization by Spain began in the early 1500s, but in 1816 Jose de San Martin led the movement for Argentine independence. The culture of Argentina has been greatly influenced by the massive European migration in the late nineteenth and early twentieth centuries, primarily from Spain and Italy. The majority of people are at least nominally Catholic, and the country has the largest Jewish population (about 300,000) in South America. From 1880 to 1930, thanks to its agricultural development, Argentina was one of the world's top ten wealthiest nations.

① Jose de San Martin이 스페인으로부터의 독립운동을 이끌었다.
② 북미 출신 이주민들이 그 문화에 많은 영향을 끼쳤다.
③ 남미지역 중에서 가장 많은 유대인들이 살고 있는 곳이다.
④ 농업의 발전으로 한때 부유한 국가였다.

25 Sonja Henie에 관한 다음 글의 내용과 가장 일치하지 않는 것은?

> Sonja Henie is famous for her skill into a career as one of the world's most famous figure skaters—in the rink and on the screen. Henie, winner of three Olympic gold medals and a Norwegian and European champion, invented a thrillingly theatrical and athletic style of figure skating. She introduced short skirts, white skates, and attractive moves. Her spectacular spins and jumps raised the bar for all competitors. In 1936, Twentieth-Century Fox signed her to star in One in a Million, and she soon became one of Hollywood's leading actresses. In 1941, the movie 'Sun Valley Serenade' received three Academy Award nominations which she played as an actress. Although the rest of Henie's films were less acclaimed, she triggered a popular surge in ice skating. In 1938, she launched extravagant touring shows called Hollywood Ice Revues. Her many ventures made her a fortune, but her greatest legacy was inspiring little girls to skate.

① 피겨 스케이터와 영화배우로서의 업적으로 유명하다.
② 올림픽과 다른 대회들에서 좋은 성적을 거두었다.
③ 출연한 영화가 1941년에 영화제에서 3개 부문에 수상했다.
④ 어린 여자아이들에게 스케이트에 대한 영감을 주었다.

정답·해석·해설 p. 180

1회 2022년 법원직 9급
모바일 자동 채점 + 성적 분석 서비스 바로 가기

QR코드를 이용해 모바일로 간편하게 채점하고 나의 실력이 어느 정도인지, 취약 부분이 어디인지 바로 파악해 보세요.

(p.166에서 전체 정답표를 확인하실 수 있습니다)

제한시간 : 25분　시작 _____시 _____분 ~ 종료 _____시 _____분　나의 점수 _____　회독수 □ □ □

01 다음 글의 내용을 한 문장으로 요약하고자 한다. 빈칸 (A)와 (B)에 들어갈 말로 가장 적절한 것은?

Microorganisms are not calculating entities. They don't care what they do to you any more than you care what distress you cause when you slaughter them by the millions with a soapy shower. The only time a pathogen cares about you is when it kills you too well. If they eliminate you before they can move on, then they may well die out themselves. This in fact sometimes happens. History, Jared Diamond notes, is full of diseases that "once caused terrifying epidemics and then disappeared as mysteriously as they had come." He cites the robust but mercifully transient English sweating sickness, which raged from 1485 to 1552, killing tens of thousands as it went, before burning itself out. Too much efficiency is not a good thing for any infectious organism.

*pathogen 병원체

⇩

The more ___(A)___ pathogens are, the faster it is likely be to ___(B)___ .

　　(A)　　　　(B)
① weaker ---- disappear
② weaker ---- spread
③ infectious ---- spread
④ infectious ---- disappear

02 밑줄 친 "drains the mind"가 위 글에서 의미하는 바로 가장 적절한 것은?

If the writing is solid and good, the mood and temper of the writer will eventually be revealed and not at the expense of the work. Therefore, to achieve style, begin by affecting none—that is, draw the reader's attention to the sense and substance of the writing. A careful and honest writer does not need to worry about style. As you become proficient in the use of language, your style will emerge, because you yourself will emerge, and when this happens you will find it increasingly easy to break through the barriers that separate you from other minds and at last, make you stand in the middle of the writing. Fortunately, the act of composition, or creation, disciplines the mind; writing is one way to go about thinking, and the practice and habit of writing drains the mind.

① to heal the mind
② to help to be sensitive
③ to satisfy his/her curiosity
④ to place oneself in the background

03 (A), (B), (C)의 각 네모 안에서 어법에 맞는 표현으로 가장 적절한 것은?

Some of our dissatisfactions with self and with our lot in life are based on real circumstances, and some are false and simply (A) (perceive / perceived) to be real. The perceived must be sorted out and discarded. The real will either fall into the changeable or the unchangeable classification. If it's in the latter, we must strive to accept it. If it's in the former, then we have the alternative to strive instead to remove, exchange, or modify it. All of us have a unique purpose in life; and all of us are gifted, just (B) (different / differently) gifted. It's not an argument about whether it's fair or unfair to have been given one, five, or ten talents; it's about what we have done with our talents. It's about how well we have invested (C) (them / those) we have been given. If one holds on to the outlook that their life is unfair, then that's really holding an offense against God.

	(A)	(B)	(C)
①	perceive	different	them
②	perceive	differently	those
③	perceived	different	them
④	perceived	differently	those

04 주어진 글 다음에 이어질 글의 순서로 가장 적절한 것은?

People assume that, by charging a low price or one lower than their competitors, they will get more customers. This is a common fallacy.

(A) It is, therefore, far better to have lower-volume, higher-margin products and services as you start; you can always negotiate to reduce your price if you are forced to, but it is rare that you will be able to negotiate an increase.

(B) It is because when you charge reduced prices compared to your competition, you attract the lower end of the customer market. These customers want more for less and often take up more time and overhead in your business. They may also be your most difficult customers to deal with and keep happy.

(C) You also, ironically, repel the better customers because they will pay a higher price for a higher level of product or service. We have seen many competitors come into the market and charge day rates that aren't sustainable. They often struggle even to fill their quota, and soon enough they give up and move on to doing something else.

*repel 쫓아 버리다

① (B) – (A) – (C)
② (B) – (C) – (A)
③ (C) – (A) – (B)
④ (C) – (B) – (A)

05 다음 글의 밑줄 친 부분 중, 어법상 가장 틀린 것은?

Children who enjoy writing are often interested in seeing ① their work in print. One informal approach is to type, print, and post their poetry. Or you can create a photocopied anthology of the poetry of many child writers. But for children who are truly dedicated and ambitious, ② submit a poem for publication is a worthy goal. And there are several web and print resources that print children's original poetry. Help child poets become familiar with the protocol for submitting manuscripts (style, format, and so forth). Let them choose ③ which poems they are most proud of, keep copies of everything submitted, and get parent permission. Then celebrate with them when their work is accepted and appear in print. Congratulate them, ④ publicly showcase their accomplishment, and spread the word. Success inspires success. And, of course, if their work is rejected, offer support and encouragement.

*anthology 문집, 선집, **protocol 규약, 의례

06 글의 흐름으로 보아, 주어진 문장이 들어가기에 가장 적절한 곳은?

With love and strength from the tribe, the tiny seeds mature and grow tall and crops for the people.

In the Pueblo indian culture, corn is to the people the very symbol of life. (①) The Corn Maiden "grandmother of the sun and the light" brought this gift, bringing the power of life to the people. (②) As the corn is given life by the sun, the Corn Maiden brings the fire of the sun into the human bodies, giving man many representations of his love and power through nature. (③) Each Maiden brings one seed of corn that is nurtured with love like that given to a child and this one seed would sustain the entire tribe forever. (④) The spirit of the Corn Maidens is forever present with the tribal people.

07 다음 빈칸에 들어갈 말로 가장 적절한 것은?

Beeches, oaks, spruce and pines produce new growth all the time, and have to get rid of the old. The most obvious change happens every autumn. The leaves have served their purpose: they are now worn out and riddled with insect damage. Before the trees bid them adieu, they pump waste products into them. You could say they are taking this opportunity to relieve themselves. Then they grow a layer of weak tissue to separate each leaf from the twig it's growing on, and the leaves tumble to the ground in the next breeze. The rustling leaves that now blanket the ground—and make such a satisfying scrunching sound when you scuffle through them—are basically _____.

① tree toilet paper
② the plant kitchen
③ lungs of the tree
④ parents of insects

08 글의 흐름상 가장 어색한 문장은?

Fiction has many uses and one of them is to build empathy. When you watch TV or see a film, you are looking at things happening to other people. Prose fiction is something you build up from 26 letters and a handful of punctuation marks, and you, and you alone, using your imagination, create a world and live there and look out through other eyes. ① You get to feel things, and visit places and worlds you would never otherwise know. ② Fortunately, in the last decade, many of the world's most beautiful and unknown places have been put in the spotlight. ③ You learn that everyone else out there is a me, as well. ④ You're being someone else, and when you return to your own world, you're going to be slightly changed.

09 다음 빈칸에 들어갈 말로 가장 적절한 것은?

The seeds of willows and poplars are so minuscule that you can just make out two tiny dark dots in the fluffy flight hairs. One of these seeds weighs a mere 0.0001 grams. With such a meagre energy reserve, a seedling can grow only 1–2 millimetres before it runs out of steam and has to rely on food it makes for itself using its young leaves. But that only works in places where there's no competition to threaten the tiny sprouts. Other plants casting shade on it would extinguish the new life immediately. And so, if a fluffy little seed package like this falls in a spruce or beech forest, the seed's life is over before it's even begun. That's why willows and poplars _____.

*minuscule 아주 작은

① prefer settling in unoccupied territory
② have been chosen as food for herbivores
③ have evolved to avoid human intervention
④ wear their dead leaves far into the winter

10 다음 글의 밑줄 친 부분 중 문맥상 낱말의 쓰임이 가장 적절하지 않은 것은?

Good walking shoes are important. Most major athletic brands offer shoes especially designed for walking. Fit and comfort are more important than style; your shoes should feel ① supportive but not tight or constricting. The uppers should be light, breathable, and flexible, the insole moisture-resistant, and the sole ② shock-absorbent. The heel wedge should be ③ lowered, so the sole at the back of the shoe is two times thicker than at the front. Finally, the toe box should be ④ spacious, even when you're wearing athletic socks.

① supportive   ② shock-absorbent
③ lowered   ④ spacious

11 다음 글의 요지로 가장 알맞은 것은?

If your kids fight every time they play video games, make sure you're close enough to be able to hear them when they sit down to play. Listen for the particular words or tones of voice they are using that are aggressive, and try to intervene before it develops. Once tempers have settled, try to sit your kids down and discuss the problem without blaming or accusing. Give each kid a chance to talk, uninterrupted, and have them try to come up with solutions to the problem themselves. By the time kids are elementary-school age, they can evaluate which of those solutions are win-win solutions and which ones are most likely to work and satisfy each other over time. They should also learn to revisit problems when solutions are no longer working.

① Ask your kids to evaluate their test.
② Make your kids compete each other.
③ Help your kids learn to resolve conflict.
④ Teach your kids how to win an argument.

12 다음 글의 요지로 가장 적절한 것은?

There's a current trend to avoid germs at all cost. We disinfect our bathrooms, kitchens, and the air. We sanitize our hands and gargle with mouthwash to kill germs. Some folks avoid as much human contact as possible and won't even shake your hand for fear of getting germs. I think it's safe to say that some people would purify everything but their minds. Remember the story of "the Boy in the Bubble"? He was born without an immune system and had to live in a room that was completely germ free, with no human contact. Of course, everyone should take prudent measures to maintain reasonable standards of cleanliness and personal hygiene, but in many cases, aren't we going overboard? When we come in contact with most germs, our body destroys them, which in turn strengthens our immune system and its ability to further fight off disease. Thus, these "good germs" actually make us healthier. Even if it were possible to avoid all germs and to live in a sterile environment, wouldn't we then be like "the Boy in the Bubble"?

① 세균에 감염되지 않도록 개인의 위생 환경 조성이 필요하다.
② 면역 능력이 상실된 채로 태어난 유아에 대한 치료가 시급하다.
③ 지역사회의 방역 능력 강화를 위해 국가의 재정 지원이 시급하다.
④ 과도하게 세균을 제거하려고 하는 것이 오히려 면역 능력을 해친다.

13 다음 글의 밑줄 친 부분을 어법상 바르게 고친 것이 아닌 것은?

① Knowing as the Golden City, Jaisalmer, a former caravan center on the route to the Khyber Pass, rises from a sea of sand, its 30-foot-high walls and medieval sandstone fort ② shelters carved spires and palaces that soar into the sapphire sky. With its tiny winding lanes and hidden temples, Jaisalmer is straight out of The Arabian Nights, and so little has life altered here ③ which it's easy to imagine yourself back in the 13th century. It's the only fortress city in India still functioning, with one quarter of its population ④ lived within the walls, and it's just far enough off the beaten path to have been spared the worst ravages of tourism. The city's wealth originally came from the substantial tolls it placed on passing camel caravans.

① Knowing → Known
② shelters → sheltering
③ which → that
④ lived → lives

14 다음 글에서 필자가 주장하는 바로 가장 적절한 것은?

The learned are neither apathetic nor indifferent regarding the world's problems. More books on these issues are being published than ever, though few capture the general public's attention. Likewise, new research discoveries are constantly being made at universities, and shared at conferences worldwide. Unfortunately, most of this activity is self-serving. With the exception of science—and here, too, only selectively—new insights are not trickling down to the public in ways to help improve our lives. Yet, these discoveries aren't simply the property of the elite, and should not remain in the possession of a select few professionals. Each person must make his and her own life's decisions, and make those choices in light of our current understanding of who we are and what is good for us. For that matter, we must find a way to somehow make new discoveries accessible to every person.

*apathetic 냉담한, 무관심한, **trickle 흐르다

① 학자들은 연구 논문을 작성할 때 주관성을 배제해야 한다.
② 새로운 연구 결과에 모든 사람이 접근할 수 있게 해야 한다.
③ 소수 엘리트 학자들의 폐쇄성을 극복할 계기를 마련해야 한다.
④ 학자들이 연구 과정에서 겪는 어려움을 극복하도록 도와야 한다.

15 다음 글의 주제로 가장 알맞은 것은?

Language gives individual identity and a sense of belonging. When children proudly learn their language and are able to speak it at home and in their neighborhood, the children will have a high self-esteem. Moreover, children who know the true value of their mother tongue will not feel like they are achievers when they speak a foreign language. With improved self-identity and self-esteem, the classroom performance of a child also improves because such a child goes to school with less worries about linguistic marginalization.

*linguistic marginalization 언어적 소외감

① the importance of mother tongue in child development
② the effect on children's foreign language learning
③ the way to improve children's self-esteem
④ the efficiency of the linguistic analysis

16 다음 글의 주제로 가장 적절한 것은?

Many animals are not loners. They discovered, or perhaps nature discovered for them, that by living and working together, they could interact with the world more effectively. For example, if an animal hunts for food by itself, it can only catch, kill, and eat animals much smaller than itself—but if animals band together in a group, they can catch and kill animals bigger than they are. A pack of wolves can kill a horse, which can feed the group very well. Thus, more food is available to the same animals in the same forest if they work together than if they work alone. Cooperation has other benefits: The animals can alert each other to danger, can find more food (if they search separately and then follow the ones who succeed in finding food), and can even provide some care to those who are sick and injured. Mating and reproduction are also easier if the animals live in a group than if they live far apart.

① benefits of being social in animals
② drawbacks of cooperative behaviors
③ common traits of animals and humans
④ competitions in mating and reproduction

17 다음 글의 밑줄 친 부분 중, 문맥상 낱말의 쓰임이 가장 적절하지 않은 것은?

My own curiosity had been encouraged by my studies in philosophy at university. The course listed the numerous philosophers that we were supposed to study and I thought at first that our task was to learn and absorb their work as a sort of secular Bible. But I was ① delighted to discover that my tutor was not interested in me reciting their theories but only in helping me to develop my own, using the philosophers of the past as stimulants not authorities. It was the key to my intellectual ② freedom. Now I had official permission to think for myself, to question anything and everything and only agree if I thought it right. A ③ good education would have given me that permission much earlier. Some, alas, never seem to have received it and go on reciting the rules of others as if they were sacrosanct. As a result, they become the unwitting ④ opponents of other people's worlds. Philosophy, I now think, is too important to be left to professional philosophers. We should all learn to think like philosophers, starting at primary school.

*sacrosanct 신성불가침의, ***unwitting 자신도 모르는

18 (A), (B), (C)의 괄호 안에서 어법에 맞는 표현으로 가장 적절한 것은?

Looking back, scientists have uncovered a mountain of evidence (A) [that / what] Mayan leaders were aware for many centuries of their uncertain dependence on rainfall. Water shortages were not only understood but also recorded and planned for. The Mayans enforced conservation during low rainfall years, tightly regulating the types of crops grown, the use of public water, and food rationing. During the first half of their three-thousand-year reign, the Mayans continued to build larger underground artificial lakes and containers (B) [stored / to store] rainwater for drought months. As impressive as their elaborately decorated temples (C) [did / were], their efficient systems for collecting and warehousing water were masterpieces in design and engineering.

*rationing 배급

	(A)		(B)		(C)
①	that	---	to store	---	were
②	what	---	stored	---	did
③	that	---	to store	---	did
④	what	---	stored	---	were

19 주어진 글 다음에 이어질 글의 순서로 가장 적절한 것은?

Religion can certainly bring out the best in a person, but it is not the only phenomenon with that property.

(A) People who would otherwise be self-absorbed or shallow or crude or simply quitters are often ennobled by their religion, given a perspective on life that helps them make the hard decisions that we all would be proud to make.

(B) Having a child often has a wonderfully maturing effect on a person. Wartime, famously, gives people an abundance of occasions to rise to, as do natural disasters like floods and hurricanes.

(C) But for day-in, day-out lifelong bracing, there is probably nothing so effective as religion: it makes powerful and talented people more humble and patient, it makes average people rise above themselves, it provides sturdy support for many people who desperately need help staying away from drink or drugs or crime.

① (B) – (A) – (C)   ② (B) – (C) – (A)
③ (C) – (A) – (B)   ④ (C) – (B) – (A)

20 주어진 글 다음에 이어질 글의 순서로 가장 적절한 것은?

More people require more resources, which means that as the population increases, the Earth's resources deplete more rapidly.

(A) Population growth also results in increased greenhouse gases, mostly from CO_2 emissions. For visualization, during that same 20th century that saw fourfold population growth, CO_2 emissions increased twelvefold.

(B) The result of this depletion is deforestation and loss of biodiversity as humans strip the Earth of resources to accommodate rising population numbers.

(C) As greenhouse gases increase, so do climate patterns, ultimately resulting in the long-term pattern called climate change.

*deplete 고갈시키다, 대폭 감소시키다

① (A) – (B) – (C)   ② (B) – (A) – (C)
③ (B) – (C) – (A)   ④ (C) – (A) – (B)

21 다음 글에서 전체 흐름과 관계없는 문장은?

Medical anthropologists with extensive training in human biology and physiology study disease transmission patterns and how particular groups adapt to the presence of diseases like malaria and sleeping sickness. ① Because the transmission of viruses and bacteria is strongly influenced by people's diets, sanitation, and other behaviors, many medical anthropologists work as a team with epidemiologists to identify cultural practices that affect the spread of disease. ② Though it may be a commonly held belief that most students enter medicine for humanitarian reasons rather than for the financial rewards of a successful medical career, in developed nations the prospect of status and rewards is probably one incentive. ③ Different cultures have different ideas about the causes and symptoms of disease, how best to treat illnesses, the abilities of traditional healers and doctors, and the importance of community involvement in the healing process. ④ By studying how a human community perceives such things, medical anthropologists help hospitals and other agencies deliver health care services more effectively.

*epidemiologist 유행[전염]병학자

22 주어진 글 다음에 이어질 글의 순서로 가장 적절한 것은?

> Sequoya (1760?–1843) was born in eastern Tennessee, into a prestigious family that was highly regarded for its knowledge of Cherokee tribal traditions and religion.

(A) Recognizing the possibilities writing had for his people, Sequoya invented a Cherokee alphabet in 1821. With this system of writing, Sequoya was able to record ancient tribal customs.

(B) More important, his alphabet helped the Cherokee nation develop a publishing industry so that newspapers and books could be printed. School-age children were thus able to learn about Cherokee culture and traditions in their own language.

(C) As a child, Sequoya learned the Cherokee oral tradition; then, as an adult, he was introduced to Euro-American culture. In his letters, Sequoya mentions how he became fascinated with the writing methods European Americans used to communicate.

① (B) – (A) – (C)
② (B) – (C) – (A)
③ (C) – (A) – (B)
④ (C) – (B) – (A)

23 Peanut Butter Drive에 관한 다음 안내문의 내용과 가장 일치하지 않는 것은?

> SPREAD THE LOVE
> Fight Hunger During the Peanut Butter Drive
>
> Make a contribution to our community by helping local families who need a little assistance. We are kicking off our 4th annual area-wide peanut butter drive to benefit children, families and seniors who face hunger in Northeast Louisiana.
>
> Peanut butter is a much needed staple at Food Banks as it is a protein-packed food that kids and adults love. Please donate peanut butter in plastic jars or funds to the Monroe Food Bank by Friday, March 29th at 4:00 pm. Donations of peanut butter can be dropped off at the food bank's distribution center located at 4600 Central Avenue in Monroe on Monday through Friday, 8:00 am to 4:00 pm. Monetary donations can be made here or by calling 427-418-4581.
>
> For other drop-off locations, visit our website at https://www.foodbanknela.org

① 배고픈 사람들에게 도움을 주려는 행사이다.
② 토요일과 일요일에도 땅콩버터를 기부할 수 있다.
③ 전화를 걸어 금전 기부를 할 수도 있다.
④ 땅콩버터를 기부하는 장소는 여러 곳이 있다.

24 다음 글에 나타난 화자의 심경으로 가장 적절한 것은?

Our whole tribe was poverty-stricken. Every branch of the Garoghlanian family was living in the most amazing and comical poverty in the world. Nobody could understand where we ever got money enough to keep us with food in our bellies. Most important of all, though, we were famous for our honesty. We had been famous for honesty for something like eleven centuries, even when we had been the wealthiest family in what we liked to think was the world. We put pride first, honest next, and after that we believed in right and wrong. None of us would take advantage of anybody in the world.

*poverty-stricken 가난에 시달리는

① peaceful and calm
② satisfied and proud
③ horrified and feared
④ amazed and astonished

25 다음 글의 내용과 가장 일치하지 않는 것은?

Despite the increasing popularity of consuming raw foods, you can still gain nutrients from cooked vegetables. For example, our body can absorb lycopene more effectively when tomatoes are cooked. (Keep in mind, however, that raw tomatoes are still a good source of lycopene.) Cooked tomatoes, however, have lower levels of vitamin C than raw tomatoes, so if you're looking to increase your levels, you might be better off sticking with the raw. Whether you decide to eat them cooked or raw, it's important not to dilute the health benefits of tomatoes. If you're buying tomato sauce or paste, choose a variety with no salt or sugar added—or better yet, cook your own sauce at home. And if you're eating your tomatoes raw, salt them sparingly and choose salad dressings that are low in calories and saturated fat.

*dilute 희석하다, 묽게 하다

① 토마토를 요리하여 먹었을 때, 우리의 몸은 리코펜을 더 효과적으로 흡수할 수 있다.
② 더 많은 비타민C를 섭취하고 싶다면 생토마토보다 조리된 토마토를 섭취하는 것이 낫다.
③ 토마토 소스를 구입하고자 한다면, 소금이나 설탕이 첨가되지 않은 것으로 골라야 한다.
④ 생토마토를 섭취 시, 소금을 적게 넣거나, 칼로리가 적은 드레싱을 선택하도록 한다.

정답·해석·해설 p. 194

2회 2021년 법원직 9급
모바일 자동 채점 + 성적 분석 서비스 바로 가기

QR코드를 이용해 모바일로 간편하게 채점하고 나의 실력이 어느 정도인지, 취약 부분이 어디인지 바로 파악해 보세요.

(p.166에서 전체 정답표를 확인하실 수 있습니다)

제한시간 : 25분　　시작 _____시 _____분 ~ 종료 _____시 _____분　　　나의 점수 _____　회독수 ☐☐☐

01 다음 밑줄 친 (A), (B), (C)의 각 괄호 안에서 문맥에 맞는 낱말로 가장 적절한 것은?

It's tempting to identify knowledge with facts, but not every fact is an item of knowledge. Imagine shaking a sealed cardboard box containing a single coin. As you put the box down, the coin inside the box has landed either heads or tails: let's say that's a fact. But as long as no one looks into the box, this fact remains unknown; it is not yet within the realm of (A) [fact / knowledge]. Nor do facts become knowledge simply by being written down. If you write the sentence 'The coin has landed heads' on one slip of paper and 'The coin has landed tails' on another, then you will have written down a fact on one of the slips, but you still won't have gained knowledge of the outcome of the coin toss. Knowledge demands some kind of access to a fact on the part of some living subject. (B) [With / Without] a mind to access it, whatever is stored in libraries and databases won't be knowledge, but just ink marks and electronic traces. In any given case of knowledge, this access may or may not be unique to an individual: the same fact may be known by one person and not by others. Common knowledge might be shared by many people, but there is no knowledge that dangles (C) [attached / unattached] to any subject.

	(A)	(B)	(C)
①	fact	with	unattached
②	knowledge	without	unattached
③	knowledge	with	attached
④	fact	without	attached

02 다음 빈칸에 들어갈 말로 가장 적절한 것은?

Impressionable youth are not the only ones subject to _____. Most of us have probably had an experience of being pressured by a salesman. Have you ever had a sales rep try to sell you some "office solution" by telling you that 70 percent of your competitors are using their service, so why aren't you? But what if 70 percent of your competitors are idiots? Or what if that 70 percent were given so much value added or offered such a low price that they couldn't resist the opportunity? The practice is designed to do one thing and one thing only—to pressure you to buy. To make you feel you might be missing out on something or that everyone else knows but you.

① peer pressure
② impulse buying
③ bullying tactics
④ keen competition

03 다음 밑줄 친 (A), (B), (C)의 각 괄호 안에서 문맥에 맞는 낱말로 가장 적절한 것은?

People with high self-esteem have confidence in their skills and competence and enjoy facing the challenges that life offers them. They (A) [willingly / unwillingly] work in teams because they are sure of themselves and enjoy taking the opportunity to contribute. However, those who have low self-esteem tend to feel awkward, shy, and unable to express themselves. Often they compound their problems by opting for avoidance strategies because they (B) [deny / hold] the belief that whatever they do will result in failure. Conversely, they may compensate for their lack of self-esteem by exhibiting boastful and arrogant behavior to cover up their sense of unworthiness. Furthermore, such individuals account for their successes by finding reasons that are outside of themselves, while those with high self-esteem (C) [attempt / attribute] their success to internal characteristics.

	(A)	(B)	(C)
①	willingly	... deny	... attempt
②	willingly	... hold	... attribute
③	unwillingly	... hold	... attempt
④	unwillingly	... deny	... attribute

04 다음 글의 제목으로 가장 적절한 것은?

To be sure, no other species can lay claim to our capacity to devise something new and original, from the sublime to the sublimely ridiculous. Other animals do build things—birds assemble their intricate nests, beavers construct dams, and ants dig elaborate networks of tunnels. "But airplanes, strangely tilted skyscrapers and Chia Pets, well, they're pretty impressive," Fuentes says, adding that from an evolutionary standpoint, "creativity is as much a part of our tool kit as walking on two legs, having a big brain and really good hands for manipulating things." For a physically unprepossessing primate, without great fangs or claws or wings or other obvious physical advantages, creativity has been the great equalizer—and more—ensuring, for now, at least, the survival of Homo sapiens.

*sublime 황당한, (터무니없이) 극단적인
*Chia Pets 잔디가 머리털처럼 자라나는 피규어

① Where Does Human Creativity Come From?
② What Are the Physical Characteristics of Primates?
③ Physical Advantages of Homo Sapiens over Other Species
④ Creativity: a Unique Trait Human Species Have For Survival

05 다음 글의 요지를 한 문장으로 요약하고자 한다. 빈칸 (A), (B)에 들어갈 말로 가장 적절한 것은?

"Most of bird identification is based on a sort of subjective impression—the way a bird moves and little instantaneous appearances at different angles and sequences of different appearances, and as it turns its head and as it flies and as it turns around, you see sequences of different shapes and angles," Sibley says, "All that combines to create a unique impression of a bird that can't really be taken apart and described in words. When it comes down to being in the fieldland looking at a bird, you don't take time to analyze it and say it shows this, this, and this; therefore it must be this species. It's more natural and instinctive. After a lot of practice, you look at the bird, and it triggers little switches in your brain. It looks right. You know what it is at a glance."

According to Sibley, bird identification is based on (A) _____ rather than (B) _____.

① instinctive impression – discrete analysis
② objective research – subjective judgements
③ physical appearances – behavioral traits
④ close observation – distant observation

06 주어진 글 다음에 이어질 글의 순서로 가장 적절한 것은?

As cars are becoming less dependent on people, the means and circumstances in which the product is used by consumers are also likely to undergo significant changes, with higher rates of participation in car sharing and short-term leasing programs.

(A) In the not-too-distant future, a driverless car could come to you when you need it, and when you are done with it, it could then drive away without any need for a parking space. Increases in car sharing and short-term leasing are also likely to be associated with a corresponding decrease in the importance of exterior car design.

(B) As a result, the symbolic meanings derived from cars and their relationship to consumer self-identity and status are likely to change in turn.

(C) Rather than serving as a medium for personalization and self-identity, car exteriors might increasingly come to represent a channel for advertising and other promotional activities, including brand ambassador programs, such as those offered by Free Car Media.

① (A) – (C) – (B)
② (B) – (C) – (A)
③ (C) – (A) – (B)
④ (C) – (B) – (A)

07 주어진 글 다음에 이어질 글의 순서로 가장 적절한 것은?

There is a wonderful story of a group of American car executives who went to Japan to see a Japanese assembly line. At the end of the line, the doors were put on the hinges, the same as in America.

(A) But something was missing. In the United States, a line worker would take a rubber mallet and tap the edges of the door to ensure that it fit perfectly. In Japan, that job didn't seem to exist.

(B) Confused, the American auto executives asked at what point they made sure the door fit perfectly. Their Japanese guide looked at them and smiled sheepishly. "We make sure it fits when we design it."

(C) In the Japanese auto plant, they didn't examine the problem and accumulate data to figure out the best solution—they engineered the outcome they wanted from the beginning. If they didn't achieve their desired outcome, they understood it was because of a decision they made at the start of the process.

① (A) – (B) – (C)
② (A) – (C) – (B)
③ (B) – (A) – (C)
④ (B) – (C) – (A)

08 다음 글의 빈칸 (A), (B)에 들어갈 말로 가장 적절한 것은?

There has been much research on nonverbal cues to deception dating back to the work of Ekman and his idea of leakage. It is well documented that people use others' nonverbal behaviors as a way to detect lies. My research and that of many others has strongly supported people's reliance on observations of others' nonverbal behaviors when assessing honesty. (A) _____, social scientific research on the link between various nonverbal behaviors and the act of lying suggests that the link is typically not very strong or consistent. In my research, I have observed that the nonverbal signals that seem to give one liar away are different than those given by a second liar. (B) _____, the scientific evidence linking nonverbal behaviors and deception has grown weaker over time. People infer honesty based on how others nonverbally present themselves, but that has very limited utility and validity.

① However   –   What's more
② As a result –   On the contrary
③ However   –   Nevertheless
④ As a result –   For instance

09 다음 글의 밑줄 친 부분 중 어법상 틀린 것은?

As soon as the start-up is incorporated it will need a bank account, and the need for a payroll account will follow quickly. The banks are very competitive in services to do payroll and related tax bookkeeping, ① starting with even the smallest of businesses. These are areas ② where a business wants the best quality service and the most "free" accounting help it can get. The changing payroll tax legislation is a headache to keep up with, especially when a sales force will be operating in many of the fifty states. And the ③ requiring reports are a burden on a company's add administrative staff. Such services are often provided best by the banker. The banks' references in this area should be compared with the payroll service alternatives such as ADP, but the future and the long-term relationship should be kept in mind when a decision is ④ being made.

10 다음 글의 밑줄 친 부분 중 어법상 틀린 것은?

Many people refuse to visit animal shelters because they find it too sad or ① depressed. They shouldn't feel so bad because so many lucky animals are saved from a dangerous life on the streets, ② where they're at risk of traffic accidents, attack by other animals or humans, and subject to the elements. Many lost pets likewise ③ are found and reclaimed by distraught owners simply because they were brought into animal shelters. Most importantly, ④ adoptable pets find homes, and sick or dangerous animals are humanely relieved of their suffering.

11 다음 밑줄 친 (A), (B), (C)의 각 괄호 안에서 문맥에 맞는 낱말로 가장 적절한 것은?

EQ testing, when performed with reliable testing methods, can provide you with very useful information about yourself. I've found, having tested thousands of people, that many are a bit surprised by their results. For example, one person who believed she was very socially responsible and often concerned about others came out with an (A) [average / extraordinary] score in that area. She was quite disappointed in her score. It turned out that she had very high standards for social responsibility and therefore was extremely (B) [easy / hard] on herself when she performed her assessment. In reality, she was (C) [more / less] socially responsible than most people, but she believed that she could be much better than she was.

	(A)	(B)	(C)
①	average	easy	less
②	average	hard	more
③	extraordinary	hard	less
④	extraordinary	easy	more

12 다음 빈칸에 들어갈 말로 가장 적절한 것은?

A person may try to _____ by using evidence to his advantage. A mother asks her son, "How are you doing in English this term?" He responds cheerfully, "Oh, I just got a ninety-five on a quiz." The statement conceals the fact that he has failed every other quiz and that his actual average is 55. Yet, if she pursues the matter no further, the mother may be delighted that her son is doing so well. Linda asks Susan, "Have you read much Dickens?" Susan responds, "Oh, *Pickwick Papers* is one of my favorite novels." The statement may disguise the fact that *Pickwick Papers* is the only novel by Dickens that she has read, and it may give Linda the impression that Susan is a great Dickens enthusiast.

① earn extra money
② effect a certain belief
③ hide memory problems
④ make other people feel guilty

13 다음 글의 내용을 한 문장으로 요약하고자 한다. 빈칸 (A), (B)에 들어갈 말로 가장 적절한 것은?

Whether we are complimented for our appearance, our garden, a dinner we prepared, or an assignment at the office, it is always satisfying to receive recognition for a job well done. Certainly, reinforcement theory sees occasional praise as an aid to learning a new skill. However, some evidence cautions against making sweeping generalizations regarding the use of praise in improving performance. It seems that while praise improves performance on certain tasks, on others it can instead prove harmful. Imagine the situation in which the enthusiastic support of hometown fans expecting victory brings about the downfall of their team. In this situation, it seems that praise creates pressure on athletes, disrupting their performance.

Whether _____(A)_____ helps or hurts a performance depends on _____(B)_____.

	(A)		(B)
①	praise	…	task types
②	competition	…	quality of teamwork
③	praise	…	quality of teamwork
④	competition	…	task types

14 다음 글의 밑줄 친 부분 중 어법상 틀린 것은?

As we consider media consumption in the context of anonymous social relations, we mean all of those occasions that involve the presence of strangers, such as viewing television in public places like bars, ① going to concerts or dance clubs, or reading a newspaper on a bus or subway. Typically, there are social rules that ② govern how we interact with those around us and with the media product. For instance, it is considered rude in our culture, or at least aggressive, ③ read over another person's shoulder or to get up and change TV channels in a public setting. Any music fan knows what is appropriate at a particular kind of concert. The presence of other people is often crucial to defining the setting and hence the activity of media consumption, ④ despite the fact that the relationships are totally impersonal.

15 다음 글의 밑줄 친 부분 중 어법상 틀린 것은?

Many of us believe that amnesia, or sudden memory loss, results in the inability to recall one's name and identity. This belief may reflect the way amnesia is usually ① portrayed in movies, television, and literature. For example, when we meet Matt Damon's character in the movie *The Bourne Identity*, we learn that he has no memory for who he is, why he has the skills he does, or where he is from. He spends much of the movie ② trying to answer these questions. However, the inability to remember your name and identity ③ are exceedingly rare in reality. Amnesia most often results from a brain injury that leaves the victim unable to form new memories, but with most memories of the past ④ intact. Some movies do accurately portray this more common syndrome; our favorite *Memento*.

16 다음 빈칸에 들어갈 말로 가장 적절한 것은?

Much is now known about natural hazards and the negative impacts they have on people and their property. It would seem obvious that any logical person would avoid such potential impacts or at least modify their behavior or their property to minimize such impacts. However, humans are not always rational. Until someone has a personal experience or knows someone who has such an experience, most people subconsciously believe "It won't happen here" or "It won't happen to me." Even knowledgeable scientists who are aware of the hazards, the odds of their occurrence, and the costs of an event _____.

① refuse to remain silent

② do not always act appropriately

③ put the genetic factor at the top end

④ have difficulty in defining natural hazards

17 다음 글의 주제로 가장 적절한 것은?

The rise of cities and kingdoms and the improvement in transport infrastructure brought about new opportunities for specialization. Densely populated cities provided full-time employment not just for professional shoemakers and doctors, but also for carpenters, priests, soldiers and lawyers. Villages that gained a reputation for producing really good wine, olive oil or ceramics discovered that it was worth their while to specialize nearly exclusively in that product and trade it with other settlements for all the other goods they needed. This made a lot of sense. Climates and soils differ, so why drink mediocre wine from your backyard if you can buy a smoother variety from a place whose soil and climate is much better suited to grape vines? If the clay in your backyard makes stronger and prettier pots, then you can make an exchange.

① how climates and soils influence the local products

② ways to gain a good reputation for local specialties

③ what made people engage in specialization and trade

④ the rise of cities and full-time employment for professionals

18 밑줄 친 the issue가 가리키는 내용으로 가장 적절한 것은?

Nine-year-old Ryan Kyote was eating breakfast at home in Napa, California, when he saw the news: an Indiana school had taken a 6-year-old's meal when her lunch account didn't have enough money. Kyote asked if that could happen to his friends. When his mom contacted the school district to find out, she learned that students at schools in their district had, all told, as much as $25,000 in lunch debt. Although the district says it never penalized students who owed, Kyote decided to use his saved allowance to pay off his grade's debt, about $74—becoming the face of a movement to end lunch-money debt. When California Governor Gavin Newsom signed a bill in October that banned "lunch shaming," or giving worse food to students with debt, he thanked Kyote for his "empathy and his courage" in raising awareness of the issue. "Heroes," Kyote points out, "come in all ages."

① The governor signed a bill to decline lunch items to students with lunch debt.

② Kyote's lunch was taken away because he ran out of money in his lunch account.

③ The school district with financial burden cut the budget failing to serve quality meals.

④ Many students in the district who could not afford lunch were burdened with lunch debt.

19 청고래에 관한 다음 글의 내용과 일치하지 않는 것은?

The biggest heart in the world is inside the blue whale. It weighs more than seven tons. It's as big as a room. When this creature is born it is 20 feet long and weighs four tons. It is way bigger than your car. It drinks a hundred gallons of milk from its mama every day and gains 200 pounds a day, and when it is seven or eight years old it endures an unimaginable puberty and then it essentially disappears from human ken, for next to nothing is known of the mating habits, travel patterns, diet, social life, language, social structure and diseases. There are perhaps 10,000 blue whales in the world, living in every ocean on earth, and of the largest animal who ever lived we know nearly nothing. But we know this: the animals with the largest hearts in the world generally travel in pairs, and their penetrating moaning cries, their piercing yearning tongue, can be heard underwater for miles and miles.

① 아기 청고래는 매일 100갤런의 모유를 마시고, 하루에 200파운드씩 체중이 증가한다.
② 청고래는 사춘기를 지나면서 인간의 시야에서 사라져서 청고래에 대해 알려진 것이 많지 않다.
③ 세계에서 가장 큰 심장을 지닌 동물이면서, 몸집이 가장 큰 동물이다.
④ 청고래는 일반적으로 혼자서 이동하고, 청고래의 소리는 물속을 관통하여 수 마일까지 전달될 수 있다.

20 다음 글의 주제로 가장 적절한 것은?

In addition to controlling temperatures when handling fresh produce, control of the atmosphere is important. Some moisture is needed in the air to prevent dehydration during storage, but too much moisture can encourage growth of molds. Some commercial storage units have controlled atmospheres, with the levels of both carbon dioxide and moisture being regulated carefully. Sometimes other gases, such as ethylene gas, may be introduced at controlled levels to help achieve optimal quality of bananas and other fresh produce. Related to the control of gases and moisture is the need for some circulation of air among the stored foods.

① The necessity of controlling harmful gases in atmosphere
② The best way to control levels of moisture in growing plants and fruits
③ The seriousness of increasing carbon footprints every year around the world
④ The importance of controlling certain levels of gases and moisture in storing foods

21 다음 글의 밑줄 친 부분 중 문맥상 낱말의 쓰임이 가장 적절하지 않은 것은?

Even if lying doesn't have any harmful effects in a particular case, it is still morally wrong because, if discovered, lying weakens the general practice of truth telling on which human communication relies. For instance, if I were to lie about my age on grounds of vanity, and my lying were discovered, even though no serious harm would have been done, I would have ① <u>undermined</u> your trust generally. In that case you would be far less likely to believe anything I might say in the future. Thus all lying, when discovered, has indirect ② <u>harmful</u> effects. However, very occasionally, these harmful effects might possibly be outweighed by the ③ <u>benefits</u> which arise from a lie. For example, if someone is seriously ill, lying to them about their life expectancy might probably give them a chance of living longer. On the other hand, telling them the truth could possibly ④ <u>prevent</u> a depression that would accelerate their physical decline.

22 글의 흐름으로 보아 아래 문장이 들어가기에 가장 적절한 곳은?

Water is also the medium for most chemical reactions needed to sustain life.

Several common properties of seawater are crucial to the survival and well-being of the ocean's inhabitants. Water accounts for 80–90% of the volume of most marine organisms. (①) It provides buoyancy and body support for swimming and floating organisms and reduces the need for heavy skeletal structures. (②) The life processes of marine organisms in turn alter many fundamental physical and chemical properties of seawater, including its transparency and chemical makeup, making organisms an integral part of the total marine environment. (③) Understanding the interactions between organisms and their marine environment requires a brief examination of some of the more important physical and chemical attributes of seawater. (④) The characteristics of pure water and seawater differ in some respects, so we consider first the basic properties of pure water and then examine how those properties differ in seawater.

23 (A), (B), (C)의 각 네모 안에서 문맥에 맞는 낱말로 가장 적절한 것은?

Here's the even more surprising part: The advent of AI didn't (A) diminish / increase the performance of purely human chess players. Quite the opposite. Cheap, supersmart chess programs (B) discouraged / inspired more people than ever to play chess, at more tournaments than ever, and the players got better than ever. There are more than twice as many grand masters now as there were when Deep Blue first beat Kasparov. The top-ranked human chess player today, Magnus Carlsen, trained with AIs and has been deemed the most computerlike of all human chess players. He also has the (C) highest / lowest human grand master rating of all time.

	(A)	(B)	(C)
①	diminish	discouraged	highest
②	increase	discouraged	lowest
③	diminish	inspired	highest
④	increase	inspired	lowest

24 다음 글의 내용을 요약할 때 빈칸에 들어갈 말로 가장 적절한 것은?

Aesthetic value in fashion objects, like aesthetic value in fine art objects, is self-oriented. Consumers have the need to be attracted and to surround themselves with other people who are attractive. However, unlike aesthetic value in the fine arts, aesthetic value in fashion is also other-oriented. Attractiveness of appearance is a way of eliciting the reaction of others and facilitating social interaction.

⇩

Aesthetic value in fashion objects is _____ _____.

① inherently only self-oriented
② just other-oriented unlike the other
③ both self-oriented and other-oriented
④ hard to define regardless of its nature

25 글의 흐름으로 보아 아래 문장이 들어가기에 가장 적절한 곳은?

The great news is that this is true whether or not we remember our dreams.

Some believe there is no value to dreams, but it is wrong to dismiss these nocturnal dramas as irrelevant. There is something to be gained in remembering. (①) We can feel more connected, more complete, and more on track. We can receive inspiration, information, and comfort. Albert Einstein stated that his theory of relativity was inspired by a dream. (②) In fact, he claimed that dreams were responsible for many of his discoveries. (③) Asking why we dream makes as much sense as questioning why we breathe. Dreaming is an integral part of a healthy life. (④) Many people report being inspired with a new approach for a problem upon awakening, even though they don't remember the specific dream.

정답·해석·해설 p. 208

3회 2020년 법원직 9급
모바일 자동 채점 + 성적 분석 서비스 바로 가기

QR코드를 이용해 모바일로 간편하게 채점하고 나의 실력이 어느 정도인지, 취약 부분이 어디인지 바로 파악해 보세요.

(p.166에서 전체 정답표를 확인하실 수 있습니다)

제한시간 : 25분   시작 _____시 _____분 ~ 종료 _____시 _____분   나의 점수 _____   회독수 □□□

01 다음 글의 밑줄 친 부분 중 어법상 틀린 것은?

Recent research reveals that some individuals are genetically ① predisposed to shyness. In other words, some people are born shy. Researchers say that between 15 and 20 percent of newborn babies show signs of shyness: they are quieter and more vigilant. Researchers have identified physiological differences between sociable and shy babies ② that show up as early as two months. In one study, two-month-olds who were later identified as shy children ③ reacting with signs of stress to stimuli such as moving mobiles and tape recordings of human voices: increased heart rates, jerky movements of arms and legs, and excessive crying. Further evidence of the genetic basis of shyness is the fact that parents and grandparents of shy children more often say that they were shy as children ④ than parents and grandparents of non-shy children.

02 다음 밑줄 친 (A), (B), (C)에서 문맥에 맞는 낱말로 가장 적절한 것은?

South Korea is one of the only countries in the world that has a dedicated goal to become the world's leading exporter of popular culture. It is a way for Korea to develop its "soft power." It refers to the (A) [tangible / intangible] power a country wields through its image, rather than through military power or economic power. Hallyu first spread to China and Japan, later to Southeast Asia and several countries worldwide. In 2000, a 50-year ban on the exchange of popular culture between Korea and Japan was partly lifted, which improved the (B) [surge / decline] of Korean popular culture among the Japanese. South Korea's broadcast authorities have been sending delegates to promote their TV programs and cultural contents in several countries. Hallyu has been a blessing for Korea, its businesses, culture and country image. Since early 1999, Hallyu has become one of the biggest cultural phenomena across Asia. The Hallyu effect has been tremendous, contributing to 0.2% of Korea's GDP in 2004, amounting to approximately USD 1.87 billion. More recently in 2014, Hallyu had an estimated USD 11.6 billion (C) [boost / stagnation] on the Korean economy.

	(A)		(B)		(C)
①	tangible	…	surge	…	stagnation
②	intangible	…	decline	…	boost
③	intangible	…	surge	…	boost
④	tangible	…	decline	…	stagnation

03 다음 글에서 전체의 흐름과 가장 관계 없는 문장은?

The immortal operatically styled single Bohemian Rhapsody by Queen was released in 1975 and proceeded to the top of the UK charts for 9 weeks. ① A song that was nearly never released due to its length and unusual style but which Freddie insisted would be played became the instantly recognizable hit. ② By this time Freddie's unique talents were becoming clear, a voice with a remarkable range and a stage presence that gave Queen its colorful, unpredictable and flamboyant personality. ③ The son of Bomi and Jer Bulsara, Freddie spent the bulk of his childhood in India where he attended St. Peter's boarding school. ④ Very soon Queen's popularity extended beyond the shores of the UK as they charted and triumphed around Europe, Japan and the USA where in 1979 they topped the charts with Freddie's song Crazy Little thing Called Love.

04 (A), (B), (C)의 각 부분에서 어법에 맞는 표현으로 가장 적절한 것은?

Mel Blanc, considered by many industry experts to be the inventor of cartoon voice acting, began his career in 1927 as a voice actor for a local radio show. The producers did not have the funds to hire many actors, so Mel Blanc resorted to (A) [create / creating] different voices and personas for the show as needed. He became a regular on The Jack Benny Program, (B) [where / which] he provided voices for many characters—human, animal, and nonliving objects such as a car in need of a tune-up. The distinctive voice he created for Porky Pig fueled his breakout success at Warner Bros. Soon Blanc was closely associated with many of the studio's biggest cartoon stars as well as characters from Hanna-Barbera Studios. His longest running voice-over was for the character Daffy Duck—about 52 years. Blanc was extremely protective of his work—screen credits reading "Voice Characterization by Mel Blanc" (C) [was / were] always under the terms of his contracts.

*personas (극·소설 등의) 등장인물

	(A)	(B)	(C)
①	create	… where	… was
②	create	… which	… were
③	creating	… where	… were
④	creating	… which	… was

With the present plummeting demand market for office buildings, resulting in many vacant properties, we need to develop plans that will enable some future exchange between residential and commercial or office functions. This vacancy has reached a historic level; at present the major towns in the Netherlands have some five million square metres of unoccupied office space, while there is a shortage of 160,000 homes. At least a million of those square metres can be expected to stay vacant, according to the association of Dutch property developers. There is a real threat of 'ghost towns' of empty office buildings springing up around the major cities. In spite of this forecast, office building activities are continuing at full tilt, as these were planned during a period of high returns. Therefore, it is now essential that

_____ .

① a new design be adopted to reduce costs for the maintenance of buildings

② a number of plans for office buildings be redeveloped for housing

③ residential buildings be converted into commercial buildings

④ we design and deliver as many shops as possible

Child psychologists concentrate their efforts on the study of the individual from birth through age eleven. Developmental psychologists study behavior and growth patterns from the prenatal period through maturity and old age. Many clinical psychologists specialize in dealing with the behavior problems of children. Research in child psychology sometimes helps shed light on work behavior. For example, one study showed that victims of childhood abuse and neglect may suffer long-term consequences. Among them are lower IQs and reading ability, more suicide attempts, and more unemployment and low-paying jobs. Many people today have become interested in the study of adult phases of human development. The work of developmental psychologists has led to widespread interest in the problems of the middle years, such as the mid-life crisis. A job-related problem of interest to developmental psychologists is why so many executives die earlier than expected after retirement.

① 아동심리학의 연구대상은 주로 사춘기 이후의 아동이다.

② 발달심리학자들은 인간의 일생의 행동과 성장을 연구한다.

③ 아동기에 학대 받은 성인의 실업률이 더 낮은 경향이 있다.

④ 임원들의 은퇴 후 조기 사망이 최근 임상심리학의 관심사이다.

07 다음 글의 내용을 한 문장으로 요약하고자 한다. 빈칸 (A), (B)에 들어갈 말로 가장 적절한 것은?

One presentation factor that can influence decision making is the contrast effect. For example, a $70 sweater may not seem like a very good deal initially, but if you learn that the sweater was reduced from $200, all of a sudden it may seem like a real bargain. It is the contrast that "seals the deal." Similarly, my family lives in Massachusetts, so we are very used to cold weather. But when we visit Florida to see my aunt and uncle for Thanksgiving, they urge the kids to wear hats when it is 60 degree outside—virtually bathing suit weather from the kids' perspective! Research even shows that people eat more when they are eating on large plates than when eating from small plates; the same portion simply looks larger on a small plate than a large plate, and we use perceived portion size as a cue that tells us when we are full.

⇩

The contrast effect is the tendency to ____(A)____ a stimulus in different ways depending on the salient comparison with _____(B)_____ .

    (A)   (B)
① perceive ⋯ previous experience
② provide ⋯ predictive future
③ perceive ⋯ unexpected events
④ provide ⋯ initial impressions

08 다음 글의 밑줄 친 부분 중 문맥상 낱말의 쓰임이 가장 적절하지 <u>않은</u> 것은?

Most of the fatal accidents happen because of over speeding. It is a natural subconscious mind of humans to excel. If given a chance man is sure to achieve infinity in speed. But when we are sharing the road with other users we will always remain behind some or other vehicle. ① <u>Increase</u> in speed multiplies the risk of accident and severity of injury during accident. Faster vehicles are more prone to accident than the slower one and the severity of accident will also be more in case of faster vehicles. ② <u>Higher</u> the speed, greater the risk. At high speed the vehicle needs greater distance to stop—i.e., braking distance. A slower vehicle comes to halt immediately while faster one takes long way to stop and also skids a ③ <u>short</u> distance because of The First Law of Motion. A vehicle moving on high speed will have greater impact during the crash and hence will cause more injuries. The ability to judge the forthcoming events also gets ④ <u>reduced</u> while driving at faster speed which causes error in judgment and finally a crash.

*severity 심함

09 다음 글의 요지로 가장 적절한 것은?

It is first necessary to make an endeavor to become interested in whatever it has seemed worth while to read. The student should try earnestly to discover wherein others have found it good. Every reader is at liberty to like or to dislike even a masterpiece; but he is not in a position even to have an opinion of it until he appreciates why it has been admired. He must set himself to realize not what is bad in a book, but what is good. The common theory that the critical faculties are best developed by training the mind to detect shortcoming is as vicious as it is false. Any carper can find the faults in a great work; it is only the enlightened who can discover all its merits. It will seldom happen that a sincere effort to appreciate good book will leave the reader uninterested.

① Give attention to a weakness which can damage the reputation of a book.

② Try to understand the value of the book while to read before judging it.

③ Read books in which you are not only interested but also uninterested.

④ Until the book is finished, keep a critical eye on the theme.

10 다음 도표의 내용과 가장 일치하지 <u>않는</u> 문장은?

Majority of Americans say organic produce is healthier than conventionally grown produce

% of U.S. adults who say organic fruits and vegetables are _____ than conventionally grown produce

■ Better for health ■ Neither better nor worse ■ Worse for health

| 55 | 41 | 3 |

■ Taste better ■ Taste about the same ■ Taste worse

| 32 | 59 | 5 |

Note: Respondents who did not give an answer are not shown.
Source: Survey conducted May 10-June 6, 2016.
"The New Food Fights: U.S. Public Divides Over Food Science"
PEW RESEARCH CENTER

Most Americans are buying organic foods because of health concerns. ① More than half of the public says that organic fruits and vegetables are better for one's health than conventionally grown produce. ② More than forty percent say organic produce is neither better nor worse for one's health and the least number of people say that organic produce is worse for one's health. ③ Fewer Americans say organic produce tastes better than conventionally grown fruits and vegetables. ④ About one-third of U.S. adults say that organic produce tastes better, and over two-thirds of people says that organic and conventionally grown produce taste about the same.

11 밑줄 친 brush them off가 다음 글에서 의미하는 바로 가장 적절한 것은?

Much of the communication between doctor and patient is personal. To have a good partnership with your doctor, it is important to talk about sensitive subjects, like sex or memory problems, even if you are embarrassed or uncomfortable. Most doctors are used to talking about personal matters and will try to ease your discomfort. Keep in mind that these topics concern many older people. You can use booklets and other materials to help you bring up sensitive subjects when talking with your doctor. It is important to understand that problems with memory, depression, sexual function, and incontinence are not necessarily normal parts of aging. A good doctor will take your concerns about these topics seriously and not brush them off. If you think your doctor isn't taking your concerns seriously, talk to him or her about your feelings or consider looking for a new doctor.

*incontinence (대소변)실금

① discuss sensitive topics with you
② ignore some concerns you have
③ feel comfortable with something you say
④ deal with uncomfortable subjects seriously

12 다음 빈칸에 들어갈 말로 가장 적절한 것은?

Although we all possess the same physical organs for sensing the world—eyes for seeing, ears for hearing, noses for smelling, skin for feeling, and mouths for tasting—our perception of the world depends to a great extent on the language we speak, according to a famous hypothesis proposed by linguists Edward Sapir and Benjamin Lee Whorf. They hypothesized that language is like a pair of eyeglasses through which we "see" the world in a particular way. A classic example of the relationship between language and perception is the word snow. Eskimo languages have as many as 32 different words for snow. For instance, the Eskimos have different words for falling snow, snow on the ground, snow packed as hard as ice, slushy snow, wind-driven snow, and what we might call "cornmeal" snow. The ancient Aztec languages of Mexico, in contrast, used only one word to mean snow, cold, and ice. Thus, if the Sapir-Whorf hypothesis is correct and we can perceive only things that we have words for, the Aztecs perceived snow, cold, and ice as _____.

① one and the same phenomenon
② being distinct from one another
③ separate things with unique features
④ something sensed by a specific physical organ

13 글의 흐름으로 보아, 주어진 문장이 들어가기에 가장 적절한 곳을 고르시오.

> "Soft power" on the contrary is "the ability to achieve goals through attraction and persuasion, rather than coercion or fee."

The concept of "soft power" was formed in the early 1990s by the American political scientist, deputy defense of the Clinton's administration, Joseph Nye, Jr. The ideas of the American Professor J. Nye allowed to take a fresh look at the interpretation of the concept of "power," provoked scientific debate and stimulated the practical side of international politics. (①) In his works he identifies two types of power: "hard power" and "soft power." (②) He defines "hard power" as "the ability to get others to act in ways that contradict their initial preferences and strategies." (③) The "soft power" of the state is its ability to "charm" other participants in the world political process, to demonstrate the attractiveness of its own culture (in a context it is attractive to others), political values and foreign policy (if considered legitimate and morally justified). (④) The main components of "soft power" are culture, political values and foreign policy.

*contradict 부인하다, 모순되다

14 다음 글의 주제로 가장 적절한 것은?

The rapidity of AI deployment in different fields depends on a few critical factors: retail is particularly suitable for a few reasons. The first is the ability to test and measure. With appropriate safeguards, retail giants can deploy AI and test and measure consumer response. They can also directly measure the effect on their bottom line fairly quickly. The second is the relatively small consequences of a mistake. An AI agent landing a passenger aircraft cannot afford to make a mistake because it might kill people. An AI agent deployed in retail that makes millions of decisions every day can afford to make some mistakes, as long as the overall effect is positive. Some smart robot technology is already happening in retail. But many of the most significant changes will come from deployment of AI rather than physical robots or autonomous vehicles.

① dangers of AI agent
② why retail is suited for AI
③ retail technology and hospitality
④ critical factors of AI development

15 다음 빈칸에 들어갈 말로 가장 적절한 것은?

"_____" is the basic understanding of how karma works. The word karma literally means "activity." Karma can be divided up into a few simple categories—good, bad, individual and collective. Depending on one's actions, one will reap the fruits of those actions. The fruits may be sweet or sour, depending on the nature of the actions performed. Fruits can also be reaped in a collective manner if a group of people together perform a certain activity or activities. Everything we say and do determines what's going to happen to us in the future. Whether we act honestly, dishonestly, help or hurt others, it all gets recorded and manifests as a karmic reaction either in this life or a future life. All karmic records are carried with the soul into the next life and body.

① It never rains but it pours
② A stitch in time saves nine
③ Many hands make light work
④ What goes around comes around

16 다음 글에서 필자가 주장하는 바로 가장 적절한 것은?

Creating a culture that inspires out-of-the-box thinking is ultimately about inspiring people to stretch and empowering them to drive change. As a leader, you need to provide support for those times when change is hard, and that support is about the example you set, the behaviors you encourage and the achievements you reward. First, think about the example you set. Do you consistently model out-of-the-box behaviors yourself? Do you step up and take responsibility and accountability, focus on solutions and display curiosity? Next, find ways to encourage and empower the people who are ready to step out of the box. Let them know that you recognize their efforts; help them refine their ideas and decide which risks are worth taking. And most importantly, be extremely mindful of which achievements you reward. Do you only recognize the people who play it safe? Or, do you also reward the people who are willing to stretch, display out-of-the-box behaviors and fall short of an aggressive goal?

*mindful 신경을 쓰는, 염두에 두는

① 책임감 있는 리더가 되기 위해서는 보편적 윤리관을 가져야 한다.
② 구성원에 따라 다양한 전략과 전술을 수립하고 적용해야 한다.
③ 팀원들의 근무 환경 개선을 위해 외부의 평가를 받아야 한다.
④ 팀원에게 창의적인 사고를 할 수 있는 토대를 만들어줘야 한다.

※ 다음 글을 읽고 물음에 답하시오.   [17~18]

The dictionary defines winning as "achieving victory over others in a competition, receiving a prize or reward for achievement." However, some of the most meaningful wins of my life were not victories over others, nor were there prizes involved. To me, winning means overcoming obstacles.

My first experience of winning occurred in elementary school gym. Nearly every day, after the warm up of push-ups and squat thrusts, we were forced to run relays. Although I suffered from asthma as a child, my team won many races. My chest would burn terribly for several minutes following these races, but it was worth it to feel so proud, not because I'd beaten others, but because I had overcome a handicap. By the way, I (A) "outgrew" my chronic condition by age eleven. In high school, I had another experience of winning. Although I loved reading about biology, I could not bring myself to dissect a frog in lab. I hated the smell of anything dead, and the idea of cutting open a frog (B) disgusted me. Every time I tried to take the scalpel to the frog, my hands would shake and my stomach would turn. Worst of all, my biology teacher reacted to my futile attempts with contempt. After an (C) amusing couple of weeks, I decided get hold of myself. I realized that I was overreacting. With determination, I swept into my next lab period, walked up to the table, and with one swift stroke, slit open a frog. After that incident, I (D) excelled in biology. I had conquered a fear of the unknown and discovered something new about myself. I had won again.

Through these experiences, I now know that I appreciate life more if have to sacrifice to overcome these impediments. This is a positive drive for me, the very spirit of winning.

*asthma 천식 *dissect 해부하다 *futile 헛된, 효과 없는

17 윗글의 제목으로 가장 적절한 것은?
① What Winning Is to Me
② The Pursuit of Happiness
③ Winners in the Second Half
④ Narratives of Positive Thinking

18 밑줄 친 (A)~(D) 중에서 문맥상 낱말의 쓰임이 가장 적절하지 않은 것은?
① (A)   ② (B)   ③ (C)   ④ (D)

19 다음 글의 내용을 요약할 때 빈칸 (A), (B)에 들어갈 말로 가장 적절한 것은?

One classic psychology study involved mothers and their twelve-month-old babies. Each mother was with her baby throughout the study, but the mothers were divided into two groups, A and B. Both groups A and B were exposed to the same situation, the only difference being that group B mothers had to positively encourage their baby to continue playing with the thing in front of them, whereas the mothers in group A just had to be themselves in response to what their baby was playing with.

What were these babies playing with? An extremely large but tame python. The study went as follows: the children from group A were placed on the floor so the python could slither among them. As the fear of snakes is innate in humans but isn't activated until approximately the age of two, these babies saw the python as a large toy. As the group A babies started playing with the live python, they looked up to see what their mothers were doing. The mothers, who were told to be themselves, naturally looked horrified. Seeing the fear on their mothers' faces, the babies burst into tears. When it was group B's turn, as instructed the mothers laughed and encouraged their babies to keep playing with the python. As a result these babies were grabbing and chewing on the python, all because their mothers were supportive of their new toy.

*slither 미끄러져 가다

⇩

_____(A)_____ are learned, usually by children watching a parent's ____(B)____ to certain things.

	(A)		(B)
①	Rules of the game	⋯	support
②	Preferences for toys	⋯	participation
③	All phobias	⋯	reaction
④	Various emotions	⋯	encouragement

20 다음 글의 밑줄 친 부분 중, 문맥상 낱말의 쓰임이 가장 적절하지 <u>않은</u> 것은?

According to the modernization theory of aging, the status of older adults declines as societies become more modern. The status of old age was low in hunting-and-gathering societies, but it ① <u>rose</u> dramatically in stable agricultural societies, in which older people controlled the land. With the coming of industrialization, it is said, modern societies have tended to ② <u>revalue</u> older people. The modernization theory of aging suggests that the role and status of older adults are ③ <u>inversely</u> related to technological progress. Factors such as urbanization and social mobility tend to disperse families, whereas technological change tends to devalue the wisdom or life experience of elders. Some investigators have found that key elements of modernization were, in fact, broadly related to the ④ <u>declining</u> status of older people in different societies.

21 다음 글의 밑줄 친 부분 중 어법상 틀린 것은?

Rice stalks lower their heads when they are mature and corn kernels remain on the shoots even when they are ripe. This may not seem strange, but, in reality, these types of rice and corn should not survive in nature. Normally, when they mature, seeds should fall down to the ground in order to germinate. However, rice and corn are mutants, and they have been modified to keep their seeds ① <u>attached</u> for the purpose of convenient and efficient harvesting. Humans have continuously selected and bred such mutants, through breeding technology, in order ② <u>for these phenomena</u> to occur. These mutant seeds have been spread intentionally, ③ <u>which</u> means that the plants have become artificial species not found in nature, ④ <u>having bred</u> to keep their seeds intact. By nurturing these cultivars, the most preferred seeds are produced.

*germinate 발아하다　**cultivar 품종

22 (A), (B), (C)에서 어법에 맞는 표현으로 가장 적절한 것은?

First impression bias means that our first impression sets the mold (A) [which / by which] later information we gather about this person is processed, remembered, and viewed as relevant. For example, based on observing Ann-Chinn in class, Loern may have viewed her as a stereotypical Asian woman and assumed she is quiet, hard working, and unassertive. (B) [Reached / Having reached] these conclusions, rightly or wrongly, he now has a set of prototypes and constructs for understanding and interpreting Ann-Chinn's behavior. Over time, he fits the behavior consistent with his prototypes and constructs into the impression (C) [that /what] he has already formed of her. When he notices her expressing disbelief over his selection of bumper stickers, he may simply dismiss it or view it as an odd exception to her real nature because it doesn't fit his existing prototype.

	(A)		(B)		(C)
①	which	…	reached	…	that
②	which	…	having reached	…	what
③	by which	…	having reached	…	that
④	by which	…	reached	…	what

23 다음 글의 밑줄 친 부분 중, 어법상 틀린 것은?

The wave of research in child language acquisition led language teachers and teacher trainers to study some of the general findings of such research with a view to drawing analogies between first and second language acquisition, and even to ① justifying certain teaching methods and techniques on the basis of first language learning principles. On the surface, it is entirely reasonable to make the analogy. All children, ② given a normal developmental environment, acquire their native languages fluently and efficiently. Moreover, they acquire them "naturally," without special instruction, ③ despite not without significant effort and attention to language. The direct comparisons must be treated with caution, however. There are dozens of salient differences between first and second language learning; the most obvious difference, in the case of adult second language learning, ④ is the tremendous cognitive and affective contrast between adults and children.

24 다음 글의 밑줄 친 부분 중 문맥상 낱말의 쓰임이 가장 적절하지 <u>않는</u> 것은?

The American physiologist Hudson Hoagland saw scientific mysteries everywhere and felt it his calling to solve them. Once, when his wife had a fever, Hoagland drove to the drugstore to get her aspirin. He was quick about it, but when he returned, his normally ① reasonable wife complained angrily that he had been slow as molasses. Hoagland wondered if her fever had ② distorted her internal clock, so he took her temperature, had her estimate the length of a minute, gave her the aspirin, and continued to have her estimate the minutes as her temperature dropped. When her temperature was back to normal he plotted the logarithm and found it was ③ linear. Later, he continued the study in his laboratory, artificially raising and lowering the temperatures of test subjects until he was certain he was right: higher body temperatures make the body clock go faster, and his wife had not been ④ justifiably cranky.

*molasses 당밀   **logarithm (수학) 로그

25 다음 빈칸에 들어갈 말로 가장 적절한 것은?

Saint Paul said the invisible must be understood by the visible. That was not a Hebrew idea, it was Greek. In Greece alone in the ancient world people were preoccupied with the visible; they were finding the satisfaction of their desires in what was actually in the world around them. The sculptor watched the athletes contending in the games and he felt that nothing he could imagine would be as beautiful as those strong young bodies. So he made his statue of Apollo. The storyteller found Hermes among the people he passed in the street. He saw the god "like a young men at that age when youth is loveliest," as Homer says. Greek artists and poets realized how splendid a man could be, straight and swift and strong. He was the fulfillment of their search for beauty. They had no wish to create some fantasy shaped in their own minds. All the art and all the thought of Greece _____.

① had no semblance of reality
② put human beings at the center
③ were concerned with an omnipotent God
④ represented the desire for supernatural power

정답·해석·해설 p. 222

4회 2019년 법원직 9급
모바일 자동 채점 + 성적 분석 서비스 바로 가기

QR코드를 이용해 모바일로 간편하게 채점하고 나의 실력이 어느 정도인지, 취약 부분이 어디인지 바로 파악해 보세요.

(p.166에서 전체 정답표를 확인하실 수 있습니다)

제한시간 : 25분   시작 _____시 _____분 ~ 종료 _____시 _____분   나의 점수 _____   회독수 □□□

01 다음 글의 주제로 가장 적절한 것은?

Short-term stress can boost your productivity and immunity. But when stress lingers, you may find yourself struggling. People show some signs when they suffer from more stress than is healthy. First, you can't concentrate. In times of stress, your body goes into fight or flight mode, pouring its efforts into keeping safe from danger. That's why it may be hard to concentrate on a single task, and you're more likely to get distracted. "The brain's response becomes all about survival", says Heidi Hanna, author of *Stressaholic: 5 Steps to Transform Your Relationship with Stress*. "The fear response takes up all the energy of the brain for how to protect yourself." Second, you tend to get pessimistic. Because you're primed for survival, your brain has more circuits to pay attention to negatives than to positives. "When you're feeling overwhelmed by the chaos of life, take time to appreciate everything that's going well. You have to be intentional about practicing positivity", Hanna says.

① Advantages of short-term stress
② Why people keep distracted
③ Dangers of pessimism
④ Signs of excessive stress

02 다음 글의 빈칸 (A), (B)에 들어갈 말로 가장 적절한 것은?

Sometimes, the meaning of analogies may not be obvious. For instance, what comes to mind when you hear the phrase "white elephant" or "black sheep"? The expression "white elephant" comes from Thailand. Long ago, in Thailand, white elephants were very rare. Whenever one was found, it was given to the king. The king would then give it as a royal "gift" to someone he did not like since the beautiful animal cost a fortune to take care of. Nobody could refuse such a present, but it could financially ruin its owner. Moreover, it was a serious crime to mistreat a present from the king. Even riding it was not allowed, so a white elephant was almost useless. The expression, introduced in England in the 18th century, turned out to be useful for describing _____(A)_____ but _____(B)_____ public buildings. Today, it is used to refer to anything that might be _____(A)_____ and _____(B)_____ .

	(A)	(B)
①	valuable	–	unprotected
②	costly	–	worthless
③	extravagant	–	appropriate
④	priceless	–	eco-friendly

03 다음 글의 밑줄 친 부분 중 문맥상 낱말의 쓰임이 적절하지 <u>않은</u> 것은?

When asked, nearly everyone says the proper response to a compliment is "Thank you". But researchers found that when actually given a compliment, only a third of people accept it so ① <u>simply</u>. The difficulty lies in the fact that every compliment ("What a nice sweater!") has two levels: a gift component (accept or reject) and a content component (agree or disagree). The recipient is confronted with a ② <u>dilemma</u>— how to respond simultaneously to both: "I must agree with the speaker and thank him for the gift of a compliment while avoiding self-praise." Interestingly, women and men are both ③ <u>less</u> likely to accept a compliment coming from a man than from a woman. When a man says, "Nice scarf," a woman is more likely to respond ④ <u>affirmatively</u>: "Thanks. My sister knitted it for me." But when one woman tells another, "That's a beautiful sweater," the recipient is likely to disagree or deflect. "It was on sale, and they didn't even have the colour I wanted."

04 다음 글의 빈칸 (A), (B)에 들어갈 말로 가장 적절한 것은?

The chairperson should seek to have a progressive discussion that leads towards a consensus view. As the discussion develops, the chairperson should be searching to find the direction in which the weight of members' views is pointing. If, _____(A)_____, there are five members and the chair senses that two want to follow course A and a third follow course B, the focus should quickly be turned towards the remaining two members. The chair turns to member 4. If he or she wants course A, the chairperson simply has the job of getting first the other neutral (member 5) and then the dissenting member 3 to assent to the fact that course A is the majority view. If, _____(B)_____, member 4 wants course B, then member 5's view is the critical one, which the chairperson must now bring in. And so, very quickly, you can sense where the balance of opinion is pointing, and lead the meeting towards unanimous assent.

*consensus 의견 일치   **unanimous 만장일치의

	(A)	(B)
①	whereas	likewise
②	for example	therefore
③	whereas	for instance
④	for example	on the other hand

As early as 525 BCE, a Greek named Theagenes, who lived in southern Italy, identified myths as scientific analogies or allegories—an attempt to explain natural occurrences that people could not understand. To him, for instance, the mythical stories of gods fighting among themselves were allegories representing the forces of nature that oppose each other, such as fire and water. This is clearly the source of a great many explanatory or "causal" myths, beginning with the accounts found in every society or civilization that explain the creation of the universe, the world, and humanity. These "scientific" myths attempted to explain seasons, the rising and setting of the sun, the course of the stars. Myths like these were, in some ways, the forerunners of science. Old mythical explanations for the workings of nature began to be replaced by a rational attempt to understand the world, especially in the remarkable era of Greek science and philosophy that began about 500 BCE.

① Myths: Basis of Scientific Inquiry
② Dispelling the Myths about Science
③ How Are Creation Myths Universal?
④ How Much Myths Affect Our World Views

Every year in early October, Helsinki's harbor changes into a lively, colorful set for the Baltic Herring Festival, first held in 1743. Fishermen from all over Finland bring their latest catch to Helsinki to take part in one of Finland's oldest festivals. Sellers in bright orange tents line the harbor and sell herring in every imaginable form: fried, pickled, smoked, in bottles, in cans, in soup, on pizza, and in sandwiches. The choices are endless. On the first day of the festival, competitions are held to select the most delicious seasoned herring and the best herring surprise. Herring surprise is a traditional dish made with herring, cheese, and onions. The winner of each competition is awarded a trophy.

① The festival has been held in every second year since 1743.
② Sellers set up orange tents along the harbor and sell herring.
③ The competition of the festival is limited to Helsinki residents.
④ A trophy is only given to the winner of the best herring surprise.

As a youngster I shared a bedroom with my older sister. Although the age difference was slight, in intellect and maturity she viewed me from across the great divide. Her serious academic and cultural pursuits contrasted sharply with my activities of closely monitoring the radio shows. Because of these ① <u>dissimilar</u> interests and the limited resource of one bedroom between us, we frequently had conflict over what constituted disturbing and inconsiderate behavior. For months, there were attempts to ② <u>compromise</u> by "splitting the difference" in our divergent viewpoints or practicing "share and share alike." Even with written schedules and agreements plus parental mediation, the controversy persisted. Ultimately the matter was ③ <u>aggravated</u> when we both came to recognize that considerable time and energy were being wasted as we maneuvered and positioned ourselves for the next mathematical compromise. With recognition of a ④ <u>common</u> interest in solving the problem for our mutual benefit, we were able to think beyond physical resources of space, hours, and materials. The satisfying solution that met both of our needs was the purchase of earphones for the radio.

08 다음 글의 빈칸에 들어갈 말로 가장 적절한 것은?

One of the most popular of computer games in the world is called Age of Empires. For several months my own ten-year-old son was all but addicted to it. Its organizing premise is that the history of the world is the history of imperial conflict. Rival political entities vie with one another to control finite resources: people, fertile land, forests, gold mines and waterways. In their endless struggles the competing empires must strike a balance between the need for economic development and the exigencies of warfare. The player who is too aggressive soon runs out of resources if he has not taken the trouble to cultivate his existing territory, to expand its population and to accumulate gold. The player who focuses too much on getting rich may find himself _____ if he meanwhile neglects his defenses.

*exigencies 긴급 사태

① immune to illness
② tolerant to change
③ vulnerable to invasion
④ addicted to entertainment

09 다음 글에서 전체 흐름과 관계 없는 문장은?

Can an old cell phone help save the rainforests? As a matter of fact, it can. Illegal logging in the rainforests has been a problems for years, but not much has been done about it because catching illegal loggers is difficult. ① To help solve this problem, an American engineer, Topher White, invented a device called RFCx with discarded cell phones. ② When the device, which is attached to a tree, picks up the sound of chainsaws, it sends an alert message to the rangers' cell phones. ③ This provides the rangers with the information they need to locate the loggers and stop the illegal logging. ④ Destruction of the rainforest is caused by logging, farming, mining, and other human activities and among these, logging is the main reason for the nature's loss. The device has been tested in Indonesia and has proven to work well. As a result, it is now being used in the rainforests in Africa and South America.

10 다음 글의 제목으로 가장 적절한 것은?

In any symphony, the composer and the conductor have a variety of responsibilities. They must make sure that the brass horns work in synch with the woodwinds, that the percussion instruments don't drown out the violas. But perfecting those relationships—important though it is—is not the ultimate goal of their efforts. What conductors and composers desire is the ability to marshal these relationships into a whole whose magnificence exceeds the sum of its parts. So it is with the high-concept aptitude of Symphony. The boundary crosser, the inventor, and the metaphor maker all understand the importance of relationships. But the Conceptual Age also demands the ability to grasp the *relationships between relationships*. This meta-ability goes by many names—systems thinking, gestalt thinking, holistic thinking.

*marshal 모으다, 결집시키다

① The Power of Music
② Seeing the Big Picture
③ The Essence of Creativity
④ Collaboration Makes a Difference

11 다음 글의 밑줄 친 부분 중 어법상 옳지 <u>않은</u> 것은?

In criminal cases, the burden of proof is often on the prosecutor to persuade the trier (whether judge or jury) ① <u>that</u> the accused is guilty beyond a reasonable doubt of every element of the crime charged. If the prosecutor fails to prove this, a verdict of not guilty is ② <u>rendered</u>. This standard of proof contrasts with civil cases, ③ <u>where</u> the claimant generally needs to show a defendant is liable on the balance of probabilities (more than 50% probable). In the USA, this is ④ <u>referring</u> to as the preponderance of the evidence.

12 다음 밑줄 친 This system이 의미하는 바로 가장 적절한 것은?

In order to meet the demands of each course, Escoffier modernized meal preparation by dividing his kitchens into five different sections. The first section made cold dishes and organized the supplies for the whole kitchen. The second section took care of soups, vegetables, and desserts. The third dealt with dishes that were roasted, grilled, or fried. The fourth section focused only on sauces, and the last was for making pastries. This allowed restaurant kitchens to make their dishes much more quickly than in the past. If a customer ordered eggs Florentine, for example, one section would cook the eggs, another would make the sauce, and yet another would make the pastry. Then, the head chef would assemble the dish before it was served to the customer. <u>This system</u> was so efficient that it is still used in many restaurants today.

① The competition of the different sections in the kitchen
② The extended room for preparing the necessary ingredients
③ The distribution of the separate dishes to the customer by the head chef
④ The kitchen being divided into different sections to prepare a meal

13 다음 글의 내용을 한 문장으로 요약하고자 한다. 빈칸 (A), (B)에 들어갈 말로 가장 적절한 것은?

McAdams makes an important point about identity: It is a story you tell about yourself to make sense out of what has happened in the past and the kind of person you are now. From this perspective, it is not essential that the story be true. I see myself as culturally adventurous (that is, high on openness). I happen to believe this is true—that is, compared with others, I would be relatively open to trying new things on a menu, taking up new activities, visiting new places, and so on. But, from McAdams's perspective, when we're talking about identity, whether our beliefs about ourselves are true or not is pretty much irrelevant.

↓

According to McAdams, our identity is a(n) __(A)__ that we create, which in itself may or may not be __(B)__ .

	(A)	(B)
①	adventure	exciting
②	image	visible
③	door	available
④	narrative	factual

14 다음 밑줄 친 단어(어구)가 가리키는 대상이 나머지 셋과 다른 것은?

Watson had been watching ① his companion intently ever since he had sat down to the breakfast table. Holmes happened to look up and catch his eye.

"Well, Watson, what are you thinking about?" he asked.

"About you."

"② Me?"

"Yes, Holmes. I was thinking how superficial are these tricks of yours, and how wonderful it is that the public should continue to show interest in them."

"I quite agree," said Holmes. "In fact, I have a recollection that I have ③ myself made a similar remark."

"Your methods," said Watson severely, "are really easily acquired."

"No doubt", Holmes answered with a smile. "Perhaps you will ④ yourself give an example of this method of reasoning."

15 다음 글의 밑줄 친 부분 중 어법상 옳지 않은 것은?

In the 1860s, the populations of Manhattan and Brooklyn were rapidly increasing, and ① so was the number of the commuters between them. Thousands of people took boats and ferries across the East River every day, but these forms of transport were unstable and frequently stopped by bad weather. Many New Yorkers wanted to have a bridge directly ② connected Manhattan and Brooklyn because it would make their commute quicker and safer. Unfortunately, because of the East River's great width and rough tides, ③ it would be difficult to build anything on it. It was also a very busy river at that time, with hundreds of ships constantly ④ sailing on it.

16 다음 글의 밑줄 친 부분 중 어법상 옳지 <u>않은</u> 것은?

In recent years, peer-peer (P2P) lending has ① <u>become</u> the poster child of the alternative finance industry. In a 2015 report Morgan Stanley predicted that such marketplace lending ② <u>would</u> command $150 billion to $490 billion globally by 2020. P2P lending is the practice of lending money to individuals or businesses through online services that match lenders-investors directly with borrowers, ③ <u>enabled</u> both parties to go around traditional providers such as banks. Lenders typically achieve better rates of return, while borrowers—individuals and SMEs (small and medium-sized enterprises)—get access to flexible and competitively priced loans. For investors, the benefits are attractive. Being ④ <u>matched</u> with a borrower can take anywhere from a few days to a few hours. And where a bank might typically earn under 2% on personal lending, P2P returns can be more than three times that.

17 다음 글에 드러난 "I"의 심경으로 가장 적절한 것은?

So when I stood at the plate in that Old Timers game, staring at a pitcher whose hair was gray, and when he threw what used to be his fastball but what now was just a pitch that floated in toward my chest, and when I swung and made contact and heard the familiar *thwock*, and I dropped my bat and began to run, convinced that I had done something fabulous, forgetting my old gauges, forgetting that my arms and legs lacked the power they once had, forgetting that you age, the walls get farther away, and when I looked up and saw what I had first thought to be a solid hit, maybe a home run, now coming down just beyond the infield toward the waiting glove of the second baseman, no more than a pop-up, a wet firecracker, a dud, and a voice in my head yelled, "Drop it! Drop it!" as that second baseman squeezed his glove around my final offering to this maddening game.

① jealous
② delighted
③ passionate
④ disappointed

18 다음 글의 밑줄 친 부분 중 문맥상 낱말의 쓰임이 적절하지 <u>않은</u> 것은?

In our daily, conscious activity we generally experience a ① <u>separation</u> between the mind and the body. We think about our bodies and our physical actions. Animals do not experience this division. When we start to learn any skill that has a physical component, this separation becomes even ② <u>less</u> apparent. We have to think about the various actions involved, the steps we have to follow. We are aware of our slowness and of how our bodies respond in an awkward way. At certain points, as we ③ <u>improve</u>, we have glimpses of how this process could function differently, of how it might feel to practice the skill fluidly, with the mind not getting in the way of the body. With such glimpses, we know what to aim for. If we take our practice far enough the skill becomes ④ <u>automatic</u>, and we have the sensation that the mind and the body are operating as one.

19 다음 글의 밑줄 친 부분 중 어법상 옳지 <u>않은</u> 것은?

In 2000, scientists at Harvard University suggested a neurological way of ① <u>explaining</u> Mona Lisa's elusive smile. When a viewer looks at her eyes, the mouth is in peripheral vision, ② <u>which</u> sees in black and white. This accentuates the shadows at the corners of her mouth, making the smile ③ <u>seems</u> broader. But the smile diminishes when you look straight at it. It is the variability of her smile, the fact that it changes when you look away from it, ④ <u>that</u> makes her smile so alive, so mysterious.

20 글의 흐름으로 보아, 주어진 문장이 들어가기에 가장 적절한 곳은?

So around about the time we are two, our brains will already have distinct and individual patterns.

When we are babies our brains develop in relationship with our earliest caregivers. Whatever feelings and thought processes they give to us are mirrored, reacted to and laid down in our growing brains. (①) When things go well, our parents and caregivers also mirror and validate our moods and mental states, acknowledging and responding to what we are feeling. (②) It is then that our left brains mature sufficiently to be able to understand language. (③) This dual development enables us to integrate our two brains, to some extent. (④) We become able to begin to use the left brain to put into language the feelings of the right.

21 글의 흐름으로 보아, 주어진 문장이 들어가기에 가장 적절한 곳은?

Nowadays, it is much easier to find out where you are and which way to go because you have one of the world's greatest inventions at your fingertips.

For thousands of years, humans had difficulty trying to figure out where they were. (①) So, they devoted a great deal of time and effort to resolving this problem. (②) They drew complicated maps, constructed great landmarks to keep themselves on the right path, and even learned to navigate by looking up at the stars. (③) As long as you have a Global Positioning System(GPS) receiver, you never have to worry about taking a wrong turn. (④) Your GPS receiver can tell you your exact location and give you directions to wherever you need to go, no matter where you are on the planet!

22 다음 글의 빈칸에 들어갈 말로 가장 적절한 것은?

A great ad is a wonderful thing; it's why you love advertising. But what you're looking at is only half of what's there, and the part you can't see has more to do with that ad's success than the part you can. Before those surface features (the terrific headline or visual or storyline or characters or voiceover or whatever) can work their wonders, the ad has to have something to say, something that matters. Either it addresses real consumer motives and real consumer problems, or it speaks to no one. To make great ads, then, you have to start where they start: with _____.

① the effective tool
② the invisible part
③ the corporate needs
④ the surface features

23 글의 흐름으로 보아, 주어진 문장이 들어가기에 가장 적절한 곳은?

Wham-O, the visionary toy company known for its Hula-Hoops bought the rights a year later and renamed the flying disc Frisbee.

Walter Fredrick Morrison and his girlfriend, Lucile Nay, discovered that flying discs were marketable when a stranger asked to buy the metal cake pan they were flipping through the air on a beach in California. (①) By 1938, the couple were selling the 5-cent pans for 25 cents a piece. (②) Later, Morrison tried his hand at developing a flying disc far better than that of a flying cake pan. (③) Together with Franscioni, he created the Pluto Platter. (④) By the mid-1960s it got so popular that you could see a Frisbee stuck on almost every roof of houses.

24 다음 글의 빈칸에 들어갈 말로 가장 적절한 것은?

Paradoxically, the initial discovery of an interest often goes unnoticed by the discoverer. In other words, when you just start to get interested in something, you may not even realize that's what's happening. The emotion of boredom is always self-conscious—you know it when you feel it—but when your attention is attracted to a new activity or experience, you may have very little reflective appreciation of what's happening to you. This means that, at the start of a new endeavor, asking yourself nervously every few days whether you've found your passion is _____.

① relevant   ② necessary
③ premature   ④ uncommon

25 다음 글의 밑줄 친 부분 중 어법상 옳지 않은 것은?

After lots of trial and error, Richard finally created a system of flashing LED lights, ① powered by an old car battery that was charged by a solar panel. Richard set the lights up along the fence. At night, the lights could be seen from outside the stable and took turns flashing, ② which appeared as if people were moving around with torches. Never again ③ lions crossed Richard's fence. Richard called his system Lion Lights. This simple and practical device did no harm to lions, so human beings, cattle, and lions were finally able to make peace with ④ one another.

정답·해석·해설 p. 237

5회 2018년 법원직 9급
모바일 자동 채점 + 성적 분석 서비스 바로 가기

QR코드를 이용해 모바일로 간편하게 채점하고 나의 실력이 어느 정도인지, 취약 부분이 어디인지 바로 파악해 보세요.

(p.166에서 전체 정답표를 확인하실 수 있습니다)

01 다음 글의 밑줄 친 부분 중 문맥상 낱말의 쓰임이 적절하지 <u>않은</u> 것은?

All living things share basic characteristics. These common threads can be explained by descent from a common ancestor. Many kinds of evidence suggest that life began with ① <u>single</u> cells and that the present rainbow of organisms evolved from this common origin over hundreds of millions of years. In other words, the process of ② <u>evolution</u> explains the unity we observe in living things. The other striking thing about life on earth is its diversity. The same coral reef contains a multitude of animal species. Yet, each body type suits a ③ <u>particular</u> lifestyle. The process of evolution, which involves changes in the genetic material and then physical modifications suited to different environments, explains the ④ <u>unity</u> we observe in living things.

02 다음 글의 빈칸에 들어갈 내용으로 가장 적절한 것은?

A biology teacher cannot teach proteins, carbohydrates, fats, and vitamins, without having understood the basics of organic chemistry. The teacher while teaching the use of a thermometer can discuss various scales of measuring temperature. If he or she says that the body temperature of a healthy human being is 37°C and a student wants to know the temperature in Kelvin or Fahrenheit, then the teacher can satisfy the student only if he or she knows the process of converting one scale of temperature to another. In the same way, a chemistry teacher when teaching proteins, enzymes, carbohydrates, and fats, etc. should have some understanding of the human digestive system to be able to explain these concepts effectively by relating the topic to the life experiences of the learners. Thus, all branches of science _____.

① cannot be taught and learned in isolation
② converge on knowledge of organic chemistry
③ are interrelated with each learner's experiences
④ should be acquired with the basics of chemistry

03 다음 글에서 밑줄 친 표현의 쓰임이 문맥상 적절하지 <u>않은</u> 것은?

Left alone, Dodge quickly ① <u>lay down</u> on the burnt soil. As the flames approached him, he covered his mouth with a wet handkerchief in order not to ② <u>breathe in</u> the smoke. As the fire surrounded him, Dodge closed his eyes and tried to breathe from the ③ <u>thick</u> layer of oxygen that remained near the ground. Several painful minutes passed, and Dodge survived the fire, unharmed. Sadly, with the ④ <u>exception</u> of two men who found shelter in a small crack in a rock, all of the other men died in the awful fire.

04 글의 흐름으로 보아 아래 문장이 들어가기에 가장 적절한 곳은?

One population of Berwick's swans wintering in England put on fat more rapidly than usual, making them ready to begin their Siberian migration early.

Wherever human light spills into the natural world, some aspect of life—breeding, feeding, migration—is affected. Some birds—blackbirds and nightingales, among others—sing at unnatural hours in the presence of artificial light. (①) Scientists have determined that long artificial days—and artificially short nights—induce early breeding in a wide range of birds. (②) And because a longer day allows for longer feeding, it can also affect migration schedules. (③) The problem with them is that migration, like most other aspects of bird behavior, is a precisely timed biological behavior. (④) Leaving early may mean arriving too soon for nesting conditions to be right.

05 (A), (B), (C)의 각 네모 안에서 어법에 맞는 표현으로 가장 적절한 것은?

Once we emerge from childhood, eye contact actually becomes a very unreliable clue to deception. Why? The answer is that eye contact is very easy to control. Much of what happens to us when we feel nervous, such as getting sweaty hands or feeling dry in the mouth, (A) is / being uncontrollable. Most of us, however, have a great deal of control over (B) which / what we're looking at. Thus, many adults have little problem looking others in the eye while lying to them. Moreover, because skilled communicators know that people (C) equate / equating the lack of eye contact with deception, they deliberately maintain normal eye contact when they lie so the other person won't get suspicious. The eyes may be the windows to the soul, as the saying goes, but eye contact is no window to honesty!

	(A)	(B)	(C)
①	is	which	equate
②	being	which	equating
③	is	what	equate
④	being	what	equating

06 다음 갈등해결을 위한 조언으로 빈칸 (A)~(D)에 적절하지 <u>않은</u> 것은?

Tips for Conflict Resolution

(A)

Maintaining and strengthening the relationship, rather than "winning" the argument, should always be your first priority. Be respectful of the other person and his or her viewpoint.

(B)

If you're holding on to old hurts and resentments, your ability to see the reality of the current situation will be impaired. Rather than looking to the past and assigning blame, focus on what you can do right now to solve the problem.

(C)

Conflicts can be draining, so it's important to consider whether the issue is really worthy of your time and energy. Maybe you don't want to yield a parking space if you've been circling for 15 minutes. But if there are dozens of spots, arguing over a single space isn't worth it.

(D)

If you can't come to an agreement, agree to disagree. It takes two people to keep an argument going. If a conflict is going nowhere, you can choose to move on.

① (A) Make the relationship your priority.
② (B) Focus on the present.
③ (C) Weigh your words before speaking.
④ (D) Know when to let something go.

07 다음 글의 빈칸에 들어갈 내용으로 가장 적절한 것은?

By "scarcity," most of us mean that goods are in short supply: there isn't enough of something to go around. While there often is no clear-cut understanding of what constitutes "enough," the simple fact is that there is more than sufficient food to sustain everyone on the planet. The same is true of land and renewable energy. The important question, then, is why the staples of life are so unequally distributed—why, for example, the United States, with a little more than 5 percent of the world's population, uses approximately 40 percent of the world's resources. What appears to be a problem of scarcity usually turns out, on closer inspection, to be a problem of distribution. But mainstream economists _____: they talk only about whether a given system is productive or efficient, and it is up to us to ask, "For whom?"

① avert their eyes from this problem
② pay attention to reducing inequality
③ cling to solving distributional issues
④ have no interest in improving efficiency

08 다음 글의 내용을 요약할 때 빈칸 (A), (B)에 들어갈 말로 가장 적절한 것은?

Injuries sometimes occur when people do not take adequate carefulness with everyday activities. Although some such injuries occur because of pure carelessness or misfortune, others happen because the person did not want others to perceive him or her as too careful. For example, many people seem to avoid wearing seat belts in automobiles, helmets on bicycles and motorcycles, and life preservers in boats because such devices convey an impression of excessive carefulness. In addition, many people seem reluctant to wear protective gear (e.g., safety goggles, gloves, and helmets) when operating power tools or dangerous machinery because they will be viewed as nervous or extremely careful. This concern emerges at a young age; anecdotally, children as young as 6 or 7 years old are sometimes unwilling to wear knee pads and helmets when rollerskating because of what other children will think of them.

↓

Why do people get injured?
1. People lack _____(A)_____ .
2. People tend to take a risk of danger rather than be viewed as _____(B)_____ .

	(A)	(B)
①	vigilance	overcautious
②	inattention	intimidated
③	prudence	audacious
④	heedlessness	vulnerable

09 다음 글의 밑줄 친 부분 중 어법상 쓰임이 적절하지 <u>않은</u> 것은?

Performing from memory is often seen ① to have the effect of boosting musicality and musical communication. It is commonly argued that the very act of memorizing can guarantee a more thorough knowledge of and intimate connection with the music. In addition, memorization can enable use of direct eye contact with an audience ② who is more convincing than reference to the score. Those who "possess" the music in this way often convey the impression that they are spontaneously and sincerely communicating from the heart, and indeed, contemporary evidence suggests that musicians who achieve this ③ are likely to find their audiences more responsive. Moreover, when performers receive and react to visual feedback from the audience, a performance can become truly interactive, ④ involving genuine communication between all concerned.

10 다음 글의 밑줄 친 부분 중 문맥상 낱말의 쓰임이 적절하지 <u>않은</u> 것은?

Even though people seek both social status and affluence, their primary goal is to attain social status. A case can be made, in particular, that their pursuit of affluence is instrumental: they pursue it not for its own sake but because ① increased affluence will enhance their social standing. Why, after all, do they want the clothes, the car, and the house they long for? In large part because ② attaining these things will impress other people. Indeed, if there were no one around to impress, few would feel driven to live a life of ③ frugality, even if they could gain that without having to work for it. Likewise, if wealthy individuals found themselves living in a culture in which people ④ despised rather than admired those who live in luxury, one imagines that they would abandon their mansion and late-model car in favor of a modest home with an old car parked in the driveway.

11 다음 글에서 전체 흐름과 관계 없는 문장은?

It is generally believed that primates first appeared on Earth approximately 80 million years ago. Unlike reptiles, they were very sociable animals, creating a large community. ① One of the many ways in which the primates built a network of social support was grooming. ② In most cases, primates have visible folds that they would not have if they had, even lightly, groomed the area. ③ For instance, apes spent a large amount of time grooming each other. ④ Interestingly, in the case of Barbary macaques, the giving of grooming resulted in more stress relief than the receiving of grooming.

12 다음 글에서 전체 흐름과 관계 없는 문장은?

Most people agree that Plato was a pretty good teacher. He frequently used stories to teach people how to think. One story Plato used to teach about the limitations of democracy was about a ship in the middle of the ocean. On this ship was a captain who was rather shortsighted and slightly deaf. ① He and his crew followed the principles of majority rule on decisions about navigational direction. ② They had a very skilled navigator who knew how to read the stars on voyages, but the navigator was not very popular and was rather introverted. ③ As you know, it's not easy to communicate with introverted people, in particular, on the ship. ④ In the panic of being lost, the captain and crew made a decision by voting to follow the most charismatic and persuasive of the crew members. They ignored and ridiculed the navigator's suggestions, remained lost, and ultimately starved to death at sea.

13 다음 글의 빈칸 (A), (B)에 들어갈 말로 가장 적절한 것은?

Before the creation of money, people used to exchange something they had for something they needed. This system of exchange is called bartering. People traded things like animal furs, shells, beads for necklaces, and cloth. Later, people realized that some items were easier to trade than others, and those items became more common in bartering. _____(A)_____, people could trade gold for almost any other item because most people knew that it was valuable and that they could easily trade it again if they needed to. After some time, certain goods became the standard goods of exchange, and everyone began to trade with the same items. Eventually, the standard goods became money—one common unit of trade most people accepted and used in business and for their daily lives. _____(B)_____, some people still use the barter system today, especially in developing countries, where people exchange different kinds of food in order to survive.

	(A)	(B)
①	Furthermore	For instance
②	In other words	Besides
③	In contrast	However
④	For example	Nevertheless

14 다음 글의 빈칸 (A), (B)에 들어갈 말로 가장 적절한 것은?

Many people find it difficult to relate to someone who has a physical disability, often because they have not had any personal interaction with anyone with a disability.   (A)   , they might be unsure what to expect from a person who has a mobility impairment and uses a wheelchair because they have never spent any time with wheelchair users. This lack of understanding can create additional challenges for people with disabilities. If society responded more adequately to people who have impairments, they would not experience nearly as many challenges and limitations. Consider office workers who happen to use wheelchairs. Provided that there is only one level or there are ramps or elevators between levels, they may need no assistance whatsoever in the workplace.   (B)   , in an adapted work environment, they do not have a disability.

	(A)		(B)
①	However	–	Thus
②	In contrast	–	Similarly
③	Furthermore	–	In addition
④	For example	–	In other words

15 다음 글에 나타난 필자의 심경 변화로 가장 적절한 것은?

I was always mad at Charles even though I couldn't ever put my finger on exactly what he was doing to make me angry. Charles was just one of those people who rubbed me the wrong way. Yet, I was constantly upset. When we began looking at anger in this class, I thought, "What's my primary feeling about Charles?" I almost hate to admit what I found out because it makes me look like I'm a lot more insecure than I feel I really am, but my primary feeling was fear. I was afraid that Charles with his brilliance and sharp tongue was going to make me look stupid in front of the other students. Last week I asked him to stay after class and I just told him how threatened I get when he pins me down on some minor point. He was kind of stunned, and said he wasn't trying to make me look bad, that he was really trying to score brownie points with me. We ended up laughing about it and I'm not threatened by him anymore. When he forgets and pins me down now, I just laugh and say, "Hey, that's another brownie point for you."

* brownie point: 윗사람의 신임 점수

① relieved	→	irritated
② uneasy	→	relieved
③ calm	→	envious
④ frightened	→	indifferent

16 다음 글의 제목으로 가장 적절한 것은?

Amid the confusion and clutter of the natural environment, predators concentrate their search on telltale signs, ignoring everything else. There is a great benefit to this: When you specialize in searching for specific details, even cryptically colored prey can seem obvious. But there is also a cost to paying too close attention, since you can become blind to the alternatives. When a bird searches intently for caterpillars that look like twigs, it misses nearby moths that look like bark. The benefit of concealing coloration is not that it provides a solid guarantee of survival, but that it consistently yields a small advantage in the chance of living through each successive threatening encounter. At a minimum, even a tiny delay between the approach of a predator and its subsequent attack can help a prey animal escape. And at best, the prey will be completely overlooked.

① Predators in Disguise
② Beauty of Concentration
③ Camouflage: A Slight Edge
④ Merits of Specialized Search

17 글의 흐름으로 보아 아래 문장이 들어가기에 가장 적절한 곳은?

But let us say that the ranger who painted the sign meant to say just the opposite.

An ambiguous term is one which has more than a single meaning and whose context does not clearly indicate which meaning is intended. For instance, a sign posted at a fork in a trail which reads "Bear To The Right" can be understood in two ways. (①) The more probable meaning is that it is instructing hikers to take the right trail, not the left. (②) He was trying to warn hikers against taking the right trail because there is a bear in the area through which it passes. (③) The ranger's language was therefore careless, and open to misinterpretation which could have serious consequences. (④) The only way to avoid ambiguity is to spell things out as explicitly as possible: "Keep left. Do not use trail to the right. Bears in the area."

18 다음 글의 제목으로 가장 적절한 것은?

River otters have webbed toes, short legs, and tapered tails. For this reason, the river otter has a streamlined body, which helps it to move through the water very easily. Sea otters are near-sighted largely because aquatic life is much more important to them than terrestrial life. As a result, the sea otter is not as well-equipped for terrestrial life as for aquatic life.

① What Is Difference Between Aquatic and Terrestrial Life?
② Are Otters Aquatic or Terrestrial Animals?
③ Physical Characteristics of Sea Otters
④ Otter: A Perfect Terrestrial Life

19 밑줄 친 it 이 가리키는 대상이 나머지 셋과 다른 하나는?

Black pepper is one of the most widely used spices in the world. At first, it was cultivated in India as a simple ingredient for cooking. However, ① it became a lot more important to some Europeans who also used it for keeping meat from going bad. Until the 15th century, some cities in Italy were the center for trading black pepper. As the Ottoman Empire in the Middle East grew stronger in the 16th century, however, ② it forced the European traders to pay them a high tax. This made black pepper so expensive that only a few rich people could afford ③ it. In some parts of Europe, black pepper was even considered as valuable as gold. The great demand for ④ it caused Europeans to search for new sea routes to India.

20 다음 글의 빈칸 (A), (B)에 들어갈 말로 가장 적절한 것은?

In addition to the problems of individual resources, there are increasing links among energy, food, and water. As a result, problems in one area can spread to another, creating a _____(A)_____ circle. For instance, Uganda experienced a prolonged drought in 2004 and 2005, threatening the food supply. The country was using so much water from massive Lake Victoria that the water level fell by a full meter, and Uganda cut back on hydroelectric power generation at the lake. Electricity prices nearly doubled, so Ugandans began to use more wood for fuel. People cut heavily into forests, which _____(B)_____ the soil. The drought that began as a threat to food sources became an electricity problem and, eventually, an even more profound food problem. Cycles like these can end in political unrest and disasters for whole populations.

	(A)	(B)
①	vicious	fertilized
②	virtuous	deteriorated
③	destructive	degraded
④	constructive	undermined

21 다음 도표의 내용과 일치하는 문장은?

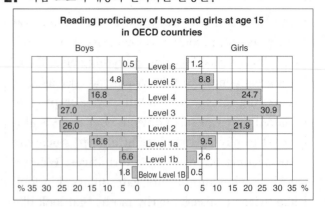

Reading proficiency of boys and girls at age 15 in OECD countries

This graph compares the percentages of male and female students in OECD countries who achieved various levels of reading proficiency at age 15. ① The percentage of girls is more than three times the percentage of boys at Below Level 1b. ② The percentage of girls is more than twice the percentage of boys at Level 5. ③ The difference between the percentages of boys and girls is smallest at Level 4 and greatest at Level 6. ④ The percentage of girls is always higher than that of boys at Level 3 and above, whereas the percentage of boys is higher than that of girls at Level 2 and below.

22 다음 글의 주제로 가장 적절한 것은?

Béla Bartók's *Duos for Two Violins* is characterized by dissonance. By employing dissonance in this work, Bartók tries to reveal the rich diversity of sounds. However, dissonance is a relative concept, and it needs to be understood in relation to consonance. Further, the dissonance prevalent in this work does not express disorder. Rather, it tries to evoke subtle harmony among individual sounds. This is mainly because dissonance can be perceived as an expression of harmonious individuality.

① ways of revealing diversity of sounds
② role of consonance in violin performance
③ importance of harmony in *Duos for Two Violins*
④ true meaning of dissonance in Béla Bartók's work

23 글의 흐름으로 보아 아래 문장이 들어가기에 가장 적절한 곳은?

> Nevertheless, Schulz believed in his work and did not change Peanuts.

These dull characters created by Charles Schulz attracted neither cartoon critics nor the people at Walt Disney, who didn't want to buy Peanuts. They said the characters did not inspire people to dream or encourage them to hope. (①) Even after it became popular in many newspapers, critics still thought the comic strip would fail, criticizing it for having uninteresting characters. (②) Some people said that Snoopy, the dog, should be taken out. (③) He even kept Snoopy, who is now one of the most loved cartoon characters of all time. (④)

24 다음 글의 밑줄 친 부분 중 어법상 옳은 것은?

Most of the time journalism cannot possibly offer anything but a fleeting record of events ① compiling in great haste. Many news stories are, at bottom, hypotheses about what happened. Science, of course, works by hypotheses, discarding them when errors are discovered, and it does so, on the whole, without blame, even when a mistake costs lives. The press, ② that lays no claim to scientific accuracy, is not easily forgiven its errors. Admittedly, the press often rushes into print with insufficient information, responding to an occasionally mindless hunger for news. A utopian society might demand that the press ③ print nothing until it had reached absolute certainty. But such a society, while waiting for some ultimate version of events, would be so rife with rumor, alarm, and lies ④ which the errors of our journalism would by comparison seem models of truth.

25 다음 빈칸에 들어갈 내용으로 가장 적절한 것은?

Children often invent novel ways to express desired meanings. In her 1995 article, linguist Clark cited such examples as a 24-month-old saying, "There comes the rat-man" and a 25-month-old saying, "Mommy just fixed this spear-page." The "rat-man" was a colleague of her father's who worked with rats in a psychology laboratory; the "spear-page" was a torn picture of a jungle tribe holding spears that her mother had taped together. Clark also cited the example of a 28-month-old saying, "You're the sworder and I'm the gunner." As these examples suggest, children's innovative uses of language are _____. They reflect rules for forming new words, such as combining words or other components that are meaningful in their own right and that, when put together, have an unambiguous meaning. Such linguistic creativity allows children to express meanings that are well beyond what their limited vocabularies would otherwise allow.

① impromptu
② quite arbitrary
③ far from random
④ results from endless drills

정답 · 해석 · 해설 p. 251

6회 2017년 법원직 9급
모바일 자동 채점 + 성적 분석 서비스 바로 가기

QR코드를 이용해 모바일로 간편하게 채점하고 나의 실력이 어느 정도인지, 취약 부분이 어디인지 바로 파악해 보세요.

(p.166에서 전체 정답표를 확인하실 수 있습니다)

제한시간 : 25분　시작 _____시 _____분 ~ 종료 _____시 _____분　**나의 점수** _____　**회독수** □ □ □

01 다음 글의 빈칸에 들어갈 말로 가장 적절한 것은?

Anthropologists believe wisdom teeth, or the third set of molars, were the evolutionary answer to our ancestor's early diet of coarse, rough food—like leaves, roots, nuts and meats—which required more chewing power and resulted in excessive wear of the teeth. The modern diet with its softer foods, along with marvels of modern technologies such as forks, spoons and knives, has made the need for wisdom teeth nonexistent. As a result, evolutionary biologists now classify wisdom teeth as vestigial organs, or body parts that have become functionless due to _____.

① dental decay　　　② evolution
③ hardness　　　　④ their shape

02 주어진 글 다음에 이어질 글의 순서로 가장 적절한 것은?

In today's technology-driven world, almost everyone, at some point in their lives, has either used or had some sort of contact with a microwave oven. Like many of the great inventions of our past, the idea behind the microwave oven was accidentally stumbled upon in 1946.

(A) Shortly after the accidental discovery, engineers at Raytheon went to work on Spencer's new idea, developing and refining it to be of practical use.

(B) Dr. Percy Spencer was working as an engineer with the Raytheon Corporation at the time, when he discovered something very unusual one day while working on a radar-related research project. While testing a new vacuum tube known as a magnetron, he discovered that a candy bar in his pocket had melted.

(C) Intrigued as he was, Spencer decided upon further experimentation. Later on, having pointed the tube at such objects as a bag of popcorn kernels and an egg, with similar results in both experiments (the popcorn popped and the egg exploded), he correctly concluded that the observed effects in each case were all attributed to exposure to low-density microwave energy.

① (A) – (C) – (B)　　② (B) – (A) – (C)
③ (B) – (C) – (A)　　④ (C) – (B) – (A)

03 다음 글의 밑줄 친 부분 중, 어법상 옳지 <u>않은</u> 것은?

To "win hands down" which means to "win easily" or "win with little or no effort" has ① <u>its</u> origins in horse racing. In a close, photo-finish race, a jockey ② <u>typically</u> strikes his horse with a bat or the reins to force it to maintain or increase speed. When the horse is leading by several lengths and a win is assured, the jockey will usually cease striking the horse or let the reins ③ <u>go</u> loose: In effect, he puts his "hands down." The expression ④ <u>was appeared</u> in the mid-19th century; by the end of the century, it was being used outside of horse racing to mean "with no trouble at all."

04 다음 밑줄 친 (A), (B), (C)에서 문맥에 맞는 낱말로 가장 적절한 것은?

In many ways, the differences between pairs of training shoe are marginal. Mr. Twitchell calls them fungible, "essentially interchangeable." But successive savvy advertising strategies turned a little Oregon sports outfitter into the globally (A) <u>dominant / dormant</u> sports giant Nike. Their swoosh logo is now one of the most recognizable images on the planet, rendering the actual name unnecessary. And while Nike may not have been the first company to seek (B) <u>celebrator / celebrity</u> plugs, its relationship with Michael Jordan is arguably the most successful endorsement in history. The release of the Just Do It motto in 1988 was a (C) <u>transparent / transformative</u> moment for the company, weaving their brand, seemingly forever, with the inspiring and dramatic physicality of sport.

	(A)	(B)	(C)
①	dominant	– celebrator	– transparent
②	dormant	– celebrator	– transformative
③	dominant	– celebrity	– transformative
④	dormant	– celebrity	– transparent

05 밑줄 친 he[him]가 가리키는 대상이 나머지 셋과 다른 하나는?

"There may be a devilish Indian behind every tree." said Goodman Brown to himself; and ① <u>he</u> glanced fearfully behind him as he added, "What if the devil himself should be at my very elbow!" His head being turned back, ② <u>he</u> passed a crook of the road, and, looking forward again, beheld the figure of a man, in grave and decent attire seated at the foot of an old tree. He arose at Goodman Brown's approach and walked onward side by side with ③ <u>him</u>. "You are late, Goodman Brown," said the man. "My wife kept me back a while," he replied, with a tremor in his voice, caused by the sudden appearance of ④ <u>him</u>, though not wholly unexpected.

06 다음 글의 밑줄 친 부분 중, 문맥상 낱말의 쓰임이 적절하지 <u>않은</u> 것은?

Our "ego" or self-conception could be pictured as a leaking balloon, forever requiring the helium of external love to remain ① <u>inflated</u>, and ever vulnerable to the smallest pinpricks of neglect. There is something at once sobering and absurd in the extent to which we are lifted by the attentions of others and sunk by their ② <u>disregard</u>. Our mood may ③ <u>brighten</u> because a colleague greets us distractedly or our telephone calls go unreturned. And we are capable of thinking life ④ <u>worthy</u> of living because someone remembers our name or sends us a fruit basket.

07 다음 글의 제목으로 가장 적절한 것은?

If a black hole has a non-zero temperature—no matter how small—the most basic and well-established physical principles would require it to emit radiation, much like a glowing poker. But black holes, as everyone knows, are black; they supposedly do not emit anything. This was the case until Hawking, in 1974, discovered something truly amazing. Black holes, Hawking announced, are not completely black. If one ignores quantum mechanics and invokes only the laws of classical general relativity, then as originally found some six decades previously, black holes certainly do not allow anything—not even light—to escape their gravitational grip. But the inclusion of quantum mechanics modifies this conclusion in a profound way, and Hawking found that black holes do emit radiation, quantum mechanically.

① What Happens inside Black Holes?
② Mystery of the Quantum World
③ The Birth of General Relativity
④ Is a Black Hole Really Black?

08 다음 글에서 전체 흐름과 관계 없는 문장은?

For the New World as a whole, the Indian population decline in the century or two following Columbus's arrival is estimated to have been as large as 95 percent. The main killers were Old World germs to which Indians had never been exposed, and against which they therefore had neither immune nor genetic resistance. ① Smallpox, measles, influenza, and typhus competed for top rank among the killers. ② For example, in 1837 the Mandan Indian tribe, with one of the most elaborate cultures in our Great Plains, contracted smallpox from a steamboat traveling up the Missouri River from St. Louis. ③ The Mandan survived mainly by hunting, farming and gathering wild plants, though some food came from trade. ④ The population of one Mandan village plummeted from 2,000 to fewer than 40 within a few weeks.

09 다음 글의 빈칸에 들어갈 말로 가장 적절한 것은?

Most of the world's great cities have grown randomly, little by little, in response to the needs of the moment; very rarely is a city planned for the remote future. The evolution of a city is like the evolution of the brain: it develops from a small center and slowly grows and changes, leaving many old parts still functioning. There is no way for evolution to remove _____ and replace it with something of more modern manufacture. The brain must function during the renovation. That is why our brain stem is surrounded by the R-complex, then the limbic system and finally the cerebral cortex. The old parts are in charge of too many fundamental functions for them to be replaced altogether. So they wheeze along, out-of-date and sometimes counterproductive, but a necessary consequence of our evolution.

* R-complex: (두뇌의) R영역
** limbic system: (두뇌의) 변연계
*** cerebral cortex: 대뇌피질

① the arrangement of new city streets
② the invasion of an alien substance
③ the advantage of natural selection
④ the ancient interior of the brain

10 주어진 글 다음에 이어질 글의 순서로 가장 적절한 것은?

> The "denotation" of a word is what the word literally means. *Blue*, for instance, means "the color of the sky on a sunny day."

(A) Likewise, We would like to have friends who are "true *blue*," to win a "*blue* ribbon", and to own "*blue*-chip stocks". But we might not like being called a "*bluenose*".

(B) As you see above, even a simple word naming a color can have a wide range of possible meanings, depending on how it's used. This is what is meant by connotation, the implied(suggested) meaning of a word.

(C) Beyond the denotation of the word, however, we also can find many other meanings in the name of the color. We usually do not like feeling *blue*, but we may enjoy hearing a great *blues* singer.

① (B) – (A) – (C) ② (B) – (C) – (A)
③ (C) – (A) – (B) ④ (C) – (B) – (A)

11 주어진 글 다음에 이어질 글의 순서로 가장 적절한 것은?

> "Begin with the End in Mind" is based on the principle that all things are created twice. There's a mental or first creation, and a physical or second creation to all things.

(A) If you want a family-centered home, you plan a family room where it would be a natural gathering place. You plan sliding doors and a patio for children to play outside. You work with ideas. You work with your mind until you get a clear image of what you want to build.

(B) Take the construction of a home, for example. You design it in every detail before you ever hammer the first nail into place. You try to get a very clear sense of what kind of house you want.

(C) Then you reduce it to blueprint and develop construction plans. All of this is done before the earth is touched. If not, then in the second creation, the physical creation, you will have to make expensive changes that may double the cost of your home.

① (A) – (C) – (B) ② (B) – (A) – (C)
③ (B) – (C) – (A) ④ (C) – (B) – (A)

12 주어진 글 다음에 이어질 글의 순서로 가장 적절한 것은?

Observations are not always undertaken with a clear sense of what data may be relevant. On a long and rough sea voyage in 1882, many of the ship's passengers were afflicted with seasickness.

(A) James speculated that seasickness must be due to some temporary disturbance of the inner ear, a problem to which the deaf mutes were not sensitive at all. Later experimentation, some carried out by James, confirmed this suspicion.

(B) This crucial clue about the causes of seasickness came thanks to James' ability to see the importance of something interesting that others had overlooked.

(C) One who was not was the American philosopher and psychologist, William James. James had the great good fortune to notice that 15 of the passengers, all of whom were deaf and mute, were completely unaffected.

① (A) – (C) – (B) ② (B) – (C) – (A)
③ (C) – (A) – (B) ④ (B) – (A) – (C)

13 다음 글의 내용을 한 문장으로 요약하고자 한다. 빈칸 (A)와 (B)에 들어갈 말로 가장 적절한 것은?

Umpires and other sports officials are the decision-makers and rulebook enforcers whose word is law on the field of play. Such authority comes with heavy responsibility to match. Sports officials must be unbiased masters of the rules and have thick skins. They must keep control of the conduct of games at all times, be good communicators, and stay cool in situations that can quickly grow heated—both on the field and in the stands. For every winner in sports there is a loser, of course, and the outcome may ride on a few crucial calls. Was that three-and-two pitch a ball or a strike? Was that last-second basket a buzzer-beater or not? While instant replay provides a fallback in professional and big-time college sports, officials at other levels are on their own. The stakes can be higher than just one game. High school athletes may hope for college scholarships, and key calls against them could hurt their chances when scouts are on hand. As one veteran high school official put it, "You never know who's in the stands."

The roles of umpires are so (A) that they can have (B) influence on players' individual future plans as well as the play at the field.

　　　　(A)　　　　　　(B)
① professional　　– slight
② expansive　　　– significant
③ ambiguous　　　– valuable
④ comprehensive　– positive

14 다음 글의 빈칸에 들어갈 말로 가장 적절한 것은?

Why would anyone be foolish enough to argue about the money supply? The more money, the merrier, right? Wrong. In slapstick movie, bumbling gangsters drop suitcases filled with bills, and bystanders dive past one another hoping to grab a few. The passer-bys always smile, but the bad guys wail and so do economists. Why do economists cry with the gangsters? A problem does not arise when just a few suitcases burst open. But if lots of luggage were to suddenly flood a town with bills, _____ might follow. If the amount of money overwhelms the capacity to produce goods, consumers, with more money to spend, bid up prices. The town is no wealthier than before; more bills do not bring a higher standard of living any more than if everyone added two zeroes to his or her salary.

① recession
② inflation
③ bankruptcy
④ unemployment

15 다음 글의 (A), (B), (C)의 각 밑줄 친 부분 중 어법상 낱말의 쓰임이 적절한 것을 바르게 나열한 것은?

Exactly how, when, why, and where the first maps came to be created is difficult to discover. Much of what was drawn in prehistoric and early historical times (A) [has / have] not survived, so what we find today may not be wholly representative of what was once there. There are other problems for the modern observer. Maps (B) [make / made] in prehistoric times cannot be accompanied by a title that explains the meaning of the drawing or that describes its content. However, we may be sure that in early times, just like today, maps were created for a variety of purposes and (C) [took / taken] a variety of forms. It may also be clear that, contrary to popular belief, of all the purposes to which maps have been put through the ages, the least important single purpose has been to find the way. Sea charts did not come into existence until the European Middle Ages, and topographical maps were not normally carried about by land travelers until the 18th century.

	(A)	(B)	(C)
①	have	make	taken
②	have	made	took
③	has	made	taken
④	has	made	took

16 글의 흐름으로 보아 주어진 문장이 들어가기에 가장 적절한 것은?

> Recordings at theaters around the world show that the pattern transcends different cultural habits and that different crowds all follow one universal curve showing how the sound rises over several seconds.

When the curtain closes at any stage theater, the audience bursts into applause. ㉠ It's usually a few clappers who hesitantly start on their own, and then others join in. ㉡ Applause is a funny thing in which each person tries to give credit to the performers, but also tries to blend into the crowd; you don't want to clap before everyone else, or to go on after others have stopped. ㉢ In fact, if you study it, you'll discover there is a pronounced pattern in the way an audience goes from silence to full volume of applause. ㉣ Even more remarkably, this curve is absolutely identical to a curve known from physics that describes how a group of atoms or molecules collectively go from one kind of behavior to another, rapidly and abruptly, because what one does depends very strongly on what others nearby do.

① ㉠
② ㉡
③ ㉢
④ ㉣

17 다음 글의 빈칸 (A), (B)에 들어갈 말로 가장 적절한 것은?

> Fifty years ago, bees lived healthy lives in our cities and rural areas because they had plenty of flowers to feed on, fewer insecticides contaminating their floral food and fewer exotic diseases and pests. Wild bees nested successfully in undisturbed soil and twigs. (A)_____, bees have trouble finding pollen and nectar sources because of the extensive use of herbicides that kill off so many flowering plants among crops and in ditches, roadsides and lawns. Flowers can be contaminated with insecticides that can kill bees directly or lead to chronic, debilitating effects on their health. (B)_____, with the increase in global trade and transportation, blood-sucking parasites, viruses and other bee pathogens have been inadvertently transmitted to bees throughout the world. These parasites and pathogens weaken bees' immune systems, making them even more susceptible to effects of poor nutrition from lack of flowers, particularly in countries with high agricultural intensity and pesticide use.

    (A)   (B)
① However – As a result
② However – In addition
③ Thus – By contrast
④ Thus – On the other hand

18 밑줄 친 (A), (B), (C)에서 문맥에 맞는 낱말로 가장 적절한 것은?

Sea foam forms when the ocean is agitated by wind and waves. Each coastal region has (A) differing / diffusing conditions governing the formation of sea foams. Algal blooms are one common source of thick sea foams. When large blooms of algae decay offshore, great amounts of decaying algal matter often wash ashore. Foam forms as this organic matter is churned up by the (B) surface / surf. Most sea foam is not harmful to humans and is often an indication of a productive ocean ecosystem. But when large harmful algal blooms decay near shore, there are potential for impacts to human health and the environment. Along Gulf coast beaches during blooms of Karenia brevis, for example, popping sea foam bubbles are one way that algal toxins become airborne. The resulting aerosol can (C) irrigate / irritate the eyes of beach goers and poses a health risk for those with asthma or other respiratory conditions.

	(A)	(B)	(C)
①	differing	– surface	– irrigate
②	diffusing	– surface	– irritate
③	diffusing	– surf	– irrigate
④	differing	– surf	– irritate

19 글의 흐름으로 보아, 주어진 문장이 들어가기에 가장 적절한 것은?

However, elevated levels and/or long term exposure to air pollution can lead to more serious symptoms and conditions affecting human health.

A variety of air pollutants have known or suspected harmful effects on human health and the environment. In most areas of Europe, these pollutants are principally the products of combustion from space heating, power generation or from motor vehicle traffic. ㉠ Pollutants from these sources may not only prove a problem in the immediate vicinity of these sources but can travel long distances. ㉡ Generally if you are young and in a good state of health, moderate air pollution levels are unlikely to have any serious short term effects. ㉢ This mainly affects the respiratory and inflammatory systems, but can also lead to more serious conditions such as heart disease and cancer. ㉣ People with lung or heart conditions may be more susceptible to the effects of air pollution.

① ㉠
③ ㉢
② ㉡
④ ㉣

20 다음 글의 빈칸 (A), (B)에 들어갈 말로 가장 적절한 것은?

Sea snakes are some of the most venomous creatures on Earth. Their venom is far deadlier than the venom of coral snakes, rattlesnakes, or even king cobras. Sea snakes use their venom to kill the fish they eat and to defend themselves against predators. It's not necessarily a good thing, however, for a sea snake to use its venom to defend itself. Venom can take a lot of energy to make—energy that could be used for growing or hunting. ____(A)____, the more often a sea snake or other venomous animal is attacked, the more likely it is to get hurt—even if it can defend itself. Like coral snakes, many sea snakes solve this problem by warning predators up front. ____(B)____, the yellow-bellied sea snake has bright, splashy colors that tell predators not to try anything. Over millions of years, predators have evolved to pay attention to this warning. Only a few kinds of sharks and sea eagles dare attack sea snakes. This keeps sea snakes from constantly having to defend themselves and increases their chances of survival.

	(A)	(B)
①	However	– In other words
②	Also	– By contrast
③	However	– In addition
④	Also	– For example

21 다음 글의 빈칸에 들어갈 말로 가장 적절한 것은?

Despite what you might think, _____ _____, according to research by psychologist Richard Wiseman. Instead, it's a result of the way lucky people think and act—which means that anyone can learn to be lucky! For instance, Wiseman found that lucky people always take notice of what's going on around them and stay open to new experiences and opportunities. Meanwhile, unlucky people tend to be tenser and too focused on certain tasks, which stops them from noticing opportunities they aren't explicitly looking for. So, next time you're heading to a party, don't go in with a goal in mind(no matter how much you want to attract someone). Instead, take things as they come and you never know what might happen. You could even make some awesome new friends.

① luck isn't matter of fate or destiny
② luck brings you closer relationships
③ luck can't be obtained at any costs
④ luck is the most precious asset for a person

22 다음 글의 빈칸에 들어갈 말로 가장 적절한 것은?

Coral reefs are some of the most diverse and valuable ecosystems on Earth. Coral reefs support more species per unit area than any other marine environment, including about 4,000 species of fish, 800 species of hard corals and hundreds of other species. Scientists estimate that there may be another 1 to 8 million undiscovered species of organisms living in and around reefs. _____ is considered key to finding new medicines for the 21st century. Many drugs are now being developed from coral reef animals and plants as possible cures for cancer, arthritis, human bacterial infections, viruses, and other diseases. Storehouses of immense biological wealth, reefs also provide economic and environmental services to millions of people. Coral reefs may provide goods and services worth $375 billion each year. This is an amazing figure for an environment that covers less than 1 percent of the Earth's surface.

① This biodiversity
② Their beauty
③ Survival skill of coral reefs
④ Food chain

23 다음 글의 목적으로 가장 적절한 것은?

Dear Charles,
It was a pleasure having lunch with you yesterday. I am very interested in the new household product you mentioned and how I might work with you develop it. I have seen nothing like it advertised in any of the trade journals, so it may be an original, one-of-a-kind product. If so, you will want to move fast to register it to protect your intellectual property rights in it. Let me know if you want to pursue this and I will have our patent associate contact you with a proposal.
Let's get together again soon.
Until then,
Frank

① 새로 구입한 가정용품을 환불하려고
② 새로 개발한 가정용품 구매를 요청하려고
③ 새로 개발한 가정용품에 대해 표창하려고
④ 새로 개발한 가정용품의 특허등록을 제안하려고

24 다음 글에서 필자가 주장하는 바로 가장 적절한 것은?

I have always taught my children that politeness, learning, and order are good things, and that something good is to be desired and developed for its own sake. But at school they learned, and very quickly, that children earn Nature Trail tickets for running the quarter-mile track during lunch recess. Or Lincoln Dollars for picking up trash on the playground or for helping a young child find the bathroom—deeds that used to be called 'good citizenship.' Why is it necessary to buy the minimal cooperation of children with rewards or treats? What disturbs me is the idea that good behavior must be reinforced with incentives. Children must be taught to perform good deeds for their own sake, not in order to receive stickers, stars, and candy bars.

① 아이들은 예절에 관한 교육을 잘 받아야 한다.
② 금전적이거나 물질적인 보상은 아이를 망친다.
③ 아이들이 보상 없이도 선행하도록 교육시켜야 한다.
④ 효과적인 교육을 위해서는 적절한 칭찬을 해주어야 한다.

25 다음 글에서 밑줄 친 낱말의 쓰임이 문맥상 적절하지 <u>않은</u> 것은?

Lead is a naturally occurring toxic metal found in the Earth's crust. Its widespread use has resulted ① <u>in</u> extensive environmental contamination, human exposure and significant public health problems in many parts of the world. Young children are particularly vulnerable to the toxic effects of lead and can suffer profound and permanent ② <u>adverse</u> health effects, particularly affecting the development of the brain and nervous system. Lead also causes long-term harm in adults, including ③ <u>decreased</u> risk of high blood pressure and kidney damage. ④ <u>Exposure</u> of pregnant women to high levels of lead can cause miscarriage, stillbirth, premature birth and low birth weight, as well as minor malformations.

정답·해석·해설 p. 265

7회 2016년 법원직 9급
모바일 자동 채점 + 성적 분석 서비스 바로 가기

QR코드를 이용해 모바일로 간편하게 채점하고 나의 실력이 어느 정도인지, 취약 부분이 어디인지 바로 파악해 보세요.

(p.166에서 전체 정답표를 확인하실 수 있습니다)

제한시간 : 25분   시작 _____시 _____분 ~ 종료 _____시 _____분   나의 점수 _____   회독수 □□□

01 밑줄 친 부분 중 의미하는 바가 아주 다른 것은?

The idea of ① using a product once or for a brief period and then replacing it runs counter to the grain of societies or individuals steeped in a heritage of poverty. Not long ago Uriel Rone, a market researcher for the French advertising agency Publicis, told me: "The French housewife ② is not used to disposable products. She likes ③ to keep things, even old things, rather than throw them away. We represented one company that wanted to introduce a kind of plastic throwaway curtain. We did a marketing study for them and found ④ the resistance too strong." This resistance, however, is dying all over the developed world.

02 다음 글에서 필자가 주장하는 바로 가장 적절한 것은?

Parents have to be optimists. They have faith in the world and its future, or they can't expect their children to have it. Without faith, it's like an Army captain muttering, "We'll never take that hill," before the battle begins. If you really feel that the world is in a hopeless mess, hide it. Whatever you say should be honest, but don't confuse honesty with total confession; not everything must be said. Don't share your uncertainties about the future with your adolescent. Allow him to explore the future on his own, with your support.

① 부모는 자녀의 능력에 관해 확신을 가지고 있어야 한다.
② 부모는 자녀에게 앞으로 생길 일들을 숨김없이 알려주어야 한다.
③ 부모는 자녀들이 자신의 미래를 스스로 개척하도록 도와주어야 한다.
④ 훌륭한 부모는 낙천적인 성격이고 미래에 대한 불안감이 전혀 없어야 한다.

03 다음 글의 밑줄 친 낱말의 쓰임이 문맥상 적절하지 <u>않은</u> 것은?

In 2009, *New York Times* reporter Matt Richtel earned a Pulitzer Prize for National Reporting with a series of articles ("Driven to Distraction") on the ① dangers of driving while texting or using cell phones. He found that distracted driving is ② responsible for 16 percent of all traffic fatalities and nearly half a million injuries annually. Even an idle phone conversation when driving takes a 40 percent bite out of your ③ focus and, surprisingly, can have the same effect as being drunk. The evidence is so ④ elusive that many states and municipalities have outlawed cell phone use while driving.

04 다음 글의 밑줄 친 부분이 의미하는 것으로 가장 적절한 것은?

Once upon a time, there was a snake that lived on a path leading from a village to a temple. The villagers were scared of it, so they threw stones at it and stepped on its home. Then the snake started to bite the villagers, and they stopped going to the temple. A monk who lived in the temple was unhappy about this, so he went to the snake and told it that it was wrong to bite people. The snake agreed and promised never to do it again. However, when the villagers realized that the snake was no longer dangerous, they started throwing stones at it and stepping on its home again. A few days later, the snake, hurt and bleeding, came to the temple to see the monk. 'What happened?' asked the monk. The snake said, 'No one is afraid of me now and the villagers treat me very badly!' The monk sighed. 'I told you not to bite,' he said. 'I didn't tell you not to hiss.'

① Using violence is okay whenever you are in trouble.
② Letting people know that you're angry doesn't help protect you and even makes a situation worse.
③ It's wrong to behave violently and hurt others, but it isn't wrong to express anger when someone treats you unfairly.
④ Just because the snake had agreed to stop biting people, that didn't mean that it was allowed to stay on a path leading to the temple.

05 다음 주어진 문장이 들어가기에 가장 적절한 곳은?

If the numbers continue to rise at the same rates, tobacco and a number of smoking-related diseases will be the world's biggest killer in just 15 years.

According to the World Health Organization (WHO), the world's biggest killer in 2030 will be something that is preventable, but voluntary. (①) Today, the WHO says that tobacco is the second major cause of death in the world, responsible for killing one in ten adults worldwide. (②) Developing countries are the most susceptible because eighty-four percent of all smokers currently live in middle to low income countries, where tobacco use has been increasing since 1970. (③) Though many governments have taken measures to ban public smoking and educate young potential smokers of health hazards, until tobacco products are entirely prohibited, it will ultimately be up to the individual to choose to take the risk or not. (④)

06 다음 글의 빈칸에 들어갈 말로 가장 적절한 것은?

The way in which we phrase our words has an enormous psychological impact on our reasoning. The most famous idiom to illustrate this point is to say that a glass is "half full" instead of "half empty." The positive connotations of a half-full glass allow for a more content and susceptible frame of mind, as opposed to the negative distancing effect of considering a glass half-empty. For instance, more people are likely to buy a box of cookies that are advertised as being 75% fat free than a box that was simply 25% fat. The subtle effects of carefully choosing our words are _____.

① selectively influential and limited
② from private and individual experiences
③ far-reaching and extraordinarily common
④ directly related to interpersonal relationships

07 글의 흐름으로 보아, 주어진 문장이 들어가기에 가장 적절한 곳은?

On the other hand, a marine mammal trainer may study and utilize knowledge from marine biology like anatomy, physiology or behavior.

We often hear people say, "I want to be a marine biologist so I can train dolphins." ① While it is true that some marine biologists do train dolphins, the descriptions for a marine biologist and a marine mammal trainer are really quite different. ② A marine biologist is someone who studies, observes, or protects marine organisms. ③ Generally, very few of these scientists train living marine mammal species themselves. ④ A marine mammal trainer is actually taught to specialize in each of these fields.

08 글의 흐름으로 보아, 주어진 문장이 들어가기에 가장 적절한 곳은?

These students may be confused after reading when their classmates can answer questions and they can't because they're not comprehending.

As they read through a short passage in a text, proficient readers accomplish many tasks; make predictions, infer information, visualize a scene, and generate questions. (①) They usually do these tasks without even realizing they are doing them. (②) But beginning readers often don't realize that they are supposed to do this, in part because they are focusing on decoding words. (③) Teachers tell the struggling readers to re-read, but they often do so with the same results. (④)

09 주어진 글 다음에 이어질 글의 순서로 가장 적절한 것은?

Most of us who have ever cleaned a house would be much happier if there was less dust. However, without dust there would be less rainfall and sunsets would be less beautiful.

(A) At the sunrise and sunset, the dust and water vapour molecules reflect the longer, red rays of light in such a way that we can see them for more time. The more dust particles in the air, the more colorful the sunrise or sunset.

(B) Thus water vapour would be much less likely to turn to rain without the dust particles. The water vapour and dust particles also reflect the rays of the sun.

(C) Rain is formed when water molecules in the air collect around particles of dust. When the collected water becomes heavy enough, the water droplets fall to the earth as rain.

① (A) − (C) − (B)　　② (B) − (A) − (C)
③ (C) − (B) − (A)　　④ (C) − (A) − (B)

10 다음 글의 내용을 한 문장으로 요약했을 때 빈칸 (A)와 (B)에 들어갈 말로 가장 적절한 것은?

Perhaps the biggest problem for men who want to do more with their children is that employers rarely make it easy for them. According to a recent study of 1,300 major corporations made by Catalyst, a career think tank for women, few companies pay more than lip service to the idea of paternal participation. More than 80 percent of the executives surveyed acknowledged that men now feel more need to share child-raising responsibilities—but nearly 40 percent also agreed that "realistically, certain positions in my firm cannot be attained by a man who combines career and parenting." While a quarter of the companies said they favored the idea of paternity leaves, fewer than one in ten actually offered them.

↓

A recent study shows that in reality it is difficult for men to share in ____(A)____ because of companies that rarely support ____(B)____ involvement in child rearing.

	(A)		(B)
①	parenting	–	paternal
②	parenting	–	executive
③	profession	–	paternal
④	profession	–	executive

11 다음 글의 밑줄 친 부분 중 어법상 틀린 것은?

Whatever route you choose, remember that climbing Kilimanjaro is a serious undertaking. While many hundreds of trekkers reach Uhuru Peak without major difficulty, many more don't make it because they ascend too quickly and suffer from altitude sickness. And every year a few trekkers die on the mountain. Come prepared with appropriate footwear and clothing, and most importantly, allow ① yourself enough time. If you're interested in reaching the top, seriously consider ② adding at least one extra day onto the 'standard' climb itinerary, no matter which route you do. ③ Despite paying an additional US$150 or so per extra day may seem like a lot when you're planning your trip, it will seem a relatively insignificant saving later on if you've gone to the expense and effort to start a trek and then need to come down without ④ having reached the top.

12 다음 글의 상황에 나타난 분위기로 가장 적절한 것은?

On a mid-September day, British climbers Rachel Kelsey and Jeremy Colenso were climbing in the Swiss Alps. They were both experienced climbers and when they left their base, the weather was good. They reached the summit, but as they started the climb down, an electric storm struck the mountain. Snow began to fall, making it difficult to see where they could put their hands and feet on the rock. After several frightening minutes, they found a narrow ledge and climbed on to it, hoping the snow would stop and they could continue their descent. The snow did not stop and the temperature dropped to −10℃.

① festive   ② mysterious
③ monotonous   ④ worrisome

13 다음 밑줄 친 it이 지칭하는 대상이 나머지 셋과 다른 것은?

One day, I looked out our dining room window to see our strawberry patch spreading its leaves and getting started with some new vines. Towards one edge of the area was one of those really spiky, thorny weeds. Figuring I'd grab ① it out of there when I had my yard-work gloves on, I got back to my housework and promptly forgot all about ② it. Time passed, and I glanced out of the window again to find a really spiky, thorny bush flourishing next to my strawberries, choking them out a bit. ③ It took a shovel to get that thing out! Why didn't I take care of it when I first saw ④ it? I guess I thought it wasn't going to get worse. It may seem silly to go after a little thing like a weed, but there is never just one little weed.

14 다음 글의 제목으로 가장 적절한 것은?

The origins of contemporary Western thought can be traced back to the golden age of ancient Greece in the sixth and fifth centuries BC, when Greek thinkers laid the foundations for modern Western politics, philosophy, science, and law. Their novel approach was to pursue rational inquiry through adversarial discussion: The best way to evaluate one set of ideas, they decided, was by testing it against another set of ideas. In the political sphere, the result was democracy, in which supporters of rival policies vied for rhetorical supremacy; in philosophy, it led to reasoned arguments and dialogues about the nature of the world; in science, it prompted the construction of competing theories to try to explain natural phenomena; in the field of law, the result was the adversarial legal system. This approach underpins the modern Western way of life, in which politics, commerce, science, and law are all rooted in orderly competition.

① Common Interests of Modern Societies
② The Importance of Adversarial Relationship
③ Contemporary Western Societies and Ancient Greece
④ The Cradle of Western Thought Based on Competition

15 주어진 글 다음에 이어질 글의 순서로 가장 적절한 것은?

The first brands were invented as a 'guarantee of quality'. Customers could feel safe that if they bought Sunlight soap, they were buying a safe and reliable product.

(A) Your preferred brand is an indication of your status. Talk to any user of an Apple computer.
(B) Today, brands have a similar function as a guarantee of quality. But brands have become more than just a simple guarantee. The brands you buy define who you are.
(C) Secretly or openly, they believe that they are different and slightly superior to Windows users. Apple, in their advertising, has reinforced this distinctive image.

① (B) − (A) − (C)　　　② (B) − (C) − (A)
③ (C) − (B) − (A)　　　④ (C) − (A) − (B)

16 주어진 글 다음에 이어질 글의 순서로 가장 적절한 것은?

Dinosaurs dominated the world 65 million years ago, until a comet 6 miles in diameter streaking 20 miles per second slammed into the Earth. The catastrophic collision instantaneously plunged the world into a very dark and cold nuclear winter that lasted for 12 months.

(A) Their flexibility allowed them to survive the Armageddon caused by the comet, and when the dust finally settled, the early mammals crawled out of their burrows, squinted at the warm sun, and evolved to become the dominant creatures of the Earth.
(B) They, though large and powerful, were cold-blooded and hairless, and proved incapable of adjusting to the radical climate changes including a sudden and sharp drop in temperature, and thus quickly died off in a mass extinction.
(C) In contrast, a group of small, furry, warm-blooded creatures (early mammals and our distant ancestors) proved to be superbly adjustable to the drastic changes.

① (B) − (A) − (C)　　　② (B) − (C) − (A)
③ (C) − (A) − (B)　　　④ (C) − (B) − (A)

17 다음 글에서 전체 흐름과 관계 없는 문장은?

It's easy to lose objectivity or to overlook errors, inconsistencies, or problems when you have focused too intensely or for too long on a particular task. You may have revised your essay so many times that you have forgotten what the question is, and your essay no longer adequately responds to it. ① Or you may have crafted what you think is a witty and clever remark, or an eloquent statement, while in reality you have just written something inappropriate. ② Also, even the best writers make grammatical and typographical errors, and spell-checking and grammar-checking software won't reveal every problem. ③ There is little possibility to misspell anything nowadays when there are computer programs available to help check grammar, spelling, punctuation and content. ④ Before typing that final version, by all means show your essays to a few other people—perhaps your peers or faculty advisor—to get their feedback.

18 다음 글에서 필자가 주장하는 바로 가장 적절한 것은?

When you ask for what you want, you're basically placing an order, just like an Amazon.com. But you have to be clear in your mind what you want. To get clear on what you want, make a list. Take out a notepad and scribble down whatever it is you want to have, do or be. Whether that's perfect health, great relationships, and awesome career, travel, or peace on Earth and goodwill to all men. Whatever you're hanging out waiting for. Just be clear in your mind what it is you want, because a confused mind creates a confusing order. And a confusing order could see Amazon.com accidentally sending you Timbaland instead of Timberlake.

① 원하는 것이 무엇인지 분명히 해라.
② 주문하기 전에 리스트를 작성해라.
③ 원하는 것이 많을 때는 기록해라.
④ 혼란스런 마음이 잘못된 주문으로 이어진다.

19 다음 글의 빈칸 (A), (B), (C)의 각 괄호 안에서 문맥에 맞는 낱말로 가장 적절한 것은?

The custom of sending greeting cards to friends and relatives for special occasions originated in England, where the practice was limited to people who could (A) [afford/attempt] to pay private messengers to carry their greetings across great distances. With the (B) [advent/abolition] of a British law that established inexpensive mail delivery, a market for sending greeting cards for birthdays, anniversaries—almost any occasion imaginable—opened up overnight. In America the card market was (C) [expanded/expended] by the founder of Hallmark Cards, whose company led the way in other products of social expression such as gift wrap, stationery, and calendars.

	(A)	(B)	(C)
①	afford	– advent	– expanded
②	afford	– abolition	– expended
③	attempt	– abolition	– expanded
④	attempt	– advent	– expended

20 다음 글의 저자가 주장하는 바로 가장 적절한 것은?

Recently I was consulting with a manufacturing company in direct competitive bid warfare with a lower-price opponent. My client was losing bid after bid. I said, "Something has to change here." They said, "It can't. We can't cut our prices any lower." I said, "If we can't come in with the lower bid, we might as well come in with an even higher bid—but let's change the rules of the game when we do it." They began changing the specifications for the bids, adding value, bundling goods and services together, extending warranties, and including delivery and completion guarantees. Then we built a "How to Compare Our Bid with Others Checklist." When it was all said and done, my client started getting projects the company had been losing to low bidders before.

① 설명서의 개선을 통하여 입찰가격을 낮출 수 있다.
② 입찰경쟁을 위해 프레젠테이션을 잘 준비해야 한다.
③ 입찰경쟁에서 이기려면 단가를 최대한 낮춰야 한다.
④ 입찰가격을 못 내리면 다른 부분의 질을 높여야 한다.

21 다음 중 글의 내용과 일치하는 것은?

By 1993 more than 56 million American households owned dogs, and consumers spent $15 billion on veterinary care, dog food, toys, accessories, and funeral arrangements. Not only do more Americans own dogs, but an unprecedented number of animals are enjoying elevated status as true members of the family. In a recent survey of ten thousand households, almost 70 percent of respondents said they would risk their own lives to save their dogs. A nearly equal number of people also said they would seek emergency medical care for their pets before obtaining it for themselves. Three-quarters of the respondents said they routinely give wrapped Christmas and birthday presents to their dogs.

① 1993년까지 5천 6백만이 넘는 미국 가구가 개를 키우고 15억 달러의 돈을 개를 돌보는데 소비했다.
② 미국에서는 많은 반려 동물들이 가족들보다 더 높은 지위를 즐기고 있다.
③ 최근 만 가구에 대한 설문 조사에서 응답자 중 약 70퍼센트가 자신보다 애완동물에게 먼저 응급 치료를 받도록 할 것이라고 말했다.
④ 전체 미국인들의 약 75%는 일상적으로 자신들의 개에게 포장된 성탄절 선물과 생일 선물을 준다고 말했다.

22 다음 글의 제목으로 가장 적절한 것은?

Web ads very frequently instruct users to *click here*. In online advertising, the imperative is an indicator of direct user addressing. As a matter of language use, these directive speech acts are not strict commands, which would be too offensive an addressing in the advertising context. Instead, they function as a kind of polite request with a reduced impact on interactants. The illocutionary force of the advertising message gives the users some space to act. In their implicit communication, it is initially the advertiser who wants something from the user, and not vice versa. Nevertheless, the use of imperatives is still far more forceful, more striking, and often shorter than a politely worded request or an indirect speech act that avoids imposing on the other. Online advertising needs to initiate an action, and for this reason, imperatives are employed. According to DoubleClick.com, the instruction *click here* tends to increase click rates by 15 percent.

① How People React to the Internet Advertising?
② Advertising DoubleClick.com for Better Sales
③ Why Internet Advertising Use Imperatives?
④ The Function of Internet Advertising

23 다음 밑줄 친 부분 중 문맥상 낱말의 쓰임이 적절하지 <u>않은</u> 것은?

Statistical studies in a broad spectrum of developing countries have provided strong support for the economic theory of fertility. For example, it has been found that high female employment opportunities outside the home and greater female school attendance, especially at the primary and secondary levels, are associated with significantly ① <u>lower</u> levels of fertility. As women become better educated, they tend to earn a larger share of household income and to produce fewer children. Moreover, these studies have confirmed the ② <u>strong</u> association between declines in child mortality and the subsequent decline in fertility. Assuming that households desire a target number of surviving children, increased female education and higher levels of income can decrease child mortality and therefore ③ <u>decrease</u> the chances that the firstborn will survive. As a result, fewer births may be necessary to attain the same number of surviving children. This fact alone ④ <u>underscores</u> the importance of educating women and improving public health and child nutrition programs in reducing fertility levels.

24 다음 글에서 Brutus가 주장하는 내용과 일치하지 <u>않는</u> 것은?

If there's anyone in this assembly, any dear friend of Caesar's, I say to him that my love for Caesar was no less than his. If, then, that friend demands to know why I rose against Caesar, this is my answer: it's not that I loved Caesar less, but that I loved Rome more. Would you prefer to die in slavery with Caesar living or would you be free with Caesar dead? As Caesar loved me, I wept for him. As he was fortunate, I rejoiced. As he was brave, I honored him. But as he was ambitious, I killed him. There are tears for his love, joy for his fortune, honor for his bravery, and death for his ambition. Who here is so base a man that he would want to be a slave? If any, speak, for I have offended him. Who here is so barbarous that he wouldn't want to be a Roman? If any, speak, for I have offended him. Who here is so wicked that he does not love his country? If any, speak, for I have offended him. I pause for a reply.

① Brutus의 Caesar에 대한 사랑은 그 어느 누구 못지않다.
② Caesar를 살해한 것은 Caesar보다 로마를 더 사랑해서이다.
③ Caesar가 죽게 되면 로마시민들은 노예의 처지에서 살게 된다.
④ Brutus는 설득력 있는 질문으로 Caesar 살해의 정당성을 주장한다.

25 다음 글의 주제로 가장 적절한 것은?

There is a widely held notion that does plenty of damage, the notion of 'scientifically proved.' It is nearly an oxymoron. The very foundation of science is to keep the door open to doubt. Precisely because we keep questioning everything, especially our own premises, we are always ready to improve our knowledge. Therefore a good scientist is never 'certain.' Lack of certainty is precisely what makes conclusions more reliable than the conclusions of those who are certain, because the good scientist will be ready to shift to a different point of view if better evidence or novel arguments emerge. Therefore certainty is not only something useless but is also in fact damaging, if we value reliability.

① Reliability values knowledge
② Scientific confidence is of no use
③ Changeable conclusions are infinite
④ Questioning worsens theoretical validity

정답·해석·해설 p. 280

(p.166에서 전체 정답표를 확인하실 수 있습니다)

01 다음 이메일의 제목으로 가장 적절한 것은?

Subject: _____

Inspired by the Special Olympics, this year's theme highlights competitive and charitable sports situations among Liz Claiborne, Inc., employees, their families, their friends. You might snap a shot of a friend or employee participating in a walkathon to raise funds, a five-mile run, or a company volleyball or soccer game. All Liz Claiborne, Inc., employees worldwide are encouraged to submit photos. The first, second, and third prizes will again be $500, $250, and $100.

Now's the time for you to start taking pictures focused on the spirit of competition for Liz Claiborne people and friends!

Because of the overwhelming number of entries last year, we're making one contest change this year. For further information call Rosemary at Extension 7645.

① The Special Olympic: Time and Place
② Annual Photography Contest of Liz Claiborne
③ Liz Claiborne's Advanced Service Quality
④ The Keynote Speech on Christmas Day

02 밑줄 친 it이 가리키는 대상이 나머지 셋과 다른 것은?

Anger makes problems for relationships when there is too much of ① it, and when people are unable to control the way they express it, and become, for instance, argumentative, aggressive, or violent. It also causes problems when people cannot express their anger and try to keep ② it hidden. It is normal, however, to feel angry at times, and it can also have useful effects. Anger can mobilize you to take action, for example, to set limits to the demands others make of you, to think about why something matters to you or to defend yourself if attacked. ③ It can be constructively expressed, and prompt you to explain what ④ it is that is distressing or alarming you, and to ask for what you need.

03 다음 글의 내용으로 보아 글의 종류로 가장 적당한 것은?

Are you embarrassed by excessive body hair or body hair in the most awkward areas? Well, you can remove unsightly, unwanted hair with laser hair removal treatment. Laser hair removal is a safe and effective medical procedure that uses laser light to remove unwanted hair painlessly within a few minutes. During the procedure, the laser passes through the skin and hits the hair follicle where hair growth originates. Thereafter, the intense heat destroys the hair follicle instantly, clearing the skin of any hair. Treat your legs, armpits, upper lip, chin, bikini line, and any other area. You can finally be free of unwanted body hair, so call our clinic today for more information.

① essay   ② novel
③ advertisement   ④ article

04 다음 글에서 필자가 주장하는 바로 가장 적절한 것은?

'Zero tolerance' is a phrase that first came to light as a description of the crackdown on trivial crime. The aim of zero tolerance is to prevent petty criminals graduating to serious crime by imposing immediate and harsh sentences for trivial offences such as under-age drinking, small-scale drug use and dealing, shoplifting or vandalism. I think 'Zero tolerance' is an innovative and effective weapon to fight against crime. It sends a clear, tough message that the state will condemn and punish rather than be soft and 'understanding'. This stance functions as an effective deterrent to potential offenders, especially potential young offenders, and also raises public confidence in the police and judiciary.

① 훈화를 통해 잘못을 개선시킴이 가장 중요하다.
② 범죄에 맞선 다양한 대처 방안이 필요하다.
③ 재활센터를 운영해 범법자가 사회에 적응할 수 있도록 도와야 한다.
④ 정부는 소소한 범죄 행위에도 강력하게 대처하여야 한다.

05 다음 글의 밑줄 친 부분 중 어법상 가장 옳지 않은 것은?

Across the nation, East Timor ① has been involved in conflicts for more than 30 years to gain independence from Indonesia. In a ② war-torn country, people with intellectual challenges are often forgotten and abandoned. Alcino Pereira, an intellectually challenged orphan from East Timor, ③ who is unable to speak, has never had access to health care. He can use one of his arms but only in a very limited way and walks with a limp. ④ Although these intellectual and physical challenges, he loves to run. In his worn-out shoes, Pereira runs every day in his home town of Dili. So he got his nickname, the "running man."

06 다음 글에 드러난 'I'의 심경으로 가장 적절한 것은?

I still remember the incident that happened last summer. We were staying at a country inn that had a small movie theater. Before every evening's presentation, my husband and I instructed our three-year-old son to sit quietly. Except for an occasional whispered question, he concentrated on the movie quietly. The soundtrack, however, was impossible to hear. That's because two children bounced on their seats, talked loudly and raced up and down the aisles. Never once did I see their parents. After several evenings of this, I followed the children to the dining room. There sat their parents enjoying a relaxed meal.

① annoyed and irritated
② regretful and apologetic
③ cold and indifferent
④ frightened and scared

07 다음 글의 제목으로 가장 적절한 것은?

A common but seriously hindering medical condition, stuttering is something that everyone wants to avoid if possible. Some people simply have a genetic predisposition towards stuttering, but there are other factors that contribute to it, though only a few are well understood. Learning a new language is often the cause for stuttering in children, but this is a rather benign form of stuttering. Some people have neurological problems that inhibit the proper brain functions regarding speech, and these problems are often the result of a stroke, accident, or some other trauma. However, the problem might be psychological, too, such as a severe lack of self-confidence or the presence of disproportionate stress. Also, behavioral disorders like autism and attention deficit disorder can lead to the speech disorder.

① The Common Symptoms of Stuttering
② Various Causes of Stuttering Conditions
③ The Factors that Aggravate Stuttering
④ The Harmful Effects of Stuttering

08 다음 글의 빈칸에 들어갈 말로 가장 적절한 것은?

Have you ever stopped and spent some time thinking about the two amazing machines located at the ends of your arms? Your hands are really incredible: they work all day, hardly ever taking a break, but they rarely get tired. And not only are your hands strong, they are also _____. Think about all the different things they do! They knock on doors and turn doorknobs. If you're hungry, they'll take the lid off a cookie jar and then put the cookies to your mouth! And if you are good at computer games, you can thank your hands for that, too. Whatever you are doing, your hands can help you.

① versatile
② tangible
③ eligible
④ genuine

09 다음 밑줄 친 단어의 쓰임이 적절하지 <u>않은</u> 것은?

Euphemisms are also problematic for English learners because they often contain more difficult words than their more direct ① counterparts. Learners of English, for instance, have to memorize that an old person can be referred to as "a senior citizen," while a police officer can be described as "a law-enforcement officer." They also have to learn to use euphemisms like "② vertically challenged" when they can get by with "short."
Despite the burden that euphemisms pose on learners of English, it is clear that euphemisms are tools which allow us to talk about all kinds of things in ③ impolite ways. As old euphemisms fall out of use and new ones come into use, English is ever ④ evolving to handle every situation, pleasant or unpleasant.

10 글의 흐름으로 보아, 주어진 문장이 들어가기에 가장 알맞은 곳은?

She recommended better meal planning, more protein and fresh vegetables, and supplements containing B vitamins, magnesium, and F-theanine.

Angie was always anxious and impatient. She regularly skipped meals and ended up driving through fast-food restaurants to eat just as her blood sugar was crashing. (①) Then she usually felt fuzzy brained and wanted to take a nap. (②) She eventually sought the advice of a nutritionally oriented physician for her bouts of fatigue. (③) Her response to eating more protein—a rotisserie chicken and steamed vegetables on the first day— was nothing short of dramatic. (④) Several months later, Angie's sister described her as a new person—she slept more soundly and woke up feeling alert and energetic.

11 다음 글의 빈칸에 들어갈 말로 가장 적절한 것은?

In a new study, it was found that species that live in restrictive environments such as the tropics cannot adapt to a changing climate as well as species in more diverse environments. The reason is _____. A species adapts to its environment and becomes better at surviving by undergoing physical and behavioral changes. These usually occur due to a gene mutation. If a species already has a more varied set of genes, it is more likely to undergo the necessary changes. However, species in the tropics have less varied sets of genes.

① destroyed environment
② isolation from their habitat
③ attack from their predators
④ the lack of variation in their genes

12 다음 글의 주제로 가장 적절한 것은?

Scientists are currently studying the navigational systems and locomotive strategies of insects to help design the next generation of autonomous robots and vehicles. Also, researchers have recently found that the flipper of the humpback whale is a more efficient wing design than the current model used by the aeronautics industry on airplanes. They are working to apply their findings to future airplane and automotive design. Similarly, engineers have used the rough skin of the shark as inspiration in developing a ridged foil coating for the wings of aircraft, a design which has resulted in six percent less friction and improved fuel efficiency.

① Borrowing from Nature
② The Wonders of Nature
③ The Future of Aerospace Industry
④ Why We Should Preserve Wild Life

13 주어진 글 다음에 이어질 글의 순서는?

President Roosevelt openly blamed the greed of many Americans for the Depression and acted to rectify the problem. At that time, people with a lot of currency or gold hoarded them and did not put them into banks because of the fear of losing their money.

(A) It also allowed the government to seize the gold of private citizens in exchange for paper money.
(B) This made the Depression worse because banks had no money and were forced to close.
(C) In response, Roosevelt enacted the "Emergency Banking Act" which worked to shut down insolvent banks so that they could be reconstructed.

① (B) − (A) − (C)　　② (B) − (C) − (A)
③ (C) − (A) − (B)　　④ (C) − (B) − (A)

14 다음 글의 목적으로 가장 적절한 것은?

Feel like a cup of tea, but don't have the time to brew one up? Take a "tea pill" instead. Indian tea scientists have produced a tea-flavored pill that can be chewed or quickly dissolved in hot or cold water. The brownish tablet weighs 0.3 grams and is composed of 80 percent tea and 20 percent their flavors. The inventors at the research center say that it peps you up just like a traditional tea. "You can suck it, chew it, or dissolve it in water the way you like to have it, and still feel the taste of a real cup of tea," they said. "As the liquid tea refreshes, this tea pill will also refresh people because it contains pure tea ingredients." They said the center had applied for a patent, and that the pill should hit the market in six months.

① 차의 성분과 효능을 알리려고
② 차의 유래와 역사를 설명하려고
③ 약 복용 시 주의사항을 알리려고
④ 새로 시판될 알약 형태의 차를 소개하려고

15 다음 중 글의 내용과 일치하지 않는 것은?

Heart attacks, which take about 550,000 lives each year, occur when the coronary arteries that supply blood to the heart muscle become obstructed. Without oxygen and other nutrients carried in the blood, heart tissue dies or is damaged. If too much tissue is affected, the heart is so weakened that it cannot pump. But even mild damage can kill by disrupting the electrical impulses that govern the heart's rhythmic beating. Each year, stroke claims another 170,000 lives, and is also caused by impeded blood flow, this time to the brain.

* coronary artery : 심장의 관상동맥

① 심장마비는 관상동맥이 막힐 때 발생한다.
② 산소가 없으면, 심장 조직이 손상을 입는다.
③ 심장 조직이 약간 손상되는 경우에는 큰 위험이 없다.
④ 뇌졸중은 매년 170,000명의 생명을 앗아간다.

16 다음 밑줄 친 부분 중, 지칭하는 대상이 나머지 셋과 다른 하나는?

It's my Aunt Grace's practice to travel by bus and to notice what ① <u>most people</u> miss. One Saturday morning the 144 bus passed a busy intersection. She saw two young girls outfitted for camping. They looked nervous. When her bus arrived at the next intersection, she saw two young men outfitted in the same manner standing by a car. They were waiting for an appointment. Grace got off the bus and approached the young men. They spoke to her in a foreign accent. Grace described the girls she had seen, and the young men left. When ② <u>the small happy band</u> returned to thank her, what she had supposed was confirmed. There had, indeed, been a mix-up! Anxious to return good for good, ③ <u>the chattering little group</u> insisted they be allowed to take her home. Grace refused. Instead, the young people crossed the avenue to gift shop and returned with a little cotton elephant. Now there is a remembrance in Grace's apartment, but there are also ④ <u>four young people</u> who are bound to remember a friendly lady.

17 다음 글의 빈칸에 들어갈 말로 가장 적절한 것은?

Despite progress in the field of child and adolescent mental health, millions of young people every year do not get proper help. Only one in five children with a serious emotional disturbance actually uses specialized mental health services. Although today, child welfare services, the juvenile justice system, and our schools often provide care to children in need, none of these institutions has as its first priority the delivery of mental health care. In addition, the complexity of promoting collaboration across agency lines of all professionals serving the same child is daunting. All too often there is no cooperation, not enough money, and limited access to trained mental health professionals—and children and their families _____.

① require their rights
② receive good health services
③ suffer the tragic consequences
④ are reluctant to go to hospitals

18 다음 글의 밑줄 친 부분 중, 어법상 가장 옳지 <u>않은</u> 것은?

People who are satisfied appreciate what they have in life and don't worry about how it compares to ① <u>which</u> others have. Valuing what you have over what you do not or cannot have ② <u>leads</u> to greater happiness. Four-year-old Alice runs to the Christmas tree and sees wonderful presents beneath it. No doubt she has received fewer presents ③ <u>than</u> some of her friends, and she probably has not received some of the things she most wanted. But at that moment, she doesn't ④ <u>stop to think</u> why there aren't more presents or to wonder what she may have asked for that she didn't get. Instead, she marvels at the treasures before her.

19 주어진 문장에 이어질 글의 순서로 가장 적절한 것은?

It would be hard to find anything more controversial than the subject of cloning. People find it either totally fantastic or totally frightening.

(A) But for most people, the cloning of humans is different. The idea of duplicating human beings the same way we make copies of book pages on a copy machine is terrible.

(B) In addition, it could be useful in increasing the world's food supply by the cloning of animals. Bigger and healthier animals could be produced.

(C) Cloning holds the promise of cures for what are now incurable diseases, sight for the blind, hearing for the deaf, new organs to replace old worn-out ones.

① (A) – (C) – (B) ② (B) – (A) – (C)
③ (C) – (A) – (B) ④ (C) – (B) – (A)

20 글의 흐름상 밑줄 친 부분이 문맥에 맞지 않는 것은?

Britain caused hardship in the Indian cloth industry by putting a 30 percent import tax on Indian cloth. This made Indian cloth too ① expensive to sell in Britain. When the Indian lost their British customers, their cloth industry was ruined. Then British cloth factories profited by selling British cloth to the Indians. The Indian people were ② discontent under British rule. In 1930 Mohandas Gandhi took up the cause of Indian independence. He encouraged Indians to protest in nonviolent ways. He encouraged them not to pay taxes to the British, and he ③ resisted a boycott of British-made product. After great struggle, both nonviolent and violent, the British ④ withdrew, and in 1947 India became a self-governing, independent country.

① expensive ② discontent
③ resisted ④ withdrew

21 다음 글의 제목으로 가장 알맞은 것은?

A study by the USA's Northwestern University provides biological evidence that people who are bilingual have a more powerful brain. Drs Viorica Marian and Nina Kraus investigated how bilingualism affects the brain. They found that studying another language "fine-tunes" people's attention span and enhances their memory. In particular they discovered that when language learners attempt to understand speech in another language, it activates and energizes the brainstem—an ancient part of the brain. Professor Kraus stated: "Bilingualism serves as enrichment for the brain and has real consequences when it comes to attention and working memory."

① The Effect of Bilingualism on Brain
② Tips for Learning Foreign Languages
③ The Negative Effect of Bilingualism
④ The Necessity of Learning Foreign Languages

22 다음 문장이 들어갈 위치로 가장 적절한 곳은?

However, poor people began making their own boxes and asking employers and customers for money in recognition of their service.

Have you ever heard of Boxing Day? It's a holiday celebrated in the United Kingdom and British Commonwealth countries on December 26 every year. (①) Some people say that the ancient Roman tradition of gift giving during the winter festival inspired Boxing Day, but no one knows for certain. (②) This gift giving eventually took the form of placing alms boxes in churches on Christmas Day so that people could drop coins into them for later distribution to poor people. These early "Christmas Boxes" were made of clay and had holes cut in their tops but no 'stoppers' at the bottoms. It was "smashing fun" opening them! (③) During the seventeenth century, the alms-box of giving stopped. (④) From that time on, it became a tradition to give money to delivery people and other service workers on Boxing Day.

23 다음 (A), (B), (C)에서 문맥에 맞는 낱말로 가장 적절한 것은?

Companies often seek the services of well-known sports or entertainment personalities to promote their products. Although this is a good practice when the person embodies wholesome qualities, it can backfire when the person engages in scandalous or (A) moral / immoral behavior. In such cases, the public comes to associate antisocial behavior with the product, and will avoid buying it. It is advisable that before deciding whom to star, a complete background check be made. If a person has exhibited (B) desirable / undesirable behavior in the past, he will probably exhibit undesirable behavior in the future. Also, the contract should cancel automatically, should the personality bring (C) credit / discredit to the product advertised.

	(A)	(B)	(C)
①	moral	– desirable	– credit
②	moral	– desirable	– discredit
③	immoral	– undesirable	– credit
④	immoral	– undesirable	– discredit

24 주어진 글 다음에 이어질 글의 순서는?

The only way for different marine animals to survive in their harsh aquatic environment is to help each other. This is especially true in the case of the clownfish and the poisonous sea anemone.

(A) Other fish, fearing the anemone's poison, won't attack the clownfish there.

(B) On the other hand, the anemone benefits by eating leftover food provided by the clownfish.

(C) In return for cleaning the anemone, the clownfish, which is not affected by the anemone's poison, lives safely among the animal's tentacles.

① (B) – (A) – (C)   ② (B) – (C) – (A)
③ (C) – (A) – (B)   ④ (C) – (B) – (A)

25 다음 글의 요지로 가장 적절한 것은?

ABC Airlines uses the same scent everywhere, for instance, in the perfume worn by its flight attendants, in its hot towels, and in other elements of its service. Among the sensory elements, using a scent is a relatively recent marketing strategy adopted by many retailers. More and more research shows that smell affects consumer behavior, which stimulates the demand for scent marketing by stores, hotels, and even museums. Advertising studies in Martin Lindstrom's book *Brand Sense* suggest that although most contemporary commercial messages are aimed at our eyes, many of the emotional moments people remember on a given day are actually prompted by smell.

① Certain scents energize us for work.

② Sense of sight is mightier than sense of smell.

③ The demand for scent marketing is increasing.

④ Our sense of smell becomes dull over the years.

정답·해석·해설 p. 294

(p.166에서 전체 정답표를 확인하실 수 있습니다)

01 다음 글의 분위기로 가장 적절한 것은?

It was weird being back at Foothills Hospital, in the same room where she rested after going through many hours of labor and finally giving birth to me. There were beautiful hand-painted pictures on the wall and a clock that ticked so loud that it sounded like a timer on an explosive. In the corner was a vase of flowers surrounded by gifts, get-well cards and stuffed animals. I sat on the left side of the bed holding her hand. "Mom," I said. "Today I bought a new watch. It has a video game built into it!" Usually, stuff like that would get me into lots of trouble, because she didn't want me to waste money on stupid things. Today was an exception, though; today, she didn't say a word. It was the only time I ever wished that I would get yelled at, but she just lay there asleep.

① merry
② gloomy
③ humorous
④ relaxing

02 다음 밑줄 친 단어가 문맥상 적절치 못한 것은?

'Pride,' observed Mary, who piqued herself upon the solidity of her reflections, is a very ① common failing I believe. By all that I have ever read, I am convinced that it is very common indeed, that human nature is particularly prone to it, and that there are very few of us who do not ② cherish a feeling of self-complacency on the score of some quality or other, real or imaginary. Vanity and pride are ③ similar things, though the words are often used synonymously. A person may be proud without being vain. Pride ④ relates more to our opinion of ourselves, vanity to what we would have others think of us.

03 다음 글에서 주인공의 심경 변화를 가장 잘 나타낸 것은?

When my eighth-grade teacher announced a graduation trip to Washington, D.C., it never crossed my mind that I would be left behind. We would visit Glen Echo Amusement Park in Maryland. My heart beating wildly, I raced home to deliver the news. But when my mother found out how much the trip cost, she just shook her head. We couldn't afford it. After feeling sad for 10 seconds, I decided to try to earn money for myself. For the next eight weeks, I sold candy bars, delivered newspapers and mowed lawns. Three days before the deadline, I'd made just barely enough. I was going!

① worried → angry → sad
② excited → disappointed → hopeful
③ hopeful → resentful → nervous
④ thrilled → sad → worried

04 밑줄 친 (A), (B), (C)에서 문맥상 맞는 표현으로 가장 적절한 것은?

It seems odd that a sound can sometimes be heard at its source and (A) vanish / appear at a distance, only to be heard again still farther away. For a long time this "zone of silence" defeated all attempts at its explanation. At length a meteorologist discovered that layers of air of different temperature interfere with sound. Since the air immediately above the ground is usually warmer than that in higher layers the sound waves are deflected diagonally upwards. The consequences are easily deduced. A certain distance from the source a sound becomes (B) inaudible / audible because it passes over our heads. At a height of about twenty-five miles, however, there is usually another layer of warm air and this deflects the sound back towards the earth. This explains why there is a region of audibility (C) within / beyond the zone of silence.

	(A)	(B)	(C)
①	appear	inaudible	within
②	appear	audible	beyond
③	vanish	inaudible	beyond
④	vanish	audible	beyond

05 다음 글의 목적으로 가장 적절한 것은?

Take high cholesterol. Anyone can have it. Here's something else that you might not know. About one-fifth of your cholesterol comes from what you eat. That's because high cholesterol often has as much to do with family genes as food. So, even if you diet and exercise you may need some help to lower it. The good news is that having Zelous can help. It can lower your total cholesterol 29% to 45%. Ask your doctor if it's right for you. Of all the cholesterol medicines, doctors prescribe Zelous the most. Learn more. Call us at 1-888-Zelous or find us on the web at www.zelous.com.

① to advertise
② to praise
③ to reject
④ to thank

06 다음 글에서 전체의 흐름과 관련이 없는 문장은?

There are subtle signals you can send to the other person that will bring the conversation to its close without hurting anyone's feelings. ① Breaking eye contact is a good way of signaling to the other person that you are ready to end the conversation. ② Another way to signal that a conversation is coming to an end is to use transition words like "Well" or "At any rate," or even statements like "It was really nice talking to you." ③ The ability to converse with those you encounter without effort is a very important element of all your personal and business relationships. ④ When you leave, it's essential to leave a positive final impression as the initial impression you made.

07 다음 글의 밑줄 친 부분 중, 어법상 틀린 것은?

A responsible tourist understands that it's much easier to protect the environment than to restore it. There are many simple things you can do ① to protect nature when you travel. Don't buy souvenirs that are made from endangered plants or animals like coral or ivory. If no one bought those items, people would stop ② killing those endangered animals. Responsible tourism also considers local resources. One five-star hotel in Goa, on the west coast of India, uses as much water as five local villages, and one person staying there ③ use 28 times more electricity than a local resident. A responsible tourist should not use more than he must. Responsible tourism also aims to lower carbon emissions in order to reduce global warming. If possible, take a train or bus instead of an airplane. For short distances, ride a bicycle or walk. Walking is best for nature, and lets you ④ get to know the place you're visiting more closely.

08 다음 밑줄 친 단어가 의미하는 것은?

Imagine that opportunities fall in the form of rain, and you are standing in that rain holding an umbrella. Even though the raindrops are abundant, you aren't catching any of them. But suppose that underneath the edges of the umbrella is a circle of buckets. As you stand holding the umbrella perfectly straight, most of the raindrops fall off the edges down into the empty buckets, with some falling in between. If these buckets have no purpose, they will have no meaning for you, and the raindrops will be wasted.

① opportunities   ② efforts
③ results   ④ purposes

09 주어진 글을 문맥이 통하도록 순서대로 바르게 배열한 것은?

(A) The concept of laissez faire is often paired with capitalism, an economic system that is based on private ownership of the factors of production. Capitalism, the foundation of market economies, operates on the belief that, on their own, producers will create the goods and services that consumers demand.

(B) Therefore, according to laissez faire capitalism, there is no need for government involvement in the marketplace. This laissez faire capitalism is a market economy in its pure form. However, there are no pure market economies—all real-world market economies have some degree of government involvement.

(C) Sometimes the government's economic role is to stay out of the marketplace. The principle that the government should not interfere in the economy is called laissez faire, a French phrase meaning "leave things alone."

① (A) − (B) − (C)   ② (A) − (C) − (B)
③ (B) − (C) − (A)   ④ (C) − (A) − (B)

10 문맥상 빈칸에 공통으로 들어 갈 단어는?

Most people think the world is (   ) to them. They allow events to pass without connecting them to other events. Whatever happens, and there's nothing else to it. Unlike most people, scientists see the world in a very orderly way. They look for what goes with what. Events and conditions are not (   ); they have cause and effect. Scientists everywhere, all the time, see connections because they are looking for connections. What happens when you throw a rock up in the air? It comes back down every time. That is the pattern, the essence of science.

① consistent   ② creative
③ random   ④ cruel

11 다음 글의 목적으로 가장 적절한 것은?

Dear Amy,

Don't give up! I know you can do this assignment. I think you need to start by changing the way you look at yourself and your metaphor. You have already come up with many things that are half one thing and half another thing.

I want you to make a list of things that are good combinations of two parts. There are lots of things that are better when they're combined with something else. Here, I'll start your list: peanut butter and jelly are better together than they are apart. And think about all those exciting varieties of hybrid roses.

If you keep on going with this list, I think you can finish the assignment by Friday. If you're still stuck, come and talk to me before then.

Mrs. Thomas

① to inform   ② to encourage
③ to warn   ④ to complain

12 다음 빈칸에 들어갈 말로 가장 적절한 것을 고르시오.

In sudden infant death syndrome (SIDS), a sleeping baby stops breathing and dies. In the United States, SIDS strikes about two of every thousand infants, usually when they are two to four months old. SIDS is less common in cultures where infants and parents sleep in the same bed, suggesting that _____ may be important. Indeed, about half of apparent SIDS cases maybe accidental suffocations caused when infants lie face down on soft surfaces. Other SIDS cases may stem from problems with brain systems regulating breathing or from exposure to cigarette smoke.

① eating habits   ② sleeping position
③ domestic violence   ④ the age of infants

13 다음 글의 제목으로 가장 적절한 것을 고르시오

We humans are not bad at smelling. We can distinguish about 10,000 different smells, and we do it in just a few milliseconds. But we use our brains for all kinds of other things, like interpreting images from our eyes and engaging in a variety of mental activities. Other animals don't have this kind of distraction, so their sense of smell is much better than ours. Sharks, for example, can smell 10,000 times better than we do. Salmon are even better. It is known that they can smell 30,000 times better than us. Many scientists believe that's how they smell their way back home when they are ready to give birth. For fish like these, the whole world must be full of patterns of scents. By contrast, for us, the world is full of patterns of sights.

① Who Smells Best?
② Smell and Birth Home
③ What Smell Means to Animals
④ The Mental Activities of Human

14 다음 글의 주제로 가장 적절한 것을 고르시오.

Some societies have a custom called the couvade. The couvade is a ceremony in which the husband acts as if he is suffering from labor pains at the same time that his wife actually gives birth. Although no one seems able to explain fully the meaning of the couvade, there are several theories. According to one, the couvade is a way of warding off evil spirits. In effect, the husband directs attention away from his wife and toward himself. Another theory speculates that the couvade is a way of publicly identifying the father so that his paternity will not be in doubt.

① the meaning of giving birth in some societies
② the theories explaining the meaning of couvade
③ the superstition some people have in giving birth
④ the importance of husband sharing the pain of giving birth

15 주어진 문장에 이어질 글의 순서로 알맞은 것은?

The Taj Mahal was designated a UNESCO World Heritage Site in 1983 because of its architectural splendor.

(A) Since the Taj Mahal is not only a famous tourist attraction but also a masterpiece in the history of architecture, the efforts to preserve it should be continued.
(B) Therefore, recently, industries have moved farther away from the site in an attempt to retain the quality of its facade.
(C) But its brilliance has faded over the years, mainly due to air pollution of the Agra area.

① (B) − (A) − (C)   ② (C) − (A) − (B)
③ (B) − (C) − (A)   ④ (C) − (B) − (A)

16 다음 글에서 필자의 태도로 가장 알맞은 것은?

Habitat for humanity is a program aimed at eliminating substandard housing homelessness around the world. Habitat employees and dedicated volunteers work together to build new homes and renovate old ones that are then sold at no profit to families in need. The *Habitat* volunteers are rewarded with a keen sense of accomplishment and strong bonds of friendship. New volunteers are needed throughout the country to continue the work of this wonderful organization. No special building skills are required. Wouldn't you like to join the thousands who have enabled more than 300,000 people around the world to live in sturdy, decent housing?

① compassionate   ② admiring
③ criticizing   ④ lighthearted

17 다음 빈칸에 들어갈 말로 가장 적절한 것을 고르시오.

Conjoined twins are usually classified into three basic categories depending on _____. Twins of the first type are conjoined in a way that never involves the heart or the midline of the body. For example, about 2 percent of all conjoined twins are attached at the head only, and about 19 percent are joined at the buttocks. Twins of the second type are always joined in a way that involves the midline of the body. Many twins joined at the midline share a heart. Around 35 percent are fused together at the upper half of the trunk. Another 30 percent are joined at the lower half of their bodies. Finally, the third major type of conjoined twins includes the very rare forms. In this category are those in which one twin is smaller, less formed, and dependent on the other, as well as the cases involving one twin born completely within the body of his or her sibling.

① the time when they are joined
② the reason why they are joined
③ the point where they are joined
④ whether they are attached at the head

18 글의 흐름상 ____친 부분이 문맥에 맞지 <u>않는</u> 것은?

We should endeavor to give our children a wholesome variety of mental food, and to cultivate their tastes and ① <u>stimulate</u> their interests, rather than to fill their minds with dry facts. The important thing is not so much that every child should be taught, as that every child should be given the wish to ② <u>learn</u>. What does it matter if the pupil knows a little more or a little less? A boy who leaves school knowing ③ <u>less</u>, but hating his lessons, will soon have forgotten almost all he ever learnt; while another who has acquired a thirst for ④ <u>knowledge</u>, even if he had learnt little, will soon teach himself more than the first ever knew.

① stimulate   ② learn
③ less   ④ knowledge

19 ____친 priorities에 해당하지 <u>않는</u> 것은?

I am honored and deeply humbled to take the oath of office as your governor for the next four years. My <u>priorities</u> are clear. We will focus on creating jobs by keeping taxes low and building an advanced transportation system. We will improve access to health-care by allowing doctors to spend more time examining patients. We will continue to invest in the education of our children, all of our children. There are other challenges before us that did not arise yesterday and that will not be solved tomorrow. All the answers may not be found this session, but we will work until they are found.

① better traffic system
② tax cut
③ investment in education
④ cost of health-care

20 다음 글의 San Francisco에 대한 내용으로 옳지 <u>않은</u> 것은?

What can you expect when you arrive in San Francisco? High rent! Rents have been rising for the last few years, and it doesn't seem as if they will come down. Everybody complains about the high cost of living in San Francisco, but few complain about the quality of life here. San Francisco is a most active city, and also many people say that it is the "most European city" in the United States. I've never seen any European city like San Francisco that can take so many different cultures so comfortably.

① People have to pay much money when renting a house.
② Many people think that the quality of life is not good.
③ The city is said to be very lively.
④ Many different cultures are mixed harmoniously.

21 ___친 (A), (B)의 표현 중, 어법에 맞는 것끼리 짝지어진 것은?

When seeking to understand a foreign culture, although we tend to focus on rituals and practices, there is also much to (A) <u>learn / be learned</u> from observing what people don't do. In this sense, knowing what people don't eat can be an integral part of a balanced comprehension of their society. Examining the motivation behind food taboos can provide us with illuminating perspective on the feelings and beliefs of people we may otherwise find strange. (B) <u>Who / What</u> we are is reflected in what we won't eat, as well as what we will.

   (A)   (B)
① learn   — What
② be learned — Who
③ learn   — Who
④ be learned — What

22 다음 글의 내용과 일치하지 <u>않는</u> 것은?

While European artists had developed a tradition of working in a realistic style, other cultures had a long tradition of abstract art form. Some native American artists also work in an abstract style. Navajo Indian artists make abstract paintings that do not use oil paints, watercolors, or any kind of wet materials. Their artworks are called sand paintings because the artist's materials are crushed charcoal, cornmeal, crushed rocks, and sand. The artist makes a sand painting by pouring these materials onto the ground according to one of hundreds of traditional designs. It is a delicate task to make this kind of artwork because, as you can imagine, once the materials are poured it is very hard to correct mistakes.

① 아메리카 원주민 예술가들은 추상적인 양식으로 작업을 한다.
② 나바호 인디언은 석탄 부순 것, 모래 등을 사용하여 예술 작품을 만든다.
③ 모래그림은 재료들을 땅에 쏟아부어 전통 문양에 맞게 그려진다.
④ 재료를 땅에 쏟은 후 잘못된 부분의 수정이 섬세하게 이루어진다.

23 다음 글의 제목으로 가장 알맞은 것은?

Thousands of discarded computers from Western Europe and the U.S.A. arrive in the ports of West Africa every day, ending up in massive toxic dumps, where children burn and pull them apart to extract metals for cash. The exportation of the developed world's electronic trash, or e-waste, is in direct violation of international legislation and is causing serious health problems for the inhabitants of the area. Apparently, dishonest waste merchants unload millions of tons of dangerous waste in the developing world by claiming that it will be used in schools and hospitals. Campaigners are calling for better policing of the ban on exports of e-waste, which can release lead, mercury, and other dangerous chemicals.

① Illegal disposal of electronic waste
② Campaign for recycling computers
③ Banning of toxic dumps in Africa
④ Benefits of discarding e-waste

24 다음 글에 드러난 필자의 심경으로 가장 적절한 것은?

Driving home through the quiet lane early one morning, my headlights picked out a shape in the middle of the road. Only at the last moment did the shape turn its head and look straight at me. The owl apparently neither heard nor saw my car coming. It was too late. There was nothing I could do. There was a horrible sound as I hit the bird head-on. I thought about stopping to see if it was lying injured yet alive by the side of the road, but decided that it wouldn't have stood a chance. I tried to put the incident out of my mind as I drove home, only to be confronted a new horror when I got out of the car. The evening had taken a distinctively dreadful turn. I discovered that the owl had gotten stuck in my radiator grill.

① bored and indifferent
② curious and anticipating
③ shocked and disgusted
④ relieved and encouraged

25 주어진 글 다음에 이어질 글의 순서로 가장 적절한 것을 고르시오.

Avalanches are among the world's most dangerous natural disasters. Fortunately, they usually occur in remote mountain areas, where they threaten neither human life nor property.

(A) Suddenly they were overtaken by an avalanche that left only a few survivors. Three members of the party were buried in the snow. When, after almost half a century, the bodies were found, they were perfectly preserved.

(B) They were so well preserved, in fact, that a surviving member of the original party, by then an old man, was able to recognize them.

(C) Occasionally, however, an avalanche can strike without warning, taking hikers and skiers by surprise. This is precisely what happened more than a century ago when a small group of mountain climbers tried to scale the huge alpine peak Mont Blanc.

① (A) — (C) — (B)   ② (B) — (A) — (C)
③ (B) — (C) — (A)   ④ (C) — (A) — (B)

정답 · 해석 · 해설 p. 307

10회 2013년 법원직 9급
모바일 자동 채점 + 성적 분석 서비스 바로 가기

QR코드를 이용해 모바일로 간편하게 채점하고 나의 실력이 어느 정도인지, 취약 부분이 어디인지 바로 파악해 보세요.

(p.167에서 전체 정답표를 확인하실 수 있습니다)

제한시간 : 25분   시작 _____시 _____분 ~ 종료 _____시 _____분   나의 점수 _____   회독수 □□□

01 다음 글을 읽고 주어진 문장의 빈칸에 가장 알맞은 것은?

The idea of public works projects as a device to prevent or control depression was designed as a means of creating job opportunities for unemployed workers and as a "pump-priming" device to aid business to revive. By 1933, the number of unemployed worker had reached about 13 million. This meant that about 59 million people—about one-third of the nation—were without means of support. At first, direct relief in the form of cash or food was provided these people. This made them recipients of government charity. In order to remove this stigma and restore to the unemployed some measure of respectability and human dignity, a plan was devised to create governmentally sponsored work projects that private industry would not or could not provide. This would also stimulate production and revive business activity.

By using the expression "pump-priming" as a description of public works projects, the author implies that it _____.

① was useless
② lowered human dignity
③ was pouring money down the drain
④ provided business with initial impetus

02 (A), (B), (C)의 각 괄호 속에서 어법에 맞는 표현으로 가장 적절한 것은?

Scientists, like other people, are always pleased to have their own ideas (A) [confirm / confirmed]. So I was gratified by a report which appeared in the August 1963 issue of the *Journal of the British Astronomical Association*. This report was written by the famous Soviet astronomer, Dr. Nikolai Kozyrev, who several years ago discovered evidence in telescopic photographs to support the belief that some of the craters on the moon are sites of presently active volcanoes. When Dr. Kozyrev first published (B) [that / what] he thought he had seen on the moon, his interpretation was doubted by many astronomers in other lands. Subsequently, however, astronomers here have seen color changes (C) [which / where] they, too, believe are signs of continuing volcanic activity on the previously supposed dead body of the moon.

	(A)	(B)	(C)
①	confirm	that	which
②	confirmed	what	which
③	confirm	that	where
④	confirmed	what	where

03 다음 빈칸에 들어갈 말로 가장 적절한 것은?

A scorpion wanted to pass the pond but it could not swim. Thus, it climbed on a frog's back, and asked the frog to take it to the other side of the pond. The frog refused because the scorpion might sting him when he swims. The scorpion promised not to do so. Though the frog knew how vicious the scorpion was, it felt that its words were correct. When they swam in the middle of the pond, the scorpion suddenly stung the frog. The heavily wounded frog yelled out, "Why did you sting me? Stinging me is not useful for you totally." "I know." the scorpion said, while sinking down. "But I'm a scorpion. I must sting you because this is my instinct." As the saying goes: _____, everyone has their own advantages and disadvantages. Therefore, we should be aware of that changing one person is limited. What we need to do is try not to eliminate these drawbacks, but to reasonably use their advantages.

① one good turn deserves another
② friends and wines improve with age
③ the leopard cannot change its spots
④ drowning men catch at a straw

04 다음 글을 쓴 사람의 심정으로 가장 적절한 것은?

My clothes were drenched. Sweat flowed in torrents from my forehead, requiring constant mopping with a bandanna to keep my glasses from steaming up to the point where I couldn't see anything. Keeping my eyes riveted to the ground wasn't enough because there was plenty to watch out for overhead too. Vines yanked my hat off. Thorns ripped at my sleeves. Trees with trunks and limbs encased in three-inch spikes threatened to impale an eyeball in a moment of carelessness. Deadly pit vipers also lurked in the trees, camouflaged bright green.

① excited   ② relieved
③ bored   ④ frightened

05 다음 글의 밑줄 친 부분 중, 문맥상 낱말의 쓰임이 적절하지 않은 것은?

Political power in Rome had traditionally rested with the aristocrats; now, it lay increasingly with the families of the new commercial class. The ① attainment of high political office became the main goal of these families because it meant prestige, power, and more wealth. Individuals ② captured office not so much on the strength of their political philosophy and policy but on the appeal of their personalities, charisma, and conquests. Rome began to be ③ dominated by men who were self-seeking, larger-than-life figures who won the support of the masses through the distribution of free food, olive oil, and wine, and the sponsoring of public entertainment. ④ Shortages that flowed to Rome from the fertile fields of its provinces overseas—Carthage, Sicily, Sardinia, and Numidia—allowed free distributions to the restless and unemployed urban proletariat.

① attainment   ② captured
③ dominated   ④ Shortages

06 (A), (B), (C)의 각 괄호 안에서 문맥에 맞는 낱말로 가장 적절한 것은?

A group of British psychologists have recently shown that the youngest children in class are more (A) [sensible / sensitive] to stress at school than their older classmates. The study examined over 20,000 school children between the ages of five and twelve in England, and symptoms were evaluated by psychopathology questionnaires (B) [competed / completed] by parents, teachers, and 10−12 year old study participants. According to the study, the youngest in each group experienced more emotional and behavioral problems at school, and this effect was (C) [observed / preserved] throughout all the age groups in the study.

(A)	(B)	(C)
① sensible	− competed	− observed
② sensible	− completed	− preserved
③ sensitive	− completed	− observed
④ sensitive	− competed	− preserved

07 다음 글의 주제로 가장 적절한 것은?

The railroad was the first institution to impose regularity on society, or to draw attention to the importance of precise timekeeping. For as long as merchants have set out their wares at daybreak and religious services have begun on the hour, people have been in rough agreement with their neighbors as to the time of day. The value of this tradition is today more apparent than ever. Were it not for public acceptance of a single yardstick of time, social life would be unbearably chaotic: the massive daily transfers of goods, services, and information would proceed in fits and starts; the very fabric of modern society would begin to unravel.

① The traditions of society are timeless.
② Certain activities have to be conducted in time.
③ Modern society judges people by the times they conduct certain activities.
④ People's agreement on the measurement of time is essential for the functioning of society.

08 다음 글 맨 뒤에 the colonel이 느낄 심경으로 가장 알맞은 것은?

Having just moved into his new office, a pompous colonel was sitting at his desk when a private knocked on the door. Conscious of his new position, the colonel told the private to enter, then quickly picked up the phone and said, "Yes, General, I'll pass along your message. In the meantime, thank you for your good wishes, sir." Feeling as though he had sufficiently impressed the young enlisted man, he asked, "What do you want?" "Nothing important, sir," the private replied. "Just here to hook up your telephone, sir."

① proud   ② satisfied
③ ashamed   ④ indifferent

09 다음 글의 빈칸 (A), (B)에 들어갈 말로 가장 적절한 것은?

Fast food is everywhere. It's available on the main corners of a busy street and in the luxury of your own home. Effects of fast food are quickly catching up with us. The nation has become a culture of fast food eating and on-the-go living, ultimately creating "fat" America.   (A)   , fast food has some advantages in the short term: people appreciate the fact that it's fast and convenient. There is no other food that you can pick up and have ready at a moment's notice. It involves no cooking, shopping, or dishwashing. In the end, you are saving an immense amount of time.   (B)   , there seems to be a direct link in America between obesity and fast food. A typical meal from a fast-food restaurant, say a serving of fries and cheeseburger, adds up to over 1,000 calories per serving. This is about half the recommended dietary allowance for an individual per day.

	(A)	(B)
①	However	— As a result
②	However	— Nevertheless
③	In addition	— As a result
④	In addition	— Nevertheless

10 다음 빈칸에 들어갈 말로 가장 적절한 것은?

Here is one scene from the drama of the differences in men's and women's ways of talking. A woman and a man return home from work. She tells everything that happened during the day: what she did, whom she met, what they said, what that made her think. Then she turns to him and asks, "How was your day?" He says, "Same fierce struggle for existence!" She feels locked out: "You don't tell me anything." He protests, "Nothing happened at work." They have different assumptions about _____.
To her, telling life's daily events and impressions means she's not alone in the world. Such talk is the essence of intimacy—evidence that she and her partner are best friends. Since he never spent time talking in this way with his friends, best or otherwise, he doesn't expect it, doesn't know how to do it, and doesn't miss it when it isn't there.

① which things are similar
② what is anything to tell
③ whether the drama is real or not
④ which words are better for them

11 다음 빈칸에 들어갈 말로 가장 적절한 것은?

Given how little we know about our inner ecology, carpet-bombing it might not always be the best idea. "I would put it very bluntly," Margulis told me. "When you advocate your soaps that say they kill all harmful bacteria, you are committing suicide." The bacteria in the intestines can take up to four years to recover from a round of antibiotics, recent studies have found, and the steady attack of detergents, preservatives, and chemicals are also harmful. The immune system builds up fewer antibodies in a clean environment; the deadliest pathogens can grow more resistant to antibiotics. All of which may explain why a number of studies have found that children raised on farms are less likely to be influenced by allergies, asthma, and autoimmune diseases. It sometimes seems _____.

* pathogen 병원균

① people avoid an healthy lifestyle
② leading a rural life boost immunity
③ pollutants can trigger allergic effects
④ as we are cleaner, we get sicker

12 (A), (B), (C)의 각 괄호 안에서 문맥에 맞는 낱말로 가장 적절한 것은?

A tornado is a dark, funnel-shaped cloud made up of violently churning winds. A tornado's width can measure from a few feet to a mile, and its track can (A) [extend / contract] from less than a mile to several hundred miles. Tornados are most often caused by giant thunderstorms. These highly powerful storms form when warm, moist air along the ground rushes upward, meeting cooler, drier air. As the rising warm air cools, the moisture it carries (B) [condenses / condescends], forming a massive thundercloud. Winds at different levels of the atmosphere (C) [feed / thwart] the updraft and cause the formation of the tornado's characteristic funnel shape.

	(A)	(B)	(C)
①	extend	– condenses	– feed
②	extend	– condescends	– thwart
③	contract	– condenses	– feed
④	contract	– condescends	– thwart

13 다음 글의 빈칸에 들어갈 말로 가장 적절한 것은?

It is crucial for parents to teach children that _____. Asians are particularly likely to believe that ability or intelligence is something you have to work for. Not surprisingly, Asian Americans work harder to achieve academic goals than European Americans. And Asians work harder after failure than after success—unlike North Americans of European descent who work harder after success than after failure. It is important to teach children that if at first you don't succeed, try again harder.

① intelligence is highly hereditary
② their intelligence is under their control
③ intelligent people are not always successful
④ success in life doesn't always guarantee happiness

14 다음 글의 제목으로 가장 적절한 것은?

The magnetic field is oddly prevalent in all kinds of animal orientation. Termites line up along its cardinal axes. Yellow eels also use the magnetic field. Homing pigeons, however, are more of a mystery. It was long thought that they, too, relied solely upon the magnetic field to find their way. In studies that disrupt the field, the pigeons' path was thrown off. But after tracking pigeons with GPS satellites for ten years, researchers announced their findings: rather than using sun for directional bearings, it turns out that the pigeons use roads they've traveled in the past as a guide. Then, three years after this study, different scientists found that iron-containing structures within the birds' beaks apparently also aid in their sense of direction. They might even have the ability to use atmospheric odors.

* cardinal axes 기본 축

① Homing Pigeons Follow Their Instinct
② Why Birds Migrate from Season to Season?
③ Constraints Birds Are Facing During Migration
④ Mysterious Sense of Direction of Homing Pigeons

15 다음 글의 요지로 가장 적절한 것은?

Most native English speakers don't actually talk in correct English. What we usually consider correct English is a set of guidelines developed over time to help standardize written expression. This standardization is a matter of use and convenience. Suppose you went to a vegetable stand and asked for a pound of peppers and the storekeeper gave you a half pound but charged you for a full one. When you complained, he said, "But that's what I call a pound." Life would be very frustrating if everyone had a different set of standards: Imagine what would happen if some states used a red light to signal "go" and a green one for "stop." Languages are not that different. In all cultures, languages have gradually developed certain general rules and principles to make communication as clear and efficient as possible.

① 규칙에 얽매인 언어 사용은 대화를 방해한다.
② 이질적인 문화는 사회생활의 불편을 초래한다.
③ 언어는 명확한 의사소통을 위해 표준화되어 왔다.
④ 외국어의 문법 규칙은 맥락 속에서 습득해야 한다.

16 글의 내용으로 보아 밑줄 친 단어의 쓰임이 적절하지 <u>않은</u> 것은?

The intangibles we attach to tangible property are still rapidly multiplying. Every day there are more legal precedents, more real-estate records, more transactional data and the like. Each piece of tangible property, therefore, contains ① <u>higher</u> component of untouchability. In advanced economies the degree of intangibility in society's property base is spiraling ② <u>upward</u>. What's more, even industrial-age manufacturing giants now depend on ③ <u>ever-growing</u> inputs of skill, R&D findings, smart management, market intelligence, etc. All this changes the tangibility ratio in the economy's property base, further ④ <u>increasing</u> the role of touchables.

① higher   ② upward
③ ever-growing   ④ increasing

17 다음 글에 드러난 'I'의 심경 변화로 가장 적절한 것은?

I cannot believe what I am seeing: plants, and trees everywhere. The scents are sweet and the air is pure and clean. I like the silence that greets me as I arrive at hotel. Upstairs, my heart is all aflutter at finding I have a good room, with a good-enough balcony view of the distant water. I take out clean clothes, shower, and, camera in hand, head downstairs to ask the attendant where I can find Moreno gardens. The man at the desk looks puzzled and says he's never heard of the Moreno gardens. He steps into the back office and comes out accompanied by a woman. She has never heard of the Moreno gardens, either. My second question, regarding the house painted by Monet, brings me no closer to the truth. Neither has heard of such a house. It makes my shoulders droop.

① bored → expectant
② worried → pleased
③ sorrowful → relieved
④ excited → disappointed

18 다음 글의 제목으로 가장 적절한 것은?

In composition, your purpose is your overall goal or aim in writing. It is basically what you hope to accomplish by writing—whether it is to promote or endorse a certain point of view, rally support for a cause, criticize a film or a book, or examine the effects of a social trend. Your purpose may or may not be expressed explicitly (in creative writing, for example, it rarely is), but in essays it is usually important that your reader understand the purpose behind your writing. An explicitly stated purpose not only helps the reader follow your argument or perspective but also helps ensure that everything you write reflects that purpose. A carefully expressed purpose will help anchor your essay and keep it from aimlessly floating all over.

① Criticism: The Goal of Writing an Essay
② Express Clearly the Purpose of Your Essay
③ Brevity: The Fundamental of Writing
④ Write Carefully, but Enjoy the Moment

19 다음 글의 목적으로 가장 적절한 것은?

The U.S. is shrinking physically. It has lost nearly 20 meters of beach from its East Coast during the 20th century. The oceans have risen by roughly 17 centimeters since 1900 through expansion (warmer water taking up more space) and the ongoing melt down of polar ice. That increase, however, is a small fraction compared with what's to come. In fact, unless greenhouse gas emissions are tamed, the seas will keep rising as the ice sheets covering mountain ranges melt away. Just how humans will adapt to a more watery world is still not known. Of today's trend, Robert Bindschadler, an emeritus scientist at NASA, notes, "We're not going to avoid this one."

① 온실가스 배출로 인한 해수면 상승을 경고하려고
② 미국의 해안가 오염문제에 대한 대책을 촉구하려고
③ 세계적인 물 부족으로 인한 대책마련의 필요성을 강조하려고
④ 빙하 감소로 인한 극지방 생물들의 멸종위기를 경고하려고

20 다음 글의 내용을 한 문장으로 요약하고자 한다. 빈칸 (A)와 (B)에 들어갈 말로 가장 적절한 것은?

In dealing with the inevitable behavior problems in their classrooms, teachers may sometimes go too far. Often, teachers will humiliate a misbehaving student in front of the entire class. Despite bringing about an immediate, temporary end to the problematic behavior, taking such action can cause long-term educational repercussions. Prominent psychologists have noted that humiliating experiences in school are correlated with a drop-off in academic performance. The students lose self-confidence and begin to believe that positive grades are out of their reach.

Because embarrassing students can ___(A)___ their educational development, teachers should consider their ___(B)___ factors for academic performance.

    (A)   (B)
① harm   – physical
② improve – physical
③ harm   – psychological
④ improve – psychological

21 다음 글의 요지를 아래와 같이 한 문장으로 요약하고자 한다. 빈칸에 들어갈 말로 가장 적절한 것은?

Soccer is the man-on-the-street's game in Europe, and the politicians, academics, and high-end journalists who would normally shun exhibitionist patriotism support their national teams as a means of proving they are really men-in-the street themselves. But it may also be that high national emotions are permissible when a soccer team is playing precisely because they are impermissible at most other times. There aren't, simply, many other places where you can sing your national anthem until you lose your voice without causing a riot.

From the passage above, it can be inferred that soccer is _____.

① an acceptable form of nationalism
② the best sport for relieving stress
③ the most popular sport ever created
④ a unique sport that unites people in harmony

22 다음 글의 빈칸에 들어갈 말로 가장 적절한 것은?

Etiquette—the sets of rules that give expression to manners—can vary from culture to culture. In Japan, you would remove your shoes before entering someone's house. If you did this in America, people would give you strange looks and hold their noses. In some Asian and Middle Eastern countries, belching and smacking your lips is a way to compliment the chef. In the United States, it's a way to get sent to your room. It's important to know the manners of the culture in which you're operating. Otherwise, an innocent, friendly gesture could _____.

① help make new friends
② be interpreted correctly
③ cause offense or embarrassment
④ make other people think highly of you

23 다음 글의 빈칸에 들어갈 말로 가장 적절한 것은?

An economist Gary Becker has applied Marshallian economics to family law and to criminal law. Becker's crime model posits criminals who apparently weigh the costs and benefits of committing offences. If we have a crime problem, Becker implies, it's because crime does pay. Economists have tried to calculate what deters criminals. Two variables seem most important: apprehension rates and severity of punishment. The deterrent effect differs for different types of crimes. For some crimes, police should concentrate on catching the criminals. For other crimes, apprehension rates do not scare offenders. Instead they are deterred by _____.

① police questioning
② higher arrest rates
③ severe punishments
④ the policy of appeasement

24 글의 흐름으로 보아, 주어진 문장이 들어가기에 가장 적절한 곳은?

But not all arguments attempt to persuade, and many attempts to persuade do not involve arguments.

Some writers define an argument as an attempt to persuade somebody of something. This is not correct. (①) An argument attempts to prove or support a conclusion. (②) When you attempt to persuade someone, you attempt to win him or her to your point of view; trying to persuade and trying to argue are logically distinct projects. (③) True, when you want to persuade somebody of something, you might use an argument. (④) In fact, giving an argument is often one of the least effective methods of persuading people—which, of course, is why so few advertisers bother with arguments.

25 글의 흐름으로 보아, 주어진 문장이 들어가기에 가장 적절한 곳은?

They weren't quite green, however.

Green buildings are not new. For thousands of years, humans have built structures with local natural materials. These structures did not use energy or damage the planet. (①) When the people who lived in them moved on, the structures usually collapsed, and their materials returned to the earth. (②) Before the 1930s, most buildings used far less energy than today's buildings. Instead of air-conditioning, they had windows that opened to let in breezes. (③) Coal-burning furnaces were used for heating. As a result, many buildings spewed dirty smoke into the air. (④) Beginning in the 1970s, in the United States and much of the world, air-pollution laws were passed to reduce or eliminate pollution given off by buildings.

정답·해석·해설 p. 319

11회 2012년 법원직 9급
모바일 자동 채점 + 성적 분석 서비스 바로 가기

QR코드를 이용해 모바일로 간편하게 채점하고 나의 실력이 어느 정도인지, 취약 부분이 어디인지 바로 파악해 보세요.

(p.167에서 전체 정답표를 확인하실 수 있습니다)

01 다음 글의 요지를 아래와 같이 한 문장으로 요약하고자 한다. 빈칸에 가장 적절한 것은?

Problems, problems! Some would-be problem solvers are so overwhelmed by the problem that they usually fail. There are others who approach the problem calmly and practically, and usually solve it. Still others—only the truly inventive— find a unique solution to the problem in order to prove a point. For example, Alexander the Great, an ancient Greek ruler, was said to have been challenged to untie the Gordian knot. In mythology, this knot was fastened to a wagon and was thought to be impossible to undo. The great ruler was able to accomplish the task easily, however. He simply cut the knot with his sword! Tradition has it that Christopher Columbus was once given a challenge, too. In 1493, he attended a banquet in his honor, where he was questioned about how he had coped with the difficulties of his voyage to the New World. Columbus replied by challenging his questioners to balance an egg. When they couldn't, he did. How? He cracked the shell to create a flat bottom!

According to the passage above, we can infer that some difficult problems _____.

① could be solved easily
② gave us questions
③ gave us challenges
④ could be solved by the science

02 다음 글의 내용을 한 문장으로 요약하고자 한다. 빈칸 (A)와 (B)에 들어갈 말로 가장 적절한 것은?

The discovery that the seeds of the coffee fruit tasted good when roasted was undoubtedly the key moment in coffee history. It marked the beginning of the transformation of coffee from an obscure medicinal herb known only in the Horn of Africa and southern Arabia to the most popular beverage in the world. A skeptic might counter that it is caffeine, not flavor that made coffee into one of the world's most important commodities. This argument is difficult to sustain, however. Tea, yerba mate, cocoa and other less famous plants also contain substances that wake us up and make us feel good. Yet none has achieved quite the same universal success as coffee. Furthermore coffee figures as important flavoring in countless candies, cookies, cakes and confections.

It is clear that the ___(A)___ has(have) a great deal to do with its triumph as the ___(B)___ in the world.

	(A)	(B)
①	aromatics of roasted coffee	most popular artificial flavor
②	aromatics of roasted coffee	most favored beverage
③	caffeine in roasted coffee	most popular artificial flavor
④	caffeine in roasted coffee	most favored beverage

03 다음 글의 내용으로 보아 밑줄 친 단어의 쓰임이 적절하지 않은 것은?

In 1953 Eisenhower appointed Earl Warren as chief justice of the Supreme Court, an appointment that began a new era in ① judicial history. The Warren Court transformed the American legal system by expanding civil rights and civil liberties. In Brown v. Board of Education of Topeka (1954), the Warren Court declared state laws establishing separate public schools for black and white students ② unconstitutional. In 1955 the Court ordered the states to desegregate schools "with all deliberate speed." However, many people resisted school ③ integration. In 1957 the governor of Arkansas, Orval Faubus, tried to ④ expedite the enrollment of nine black students into Little Rock High School. In response, Eisenhower sent federal troops to desegregate the school. The Brown decision began a new era in civil rights.

① judicial
② unconstitutional
③ integration
④ expedite

04 다음 글의 빈칸에 들어갈 말로 가장 적절한 것은?

Governments become more vulnerable when economies falter; in fact, the credibility of government is often thought to be linked very closely to _____. In the early stages of the 2008 crisis, the governments of Belgium, Iceland, and Latvia fell. In 2009, the government of Kuwait dismissed the parliament after a dispute over the handling of the financial crisis. The Hungarian government collapsed in 2009 for similar reasons. So did that of the Czech Republic, leaving the rotating presidency of the European Union in chaos. There are many historic examples of government collapse in the wake of financial disaster.

① cultural conflict management
② historical analysis on the past
③ effective economic performance
④ democratic system in government

05 글의 흐름으로 볼 때 다음 문장이 들어가기에 가장 적절한 곳은?

They believe that executing a criminal is the only way to protect society from further crime.

Capital punishment is the legal infliction of death as the penalty for violating capital laws. It is also known as the death penalty, and it is one of the most controversial practices in the modern world. (①) Arguments both for and against the practice are often based on religion and emotions. (②) Those in favor of capital punishment believe that it deters crime and offers closure or a sense of justice for the family of the victim. (③) On the other hand, those opposed believe that it is barbaric and allows government to sink to the level of the criminal. (④) There is also the possibility that the person being executed is really innocent, even with extensive background checks, and investigations.

06 내용상 (A), (B)에 들어갈 말로 가장 적절한 것끼리 짝지은 것은?

On 26 April 2003, the civil courts of the English legal system are to undergo a huge change. A new set of rules is being brought in to simplify and streamline procedures, in an attempt to make litigation quicker, cheaper and simpler. An 800-page document published by the Lord Chancellor's Department abandons traditions in favor of new procedures that give judges an active role in managing cases and dictating the pace of litigation. One of the more significant changes is that of ＿＿＿(A)＿＿＿. For the first time, people outside the legal system have been involved in the process of drawing up the rules. As a result, many common but ＿＿(B)＿＿ legal terms have been discarded, to be replaced by simple English, or at least English that is as simple to understand as possible in such a complex field. The Plain English Campaign, which has been fighting for 20 years to change legal language, is delighted: "This may be our greatest victory yet," its founder, Chrissie Maher, is quoted as saying.

	(A)	(B)
①	language	– obscure
②	language	– obvious
③	behavior	– obscure
④	behavior	– obvious

07 다음 글의 주제로 가장 적절한 것은?

There is a small amount of scientific evidence for an increase in certain types of rare tumors(cancer) in long-time, heavy mobile phone users. More recently a pan-European study provided significant evidence of genetic damage under certain conditions. Some researchers also report the mobile phone industry has interfered with further research on health risks. So far, however, the World Health Organization Task Force on EMF effects on health has no definitive conclusion on the veracity of these allegations. It is generally thought, however, that RF is incapable of producing any more than heating effects, as it is considered Non-ionizing Radiation; in other words, it lacks the energy to disrupt molecular bonds such as occurs in genetic mutations.

① the benefits of using mobile phones
② the health effects of using mobile phones
③ the radiation characteristics of mobile phones
④ the need for precautions for the use of mobile phones

08 다음 글의 밑줄 친 부분이 어법상 바르지 <u>않은</u> 것은?

Code talkers was a term used to describe people ① <u>who</u> talk using a coded language. It is frequently used to describe Native Americans who served in the United States Marine Corps ② <u>which</u> primary job was the transmission of secret tactical messages. Code talkers transmitted these messages over military telephone or radio communications nets ③ <u>using</u> formal or informally developed codes built upon their native languages. Their service was very valuable because it enhanced the communications security of vital front line operations ④ <u>during</u> World War II.

① who	② which
③ using	④ during

09 다음 글의 목적으로 가장 적절한 것은?

Every hour of every day, one thousand children, women and men die from preventable illness. While life expectancy has continued to climb in the world's most affluent countries, it is decreasing in many of the poorest countries. That is simply not right. And the world has means to address this injustice. For more than 30 years, we have worked to see that these means are put into action. Tremendous strides have been made but much is left to accomplish. You can help us as we work with governments and multilateral agencies to ensure that adequate resources and sound policies are applied to global health. Your support also enables us to make sure that effective, low-cost health-care practices are recognized and promoted. Your financial support helps us save lives. Not dozens or even hundreds of lives, but millions.

① 빈곤 퇴치를 위한 정부의 정책을 홍보하려고
② 저소득층의 기대 수명 연장 방안을 공모하려고
③ 세계적 보건문제 해결을 위한 기금을 모으려고
④ 경제 위기 극복을 위한 국제적 협력을 촉구하려고

10 (A), (B), (C)의 각 괄호 안에서 어법에 맞는 표현으로 가장 적절한 것은?

A natural habitat can change for natural reasons or unnatural reasons. As regards to the former, climate change is a major possibility. Natural grasslands are the result of a specific set of climatic characteristics. So if those climatic factors change, you would expect grasslands (A) [change / to change], too. Now ample evidence exists of climate change in Africa. But the nature and extent of it is insufficient to explain the wholesale disappearance of grasslands over the wide area (B) [indicated / indicating] on the map. So climate is not the culprit. Instead, the fault lies elsewhere and mainly (C) [take / takes] the form of human beings.

	(A)	(B)	(C)
①	change	– indicated	– take
②	change	– indicating	– takes
③	to change	– indicated	– take
④	to change	– indicated	– takes

11 글의 흐름으로 볼 때 다음 문장이 들어가기에 가장 적절한 곳은?

But what are the causes of this trend?

Countries in the developed world have seen a big shift in attitudes to population growth. Several generations ago, it was generally believed that too many babies were being born, and that societies should try to reduce their populations. (①) Nowadays, however, the concern is the reverse—that birthrates are falling too low and that urgent action is needed to encourage people to have more children. (②) And how much are the attitudes and lifestyles of young people to blame? (③) This essay will consider a number of explanations for the so-called "baby crash." (④) My argument will be that to hold young people responsible is neither valid nor helpful. The best explanation, I believe, is to be found in the condition of increased economic insecurity faced by the young.

12 다음 글의 주제로 가장 적절한 것은?

The light rays from the sun are refracted by the atmosphere. The closer the sun is to the horizon, the more this refraction is. Consider the sun when its lower edge appears to be on the horizon. Were it not for the refraction, the sun would just then actually have its lower edge a little more than half a degree below the horizon. The upper edge, in the meantime, appears to be slightly less than half a degree from where it would be if there were no refraction. As a result, the vertical width of the sun appears to be somewhat less than it would be with the sun overhead. The horizontal width suffers very little shortening due to refraction. Thus, when the sun is on the horizon, it appears to be an ellipse.

① why does refraction occur
② the laws of the refraction of light
③ what makes the swelling of the sun
④ the cause of the flattening of the sun

13 다음 글의 빈칸에 들어갈 말로 가장 적절한 것은?

In Bootle, England, a city of 55,000, people were bombed nightly for a week during World War II with only 10 percent of the houses escaping serious damage. Yet one-fourth of the population remained asleep in their homes during the raids. Only 37 percent of the London mothers and children who were eligible for evacuation left the city during the war crisis. Furthermore, even during periods of heavy bombing in London, evacuees drifted back nearly as rapidly as they were being evacuated. Similar findings are on record for Germany and Japan during World War II. This should not be surprising. Human beings have a very strong tendency to _____.

① continue with their established behavior patterns
② play a definite role within their group
③ run away in a panic during emergency situations
④ initiate new courses of action

14 다음 글에서 밑줄 친 부분 중 어법상 어색한 것은?

It is common these days to eat a healthy and balanced diet. This means watching ① what you eat. A variety of foods are great for maintaining a good body. Of course, the healthier your body, ② the less likely you are to encounter disease. Most people who become overweight or get heart attacks are unhealthy ③ because they eat too much food with the wrong types of fat. Therefore, the best way to avoid problems ④ are to eat the right balance of meat, fish, vegetables and dairy products.

15 다음 글에서 밑줄 친 부분 중 어법상 틀린 것은?

We solve problems every day. For a computer to solve a problem, not only must the solution ① be very detailed, it must be written in a form the computer can understand. An algorithm is a procedure for solving a problem. It is a step-by-step set of instructions that, if ② carried out, exactly solves the problem. While a computer follows instructions very rapidly, it does only and exactly what it ③ tells. Algorithm are used to ④ design these very specific instructions.

16 다음 글의 빈칸에 들어갈 속담으로 가장 적절한 것은?

The saying goes: _____
_____. In language teaching, teachers can provide all the necessary circumstances and input, but learning can only happen if learners are willing to contribute. Their passive presence will not suffice. In order for learners to be actively involved in the learning process, they first need to realize and accept that success in learning depends as much on the student as on the teacher. That is, they share responsibility for the outcome. In other words, success in learning very much depends on learners having a responsible attitude.

① learn to walk before you run

② burn not your house to fright the mouse away

③ do as most men do, then most men will speak well of you

④ you can bring the horse to water, but you cannot make him drink

17 Bernice의 심경으로 가장 적절한 것은?

When Marjorie and Bernice reached home at half past midnight, they said good night at the top of the stairs. Although they were cousins, they were not close friends. In fact, Marjorie had no female friends—she considered girls stupid. Bernice, on the other hand, had hoped that she and Marjorie would share their secrets. She had looked forward to long talks full of girlish laughter and tears. For her these were an important part of all feminine conversation. However, she found Marjorie rather cold. For Bernice it was as difficult to talk to Marjorie as it was to talk to men.

① satisfied and happy

② relieved and rested

③ terrified and panicked

④ uncomfortable and awkward

18 다음 글에서 전체 흐름과 관계 없는 문장은?

Friendship is a long conversation. I suppose I could imagine a nonverbal friendship revolving around shared physical work or sport, but for me, good talk is the point of the thing. (A) Indeed, the ability to generate conversation by the hour is the most promising indication, during the uncertain early stages, that a possible friendship will take hold. (B) In the first few conversations there may be an exaggeration of agreement, as both parties angle for adhesive surfaces. (C) Friendship based on utility and pleasure are founded on circumstances that could easily change. (D) But later on, trust builds through the courage to assert disagreement, through the tactful acceptance that differences of opinion will have to remain.

① (A)   ② (B)

③ (C)   ④ (D)

19 밑줄 친 단어의 뜻을 가장 잘 나타낸 것은?

Victor didn't know what to say. The teacher wet his lips and asked something else in French. The room grew silence. Victor felt all eyes staring at him. He tried to bluff his way out by making noises that sounded French.

① deceive   ② lament

③ avoid   ④ investigate

20 다음 글에서 전체 글의 흐름과 관계가 없는 문장은?

A child born into society must be fed and looked after. In many societies, the parents of the child are responsible for his welfare and therefore perform a function for society by looking after the next generation. ① As the child grows up, surrounded by brothers and sisters, his parents and sometimes by a member of the extended family group, he gradually learns things about the society in which he lives. ② For example, he will learn its language, its idea about right and wrong, its ideas about what is funny and what is serious and so on. ③ Census estimates the number of unmarried heterosexual couples who cohabit has reached a startling 6.4 million couples in 2007. ④ In other words, the child will learn the culture of his society through his contact with, at first, the members of his family.

21 빈칸에 들어갈 말로 가장 적절한 것은?

Global food prices are going through the roof, threatening to push the world into a war over food. Earlier this month, the U.N. Food and Agricultural Organization said world food prices hit their highest level ever recorded in January and _____ in the months to come. It is a strong signal that a severe global food crisis is imminent or under way.

① were set to keep rising ② have set to keep raising
③ have set to keep rising ④ were set to keep raising

22 다음 글에서 밑줄 친 부분 중 어법상 틀린 것은?

The works of discovery in every age ① shape— and shake up—the thinking of the whole literate community. And this effect has multiplied with the rise of democracy and literacy. The familiar example, of course, is ② how the works of Copernicus(1473–1543) and his followers disturbed Western culture with the realization that the earth was no longer the center. More ③ recently examples are the impact of Darwinian biology and Freudian psychology. Nowadays, the space sciences, arcane and specialized ④ though they have become, continue to have a profound and wide influence on the whole community's thinking.

23 다음 글의 밑줄 친 부분 중 어법상 바르지 않은 것은?

One of your greatest mental powers ① is imagination. You can visualize anything you want and you can embellish and exaggerate your imagery as ② much as you want. For example, you could imagine the free fatty acids ③ being burned for energy in the "cellular powerhouse"— the mitochondria—and you could imagine the mitochondria as a fiery furnace... "incinerating" the fat! I think it's a pretty cool idea to "see" your fat cells shrinking and ④ visualizing your body as a "fat burning furnace."

① is   ② much
③ being burned   ④ visualizing

With the publication in 1789 of the *Elements of Chemistry* by Lavoisier, the science of chemistry served its remaining connections with the alchemical past and assumed a modern form. Lavoisier stressed the importance of quantitative methods of investigation in chemistry, and in this connection he introduced the principle of the _____ of matter which stated that nothing was lost or gained during the course of a chemical reaction, the weight of the products equalling the weight of the starting materials.

① reduction ② deprivation
③ conservation ④ accumulation

25 다음 글의 빈칸에 들어갈 말로 가장 적절한 것은?

Ideas are created by integrating previous ideas and sensory input. Due to this dependency of ideas on previous ideas or sensory input, we know that knowledge is _____. Every higher level concept is based on a lower level information. At the root of all of this, of course, is perception. The very first concepts are derived directly from perceptions, via reason. Future concepts can then use the first concepts as part of their base, but the foundation is always there.

① horizontal ② hierarchical
③ goal-oriented ④ multidirectional

정답·해석·해설 p. 332

12회 2011년 법원직 9급
모바일 자동 채점 + 성적 분석 서비스 바로 가기

QR코드를 이용해 모바일로 간편하게 채점하고 나의 실력이 어느 정도인지,
취약 부분이 어디인지 바로 파악해 보세요.

(p.167에서 전체 정답표를 확인하실 수 있습니다)

01 새로운 오토바이의 특성 중의 하나가 아닌 것은?

> **Jetway's New Bike Hits the Mark!**
> Jetway's new 2010 Jetway MX200 is the fastest motorbike available and can be ridden by the widest range of riders, including those with a little experience. The new 2010 Jetway MX200 is available in four different color schemes. It also looks better than previous motorcycles from this company and appears to have a sleeker and more curvaceous look. Thanks to new fully adjustable suspension technology, the handling of each motorcycle can be individually adjusted to a rider's weight or the street environment. This can greatly improve a rider's ability to drive it. The onboard computer fan also automatically adjust speed, acceleration and braking forces in order to keep the bike's handling optimal. The tires designed for this bike are capable of performing well in all types of road conditions and prevent slipping better than any other bike available on the market.

① It is more fuel-efficient than other models.
② It handles very well on the road in all conditions.
③ It is more attractive to riders than other models.
④ It can be customized to each rider's preferences.

02 다음 밑줄 친 것 중 의미하는 바가 다른 것은?

> When I was a boy, my father decided to build a basketball court for my brother and me. He made a cement driveway, put a backboard on the garage and was just getting ready to put up ① the basket when he was called away on an emergency. He promised to put up the hoop as soon as he returned. "No problem," I thought. "I have a brand-new basketball and ② a new cement driveway on which to dribble it." For a few minutes I bounced the ball on the cement. Soon that became boring, so I threw the ball up against the back board—once. I let the ball run off the court and didn't pick it up again until Dad returned to put up the rim. Why? It's no fun playing basketball without ③ a goal. How true that is to life! The joy is in having ④ something to aim for and strive for.

03 밑줄 친 부분에 들어갈 말로 가장 적절한 것끼리 짝지은 것은?

> If an expectant mother knew that dangerous creatures lurked around her, and knew also that she wouldn't be around to take care of her young, she might be _____ . And if she had a way to warn her young before they were born, surely she would. Human mothers cannot do this, to the best of our knowledge. But pregnant crickets, it appears, do have the ability to _____ . This is especially useful since crickets abandon their young after birth.

① stressed – forewarn　② delighted – forewarn
③ stressed – bear　④ delighted – bear

Scientists working in Central America have discovered ruins of one of the largest and most important palaces built by the ancient Mayan people at Cancun, Guatemala. It was built about 1,300 years ago. Jungle plants have covered the ruins for hundreds of years, and the area looks like a huge hill covered by jungle. The palace has 170 rooms built around 11 open areas. The discovery of the ruins will certainly increase historians' understanding of the political life of the Mayan people, who were at the height of power in Central America and Mexico more than one thousand years ago. Writings on the newly found palace walls say it was built by King Tah ak Chaan, who ruled Cancun for about fifty years beginning in the year 740 A.D.

① One of the largest and most important palaces was built about 1,300 years ago.

② The area looks like a huge hill covered by jungle.

③ The palace was built by a Mayan king in the 7th century.

④ The Mayan people was at the height of power in Central America and Mexico.

The ① 35-year-old federal law regulating tap water is so out of date ② <u>which</u> the water Americans drink can pose what scientists say are serious health risks—and still be legal. Only 91 contaminants are regulated by the Safe Drinking Water Act, yet more than 60,000 chemicals ③ <u>are used</u> within the United States, according to Environmental Protection Agency estimates. Government and independent scientists have scrutinized thousands of ④ <u>those</u> chemicals in recent decades, and identified hundreds associated with a risk of cancer and other diseases at small concentrations in drinking water, according to an analysis of government records by The New York Times.

① 35-year-old   ② which

③ are used   ④ those

If solar energy can be produced cheaply, it will benefit both the environment and the world's economies. At this time a major economic obstacle for poorer nations is the cost of electricity. It is impossible to run factories and communications systems without electric power. So when poor nations try to build up their economies, they are forced to use the cheapest fossil fuels available, and this can cause environmental and health problems. The prospect of cheap and clean solar electricity means that economic development around the world will not _____. Some people think large-scale use of solar energy is a kind of fantasy, but many great inventions in history, including the airplane, seemed impossible initially.

① continue without any barrier

② guarantee eco-friendly policy

③ create environmental disasters

④ affect heating and cooling system

Defying the Odds at Craig's Records

Craig's Records has experienced remarkable growth over the last few years, having opened an additional ten stores across the country in the last five years. When Craig Milligan, the owner of the chain was asked what the secret of his success was,

(A) From the beginning, he wanted to restore the feeling of a neighborhood record store where people could enjoy spending countless hours.

(B) he responded that it was probably the atmosphere of the store.

(C) That was why when he expanded nationwide he kept the same design at every new location.

A tiny store where the staff could get to know all the customers and their music preferences. The formula seems to have paid off for him as profits have increased 45% this year alone.

① (A) − (B) − (C)   ② (A) − (C) − (B)

③ (B) − (C) − (A)   ④ (B) − (A) − (C)

08 (A), (B), (C)의 각 괄호 안에서 문맥에 맞는 낱말로 가장 적절한 것은?

The tsunami of December 2004 resulted in a severe loss of life and property along coastal Tamil Nadu in southern India. For 15 years now, residents of that district have been trying to persuade coastal communities not to destroy the mangrove forests along the coast. But the coastal people's preoccupation with their livelihood did not allow them to (A) [ignore / heed] that request. The tsunami miraculously changed their outlook. Villages (B) [adjoining / conjoining] thick mangrove forests were saved from the fury of the tsunami because of the wave breaking role played by the mangroves. But in nearby villages, where mangroves had been (C) [conserved / destroyed] either for fuel wood or to create fish ponds, several hundred fishermen died.

	(A)	(B)	(C)
①	ignore	– adjoining	– conserved
②	heed	– adjoining	– destroyed
③	heed	– conjoining	– conserved
④	ignore	– conjoining	– destroyed

09 빈칸에 들어갈 말로 가장 적절한 것은?

In fluid dynamics, Bernoulli's principle states that for an inviscid flow, an increase in the speed of the fluid occurs simultaneously with a decrease in pressure or a decrease in the fluid's potential energy. Bernouilli's principle also tells us why windows tend to explode, rather than implode in hurricanes: the very high speed of the air just outside the window causes the pressure just outside to be much less than the pressure inside, where the air is still. The difference in force pushes the windows _____, and hence explode. If you know that a hurricane is coming it is therefore better to open as many windows as possible, to equalize the pressure inside and out.

① itself　　　　② bottom
③ inward　　　④ outward

10 When will the court order be removed?

CLOSED BY COURT ORDER

This building has been closed and sealed by the Sheriff pursuant to an Order issued by Judge B. R. O'Reilly, 3rd District Magistrate's Court, and may not be entered into, demolished, or materially altered in any manner. Violation may result in severe criminal penalties including fine and imprisonment.

This order shall stand and be effective until removed by Order of the same Court. Such a removal Order will be issued only upon presentation to the Court of Proof of Payment of the amount of Seven Thousand Three Hundred and Twenty Four Dollars ($7,324) in property tax arrears by the deeded owner of the property, Peter Paltram Holdings Inc., or its representative.

In the event that such payment is not made within Ninety (90) days of the posting of this Order, the property may be seized by the City of Hamston and sold at auction with any proceeds in excess of the stated tax arrears (plus any costs of sale) being remitted to the deeded owner.

① In ninety days
② When the taxes have been paid
③ After sale costs have been paid
④ After the building owner is fined

11 다음 글의 빈칸에 들어갈 가장 적절한 것은?

Everyday life in the British colonies of North America may now seem to have been glamorous, especially as reflected in antique shops. But judged by modern standards, it was quite a(n) _____. For most people, the labor was heavy and constant from daybreak to nightfall. Basic comforts now taken for granted were lacking. Public buildings were often not heated at all. Drafty homes were heated only by inefficient fireplaces. There was no running water or indoor plumbing. The flickering light of candles and whale oil lamps provided inadequate illumination. There was no sanitation service to dispose of garbage; instead, long-snouted hogs were allowed to roam the streets, consuming refuse.

* long-snouted 긴 주둥이가 달린

① outdated style
② ingenious living
③ perfect way of life
④ miserable existence

12 밑줄 친 부분에 들어갈 가장 알맞은 말은?

Mount Everest is legendary. Massive snow and ice avalanches are a constant threat to all expeditions, sometimes burying valleys, glaciers, and climbing routes. Hurricane-force winds are a well-known hazard on Everest, and many people have been killed when their tents were ripped to shreds by the gales. _____, the dramatic loss of body heat, is also a major and debilitating problem in this region of high winds and low temperatures.

① Hypothermia
② Hyperthermia
③ Hypertrophy
④ Nervous breakdown

13 밑줄 친 (A), (B) 부분에 알맞은 말은 어느 것인가?

Asahi Breweries canceled its plan to sell beer in plastic bottles, following objections from environmental groups. Asahi had planned to launch Japan's first plastic beer container as part of its strategy to promote the drink for younger consumers (A) _____ value convenience and style. However, Greenpeace Japan led a campaign against the plan claiming that the introduction of plastic bottles would create waste disposal problems. Greenpeace said that the beer industry should stick to existing glass bottles, (B) _____ a recycling system exists.

① which — for which
② what — in which
③ who — in which
④ who — for which

14 밑줄 친 곳에 들어갈 말로 가장 알맞은 것은?

As more women gain the work experience and education necessary to qualify for leadership positions, the supply of capable women leaders grows. Organizations are subsequently called on to reestablish and expand their notions of what constitutes effective leadership as it relates to gender stereotype, and role expectations. If traditional perspectives of leadership center on masculine-oriented concepts of authoritarian and task-oriented behavior, then these same perspectives may contribute to a '_____' prohibiting relationship-oriented (i.e. feminine) leadership behaviors from being integrated into organization management structures.

① task-oriented leadership
② glass ceiling
③ high-speed growth
④ feminine behavior

15 다음 밑줄 친 단어의 사용이 어색한 것은?

The pressure is almost as heavy on students who just want to graduate and get a job. Long gone are the days of the "gentleman's C," when students ① journeyed through college with a certain relaxation, ② sampling a wide variety of courses that would send them out as liberally ③ educated men and women. If I were an employer I would rather employ graduates who have this range and curiosity than those who narrowly pursued safe subjects and high grades. I know countless students whose inquiring minds ④ exhaust me. I like to hear the play of their ideas. I don't know if they are getting As or Cs, and I don't care.

① journeyed ② sampling
③ educated ④ exhaust

16 다음 문장이 들어가기에 가장 적절한 곳은?

But nothing seems to work.

Korean police have a very hard time trying to control the situation. (①) They've tried everything from policemen dummies to hidden cameras to crackdowns. (②) Drivers soon figure out where the dummies are and then just ignore them. (③) They memorize where the cameras are hidden, so they slow down before they get to them and speed up again as soon as they pass. (④)

17 다음 글에서 전체 흐름과 관계 없는 문장은?

Government authorities in the United States have no control over what is published. The freedom has allowed the development of a fiercely independent and diverse communications industry. One result is the press exerts more influence in the United States than any other country. Often this influence is a force for reform, uncovering shortcomings in society and providing information that people in powerful positions are sometimes reluctant to divulge. Anyone who does not want his article to get censored must then start his or her own newspaper. ① Many people argue that censoring is unconstitutional and an infringement on the right of press. ② Another result, however, is a tendency to ignore, as much as possible, the occasional errors, excesses and lapses in fairness by the press itself. ③ For many decades attacks on specific flaws were regarded as undermining the basic freedom of the press— particularly when the attacks came from outside. ④ Inside, the general practice was silence.

18 다음 글에서 전체 흐름과 관계 없는 문장은?

Many birds pursue prey by swimming under water, but none is so superbly adapted to the task as the penguins. (A) The entire anatomy of the penguin wing has been modified so that it is a stiff, oar-like flipper like that of a dolphin. (B) Awkward on land, penguins use their wings for underwater propulsion as efficiently as other birds use wings for flying. (C) Although all birds share a generally similar body plan, they vary greatly in size and proportions, being adapted to so many ways of life. (D) Most other underwater swimmers—such as loons, cormorants and some ducks—are propelled by their powerful feet, although some use their wings for balance.

① (A) ② (B) ③ (C) ④ (D)

We are now beginning to realize that the great age of expansion of man over the face of this planet is rapidly drawing to a close. There are no great open spaces any more and we are forced to recognize the very limited nature of the earth's resources. The geological capital in the shape of fuel and minerals which has made our present achievements possible will have been exhausted and is unlikely to be renewed. Man's voyages to the moon, and later no doubt to other planets, are not likely to open up any new resources, simply because of the enormous energy requirement for transportation. The whole space enterprise is more likely to be resource using than resource-finding. It will eventually bring us face to face with the realization that the earth is all we have, and that this precious beautiful, blue-green planet must be cherished and preserved if we are to continue to inhabit it.

① necessity of developing universe
② necessity of preserving Earth
③ limitation of human history
④ energy of developing civilization

20 주어진 글 다음에 이어질 글의 순서로 가장 적절한 것은?

Exhausted from studying for final exams, he returned one December day to his rented, off-campus room and fell into a deep sleep.

(A) An incredibly heavy weight compressed his rib cage. Breathing became difficult, and he felt a pair of hands encircle his neck and start to squeeze.

(B) An hour later, he awoke with a start to the sound of the bedroom door creaking open— the same door he had locked before going to bed. He then heard footsteps moving toward his bed and felt an evil presence.

(C) It gripped the young man, who couldn't move a muscle, his eyes wide open. Without warning, the evil entity, whatever it was, jumped onto his chest.

① (A) – (B) – (C)　　② (A) – (C) – (B)
③ (B) – (C) – (A)　　④ (C) – (A) – (B)

21 다음 글의 주제로 가장 적절한 것은?

Obesity has a strong genetic component, and this plays an important role in explaining why a given individual is obese. But genetic characteristics in the population change very slowly, and so they clearly cannot explain why obesity has increased so rapidly in recent decades. Researchers have instead sought to explain obesity by looking at technological changes, changes in consumer habits, and changes in the social environment. Economists have taken the lead in these efforts. According to them, technological advances in agriculture have caused grocery prices to fall, and these declines have caused consumers to demand more groceries. The increase of food consumption has contributed to a surge in caloric intake that can account for as much as 40 percent of the increase in the body mass index of adults since 1980.

① reasons for recent rapid growth in obesity
② worldwide efforts to reduce caloric intake
③ risks overweight people might struggle with
④ the main culprit of increased food consumption

22 글의 흐름으로 보아, 주어진 문장이 들어가기에 가장 적절한 곳은?

However, people growing up in different cultures have very different ideas about what is natural and very different assumptions about human nature.

We tend to feel that the way we do things, say things, and think about things is only logical. (①) The level of aggression that seems appropriate, and ways of expressing agreement or disagreement, come to seem natural. (②) Observing how people in other cultures deal with conflict, disagreement, and aggression can give new perspectives in our attempts to manage conflict and use opposition in positive rather than negative ways. (③) Such a newly-acquired view suggests possibilities—for example, of how similar ends can be achieved with different means. (④)

23 글의 흐름으로 보아, 주어진 문장이 들어가기에 가장 적절한 곳은?

> Yet even the most superficial look into history shakes such an opinion.

The price of art attracts more public attention than any other commodity—except perhaps oil. (①) The ups and downs of the price are debated by those both inside and outside the business. (②) An exceptionally high price attracts wide media coverage together with a public response that ranges from outrage and ridicule to admiration. (③) The orthodox view is that this situation is not only new but bad and that art is not subject to financial speculators. (④) Holland, a rich and powerful imperial nation in the seventeenth century, traded and speculated in art. A historian records that it was quite usual to find Dutch farmers paying the equivalent of up to £3,000 for painting and then reselling them at 'very great gains.'

24 다음 글을 쓴 목적은 무엇인가?

In the past few decades, biochemistry has come a long way towards explaining how the cell produces all its various proteins. But as to the breaking down of proteins, not so many researchers were interested. Aaron Ciechanover, Avram Hershko and Irwin Rose went against the stream and at the beginning of the 1980s discovered one of the cell's most important cyclical processes—regulated protein degradation. For going against the tide with their bold research, they were rewarded with this year's Nobel Prize in Chemistry. The work of the three laureates has brought us to realize that the cell functions as a highly-efficient checking station where proteins are built up and broken down at a furious rate.

① 어떻게 단백질이 분해되는지를 설명하기 위해
② 세포가 어떻게 다양한 단백질을 생산해 내는지 설명하기 위해
③ 생화학에서 시류를 따르지 않았던 비주류 연구자들의 업적을 설명하기 위해
④ 노벨물리학상 수상자들의 연구로 노벨상이 더욱 빛이 남을 알리기 위하여

25 밑줄 친 단어의 쓰임이 어법상 바르지 않은 것은?

On the morning of December 7, 1941, Japanese submarines and carrier planes ① launched an attack of the U.S. Pacific Fleet at Pearl Harbor. Two hundred American ② aircrafts were destroyed, eight ③ battleships were sunk, and approximately eight thousand naval and military personnel were killed or wounded. This savage attack and ④ its horrifying consequences propelled the United States into World War II.

① launched   ② aircrafts
③ battleships   ④ its

정답 · 해석 · 해설 p. 344

13회 2010년 법원직 9급
모바일 자동 채점 + 성적 분석 서비스 바로 가기

QR코드를 이용해 모바일로 간편하게 채점하고 나의 실력이 어느 정도인지, 취약 부분이 어디인지 바로 파악해 보세요.

(p.167에서 전체 정답표를 확인하실 수 있습니다)

제한시간 : 25분   시작 _____시 _____분 ~ 종료 _____시 _____분   나의 점수 _____ 회독수 ☐ ☐ ☐

---

01 주어진 문장 다음에 이어질 글의 순서로 올바른 것은?

"Cloud seeding" is a process used by several western state governments and private businesses, such as ski resorts, to increase the amount of rainfall or snow over a certain area.

(A) Then they measure a storm's clouds for temperature, wind, and composition. When the meteorologists determine that conditions are right, pilots are sent to "seed" the clouds with dry ice (frozen carbon dioxide). An aircraft flies above the clouds and dry ice pellets are dropped directly into them. Almost immediately, the dry ice begins attracting the clouds' moisture, which freezes to the dry ice's crystalline structure.
(B) Meteorologists use radar, satellites, and weather stations to track storm fronts.
(C) Precipitation drops from the clouds to the earth in the form of rain or snow.

① (C) − (B) − (A) ② (B) − (C) − (A)
③ (B) − (A) − (C) ④ (A) − (B) − (C)

---

02 다음 밑줄 친 단어 (A)와 뜻이 통하지 <u>않는</u> 단어는?

Any headache can make you miserable, but a migraine can be excruciating. More than 28 million Americans suffer from migraine headaches. Their frequency and severity varies from person to person, but they strike women three times more often than men. And if there is a history of migraine in your family, there is an 80 percent chance you will have them as well. It's important for migraine sufferers to avoid certain triggers, smoking, or certain foods that may have triggered their headaches in the past. Regular aerobic exercise is highly recommended to reduce (A) <u>tension</u> and to help prevent migraines.

① strain   ② anxiety
③ calmness   ④ nervousness

---

03 다음 각 문장 중 밑줄 친 단어의 쓰임이 적절치 않은 것은?

① I can watch TV and talk on the phone at the <u>same time</u>.
(나는 동시에 TV도 보고 전화도 할 수 있어.)
② We offer a wide <u>arrange</u> of skincare products.
(저희는 다양한 종류의 스킨 케어 제품들을 보유하고 있습니다.)
③ I am sorry to <u>bother</u> you, but what time do you think you'll be done with your work?
(귀찮게 해서 미안하지만, 몇 시쯤 일이 끝날 거 같아?)
④ Can you make <u>sure</u> he gets the message?
(그 사람에게 메시지를 꼭 전달해 주시겠습니까?)

04 다음 주어진 문장들을 문맥상 가장 적절한 순서로 배열한 것은?

ⓐ It is caused by factories that burn coal, oil or gas.

ⓑ The wind often carries the smoke far from these factories.

ⓒ Acid rain is a kind of air pollution.

ⓓ These factories send smoke high into the air.

① ⓒ → ⓐ → ⓓ → ⓑ ② ⓑ → ⓐ → ⓒ → ⓓ

③ ⓒ → ⓓ → ⓑ → ⓐ ④ ⓑ → ⓒ → ⓐ → ⓓ

05 다음 글의 밑줄 친 ①~④ 중 어법상 잘못된 것은?

Among the most tragic accidents are ① those involving guns. Each year, about five thousand people under the age of twenty die because of firearms. One in ten of these deaths is said to be accidental, many of them caused by children who find ② loading guns in their homes. Nearly half of all American households have guns, and often, instead of being locked up, they are just hidden or even left in a drawer, filled with ammunition. Accidental gun injuries have become so ③ prevalent that the American Medical Association advises doctors to make a point of talking with patients who are gun owners about using safety locks on their guns and storing ammunition ④ separately.

① those involving ② loading guns
③ prevalent ④ separately

06 빈칸에 어울리는 속담으로 가장 적절한 것은?

You're aware of the health benefits of eating fresh vegetables, you have the space for a small garden, but just don't know where to start? Look no further. Here's all you need to know to put fresh, crisp vegetables on your dinner table.

First, think small. _____ It's like starting out an exercise program by running five miles the first day. You get tired, sore and you quit. Likewise, if you plant a huge garden the first year, you'll curse, cuss and turn your sore back on gardening for good. So, if you're new to gardening, start off with a garden no larger than 8' X 10'. You can always expand later if you can't get enough of those fresh, crispy vegetables.

Choose a location that receives as much sun as possible throughout the day. Northern gardeners should insist on full sun. Now you're ready to work up the soil. You can rent a rear tine tiller or borrow one from a friend or neighbor for this task.

① The grass is always greener on the other side of the fence.

② Scratch my back and I'll scratch yours.

③ You reap what you sow.

④ Don't bite off more than you can chew.

07 다음 글을 쓴 사람의 심정으로 가장 알맞은 것은?

Rainforests are home to more than half of the world's plants and animals. Rainforests used to cover as much as 14% of the Earth's land. Now they cover less than 6%. The problem is that the rainforests are being destroyed. The amount being destroyed each minute would fill 20 football fields. And about 50,000 species of rainforest animals and plants are disappearing every year. This means they will all be gone by the time you grow up unless we save them with your help!

① exited ② pleasant
③ relieved ④ worried

08 다음 글의 전개 방식으로 가장 적절한 것은?

With the arrival of twentieth-century technology, medical professions were able to think seriously about creating artificial replacements for damaged human hearts that no longer functioned effectively. In 1957, Dr. Willem Kolff created the first artificial heart and implanted it in a dog, who promptly died from the experiment. Still, animal research continued, and, in 1969, Dr. Denton Cooley implanted the first artificial heart into the body of a human. The device, made largely of plastic, only had to function for a brief period of time, while the patient awaited a transplanted human heart. In 1979, Dr. Robert Jarvik patented the first artificial heart. Three years later, the Jarvik heart, as it came to be called, was implanted in the body of Barney Clark, a retired dentist dying of heart disease. Clark lived for 112 days after the surgery, and his survival raised hopes for the future success of artificial hearts.

① time order
② cause and effect
③ classification
④ definition

09 밑줄 친 빈칸에 들어가기에 가장 적절한 단어는?

Q: When praised, Koreans often insist they did nothing deserving of praise. Why do you do this instead of accepting the praise and saying Thank you?

A: This is done out of _____; in other words, we feel like we are not deserving of so much praise. However, don't think that Koreans really dislike being praised. Even though we react this way, we very much appreciate the compliment.

① responsibility
② modesty
③ condemnation
④ confidence

10 다음 글에서 밑줄 친 This가 가리키는 것으로 가장 적절한 것은?

This is a gift given by physical or legal persons, typically for charitable purposes and/or to benefit a cause. This may take various forms, including cash, services, new or used goods including but not limited to clothing, toys, food, vehicles, it also may consist of emergency, relief or humanitarian aid items, development aid support, and can also relate to medical care needs as i.e. blood or organs for transplant. Charitable gifts of goods or services are also called gifts in kind.

① operation
② donation
③ fund
④ volunteering

11 글의 흐름상 다음 문장이 들어갈 곳으로 가장 적절한 곳은?

This is the keystone.

The Romans have just invented a new building technique: the arch. It is the strongest way to support walls and bridges. A master builder explains the process. ㉮ "First, take some stone blocks and shape them as wedges. ㉯ Take another stone and shape it to fit perfectly in the middle of the arch. ㉰ Use wood to hold the wedges together until the keystone can be placed in the middle. ㉱ Finally, put stones on top of the wedges and build up the entire wall."

① ㉮
② ㉯
③ ㉰
④ ㉱

12 다음 글의 빈칸에 들어갈 말로 가장 적절한 것은?

Increasing numbers of Americans are turning to hypnosis to stop smoking or to lose weight. Similarly, arthritis sufferers are using acupuncture, an ancient method of Chinese healing, to gain some relief from their pain. Cancer patients have also been using nontraditional treatments like creative visualization to fight their disease. Some cancer sufferers, for example, imagine themselves as huge and powerful sharks. They imagine their cancer cells as much smaller fish that easily fall prey to the larger and more dangerous sharks. Even some businesses are supporting nontraditional medical treatments and encouraging employees to use _____ to ward off migraine headaches and high blood pressure.

① mediation
② meditation
③ mutilation
④ medication

13 다음 글의 주제로 가장 적절한 것은?

Infants spend most of their days fast asleep. In the period immediately after birth, newborns sleep an average of sixteen hours per day. But the amount they sleep decreases steadily with each passing month. By the age of six months, babies average about thirteen to fourteen hours of sleep per day. By twenty-four months, they average only eleven or twelve hours per day. In short, babies sleep a lot, but the amount of sleep they need decreases over time.

① reasonable amount of sleep
② the sleep patterns of infants
③ the habits of newborns
④ the development of infants

14 밑줄 친 부분의 어법상 쓰임이 바르지 <u>않은</u> 것은?

For instance, American college students expect to live longer, stay ① <u>married</u> longer, and travel to Europe more often than average. They believe they are more likely to have a gifted child, ② <u>to own</u> their own home, and to appear in the newspaper, and less likely to have a heart attack, venereal disease, a drinking problem, an auto accident, a broken bone, or gum disease. Americans of all ages expect their futures to be an improvement on their presents, and although citizens of other nations are not quite optimistic as Americans, they also tend to imagine that their futures will be brighter than ③ <u>that</u> of their peers. These overly optimistic expectations about our personal futures are not easily ④ <u>undone</u>: Experiencing an earthquake causes people to become temporarily realistic about their risk of dying in a future disaster, but within a couple of weeks even earthquake survivors return to their normal level of unfounded optimism.

① married
② to own
③ that
④ undone

15 다음 글의 밑줄 친 칸에 들어가기에 적절한 단어는?

Take the case of two people who are watching a football game. One person, who has very little understanding of football, sees merely a bunch of grown men hitting each other for no apparent reason. _____ person, who loves football, sees complex play patterns, daring coaching strategies, effective blocking and tackling techniques, and zone defenses with "seams" that the receivers are trying to "split." Both persons have their eyes glued to the same event, but they are perceiving two entirely different situations. The perceptions differ because each person is actively selecting, organizing, and interpreting the available stimuli in different ways.

① Other
② Some
③ The other
④ This one

16 필자가 주장하는 바로 가장 적절한 것은?

Among life's cruelest truths is this one: Wonderful things are especially wonderful the first time they happen, but their wonderfulness wanes with repetition. Just compare the first and last time your child said "Mama" or your partner said "I love you" and you'll know exactly what I mean. When you have an experience—hearing a particular sonata, making love with a particular person, watching the sun set from a particular window of a particular room—on successive occasions, we quickly begin to adapt to it, and the experience yields less pleasure each time. Psychologists call this habituation, economists call it declining marginal utility, and the rest of us call it marriage.

① 성공적인 대화는 공감을 바탕으로 이루어진다.
② 아무리 좋은 일도 반복되면 식상해 진다.
③ 치밀한 계획을 세우자.
④ 성공은 좌절을 극복함으로써 얻을 수 있다.

17 (A), (B), (C)에 들어갈 말로 가장 적절하게 짝지어진 것은?

Clouds darken from a pleasant soft white just before rain begins to fall because they absorb more light. Clouds normally appear white when the light that strikes them is (A) concentrated / scattered by the small ice or water particles from which they are composed. However, when the size of these ice and water particles (B) decreases / increases—as it does just before clouds begin to deposit rain—this scattering of light is increasingly (C) replaced / developed by absorption. As a result, much less light reaches the observer on the ground below and the clouds look darker.

	(A)	(B)	(C)
①	concentrated	– decreases	– developed
②	scattered	– increases	– replaced
③	concentrated	– increases	– developed
④	scattered	– decreases	– replaced

18 다음 글의 흐름으로 보아 밑줄 친 단어의 쓰임이 적절하지 않은 것은?

For everywhere we look, there is work to be done. The state of the economy ① calls for action, bold and swift, and we will act not only to create new jobs, but to lay a new foundation for growth. We will build the roads and bridges, the electric grids and digital lines that ② bolster our commerce and bind us together. We will restore science to its rightful place, and wield technology's wonders to ③ erode health care's quality and lower its cost. We will harness the sun and the winds and the soil to fuel our cars and ④ run our factories. And we will transform our schools and colleges and universities to meet the demands of a new age. All this we can do. And all this we will do.

① calls for   ② bolster
③ erode   ④ run

19 다음 글의 빈칸에 들어갈 연결어로 가장 적절한 것은?

In order to live well after you stop working, you should begin saving for retirement early. Experts suggest that after you retire, you will need 75 percent to 80 percent of your salary to live on every month. _____, if you make $3,000 per month while working, you will need between $2,250 and $2,400 per month to live on during retirement. This calculation assumes that you have no mortgage on a house to continue paying, or any other major expenses. However, many retired people now rent their housing, and so they will pay more money in housing costs over time. Older people now also have to spend more on health care because they live longer; many people in developed countries now live into their eighties or nineties.

① Conversely   ② Likewise
③ In other words   ④ Furthermore

20 다음 글의 밑줄 친 빈칸에 들어가기에 가장 적절한 것은?

We normally think of the expressions on our face as the reflection of an inner state. I feel happy, so I smile. I feel sad, so I frown. Emotion goes inside-out. Emotional contagion, though, suggests that the opposite is also true. If I can make you smile, I can make you happy. If I can make you frown, I can make you sad. Emotion, in this sense, goes outside-in. If we think about emotion this way—as outside-in, not inside-out—it is possible to understand how some people can have an enormous amount of _____ over others. Some of us, after all, are very good at expressing emotions and feelings, which means that we are far more emotionally contagious than the rest of us.

① feelings
② actions
③ fluency
④ influence

21 밑줄 친 (A)가 가리키는 바를 본문에서 바르게 찾은 것은?

In discussing the relative difficulties of analysis which the exact and inexact sciences face, let me begin with an analogy. Would you agree that (A) swimmers are less skillful athletes than runners because swimmers do not move as fast as runners? You probably would not. You would quickly point out that water offers greater resistance to swimmers than the air and ground do to runners. Agreed, that is just the point. In seeking to solve their problems, the social scientists encounter greater resistance than the physical scientists. By that I do not mean to belittle the great accomplishments of physical scientists who have been able, for example, to determine the structure of atom without seeing it. That is a tremendous achievement; yet in many ways it is not so difficult as what the social scientists are expected to do.

① runners
② social scientists
③ physical scientists
④ athletes

22 다음 글의 마지막에 느꼈을 I의 심경으로 가장 적절한 것은?

To my mother, it was a big occasion to give me a ride to the college for my freshman year. She wore one of her "outfits"—a purple pantsuit, a scarf, high heels, and sunglasses, and she insisted that I wear a white shirt and a necktie. "You're starting college, not going fishing," she said. Together we would have stood out badly enough in Pepperville Beach, but remember, this was college in the mid-60s, where the less correctly you were dressed, the more you were dressed correctly. So when we finally got to campus and stepped out of our Chevy station wagon, we were surrounded by young women in sandals and peasant skirts, and young men in tank tops and shorts, their hair worn long over their ears. And there we were, a necktie and a purple pantsuit, and I felt, once more, that my mother was shining ridiculous light on me.

① fascinated
② delighted
③ embarrassed
④ indifferent

23 다음 글의 어조로 가장 알맞은 것은?

Will you get more sick if you exercise while you have a cold? In one experiment, a team of researchers injected a group of fifty students with rhinovirus, and then had part of the group run, climb stairs, or cycle at moderate intensity for forty minutes every other day, while the second group remained relatively sedentary. They found that the exercise regimen neither eased nor worsened symptoms of the common cold. Several similar studies conducted elsewhere have found the same thing. Doctors refer to a good rule of thumb as the neck check. It's safe to exercise if you have only "above the neck" symptoms, like a runny nose or sneezing. If your symptoms are "below the neck"— a fever or diarrhea—you're better off sitting it out for a few days.

* rhinovirus 감기의 주된 바이러스

① humorous
② emotional
③ persuasive
④ informative

24 다음 글의 목적으로 가장 적절한 것은?

I was not aware that the quality of university education in England is in decline until I read your article. The situation appears similar in Japan, where I lecture in English. I find many students ill-prepared for university education. Many lack the necessary intellectual abilities, while many more have very little interest in actually learning anything. Why do parents pay so much money for an education when their children are too lazy to study? Parents often force their children into university not to challenge them academically but simply for the social prestige and reputation associated with certain universities.

① 대학생들의 적극적인 수업 참여도를 높이려고
② 자녀교육에 대한 부모의 잘못된 가치관을 지적하려고
③ 고등교육의 질을 향상시키는 프로그램을 제안하려고
④ 사회적 신분과 대학 순위 간의 상관관계를 설명하려고

25 다음 글의 제목으로 가장 적절한 것은?

Are you keen to discover new music, but put off by most of the stuff you hear? Then visit MusicAll. It's a cunning website that allows users to recommend music to one another based on shared tastes. As a member you upload a playlist of your own favorite tunes: the site then makes recommendations based on the music enjoyed by other people who also like those tracks. It will also make suggestions based on what you're listening to at the time; you can listen to clips of the recommendations to see whether they appeal. If so, you can download them for free. The more you put into the site, the more useful it becomes.

① Music Can Contribute To Your Life
② What You'd Like To Recommend For A Change
③ Share Opinions about Music at the Website
④ How To Make An Appealing Website

정답 · 해석 · 해설 p. 357

14회 2009년 법원직 9급
모바일 자동 채점 + 성적 분석 서비스 바로 가기

QR코드를 이용해 모바일로 간편하게 채점하고 나의 실력이 어느 정도인지, 취약 부분이 어디인지 바로 파악해 보세요.

(p.167에서 전체 정답표를 확인하실 수 있습니다)

제한시간 : 25분　　시작 _____시 _____분 ~ 종료 _____시 _____분　　　　나의 점수 _____　회독수 ☐☐☐

01 다음 글의 밑줄 친 부분에 함축된 뜻은?

It was in the spring of his thirty-fifth year that father married my mother, then a country school teacher, and in the following spring I came crying into the world. Something happened to the two people. They became ambitious. The American passion for getting up in the world took possession of them. It may have been that mother was responsible. Being a school teacher, she had no doubt read books and magazines. She had, I suppose, read of Garfield, Lincoln, and other Americans rose from poverty to fame and greatness and <u>as I lay beside she may have dreamed that I would some day rule men and cities.</u>

① 위대한 어머니에 대한 나의 존경심
② 나의 출세에 대한 어머니의 야심
③ 아버지와 어머니 사이의 깊은 사랑
④ 행복하고 평화로운 나의 어린시절

02 다음 글의 문맥상 주어진 문장이 들어가야 할 가장 적절한 곳은?

But nature has solved this problem for the flounder.

The flounder is a kind of flatfish. The odd thing about this fish is that both its eyes are on the same side of its head. (①) Flounder are not born that way, though. When a flounder hatched, it looks like any other fish. As it grows, however, its body becomes flattened. (②) One side of the fish is white and the other is a sandy color. The flounder lies on its white side on the ocean floor. Its sandy-colored side faces up. (③) This makes the flounder blend in with the sand, so it can't be easily seen. For any other fish, this would cause a problem. One eye would be looking right into the sand. (④) As the fish grows, the eye on the bottom moves to the upper side.

03 다음 글을 읽고 아래 질문의 답을 고르시오.

The common plant starch—found in flour, cereal grains and potatoes—is built of glucose. Starch can be split in several ways and eventually yields glucose. Digestion is one such way. After digestion takes place the glucose goes into the blood and is burned. Some glucose may not be burned. The liver takes it and converts it to glycogen. The body then stores this glycogen until the body is hungry, at which time it is digested again.

* When is glycogen used by the body?
① After it has been split.
② Shortly after being burned.
③ Once the body has stored it.
④ When the body needs energy.

Hibernation of bears presents several wonders to us. Although they are mammals, their life is a repetition of winter sleep and a preparation period unlike humans. Basically, the bear stocks up energy before winter and expends it during hibernation. In the process, the bear's body goes through drastic change. The preparation for hibernation starts as early as summer. Bears gain weight up to 15kg to 20kg per week by eating everything available. The energy is stored in the form of fat under the skin, which grows inches thick at its peak.

As winter approaches, the bear slows down its activity and eventually goes into a winter sleep in its cave. The bear sleeps until winter is over unless it gets disturbed. During the winter, the bear does not eat or drink for almost 100 days, and it loses between 15% to 40% of its weight just by sleeping. Despite the tremendous change in the body, virtually every single bear survives this long starvation period. In late spring, when the food is in great supply again, the bear walks out from the cave and resumes its life.

① 곰은 겨울에 엄청난 양의 음식을 섭취한다.
② 다수의 곰이 겨울에 영양실조로 사망한다.
③ 곰은 늦은 겨울에 이미 잠에서 깨어난다.
④ 곰의 겨울잠 준비는 여름부터 시작된다.

Many experts think that the artists in prehistoric times believed they captured the animal's soul when they painted it. ① This could be why the images are so lifelike. ② According to their belief, if the artists captured an animal's true likeness, they would be sure to capture the real thing during the hunt. ③ Prehistoric men hunted bulls, bison and mammoths for their survival. ④ Whatever the paintings meant, surely no one would have crawled so deep into these caves to paint had the pictures not had a special meaning. The dark caves were sacred places for prehistoric people, and this art was part of their beliefs.

The candidate vowed to _____ public schools with new textbooks and cutbacks in taxes but failed to act on either promise once he was elected.

① purchase   ② sell
③ address   ④ provide

07 다음 글의 ＿＿ 부분에 들어갈 어법에 맞는 표현은?

> Although ＿＿＿＿＿＿＿＿＿＿＿＿＿＿＿
> instant critical acclaim in 1952, he never
> completed a second novel, publishing many short
> works instead.

① *Invisible Man* was the first novel by Ralph Ellison
received

② first received by Ralph Ellison, the novel *Invisible Man* was

③ Ralph Ellison's first novel, *Invisible Man*, received

④ Ralph Ellison's first novel, *Invisible Man*, was received

08 다음 글의 밑줄 친 ①~④ 중 어법상 잘못된 것은?

> Teach your teen that the family phone ① is for the whole family. If your child talks on the family's telephone excessively, tell him he can talk for 15 minutes, but then ② he must stay off the phone for at least an equal amount of time. This not only frees up the line so that other family members can make and receive calls, ③ but teaching your teen moderation and discipline. Or if you are not open to the idea, allow your talkative teen his own phone ④ that he pays for with his allowance or a part-time jobs.

09 다음 글의 내용을 가장 잘 표현한 속담은?

> Mr. Jones, the owner of a small company, wanted to bring his nephew Carl, into the business. At first he sent Carl out on the road selling, but he didn't make many sales. Then he tried Carl in the manufacturing department, but Carl was too thorough and took too much time. Then he tried Carl in human resources, but Carl was too kind and the other employees took advantage of him. Finally, Mr. Jones put Carl in customer relations, and he was wonderful! He was kind to all who called, and made everyone happy. The customers were pleased and spread the word to all their friends about Mr. Jones' great company.

① Where there is a will, there is a way.
② Every man has his own trade.
③ One man's music is another man's noise.
④ Everybody's business is nobody's business.

10 다음 글의 내용을 한 문장으로 요약하고자 한다. 빈칸 (A)와 (B)에 들어갈 말로 적절한 것은?

In 1960, presidential candidates Richard M. Nixon and John F. Kennedy agreed to a series of debates, which were broadcast simultaneously on television and radio. According to surveys, most radio listeners felt that Nixon had won the debates, while television viewers picked the younger, more photogenic Kennedy.

Kennedy went on to win the general election that fall. Television coverage was also influential during the Vietnam War. By the mid-1960s, major networks were broadcasting daily images of the war into virtually every home in the United States. For many viewers, the horrors they saw on television were more significant than the optimistic reports of impending victory issued by government officials and repeated in print accounts.

In the 1960s in the United States, (A) _____ had a more profound effect on some (B) _____ issues than any other media.

	(A)	(B)
①	television	political
②	radio	economical
③	newspapers	political
④	television	economical

11 (A), (B), (C)의 각 괄호 안에서 문맥에 맞는 낱말로 가장 적절한 것은?

School uniforms are becoming more and more popular. That's no surprise, because they offer many benefits. They instantly end the powerful social sorting and labeling that come from clothing. If all students are dressed in the same way, they will not be (A) (distracted / contracted) by fashion competition. Some students will also not be excluded or laughed at because they wear the "wrong" clothes. Some people (B) (object / subject) to the "regimentation" of school uniforms, but they do not realize that students already accept a kind of regimentation—wanting to look just like their friends. The difference is that the clothing students choose for themselves creates social barrier; school uniform (C) (wear / tear) those barriers down.

	(A)	(B)	(C)
①	contracted	object	tear
②	contracted	subject	tear
③	distracted	subject	wear
④	distracted	object	tear

12 다음 글을 아래와 같이 요약할 때 ___ 부분에 가장 적절한 말은?

For the normal emotional and physical development of infants, sensory and perceptual stimulation is necessary. Healthy babies experience this stimulation while in contact with the mother or other adults who feed, diaper, or wash the infant. However, infants who are born prematurely or are sick miss these experiences during the early weeks of their lives when they live in incubators, an artificial environment devoid of normal stimuli. These babies tend to become listless and seem uninterested in their surroundings. However, when they are stimulated by being handled and spoken to and by being provided with bright objects such as hanging mobiles or pictures, they began to respond by smiling, becoming more active physically, and gaining weight more rapidly.

According to the passage, premature infants cared for in incubators, when compared with full-term infants, are likely to _____.

① gain weight more rapidly
② receive more natural stimulation
③ respond more to bright objects
④ be less active physically

13 다음 글 바로 앞에 올 수 있는 내용으로 가장 적절한 것은?

You can see this in the way Americans treat their children. Even very young children are given opportunities to make their own choices and express their opinions. A parent will ask a one-year-old child what color balloon he or she wants, which candy bar he or she would prefer, or whether he or she wants to sit next to mommy or daddy. The child's preference will normally be accepted. Through this process, Americans come to consider themselves as equal beings with the right to have their own individual opinions and decisions respected. At the same time, they are also taught to respect the opinions and decisions of others.

① 개인의 의사가 존중되는 미국 사회의 특성
② 미국 사회 특유의 자녀 교육 방법
③ 미국 사회에 있어서 부모의 역할의 중요성
④ 다수결 원칙에 입각한 의사 결정의 필요성

14 다음 글을 읽고 아래 질문의 답을 고르시오.

Dear Ms. Larson,

Thank you for inquiry of 12 September asking for the latest edition of our catalogue. We are pleased to enclose our latest brochure. Purchases can be made online by visiting our website at mortmonbros.com. We would also like to inform you that we are having a special sale on HP printers all throughout the month and have already included in this mailing an order sheet. Orders can be filled out on paper and sent by post or filled in on our website and submitted electrically. The phone ordering method will take three extra days for shopping but no additional costs will be attached. Our company policy is that all first time customers receive free shipping and handling for their first three months for business, so the new printers would have no extra costs.

We look forward to welcoming you as our customer.

Your sincerely,
John Mortmon
Marketing Director of Mortmon Brothers

* What is the benefit for the first time customers?

① They win a free printer from the company.
② They get free delivery for a few months.
③ They can submit orders through the internet.
④ They can receive a brochure listing new items.

15 빈칸 (A), (B)에 들어갈 단어로 가장 적절한 것은?

When you want to remind yourself to do something, link that activity to another event that you know will take place. Say you're walking to work and suddenly you realize that your books are (A) _____ at the library tomorrow. Switch your watch from your left to your right wrist. Every time you look at your watch it becomes a (B) _____ that you were supposed to remember something. If you empty your pockets every night, put an unusual item in your pocket to remind yourself to do something before you go to bed. To remember to call your sister for her birthday, pick an object from the kitchen—a fork, perhaps—and put it in your pocket.

	(A)		(B)
①	due	–	reminder
②	due	–	recliner
③	ready	–	reminder
④	ready	–	recliner

16 다음 문장의 밑줄 친 단어의 의미를 아래에 주어진 사전 뜻풀이 가운데에서 고를 때 가장 적절한 것은?

* Ignorance <u>breeds</u> prejudice.

> breed v.
> 1. to have sex and produce young : *Many animals breed only at certain times of the year.*
> 2. to keep animals or plants in order to produce young ones in a controlled way : *The rabbits are bred for their long coats.*
> 3. to be the cause of something : *Nothing breeds success like success.*
> 4. to educate somebody in a particular way as they are growing up : *Fear of failure was bred into him at an early age.*

① 1.   ② 2.
③ 3.   ④ 4.

17 다음 글의 제목으로 가장 적절한 것은?

> Personal qualities generally have either positive or negative connotations. Our attitudes toward such personal qualities are partly personal, partly social, and partly cultural. Some people also feel that gender plays a role, with some qualities being more positively valued by women than by men and vice versa. Such attitudes are not always static, and they can change with changing economic and social circumstances. In some places, during the 1970s, ambition was seen to be bad, and then, during the 1980s, it was seen to be good. During the harsh economic times of the 1990s, a high value was placed on generosity and compassion.

① How Personal Qualities Form
② Changeable Standards of Value on Personal Qualities
③ The Meaning of Personal Qualities
④ Why Some Personal Qualities Have Positive Connotations

18 다음 글의 문맥상 밑줄 친 단어의 의미로 가장 가까운 것은?

> The time it takes a planet to make one orbit is related to its <u>proximity</u> to the sun.

① closeness to   ② attachment to
③ variance from   ④ reflection from

19 다음 글의 주제로 가장 적절한 것은?

> Recently, scientists have discovered that ancient Egyptians mummified animals. Some of the animals found in tombs were pets such as cats, dogs, and rabbits. Scientists believe that animals were mummified using the same technique as for humans. Apparently, the early Egyptians had many household pets and were quite fond of them. They believed their pets would live on into the afterlife to protect and comfort their masters. In addition, other animals have also been discovered. In other tombs, mummified bulls and crocodiles were found. For the ancient Egyptians, these animals were sacred and were the living spirits of gods. The Egyptians took good care of them while they were alive, and when they died, they buried them like kings.

① sacred animal tombs in ancient Egypt
② animal worship in ancient Egyptian funerals
③ the relationship between humans and animals
④ the reasons for animal mummification in ancient Egypt

20 다음 글의 필자가 느끼는 심정으로 가장 적절한 것은?

"I work at home for my children's sake!" I repeat this to myself until maybe I can believe it. Too often lately I feel like the worst parent on the planet. As a freelance writer, I make my own hours and can work at home with my kids. A good deal, right? Not always. Some days I take four-year-old Hewson to the park. The older kids are at school, I'm staring at a deadline, but I'm eaten up with guilt because I'm not spending time with him. Then I think, Hey, I'm my own boss! We can go to the park! I can work while he plays—the best of both worlds. I grab my cell phone and my laptop, and pull into the park, thinking, Yes! You can have it all! The next thing I know, I'm sitting on a park bench with my laptop balanced on my knees while other mothers keep an eye on my son.

① excited
② bored
③ lonely
④ guilty

21 다음 글의 흐름에 맞게 ( )에 적합한 연결어는?

The scientists are convinced that they, as scientists, possess a number of very admirable human qualities, such as accuracy, observation, reasoning power, intellectual curiosity, tolerance and even humility. ( ), they suppose that these qualities can be imparted to other people, to a certain extent, by teaching them science.

① However   ② Furthermore
③ Contrarily   ④ Nevertheless

22 다음 문장과 의미상 가장 가까운 것은?

Taking notes, even incomplete ones is usually more efficient than relying on one's memory.

① It is usually more efficient to take incomplete notes than to rely on one's memory.
② Because notes are usually incomplete, it is more efficient to rely on one's memory.
③ Taking incomplete notes is usually less efficient than relying on one's memory.
④ One's memory is usually more efficient than incomplete notes.

23 (A), (B), (C)에 들어갈 어법에 맞는 표현을 골라 짝지은 것은?

In some areas, the use of English in schools and in the media has contributed (A) (to / for) the decline of minority languages. There (B) (were / have been) about 69,000 speakers of Gaelic in Scotland in 1991, according to that year's census. The language is still used in some schools but speakers have limited legal rights. It is not used in courts, and (C) (plays / playing) no part in the national government.

(A)	(B)	(C)
① to	– have been	– plays
② to	– were	– plays
③ for	– were	– playing
④ for	– have been	– playing

24 다음 글에서 "cloning"에 대한 필자의 태도로 가장 적절한 것은?

People seem to forget that nature has been "cloning" since the beginning of time. Identical twins are exactly the same cell—split into two. Despite this, they are different human beings with different "souls". Similarly, through technology we may create a being with identical attributes but cannot clone a soul. If, through cloning, we can eliminate many genetic disorders, then surely this should be welcomed as a wonderful opportunity. Though perfected, there may still be risks, as there are in choosing to vaccinate your child. But the potential benefits may far outweigh the risks. How can we allow ourselves and our children to suffer when there could be a solution?

① neutral   ② critical

③ supportive   ④ concerned

25 다음 글의 빈칸에 들어갈 말로 가장 적절한 것은?

The second great force behind immigration has been _____. America has always been a refuge from tyranny. As a nation conceived in liberty, it has held out to the world the promise of respect for human rights.
Every time a revolution has failed in Europe, every time a nation has succumbed to tyranny, men and women who love freedom have assembled their families and their belongings and set sail across the sea.

① political oppression

② economic factor

③ flight from poverty

④ the search for freedom of worship

정답·해석·해설 p. 369

(p.167에서 전체 정답표를 확인하실 수 있습니다)

gosi.Hackers.com

정답
한눈에 보기

1회 2022년 법원직 9급   p.30

01	①	11	①	21	③
02	①	12	③	22	②
03	①	13	①	23	③
04	③	14	②	24	②
05	④	15	④	25	③
06	④	16	②		
07	①	17	③		
08	③	18	①		
09	③	19	①		
10	④	20	②		

2회 2021년 법원직 9급   p.40

01	④	11	③	21	②
02	④	12	④	22	③
03	④	13	④	23	②
04	②	14	②	24	②
05	②	15	①	25	②
06	④	16	①		
07	①	17	④		
08	②	18	①		
09	①	19	②		
10	②	20	②		

3회 2020년 법원직 9급   p.50

01	②	11	②	21	④
02	①	12	②	22	③
03	②	13	①	23	②
04	④	14	③	24	③
05	①	15	③	25	④
06	①	16	②		
07	①	17	③		
08	①	18	④		
09	③	19	④		
10	①	20	④		

4회 2019년 법원직 9급   p.60

01	③	11	②	21	④
02	③	12	①	22	③
03	③	13	③	23	③
04	③	14	②	24	④
05	②	15	④	25	②
06	②	16	④		
07	①	17	①		
08	③	18	③		
09	③	19	③		
10	④	20	②		

5회 2018년 법원직 9급   p.72

01	④	11	④	21	③
02	②	12	④	22	②
03	③	13	④	23	④
04	④	14	④	24	④
05	①	15	②	25	③
06	②	16	③		
07	③	17	④		
08	③	18	②		
09	④	19	③		
10	②	20	②		

6회 2017년 법원직 9급   p.81

01	④	11	②	21	④
02	①	12	③	22	④
03	③	13	④	23	③
04	③	14	④	24	③
05	③	15	②	25	③
06	③	16	③		
07	①	17	②		
08	①	18	②		
09	②	19	④		
10	③	20	③		

7회 2016년 법원직 9급   p.90

01	②	11	②	21	①
02	③	12	③	22	①
03	④	13	②	23	④
04	③	14	②	24	③
05	④	15	④	25	③
06	③	16	④		
07	④	17	②		
08	③	18	④		
09	④	19	③		
10	③	20	④		

8회 2015년 법원직 9급   p.101

01	①	11	③	21	③
02	③	12	④	22	③
03	③	13	③	23	③
04	③	14	④	24	③
05	②	15	①	25	②
06	③	16	②		
07	④	17	③		
08	③	18	①		
09	③	19	①		
10	①	20	④		

9회 2014년 법원직 9급   p.110

01	②	11	④	21	①
02	④	12	①	22	④
03	③	13	②	23	④
04	④	14	④	24	③
05	④	15	③	25	③
06	①	16	①		
07	②	17	③		
08	①	18	①		
09	③	19	④		
10	③	20	③		

10회 2013년 법원직 9급   p.117

1	②	11	②	21	②
2	③	12	②	22	④
3	②	13	①	23	①
4	③	14	②	24	③
5	①	15	④	25	④
6	③	16	④		
7	③	17	③		
8	①	18	③		
9	④	19	④		
10	③	20	②		

11회 2012년 법원직 9급   p.124

1	④	11	④	21	①
2	②	12	①	22	③
3	③	13	②	23	③
4	④	14	④	24	④
5	④	15	③	25	③
6	③	16	④		
7	④	17	④		
8	③	18	②		
9	②	19	①		
10	②	20	③		

12회 2011년 법원직 9급   p.133

1	①	11	②	21	①
2	②	12	④	22	③
3	④	13	①	23	④
4	③	14	④	24	③
5	③	15	③	25	②
6	①	16	④		
7	②	17	④		
8	②	18	③		
9	③	19	①		
10	④	20	③		

13회 2010년 법원직 9급   p.141

1	①	11	④	21	①
2	②	12	①	22	②
3	①	13	④	23	④
4	③	14	②	24	③
5	②	15	④	25	②
6	③	16	②		
7	④	17	①		
8	②	18	③		
9	④	19	②		
10	②	20	③		

14회 2009년 법원직 9급   p.148

1	③	11	③	21	②
2	③	12	②	22	③
3	②	13	②	23	④
4	①	14	③	24	②
5	②	15	③	25	③
6	④	16	②		
7	④	17	②		
8	①	18	③		
9	②	19	③		
10	②	20	④		

15회 2008년 법원직 9급   p.155

1	②	11	④	21	②
2	④	12	④	22	①
3	④	13	①	23	②
4	④	14	②	24	③
5	③	15	①	25	①
6	④	16	③		
7	③	17	②		
8	③	18	①		
9	②	19	④		
10	①	20	④		

gosi.Hackers.com

해커스법원직 15개년 기출문제집 영어

답안지

답안지 활용 방법

1. 맞은 것은 ○, 찍었는데 맞은 것은 △, 틀린 것은 x를 문번에 표시하며 채점합니다.
2. △, x가 표시된 문제는 반드시 해설로 개념을 익히고, 회독을 통해 확실하게 학습합니다.
   회독을 할 때는 해커스공무원(gosi.Hackers.com) ▶ 사이트 상단의 [교재정보] ▶ [무료 학습 자료]에서 회독용 답안지를 다운받아 진행하실 수 있습니다.
3. 점선을 따라 답안지를 잘라내어 사용하실 수도 있습니다.

___ 회

문번	제 2 과목			
01	①	②	③	④
02	①	②	③	④
03	①	②	③	④
04	①	②	③	④
05	①	②	③	④
06	①	②	③	④
07	①	②	③	④
08	①	②	③	④
09	①	②	③	④
10	①	②	③	④
11	①	②	③	④
12	①	②	③	④
13	①	②	③	④
14	①	②	③	④
15	①	②	③	④
16	①	②	③	④
17	①	②	③	④
18	①	②	③	④
19	①	②	③	④
20	①	②	③	④
21	①	②	③	④
22	①	②	③	④
23	①	②	③	④
24	①	②	③	④
25	①	②	③	④

O: 개 △: 개 X: 개

___ 회

문번	제 2 과목			
01	①	②	③	④
02	①	②	③	④
03	①	②	③	④
04	①	②	③	④
05	①	②	③	④
06	①	②	③	④
07	①	②	③	④
08	①	②	③	④
09	①	②	③	④
10	①	②	③	④
11	①	②	③	④
12	①	②	③	④
13	①	②	③	④
14	①	②	③	④
15	①	②	③	④
16	①	②	③	④
17	①	②	③	④
18	①	②	③	④
19	①	②	③	④
20	①	②	③	④
21	①	②	③	④
22	①	②	③	④
23	①	②	③	④
24	①	②	③	④
25	①	②	③	④

O: 개 △: 개 X: 개

___ 회

문번	제 2 과목			
01	①	②	③	④
02	①	②	③	④
03	①	②	③	④
04	①	②	③	④
05	①	②	③	④
06	①	②	③	④
07	①	②	③	④
08	①	②	③	④
09	①	②	③	④
10	①	②	③	④
11	①	②	③	④
12	①	②	③	④
13	①	②	③	④
14	①	②	③	④
15	①	②	③	④
16	①	②	③	④
17	①	②	③	④
18	①	②	③	④
19	①	②	③	④
20	①	②	③	④
21	①	②	③	④
22	①	②	③	④
23	①	②	③	④
24	①	②	③	④
25	①	②	③	④

O: 개 △: 개 X: 개

___ 회

문번	제 2 과목			
01	①	②	③	④
02	①	②	③	④
03	①	②	③	④
04	①	②	③	④
05	①	②	③	④
06	①	②	③	④
07	①	②	③	④
08	①	②	③	④
09	①	②	③	④
10	①	②	③	④
11	①	②	③	④
12	①	②	③	④
13	①	②	③	④
14	①	②	③	④
15	①	②	③	④
16	①	②	③	④
17	①	②	③	④
18	①	②	③	④
19	①	②	③	④
20	①	②	③	④
21	①	②	③	④
22	①	②	③	④
23	①	②	③	④
24	①	②	③	④
25	①	②	③	④

O: 개 △: 개 X: 개

___ 회

문번	제 2 과목			
01	①	②	③	④
02	①	②	③	④
03	①	②	③	④
04	①	②	③	④
05	①	②	③	④
06	①	②	③	④
07	①	②	③	④
08	①	②	③	④
09	①	②	③	④
10	①	②	③	④
11	①	②	③	④
12	①	②	③	④
13	①	②	③	④
14	①	②	③	④
15	①	②	③	④
16	①	②	③	④
17	①	②	③	④
18	①	②	③	④
19	①	②	③	④
20	①	②	③	④
21	①	②	③	④
22	①	②	③	④
23	①	②	③	④
24	①	②	③	④
25	①	②	③	④

O: 개 △: 개 X: 개

___ 회

문번	제 2 과목			
01	①	②	③	④
02	①	②	③	④
03	①	②	③	④
04	①	②	③	④
05	①	②	③	④
06	①	②	③	④
07	①	②	③	④
08	①	②	③	④
09	①	②	③	④
10	①	②	③	④
11	①	②	③	④
12	①	②	③	④
13	①	②	③	④
14	①	②	③	④
15	①	②	③	④
16	①	②	③	④
17	①	②	③	④
18	①	②	③	④
19	①	②	③	④
20	①	②	③	④
21	①	②	③	④
22	①	②	③	④
23	①	②	③	④
24	①	②	③	④
25	①	②	③	④

O: 개 △: 개 X: 개

___ 회

문번	제 2 과목			
01	①	②	③	④
02	①	②	③	④
03	①	②	③	④
04	①	②	③	④
05	①	②	③	④
06	①	②	③	④
07	①	②	③	④
08	①	②	③	④
09	①	②	③	④
10	①	②	③	④
11	①	②	③	④
12	①	②	③	④
13	①	②	③	④
14	①	②	③	④
15	①	②	③	④
16	①	②	③	④
17	①	②	③	④
18	①	②	③	④
19	①	②	③	④
20	①	②	③	④
21	①	②	③	④
22	①	②	③	④
23	①	②	③	④
24	①	②	③	④
25	①	②	③	④

O: 개 △: 개 X: 개

___ 회

문번	제 2 과목			
01	①	②	③	④
02	①	②	③	④
03	①	②	③	④
04	①	②	③	④
05	①	②	③	④
06	①	②	③	④
07	①	②	③	④
08	①	②	③	④
09	①	②	③	④
10	①	②	③	④
11	①	②	③	④
12	①	②	③	④
13	①	②	③	④
14	①	②	③	④
15	①	②	③	④
16	①	②	③	④
17	①	②	③	④
18	①	②	③	④
19	①	②	③	④
20	①	②	③	④
21	①	②	③	④
22	①	②	③	④
23	①	②	③	④
24	①	②	③	④
25	①	②	③	④

O: 개 △: 개 X: 개

gosi.Hackers.com

해커스법원직 15개년 기출문제집 영어

답안지

답안지 활용 방법

1. 맞은 것은 ○, 찍었는데 맞은 것은 △, 틀린 것은 x를 문번에 표시하며 채점합니다.
2. △, x가 표시된 문제는 반드시 해설로 개념을 익히고, 회독을 통해 확실하게 학습합니다.
   회독을 할 때는 해커스공무원(gosi.Hackers.com) ▶ 사이트 상단의 [교재정보] ▶ [무료 학습 자료]에서 회독용 답안지를 다운받아 진행하실 수 있습니다.
3. 점선을 따라 답안지를 잘라내어 사용하실 수도 있습니다.

___ 회

문번	제 2 과목			
01	①	②	③	④
02	①	②	③	④
03	①	②	③	④
04	①	②	③	④
05	①	②	③	④
06	①	②	③	④
07	①	②	③	④
08	①	②	③	④
09	①	②	③	④
10	①	②	③	④
11	①	②	③	④
12	①	②	③	④
13	①	②	③	④
14	①	②	③	④
15	①	②	③	④
16	①	②	③	④
17	①	②	③	④
18	①	②	③	④
19	①	②	③	④
20	①	②	③	④
21	①	②	③	④
22	①	②	③	④
23	①	②	③	④
24	①	②	③	④
25	①	②	③	④

○: 개 △: 개 X: 개

___ 회

문번	제 2 과목			
01	①	②	③	④
02	①	②	③	④
03	①	②	③	④
04	①	②	③	④
05	①	②	③	④
06	①	②	③	④
07	①	②	③	④
08	①	②	③	④
09	①	②	③	④
10	①	②	③	④
11	①	②	③	④
12	①	②	③	④
13	①	②	③	④
14	①	②	③	④
15	①	②	③	④
16	①	②	③	④
17	①	②	③	④
18	①	②	③	④
19	①	②	③	④
20	①	②	③	④
21	①	②	③	④
22	①	②	③	④
23	①	②	③	④
24	①	②	③	④
25	①	②	③	④

○: 개 △: 개 X: 개

___ 회

문번	제 2 과목			
01	①	②	③	④
02	①	②	③	④
03	①	②	③	④
04	①	②	③	④
05	①	②	③	④
06	①	②	③	④
07	①	②	③	④
08	①	②	③	④
09	①	②	③	④
10	①	②	③	④
11	①	②	③	④
12	①	②	③	④
13	①	②	③	④
14	①	②	③	④
15	①	②	③	④
16	①	②	③	④
17	①	②	③	④
18	①	②	③	④
19	①	②	③	④
20	①	②	③	④
21	①	②	③	④
22	①	②	③	④
23	①	②	③	④
24	①	②	③	④
25	①	②	③	④

○: 개 △: 개 X: 개

___ 회

문번	제 2 과목			
01	①	②	③	④
02	①	②	③	④
03	①	②	③	④
04	①	②	③	④
05	①	②	③	④
06	①	②	③	④
07	①	②	③	④
08	①	②	③	④
09	①	②	③	④
10	①	②	③	④
11	①	②	③	④
12	①	②	③	④
13	①	②	③	④
14	①	②	③	④
15	①	②	③	④
16	①	②	③	④
17	①	②	③	④
18	①	②	③	④
19	①	②	③	④
20	①	②	③	④
21	①	②	③	④
22	①	②	③	④
23	①	②	③	④
24	①	②	③	④
25	①	②	③	④

○: 개 △: 개 X: 개

___ 회

문번	제 2 과목			
01	①	②	③	④
02	①	②	③	④
03	①	②	③	④
04	①	②	③	④
05	①	②	③	④
06	①	②	③	④
07	①	②	③	④
08	①	②	③	④
09	①	②	③	④
10	①	②	③	④
11	①	②	③	④
12	①	②	③	④
13	①	②	③	④
14	①	②	③	④
15	①	②	③	④
16	①	②	③	④
17	①	②	③	④
18	①	②	③	④
19	①	②	③	④
20	①	②	③	④
21	①	②	③	④
22	①	②	③	④
23	①	②	③	④
24	①	②	③	④
25	①	②	③	④

○: 개 △: 개 X: 개

___ 회

문번	제 2 과목			
01	①	②	③	④
02	①	②	③	④
03	①	②	③	④
04	①	②	③	④
05	①	②	③	④
06	①	②	③	④
07	①	②	③	④
08	①	②	③	④
09	①	②	③	④
10	①	②	③	④
11	①	②	③	④
12	①	②	③	④
13	①	②	③	④
14	①	②	③	④
15	①	②	③	④
16	①	②	③	④
17	①	②	③	④
18	①	②	③	④
19	①	②	③	④
20	①	②	③	④
21	①	②	③	④
22	①	②	③	④
23	①	②	③	④
24	①	②	③	④
25	①	②	③	④

○: 개 △: 개 X: 개

___ 회

문번	제 2 과목			
01	①	②	③	④
02	①	②	③	④
03	①	②	③	④
04	①	②	③	④
05	①	②	③	④
06	①	②	③	④
07	①	②	③	④
08	①	②	③	④
09	①	②	③	④
10	①	②	③	④
11	①	②	③	④
12	①	②	③	④
13	①	②	③	④
14	①	②	③	④
15	①	②	③	④
16	①	②	③	④
17	①	②	③	④
18	①	②	③	④
19	①	②	③	④
20	①	②	③	④
21	①	②	③	④
22	①	②	③	④
23	①	②	③	④
24	①	②	③	④
25	①	②	③	④

○: 개 △: 개 X: 개

___ 회

문번	제 2 과목			
01	①	②	③	④
02	①	②	③	④
03	①	②	③	④
04	①	②	③	④
05	①	②	③	④
06	①	②	③	④
07	①	②	③	④
08	①	②	③	④
09	①	②	③	④
10	①	②	③	④
11	①	②	③	④
12	①	②	③	④
13	①	②	③	④
14	①	②	③	④
15	①	②	③	④
16	①	②	③	④
17	①	②	③	④
18	①	②	③	④
19	①	②	③	④
20	①	②	③	④
21	①	②	③	④
22	①	②	③	④
23	①	②	③	④
24	①	②	③	④
25	①	②	③	④

○: 개 △: 개 X: 개

해커스법원직 15개년 기출문제집 영어

답안지

답안지 활용 방법

1. 맞은 것은 O, 찍었는데 맞은 것은 △, 틀린 것은 x를 문번에 표시하며 채점합니다.
2. △, x가 표시된 문제는 반드시 해설로 개념을 익히고, 회독을 통해 확실하게 학습합니다.
   회독을 할 때는 해커스공무원(gosi.Hackers.com) ▶ 사이트 상단의 [교재정보] ▶ [무료 학습 자료]에서 회독용 답안지를 다운받아 진행하실 수 있습니다.
3. 점선을 따라 답안지를 잘라내어 사용하실 수도 있습니다.

___ 회

문번	제 2 과목			
01	①	②	③	④
02	①	②	③	④
03	①	②	③	④
04	①	②	③	④
05	①	②	③	④
06	①	②	③	④
07	①	②	③	④
08	①	②	③	④
09	①	②	③	④
10	①	②	③	④
11	①	②	③	④
12	①	②	③	④
13	①	②	③	④
14	①	②	③	④
15	①	②	③	④
16	①	②	③	④
17	①	②	③	④
18	①	②	③	④
19	①	②	③	④
20	①	②	③	④
21	①	②	③	④
22	①	②	③	④
23	①	②	③	④
24	①	②	③	④
25	①	②	③	④
O: 개 △: 개 X: 개				

___ 회

문번	제 2 과목			
01	①	②	③	④
02	①	②	③	④
03	①	②	③	④
04	①	②	③	④
05	①	②	③	④
06	①	②	③	④
07	①	②	③	④
08	①	②	③	④
09	①	②	③	④
10	①	②	③	④
11	①	②	③	④
12	①	②	③	④
13	①	②	③	④
14	①	②	③	④
15	①	②	③	④
16	①	②	③	④
17	①	②	③	④
18	①	②	③	④
19	①	②	③	④
20	①	②	③	④
21	①	②	③	④
22	①	②	③	④
23	①	②	③	④
24	①	②	③	④
25	①	②	③	④
O: 개 △: 개 X: 개				

___ 회

문번	제 2 과목			
01	①	②	③	④
02	①	②	③	④
03	①	②	③	④
04	①	②	③	④
05	①	②	③	④
06	①	②	③	④
07	①	②	③	④
08	①	②	③	④
09	①	②	③	④
10	①	②	③	④
11	①	②	③	④
12	①	②	③	④
13	①	②	③	④
14	①	②	③	④
15	①	②	③	④
16	①	②	③	④
17	①	②	③	④
18	①	②	③	④
19	①	②	③	④
20	①	②	③	④
21	①	②	③	④
22	①	②	③	④
23	①	②	③	④
24	①	②	③	④
25	①	②	③	④
O: 개 △: 개 X: 개				

___ 회

문번	제 2 과목			
01	①	②	③	④
02	①	②	③	④
03	①	②	③	④
04	①	②	③	④
05	①	②	③	④
06	①	②	③	④
07	①	②	③	④
08	①	②	③	④
09	①	②	③	④
10	①	②	③	④
11	①	②	③	④
12	①	②	③	④
13	①	②	③	④
14	①	②	③	④
15	①	②	③	④
16	①	②	③	④
17	①	②	③	④
18	①	②	③	④
19	①	②	③	④
20	①	②	③	④
21	①	②	③	④
22	①	②	③	④
23	①	②	③	④
24	①	②	③	④
25	①	②	③	④
O: 개 △: 개 X: 개				

___ 회

문번	제 2 과목			
01	①	②	③	④
02	①	②	③	④
03	①	②	③	④
04	①	②	③	④
05	①	②	③	④
06	①	②	③	④
07	①	②	③	④
08	①	②	③	④
09	①	②	③	④
10	①	②	③	④
11	①	②	③	④
12	①	②	③	④
13	①	②	③	④
14	①	②	③	④
15	①	②	③	④
16	①	②	③	④
17	①	②	③	④
18	①	②	③	④
19	①	②	③	④
20	①	②	③	④
21	①	②	③	④
22	①	②	③	④
23	①	②	③	④
24	①	②	③	④
25	①	②	③	④
O: 개 △: 개 X: 개				

___ 회

문번	제 2 과목			
01	①	②	③	④
02	①	②	③	④
03	①	②	③	④
04	①	②	③	④
05	①	②	③	④
06	①	②	③	④
07	①	②	③	④
08	①	②	③	④
09	①	②	③	④
10	①	②	③	④
11	①	②	③	④
12	①	②	③	④
13	①	②	③	④
14	①	②	③	④
15	①	②	③	④
16	①	②	③	④
17	①	②	③	④
18	①	②	③	④
19	①	②	③	④
20	①	②	③	④
21	①	②	③	④
22	①	②	③	④
23	①	②	③	④
24	①	②	③	④
25	①	②	③	④
O: 개 △: 개 X: 개				

___ 회

문번	제 2 과목			
01	①	②	③	④
02	①	②	③	④
03	①	②	③	④
04	①	②	③	④
05	①	②	③	④
06	①	②	③	④
07	①	②	③	④
08	①	②	③	④
09	①	②	③	④
10	①	②	③	④
11	①	②	③	④
12	①	②	③	④
13	①	②	③	④
14	①	②	③	④
15	①	②	③	④
16	①	②	③	④
17	①	②	③	④
18	①	②	③	④
19	①	②	③	④
20	①	②	③	④
21	①	②	③	④
22	①	②	③	④
23	①	②	③	④
24	①	②	③	④
25	①	②	③	④
O: 개 △: 개 X: 개				

___ 회

문번	제 2 과목			
01	①	②	③	④
02	①	②	③	④
03	①	②	③	④
04	①	②	③	④
05	①	②	③	④
06	①	②	③	④
07	①	②	③	④
08	①	②	③	④
09	①	②	③	④
10	①	②	③	④
11	①	②	③	④
12	①	②	③	④
13	①	②	③	④
14	①	②	③	④
15	①	②	③	④
16	①	②	③	④
17	①	②	③	④
18	①	②	③	④
19	①	②	③	④
20	①	②	③	④
21	①	②	③	④
22	①	②	③	④
23	①	②	③	④
24	①	②	③	④
25	①	②	③	④
O: 개 △: 개 X: 개				

gosi.Hackers.com

해커스법원직 15개년 기출문제집 영어

답안지

답안지 활용 방법

1. 맞은 것은 O, 찍었는데 맞은 것은 △, 틀린 것은 x를 문번에 표시하며 채점합니다.
2. △, x가 표시된 문제는 반드시 해설로 개념을 익히고, 회독을 통해 확실하게 학습합니다.
   회독을 할 때는 해커스공무원(gosi.Hackers.com) ▶ 사이트 상단의 [교재정보] ▶ [무료 학습 자료]에서 회독용 답안지를 다운받아 진행하실 수 있습니다.
3. 점선을 따라 답안지를 잘라내어 사용하실 수도 있습니다.

___ 회

문번	제 2 과목			
01	①	②	③	④
02	①	②	③	④
03	①	②	③	④
04	①	②	③	④
05	①	②	③	④
06	①	②	③	④
07	①	②	③	④
08	①	②	③	④
09	①	②	③	④
10	①	②	③	④
11	①	②	③	④
12	①	②	③	④
13	①	②	③	④
14	①	②	③	④
15	①	②	③	④
16	①	②	③	④
17	①	②	③	④
18	①	②	③	④
19	①	②	③	④
20	①	②	③	④
21	①	②	③	④
22	①	②	③	④
23	①	②	③	④
24	①	②	③	④
25	①	②	③	④

O: 개 △: 개 X: 개

___ 회

문번	제 2 과목			
01	①	②	③	④
02	①	②	③	④
03	①	②	③	④
04	①	②	③	④
05	①	②	③	④
06	①	②	③	④
07	①	②	③	④
08	①	②	③	④
09	①	②	③	④
10	①	②	③	④
11	①	②	③	④
12	①	②	③	④
13	①	②	③	④
14	①	②	③	④
15	①	②	③	④
16	①	②	③	④
17	①	②	③	④
18	①	②	③	④
19	①	②	③	④
20	①	②	③	④
21	①	②	③	④
22	①	②	③	④
23	①	②	③	④
24	①	②	③	④
25	①	②	③	④

O: 개 △: 개 X: 개

___ 회

문번	제 2 과목			
01	①	②	③	④
02	①	②	③	④
03	①	②	③	④
04	①	②	③	④
05	①	②	③	④
06	①	②	③	④
07	①	②	③	④
08	①	②	③	④
09	①	②	③	④
10	①	②	③	④
11	①	②	③	④
12	①	②	③	④
13	①	②	③	④
14	①	②	③	④
15	①	②	③	④
16	①	②	③	④
17	①	②	③	④
18	①	②	③	④
19	①	②	③	④
20	①	②	③	④
21	①	②	③	④
22	①	②	③	④
23	①	②	③	④
24	①	②	③	④
25	①	②	③	④

O: 개 △: 개 X: 개

___ 회

문번	제 2 과목			
01	①	②	③	④
02	①	②	③	④
03	①	②	③	④
04	①	②	③	④
05	①	②	③	④
06	①	②	③	④
07	①	②	③	④
08	①	②	③	④
09	①	②	③	④
10	①	②	③	④
11	①	②	③	④
12	①	②	③	④
13	①	②	③	④
14	①	②	③	④
15	①	②	③	④
16	①	②	③	④
17	①	②	③	④
18	①	②	③	④
19	①	②	③	④
20	①	②	③	④
21	①	②	③	④
22	①	②	③	④
23	①	②	③	④
24	①	②	③	④
25	①	②	③	④

O: 개 △: 개 X: 개

___ 회

문번	제 2 과목			
01	①	②	③	④
02	①	②	③	④
03	①	②	③	④
04	①	②	③	④
05	①	②	③	④
06	①	②	③	④
07	①	②	③	④
08	①	②	③	④
09	①	②	③	④
10	①	②	③	④
11	①	②	③	④
12	①	②	③	④
13	①	②	③	④
14	①	②	③	④
15	①	②	③	④
16	①	②	③	④
17	①	②	③	④
18	①	②	③	④
19	①	②	③	④
20	①	②	③	④
21	①	②	③	④
22	①	②	③	④
23	①	②	③	④
24	①	②	③	④
25	①	②	③	④

O: 개 △: 개 X: 개

___ 회

문번	제 2 과목			
01	①	②	③	④
02	①	②	③	④
03	①	②	③	④
04	①	②	③	④
05	①	②	③	④
06	①	②	③	④
07	①	②	③	④
08	①	②	③	④
09	①	②	③	④
10	①	②	③	④
11	①	②	③	④
12	①	②	③	④
13	①	②	③	④
14	①	②	③	④
15	①	②	③	④
16	①	②	③	④
17	①	②	③	④
18	①	②	③	④
19	①	②	③	④
20	①	②	③	④
21	①	②	③	④
22	①	②	③	④
23	①	②	③	④
24	①	②	③	④
25	①	②	③	④

O: 개 △: 개 X: 개

___ 회

문번	제 2 과목			
01	①	②	③	④
02	①	②	③	④
03	①	②	③	④
04	①	②	③	④
05	①	②	③	④
06	①	②	③	④
07	①	②	③	④
08	①	②	③	④
09	①	②	③	④
10	①	②	③	④
11	①	②	③	④
12	①	②	③	④
13	①	②	③	④
14	①	②	③	④
15	①	②	③	④
16	①	②	③	④
17	①	②	③	④
18	①	②	③	④
19	①	②	③	④
20	①	②	③	④
21	①	②	③	④
22	①	②	③	④
23	①	②	③	④
24	①	②	③	④
25	①	②	③	④

O: 개 △: 개 X: 개

___ 회

문번	제 2 과목			
01	①	②	③	④
02	①	②	③	④
03	①	②	③	④
04	①	②	③	④
05	①	②	③	④
06	①	②	③	④
07	①	②	③	④
08	①	②	③	④
09	①	②	③	④
10	①	②	③	④
11	①	②	③	④
12	①	②	③	④
13	①	②	③	④
14	①	②	③	④
15	①	②	③	④
16	①	②	③	④
17	①	②	③	④
18	①	②	③	④
19	①	②	③	④
20	①	②	③	④
21	①	②	③	④
22	①	②	③	④
23	①	②	③	④
24	①	②	③	④
25	①	②	③	④

O: 개 △: 개 X: 개

MEMO

레벨별 교재 확인 및
수강신청은 여기서!
gosi.Hackers.com

* 커리큘럼은 과목별·선생님별로 상이할 수 있으며, 자세한 내용은 해커스공무원 사이트에서 확인하세요.

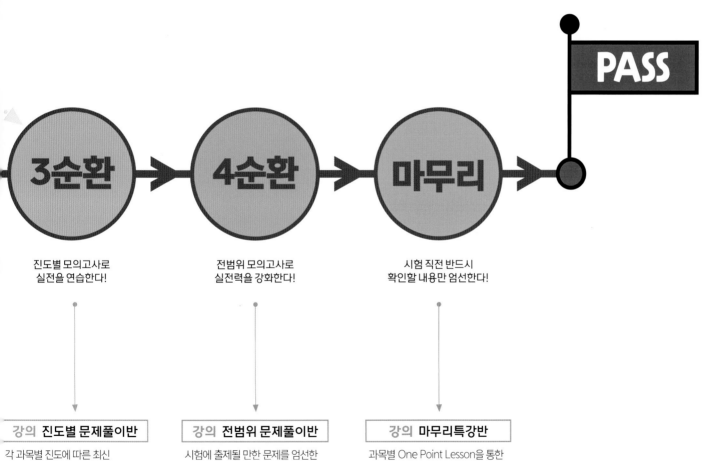

PASS

3순환	4순환	마무리

진도별 모의고사로
실전을 연습한다!

전범위 모의고사로
실전력을 강화한다!

시험 직전 반드시
확인할 내용만 엄선한다!

강의 **진도별 문제풀이반**

각 과목별 진도에 따른 최신
문제를 풀이하며 본인의 취약영역을
파악 및 보완하는 강의

강의 **전범위 문제풀이반**

시험에 출제될 만한 문제를 엄선한
전범위 예상 문제풀이를 통해
실전력을 강화하는 강의

강의 **마무리특강반**

과목별 One Point Lesson을 통한
자기주도 마무리 및 반복학습으로
최종 점검할 수 있는 강의

회독 학습 점검표

회독이 끝나면 □박스에 체크하고 틀린 문항의 번호는 적어서 복습해 보세요.

회차	다시 풀어볼 문항 체크		
	1 회독	2 회독	3 회독
예시	□ 5, 9, 10, 14	□ 5, 9	□ 9
1회	□	□	□
2회	□	□	□
3회	□	□	□
4회	□	□	□
5회	□	□	□
6회	□	□	□
7회	□	□	□
8회	□	□	□
9회	□	□	□
10회	□	□	□
11회	□	□	□
12회	□	□	□
13회	□	□	□
14회	□	□	□
15회	□	□	□

해커스법원직

15개년 기출문제집
영어

해설집

정답

p.30

01	① 문법 – 수 일치 &to 부정사&관계절	11	① 문법 – 명사절&시제 &능동태·수동태	21	③ 독해 – 논리적 흐름 파악
02	① 독해 – 전체내용 파악	12	③ 독해 – 추론	22	② 독해 – 전체내용 파악
03	① 독해 – 전체내용 파악	13	① 독해 – 논리적 흐름 파악	23	③ 독해 – 전체내용 파악
04	③ 독해 – 논리적 흐름 파악	14	② 독해 – 논리적 흐름 파악	24	② 독해 – 세부내용 파악
05	④ 독해 – 세부내용 파악	15	④ 문법 – 수 일치	25	③ 독해 – 세부내용 파악
06	④ 독해 – 추론	16	② 독해 – 전체내용 파악		
07	① 독해 – 세부내용 파악	17	③ 독해 – 추론		
08	③ 독해 – 논리적 흐름 파악	18	① 문법 – 병치·도치· 강조 구문		
09	③ 독해 – 전체내용 파악	19	① 문법 – 조동사		
10	④ 독해 – 논리적 흐름 파악	20	② 독해 – 추론		

취약영역 분석표

영역	세부 유형	문항 수	소계
문법	수 일치&to 부정사&관계절	1	/5
	명사절&시제&능동태·수동태	1	
	수 일치	1	
	병치·도치·강조 구문	1	
	조동사	1	
독해	전체내용 파악	6	/20
	세부내용 파악	4	
	추론	4	
	논리적 흐름 파악	6	
총계			/25

· 자신이 취약한 영역은 '법원직 9급 영어, 이렇게 출제된다!'(문제집 p.8)를 통해 다시 한번 확인하고 학습하시기 바랍니다.

---

01 문법 수 일치&to 부정사&관계절　　난이도 ★★☆

해석　일이나 직무에 적합한 보호복의 선택은 보통 야기되는 위험에 대한 분석 또는 평가에 의해 좌우된다. 노출의 빈도와 유형에 더하여 착용자에게 예상되는 활동이 이 결정에 입력되는 전형적인 변수이다. 예를 들어, 소방관은 다양한 연소 물질에 노출된다. 따라서 특수한 여러 겹의 직물 조직이 야기되는 열 문제에 대처하기 위해 사용된다. 이것은 보통 상당히 무겁고 어떤 화재 상황에도 대비하여 근본적으로 최고 수준의 보호를 제공하는 보호 장비가 된다. 대조적으로, 돌발적인 화재의 가능성이 있는 지역에서 일해야 하는 산업 근로자는 매우 다른 일련의 위험 요소와 필요 조건을 갖게 될 것이다. 많은 경우에, 면으로 된 작업복 위에 착용하는 방염 작업복은 충분히 위험에 대처할 수 있다.

해설　(A) 주어와 동사의 수 일치 주어 자리에 단수 명사 The selection이 왔으므로 단수 동사 is를 써야 한다.
(B) to 부정사의 역할 문맥상 '대처하기 위해'라는 의미가 되어야 자연스러우므로 부사처럼 목적을 나타낼 수 있는 to 부정사 to meet을 써야 한다.
(C) 관계부사와 관계대명사 비교 관계사 뒤에 완전한 절(the possibility ~ requirements)이 왔으므로 관계대명사 which가 아닌 관계부사 where를 써야 한다.
따라서 ① (A) is – (B) to meet – (C) where가 정답이다.

어휘　appropriate 적합한　dictate ~을 좌우하다　assessment 평가
hazard 위험 (요소)　present (문제 등을) 야기하다, 제시하다
frequency 빈도　exposure 노출　typical 전형적인
variable 변수　meet 대처하다, 만나다　protective 보호의, 방어적인
fairly 상당히, 꽤　flash fire 돌발적인 화재
flame-resistant 방염의, 내염성의(불에 잘 타지 않는)

👍 이것도 알면 합격!

관계부사(when, where, why, how)는 '전치사 + 관계대명사'의 형태로 바꾸어 쓸 수 있고 뒤에는 완전한 절이 온다는 것을 알아두자.
ex The protesters weren't entirely clear about the reasons why (= for which) they were demonstrating.
그 시위자들은 왜 그들이 시위에 참여하고 있는지 완전히 확실하지는 않았다.

---

02 독해 전체내용 파악 (문단 요약)　　난이도 ★★☆

끊어읽기 해석

In India, / approximately 360 million people / —one-third of the population— / live in or very close to the forests.
인도에서는 / 약 3억 6천만 명이 / 인구의 3분의 1인 / 숲속이나 숲과 매우 가까이에 살고 있다

More than half of these people / live below the official poverty line, / and consequently / they depend crucially / on the resources / they obtain from the forests.
이러한 사람들 중 절반 이상이 / 공식적인 빈곤선 이하에서 살고 있다 / 그리고 그 결과 / 그들은 결정적으로 의존한다 / 자원에 / 그들이 숲에서 얻는

The Indian government now runs / programs aimed at improving their lot / by involving them / in the commercial management of their forests, / in this way / allowing them to continue / to obtain the food and materials / they need, / but at the same time / to sell forest produce.
인도 정부는 현재 운영한다 / 그들 지역의 가치를 높이는 것을 목적으로 하는 프로그램을 / 그들을 참여시킴으로써 / 숲의 상업적 관리에 / 이 방식으로 / 그들이 계속 ~하는 것을 가능하게 한다 / 필요한 식량과 재료를 얻는 것을 / 그들이 필요한 / 그러나 동시에 / 임산물을 판매하는 것을

If the programs succeed, / forest dwellers will be more prosperous, / but they will be able to preserve / their

traditional way of life and culture, / and the forest will be managed sustainably, / so the wildlife is not depleted.
만약 그 프로그램이 성공하면 / 숲에 사는 사람들은 더 부유해지겠지만 / 그들은 보존할 수 있을 것이고 / 그들의 전통적인 생활양식과 문화를 / 그리고 숲이 지속 가능하게 관리되어서 / 야생동물은 대폭 감소하지 않을 것이다

해석 인도에서는, 인구의 3분의 1인 약 3억 6천만 명이 숲속이나 숲과 매우 가까이에 살고 있다. 이러한 사람들 중 절반 이상이 공식적인 빈곤선 이하에서 살고 있고, 그 결과 그들은 그들이 숲에서 얻는 자원에 결정적으로 의존한다. 인도 정부는 현재 그들을 숲의 상업적 관리에 참여시킴으로써 그들 지역의 가치를 높이는 것을 목적으로 하는 프로그램을 운영하는데, 이 방식으로 그들이 필요한 식량과 재료를 계속 얻게 하면서 동시에 임산물을 판매하는 것을 가능하게 한다. 만약 그 프로그램이 성공하면, 숲에 사는 사람들은 더 부유해지겠지만, 그들은 그들의 전통적인 생활양식과 문화를 보존할 수 있을 것이고, 숲이 지속 가능하게 관리되어서, 야생동물은 대폭 감소하지 않을 것이다.
⇒ 인도 정부는 숲을 (B) 파괴하는 것 없이 숲 근처에 사는 가난한 사람들의 삶을 (A) 개선하려 하고 있다.

	(A)	(B)
①	개선하다	파괴하는 것
②	통제하다	보존하는 것
③	개선하다	제한하는 것
④	통제하다	확대하는 것

해설 지문 중간에 인도 정부가 숲이나 그 근처에 사는 사람들을 숲의 상업적 관리에 참여시킴으로써 그들 지역의 가치를 높이기 위한 프로그램을 운영한다는 내용이 있고, 지문 마지막에 그 프로그램이 성공한다면 숲에 사는 사람들이 더 부유해지면서도 숲이 지속 가능하게 관리되어 야생동물이 대폭 감소하지 않을 것이라는 내용이 있으므로, (A)와 (B)에 인도 정부는 숲을 파괴하는 것(ruining) 없이 숲 근처에 사는 가난한 사람들의 삶을 개선하려(improve) 하고 있다는 내용이 와야 적절하다. 따라서 ① improve – ruining이 정답이다.

어휘 poverty line 빈곤선(빈곤의 여부를 구분하는 최저 수입)
depend 의존하다 obtain 얻다 aim at ~을 목적으로 하다
lot 지역, 다량 forest produce 임산물
dweller ~에 사는 사람, 거주자 prosperous 부유한
preserve 보존하다 sustainably 지속 가능하게
deplete 대폭 감소시키다, 고갈시키다 ruin 파괴하다, 망치다
enlarge 확대하다

03 독해 전체내용 파악 (문단 요약) 난이도 ★★☆

끊어읽기 해석

In the absence of facial cues or touch / during pandemic, / there is a greater need / to focus on other aspects of conversation, / including more emphasis on tone and inflection, / slowing the speed, / and increasing loudness / without sounding annoying.
얼굴을 사용하는 신호나 접촉이 없어서 / 팬데믹 중에는 / 필요성이 더욱 크다 / 대화의 다른 측면들에 집중할 / 어조와 억양을 더 강조하는 것을 포함하여 / 속도를 낮추는 것 / 음량을 높이는 것 / 성가시게 들리지 않게

Many nuances of the spoken word / are easily missed / without facial expression, / so eye contact will assume / an even greater importance.
구어의 많은 뉘앙스는 / 놓치기 쉬워서 / 얼굴 표정이 없으면 / 눈맞춤이 나타낼 것이다 / 더욱 큰 중요성을

Some hospital workers / have developed innovative ways / to try to solve this problem.
일부 병원 근로자들은 / 혁신적인 방법을 개발했다 / 이 문제를 해결하려고 시도하기 위해

One of nurse specialists was deeply concerned / that her chronically sick young patients / could not see her face, / so she printed off a variety of face stickers / to get children to point towards.
전문 간호사들 중 한 명은 깊은 관심을 가졌다 / 그녀의 만성적으로 아픈 어린 환자들이 / 그녀의 얼굴을 볼 수 없다는 것에 / 그래서 그녀는 다양한 얼굴 스티커를 인쇄했다 / 아이들이 가리키게 하기 위해

Some hospitals / now also provide their patients / with 'face-sheets' / that permit easier identification / of staff members, / and it is always useful / to reintroduce yourself and colleagues / to patients / when wearing masks.
일부 병원들은 / 오늘날 또한 환자들에게 제공한다 / '페이스 시트'를 / 더 쉬운 신원 확인을 가능하게 하는 / 직원의 / 그리고 그것은 항상 유용하다 / 당신 자신과 동료들을 다시 소개하는 데 / 환자들에게 / 마스크를 착용하고 있을 때

해석 팬데믹 중에는 얼굴을 사용하는 신호(표정)나 접촉이 없어서, 어조와 억양을 더 강조하는 것, 속도를 낮추는 것, 성가시게 들리지 않게 음량을 높이는 것을 포함하여 대화의 다른 측면들에 집중할 필요성이 더욱 크다. 구어의 많은 뉘앙스는 얼굴 표정이 없으면 놓치기 쉬워서, 눈맞춤이 더욱 큰 중요성을 나타낼 것이다. 일부 병원 근로자들은 이 문제를 해결하려고 시도하기 위해 혁신적인 방법을 개발했다. 전문 간호사들 중 한 명은 그녀의 만성적으로 아픈 어린 환자들이 그녀의 얼굴을 볼 수 없다는 것에 깊은 관심을 가졌고, 그래서 그녀는 아이들이 가리키게 하기 위해 다양한 얼굴 스티커를 인쇄했다. 오늘날 일부 병원들은 또한 환자들에게 직원의 더 쉬운 신원 확인을 가능하게 하는 '페이스 시트'를 제공하고 있는데, 그것은 마스크를 착용하고 있을 때 환자들에게 당신 자신과 동료들을 다시 소개하는 데 항상 유용하다.

일부 병원과 근로자들은 팬데믹 중에 환자들과의 대화를 (B) 보완하기 위한 (A) 대안적인 방법들을 찾고 있다.

	(A)	(B)
①	대안적인	보완하다
②	성가신	분석하다
③	효과적인	방해하다
④	방해하는	개선하다

해설 지문 중간에서 전문 간호사들 중 한 명이 환자들이 자신의 얼굴을 볼 수 없다는 것에 깊은 관심을 가지게 되어 환자들이 가리킬 수 있는 얼굴 스티커를 인쇄했다고 하였고, 오늘날 일부 병원들은 마스크를 착용하고 있을 때 환자가 직원을 쉽게 확인할 수 있도록 '페이스 시트'를 제공한다고 설명하고 있으므로, (A)와 (B)에 일부 병원과 근로자들은 팬데믹 중에 환자들과의 대화를 보완하기(complement) 위한 대안적인(alternative) 방법들을 찾고 있다는 내용이 와야 적절하다. 따라서 ① alternative – complement가 정답이다.

어휘 in the absence of ~이 없어서, ~이 없을 때 cue 신호, 단서
pandemic 팬데믹(전 세계적인 유행병) inflection 억양, 굴절
annoying 성가신 assume (특질 등을) 나타내다, 추정하다
chronically 만성적으로 permit 가능하게 하다
identification 신원 확인, 인지 alternative 대안적인
complement 보완하다 bothering 성가신 analyze 분석하다
hinder 방해하다 disturb 방해하다, 불안하게 하다

끊어읽기 해석

Once they leave their mother, / primates have to keep on making decisions / about whether new foods they encounter / are safe and worth collecting.
일단 그들이 어미 곁을 떠나면 / 영장류는 계속 결정해야 한다 / 그들이 접하게 되는 새로운 음식이 ~인지에 대해 / 안전하고 채집할 가치가 있는

(A) By the same token, / if the sampler feels fine, / it will reenter the tree / in a few days, / eat a little more, / then wait again, / building up to a large dose slowly.
같은 이유로 / 만약 그 시식자가 괜찮다고 느낀다면 / 그것은 다시 나무에 들어갈 것이다 / 며칠 내로 / 좀 더 먹고 / 그 후 다시 기다린다 / 많은 양으로 천천히 늘려가면서

Finally, / if the monkey remains healthy, / the other members figure / this is OK, / and they adopt the new food.
마침내 / 그 원숭이가 건강을 유지하면 / 다른 구성원들은 생각한다 / 이것이 괜찮다고 / 그래서 그들은 그 새로운 음식을 채택한다

(B) If the plant harbors / a particularly strong toxin, / the sampler's system will try / to break it down, / usually making the monkey sick / in the process.
만약 그 식물이 숨기고 있는 경우 / 특히 강한 독소를 / 그 시식자의 몸은 시도할 것이다 / 그것을 분해하려고 / 보통은 그 원숭이를 병들게 한다 / 그 과정에서

"I've seen this happen," / says Glander.
"저는 이것이 일어나는 것을 본 적이 있습니다" / 라고 Glander는 말한다

"The other members of the troop are watching / with great interest / —if the animal gets sick, / no other animal / will go into that tree.
"무리의 다른 구성원들은 지켜보고 있습니다 / 아주 흥미롭게 / 만약 그 동물이 병든다면 / 다른 어떤 동물들도 / 그 나무로 가지 않으려 할 것입니다

There's a cue being given / —a social cue."
거기에는 주어진 신호가 있습니다 / 바로 사회적 신호입니다"

(C) Using themselves / as experiment tools / is one option, / but social primates have found a better way.
그들 스스로를 사용하는 것은 / 실험 도구로 / 하나의 선택지이다 / 하지만 사회적인 영장류는 더 나은 방법을 찾았다

Kenneth Glander calls it "sampling."
Kenneth Glander는 그것을 '샘플링'이라고 부른다

When howler monkeys move / into a new habitat, / one member of the troop will go to a tree, / eat a few leaves, / then wait a day.
짖는원숭이가 이동할 때 / 새로운 서식지로 / 무리의 한 구성원이 나무로 갈 것이다 / 약간의 이파리를 먹는다 / 그 후 하루를 기다린다

해석 영장류는 일단 어미 곁을 떠나면 그들이 접하게 되는 음식이 안전하고 채집할 가치가 있는지에 대해 계속 결정해야 한다.

(C) 그들 스스로를 실험 도구로 사용하는 것도 하나의 선택지이지만, 사회적인 영장류는 더 나은 방법을 찾았다. Kenneth Glander는 그것을 '샘플링'이라고 부른다. 짖는원숭이가 새로운 서식지로 이동할 때, 무리의 한 구성원이 나무로 가서 약간의 이파리를 먹은 후 하루를 기다릴 것이다.

(B) 만약 그 식물이 특히 강한 독소를 숨기고 있는 경우, 그 시식자의 몸은 그것을 분해하려고 시도할 것이고, 보통은 그 과정에서 그 원숭이를 병들게 한다. "저는 이것이 일어나는 것을 본 적이 있습니다"라고 Glander는 말한다. "무리의 다른 구성원들은 아주 흥미롭게 지켜보고 있습니다. 만약 그 동물이 병든다면, 다른 어떤 동물들도 그 나무로 가지 않으려 할 것입니다.

거기에는 주어진 신호가 있는데, 바로 사회적 신호입니다."
(A) 같은 이유로, 만약 그 시식자가 괜찮다고 느낀다면, 그것은 며칠 내로 다시 나무에 들어가서 좀 더 먹은 후 많은 양으로 천천히 늘려가면서 다시 기다릴 것이다. 마침내, 그 원숭이가 건강을 유지하면 다른 구성원들은 이것이 괜찮다고 생각해서 그 새로운 음식을 채택한다.

해설 주어진 문장에서 영장류가 어미 곁을 떠나면 그들이 접하게 되는 음식이 안전하고 채집할 가치가 있는지를 계속 결정해야 한다고 한 뒤, (C)에서 사회적 영장류가 그들 스스로를 실험 도구로 사용하는 것보다 더 나은 방법인 '샘플링'이라는 방법을 사용한다고 설명하면서 짖는원숭이가 서식지를 이동할 때 한 구성원이 약간의 이파리를 먹고 하루 지켜보는 것을 예시로 들고 있다. 이어서 (B)에서 만약 원숭이가 먹은 그 식물(the plant)이 독소를 숨기고 있어 시식자인 그 원숭이가 병든다면 다른 동물들도 그 나무로 가지 않으려 할 것이라고 하며 이것이 바로 사회적 신호라고 설명한 뒤, (A)에서 이와 같은 이유로(By the same token) 만약 시식자가 건강을 유지하면 다른 구성원들도 이것이 괜찮다고 생각하여 그 새로운 음식을 채택하게 된다고 결론짓고 있다.

어휘 primates 영장류 encounter 접하다
by the same token 같은 이유로 dose 양 harbor 숨기다, 품다
toxin 독소 break down 분해하다, 부수다 troop 무리, 부대
cue 신호 experiment 실험 habitat 서식지

끊어읽기 해석

Following Japan's defeat / in World War II, / the majority of ethnic Koreans (1–1.4 million) left Japan.
일본의 패배 후 / 제 2차 세계대전에서의 / 한국 교포(100에서 140만 명) 대다수가 일본을 떠났다

By 1948, / the population of ethnic Koreans settled / around 600,000.
1948년까지 / 한국 교포 인구는 정착했다 / 약 60만 명이

These Koreans and their descendants are commonly referred to as Zainichi / (literally "residing in Japan"), / a term that appeared / in the immediate postwar years.
이 한국인들과 그 후손들은 흔히 Zainichi라고 일컬어진다 / (문자 그대로 '일본에 거주하는') / 이 용어는 나타났다 / 종전 직후에

Ethnic Koreans / who remained in Japan / did so / for diverse reasons.
한국 교포들은 / 일본에 남은 / 그렇게 했다 / 여러 가지 이유로

Koreans / who had achieved successful careers / in business, the imperial bureaucracy, and the military / during the colonial period / or who had taken advantage of economic opportunities / that opened up immediately / after the war / —opted to maintain / their relatively privileged status / in Japanese society / rather than risk returning / to an impoverished and politically unstable post-liberation Korea.
한국인들은 / 성공적인 경력을 쌓아온 / 기업, 제국의 관료 체제와 군대에서 / 식민지 시대에 / 또는 경제적 기회에 편승한 / 즉시 열린 / 전후에 / 유지하는 것을 선택했다 / 그들의 상대적으로 특권이 있는 지위를 / 일본 사회에서의 / 돌아가는 위험을 무릅쓰기보다는 / 빈곤하고 정치적으로 불안정한 해방 후의 한국으로

Some Koreans / who repatriated / were so repulsed / by the poor conditions / they observed / that they decided to return / to Japan.
몇몇 한국인들은 / 본국으로 송환된 / 매우 혐오감을 느껴서 / 열악한 환경에 / 그들이 본 / 그들은 돌아가기로 결심했다 / 일본으로

Other Koreans / living in Japan / could not afford the train fare / to one of the departure ports, / and among them / who had ethnic Japanese spouses / and Japanese-born, Japanese-speaking children, / it made more sense / to stay in Japan / rather than to navigate the cultural and linguistic challenges / of a new environment.

또 다른 한국인들은 / 일본에 살고 있던 / 기차 요금을 낼 여유가 없었다 / 출국항 중 하나로 가기 위한 / 그들 사이에서 / 일본인 배우자를 두거나 / 일본에서 태어난, 일본어를 하는 자녀를 둔 / 더 타당했다 / 일본에 머무르는 것이 / 문화 및 언어적인 문제를 처리하는 것보다 / 새로운 환경의

해석 제 2차 세계대전에서의 일본의 패배 후, 한국 교포(100에서 140만 명) 대다수가 일본을 떠났다. 1948년까지, 한국 교포 인구는 약 60만 명이 정착했다. 이 한국인들과 그 후손들은 흔히 Zainichi(문자 그대로 '일본에 거주하는')라고 일컬어지는데, 이 용어는 종전 직후 나타났다. 일본에 남은 한국 교포들은 여러 가지 이유로 그렇게 했다. 식민지 시대에 기업, 제국의 관료 체제와 군대에서 성공적인 경력을 쌓아 왔거나, 전후 즉시 열린 경제적 기회에 편승한 한국인들은 빈곤하고 정치적으로 불안정한 해방 후의 한국으로 돌아가는 위험을 무릅쓰기보다는 일본 사회에서의 상대적으로 특권이 있는 지위를 유지하는 것을 선택했다. 본국으로 송환된 몇몇 한국인들은 그들이 본 열악한 환경에 매우 혐오감을 느껴 일본으로 돌아가기로 결심했다. 일본에 살고 있던 또 다른 한국인들은 출국항 중 하나로 가기 위한 기차 요금을 낼 여유가 없었고, 그들 사이에서 일본인 배우자나 일본에서 태어난, 일본어를 하는 자녀를 둔 이들은 새로운 환경의 문화 및 언어적인 문제를 처리하는 것보다 일본에 머무르는 것이 더 타당했다.

해설 지문 마지막에서 일본에 살고 있던 또 다른 한국인들은 출국항으로 가기 위한 기차 요금을 낼 여유가 없었고, 그들 사이에서 일본인 배우자나 일본에서 태어난 자녀를 둔 이들은 일본에 머무르는 것이 더 타당했다고 했으므로, '④ 한국으로 돌아갈 교통비를 마련하지 못한 사람들은 일본인과 결혼했다'는 것은 지문의 내용과 일치하지 않는다.

어휘 defeat 패배 ethnic Koreans 한국 교포 settle 정착하다
descendant 후손 refer to as ~라고 일컫다
reside 거주하다, 살다 postwar 종전 후 imperial 제국의
bureaucracy 관료 체제 colonial period 식민지 시대
take advantage of ~에 편승하다 opt to ~하기로 선택하다
privileged 특권이 있는 impoverished 빈곤한
unstable 불안정한 post-liberation 해방 후
repulse 혐오감을 주다 fare 요금 departure port 출국항
spouse 배우자 navigate 처리하다, 항해하다

06 독해 추론 (빈칸 완성 - 구)   난이도 ★★☆

끊어읽기 해석

There are a few jobs / where people have had to develop their signing / a bit more fully.
몇몇 직업이 있다 / 사람들이 손짓 언어를 개발해야 하는 / 좀 더 충분히

We see referees and umpires / using their arms and hands / to signal directions / to the players / —as in cricket, / where a single finger upwards means / that the batsman is out / and has to leave the wicket.
우리는 (농구, 축구 등의) 심판과 (테니스, 야구 등의) 심판을 본다 / 팔과 손을 사용하는 것을 / 방향을 제시하기 위해 / 선수들에게 / 크리켓에서처럼 / 여기에서(크리켓에서) 한 손가락을 위로 향하는 것은 의미한다 / 타자가 아웃이 된 것을 / 그리고 삼주문(투구장)을 떠나야 한다는 것을

Orchestra conductors control the musicians / through their movements.
오케스트라 지휘자는 연주자들을 통제한다 / 그들의 동작을 통해

People working at a distance / from each other / have to invent special signals / if they want to communicate.
멀리 떨어져서 일하는 사람들은 / 서로 / 특별한 신호를 만들어야 한다 / 그들이 의사소통하고 싶은 경우

So do people working in a noisy environment, / such as in a factory / where the machines are very loud, / or lifeguards around a swimming pool / full of school children.
시끄러운 환경에서 일하는 사람들도 그렇게 한다(특별한 신호를 만들어 의사소통한다) / 공장에서처럼 / 기계 소리가 매우 시끄러운 / 또는 수영장 주변의 안전요원들도 / 학생들로 가득 찬

해석 손짓 언어를 좀 더 충분히 개발해야 하는 몇몇 직업이 있다. 우리는 크리켓에서처럼 (농구, 축구 등의) 심판과 (테니스, 야구 등의) 심판이 선수들에게 방향을 제시하기 위해 팔과 손을 사용하는 것을 보는데, 여기에서(크리켓에서) 한 손가락을 위로 향하는 것은 타자가 아웃이 되어 삼주문(투구장)을 떠나야 한다는 것을 의미한다. 오케스트라 지휘자는 그들의 동작을 통해 연주자들을 통제한다. 서로 멀리 떨어져서 일하는 사람들은 의사소통하고 싶은 경우 특별한 신호를 만들어야 한다. 기계 소리가 매우 시끄러운 공장에서처럼, 시끄러운 환경에서 일하는 사람들이나 학생들로 가득 찬 수영장 주변의 안전요원들도 그렇게 한다(특별한 신호를 만들어 의사소통한다).

① 부모와 아이들을 지원하다
② 완전히 새로운 근무 방식에 적응하다
③ 기본적인 인권을 위해 법정에서 싸우다
④ 손짓 언어를 좀 더 충분히 개발하다

해설 지문 전반에 걸쳐 크리켓의 심판, 오케스트라 지휘자, 공장과 같은 시끄러운 환경에서 일하는 사람 등을 예시로 들며 몇몇 직업을 가진 사람들은 의사소통을 위해 특별한 신호를 만들어야 한다고 설명하고 있으므로, 빈칸에는 '④ 손짓 언어를 좀 더 충분히 개발하다'가 들어가는 것이 적절하다.

어휘 referee (농구, 축구 등의) 심판 umpire (테니스, 야구 등의) 심판
conductor 지휘자 adapt to ~에 적응하다

07 독해 세부내용 파악 (내용 불일치 파악)   난이도 ★★☆

끊어읽기 해석

Opponents of the use of animals / in research / also oppose use of animals / to test the safety / of drugs or other compounds.
동물을 사용하는 것을 반대하는 사람들은 / 연구에서 / 동물을 사용하는 것 또한 반대한다 / 안전성을 검사하기 위해 / 약물이나 다른 화합물의

Within the pharmaceutical industry, / it was noted that / out of 19 chemicals / known to cause cancer in humans / when taken, / only seven caused cancer / in mice and rats / using standards / set by the National Cancer Instituted / (Barnard and Koufman, 1997).
제약 업계 내에서는 / ~라는 점이 주목되었다 / 19개의 화학 물질 중 / 인간에게 암을 유발하는 것으로 알려진 / 섭취되었을 때 / 오직 7개만이 암을 유발했다는 것이 / 생쥐와 쥐들에게 / 기준을 사용했을 때 / 미국 국립 암 연구소에 의해 정해진 / (1997년 Barnard와 Koufman이 설립)

For example, / and antidepressant, nomifensin, / had minimal toxicity / in rats, rabbits, dogs, and monkeys / yet caused liver toxicity and anemia / in humans.
예를 들어 / 항우울제인 노미펜신은 / 아주 적은 독성을 가지고 있었다 / 쥐, 토끼, 개, 그리고 원숭이에게는 / 그러나 간독성과 빈혈을 유발했다 / 인간에게는

In these and other cases, / it has been shown that / some compounds have serious adverse reactions / in humans /

that were not predicted by animal testing / resulting in conditions / in the treated humans / that could lead to disability, / or even death.
이와 다른 경우에는 ~인 것으로 보인다 / 일부 화합물에 심각한 부작용이 있다는 / 인간에게 / 동물 실험에서는 예측할 수 없었던 / 상태를 초래한다 / 치료 받은 인간에게 / 장애에 이를 수 있는 / 심지어 죽음에까지

And researchers / who are calling for an end / to animal research / state that they have better methods available / such as human clinical trials, / observation aided by laboratory of autopsy tests.
그리고 연구자들은 / 중단을 요구하고 있는 / 동물 연구에 대한 / 더 나은 방법이 있다고 말한다 / 인간의 임상 실험처럼 / 해부 검사 실험실의 도움을 받는 관찰

해석 연구에서 동물을 사용하는 것을 반대하는 사람은 약물이나 다른 화합물의 안전성을 검사하기 위해 동물을 사용하는 것 또한 반대한다. 제약 업계 내에서는, 섭취되었을 때 인간에게 암을 유발하는 것으로 알려진 19개의 화학 물질 중 오직 7개만이 미국 국립 암 연구소(1997년 Barnard와 Koufman이 설립)에 의해 정해진 기준을 사용했을 때 생쥐들과 쥐들에게 암을 유발했다는 점이 주목되었다. 예를 들어, 항우울제인 노미펜신은 쥐, 토끼, 개, 그리고 원숭이에게는 아주 적은 독성을 가지고 있었지만 인간에게는 간독성과 빈혈을 유발했다. 이와 다른 경우에는, 일부 화합물에 동물 실험에서는 예측할 수 없었던 심각한 부작용이 있는 것으로 보이며, 이는 치료 받은 인간에게 장애나 심지어 죽음에까지 이를 수 있는 상태를 초래할 수 있다. 그리고 동물 연구에 대한 중단을 요구하고 있는 연구자들은 인간의 임상 실험이나 해부 검사 실험실의 도움을 받는 관찰 등 더 나은 방법이 있다고 말한다.

*세 번째 문장의 and는 an의 오타이므로, 해석하지 않았습니다.

해설 지문 처음에서 섭취되었을 때 인간에게 암을 유발하는 것으로 알려진 화학 물질 19개 중 오직 7개만이 미국 국립 암 연구소에 의해 정해진 기준을 사용했을 때 생쥐들과 쥐들에게 암을 유발했다는 점이 제약 업계에서 주목되었다고 했으므로, '① 한 기관의 실험 결과 동물과 달리 19개의 발암물질 중에 7개는 인간에게 영향을 미쳤다'는 것은 지문의 내용과 일치하지 않는다.

어휘 opponent 반대하는 사람 compounds 화합물
pharmaceutical 제약의 chemicals 화학 물질 standard 기준
antidepressant 항우울제 toxicity 독성
adverse reaction 부작용 disability 장애 call for ~을 요구하다
aid 돕다 autopsy 해부, 부검

08 독해 논리적 흐름 파악 (문맥상 부적절한 어휘) 난이도 ★★☆

끊어읽기 해석

Cold showers are any showers / with a water temperature below 70°F.
찬물 샤워는 모든 샤워이다 / 화씨 70도 이하 온도의 물로 하는

They may have health benefits.
그것들에는 건강상의 이점이 있을지도 모른다

For people with depression, / cold showers can work / as a kind of gentle electroshock therapy.
우울증이 있는 사람들에게 / 찬물 샤워는 작용할 수 있다 / 일종의 가벼운 전기 충격 요법으로서

The cold water sends many electrical impulses / to your brain.
차가운 물은 많은 전기적 자극을 보낸다 / 당신의 뇌에

They jolt your system / to ① increase / alertness, clarity, and energy levels.

그것들(전기적 자극)은 당신의 몸이 갑자기 덜컥 움직이게 한다 / ① 향상시키도록 / 각성도, 명확성과 활력 수준을

Endorphins, / which are sometimes called happiness hormones, / are also released.
엔도르핀 / 때때로 행복 호르몬이라고 불리기도 하는 / 또한 방출이 된다

This effect leads to / feelings of well-being and ② optimism.
이 효과는 이어진다 / 행복감과 ② 낙관주의로

For people that are obese, / taking a cold shower / 2 or 3 times per week / may contribute / to increased metabolism.
비만인 사람들에게 / 찬물 샤워하는 것은 / 일주일에 두세 번 / 기여할지도 모른다 / 신진대사 향상에

It may help fight obesity / over time.
그것은 비만과 싸우는 데 도움이 될지도 모른다 / 시간이 지남에 따라

The research about / how exactly cold showers help people / lose weight / is ③ clear.
~에 대한 연구는 / 정확하게 어떻게 찬물 샤워가 사람들을 돕는지 / 체중 감량을 하도록 / ③ 분명하다.

However, / it does show / that cold water can even out certain hormone levels / and heal the gastrointestinal system.
그러나 / 그것은 보여준다 / 찬물이 특정 호르몬 수준을 안정되게 할 수 있다는 것을 / 그리고 위장계를 치료하는 것을

These effects may add / to the cold shower's ability / to lead to weight loss.
이러한 효과들이 증가시키는 것일지도 모른다 / 찬물 샤워의 능력을 / 체중 감량으로 이어지는

Furthermore, / when taken regularly, / cold showers can make our circulatory system / more efficient.
게다가 / 정기적으로 (찬물 샤워가) 행해진다면 / 찬물 샤워는 우리의 순환계를 만들 수 있다 / 더욱 효율적으로

Some people also report / that their skin looks better / as a result of cold showers, / probably because of better circulation.
어떤 사람들은 또한 전한다 / 그들의 피부가 더 보기 좋아졌다는 것을 / 찬물 샤워의 결과로 / 이는 아마도 더 나은 혈액 순환 때문일 것이다

Athletes have known this benefit / for years, / even if we have only ④ recently seen data / that supports cold water / for healing after a sport injury.
운동선수들은 이 장점을 알고 있었다 / 몇 년 전부터 / 우리는 불과 ④ 최근에 자료를 봤지만 / 찬물을 지지하는 / 스포츠 부상 이후의 치료를 위한

해석 찬물 샤워는 화씨 70도 이하 온도의 물로 하는 모든 샤워이다. 그것들에는 건강상의 이점이 있을지도 모른다. 우울증이 있는 사람들에게, 찬물 샤워는 일종의 가벼운 전기 충격 요법으로서 작용할 수 있다. 차가운 물은 당신의 뇌에 많은 전기적 자극을 보낸다. 그것들(전기적 자극)은 당신의 몸이 각성도, 명확성과 활력 수준을 ① 향상시키도록 갑자기 덜컥 움직이게 한다. 때때로 행복 호르몬이라고 불리기도 하는 엔도르핀 또한 방출이 된다. 이 효과는 행복감과 ② 낙관주의로 이어진다. 비만인 사람들에게, 일주일에 두세 번 찬물 샤워하는 것은 신진대사 향상에 기여할지도 모른다. 그것은 시간이 지남에 따라 비만과 싸우는 데 도움이 될지도 모른다. 정확하게 어떻게 찬물 샤워가 사람들의 체중 감량을 돕는지에 대한 연구는 ③ 분명하다. 그러나, 그것은 찬물이 특정 호르몬 수준을 안정되게 해서 위장계를 치료할 수 있다는 것을 보여준다. 이러한 효과들이 체중 감량으로 이어지는 찬물 샤워의 능력을 증가시키는 것일지도 모른다. 게다가, 정기적으로 (찬물 샤워가) 행해진다면, 찬물 샤워는 우리의 순환계를 더욱 효율적으로 만들 수 있다. 어떤 사람들은 또한 그들의 피부가 찬물 샤워의 결과로 더 보기 좋아졌다고 전하는데, 이는 아마도 더 나은 혈액 순환 때문일 것이다. 우리는 스포츠 부상 이후의 치료를 위한 찬물을 뒷받침하

는 자료를 불과 ④ <u>최근</u>에 봤지만, 운동선수들은 몇 년 전부터 이 장점을 알고 있었다.

해설 지문 중간에 일주일에 두세 번의 찬물 샤워가 신진대사 향상에 기여할지도 모르며, 그것이 시간이 지남에 따라 비만과 싸우는 데 도움이 될지도 모른다는 내용이 있고, ③번 뒤 문장에 그러나 (However) 찬물이 특정 호르몬 수준을 안정되게 해서 위장계를 치료할 수 있다는 것을 보여준다는 내용이 있으므로, 정확하게 어떻게 찬물 샤워가 사람들의 체중 감량을 돕는지에 대한 연구가 '③ 분명하다(clear)'는 것은 문맥상 적절하지 않다. 주어진 clear 를 대신할 수 있는 어휘로는 '불분명하다'라는 의미의 unclear 등 이 있다.

어휘 temperature 온도 depression 우울증 electroshock 전기 충격 impulse 자극 alertness 각성도 clarity 명확성 optimism 낙관주의 obese 비만인, 뚱뚱한 contribute to ~에 기여하다 metabolism 신진대사 even out 안정되다 heal 치료하다 circulatory system 순환계 efficient 효율적인

09 독해 전체내용 파악 (문단 요약) 난이도 ★★☆

끊어읽기 해석

Researchers have been interested / in the habitual ways / a single individual copes with conflict / when it occurs.
연구원들은 흥미를 느꼈다 / 습관적인 방법들에 / 한 개인이 갈등에 대처하는 / 그것이 발생했을 때

They've called this approach / conflict styles.
그들은 이 접근법을 불러왔다 / 갈등 방식이라고

There are several apparent conflict styles, / and each has its pros and cons.
몇 가지 분명한 갈등 방식이 있다 / 그리고 각각 장단점이 있다

The collaborating style tends / to solve problems / in ways that maximize the chances / that the best result is provided / for all involved.
협력 방식은 경향이 있다 / 문제를 해결하는 / 가능성을 최대화하는 방식으로 / 최상의 결과가 제공될 / 관련된 모두에게

The pluses of a collaborating style include / creating trust, maintaining positive relationship, and building commitment.
협력 방식의 이점은 포함한다 / 신뢰를 형성하는 것, 긍정적인 관계를 유지하는 것, 그리고 참여를 만들어 내는 것을

However, / it's time consuming / and it takes a lot of energy / to collaborate with another / during conflict.
그러나 / 그것은 시간이 걸린다 / 그리고 많은 에너지를 필요로 한다 / 다른 사람과 협력하는 것은 / 갈등 중에

The competing style may develop hostility / in the person / who doesn't achieve their goals.
경쟁 방식은 적대감이 생기게 할 수도 있다 / 사람에게 / 목표를 달성하지 못한

However, / the competing style tends / to resolve a conflict quickly.
그러나 / 경쟁 방식은 경향이 있다 / 갈등을 빠르게 해결하는

해석 연구원들은 갈등이 발생했을 때 한 개인이 그에 대처하는 습관적인 방법들에 흥미를 느껴왔다. 그들은 이 접근법을 갈등 방식이라고 불러왔다. 몇 가지 분명한 갈등 방식이 있으며, 각각 장단점이 있다. 협력 방식은 관련된 모두에게 최상의 결과가 제공될 가능성을 최대화하는 방식으로 문제를 해결하는 경향이 있다. 협력 방식의 이점은 신뢰를 형성하는 것, 긍정적인 관계를 유지하는 것, 그리고 참여를 만들어 내는 것을 포함한다. 그러나, 그것은 시간이 걸리고 갈등 중에 다른 사람과 협력하는 것은 많은 에너지를 필요

로 한다. 경쟁 방식은 목표를 달성하지 못한 사람에게 적대감이 생기게 할 수도 있다. 그러나, 경쟁 방식은 갈등을 빠르게 해결하는 경향이 있다.

> 협력 방식은 (A) <u>상호 이해</u>에 큰 가치를 부여하는 사람에 의해 사용될 수 있는 반면, (B) <u>시간 효율</u>을 선호하는 사람은 경쟁 방식을 선택할 것이다.

	(A)	(B)
①	재정적 능력	상호작용
②	시간 절약	평화로움
③	상호 이해	시간 효율
④	유효성	일관성

해설 지문 중간에 협력 방식은 관련된 모두에게 최상의 결과가 제공될 가능성을 최대화하는 방식으로 문제를 해결하는 경향이 있다는 내용이 있고, 지문 후반에 다른 사람과 협력하는 데는 시간이 걸리고 많은 에너지가 필요하며, 경쟁 방식이 갈등을 빠르게 해결하는 경향이 있다는 내용이 있으므로, (A)와 (B)에 협력 방식은 상호 이해(mutual understanding)에 큰 가치를 부여하는 사람에 의해 사용될 수 있는 반면, 시간 효율(time efficiency)을 선호하는 사람은 경쟁 방식을 선택할 것이라는 내용이 와야 적절하다. 따라서 ③ (A) mutual understanding – (B) time efficiency 가 정답이다.

어휘 habitual 습관적인 cope with ~에 대처하다 conflict 갈등 apparent 분명한 pros and cons 장단점 collaborate 협력하다 maximize 최대화하다 plus 이점 maintain 유지하다 commitment 참여, 약속 time consuming 시간이 걸리는 compete 경쟁하다 hostility 적대감, 적의 prefer 선호하다 interaction 상호작용 mutual 상호의, 서로의 efficiency 효율, 능률 effectiveness 유효성 consistency 일관성

10 독해 논리적 흐름 파악 (문단 순서 배열) 난이도 ★★★

끊어읽기 해석

The historical evolution of Conflict Resolution / gained momentum / in the 1950s and 1960s, / at the height of the Cold War, / when the development of nuclear weapons and conflict between the superpowers / seemed to threaten human survival.
분쟁 해결의 역사적 발전이 / 탄력을 받게 되었다 / 1950년대와 1960년대에 / 냉전이 한창이었던 / 그 당시에는 핵무기 개발과 초강대국 간 분쟁이 / 인류의 생존을 위협하는 것처럼 보였다

(A) The combination of analysis and practice / implicit in the new ideas / was not easy / to reconcile with traditional scholarly institutions / or the traditions of practitioners / such as diplomats and politicians.
분석과 실천의 조합은 / 그 새로운 발상에 내재된 / 쉽지 않았다 / 전통적인 학술기관과 조화시키기가 / 혹은 전문직 종사자들의 관례와 / 외교관 및 정치인과 같은

(B) However, / they were not taken seriously / by some.
그러나 / 그들은 진지하게 받아들여지지 않았다 / 일부 사람들에게

The international relations profession had its own understanding / of international conflict / and did not see value / in the new approaches / as proposed.
국제 관계 전문가는 고유한 이해를 갖고 있었다 / 국제 분쟁에 대한 / 그리고 가치를 찾지 못했다 / 새로운 접근법에서 / 제안된 것과 같은

(C) A group of pioneers / from different disciplines / saw the value of studying conflict / as a general phenomenon, / with similar properties, / whether it occurs / in international

relations, domestic politics, industrial relations, communities, / or between individuals.
선구자 집단은 / 서로 다른 학문의 / 분쟁을 연구하는 것의 가치를 이해했다 / 일반적인 현상으로써 / 유사한 특성들을 갖는 / 그것(분쟁)이 발생하는지 관계없이 / 국제 관계, 국내 정치, 산업 관계, 지역사회 / 또는 개인들 사이에

해석 | 냉전이 한창이었던 1950년대와 1960년대에 분쟁 해결의 역사적 발전이 탄력을 받게 되었는데, 그 당시에는 핵무기 개발과 초강대국 간 분쟁이 인류의 생존을 위협하는 것처럼 보였다.

(C) 서로 다른 학문의 선구자 집단은 그것(분쟁)이 국제 관계, 국내 정치, 산업 관계, 지역사회, 또는 개인들 사이에 발생하는지와 관계없이 분쟁을 유사한 특성들을 갖는 일반적인 현상으로써 연구하는 것의 가치를 이해했다.

(B) 그러나, 그들은 일부 사람들에게 진지하게 받아들여지지 않았다. 국제 관계 전문가는 국제 분쟁에 대해 고유한 이해를 갖고 있었고 제안된 것과 같은 새로운 접근법에서 가치를 찾지 못했다.

(A) 그 새로운 발상에 내재된 분석과 실천의 조합은 전통적인 학술 기관이나 외교관 및 정치인과 같은 전문직 종사자들의 관례와 조화시키기가 쉽지 않았다.

해설 주어진 문장에서 냉전이 한창이던 1950년대와 1960년대에 분쟁 해결의 역사적 발전이 탄력을 받게 되었다고 한 뒤, (C)에서 서로 다른 학문의 선구자 집단이 분쟁을 일반적인 현상으로써 연구하는 것의 가치를 이해했다고 하면서 분쟁에 관한 새로운 발상을 설명하고 있다. 이어서 (B)에서 그러나(However) 그들(they)이 일부 사람들에게는 진지하게 받아들여지지 않았다고 하며 국제 관계 전문가들은 그러한 새로운 접근법에서 가치를 찾지 못했다고 한 뒤, (A)에서 그 새로운 발상에 내재된 내용은 전통적인 학술기관이나 외교관 및 정치인과 같은 전문직 종사자들의 관례와 조화시키기가 쉽지 않았다고 하며 분쟁에 관한 새로운 발상이 직면하게 된 문제를 설명하고 있다.

어휘 resolution 해결 momentum 탄력, 가속도
at the height of ~이 한창일 때 superpower 초강대국
threaten 위협하다 combination 조합 analysis 분석
implicit 내재된, 암시된 reconcile 조화시키다, 화해시키다
scholarly 학술의, 학문적인
practitioner 전문직 종사자, 실천하는 사람 diplomat 외교관
pioneer 선구자 disciplines 학문 phenomenon 현상
properties 특성, 성질 domestic 국내의

---

11 문법 명사절 & 시제 & 능동태·수동태 난이도 ★★☆

해석 경제학을 이해하는 비결은 항상 의도하지 않은 결과가 있다는 것을 받아들이는 것이다. 사람들이 자신만의 타당한 이유들로 취하는 행동들은 그들이 상상하지 못하거나 의도치 않은 결과를 낳는다. 지정학에 있어서도 마찬가지이다. 기원전 7세기에 확장을 시작한 로마의 마을이 500년 이후의 지중해 권역 정복에 관한 기본 계획을 가지고 있었는지는 의문이다. 하지만 인근 마을에 대해 그곳의 주민들이 취했던 가장 첫 번째 행동은 현실에 제약받았을 뿐만 아니라 의도치 않은 결과로 가득 찼던 과정을 촉발했다. 로마는 계획되지 않았고, 그저 우연히 일어난 것 또한 아니었다.

해설 (A) what vs. that 완전한 절(there are ~ consequences)을 이끌면서 동명사 accepting의 목적어 자리에 올 수 있는 명사절 접속사 that을 써야 한다.
(B) 과거 시제 문맥상 '로마의 마을이 기본 계획을 가지고 있었는지'라는 의미가 되어야 자연스럽고 특정 과거 시점을 나타내

는 표현(in the seventh century BC)이 왔으므로 과거 동사 had를 써야 한다.
(C) 능동태·수동태 구별 동사 fill 뒤에 목적어가 없고, 관계절의 선행사(a process)와 동사가 '의도치 않은 결과로 가득 찬 과정'이라는 의미의 수동 관계이므로 be동사(was) 뒤에서 수동태를 완성하는 과거분사 filled를 써야 한다.
따라서 ① (A) that – (B) had – (C) filled가 정답이다.

어휘 key 비결, 열쇠 unintended 의도하지 않은 consequence 결과
envision 상상하다 expansion 확장 conquer 정복하다
Mediterranean 지중해의 inhabitant 주민, 거주자
set in motion 촉발하다, 움직이게 하다
constrain 제약하다, 제한하다

🔖 이것도 알면 **합격!**

능동태 문장의 목적어가 수동태 문장의 주어가 되므로, 목적어를 갖지 않는 자동사는 수동태가 될 수 없다.

ex An ominous set of storm clouds ~~was appeared~~ (→ appeared) on the horizon last week.
불길한 폭풍우 구름 떼가 저번 주 지평선 위에 나타났다.

---

12 독해 추론 (빈칸 완성 - 구) 난이도 ★★☆

끊어읽기 해석

Water and civilization go hand-in-hand.
물과 문명은 밀접하게 관련되어 있다

The idea of a "hydraulic civilization" argues / that water is the unifying context and justification / for many large-scale civilizations / throughout history.
'수력학의 문명'이라는 발상은 주장한다 / 물이 통합적인 배경이자 타당한 이유라는 것을 / 많은 대규모 문명에 대한 / 역사를 통틀어

For example, / the various multi-century Chinese empires survived / as long as they did / in part / by controlling floods / along the Yellow River.
예를 들어 / 여러 세기에 걸친 다양한 중국 제국은 살아남았다 / 그들이 그랬던 만큼 오래 / 부분적으로 / 홍수를 제어함으로써 / 황하를 따라

One interpretation of the hydraulic theory / is that the justification / for gathering populations / into large cities / is to manage water.
수력학 이론 중 한 가지 해석은 / 타당한 이유가 ~라는 것이다 / 인구를 모으는 것에 대한 / 대도시로 / 물을 관리하기 위해서다

Another interpretation suggests / that large water projects enable / the rise of big cities.
또 다른 해석은 시사한다 / 대규모 치수 사업이 가능하게 한다는 것을 / 대도시들의 발생을

The Romans understood / the connections between water and power, / as the Roman Empire built / a vast network of aqueducts / throughout land they controlled, / many of which remain intact.
로마인들은 이해하고 있었다 / 물과 권력의 관련성을 / 로마 제국이 건설했다는 점에서 / 송수로의 광활한 망을 / 그들이 지배하는 땅의 도처에 / 그것들(송수로)의 대부분은 온전히 남아 있다

For example, / Pont du Gard in southern France stands today / as a testament to humanity's investment / in its water infrastructure.
예를 들어 / 프랑스 남부에 있는 가르 수도교는 오늘날 세워져 있다 / 인류의 투자의 증거로서 / 그것의 물 기반 시설에 대한

Roman governors / built roads, bridges, and water systems / as a way of concentrating and strengthening / their authority.

로마의 지배자들은 / 도로, 다리, 그리고 상수도를 건설했다 / 집중하고 강화하는 방법으로서 / 그들의 권한을

해석 물과 문명은 밀접하게 관련되어 있다. '수력학의 문명'이라는 발상은 물이 역사를 통틀어 많은 대규모 문명에 대한 통합적인 배경이자 타당한 이유라고 주장한다. 예를 들어, 여러 세기에 걸친 다양한 중국 제국은 부분적으로 황하를 따라 홍수를 제어함으로써 그들이 그랬던 만큼 오래 살아남았다. 수력학 이론 중 한 가지 해석은 대도시로 인구를 모으는 것에 대한 타당한 이유가 물을 관리하기 위해서라는 것이다. 또 다른 해석은 대규모 치수 사업이 대도시들의 발생을 가능하게 한다는 것을 시사한다. 로마 제국이 그들이 지배하는 땅의 도처에 송수로의 광활한 망을 건설했다는 점에서, 로마인들은 물과 권력의 관련성을 이해하고 있었던 것이고, 그것들(송수로)의 대부분은 온전히 남아 있다. 예를 들어, 프랑스 남부에 있는 가르 수도교는 오늘날 그것(인류)의 물 기반 시설에 대한 인류의 투자의 증거로서 세워져 있다. 로마의 지배자들은 그들의 권한을 집중하고 강화하는 방법으로서 도로, 다리, 그리고 상수도를 건설했다.

① 젊은이들을 교육하는 데 초점을 맞추는
② 현지 시장에서 자유 무역을 금지하는
③ 그들의 권한을 집중하고 강화하는
④ 다른 나라들에 그들의 토지를 넘겨주는

해설 지문 중간에서 수력학 이론의 또 다른 해석은 대규모 치수 사업이 대도시들의 발생을 가능하게 한다는 것이라는 것을 시사한다고 하며 로마 제국이 지배하는 땅의 도처에 송수로의 광활한 망을 건설했다는 점에서 로마인들이 물과 권력의 관련성을 이해하고 있었던 것이라고 설명하고 있으므로, 빈칸에는 로마의 지배자들이 '③ 그들의 권한을 집중하고 강화하는' 방법으로서 도로, 다리, 그리고 상수로를 건설했다는 내용이 들어가야 적절하다.

어휘 civilization 문명 go hand-in-hand 밀접하게 관련되어 있다
unify 통합하다, 통일하다 justification 타당한 이유, 정당화
interpretation 해석 gather 모으다 intact 온전한
Pont du gard 가르 수도교(프랑스 남부에 있는 고대 로마의 수도교)
testament 증거 infrastructure 기반 시설
governor 지배자, 통치자 prohibit 금지하다
concentrate 집중하다 strengthen 강화하다 authority 권한
give up ~을 넘겨주다 property 토지, 소유지

13 독해 논리적 흐름 파악 (문단 순서 배열) 난이도 ★☆☆

끊어읽기 해석

Ambiguity is so uncomfortable / that it can even turn / good news into bad.
모호함은 매우 불쾌해서 / 심지어 바꿀 수 있다 / 좋은 소식을 나쁜 소식으로

You go to your doctor / with a persistent stomachache.
당신은 의사에게 간다 / 계속되는 복통으로

Your doctor can't figure out / what the reason is, / so she sends you / to the lab for tests.
당신의 담당 의사는 알아내지 못한다 / 이유가 무엇인지를 / 그래서 그녀는 당신을 보낸다 / 검사를 위해 연구실로

(A) And what happens?
그리고 어떤 일이 일어날까?

Your immediate relief may be replaced / by a weird sense of discomfort.
당신의 즉각적인 안도감이 대체될지도 모른다 / 이상한 불편함으로

You still don't know / what the pain was!
당신은 아직도 모른다 / 그 고통이 무엇이었는지!

There's got to be an explanation / somewhere.
설명이 있어야만 한다 / 어딘가에

(B) A week later / you're called back / to hear the results.
일주일 후 / 당신은 다시 호출된다 / 결과를 듣기 위해

When you finally get into her office, / your doctor smiles / and tells you the tests were all negative.
마침내 그녀의 진료실에 들어섰을 때 / 당신의 의사는 웃는다 / 그리고 검사 결과가 모두 음성이었다고 당신에게 말한다

(C) Maybe it is cancer / and they've just missed it.
어쩌면 암일지도 모른다 / 그리고 그것들(검사 결과)이 그것을 놓쳤다

Maybe it's worse. // Surely / they should be able to find a cause.
더 나쁠 수도 있다. // 분명 / 그것들은 원인을 찾을 수 있어야만 한다

You feel frustrated / by the lack of a definitive answer.
당신은 좌절감을 느낀다 / 명확한 답이 없는 것에

해석 모호함은 매우 불쾌해서 심지어 좋은 소식을 나쁜 소식으로 바꿀 수 있다. 당신은 계속되는 복통으로 의사에게 간다. 당신의 담당 의사는 이유가 무엇인지를 알아내지 못해서, 그녀는 검사를 위해 연구실로 당신을 보낸다.

(B) 일주일 후 당신은 결과를 듣기 위해 다시 호출된다. 마침내 그녀의 진료실에 들어섰을 때, 당신의 의사는 웃으면서 검사 결과가 모두 음성이었다고 당신에게 말한다.

(A) 그리고 어떤 일이 일어날까? 당신의 즉각적인 안도감이 이상한 불편함으로 대체될지도 모른다. 당신은 아직도 그 고통이 무엇이었는지 모른다! 어딘가에 설명이 있어야만 한다.

(C) 어쩌면 암일지도 모르고 그것들(검사 결과)이 그것을 놓쳤을지도 모른다. 더 나쁠 수도 있다. 분명 그것들은 원인을 찾을 수 있어야만 한다. 당신은 명확한 답이 없는 것에 좌절감을 느낀다.

해설 주어진 글에서 모호함은 매우 불쾌해서 심지어 좋은 소식을 나쁜 소식으로 바꿀 수 있다고 하며 계속되는 복통으로 의사에게 갔지만 의사가 이유를 알아내지 못해 검사를 위해 연구실로 보내는 상황을 예시로 들고 있다. 이어서 (B)에서 일주일 후 결과를 듣기 위해 다시 호출되었고 의사를 만나 검사 결과가 음성이었다는 이야기를 듣는 상황을 설명한다. 뒤이어 (A)에서 그리고(And) 어떤 일이 일어날지 물어보면서 안도감이 이상한 불편함으로 대체된다고 한 뒤, (C)에서 어쩌면 암일지도 모르는 것을 검사 결과가 놓쳤을지도 모른다고 하며 당신은 명확한 답이 없는 것에 대해 좌절감을 느끼게 된다고 설명하고 있다.

어휘 ambiguity 모호함 persistent 계속되는 stomachache 복통
lab(=laboratory) 연구실 immediate 즉각적인
replace 대체하다 weird 이상한 discomfort 불편함
explanation 설명 negative 음성의 cancer 암
frustrated 좌절감을 느끼는 definitive 명확한, 결정적인

14 독해 논리적 흐름 파악 (문장 삽입) 난이도 ★☆☆

끊어읽기 해석

The effect, however, was just the reverse.
그러나, 효과는 그 반대였다

How we dress for work / has taken on a new element of choice, / and with it, new anxieties.
우리가 일할 때 어떻게 옷을 입을 것인가 하는 것은 / 새로운 선택 요소를 띠게 되었다 / 그리고 그로 인해, 새로운 불안감을 떠안게 되었다

(①) The practice of having a "dress-down day" or

"casual day," / which began to emerge / a decade or so ago, / was intended to make life easier / for employees, / to enable them to save money / and feel more relaxed / at the office.

'자유 복장으로 근무하는 날'이나 '평상복의 날'의 관행은 / 그것이 부각되기 시작했던 / 10여 년 전 / 생활을 더 편안하게 하기 위해 의도되었다 / 직원들이 / 돈을 절약할 수 있게 하다 / 그리고 더 편안함을 느낄 수 있도록 / 사무실에서

(②) In addition to the normal workplace wardrobe, / employees had to create / a "workplace casual" wardrobe.

표준적인 직장 옷뿐만 아니라 / 직원들은 만들어 낼 필요가 있었다 / '직장 평상복' 옷을

(③) It couldn't really be the sweats and T-shirts / you wore around the house / on the weekend.

그것이 운동복이나 티셔츠였을 리는 없다 / 당신이 집안에서 입던 / 주말에

(④) It had to be a selection of clothing / that sustained a certain image / — relaxed, but also serious.

그것은 엄선된 옷이어야 했다 / 특정 이미지를 유지하는 / 편안하지만 진지하기도 한

해석 우리가 일할 때 어떻게 옷을 입을 것인가 하는 것은 새로운 선택 요소를 띠게 되었고, 그로 인해 새로운 불안감을 띠게 되었다. 10여 년 전 부각되기 시작했던 '자유 복장으로 근무하는 날'이나 '평상복의 날'의 관행은 직원들이 돈을 절약할 수 있게 하고 사무실에서 더 편안함을 느낄 수 있도록 하여 생활을 더 편안하게 하기 위해 의도되었다. ② 그러나, 효과는 그 반대였다. 표준적인 직장 옷뿐만 아니라, 직원들은 '직장 평상복' 옷을 만들어 낼 필요가 있었다. 그것이 주말에 당신이 집안에서 입던 운동복이나 티셔츠였을 리는 없다. 그것은 편안하지만 진지하기도 한 특정 이미지를 유지하는 엄선된 옷이어야 했다.

해설 ②번 앞 문장에 10여 년 전 '자유 복장으로 근무하는 날'이나 '평상복의 날'의 관행이 직원들의 생활을 더 편안하게 하기 위해 의도되었다는 내용이 있고, ②번 뒤 문장에 표준적인 직장 옷뿐만 아니라, 직원들은 '직장 평상복' 옷을 만들어 낼 필요가 있었으며 그것은 편안하지만 진지하기도 한 특정 이미지를 유지하는 엄선된 옷이어야 했다는 처음 의도와 반대되는 내용이 있으므로 ②번 자리에 그러나(however) 효과는 그 반대였다는 주어진 문장이 들어가야 지문이 자연스럽게 연결된다.

어휘 reverse 반대 take on (특질·모습 등) 띠다, (책임 등을) 떠맡다
anxiety 불안감, 염려 practice 관행, 관습
emerge 부각되다, 부상하다 intend 의도하다, 작정하다
wardrobe 옷, 옷장 sustain 유지하다, 지탱하다

15 문법 수 일치 난이도 ★★☆

해석 당신은 당신이 원하는 결과에 가장 적합한 연구 방법을 선택해야 한다. 당신은 수많은 사람들에게 질문하고 보고서 형식으로 완전한 분석을 할 수 있게 하는 온라인 설문을 진행할 수 있으며, 아니면 당신은 일대일로 질문을 하는 것이 더 적은 시험 선발 인원으로부터 당신이 필요한 답변을 얻기 위한 더 좋은 방법이라고 생각할 수도 있다. 당신이 어느 방법을 선택하든, 동일한 것끼리 비교해야 한다. 사람들에게 동일한 질문을 하고 답을 비교하라. 유사점과 차이점을 모두 찾아라. 양식과 추세를 찾아라. 데이터를 기록하고 분석하는 방법을 결정하는 것은 중요하다. 스스로 작성한 간단한 스프레드시트라면 기본적인 조사 데이터를 기록하는 데 아마도 충분할 것이다.

해설 ④ 주어와 동사의 수 일치 동명사(Deciding) 주어는 단수 취급하므로 복수 동사 are를 단수 동사 is로 고쳐야 한다. 참고로, 주

어와 동사 사이의 수식어 거품(on ~ the data)은 동사의 수 결정에 영향을 주지 않는다.

오답분석 ① 관계대명사 that 선행사(the research method)가 사물이고 관계절 내에서 동사 suits의 주어 역할을 하므로 주격 관계대명사 that이 올바르게 쓰였다.
② 주격 관계절의 수 일치 주격 관계절(provides ~ format)의 동사는 선행사(a survey)에 수 일치시켜야 하는데, 선행사가 단수 명사이므로 단수 동사 provides가 올바르게 쓰였다. 참고로, 해당 문장은 관계대명사 that 뒤에 주격 관계절이 접속사 and로 연결된 병치 구문이다.
③ 명사절 접속사 4: 복합관계대명사 복합관계형용사를 쓸지 의문사를 쓸지는 문맥에 따라 결정되는데, 문맥상 '당신이 어느 방법을 선택하든'이라는 의미가 되어야 자연스러우므로 명사 way를 수식하는 복합관계형용사 Whichever가 올바르게 쓰였다.

어휘 suit 적합하다 compare 비교하다 analyse[analyze] 분석하다

👍 이것도 알면 합격!

주어와 동사 사이의 수식어 거품은 동사의 수 결정에 영향을 주지 않는다는 것을 알아두자.

ex The song playing on the radio was my favorite when I was
단수 주어   수식어 거품   단수 동사
growing up.
라디오에서 흘러나오는 그 노래는 내가 자랄 때 가장 좋아했던 노래이다.

16 독해 전체내용 파악 (요지 파악) 난이도 ★☆☆

끊어읽기 해석

Some criminal offenders may engage in illegal behavior / because they love the excitement and thrills / that crime can provide.
일부 범죄자들은 불법 행위에 관여할지도 모른다 / 흥분과 스릴을 대단히 즐기기 때문에 / 범죄가 줄 수 있는

In his highly influential work Seductions of Crime, / sociologist Jack Katz argues / that there are immediate benefits / to criminality / that "seduce" people / into a life of crime.
그의 매우 영향력 있는 작품인 「범죄의 유혹」에서 / 사회학자 Jack Katz는 주장한다 / 즉각적인 이익이 있다는 것을 / 범행에 / 사람들을 '유혹'하는 / 범죄의 삶으로

For some people, / shoplifting and vandalism are attractive / because getting away with crime is a thrilling demonstration / of personal competence.
일부 사람들에게 / 물건을 훔치는 것과 기물 파손은 매력적이다 / 이는 범죄를 저지르고도 처벌을 모면하는 것이 스릴 있는 증명이기 때문이다 / 개인 능력의

The need for excitement may counter / fear of apprehension and punishment.
흥분에 대한 욕구는 역행할지도 모른다 / 불안과 형벌에 대한 두려움에

In fact, / some offenders will deliberately seek out / especially risky situations / because of the added "thrill".
실제로 / 일부 범죄자들은 의도적으로 추구할 것이다 / 특히 위험한 상황을 / 더해진 '스릴'로 인해

The need for excitement is a significant predictor / of criminal choice.
흥분에 대한 욕구는 중요한 예측 변수이다 / 범죄 선택의

해석 일부 범죄자들은 범죄가 줄 수 있는 흥분과 스릴을 대단히 즐기기 때문에 불법 행위에 관여할지도 모른다. 사회학자 Jack Katz는 그

의 매우 영향력 있는 작품인 「범죄의 유혹」에서 사람들을 범죄의 삶으로 '유혹'하는 범행들에는 즉각적인 이익이 있다고 주장한다. 일부 사람들에게, 범죄를 저지르고도 처벌을 모면하는 것이 개인 능력의 스릴 있는 증명이기 때문에 물건을 훔치는 것과 기물 파손은 매력적이다. 흥분에 대한 욕구는 불안과 형벌에 대한 두려움에 역행할지도 모른다. 실제로, 일부 범죄자들은 더해진 '스릴'로 인해 특히 위험한 상황을 의도적으로 추구할 것이다. 흥분에 대한 욕구는 범죄 선택의 중요한 예측 변수이다.

해설　지문 처음에서 일부 범죄자들은 범죄가 줄 수 있는 흥분과 스릴을 대단히 즐기기 때문에 불법 행위에 관여할지도 모른다고 한 뒤, 지문 전반에 걸쳐 범죄자들이 흥분에 대한 욕구로 범죄를 저지르는 것에 대해 설명하고 있으므로, '② 범죄 행위에서 생기는 흥분과 쾌감이 범죄를 유발할 수 있다'가 이 지문의 요지이다.

어휘　criminal offender 범죄자　engage in ~에 관여하다
illegal 불법의　seduction 유혹
shoplifting 물건을 훔치는 것, 좀도둑질
get away with 처벌을 모면하다, ~을 잘 해내다
demonstration 증명, 증거　competence 능력
counter ~에 역행하다　apprehension 불안, 우려
deliberately 의도적으로　predictor 예측 변수, 예언자

17　독해　추론 (빈칸 완성 - 단어)　난이도 ★☆☆

끊어읽기 해석

> In one classic study / showing the importance of attachment, / Wisconsin University psychologists Harry and Margaret Harlow investigated the responses / of young monkeys.
> 한 고전적인 연구에서 / 애착의 중요성을 보여주는 / 위스콘신 대학의 심리학자 Harry와 Margaret Harlow는 반응을 조사했다 / 어린 원숭이들의
>
> The infants were separated / from their biological mothers, / and two surrogate mothers were introduced / to their cages.
> 새끼들은 분리되었다 / 그것들의 생모로부터 / 그리고 두 명의 대리모가 놓여졌다 / 그것들의 우리에
>
> One, the wire mother, / consisted of a round wooden head, / a mesh of cold metal wires, and a bottle of milk / from which the baby monkey could drink.
> 하나는 철사 어미이다 / 둥근 나무 머리로 이루어진 / 차가운 금속 철사 그물망 / 그리고 우유병으로 / 새끼 원숭이가 마실 수 있는
>
> The second mother was a foam-rubber form / wrapped in a heated terry-cloth blanket.
> 두 번째 어미는 스펀지 고무 형태였다 / 데워진 테리 직물 담요로 감싸진
>
> The infant monkeys went to the wire mother / for food, / but they overwhelmingly preferred / and spent significantly more time / with the warm terry-cloth mother.
> 새끼 원숭이들은 철사 어미에게 갔다 / 먹을 것을 찾아 / 그렇지만 그것들은 (따뜻한 테리 직물 어미를) 압도적으로 선호했다 / 그리고 더 많은 시간을 보냈다 / 따뜻한 테리 직물 어미와
>
> The warm terry-cloth mother / provided no food, / but did provide comfort.
> 따뜻한 테리 직물 어미는 / 먹이를 주지는 않았다 / 그렇지만 안락함을 주었다

해석　애착의 중요성을 보여주는 한 고전적인 연구에서, 위스콘신 대학의 심리학자 Harry와 Margaret Harlow는 어린 원숭이들의 반응을 조사했다. 새끼들은 그것들의 생모로부터 분리되었고, 두 명의 대리모가 우리에 놓여졌다. 하나는 철사 어미로, 둥근 나무 머리, 차가운 금속 철사 그물망, 그리고 새끼 원숭이가 마실 수 있는 우유병으로 이루어졌다. 두 번째 어미는 데워진 테리 직물 담요로 감

싸진 스펀지 고무 형태였다. 새끼 원숭이들은 먹을 것을 찾아 철사 어미에게 갔지만, 그것들은 (따뜻한 테리 직물 어미를) 압도적으로 선호했고 따뜻한 테리 직물 어미와 더 많은 시간을 보냈다. 따뜻한 테리 직물 어미는 음식을 제공하지는 않았지만, 안락함을 주었다.

① 일　　　　　　　② 약물
③ 안락함　　　　　④ 교육

해설　지문 전반에 걸쳐 생모로부터 분리된 새끼 원숭이들이 우유병을 가진 철사 어미보다 따뜻한 테리 직물 담요로 감싸진 스펀지 고무 형태의 어미를 압도적으로 선호했고 더 많은 시간을 보냈다고 하며 애착의 중요성을 보여주는 한 연구 결과에 대해 설명하고 있으므로, 빈칸에는 따뜻한 테리 직물 어미는 음식을 제공하지는 않았지만 '③ 안락함'을 주었다는 내용이 들어가야 적절하다.

어휘　attachment 애착　investigate 조사하다　infant 새끼, 유아
separate 분리하다　biological mother 생모　wire 철사
consist of ~으로 이루어지다　mesh 그물망
foam-rubber 스펀지 고무　wrap 감싸다
terry-cloth 테리 직물(일반적으로 타월이라고 불리는 면직물)
overwhelmingly 압도적으로　prefer 선호하다　comfort 안락함

18　문법　병치·도치·강조 구문　난이도 ★★☆

해석　나는 입양을 위해 내 친부모로부터 포기되었고, 내 인생의 첫 10년을 보육원에서 보냈다. 나는 나에게 뭔가 문제가 있다고 생각하며 몇 년을 보냈다. 만약 나의 부모님이 나를 원하지 않았다면, 누가 그러겠는가(원하겠는가)? 나는 내가 무엇을 잘못했고 왜 그렇게 많은 사람들이 나를 쫓아 보냈는지 알아내려고 노력했다. 만약에 내가 그렇게 하면(친해지면) 그들이 나를 떠날지도 모르기 때문에 나는 지금 그 누구와도 친해지지 않는다. 나는 어렸을 때 살아남기 위해 나 자신을 감정적으로 고립시켜야 했고, 여전히 내가 어렸을 때 했었던 가정을 가지고 행동한다. 나는 버림받는 것이 너무 무서워서 모험을 하지 않을 것이고 최소한의 위험도 감수하지 않을 것이다. 나는 지금 40살이지만, 아직 아이인 것처럼 느낀다.

해설　① 병치 구문　접속사(and)로 연결된 병치 구문에서 같은 품사끼리 연결되어야 하고, 이때 동사끼리 수·시제가 일치해야 하므로 현재 시제 동사 spend를 과거 시제 동사 spent로 고쳐야 한다.

오답
분석　② 명사절 접속사 3: 의문사　목적어가 없는 불완전한 절(I had done wrong)을 이끌며 전치사 out 뒤의 목적어 자리에 올 수 있는 명사절 접속사 what이 올바르게 쓰였다.
③ 재귀대명사　동사(isolate)의 목적어가 지칭하는 대상이 문장의 주어(I)와 동일하므로 동사 isolate의 목적어 자리에 재귀대명사 myself가 올바르게 쓰였다.
④ 부사절 접속사 2: 기타　문맥상 '나는 버림받는 것이 너무 무서워서 ~하지 않을 것이다'라는 의미가 되어야 자연스러우므로 부사절 접속사 so ~ that(너무 ~해서 -하다)가 와야 한다. 따라서 부사절 접속사 that이 올바르게 쓰였다.

어휘　release 포기하다, 방출하다　adoption 입양　orphanage 보육원
send away 쫓아 보내다　assumption 가정　deserted 버림받은
venture 모험하다

👍 이것도 알면 합격!
병치 구문에서는 같은 구조끼리 연결되어야 한다는 것을 알아두자.
(ex) Please set the table and arrange the decorations.
　　　　동사구　　　　　　　　동사구
　식탁을 차리고 장식물을 배치해주세요.

19 문법 조동사 난이도 ★★☆

해석 음악은 일상생활에 전할 수 있는 심리 요법의 효과를 가져올 수 있다. 많은 학자들은 사람들에게 음악을 심리 요법의 동인으로 사용할 것을 제안했다. 음악 요법은 '개인의 심리적, 신체적, 인지적, 또는 사회적 기능을 높이기 위한 치료나 재활의 부가물로서의 음악의 사용'으로 널리 정의될 수 있다. 음악으로부터의 긍정적인 감정의 경험은 치료 과정을 개선해서 전통적인 인지적/행동적 방법과 일상 목표로의 이전을 강화할 수도 있다. 이것은 부분적으로는 음악과 일상적인 행동에 의해 유발되는 감정의 경험이 긍정적인 감정과 자극을 담당하는 서로 중복되는 신경학적 경로를 공유하고 있기 때문일 수도 있다.

해설 ① 조동사 should의 생략 문맥상 '많은 학자들이 ~ 제안했다'라는 의미가 되어야 자연스럽고 제안을 나타내는 동사 suggest가 주절에 나오면 종속절에 '(should +) 동사원형'의 형태가 와야 하므로 to 부정사 to use를 (should) use로 고쳐야 한다. 참고로, 동사 suggest는 that절을 목적어로 취하는 3형식 동사이므로 5형식 동사와 같이 '목적어 + 목적격 보어(to 부정사)'를 취할 수 없다.

오답분석 ② 목적어 자리 동사 enhance의 목적어 자리에 올 수 있는 것은 명사 역할을 하는 것들이므로 동명사 functioning이 목적어 자리에 올바르게 쓰였다.
③ 병치 구문 접속사(and)로 연결된 병치 구문에서는 같은 구조끼리 연결되어야 하는데 and 앞에 동사구(improve ~ process)가 왔으므로 and 뒤에도 동사구(strengthen ~ goals)를 이끄는 동사 strengthen이 올바르게 쓰였다.
④ 주어와 동사의 수 일치 주어 자리에 복수 명사(emotional experiences)가 왔으므로 복수 동사 share가 올바르게 쓰였다. 참고로, 주어와 동사 사이의 수식어 거품(elicited by ~ behaviors)은 동사의 수 결정에 영향을 주지 않는다.

어휘 transfer 전하다, 이동하다
agent 동인(사물을 발동하여 일으키게 하는 원인) define 정의하다
adjunct 부가물, 부속물 rehabilitation 재활 enhance 높이다
therapeutic 치료(상)의 strengthen 강화하다
behavioral 행동적인, 행동의 partially 부분적으로
elicit 유발하다, 끌어내다 overlap 중복되다, 겹치다
neurological 신경학적인, 신경학의 pathway 경로, 길

👉 이것도 알면 **합격!**

주절에 아래와 같은 제안·의무·요청·주장을 나타내는 동사나 형용사가 나오면, 종속절에는 '(should +) 동사원형'이 와야 한다는 것을 알아두자.

동사	require 요구하다	request 요청하다
	suggest 제안하다	recommend 추천하다
	order 명령하다	insist 주장하다
	demand 요구하다	move 제의하다
형용사	necessary 필수적인	imperative 필수적인
	essential 필수적인	important 중요한

20 독해 추론 (빈칸 완성 - 단어) 난이도 ★★☆

끊어읽기 해석

Cultural interpretations are usually made / on the basis of prejudice / rather than measurable evidence.
문화적 해석은 대개 만들어진다 / 편견을 토대로 하여 / 측정 가능한 증거보다는

The arguments / tend to be circular.
그 주장들은 / 순환적인 경향이 있다

People are poor / because they are lazy.
사람들은 가난하다 / 그들이 게으르기 때문에

How do we "know" / they are lazy? // Because they are poor.
우리가 어떻게 '알까' / 그들이 게으르다는 것을? // 왜냐하면 그들이 가난하기 때문이다

Promoters of these interpretations / rarely understand / that low productivity results / not from laziness and lack of effort / but from lack of capital inputs / to production.
이러한 해석의 옹호자들은 / 좀처럼 이해하지 못한다 / 낮은 생산성이 온다고 / 게으름과 노력의 부족에서가 아니라 / 자본 투입의 부족에서 / 생산에 대한

African farmers are not lazy, / but they do lack / soil nutrients, tractors, feeder roads, irrigated plots, storage facilities, / and the like.
아프리카 농부들은 게으르지 않다 / 하지만 그들은 정말 부족하다 / 토양 영양분, 트랙터, 지선 도로, 관개된 토지, 저장 시설 / 같은 것들이

Stereotypes / that Africans work little / and therefore are poor / are put to rest immediately / by spending a day in a village, / where backbreaking labor by men and women is the norm.
고정관념은 / 아프리카 사람들이 일을 거의 하지 않는다는 / 그래서 가난하다는 / 즉시 잠재워진다 / 마을에서 하루를 보냄으로써 / 남성과 여성의 몹시 힘든 노동이 일반적인

해석 문화적 해석은 대개 측정 가능한 증거보다는 편견을 토대로 하여 만들어진다. 그 주장들은 순환적인 경향이 있다. 사람들은 그들이 게으르기 때문에 가난하다. 그들이 게으르다는 것을 우리가 어떻게 '알까'? 왜냐하면 그들이 가난하기 때문이다. 이러한 해석의 옹호자들은 낮은 생산성이 게으름과 노력의 부족에서가 아니라 생산에 대한 자본 투입의 부족에서 온다는 것을 좀처럼 이해하지 못한다. 아프리카 농부들은 게으르지 않지만, 그들은 토양 영양분, 트랙터, 지선 도로, 관개된 토지, 저장 시설 같은 것들이 정말 부족하다. 아프리카 사람들이 일을 거의 하지 않아서 가난하다는 고정관념은 남성과 여성의 몹시 힘든 노동이 일반적인 마을에서 하루를 보냄으로써 즉시 잠재워진다.

① 통계
② 편견
③ 겉모습
④ 환경

해설 지문 처음에 밑줄이 있는 문장에서 문화적 해석이 대개 측정 가능한 증거보다는 다른 어떤 것을 토대로 이루어진다는 내용이 있고, 지문 전반에 걸쳐 가난한 사람들이 게으르기 때문에 가난하다는 해석을 옹호하는 사람들에 대해 아프리카 농부들을 예시로 들며 그들이 일을 거의 하지 않기 때문에 가난하다는 고정관념(stereotype)은 몹시 힘든 노동이 일반적인 마을에서 하루를 보냄으로써 즉시 잠재워진다고 설명하고 있다. 따라서 빈칸에는 '② 편견'이 들어가야 적절하다.

어휘 interpretation 해석 on the basis of ~를 토대로 하여
measurable 측정 가능한 circular 순환적인 lazy 게으른
promoter 옹호자, 기획자 capital 자본 soil 토양
tractor 트랙터(견인차) irrigate 관개하다(토지에 물을 대다)
plot 토지, 작은 땅 조각 storage 저장 facility 시설
stereotype 고정관념 put to rest 잠재우다
backbreaking 몹시 힘든, 고된 statistics 통계 prejudice 편견
appearance 겉모습 circumstance 환경, 상황

끊어읽기 해석

> But the demand for food isn't elastic; / people don't eat more / just because food is cheap.
> 하지만 음식에 대한 수요는 탄력적이지 않다 / 사람들은 더 많이 먹지 않는다 / 그저 음식이 싸다고 해서
>
> The free market has never worked / in agriculture / and it never will.
> 자유 시장은 결코 잘 된 적이 없다 / 농업에서 / 앞으로도 그럴 것이다
>
> (①) The economics of a family farm are very different / than a firm's:
> 가족 농장의 경제는 매우 다르다 / 회사의 그것과
>
> When prices fall, / the firm can lay off people / and idle factories.
> 가격이 떨어지면 / 회사는 사람들을 해고할 수 있다 / 그리고 공장을 놀게 한다
>
> (②) Eventually the market finds a new balance / between supply and demand.
> 결국 시장은 새로운 균형을 찾는다 / 수요와 공급 사이의
>
> (③) And laying off farmers doesn't help / to reduce supply.
> 그리고 농부들을 해고하는 것은 도움이 되지 않는다 / 공급을 줄이는 데
>
> (④) You can fire me, / but you can't fire my land, / because some other farmer / who needs more cash flow / or thinks he's more efficient / than I am / will come in and farm it.
> 당신은 나를 해고할 수는 있다 / 하지만 당신은 나의 땅을 해고할 수는 없다 / 왜냐하면 다른 어떤 농부가 / 더 많은 현금 유동성이 필요한 / 또는 그 자신이 더 효율적이라고 생각하는 / 내가 그러한 것보다 / 와서 농사를 지을 것이기 때문이다

해석 자유 시장은 농업에서 결코 잘 된 적이 없으며 앞으로도 그럴 것이다. 가족 농장의 경제는 회사의 그것과 매우 다르다. 가격이 떨어지면, 회사는 사람들을 해고하고 공장을 놀게 할 수 있다. 결국 시장은 수요와 공급 사이의 새로운 균형을 찾는다. ③ 하지만 음식에 대한 수요는 탄력적이지 않은데, 사람들은 그저 음식이 싸다고 해서 더 많이 먹지 않는다. 그리고 농부들을 해고하는 것은 공급을 줄이는 데 도움이 되지 않는다. 당신은 나를 해고할 수는 있지만 나의 땅을 해고할 수는 없는데, 왜냐하면 더 많은 현금 유동성이 필요하거나 내가 그러한 것보다 그 자신이 더 효율적이라고 생각하는 다른 어떤 농부가 와서 농사를 지을 것이기 때문이다.

해설 지문 처음에 농업에서는 자유 시장이 잘 된 적이 없다고 하며 가족 농장과 회사의 경제가 다르다는 내용이 있다. ③번 앞부분에 회사는 가격이 떨어지더라도 해고를 하거나 공장을 멈춰서 시장이 수요와 공급 사이의 새로운 균형을 찾는다는 내용이 있고, ③번 뒤 문장에 그리고(And) 농부들을 해고하는 것은 공급을 줄이는 데 도움이 되지 않는다는 내용이 있으므로, ③번 자리에 하지만(But) 음식에 대한 수요는 탄력적이지 않다고 하며 자유 시장이 농업에서 실패하는 이유에 대한 주어진 문장이 들어가야 지문이 자연스럽게 연결된다.

어휘 demand 수요 agriculture 농업 firm 회사 lay off 해고하다
idle (노동자 등을) 놀게 하다 supply 수요 reduce 줄이다
cash flow 현금 유동성 efficient 효율적인

끊어읽기 해석

> Daily training creates special nutritional needs / for an athlete, / particularly the elite athlete / whose training commitment is almost a fulltime job.
> 매일의 훈련은 만들어낸다 특별한 영양적 필요를 / 운동선수에게 / 특히 선발된 운동선수에게 / 훈련에 전념하는 것이 거의 전업인
>
> But even recreational sport will create nutritional challenges.
> 하지만 오락적인 스포츠조차도 영양 문제를 일으킬 것이다
>
> And whatever your level of involvement in sport, / you must meet these challenges / if you're to achieve the maximum return / from training.
> 그리고 스포츠에 대한 당신의 관여 수준이 어느 정도이든 / 당신은 이러한 도전들을 반드시 잘 대처해야 한다 / 만약 당신이 최대한의 이익을 얻고자 한다면 / 훈련으로부터
>
> Without sound eating, / much of the purpose of your training might be lost.
> 건강한 식사 없이는 / 당신 훈련 목적의 상당 부분을 잃게 될 수도 있다
>
> In the worst-case scenario, / dietary problems and deficiencies / may directly impair / training performance.
> 최악의 경우 / 식습관 문제와 영양 부족은 / 직접적으로 손상시킬 수도 있다 / 훈련 성과를
>
> In other situations, / you might improve, / but at a rate / that is below your potential / or slower than your competitors.
> 다른 상황에서 / 당신은 향상될 수도 있다 / 하지만 속도로 / 당신의 잠재력보다 낮은 / 또는 당신의 경쟁자보다 느린
>
> However, / on the positive side, / with the right everyday eating plan / your commitment to training will be fully rewarded.
> 그러나 / 긍정적인 측면에서 / 매일 올바른 식사 계획과 함께 / 훈련에 대한 당신의 전념은 충분히 보상받을 것이다

해석 매일의 훈련은 운동선수, 특히 훈련에 전념하는 것이 거의 전업인 선발된 운동선수에게 특별한 영양적 필요를 만들어낸다. 하지만 오락적인 스포츠조차도 영양 문제를 일으킬 것이다. 그리고 스포츠에 대한 당신의 관여 수준이 어느 정도이든, 만약 당신이 훈련으로부터 최대한의 이익을 얻고자 한다면 당신은 이러한 문제를 반드시 잘 대처해야 한다. 건강한 식사 없이는, 당신의 훈련 목적의 상당 부분을 잃게 될 수 있다. 최악의 경우, 식습관 문제와 영양 부족은 훈련 성과를 직접적으로 손상시킬 수 있다. 다른 상황에서, 당신은 실력이 향상될 수도 있지만, 당신의 잠재력보다 낮거나 당신의 경쟁자보다 느린 속도로 향상될 수도 있다. 하지만, 긍정적인 측면에서, 매일 올바른 식사 계획과 함께 훈련에 대한 당신의 전념은 충분히 보상받을 것이다.

① 신체의 유연성을 향상시키는 방법
② 운동에서 잘 먹는 것의 중요성
③ 과도한 식사로 인해 발생하는 건강 문제
④ 지속적인 훈련을 통한 기술 향상

해설 지문 전반에 걸쳐 운동선수뿐만 아니라 오락적인 스포츠를 하는 경우에도 특별한 영양적 필요가 발생한다고 하며 건강한 식사 없이는 훈련 목적의 상당 부분을 잃게 될 수 있고 식습관 문제와 영양 부족은 훈련 성과를 직접적으로 손상시킬 수 있다고 설명하고 있다. 또한, 지문 마지막에서 매일 올바른 식사 계획을 하는 것의 중요성에 대해 언급하고 있다. 따라서 '② 운동에서 잘 먹는 것의 중요성'이 이 글의 주제이다.

어휘 nutritional 영양적인 athlete 운동선수 elite 선발의
commitment 전념, 헌신 recreational 오락적인
involvement 관여, 몰두 sound 건강한; 소리

dietary 식습관의, 음식물의 deficiency 영양 부족, 결함
impair 손상시키다, 해치다 rate 속도, 비율 potential 잠재력
reward 보상하다

끊어읽기 해석

A very well-respected art historian / called Ernst Gombrich / wrote about something / called "the beholder's share".
매우 존경받는 미술사가는 / 에른스트 곰브리치라는 이름의 / 무언가에 대해 썼다 / '관람자의 몫'이라고 불렸던

It was Gombrich's belief / that a viewer "completed" the artwork, / that part of an artwork's meaning came / from the person viewing it.
그것은 곰브리치의 믿음이었다 / 보는 사람이 미술작품을 '완성'한다는 / 미술작품의 의미 중 일부는 나온다는 / 그것을 관찰하는 사람으로부터

So you see— / there really are no wrong answers / as it is you, / as the viewer / who is completing the artwork.
알다시피 / 오답은 정말로 없다 / 당신이기 때문에 / 관찰자로서의 / 미술작품을 완성하는

If you're looking at art / in a gallery, / read the wall text / at the side of the artwork.
만약 당신이 미술품을 보고 있다면 / 갤러리에서 / 벽의 글을 읽어 보아라 / 미술작품의 측면에 있는

If staff are present, / ask questions. // Ask your fellow visitors / what they think.
만약 직원이 있다면 / 질문을 하라 // 동행한 방문객들에게 물어보아라 / 어떻게 생각하는지

Asking questions is the key / to understanding more / —and that goes for anything in life— / not just art.
질문을 하는 것은 비결이다 / 더 많은 것을 이해하는 / 인생의 어떤 것에라도 해당되는 / 미술(을 이해하는 것)뿐만이 아니라

But above all, / have confidence / in front of an artwork.
하지만 무엇보다도 / 자신감을 가져라 / 미술작품 앞에서

If you are contemplating an artwork, / then you are the intended viewer / and what you think matters.
만약 당신이 미술작품을 감상하고 있다면 / 당신은 의도된 관찰자이며 / 당신의 생각이 어떤지가 중요하다

You are the only critic / that counts.
오직 당신만이 비평가이다 / 중요한

해석 에른스트 곰브리치라는 이름의 매우 존경받는 미술사가는 '관람자의 몫'이라고 불렸던 무언가에 대해 썼다. 그것은 보는 사람이 미술작품을 '완성'한다는, 즉 미술작품의 의미 중 일부는 그것을 관찰하는 사람으로부터 나온다는 곰브리치의 믿음이었다. 알다시피 미술작품을 완성하는 것은 관찰자로서의 당신이기 때문에 오답은 정말로 없다. 만약 당신이 갤러리에서 미술품을 보고 있다면, 미술작품의 측면에 있는 벽의 글을 읽어 보아라. 만약 직원이 있다면, 질문을 하라. 동행한 방문객들에게 어떻게 생각하는지 물어보아라. 질문을 하는 것은 미술(을 이해하는 것)뿐만이 아니라 인생의 어떤 것에라도 해당되는, 더 많은 것을 이해하는 비결이다. 하지만 무엇보다도, 미술작품 앞에서 자신감을 가져라. 만약 당신이 미술작품을 감상하고 있다면, 당신은 의도된 관찰자이며 당신의 생각이 어떤지가 중요하다. 오직 당신만이 중요한 비평가이다.

해설 지문 처음에서 존경받는 미술사가인 곰브리치가 미술작품의 의미 중 일부는 그것을 관찰하는 사람으로부터 나온다는 믿음을 가졌다고 했고, 지문 마지막에서 만약 미술작품을 감상하고 있다면 당신은 의도된 관찰자이며, 당신의 생각이 어떤지가 중요하다고 언급하면서 오직 당신만이 중요한 비평가라고 했으므로, '③ 미술작

품은 감상하는 사람으로 인하여 비로소 완성된다'가 이 글의 주제이다.

어휘 well-respected 존경받는 beholder 관람자, 구경꾼
share 몫, 지분 fellow 동행하는, 동료의
contemplate 감상하다, 곰곰이 생각하다 intend 의도하다, 작정하다
matter 중요하다 critic 비평가 count 중요하다

끊어읽기 해석

Argentina is the world's eighth largest country, / comprising almost the entire southern half / of South America.
아르헨티나는 세계에서 여덟 번째로 큰 나라이다 / 거의 남쪽 전체를 차지하는 / 남아메리카의

Colonization by Spain began / in the early 1500s, / but in 1816 Jose de San Martin led the movement / for Argentine independence.
스페인에 의한 식민지화는 시작되었다 / 1500년대 초반에 / 하지만 1816년에 호세 데 산 마르틴이 운동을 이끌었다 / 아르헨티나 독립을 위한

The culture of Argentina / has been greatly influenced / by the massive European migration / in the late nineteenth and early twentieth centuries, / primarily from Spain and Italy.
아르헨티나의 문화는 / 크게 영향을 받아 왔다 / 유럽인들의 대규모 이주로 인해 / 19세기 후반과 20세기 초에 있었던 / 주로 스페인과 이탈리아로부터의

The majority of people are at least nominally Catholic, / and the country has the largest Jewish population (about 300,000) / in South America.
대다수의 사람들은 적어도 명목상으로는 가톨릭 신자이다 / 그리고 그 나라는 가장 많은 유대인 인구(약 30만 명)를 가지고 있다 / 남아메리카에서

From 1880 to 1930, / thanks to its agricultural development, / Argentina was one of the world's top ten wealthiest nations.
1880년부터 1930년까지 / 농업 개발 덕분에 / 아르헨티나는 세계에서 가장 부유한 10개 국가 중 하나였다

해석 아르헨티나는 남아메리카의 거의 남쪽 전체를 차지하는 세계에서 여덟 번째로 큰 나라이다. 스페인에 의한 식민지화는 1500년대 초반에 시작되었지만, 1816년에 호세 데 산 마르틴이 아르헨티나 독립을 위한 운동을 이끌었다. 아르헨티나의 문화는 19세기 후반과 20세기 초에 있었던 주로 스페인과 이탈리아로부터의 유럽인들의 대규모 이주로 인해 크게 영향을 받아 왔다. 대다수의 사람들은 적어도 명목상으로는 가톨릭 신자이고, 그 나라는 남아메리카에서 가장 많은 유대인 인구(약 30만 명)를 가지고 있다. 1880년부터 1930년까지, 농업 개발 덕분에, 아르헨티나는 세계에서 가장 부유한 10개 국가 중 하나였다.

해설 지문 중간에서 아르헨티나의 문화는 19세기 후반과 20세기 초에 있었던 주로 스페인과 이탈리아로부터의 유럽인들의 대규모 이주로 인해 크게 영향을 받아 왔다고 했으므로, '② 북미 출신 이주민들이 그 문화에 많은 영향을 끼쳤다'는 것은 지문의 내용과 일치하지 않는다.

어휘 comprise 차지하다, 구성하다 entire 전체의, 완전한
colonization 식민지화 massive 대규모의, 대량의
migration 이주, 이동 primarily 주로 nominally 명목상으로
Jewish 유대인의 agricultural 농업의

끊어읽기 해석

Sonja Henie is famous / for her skill into a career / as one of the world's most famous figure skaters / —in the rink and on the screen.
소냐 헤니는 유명하다 / 경력에서 그녀의 기술로 / 세계에서 가장 유명한 피겨 스케이팅 선수 중 한 명으로서 / 스케이트장과 스크린에서

Henie, winner of three Olympic gold medals / and a Norwegian and European champion, / invented a thrillingly theatrical and athletic style of figure skating.
올림픽 금메달 3관왕인 헤니는 / 그리고 노르웨이와 유럽 챔피언인 / 황홀하게 극적이며 활발한 스타일의 피겨 스케이팅을 만들어냈다

She introduced / short skirts, white skates, and attractive moves.
그녀는 도입했다 / 짧은 치마, 하얀 스케이트와 매력적인 동작들을

Her spectacular spins and jumps raised the bar / for all competitors.
그녀의 화려한 스핀과 점프는 기대치를 높였다 / 모든 경쟁자들에 대한

In 1936, / Twentieth-Century Fox signed her / to star in One in a Million, / and she soon became / one of Hollywood's leading actresses.
1936년에 / 20세기 폭스는 그녀와 계약했다 / 「One in a Million」에 출연시키기로 / 그리고 그녀는 곧 되었다 / 할리우드의 주연 여배우들 중 한 명이

In 1941, / the movie 'Sun Valley Serenade' received three Academy Award nominations / which she played as an actress.
1941년에 / 영화 「Sun Valley Serenade」는 아카데미상 후보에 세 번 올랐다 / 그녀가 여배우로 연기한

Although the rest of Henie's films were less acclaimed, / she triggered a popular surge / in ice skating.
비록 헤니의 나머지 영화들은 덜 칭송받았지만 / 그녀는 대중적인 급증을 일으켰다 / 아이스 스케이팅의

In 1938, / she launched extravagant touring shows / called Hollywood Ice Revues.
1938년에 / 사치스러운 투어 쇼를 시작했다 / 'Hollywood Ice Revues' 라고 불린

Her many ventures made her a fortune, / but her greatest legacy was inspiring little girls / to skate.
그녀의 많은 모험들은 그녀가 부자가 되게 했다 / 하지만 그녀의 가장 큰 유산은 어린 소녀들에게 영감을 준 것이었다 / 스케이트를 타도록

해석　소냐 헤니는 세계에서 가장 유명한 피겨 스케이팅 선수 중 한 명으로서 스케이트장과 스크린에서의 경력에서 그녀의 기술로 유명하다. 올림픽 금메달 3관왕이자 노르웨이와 유럽 챔피언인 헤니는, 황홀하게 극적이며 활발한 스타일의 피겨 스케이팅을 만들어냈다. 그녀는 짧은 치마, 하얀 스케이트와 매력적인 동작들을 도입했다. 그녀의 화려한 스핀과 점프는 모든 경쟁자들에 대한 기대치를 높였다. 1936년에, 20세기 폭스는 그녀를 「One in a Million」에 출연시키기로 계약했고, 그녀는 곧 할리우드의 주연 여배우들 중 한 명이 되었다. 1941년에, 그녀가 여배우로 연기한 영화 「Sun Valley Serenade」는 아카데미상 후보에 세 번 올랐다. 비록 헤니의 나머지 영화들은 덜 칭송받았지만, 그녀는 아이스 스케이팅의 대중적인 급증을 일으켰다. 1938년에, 그녀는 'Hollywood Ice Revues'라고 불린 사치스러운 투어 쇼를 시작했다. 그녀의 많은 모험들은 그녀가 부자가 되게 했지만, 그녀의 가장 큰 유산은 어린 소녀들에게 스케이트를 타도록 영감을 준 것이었다.

해설　지문 뒷부분에서 1941년에 그녀가 여배우로 연기한 영화 「Sun Valley Serenade」는 아카데미상 후보에 세 번 올랐다고 했으므로, '③ 출연한 영화가 1941년에 영화제에서 3개 부문에 수상했다'는 것은 지문의 내용과 일치하지 않는다.

어휘　rink 스케이트장　invent 만들어내다, 발명하다　theatrical 극적인
athletic 활발한　spectacular 화려한, 장관의
raise the bar 기대치를 높이다　competitor 경쟁자
nomination 후보　acclaim 칭송하다　trigger 일으키다
surge 급증, 쇄도　launch 시작하다, 개시하다
extravagant 사치스러운, 낭비하는
make a fortune 부자가 되다, 재산을 모으다　legacy 유산
inspire 영감을 주다

정답
p.40

01	④ 독해 - 전체내용 파악	11	③ 독해 - 전체내용 파악	21	② 독해 - 논리적 흐름 파악	
02	④ 독해 - 세부내용 파악	12	④ 독해 - 전체내용 파악	22	② 독해 - 논리적 흐름 파악	
03	④ 문법 - 병치·도치·강조 구문 & 형용사와 부사 & 대명사	13	④ 문법 - 분사	23	② 독해 - 세부내용 파악	
04	② 독해 - 논리적 흐름 파악	14	② 독해 - 전체내용 파악	24	② 독해 - 전체내용 파악	
05	② 문법 - 주어·동사/목적어·보어/수식어	15	① 독해 - 전체내용 파악	25	② 독해 - 세부내용 파악	
06	④ 독해 - 논리적 흐름 파악	16	① 독해 - 전체내용 파악			
07	① 독해 - 추론	17	④ 독해 - 논리적 흐름 파악			
08	② 독해 - 논리적 흐름 파악	18	① 문법 - 명사절 & to 부정사 & 주어·동사/목적어·보어/수식어			
09	① 독해 - 추론	19	② 독해 - 논리적 흐름 파악			
10	③ 독해 - 논리적 흐름 파악	20	② 독해 - 논리적 흐름 파악			

취약영역 분석표

영역	세부 유형	문항 수	소계
문법	병치·도치·강조 구문 & 형용사와 부사 & 대명사	1	/4
	주어·동사/목적어·보어/ 수식어	1	
	분사	1	
	명사절 & to 부정사 & 주어· 동사/목적어·보어/수식어	1	
독해	전체내용 파악	7	/21
	세부내용 파악	3	
	추론	2	
	논리적 흐름 파악	9	
총계			/25

· 자신이 취약한 영역은 '법원직 9급 영어, 이렇게 출제된다!'(문제집 p.8)를 통해 다시 한번 확인하고 학습하시기 바랍니다.

---

01 독해 전체내용 파악 (문단 요약)
난이도 ★★☆

끊어읽기 해석

Microorganisms are not calculating entities.
미생물들은 계산적인 존재들이 아니다.

They don't care / what they do to you / any more than you care / what distress you cause / when you slaughter them / by the millions / with a soapy shower.
그것들은 상관하지 않는다 / 무엇을 그것들이 당신에게 하는지를 / 당신이 신경 쓰지 않듯이 / 당신이 어떤 고통을 유발하는지를 / 당신이 그것들을 학살할 때 / 수백만씩 / 비누투성이의 샤워로

The only time / a pathogen cares about you / is when it kills you / too well.
유일한 때는 / 병원체가 당신에 대해 신경 쓰는 / 그것이 당신을 죽이는 때이다 / 대단히 잘

If they eliminate you / before they can move on, / then they may well die out themselves.
만약 그것들이 당신을 없앤다면 / 그것들이 이동할 수 있기 전에 / 그러면 그것들은 스스로 아마 소멸할 것이다

This in fact sometimes happens.
이것은 실제로 가끔 발생한다.

History, / Jared Diamond notes, / is full of diseases / that "once caused terrifying epidemics / and then disappeared / as mysteriously as they had come."
역사는 / Jared Diamond가 언급한다 / 질병들로 가득하다 / '한때 무서운 유행병들을 유발했던 / 그러고는 사라진 / 그것들이 나타났던 것처럼 기이하게'

He cites / the robust but mercifully transient English sweating sickness, / which raged from 1485 to 1552, / killing tens of thousands / as it went, / before burning itself out.
그는 예로 든다 / 강력하지만 다행히도 일시적이었던 영국 발한병을 / 그것은 1485년부터 1552년까지 창궐했다 / 수만 명을 죽이면서 / 그것이 지나가면서 / 그것 스스로를 소멸시키기 전까지

Too much efficiency / is not a good thing / for any infectious organism.
과도한 효율은 / 좋은 것이 아니다 / 어떤 전염성이 있는 미생물에게도

해석 미생물들은 계산적인 존재들이 아니다. 당신이 비누투성이의 샤워로 수백만씩 그것들(미생물들)을 학살할 때, 당신이 그것들(미생물들)에게 어떤 고통을 유발하는지를 신경 쓰지 않는 것처럼 그것들(미생물들)은 그들이 당신에게 무엇을 하는지를 상관하지 않는다. 병원체가 당신에 대해 신경 쓰는 유일한 때는 그것(병원체)이 당신을 대단히 잘 죽일 때이다. 만약 그것들(병원체)이 이동할 수 있기 전에 그것들이 당신을 없앤다면, 그것들은 아마 스스로 소멸할 것이다. 이것은 실제로 가끔 발생한다. Jared Diamond는 역사가 '한때 무서운 유행병들을 유발하고는 그것들(유행병들)이 일어났던 것처럼 기이하게 사라진' 질병들로 가득하다고 언급한다. 그는 강력하지만 다행히도 일시적이었던 영국 발한병을 예로 드는데, 그 병은 그것 스스로를 소멸시키기 전까지 지나가면서 수만 명을 죽이면서 1485년부터 1552년까지 창궐했다. 어떤 전염성이 있는 미생물에게도 과도한 효율은 좋은 것이 아니다.

병원체들이 더 (A) 전염성이 있을수록, 그것(병원체)은 더 빨리 (B) 사라질 가능성이 있다.

	(A)		(B)
①	더 약한	----	사라지다
②	더 약한	----	퍼지다
③	전염성이 있는	----	퍼지다
④	전염성이 있는	----	사라지다

해설 지문 중간에서 병원체들은 그것들이 이동할 수 있기 전에 인간을 없앤다면 병원체들 스스로 소멸할 것이라고 한 뒤, 지문 뒷부분에서 수만 명을 죽일 정도로 강력했지만 일시적이었던 영국 발한병을 예로 들며 어떤 전염성 미생물에게도 과도한 효율은 좋은

것이 아니라고 설명하고 있으므로, (A)와 (B)에 병원체들이 더 전염성이 있을수록(infectious) 그것이 더 빨리 사라진다(disappear)는 내용이 와야 적절하다.

따라서, ④ (A) infectious – (B) disappear가 정답이다.

어휘 **microorganism** 미생물 **entity** 존재
not A any more than B A가 아닌 것처럼 B도 아니다
distress 고통 **slaughter** 학살하다 **epidemic** 유행병
cite 예로 들다 **robust** 강력한 **mercifully** 다행히도
transient 일시적인 **burn out** 소멸하다 **infectious** 전염성이 있는

02 독해 세부내용 파악 (지칭 대상 파악) 난이도 ★★★

끊어읽기 해석

> If the writing is solid and good, / the mood and temper of the writer / will eventually be revealed / and not at the expense of the work.
> 만약 글이 기초가 탄탄하고 좋으면 / 작가의 분위기와 성향은 / 결국 드러날 것이다 / 그리고 그 작품을 훼손시키지 않으면서
>
> Therefore, / to achieve style, / begin by affecting none / —that is, draw the reader's attention / to the sense and substance of the writing.
> 그러므로 / 문체를 획득하기 위해서는 / 아무것도 영향을 주지 않는 것으로 시작해라 / 즉, 독자의 관심을 끌어라 / 글의 느낌과 요지로
>
> A careful and honest writer / does not need to worry / about style.
> 세심하고 솔직한 작가는 / 걱정할 필요가 없다 / 문체에 대해
>
> As you become proficient / in the use of language, / your style will emerge, / because you yourself will emerge, / and when this happens / you will find it increasingly easy / to break through the barriers / that separate you / from other minds / and at last, make you stand / in the middle of the writing.
> 당신이 능숙해짐에 따라 / 언어 사용에 / 당신의 문체가 드러날 것이다 / 당신 자신이 드러날 것이기 때문에 / 그리고 이것이 발생할 때 / 당신은 갈수록 더 쉽다는 것을 알게 될 것이다 / 장벽들을 돌파하는 것이 / 당신을 분리하는 / 다른 (사람들의) 마음으로부터 / 그리고 마침내 당신을 서게 만드는 것이 / 글의 한가운데에
>
> Fortunately, / the act of composition, or creation, / disciplines the mind; / writing is one way / to go about thinking, / and the practice and habit of writing / drains the mind.
> 다행히도 / 작문이나 창작의 행위는 / 마음을 단련시킨다 / 글쓰기는 한 가지 방법이다 / 생각을 시작하는 / 그리고 글쓰기의 연습과 습관은 / 생각을 비운다

해석 만약 글이 기초가 탄탄하고 좋으면, 작가의 분위기와 성향은 그 작품을 훼손시키지 않으면서 결국 드러날 것이다. 그러므로, 문체를 획득하기 위해서는 아무것도 영향을 주지 않는 것으로 시작해라. 즉, 글의 느낌과 요지로 독자의 관심을 끌어라. 세심하고 솔직한 작가는 문체에 대해 걱정할 필요가 없다. 당신이 언어 사용에 능숙해짐에 따라, 당신 자신이 드러날 것이기 때문에 문체가 드러날 것이고, 이것(문체가 드러나는 것)이 발생할 때 당신은 다른 (사람들의) 마음으로부터 당신을 분리하는 장벽들을 돌파하고, 마침내 당신을 글의 한가운데에 서게 만드는 것이 갈수록 더 쉽다는 것을 알게 될 것이다. 다행히도, 작문이나 창작의 행위는 마음을 단련시킨다. 글쓰기는 생각을 시작하는 한 가지 방법이고, 글쓰기의 연습과 습관은 생각을 비운다.

① 마음을 치유하는 것
② 감성적 이도록 돕는 것
③ 그 또는 그녀의 호기심을 만족시키는 것
④ 스스로를 배경에 두는 것

해설 지문 중간에서 세심하고 솔직한 작가는 언어 사용에 능숙해짐에 따라 작가 자신이 드러나기 때문에 문체도 드러나는데, 이것은 작가가 다른 사람들의 마음과 자신을 분리하는 장벽을 돌파하고 글의 한가운데에 서게 만든다고 설명하고 있다. 밑줄이 있는 문장에서 작문이나 창작의 행위는 마음을 단련시킨다고 했으므로, 작가가 솔직하게 스스로를 드러내서 글의 한가운데에 서는 것과 비슷한 맥락인 '④ 스스로를 배경에 두는 것'이 drains the mind의 의미로 가장 적절하다.

어휘 **solid** 기초가 탄탄한, 견고한 **temper** 성향
at the expense of ~을 훼손하면서
draw one's attention ~의 관심을 끌다 **sense** 느낌, 의미
substance 요지 **proficient** 능숙한 **composition** 작문
discipline 단련하다 **go about** 시작하다 **drain** 비우다, 소진시키다

03 문법 병치·도치·강조 구문 & 형용사와 부사 & 대명사 난이도 ★★☆

해석 자신 그리고 삶에서 우리의 운명에 대한 불만족들 중 일부는 실제 상황들에 근거하는데, 일부는 거짓이고 그저 진짜로 인식된 것이다. (거짓인데 진짜인 것처럼) 인식된 것(불만족)은 정리되고 버려져야 한다. 진짜인 것(불만족)은 바뀔 수 있거나 바뀔 수 없는 유형 중 하나로 나뉠 것이다. 만약 그것(불만족)이 후자(바뀔 수 없는 유형)에 속한다면, 우리는 그것을 받아들이려고 노력해야 한다. 만약 그것(불만족)이 전자(바뀔 수 있는 유형)에 속한다면, 그런 경우 우리는 대신 그것(불만족)을 제거하고 교환하거나 변경하기 위해 노력하는 대안이 있다. 우리 모두는 삶에서 고유한 목적을 가지며, 단지 다르게 타고난 재능일 뿐, 우리 모두는 타고난 재능이 있다. 이것은 주어진 한 가지, 다섯 가지, 또는 열 가지 재능이 공평한지 불공평한지에 대한 논쟁이 아니다. 이것은 우리가 우리의 재능으로 무엇을 했는지에 대한 것이다. 이것은 우리가 우리에게 주어진 그것들(재능)을 얼마나 잘 투자했는지에 대한 것이다. 만약 누군가가 그들의 삶이 불공평하다는 견해를 고수한다면, 그것은 정말 신에 반항하여 모욕하는 것이다.

해설 (A) 병치 구문 접속사(and)로 연결된 병치 구문에서는 같은 품사끼리 연결되어야 하는데 and 앞에 형용사(false)가 왔으므로 형용사 역할을 하는 과거분사 perceived를 써야 한다.
(B) 부사 자리 형용사(gifted)를 수식할 수 있는 것은 부사이므로 부사 differently를 써야 한다.
(C) 지시대명사 앞에 나온 복수 명사 talents를 대신하면서, 관계절(we have been given)의 꾸밈을 받을 수 있는 것은 지시대명사 those이므로 빈칸에는 those를 써야 한다.

따라서 ④ (A) perceived – (B) differently – (C) those가 정답이다.

어휘 **dissatisfaction** 불만족 **lot** 운명 **perceive** 인식하다
sort out 정리하다, 처리하다 **discard** 버리다 **fall into** ~으로 나뉘다
strive 노력하다 **alternative** 대안 **modify** 변경하다
gifted 타고난 재능이 있는 **hold on to** ~을 고수하다 **outlook** 견해
offense 모욕

👍 이것도 알면 **합격!**

지시대명사 those는 '~한 사람들'이라는 뜻으로, 반드시 뒤에서 수식어(전치사구, 관계절, 분사)의 꾸밈을 받는다는 것을 기억하자.

(ex) Those living in storm damaged homes will be given money
　　　　　　수식어(분사)
by the government.
폭풍으로 피해를 입은 집에 사는 사람들은 정부에게 돈을 받을 것이다.

끊어읽기 해석

People assume / that, by charging a low price / or one lower than their competitors, / they will get more customers.
사람들은 추정한다 / 낮은 가격을 청구함으로써 / 또는 그들의 경쟁자들보다 더 낮은 금액을 / 그들이 더 많은 고객들을 얻을 것이라고

This is a common fallacy.
이것은 흔한 오류이다.

(A) It is, therefore, far better / to have lower-volume, higher-margin products and services / as you start; / you can always negotiate / to reduce your price / if you are forced to, / but it is rare / that you will be able to negotiate an increase.
그러므로 훨씬 더 낫다 / 더 적은 양, 더 높은 판매 수익의 제품과 서비스들을 가지는 것이 / 당신이 시작할 때 / 당신은 언제나 협상할 수 있다 / 당신의 가격을 낮추도록 / 만약 당신이 하는 수 없이 해야 한다면 / 그러나 드물다 / 당신이 인상을 협상할 수 있게 되는 것은

(B) It is because / when you charge reduced prices / compared to your competition, / you attract the lower end / of the customer market.
이것은 왜냐하면 / 당신이 할인된 가격을 청구할 때 / 당신의 경쟁 상대에 비해 / 당신은 더 낮은 몫을 끌어모으기 때문이다 / 고객 시장의

These customers want more for less / and often take up more time and overhead / in your business.
이러한 고객들은 적은 것으로 더 많은 것을 원한다 / 그리고 종종 더 많은 시간과 간접비를 차지한다 / 당신의 회사에서

They may also be your most difficult customers / to deal with and keep happy.
그들은 또한 당신의 가장 어려운 고객들일 수 있다 / 상대하고 계속 기쁘게 하기에

(C) You also, ironically, / repel the better customers / because they will pay a higher price / for a higher level of product or service.
당신은 또한 역설적이게도 / 더 나은 고객들을 쫓아 버린다 / 그들이 더 높은 가격을 지불할 것이기 때문에 / 더 높은 수준의 제품이나 서비스에

We have seen many competitors / come into the market / and charge day rates / that aren't sustainable.
우리는 많은 경쟁자들을 봤다 / 시장에 들어오는 것을 / 그리고 일급을 청구하는 것을 / 지속 가능하지 않은

They often struggle even / to fill their quota, / and soon enough / they give up / and move on to doing something else.
그들은 심지어 종종 애쓴다 / 그들의 할당량을 채우기 위해 / 그리고 오래지 않아 / 그들은 포기한다 / 그리고 또 다른 것을 하는 것으로 넘어간다

해석   사람들은 낮은 가격을 청구하거나 그들의 경쟁자들보다 더 낮은 금액을 청구함으로써 그들이 더 많은 손님들을 얻을 것이라고 추정한다. 이것은 흔한 오류이다.
(B) 이것은 당신이 경쟁 상대에 비해 할인된 가격을 청구하면 고객 시장의 더 낮은 몫을 끌어모으기 때문이다. 이러한 고객들은 적은 것으로 더 많은 것을 원하고, 종종 당신의 회사에서 더 많은 시간과 간접비를 차지한다. 그들은 또한 당신이 상대하고 계속 기쁘게 하기에 가장 어려운 고객들일 수 있다.
(C) 당신은 또한 역설적이게도, 그들(더 나은 고객들)이 더 높은 수준의 제품이나 서비스에 더 높은 가격을 지불할 것이기 때문에 더 나은 고객들을 쫓아 버린다. 우리는 많은 경쟁자들이 시장에 들어와 지속 가능하지 않은 일급을 청구하는 것을 봤다. 그들(경쟁자들)은 심지어 종종 그들의 할당량을 채우기 위해 애쓰고, 오래지 않아 포기하고 또 다른 것을 하는 것으로 넘어간다.

(A) 그러므로, 당신이 (사업을) 시작할 때 더 적은 양, 더 높은 판매 수익의 제품과 서비스들을 가지는 것이 훨씬 더 낫다. 만약 하는 수 없다(가격을 낮춰야 한다)면 당신은 언제나 가격을 낮추도록 협상할 수는 있지만, 당신이 인상을 협상할 수 있게 되는 것은 드물다.

해설   주어진 문장에서 사람들이 경쟁자보다 낮은 가격을 청구함으로써 더 많은 고객들을 얻을 수 있다고 추정하는 것은 흔한 오류라고 한 뒤, (B)에서 이(흔한 오류)는 할인된 가격을 청구할수록 고객 시장에서 더 낮은 몫을 끌어모으기 때문이라며 그 이유를 설명하고 있다. 이어서 (C)에서 더 나은 고객들은 더 높은 수준의 제품이나 서비스에 더 높은 가격을 지불할 것이기 때문에 당신의 할인된 가격을 청구하는 가격 방식이 역설적이게도(ironically) 더 나은 고객들을 쫓아버린다고 하며 하며 추가 이유를 제시한 뒤, (A)에서 그러므로(therefore) 사업을 시작할 때 더 높은 수익의 제품과 서비스를 가지는 것이 낫다고 결론짓고 있다.

어휘   fallacy 오류   volume 양, 부피   be forced to 하는 수 없이 ~하다   charge 청구하다   end 몫   take up 차지하다   overhead 간접비   deal with ~를 상대하다   ironically 역설적이게도   come into 들어오다[가다]   sustainable 지속 가능한   quota 할당량   move on to ~으로 넘어가다

---

05 **문법** 주어·동사/목적어·보어/수식어   난이도 ★☆☆

해석   글쓰기를 즐기는 아이들은 보통 그들의 작품을 인쇄물로 보는 것에 관심이 있다. 한 가지 비공식적인 접근은 그들의 시를 타이핑하고, 인쇄하여 게시하는 것이다. 아니면 당신은 많은 아동 작가들의 시를 복사한 문집을 만들 수도 있다. 하지만 진정으로 열심이고 야심 있는 아이들에게, 출판을 위한 시를 제출하는 것은 가치 있는 목표이다. 그리고 아이들의 독창적인 시를 발행하는 몇몇 웹과 인쇄 수단이 있다. 아동 시인들이 원고를 제출하는 것에 대한 규약(양식, 형식 등)에 익숙해지도록 도와라. 그들(아이들)이 가장 자랑스러워 하는 시를 고르게 하고, 제출된 모든 것들의 복사본들을 보관하고, 부모의 허락을 받아라. 그러고 나서 그들의 작품이 받아들여져서 인쇄되어 나오면 그들과 함께 기념해라. 그들을 축하해주고, 그들의 업적을 공개적으로 전시하고, 소문을 퍼뜨려라. 성공은 성공에 영감을 준다. 그리고 물론, 만약 그들의 작품이 (출판사에 의해) 거절된다면, 응원과 격려를 해주어라.

해설   ② 주어 자리 주어 자리에는 명사 역할을 하는 것이 와야 하므로 동사원형 submit을 동명사 submitting으로 고쳐야 한다.

오답 분석   ① 인칭대명사 명사(work) 앞에서 소유의 의미를 나타내기 위해서는 소유격 대명사가 와야 하는데, 대명사가 지시하는 명사(Children)가 3인칭 복수 명사이므로 3인칭 복수 소유격 대명사 their가 올바르게 쓰였다.
③ 명사절 접속사 3: 의문사 의문형용사 which가 뒤에 나온 명사(poems)를 꾸미면서 '의문형용사 + 명사'(which poems) 형태로 명사절 내의 전치사 of의 목적어 역할을 하고 있으므로 의문형용사 which가 올바르게 쓰였다.
④ 부사 자리 동사를 앞에서 수식하는 것은 부사이므로 부사 publicly가 동사 showcase 앞에 올바르게 쓰였다.

어휘   informal 비공식적인   dedicated 열심인, 헌신적인   ambitious 야심 있는   resource 수단, 방안   showcase 전시하다   spread the word 소문을 퍼뜨리다   inspire 영감을 주다   reject 거절하다, 불합격시키다   encouragement 격려

이것도 알면 합격!

명사가 a/the/some/many와 함께 쓰여 소유의 의미를 나타낼 때는, 'a/the/some/many + 명사 + of + 소유대명사'의 형태로 쓴다.

(ex) Mary went swimming with a friend of hers.
Mary는 그녀의 친구들 중 한 명과 수영을 갔다.

---

06 독해 논리적 흐름 파악 (문장 삽입) 난이도 ★☆☆

끊어읽기 해석

With love and strength / from the tribe, / the tiny seeds mature / and grow tall / and crops for the people.
사랑과 힘으로 / 부족으로부터의 / 그 아주 작은 씨앗들은 성숙해지고 / 크게 자라고 / 그리고 사람들을 위한 작물들도

In the Pueblo indian culture, / corn is to the people / the very symbol of life.
푸에블로 인디언 문화에서 / 옥수수는 사람들에게 ~이다 / 바로 삶의 상징

(①) The Corn Maiden / "grandmother of the sun and the light" / brought this gift, / bringing the power of life / to the people.
Corn Maiden은 / '태양과 빛의 할머니'인 / 이 선물을 가져왔다 / 생명의 힘을 가져오면서 / 사람들에게

(②) As the corn is given life / by the sun, / the Corn Maiden brings the fire of the sun / into the human bodies, / giving man many representations of his love and power / through nature.
옥수수에 생명이 주어짐에 따라 / 태양에 의해 / Corn Maiden은 태양의 불꽃을 가져온다 / 인체로 / 인간에게 그의 사랑과 힘의 많은 표현들을 주면서 / 자연을 통해

(③) Each Maiden brings one seed of corn / that is nurtured with love / like that given to a child / and this one seed would sustain / the entire tribe forever.
각각의 Maiden은 하나의 옥수수 씨앗을 가져온다 / 사랑으로 키워진 / 아이에게 주어진 것과 같은 / 그리고 이 하나의 씨앗은 살아가게 할 것이다 / 전체의 부족을 영원히

(④) The spirit of the Corn Maidens is forever present / with the tribal people.
Corn Maiden의 정신은 영원히 존재한다 / 부족의 사람들과 함께

해석 푸에블로 인디언 문화에서, 사람들에게 옥수수는 바로 삶의 상징이다. '태양과 빛의 할머니'인 Corn Maiden은 사람들에게 생명의 힘을 가져오면서 이 선물(옥수수)을 가져왔다. 태양에 의해 옥수수에 생명이 주어짐에 따라, Corn Maiden은 자연을 통해 인간에게 그의 사랑과 힘의 많은 표현들을 주면서 인체로 태양의 불꽃을 가져온다. 각각의 Maiden은 아이에게 주어진 것과 같은 사랑으로 키워진 하나의 옥수수 씨앗을 가져오는데, 이 하나의 씨앗은 전체의 종족을 영원히 살아가게 할 것이다. ④ 부족으로부터 받은 사랑과 힘으로, 아주 작은 씨앗들은 성숙해지고 크면서 사람들을 위한 작물들도 자란다. Corn Maiden의 정신은 부족의 사람들과 함께 영원히 존재한다.

해설 ④번 앞 문장에 사랑으로 키워진 하나의 옥수수 씨앗(this one seed)이 부족 전체를 영원히 살아가게 한다는 내용이 있으므로, ④번 자리에 부족의 사랑과 힘으로 그 아주 작은 씨앗들은(the tiny seeds)은 성숙해지고 크면서 사람들을 위한 작물들이 자란다는 주어진 문장이 들어가야 지문이 자연스럽게 연결된다.

어휘 tribe 부족 mature 성숙해지다, 익다 nurture 키우다, 양육하다
sustain 살아가게 하다, 지탱하다

---

07 독해 추론 (빈칸 완성 - 구) 난이도 ★★☆

끊어읽기 해석

Beeches, oaks, spruce and pines / produce new growth all the time, / and have to get rid of the old.
너도밤나무, 참나무, 가문비나무 그리고 소나무는 / 항상 새로운 가지를 만들어 낸다 / 그리고 오래된 것을 제거해야 한다

The most obvious change / happens every autumn.
가장 분명한 변화는 / 매 가을마다 일어난다

The leaves have served their purpose : / they are now worn out / and riddled with insect damage.
나뭇잎들은 그것들(나뭇잎들)의 목적을 채웠다 / 그것들은 이제 닳아서 못쓰게 되었다 / 그리고 충해로 인해 구멍이 뚫렸다

Before the trees bid them adieu, / they pump waste products into them.
나무들이 그것들에게 이별을 고하기 전에 / 그것들은 그것들(나무들)에 노폐물을 쏟아붓는다

You could say / they are taking this opportunity / to relieve themselves.
당신은 말할 수 있다 / 그것들(나무들)이 이 기회를 이용하고 있다고 / 볼일을 보기 위해

Then they grow / a layer of weak tissue / to separate each leaf / from the twig / it's growing on, / and the leaves tumble to the ground / in the next breeze.
그리고 나서 그것들은 기른다 / 한 겹의 약한 조직을 / 각각의 나뭇잎을 분리하기 위한 / 잔가지로부터 / 그것이 자라나고 있는 / 그리고 나뭇잎들은 땅으로 굴러떨어진다 / 다음 미풍에

The rustling leaves / that now blanket the ground / —and make such a satisfying scrunching sound / when you scuffle through them / —are basically tree toilet paper.
바스락거리는 나뭇잎들은 / 이제는 땅을 뒤덮는 / 그리고 아주 만족스러운 뽀드득뽀드득하는 소리를 내는 / 당신이 그것들 사이로 움직이며 돌아다닐 때 / 실은 나무 화장지이다

해석 너도밤나무, 참나무, 가문비나무 그리고 소나무는 항상 새로운 가지를 만들어 내고 오래된 것(가지)을 제거해야 한다. 가장 분명한 변화는 가을마다 일어난다. 나뭇잎들은 그것들의 목적을 채웠다. 그것들(나뭇잎들)은 이제 닳아서 못쓰게 되었고 충해로 인해 구멍이 뚫렸다. 나무들이 그것들(나뭇잎들)에게 이별을 고하기 전에 그것들(나무들)은 그것들(나뭇잎들)에 노폐물을 쏟아붓는다. 당신은 그것들(나무들)이 볼일을 보기 위해 기회를 이용하고 있다고 말할 수 있다. 그리고 나서 그것들(나무들)은 그것(조직)이 자라나고 있는 잔가지로부터 각각의 나뭇잎을 분리하기 위해 한 겹의 약한 조직을 기르고 나뭇잎들은 다음 미풍에 땅으로 굴러떨어진다. 이제 땅을 뒤덮고 당신이 그것(나뭇잎)들 사이로 움직이며 돌아다닐 때 아주 만족스러우면서 뽀드득뽀드득하는 소리를 내는, 바스락거리는 나뭇잎들은 실은 나무 화장지이다.

해설 지문 중간에서 나무들은 오래된 나뭇잎들을 제거하기 위해 그것들에 노폐물을 쏟아붓는데, 이는 나무들이 볼일을 보는 것과 같다고 언급하며 나무들이 오래된 나뭇잎들을 어떻게 처리하는 지를 단계별로 설명하고 있으므로, 빈칸에 바스락거리는 나뭇잎들은 실은 '① 나무 화장지'라는 내용이 들어가야 한다.

어휘 beech 너도밤나무 oak 참나무 spruce 가문비나무
growth 가지, 성장 get rid of ~을 제거하다
worn out 닳아서 못쓰게 된 riddle 구멍을 뚫다, 벌집같이 만들다
bid adieu 이별을 고하다 relieve oneself 볼일을 보다, 대소변을 보다
twig 잔가지 tumble 굴러떨어지다 rustle 바스락거리다
scrunch 뽀드득뽀드득 소리를 내다
scuffle 움직이며 돌아다니다, 발을 질질 끌다
basically 실은, 기본적으로

끊어읽기 해석

Fiction has many uses / and one of them / is to build empathy.
소설은 많은 용도가 있다 / 그리고 그것들 중 하나는 / 공감을 형성하는 것이다

When you watch TV or see a film, / you are looking at things / happening to other people.
당신이 TV를 보거나 영화를 볼 때 / 당신은 ~한 것들을 보고 있다 / 다른 사람들에게 일어나는

Prose fiction is something you build up / from 26 letters / and a handful of punctuation marks, / and you, and you alone, / using your imagination, / create a world and live there / and look out through other eyes.
산문 소설은 당신이 창조하는 무언가이다 / 26개의 글자들로부터 / 그리고 몇 안 되는 구두점들로부터 / 그리고 당신, 당신 혼자서 / 당신의 상상력을 사용하면서 / 세상을 창조하고 그곳에 산다 / 그리고 다른 눈을 통해 내다본다

① You get to feel things, / and visit places and worlds / you would never otherwise know.
당신은 무언가를 느끼기 시작한다 / 그리고 장소와 세상들을 방문한다 / 그렇지 않으면 당신이 절대 알지 못했을

② Fortunately, / in the last decade, / many of the world's most beautiful and unknown places / have been put in the spotlight.
다행히도 / 지난 10년 동안 / 세계의 가장 아름답고 알려지지 않은 많은 장소들이 / 주목을 받아왔다

③ You learn / that everyone else out there is a me, / as well.
당신은 알게 된다 / 저 바깥의 다른 모든 사람들이 나라는 것을 / 또한

④ You're being someone else, / and when you return / to your own world, / you're going to be slightly changed.
당신은 다른 누군가가 되어있는 것이다 / 그리고 당신이 돌아오면 / 당신의 세상으로 / 당신은 조금 바뀌게 될 것이다

해석 소설은 많은 용도가 있고 그것들 중 하나는 공감을 형성하는 것이다. 당신이 TV를 보거나 영화를 볼 때, 당신은 다른 사람들에게 일어나는 것들을 보고 있다. 산문 소설은 26개의 글자들과 몇 안 되는 구두점들로부터 당신이 창조하는 것이고 당신, (즉) 당신 혼자서 당신의 상상력을 사용하면서 세상을 창조하고 그곳(세상)에 살며 다른 눈을 통해 내다본다. ① 당신은 무언가를 느끼기 시작하고 그렇지 않으면 절대 알지 못했을 장소들과 세상들을 방문한다. ② 다행히도, 지난 10년 동안 세계의 많은 가장 아름답고 알려지지 않은 장소들이 주목을 받아왔다. ③ 당신은 저 바깥의 다른 모든 사람들도 또한 나라는 것을 알게 된다. ④ 당신은 다른 누군가가 되어있는 것이고, 당신의 세상으로 다시 돌아오면 당신은 조금 바뀌게 될 것이다.

해설 지문의 처음에서 소설은 당신이 혼자 상상력을 사용해 세상을 창조하고 다른 눈을 통해 그 세상을 보는 것이라고 언급한 뒤, 이어서 ①, ③, ④번에서 소설을 통해서 당신이 알고 느낄 수 있는 현상들에 대해서 설명하고 있다. 그러나 ②번은 세계의 많은 장소들이 지난 10년 동안 주목을 받아왔다는 내용으로, 지문 처음의 내용과 관련이 없다.

어휘 empathy 공감 prose 산문의, 산문 a handful of 몇 안 되는, 한 줌의 get to ~을 시작하다

끊어읽기 해석

The seeds of willows and poplars / are so minuscule / that you can just make out / two tiny dark dots / in the fluffy flight hairs.
버드나무와 포플러 나무의 씨앗들은 / 아주 작다 / 그래서 당신은 딱 알아볼 수 있다 / 두 개의 아주 작고 검은 점들을 / 솜털로 뒤덮여 날아다니는 털에서

One of these seeds / weighs a mere 0.0001 grams.
이 씨앗들 중 하나는 / 무게가 겨우 0.0001그램에 불과하다

With such a meagre energy reserve, / a seedling can grow / only 1–2 millimetres / before it runs out of steam / and has to rely on food / it makes for itself / using its young leaves.
아주 빈약한 에너지 비축량으로 / 묘목은 자랄 수 있다 / 겨우 1–2밀리미터만 / 이것이 수증기를 다 써버리기 전에 / 그리고 식량에 의존해야 한다 / 이것이 스스로 만드는 / 이것의 어린잎들을 이용해서

But that only works in places / where there's no competition / to threaten the tiny sprouts.
하지만 그것은 장소들에서만 효과가 있다 / 경쟁이 없는 / 아주 작은 새싹들을 위협하는

Other plants casting shade on it / would extinguish the new life immediately.
이것 위에 그림자를 드리우는 다른 식물들은 / 즉시 그 새로운 생명을 없앨 것이다

And so, / if a fluffy little seed package / like this / falls in a spruce or beech forest, / the seed's life is over / before it's even begun.
그래서 / 만약 솜털로 뒤덮인 작은 씨앗 꾸러미가 / 이것과 같이 / 가문비나무나 너도밤나무 숲에 떨어지면 / 씨앗의 삶은 끝난다 / 그것이 시작되기도 전에

That's why / willows and poplars prefer settling / in unoccupied territory.
그것이 이유이다 버드나무와 포플러 나무들이 정착하는 것을 선호하는 / 점유되지 않은 영역에

해석 버드나무와 포플러 나무의 씨앗들은 아주 작아서 당신은 솜털로 뒤덮여 날아다니는 털에서 두 개의 작고 검은 점들을 딱 알아볼 수 있다. 이 씨앗들 중 하나는 무게가 겨우 0.0001그램에 불과하다. 아주 빈약한 에너지 비축량으로 묘목은 수증기를 다 써버리기 전에 겨우 1–2밀리미터만 자랄 수 있고, 이것(묘목)은 어린 잎들을 이용해서 이것(묘목) 스스로 만드는 식량에 의존해야 한다. 하지만 이것(묘목이 어린잎들을 이용해 만든 식량에 의존하며 자라는 것)은 아주 작은 새싹들을 위협하는 경쟁이 없는 장소들에서만 효과가 있다. 이것(묘목) 위에 그림자를 드리우는 다른 식물들이 즉시 그 새로운 생명을 없앨 것이다. 그래서, 만약 이것(묘목)과 같이 솜털같은 작은 씨앗 꾸러미가 가문비나무나 너도밤나무 숲에 떨어진다면, 씨앗의 삶은 시작되기도 전에 끝난다. 그것이 버드나무와 포플러 나무들이 점유되지 않은 영역에 정착하는 것을 선호하는 이유이다.

① 점유되지 않은 영역에 정착하는 것을 선호하는
② 초식 동물들의 먹이로 채택된
③ 인간의 간섭을 피하기 위해 진화해온
④ 먼 겨울까지 그들의 죽은 잎을 간직하고 있는

해설 지문 중간에 새싹이 존재하기 위해서는 새싹 위에 그림자를 드리우는 다른 식물들과 같이 새싹을 위협하는 경쟁이 없어야 한다고 했으므로, 빈칸에는 '① 점유되지 않은 영역에 자리를 잡는 것을 선호하는'이 들어가야 한다.

어휘 willow 버드나무 poplar 포플러 나무 make out ~을 알아보다 fluffy 솜털로 뒤덮인 meagre 빈약한 reserve 비축량 seedling 묘목 run out of ~을 다 써버리다 sprout 새싹

cast (그림자를) 드리우다　extinguish 없애다　beech 너도밤나무
unoccupied 점유되지 않은　herbivore 초식 동물
intervention 간섭

10 독해 논리적 흐름 파악 (문맥상 부적절한 어휘) 난이도 ★☆☆

끊어읽기 해석

Good walking shoes / are important.
좋은 워킹화는 / 중요하다

Most major athletic brands / offer shoes / especially designed for walking.
대부분의 주요 스포츠 브랜드들은 / 신발을 내놓는다 / 걷기를 위해 특별히 디자인된

Fit and comfort / are more important than style; / your shoes should feel ① supportive / but not tight or constricting.
몸에 꼭 맞는 것과 편안함은 / 스타일보다 더 중요하다 / 당신의 신발은 ① 지탱하는 느낌이 들어야 한다 / 하지만 딱 붙거나 조이지는 않는

The uppers should be light, breathable, and flexible, / the insole moisture-resistant, / and the sole ② shock-absorbent.
윗부분은 가볍고, 통기성이 있고, 신축성이 있어야 한다 / 안창은 습기에 잘 견딜 수 있어야 한다 / 그리고 밑창은 ② 충격 흡수력이 있어야 한다

The heel wedge should be ③ lowered, / so the sole at the back of the shoe / is two times thicker than at the front.
굽의 쐐기는 ③ 낮춰져야 한다 / 그래서 신발 뒤쪽의 안창이 / 앞쪽보다 두 배 더 두껍도록

Finally, / the toe box should be ④ spacious, / even when you're wearing athletic socks.
마지막으로 / 앞심은 ④ 넓어야 한다 / 당신이 운동용 양말을 신고 있을 때조차도

해석 좋은 워킹화는 중요하다. 대부분의 주요 스포츠 브랜드들은 걷기를 위해 특별히 디자인된 신발을 내놓는다. 몸에 꼭 맞는 것과 편안함은 스타일보다 더 중요하다. 당신의 신발은 ① 지탱하는 느낌이 들어야 하지만 딱 붙거나 조이지는 않아야 한다. 윗부분은 가볍고, 통기성이 있고, 신축성이 있어야 하고, 안창은 습기에 잘 견딜 수 있어야 하며 밑창은 ② 충격 흡수력이 있어야 한다. 신발 뒤쪽의 밑창이 앞쪽보다 두 배 더 두껍도록 굽의 쐐기는 ③ 낮춰져야 한다. 마지막으로, 당신이 운동용 양말을 신고 있을 때조차도 앞심은 ④ 넓어야 한다.

① 지탱하는　　　　　② 충격 흡수력이 있는
③ 낮춰진　　　　　　④ 넓은

해설 지문 전반적으로 좋은 워킹화의 특징에 대해 이야기하고 있고, 지문 중간에서 신발 뒤쪽의 안창이 앞쪽보다 두 배 더 두꺼워야 한다고 하고 있으므로, 굽의 쐐기가 '③ 낮춰져야(lowered)' 한다는 것은 문맥상 적절하지 않다. 주어진 lowered를 대신할 수 있는 어휘는 '올려진'이라는 의미의 raised가 있다.

어휘 supportive 지탱하는　constricting 조이는　insole 안창
resistant ~에 잘 견디는　sole 밑창　absorbent 흡수력이 있는
toe box 앞심　spacious 넓은

11 독해 전체내용 파악 (요지 파악) 난이도 ★★☆

끊어읽기 해석

If your kids fight / every time they play video games, / make sure you're close enough / to be able to hear them / when they sit down to play.
만약 당신의 아이들이 싸운다면 / 그들이 비디오 게임을 할 때마다 / 반드

시 당신이 충분히 가까이 있도록 해라 / 그들의 소리를 들을 수 있을 정도로 / 그들이 게임을 하기 위해 앉을 때

Listen for the particular words or tones of voice / they are using / that are aggressive, / and try to intervene / before it develops.
특정한 단어나 목소리의 어조들을 들어라 / 그들이 사용하고 있는 / 공격적인 / 그리고 개입하려고 해라 / 그것이 (싸움으로) 발전하기 전에

Once tempers have settled, / try to sit your kids down / and discuss the problem / without blaming or accusing.
일단 화가 진정되면 / 아이들을 앉히려고 해라 / 그리고 문제에 대해 논의해라 / 탓하거나 비난하지 말고

Give each kid a chance to talk, / uninterrupted, / and have them try to come up with solutions / to the problem themselves.
각각의 아이에게 말할 기회를 주어라 / 방해받지 않고 / 그리고 그들이 해결책을 제시하도록 노력하게 해라 / 문제에 대해 그들 스스로

By the time kids are elementary-school age, / they can evaluate / which of those solutions are win-win solutions / and which ones are most likely to work / and satisfy each other / over time.
아이들이 초등학생의 나이가 될 때쯤 / 그들은 평가할 수 있다 / 그 해결책들 중 어떤 것들이 서로에게 유리한 해결책인지를 / 그리고 어떤 것들이 가장 효과가 있을 가능성이 큰지를 / 그리고 서로를 만족시킬지를 / 시간이 지나면서

They should also learn / to revisit problems / when solutions are no longer working.
그들은 또한 배워야 한다 / 문제들을 다시 논의하는 것을 / 해결책들이 더 이상 효과가 없을 때

해석 만약 당신의 아이들이 비디오 게임을 할 때마다 싸운다면, 그들이 게임을 하기 위해 앉을 때 그들(아이들)의 소리를 들을 수 있을 정도로 반드시 당신이 충분히 가까이 있도록 해라. 그들이 사용하고 있는 공격적인 특정 단어들이나 목소리의 어조들을 듣고, 그것이 (싸움으로) 발전하기 전에 개입하려고 해라. 일단 화가 진정되면 아이들을 앉히려고 하고, 탓하거나 비난하지 말고 문제에 대해 논의하려고 해라. 각각의 아이에게 방해받지 않고 말할 기회를 주고, 그들이 문제에 대해 그들 스스로 해결책을 제시하도록 노력하게 해라. 아이들이 초등학생의 나이가 될 때쯤, 그들(아이들)은 그 해결책들 중 어떤 것들이 서로에게 유리한 해결책인지 그리고 시간이 지나면서 어떤 것들이 가장 효과가 있고 서로를 만족시킬 가능성이 큰지를 평가할 수 있다. 그들(아이들)은 또한 해결책들이 더 이상 효과가 없을 때 문제들을 다시 논의하는 것을 배워야 한다.

① 당신의 아이들에게 그들의 시험을 평가하도록 요청해라.
② 당신의 아이들이 서로 경쟁하게 만들어라.
③ 당신의 아이들이 갈등을 해결하는 것을 배우도록 도와줘라.
④ 당신의 아이들에게 어떻게 논쟁에서 이기는지를 가르쳐라.

해설 지문 처음에서 아이들이 이야기하는 것을 듣고 싸우기 전에 개입해서 싸움이 번지지 않도록 하라고 한 뒤, 아이들의 화가 가라 앉으면 탓하거나 비난하지 말고 그들과 문제에 대해 논의하고, 아이들이 방해 없이 스스로 문제에 대한 해결책을 제시할 기회를 주면 아이들은 초등학생쯤에 어떤 해결책이 서로에게 유리한지 등을 알게 된다고 하고 있으므로, '③ 당신의 아이들이 갈등을 해결하는 것을 배우도록 도와줘라'가 이 글의 요지이다.

어휘 aggressive 공격적인　intervene 개입하다　temper 화
settle 진정되다　accuse 비난하다　uninterrupted 방해받지 않는
come up with 제시하다　revisit 다시 논의하다　resolve 해결하다

끊어읽기 해석

There's a current trend / to avoid germs / at all cost. // We disinfect / our bathrooms, kitchens, and the air.
현재의 추세가 있다 / 세균을 피하는 / 무슨 수를 써서라도 // 우리는 소독한다 / 우리의 화장실, 부엌 그리고 공기를

We sanitize our hands / and gargle with mouthwash / to kill germs.
우리는 우리의 손을 살균한다 / 그리고 구강 세정제로 가글한다 / 세균을 죽이기 위해

Some folks avoid / as much human contact as possible / and won't even shake your hand / for fear of getting germs.
몇몇 사람들은 피한다 / 되도록 사람 간의 접촉을 / 그리고 심지어 당신과 악수를 하지도 않을 것이다 / 세균이 옮는 것을 두려워해서

I think it's safe to say / that some people would purify everything / but their minds.
나는 ~라고 말해도 무방하다고 생각한다 / 몇몇 사람들이 모든 것을 정화할 것이라고 / 그들의 생각을 제외하고

Remember the story / of "the Boy in the Bubble"?
이야기를 기억하는가? / 「거품 속의 소년」의

He was born / without an immune system / and had to live / in a room / that was completely germ free, / with no human contact.
그는 태어났다 / 면역 체계 없이 / 그리고 살아야 했다 / 방에서 / 완전히 세균이 없었던 / 사람의 접촉 없이

Of course, / everyone should take prudent measures / to maintain reasonable standards / of cleanliness and personal hygiene, / but in many cases, / aren't we going overboard?
물론 / 모든 사람들은 신중한 조치를 취해야 한다 / 적정한 수준을 유지하기 위해 / 깨끗함과 개인위생의 / 그러나 많은 경우에 / 우리는 도를 지나치고 있지 않은가?

When we come in contact with most germs, / our body destroys them, / which in turn strengthens / our immune system and its ability / to further fight off disease.
우리가 대부분의 세균들과 접촉하면 / 우리 몸은 그것들을 파괴한다 / 그리고 그것은 결과적으로 강화한다 / 우리 면역 체계와 그것의 능력을 / 더 나아가 병을 물리치는

Thus, / these "good germs" / actually make us healthier.
따라서 / 이러한 '좋은 세균들'은 / 사실 우리를 더 건강하게 만든다

Even if it were possible / to avoid all germs / and to live in a sterile environment, / wouldn't we then be like "the Boy in the Bubble"?
만약 가능하더라도 / 모든 세균을 피하는 것이 / 그리고 무균 환경에 사는 것이 / 우리는 그러면 「거품 속의 소년」처럼 되지 않을까

해석 무슨 수를 써서라도 세균을 피하는 현재의 추세가 있다. 우리는 우리의 화장실, 부엌 그리고 공기를 소독한다. 우리는 세균을 죽이기 위해 우리의 손을 살균하고 구강 세정제로 가글한다. 몇몇 사람들은 되도록 사람 간의 접촉을 피하고 세균이 옮는 것을 두려워해서 심지어 당신과 악수를 하지도 않을 것이다. 나는 몇몇 사람들이 그들의 마음을 제외한 모든 것을 정화할 것이라고 말해도 무방하다고 생각한다. 「거품 속의 소년」의 이야기를 기억하는가? 그는 면역 체계 없이 태어났고 사람의 접촉 없이 완전히 세균이 없는 방에서 살아야 했다. 물론, 모든 사람들은 깨끗함과 개인위생의 적정한 수준을 유지하기 위해 신중한 조치를 취해야 하지만, 많은 경우에 우리는 도를 지나치고 있지 않은가? 우리가 대부분의 세균들과 접촉하면, 우리 몸은 그것들을 파괴하는데, 이것은 결과적으로 우리 면역 체계와 더 나아가 병을 물리치는 그것(면역 체계)의 능력을 강화한다. 따라서, 이러한 '좋은 세균들'은 사실 우리를 더 건강하

게 만든다. 만약 모든 세균을 피하고 무균 환경에 사는 것이 가능하더라도, 우리는 그러면 「거품 속의 소년」처럼 되지 않을까?

해설 지문 중간에서 모든 사람들은 적정한 위생 수준을 유지하기 위해 신중한 조치를 취해야 하지만, but(하지만) 뒤에서 많은 경우에 그 정도가 지나치다고 했고, 이어서 대부분의 세균과 접촉하면 결과적으로 우리 몸은 면역 체계를 강화하고 더 나아가 병을 물리치는 능력을 강화한다고 했으므로, '④ 과도하게 세균을 제거하려고 하는 것이 오히려 면역 능력을 해친다'가 이 글의 요지이다.

어휘 germ 세균 at all cost 무슨 수를 써서라도 disinfect 소독하다
sanitize 살균하다 folk 사람들
for fear of ~하는 것을 두려워하며, ~할까 봐
safe to say ~이라고 말해도 무방하다 purify 정화하다
take measures 조치를 취하다 prudent 신중한
go overboard 도를 지나치다, 열중하다
come in contact with ~와 접촉하다 fight off 물리치다
sterile 무균의, 불임의

해석 Golden City로 알려진, 카이버 고개로 향하는 길목에 있는 이전의 캐러밴 중심지였던 자이살메르는 그곳의 30피트 높이의 성벽들과 중세 사암으로 된 요새가 사파이어색의 하늘로 치솟는 조각된 첨탑과 궁전들을 보호하며 모래 바다에 우뚝 솟아 있다. 그것의 아주 작고 구불구불한 길과 숨겨진 사원들 때문에, 자이살메르는 아라비안 나이트에서 바로 나온 것 같이 생겼고, 이곳(자이살메르)의 삶은 거의 변하지 않아서 과거 13세기의 당신 스스로를 상상하기 쉽다. 이곳은 인구의 4분의 1이 성벽 안에 살고 있으면서 여전히 기능하고 있는 인도의 유일한 요새 도시이고, 이곳(자이살메르)은 (사람들이) 자주 다니는 길목에서 충분히 꽤 멀어서 관광업으로 인한 최악의 파괴를 모면할 수 있었다. 그 도시의 재산은 본래 그곳(그 도시)을 지나가는 낙타 캐러밴들에 부과되었던 상당한 통행료에서 나왔다.

해설 ④ 분사구문의 관용 표현 동시에 일어나는 상황은 'with + 명사 + 분사'의 형태로 나타낼 수 있는데, 명사(one quarter of its population)와 분사가 '인구의 4분의 1이 살고 있다'라는 의미의 능동 관계이므로 과거분사 lived를 현재분사 living으로 고쳐야 한다.

오답 분석
① 분사구문의 형태 주절의 주어(Jaisalmer)와 분사구문이 '자이살메르가 Golden City로 알려졌다'라는 의미의 수동 관계이므로 현재분사 Knowing을 과거분사 Known으로 올바르게 고쳤다.
② 분사구문의 형태 문장 내에 이미 동사(rises)가 있으므로 동사 shelters를 명사(its 30-foot-high ~ fort)를 뒤에서 수식하는 분사로 고쳐야 하는데 수식받는 명사와 분사가 '성벽들과 요새가 보호한다'라는 의미의 능동 관계이므로 동사 shelters를 현재분사 sheltering으로 올바르게 고쳤다.
③ 부사절 접속사 2: 기타 문맥상 '이곳의 삶은 거의 변하지 않아서 13세기의 당신 스스로를 상상하기 쉽다'라는 의미가 되어야 자연스러우므로 부사절 접속사 so ~ that(매우 ~해서 -하다)을 사용해 관계대명사 which를 부사절 접속사 that으로 올바르게 고쳤다.

어휘 caravan 캐러밴, 이동식 주택 medieval 중세의 fort 요새
shelter 보호하다 spire 첨탑 soar 우뚝 솟아 있다
winding 구불구불한 alter 변하다 beaten path 자주 다니는 길목
spare 모면하다 ravage 파괴 substantial 상당한 toll 통행료

---

14 독해 전체내용 파악 (요지 파악) 난이도 ★★☆

끊어읽기 해석

The learned / are neither apathetic nor indifferent / regarding the world's problems.
배운 사람들은 / 냉담하지도 무관심하지도 않다 / 세상의 문제에 대해

More books / on these issues / are being published than ever, / though few capture the general public's attention.
더 많은 책들이 / 이러한 문제에 대한 / 여느 때보다 더 출판되고 있다 / 비록 대중들의 주의를 사로잡는 것은 거의 없지만

Likewise, / new research discoveries are constantly being made / at universities, / and shared at conferences worldwide.
마찬가지로 / 새로운 연구 결과들이 계속해서 만들어지고 있다 / 대학들에서 / 그리고 전 세계의 학회에서 공유된다

Unfortunately, / most of this activity is self-serving.
유감스럽게도 / 이 활동의 대부분은 자기 이익만을 도모한다

With the exception of science / —and here, too, / only selectively— / new insights are not trickling down / to the public / in ways to help improve our lives.
과학을 제외하고 / 그리고 이것 또한 / 오직 선택적으로 / 새로운 견해들은 흘러내리고 있지 않다 / 대중에게 / 우리의 삶을 향상시키도록 돕는 방식들로

Yet, / these discoveries aren't simply the property of the elite, / and should not remain / in the possession of a select few professionals.
그러나 / 이러한 발견들은 단지 최상류층의 소유물이 아니다 / 그리고 남아선 안 된다 / 선택된 몇몇 전문가들의 소유물로

Each person / must make his and her own life's decisions, / and make those choices / in light of our current understanding / of who we are / and what is good for us.
각각의 사람은 / 그 사람 자신의 인생의 결정들을 내려야 한다 / 그리고 그러한 선택들을 한다 / 우리의 현재의 이해를 고려하여 / 우리가 누구인지에 대한 / 그리고 무엇이 우리에게 좋은지

For that matter, / we must find a way / to somehow make new discoveries accessible / to every person.
그 점에 있어서 / 우리는 방법을 찾아야 한다 / 어떻게든 새로운 발견들이 접근 가능하게 하기 위한 / 모든 사람에게

해석 배운 사람들은 세계의 문제에 대해 냉담하지도 무관심하지도 않다. 비록 대중들의 주의를 사로잡는 것은 거의 없지만, 이러한 문제에 대해 여느 때보다 더 많은 책들이 더 출판되고 있다. 마찬가지로, 새로운 연구 결과들이 대학들에서 계속해서 만들어지고 있고 전 세계의 학회에서 공유되고 있다. 유감스럽게도, 이 활동의 대부분은 자기 이익만을 도모한다. 이것(과학) 또한 오직 선택적으로, 과학을 제외하고, 새로운 견해들은 우리의 삶을 향상시키도록 돕는 방식들로 대중들에게 흘러내리고 있지 않다. 그러나 이러한 발견들은 단지 최상류층의 소유물이 아니며, 선택된 몇몇 전문가들의 소유로 남아선 안 된다. 각각의 사람은 자신의 인생의 결정을 내리고, 우리가 누구인지와 우리에게 무엇이 좋은지에 대한 현재 우리의 이해를 고려하여 선택을 해야 한다. 그 점에 있어서 우

리는 어떻게든 새로운 발견들이 모든 사람에게 접근 가능하게 만들기 위한 방법을 찾아야 한다.

해설 지문 중간에서 새로운 연구 결과들은 Unfortunately(유감스럽게도) 자기 이익만을 도모하고 대중들에게 흘러내려오지 않기 때문에, 모든 사람이 새로운 발견에 접근 가능하게 만들기 위한 방법을 찾아야 한다고 하고 있으므로, '② 새로운 연구 결과에 모든 사람이 접근할 수 있게 해야 한다'가 이 필자가 주장하는 바이다.

어휘 indifferent 무관심한 capture (흥미를) 사로잡다 self-serving 자기 이익을 도모하는 selectively 선택적으로 property 소유물 possession 소유 in light of ~을 고려하여 accessible 접근 가능한

---

15 독해 전체내용 파악 (주제 파악) 난이도 ★★☆

끊어읽기 해석

Language gives individual / identity and a sense of belonging.
언어는 개인에게 준다 / 정체성과 소속감을

When children proudly learn their language / and are able to speak it / at home and in their neighborhood, / the children will have a high self-esteem.
아이들이 자랑스럽게 그들의 언어를 배울 때 / 그리고 그것을 말할 수 있을 때 / 가정과 그들의 이웃에서 / 아이들은 높은 자존감을 가질 것이다

Moreover, / children who know the true value / of their mother tongue / will not feel / like they are achievers / when they speak a foreign language.
게다가 / 진정한 가치를 아는 아이들은 / 그들의 모국어의 / 느끼지 않을 것이다 / 그들이 성공한 사람인 것처럼 / 그들이 외국어로 말할 때

With improved self-identity and self-esteem, / the classroom performance of a child also improves / because such a child goes to school / with less worries / about linguistic marginalization.
향상된 자아 정체성과 자존감 덕분에 / 아이의 학급 성적 또한 향상된다 / 그러한 아이가 학교에 가기 때문에 / 걱정을 덜 가지고 / 언어적 소외감에 대한

해석 언어는 개인에게 정체성과 소속감을 준다. 아이들이 자랑스럽게 그들의 언어를 배우고 가정과 그들의 이웃에서 그것(모국어)을 말할 수 있을 때, 아이들은 높은 자존감을 가질 것이다. 게다가, 그들의 모국어의 진정한 가치를 아는 아이들은 그들이 외국어로 말할 때 성공한 사람인 것처럼 느끼지 않을 것이다. 향상된 자아 정체성과 자존감 덕분에, 아이의 학급 성적 또한 향상되는데, 이것은 그러한 아이가 언어적 소외감에 대한 걱정을 덜 가지고 학교에 가기 때문이다.

① 아이의 성장에서의 모국어의 중요성
② 아이들의 외국어 학습에 대한 영향
③ 아이들의 자존감을 향상시키는 방법
④ 언어학적 분석의 효율성

해설 지문 전반적으로 언어는 개인에게 정체성과 소속감을 주기 때문에 아이들이 자랑스럽게 그들의 언어를 배우고 말할 수 있을 때 높은 자존감을 가지게 되고, 아이가 언어적 소외감에 대한 걱정을 덜 갖고 학교에 가기 때문에 아이의 학급 성적 또한 향상된다고 했으므로, '① 아이의 성장에서의 모국어의 중요성'이 이 글의 주제이다.

어휘 identity 정체성 a sense of belonging 소속감 mother tongue 모국어 efficiency 효율성

끊어읽기 해석

Many animals are not loners.
많은 동물들은 외톨이가 아니다.

They discovered, / or perhaps nature discovered for them, / that by living and working together, / they could interact with the world / more effectively.
그것들은 발견했다 / 혹은 어쩌면 자연이 그것들을 위해 발견했을지도 모른다 / 함께 살고 일함으로써 / 그들이 세상과 상호작용 할 수 있다는 것을 / 더 효과적으로

For example, / if an animal hunts for food / by itself, / it can only catch, kill, and eat / animals much smaller than itself / —but if animals band together / in a group, / they can catch and kill / animals bigger than they are.
예를 들어 / 만약 동물이 먹이를 사냥한다면 / 혼자서 / 그것은 오직 잡고 죽이고 먹을 수 있다 / 자신보다 훨씬 더 작은 동물들을 / 하지만 만약 동물들이 함께 뭉친다면 / 무리를 지어 / 그것들은 잡고 죽일 수 있다 / 그것들보다 더 큰 동물들을

A pack of wolves / can kill a horse, / which can feed the group very well.
한 떼의 늑대는 / 말 한 마리를 죽일 수 있다 / 그리고 이는 무리를 아주 잘 먹여 살릴 수 있다

Thus, / more food is available to the same animals / in the same forest / if they work together / than if they work alone.
따라서 / 더 많은 먹이가 동일한 동물들에게 구해질 수 있다 / 같은 숲에 있는 / 만약 그것들이 함께 움직이면 / 그것들이 혼자 움직일 때보다

Cooperation has other benefits: / The animals can alert each other to danger, / can find more food / (if they search separately / and then follow the ones / who succeed in finding food), / and can even provide some care / to those who are sick and injured.
협력은 다른 장점들도 있다 / 동물들은 서로에게 위험을 알릴 수 있다 / 더 많은 먹이를 찾을 수 있다 / (만약 그것들이 따로따로 수색한다면 / 그리고 그것들을 따라간다면 / 음식을 찾는 것에 성공한) / 그리고 심지어 보살핌을 제공할 수 있다 / 병들거나 부상을 입은 것들에게

Mating and reproduction are also easier / if the animals live in a group / than if they live far apart.
짝짓기와 번식은 또한 더 쉽다 / 만약 동물들이 무리 지어 살면 / 그것들이 멀리 떨어져서 살 때보다

해석 많은 동물들은 외톨이가 아니다. 그것들(동물들)은 혹은 어쩌면 자연이 그것들(동물들)을 위해 발견했을지도 모르지만, 함께 살고 일함으로써 세상과 더 효과적으로 상호작용 할 수 있다는 것을 발견했다. 예를 들어, 만약 동물이 혼자서 먹이를 사냥한다면, 그것은 자신보다 훨씬 더 작은 동물들만 잡고 죽이고 먹을 수 있지만, 만약 동물들이 무리를 지어 함께 뭉친다면, 그것들(무리 지어 함께 뭉친 동물들)은 그것들보다 더 큰 동물들을 잡고 죽일 수 있다. 한 떼의 늑대는 말 한 마리를 죽일 수 있고, 이는 무리를 아주 잘 먹여 살릴 수 있다. 따라서 만약 그것들(동물들)이 함께 움직이면 그것들이 혼자 움직일 때보다 같은 숲에 있는 동일한 동물들이 더 많은 먹이를 구할 수 있다. 협력은 다른 장점들도 있다. 동물들은 서로에게 위험을 알릴 수 있고, (만약 그것들(동물들)이 따로따로 수색하고 나서 음식을 찾는 것에 성공한 것들(동물들)을 따라간다면) 더 많은 먹이를 찾을 수 있고, 심지어 병들거나 부상을 입은 것들(동물들)에게 보살핌을 제공할 수 있다. 만약 동물들이 무리 지어 살면 짝짓기와 번식 또한 그들이 멀리 떨어져서 살 때보다 더 쉽다.

① 동물들이 사회적인 것의 장점
② 협력적인 행동들의 결점
③ 동물들과 사람들의 공통적인 특성
④ 짝짓기와 번식에서의 경쟁

해설 지문 처음에서 동물들이 함께 살고 일함으로써 세상과 더 효과적으로 상호작용할 수 있다는 것을 발견했다고 한 뒤, 무리를 지어 사냥하면 자신보다 더 큰 동물들을 잡을 수 있고, 서로에게 위험을 알리거나 더 많은 먹이를 찾는 것 등과 같은 이점들을 가진다고 했으므로, '① 동물들이 사회적인 것의 장점'이 이 글의 주제이다.

어휘 loner 외톨이 interact 상호작용하다 band together 함께 뭉치다
pack 떼, 무리 mating 짝짓기 reproduction 번식
drawback 결점 trait 특성

끊어읽기 해석

My own curiosity had been encouraged / by my studies in philosophy / at university.
내 자신의 호기심은 촉진되어왔었다 / 내 철학 공부에 의해 / 대학에서

The course listed / the numerous philosophers / that we were supposed to study / and I thought at first / that our task / was to learn and absorb their work / as a sort of secular Bible.
그 강좌는 목록에 포함했다 / 많은 철학자들을 / 우리가 공부하기로 되어 있던 / 그리고 나는 처음에는 생각했다 / 우리의 일이 / 그들의 연구를 배우고 받아들이는 것이라고 / 일종의 비종교적인 성서처럼

But I was ① delighted to discover / that my tutor was not interested in me / reciting their theories / but only in helping me / to develop my own, / using the philosophers / of the past / as stimulants not authorities.
그러나 나는 알게 되어 ① 기뻤다 / 나의 교수가 나에게 관심이 없었다는 것을 / 그들의 이론들을 암송하는 / 그러나 오직 나를 돕는 것에만 / 내 자신의 것을 개발하도록 / 철학자들을 활용하여 / 과거의 / 권위자가 아닌 자극제로서

It was the key / to my intellectual ② freedom.
그것이 비결이었다 / 내 지적 ② 자유의

Now I had official permission / to think for myself, / to question anything and everything / and only agree / if I thought it right.
이제 나는 공식적인 허락을 받았다 / 나 자신을 위해서 생각할 / 어떤 것이든 그리고 모든 것을 의심할 / 그리고 동의할 / 내가 그것이 옳다고 생각할 때만

A ③ good education / would have given me / that permission much earlier.
③ 좋은 교육은 / 나에게 주었을 것이다 / 그 허락을 훨씬 더 일찍

Some, alas, never seem to have received it / and go on reciting / the rules of others / as if they were sacrosanct.
아아, 몇몇 사람들은 그것을 받지 못한 것처럼 보인다 / 그리고 암송하는 것을 계속한다 / 다른 사람들의 원칙들을 / 마치 그것들이 신성 불가침한 것처럼

As a result, / they become the unwitting ④ opponents / of other people's worlds.
그 결과 / 그들은 무의식중에 ④ 반대자들이 된다 / 다른 사람들의 세상에 대한

Philosophy, I now think, / is too important to be left / to professional philosophers.
내가 지금 생각하기에 철학은 / 맡겨지기에는 너무 중요하다 / 전문 철학자들에게

We should all learn / to think like philosophers, / starting at primary school.
우리는 모두 배워야 한다 / 철학자들처럼 생각하는 것을 / 초등학교 때부터 시작해서

해석 내 자신의 호기심은 대학에서 내 철학 공부에 의해 촉진되어왔었다. 그 강좌는 우리가 공부하기로 되어 있던 많은 철학자들을 목록

에 포함했고 나는 처음에는 우리의 일이 일종의 비종교적인 성서처럼 그들의 연구를 배우고 받아들이는 것이라고 생각했다. 그러나 나는 나의 교수가 그들의 이론들을 암송하는 내가 아니라 과거의 철학자들을 권위자가 아닌 자극제로서 사용하며 내 자신의 것을 개발하도록 오직 나를 돕는 것에만 관심이 있다는 것을 알게 되어 ① 기뻤다. 그것이 내 지적 ② 자유의 비결이었다. 이제 나는 나 자신을 위해서 생각하고, 어떤 것이든 그리고 모든 것을 의심하고, 내가 그것이 옳다고 생각할 때만 동의할 공식적인 허락을 받았다. ③ 좋은 교육은 그 허락을 훨씬 더 일찍 나에게 주었을 것이다. 아아, 몇몇 사람들은 그것을 받지 못한 것처럼 보이고 마치 그것들(다른 사람들의 원칙들)이 신성 불가침한 것처럼 다른 사람들의 원칙들을 암송하는 것을 계속한다. 그 결과, 그들은 무의식중에 다른 사람들의 세상에 대한 ④ 반대자들이 된다. 내가 지금 생각하기에, 철학은 전문적인 철학자들에게 맡겨지기에는 너무 중요하다. 우리는 모두 초등학교 때부터 시작해서 철학자들처럼 생각하는 것을 배워야 한다.

해설 지문 중간에서 화자가 대학에서 공부를 하며 자신을 위해서 생각하고, 어떤 것이든 자신이 옳다고 생각할 때만 동의한다는 공식적인 허락을 받았다고 한 뒤, 몇몇 사람들은 그러한 허락을 받지 못해 다른 사람들의 원칙을 마치 그것들이 신성불가침한 것처럼 암송만 한다고 했으므로, 다른 사람들의 세상에 무의식중에 '④ 반대자(opponents)'가 된다는 것은 문맥상 적절하지 않다. 주어진 opponents를 대신할 수 있는 어휘로는 '지지자'라는 의미의 proponents가 있다.

어휘 philosophy 철학 be supposed to ~하기로 되어 있다
absorb 받아들이다, 흡수하다 secular 비종교적인, 속세의
delighted 기뻐하는 recite 암송하다, 나열하다 stimulant 자극제
authority 권위자 intellectual 지적인
alas 아아(슬픔·염려 등을 나타내는 소리) unwitting 무의식중의
opponent 반대자

18 문법 명사절 & to 부정사 & 주어 · 동사 · 목적어 · 보어 / 수식어
난이도 ★ ★ ☆

해석 되돌아보면, 과학자들은 마야의 지도자들이 강우에 대한 불안정한 그들의 의존성을 수 세기 동안 알고 있었다는 많은 증거를 알아냈다. 물 부족은 이해되었을 뿐만 아니라 기록되었고 그것(물 부족)을 위한 계획이 세워졌다. 마야인들은 강수가 적은 해 동안 재배되는 작물들의 종류, 공공 용수의 사용과 식량 배급을 통제하며 절약을 시행했다. 그들의 3천 년 통치 기간의 처음 절반 동안, 마야인들은 가뭄 달을 대비한 빗물을 저장하기 위해 더 큰 지하 인공 호수와 저장 장치를 건설하는 것을 계속했다. 비록 그들의 정교하게 장식된 사원도 인상적이었지만, 물을 모으고 보관하기 위한 그들의 효율적인 시스템은 설계와 공학의 걸작이었다.

해설 (A) what vs. that 완전한 절(Mayan leaders ~ rainfall)을 이끌면서 evidence의 형용사 자리에 올 수 있는 명사절 접속사 that을 써야 한다.
(B) to 부정사의 역할 '저장하기 위해'라는 의미를 표현하기 위해 부사처럼 목적을 나타낼 수 있는 to 부정사 to store를 써야 한다.
(C) 보어 자리 보어 자리에 형용사 역할을 하는 impressive가 왔으므로 주격 보어를 취하는 be동사 were를 써야 한다. 참고로, as가 '비록 ~이지만'이라는 의미의 양보를 나타내는 부사절 접속사로 쓰이면 'as + 보어(impressive) + as + 주어(their ~ temples) + 동사'의 어순이 된다.
따라서 ① (A) that – (B) to store – (C) were가 정답이다.

어휘 look back 되돌아보다 uncover 알아내다 a mountain of 많은
uncertain 불안정한, 불확실한 dependence 의존성
enforce 시행하다 conservation 절약 reign 통치 기간

---

artificial 인공의 drought 가뭄 elaborately 정교하게
warehouse 보관하다 masterpiece 걸작, 명작

👍 이것도 알면 합격!

as가 '비록 ~이지만'이라는 의미로 쓰이고, 양보의 부사절 내의 보어나 부사가 as 앞에 와서 '보어/부사 + as + 주어 + 동사' 형태를 이루는 경우, 부사절 접속사 as 대신에 though를 사용할 수도 있다.

(ex) Dangerous **as** smoking is, many people still do it.
비록 흡연은 위험하지만, 많은 사람들이 여전히 그것(흡연)을 한다.
= Dangerous **though** smoking is, many people still do it.

19 독해 논리적 흐름 파악 (문단 순서 배열)
난이도 ★ ★ ☆

끊어읽기 해석

Religion can certainly bring out / the best in a person, / but it is not the only phenomenon / with that property.
종교는 분명히 끌어낼 수 있다 / 한 사람에게서 최고의 것을 / 하지만 그것이 유일한 현상은 아니다 / 그 속성을 동반하는

(A) People who would otherwise be self-absorbed / or shallow / or crude / or simply quitters / are often ennobled / by their religion, / given a perspective on life / that helps them make the hard decisions / that we all would be proud to make.
그렇지 않았다면 자아도취 할 사람들은 / 또는 천박한 / 또는 미숙한 / 또는 쉽게 포기할 / 종종 고상해진다 / 그들의 종교에 의해 / 삶에 대한 통찰력이 주어질 때 / 그들이 어려운 결정을 하는 것을 돕는 / 우리 모두가 자랑스러워할

(B) Having a child / often has a wonderfully maturing effect / on a person.
아이를 가지는 것은 / 종종 아주 성숙해지는 효과가 있다 / 한 사람에게

Wartime, famously, / gives people an abundance of occasions to rise to, / as do natural disasters / like floods and hurricanes.
유명하게 전시는 / 사람들에게 대처해야 할 많은 위기를 제공한다 / 자연재해들이 하는 것처럼 / 홍수와 허리케인과 같은

(C) But for day-in, day-out lifelong bracing, / there is probably nothing so effective as religion: / it makes powerful and talented people / more humble and patient, / it makes average people / rise above themselves, / it provides sturdy support / for many people / who desperately need help / staying away from drink or drugs or crime.
하지만 하루도 빠짐없이, 평생 동안의 대비를 위해서 / 종교만큼 효과적인 것은 없을 것이다 / 그것은 영향력 있고 재능 있는 사람들을 만든다 / 더 겸손하고 참을성 있게 / 그것은 보통의 사람들을 만든다 / 그들 자신을 넘어서도록 / 그것은 견고한 도움을 제공한다 / 많은 사람들에게 / 필사적으로 도움을 필요로 하는 / 술, 마약 또는 범죄를 가까이하지 않는 것에

해석 종교는 분명히 한 사람에게서 최고의 것을 끌어낼 수 있지만, 그것이 그 속성을 동반하는 유일한 현상은 아니다.

(B) 아이를 가지는 것은 한 사람에게 종종 아주 성숙해지는 효과가 있다. 유명하게, 전시는 홍수와 허리케인과 같은 자연재해들이 하는 것처럼 대처해야 할 많은 위기들을 사람들에게 제공한다.

(C) 하지만 하루도 빠짐없이, 평생 동안의 대비를 위해서 종교만큼 효과적인 것은 없을 것이다. 그것(종교)은 영향력 있고 재능 있는 사람들을 더 겸손하고 참을성 있게 만들고, 보통의 사람들이 그들 자신을 넘어서도록 만들며, 술, 마약 또는 범죄를 가까이하지 않는 것에 필사적으로 도움을 필요로 하는 많은 사람들에게 견고한 도움을 제공한다.

(A) 우리 모두가 자랑스러워할 어려운 결정을 하는 것을 돕는 삶에 대한 통찰력이 주어질 때 그렇지 않았다면(종교가 아니었다면) 자아도취 하거나, 천박하거나, 미숙하거나 쉽게 포기할 사람들은 그들의 종교에 의해 종종 고상해진다.

해설 주어진 문장에서 종교가 사람으로부터 최고의 것을 끌어내는 유일한 현상은 아니라고 한 뒤, (B)에서 아이를 가지는 것이나 전쟁, 자연재해도 사람에게 성숙해지는 효과가 있다고 설명하고 있다. 이어서 (C)에서 하지만(But) 평생 동안의 준비에는 종교만큼 효과적인 것이 없다고 이야기하며 (A)에서 종교가 아니었다면(otherwise) 자아도취 하거나 천박할 사람들도 종교에 의해 삶에 대한 통찰력을 얻게 되면 고상해진다고 설명하고 있다.

어휘 bring out ~을 끌어내다 property 속성
self-absorbed 자아도취 하는 shallow 천박한 crude 미숙한
ennoble 고상하게 하다 perspective 통찰력 wonderfully 아주
an abundance of 많은 rise to occasion 위기에 대처하다
day-in, day-out 하루도 빠짐없이 brace 대비하다, 버티다
sturdy 견고한, 완강한 desperately 필사적으로
stay away from ~을 가까이하지 않다

20 독해 논리적 흐름 파악 (문단 순서 배열) 난이도 ★★☆

끊어읽기 해석

More people require more resources, / which means / that as the population increases, / the Earth's resources deplete more rapidly.
더 많은 사람들이 더 많은 자원을 필요로 한다 / 그리고 이것은 의미한다 / 인구가 증가함에 따라 / 지구의 자원이 더 빠르게 고갈된다는 것을

(A) Population growth also results in / increased greenhouse gases, / mostly from CO_2 emissions.
인구 증가는 또한 야기한다 / 늘어난 온실가스를 / 주로 이산화탄소 배출로부터 나오는

For visualization, / during that same 20th century / that saw fourfold population growth, / CO_2 emissions increased twelvefold.
가시화해보면 / 같은 그 20세기 동안에 / 4배의 인구 성장을 보인 / 이산화탄소 배출은 12배 증가했다

(B) The result of this depletion / is deforestation / and loss of biodiversity / as humans strip the Earth of resources / to accommodate rising population numbers.
이러한 고갈의 결과는 / 삼림 파괴이다 / 그리고 생물 다양성의 감소이다 / 사람들이 지구의 자원을 없애기 때문에 / 증가하는 인구수를 수용하기 위해

(C) As greenhouse gases increase, / so do climate patterns, / ultimately resulting in the long-term pattern / called climate change.
온실가스가 증가하듯이 / 기후 패턴들 또한 그러하다 / 결국 장기적인 패턴을 야기한다 / 기후 변화라고 불리는

해석 더 많은 사람들이 더 많은 자원을 필요로 하는데, 이것은 인구가 증가함에 따라 지구의 자원이 더 빠르게 고갈된다는 것을 의미한다.

(B) 사람들이 증가하는 인구수를 수용하기 위해 지구의 자원을 없애기 때문에 이러한 고갈의 결과는 삼림 파괴와 생물 다양성의 감소이다.
(A) 인구 증가는 또한 주로 이산화탄소 배출로부터 나오는 늘어난 온실가스를 야기한다. 가시화해보면, 4배의 인구 성장을 보인 같은 그 20세기 동안에, 이산화탄소 배출은 12배 증가했다.

(C) 온실가스가 증가하듯이 기후 패턴 또한 그러한데(늘어나는데), 이것은 결국 기후 변화라고 불리는 장기적인 패턴을 야기한다.

해설 주어진 문장에서 인구가 증가함에 따라 지구의 자원이 더 빠르게 고갈되고(deplete) 있다고 한 뒤, (B)에서 이러한 고갈(this depletion)의 결과로 삼림 파괴와 생물 다양성이 감소가 나타났음을 설명하고 있다. 이어서 (A)에서 인구 증가는 또한(also) 늘어난 온실가스를 야기했다고 하고, (C)에서 온실가스 증가로 인해 기후 패턴들 또한 변화하고 있음을 설명하고 있다.

어휘 emission 배출 visualization 가시화, 시각화 fold 배, 겹
deforestation 삼림 파괴 strip 없애다 accommodate 수용하다
ultimately 결국

21 독해 논리적 흐름 파악 (무관한 문장 삭제) 난이도 ★★☆

끊어읽기 해석

Medical anthropologists / with extensive training / in human biology and physiology / study disease transmission patterns / and how particular groups adapt / to the presence of diseases / like malaria and sleeping sickness.
의학 인류학자들은 / 광범위한 교육을 받은 / 인간 생물학과 생리학의 / 질병 전파 패턴들을 연구한다 / 그리고 어떻게 특정한 집단들이 적응하는지를 / 질병들의 존재에 대해 / 말라리아나 수면병과 같은

① Because the transmission / of viruses and bacteria / is strongly influenced / by people's diets, sanitation, and other behaviors, / many medical anthropologists work / as a team with epidemiologists / to identify cultural practices / that affect the spread of disease.
전파가 ~하기 때문에 / 바이러스와 세균의 / 강하게 영향받는다 / 사람들의 식습관, 공중위생과 다른 행동들에 의해 / 많은 의학 인류학자들은 일한다 / 유행병학자들과 한 조로 / 문화적 관습을 확인하기 위해 / 질병의 전파에 영향을 주는

② Though it may be a commonly held belief / that most students enter medicine / for humanitarian reasons / rather than for the financial rewards / of a successful medical career, / in developed nations / the prospect of status and rewards / is probably one incentive.
비록 일반적으로 받아들여지는 믿음일지라도 / 대다수의 학생들이 의학을 시작한다는 것이 / 인도주의적인 이유로 / 금전적인 보상보다는 / 성공적인 의학 경력에 대한 것으로서 / 선진국들에서 / 지위와 보상에 대한 전망은 / 아마도 하나의 자극일 것이다

③ Different cultures have different ideas / about the causes and symptoms of disease, / how best to treat illnesses, / the abilities of traditional healers and doctors, / and the importance of community involvement / in the healing process.
각각 다른 문화권들은 다른 생각들을 가진다 / 병의 원인과 증상들에 대해 / 어떻게 가장 잘 질병을 치료할 수 있을지에 대해 / 전통적인 신앙 요법가와 의사들의 능력 / 그리고 지역 사회 참여의 중요성에 대해 / 치료 과정에서

④ By studying / how a human community perceives such things, / medical anthropologists help / hospitals and other agencies / deliver health care services more effectively.
연구함으로써 / 어떻게 인간 공동체가 그러한 것들을 인식하는지를 / 의학 인류학자들은 도와준다 / 병원과 다른 기관들이 / 보건 의료 서비스를 더 효과적으로 제공하는 것을

해석 인간 생물학과 생리학에서 광범위한 교육을 받은 의학 인류학자들은 질병 전파 패턴들과 특정한 집단들이 말라리아나 수면병과 같은 질병의 존재에 대해 어떻게 적응하는지를 연구한다. ① 바이러스와 세균의 전파가 사람들의 식습관, 공중위생과 다른 행동들에

의해 강하게 영향받기 때문에, 많은 의학 인류학자들은 질병의 전파에 영향을 주는 문화적 관습을 확인하기 위해 유행병학자들과 한 조로 일한다. ② 비록 대다수의 학생들이 성공적인 의학 경력에 대한 보상으로서 금전적인 보상보다는 인도주의적인 이유들로 의학을 시작한다는 것이 일반적으로 받아들여지는 믿음일지라도, 선진국들에서의 지위와 보상에 대한 전망은 아마도 (의학을 시작하는) 하나의 자극일 것이다. ③ 질병의 원인과 증상, 질병을 어떻게 가장 잘 치료할 수 있을지, 그리고 전통적인 신앙 요법가와 의사들의 능력과 치료 과정에서 지역 사회 참여의 중요성에 대해 서로 다른 문화들은 다른 생각들을 가진다. ④ 어떻게 인간 공동체가 그러한 것들을 인식하는지를 연구함으로써 의학 인류학자들은 병원과 다른 기관들이 보건 의료 서비스를 더 효과적으로 제공하는 것을 도와준다.

해설 지문 처음에서 의학 인류학자들은 질병 전파 패턴들과 특정 집단이 질병에 어떻게 적응하는지에 대해 연구한다고 언급한 뒤, ①번에서 질병 전파에 영향을 주는 문화적 관습을 찾기 위해 의학 인류학자들은 유행병학자들과 함께 일한다고 언급하고 있다. 이어서 ③번에서 각 문화권들은 질병의 원인과 최적의 치료법 등에 대해 다른 생각을 가진다고 한 뒤, ④번에서 인간 공동체가 이러한 것들(such things)을 어떻게 인식하는지를 연구한다고 하며 이에 대한 의학 인류학자들의 역할에 대해서 설명하고 있다. 그러나 ②번은 학생들이 의학을 시작하는 이유에 대한 내용으로, 지문 처음의 내용과 관련이 없다.

어휘 anthropologist 인류학자 physiology 생리학
transmission 전파 adapt 적응하다 presence 존재
sanitation 공중위생 identify 확인하다
humanitarian 인도주의적인 prospect 전망 incentive 자극
treat 치료하다 healer 신앙 요법가

22 독해 논리적 흐름 파악 (문단 순서 배열) 난이도 ★★☆

끊어읽기 해석

Sequoya (1760?–1843) was born / in eastern Tennessee, / into a prestigious family / that was highly regarded / for its knowledge / of Cherokee tribal traditions and religion.
Sequoya(1760?–1843)는 태어났다 / 테네시주 동부에서 / 명망 있는 가문에 / 높이 평가되었던 / 그것의 지식으로 / 체로키 부족의 전통과 종교에 대한

(A) Recognizing the possibilities / writing had / for his people, / Sequoya invented a Cherokee alphabet / in 1821.
가능성들을 알아보았기 때문에 / 글자가 가지는 / 그의 민족에게 / Sequoya는 체로키 알파벳을 발명했다 / 1821년에

With this system of writing, / Sequoya was able to record / ancient tribal customs.
이 표기 체계를 가지고 / Sequoya는 기록할 수 있었다 / 고대 부족의 관습들을

(B) More important, / his alphabet helped the Cherokee nation / develop a publishing industry / so that newspapers and books could be printed.
더 중요한 것은 / 그의 알파벳이 체로키 민족을 도왔다는 것이다 / 출판 산업을 발전시키도록 / 그래서 신문과 책이 인쇄될 수 있었다

School-age children / were thus able to learn / about Cherokee culture and traditions / in their own language.
취학 연령의 아이들은 / 따라서 배울 수 있었다 / 체로키 문화와 전통에 대해 / 그들만의 언어로

(C) As a child, / Sequoya learned the Cherokee oral tradition; / then, as an adult, / he was introduced to Euro-American culture.
어릴 적에 / Sequoya는 체로키 구전을 배웠다 / 그리고 나서 어른이 되어서 / 그는 유럽계 미국의 문화를 처음으로 경험하게 되었다

In his letters, / Sequoya mentions / how he became fascinated / with the writing methods / European Americans used to communicate.
그의 편지들에서 / Sequoya는 언급한다 / 그가 어떻게 매료되었는지 / 표기법들에 / 유럽계 미국인들이 의사소통을 하던

해석
> Sequoya(1760?–1843)는 테네시주 동부에서 체로키 부족의 전통과 종교에 대한 지식으로 높이 평가되었던 명망 있는 가문에 태어났다.

(C) 어릴 적에 Sequoya는 체로키 구전을 배웠고, 그리고 나서 어른이 되어서 그는 유럽계 미국의 문화를 처음으로 경험하게 되었다. 그의 편지들에서 Sequoya는 그가 어떻게 유럽계 미국인들이 의사소통을 하던 표기법에 매료되었는지 언급한다.

(A) 그(Sequoya)의 민족에게 글자가 가지는 가능성을 알아보았기 때문에, Sequoya는 1821년에 체로키 알파벳을 발명했다. 이 표기 체계를 가지고 Sequoya는 고대 부족의 관습들을 기록할 수 있었다.

(B) 더 중요한 것은 그의 알파벳이 체로키 민족이 출판 산업을 발전시키도록 도와서 신문과 책이 인쇄될 수 있었다는 것이다. 따라서 취학 연령의 아이들은 그들만의 언어로 체로키 문화와 전통에 대해 배울 수 있었다.

해설 주어진 문장에서 Sequoya에 대해 소개한 뒤, (C)에서 어른이 된 Sequoya가 유럽계 미국 문화를 처음으로 경험한 후, 그들의 의사소통 표기법에 매료되었다고 설명하고 있다. 이어서 (A)에서 글자가 가지는 가능성을 알아본 Sequoya가 체로키 알파벳을 발명했다(invented)고 하고, (B)에서 그의 알파벳(his alphabet)이 결과적으로 체로키 민족을 도왔음을 설명하고 있다.

어휘 prestigious 명망 있는 family 가문 nation 민족
oral tradition 구전 introduce 처음으로 경험하다, 도입하다
fascinated 매료된

23 독해 세부내용 파악 (내용 불일치 파악) 난이도 ★☆☆

끊어읽기 해석

SPREAD THE LOVE
사랑을 나눠주세요

Fight Hunger / During the Peanut Butter Drive
굶주림과 싸워보자 / 땅콩버터 운동 동안에

Make a contribution / to our community / by helping local families / who need a little assistance.
공헌하세요 / 우리 지역 사회에 / 지역의 가정들을 도움으로써 / 약간의 도움을 필요로 하는

We are kicking off / our 4th annual area-wide peanut butter drive / to benefit children, families and seniors / who face hunger / in Northeast Louisiana.
저희는 시작합니다 / 우리의 네 번째 연간 광역 땅콩버터 운동을 / 아이들, 가족들과 고령자들에게 도움이 되기 위해 / 굶주림에 직면한 / 루이지애나주 북동쪽의

Peanut butter is a much needed staple / at Food Banks / as it is a protein-packed food / that kids and adults love.
땅콩버터는 매우 필요한 주식이다 / 푸드 뱅크에서 / 그것이 단백질로 가득 찬 식품이기 때문에 / 아이들과 어른들이 좋아하는

Please donate peanut butter / in plastic jars / or funds to the Monroe Food Bank / by Friday, March 29th at 4:00 pm.

땅콩버터를 기부해 주세요 / 플라스틱병에 담긴 / 또는 Monroe 푸드 뱅크
에 기금을 / 3월 29일 금요일 오후 4 시까지

Donations of peanut butter / can be dropped off / at the
food bank's distribution center / located at 4600 Central
Avenue in Monroe / on Monday through Friday, / 8:00 am to
4:00 pm.
땅콩버터 기증품은 / 전달될 수 있습니다 / 푸드 뱅크의 배급 센터에서 /
Monroe에 있는 4600 Central Avenue에 위치한 / 월요일부터 금요일
까지 / 오전 8시에서 오후 4시까지

Monetary donations can be made here / or by calling 427-
418-4581.
금전적인 기부는 이곳에서 이루어질 수 있습니다 / 또는 427-418-4581
로 전화함으로써

For other drop-off locations, / visit our website / at https://
www.foodbanknela.org
다른 전달 장소들에 대해서는 / 우리 웹사이트를 방문하세요 / https://
www.foodbanknela.org

해석 사랑을 나눠주세요

땅콩버터 운동 동안에 굶주림과 싸워보자

약간의 도움을 필요로 하는 지역의 가정들을 도움으로써 우리 지
역 사회에 공헌하세요. 저희는 루이지애나주 북동쪽의 굶주림에
직면한 아이들, 가족들과 고령자들에게 도움이 되기 위한 우리의
네 번째 연간 광역 땅콩버터 운동을 시작합니다.

땅콩버터는 푸드 뱅크에서 매우 필요한 주식인데, 그것(땅콩 버터)
이 아이들과 어른들이 좋아하는 단백질로 가득 찬 식품이기 때문
입니다. 3월 29일 금요일 오후 4시까지 플라스틱병에 담긴 땅콩
버터나 기금을 Monroe 푸드 뱅크에 기부해 주세요. 땅콩버터 기
증품은 월요일부터 금요일 오전 8시에서 오후 4시까지 Monroe에
있는 4600 Central Avenue에 위치한 푸드 뱅크의 배급 센터에서
전달될 수 있습니다. 금전적인 기부는 이곳(푸드 뱅크)에서 또는
427-418-4581로 전화함으로써 이루어질 수 있습니다.

다른 전달 장소들에 대해서는 우리 웹사이트(인) https://www.
foodbanknela.org를 방문하세요.

해설 지문 중간에서 땅콩버터의 기부는 월요일부터 금요일까지만 받는
다고 했으므로, '② 토요일과 일요일에도 땅콩버터를 기부할 수
있다'는 지문의 내용과 다르다.

어휘 make a contribution 공헌하다, 기부하다 assistance 도움
kick off 시작하다 benefit 도움이 되다 staple 주식, 기본 식료품
packed ~이 가득 찬 drop off 전달하다, 갖다 놓다
distribution 배급, 유통 monetary 금전적인

24 독해 전체내용 파악 (글의 감상) 난이도 ★★☆

끊어읽기 해석

Our whole tribe was poverty-stricken.
우리 부족 전체는 가난에 시달렸다.

Every branch / of the Garoghlanian family / was living / in the
most amazing and comical poverty / in the world.
모든 일가는 / Garoghlanian 가문의 / 살고 있었다 / 가장 놀랍고 우스꽝
스러운 가난 속에서 / 세상에서

Nobody could understand / where we ever got money /
enough to keep us / with food in our bellies.
아무도 이해할 수 없었다 / 우리가 도대체 어디에서 돈을 구했는지 / 우리
가 유지하기에 충분한 / 우리의 뱃속에 음식을 지닌 채로

Most important of all, though, / we were famous for our
honesty.

하지만 무엇보다도 가장 중요한 것은 / 우리가 우리의 정직함으로 유명했
다는 것이다

We had been famous for honesty / for something like eleven
centuries, / even when we had been the wealthiest family / in
what we liked to think was the world.
우리는 정직함으로 유명했었다 / 약 11세기 동안 / 우리가 가장 부유한 가
족이었을 때조차 / 우리가 세상이었다고 생각하고 싶었던 곳에서

We put pride first, / honest next, / and after that / we
believed in right and wrong.
우리는 가장 중시한다 자부심을 / 다음으로 정직함을 / 그리고 그다음에 /
우리는 옳고 그름을 믿었다.

None of us / would take advantage of anybody / in the
world.
우리들 중 그 아무도 / 누군가를 이용하지 못했을 것이다 / 이 세상에서

해석 우리 부족 전체는 가난에 시달렸다. Garoghlanian 가문의 모든 일
가는 세상에서 가장 놀랍고 우스꽝스러운 가난 속에서 살고 있었
다. 우리의 뱃속에 음식을 지닌 채로 유지하기에 충분한 돈을 우리
가 도대체 어디서 구했는지 아무도 이해할 수 없었다. 하지만 무
엇보다도 가장 중요한 것은 우리가 우리의 정직함으로 유명했다
는 것이다. 약 11세기 동안 우리는 우리(자체)가 세상이었다고 생
각하고 싶었던 곳에서 가장 부유한 가문이었을 때조차 정직함으로
유명했다. 우리는 자부심을 가장 중시하고, 다음으로 정직함을
(우선시하고), 그다음으로 우리는 옳고 그름을 믿었다. 우리들 중
그 아무도 이 세상에서 누군가를 이용하지 못했을 것이다.

① 평화롭고 차분한
② 만족해하고 자랑스러워하는
③ 겁에 질리고 무서워하는
④ 경악하고 깜짝 놀란

해설 지문 전반에 걸쳐 화자는 자신의 부족이 가난했지만 정직함으로
유명했다고 하고 있고, 지문 뒷부분에서 화자의 부족은 자부심과
정직함을 중시하며 옳고 그름을 믿으며 세상에서 자신들은 그 누
구도 이용하지 못했을 것이라고 했으므로, '② 만족해하고 자랑스
러워하는'이 화자의 심경으로 적절하다.

어휘 branch 일가, 가족 comical 우스꽝스러운
put A first A를 가장 중시하다 take advantage of ~을 이용하다
horrified 겁에 질린 astonished 깜짝 놀란

25 독해 세부내용 파악 (내용 불일치 파악) 난이도 ★★☆

끊어읽기 해석

Despite the increasing popularity / of consuming raw foods, /
you can still gain nutrients / from cooked vegetables.
더욱더 늘어나는 인기에도 불구하고 / 날음식을 먹는 것의 / 당신은 여전히
영양소를 얻을 수 있다 / 익힌 채소들로부터

For example, / our body can absorb lycopene / more
effectively / when tomatoes are cooked.
예를 들어 / 우리의 몸은 리코펜을 흡수할 수 있다 / 더 효과적으로 / 토마
토들이 익혀지면

(Keep in mind, however, / that raw tomatoes are still a good
source of lycopene.)
(그러나 명심해라 / 날것의 토마토들도 여전히 좋은 리코펜의 원천이라는
것을)

Cooked tomatoes, / however, / have lower levels of vitamin C
/ than raw tomatoes, / so if you're looking to increase your
levels, / you might be better off / sticking with the raw.
익힌 토마토들은 / 그러나 / 더 낮은 수치의 비타민 C를 가지고 있다 / 날것
의 토마토들보다 / 그래서 만약 당신이 당신의 수치를 늘리는 것을 기대하
고 있다면 / 당신은 더 나을지도 모른다 / 날것을 고수하는 것이

Whether you decide / to eat them cooked or raw, / it's important / not to dilute / the health benefits of tomatoes.
당신이 결정하든지 간에 / 그것들을 익혀서 혹은 날것으로 먹을지 / 중요하다 / 약화시키지 않는 것이 / 토마토가 주는 건강상의 이익들을

If you're buying tomato sauce or paste, / choose a variety / with no salt or sugar added / —or better yet, / cook your own sauce at home.
만약 당신이 토마토소스나 페이스트를 산다면 / 종류를 선택해라 / 소금이나 설탕이 첨가되지 않은 상태의 / 아니면 그보다 좋은 (것은) / 집에서 당신 자신의 소스를 요리해라

And if you're eating / your tomatoes raw, / salt them sparingly / and choose salad dressings / that are low in calories and saturated fat.
그리고 만약 당신이 먹고 있다면 / 당신의 토마토들을 날것으로 / 그것들에 소금을 조금만 뿌려라 / 그리고 샐러드 소스들을 골라라 / 열량과 포화 지방이 낮은

해석 날음식을 먹는 것의 더욱더 늘어나는 인기에도 불구하고, 당신은 여전히 익힌 채소들로부터 영양소를 얻을 수 있다. 예를 들어, 토마토가 익혀지면 우리의 몸은 더 효과적으로 리코펜을 흡수할 수 있다. (그러나, 날것의 토마토들도 여전히 좋은 리코펜의 원천이라는 것을 명심해라.) 그러나, 익힌 토마토들은 날것의 토마토들보다 더 낮은 수치의 비타민 C를 가지고 있으므로, 당신의 (비타민 C) 수치를 늘리는 것을 기대하고 있다면, 당신은 날것을 고수하는 것이 더 나을지도 모른다. 당신이 그것들을 익혀서 혹은 날것으로 먹을지 결정하든지 간에, 토마토가 주는 건강상의 이익들을 약화시키지 않는 것이 중요하다. 만약 당신이 토마토소스나 페이스트를 산다면, 소금이나 설탕이 첨가되지 않은 상태의 종류를 선택하고, 아니면 그보다 좋은 (것은) 집에서 당신 자신의 소스를 요리해라. 그리고 만약 당신이 토마토들을 날것으로 먹고 있다면, 그것들(토마토들)에 소금을 조금만 뿌리고 열량과 포화 지방이 낮은 샐러드 소스들로 골라라.

해설 지문 중간에서 당신의 비타민 C 수치를 늘리는 것을 기대하고 있다면 날것의 토마토를 고수하는 것이 더 나을지도 모른다고 했으므로, '② 더 많은 비타민 C를 섭취하고 싶다면 생토마토보다 조리된 토마토를 섭취하는 것이 낫다'는 것은 지문의 내용과 다르다.

어휘 popularity 인기 consume 먹다 look to 기대하다
be better off 더 낫다 stick with ~을 고수하다
variety 종류, 다양성 sparingly 조금만 saturated fat 포화 지방

정답

p.50

01	② 독해 – 논리적 흐름 파악	**11**	② 독해 – 논리적 흐름 파악	**21**	④ 독해 – 논리적 흐름 파악
02	① 독해 – 추론	**12**	② 독해 – 추론	**22**	② 독해 – 논리적 흐름 파악
03	② 독해 – 논리적 흐름 파악	**13**	① 독해 – 전체내용 파악	**23**	③ 독해 – 논리적 흐름 파악
04	④ 독해 – 전체내용 파악	**14**	③ 문법 – 병치·도치·강조 구문	**24**	③ 독해 – 전체내용 파악
05	① 독해 – 전체내용 파악	**15**	② 문법 – 수 일치	**25**	④ 독해 – 논리적 흐름 파악
06	① 독해 – 논리적 흐름 파악	**16**	② 독해 – 추론		
07	① 독해 – 논리적 흐름 파악	**17**	③ 독해 – 전체내용 파악		
08	① 독해 – 추론	**18**	④ 독해 – 세부내용 파악		
09	③ 문법 – 분사	**19**	④ 독해 – 세부내용 파악		
10	① 문법 – 분사	**20**	④ 독해 – 전체내용 파악		

취약영역 분석표

영역	세부 유형	문항 수	소계
어휘	어휘 & 표현	0	/0
	생활영어	0	
문법	분사	2	/4
	병치·도치·강조 구문	1	
	수 일치	1	
독해	전체내용 파악	6	/21
	세부내용 파악	2	
	추론	4	
	논리적 흐름 파악	9	
총계			**/25**

· 자신이 취약한 영역은 '법원직 9급 영어, 이렇게 출제된다!'(문제집 p.8)를 통해 다시 한번 확인하고 학습하시기 바랍니다.

---

01 독해 논리적 흐름 파악 (문맥상 적절한 어휘)
난이도 ★★★

끊어읽기 해석

It's tempting / to identify knowledge with facts, / but not every fact is an item / of knowledge.
솔깃한 일이다 / 지식과 사실을 동일시하는 것은 / 하지만 모든 사실이 항목인 것은 아니다 / 지식의

Imagine / shaking a sealed cardboard box / containing a single coin.
상상해 보라 / 밀봉된 판지 상자를 흔드는 것을 / 동전 한 개가 들어 있는

As you put the box down, / the coin inside the box has landed / either heads or tails: / let's say that's a fact.
당신이 상자를 내려놓을 때 / 상자 안에 있는 동전이 떨어졌다 / 앞면이나 뒷면 둘 중 하나로 / 그것이 사실이라고 하자

But / as long as no one looks into the box, / this fact remains unknown; / it is not yet / within the realm of **(A)** knowledge.
그러나 / 아무도 그 상자를 들여다보지 않는 한 / 이 사실은 계속 알 수 없는 것이다 / 그것은 아직 ~있지 않다 / (A) 지식의 영역 안에

Nor do facts become knowledge / simply by being written down.
사실이 지식이 되는 것도 아니다 / 단순히 기록됨으로써

If you write the sentence / 'The coin has landed heads' / on one slip of paper / and 'The coin has landed tails' / on another, / then you will have written down a fact / on one of the slips, / but you still won't have gained / knowledge of the outcome / of the coin toss.
만약 당신이 문장을 쓴다면 / '동전이 앞면으로 떨어졌다'라는 / 한 쪽 종이에 / 그리고 '동전이 뒷면으로 떨어졌다'라는 / 다른 쪽에는 / 그랬다면 당신은 사실을 적었을 것이다 / 그 두 쪽 중 하나에 / 하지만 당신은 여전히 얻지 못했을 것이다 / 결과에 대한 지식은 / 동전 던지기의

Knowledge demands / some kind of access / to a fact / on the part of some living subject.
지식은 요구한다 / 일종의 접근을 (할 것을) / 사실에 / 몇몇 현존하는 대상에 관한

(B) Without a mind / to access it, / whatever is stored / in libraries and databases / won't be knowledge, / but just ink marks and electronic traces.
의도가 (B) 없다면 / 이것에 접근하려는 / 저장되어 있는 것은 무엇이든지 / 도서관이나 데이터베이스에 / 지식이 아닐 것이다 / 단지 잉크 자국이나 전자 기록일 것이다

In any given case of knowledge, / this access may or may not be unique / to an individual: / the same fact / may be known by one person and not by others.
어떤 지식의 경우라도, / 이러한 접근은 유일할 수도 있고 아닐 수도 있다 / 한 개인에게 / 동일한 사실은 / 한 사람이 알고 다른 사람들이 알지 못할 수도 있다

Common knowledge might be shared / by many people, / but there is no knowledge that dangles / **(C)** unattached to any subject.
상식은 공유될 수도 있다 / 많은 사람들에 의해 / 하지만 매달리는 지식은 없다 / 어떤 대상에도 (C) 소속되지 않은 채

해석 지식과 사실을 동일시하는 것은 솔깃한 일이지만, 모든 사실이 지식의 항목인 것은 아니다. 동전 한 개가 들어 있는 밀봉된 판지 상자를 흔드는 것을 상상해 보라. 당신이 상자를 내려놓을 때, 상자 안에 있는 동전이 앞면이나 뒷면 둘 중 하나로 떨어졌고, 그것이 사실이라고 하자. 그러나 아무도 그 상자를 들여다보지 않는 한 이 사실은 계속 알 수 없는 것이며, 그것은 아직 (A) 지식의 영역 안에 있지 않다. 사실이 단순히 기록됨으로써 지식이 되는 것도 아니다. 만약 당신이 한 쪽 종이에 '동전이 앞면으로 떨어졌다'라는 문장을 쓰고 다른 쪽에는 '동전이 뒷면으로 떨어졌다'라는 문장을 쓴다면, 당신은 그 두 쪽 중 하나에 사실을 적었을 것이지만, 당신은 여전히 동전 던지기의 결과에 대한 지식은 얻지 못했을 것이다. 지식은 몇몇 현존하는 대상에 관한 사실에 일종의 접근을 (할 것을) 요구한다. 이것(몇몇 현존하는 대상에 관한 사실)에 접근하려는 의도가 (B) 없다면, 도서관이나 데이터베이스에 저장되어 있는 것은 무엇이든지, 지식이 아니라 단지 잉크 자국이나 전자 기록일 것이다. 어떤 지식의 경우라도, 이러한 접근은 한 개인에게 유일할 수도 있

고 아닐 수도 있다. 동일한 사실은 한 사람이 알고 다른 사람들이 알지 못할 수도 있다. 상식은 많은 사람들에 의해 공유될 수도 있지만, 어떤 대상에도 (C) 소속되지 <u>않은</u> 채 매달리는 지식은 없다.

	(A)	(B)	(C)
①	사실	~를 가지고	소속되지 않은
②	지식	~ 없이	소속되지 않은
③	지식	~를 가지고	소속된
④	사실	~ 없이	소속된

해설 (A) 빈칸이 있는 문장에서 상자 속 동전이 떨어진 것을 사실이라고 했을 때, 아무도 상자를 들여다보지 않는 한, 동전 던지기에 관한 사실은 여전히 알 수 없는 것이라고 했으므로, 빈칸에는 이 사실은 아직 '지식'의 영역 안에 있지 않다는 내용이 들어가야 적절하다. (B) 빈칸 앞 문장에서 지식은 현존하는 대상에 관한 사실에 일종의 접근을 할 것을 요구한다고 했고, 빈칸이 있는 문장에서 이것(몇몇 현존하는 대상에 관한 사실)에 접근하려는 의도가 어떠하면 도서관이나 데이터베이스에 저장되어 있는 것은 지식이 아니라 단지 기록일 것이라고 했으므로, 빈칸에는 이것(몇몇 현존하는 대상에 관한 사실)에 접근하려는 의도가 '없다면'이라는 내용이 들어가야 적절하다. (C) 빈칸 앞부분에서 지식은 현존하는 대상에 관한 사실에 접근할 것을 요구한다고 했으므로, 어떤 대상에도 '소속되지 않은'(unattached) 채 매달리는 지식은 없다는 내용이 들어가야 적절하다.
따라서 ② (A) knowledge(지식) – (B) Without(~ 없이) – (C) unattached(소속되지 않은)가 정답이다.

어휘 identify A with B A와 B를 동일시하다 sealed 밀봉된
land 떨어지다, 착지하다 look into 들여다보다 realm 영역
trace 기록 any given 어떤 ~도, 어느 ~도
common knowledge 상식 dangle 매달리다
unattached 소속되지 않은, 붙어 있지 않은

02 독해 추론 (빈칸 완성 - 구) 난이도 ★★☆

끊어읽기 해석

Impressionable youth are not the only ones / subject to peer pressure.
쉽게 외부의 영향을 받는 젊은이들이 ~인 유일한 사람은 아니다 / 동료집단으로부터 받는 압력의 영향을 받기 쉬운

Most of us / have probably had an experience / of being pressured / by a salesman.
우리 중 대부분은 / 아마도 경험이 있을 것이다 / 압박을 받은 / 판매원으로부터

Have you ever had / a sales rep try to sell you / some "office solution" / by telling you / that 70 percent of your competitors / are using their service, / so why aren't you?
당신은 겪어본 적이 있는가 / 영업 사원이 당신에게 판매하려고 노력하는 것을 / '사무용 솔루션'을 / 당신에게 말함으로써 / 당신의 경쟁자들 중 70퍼센트가 / 그들의 서비스를 이용하고 있다고 / 그렇다면 왜 당신은 사용하지 않고 있냐며

But what if / 70 percent of your competitors are idiots?
하지만 ~라면 어떨까 / 경쟁자들 중 70퍼센트가 바보이다

Or what if / that 70 percent were given so much value added / or offered such a low price / that they couldn't resist the opportunity?
아니면 ~라면 어떨까 / 70퍼센트가 너무 많은 부가가치를 받았다 / 또는 너무 낮은 가격을 제시 받았다 / 그래서 그들이 그 기회를 참을 수 없었다

The practice is designed / to do one thing and one thing only / —to pressure you to buy.
그 관행은 고안되었다 / 한 가지, 오로지 한 가지의 일을 하기 위해 / (물건을) 구입하도록 당신에게 압력을 가하는

To make you feel / you might be missing out on something / or that everyone else knows / but you.
당신이 느끼게 하기 위해서이다 / 당신이 무언가를 놓치고 있을지도 모른다고 / 또는 다른 모든 사람들이 알고 있다고 / 당신을 제외한

해석 쉽게 외부의 영향을 받는 젊은이들이 동료집단으로부터 받는 압력의 영향을 받기 쉬운 유일한 사람은 아니다. 우리 중 대부분은 아마도 판매원으로부터 압박을 받은 경험이 있을 것이다. 당신은 경쟁자들 중 70퍼센트가 그들의 서비스를 이용하고 있는데, 그렇다면 왜 당신은 사용하지 않고 있냐고 말함으로써 영업사원이 '사무용 솔루션'을 당신에게 판매하려고 노력하는 것을 겪어본 적이 있는가? 하지만 경쟁자들 중 70퍼센트가 바보라면 어떨까? 아니면 그 (경쟁자 중) 70퍼센트가 너무 많은 부가가치를 받았거나 너무 낮은 가격을 제시받아서 그 기회를 참을 수 없었다면 어떨까? 그 관행은 한 가지, (물건을) 구입하도록 당신에게 압력을 가하는 오로지 그 한 가지의 일을 하기 위해 고안되었다. 당신이 무언가를 놓치고 있을 지도 모른다고 느끼거나 당신을 제외한 다른 모든 사람들이 알고 있다고 느끼게 하기 위해서이다.

① 동료집단으로부터 받는 압력
② 충동 구매
③ 괴롭히기 작전
④ 격렬한 경쟁

해설 빈칸이 있는 문장을 통해 빈칸에 쉽게 외부의 영향을 받는 젊은이들이 무엇에 영향을 받기 쉬운 유일한 사람은 아닌지에 대한 내용이 나와야 적절하다는 것을 알 수 있다. 지문 전반에 걸쳐 우리 중 대부분이 영업사원에게 경쟁자의 70퍼센트가 이용하고 있는 서비스를 왜 사용하지 않냐는 말을 들은 경험이 있을 것이라고 하며 이러한 관행은 우리에게 물건을 구입하도록 압력을 가해 당신이 무언가를 놓치고 있을지 모른다고 느끼게 하기 위해 고안되었다는 내용이 있으므로, 쉽게 외부의 영향을 받는 젊은이들이 '동료집단으로부터 받는 압력'에 영향을 받기 쉬운 유일한 사람은 아니라고 한 ①번이 정답이다.

어휘 impressionable 쉽게 외부의 영향을 받는
subject to ~의 영향을 받기 쉬운, ~에 시달리게 만들다
sale rep 영업 사원 solution 솔루션(전산 기기에서 다양한 기능을 관리하고 문제를 처리하며 서로 간에 연동이 가능한 하드웨어나 소프트웨어)
value added 부가가치 practice 관행 impulse 충동적인, 충동
tactic 작전, 전략 keen 격렬한, 예리한

03 독해 논리적 흐름 파악 (문맥상 적절한 어휘) 난이도 ★★☆

끊어읽기 해석

People with high self-esteem / have confidence / in their skills and competence / and enjoy facing the challenges / that life offers them.
자존감이 높은 사람들은 / 자신감을 가지고 있다 / 그들의 실력과 능력에 / 그리고 도전에 직면하는 것을 즐긴다 / 인생이 그들에게 주는

They (A) willingly work in teams / because they are sure of themselves / and enjoy taking the opportunity / to contribute.
그들은 (A) 기꺼이 팀을 이루어 일한다 / 스스로에게 확신을 가지고 있기 때문이다 / 그리고 기회를 잡는 것을 즐긴다 / 기여할

However, / those who have low self-esteem / tend to feel awkward, shy, / and unable to express themselves.
그러나 / 자존감이 낮은 사람들은 / 어색해하고 수줍어하는 경향이 있다 / 그리고 자기 자신을 표현하지 못한다

Often they compound their problems / by opting for avoidance strategies / because they (B) hold the belief / that whatever they do will result in failure.

그들은 종종 그들의 문제를 악화시킨다 / 회피 전략을 선택함으로써 / 그들은 생각을 (B) 가지고 있기 때문이다 / 그들이 하는 것이 무엇이든지 실패로 끝날 것이라는

Conversely, / they may compensate / for their lack of self-esteem / by exhibiting boastful and arrogant behavior / to cover up their sense of unworthiness.
반대로 / 그들은 보완할 수도 있다 / 자존감의 결여를 / 허풍을 떨고 거만한 행동을 보여줌으로써 / 하찮다는 기분을 감추기 위해

Furthermore, / such individuals account for their successes / by finding reasons / that are outside of themselves, / while those with high self-esteem (C) attribute their success / to internal characteristics.
게다가 / 그러한 사람들은 그들의 성공을 설명한다 / 이유를 찾아냄으로써 / 자신들 외부에 있는 / 자존감이 높은 사람들은 그들의 성공을 ~의 (C) 덕분으로 보는 반면에 / 내면적인 특성의

해석 자존감이 높은 사람들은 그들의 실력과 능력에 자신감을 가지고 있으며 인생이 그들에게 주는 도전에 직면하는 것을 즐긴다. 그들은 스스로에게 확신을 가지고 있고 기여할 기회를 잡는 것을 즐기기 때문에 (A) 기꺼이 팀을 이루어 일한다. 그러나, 자존감이 낮은 사람들은 어색해하고 수줍어하며, 자기 자신을 표현하지 못하는 경향이 있다. 그들이 하는 것이 무엇이든지 실패로 끝날 것이라는 생각을 (B) 가지고 있기 때문에 그들은 회피 전략을 선택함으로써 종종 그들의 문제를 악화시킨다. 반대로, 그들은 하찮다는 기분을 감추기 위해 허풍을 떨고 거만한 행동을 보여줌으로써 자존감의 결여를 보완할 수도 있다. 게다가, 그러한 사람들은 자신들 외부에 있는 이유를 찾아냄으로써 그들의 성공을 설명하는 반면, 자존감이 높은 사람들은 그들의 성공을 내면적인 특성의 (C) 덕분으로 본다.

	(A)	(B)	(C)
①	기꺼이	부인하다	시도하다
②	기꺼이	가지다	(~을 -의) 덕분으로 보다
③	마지못해	가지다	시도하다
④	마지못해	부인하다	(~을 -의) 덕분으로 보다

해설 (A) 빈칸이 있는 문장에서 자존감이 높은 사람들은 스스로에게 확신을 가지고 있고 기여할 기회를 잡는 것을 즐긴다고 했으므로, 빈칸에는 '기꺼이'(willingly) 팀을 이루어 일한다는 내용이 들어가야 적절하다. (B) 빈칸이 있는 문장에서 자존감이 낮은 사람들은 회피 전략을 선택함으로써 종종 그들의 문제를 악화시킨다고 했으므로, 빈칸에는 자존감이 낮은 사람들은 그들이 하는 것이 무엇이든지 실패로 끝날 것이라는 믿음을 '가지고'(hold) 있다는 내용이 들어가야 적절하다. (C) 빈칸이 있는 문장에서 자존감이 낮은 사람들은 그들의 외부에 있는 이유를 찾아냄으로써 성공을 설명한다고 했으므로, 빈칸에는 자존감이 높은 사람들은 그들의 성공을 그들의 내면적인 특성의 '덕분으로 본다'(attribute)라는 내용이 들어가야 적절하다.
따라서 ② (A) willingly(기꺼이) - (B) hold(가지다) - (C) attribute(덕분으로 보다)가 정답이다.

어휘 self-esteem 자존감 confidence 자신감 competence 능력
willingly 기꺼이 unwillingly 마지못해
be sure of ~에 확신을 가지다 awkward 어색한
compound 악화시키다 opt for ~를 선택하다 deny 부인하다
hold (신념, 의견 등을) 가지다 conversely 반대로
compensate 보완하다 lack 결여, 결핍 exhibit 보이다, 드러내다
boastful 허풍을 떠는 arrogant 거만한 unworthiness 하찮음
account for 설명하다 attribute (~을 -의) 덕분으로 보다
internal 내면적인

끊어읽기 해석

To be sure, / no other species can lay claim to our capacity / to devise something new and original, / from the sublime to the sublimely ridiculous.
확실히 / 다른 어떠한 종도 우리의 능력에 대한 소유권을 주장할 수 없다 / 새롭고 독창적인 무언가를 고안하는 / 황당한 것에서부터 완전히 우스꽝스러운 것에 이르기까지(극단에서 극단으로)

Other animals do build things / —birds assemble their intricate nests, / beavers construct dams, / and ants dig elaborate networks of tunnels.
다른 동물들은 무언가를 짓는다 / 새들은 그들의 복잡한 둥지를 조립한다 / 비버는 댐을 건설한다 / 그리고 개미는 정교한 터널 망을 판다

"But airplanes, strangely tilted skyscrapers and Chia Pets, / well, they're pretty impressive," / Fuentes says, / adding that / from an evolutionary standpoint, / "creativity is as much a part of our tool kit / as walking on two legs, / having a big brain and really good hands / for manipulating things."
"그러나 비행기, 묘하게 기울어진 고층빌딩과 잔디가 머리털처럼 자라나는 피규어는 / 음, 그들은 매우 인상적이다" / 푸엔테스는 말한다 / ~라고 덧붙이며 / 진화의 관점에서 보면 / "창조성은 ~만큼이나 우리의 도구의 일부분이다 / 두 다리로 걷는 것(만큼이나) / 큰 두뇌와 정말 좋은 손을 가지는 것 / 사물을 조작하기 위한"

For a physically unprepossessing primate, / without great fangs / or claws or wings / or other obvious physical advantages, / creativity has been the great equalizer / —and more— / ensuring, / for now, at least, / the survival of Homo sapiens.
신체적으로 매력적이지 않은 영장류에게 / 큰 송곳니가 없는 / 또는 발톱이나 날개 / 또는 다른 분명한 신체적 이점 / 창조성은 정말 좋은 균형 장치이다 / 그리고 게다가 / 보장해왔다 / 적어도 지금으로서는 / 호모 사피엔스의 생존을

해석 확실히, 다른 어떠한 종도, 황당한 것에서부터 완전히 우스꽝스러운 것에 이르기까지(극단에서 극단으로), 새롭고 독창적인 무언가를 고안하는 우리의 능력에 대한 소유권을 주장할 수 없다. 다른 동물들은 무언가를 짓는다. 새들은 그들의 복잡한 둥지를 조립하고, 비버는 댐을 건설하며, 개미는 정교한 터널 망을 판다. 푸엔테스는 "그러나 비행기, 묘하게 기울어진 고층빌딩과 잔디가 머리털처럼 자라나는 피규어는, 음, 매우 인상적이다"라고 말하며, 진화의 관점에서 보면 "창조성은 두 다리로 걷는 것, 큰 두뇌와 사물을 조작하기 위한 정말 좋은 손을 가지는 것만큼이나 우리의 도구의 일부분이다"라고 덧붙였다. 큰 송곳니나 발톱, 날개, 또는 다른 분명한 신체적 이점이 없는, 신체적으로 매력적이지 않은 영장류에게, 창조성은 정말 좋은 균형 장치이며, 게다가, 적어도 지금으로서는 호모 사피엔스의 생존을 보장해왔다.

① 인간의 창조성은 어디로부터 오는가?
② 영장류의 신체적 특징은 무엇인가?
③ 다른 종에 비해 호모 사피엔스가 가진 신체적 이점
④ 창조성: 생존을 위해 인류가 지닌 유일한 특성

해설 지문 처음에서 다른 어떠한 종도 인간이 새롭고 독창적인 무언가를 고안해내는 능력에 대한 소유권을 주장할 수 없다고 하고, 지문 뒷부분에서 창조성은 신체적으로 매력적이지 않은 영장류에게 좋은 균형 장치이며 적어도 지금으로서는 호모 사피엔스의 생존을 보장해왔다고 설명하고 있다. 따라서 지문의 제목을 '창조성: 생존을 위해 인류가 지닌 유일한 특성'이라고 표현한 ④번이 정답이다.

어휘 to be sure 확실히 lay claim to ~에 대한 소유권을 주장하다
sublimely 완전히 ridiculous 우스꽝스러운 assemble 조립하다

intricate 복잡한 tilt 기울다 skyscraper 고층빌딩
standpoint 관점 creativity 창조성, 창의력
tool kit 도구, 연장 키트 manipulate 조작하다
unprepossessing 매력적이지 않은 fang 송곳니 claw 발톱
equalizer 균형 장치, 동등하게 만드는 것 ensure 보장하다

05 독해 전체내용 파악 (문단 요약)   난이도 ★★☆

끊어읽기 해석

> "Most of bird identification / is based on a sort of subjective impression / —the way a bird moves / and little instantaneous appearances / at different angles / and sequences of different appearances, / and as it turns its head / and as it flies / and as it turns around, / you see sequences of different shapes and angles," / Sibley says, / "All that combines to create a unique impression of a bird / that can't really be taken apart and described in words.
> 대부분의 조류 식별은 / 일종의 주관적인 인상에 근거한다 / 새가 움직이는 방식 / 그리고 찰나의 순간적인 모습들 / 서로 다른 각도에서 본 / 그리고 연속적인 서로 다른 모습들 / 그리고 그들이 머리를 돌릴 때 / 그리고 그들이 날아다닐 때 / 그리고 그들이 방향을 바꿀 때 / 당신은 연속적인 서로 다른 모양과 각도를 보게 된다 / ~라고 Sibley는 말한다 / "그 모든 것이 결합되어 새에 대한 독특한 인상을 준다 / 사실상 분리될 수 없고 말로 설명될 수 없는
>
> When it comes down to being in the fieldland / looking at a bird, / you don't take time / to analyze it and say / it shows this, this, and this; / therefore it must be this species.
> 요컨대 들판에 있을 때 / 새를 바라보며 / 당신은 시간이 걸리지 않는다 / 그것을 분석하는 데 / 그리고 말하는 데 / 이것은 이것, 이것, 그리고 이것을 나타낸다고 / 그러므로 이것은 이러한 종(種)임에 틀림없다고
>
> It's more natural and instinctive.
> 이것이 더 자연스럽고 본능적이다.
>
> After a lot of practice, / you look at the bird, / and it triggers little switches / in your brain.
> 많은 연습 이후 / 당신이 새를 본다 / 그리고 그것은 작은 스위치를 작동시킨다 / 당신의 뇌에 있는
>
> It looks right. // You know what it is / at a glance."
> 그것이 맞다. // 당신은 그것이 무엇인지 안다 / 한눈에"

해석 "대부분의 조류 식별은 새가 움직이는 방식, 서로 다른 각도에서 본 찰나의 순간적인 모습들, 그리고 연속적인 서로 다른 모습들과 같은 일종의 주관적인 느낌에 근거한다. 그리고 그들이 머리를 돌려서 날아다니며 방향을 바꿀 때, 당신은 연속적인 서로 다른 모양과 각도를 보게 된다"라고 Sibley는 말한다. "그 모든 것이 결합되어 새에 대한, 사실상 분리될 수 없고 말로 설명될 수도 없는, 독특한 인상을 준다. 요컨대 새를 바라보며 들판에 있을 때, 당신은 그것을 분석하고 이것은 이것, 이것, 그리고 이것을 나타내므로 이것은 이러한 종(種)임에 틀림없다라고 말하는 데 시간이 걸리지 않는다. 이것이 더 자연스럽고 본능적이다. 많은 연습 이후, 당신이 새를 보면 그것은 당신의 뇌에 있는 작은 스위치를 작동시킨다. 그것이 맞다. 당신은 한눈에 그것이 무엇인지 알 것이다."

> Sibley에 따르면, 조류 식별은 (B) 개별적인 분석보다는 (A) 본능적인 느낌에 근거한다.

① 본능적인 느낌 - 개별적인 분석
② 객관적인 연구 - 주관적인 판단
③ 신체적 외모 - 행동적 특성
④ 밀접한 관찰 - 원거리 관찰

해설 지문 처음에서 걸쳐 Sibley는 조류 식별이 일종의 주관적인 느낌에 근거한다고 설명한다. 이어서 그는 새의 서로 다른 모습들은 결

합되어 사실상 분리될 수 없고 말로 설명될 수도 없는 독특한 인상을 주고, 많은 연습 이후에 우리가 새를 보면 한눈에 무엇인지 알 것이라고 설명하고 있으므로, (A)와 (B)에는 Sibley에 따르면 조류 식별은 '개별적인 분석'보다는 '본능적인 느낌'에 근거한다는 내용이 와야 적절하다.
따라서 ① (A) instinctive impression(본능적인 느낌) – (B) discrete analysis(개별적인 분석)가 정답이다.

어휘 identification 식별 subjective 주관적인
instantaneous 순간적인 come down to 요컨대 ~이 되다
instinctive 본능적인 trigger (장치를) 작동시키다
at a glance 한눈에 discrete 개별적인 objective 객관적인

06 독해 논리적 흐름 파악 (문단 순서 배열)   난이도 ★★☆

끊어읽기 해석

> As cars are becoming less dependent / on people, / the means and circumstances / in which the product is used / by consumers / are also likely to / undergo significant changes, / with higher rates of participation / in car sharing and short-term leasing programs.
> 자동차가 덜 의존함에 따라 / 사람에 / 수단과 환경 / 제품이 사용되는 / 소비자에 의해 / 또한 ~일 것 같다 / 상당한 변화를 겪을 / 참여율이 높아지면서 / 카셰어링과 단기 임대 프로그램에 대한
>
> (A) In the not-too-distant future, / a driverless car could come to you / when you need it, / and when you are done with it, / it could then drive away / without any need for a parking space.
> 머지않은 미래에 / 운전자가 없는 그것(차)이 당신에게 올 수 있다 / 당신이 그것을 필요로 할 때 / 그리고 당신이 그것을 다 쓰면 / 그 다음에 그것은 떠날 수 있다 / 주차 공간이 전혀 필요 없이
>
> Increases in car sharing and short-term leasing / are also likely to be associated with / a corresponding decrease / in the importance of exterior car design.
> 카셰어링과 단기 임대의 증가는 / 또한 ~와 관련될 것 같다 / 상응하는 감소 / 자동차 외부 디자인의 중요성의
>
> (B) As a result, / the symbolic meanings / derived from cars / and their relationship / to consumer self-identity and status / are likely to change / in turn.
> 결과적으로 / 상징적 의미는 / 자동차에서 파생된 / 그리고 그것들(상징적 의미)의 관계는 / 소비자의 자아 정체성 그리고 지위와 / 변화할 것 같다 / 차례로
>
> (C) Rather than serving as a medium / for personalization and self-identity, / car exteriors might increasingly come to represent a channel / for advertising and other promotional activities, / including brand ambassador programs, / such as those offered by Free Car Media.
> 매개체의 역할을 하기보다는 / 개인화와 자아 정체성을 위한 / 자동차 외관은 점점 더 수단에 해당하게 될지도 모른다 / 광고 및 기타 홍보 활동을 위한 / 브랜드 홍보대사 프로그램을 포함해 / Free Car Media에서 제공되는 것들과 같은

해석
> 자동차가 사람에 덜 의존함에 따라, 카셰어링과 단기 임대 프로그램에 대한 참여율이 높아지면서 제품이 소비자에 의해 사용되는 수단과 환경 또한 상당한 변화를 겪을 것 같다.

(A) 머지않은 미래에, 당신이 운전자가 없는 차가 필요할 때 그것(차)이 당신에게 올 수 있고, 당신이 그것을 다 쓰면 그 다음에 그것은 떠날 수 있으며 주차 공간을 전혀 필요로 하지 않는다. 카셰어링과 단기 임대의 증가는 또한, 상응하는 자동차 외부 디자인의 중요성의 감소와 관련될 것 같다.

(C) 자동차 외관은 개인화와 자아 정체성을 위한 매개체의 역할을 하기보다는, 점점 더 Free Car Media에서 제공되는 것들과 같은 브랜드 홍보대사 프로그램을 포함해, 광고 및 기타 홍보 활동을 위한 수단에 해당하게 될지도 모른다.

(B) 결과적으로, 자동차에서 파생된 상징적 의미와 소비자의 자아 정체성 그리고 지위와 그것들(상징적 의미)의 관계는 차례로 변화할 것 같다.

해설 주어진 문장에서 자동차가 사람에 덜 의존하여 자동차가 소비자에 의해 사용되는 수단과 환경도 상당한 변화를 겪을 것 같다고 설명한 뒤, (A)에서 미래의 상황에 대해 이야기하며 카셰어링과 단기 임대의 증가가 자동차 외부 디자인의 중요성의 감소와 관련될 것 같다고 설명하고 있다. 이어서 (C)에서 자동차 외관은 개인화와 자아 정체성을 위한 매개체 역할보다는 광고 및 기타 홍보 활동을 위한 수단에 해당하게 될지도 모른다고 하고, (B)에서 결과적으로(As a result) 자동차에서 파생된 상징적 의미와 소비자의 자아 정체성, 지위와 그것들(상징적 의미)의 관계가 변화할 것 같다고 설명하고 있다. 따라서 ① (A) – (C) – (B)가 정답이다.

어휘 **means** 수단 **circumstance** 환경 **undergo** 겪다
significant 상당한 **not-too-distant** 머지않은
be associated with ~와 관련되다 **corresponding** 상응하는
derive from ~에서 파생하다 **self-identity** 자아 정체성
medium 매개체 **personalization** 개인화
channel 수단, 방법 **promotional** 홍보의

---

07 독해 논리적 흐름 파악 (문단 순서 배열) 난이도 ★★☆

끊어읽기 해석

There is a wonderful story / of a group of American car executives / who went to Japan / to see a Japanese assembly line.
멋진 이야기가 있다 / 미국 자동차 (회사의) 경영진들의 / 일본을 방문했던 / 일본의 조립 라인을 보기 위해

At the end of the line, / the doors were put on the hinges, / the same as in America.
(조립) 라인의 끝에는 / 문들이 경첩에 달렸다 / 미국에서와 똑같이

(A) But something was missing.
그러나 무언가가 빠져 있었다.

In the United States, / a line worker would take a rubber mallet / and tap the edges of the door / to ensure that it fit perfectly.
미국에서 / 조립 공정 노동자는 고무 망치를 쥐곤 했다 / 그리고 문 가장자리를 두드리곤 했다 / 그것(문)이 반드시 완벽하게 맞게 하기 위해

In Japan, / that job didn't seem to exist.
일본에서는 / 그 작업이 존재하지 않는 것 같았다

(B) Confused, / the American auto executives asked / at what point they made sure / the door fit perfectly.
당황해하며 / 미국 자동차 (회사) 경영진들은 물었다 / 어느 시점에 그들(일본인 직원들)이 확인하는지 / 문이 완벽히 맞는 것을

Their Japanese guide looked at them / and smiled sheepishly.
그들의 일본인 가이드는 그들을 바라보았다 / 그리고 겸연쩍게 웃었다

"We make sure it fits / when we design it."
"우리는 이것이 꼭 맞도록 확인한다 / 우리가 이것을 디자인할 때"

(C) In the Japanese auto plant, / they didn't examine the problem and accumulate data / to figure out the best solution / —they engineered the outcome / they wanted / from the beginning.
일본의 자동차 공장에서 / 그들(일본인 직원들)은 문제를 조사하며 데이터를 축적하지 않았다 / 최선의 해결책을 알아내기 위해 / 그들은 결과물을

설계했다 / 그들이 원하는 / 처음부터

If they didn't achieve / their desired outcome, / they understood / it was because of a decision / they made at the start of the process.
만약 그들이 얻지 못했다면 / 그들의 바라던 결과를 / 그들은 생각했다 / 그것이 결정 때문이라고 / 그들이 그 과정의 시작에서 내린

해석 일본의 조립 라인을 보기 위해 일본을 방문했던 미국 자동차 (회사의) 경영진들의 멋진 이야기가 있다. 조립 라인의 끝에는, 미국에서와 똑같이, 문들이 경첩에 달렸다.

(A) 그러나 무언가가 빠져 있었다. 미국에서 조립 공정 노동자는 그것(문)이 반드시 완벽하게 맞게 하기 위해 고무 망치를 쥐고 문 가장자리를 두드리곤 했다. 일본에서는 그 작업이 존재하지 않는 것 같았다.

(B) 당황해하며, 미국 자동차 (회사) 경영진들은 어느 시점에 그들(일본인 직원들)이 문이 완벽히 맞는 것을 확인하는지 물었다. 그들의 일본인 가이드는 그들을 바라보았고 겸연쩍게 웃었다. "우리는 이것(문)을 디자인할 때 이것이 꼭 맞도록 확인합니다."

(C) 일본의 자동차 공장에서, 그들(일본인 직원들)은 최선의 해결책을 알아내기 위해 문제를 조사하며 데이터를 축적하지 않았다. 그들은 처음부터 그들이 원하는 결과물을 설계했다. 만약 그들이 바라던 결과를 얻지 못했다면, 그들은 그것이 그 과정의 시작에서 내린 결정 때문이라고 생각했다.

해설 주어진 문장에서 일본의 조립 라인을 보기 위해 미국 자동차 (회사의) 경영진들이 일본을 방문하였는데, 조립 라인의 끝에는 미국에서 그러한 것처럼 문들이 경첩에 달렸다고 하고, (A)에서 그러나(But) 미국과 달리 문이 완벽하게 맞도록 하기 위한, 문 가장자리를 두드리는 작업이 존재하지 않는 것 같았다고 언급했다. 이어서 (B)에서, 당황한 경영진들이 어느 시점에 문이 완벽히 맞는 것을 확인하는지 물었고, 일본인 가이드는 그들(일본인 직원들)이 디자인할 때 그것(문이 완벽히 맞는 것)을 확인한다고 대답했으며 (C)에서 일본의 자동차 공장은 최선의 해결책을 알아내기 위해 문제를 조사하며 데이터를 축적하는 것이 아니라, 처음부터 그들이 원하는 결과를 설계한다고 설명하고 있다. 따라서 ① (A) – (B) – (C)가 정답이다.

어휘 **executive** 경영진, 임원 **assembly** 조립 **hinge** 경첩
rubber mallet 고무 망치 **sheepishly** 겸연쩍게, 소심하게
engineer 설계하다

---

08 독해 추론 (빈칸 완성 - 연결어) 난이도 ★★☆

끊어읽기 해석

There has been much research / on nonverbal cues to deception / dating back to / the work of Ekman and his idea of leakage.
많은 연구가 있었다 / 속임수의 비언어적인 단서와 관련된 / 거슬러 올라가는 / 에크만의 연구와 누설에 관한 그의 생각까지

It is well documented / that people use others' nonverbal behaviors / as a way to detect lies.
문서로 잘 증명되어 있다 / 사람들이 다른 이들의 비언어적인 행동을 활용한다는 것은 / 거짓말을 알아내기 위한 방법으로

My research and that of many others / has strongly supported / people's reliance / on observations of others' nonverbal behaviors / when assessing honesty.
나의 연구와 다른 많은 사람들의 그것(연구)은 / 강력하게 뒷받침해왔다 / 사람들이 의존한다는 것을 / 다른 이들의 비언어적인 행동을 관찰한 것에 / 정직함을 판단할 때

(A) Hptsd Howe<u>ver</u>, / social scientific research / on the link / between various nonverbal behaviors and the act of lying / suggests that / the link is typically not very strong or consistent.
(A) 하지만 / 사회 과학적 연구는 / 관계에 대한 / 다양한 비언어적 행동과 거짓말을 하는 행위 사이의 / ~라는 것을 시사한다 / 그 관계는 일반적으로 매우 견고하거나 일관되지 않다

In my research, / I have observed / that the nonverbal signals / that seem to give one liar away / are different than / those given by a second liar.
나의 연구에서, / 나는 발견했다 / 비언어적 신호는 / 한 거짓말쟁이의 비밀을 누설하는 것처럼 보이는 / ~와 다르다는 것을 / 두 번째 거짓말쟁이가 전하는 것들(신호)

(B) What's more, / the scientific evidence / linking nonverbal behaviors and deception / has grown weaker / over time.
(B) 더군다나 / 과학적 증거는 / 비언어적 행동과 속임수를 관련 짓는 / 더욱 설득력이 없어졌다 / 시간이 지나면서

People infer honesty / based on how others nonverbally present themselves, / but that has very limited utility and validity.
사람들은 정직함을 추측한다 / 다른 사람들이 그들 자신을 비언어적으로 보여주는 방식에 근거하여 / 하지만 그것은 매우 제한된 유용성과 타당성이 있다.

해석 에크만의 연구와 누설에 관한 그의 생각까지 거슬러 올라가는, 속임수의 비언어적인 단서와 관련된 많은 연구가 있었다. 사람들이 거짓말을 알아내기 위한 방법으로 다른 이들의 비언어적인 행동을 활용한다는 것은 문서로 잘 증명되어 있다. 나의 연구와 다른 많은 사람들의 그것(연구)은 사람들이 정직함을 판단할 때 다른 이들의 비언어적인 행동을 관찰한 것에 의존한다는 것을 강력하게 뒷받침해왔다. (A) 하지만, 다양한 비언어적 행동과 거짓말을 하는 행위 사이의 관계에 대한 사회 과학적 연구는 그 관계가 일반적으로 매우 견고하거나 일관되지 않다는 것을 시사한다. 나의 연구에서, 나는 한 거짓말쟁이의 비밀을 누설하는 것처럼 보이는 비언어적 신호는 두 번째 거짓말쟁이가 전하는 것들(신호)과 다르다는 것을 발견했다. (B) 더군다나, 비언어적 행동과 속임수를 관련 짓는 과학적 증거는 시간이 지나면서 더욱 설득력이 없어졌다. 사람들은 다른 사람들이 그들 자신을 비언어적으로 보여주는 방식에 근거하여 정직함을 추측하지만, 그것은 매우 제한된 유용성과 타당성이 있다.

① 하지만 - 더군다나
② 그 결과 - 대조적으로
③ 하지만 - 그럼에도 불구하고
④ 그 결과 - 예를 들어

해설 (A) 빈칸 앞부분은 거짓말을 알아내기 위한 방법으로 비언어적인 행동을 활용한다는 내용이고, 빈칸이 있는 문장은 비언어적 행동과 거짓말을 하는 행위 사이의 관계가 매우 견고하거나 일관되지 않다는 대조적인 내용이다. 따라서 대조를 나타내는 연결어인 However(하지만)가 나와야 적절하다. (B) 빈칸 앞 문장은 거짓말쟁이들의 비언어적 신호들이 서로 다르다는 것을 발견했다는 내용이고, (B) 빈칸이 있는 문장은 비언어적 행동과 속임수를 관련 짓는 과학적 증거가 더욱 설득력이 없어졌다는 첨가하는 내용이다. 따라서 첨가를 나타내는 연결어인 What's more(더군다나)가 나와야 적절하다.
따라서 ① (A) However(하지만) – (B) What's more(더군다나)가 정답이다.

어휘 nonverbal 비언어적인, 말을 사용하지 않는 cue 단서, 신호
deception 속임수, 기만 leakage 누설, 누출
document 문서로 증명하다, 기록하다
detect 알아내다, 감지하다 reliance 의존, 신용

observation 관찰, 주목 assess 판단하다, 평가하다
honesty 정직함, 솔직함 consistent 일관된, 지속적인
give away (비밀 등을) 누설하다 utility 유용성, 효용성
validity 타당성, 확실(성)

09 문법 분사 · 난이도 ★☆☆

해석 신생 기업이 법인이 되자마자, 그것은 은행 계좌가 필요할 것이며, 임금대장 계좌의 필요성이 곧 뒤따를 것이다. 은행은 급여를 지불하고 관련 세금 회계 장부를 기록하는 서비스에서 매우 경쟁적이며, 심지어 가장 규모가 작은 기업들을 상대로 (서비스를) 시작한다. 이러한 것들은 한 기업이 그들이 받을 수 있는 최상의 서비스와 대부분 '무료인' 회계 관련 지원을 원하는 분야이다. 변화하는 지불 급여세 법률은, 특히 50개의 주 중 여러 곳에서 영업 인력이 운영될 예정일 경우, 뒤떨어지지 않도록 따라가야 하는 골칫거리이다. 그리고 요구되는 보고서들은 회사의 사무직의 부담이 된다. 그러한 서비스들은 대개 은행 직원에 의해 가장 잘 제공된다. 이 분야에 있는 은행들의 참고 자료는 ADP와 같은 급여 지불 대체 서비스와 비교되어야 하지만, 결정을 내릴 때는 장래의 그리고 장기적인 관계를 명심해야 한다.

*13번째 줄의 add는 오타이므로, 해석하지 않았습니다.

해설 ③ 현재분사 vs. 과거분사 수식받는 명사(reports)와 분사가 '보고서들이 요구되다(요구되는 보고서들)'라는 의미의 수동 관계이므로 현재분사 requiring을 과거분사 required로 고쳐야 한다.

오답 분석 ① 분사구문의 형태 주절의 주어(The banks)와 분사구문이 '은행이 시작하다'라는 의미의 능동 관계이므로 현재분사 starting이 올바르게 쓰였다.
② 관계부사 선행사 areas가 장소를 나타내고 관계사 뒤에 완전한 절(a business ~ get)이 왔으므로 장소를 나타내는 선행사와 함께 쓰이는 관계부사 where가 올바르게 쓰였다. 참고로, it can get은 목적격 관계대명사 which/that이 생략된 관계절이며 선행사 service와 help를 수식한다.
④ 능동태·수동태 구별 주어(a decision)와 동사가 '결정이 내려지다(결정을 내리다)'라는 의미의 수동 관계이므로 수동태가 와야 하고, 수동태의 진행형은 'be being + p.p.'의 형태를 취하므로 과거분사 made 앞에 being이 올바르게 쓰였다.

어휘 start-up 신생 기업 incorporate 법인으로 만들다, 설립하다
payroll 임금대장, 급여 대상자 명단
competitive 경쟁적인, 경쟁으로 결정되는
legislation 법률, 법률 제정
keep up with 뒤떨어지지 않도록 따라가다
administrative 사무의, 행정의 reference 참고 자료
alternative 대체의, 대체 가능한
keep in mind 명심하다, 잊지 않고 있다

👍 이것도 알면 **합격!**

관계부사(when, where, why, how)는 '전치사 + 관계대명사'의 형태로 바꾸어 쓸 수 있고, 관계부사 뒤에는 완전한 절이 온다는 것을 기억하자.
ⓔ️ⓧ The Middle East is the region <u>where</u>(= in which) most of the world's oil is produced.
중동은 전 세계 대부분의 석유가 생산되는 지역이다.

10 문법 분사   난이도 ★☆☆

해석 많은 사람들은 그것(동물 보호소를 방문하는 것)이 너무 슬프거나 우울하게 하기 때문에 동물 보호소를 방문하려고 하지 않는다. 너무나 많은 운이 좋은 동물들이 교통사고, 그리고 다른 동물이나 인간의 공격을 받을 위험이 있으며 악천후의 영향을 받기 쉬운 길거리에서의 위험한 생활에서 구조되었기 때문에 그들은 그렇게 낙담하지 않아야 한다. 마찬가지로 많은 실종된 반려동물들도 그들이 동물 보호소로 이동되었다는 이유만으로 마음이 산란하면 주인들에게 발견되고 되찾아진다. 가장 중요한 것은, 입양할 수 있는 반려동물들은 집을 찾으며, 아프고 위험에 처한 동물들은 인도적으로 고통을 덜게 된다.

해설 ① 현재분사 vs. 과거분사 감정을 나타내는 동사(depress)의 경우 주어가 감정의 원인이면 현재분사를, 감정을 느끼는 주체이면 과거분사를 써야 하는데, 문맥상 주어(it)가 우울한 감정의 원인이므로 과거분사 depressed를 현재분사 depressing으로 고쳐야 한다.

오답분석 ② 관계부사 선행사 the streets가 장소를 나타내고 관계사 뒤에 완전한 절(they're ~ the elements)이 왔으므로 장소를 나타내는 관계부사 where이 올바르게 쓰였다.
③ 능동태·수동태 구별 동사 are found 뒤에 목적어가 없고 주어(Many lost pets)와 동사가 '많은 실종된 반려동물들이 발견되다'라는 의미의 수동 관계이므로 수동태 are found가 올바르게 쓰였다.
④ 형용사 자리 문맥상 '입양할 수 있는 반려동물들'이라는 의미가 되어야 자연스러우므로 명사를 수식할 수 있는 형용사 adoptable이 명사(pets) 앞에 올바르게 쓰였다.

어휘 refuse ~하려고 하지 않다 shelter 보호소, 피난처 at risk 위험이 있는 subject to ~의 영향을 받기 쉬운 elements 악천후 likewise 마찬가지로 reclaim 되찾다, 매립하다 distraught (근심 따위로) 마음이 산란해진 relieve ~을 덜게 하다, 편안하게 하다 suffering 고통, 괴로움

👍 이것도 알면 합격!

형용사는 명사를 주로 앞에서 수식하지만, -able, -ible로 끝나는 형용사는 명사를 뒤에서 수식할 수 있으며, -where, -thing, -one, -body로 끝나는 명사는 항상 뒤에서 수식한다는 것을 알아두자.

11 독해 논리적 흐름 파악 (문맥상 적절한 어휘)   난이도 ★★☆

끊어읽기 해석

EQ testing, / when performed with reliable testing methods, / can provide you with very useful information / about yourself.
감성지수 테스트는 / 신뢰할 수 있는 검사 방법으로 실시될 때 / 매우 유용한 정보를 당신에게 제공할 수 있다 / 당신 스스로에 대한

I've found, / having tested thousands of people, / that many are a bit surprised / by their results.
나는 발견해왔다 / 수천 명의 사람들을 검사해오면서 / 많은 사람들이 약간 놀란다는 것을 / 그들의 결과에

For example, / one person / who believed / she was very socially responsible / and often concerned about others / came out with an (A) average score / in that area.
예를 들어 / 한 사람은 / ~라고 여긴 / 그녀 자신이 사회적으로 매우 책임감이 있다고 / 그리고 종종 다른 사람들을 걱정한다고 / (A) 보통 수준의 점수를 보여주었다 / 그 부분에서

She was quite disappointed / in her score.
그녀는 상당히 실망했다 / 그녀의 점수에

It turned out that / she had very high standards / for social responsibility / and therefore was extremely (B) hard on herself / when she performed her assessment.
~인 것으로 밝혀졌다 / 그녀는 매우 높은 기준을 가졌다 / 사회적 책임에 대한 / 그래서 그녀 스스로에게 매우 (B) 엄격했다 / 그녀가 그녀의 평가를 실시했을 때

In reality, / she was (C) more socially responsible / than most people, / but she believed / that she could be much better / than she was.
실제로 / 그녀는 사회적으로 책임감이 (C) 더 많이 있었다 / 대다수의 사람들보다 / 하지만 그녀는 생각했다 / 그녀는 훨씬 더 잘할 수 있었다고 / 그녀가 그랬던 것보다

해석 감성지수 테스트는 신뢰할 수 있는 검사 방법으로 실시될 때 당신 스스로에 대한 매우 유용한 정보를 당신에게 제공할 수 있다. 나는 수천 명의 사람들을 검사해오면서, 많은 사람들이 그들의 결과에 약간 놀란다는 것을 발견해왔다. 예를 들어, 그녀 자신이 사회적으로 매우 책임감이 있고 종종 다른 사람들을 걱정한다고 여긴 한 사람은 그 부분에서 (A) 보통 수준의 점수를 보여주었다. 그녀는 그녀의 점수에 상당히 실망했다. 그녀는 사회적 책임에 대한 매우 높은 기준을 가지고 있어서 그녀가 그녀의 평가를 실시했을 때 그녀 스스로에게 매우 (B) 엄격했던 것으로 밝혀졌다. 실제로, 그녀는 대다수의 사람들보다 사회적으로 책임감이 (C) 더 많이 있었지만, 그녀는 그녀가 그랬던 것보다 훨씬 더 잘할 수 있었다고 생각했다.

	(A)	(B)	(C)
①	보통 수준의	관대한	더 적게
②	보통 수준의	엄격한	더 많이
③	보기 드문	엄격한	더 적게
④	보기 드문	관대한	더 많이

해설 (A) 빈칸이 있는 문장에서 그녀 자신이 사회적으로 매우 책임감이 있고 다른 사람들을 걱정한다고 여긴다는 내용이 있고, 빈칸 뒤 문장에서 그녀는 자신의 감성지수 테스트 점수에 실망했다고 했으므로, 빈칸에는 그 부분에서 '보통 수준의'(average) 점수를 보여주었다는 내용이 들어가야 적절하다. (B) 빈칸이 있는 문장에서 그녀는 사회적 책임에 대한 매우 높은 기준을 가졌다고 했으므로, 빈칸에는 스스로에게 매우 '엄격했다'(hard)는 내용이 들어가야 적절하다. (C) 빈칸이 있는 문장에서 하지만 그녀는 자신이 훨씬 더 잘할 수 있었다고 생각했다고 했으므로, 빈칸에는 실제로 책임감이 '더 많이'(more) 있었다는 내용이 들어가야 적절하다.
따라서 ② (A) average(보통 수준의) – (B) hard(엄격한) – (C) more(더 많이)가 정답이다.

어휘 EQ(Emotional Quotient) 감성지수 reliable 신뢰할 수 있는 responsible 책임이 있는 come out with ~을 보여주다 average 보통 수준의; 평균 extraordinary 보기 드문, 비범한 disappointed 실망한 responsibility 책임, 의무 easy[hard] on ~에 관대한[엄격한] assessment 평가

12 독해 추론 (빈칸 완성 - 구)   난이도 ★★☆

끊어읽기 해석

A person may try to effect a certain belief / by using evidence / to his advantage.
사람은 특정한 믿음을 초래하려고 노력할지도 모른다 / 증거를 사용함으로써 / 그에게 유리하게

A mother asks her son, / "How are you doing in English this term?"
한 엄마가 그녀의 아들에게 묻는다 / "너 이번 학기 영어 어떻게 하고 있어?"

He responds cheerfully, / "Oh, I just got a ninety-five on a quiz."
그는 명랑하게 대답한다 / "아, 저는 한 퀴즈에서 간신히 95점 받았어요."

The statement conceals the fact / that he has failed every other quiz / and that his actual average is 55.
이 한 마디의 말은 사실을 숨긴다 / 그가 다른 모든 퀴즈를 불합격했다는 / 그리고 그의 실제 평균 성적은 55점이라는

Yet, / if she pursues the matter no further, / the mother may be delighted / that her son is doing so well.
하지만 / 만약 그녀가 그 일에 대해 더 이상 계속해서 말하지 않으면 / 그 엄마는 기뻐할지도 모른다 / 그녀의 아들이 그렇게 잘하고 있다는 것에 대해

Linda asks Susan, / "Have you read much Dickens?"
Linda가 Susan에게 묻는다 / "너 디킨스 책 많이 읽었어?"

Susan responds, / "Oh, *Pickwick Papers* is one of my favorite novels."
Susan은 대답한다 / "아, 『픽윅 보고서』가 제가 제일 좋아하는 소설 중 하나예요."

The statement may disguise the fact / that *Pickwick Papers* is the only novel by Dickens / that she has read, / and it may give Linda the impression / that Susan is a great Dickens enthusiast.
이 한 마디의 말은 사실을 숨길 수도 있다 / 『픽윅 보고서』가 디킨스의 유일한 소설이라는 / 그녀가 읽은 / 그리고 그것은 Linda에게 인상을 줄 수도 있다 / Susan이 엄청나게 열광적인 디킨스의 팬이라는

해석 사람은 그에게 유리하게 증거를 사용함으로써 특정한 믿음을 초래하려고 노력할지도 모른다. 한 엄마가 그녀의 아들에게 "너 이번 학기 영어 어떻게 하고 있어?"라고 묻는다. 그는 명랑하게 "아, 저는 한 퀴즈에서 간신히 95점 받았어요."라고 대답한다. 이 한 마디의 말은 그가 다른 모든 퀴즈를 불합격했고 그의 실제 평균 성적은 55점이라는 사실을 숨긴다. 하지만, 만약 그녀가 그 일에 대해 더 이상 계속해서 말하지 않으면, 그 엄마는 그녀의 아들이 그렇게 잘하고 있다는 것에 대해 기뻐할지도 모른다. Linda가 Susan에게 "너 디킨스 책 많이 읽었어?"라고 묻는다. Susan은 "아, 『픽윅 보고서』가 제가 제일 좋아하는 소설 중 하나예요."라고 대답한다. 이 한 마디의 말은 『픽윅 보고서』가 그녀가 읽은 디킨스의 유일한 소설이라는 사실을 숨길 수도 있고, 그것은 Linda에게 Susan이 엄청나게 열광적인 디킨스의 팬이라는 인상을 줄 수도 있다.

① 여분의 돈을 벌다
② 특정한 믿음을 초래하다
③ 기억력 문제를 숨기다
④ 다른 사람들이 죄책감이 들도록 만들다

해설 빈칸이 있는 문장을 통해 빈칸에 사람은 자신에게 유리하게 증거를 사용함으로써 어떻게 하려고 노력할지도 모르는지에 대한 내용이 나와야 적절하다는 것을 알 수 있다. 빈칸 뒷부분의 예시에서 아들과 Susan이 다른 사실은 숨기고 자신들에게 유리한 내용만 말함으로써 엄마는 자신의 아들이 영어를 잘하고 있다고 생각하며 기뻐할 수도 있고, Linda에게 Susan이 디킨스의 열광적인 팬이라는 인상을 줄 수도 있다는 내용이 있으므로, 사람은 유리하게 증거를 사용함으로써 '특정한 믿음을 초래'하려고 노력할지도 모른다고 한 ②번이 정답이다.

어휘 evidence 증거 to one's advantage ~에게 유리하게
statement 한 마디 말, 진술 conceal 숨기다, 감추다
pursue 계속해서 말하다 delighted 기뻐하는
disguise 숨기다, 위장하다 impression 인상
enthusiast 열광적인 팬 earn 벌다, 얻다
effect 초래하다, ~을 만들다 hide 숨기다, 감추다
guilty 죄책감이 드는

---

13 독해 전체내용 파악 (문단 요약)

끊어읽기 해석

Whether we are complimented / for our appearance, our garden, a dinner we prepared, or an assignment at the office, / it is always satisfying / to receive recognition / for a job well done.
우리가 칭찬을 받든지 간에 / 우리의 외모, 우리의 정원, 우리가 준비한 저녁 식사, 또는 회사에서의 업무로 / 항상 만족스럽다 / 인정을 받는 것은 / 잘 처리된 일로

Certainly, / reinforcement theory sees / occasional praise as an aid / to learning a new skill.
분명히 / 강화이론은 여긴다 / 가끔의 칭찬을 도움이 되는 것으로 / 새로운 기술 학습으로 향하는 데

However, / some evidence cautions / against making sweeping generalizations / regarding the use of praise / in improving performance.
하지만 / 몇몇 증거는 경고한다 / 지나치게 포괄적인 일반화를 하는 것을 / 칭찬을 하는 것과 관련하여 / 성과를 향상시킴에 있어

It seems that / while praise improves performance / on certain tasks, / on others / it can instead prove harmful.
~인 것 같다 / 칭찬은 성과를 향상시키는 반면 / 특정 업무에 대한 / 다른 업무에 있어서 / 그것은 오히려 해가 되는 것으로 밝혀질 수도 있다

Imagine the situation / in which the enthusiastic support of hometown fans / expecting victory / brings about the downfall / of their team.
상황을 상상해보라 / 출신 도시 팬들의 열렬한 지지가 / 승리를 예상하는 / 급격한 전락을 초래하는 / 그들의 팀의

In this situation, / it seems that / praise creates pressure / on athletes, / disrupting their performance.
이러한 상황에서 / ~인 것 같다 / 칭찬은 부담을 준다 / 운동선수들에게 / 그 결과 그들의 성과에 지장을 준다

해석 우리가 우리의 외모, 우리의 정원, 우리가 준비한 저녁 식사, 또는 회사에서의 업무로 칭찬을 받든지 간에, 잘 처리된 일로 인정을 받는 것은 항상 만족스럽다. 분명히, 강화이론은 가끔의 칭찬을 새로운 기술 학습으로 향하는 데 도움이 되는 것으로 여긴다. 하지만, 몇몇 증거는 성과를 향상시킴에 있어 칭찬을 하는 것과 관련하여 지나치게 포괄적인 일반화를 하는 것을 경고한다. 칭찬은 특정 업무에 대한 성과를 향상시키는 반면, 다른 업무에 있어서 그것은 오히려 해가 되는 것으로 밝혀질 수도 있는 것 같다. 승리를 예상하는 출신 도시 팬들의 열렬한 지지가 그들의 팀의 급격한 전락을 초래하는 상황을 상상해보라. 이러한 상황에서, 칭찬은 운동선수들에게 부담을 주며, 그 결과 그들의 성과에 지장을 주는 것 같다.

> (A) 칭찬이 성과에 도움이 되는지 지장을 주는지는 (B) 업무의 종류에 달렸다.

	(A)	(B)
①	칭찬	업무의 종류
②	경쟁	팀워크의 질
③	칭찬	팀워크의 질
④	경쟁	업무의 종류

해설 지문 중간에서 몇몇 증거는 칭찬이 성과를 향상시킴에 있어 도움이 된다고 지나치게 일반화하는 것을 경고한다고 하고, 특정 업무에서는 칭찬이 성과를 향상시키지만 다른 업무에서는 오히려 해가 되는 것 같다고 설명하고 있으므로, (A)와 (B)에는 '칭찬'이 성과에 도움이 되는지 지장을 주는지는 '업무의 종류'에 달렸다는 내용이 와야 적절하다.
따라서 ① (A) praise(칭찬) – (B) task types(업무의 종류)가 정답이다.

compliment 칭찬하다 appearance 외모 recognition 인정
reinforcement 강화 occasional 가끔의, 때때로의
praise 칭찬; 칭찬하다 aid 도움이 되는 것; 돕다 caution 경고하다
sweeping (지나치게) 포괄적인, 광범위한 generalization 일반화
prove 밝혀지다 enthusiastic 열렬한 bring about 초래하다
downfall (급격한) 전락, 실패 disrupt 지장을 주다, 방해하다

14 문법 병치·도치·강조 구문 　난이도 ★☆☆

해석 우리가 매체를 이용하는 것을 익명의 사회적 관계라는 맥락에서
고려할 때, 우리는 바와 같은 공공 장소에서 텔레비전을 보는 것,
콘서트나 댄스 클럽에 가는 것, 또는 버스나 지하철에서 신문을 읽
는 것과 같이 낯선 사람의 존재를 수반하는 그러한 모든 경우를 의
미한다. 일반적으로, 우리가 우리 주변의 사람들 그리고 대중매체
상품과 상호작용하는 방법을 좌우하는 사회적 규칙들이 있다. 예
를 들어, 우리의 문화에서는 다른 사람의 어깨 너머로 읽거나 공공
장소에서 일어나서 텔레비전 채널을 바꾸는 것은 무례하거나, 최
소한 공격적이라고 여겨진다. 음악을 좋아하는 사람은 누구든지
특정한 종류의 콘서트에서 무엇이 적절한 것인지를 안다. 타인의
존재는, 비록 그 관계가 전적으로 개인적인 정을 나누지 않는다는
사실에도 불구하고, 종종 환경을 규정하는 데 결정적이며, 따라서
매체를 이용하는 행위에도 결정적이다.

해설 ③ 병치 구문 접속사(or)로 연결된 병치 구문에서는 같은 구조끼
리 연결되어야 하는데, or 뒤에 to 부정사구(to get up ~ public
setting)가 왔으므로 or 앞에도 to 부정사구가 와야 한다. 따라서
동사원형 read를 to 부정사 to read로 고쳐야 한다. 참고로, 해당
문장은 가주어 it이 길이가 긴 진짜 주어 to 부정사구(to read ~
public setting) 대신 주어 자리에 쓰인 형태이다.

오답
분석
① 병치 구문 접속사(or)로 연결된 병치 구문에서는 같은 구조끼
리 연결되어야 하는데, or 앞뒤에 동명사구(viewing ~ bars,
reading ~ subway)가 콤마(,)로 연결되어 나열되고 있으므
로 or 앞에도 동명사 going이 올바르게 쓰였다.
② 주격 관계절의 수 일치 주격 관계절(that ~ product) 내의 동
사는 선행사(social rules)에 수 일치시켜야 하는데, 선행사가
복수 명사이므로 복수 동사 govern이 올바르게 쓰였다.
④ 전치사 4: 양보 명사(the fact) 앞에 올 수 있는 것은 전치사
이고, 문맥상 '사실에도 불구하고'라는 의미가 되어야 자연스
러우므로 양보를 나타내는 전치사 despite(~에도 불구하고)가
올바르게 쓰였다.

어휘 anonymous 익명의, 특성이 없는 occasion 경우, 때
involve 수반하다, 포함하다 presence 존재, 있음
govern 좌우하다, 결정하다 rude 무례한 aggressive 공격적인
particular 특정한 crucial 결정적인, 중대한
impersonal 개인적인 정을 나누지 않는, 비인격적인

👍 이것도 알면 합격!

가주어 it은 to 부정사구, that절 같은 긴 주어를 대신해서 주어 자리
에 쓰이고 진짜 주어는 문장 맨 뒤로 보낸다는 것을 기억하자.

15 문법 수 일치 　난이도 ★★☆

해석 우리 대부분은 기억 상실증, 즉 갑작스러운 기억 상실의 결과 사람
의 이름과 신분을 기억해내지 못하게 된다고 믿는다. 이러한 믿음
은 기억 상실증이 보통 영화, 텔레비전, 그리고 문학 작품에서 묘
사되는 방식을 반영할지도 모른다. 예를 들어, 우리가 영화 『본 아
이덴티티』에서 맷 데이먼의 캐릭터를 본다면, 그는 그가 누구인

지, 왜 그가 가진 기술을 갖고 있는지, 또는 그가 어디 출신인지에
대한 기억이 없다는 것을 우리는 알게 된다. 그는 영화의 대부분을
이러한 질문에 대답하는 데 애쓰며 보낸다. 하지만, 당신의 이름과
신분을 기억하지 못하는 것은 실제로는 몹시 드물다. 대개 기억 상
실증은 피해자들이 새로운 기억을 형성할 수 없게 만드는 뇌 손상
이 원인이지만, 대부분의 과거 기억은 온전한 상태이다. 우리가 가
장 좋아하는 『메멘토』 같은 일부 영화에서는 이러한 더욱 일반적
인 증상을 그대로 묘사한다.

해설 ③ 주어와 동사의 수 일치 주어 자리에 단수 취급하는 불가산 명
사 the inability가 왔으므로 복수 동사 are를 단수 동사 is로 고쳐
야 한다. 참고로, 주어와 동사 사이의 수식어 거품(to remember
~ identity)은 동사의 수 결정에 영향을 주지 않는다.

오답
분석
① 능동태·수동태 구별 동사 is portrayed 뒤에 목적어가 없고,
주어(amnesia)와 동사가 '기억 상실증이 묘사되다'라는 의미
의 수동 관계이므로 be동사(is) 뒤에서 수동태를 완성하는 과
거분사 portrayed가 올바르게 쓰였다.
② 동명사 관련 표현 '~하는 데 애쓰며 보내다'는 동명사구 관용
표현 'spend + 시간/돈 + -ing'(~하는 데 시간/돈을 쓰다)를
사용하여 나타낼 수 있으므로 동명사 trying이 올바르게 쓰였
다.
④ 분사구문의 관용 표현 동시에 일어나는 상황은 'with + 명사
(most memories of the past) + 분사(being intact)'의 형
태로 나타낼 수 있는데, 'being + 보어'로 이루어진 분사구문
에서 being은 생략할 수 있으므로 intact가 올바르게 쓰였다.

어휘 amnesia 기억 상실(증) recall 기억해내다, 상기하다
reflect 반영하다, 반사하다 portray 묘사하다, 보여주다
exceedingly 몹시 rare 드문, 보기 힘든
intact 온전한, 손상되지 않은 accurately 그대로

👍 이것도 알면 합격!

동명사구 관용 표현을 알아두자.

- have difficulty[trouble, a problem] -ing ~하는 데 어려움을 겪다
- cannot help -ing ~하지 않을 수 없다
  (= have no choice but + to 부정사)
- It's no use[good] -ing ~해도 소용 없다
- be busy -ing ~하느라 바쁘다　　· on[upon] -ing ~하자마자
- end up -ing 결국 ~하다　　· keep (on) -ing 계속 ~하다
- go -ing ~하러 가다　　· be worth -ing ~할 가치가 있다

16 독해 추론 (빈칸 완성 - 구) 　난이도 ★★☆

끊어읽기 해석

Much is now known / about natural hazards and the negative
impacts / they have / on people and their property.
오늘날 많이 알려져 있다 / 자연의 위험 요소와 그 부정적인 영향은 / 그것
들이 미치는 / 사람들과 그들의 재산에

It would seem obvious / that any logical person would
avoid / such potential impacts / or at least modify their
behavior or their property / to minimize such impacts.
분명해 보이는 듯하다 / 논리적인 사람이라면 누구든 피할 것이라는 것
이 / 그러한 일어날 가능성이 있는 영향을 / 또는 최소한 그들의 행동이나
소유물을 조정할 것이다 / 그러한 영향을 최소화하기 위해

However, / humans are not always rational.
하지만 / 인간은 언제나 합리적이지는 않다

Until someone has a personal experience / or knows
someone / who has such an experience, / most people

subconsciously believe / "It won't happen here" / or "It won't happen to me."
어떤 사람이 개인적인 경험을 할 때까지 / 또는 누군가를 알게 될 때까지 / 그러한 경험을 한 / 대부분의 사람들은 잠재의식적으로 믿는다 / "그것은 여기에서 일어나지 않을 거야"라고 / 또는 "그것은 나에게 일어나지 않을 거야."라고

Even knowledgeable scientists / who are aware of / the hazards, the odds of their occurrence, and the costs of an event / do not always act appropriately.
심지어 총명한 과학자들도 / 인지하고 있는 / 위험 요소, 사건이 일어날 가능성 그리고 어떠한 사건의 손실을 / 항상 적절하게 행동하는 것은 아니다

해석　오늘날 자연의 위험 요소와 그것들이 사람들과 그들의 재산에 미치는 부정적인 영향은 많이 알려져 있다. 논리적인 사람이라면 누구든 그러한 일어날 가능성이 있는 영향을 피하거나 그러한 영향을 최소화하기 위해 최소한 그들의 행동이나 소유물을 조정할 것이라는 것이 분명해 보이는 듯하다. 하지만, 인간은 언제나 합리적이지는 않다. 어떤 사람이 개인적인 경험을 하거나 그러한 경험을 한 누군가를 알게 될 때까지, 대부분의 사람들은 잠재의식적으로 "그것은 여기에서 일어나지 않을 거야"라거나 "그것은 나에게 일어나지 않을 거야"라고 믿는다. 심지어 위험 요소, 사건이 일어날 가능성 그리고 어떠한 사건의 손실을 인지하고 있는 총명한 과학자들도 항상 적절하게 행동하는 것은 아니다.

① 침묵을 지키지 않는다
② 항상 적절하게 행동하는 것은 아니다
③ 유전적인 요소를 가장 높은 목표로 둔다
④ 자연의 위험 요소를 규정하는 데 어려움을 겪는다

해설　빈칸이 있는 문장을 통해 빈칸에 심지어 총명한 과학자들도 어떻게 하는지에 대한 내용이 나와야 적절하다는 것을 알 수 있다. 지문 앞부분에서 논리적인 사람이라면 부정적인 영향을 피하려고 할 것이 분명한 듯하다고 하지만, 인간이 언제나 합리적이지는 않다고 했으므로, 심지어 위험 요소, 사건이 일어날 가능성 그리고 어떠한 사건의 손실을 인지하고 있는 총명한 과학자들도 '항상 적절하게 행동하는 것은 아니다'라고 한 ②번이 정답이다.

어휘　hazard 위험 (요소)　impact 영향　property 재산, 소유물
obvious 분명한, 명백한　potential 일어날 가능성이 있는, 잠재적인
modify 조정하다, 수정하다　minimize 최소화하다, 축소하다
rational 합리적인, 이성적인　subconsciously 잠재의식적으로
knowledgeable 총명한, 아는 것이 많은
odds (어떤 일이 있을) 가능성　occurrence 사건, 발생
silent 침묵을 지키는, 조용한　end 목표

17　**독해**　**전체내용 파악 (주제 파악)**　난이도 ★☆☆

끊어읽기 해석

The rise of cities and kingdoms and the improvement in transport infrastructure / brought about new opportunities / for specialization.
도시와 왕국의 번영과 운송 기반시설의 발전은 / 새로운 기회들이 생기게 했다 / 전문화를 위한

Densely populated cities / provided full-time employment / not just for professional shoemakers and doctors, / but also for carpenters, priests, soldiers and lawyers.
인구가 밀집된 도시들은 / 정규직을 제공했다 / 전문 구두장이, 의사뿐만 아니라 / 목수, 사제, 군인 그리고 변호사에게도

Villages / that gained a reputation / for producing really good wine, olive oil or ceramics / discovered / that it was worth their while / to specialize nearly exclusively in that product and trade it / with other settlements / for all the other goods /

---

they needed.
마을들은 / 명성을 얻은 / 매우 좋은 와인, 올리브 오일, 또는 도자기를 생산하는 것으로 / 깨달았다 / ~할 가치가 있다는 것을 / 거의 독점적으로 그 제품을 전문적으로 다루고 그것을 거래할 / 다른 촌락들과 / 모든 다른 제품들을 위해서 / 그들이 필요했던

This made a lot of sense.
이것은 정말 그럴 듯하다.

Climates and soils differ, / so why drink mediocre wine / from your backyard / if you can buy a smoother variety / from a place / whose soil and climate is much better suited / to grape vines?
기후와 토양이 서로 다르다 / 그런데 왜 그저 그런 와인을 마시는가 / 당신의 뒷마당에서 온 / 당신이 더 부드러운 종류를 살 수 있다면 / 지역에서 온 / 토양과 기후가 훨씬 더 안성맞춤인 / 포도 나무에

If the clay / in your backyard / makes stronger and prettier pots, / then you can make an exchange.
만약 흙이 (~한다면) / 당신의 뒷마당의 / 더 단단하고 예쁜 도자기를 만든다면 / 그럼 당신은 거래를 할 수 있다

해석　도시와 왕국의 번영과 운송 기반시설의 발전은 전문화를 위한 새로운 기회들이 생기게 했다. 인구가 밀집된 도시들은 전문 구두장이, 의사뿐만 아니라 목수, 사제, 군인 그리고 변호사에게도 정규직을 제공했다. 매우 좋은 와인, 올리브 오일, 또는 도자기를 생산하는 것으로 명성을 얻은 마을들은 거의 독점적으로 그 제품을 전문적으로 다루고 그들이 필요했던 모든 다른 제품들을 위해서 다른 촌락들과 그것을 거래할 가치가 있다는 것을 깨달았다. 이것은 정말 그럴 듯 하다. 기후와 토양이 서로 다른데, 당신이 토양과 기후가 포도 나무에 훨씬 더 안성맞춤인 지역에서 온 더 부드러운 종류를 살 수 있다면 왜 당신의 뒷마당에서 온 그저 그런 와인을 마시는가? 만약 당신의 뒷마당의 흙이 더 단단하고 예쁜 도자기를 만든다면, 그럼 당신은 거래를 할 수 있다.

① 어떻게 기후와 토양이 지역 특산물에 영향을 미치는지
② 지역 특산품에 좋은 평판을 얻는 방법
③ 무엇이 사람들을 전문화와 거래에 참여하게 만드는지
④ 도시의 번영과 전문직을 위한 정규직

해설　지문 처음에서 도시의 번영과 운송 기반시설의 발전은 전문화를 위한 새로운 기회들이 생기게 했다고 한 뒤, 지문 마지막에서 그 예시로 자신의 뒷마당에서 온 그저 그런 와인을 마시는 것보다는 포도 나무에 훨씬 더 안성맞춤인 기후와 토양에서 온 와인을 마시는 것이 좋으며, 뒷마당의 흙이 도자기 만들기에 적합하다면 거래를 할 수 있다는 것을 설명하고 있다. 따라서 이 지문의 주제를 '무엇이 사람들을 전문화와 거래에 참여하게 만드는지'라고 표현한 ③번이 정답이다.

어휘　transport 운송　infrastructure 기반시설　specialization 전문화
densely populated 인구가 밀집된　exclusively 독점적으로
settlement 촌락　mediocre 그저 그런　variety 종류
well suited 안성맞춤인, 적절한　grape vines 포도 나무

18　**독해**　**세부내용 파악 (지칭 대상 파악)**　난이도 ★☆☆

끊어읽기 해석

Nine-year-old Ryan Kyote / was eating breakfast / at home in Napa, California, / when he saw the news: / an Indiana school had taken a 6-year-old's meal / when her lunch account didn't have enough money.
9살의 Ryan Kyote는 / 아침을 먹고 있었다 / 캘리포니아 나파에 위치한 집에서 / 그가 뉴스를 봤을 때 / 인디애나 주의 한 학교가 6살 아이의 식사를 빼앗았다 / 그녀의 점심 계좌에 충분한 돈이 없자

Kyote asked / if that could happen / to his friends.
Kyote는 물어보았다 / 이런 일이 일어날 수 있는지 / 그의 친구들에게

When his mom contacted the school district / to find out, / she learned / that students / at schools in their district / had, all told, as much as $25,000 / in lunch debt.
그의 엄마가 교육청에 연락했을 때 / 알아보기 위해서 / 그녀는 알았다 / 그 학생들은 / 그들 지역에 있는 학교의 / 모두 합해서 2만 5천 달러만큼 있었다 / 점심값 빚이

Although the district says / it never penalized students who owed, / Kyote decided to use / his saved allowance / to pay off his grade's debt, / about $74 —becoming the face of a movement to end lunch-money debt.
비록 교육청은 ~라고 말하지만 / 빚이 있는 학생들을 절대 불리하게 만들지는 않았다 / Kyote는 / 사용하기로 결심했다 / 모아둔 용돈을 / 그의 학년의 빚을 갚기 위해 / 약 74 달러의 / 점심값 빚을 청산하기 위한 운동의 양상이 되었다

When California Governor Gavin Newsom signed a bill / in October / that banned "lunch shaming," / or giving worse food / to students with debt, / he thanked Kyote / for his "empathy and his courage" / in raising awareness of <u>the issue</u>.
캘리포니아 주지사 Gavin Newsom이 법안에 서명을 했을 때 / 10월에 / '점심 창피 주기'를 금지하는 / 또는 좋지 않은 음식을 주는 것을 / 빚이 있는 학생들에게 / 그는 Kyote에게 고마워했다 / 그의 '공감과 용기'에 / <u>이 문제</u>에 대한 인식을 높이기 위한

"Heroes," / Kyote points out, "come in all ages."
"'영웅들은' / Kyote는 언급했다 / "모든 연령대에서 나온다"

해석 9살의 Ryan Kyote가 인디애나 주의 한 학교가 그녀의 점심 계좌에 충분한 돈이 없자 6살 아이의 식사를 빼앗았다는 뉴스를 봤을 때, 그는 캘리포니아 나파에 위치한 집에서 아침을 먹고 있었다. Kyote는 그의 친구들에게 이런 일이 일어날 수 있는지 물어보았다. 그의 엄마가 알아보기 위해서 교육청에 연락했을 때, 그녀는 그들 지역에 있는 학교의 학생들은 점심값 빚이 모두 합해서 2만 5천 달러만큼 있었다는 것을 알았다. 비록 교육청은 빚이 있는 학생들을 절대 불리하게 만들지는 않았다고 말하지만, Kyote는 그의 학년의 빚을 갚기 위해, 약 74 달러의 모아둔 용돈을 사용하기로 결심했고 이것은 점심값 빚을 청산하기 위한 운동의 양상이 되었다. 10월에 캘리포니아 주지사 Gavin Newsom이 빚이 있는 학생들에게 '점심 창피 주기'나 좋지 않은 음식을 주는 것을 금지하는 법안에 서명을 했을 때, 그는 Kyote에게 이 문제에 대한 인식을 높이기 위한 그의 '공감과 용기'에 고마워했다. Kyote는 "영웅들은 모든 연령대에서 나온다"라고 언급했다.

① 주지사는 점심값 빚이 있는 학생들에게 점심 제공을 거부하는 법안에 서명했다.
② Kyote는 그의 점심 계좌의 돈을 다 써버려서 점심을 빼앗겼다.
③ 경제적 부담이 있는 교육청은 예산을 절감해서 좋은 질의 식사를 제공하지 못했다.
④ 이 지역구의 점심값을 낼 형편이 되지 않는 많은 학생들은 점심값 빚을 지고 있었다.

해설 밑줄 친 the issue가 있는 문장을 통해 Kyote가 인식을 높인 문제가 무엇인지를 지문에서 추론해야 한다는 것을 알 수 있다. 지문 전반에 걸쳐 Kyote는 점심 계좌에 돈이 없어 점심 식사를 빼앗긴 6살 아이에 대한 뉴스를 보고, 동일하게 점심값 빚이 있는 자신과 같은 학년의 학생들을 위해 자신의 용돈을 사용하기로 결정함으로써 이것이 점심값 빚을 청산하기 위한 운동의 양상이 되었다고 했으므로, the issue의 의미를 '이 지역구의 점심값을 낼 형편이 되지 않는 많은 학생들은 점심값 빚을 지고 있었다'라고 한 ④번이 정답이다.

어휘 all told 모두 합해서 penalize 불리하게 만들다 owe 빚이 있다 allowance 용돈 pay off 갚다 empathy 공감 decline 거부하다 run out of ~을 다 써버리다 afford ~할 형편이 되다

끊어읽기 해석

The biggest heart / in the world / is inside the blue whale. // It weighs / more than seven tons. // It's as big as a room.
가장 큰 심장은 / 세계에서 / 청고래 안에 있다 // 그것은 무게가 ~이다 / 7톤 이상 // 그것은 방만큼 크다.

When this creature is born / it is 20 feet long and weighs four tons. // It is way bigger / than your car.
이 생물체가 태어날 때 / 이것은 길이가 20피트이고 무게는 4톤이다 // 이것은 훨씬 더 크다 / 당신의 자동차보다

It drinks a hundred gallons of milk / from its mama every day / and gains 200 pounds a day, / and when it is seven or eight years old / it endures an unimaginable puberty / and then it essentially disappears / from human ken, / for next to nothing is known / of the mating habits, travel patterns, diet, social life, language, social structure and diseases.
그것은 100갤런의 젖을 먹는다 / 매일 그들의 엄마에게서 / 그리고 날마다 200파운드가 증가한다 / 그리고 7살이나 8살이 되면 / 그것은 상상할 수 없는 사춘기를 겪는다 / 그리고 그 후에 그것은 반드시 사라진다 / 인간의 시야에서 / 그래서 거의 아무것도 알려져 있지 않다 / 짝짓기 습관, 이동 패턴, 식단, 사교 생활, 언어, 사회적 구조 그리고 질병에 대해

There are perhaps 10,000 blue whales / in the world, / living in every ocean on earth, / and of the largest animal / who ever lived / we know nearly nothing.
아마 1만 마리의 청고래가 있을 것이다 / 세계에 / 지구의 모든 바다에 사는 / 그런데도 그 가장 큰 동물에 대해서 / 지금까지 살았던 / 우리는 거의 아무것도 모른다

But we know this: / the animals with the largest hearts / in the world / generally travel in pairs, / and their penetrating moaning cries, / their piercing yearning tongue, / can be heard underwater / for miles and miles.
그러나 우리는 이것을 알고 있다 / 가장 큰 심장을 가진 그 동물이 / 세계에서 / 주로 짝지어서 이동한다 / 그리고 그들의 날카로운 신음 소리는 / 그들의 귀청을 찢는 듯한 갈망하는 언어인 / 물속에서 들릴 수 있다 / 수 마일에 걸쳐서

해석 세계에서 가장 큰 심장은 청고래 안에 있다. 그것은 무게가 7톤 이상이다. 그것은 방만큼 크다. 이 생물체가 태어날 때 이것은 길이가 20피트이고 무게는 4톤이다. 이것은 당신의 자동차보다 훨씬 더 크다. 그것은 매일 그것의 엄마에게서 100갤런의 젖을 먹고 날마다 200파운드가 증가하고, 7살이나 8살이 되면 그들은 상상할 수 없는 사춘기를 겪으며, 그 후에 인간의 시야에서 반드시 사라지는데, 그래서 짝짓기 습관, 이동 패턴, 식단, 사교 생활, 언어, 사회적 구조 그리고 질병에 대해 거의 아무것도 알려져 있지 않다. 아마 지구의 모든 바다에 사는 1만 마리의 청고래가 세계에 있을 것인데도, 지금까지 살았던 그 가장 큰 동물에 대해서 우리는 거의 아무것도 모른다. 그러나 세계에서 가장 큰 심장을 가진 그 동물이 주로 짝지어서 이동하며, 귀청을 찢는 듯한 갈망하는 언어인 그들의 날카로운 신음 소리는 수 마일에 걸쳐서 물속에서 들릴 수 있다는 것을 우리는 알고 있다.

해설 지문 마지막에서 청고래는 주로 짝지어서 이동하며, 그들의 목소리는 수 마일에 걸쳐 들린다는 내용이 있으므로, 청고래가 일반적으로 혼자서 이동한다는 것은 지문의 내용과 반대이다. 따라서 ④번이 정답이다.

어휘   creature 생물체   unimaginable 상상할 수 없는
      puberty 사춘기, 성숙기   ken 시야   mating 짝짓기
      in pairs 짝지어서   penetrating 날카로운   moan 신음하다
      piercing 귀청을 찢는 듯한   yearn 갈망하다

20   독해   전체내용 파악 (주제 파악)   난이도 ★★☆

끊어읽기 해석

In addition to controlling temperatures / when handling fresh produce, / control of the atmosphere is important.
온도를 조절하는 것과 더불어 / 신선한 농산물을 다룰 때는 / 대기를 조절하는 것이 중요하다

Some moisture is needed / in the air / to prevent dehydration / during storage, / but too much moisture can encourage / growth of molds.
약간의 습기는 필요하다 / 대기에 / 건조를 예방하기 위해 / 보관하는 동안 / 그러나 너무 많은 습기는 촉진할 수 있다 / 곰팡이의 성장을

Some commercial storage units / have controlled atmospheres, / with the levels of both carbon dioxide and moisture / being regulated carefully.
몇몇 상업적인 보관 장치는 / 대기를 조절한다 / 이산화탄소의 농도와 습도 모두 / 세심하게 조절되면서

Sometimes other gases, / such as ethylene gas, / may be introduced / at controlled levels / to help achieve optimal quality / of bananas and other fresh produce.
때때로 다른 가스가 / 에틸렌 가스와 같은 / 주입될 수도 있다 / 제한된 농도로 / 최상의 품질을 얻는 것을 돕기 위해 / 바나나와 다른 신선한 농산물이

Related to the control of gases and moisture is / the need for some circulation of air / among the stored foods.
가스와 습기의 조절과 관련되어 있다 / 약간의 공기 순환의 필요성은 / 저장된 음식 사이에서

해석   신선한 농산물을 다룰 때는, 온도를 조절하는 것과 더불어 대기를 조절하는 것이 중요하다. 보관하는 동안 건조를 예방하기 위해 대기에 약간의 습기가 필요하지만, 너무 많은 습기는 곰팡이의 성장을 촉진할 수 있다. 몇몇 상업적인 보관 장치는 이산화탄소의 농도와 습도 모두 세심하게 조절되면서 대기를 조절한다. 때때로 에틸렌 가스와 같은 다른 가스가 바나나와 다른 신선한 농산물이 최상의 품질을 얻는 것을 돕기 위해 제한된 농도로 주입될 수도 있다. 저장된 음식 사이에서 약간의 공기 순환의 필요성은 가스와 습기의 조절과 관련되어 있다.

   ① 대기 중의 유해한 가스를 조절하는 것의 필요성
   ② 식물과 과일을 재배하는 동안 습도를 조절하는 가장 좋은 방법
   ③ 전 세계에서 매년 증가하는 탄소 발자국의 심각성
   ④ 음식을 저장함에 있어 특정 농도의 가스와 습도를 조절하는 것의 중요성

해설   지문 처음에서 신선한 농산물을 다룰 때는 대기 조절이 중요하고 약간의 습기가 필요하지만, 너무 많은 습기는 곰팡이의 성장을 촉진할 수 있다고 했다. 이어서 지문 마지막에서 저장된 음식 사이에서 약간의 공기 순환의 필요성은 가스와 습기의 조절과 관련되어 있다고 설명하고 있다. 따라서, 이 지문의 제목을 '음식을 저장함에 있어 특정 농도의 가스와 습도를 조절하는 것의 중요성'이라고 표현한 ④번이 정답이다.

어휘   produce 농산물; 생산하다   atmosphere 대기, 분위기
      dehydration 건조   storage 보관   mold 곰팡이   unit 장치
      regulate 조절하다, 규제하다   optimal 최상의   circulation 순환
      necessity 필요성   carbon footprint 탄소 발자국(개인 또는 단체가 발생시키는 온실가스의 총량)

21   독해   논리적 흐름 파악 (문맥상 부적절한 어휘)   난이도 ★★☆

끊어읽기 해석

Even if lying doesn't have any harmful effects / in a particular case, / it is still morally wrong / because, if discovered, / lying weakens the general practice / of truth telling / on which human communication relies.
설사 거짓말이 어떤 해로운 영향을 끼치지 않더라도 / 특정 경우에 / 그것은 여전히 도덕적으로 잘못된 것이다 / 만약 밝혀지면 ~이기 때문에 / 거짓말은 일반적인 관행을 약화시킨다 / 진실을 말하는 / 인간의 의사소통이 따르고 있는

For instance, / if I were to lie / about my age / on grounds of vanity, / and my lying were discovered, / even though no serious harm would have been done, / I would have ① undermined your trust generally.
예를 들어 / 내가 거짓말을 하면 / 나의 나이에 대해서 / 허영심을 이유로 / 그리고 내 거짓말이 밝혀지면 / 비록 아무런 심각한 피해가 없었더라도 / 전반적으로 당신의 신뢰를 ① 약화시켰을 것이다

In that case / you would be far less likely to believe anything / I might say / in the future.
그 경우에 / 당신은 어떤 것이든 훨씬 덜 신뢰할 것이다 / 내가 말할지도 모르는 / 앞으로

Thus all lying, / when discovered, / has indirect ② harmful effects.
그러므로 모든 거짓말은 / 밝혀지면 / 간접적인 ② 해로운 영향이 있다

However, / very occasionally, / these harmful effects might possibly be outweighed / by the ③ benefits / which arise from a lie.
하지만 / 아주 가끔 / 아마 이러한 해로운 영향의 결점을 메우기에 충분할지도 모른다 / ③ 장점으로 / 거짓말로 인해 생기는

For example, / if someone is seriously ill, / lying to them / about their life expectancy / might probably give them a chance / of living longer.
예를 들어 / 만약 누군가가 심각하게 아프면 / 그들에게 거짓말 하는 것은 / 그들의 기대 수명에 대해서 / 아마 그들에게 기회를 줄지도 모른다 / 더 오래 살

On the other hand, / telling them the truth / could possibly ④ prevent a depression / that would accelerate their physical decline.
반면에 / 그들에게 진실을 말하는 것은 / 아마 우울증을 ④ 예방할 수 있다 / 그들의 육체적 쇠약을 가속화 할

해석   설사 거짓말이 특정 경우에 어떤 해로운 영향을 끼치지 않더라도, 만약 밝혀지면 거짓말은 인간의 의사소통이 따르고 있는, 진실을 말하는 일반적인 관행을 약화시키기 때문에 그것은 여전히 도덕적으로 잘못된 것이다. 예를 들어, 내가 허영심을 이유로 나의 나이에 대해서 거짓말을 하고 내 거짓말이 밝혀지면, 비록 아무런 심각한 피해가 없었더라도, 전반적으로 당신의 신뢰를 ① 약화시켰을 것이다. 그 경우에 당신은 앞으로 내가 말할지도 모르는 어떤 것이든 훨씬 덜 신뢰할 것이다. 그러므로 모든 거짓말은 밝혀지면 간접적인 ② 해로운 영향이 있다. 하지만, 아주 가끔, 거짓말로 인해 생기는 ③ 장점으로 아마 이러한 해로운 영향의 결점을 메우기에 충분할지도 모른다. 예를 들어, 만약 누군가가 심각하게 아프면, 그들의 기대 수명에 대해서 거짓말 하는 것은 아마 그들에게 더 오래 살 기회를 줄지도 모른다. 반면에, 그들에게 진실을 말하는 것은 아마 그들의 육체적 쇠약을 가속화 할 우울증을 ④ 예방할 수 있다.

해설   지문 마지막에서 심각하게 아픈 사람에게 기대 수명에 대해서 거짓말 하는 것이 그들에게 더 오래 살 수 있는 기회를 줄지도 모른다고 했으므로, 그들에게 진실을 말하는 것이 육체적 쇠약을 가속화할 우울증을 예방할(prevent) 수 있다고 하는 것은 문맥상 적절하지 않다. 따라서 ④ prevent가 정답이다. 참고로, 주어

진 prevent를 대신할 수 있는 어휘로는 '야기하다'라는 의미의 cause, induce 등이 있다.

어휘 **morally** 도덕적으로 **on grounds of** ~을 이유로 **vanity** 허영심 **undermine** 약화시키다 **outweigh** ~의 결점을 메우기에 충분하다 **life expectancy** 기대 수명 **accelerate** 가속화하다 **decline** 쇠약; 감소하다

---

22 독해 논리적 흐름 파악 (문장 삽입) 난이도 ★★☆

끊어읽기 해석

> Water is also the medium / for most chemical reactions / needed to sustain life.
> 물은 또한 매개물이다 / 대부분의 화학 반응의 / 생명을 유지하기 위해 필요한
>
> Several common properties of seawater / are crucial / to the survival and well-being / of the ocean's inhabitants.
> 바닷물의 여러 공통적인 특징들은 / 필수적이다 / 생존과 안녕에 / 바다의 서식 동물들의
>
> Water accounts for 80–90% / of the volume of most marine organisms.
> 물은 80-90퍼센트를 차지한다 / 대부분의 해양 생물들의 부피의
>
> (①) It provides buoyancy and body support / for swimming and floating organisms / and reduces the need / for heavy skeletal structures.
> 그것은 부력과 신체 지지력를 제공한다 / 헤엄치며 떠있는 생물들에게 / 그리고 필요성을 줄여준다 / 무거운 골격 구조에 대한
>
> (②) The life processes / of marine organisms / in turn / alter many fundamental physical and chemical properties / of seawater, / including its transparency and chemical makeup, / making organisms an integral part / of the total marine environment.
> 삶의 과정은 / 해양 생물들의 / 차례로 / 많은 기본적인 물리적 및 화학적 특징들을 바꾼다 / 바닷물의 / 그것의 투명도와 화학적 구조를 포함한 / 이는 생물이 구성 요소가 되도록 한다 / 전체적인 해양 환경의
>
> (③) Understanding the interactions / between organisms and their marine environment / requires a brief examination / of some of the more important physical and chemical attributes / of seawater.
> 상호작용을 이해하는 것은 / 생물들과 그들의 해양 환경 사이의 / 간단한 조사를 필요로 한다 / 더 중요한 물리적 그리고 화학적 특징 중 몇몇에 대한 / 바닷물의
>
> (④) The characteristics / of pure water and seawater / differ in some respects, / so we consider first the basic properties / of pure water / and then examine / how those properties differ / in seawater.
> 특징들은 / 순수한 물과 바닷물의 / 어떤 점에서는 다르다 / 그래서 우리는 우선 기본적인 특징들을 고려한다 / 순수한 물의 / 그리고 나서 조사한다 / 그러한 특징들이 어떻게 다른지 / 바닷물에서

해석 바닷물의 여러 공통적인 특징들은 바다의 서식 동물들의 생존과 안녕에 필수적이다. 물은 대부분의 해양 생물들의 부피의 80-90퍼센트를 차지한다. 그것은 헤엄치며 떠있는 생물들에게 부력과 신체 지지력을 제공하고 무거운 골격 구조에 대한 필요성을 줄여준다. ② 물은 또한 생명을 유지하기 위해 필요한 대부분의 화학 반응의 매개물이다. 해양 생물들의 삶의 과정은 차례로 바닷물의 투명도와 화학적 구조를 포함한, 많은 기본적인 물리적 및 화학적 특징들을 바꾸고, 이는 생물들이 전체적인 해양 환경의 구성 요소가 되도록 한다. 생물들과 그들의 해양 환경 사이의 상호작용을 이해하는 것은 바닷물의 더 중요한 물리적 그리고 화학적 특징 중 몇몇에 대한 간단한 조사를 필요로 한다. 순수한 물과 바닷물의 특징들은 어떤 점에서는 달라서, 우리는 우선 순수한 물의 기본적인 특

징들을 고려하고 나서 바닷물에서 그러한 특징들이 어떻게 다른지 조사한다.

해설 ②번 앞 문장에 물은 헤엄치며 떠있는 생물들에게 부력과 신체 지지력을 제공하고 무거운 골격 구조에 대한 필요성을 줄여준다는 내용이 있고, ②번 뒤 문장에 해양 생물들의 삶의 과정은 차례로 바닷물의 투명도와 화학적 구조(chemical makeup)를 포함한 많은 기본적인 물리적 및 화학적 특징(chemical properties)들을 바꾼다는 내용이 있으므로, ②번 자리에 물은 또한(also) 생명을 유지하기 위해 필요한 대부분의 화학 반응(chemical reactions)의 매개물이다라는 내용의 주어진 문장이 나와야 지문이 자연스럽게 연결된다. 따라서 ②번이 정답이다.

어휘 **medium** 매개 **sustain** 유지하다 **well-being** 안녕, 행복 **inhabitants** 서식 동물 **buoyancy** 부력 **skeletal** 골격의 **alter** 바꾸다 **transparency** 투명도 **brief** 간단한, 짧은 **examination** 조사 **attribute** 특징

---

23 독해 논리적 흐름 파악 (문맥상 적절한 어휘) 난이도 ★★☆

끊어읽기 해석

> Here's the even more surprising part: / The advent of AI / didn't (A) diminish the performance / of purely human chess players.
> 여기 심지어 더 놀라운 부분이 있다 / AI의 출현은 / 실력을 (A) 약화시키지 않았다 / 완전히 인간인 체스 기사들의
>
> Quite the opposite.
> 정반대이다.
>
> Cheap, supersmart chess programs (B) inspired / more people than ever to play chess, / at more tournaments than ever, / and the players got better than ever.
> 저렴하면서 매우 똑똑한 체스 프로그램은 (B) 고취시켰다 / 여느 때보다도 더 많은 사람이 체스를 하도록 / 여느 때보다 더 많은 시합에서 / 그리고 그 선수들은 여느 때보다 더 발전했다
>
> There are more than twice as many grand masters now / as there were / when Deep Blue first beat Kasparov.
> 현재 두 배 이상의 그랜드 마스터들이 있다 / (그랜드 마스터들이) 있었던 것보다 / Deep blue가 처음으로 Kasparov를 이겼을 때
>
> The top-ranked human chess player today, / Magnus Carlsen, / trained with AIs / and has been deemed the most computerlike / of all human chess players.
> 오늘날 최고의 인간 체스 기사인 / Magnus Carlsen은 / 인공지능과 훈련했다 / 그리고 가장 컴퓨터 같다고 여겨져 왔다 / 모든 인간 체스 기사들 중에서
>
> He also has / the (C) highest human grand master rating / of all time.
> 그는 또한 가지고 있다 / (C) 가장 높은 인간 그랜드 마스터 등급을 / 역대

해석 여기 심지어 더 놀라운 부분이 있다. AI의 출현은 완전히 인간인 체스 기사들의 실력을 (A) 약화시키지 않았다. 정반대이다. 저렴하면서 매우 똑똑한 체스 프로그램은 여느 때보다 더 많은 사람들이 여느 때보다 더 많은 시합에서 체스를 하도록 (B) 고취시켰고, 그 선수들은 여느 때보다 더 발전했다. Deep Blue가 처음으로 Kasparov를 이겼을 때 (그랜드 마스터들이) 있었던 것보다 현재 두 배 이상의 그랜드 마스터들이 있다. 오늘날 최고의 인간 체스 기사인 Magnus Carlsen은 인공지능과 훈련했고 모든 인간 체스 기사들 중에서 가장 컴퓨터 같다고 여겨져 왔다. 그는 또한 역대 (C) 가장 높은 인간 그랜드 마스터 등급을 가지고 있다.

	(A)	(B)	(C)
①	약화시키다	의욕을 꺾었다	가장 높은
②	증가시키다	의욕을 꺾었다	가장 낮은

③ 약화시키다　고취시켰다　가장 높은
④ 증가시키다　고취시켰다　가장 낮은

해설　(A) 빈칸 뒤 문장에서 정반대라고 하며 선수들은 여느 때보다 더 발전했다고 했으므로, AI의 출현이 체스 기사들의 실력을 '약화시키지'(diminish) 않았다는 내용이 들어가야 적절하다. (B) 빈칸 뒤 문장에서 Deep Blue가 Kasparov를 이겼을 때보다 현재 두 배 이상의 그랜드 마스터들이 있다고 했으므로, 더 많은 시합에서 체스를 하도록 '고취시켰다'(inspired)는 내용이 들어가야 적절하다. (C) 빈칸 앞 문장에서 Magnus Carlsen이 오늘날 최고의 인간 체스 기사라고 했으므로 '가장 높은'(highest) 인간 그랜드 마스터 등급을 가지고 있다는 내용이 들어가야 적절하다.
따라서 ③ (A) diminish(약화시키다) – (B) inspired(고취시켰다) – (C) highest(가장 높은)가 정답이다.

어휘　advent 출현　diminish 약화시키다　purely 완전히, 전적으로
beat 이기다　deem 여기다　computerlike 컴퓨터 같은

24　독해　전체내용 파악 (문단 요약)　난이도 ★☆☆

끊어읽기 해석

Aesthetic value / in fashion objects, / like aesthetic value / in fine art objects, / is self-oriented.
미적 가치는 / 패션 물품의 / 미적 가치처럼 / 순수 미술 작품에서의 / 자기 중심적이다

Consumers have the need / to be attracted / and to surround themselves with other people / who are attractive.
소비자들은 욕구를 갖고 있다 / 매력을 느끼려 하는 / 그리고 다른 사람들을 항상 자신의 주변에 두려는 / 매력적인

However, / unlike aesthetic value / in the fine arts, / aesthetic value / in fashion / is also other-oriented.
그러나 / 미적 가치와는 달리 / 순수 미술 작품의 / 미적 가치 / 패션에서의 / 또한 타인 지향적이다

Attractiveness of appearance / is a way / of eliciting the reaction of others / and facilitating social interaction.
외모의 끌어 당기는 힘은 / 하나의 방법이다 / 다른 사람들의 반응을 끌어내는 / 그리고 사회적 상호작용을 용이하게 하는

해석　패션 물품의 미적 가치는 순수 미술 작품에서의 미적 가치처럼 자기 중심적이다. 소비자들은 매력을 느끼려 하고 매력적인 다른 사람들을 항상 자신의 주변에 두려는 욕구를 갖고 있다. 그러나, 순수 미술 작품의 미적 가치와는 달리, 패션에서의 미적 가치는 또한 타인 지향적이다. 외모의 끌어 당기는 힘은 다른 사람들의 반응을 끌어내고 사회적 상호작용을 용이하게 하는 하나의 방법이다.

> 패션 물품에서 미적 가치는 자기 중심적이기도 하고 타인 지향적이기도 하다.

① 본질적으로 오직 자기 중심적인
② 다른 것과 달리 단지 타인 지향적인
③ 자기 중심적이기도 하고 타인 지향적이기도 한
④ 그것의 본질과 관계 없이 정의하기 어려운

해설　지문 처음에서 패션 물품의 미적 가치는 순수 미술 작품처럼 자기 중심적이라고 한 뒤, 지문 중간에서 패션 물품에서의 미적 가치는 또한 타인 지향적이기도 하다고 설명하고 있으므로, 빈칸에는 '자기 중심적이기도 하고 타인 지향적이기도 한'이라는 내용이 와야 적절하다. 따라서 ③번이 정답이다.

어휘　aesthetic 미적인, 감각적인　value 가치
self-oriented 자기 중심적인　surround ~을 항상 자신의 주변에 두다
attractiveness 끌어 당기는 힘　elicit 끌어내다
facilitate 용이하게 하다　inherently 본질적으로

25　독해　논리적 흐름 파악 (문장 삽입)　난이도 ★★☆

끊어읽기 해석

The great news is / that this is true / whether or not we remember our dreams.
좋은 소식은 ~이다 / 이것이 사실이라는 것이다 / 우리가 우리의 꿈을 기억하든지 못하든지

Some believe / there is no value to dreams, / but it is wrong / to dismiss these nocturnal dramas / as irrelevant.
몇몇은 믿는다 / 꿈에는 의미가 없다고 / 그러나 잘못된 것이다 / 밤에 일어나는 이러한 드라마를 일축하는 것은 / 무의미한 것으로

There is something / to be gained / in remembering.
(어떤) 것이 있다 / 얻어지는 / 기억하는 것에서

(①) We can feel / more connected, / more complete, / and more on track.
우리는 느낄 수 있다 / 더 연결되어 있다고 / 더 완벽하다고 / 그리고 더 제대로 진행되고 있다고

We can receive / inspiration, information, and comfort.
우리는 받아들일 수 있다 / 영감, 정보, 그리고 편안함을

Albert Einstein stated / that his theory of relativity was inspired / by a dream.
알버트 아인슈타인은 말했다 / 그의 상대성 이론이 영감을 받았다고 / 꿈에서

(②) In fact, / he claimed / that dreams were responsible for / many of his discoveries.
사실 / 그는 주장했다 / 꿈들이 ~에 책임이 있다고 / 그의 많은 발견들

(③) Asking why we dream / makes as much sense as / questioning why we breathe.
우리가 왜 꿈꾸는지 물어보는 것은 / ~만큼 타당하다 / 우리가 왜 숨쉬는지 질문하는 것

Dreaming is an integral part / of a healthy life.
꿈꾸는 것은 필수적인 요소이다 / 건강한 삶의

(④) Many people report / being inspired with a new approach / for a problem / upon awakening, / even though they don't remember / the specific dream.
많은 사람들은 말한다 / 새로운 접근법의 영감을 얻는다고 / 어떤 문제에 대한 / 깨자마자 / 비록 그들이 기억하진 못하지만 / 그 특정한 꿈을

해석　몇몇은 꿈에는 의미가 없다고 믿지만, 밤에 일어나는 이러한 드라마를 무의미한 것으로 일축하는 것은 잘못된 것이다. 기억하는 것에는 얻어지는 것이 있다. 우리는 더 연결되어 있고, 더 완벽하고, 더 제대로 진행되고 있다고 느낄 수 있다. 우리는 영감, 정보, 그리고 편안함을 받아들일 수 있다. 알버트 아인슈타인은 그의 상대성 이론이 꿈에서 영감을 받았다고 말했다. 사실, 그는 꿈들이 그의 많은 발견들에 책임이 있다고 주장했다. 우리가 왜 꿈꾸는지 물어보는 것은 우리가 왜 숨쉬는지 질문하는 것만큼 타당하다. 꿈꾸는 것은 건강한 삶의 필수적인 요소이다. ④ 좋은 소식은 우리가 우리의 꿈을 기억하든지 못하든지 이것이 사실이라는 것이다. 많은 사람들은 비록 그들이 그 특정한 꿈을 기억하진 못하지만, 깨자마자 어떤 문제에 대한 새로운 접근법의 영감을 얻는다고 말한다.

해설　④번 앞 문장에 꿈꾸는 것은 건강한 삶의 필수 요소라는 내용이 있고, ④번 뒤 문장에 사람들이 특정한 꿈을 기억하진 못하지만, 어떤 문제에 대한 새로운 접근법의 영감을 얻는다는 내용이 있으므로 ④번 자리에 좋은 소식은 우리가 꿈을 기억하든지 못하든지 이것이(this) 사실이라는 주어진 문장이 나와야 지문이 자연스럽게 연결된다. 따라서 ④번이 정답이다.

어휘　dismiss 일축하다　nocturnal 밤에 일어나는, 야행성의
irrelevant 무의미한　on track 제대로 진행되고 있는
relativity 상대성　integral 필수적인　awaken 깨다

정답

p.60

01	③ 문법 - 주어·동사/목적어·보어/수식어	11	② 독해 - 세부내용 파악	21	④ 문법 - 분사
02	③ 독해 - 논리적 흐름 파악	12	① 독해 - 추론	22	③ 문법 - 관계절&분사
03	③ 독해 - 논리적 흐름 파악	13	③ 독해 - 논리적 흐름 파악	23	③ 문법 - 부사절
04	③ 문법 - 전치사&관계절&수 일치	14	② 독해 - 전체내용 파악	24	④ 독해 - 논리적 흐름 파악
05	② 독해 - 추론	15	④ 독해 - 추론	25	② 독해 - 추론
06	② 독해 - 세부내용 파악	16	④ 독해 - 전체내용 파악		
07	① 독해 - 전체내용 파악	17	① 독해 - 전체내용 파악		
08	③ 독해 - 논리적 흐름 파악	18	③ 독해 - 논리적 흐름 파악		
09	② 독해 - 전체내용 파악	19	③ 독해 - 전체내용 파악		
10	④ 독해 - 세부내용 파악	20	② 독해 - 논리적 흐름 파악		

취약영역 분석표

영역	세부 유형	문항 수	소계
어휘	어휘 & 표현	0	/0
	생활영어	0	
문법	주어·동사/목적어·보어/수식어	1	/5
	전치사 & 관계절 & 수 일치	1	
	분사	1	
	관계절 & 분사	1	
	부사절	1	
독해	전체내용 파악	6	/20
	세부내용 파악	3	
	추론	4	
	논리적 흐름 파악	7	
총계			/25

· 자신이 취약한 영역은 '법원직 9급 영어, 이렇게 출제된다!'(문제집 p.8)를 통해 다시 한번 확인하고 학습하시기 바랍니다.

---

01 문법 주어·동사/목적어·보어/수식어 난이도 ★★☆

해석 최근 연구는 어떤 사람들은 유전적으로 수줍어하는 성향을 갖게 된다고 밝힌다. 다시 말하면, 어떤 사람들은 내성적으로 태어난다. 연구원들은 15퍼센트에서 20퍼센트 사이의 신생아들이 수줍음의 징후를 보인다고 말하는데, 그들은 더 조용하고 더 경계한다. 연구원들은 생후 2개월 만에 나타나는 사교적인 아기와 내성적인 아기들 간의 생리학적인 차이점들을 확인했다. 한 연구에서, 이후 내성적인 아이들로 확인된 2개월 된 아기들은 움직이는 모빌과 사람의 목소리 녹음 테이프와 같은 자극에 대해 스트레스 징후를 보이며 반응했는데, 스트레스 징후에는 증가된 심장 박동, 팔다리의 요동치는 움직임과 지나친 울음이 있었다. 수줍음과 관련된 유전적 근거에 대한 추가 증거는 내성적인 아이들의 부모나 조부모들은 그들이 어렸을 때 내성적이었다는 것을 내성적이지 않은 아이들의 부모나 조부모들보다 더 자주 말한다는 사실이다.

해설 ③ 동사 자리 절에는 반드시 주어와 동사가 있어야 하고, 동사 자리에는 동사나 '조동사 + 동사원형'이 와야 하므로 동명사 reacting을 과거 동사 reacted로 고쳐야 한다.

오답 분석 ① 능동태·수동태 구별 동사 predispose(~하는 성향을 갖게 하다) 뒤에 목적어가 없고 주어(some individuals)와 동사가 '어떤 사람들이 ~하는 성향을 갖게 된다'라는 의미의 수동 관계이므로 be동사(are) 뒤에서 수동태를 완성하는 과거분사 predisposed가 올바르게 쓰였다.
② 관계대명사 that 선행사 physiological differences가 사물이고 관계절 내에서 동사(show up)의 주어 역할을 하므로 사물을 가리키는 주격 관계대명사 that이 올바르게 쓰였다.
④ 비교급 비교급 표현은 '부사의 비교급(more often) + than'의 형태로 나타낼 수 있으므로 than이 올바르게 쓰였다.

어휘 reveal 밝히다 individual 사람, 개인 genetically 유전적으로 predispose ~하는 성향을 갖게 하다 vigilant 경계하는 identify 확인하다 physiological 생리학적인 jerky movement 요동치는 움직임 excessive 지나친, 과도한

👍 이것도 알면 합격!

③번 밑줄이 있는 문장의 주어인 two-month-olds(2개월 된 아기들)처럼 '수사 + 하이픈(-) + 단위 표현'은 명사로 쓰일 수 있으며, 의미에 따라 단위 표현이 복수형으로도 쓰인다는 것을 알아두자.

형용사로 쓰인 경우	a two-month-old baby 2개월 된 아기
복수 명사로 쓰인 경우	two-month-olds 2개월 된 아기들

---

02 독해 논리적 흐름 파악 (문맥상 적절한 어휘) 난이도 ★★★

끊어읽기 해석

South Korea is one of the only countries / in the world / that has a dedicated goal / to become the world's leading exporter / of popular culture.
한국은 유일한 국가들 중 하나이다 / 세계에서 / 헌신적인 목표를 가진 / 전 세계의 선두적인 수출국가가 되겠다는 / 대중문화의

It is a way / for Korea / to develop its "soft power."
이것은 방법이다 / 한국이 / 그것의 '소프트 파워'를 발전시키는

It refers to / the (A) intangible power / a country wields / through its image, / rather than / through military power or economic power.
이것은 ~을 가리킨다 / (A) 무형의 힘을 / 국가가 행사하는 / 그것(국가)의 이미지를 통해 / ~보다는 / 군사적 힘 또는 경제적 힘을 통해서

Hallyu first spread / to China and Japan, / later to Southeast Asia and several countries / worldwide.
한류는 처음으로 퍼졌다 / 중국과 일본에 / 이후 동남아시아와 여러 국가들에 / 전 세계의

In 2000, / a 50-year ban / on the exchange / of popular culture / between Korea and Japan / was partly lifted, / which improved the (B) surge / of Korean popular culture / among the Japanese.
2000년에 / 50년간의 금지가 / 교류에 대한 / 대중문화의 / 한국과 일본

간의 / 부분적으로 해제되었다 / 그리고 이것은 (B) 상승을 향상시켰다 / 한국 대중문화의 / 일본인들 사이에서

South Korea's broadcast authorities / have been sending delegates / to promote their TV programs and cultural contents / in several countries.
한국의 방송 관계자들은 / 대표단을 파견해오고 있다 / 그들의 TV 프로그램과 문화 콘텐츠를 홍보하기 위해 / 여러 나라에서

Hallyu has been a blessing / for Korea, its businesses, culture and country image.
한류는 축복이 되어왔다 / 한국, 그것(한국)의 기업들, 문화 그리고 국가 이미지에

Since early 1999, / Hallyu has become one of the biggest cultural phenomena / across Asia.
1999년 초부터 / 한류는 가장 큰 문화적 현상들 중 하나가 되어왔다 / 아시아 전역에 걸쳐

The Hallyu effect has been tremendous, / contributing to 0.2% / of Korea's GDP in 2004, / amounting to approximately USD 1.87 billion.
한류 효과는 엄청났다 / 0.2퍼센트를 기여했으며 / 2004년 한국의 GDP에 / 대략적으로 미화 18억 7천만 달러에 상당했다

More recently in 2014, / Hallyu had / an estimated USD 11.6 billion (C) boost / on the Korean economy.
더 최근인 2014년에 / 한류는 주었다 / 어림잡아 미화 116억 달러의 (C) 증가를 / 한국 경제에서

해석 한국은 전 세계의 선두적인 대중문화의 수출국가가 되겠다는 헌신적인 목표를 가진 세계에서 유일한 국가들 중 하나이다. 이것은 한국이 그것의 '소프트 파워'를 발전시키는 방법이다. 이것은 국가가 군사적 힘 또는 경제적 힘을 통해서 보다는 그것(국가)의 이미지를 통해 행사하는 (A) 무형의 힘을 가리킨다. 한류는 처음으로 중국과 일본에 퍼졌고, 이후 동남아시아와 전 세계의 여러 국가들에 퍼졌다. 2000년에, 한국과 일본 간의 대중문화의 교류에 대한 50년간의 금지가 부분적으로 해제되었고, 이것은 일본인들 사이에서 한국 대중문화의 (B) 상승을 향상시켰다. 한국의 방송 관계자들은 여러 나라에서 그들의 TV 프로그램과 문화 콘텐츠를 홍보하기 위해 대표단을 파견해오고 있다. 한류는 한국, 그것(한국)의 기업들, 문화 그리고 국가 이미지에 축복이 되어왔다. 1999년 초부터, 한류는 아시아 전역에 걸쳐 가장 큰 문화적 현상들 중 하나가 되어왔다. 한류 효과는 엄청났는데, 2004년 한국의 GDP에 0.2퍼센트를 기여했으며, 이는 대략적으로 미화 18억 7천만 달러에 상당했다. 더 최근인 2014년에, 한류는 한국 경제에서 어림잡아 미화 116억 달러의 (C) 증가를 주었다.

	(A)	(B)	(C)
①	유형의	상승	침체
②	무형의	하락	증가
③	무형의	상승	증가
④	유형의	하락	침체

해설 (A) 빈칸이 있는 문장에서 이것(소프트 파워)은 국가가 군사적 힘 또는 경제적 힘을 통해서 보다는 국가의 이미지를 통해 행사하는 힘을 가리킨다고 했으므로, 빈칸에는 '무형의'(intangible)라는 내용이 들어가야 적절하다. (B) 빈칸이 있는 문장에서 2000년에 한국과 일본 간의 대중문화의 교류에 대한 50년간의 금지가 부분적으로 해제되었고 이것이 일본인들 사이에서 한국 대중 문화의 무언가를 향상시켰다고 했으므로, 빈칸에는 '상승'(surge)이라는 내용이 들어가야 적절하다. (C) 빈칸 앞 문장에서 한류 효과는 엄청났는데, 2004년 한국의 GDP에 0.2퍼센트를 기여했고, 이는 미화 18억 7천만 달러에 상당했다고 했으므로, 빈칸에는 더 최근인 2014년에, 한류는 한국 경제에 어림잡아 미화 116억 달러의 '증가'(boost)를 주었다는 내용이 들어가야 적절하다.

따라서 ③ (A) intangible(무형의) - (B) surge(상승) - (C) boost(증가)가 정답이다.

어휘 dedicated 헌신적인 popular culture 대중문화 tangible 유형의 intangible 무형의 wield 행사하다 military 군사적인 spread 퍼지다 ban 금지 lift (제재를) 해제하다 surge 상승 decline 하락 delegate 대표단 promote 홍보하다 tremendous 엄청난 amount ~에 상당하다 estimated 어림잡은 stagnation 침체, 불경기

03 독해 논리적 흐름 파악 (무관한 문장 삭제) 난이도 ★★☆

끊어읽기 해석

The immortal operatically styled single Bohemian Rhapsody / by Queen / was released / in 1975 / and proceeded to the top of the UK charts / for 9 weeks.
불멸의 오페라 풍 스타일의 싱글 앨범 『Bohemian Rhapsody』는 / Queen의 / 발매되었다 / 1975년에 / 그리고 영국 음악차트에서 계속해서 1위를 했다 / 9주 동안

① A song / that was nearly never released / due to its length and unusual style / but which Freddie insisted would be played / became the instantly recognizable hit.
노래는 / 하마터면 발매되지 않을 뻔했던 / 그것의 길이와 독특한 스타일 때문에 / 그러나 Freddie가 (사람들에 의해) 들려지게 될 것이라고 강력히 주장했던 / 즉시 눈에 띄는 히트곡이 되었다

② By this time / Freddie's unique talents were becoming clear, / a voice with a remarkable range / and a stage presence / that gave Queen / its colorful, unpredictable and flamboyant personality.
이 때쯤에 / Freddie의 독특한 재능은 분명해지고 있었다 / 놀랄 만한 음역대의 목소리 / 그리고 무대 장악력 / Queen에게 준 / 그것의 다채롭고, 예측할 수 없으며 이색적인 개성을

③ The son of Bomi and Jer Bulsara, / Freddie spent the bulk of his childhood / in India / where he attended St. Peter's boarding school.
Bomi와 Jer Bulsara의 아들인 / Freddie는 그의 어린 시절의 상당 부분을 보냈다 / 인도에서 / 그가 St. Peter 기숙 학교를 다녔던

④ Very soon / Queen's popularity extended / beyond the shores of the UK / as they charted and triumphed / around Europe, Japan and the USA / where in 1979 they topped the charts / with Freddie's song Crazy Little thing Called Love.
머지 않아 / Queen의 인기는 뻗어 나갔다 / 영국의 해안을 넘어 / 그들이 차트에 올라 성공하면서 / 유럽 전역, 일본 그리고 미국에서 / 1979년에 차트에서 1위를 차지한 / Freddie의 노래 「Crazy Little thing Called Love」로

해석 Queen의 불멸의 오페라 풍 스타일의 싱글 앨범 『Bohemian Rhapsody』는 1975년에 발매되었고 영국 음악차트에서 9주 동안 계속해서 1위를 했다. ① 그것의 길이와 독특한 스타일 때문에 하마터면 발매되지 않을 뻔했으나 Freddie가 (사람들에 의해) 들려지게 될 것이라고 강력히 주장했던 노래는 즉시 눈에 띄는 히트곡이 되었다. ② 이 때쯤에 Freddie의 독특한 재능은 분명해지고 있었는데, 그것들은 놀랄 만한 음역대의 목소리와 Queen에게 그것의 다채롭고, 예측할 수 없으며 이색적인 개성을 준 무대 장악력이었다. ③ Bomi와 Jer Bulsara의 아들인 Freddie는 그의 어린 시절의 상당 부분을 그가 St. Peter 기숙 학교를 다녔던 인도에서 보냈다. ④ 머지 않아 그들이 유럽 전역, 일본 그리고 Freddie의 노래 「Crazy Little thing Called Love」로 1979년 차트에서 1위를 차지한 미국에서 차트에 올라 성공하면서 Queen의 인기는 영국의 해안을 넘어 뻗어 나갔다.

해설 첫 문장에서 Queen의 싱글 앨범 『Bohemian Rhapsody』는

1975년에 발매되었고 영국 음악차트에서 9주 동안 계속해서 1위를 했다고 언급한 뒤, ①, ②, ④번에서 Queen의 인기 비결과 그들의 성공적이었던 음악 활동들에 대해 설명하고 있으므로 지문의 앞부분과 관련이 있다. 그러나 ③번은 'Freddie의 어린 시절'에 대한 내용으로, 지문 앞부분의 내용과 관련이 없으므로 ③번이 정답이다.

어휘 immortal 불멸의 operatically 오페라 풍으로 release 발매하다
proceed 계속 ~이 되다 length 길이 insist 강력히 주장하다
instantly 즉시 recognizable 눈에 띄는, 알아볼 수 있는
stage presence 무대 장악력 flamboyant 이색적인
personality 개성 triumph 성공하다, 승리를 거두다

---

04 문법 전치사 & 관계절 & 수 일치 난이도 ★★☆

해석 많은 업계의 전문가들에 의해 만화 목소리 연기의 창시자로 여겨지는 Mel Blanc는 1927년에 지역 라디오 쇼의 목소리 배우로서 그의 경력을 시작했다. 제작자들은 많은 배우들을 고용할 수 있는 자금을 가지고 있지 않아서 Mel Blanc은 필요에 따라 쇼를 위해 여러 가지 목소리와 등장인물들을 만들어내는 것에 의지했다. 그는 The Jack Benny Program의 고정 출연자가 되었는데, 이 프로그램에서 그는 인간, 동물, 그리고 엔진 조정이 필요한 자동차와 같이 생명이 없는 물체들 등의 많은 등장인물들에 대한 목소리를 제공했다. Porky Pig를 위해 그가 만들어낸 독특한 목소리는 Warner Bros에서의 그의 큰 성공에 연료를 공급했다. 머지 않아 Blanc는 Hanna-Barbera Studios의 등장인물뿐만 아니라 많은 스튜디오의 초대형 만화 스타들과 밀접한 관계를 맺게 되었다. 그의 가장 오래 진행한 목소리 연기는 약 52년간 Daffy Duck이라는 등장인물을 위해 한 것이었다. Blanc는 그의 작업을 매우 보호하려고 했으며 'Mel Blanc의 목소리 연기'라고 쓰인 스크린 크레딧이 항상 그의 계약 조건의 항목에 있었다.

해설 (A) 전치사 자리 resort to(~에 의지하다)에서 전치사 to 뒤에는 명사 역할을 하는 것이 와야 하므로 동사원형 create가 아닌 동명사 creating을 써야 한다.
   (B) 관계부사와 관계대명사 비교 관계사 뒤에 완전한 절(he ~ many characters)이 왔으므로 관계대명사 which가 아닌 관계부사 where를 써야 한다.
   (C) 주어와 동사의 수 일치 주어 자리에 복수 명사 screen credits가 왔으므로 단수 동사 was가 아닌 복수 동사 were를 써야 한다. 참고로, 주어와 동사 사이의 수식어 거품(reading ~ Mel Blanc)은 동사의 수 결정에 영향을 주지 않는다.
   따라서 ③ (A) creating – (B) where – (C) were가 정답이다.

어휘 expert 전문가 inventor 창시자 resort to ~에 의지하다
regular 고정 출연자 nonliving 생명이 없는 tune-up 엔진 조정
distinctive 독특한 breakout success 큰 성공
protective 보호하는 term 조건

👍 이것도 알면 **합격!**

관계부사(when, where, why, how)는 '전치사 + 관계대명사'의 형태로 바꾸어 쓸 수 있고, 관계부사 뒤에는 완전한 절이 온다는 것을 기억하자.

(ex) August is the month when(= in which) most Parisians leave the city for vacation.
8월은 대부분의 파리의 주민들이 휴가를 위해 그 도시를 떠나는 달이다.

---

05 독해 추론 (빈칸 완성 - 구) 난이도 ★★☆

끊어읽기 해석

With the present plummeting demand market / for office buildings, / resulting in many vacant properties, / we need to develop plans / that will enable some future exchange / between residential and commercial or office functions.
현재의 급락하는 수요 시장으로 인해 / 사무실용 빌딩에 대한 / 많은 비어 있는 건물들을 초래한 / 우리는 계획을 개발하는 것이 필요하다 / 미래에 있을 맞바꿈을 가능하게 할 / 주거 기능과 상업적 또는 사무실 기능 간에

This vacancy has reached / a historic level; / at present / the major towns / in the Netherlands / have some five million square metres / of unoccupied office space, / while / there is a shortage / of 160,000 homes.
이러한 공실들이 이르렀다 / 역사적인 수준에 / 현재 / 주요 도시들은 / 네덜란드의 / 약 500만 제곱미터의 ~을 가지고 있다 / 비어 있는 사무실을 / 반면 / 부족하다 / 16만 주택이

At least / a million of those square metres can be expected / to stay vacant, / according to the association of Dutch property developers.
적어도 / 그중 100만 제곱미터는 예상될 수 있다 / 비어있는 상태를 유지할 것으로 / 네덜란드 부동산 개발협회에 따르면

There is a real threat / of 'ghost towns' / of empty office buildings / springing up / around the major cities.
실질적인 위협이 있다 / '유령 도시'에 대한 / 빈 사무실용 빌딩들로 이루어진 / 생겨나는 / 주요 도시들의 주변에서

In spite of this forecast, / office building activities are continuing / at full tilt, / as these were planned / during a period of high returns.
이러한 예상에도 불구하고 / 사무실 건설 활동들은 계속되고 있다 / 전속력으로 / 이것들이 계획되었기 때문이다 / 높은 수익률의 시기 동안에

Therefore, / it is now essential / that a number of plans / for office buildings / be redeveloped / for housing.
그러므로 / 이제는 필수적이다 / 많은 계획들이 / 사무실용 빌딩에 대한 / 재개발되어야 한다는 것이 / 주택을 위한 것으로

해석 많은 비어있는 건물들을 초래한 사무실용 빌딩에 대한 현재의 급락하는 수요 시장으로 인해, 우리는 주거 기능과 상업적 또는 사무실 기능 간에 미래에 있을 맞바꿈을 가능하게 할 계획을 개발하는 것이 필요하다. 이러한 공실들이 역사적인 수준에 이르렀고, 현재 네덜란드의 주요 도시들은 16만 주택이 부족한 반면 약 500만 제곱미터의 비어 있는 사무실을 가지고 있다. 네덜란드 부동산 개발협회에 따르면, 그중 적어도 100만 제곱 미터는 비어있는 상태를 유지할 것으로 예상될 수 있다. 주요 도시들의 주변에서 생겨나는 빈 사무실용 빌딩들로 이루어진 '유령 도시'에 대한 실질적인 위협이 있다. 이러한 예상에도 불구하고, 사무실 건설 활동들은 전속력으로 계속되고 있는데, 이것들이 높은 수익률의 시기 동안에 계획되었기 때문이다. 그러므로, 이제는 <u>사무실용 빌딩에 대한 많은 계획들이 주택을 위한 것으로 재개발되어야 한다</u>는 것이 필수적이다.

① 건물 유지 비용을 줄이기 위해 새로운 디자인이 채택되어야 한다
② 사무실용 빌딩에 대한 많은 계획들이 주택을 위한 것으로 재개발되어야 한다
③ 거주용 빌딩들은 상업용 빌딩으로 변경되어야 한다
④ 우리는 가능한 한 많은 상점들을 설계하고 넘겨주어야 한다

해설 빈칸이 있는 문장을 통해 빈칸에 무엇이 필수적인지에 대한 내용이 나와야 적절하다는 것을 알 수 있다. 지문 처음에 많은 비어있는 건물들을 초래한 사무실용 빌딩에 대한 현재의 급락하는 수요 시장으로 인해, 주거 기능과 상업적 또는 사무실 기능 간에 맞바꿈을 가능하게 할 계획을 개발하는 것이 필요하다는 내용이 있고, 빈칸 앞 문장에 수익률이 높은 시기에 계획된 사무실 건설 활동들이 계속되고 있다는 내용이 있으므로, 이제는 '사무실용 빌딩에 대

한 많은 계획들이 주택을 위한 것으로 재개발되어야 한다'는 것이 필수적이라고 한 ②번이 정답이다.

어휘 plummet 급락하다 demand 수요 vacant 비어있는, 공석인
property 건물, 재산 exchange 맞바꿈, 교환
residential 주거용의 commercial 상업적인
unoccupied 비어있는 shortage 부족
spring up (갑자기) 생겨나다 at full tilt 전속력으로, 쏜살같이
return 수익(률) adopt 채택하다, 쓰다
maintenance 유지, 보수관리 convert 변경하다, 개조하다

06 독해 세부내용 파악 (내용 일치 파악) 난이도 ★★☆

끊어읽기 해석

①Child psychologists concentrate their efforts / on the study of the individual / from birth through age eleven.
아동 심리학자들은 그들의 노력을 집중한다 / 개인에 대한 연구에 / 출생부터 11세까지의

② Developmental psychologists study / behavior and growth patterns / from the prenatal period / through maturity and old age.
발달 심리학자들은 연구한다 / 행동과 성장 유형을 / 태아기부터 / 성인기와 노년기까지

Many clinical psychologists specialize in / dealing with the behavior problems of children.
많은 임상 심리학자들은 전문으로 한다 / 아동의 행동 문제들을 다루는 것을

Research in child psychology sometimes helps / shed light on work behavior.
아동 심리학에서의 연구는 종종 도움이 된다 / 업무 행동을 설명하는 데

③For example, / one study showed / that victims of childhood abuse and neglect / may suffer long-term consequences.
예를 들어 / 한 연구는 보여주었다 / 아동 학대와 방치의 피해자들이 / 장기간의 영향을 겪는지도 모른다는 것을

③Among them are / lower IQs and reading ability, / more suicide attempts, / and more unemployment and low-paying jobs.
그것들 중에서는 있다 / 낮은 IQ와 읽기 능력이 / 더 많은 자살 시도 / 그리고 더 높은 실업률과 더 많은 저임금 직업들이

Many people / today / have become interested / in the study of adult phases / of human development.
많은 사람들이 / 오늘날 / 관심을 갖게 되었다 / 성인기 연구에 / 인간 발달 단계 중

The work of developmental psychologists / has led to widespread interest / in the problems of the middle years, / such as the mid-life crisis.
발달 심리학자들의 연구는 / 폭넓은 관심을 이끌었다 / 중년의 문제들에 대한 / 중년의 위기와 같은

④A job-related problem / of interest to developmental psychologists / is why so many executives die earlier / than expected / after retirement.
직업과 관련된 문제는 / 발달 심리학자들에게 흥미로운 / 왜 그렇게 많은 임원들이 더 일찍 죽는지이다 / 예상된 것보다 / 은퇴 후에

해석 아동 심리학자들은 출생부터 11세까지의 개인에 대한 연구에 그들의 노력을 집중한다. 발달 심리학자들은 태아기부터 성인기와 노년기까지 행동과 성장 유형을 연구한다. 많은 임상 심리학자들은 아동의 행동 문제들을 다루는 것을 전문으로 한다. 아동 심리학에서의 연구는 종종 업무 행동을 설명하는 데 도움이 된다. 예를 들어, 한 연구는 아동 학대와 방치의 피해자들이 장기간의 영향을 겪는지도 모른다는 것을 보여주었다. 그것들 중에서는 낮은 IQ와 읽기 능력, 더 많은 자살 시도와 더 높은 실업률과 더 많은 저임금 직

업들이 있다. 오늘날 많은 사람들이 인간 발달 단계 중 성인기 연구에 관심을 갖게 되었다. 발달 심리학자들의 연구는 중년의 위기와 같은 중년의 문제들에 대한 폭넓은 관심을 이끌었다. 발달 심리학자들에게 흥미로운 직업과 관련된 문제는 왜 그렇게 많은 임원들이 은퇴 후에 예상된 것보다 더 일찍 죽는지 이다.

해설 지문 앞부분에서 발달 심리학자들은 태아기부터 성인기와 노년기까지 행동과 성장 유형을 연구한다는 내용이 있으므로, 발달 심리학자들은 인간의 일생의 행동과 성장을 연구한다는 것을 알 수 있다. 따라서 ②번이 정답이다.

오답
분석
① 아동 심리학자들은 출생부터 11세까지의 개인에 대한 연구에 집중한다는 내용이 있으므로, 아동심리학의 연구대상이 주로 사춘기 이후의 아동이라는 것은 지문의 내용과 다르다.
③ 한 연구는 아동 학대와 방치의 피해자들이 더 많은 실업률을 겪을 수 있다는 것을 보여 준다고 했으므로, 아동기에 학대 받은 성인의 실업률이 더 낮은 경향이 있다는 것은 지문의 내용과 다르다.
④ 발달 심리학자들이 흥미를 갖는 직업과 관련된 문제는 많은 임원들이 은퇴 후에 예상된 것보다 더 일찍 죽는 이유라는 내용이 있으므로, 임원들의 은퇴 후 조기 사망이 최근 임상 심리학의 관심사라는 것은 지문의 내용과 다르다.

어휘 psychologist 심리학자 concentrate 집중하다
developmental 발달의 prenatal period 태아기 clinical 임상의
specialize in ~을 전문으로 하다 shed light on 설명하다
victim 피해자, 희생자 abuse 학대 neglect 방치, 유기
long-term 장기간의 consequence 영향, 결과 suicide 자살
attempt 시도, 노력 executive 임원, 관리자 retirement 은퇴

07 독해 전체내용 파악 (문단 요약) 난이도 ★★☆

끊어읽기 해석

One presentation factor / that can influence decision making / is the contrast effect.
한 가지 설명 요소는 / 의사 결정에 영향을 줄 수 있는 / 대비 효과이다

For example, / a $70 sweater may not seem / like a very good deal / initially, / but / if you learn / that the sweater was reduced from $200, / all of a sudden / it may seem / like a real bargain.
예를 들어 / 70달러짜리 스웨터는 아마 보이지 않을 것이다 / 아주 좋은 거래처럼 / 처음에는 / 하지만 / 당신이 알게 된다면 / 그 스웨터가 200달러에서 할인되었다는 것을 / 갑자기 / 그것은 아마 보일 것이다 / 매우 싸게 산 물건처럼

It is the contrast / that "seals the deal."
바로 대비이다 / '거래를 성사시킨' 것은

Similarly, / my family lives in Massachusetts, / so we are very used to cold weather.
유사하게 / 우리 가족은 매사추세츠에 산다 / 그래서 우리는 추운 날씨에 매우 익숙하다

But / when we visit Florida / to see my aunt and uncle / for Thanksgiving, / they urge the kids / to wear hats / when it is 60 degree outside / —virtually / bathing suit weather / from the kids' perspective!
그러나 / 우리가 플로리다를 방문하면 / 이모와 삼촌을 보기 위해 / 추수감사절에 / 그들은 아이들에게 재촉한다 / 모자를 쓸 것을 / 밖이 60도(섭씨 15도)일 때 / 사실상 / 수영할 날씨인 / 아이들의 관점에서는

Research even shows / that people eat more / when they are eating / on large plates / than when eating / from small plates; / the same portion simply looks larger / on a small plate / than a large plate, / and we use perceived portion size / as a cue / that tells us / when we are full.

연구는 심지어 보여준다 / 사람들이 더 많이 먹는다는 것을 / 그들이 먹을 때 / 큰 접시에 / 먹을 때 보다 / 작은 접시에 / 같은 양도 단순히 더 많게 보인다 / 작은 접시에서 / 큰 접시에서 보다 / 그리고 우리는 인식된 분량을 사용한다 / 신호로 / 우리에게 말해주는 / 언제 우리가 배부른지

해석 의사 결정에 영향을 줄 수 있는 한 가지 설명 요소는 대비 효과이다. 예를 들어, 70달러짜리 스웨터는 처음에는 아마 아주 좋은 거래처럼 보이지 않을 것이지만 당신이 그 스웨터가 200달러에서 할인되었다는 것을 알게 된다면 아마 그것은 갑자기 매우 싸게 산 물건처럼 보일 것이다. '거래를 성사시킨' 것은 바로 대비이다. 유사하게, 우리 가족은 매사추세츠에 살아서 우리는 추운 날씨에 매우 익숙하다. 그러나 우리가 추수감사절에 이모와 삼촌을 보기 위해 플로리다를 방문하면, 그들은 밖이 아이들의 관점에서는 사실상 수영할 날씨인 60도(섭씨 15도)일 때 아이들에게 모자를 쓸 것을 재촉한다. 연구는 심지어 사람들이 작은 접시에 먹을 때 보다 큰 접시에 먹을 때 그들이 더 많이 먹는다는 것을 보여준다. 같은 양도 단순히 큰 접시에서 보다 작은 접시에서 더 많게 보이고, 우리는 인식된 분량을 언제 우리가 배부른지 우리에게 말해주는 신호로 사용한다.

> 대비 효과는 (B) 이전의 경험과의 가장 두드러진 비교에 따라 여러 가지 방식으로 자극을 (A) 인식하는 경향이다.

	(A)	(B)
①	인식하다	이전의 경험
②	제공하다	예측된 미래
③	인식하다	뜻밖의 사건들
④	제공하다	첫 인상들

해설 지문의 처음에서 의사 결정에 영향을 줄 수 있는 한 가지 설명 요소는 대비 효과라고 한 뒤, 처음에는 비싸다고 느낀 물건이 원래 가격에서 크게 할인된 가격에 판매되고 있음을 알게 되면 저렴한 물건이라고 느낀다는 점, 플로리다 사람은 추운 지방인 매사추세츠에 사는 사람들이 수영을 할 수 있을 온도를 춥다고 느낀다는 점, 접시 크기에 따라 사람이 배부르다고 인식하는 음식의 양이 달라진다는 점을 예로 들어 대비 효과에 대해 설명하고 있으므로, (A)와 (B)에는 대비 효과는 '이전의 경험'과의 가장 두드러진 비교에 따라 여러 가지 방식으로 자극을 '인식하는' 경향이라는 내용이 와야 적절하다.
따라서 ① (A) perceive(인식하다) – (B) previous experience (이전의 경험)가 정답이다.

어휘 presentation 설명 factor 요소 contrast 대비, 대조 deal 거래 initially 처음에는 bargain 싸게 산 물건 seal the deal 거래를 성사시키다 urge 재촉하다, 강요하다 virtually 사실상 perspective 관점 plate 접시 portion 양, 분량 perceive 인식하다 cue 신호 salient 가장 두드러진 previous 이전의 predictive 예측의 unexpected 뜻밖의

08 독해 논리적 흐름 파악 (문맥상 부적절한 어휘) 난이도 ★★★

끊어읽기 해석

Most of the fatal accidents happen / because of over speeding.
치명적인 사고의 대부분은 일어난다 / 과속 때문에

It is a natural subconscious mind / of humans / to excel.
자연스러운 잠재의식이다 / 인간의 / (남을) 능가하려고 하는 것은

If given a chance / man is sure to achieve / infinity in speed.
만약 기회가 주어진다면 / 인간은 반드시 달성할 것이다 / 속도에서 무한대를

But / when we are sharing the road / with other users / we will always remain / behind some or other vehicle.

그러나 / 우리가 도로를 공유하고 있을 때 / 다른 이용자들과 / 우리는 항상 남아있을 것이다 / 어느 차량의 뒤에

① Increase in speed multiplies / the risk of accident / and severity of injury / during accident.
속도의 ① 증가는 크게 증가시킨다 / 사고의 위험성을 / 그리고 부상의 심함을 / 사고 동안

Faster vehicles are more prone to accident / than the slower one / and the severity of accident / will also be more / in case of faster vehicles.
빠른 차량들은 사고를 당하기 더 쉽다 / 느린 것보다 / 그리고 사고의 심함도 / 또한 더 클 것이다 / 빠른 차량의 경우에

② Higher the speed, / greater the risk.
속도가 ② 더 높을수록 / 위험은 더 크다

At high speed / the vehicle needs greater distance / to stop / —i.e., braking distance.
고속에서 / 차량은 더 긴 거리가 필요하다 / 정지하기 위해 / 즉, 제동 거리가

A slower vehicle comes to halt immediately / while faster one takes long way / to stop / and also skids a ③ short distance / because of The First Law of Motion.
느린 차량은 즉시 정지한다 / 반면 빠른 것은 긴 거리가 있어야 한다 / 정지하기 위해 / 그리고 또한 ③ 짧은 거리를 미끄러진다 / 운동 제1법칙 때문에

A vehicle / moving on high speed / will have greater impact / during the crash / and hence / will cause more injuries.
차량은 / 고속으로 움직이는 / 큰 충격을 갖게 될 것이다 / 충돌하는 동안 / 그리고 따라서 / 더 많은 부상을 초래할 것이다

The ability to judge the forthcoming events / also gets ④ reduced / while driving / at faster speed / which causes error in judgment / and finally a crash.
다가오는 사건들을 판단하는 능력은 / 또한 ④ 줄어들게 된다 / 운전하는 동안 / 빠른 속도로 / 판단의 오류를 일으키는 / 그리고 결국 충돌을

해석 치명적인 사고의 대부분은 과속 때문에 일어난다. (남을) 능가하려고 하는 것은 인간의 자연스러운 잠재의식이다. 만약 기회가 주어진다면 인간은 반드시 속도에서 무한대를 달성할 것이다. 그러나 우리가 다른 이용자들과 도로를 공유하고 있을 때 우리는 항상 어느 차량의 뒤에 남아있을 것이다. 속도의 ① 증가는 사고의 위험성과 사고 동안 부상의 심함을 크게 증가시킨다. 빠른 차량들은 느린 것보다 사고를 당하기 더 쉽고 빠른 차량의 경우에 사고의 심함도 또한 더 클 것이다. 속도가 ② 더 높을수록, 위험은 더 크다. 고속에서 차량은 정지하기 위해 더 긴 거리 즉, 제동 거리가 필요하다. 빠른 것(차량)은 정지하기 위해 긴 거리가 있어야 하고, 또한 운동 제1법칙 때문에 ③ 짧은 거리를 미끄러지는 반면 느린 차량은 즉시 정지한다. 고속으로 움직이는 차량은 충돌하는 동안 큰 충격을 갖게 될 것이고 따라서 더 많은 부상을 초래할 것이다. 판단의 오류와 결국 충돌을 일으키는 빠른 속도로 운전하는 동안 다가오는 사건들을 판단하는 능력은 또한 ④ 줄어들게 된다.

해설 지문 중간에서 차량은 고속에서 정지하기 위해 제동 거리가 필요하고, 빠른 차량은 정지하기 위해 긴 거리가 있어야 한다고 했으므로, 운동의 제1법칙 때문에 짧은(short) 거리를 미끄러진다고 하는 것은 문맥상 적절하지 않다. 따라서 ③ short가 정답이다. 참고로, 주어진 short를 대신할 수 있는 어휘로는 '긴'이라는 의미의 long 등이 있다.

어휘 fatal 치명적인 over speeding 과속 natural 자연스러운, 당연한 subconscious 잠재의식의 excel (남을) 능가하다, 뛰어 나다 achieve 달성하다, 성취하다 infinity 무한대 multiply 크게 증가시키다 braking distance 제동 거리 halt 정지하다 immediately 즉시 skid 미끄러지다 forthcoming 다가오는

끊어읽기 해석

It is first necessary / to make an endeavor / to become interested in / whatever it has seemed worth while / to read.
우선 필요하다 / 노력하는 것이 / ~에 관심을 가지기 위해 / 가치가 있는 것으로 보이는 것은 무엇이든 / 읽을

The student should try earnestly / to discover / wherein others have found it good.
학생은 진지하게 노력해야 한다 / 알아내기 위해 / 어떤 점에서 다른 사람들이 그것을 좋다고 생각하는지

Every reader is at liberty / to like or to dislike / even a masterpiece; / but he is not in a position / even to have an opinion of it / until he appreciates / why it has been admired.
모든 독자는 자유가 있다 / 좋아하거나 싫어할 / 걸작이라도 / 하지만 그는 ~할 입장은 아니다 / 그것에 대한 의견을 가질 / 그가 진가를 알아볼 때까지 / 왜 그것이 찬사를 받아왔는지

He must set himself / to realize / not what is bad / in a book, / but what is good.
그는 반드시 노력해야 한다 / 깨닫기 위해 / 무엇이 나쁜지가 아니라 / 책에서 / 무엇이 좋은지를

The common theory / that the critical faculties are best developed / by training the mind / to detect shortcoming / is as vicious as it is false.
일반적인 이론은 / 비판적인 능력이 가장 잘 발달된다는 / 정신을 훈련시킴으로써 / 단점을 발견하기 위해 / 그것이 거짓인 것만큼 잔인하다

Any carper can find the faults / in a great work; / it is only the enlightened / who can discover / all its merits.
어느 트집쟁이든 결점을 찾을 수 있다 / 위대한 작품에서 / 오직 계몽된 사람이다 / 발견할 수 있는 것은 / 그것의 모든 가치를

It will seldom happen / that a sincere effort / to appreciate good book / will leave the reader uninterested.
거의 일어나지 않을 것이다 / 진정한 노력이 / 좋은 책의 진가를 알아보기 위한 / 독자를 흥미가 없도록 만드는 일은

해석 읽을 가치가 있는 것으로 보이는 것은 무엇이든 관심을 가지기 위해 노력하는 것이 우선 필요하다. 학생은 어떤 점에서 다른 사람들이 그것을 좋다고 생각하는지 알아내기 위해 진지하게 노력해야 한다. 모든 독자는 걸작이라도 좋아하거나 싫어할 자유가 있지만, 왜 그것이 찬사를 받아왔는지 진가를 알아볼 때까지 그는 그것에 대한 의견을 가질 입장은 아니다. 그는 책에서 무엇이 나쁜지가 아니라, 무엇이 좋은지를 깨닫기 위해 반드시 노력해야 한다. 단점을 발견하기 위해 정신을 훈련시킴으로써 비판적인 능력이 가장 잘 발달된다는 일반적인 이론은 그것이 거짓인 것만큼 잔인하다. 어느 트집쟁이든 위대한 작품에서 결점을 찾을 수 있다. 그것의 모든 가치를 발견할 수 있는 것은 오직 계몽된 사람이다. 좋은 책의 진가를 알아보기 위한 진정한 노력이 독자를 흥미가 없도록 만드는 일은 거의 일어나지 않을 것이다.
① 한 책의 평판을 훼손할 수 있는 결점에 주목해라.
② 작품을 평가하기 전 읽어보려고 노력하면서 그것의 가치를 이해하려고 노력해라.
③ 관심이 가는 책뿐만 아니라 무관심한 책도 읽어라.
④ 책을 다 읽기 전까지는 주제를 비판적으로 바라봐라.

해설 지문 처음에서 읽을 가치가 있어 보이는 것에 관심을 가지기 위해 노력하는 것이 우선 필요하다고 하고, 지문 중간에서 독자는 걸작이라도 좋아하거나 싫어할 자유가 있지만 걸작의 진가를 알아볼 때까지 그것에 대한 의견을 가질 입장은 아니라고 하며 책에서 무엇이 나쁜지가 아니라 무엇이 좋은지를 깨닫기 위해 노력해야 한다고 설명하고 있다. 따라서 이 지문의 요지를 '작품을 평가하기

전 읽어보려고 노력하면서 그것의 가치를 이해하려고 노력해라'라고 표현한 ②번이 정답이다.

어휘 endeavor 노력 worth while 가치가 있는 earnestly 진지하게 be at liberty to ~할 자유가 있다 masterpiece 걸작 appreciate (진가를) 알아보다, 인정하다 critical 비판적인 faculty 능력, 기능 detect 발견하다 shortcoming 단점 vicious 잔인한, 악랄한 carper 트집쟁이, 혹평가 fault 결점 enlightened 계몽된 merit 가치

끊어읽기 해석

Most Americans are buying / organic foods / because of health concerns.
대부분의 미국인들은 구매하고 있다 / 유기농 식품을 / 건강에 대한 관심 때문에

① More than half of the public says / that organic fruits and vegetables are better / for one's health / than conventionally grown produce.
① 절반 이상의 대중들은 말한다 / 유기농 과일과 야채가 더 좋다고 / 건강에 / 전통적으로 재배된 농산물보다

② More than forty percent say / organic produce is neither better nor worse / for one's health / and the least number of people say / that organic produce is worse / for one's health.
② 40퍼센트 이상은 말한다 / 유기농 농산물은 더 좋지도 더 나쁘지도 않다고 / 건강에 / 그리고 가장 적은 수의 사람들은 말한다 / 유기농 농산물이 더 나쁘다고 / 건강에

③ Fewer Americans say / organic produce tastes better / than conventionally grown fruits and vegetables.
③ 보다 소수의 미국인들은 말한다 / 유기농 농산물이 맛이 더 좋다고 / 전통적으로 재배된 과일과 야채들보다

④ About one-third of U.S. adults say / that organic produce tastes better, / and over two-thirds of people says / that organic and conventionally grown produce / taste about the same.
④ 미국 성인들의 약 3분의 1은 말한다 / 유기농 농산물이 맛이 더 좋다고 / 그리고 3분의 2 이상의 사람들은 말한다 / 유기농과 전통적으로 재배된 농산물이 / 거의 맛이 비슷하다고

해석 대부분의 미국인들은 유기농 식품을 건강에 대한 관심 때문에 구매하고 있다. ① 절반 이상의 대중들은 유기농 과일과 야채가 전통적으로 재배된 농산물보다 건강에 더 좋다고 말한다. ② 40퍼센트 이상은 유기농 농산물은 건강에 더 좋지도 더 나쁘지도 않다고 말하고 가장 적은 수의 사람들은 유기농 농산물이 건강에 더 나쁘다고 말한다. ③ 보다 소수의 미국인들은 전통적으로 재배된 과일과 야채들보다 유기농 농산물이 맛이 더 좋다고 말한다. ④ 미국 성인들의 약 3분의 1은 유기농 농산물이 맛이 더 좋다고 말하고, 3분의 2 이상의 사람들은 유기농과 전통적으로 재배된 농산물이 거의 맛이 비슷하다고 말한다.

해설 제시된 도표를 보면, 유기농과 전통적으로 재배된 농산물이 맛이 비슷하다고 말한 사람들은 59퍼센트이므로, 3분의 2 이상의 사람들이 유기농과 전통적으로 재배된 농산물이 거의 맛이 비슷하다고 말했다는 것은 도표의 내용과 다르다. 따라서 ④번이 정답이다.

어휘 organic 유기농의 concern 관심, 걱정 conventionally 전통적으로 produce 농산물

끊어읽기 해석

> Much of the communication / between doctor and patient / is personal.
> 많은 대화는 / 의사와 환자 사이의 / 사적이다
>
> To have a good partnership / with your doctor, / it is important / to talk about sensitive subjects, / like sex or memory problems, / even if you are embarrassed or uncomfortable.
> 좋은 관계를 갖기 위해서는 / 당신의 의사와 / 중요하다 / 민감한 주제들에 대해 이야기 하는 것이 / 섹스나 기억력 문제와 같은 / 비록 당신이 쑥스럽거나 불편할지라도
>
> Most doctors are used to / talking about personal matters / and will try to ease / your discomfort.
> 대부분의 의사들은 익숙하다 / 사적인 문제들에 대해 이야기 하는 것에 / 그리고 덜어주기 위해 노력할 것이다 / 당신의 불편함을
>
> Keep in mind / that these topics concern / many older people.
> 명심해라 / 이러한 주제들은 관련이 있다는 것을 / 다수의 노인들과
>
> You can use booklets and other materials / to help you bring up sensitive subjects / when talking / with your doctor.
> 당신은 소책자나 다른 자료들을 사용할 수 있다 / 당신이 민감한 주제를 꺼내도록 도와주는 / 이야기 할 때 / 당신의 의사와
>
> It is important to understand / that problems / with memory, depression, sexual function, and incontinence / are not necessarily normal parts of aging.
> 이해하는 것은 중요하다 / 문제들은 / 기억, 우울증, 성 기능 그리고 요실금에 대한 / 반드시 노화의 보편적인 부분들이 아니라는 것을
>
> A good doctor will take your concerns / about these topics / seriously / and not brush them off.
> 좋은 의사는 당신의 걱정들을 받아들일 것이다 / 이러한 주제들에 대한 / 진지하게 / 그리고 그것들을 무시하지 않을 것이다
>
> If you think / your doctor isn't taking your concerns / seriously, / talk to him or her / about your feelings / or consider looking for a new doctor.
> 만약 당신이 생각한다면 / 당신의 의사가 당신의 걱정들을 받아들이고 있지 않다고 / 진지하게 / 그 또는 그녀에게 이야기 해라 / 당신의 기분에 대해 / 혹은 새로운 의사를 찾는 것을 고려해봐라

해석 의사와 환자 사이의 많은 대화는 사적이다. 당신의 의사와 좋은 관계를 갖기 위해서는, 비록 당신이 쑥스럽거나 불편할지라도, 섹스나 기억력 문제와 같은 민감한 주제들에 대해 이야기 하는 것이 중요하다. 대부분의 의사들은 사적인 문제들에 대해 이야기 하는 것에 익숙하고 당신의 불편함을 덜어주기 위해 노력할 것이다. 이러한 주제들은 다수의 노인들과 관련이 있다는 것을 명심해라. 당신은 당신은 의사와 이야기 할 때 당신이 민감한 주제를 꺼내도록 도와주는 소책자나 다른 자료들을 사용할 수 있다. 기억, 우울증, 성 기능 그리고 요실금에 대한 문제들은 반드시 노화의 보편적인 부분들이 아니라는 것을 이해하는 것은 중요하다. 좋은 의사는 이러한 주제들에 대한 당신의 걱정들을 진지하게 받아들일 것이고 그것들을 무시하지 않을 것이다. 만약 당신의 의사가 당신의 걱정들을 진지하게 받아들이고 있지 않다고 생각한다면, 그 또는 그녀에게 당신의 기분에 대해 이야기하거나 새로운 의사를 찾는 것을 고려해봐라.

① 당신과 민감한 문제에 대해 이야기하다
② 당신이 가진 어떤 걱정을 무시하다
③ 당신이 말한 것에 대해 편안하게 느끼다
④ 불편한 문제를 진지하게 다루다

해설 밑줄 친 brush them off가 있는 문장을 통해 좋은 의사는 당신의 걱정들을 진지하게 받아들일 것이고 어떻게 하지 않을 것인

지를 지문에서 추론해야 한다는 것을 알 수 있다. 지문 마지막에서 만약 당신의 의사가 당신의 걱정들을 진지하게 받아들이고 있지 않다고 생각한다면, 그 또는 그녀에게 당신의 기분에 대해 이야기하거나 새로운 의사를 찾는 것을 고려해보라고 하고 있으므로, brush them off의 의미를 '당신이 가진 어떤 걱정을 무시하다'라고 한 ②번이 정답이다.

어휘 personal 사적인, 개인적인   sensitive 민감한
embarrassed 쑥스러운   uncomfortable 불편한
ease (불편함을) 덜어주다   discomfort 불편함
seriously 진지하게, 심각하게   brush off 무시하다

12 독해 추론 (빈칸 완성 - 구)   난이도 ★★☆

끊어읽기 해석

> Although we all possess / the same physical organs / for sensing the world / —eyes for seeing, / ears for hearing, / noses for smelling, / skin for feeling, / and mouths for tasting / —our perception of the world / depends to a great extent / on the language / we speak, / according to a famous hypothesis / proposed by linguists Edward Sapir and Benjamin Lee Whorf.
> 비록 우리는 모두 가지고 있지만 / 같은 신체 기관을 / 세상을 느끼기 위한 / 시각을 위한 눈 / 청각을 위한 귀 / 후각을 위한 코 / 촉감을 위한 피부 / 그리고 미각을 위한 입인 / 세상에 대한 우리의 인식은 / 상당 부분 달려 있다 / 언어에 / 우리가 말하는 / 유명한 가설에 따르면 / 언어학자 Edward Sapir와 Benjamin Lee Whorf에 의해 제시된
>
> They hypothesized / that language is like a pair of eyeglasses / through which we "see" the world / in a particular way.
> 그들은 가설을 세웠다 / 언어는 한 쌍의 안경과 같다고 / 우리가 그것(안경)을 통해 세상을 '보는' / 특정한 방식으로
>
> A classic example of the relationship / between language and perception / is the word snow.
> 관계에 대한 전형적인 사례는 / 언어와 인식 사이의 / 눈이라는 단어이다
>
> Eskimo languages have / as many as 32 different words / for snow.
> 에스키모 언어는 가지고 있다 / 무려 32가지나 되는 각양각색의 단어들을 / 눈에 대한
>
> For instance, / the Eskimos have / different words / for falling snow, / snow on the ground, / snow packed as hard as ice, / slushy snow, / wind-driven snow, / and what we might call "cornmeal" snow.
> 예를 들어 / 에스키모인들은 가지고 있다 / 여러 가지 단어들을 / 떨어지는 눈에 대한 / 땅 위의 눈 / 얼음처럼 단단히 뭉쳐진 눈 / 질척거리는 눈 / 바람에 날리는 눈 / 그리고 우리가 '옥수숫가루' 눈이라고 부를지도 모르는 것
>
> The ancient Aztec languages of Mexico, / in contrast, / used only one word / to mean snow, cold, and ice.
> 멕시코의 고대 아즈텍 언어는 / 반면에 / 오직 한 가지 단어를 사용했다 / 눈, 추위, 그리고 얼음을 의미하는
>
> Thus, / if the Sapir-Whorf hypothesis is correct / and we can perceive / only things that we have words for, / the Aztecs perceived / snow, cold, and ice / as one and the same phenomenon.
> 따라서 / 만약 Sapir-Whorf의 가설이 정확하다면 / 그리고 우리는 인식할 수 있다면 / 우리가 단어로 가진 것들만 / 아즈텍인들은 인식했다 / 눈, 추위, 그리고 얼음을 / 단일의 동일한 현상으로

해석 언어학자 Edward Sapir와 Benjamin Lee Whorf에 의해 제시된 유명한 가설에 따르면, 비록 우리는 모두 세상을 느끼기 위한 시각을 위한 눈, 청각을 위한 귀, 후각을 위한 코, 촉감을 위한 피부, 그리고 미각을 위한 입인 같은 신체 기관을 가지고 있지만, 세상에 대한 우리의 인식은 우리가 말하는 언어에 상당 부분 달려 있다. 그들은 언어는 우리가 그것(안경)을 통해 특정한 방식으로 세상

을 '보는' 한 쌍의 안경과 같다고 가설을 세웠다. 언어와 인식 사이의 관계에 대한 전형적인 사례는 눈이라는 단어이다. 에스키모 언어는 무려 32가지나 되는 눈에 대한 각양각색의 단어들을 가지고 있다. 예를 들어, 에스키모인들은 떨어지는 눈, 땅 위의 눈, 얼음처럼 단단히 뭉쳐진 눈, 질척거리는 눈, 바람에 날리는 눈, 그리고 우리가 '옥수숫가루' 눈이라고 부를 지도 모르는 것에 대한 여러 가지 단어들을 가지고 있다. 반면에, 멕시코의 고대 아즈텍 언어는 눈, 추위, 그리고 얼음을 의미하는 오직 한 가지 단어를 사용했다. 따라서, 만약 Sapir-Whorf의 가설이 정확하고 우리는 우리가 단어로 가진 것들만 인식할 수 있다면, 아즈텍인들은 눈, 추위, 그리고 얼음을 <u>단일의 동일한 현상</u>으로 인식했다.

① 단일의 동일한 현상
② 서로 별개의 것
③ 각자 특성을 가진 분리된 것
④ 특수한 신체 기관을 통해서 느껴지는 어떤 것

해설 빈칸이 있는 문장을 통해 빈칸에 아즈텍인들은 눈, 추위, 그리고 얼음을 어떻게 인식했는지에 대한 내용이 나와야 적절하다는 것을 알 수 있다. 지문 중간에서 에스키모 언어는 눈에 대한 여러 가지의 단어를 32개만큼 가지고 있는 반면에 멕시코의 고대 아즈키모 언어는 눈, 추위, 얼음을 의미하는 오직 한 가지 단어를 사용했다고 하고, 빈칸 앞부분에서 Sapir-Whorf의 가설이 정확하고 우리가 단어로 가진 것들만 인식하는 상황을 가정하고 있으므로, 아즈텍인들은 눈, 추위와 얼음을 '단일의 동일한 현상'으로 인식했다고 한 ①번이 정답이다.

어휘 organ 기관, 장기 sense 느끼다 perception 인식
hypothesis 가설 linguist 언어학자 hypothesize 가설을 세우다
phenomenon 현상 distinct 별개의, 뚜렷한 separate 분리된

---

13 독해 논리적 흐름 파악 (문장 삽입) 난이도 ★☆☆

끊어읽기 해석

"Soft power" / on the contrary / is "the ability / to achieve goals / through attraction and persuasion, / rather than coercion or fee."
'소프트 파워'는 / 반대로 / 능력이다 / 목표에 도달하는 / 유인과 설득을 통해 / 강제나 요금보다는

The concept of "soft power" / was formed / in the early 1990s / by the American political scientist, / deputy defense / of the Clinton's administration, / Joseph Nye, Jr.
'소프트 파워'의 개념은 / 만들어졌다 / 1990년대 초에 / 미국 정치학자이자 / 국방부 차관이었던 / 클린턴 행정부의 / Joseph Nye, Jr.에 의해

The ideas of the American Professor J. Nye / allowed to take a fresh look / at the interpretation / of the concept of "power," / provoked scientific debate / and stimulated the practical side / of international politics.
미국인 교수 J. Nye의 의견은 / 새롭게 바라볼 수 있게 했다 / 해석을 / '힘'의 개념에 대한 / 과학적인 논쟁을 유발했다 / 그리고 실용적인 측면을 자극했다 / 국제정치의

(①) In his works / he identifies two types of power: / "hard power" and "soft power."
그의 연구에서 / 그는 두 종류의 힘을 확인한다 / '하드 파워'와 '소프트 파워'로

(②) He defines "hard power" / as "the ability / to get others to act / in ways / that contradict their initial preferences and strategies."
그는 '하드 파워'를 정의한다 / '능력으로 / 다른 사람들이 행동하도록 하는 / 방법으로 / 그들의 처음 선호와 전략들에 모순되는'

(③) The "soft power" / of the state / is its ability / to "charm" other participants / in the world political process, / to demonstrate the attractiveness / of its own culture / (in a context / it is attractive / to others), / political values and foreign policy / (if considered / legitimate and morally justified).
'소프트 파워'는 / 국가의 / 그것(국가)의 능력이다 / 다른 참여자들을 '매혹시키는' / 전 세계의 정치 과정에서 / 매력을 입증하는 / 그것의 고유한 문화의 / (맥락에서 / 그것이 매력적이라는 / 다른 사람들에게) / 정치적 가치와 외교 정책 / (만약 여겨진다면 / 합법적이고 도덕적으로 정당하다고)

(④) The main components / of "soft power" / are culture, political values and foreign policy.
주요 구성 요소는 / '소프트 파워'의 / 문화, 정치적 가치 그리고 외교 정책이다

해석 '소프트 파워'의 개념은 1990년대 초에 미국 정치학자이자 클린턴 행정부의 국방부 차관이었던 Joseph Nye, Jr.에 의해 만들어졌다. 미국인 교수 J. Nye의 의견은 '힘'의 개념에 대한 해석을 새롭게 바라볼 수 있게 했고, 과학적인 논쟁을 유발했으며 국제정치의 실용적인 측면을 자극했다. 그의 연구에서 그는 '하드 파워'와 '소프트 파워'로 두 종류의 힘을 확인한다. 그는 '하드 파워'를 '그들의 처음 선호와 전략들에 모순되는 방법으로 다른 사람들이 행동하도록 하는 능력'으로 정의한다. ③ 반대로 '소프트 파워'는 강제나 요금 보다는 유인과 설득을 통해 목표에 도달하는 능력이다. 국가의 '소프트 파워'는 전 세계의 정치 과정에서 다른 참여자들을 '매혹시키고' 그것의 고유한 문화 (그것이 다른 사람들에게 매력적이라는 맥락에서), 정치적 가치와 외교 정책 (만약 합법적이고 도덕적으로 정당하다고 여겨진다면)의 매력을 입증하는 그것(국가)의 능력이다. '소프트 파워'의 주요 구성 요소는 문화, 정치적 가치 그리고 외교 정책이다.

해설 ③번 앞 문장에 그(J. Nye)는 그의 연구에서 '하드 파워'로 '소프트 파워'로 두 종류의 힘을 확인하는데, '하드 파워'를 그들의 처음 선호와 전략들에 모순되는 방법으로 다른 사람들이 행동하도록 하는 능력으로 정의한다는 내용이 있으므로, ③번 자리에 반대로 '소프트 파워'는 강제나 요금 보다는 유인과 설득을 통해 목표에 도달하는 능력이라는 주어진 문장이 나와야 지문이 자연스럽게 연결된다. 따라서 ③번이 정답이다.

어휘 attraction 유인 persuasion 설득 coercion 강제
political scientist 정치학자 interpretation 해석
provoke 유발하다 stimulate 자극하다 practical 실용적인
define 정의하다 preference 선호 demonstrate 입증하다
legitimate 합법적인 morally 도덕적으로 justified 정당한

---

14 독해 전체내용 파악 (주제 파악) 난이도 ★★☆

끊어읽기 해석

The rapidity / of AI deployment / in different fields / depends on a few critical factors: / retail is particularly suitable / for a few reasons.
속도는 / 인공지능이 배치되는 / 다양한 분야에 / 몇 가지 중요한 요소들에 달려있다 / 소매업이 특히 적절하다 / 몇 가지 이유 때문에

The first is the ability / to test and measure.
첫 번째는 능력이다 / 시험하고 측정하는

With appropriate safeguards, / retail giants can deploy AI / and test and measure / consumer response.
적절한 안전장치와 함께 / 소매 업체는 인공지능을 배치할 수 있다 / 그리고 시험하고 측정할 수 있다 / 소비자 반응을

They can also directly measure the effect / on their bottom line / fairly quickly.

그들은 또한 직접적으로 영향을 측정할 수 있다 / 순이익에 대한 / 상당히 빠르게

The second is the relatively small consequences / of a mistake.
둘째는 상대적으로 작은 결과들이다 / 실수로 인한

An AI agent / landing a passenger aircraft / cannot afford to make a mistake / because it might kill people.
인공지능은 / 여객기를 착륙시키는 / 실수를 해서는 안 된다 / 그것은 사람들을 죽일 수도 있기 때문에

An AI agent / deployed in retail / that makes millions of decisions every day / can afford to make some mistakes, / as long as the overall effect is positive.
인공지능은 / 소매업에 배치된 / 매일 수백만의 결정을 내리는 / 실수를 할 여유가 있다 / 전반적인 결과가 긍정적이기만 하면

Some smart robot technology / is already happening / in retail.
일부 똑똑한 로봇 기술은 / 이미 일어나고 있는 중이다 / 소매업에서

But / many of the most significant changes / will come / from deployment of AI / rather than physical robots or autonomous vehicles.
그러나 / 대부분의 중요한 변화들 중 다수는 / 올 것이다 / 인공지능의 배치로부터 / 물리적 로봇이나 자율주행 차량 보다는

해석 다양한 분야에 인공지능이 배치되는 속도는 몇 가지 중요한 요소들에 달려있고 몇 가지 이유 때문에 소매업이 특히 적절하다. 첫 번째는 시험하고 측정하는 능력이다. 적절한 안전장치와 함께, 소매 업체는 인공지능을 배치할 수 있고 소비자 반응을 시험하고 측정할 수 있다. 그들은 또한 직접적으로 순이익에 대한 영향을 상당히 빠르게 측정할 수 있다. 둘째는 실수로 인한 상대적으로 작은 결과들이다. 여객기를 착륙시키는 인공지능은 사람들을 죽일 수도 있기 때문에 실수를 해서는 안 된다. 소매업에 배치된 매일 수백만의 결정을 내리는 인공지능은 전반적인 결과가 긍정적이기만 하면 실수를 할 여유가 있다. 일부 똑똑한 로봇 기술은 소매업에서 이미 일어나고 있는 중이다. 그러나 대부분의 중요한 변화들 중 다수는 물리적 로봇이나 자율주행 차량 보다는 인공지능의 배치로부터 올 것이다.

① 인공지능 에이전트의 위험
② 소매업이 인공지능에 적합한 이유
③ 소매 기술과 수용력
④ 인공지능 발달의 중요 요소

해설 지문 앞부분에서 인공지능이 배치되는 속도는 몇 가지 중요한 요소들에 달려있고 몇 가지 이유 때문에 소매업이 적절하다고 한 뒤, 소매 업체는 인공지능을 배치하여 소비자 반응을 시험하고 측정할 수 있고, 소매업에 배치된 인공지능은 전반적인 결과가 긍정적이기만 하면 실수를 할 여유가 있다고 하며 그 장점을 설명하고 있다. 따라서 이 지문의 주제를 '소매업이 인공지능에 적합한 이유'라고 표현한 ②번이 정답이다.

어휘 **rapidity** 속도 **deployment** 배치 **suitable** 적절한
measure 측정하다 **appropriate** 적절한 **safeguard** 안전장치
bottom line 순이익 **fairly** 상당히 **relatively** 상대적으로
consequence 결과 **passenger aircraft** 여객기
autonomous 자율적인 **hospitality** 수용력, 환대

끊어읽기 해석

"What goes around comes around" is the basic understanding / of how karma works.
'뿌린 대로 거둔다'는 기본적인 이해이다 / 카르마가 어떻게 작동하는가에 대한

The word karma / literally means "activity."
카르마라는 단어는 / 글자 그대로 '행동'을 의미한다

Karma can be divided up / into a few simple categories / —good, bad, individual and collective.
카르마는 나뉠 수 있다 / 몇 가지 단순한 범주들로 / 선, 악, 개인과 집단이라는

Depending on one's actions, / one will reap / the fruits of those actions.
한 사람의 행동에 따라 / 그 사람은 거둘 것이다 / 그 행동들의 결과를

The fruits may be sweet or sour, / depending on the nature / of the actions / performed.
결과는 달콤하거나 시큼할 수도 있다 / 본질에 따라 / 행동들의 / 했던

Fruits can also be reaped / in a collective manner / if a group of people / together perform a certain activity or activities.
결과는 거두어 질 수 있다 / 집단적인 방식으로 / 만약 한 무리의 사람들이 / 특정 활동이나 활동들을 함께 한다면

Everything / we say and do / determines / what's going to happen / to us / in the future.
모든 것은 / 우리가 말하고 행동하는 / 결정한다 / 일어날 일을 / 우리에게 / 미래에

Whether we act / honestly, dishonestly, / help or hurt others, / it all gets recorded and manifests / as a karmic reaction / either in this life or a future life.
우리가 행동하든지 / 정직하게 / 정직하지 못하게 / 다른 사람들을 돕든지 해를 입히든지 / 그것은 모두 기록되고 나타난다 / 카르마적인 반응으로 / 이번 생이나 다음 생에서

All karmic records are carried / with the soul / into the next life and body.
모든 카르마적인 기록은 전달된다 / 영혼과 함께 / 다음 생과 육체에

해석 '뿌린 대로 거둔다'는 카르마가 어떻게 작동하는가에 대한 기본적인 이해이다. 카르마라는 단어는 글자 그대로 '행동'을 의미한다. 카르마는 선, 악, 개인과 집단이라는 몇 가지 단순한 범주들로 나뉠 수 있다. 한 사람의 행동에 따라, 그 사람은 그 행동들의 결과를 거둘 것이다. 했던 행동들의 본질에 따라 결과는 달콤하거나 시큼할 수도 있다. 만약 한 무리의 사람들이 특정 활동이나 활동들을 함께 한다면 결과는 집단적인 방식으로 거두어 질 수 있다. 우리가 말하고 행동하는 모든 것은 미래에 우리에게 일어날 일을 결정한다. 우리가 정직하게, 정직하지 못하게 행동하든지, 다른 사람을 돕든지 해를 입히든지, 그것은 모두 기록되고 이번 생이나 다음 생에서 카르마적인 반응으로 나타난다. 모든 카르마적인 기록은 다음 생과 육체에 영혼과 함께 전달된다.

① 불운은 한꺼번에 닥친다
② 호미로 막을 데 가래로 막는다
③ 백지장도 맞들면 낫다
④ 뿌린 대로 거둔다

해설 빈칸이 있는 문장을 통해 빈칸에 카르마가 어떻게 작동하는가에 대한 기본적인 이해에 대한 내용이 나와야 한다는 것을 알 수 있다. 지문 중간에서 한 사람의 행동에 따라 그 사람은 그 행동들의 결과를 거둘 것이라고 하고, 지문 마지막에서 우리가 하는 행동들은 모두 기록되고 이번 생이나 다음 생에서 카르마적인 반응으로 나타난다고 했으므로, '뿌린 대로 거둔다'는 어떻게 카르마가 작동하는가에 대한 기본적인 이해라고 한 ④번이 정답이다.

16 독해 전체내용 파악 (요지 파악) 난이도 ★★★

끊어읽기 해석

Creating a culture / that inspires out-of-the-box thinking /
is ultimately about / inspiring people / to stretch / and
empowering them / to drive change.
문화를 만드는 것은 / 틀을 깨는 생각에 영감을 주는 / 궁극적으로는 ~에
대한 것이다 / 사람들에게 영감을 주는 것 / 더 나아가도록 / 그리고 그들
에게 권한을 부여하는 것 / 변화를 추진하기 위해

As a leader, / you need to provide support / for those
times / when change is hard, / and that support is about the
example / you set, the behaviors / you encourage / and the
achievements / you reward.
리더로서 / 당신은 힘을 보태야 한다 / ~한 시기에 / 변화가 어려운 / 그
리고 그 지지는 본보기에 대한 것이다 / 당신이 설정한 / 행동들과 / 당신이
격려한 / 그리고 성과들에 / 당신이 보상한

First, / think about the example / you set.
먼저 / 본보기에 대해 생각해라 / 당신이 설정한

Do you consistently model / out-of-the-box behaviors /
yourself?
당신은 일관되게 훌륭한 사례를 만드는가 / 틀을 깨는 행동들의 / 스스로?

Do you step up / and take responsibility and accountability, /
focus on solutions / and display curiosity?
당신은 앞으로 나가는가 / 그리고 책임과 의무를 지고 / 해결책에 집중하
고 / 그리고 호기심을 보여주는가?

Next, / find ways / to encourage and empower the people /
who are ready / to step out of the box.
다음은 / 방법을 찾아라 / 사람들에게 격려하고 권한을 부여하는 / 준비가
된 / 틀에서 벗어날

Let them know / that you recognize their efforts; / help them
refine their ideas / and decide / which risks are worth taking.
그들에게 알려주어라 / 당신이 그들의 노력을 인정한다는 것을 / 그들이
그들의 아이디어를 개선하는 것을 도와줘라 / 그리고 결정하는 것을 / 어떤
위험들이 감수할 가치가 있는 것인지

And most importantly, / be extremely mindful / of which
achievements you reward.
그리고 가장 중요한 것은 / 깊이 신경을 써라 / 어떤 성과를 당신이 보상할
것인지

Do you only recognize / the people / who play it safe?
당신은 오직 인정하는가 / 사람들을 / 안전책을 강구하는?

Or, / do you also reward / the people / who are willing to
stretch, / display out-of-the-box behaviors / and fall short of
an aggressive goal?
아니면 / 당신은 또한 보상하는가 / 사람들을 / 기꺼이 더 나아가려고 하는 /
틀을 깨는 행동을 보여주며 / 그리고 과감한 목표에 미치지 못한

해석 틀을 깨는 생각에 영감을 주는 문화를 만드는 것은 궁극적으로는
사람들에게 더 나아가도록 영감을 주고 변화를 추진하기 위해 그
들에게 권한을 부여하는 것에 대한 것이다. 리더로서, 당신은 변화
가 어려운 시기에 힘을 보태야 하고, 그 지지는 당신이 설정한 본
보기, 당신이 격려한 행동들과 당신이 보상한 성과들에 대한 것이
다. 먼저, 당신이 설정한 본보기에 대해 생각해라. 당신은 스스로
일관되게 틀을 깨는 행동들의 훌륭한 사례를 만드는가? 당신은 앞
으로 나가 책임과 의무를 지고 해결책에 집중하고 호기심을 보여
주는가? 다음은, 틀에서 벗어날 준비가 된 사람들에게 격려하고
권한을 부여하는 방법을 찾아라. 그들에게 당신이 그들의 노력을
인정한다는 것을 알려주고, 그들이 그들의 아이디어를 개선하고

어떤 위험들이 감수할 가치가 있는 것인지 결정하는 것을 도와줘
라. 그리고 가장 중요한 것은, 어떤 성과를 당신이 보상할 것인지
깊이 신경을 써라. 당신은 오직 안전책을 강구하는 사람들을 인정
하는가? 아니면, 당신은 또한 기꺼이 더 나아가려고 하고, 틀을 깨
는 행동을 보여주며 과감한 목표에 미치지 못한 사람들을 보상하
는가?

해설 지문 앞부분에서 필자는 틀을 깨는 생각에 영감을 주는 문화를 만
드는 것은 사람들에게 더 나아가도록 영감을 주고 변화를 추진하
기 위해 그들에게 권한을 부여한다고 하며 리더로서 변화가 어려
운 시기에 힘을 보태야 한다고 주장하고 있다. 따라서 필자가 주
장하는 바를 '팀원에게 창의적인 사고를 할 수 있는 토대를 만들
어줘야 한다'라고 표현한 ④번이 정답이다.

어휘 inspire 영감을 주다 ultimately 궁극적으로
stretch 더 나아가다 empower 권한을 부여하다
example 본보기 achievement 성과 consistently 일관되게
responsibility 책임 accountability 의무 curiosity 호기심
recognize 인정하다 refine 개선하다
play it safe 안전책을 강구하다 fall short of ~에 미치지 못하다
aggressive 과감한, 공격적인

17-18

끊어읽기 해석

The dictionary defines winning / as "achieving victory / over
others / in a competition, / receiving a prize or reward / for
achievement."
사전에서는 승리를 정의한다 / '승리를 성취하는 것으로 / 다른 사람을 누
르고 / 경쟁에서 / 상 또는 보상을 받는 것 / 성취에 대한'

However, / some of the most meaningful wins / of my life /
were not victories / over others, / nor were there prizes /
involved.
그러나, / 가장 의미 있는 승리 중 일부는 / 내 인생에서 / 승리가 아니었
다 / 다른 사람을 누른 / 상이 있었던 것도 아니었다 / 관련된

[17] To me, / winning means / overcoming obstacles.
나에게 / 승리는 의미한다 / 장애를 극복하는 것을

My first experience / of winning / occurred / in elementary
school gym.
나의 첫 경험은 / 승리의 / 일어났다 / 초등학교 체육관에서

Nearly every day, / after the warm up / of push-ups and squat
thrusts, / we were forced to run relays.
거의 매일 / 준비운동 후에 / 팔굽혀 펴기와 스쿼트 스러스트의 / 우리는 이
어달리기를 억지로 하게 되었다

Although I suffered from asthma / as a child, / my team won
many races.
비록 나는 천식을 겪었지만 / 어렸을 때 / 우리 팀은 많은 경주에서 이겼다

My chest would burn / terribly / for several minutes /
following these races, / but it was worth it / to feel so proud, /
not because I'd beaten others, / but because I had overcome
a handicap.
나의 가슴은 열이 났다 / 심하게 / 몇 분 동안에 / 이러한 경주 이후에 / 하지
만 가치 있는 것이었다 / 매우 자랑스럽게 느끼는 것은 / 내가 다른 사람들
을 이겼기 때문이 아니라 / 내가 장애를 극복했기 때문에

By the way, / I (A) "outgrew" / my chronic condition / by age
eleven.
어쨌든, / 나는 (A) '극복했다' / 나의 만성적인 질병을 / 11살에

In high school, / I had another experience / of winning.
고등학교에서 / 나는 또 다른 경험을 했다 / 승리의

Although I loved reading / about biology, / I could not bring
myself to dissect a frog / in lab.
비록 나는 읽는 것을 좋아했지만 / 생물학에 대해 / 나는 개구리를 해부하는
것을 할 수 없었다 / 실험실에서

비록 나는 읽는 것은 좋아했지만 / 생물학에 관해 / 나는 개구리를 해부를 할 수가 없었다 / 실험실에서

I hated the smell / of anything dead, / and the idea / of cutting open a frog / (B) disgusted me.
나는 냄새를 싫어했다 / 어떤 것이든 죽은 것의 / 그리고 ~라는 생각은 / 개구리를 잘라서 여는 / 나를 (B) 역겹게 만들었다

[18] **Every time I tried / to take the scalpel / to the frog, / my hands would shake / and my stomach would turn.**
내가 시도할 때마다 / 메스를 갖다 대려고 / 개구리에게 / 나의 손은 떨렸고 / 나의 속은 뒤집혔다

Worst of all, / my biology teacher reacted / to my futile attempts / with contempt.
최악이었던 것은 / 나의 생물학 선생님이 반응했다 / 나의 헛된 시도들에 / 무시하듯이

After an (C) amusing couple of weeks, / I decided / get hold of myself.
(C) 즐거운 몇 주가 지난 후에 / 나는 결심했다 / 침착하기로

I realized / that I was overreacting.
나는 깨달았다 / 내가 과민반응을 하고 있다는 것을

With determination, / I swept into my next lab period, / walked up to the table, / and with one swift stroke, / slit open a frog.
결심을 하여 / 나는 다음 실험 시간에 당당히 들어갔고 / 테이블까지 걸어 갔다 / 그리고 한 번의 재빠른 타격으로 / 개구리를 자르고 열었다

After that incident, / I (D) excelled / in biology.
그 사건 이후로, / 나는 (D) 뛰어나게 잘했다 / 생물학에서

I had conquered a fear / of the unknown / and discovered / something new / about myself.
나는 두려움을 정복했다 / 알려지지 않은 것에 대한 / 그리고 발견했다 / 새로운 무언가를 / 나 자신에 대한

I had won / again.
나는 승리했다 / 다시

Through these experiences, / I now know / that I appreciate life more / if have to sacrifice / to overcome / these impediments.
이러한 경험들을 통해 / 나는 이제 안다 / 내가 삶을 더 많이 고맙게 여기는 것을 / 희생해야 할지라도 / 극복하기 위해 / 이러한 장애들을

This is a positive drive / for me, / the very spirit / of winning.
이것은 긍정적인 동기이며 / 나에게 / 다름 아닌 정신이다 / 승리의

해석　사전에서는 승리를 '경쟁에서 다른 사람을 누르고 승리를 성취하고, 성취에 대한 상 또는 보상을 받는 것'으로 정의한다. 그러나, 내 인생에서 가장 의미 있는 승리 중 일부는 다른 사람을 누른 승리가 아니었고, 관련된 상이 있었던 것도 아니었다. 나에게, 승리는 장애를 극복하는 것을 의미한다. 나의 첫 승리의 경험은 초등학교 체육관에서 일어났다. 거의 매일, 팔굽혀 펴기와 스쿼트 스러스트의 준비운동 후에, 우리는 이어달리기를 억지로 하게 되었다. 비록 나는 어렸을 때 천식을 겪었지만, 우리 팀은 많은 경주에서 이겼다. 나의 가슴은 이러한 경주 이후에 몇 분 동안 심하게 열이 났지만, 자랑스럽게 느끼는 것은 내가 다른 사람들을 이겼기 때문이 아니라 내가 장애를 극복했기 때문에 가치 있는 것이었다. 어쨌든, 나는 11살에 나의 만성적인 질병을 (A) '극복했다'. 고등학교에서, 나는 또 다른 승리의 경험을 했다. 비록 나는 생물학에 관해 읽는 것은 좋아했지만, 실험실에서 개구리를 해부할 수가 없었다. 나는 어떤 것이든 죽은 것의 냄새를 싫어했고, 개구리를 잘라서 여는 생각은 나를 (B) 역겹게 만들었다. 내가 개구리에게 메스를 갖다 대려고 시도할 때마다 나의 손은 떨렸고 나의 속은 뒤집혔다. 최악이었던 것은, 나의 생물학 선생님이 나의 헛된 시도들에 무시하듯이 반응했다. (C) 즐거운 몇 주가 지난 후에, 나는 침착하기로 결심했다. 나는 내가 과민반응을 하고 있다는 것을 깨달았다. 결심을 하여 나는 다음 실험 시간에 당당히 들어갔고 테이블까지 걸어 가서 한 번

의 재빠른 타격으로 개구리를 자르고 열었다. 그 사건 이후로, 나는 생물학에서 (D) 뛰어나게 잘했다. 나는 알려지지 않은 것에 대한 두려움을 정복했고 나 자신에 대한 새로운 무언가를 발견했다. 나는 다시 승리했다. 이러한 경험들을 통해, 나는 이러한 장애들을 극복하기 위해 희생해야 할지라도 내가 삶을 더 많이 고맙게 여기는 것을 이제 안다. 이것은 나에게 긍정적인 동기이며 다름 아닌 승리의 정신이다.

어휘　**dictionary** 사전　**overcome** 극복하다　**obstacle** 장애　**occur** 일어나다　**beat** 이기다　**handicap** 장애　**outgrow** 극복하다　**chronic** 만성적인　**scalpel** 메스　**futile** 헛된　**contempt** 무시　**get hold of oneself** 침착하다　**overreact** 과민반응하다　**determination** 결심　**sweep** 당당히 들어가다　**slit** 자르다　**incident** 사건　**excel** 뛰어나게 잘하다　**conquer** 정복하다　**unknown** 알려지지 않은　**appreciate** 고마워하다　**sacrifice** 희생하다　**impediment** 장애

17　독해　전체내용 파악 (제목 파악)　난이도 ★★☆

해석　① 나에게 승리란 무엇인가
② 행복 추구
③ 후반기의 승자
④ 긍정적 사고에 대한 이야기

해설　지문 앞부분에서 나에게 승리는 장애를 극복하는 것을 의미한다고 하고, 지문 전반에 걸쳐 두려움을 정복하고 자신에 대해 새로운 무언가를 발견한 경험을 설명하고 있다. 따라서 지문의 제목을 '나에게 승리란 무엇인가'라고 표현한 ①번이 정답이다.

어휘　**pursuit** 추구　**second half** 후반기, 하반기

18　독해　논리적 흐름 파악 (문맥상 부적절한 어휘 파악)　난이도 ★★☆

해설　지문 중간에서 화자는 개구리에게 메스를 갖다 대려고 시도할 때마다 손이 떨렸고 속이 뒤집혔다고 한 뒤, 최악이었던 것은 자신의 생물학 선생님이 자신을 무시하듯이 반응했던 때라고 했으므로, '즐거운' 몇 주가 지난 후에라는 것은 문맥상 적절하지 않다. 따라서 ③번이 정답이다. 참고로, 주어진 amusing을 대신할 수 있는 어휘로는 '힘든'이라는 의미의 tough 등이 있다.

19　독해　전체내용 파악 (문단 요약)　난이도 ★☆☆

끊어읽기 해석

One classic psychology study involved / mothers and their twelve-month-old babies.
한 대표적인 심리학 연구는 참여시켰다 / 엄마들과 그들의 12개월 된 아기들을

Each mother was with her baby / throughout the study, / but the mothers were divided / into two groups, / A and B.
각각의 엄마는 그녀의 아기와 함께 있었다 / 연구 내내 / 그러나 엄마들은 나뉘어졌다 / 2개의 그룹으로 / A와 B의

Both groups A and B were exposed / to the same situation, / the only difference / being that group B mothers / had to positively encourage / their baby to continue playing / with the thing in front of them, / whereas the mothers in group A / just had to be themselves / in response to / what their baby was playing with.
A와 B그룹 모두 노출되었다 / 같은 상황에 / 유일한 차이는 / B그룹 엄마들은 / 긍정적으로 격려해야 했다 / 그들의 아기가 계속해서 놀도록 / 그들의 앞에 있는 것을 가지고 / 반면 A그룹의 엄마들은 / 단지 그들 모습 그대

로 있어야 했다 / ~에 반응하여 / 그들의 아기가 가지고 노는 것에

What / were these babies / playing with? // An extremely large / but tame python.
무엇을 / 이 아기들이 / 가지고 놀았을까? // 매우 큰 / 그러나 길들여진 비단뱀이었다

The study went as follows: / the children / from group A / were placed on the floor / so the python could slither / among them.
연구는 다음과 같이 진행됐다 / 아이들은 / A그룹의 / 바닥에 놓여졌다 / 그래서 비단뱀이 미끄러지듯이 나아갈 수 있도록 / 그들 사이에서

As the fear of snakes is innate / in humans / but isn't activated / until approximately the age of two, / these babies saw the python / as a large toy.
뱀에 대한 공포는 선천적이기 때문에 / 인간에게는 / 그러나 활성화되지 않는다 / 약 2살의 나이까지 / 이러한 아기들은 비단뱀을 보았다 / 큰 장난감으로

As the group A babies started playing / with the live python, / they looked up / to see / what their mothers were doing.
A그룹 아기들이 놀기 시작하면서 / 살아있는 비단뱀과 / 그들은 쳐다보았다 / 보기 위해 / 그들의 엄마들이 하고 있던 것을

The mothers, / who were told to be themselves, / naturally looked horrified.
엄마들은 / 그들 모습 그대로 있도록 당부받은 / 당연히 겁에 질려 보였다

Seeing the fear / on their mothers' faces, / the babies burst into tears.
공포를 보자 / 그들의 엄마들의 얼굴의 / 아기들은 울음을 터뜨렸다

When it was group B's turn, / as instructed / the mothers laughed and encouraged / their babies to keep playing / with the python.
B그룹의 차례가 되었을 때 / 지시 받은 대로 / 그 엄마들은 웃으며 격려했다 / 그들의 아기들이 계속 놀도록 / 비단뱀과

As a result / these babies were grabbing and chewing on the python, / all because their mothers were supportive / of their new toy.
그 결과 / 이 아기들은 비단뱀을 움켜쥐고 입에 물었다 / 모두 그들의 엄마들이 격려했기 때문에 / 그들의 새로운 장난감을

해석 한 대표적인 심리학 연구는 엄마들과 그들의 12개월 된 아기들을 참여시켰다. 각각의 엄마는 연구 내내 그녀의 아기와 함께 있었으나, 엄마들은 A와 B의 2개의 그룹으로 나뉘어졌다. A와 B 그룹 모두 같은 상황에 노출되었고 유일한 차이는 B그룹 엄마들은 그들의 아기가 그들의 앞에 있는 것을 가지고 계속해서 놀도록 긍정적으로 격려해야 했던 반면, A그룹의 엄마들은 그들의 아기가 가지고 노는 것에 반응하여 단지 그들 모습 그대로 있어야 했다.

이 아기들이 무엇을 가지고 놀았을까? 매우 크지만 길들여진 비단뱀이었다. 연구는 다음과 같이 진행됐다. A그룹의 아이들은 비단뱀이 그들 사이에서 미끄러지듯 나아갈 수 있도록 바닥에 놓여졌다. 인간에게는 뱀에 대한 공포는 선천적이나 약 2살의 나이까지 활성화되지 않기 때문에, 이러한 아기들은 비단뱀을 큰 장난감으로 보았다. A그룹 아기들이 살아있는 비단뱀과 놀기 시작하면서 그들은 그들의 엄마들이 하고 있던 것을 보기 위해 쳐다보았다. 그들 모습 그대로 있도록 당부받은 엄마들은 당연히 겁에 질려 보였다. 그들의 엄마들의 얼굴의 공포를 보자, 아기들은 울음을 터뜨렸다. B그룹의 차례가 되었을 때, 그 엄마들은 지시 받은 대로 그들의 아기들이 비단뱀과 계속 놀도록 웃으며 격려했다. 그 결과 모두 그들의 엄마들이 그들의 새로운 장난감을 격려했기 때문에 이 아기들은 비단뱀을 움켜쥐고 입에 물었다.

(A) 모든 공포증은 보통 아이들이 어떤 것들에 대한 부모의
(B) 반응을 관찰함으로써 학습된다.

	(A)	(B)
①	게임의 규칙들	지지
②	장난감에 대한 선호	참여
③	모든 공포증	반응
④	다양한 감정	격려

해설 지문 후반에서 A그룹의 아기들이 살아있는 비단뱀과 놀기 시작하면서 엄마들을 쳐다보았는데, 엄마들이 겁에 질린 것을 보자 울음을 터뜨렸다고 한 후, B그룹의 엄마들은 아기들이 비단뱀과 놀도록 웃으며 격려했고, 아이들은 비단뱀을 움켜쥐고 입에 물었다고 했으므로, (A)와 (B)에 '모든 공포증'은 보통 아이들이 어떤 것들에 대한 부모의 '반응'을 관찰함으로써 학습된다는 내용이 와야 적절하다.
따라서 ③ (A) All phobias(모든 공포증) – (B) reaction(반응)이 정답이다.

어휘 classic 대표적인, 전형적인 involve 참여시키다 expose 노출하다
situation 상황 positively 긍정적으로
in response to ~에 반응하여 extremely 매우 tame 길들여진
python 비단뱀 slither 미끄러지듯이 나아가다 fear 공포, 두려움
innate 선천적인 activated 활성화 된
naturally 당연히, 자연스럽게 burst into tears 울음을 터뜨리다
grab 움켜쥐다 chew on ~을 입에 물다 supportive 격려하는
preference 선호 participation 참여 phobia 공포증

20 독해 논리적 흐름 파악 (문맥상 부적절한 어휘) 난이도 ★★☆

끊어읽기 해석

According to the modernization theory / of aging, / the status of older adults declines / as societies become more modern.
근대화 이론에 따르면 / 고령화에 대한 / 노년층의 지위는 약화된다 / 사회가 더 현대화 되면서

The status of old age was low / in hunting-and-gathering societies, / but it ① rose dramatically / in stable agricultural societies, / in which older people controlled the land.
노인들의 지위는 낮았다 / 수렵채집 사회에서 / 하지만 그것은 급격하게 ① 상승했다 / 안정적인 농업사회에서 / 노인들이 토지를 통제했던

With the coming of industrialization, / it is said, / modern societies have tended / to ② revalue older people.
산업화의 도래와 함께 / 말해진다 / 현대 사회가 경향이 있다고 / 노인을 ② 재평가하는

The modernization theory / of aging / suggests / that the role and status of older adults / are ③ inversely related / to technological progress.
근대화 이론은 / 고령화에 대한 / 시사한다 / 노년층의 역할과 지위는 / ③ 반비례적으로 관계가 있다고 / 기술 발전과

Factors / such as urbanization and social mobility / tend to disperse families, / whereas technological change / tends to devalue / the wisdom or life experience / of elders.
요소들이 / 도시화와 사회적 유동성과 같은 / 가족들을 흩어지게 하는 경향이 있다 / 반면 기술적인 변화는 / 낮게 평가하는 경향이 있다 / 지혜와 인생 경험을 / 노인들의

Some investigators have found / that key elements of modernization were, / in fact, / broadly related / to the ④ declining status of older people / in different societies.
몇몇 연구자들은 발견했다 / 근대화의 핵심 요소들이 ~라는 것을 / 사실상 / 폭넓게 연관되어 있다 / 노인들의 ④ 쇠퇴하는 지위와 / 다양한 사회에서

해설 고령화에 대한 근대화 이론에 따르면, 사회가 더 현대화 되면서 노년층의 지위는 약화된다. 수렵채집 사회에서 노인들의 지위는 낮

앉지만, 그것은 노인들이 토지를 통제했던 안정적인 농업사회에서 급격하게 ① 상승했다. 산업화의 도래와 함께, 현대 사회가 노인을 ② 재평가하는 경향이 있다고 말해진다. 고령화에 대한 근대화 이론은 노년층의 역할과 지위는 기술 발전과 ③ 반비례적으로 관계가 있다고 시사한다. 도시화와 사회적 유동성과 같은 요소들이 가족들을 흩어지게 하는 경향이 있는 반면, 기술적인 변화는 노인들의 지혜와 인생 경험을 낮게 평가하는 경향이 있다. 몇몇 연구자들은 근대화의 핵심 요소들이 사실상 다양한 사회에서 노인들의 ④ 쇠퇴하는 지위와 폭넓게 연관되어 있다는 것을 발견했다.

해설 지문 앞부분에서 고령화에 대한 근대화 이론에 따르면 사회가 더 현대화 되면서 노년층의 지위가 약화된다고 한 뒤, 지문 중간에서 고령화에 대한 근대화 이론은 노년층의 역할과 지위가 기술 발전과 반비례적으로 관계가 있다고 시사한다고 했으므로 산업화의 도래와 함께 현대 사회가 노인을 '재평가하는'(revalue) 경향이 있다고 말해진다는 것은 문맥상 적절하지 않다. 따라서 ② revalue가 정답이다. 참고로, 주어진 revalue를 대신할 수 있는 어휘로는 '가치를 낮춰보다'라는 의미의 devalue가 있다.

어휘 modernization 근대화 status 지위 decline 약화되다, 쇠퇴하다
rise 상승하다 dramatically 급격하게 stable 안정적인
control 통제하다 industrialization 산업화 revalue 재평가하다
inversely 반비례적으로 urbanization 도시화 mobility 유동성
disperse 흩어지게 하다 investigator 연구자 broadly 폭넓게

21 문법 분사 난이도 ★★☆

해석 벼 줄기는 익으면 고개를 숙이고, 옥수수 낟알은 익었을 때조차도 새싹의 위에 남아 있다. 이것은 이상하게 보이지 않을 수도 있지만, 실제로 이러한 종류의 쌀과 옥수수는 자연에서 살아남으면 안 된다. 보통, 그것들(쌀과 옥수수)이 익으면, 씨앗들은 발아하기 위해 땅으로 떨어져야 한다. 그러나, 쌀과 옥수수는 돌연변이이며, 그것들은 편리하고 효율적인 수확의 목적을 위해 그것들의 씨앗들이 계속 부착되어 있도록 하기 위해 변형되어 왔다. 인간들은 이러한 현상이 발생하도록 하기 위해 재배 기술을 통해 지속적으로 그러한 돌연변이를 고르고 재배했다. 이러한 돌연변이 씨앗들은 의도적으로 퍼져나갔고, 이것은 그 식물들이 그것들의 씨앗들을 온전하게 유지하기 위해 개량된 후, 자연에서 발견되지 않는 인공적인 종이 되었다는 것을 의미한다. 이러한 품종들을 키움으로써, 가장 선호되는 씨앗들이 생산된다.

해설 ④ 분사구문의 형태 주절의 주어(the plants)와 분사구문이 '식물들이 개량되다'라는 의미의 수동 관계이고, 식물이 '개량된 것'이 '인공적인 종이 된 것'보다 이전 시점에 일어났으므로 분사구문의 완료 수동형을 써야 한다. 따라서 분사구문의 완료형 having bred를 완료 수동형 having been bred로 고쳐야 한다.

오답분석 ① 5형식 동사 동사 keep은 '~을 (어떤 상태로) 두다'라는 의미를 나타낼 때 목적어와 목적격 보어를 취하는 5형식 동사인데, 목적어(their seeds)와 목적격 보어가 '그것들의 씨앗들이 부착되어 있다'라는 의미의 수동 관계이므로 과거분사 attached가 올바르게 쓰였다.

② to 부정사의 의미상 주어 to 부정사가 목적을 나타낼 때는 to 대신 in order to를 쓸 수 있는데, 문장의 주어(Humans)와 to 부정사의 행위 주체(these phenomena)가 달라서 to 부정사의 의미상 주어가 필요할 경우 'for + 명사'를 to 부정사(to occur) 앞에 써야 하므로 for these phenomena가 올바르게 쓰였다.

③ 관계절의 용법 관계절이 콤마(,) 뒤에서 계속적 용법으로 쓰여 선행사(These mutant seeds ~ intentionally)에 대한 부가 설명을 하고 관계절 내에서 동사 means의 주어 역할을 하

고 있으므로 계속적 용법으로 쓰일 수 있는 주격 관계대명사 which가 올바르게 쓰였다.

어휘 stalk (식물의) 줄기 kernel (작은) 낟알 shoot 싹 ripe 익은
mutant 돌연변이 modify 변형하다
breed (품종을) 개량하다, 재배하다 intact 온전한 nurture 키우다

👍 이것도 알면 **합격!**

동명사의 의미상의 주어는 '명사의 소유격' 또는 '소유격 대명사'를 동명사 앞에 써서 나타내며, 분사구문의 의미상 주어는 '명사' 또는 '주격 대명사'를 분사구문 앞에 써서 나타낸다는 것을 함께 알아두자.

동명사	Becca was embarrassed by her **mother's** calling her "pumpkin" in public. Becca는 엄마가 공공 장소에서 그녀를 '호박(귀여운 아이)'이라고 부르는 것 때문에 부끄러웠다.
분사	**The seas** getting rough, the sailors tried to find a safe place to dock. 바다가 거칠어졌기 때문에, 선원들은 정박할 안전한 장소를 찾으려고 애썼다.

---

22 문법 관계절&분사 난이도 ★★☆

해석 첫인상 편향이란 우리의 첫인상이 이 사람에 대해 우리가 수집한 후속 정보가 처리되고, 기억되고, 적절하다고 보여지는 틀을 만든다는 것을 의미한다. 예를 들어, 수업 중인 Ann-Chinn을 관찰한 것을 기반으로, Loern은 그녀를 전형적인 아시아 여성으로 보고 그녀는 조용하고, 성실하며 내성적이라고 가정했을지도 모른다. 옳건 틀리건, 이러한 결론에 도달한 채, 그는 이제 Ann-Chinn의 행동을 이해하고 해석하는 데 있어 일련의 원형과 생각을 가진다. 시간이 흐르면서, 그는 그의 원형과 생각에 일치하는 행동을 그가 이미 그녀에 대해 만들어 놓은 인상에 맞춘다. 그녀가 그의 범퍼스티커의 선택지에 대해 불신을 표현하는 것을 그가 알게 될 때, 그는 그의 그것이 기존 원형과 맞지 않기 때문에 단순히 그것을 무시하거나 그녀의 실제 본성에 대한 특이한 예외로 볼 것이다.

해설 (A) 전치사+관계대명사 관계사 뒤에 완전한 절(later information ~ relevant)이 왔고, 선행사 the mold가 사물을 나타내며 문맥상 '틀에 의해 후속 정보가 처리되다'라는 의미가 되어야 자연스러우므로 관계대명사 which가 아닌 전치사 by(~에 의해)를 사용한 by which를 써야 한다.

(B) 분사구문의 형태 주절의 주어(he)와 분사구문이 '그가 결론에 도달하다'라는 의미의 능동 관계이므로 현재분사를 써야 하는데, '결론에 도달한' 시점이 '그가 원형과 생각을 가진' 시점보다 이전에 일어난 일이므로 분사구문의 완료형 Having reached를 써야 한다.

(C) 관계절 자리와 쓰임 명사(the impression)를 수식하기 위해 형용사 역할을 하는 관계절이 와야 하는데, 선행사 the impression이 사물이고 관계절 내에서 동사 has formed의 목적어 역할을 하므로 명사절 접속사 what이 아닌 목적격 관계대명사 that을 써야 한다.

따라서 ③ (A) by which – (B) Having reached – (C) that이 정답이다.

어휘 impression 인상 mold 틀 gather 수집하다 observe 관찰하다
stereotypical 전형적인 assume 가정하다
unassertive 내성적인 conclusion 결론 prototype 원형
construct 생각 interpret 해석하다 disbelief 불신
bumper sticker 범퍼스티커(자동차 범퍼에 붙인 광고 스티커)
dismiss 무시하다 exception 예외 existing 기존의, 현존하는

이것도 알면 **합격!**

분사구문의 의미를 분명하게 하기 위해 부사절 접속사가 분사구문 앞에 올 수 있다는 것을 알아두자.

ex Before landing, the crew members made sure all the passengers were seated.
착륙하기 전에, 승무원들은 모든 승객이 자리에 앉아있도록 했다.

---

23 문법 부사절 　　　　　　　　　　난이도 ★★☆

해석 아동 언어 습득에 대한 연구의 물결은 제1언어와 제2언어 습득 사이의 유사점을 도출하고, 심지어 제1언어 학습 원리에 근거한 특정 교수법과 기술들을 정당화할 목적으로 언어교사와 교사 교육 담당자들이 이러한 연구의 일반적인 결과들 중 일부를 연구하도록 이끌었다. 표면적으로는, 유추를 하는 것은 전적으로 타당하다. 정상적인 발달 환경이 주어진 모든 아이들은 그들의 모국어를 유창하고 효율적으로 습득한다. 게다가, 그들이 언어에 대한 상당한 노력과 집중이 없는 것은 아니지만, 그것들을 특별한 교육 없이 '자연스럽게' 습득한다. 그러나, 직접적인 비교는 신중하게 다루어져야 한다. 제1언어와 제2언어 학습 사이에는 수십 가지의 두드러진 차이가 있는데, 성인의 제2언어 학습의 경우 가장 분명한 차이는 어른과 아이들 사이의 인지적, 정서적 대조가 엄청나다는 것이다.

해설 ③ 부사절 자리와 쓰임 전치사(despite)의 목적어 자리에는 명사 역할을 하는 것이 와야 하는데, 뒤에 전치사구(not without ~ language)가 왔고, 전치사구(not without ~ language)는 '주어 + 동사'(they acquire)가 생략된 부사절에서 동사 acquire를 수식하는 부사 역할을 하고 있으므로 전치사 despite를 전치사구 앞에 올 수 있는 부사절 접속사 although 또는 though로 고쳐야 한다.

오답 분석 ① 병치 구문 접속사(and)로 연결된 병치 구문에서는 같은 구조끼리 연결되어야 하는데, and 앞에 전치사구(to drawing ~ acquisition)가 왔으므로, and 뒤에도 전치사구를 완성하는 justifying이 올바르게 쓰였다. 참고로, 전치사(to) 뒤에는 명사 역할을 하는 것이 와야 하므로 동명사 drawing과 justifying이 쓰였다.
② 분사구문의 형태 주절의 주어(All children)와 분사구문이 '모든 아이들이 주어지다'라는 의미의 수동 관계이므로 과거분사 given이 올바르게 쓰였다.
④ 주어와 동사의 수 일치 주어 자리에 단수 명사 the most obvious difference가 왔으므로 단수 동사 is가 올바르게 쓰였다. 참고로, 주어와 동사 사이의 수식어 거품(in ~ learning)은 동사의 수 결정에 영향을 주지 않는다.

어휘 acquisition 습득 general 일반적인 finding 결과
draw 도출하다 analogy 유사점, 유추 justify 정당화하다
principle 원리 surface 표면 entirely 전적으로
reasonable 타당한 environment 환경 fluently 유창하게
attention 집중 salient 두드러진, 눈에 띄는 tremendous 엄청난
cognitive 인지의 affective 정서적인

이것도 알면 **합격!**

③번에서와 같이 부사절 접속사(though/although)가 이끄는 부사절의 동사가 be동사일 경우, 부사절 접속사 뒤의 '주어 + 동사'는 생략할 수 있다. 의미는 유사하지만, even though가 온 경우에는 '주어 + 동사'를 생략할 수 없다는 것도 함께 기억해두자.

(생략) though/although (it is) not without significant effort and attention to language.
그들이 언어에 대한 상당한 노력과 집중이 없는 것은 아니지만 (생략)

---

24 독해 논리적 흐름 파악 (문맥상 부적절한 어휘) 　난이도 ★★☆

끊어읽기 해석

The American physiologist Hudson Hoagland saw / scientific mysteries / everywhere / and felt it his calling / to solve them.
미국 생리학자 Hudson Hoagland는 목격했다 / 과학적인 미스터리를 / 도처에서 / 그리고 그의 소명이라고 느꼈다 / 그것들을 해결하는 것이

Once, / when his wife had a fever, / Hoagland drove / to the drugstore / to get her aspirin.
한번은 / 그의 아내가 열이 났을 때 / Hoagland는 차를 몰고 갔다 / 약국에 / 그녀에게 아스피린을 주기 위해

He was quick about it, / but when he returned, / his normally ① reasonable wife complained / angrily / that he had been slow as molasses.
그는 그것을 빨리 처리했다 / 하지만 그가 돌아왔을 때 / 평소에는 ① 이성적인 그의 아내가 불평했다 / 화를 내며 / 그가 몹시 느렸다고

Hoagland wondered / if her fever had ② distorted / her internal clock, / so he took her temperature, / had her estimate / the length of a minute, / gave her the aspirin, / and continued to have her estimate / the minutes / as her temperature dropped.
Hoagland는 궁금했다 / 그녀의 열이 ② 왜곡시켰는지 / 그녀의 생체 시계를 / 그래서 그는 아내의 체온을 측정했고 / 그녀에게 추측하도록 시켰고 / 1분의 길이를 / 그녀에게 아스피린을 주었다 / 그리고 계속해서 그녀에게 추측하도록 시켰다 / 시간을 / 그녀의 체온이 내려가는 동안에

When her temperature was back / to normal / he plotted the logarithm / and found it was ③ linear.
그녀의 체온이 돌아왔을 때 / 정상으로 / 그는 로그 그래프를 그렸다 / 그리고 그것이 ③ 직선인 것을 발견했다

Later, / he continued the study / in his laboratory, / artificially raising and lowering / the temperatures of test subjects / until he was certain / he was right: / higher body temperatures make / the body clock go faster, / and his wife had not been ④ justifiably cranky.
후에 / 그는 연구를 계속했다 / 그의 실험실에서 / 인위적으로 올리고 내리면서 / 피실험자들의 체온을 / 그가 확신할 때까지 / 그가 맞다고 / 높은 체온은 만들었다 / 생체 시계가 더 빨리 가도록 / 그리고 그의 아내는 ④ 정당하게 짜증을 낸 것이 아니었다

해석 미국 생리학자 Hudson Hoagland는 도처에서 과학적인 미스터리를 목격했고 그것들을 해결하는 것이 그의 소명이라고 느꼈다. 한번은 그의 아내가 열이 났을 때, 그녀에게 아스피린을 주기 위해 Hoagland는 차를 몰고 약국에 갔다. 그는 그것을 빨리 처리했지만 그가 돌아왔을 때, 평소에는 ① 이성적인 그의 아내가 그가 몹시 느렸다고 화를 내며 불평했다. Hoagland는 그녀의 열이 그녀의 생체 시계를 ② 왜곡시켰는지 궁금해서 그는 아내의 체온을 측정했고, 그녀에게 1분의 길이를 추측하도록 시켰으며, 그녀에게 아스피린을 주었고 그녀의 체온이 내려가는 동안에 그녀에게 시간을 추측하도록 계속해서 시켰다. 그녀의 체온이 정상으로 돌아왔을 때 그는 로그 그래프를 그렸고 그것이 ③ 직선인 것을 발견했다. 후에, 그는 피실험자들의 체온을 인위적으로 올리고 내리면서, 그가 맞다고 확신할 때까지 그의 실험실에서 연구를 계속했다. 높은 체온은 생체 시계가 더 빨리 가도록 만들었고 그의 아내는 ④ 정당하게 짜증을 낸 것이 아니었다.

해설 지문 처음에서 평소에는 이성적인 Hoagland의 아내가 열이 났을 때는 Hoagland가 빨리 처리했음에도 몹시 느리게 돌아왔다고 불평했다고 하고, 지문 마지막에서 높은 체온이 생체 시계가 더 빨리 가도록 만들었다고 했으므로 그의 아내가 '정당하게'(justifiably) 짜증을 낸 것이 아니었다는 것은 문맥상 적절하지 않다. 따라서 ④ justifiably가 정답이다. 참고로, 주어진 justifiably를 대신할 수 있는 어휘로는 '이치에 맞지 않게'라는 의

미의 unjustifiably가 있다.

어휘 **physiologist** 생리학자 **calling** 소명 **drugstore** 약국
reasonable 이성적인 **slow as molasses** (동작 등이) 몹시 느린
distort 왜곡하다 **internal clock** 생체 시계
temperature 체온, 온도 **estimate** 추측하다, 어림잡다
drop 내려가다, 떨어지다 **plot** 그래프를 그리다 **linear** 직선의
laboratory 실험실 **artificially** 인위적으로 **test subject** 피실험자
justifiably 정당하게 **cranky** 짜증을 내는

---

25 독해 추론 (빈칸 완성 - 구)   난이도 ★★★

끊어읽기 해석

Saint Paul said / the invisible must be understood / by the visible.
Saint Paul은 말했다 / 눈에 보이지 않은 것은 이해되어야 한다고 / 눈에 보이는 것에 의해

That was not a Hebrew idea, / it was Greek.
그것은 유대인의 생각이 아닌 / 그리스인의 것이었다

In Greece alone / in the ancient world / people were preoccupied / with the visible; they were finding / the satisfaction of their desires / in what was actually / in the world / around them.
그리스에서만 / 고대 사회에서 / 사람들은 사로잡혔다 / 눈에 보이는 것에 / 그들은 찾고 있었다 / 그들의 욕구에 대한 만족을 / 실제로 있는 것에서 / 세계에 / 그들 주위의

The sculptor watched / the athletes contending / in the games / and he felt / that nothing / he could imagine / would be as beautiful as / those strong young bodies.
조각가는 보았고 / 운동 선수들이 겨루는 것을 / 경기에서 / 그리고 그는 생각했다 / 어떤 것도 ~하지 않다고 / 그가 상상할 수 있는 / ~만큼 아름답지 / 그렇게 튼튼한 젊은 신체만큼

So he made / his statue of Apollo.
그래서 그는 만들었다 / 그의 아폴로 조각상을

The storyteller found Hermes / among the people / he passed / in the street.
이야기꾼은 헤르메스를 발견했다 / 사람들 사이에서 / 그가 지나쳤던 / 거리의

He saw the god / "like a young men / at that age / when youth is loveliest," / as Homer says.
그는 신을 보았다 / '젊은 인간들과 똑같이 / 그 나이의 / 젊음이 가장 아름다운' / 호머가 말한 것처럼

Greek artists and poets realized / how splendid / a man could be, / straight and swift / and strong.
그리스의 예술가들과 시인들은 깨달았다 / 얼마나 눈부시고 / 인간이 ~할 수 있는지 / 곧고 재빠르며 / 그리고 강인한

He was the fulfillment / of their search for beauty.
그는 완성이었다 / 그들의 미에 대한 탐색의

They had no wish / to create some fantasy / shaped in their own minds.
그들은 소망이 없었다 / 멋진 환상을 만들어 내는 / 그들의 마음에 형성된

All the art and all the thought / of Greece / <u>put human beings / at the center.</u>
모든 예술과 생각은 / 그리스의 / <u>인간을 두었다 / 그 중심에</u>

해석 Saint Paul은 눈에 보이지 않는 것은 눈에 보이는 것에 의해 이해되어야 한다고 말했다. 그것은 유대인의 생각이 아닌 그리스인의 것이었다. 고대 사회에서 그리스에서만 사람들은 눈에 보이는 것에 사로잡혔다. 그들은 그들 주위의 세계에 실제로 있는 것에서 그들의 욕구에 대한 만족을 찾고 있었다. 조각가는 경기에서 운동 선수들이 겨루는 것을 보았고 그가 상상할 수 있는 어떤 것도 그렇게

튼튼한 젊은 신체만큼 아름답지 않다고 생각했다. 그래서 그는 그의 아폴로 조각상을 만들었다. 이야기꾼은 거리에서 그가 지나쳤던 사람들 사이에서 헤르메스를 발견했다. 그는 호머가 말한 것처럼 신을 '젊음이 가장 아름다운 그 나이의 젊은 인간들과 똑같이' 보았다. 그리스의 예술가들과 시인들은 인간이 얼마나 눈부시고, 곧고 재빠르며 강인할 수 있는지 깨달았다. 그는 그들의 미에 대한 탐색의 완성이었다. 그들은 그들의 마음에 형성된 멋진 환상을 만들어 내는 소망이 없었다. 그리스의 모든 예술과 생각은 <u>인간을 그 중심에 두었다.</u>

① 현실의 모습을 가지고 있지 않았다
② 인간을 그 중심에 두었다
③ 전능한 신과 관련이 있었다
④ 초자연적인 힘에 대한 욕망을 나타냈다

해설 빈칸이 있는 문장을 통해 빈칸에 그리스의 모든 예술과 생각은 어떠했는지에 대한 내용이 나와야 적절하다는 것을 알 수 있다. 지문 중간에서 조각가는 운동 선수들의 튼튼한 신체가 제일 아름답다고 했고, 이야기꾼은 사람들 사이에서 헤르메스를 발견하고 신을 젊음이 가장 아름다운 그 나이의 젊은 인간들과 똑같이 보았다고 했으며, 그리스의 예술가들과 시인들은 인간이 얼마나 눈부시고, 곧고 재빠르며 강인할 수 있는지 깨달았다고 설명하고 있다. 따라서 그리스의 모든 예술과 생각은 '인간을 그 중심에 두었다'라고 한 ②번이 정답이다.

어휘 **invisible** 눈에 보이지 않는 것; (눈에) 보이지 않는
visible 눈에 보이는 것; (눈에) 보이는 **ancient** 고대의
preoccupy 사로잡다 **satisfaction** 만족 **sculptor** 조각가
athlete 운동 선수 **contend** 겨루다, 다투다 **splendid** 눈부신
straight 곧은, 정직한 **swift** 재빠른 **fulfillment** 완성, 성취
semblance 모습 **omnipotent** 전능한 **supernatural** 초자연적인

정답

p.72

01	④ 독해 - 전체내용 파악	11	④ 문법 - 능동태·수동태	21	③ 독해 - 논리적 흐름 파악		
02	② 독해 - 추론	12	④ 독해 - 세부내용 파악	22	② 독해 - 추론		
03	③ 독해 - 논리적 흐름 파악	13	④ 독해 - 전체내용 파악	23	④ 독해 - 논리적 흐름 파악		
04	④ 독해 - 추론	14	④ 독해 - 세부내용 파악	24	③ 독해 - 추론		
05	① 독해 - 전체내용 파악	15	② 문법 - 분사	25	③ 문법 - 병치·도치·강조 구문		
06	② 독해 - 세부내용 파악	16	③ 문법 - 분사				
07	③ 독해 - 논리적 흐름 파악	17	④ 독해 - 전체내용 파악				
08	③ 독해 - 추론	18	② 독해 - 논리적 흐름 파악				
09	④ 독해 - 논리적 흐름 파악	19	③ 문법 - 동사의 종류				
10	② 독해 - 전체내용 파악	20	② 독해 - 논리적 흐름 파악				

취약영역 분석표

영역	세부 유형	문항 수	소계
어휘	어휘&표현	0	/0
	생활영어	0	
문법	능동태·수동태	1	/5
	분사	2	
	동사의 종류	1	
	병치·도치·강조 구문	1	
독해	전체내용 파악	5	/20
	세부내용 파악	3	
	추론	5	
	논리적 흐름 파악	7	
총계			/25

· 자신이 취약한 영역은 '법원직 9급 영어, 이렇게 출제된다!'(p.8)를 통해 다시 한번 확인하고 학습하시기 바랍니다.

---

01 독해 전체내용 파악 (주제 파악)   난이도 ★☆☆

끊어읽기 해석

Short-term stress can boost / your productivity and immunity.
단기적인 스트레스는 증대시킬 수 있다 / 당신의 생산성과 면역력을

But when stress lingers, / you may find / yourself struggling.
그러나 스트레스가 계속되면 / 당신은 발견할 수 있다 / 스스로가 힘겨워 하는 것을

People show / some signs / when they suffer from more stress / than is healthy.
사람들은 보인다 / 몇몇 징후들을 / 그들이 더 많은 스트레스로 고통받을 때 / 정상적인 것보다

First, / you can't concentrate.
첫 번째로 / 당신은 집중하지 못한다

In times of stress, / your body goes into fight or flight mode, / pouring its efforts / into keeping safe / from danger.
스트레스를 받을 때 / 당신의 몸은 투쟁 혹은 도피 상태가 된다 / 노력을 쏟으며 / 안전을 유지하는 데 / 위험으로부터

That's why / it may be hard to concentrate / on a single task, / and you're more likely to get distracted.
그것이 바로 이유이다 / 집중하는 것이 어려울 수 있는 / 단 하나의 일에 / 그리고 당신이 더 산만해질 가능성이 높은

"The brain's response becomes / all about survival", / says Heidi Hanna, / author of *Stressaholic: 5 Steps to Transform Your Relationship with Stress*.
"뇌의 반응은 됩니다 / 모두 생존에 관한 것이" / ~라고 Heidi Hanna는 말한다 / 『Stressaholic: 스트레스와 당신의 관계를 바꿔놓을 5단계』의 저자인

"The fear response takes up / all the energy of the brain / for how to protect yourself."
"두려움의 반응은 씁니다 / 뇌의 모든 에너지를 / 어떻게 스스로를 보호할지에"

Second, / you tend to get pessimistic.
두 번째로 / 당신은 비관적이게 되는 경향이 있다

Because you're primed for survival, / your brain has more circuits / to pay attention / to negatives / than to positives.
당신이 생존을 위해 준비되었기 때문에 / 당신의 뇌는 더 많은 회로가 있다 / 주의를 기울이기 위한 / 부정적인 것에 / 긍정적인 것보다

"When you're feeling overwhelmed / by the chaos of life, / take time / to appreciate everything / that's going well.
"당신이 압도되었다고 느낄 때 / 삶의 혼돈에 / 시간을 가져보세요 / 모든 것들에 감사하는 / 잘 진행되고 있는

You have to be intentional / about practicing positivity", / Hanna says.
당신은 의도적이어야 합니다 / 긍정을 연습하는 것에 대해" / Hanna는 ~라고 말한다

해석 단기적인 스트레스는 당신의 생산성과 면역력을 증대시킬 수 있다. 그러나 스트레스가 계속되면, 당신은 스스로가 힘겨워 하는 것을 발견할 수 있다. 사람들은 정상적인 것보다 그들이 더 많은 스트레스로 고통받을 때 몇몇 징후들을 보인다. 첫 번째로, 당신은 집중하지 못한다. 스트레스를 받을 때, 당신의 몸은 투쟁 혹은 도피 상태가 되며, 위험으로부터 안전을 유지하는 데 노력을 쏟는다. 그것이 바로 단 하나의 일에 집중하는 것이 어려울 수도 있으며, 당신이 더 산만해질 가능성이 높은 이유이다. "뇌의 반응은 모두 생존에 관한 것이 됩니다"라고 『Stressaholic: 스트레스와 당신의 관계를 바꿔놓을 5단계』의 저자인 Heidi Hanna는 말한다. "두려움의 반응은 스스로를 어떻게 보호할지에 뇌의 모든 에너지를 씁니다." 두 번째로, 당신은 비관적이게 되는 경향이 있다. 당신이 생존을 위해 준비되었기 때문에, 당신의 뇌는 긍정적인 것보다 부정적인 것에 주의를 기울이기 위한 더 많은 회로가 있다. "당신이 삶의 혼돈에 압도되었다고 느낄 때, 잘 진행되고 있는 모든 것들에 감사하는 시간을 가져보세요. 당신은 긍정을 연습하는 것에 대해 의도적이어야 합니다"라고 Hanna는 말한다.

① 단기적인 스트레스의 이점들
② 사람들이 계속 산만한 이유
③ 비관주의의 위험성

④ 과도한 스트레스의 징후

해설 지문 처음에서 사람들은 정상적인 것보다 더 많은 스트레스로 고통받을 때 몇몇 징후들을 보인다고 하고, 이어서 그 징후들을 차례로 설명하고 있으므로, 이 지문의 주제를 '과도한 스트레스의 징후'라고 표현한 ④번이 정답이다.

어휘 short-term 단기적인 boost 증대시키다, 신장시키다
productivity 생산성 immunity 면역력 linger 계속되다
struggle 힘겨워하다 suffer from ~로 고통 받다 pour 쏟다
distract 산만하게 하다 take up ~를 쓰다, 차지하다
pessimistic 비관적인 prime 준비시키다
pay attention to ~에 주의를 기울이다 overwhelm 휩싸다
chaos 혼돈 intentional 의도적인

02 독해 추론 (빈칸 완성 - 단어) 난이도 ★★☆

끊어읽기 해석

Sometimes, / the meaning of analogies / may not be obvious.
때때로 / 비유의 의미는 / 분명하지 않을 수도 있다

For instance, / what comes to mind / when you hear / the phrase "white elephant" or "black sheep"?
예를 들어 / 무엇이 떠오르는가 / 당신이 들으면 / '하얀 코끼리' 혹은 '검은 양'과 같은 문구를

The expression "white elephant" / comes from Thailand.
'하얀 코끼리'라는 표현은 / 태국에서 왔다

Long ago, / in Thailand, / white elephants were very rare.
오래 전 / 태국에서는 / 하얀 코끼리가 매우 귀했다

Whenever one was found, / it was given / to the king.
한 마리가 발견될 때 마다 / 그것은 주어졌다 / 왕에게

The king would then give it / as a royal "gift" / to someone / he did not like / since the beautiful animal / cost a fortune / to take care of.
그러면 왕은 그것을 주었다 / 국왕의 '선물'로 / 누군가에게 / 그가 좋아하지 않는 / 그 아름다운 동물은 ~하기 때문에 / 엄청난 비용이 들기 / 돌보는 데

Nobody could refuse such a present, / but it could financially ruin / its owner.
누구도 그러한 선물을 거부할 수 없었다 / 하지만 그것은 재정적으로 파산시킬 수 있었다 / 그것의 소유주를

Moreover, / it was a serious crime / to mistreat a present / from the king.
게다가 / 중죄였다 / 선물을 홀대하는 것은 / 왕으로부터 (받은)

Even riding it was not allowed, / so a white elephant was almost useless.
심지어 그것을 타는 것도 허용되지 않았다 / 그래서 하얀 코끼리는 거의 쓸모가 없었다

The expression, / introduced in England / in the 18th century, / turned out to be useful for describing / (A) costly but (B) worthless public buildings.
이 표현은 / 영국에 소개된 / 18세기에 / 묘사하는 데 유용한 것으로 드러났다 / (A) 비싸지만 (B) 가치 없는 공공건물들을

Today, / it is used / to refer to anything / that might be (A) costly and (B) worthless.
오늘날 / 그것은 사용된다 / 무언가를 나타내는 데 / (A) 비싸고 (B) 가치 없을 수 있는

해석 때때로, 비유의 의미는 분명하지 않을 수도 있다. 예를 들어, 당신이 '하얀 코끼리' 혹은 '검은 양'과 같은 문구를 들으면 무엇이 떠오르는가? '하얀 코끼리'라는 표현은 태국에서 왔다. 오래 전, 태국에서는 하얀 코끼리가 매우 귀했다. 한 마리가 발견될 때마다, 그

것은 왕에게 주어졌다. 그러면 왕은 그것을 국왕의 '선물'로 그(왕)가 좋아하지 않는 누군가에게 주었는데, 그 아름다운 동물은 돌보는 데 엄청난 비용이 들기 때문이었다. 누구도 그러한 선물을 거부할 수 없었지만, 그것은 재정적으로 그것의 소유주를 파산시킬 수 있었다. 게다가, 왕으로부터 받은 선물을 홀대하는 것은 중죄였다. 심지어 그것을 타는 것도 허용되지 않아서, 하얀 코끼리는 거의 쓸모가 없었다. 18세기에 영국에 소개된 이 표현은 (A) 비싸지만 (B) 가치 없는 공공건물들을 묘사하는 데 유용한 것으로 드러났다. 오늘날, 그것은 (A) 비싸고 (B) 가치 없을 수 있는 무언가를 나타내는 데 사용된다.

	(A)	(B)
①	귀중한	보호받지 못하는
②	비싼	가치 없는
③	낭비하는	적절한
④	아주 귀중한	환경친화적인

해설 (A), (B) 빈칸이 있는 문장을 통해 빈칸에 18세기에 영국에 소개된 이 표현(하얀 코끼리)이 어떤 공공건물들을 묘사하는 데 유용한지, 오늘날 그것이 무엇을 나타낼 때 사용되는지에 대한 내용이 나와야 적절하다는 것을 알 수 있다. 지문 중간에 하얀 코끼리는 돌보는 데 엄청나게 많은 비용이 든다는 내용이 있고, 지문 마지막에 하얀 코끼리는 거의 쓸모가 없었다는 내용이 있으므로, '비싸지만 가치 없는'(costly but worthless) 공공건물들을 묘사하는 데 유용하고, 오늘날 그것이 '비싸고 가치 없는'(costly and worthless) 무언가를 나타내는 데 사용된다는 내용이 들어가는 것이 적절하다.
따라서 ② costly(비싼) – worthless(가치 없는)가 정답이다.

어휘 analogy 비유 obvious 분명한, 명백한
come to mind (생각이) 떠오르다 phrase 문구, 구절
rare 귀한, 드문 cost a fortune 엄청난 비용이 들다
financially 재정적으로 ruin 파산시키다
mistreat 홀대하다, 학대하다 useless 쓸모 없는
turn out ~인 것으로 드러나다 refer to ~을 나타내다, ~을 가리키다
valuable 귀중한, 가치가 큰 unprotected 보호받지 못하는, 무방비의
costly 비싼 worthless 가치 없는
extravagant 낭비하는, 사치스러운 appropriate 적절한
priceless 아주 귀중한 eco-friendly 환경친화적인

03 독해 논리적 흐름 파악 (문맥상 부적절한 어휘) 난이도 ★★☆

끊어읽기 해석

When asked, / nearly everyone says / the proper response / to a compliment / is "Thank you".
질문을 받았을 때 / 거의 모든 사람은 말한다 / 적절한 반응이 / 칭찬에 대한 / '감사합니다'라고

But researchers found / that when actually given a compliment, / only a third of people / accept it so ① simply.
하지만 연구원들은 알아냈다 / 실제로 칭찬을 받았을 때 / 사람들의 3분의 1만이 / 그것을 정말로 ① 단순하게 받아들인다는 것을

The difficulty lies / in the fact / that every compliment ("What a nice sweater!") has two levels: / a gift component (accept or reject) and a content component (agree or disagree).
어려움은 ~에 있다 / 사실에 / 모든 칭찬이("스웨터가 참 멋지구나!") 두 가지 관점을 가지고 있다는 / 선물 요소(수락하거나 거절하거나)와 내용 요소(동의하거나 반대하거나)의

The recipient is confronted / with a ② dilemma / — how to respond simultaneously to both: / "I must agree with the speaker / and thank him / for the gift of a compliment / while avoiding self-praise."

(칭찬을) 받는 사람은 직면한다 / ② 딜레마에 / 어떻게 그 두 가지에 동시에 대답할지 / "나는 말하는 사람에게 동의해야 한다 / 그리고 그에게 감사를 표해야 한다 / 칭찬이라는 선물에 대한 / 자화자찬을 피하면서"

Interestingly, / women and men are both / ③ less likely to accept / a compliment coming from a man / than from a woman.
흥미롭게도 / 여성들과 남성들은 양쪽 다 / ③ 덜 받아들이는 경향이 있다 / 남성으로부터의 칭찬을 / 여성으로부터의 (칭찬) 보다

When a man says, "Nice scarf," / a woman is more likely to respond ④ affirmatively: / "Thanks. // My sister knitted it for me."
남자가 "멋진 스카프네요"라고 말할 때 / 여자는 더 ④ 긍정적으로 대답하는 경향이 있다 / "고맙습니다 // 여동생이 저를 위해 떠 줬어요."

But when one woman tells another, / "That's a beautiful sweater," / the recipient is likely to disagree or deflect.
그러나 여자가 다른 여자에게 말할 때 / "참 아름다운 스웨터네요"라고 / (칭찬) 받는 사람은 동의하지 않거나 회피하기 쉽다

"It was on sale, / and they didn't even have the colour I wanted."
"할인 중이었어요 / 그리고 심지어 제가 원했던 색깔도 없었어요"

해석 질문을 받았을 때, 거의 모든 사람은 칭찬에 대한 적절한 반응이 '감사합니다'라고 말한다. 하지만 연구원들은 실제로 칭찬을 받았을 때, 사람들의 3분의 1만이 그것을 정말로 ① 단순하게 받아들인다는 것을 알아냈다. 어려움은 모든 칭찬이("스웨터가 참 멋지구나!") 선물 요소(수락하거나 거절하거나)와 내용 요소(동의하거나 반대하거나)의 두 가지 관점을 가지고 있다는 사실에 있다. (칭찬을) 받는 사람은 어떻게 그 두 가지에 동시에 대답할지에 대한 ② 딜레마에 직면한다. 즉, "나는 말하는 사람에게 동의해야 하고, 자화자찬을 피하면서 그에게 칭찬이라는 선물에 대한 감사를 표해야 한다." 흥미롭게도, 여성들과 남성들은 양쪽 다 여성보다 남성으로부터의 칭찬을 ③ 덜 받아들이는 경향이 있다. 남자가 "멋진 스카프네요."라고 말할 때, 여자는 "고맙습니다. 여동생이 저를 위해 떠 줬어요."와 같이 더 ④ 긍정적으로 대답하는 경향이 있다. 그러나 여자가 다른 여자에게 "참 아름다운 스웨터네요."라고 말할 때, (칭찬을) 받는 사람은 "할인 중이었고, 심지어 제가 원했던 색깔도 없었어요."와 같이 동의하지 않거나 회피하기 쉽다.

해설 지문 뒷부분에 칭찬을 받는 사람은 남자가 칭찬할 때는 긍정적으로 대답하고, 여자가 칭찬할 때는 동의하지 않거나 회피하기 쉽다는 내용이 있으므로, 흥미롭게도 여성들과 남성들은 양쪽 다 여성보다 남성으로부터의 칭찬을 '덜'(less) 받아들이는 경향이 있다는 것은 문맥상 적절하지 않다. 따라서 ③ less가 정답이다. 참고로, 주어진 less를 대신할 수 있는 어휘로는 '더'라는 의미의 more가 있다.

어휘 compliment 칭찬 level 관점, 수준 reject 거절하다
confront 직면하다 dilemma 딜레마 simultaneously 동시에
affirmatively 긍정적으로 deflect 회피하다, 모면하다

04 독해 추론 (빈칸 완성 - 연결어) 난이도 ★★☆

끊어읽기 해석

The chairperson should seek / to have a progressive discussion / that leads / towards a consensus view.
의장은 추구해야 한다 / 진보적인 토론을 하는 것을 / 나아가는 / 일치된 의견으로

As the discussion develops, / the chairperson should be searching / to find the direction / in which the weight of members' views is pointing.
토론이 전개됨에 따라 / 의장은 자세히 살펴야 한다 / 방향을 찾기 위해 /

구성원들의 의견의 무게가 가리키는

If, / (A) for example, / there are five members / and the chair senses / that two want / to follow course A and a third follow course B, / the focus should quickly be turned / towards the remaining two members.
만약 / (A) 예를 들어 / 다섯 명의 구성원들이 있다 / 그리고 의장이 알아챈 다면 / 두 명은 원한다는 것을 / 과정 A를 따르기를 / 그리고 세 번째 구성원은 과정 B를 따르기를 / 초점은 빠르게 향해져야 한다 / 남은 두 명의 구성원에게로

The chair turns to member 4.
의장은 네 번째 구성원에게로 고개를 돌린다.

If he or she wants course A, / the chairperson simply has the job / of getting first the other neutral (member 5) / and then the dissenting member 3 / to assent to the fact / that course A is the majority view.
만약 그 또는 그녀가 과정 A를 원한다면 / 의장은 그저 일을 맡는다 / 먼저 다른 중립적인 한 명(다섯 번째 구성원)이 ~하도록 만드는 / 그 이후에 반대하는 세 번째 구성원이 / 사실에 동의하게 / 과정 A가 다수의 의견이라는

If, / (B) on the other hand, / member 4 wants course B, / then member 5's view is the critical one, / which the chairperson must now bring in.
만약 / (B) 반면에 / 네 번째 구성원이 과정 B를 원한다 / 그러면 다섯 번째 구성원의 의견이 결정적인 것이다 / 이는 의장이 이제 끌어내야 하는 것이다

And so, very quickly, / you can sense / where the balance of opinion is pointing, / and lead the meeting / towards unanimous assent.
그래서 매우 신속히 / 당신은 알아챌 수 있다 / 의견의 균형이 어디를 향하고 있는지를 / 그리고 회의를 이끌 수 있다 / 만장일치의 동의로

해석 의장은 일치된 의견으로 나아가는 진보적인 토론을 하는 것을 추구해야 한다. 토론이 전개됨에 따라, 의장은 구성원들의 의견의 무게가 가리키는 방향을 찾기 위해 자세히 살펴야 한다. (A) 예를 들어, 만약 다섯 명의 구성원들이 있고, 의장이 두 명은 과정 A를 따르기를 원하고 세 번째 구성원은 과정 B를 따르기를 원한다는 것을 알아챈다면, 초점은 빠르게 남은 두 명의 구성원에게로 향해져야 한다. 의장은 네 번째 구성원에게로 고개를 돌린다. 만약 그 또는 그녀가 과정 A를 원한다면, 의장은 그저 먼저 다른 중립적인 한 명(다섯 번째 구성원), 그 이후에 반대하는 세 번째 구성원이 과정 A가 다수의 의견이라는 사실에 동의하도록 만드는 일을 맡는다. (B) 반면에, 만약 네 번째 구성원이 과정 B를 원한다면, 다섯 번째 구성원의 의견이 결정적인 것인데, 이는 의장은 이제 끌어내야 하는 것이다. 그래서 매우 신속히, 당신은 의견의 균형이 어디를 향하고 있는지를 알아채고 만장일치의 동의로 회의를 이끌 수 있다.

	(A)	(B)
①	반면에	마찬가지로
②	예를 들어	그러므로
③	반면에	예를 들어
④	예를 들어	반면에

해설 (A) 빈칸 앞 문장은 의장이 구성원들의 의견의 무게가 가리키는 방향을 찾기 위해 자세히 살펴야 한다는 내용이고, 빈칸 뒤 문장은 만약 다섯 명의 구성원이 있고, 그중 2명과 1명의 의견이 다르다는 것을 의장이 알아챈다면 남은 구성원에게 초점을 빠르게 이동시켜야 한다는 토론 진행 방식의 예시를 드는 내용이다. 따라서 예시를 나타내는 연결어인 for example(예를 들어)이 나와야 적절하다. (B) 빈칸 앞 문장은 네 번째 구성원이 다른 두 명과 동일하게 과정 A를 원하는 상황에 대한 설명이고, 빈칸 뒤 문장은 네 번째 구성원이 과정 B를 원하는 상황에 대해 묘사하는 대조적인 내용이다. 따라서 대조를 나타내는 연결어인 on the other hand(반면에)가 나와야 적절하다.

따라서 ④ (A) for example(예를 들어) – (B) on the other hand(반면에)가 정답이다.

어휘 **chairperson** 의장, 회장 **progressive** 진보적인
lead toward ~로 나아가다 **view** 의견, 견해
develop 전개하다, 진전시키다 **point** 가리키다 **sense** 감지하다
neutral 중립적인 **dissent** 반대하다 **critical** 결정적인, 중대한
assent 동의

05 독해 전체내용 파악 (제목 파악) 난이도 ★☆☆

끊어읽기 해석

As early as 525 BCE, / a Greek named Theagenes, / who lived / in southern Italy, / identified myths as scientific analogies or allegories / —an attempt / to explain natural occurrences / that people could not understand.
일찍이 기원전 525년에 / Theagenes라는 이름의 그리스인은 / 살았던 / 이탈리아 남부에 / 신화가 과학적인 비유 혹은 우화임을 확인했다 / 시도인 / 자연 현상들을 설명하려는 / 사람들이 이해할 수 없었던

To him, / for instance, / the mythical stories of gods / fighting among themselves / were allegories / representing the forces of nature / that oppose each other, / such as fire and water.
그에게 / 예를 들어 / 신들에 대한 신화 속의 이야기들은 / 자기들끼리 싸우는 / 우화였다 / 자연의 힘들을 나타내는 / 서로 반대되는 / 불과 물처럼

This is clearly the source / of a great many explanatory or "causal" myths, / beginning with the accounts / found in every society or civilization / that explain the creation / of the universe, the world, and humanity.
이것은 분명 근원이다 / 설명적인 혹은 '가벼운' 수많은 신화의 / 이야기들로 시작하는 / 모든 사회나 문명에서 발견되는 / 창조를 설명하는 / 우주, 세계, 그리고 인류의

These "scientific" myths / attempted to explain / seasons, the rising and setting of the sun, the course of the stars.
이러한 '과학적인' 신화들은 / 설명하려 시도했다 / 계절, 태양이 뜨고 지는 것, 별들의 행로를

Myths like these were, / in some ways, / the forerunners of science.
이런 신화들은 ~이었다 / 어떤 면에서는 / 과학의 전신

Old mythical explanations / for the workings of nature / began to be replaced / by a rational attempt / to understand the world, / especially in the remarkable era of Greek science and philosophy / that began about 500 BCE.
오래된 신화적 설명들은 / 자연의 작용에 대한 / 대체되기 시작했다 / 합리적인 시도에 의해 / 세상을 이해하려는 / 특히 그리스의 과학과 철학의 놀라운 시대에 / 약 기원전 500년에 시작되었던

해석 일찍이 기원전 525년에, 이탈리아 남부에 살았던 Theagenes라는 이름의 그리스인은 신화가 과학적인 비유 혹은 우화 즉, 사람들이 이해할 수 없었던 자연 현상들을 설명하려는 시도였음을 확인했다. 예를 들어, 그에게 자기들끼리 싸우는 신들에 대한 신화 속의 이야기들은 불과 물처럼 서로 반대되는 자연의 힘들을 나타내는 우화였다. 이것은 분명 우주, 세계, 그리고 인류의 창조를 설명하는, 모든 사회나 문명에서 발견되는 이야기들로 시작하는, 설명적인 혹은 '가벼운' 수많은 신화의 근원이다. 이러한 '과학적인' 신화들은 계절, 태양이 뜨고 지는 것, 별들의 행로를 설명하려고 시도했다. 이런 신화들은 어떤 면에서는 과학의 전신이었다. 자연의 작용에 대한 오래된 신화적 설명들은 특히 약 기원전 500년에 시작되었던 그리스의 과학과 철학의 놀라운 시대에, 세상을 이해하려는 합리적인 시도에 의해 대체되기 시작했다.

① 신화: 과학적 연구의 기초
② 과학에 대한 근거 없는 믿음 없애기
③ 창조 신화는 어떻게 보편적인가?
④ 신화는 우리의 세계관에 얼마나 많은 영향을 미치는가

해설 지문 처음에서 그리스인 Theagenes가 신화는 자연 현상에 대한 과학적 비유 또는 우화임을 확인했다고 하고, 지문 중간에서 과학적인 신화는 계절, 태양이 뜨고 지는 것, 별들의 행로를 설명하려고 시도했으며, 이런 신화는 어떤 면에서는 과학의 전신이었다고 설명하고 있다. 따라서 이 지문의 제목을 '신화: 과학적 연구의 기초'라고 표현한 ①번이 정답이다.

어휘 **identify** 확인하다, 식별하다 **analogy** 비유 **allegory** 우화
natural occurrence 자연 현상 **represent** 나타내다
oppose 반대하다 **explanatory** 설명적인, 설명하기 위한
causal 가벼운, 우발적인 **account** 이야기, 말
forerunner 전신, 선구자 **rational** 합리적인 **remarkable** 놀라운
era 시대 **philosophy** 철학 **inquiry** 연구
dispel 없애다, 떨쳐 버리다 **universal** 보편적인, 전 세계적인
world view 세계관

06 독해 세부내용 파악 (내용 일치 파악) 난이도 ★★☆

끊어읽기 해석

①Every year / in early October, / Helsinki's harbor changes / into a lively, colorful set, / for the Baltic Herring Festival, / first held / in 1743.
매년 / 10월 초에 / 헬싱키의 항구는 변한다 / 활기차고 화려한 세트장으로 / 발트해 청어 축제를 위한 / 처음 개최된 / 1743년에

Fishermen / from all over Finland / bring their latest catch / to Helsinki / to take part in one of Finland's oldest festivals.
어부들은 / 핀란드 전역에서 온 / 그들이 가장 최근에 잡은 것을 가지고 온다 / 헬싱키로 / 핀란드의 가장 오래된 축제 중 하나에 참가하기 위해

②Sellers / in bright orange tents / line the harbor / and sell herring / in every imaginable form: / fried, pickled, smoked, in bottles, in cans, in soup, on pizza, and in sandwiches.
판매자들은 / 밝은 오렌지색 텐트에 있는 / 항구를 따라 늘어선다 / 그리고 청어를 판매한다 / 상상할 수 있는 모든 형태로 / 튀겨진, 절여진, 훈제된, 병에 든, 캔에 든, 수프에 넣은, 피자 위에 얹은, 그리고 샌드위치 안에 넣은 형태

The choices are endless.
선택권들은 끝이 없다.

On the first day of the festival, / competitions are held / to select the most delicious seasoned herring / and the best herring surprise.
축제의 첫째 날에 / 대회들이 개최된다 / 가장 맛있는 양념된 청어를 선발하기 위해 / 그리고 최고의 청어 서프라이즈를 (선발하기 위해)

Herring surprise is a traditional dish / made with herring, cheese, and onions.
청어 서프라이즈는 전통 요리이다 / 청어, 치즈 그리고 양파로 만들어진

④The winner of each competition is awarded a trophy.
각 대회의 우승자는 트로피를 수여받는다.

해석 매년 10월 초에 헬싱키의 항구는 1743년에 처음 개최된 발트해 청어 축제를 위한 활기차고 화려한 세트장으로 변한다. 핀란드 전역에서 온 어부들이 핀란드의 가장 오래된 축제 중 하나에 참가하기 위해 그들이 가장 최근에 잡은 것을 헬싱키로 가지고 온다. 밝은 오렌지색 텐트에 있는 판매자들은 항구를 따라 늘어서고 튀겨진, 절여진, 훈제된, 병에 든, 캔에 든, 수프에 넣은, 피자 위에 얹은, 그리고 샌드위치 안에 넣은 상상할 수 있는 모든 형태로 청어를 판매한다. 선택권들은 끝이 없다. 축제의 첫째 날에, 가장 맛있는 양념된 청어와 최고의 청어 서프라이즈를 선발하기 위해 대회들이 개최된다. 청어 서프라이즈는 청어, 치즈, 그리고 양파로 만들어진 전통 요리이다. 각 대회의 우승자는 트로피를 수여받는다.

① 이 축제는 1743년 이후로 2년에 한번씩 개최되었다.

② 판매자들은 항구를 따라 오렌지색 텐트를 설치하고 청어를 판매한다.

③ 이 축제의 대회는 헬싱키 거주자들에게 한정된다.

④ 트로피는 최고의 청어 서프라이즈의 우승자에게만 주어진다.

해설   지문 중간에서 밝은 오렌지색 텐트에 있는 판매자들이 항구를 따라 늘어서서 다양한 형태로 된 청어를 판매한다고 했으므로, 판매자들이 항구를 따라 오렌지색 텐트를 설치하고 청어를 판매한다는 것을 알 수 있다. 따라서 ②번이 정답이다.

오답 분석
① 매년 10월 초에 헬싱키의 항구는 1743년에 처음 개최된 발트해 청어 축제를 위한 활기차고 화려한 세트장으로 변한다고 했으므로, 이 축제가 1743년 이후로 2년에 한 번씩 개최되었다는 것은 지문의 내용과 다르다.

③ 이 축제의 대회가 헬싱키 거주자들에게 한정되는지에 대해서는 언급되지 않았다.

④ 각 대회의 우승자가 트로피를 수여받는다고 했으므로, 트로피는 최고의 청어 서프라이즈의 우승자에게만 주어진다는 것은 지문의 내용과 다르다.

어휘   harbor 항구   lively 활기찬   herring 청어   catch 잡은 것, 어획(량)
take part in ~에 참가하다   line ~를 따라 늘어서다
imaginable 상상할 수 있는   pickle 절이다   smoke 훈제하다
season 양념하다   award 수여하다   set up 설치하다

07   독해   논리적 흐름 파악 (문맥상 부적절한 어휘)   난이도 ★★☆

끊어읽기 해석

As a youngster / I shared a bedroom / with my older sister.
아이였을 때 / 나는 침실을 같이 썼다 / 언니와

Although the age difference was slight, / in intellect and maturity / she viewed me / from across the great divide.
비록 나이 차는 적었지만 / 지적 능력과 성숙함에 있어 / 그녀는 나를 바라보았다 / 거대한 분수령 너머에서

Her serious academic and cultural pursuits / contrasted sharply / with my activities / of closely monitoring the radio shows.
그녀의 진지한 학문적 그리고 문화적 추구는 / 뚜렷하게 대조를 이루었다 / 내 행동과 / 라디오 쇼를 열심히 모니터링하는

Because of these ① dissimilar interests / and the limited resource of one bedroom / between us, / we frequently had conflict / over what constituted disturbing and inconsiderate behavior.
이러한 ① 다른 관심사 때문에 / 그리고 하나의 침실이라는 제한된 자원 (때문에) / 우리 사이에 / 우리는 자주 갈등을 겪었다 / 무엇이 방해가 되고 사려 깊지 못한 행동이 되는지에 관해

For months, / there were attempts / to ② compromise / by "splitting the difference" / in our divergent viewpoints / or practicing "share and share alike."
몇 달 동안 / 시도들이 있었다 / ② 타협하려는 / '절반씩 절충해서 합의를 봄'으로써 / 우리의 다른 관점에 있어서 / 혹은 '모두 똑같이 공평하게 분배하는 것'을 실천함으로써

Even with written schedules and agreements / plus parental mediation, / the controversy persisted.
심지어 서면으로 된 일정과 협정이 있었지만 / 부모님의 중재뿐만 아니라 / 언쟁은 계속되었다

Ultimately the matter was ③ aggravated / when we both came to recognize / that considerable time and energy were being wasted / as we maneuvered and positioned ourselves / for the next mathematical compromise.
결국 그 문제는 ③ 악화되었다 / 우리 둘 모두가 깨닫게 되었을 때 / 상당한

시간과 에너지가 낭비되고 있다는 것을 / 우리가 책략을 짜고 스스로의 위치를 정하며 / 다음 번의 수학적 타협을 위해

With recognition of a ④ common interest / in solving the problem / for our mutual benefit, / we were able to think beyond physical resources / of space, hours, and materials.
④ 공통의 관심사를 인식하면서 / 문제를 해결하는 것에 대한 / 우리의 상호 이익을 위해 / 우리는 물리적인 자원을 넘어서 생각할 수 있었다 / 공간, 시간, 그리고 물질의

The satisfying solution / that met both of our needs / was the purchase of earphones / for the radio.
만족스러운 해결책은 / 우리의 요구를 모두 충족시키는 / 이어폰의 구입이었다 / 라디오용의

해석   아이였을 때 나는 언니와 침실을 같이 썼다. 비록 나이 차는 적었지만, 지적 능력과 성숙함에 있어서 그녀는 거대한 분수령 너머에서 나를 바라보았다(아주 멀고 높은 곳에서 멀리를 보듯 바라보았다). 그녀의 진지한 학문적이고 문화적인 추구는 라디오 쇼를 열심히 모니터링하는 내 행동과 뚜렷하게 대조를 이루었다. 이러한 ① 다른 관심사와 우리 사이에 하나의 침실이라는 제한된 자원 때문에, 우리는 무엇이 방해가 되고 사려 깊지 못한 행동이 되는지에 관해 자주 갈등을 겪었다. 몇 달 동안, 우리의 다른 관점에 있어서 '절반씩 절충해서 합의를 봄'으로써 혹은 '모두 똑같이 공평하게 분배하는 것'을 실천함으로써 ② 타협하려는 시도들이 있었다. 심지어 부모님의 중재뿐만 아니라 서면으로 된 일정과 협정이 있었지만, 언쟁은 계속되었다. 우리가 다음 번의 수학적 타협을 위해 책략을 짜고 스스로의 위치를 정하며 상당한 시간과 에너지가 낭비되고 있다는 것을 우리 둘 모두가 깨닫게 되었을 때, 결국 그 문제는 ③ 악화되었다. 우리의 상호 이익을 위해 문제를 해결하는 것에 대한 ④ 공통의 관심사를 인식하면서, 우리는 공간, 시간, 그리고 물질의 물리적인 자원을 넘어서 생각할 수 있었다. 우리의 요구를 모두 충족시키는 만족스러운 해결책은 라디오용 이어폰의 구입이었다.

해설   지문 마지막에서 상호 이익을 위해 문제를 해결하는 것에 대한 공통의 관심사를 인식하면서 화자와 언니는 물리적인 자원을 넘어서 생각할 수 있었다고 했으므로, 결국 그 문제가 '악화되었다'(aggravated)는 것은 문맥상 적절하지 않다. 따라서 ③ aggravated가 정답이다. 참고로, 주어진 aggravated를 대신할 수 있는 어휘로는 '해결되었다'라는 의미의 settled가 있다.

어휘   youngster 아이, 청소년   intellect 지적 능력   maturity 성숙함
pursuit 추구, 좇음   contrast 대조를 이루다   sharply 뚜렷하게
dissimilar 다른   constitute ~가 되다   disturbing 방해가 되는
inconsiderate 사려 깊지 못한   compromise 타협하다
split the difference 절반씩 절충해서 합의를 보다   divergent 다른
share and share alike 모두 똑같이 공평하게 분배하다
agreement 협정, 계약   mediation 중재, 조정
controversy 언쟁, 싸움   persist 계속되다
ultimately 결국, 궁극적으로   aggravate 악화시키다
considerable 상당한   maneuver 책략을 짜다
position 위치를 정하다   mathematical 수학적인
mutual 상호의

08   독해   추론 (빈칸 완성 - 구)   난이도 ★☆☆

끊어읽기 해석

One of the most popular of computer games / in the world / is called Age of Empires.
가장 인기 있는 컴퓨터 게임 중의 하나는 / 세계에서 / Age of Empires라고 불린다

For several months / my own ten-year-old son / was all but addicted to it.
몇 달 동안 / 나 자신의 열 살배기 아들은 / 그것에

몇 달 동안 / 나의 10살 짜리 아들은 / 거의 그것에 중독되어 있었다

Its organizing premise is / that the history of the world is / the history of imperial conflict.
그것의 구성 전제는 / 세계의 역사가 ~라는 것이다 / 제국의 갈등의 역사

Rival political entities vie with one another / to control finite resources: / people, fertile land, forests, gold mines and waterways.
경쟁하는 정치적 독립체들은 서로와 경쟁한다 / 한정된 자원들을 통제하기 위해 / 사람, 비옥한 영토, 숲, 금광, 그리고 수로와 같은

In their endless struggles / the competing empires must strike a balance / between / the need for economic development / and the exigencies of warfare.
그들의 끊임없는 투쟁 동안 / 경쟁하는 제국들은 균형을 유지해야 한다 / ~ 사이에서 / 경제적인 발전에 대한 필요 / 그리고 전쟁이라는 긴급 사태

The player / who is too aggressive / soon runs out of resources / if he has not taken the trouble / to cultivate his existing territory, / to expand its population / and to accumulate gold.
플레이어는 / 지나치게 공격적인 / 곧 자원을 다 써버린다 / 그가 수고를 들이지 않으면 / 자신의 기존 영토를 경작하고 / 인구를 늘리고 / 금을 축적하는

The player / who focuses too much / on getting rich / may find himself vulnerable to invasion / if he meanwhile neglects his defenses.
플레이어는 / 너무 많이 집중하는 / 부자가 되는 것에 / 스스로가 침략에 취약하다는 것을 알게 될지도 모른다 / 그가 그동안에 그의 방어를 소홀히 한다면

해석 세계에서 가장 인기 있는 컴퓨터 게임 중의 하나는 Age of Empires라고 불린다. 몇 달 동안 나의 10살짜리 아들은 거의 그것에 중독되어 있었다. 그것의 구성 전제는 세계의 역사가 제국의 갈등의 역사라는 것이다. 경쟁하는 정치적 독립체들은 사람, 비옥한 영토, 숲, 금광, 그리고 수로와 같은 한정된 자원들을 통제하기 위해 서로와 경쟁한다. 그들의 끊임없는 투쟁 동안, 경쟁하는 제국들은 경제적인 발전에 대한 필요와 전쟁이라는 긴급 사태 사이에서 균형을 유지해야 한다. 지나치게 공격적인 플레이어는 그가 자신의 기존 영토를 경작하고, 인구를 늘리고, 금을 축적하는 수고를 들이지 않으면 곧 자원을 다 써버린다. 부자가 되는 것에 너무 많이 집중하는 플레이어는 그가 그동안에 그의 방어를 소홀히 한다면 스스로가 침략에 취약하다는 것을 알게 될지도 모른다.

① 병에 면역이 된
② 변화를 용인하는
③ 침략에 취약한
④ 오락에 중독된

해설 빈칸이 있는 문장을 통해 빈칸에 부자가 되는 것에 너무 많이 집중하는 플레이어는 스스로가 어떠하다는 것을 알게 될지도 모르는지에 대한 내용이 나와야 적절하다는 것을 알 수 있다. 지문 중간에서 끊임없는 투쟁 동안, 경쟁하는 제국들은 경제적인 발전에 대한 필요와 전쟁이라는 긴급 사태 사이에서 균형을 유지해야 한다고 했으므로, 부자가 되는 것에 너무 많이 집중하는 플레이어는 그가 그동안에 그의 방어를 소홀히 한다면 스스로가 '침략에 취약하다는' 것을 알게 될지도 모른다고 한 ③번이 정답이다.

어휘 all but 거의 addict 중독되게 하다 premise 전제
imperial 제국의 entity 독립체 vie with ~와 경쟁하다
finite 한정된, 유한한 fertile 비옥한 gold mine 금광
waterway 수로 struggle 투쟁, 싸움
strike a balance 균형을 유지하다 exigency 긴급 사태
warfare 전쟁 aggressive 공격적인 run out of ~을 다 써버리다
take the trouble to 수고를 아끼지 않다 cultivate 경작하다
existing 기존의 territory 영토 expand 늘리다, 팽창시키다
accumulate 축적하다 meanwhile 그동안에

---

neglect 소홀히 하다, 등한하다 immune ~에 면역이 된
tolerant 용인하는, 관대한 vulnerable ~에 취약한

09 독해 논리적 흐름 파악 (무관한 문장 삭제) 난이도 ★★☆

끊어읽기 해석

Can an old cell phone / help save the rainforests?
오래된 휴대 전화가 / 열대 우림을 구하는 것을 도울 수 있을까?

As a matter of fact, / it can.
사실 / 그것은 할 수 있다

Illegal logging / in the rainforests / has been a problems / for years, / but not much has been done / about it / because catching illegal loggers is difficult.
불법 벌목은 / 열대 우림에서의 / 문제가 되어왔다 / 수년 동안 / 하지만 많은 것(조치)이 취해지지 않았다 / 그것에 대해 / 불법 벌목꾼을 잡는 것이 어렵기 때문에

① To help solve this problem, / an American engineer, Topher White, / invented a device / called RFCx / with discarded cell phones.
이 문제를 해결하는 것을 돕기 위해서 / 미국인 기술자인 Topher White가 / 장치를 발명했다 / RFCx라고 불리는 / 버려진 휴대폰들로

② When the device, / which is attached to a tree, / picks up the sound of chainsaws, / it sends an alert message / to the rangers' cell phones.
이 장치가 / 나무에 부착된 / 사슬톱의 소리를 듣게 되면 / 그것은 경보 메시지를 보낸다 / 삼림 관리원의 휴대폰으로

③ This provides the rangers / with the information / they need / to locate the loggers / and stop the illegal logging.
이는 삼림 관리원에게 제공한다 / 정보를 / 그들이 필요한 / 벌목꾼의 위치를 찾아내는 데 / 그리고 불법 벌목을 중단시키는 데

④ Destruction of the rainforest is caused / by logging, farming, mining, and other human activities / and among these, / logging is the main reason / for the nature's loss.
열대 우림의 파괴는 야기된다 / 벌목, 농사, 채굴, 그리고 다른 인간의 행위들로 인해 / 그리고 이러한 것들 중 / 벌목이 주요 원인이다 / 자연 손실의

The device has been tested / in Indonesia / and has proven to work well.
이 장치는 테스트되었다 / 인도네시아에서 / 그리고 잘 작동하는 것으로 드러났다

As a result, / it is now being used / in the rainforests / in Africa and South America.
그 결과 / 그것은 현재 사용되고 있다 / 열대 우림에서 / 아프리카와 남아메리카의

해석 오래된 휴대 전화가 열대 우림을 구하는 것을 도울 수 있을까? 사실, 그것은 할 수 있다. 열대 우림에서 불법 벌목은 수년 동안 문제가 되어왔지만, 불법 벌목꾼을 잡는 것이 어렵기 때문에 그것에 대해 많은 것(조치)이 취해지지 않았다. ① 이 문제를 해결하는 것을 돕기 위해서, 미국인 기술자인 Topher White가 버려진 휴대폰들로 RFCx라고 불리는 장치를 발명했다. ② 나무에 부착된 이 장치가 사슬톱의 소리를 듣게 되면, 그것은 삼림 관리원의 휴대폰으로 경보 메시지를 보낸다. ③ 이는 삼림 관리원에게 그들이 벌목꾼의 위치를 찾아내고 불법 벌목을 중단시키는 데 필요한 정보를 제공한다. ④ 열대 우림의 파괴는 벌목, 농사, 채굴 그리고 다른 인간의 행위들로 인해 야기되고, 이러한 것들 중 벌목이 자연 손실의 주요 원인이다. 이 장치는 인도네시아에서 테스트되었고, 잘 작동하는 것으로 드러났다. 그 결과, 그것은 현재 아프리카와 남아메리카의 열대 우림에서 사용되고 있다.

해설 지문 앞 부분에서 휴대 전화가 열대 우림을 구하는 것을 도울 수 있다고 언급한 뒤, ①, ②, ③번에서 열대 우림에서의 불법 벌목

문제를 해결하기 위해 발명된 장치인 RFCx의 작동 방식에 대해 설명하고 있으므로 모두 지문의 앞 부분과 관련이 있다. 그러나 ④번은 '열대 우림 파괴의 주요 원인인 벌목'에 대한 내용으로, 지문 앞부분의 내용과 관련이 없으므로 ④번이 정답이다.

어휘 rainforest 열대 우림 as a matter of fact 사실 logging 벌목
discard 버리다 attach 부착하다 pick up ~를 듣게 되다
chainsaw 사슬톱 alert 경보 ranger 삼림 관리원
locate 위치를 찾아내다 mining 채굴 loss 손실 prove 드러나다

---

10 독해 전체내용 파악 (제목 파악) 난이도 ★★☆

끊어읽기 해석

In any symphony, / the composer and the conductor / have a variety of responsibilities.
어떤 교향곡에서든 / 작곡가와 지휘자는 / 다양한 책임을 지닌다

They must make sure / that the brass horns work / in synch with the woodwinds, / that the percussion instruments don't drown out the violas.
그들은 반드시 확실히 해야 한다 / 금관악기 호른이 작동(연주)되는지 / 목관악기에 맞춰서 / 타악기가 비올라 소리를 막지 않는지를

But perfecting those relationships / —important though it is— / is not the ultimate goal / of their efforts.
그러나 그러한 관계를 완벽하게 하는 것이 / 중요하기는 하지만 / 궁극적인 목적은 아니다 / 그들이 하는 노력의

What conductors and composers desire / is the ability / to marshal these relationships / into a whole / whose magnificence exceeds / the sum of its parts.
지휘자들과 작곡가들이 바라는 것은 / 능력이다 / 이러한 관계를 모으는 / 하나의 전체로 / 그것(전체)의 웅장함이 넘어서는 / 각 부분들의 합을

So it is with the high-concept aptitude of Symphony.
따라서 그것이 바로 관객에게 폭넓은 호소력을 갖는 교향곡의 성질이다.

The boundary crosser, the inventor, and the metaphor maker all / understand the importance of relationships.
경계를 넘는 사람, 발명가, 그리고 은유를 만드는 사람 모두 / 관계의 중요성을 이해한다

But the Conceptual Age also demands / the ability / to grasp the *relationships between relationships*.
그러나 Conceptual Age(개념 시대)는 또한 요구한다 / 능력을 / '관계들 사이의 관계들'을 파악하는

This meta-ability goes / by many names / —systems thinking, gestalt thinking, holistic thinking.
이러한 메타(초월) 능력은 통한다 / 많은 이름들로 / 시스템 사고, 게슈탈트 사고, 전체론적 사고와 같은

해석 어떤 교향곡에서든, 작곡가와 지휘자는 다양한 책임을 지닌다. 그들은 반드시 금관악기 호른이 목관악기에 맞춰서 작동(연주)되고, 타악기가 비올라 소리를 막지 않는지를 반드시 확실히 해야 한다. 그러나 그러한 관계를 완벽하게 하는 것이 중요하기는 하지만, 그들이 하는 노력의 궁극적인 목적은 아니다. 지휘자들과 작곡가들이 바라는 것은 이러한 관계를 그것(전체)의 웅장함이 각 부분들의 합을 넘어서는 하나의 전체로 모으는 능력이다. 따라서 그것이 바로 관객에게 폭넓은 호소력을 갖는 교향곡의 성질이다. 경계를 넘는 사람, 발명가, 그리고 은유를 만드는 사람 모두 관계의 중요성을 이해한다. 그러나 Conceptual Age(개념 시대)는 또한 '관계들 사이의 관계들'을 파악하는 능력을 요구한다. 이러한 메타(초월) 능력은 시스템 사고, 게슈탈트 사고, 전체론적 사고와 같은 많은 이름들로 통한다.

① 음악의 힘
② 큰 그림 보기
③ 창조성의 본질
④ 공동 작업은 차이를 만든다

해설 지문 중간에서 지휘자들과 작곡가들이 바라는 것은 악기들의 관계를 전체의 웅장함이 각 부분들의 합을 넘어서는 하나의 전체로 모으는 능력이라고 하고, 지문 마지막에서 Conceptual Age(개념 시대)는 '관계들 사이의 관계들'을 파악하는 능력을 요구한다고 설명하고 있다. 따라서 이 지문의 제목을 '큰 그림 보기'라고 표현한 ②번이 정답이다.

어휘 symphony 교향곡 composer 작곡가 conductor 지휘자
brass horn 금관악기 호른 in synch with ~에 맞춰서
woodwind 목관악기 percussion 타악기
drown out (소리를) 막다, ~가 들리지 않게 하다
perfect 완벽하게 하다 ultimate 궁극적인
marshal 모으다, 결집시키다 magnificence 웅장함
exceed 넘어서다, 초월하다 sum 합
high-concept 관객에게 폭넓은 호소력을 갖는 aptitude 성질, 성향
boundary 경계(선) metaphor 은유, 비유 conceptual 개념의
grasp 파악하다, 이해하다 holistic 전체론적인 essence 본질

---

11 문법 능동태·수동태 난이도 ★★☆

해석 형사 소송에서, 입증 책임은 종종 판결을 내리는 사람(판사가 되었든 배심원이 되었든)에게 기소된 범죄의 모든 요소에 대한 합리적인 의심을 넘어서서 피고가 유죄라는 것을 납득시키는 검사에게 있다. 만약 검사가 이것을 증명하지 못하면, 유죄가 아니라는 판결이 내려진다. 이러한 증명 기준은 민사 소송과는 대조를 이루는데, 이는 청구인이 일반적으로 피고가 개연성의 균형(50퍼센트 이상 개연적인)에서 법적 책임이 있다는 것을 보여줄 필요가 있다. 미국에서 이것은 증거의 우세라고 불린다.

해설 ④ 능동태·수동태 구별 | 동사구의 수동태 동사구 refer to 뒤에 목적어가 없고, 주어(this)와 동사가 '이것이 증거의 우세라고 불리다'라는 의미의 수동 관계이므로 현재분사 referring을 be동사(is) 뒤에서 수동태를 완성하는 과거분사 referred로 고쳐야 한다. 참고로, '자동사 + 전치사' 형태의 동사구가 수동태가 되어 목적어(this)가 주어가 된 경우, 목적어 뒤에 쓰인 전치사 as가 수동태 동사 뒤에 그대로 남는다.

오답 분석
① 4형식 동사 동사 persuade는 'persuade + 간접 목적어(the trier) + 직접 목적어(that절/의문사절)'의 형태를 취하는 4형식 동사이므로 persuade the trier 뒤에 that절을 이끄는 명사절 접속사 that이 올바르게 쓰였다.
② 능동태·수동태 구별 동사 is rendered 뒤에 목적어가 없고 주어(a verdict of not guilty)와 동사가 '유죄가 아니라는 판결이 내려지다'라는 의미의 수동 관계이므로 be동사(is) 뒤에서 수동태를 완성하는 과거분사 rendered가 올바르게 쓰였다.
③ 관계부사 선행사 civil cases가 장소나 상황을 나타내고 관계사 뒤에 완전한 절(the claimant generally ~ of probabilities)이 왔으므로 장소를 나타내는 관계부사 where가 올바르게 쓰였다. 참고로, 관계부사 where는 in which로도 바꾸어 쓸 수 있다.

어휘 criminal case 형사 소송 burden of proof 입증 책임
prosecutor 검사 persuade 납득시키다 trier 판결을 내리는 사람
judge 판사 jury 배심원 the accused 피고 guilty 유죄의
reasonable 합리적인 doubt 의심 charge 기소하다
verdict 판결, 결정 render (판결을) 내리다 civil case 민사 소송
claimant 청구인 defendant 피고 liable 법적 책임이 있는
probability 개연성 preponderance 우세(함) evidence 증거

①번의 보기가 포함된 문장에서 persuade the trier (whether judge or jury) that the accused is guilty처럼 that절이나 의문사절을 직접 목적어로 갖는 4형식 동사를 알아두자.

convince 확신시키다 assure 납득시키다 tell 말하다 inform 알리다	+ 간접 목적어 (~에게)	+ 직접 목적어 (that절/의문사절)

---

12 독해 세부내용 파악 (지칭 대상 파악) 난이도 ★☆☆

끊어읽기 해석

In order to meet the demands of each course, / Escoffier modernized meal preparation / by dividing his kitchens / into five different sections.
각각의 코스에 대한 수요를 충족시키기 위해 / Escoffier는 식사 준비를 현대화했다 / 그의 주방을 나눔으로써 / 다섯 개의 다른 부분으로

The first section made cold dishes / and organized the supplies / for the whole kitchen.
첫 번째 부분은 차가운 요리를 만들었다 / 그리고 용품을 정리했다 / 주방 전체를 위한

The second section took care of / soups, vegetables, and desserts.
두 번째 부분은 책임졌다 / 수프, 야채, 그리고 디저트를

The third dealt with dishes / that were roasted, grilled, or fried.
세 번째는 요리들을 다루었다 / 구워지거나, 석쇠에 구워지거나, 혹은 튀겨진

The fourth section focused / only on sauces, / and the last was for making pastries.
네 번째 부분은 집중했다 / 오직 소스에만 / 그리고 마지막은 페스트리를 만들기 위한 곳이었다

This allowed restaurant kitchens to make their dishes / much more quickly / than in the past.
이것은 식당 주방이 요리를 만들게 했다 / 훨씬 더 빨리 / 과거보다

If a customer ordered eggs Florentine, / for example, / one section would cook the eggs, / another would make the sauce, / and yet another would make the pastry.
만약 고객이 달걀 플로렌타인을 주문하면 / 예를 들어 / 한 부분은 달걀을 요리하고 / 다른 부분은 소스를 만들고 / 또 다른 부분은 페스트리를 만들 것이다

Then, / the head chef would assemble the dish / before it was served / to the customer.
그러고 나서 / 수석 주방장이 요리를 조합할 것이다 / 그것이 내어지기 전에 / 손님에게

This system was so efficient / that it is still used / in many restaurants today.
이 체계는 너무도 효율적이어서 / 그것은 여전히 사용된다 / 오늘날 많은 식당에서

해석 각각의 코스에 대한 수요를 충족시키기 위해, Escoffier는 다섯 개의 다른 부분으로 그의 주방을 나눔으로써 식사 준비를 현대화했다. 첫 번째 부분은 차가운 요리를 만들었고 주방 전체를 위한 용품을 정리했다. 두 번째 부분은 수프, 야채, 그리고 디저트를 책임졌다. 세 번째는 구워지거나, 석쇠에 구워지거나, 혹은 튀겨진 요리들을 다루었다. 네 번째 부분은 오직 소스에만 집중했고, 마지막은 페스트리를 만들기 위한 곳이었다. 이것은 식당 주방이 과거보다 요리를 훨씬 더 빨리 만들게 했다. 예를 들어, 만약 고객이 달걀 플로렌타인을 주문하면, 한 부분은 달걀을 요리하고, 다른 부분은

소스를 만들고, 또 다른 부분은 페스트리를 만들 것이다. 그러고 나서, 수석 주방장이 손님에게 그것이 내어지기 전에 요리를 조합할 것이다. 이 체계는 너무도 효율적이어서 그것은 오늘날 많은 식당에서 여전히 사용된다.

① 주방에서 다른 부분들의 경쟁
② 필요한 재료를 준비하기 위한 확장된 공간
③ 수석 주방장의 고객을 위한 별개의 요리 분배
④ 식사를 준비하기 위해 다른 부분들로 나뉘어져 있는 주방

해설 밑줄 친 This system이 있는 문장을 통해 너무도 효율적이어서 여전히 많은 식당에서 사용되는 이 체계가 무엇인지를 지문에서 추론해야 한다는 것을 알 수 있다. 지문 처음에서 Escoffier는 각 코스에 대한 수요를 충족시키기 위해 그의 주방을 다섯 개의 부분으로 나누어 식사 준비를 현대화했다고 한 뒤, 각각의 부분에서 담당하는 역할을 설명하고 있다. 따라서 This system의 의미를 '식사를 준비하기 위해 다른 부분들로 나뉘어져 있는 주방'이라고 한 ④번이 정답이다.

어휘 meet the demand 수요를 충족시키다 modernize 현대화하다 organize 정리하다, 준비하다 supply 용품, 비품 take care of ~를 책임지다 deal with ~를 다루다 roast 굽다 grill 그릴(석쇠)에 굽다 fry 튀기다 pastry 페스트리 head chef 주방장 assemble 조합하다 serve (요리를) 내다 efficient 효율적인 ingredient 재료, 성분 distribution 분배, 배급 separate 별개의, 분리된

---

13 독해 전체내용 파악 (문단 요약) 난이도 ★★☆

끊어읽기 해석

McAdams makes an important point / about identity: / It is a story / you tell about yourself / to make sense out of / what has happened / in the past / and the kind of person you are now.
McAdams는 중요한 지적을 한다 / 정체성에 대한 / 그것은 이야기라고 / 당신이 스스로에 대해 말하는 / 이해하기 위해 / 무엇이 일어났는지를 / 과거에 / 그리고 현재 당신이 어떤 사람인지를

From this perspective, / it is not essential / that the story be true.
이러한 관점에서 / 반드시 ~일 필요는 없다 / 그 이야기가 진실일

I see myself / as culturally adventurous (that is, high on openness).
나는 나 자신이 생각한다 / 문화적으로 모험을 즐긴다고 (말하자면, 개방성에 열광하는)

I happen to believe / this is true / —that is, / compared with others, / I would be relatively open to / trying new things on a menu, / taking up new activities, / visiting new places, / and so on.
나는 믿게 되었다 / 이것이 진실이라고 / 즉 / 다른 사람과 비교했을 때 / 나는 상대적으로 ~에 열려 있을 것이다 / 메뉴에 있는 새로운 것을 시도하는 것 / 새로운 활동들을 시작하는 것 / 새로운 장소를 방문하는 것 / 등등

But, / from McAdams's perspective, / when we're talking about identity, / whether our beliefs about ourselves are true or not / is pretty much irrelevant.
그러나 / McAdams의 관점에서 보면 / 우리가 정체성에 대해 이야기할 때 / 스스로에 대한 우리의 믿음이 진실인지 아닌지는 / 거의 상관이 없다

해석 McAdams는 정체성에 대한 중요한 지적을 하는데, 그것은 과거에 무엇이 일어났는지와 현재 당신이 어떤 사람인지를 이해하기 위해 당신이 스스로에 대해 말하는 이야기라는 것이다. 이러한 관점에서, 그 이야기가 반드시 진실일 필요는 없다. 나는 나 자신이 문화

적으로 모험을 즐긴다고(말하자면, 개방성에 열광하는) 생각한다. 나는 이것이 진실이라고 믿게 되었는데, 즉 다른 사람과 비교했을 때, 나는 메뉴에 있는 새로운 것을 시도하고, 새로운 활동들을 시작하고, 새로운 장소를 방문하는 것 등등에 상대적으로 열려 있을 것이다. 그러나 McAdams의 관점에서 보면, 우리가 정체성에 대해 이야기할 때, 스스로에 대한 우리의 믿음이 진실인지 아닌지는 거의 상관이 없다.

> McAdams에 따르면, 우리의 정체성은 우리가 만들어 내는 (A) 이야기이며, 그것은 본질적으로 (B) 사실일 수도 있고 아닐 수도 있다.

	(A)	(B)
①	모험	신나는
②	모습	눈에 보이는
③	문	이용할 수 있는
④	이야기	사실의

해설 지문 앞부분에서 정체성은 당신이 스스로에 대해 말하는 이야기이며, 이러한 관점에서 그 이야기가 반드시 진실일 필요는 없다고 하고, 지문 뒷부분에서 정체성에 대해 이야기할 때 스스로에 대한 믿음이 진실인지 아닌지는 거의 상관이 없다고 했으므로, (A)와 (B)에는 우리의 정체성은 우리가 만들어 내는 '이야기'이며, 그것은 본질적으로 '사실일' 수도 있고 아닐 수도 있다는 내용이 와야 적절하다.
따라서 ④ (A) narrative(이야기) – (B) factual(사실의)이 정답이다.

어휘 identity 정체성 make sense out of ~를 이해하다
perspective 관점 essential 반드시 필요한, 필수의
culturally 문화적으로 adventurous 모험을 즐기는
openness 개방성, 솔직함 relatively 상대적으로
take up ~를 시작하다 irrelevant 상관이 없는, 무관한
visible 눈에 보이는 narrative 이야기 factual 사실의

14 독해 세부내용 파악 (지칭 대상 파악) 난이도 ★☆☆

끊어읽기 해석

Watson had been watching / ① his companion intently / ever since he had sat down / to the breakfast table.
왓슨은 바라보고 있었다 / ① 그의 친구를 골똘히 / 그가 앉은 후부터 / 아침 식사용 식탁에

Holmes happened to look up / and catch his eye.
홈스는 우연히 올려다봤다 / 그리고 그의 시선을 붙잡았다

"Well, Watson, what are you thinking about?" / he asked.
"음, 왓슨, 자네 무얼 생각하고 있나?" / 그가 물었다

"About you." // "② Me?" // "Yes, Holmes. / I was thinking / how superficial are these tricks of yours, / and how wonderful it is / that the public should continue to show interest / in them."
"자네에 관해." // "② 나?" // "그래, 홈스 / 나는 생각하고 있었네 / 자네의 이러한 속임수들이 얼마나 피상적인지 / 그리고 얼마나 놀라운지 / 사람들이 계속해서 관심을 보이는 것이 / 그것들에"

"I quite agree," / said Holmes. // "In fact, / I have a recollection / that I have ③ myself made a similar remark."
"나도 꽤 동의하네" / 홈스가 말했다 // "사실 / 나는 기억이 있네 / ③ 나 스스로 비슷한 발언을 했던"

"Your methods," / said Watson severely, / "are really easily acquired."
"자네의 방식들은" / 왓슨이 심각하게 말했다 / "정말 쉽게 얻을 수 있네"

"No doubt", / Holmes answered / with a smile. // "Perhaps you will ④ yourself give an example / of this method of reasoning."

"당연하지"라고 / 홈스가 대답했다 / 미소를 띠고 // "아마도 자네도 ④ 자네 스스로 예를 들 수 있을 것이네 / 이러한 추리의 방식의"

해석 왓슨은 아침 식사용 식탁에 앉은 후부터 ① 그의 친구를 골똘히 바라보고 있었다. 홈스는 우연히 올려다보고는 그의 시선을 붙잡았다. "음, 왓슨, 자네 무얼 생각하고 있나?" 그가 물었다. "자네에 관해." "② 나?" "그래, 홈스. 나는 자네의 이러한 속임수들이 얼마나 피상적인지, 그리고 사람들이 그것들에 계속해서 관심을 보이는 것이 얼마나 놀라운지 생각하고 있었어." "나도 꽤 동의하네" 홈스가 말했다. "사실, 나는 ③ 나 스스로 비슷한 발언을 했던 기억이 있네." "자네의 방식들은 정말 쉽게 얻을 수 있네." 왓슨이 심각하게 말했다. "당연하지", 홈스는 미소를 띠고 대답했다. "아마도 자네도 ④ 자네 스스로 이러한 추리의 방식의 예를 들 수 있을 것이네."

해설 ①, ②, ③번 모두 홈스를 지칭하지만, ④번은 왓슨을 지칭하므로 ④번이 정답이다.

어휘 companion 친구, 동반자 intently 골똘히
happen to 우연히 ~하다 look up 올려다보다 catch 붙잡다
superficial 피상적인, 깊이 없는 trick 속임수 recollection 기억
make a remark 발언을 하다 severely 심각하게
acquire 얻다, 습득하다 reasoning 추리, 추론

15 문법 분사 난이도 ★★☆

해석 1860년대에 맨해튼과 브루클린의 인구가 급속히 증가하고 있었고, 그곳들 사이의 통근자 수도 마찬가지였다(급속히 증가했다). 수천 명의 사람들이 보트와 페리를 타고 매일 이스트강을 건넜지만, 이러한 형태의 운송 수단들은 불안정했고 나쁜 날씨로 인해 자주 중단되었다. 많은 뉴욕 시민들은 맨해튼과 브루클린을 직접 연결하는 다리를 갖고 싶어 했는데, 이는 그것이 그들의 통근을 더 빠르고 더 안전하게 만들 것이기 때문이었다. 유감스럽게도, 이스트강의 넓은 폭과 거친 파도 때문에 그(이스트강) 위에 어떤 것이든 짓는 것이 어려웠다. 또한 끊임없이 그 위를 항해하는 수백 척의 배들 때문에 그것은 그 당시 매우 번잡한 강이었다.

해설 ② 현재분사 vs. 과거분사 수식받는 명사(a bridge)와 분사가 '다리가 연결하다'라는 의미의 능동 관계이므로, 과거분사 connected를 현재분사 connecting으로 고쳐야 한다.

오답분석 ① 도치 구문: 기타 도치 | 수량 표현의 수 일치 부사 so가 '~역시 그렇다'라는 의미로 쓰여 문장 앞에 오면 주어와 동사가 도치되어 '(조)동사(was) + 주어(the number ~ them)'의 어순이 되어야 하고, 주어 자리에 단수 취급하는 수량 표현(the number of)이 왔으므로 단수 동사 was가 올바르게 쓰였다.
③ 가짜 주어 구문 to 부정사구(to build anything on it)와 같이 긴 주어가 오면 진주어인 to 부정사구를 문장 맨 뒤로 보내고 가주어 it이 주어 자리에 대신해서 쓰이므로 가주어 it이 올바르게 쓰였다.
④ 분사구문의 관용 표현 이유를 나타낼 때는 'with + 명사 + 분사'의 형태로 나타낼 수 있는데, 명사(hundreds of ships)와 분사가 '수백 척의 배가 항해하다'라는 의미의 능동 관계이므로 현재분사 sailing이 올바르게 쓰였다.

어휘 population 인구 rapidly 급속히 commuter 통근자
transport 운송 수단 unstable 불안정한 frequently 자주
width 폭, 너비 rough 거친 tide 조수 sail 항해하다

16　문법　분사　난이도 ★★☆

해석　최근에 P2P 대출이 대체 금융 산업의 전형적인 것이 되어 왔다. 2015년 보고서에서 Morgan Stanley는 그러한 시장 대출이 2020년까지 전 세계적으로 천오백억 달러에서 사천구백억 달러를 장악할 것이라고 예측했다. P2P 대출은 대출해 주는 사람들, 즉 투자자들을 대출자들과 직접적으로 연결시키는 온라인 서비스를 통해 돈을 개인 혹은 사업체에게 빌려주는 관행이며, 이는 양측 모두가 은행과 같은 전통적인 공급자들을 그냥 지나칠 수 있게 한다. 대출기관은 전형적으로 더 좋은 수익률을 가지는 반면 대출받는 사람들, 즉 개인들이나 SME(중소기업들)는 유동적이고 경쟁적으로 값이 매겨진 대출에 접근한다. 투자자들에게 수익은 매력적이다. 차용자와 연결되는 것은 며칠에서 몇 시간 어디든 걸릴 수 있다. 그리고 은행이 개인 대출로는 전형적으로 2퍼센트 미만의 수익을 얻는 곳에서, P2P 수익은 그것의 3배 이상일 수 있다.

해설　③ 분사구문의 형태　분사구문의 생략된 주어(P2P lending)와 분사가 'P2P 대출이 ~할 수 있게 하다'라는 의미의 능동 관계이므로 과거분사 enabled를 현재분사 enabling으로 고쳐야 한다.

오답분석　① 현재완료 시제　문맥상 '대체 금융 산업의 전형적인 것이 되어 왔다'라는 의미로 과거에 발생한 일이 현재까지 계속되는 것을 나타내고 있으므로 조동사 have(has) 뒤에서 현재완료 시제를 완성하는 과거분사 become이 올바르게 쓰였다.
　② 조동사 will　문맥상 '천오백억 달러에서 사천구백억 달러를 장악할 것이다'라는 의미가 되어야 자연스러우므로 약한 추측을 나타내는 조동사 would(~할 것이다)가 올바르게 쓰였다.
　④ 동명사의 형태　동명사의 의미상 주어(investors)와 동명사가 '투자자들이 연결되다'라는 의미의 수동 관계이므로 being 뒤에서 동명사의 수동형을 완성하는 과거분사 matched가 올바르게 쓰였다.

어휘　lending 대출　poster child 전형적인 것(인물)
alternative 대체 가능한　finance 금융, 재정　predict 예측하다
command 장악하다　globally 전세계적으로　practice 관행
match 연결시키다　party (계약·거래의) 당사자
go around (그냥) 지나치다　rate of return 수익률
get access 접근하다　flexible 유동적인, 유연한
competitively 경쟁적으로　price 값을 매기다　loan 대출
typically 전형적으로　earn (이자·수익 등을) 얻다, 올리다

17　독해　전체내용 파악 (글의 감상)　난이도 ★★☆

끊어읽기 해석

So when I stood / at the plate / in that Old Timers game, / staring at a pitcher / whose hair was gray, / and when he threw / what used to be his fastball / but what now was just a pitch / that floated in / toward my chest, / and when I swung / and made contact / and heard the familiar *thwock*, / and I dropped my bat / and began to run, / convinced that / I had done something fabulous, / forgetting my old gauges, / forgetting that my arms and legs lacked the power / they once had, / forgetting that you age, / the walls get farther away, / and when I looked up and saw / what I had first thought to be a solid hit, / maybe a home run, / now coming down / just beyond the infield / toward the waiting glove / of the second baseman, / no more than a pop-up, a wet firecracker, a dud, / and a voice in my head yelled, / "Drop it! Drop it!" / as that second baseman squeezed his glove / around my final offering / to this maddening game.

그래서 내가 서 있었을 때 / 본루에 / 그 Old Timers 게임에서 / 투수를 바라보며 / 머리가 회색이었던 / 그리고 그가 던졌을 때 / 예전에는 속구였던 것을 / 하지만 이제는 투구에 불과한 것을 / 미끄러지듯 오는 / 내 가슴 쪽으로 / 그리고 나는 팔을 휘둘러 / (공에) 닿았고 / '탁'치는 익숙한 소리를 들었을 때 / 나는 야구 방망이를 던지고 / 달리기 시작하며 / 확신했다 / 내가 기막히게 멋진 것을 해냈다고 / 내 예전의 한계치를 잊고 / 내 팔과 다리가 힘을 잃었다는 것을 잊고 / (그것들이) 한 때 갖고 있던 / 나이 들어간다는 것을 잊고 / 벽은 더 멀어지고 / 그리고 내가 위를 올려다보며 보았을 때 / 내가 처음에는 확실한 강타라고 생각했던 것을 / 아마도 홈런이라고 / 이제 (그것은) 내려오고 있는데 / 바로 내야를 넘어서 / 기다리고 있는 글러브 쪽으로 / 2루수의 / 고작 뜬 공이며, 젖은 폭죽이고, 불발탄일 뿐이었고 / 내 머릿속의 목소리는 소리쳤다 / '떨어트려! 떨어트려!'라고 / 그 2루수가 그의 글러브로 꽉 쥐었을 때 / 내가 마지막으로 친 것을 / 이 미치게 하는 게임에

해석　그래서 내가 그 Old Timers 게임에서 본루에 서서 머리가 회색이었던 투수를 뚫어지게 바라보고 있었을 때, 그리고 그가 예전에는 속구였지만 이제는 내 가슴 쪽으로 미끄러지듯 오는 투구에 불과한 것을 던졌을 때, 그리고 내가 팔을 휘둘러 (공에) 닿아 '탁'치는 익숙한 소리를 들었을 때, 나는 야구 방망이를 던지고 달리기 시작하며 내가 기막히게 멋진 것을 해냈다고 확신했고, 내 예전의 한계치를 잊었으며, 내 팔과 다리가 한 때 갖고 있던 힘을 잃었다는 것을 잊고, 나이 들어간다는 것을 잊고, 벽은 더 멀어지고, 내가 위를 올려다 보며 처음에는 확실한 강타, 아마도 홈런이라고 생각했던 것을 보았을 때, 이제 (그것은) 2루수의 기다리고 있는 글러브 쪽으로 바로 내야를 넘어서 내려오고 있는데, 그것은 고작 뜬 공이며, 젖은 폭죽이고, 불발탄일 뿐이었고, 이 미치게 하는 게임에 내가 마지막으로 친 것을 그 2루수가 그의 글러브로 꽉 쥐었을 때 내 머릿속의 목소리는 '떨어트려! 떨어트려!'라고 소리쳤다.

① 질투하는　　　　　② 아주 기뻐하는
③ 열정적인　　　　　④ 실망한

해설　지문 전반에 걸쳐 필자는 투수의 공을 친 후 그것이 아마도 홈런일 것이라고 생각했지만 공이 2루수의 글러브에 들어간 것을 확인하고 실망했다는 일화를 소개하고 있다. 따라서 지문에서 I(나)가 느꼈을 심경을 '실망한'이라고 표현한 ④번이 정답이다.

어휘　plate 본루　stare at ~를 뚫어지게 바라보다, 응시하다　pitcher 투수
fastball 속구　float 미끄러지다; 뜨다　swing (팔 등을) 휘두르다
make contact ~에 닿다　bat 야구 배트　fabulous 기막히게 멋진
gauge 한계, 범위　lack ~가 없다, 부족하다　age 나이를 먹다
farther 더 멀리　hit 강타, 타격　infield 내야　pop-up 뜬 공
firecracker 폭죽　dud 불발탄, 실패　yell 소리치다
squeeze 꽉 쥐다　offering 제공된(내놓은) 것
madden ~를 미치게 하다

끊어읽기 해석

In our daily, conscious activity / we generally experience a
① separation / between the mind and the body.
우리의 일상적이고 의식적인 활동에서 / 우리는 일반적으로 ① 분리를 경험
한다 / 정신과 육체 사이의

We think / about our bodies and our physical actions.
우리는 생각한다 / 우리의 육체와 육체적인 행위들에 대해

Animals do not experience / this division.
동물들은 경험하지 않는다 / 이 구분을

When we start to learn any skill / that has a physical
component, / this separation becomes even ② less apparent.
우리가 어떤 기술을 배우기 시작할 때 / 육체적인 요소를 가지고 있는 / 이
러한 분리는 훨씬 ② 덜 명백해진다

We have to think / about the various actions / involved, / the
steps / we have to follow.
우리는 생각해야 한다 / 다양한 행동에 대해 / 관련된 / 단계들(에 대해) /
우리가 따라야 하는

We are aware of our slowness / and of how our bodies
respond / in an awkward way.
우리는 우리의 느낌에 대해 인지하고 있다 / 그리고 우리의 육체가 어떻게
반응하는지에 대해 / 서투르게

At certain points, / as we ③ improve, / we have glimpses /
of how this process could function differently, / of how it
might feel to practice the skill fluidly, / with the mind not
getting in the way of the body.
특정 시점에는 / 우리가 ③ 개선되면서 / 우리는 어렴풋이 안다 / 이 과정
이 어떻게 다르게 기능할 수 있는지를 / 그 기술을 유동적으로 실행하는 것
이 어떤 느낌일지를 (알게 된다) / 정신이 육체를 방해하지 않는 상태로

With such glimpses, / we know / what to aim for.
그러한 짧은 경험을 통해 / 우리는 안다 / 무엇을 목표로 해야 하는지

If we take our practice far enough / the skill becomes
④ automatic, / and we have the sensation / that the mind
and the body are operating / as one.
만약 우리가 충분히 연습한다면 / 그 기술은 ④ 무의식적인 것이 되고 / 우
리는 느낌을 갖는다 / 정신과 육체가 작용하고 있다는 / 하나로서

해석 우리의 일상적이고 의식적인 활동에서, 우리는 일반적으로 정신과
육체 사이의 ① 분리를 경험한다. 우리는 우리의 육체와 육체적인
행위들에 대해 생각한다. 동물들은 이 구분을 경험하지 않는다. 우
리가 육체적인 요소를 가지고 있는 어떤 기술을 배우기 시작할 때,
이러한 분리는 훨씬 ② 덜 명백해진다. 우리는 관련된 다양한 행동
과 우리가 따라야 하는 단계들에 대해 생각해야 한다. 우리는 우리
의 느낌과 우리의 육체가 어떻게 서투르게 반응하는지에 대해 인
지하고 있다. 우리가 ③ 개선되면서, 특정 시점에는, 우리는 이 과
정이 어떻게 다르게 기능할 수 있는지, 정신이 육체를 방해하지 않
는 상태로 그 기술을 유동적으로 실행하는 것이 어떤 느낌일지를
어렴풋이 안다. 그러한 짧은 경험을 통해 우리는 무엇을 목표로 해
야 하는지 안다. 만약 우리가 충분히 연습한다면 그 기술은 ④ 무
의식적인 것이 되고 우리는 정신과 육체가 하나로서 작용하고 있
다는 느낌을 갖는다.

해설 지문 전반에 걸쳐 우리는 우리의 느낌과 우리의 육체가 어떻게 서
투르게 반응하는지를 인지하지만, 우리가 충분히 연습한다면 그
기술은 무의식적인 것이 된다고 했으므로, 우리가 육체적인 요소
를 가지고 있는 어떤 기술을 배우기 시작할 때 이러한 분리가 훨
씬 '덜'(less) 명백해진다는 것은 문맥상 적절하지 않다. 따라서
② less가 정답이다. 참고로, 주어진 less를 대신할 수 있는 어휘
로는 '더'라는 의미의 more가 있다.

어휘 conscious 의식적인   separation 분리   physical 육체의, 신체의
division 구분   component 요소   apparent 명백한, 분명한
slowness 느림   awkward 서투른, 어색한
have a glimpse of ~를 어렴풋이 알다   function 기능하다, 작용하다
fluidly 유동적으로   automatic 무의식적인, 반사적인
sensation 느낌, 감각   operate 작용하다

19 문법 동사의 종류   난이도 ★★☆

해석 2000년에 하버드 대학교의 과학자들은 모나리자의 규정하기 힘
든 미소를 설명하는 신경학적인 방법을 제시했다. 관찰자가 그녀
의 눈을 바라볼 때, 입은 흑백으로 보이는 주변 시야에 있다. 이것
은 그녀의 입 가장자리에 있는 그늘을 두드러지게 하며, 미소가 더
넓어 보이게 한다. 그러나 당신이 그것을 똑바로 바라보면, 미소는
줄어든다. 그녀의 미소를 너무도 생생하고 신비하게 만드는 것은
바로 그녀의 미소의 가변성, 즉 당신이 그것으로부터 눈길을 돌리
면 그것이 변한다는 사실이다.

해설 ③ 5형식 동사 사역동사 make(making)는 동사원형을 목적격
보어로 취하는 5형식 동사이므로 3인칭 단수 동사 seems를 동
사원형 seem으로 고쳐야 한다.

오답
분석
① 동명사의 역할 전치사(of) 뒤에는 명사 역할을 하는 것이 와야
하므로 동명사 explaining이 올바르게 쓰였다.
② 관계대명사 선행사 peripheral vision이 사물이고 관계절 내
에서 동사 sees의 주어 역할을 하므로 사물을 가리키는 주격
관계대명사 which가 올바르게 쓰였다.
④ It – that 강조 구문 문맥상 '미소를 너무도 생생하고 신비하게
만드는 것은 바로 미소의 가변성이다'라는 의미가 되어야 자연
스러운데, '~한 것은 바로 ~이다'는 It – that 강조 구문을 사
용하여 나타낼 수 있으므로 that이 올바르게 쓰였다.

어휘 neurological 신경학적인, 신경학의   elusive 규정하기 힘든
peripheral 주변적인   accentuate 두드러지게 하다
corner 가장자리, 모서리   broad 넓은   diminish 줄어들다, 약해지다
straight 똑바로   variability 가변성
look away from ~로부터 눈길을 돌리다   alive 생생한, 살아있는
mysterious 신비한

👍 이것도 알면 **합격!**

It – that 강조 구문에서 강조되는 내용이 사람일 경우 that 대신
who(m), 사물이나 동물일 경우 which, 시간일 경우 when, 장소일
경우 where를 쓸 수 있다는 것을 알아두자.

ex It is the security guard **who** lets guests into the building.
    강조된 내용(사람)
손님들을 건물 안으로 들인 사람은 바로 보안 요원이다.

It is the day **when** children get their parents gifts.
강조된 내용(시간)
아이들이 부모에게 선물을 주는 때는 바로 그날이다.

20 독해 논리적 흐름 파악 (문장 삽입)   난이도 ★★☆

끊어읽기 해석

So around about the time we are two, / our brains will already
have / distinct and individual patterns.
그래서 우리가 두 살 정도가 될 즈음에 / 우리의 뇌는 이미 갖게 될 것이
다 / 뚜렷하고 개인적인 패턴을

When we are babies / our brains develop / in relationship /
with our earliest caregivers.

우리가 아기일 때 / 우리의 뇌는 발달한다 / 관계 속에서 / 우리를 처음 돌봐주는 사람과의

Whatever feelings and thought processes / they give to us / are mirrored, reacted to and laid down / in our growing brains.
감정과 사고 과정이 무엇이든 / 그들이 우리에게 주는 / 반영되고, 반응되고, 그리고 축적된다 / 우리의 성장하는 뇌에

(①) When things go well, / our parents and caregivers also mirror and validate / our moods and mental states, / acknowledging and responding / to what we are feeling.
상황이 잘 되어가면 / 우리의 부모님과 돌봐주는 사람 또한 반영하고 입증한다 / 우리의 기분과 정신적인 상태를 / 인정하고 대응하면서 / 우리가 느끼는 것을

(②) It is then / that our left brains mature sufficiently / to be able to understand language.
그러고 나서 / 우리의 좌뇌는 충분히 성숙한다 / 언어를 이해할 수 있을 만큼

(③) This dual development / enables us to integrate our two brains, / to some extent.
이러한 이중 발달은 / 우리가 두 개의 뇌를 통합할 수 있게 한다 / 어느 정도까지

(④) We become able to begin / to use the left brain / to put / into language / the feelings of the right.
우리는 시작할 수 있게 된다 / 좌뇌를 사용하는 것을 / 더하기 위해 / 언어에 / 우뇌의 감정을

해석 우리가 아기일 때, 우리의 뇌는 우리를 처음 돌봐주는 사람과의 관계 속에서 발달한다. 그들이 우리에게 주는 감정과 사고 과정이 무엇이든, 우리의 성장하는 뇌에 반영되고, 반응되고, 그리고 축적된다. 상황이 잘 되어가면, 우리의 부모님과 돌봐주는 사람 또한 우리의 기분과 정신적인 상태를 반영하고 입증하며, 우리가 느끼는 것을 인정하고 (그것에) 대응한다. ② 그래서 우리가 두 살 정도가 될 즈음에, 우리의 뇌는 이미 뚜렷하고 개인적인 패턴을 갖게 될 것이다. 그러고 나서 우리의 좌뇌는 언어를 이해할 수 있을 만큼 충분히 성숙한다. 이러한 이중 발달은 우리가 두 개의 뇌를 어느 정도까지 통합할 수 있게 한다. 우리는 우뇌의 감정을 언어에 더하기 위해 좌뇌를 사용하는 것을 시작할 수 있게 된다.

해설 ②번 앞 문장에 우리의 부모님과 돌봐주는 사람 또한 우리의 기분과 정신적인 상태를 반영하고 입증하며, 우리가 느끼는 것을 인정하고 그것에 대응한다는 내용이 있고, ②번 뒤 문장에는 그러고 나서 우리의 좌뇌는 언어를 이해할 수 있을 만큼 충분히 성숙한다는 내용이 있으므로, ②번 자리에 그래서 우리가 두 살 정도가 될 즈음에, 우리의 뇌는 이미 뚜렷하고 개인적인 패턴을 갖게 될 것이라는 주어진 문장이 나와야 지문이 자연스럽게 연결된다. 따라서 ②번이 정답이다.

어휘 distinct 뚜렷한 individual 개인적인 caregiver 돌봐주는 사람
mirror 반영하다 go well 잘 되어가다 validate 입증하다
state 상태 acknowledge 인정하다 sufficiently 충분히
dual 이중의 integrate 통합하다 to some extent 어느 정도까지
put into ~에 더하다

21 독해 논리적 흐름 파악 (문장 삽입) 난이도 ★☆☆

끊어읽기 해석

Nowadays, / it is much easier / to find out / where you are / and which way to go / because you have one of the world's greatest inventions / at your fingertips.
요즘에는 / 훨씬 쉽다 / 알아내는 것이 / 당신이 어디에 있는지 / 그리고 어느 길로 가야 하는지를 / 당신이 세계에서 가장 위대한 발명품 중 하나를 이용하기 때문에 / 자유자재로

For thousands of years, / humans had difficulty trying to figure out / where they were.
수 천년 동안 / 인간은 알아내는 데 어려움을 겪었다 / 그들이 어디에 있는지를

(①) So, / they devoted a great deal of time and effort / to resolving this problem.
그래서 / 그들은 많은 시간과 노력을 쏟았다 / 이 문제를 해결하는 것에

(②) They drew complicated maps, / constructed great landmarks / to keep themselves on the right path, / and even learned to navigate / by looking up at the stars.
그들은 복잡한 지도들을 그렸고 / 큰 주요 지형지물들을 건설했다 / 계속 올바른 길로 가기 위해 / 그리고 심지어 방향을 읽는 것을 배웠다 / 별들을 올려다보고

(③) As long as you have a Global Positioning System(GPS) receiver, / you never have to worry / about taking a wrong turn.
당신이 GPS 수신기를 가지고 있는 한 / 당신은 걱정할 필요가 전혀 없다 / 길을 잘못 드는 것에 대해

(④) Your GPS receiver can tell you / your exact location / and give you directions / to wherever you need to go, / no matter where you are / on the planet!
당신의 GPS 수신기는 당신에게 알려줄 수 있다 / 당신의 정확한 위치를 / 그리고 당신에게 방향을 줄 수 있다 / 당신이 가야 하는 어느 곳으로든 / 당신이 어디에 있는지 / 이 지구상의!

해석 수 천년 동안 인간은 그들이 어디에 있는지를 알아내는 데 어려움을 겪었다. 그래서, 그들은 이 문제를 해결하는 것에 많은 시간과 노력을 쏟았다. 그들은 복잡한 지도들을 그렸고, 계속 올바른 길로 가기 위해 큰 주요 지형지물들을 건설했으며, 심지어 별들을 올려다보고 방향을 읽는 것을 배웠다. ③ 요즘에는 당신이 세계에서 가장 위대한 발명품 중 하나를 자유자재로 이용하기 때문에, 당신이 어디에 있고 어느 길로 가야 하는지를 알아내는 것이 훨씬 쉽다. 당신이 GPS 수신기를 가지고 있는 한, 당신은 길을 잘못 드는 것에 대해 걱정할 필요가 전혀 없다. 당신의 GPS 수신기는 당신의 정확한 위치를 알려 줄 수 있고, 당신이 이 지구상의 어디에 있든지, 당신이 가야 하는 어느 곳으로든 당신에게 방향을 줄 수 있다!

해설 ③번 앞 문장에 인간은 복잡한 지도들을 그렸고, 계속 올바른 길로 가기 위해 큰 주요 지형지물들을 건설했으며, 심지어 별들을 올려다보고 방향을 읽는 것을 배웠다는 내용이 있으므로, ③번 자리에 요즘에는 세계에서 가장 위대한 발명품 중 하나인 GPS 수신기를 사용하여 당신이 어디에 있고 어느 길로 가야 하는지를 알아내는 것이 훨씬 쉽다는 주어진 문장이 나와야 지문이 자연스럽게 연결된다. 따라서 ③번이 정답이다.

어휘 find out ~를 알아내다 invention 발명(품)
devote (몸·노력·시간·돈을) ~에 쏟다 resolve 해결하다
complicated 복잡한 construct 건설하다
landmark 주요 지형지물, 랜드마크 path 길 navigate 방향을 읽다
receiver 수신기 take a wrong turn 길을 잘못 들다
the planet 지구

22 독해 추론 (빈칸 완성 - 구) 난이도 ★☆☆

끊어읽기 해석

A great ad is a wonderful thing; / it's why / you love advertising.
훌륭한 광고는 멋진 것이며 / 그것이 이유이다 / 당신이 광고를 사랑하는

But what you're looking at / is only half of what's there, / and the part / you can't see / has more to do with that ad's success / than the part / you can.

그러나 당신이 바라보고 있는 것은 / 존재하는 것의 절반에 지나지 않는다 / 그리고 부분이 / 당신이 볼 수 없는 / 그 광고의 성공과 더 관련이 있다 / 부분보다 / 당신이 볼 수 있는

Before those surface features (the terrific headline or visual or storyline or characters or voiceover or whatever) / can work their wonders, / the ad has to have something to say, / something / that matters.
그러한 표면적 특징들(아주 멋진 표제나 시각자료, 혹은 줄거리, 등장인물, 해설 목소리, 혹은 무엇이든 간에)이 / 놀랄만한 효과를 가져오기 전에 / 광고는 할 말을 갖고 있어야 한다 / 무언가를 / 중요한

Either it addresses real consumer motives and real consumer problems, / or it speaks to no one.
그것은 진짜 소비자의 동기와 진짜 소비자의 문제를 다룬다 / 아니면 아무에게도 말하지 않는다

To make great ads, / then, / you have to start / where they start: / with the invisible part.
훌륭한 광고를 만들기 위해서 / 그러므로 / 당신은 시작해야 한다 / 그것들이 시작하는 곳에서 / 그 곳은 보이지 않는 부분이다

해석 훌륭한 광고는 멋진 것이며, 그것이 당신이 광고를 사랑하는 이유이다. 그러나 당신이 바라보고 있는 것은 존재하는 것의 절반에 지나지 않으며, 당신이 볼 수 있는 부분보다 당신이 볼 수 없는 부분이 그 광고의 성공과 더 관련이 있다. 그러한 표면적 특징들(아주 멋진 표제나 시각자료, 혹은 줄거리, 등장인물, 해설 목소리, 혹은 무엇이든 간에)이 놀랄만한 효과를 가져오기 전에, 광고는 할 말을, 중요한 무언가를 갖고 있어야 한다. 그것은 진짜 소비자의 동기와 진짜 소비자의 문제를 다루거나, 아니면 아무에게도 말하지 않는다. 그러므로, 훌륭한 광고를 만들기 위해서 당신은 그것들이 시작하는 곳에서 시작해야 하는데, 그 곳은 보이지 않는 부분이다.

① 효과적인 도구
② 보이지 않는 부분
③ 기업의 요구사항
④ 표면적인 특징들

해설 빈칸이 있는 문장을 통해 빈칸에 훌륭한 광고를 만들기 위해서 어떤 곳에서 시작해야 하는지에 대한 내용이 나와야 적절하다는 것을 알 수 있다. 지문 앞부분에서 당신이 볼 수 있는 부분보다 당신이 볼 수 없는 부분이 그 광고의 성공과 더 관련이 있다고 했으므로, 훌륭한 광고를 만들기 위해서 당신은 그것들이 시작하는 곳인 '보이지 않는 부분'에서 시작해야 한다고 한 ②번이 정답이다.

어휘 ad 광고 surface 표면의; 표면 have to do with ~와 관련이 있다
feature 특징 terrific 아주 멋진 headline 표제
voiceover 해설 목소리 work wonders 놀랄만한 효과를 가져오다
matter 중요하다 address 다루다 motive 동기
invisible 보이지 않는 corporate 기업의

23 독해 논리적 흐름 파악 (문장 삽입) 난이도 ★★☆

끊어읽기 해석

Wham-O, the visionary toy company / known for its Hula-Hoops / bought the rights a year later / and renamed the flying disc Frisbee.
선견지명이 있는 장난감 회사인 Wham-O는 / 그것의 훌라후프로 알려진 / 1년 후 그 권리를 매수하여 / 그 비행 원반을 Frisbee라는 이름으로 개명했다

Walter Fredrick Morrison and his girlfriend, Lucile Nay, / discovered / that flying discs were marketable / when a stranger asked to buy the metal cake pan / they were flipping / through the air / on a beach / in California.

Walter Fredrick Morrison과 그의 여자친구 Lucile Nay는 / 발견했다 / 비행 원반이 시장성이 있다는 것을 / 한 낯선 사람이 금속 케이크 팬을 살 수 있는지 물어봤을 때 / 그들이 툭 던지고 있었던 / 공중으로 / 한 해변에서 / 캘리포니아의

(①) By 1938, / the couple were selling the 5-cent pans / for 25 cents / a piece.
1938년에 / 이 커플은 5센트짜리 팬을 팔았다 / 25센트에 / 개당

(②) Later, / Morrison tried his hand / at developing a flying disc / far better than that of a flying cake pan.
나중에 / Morrison은 시도해 보았다 / 비행 원반을 개발하려고 / 비행 케이크 팬 원반보다 훨씬 더 좋은

(③) Together with Franscioni, / he created the Pluto Platter.
Franscioni와 함께 / 그는 Pluto Platter를 만들어 냈다

(④) By the mid-1960s / it got so popular / that you could see a Frisbee stuck / on almost every roof / of houses.
1960대 중반에/ 그것은 너무 인기가 많아져서 / 당신은 Frisbee가 끼여있는 것을 볼 수 있었다 / 거의 모든 지붕에 / 집들의

해석 Walter Fredrick Morrison과 그의 여자친구 Lucile Nay는 한 낯선 사람이 캘리포니아의 한 해변에서 그들이 공중으로 툭 던지고 있었던 금속 케이크 팬을 살 수 있는지 물어봤을 때 비행 원반이 시장성이 있다는 것을 발견했다. 1938년에 이 커플은 5센트짜리 팬을 개당 25센트에 팔았다. 나중에, Morrison은 비행 케이크 팬 원반보다 훨씬 더 좋은 비행 원반을 개발하려고 시도해 보았다. Franscioni와 함께 그는 Pluto Platter를 만들어 냈다. ④ 그것의 훌라후프로 알려진 선견지명이 있는 장난감 회사인 Wham-O가 1년 후 그 권리를 매수하여 그 비행 원반을 Frisbee라는 이름으로 개명했다. 1960대 중반에, 그것은 너무 인기가 많아져서 당신은 거의 모든 집들의 지붕에 Frisbee가 끼여있는 것을 볼 수 있었다.

해설 ④번 앞 문장에 Morrison이 Franscioni와 함께 Pluto Platter를 만들어 냈다는 내용이 있고, ④번 뒤 문장에는 그것은 너무 인기가 많아져서 거의 모든 집들의 지붕에 Frisbee가 끼여있는 것을 볼 수 있었다는 내용이 있으므로, ④번 자리에 선견지명이 있는 장난감 회사 Wham-O가 그 권리를 매수하여 그 비행 원반을 Frisbee라는 이름으로 개명했다는 주어진 문장이 나와야 지문이 자연스럽게 연결된다. 따라서 ④번이 정답이다.

어휘 visionary 선견지명이 있는 right 권리 rename 개명하다
disc 원반 marketable 시장성이 있는 metal 금속의
flip 툭 던지다 try one's hand at ~를 시도해보다
stuck ~에 끼인, 꼼짝 못하는

24 독해 추론 (빈칸 완성 - 단어) 난이도 ★★☆

끊어읽기 해석

Paradoxically, / the initial discovery / of an interest / often goes unnoticed / by the discoverer.
역설적이지만 / 초기의 발견은 / 어떤 관심사에 대한 / 종종 간과된다 / 발견한 사람에 의해

In other words, / when you just start to get interested / in something, / you may not even realize / that's what's happening.
다시 말해서 / 당신이 막 관심을 가지기 시작할 때 / 무언가에 / 당신은 심지어 인식하지 못할 수도 있다 / 무엇이 일어나고 있는지

The emotion / of boredom / is always self-conscious / —you know it / when you feel it— / but when your attention is attracted / to a new activity or experience, / you may have very little reflective appreciation / of what's happening to you.

감정은 / 지루함의 / 늘 의식적이다 / 당신이 알기 때문에 / 당신이 그것을 느낄 때 / 하지만 당신의 관심이 이끌릴때 / 새로운 행동이나 경험에 / 당신은 사색적인 감상을 거의 갖지 못할 수도 있다 / 당신에게 일어나고 있는 것에 대한

This means that, / at the start of a new endeavor, / asking yourself nervously every few days / whether you've found your passion / is premature.

이것은 의미한다 / 새로운 노력의 시작에서 / 당신 스스로에게 초조하게 며칠마다 물어보는 것은 / 당신이 당신의 열정을 찾았는지 / 너무 이르다는 것을

해석 역설적이지만, 어떤 관심사에 대한 초기의 발견은 발견한 사람에 의해 종종 간과된다. 다시 말해서, 당신이 무언가에 막 관심을 가지기 시작할 때, 당신은 심지어 무엇이 일어나고 있는지 인식하지 못할 수도 있다. 지루함의 감정은, 당신이 그것을 느낄 때 당신이 알기 때문에, 늘 의식적이지만, 당신의 관심이 새로운 행동이나 경험에 이끌릴 때, 당신은 당신에게 일어나고 있는 것에 대한 사색적인 감상을 거의 갖지 못할 수도 있다. 이것은 새로운 노력의 시작에서, 당신 스스로에게 초조하게 며칠마다 당신이 당신의 열정을 찾았는지 물어보는 것은 너무 이르다는 것을 의미한다.

① 관련 있는　　　　　② 필요한
③ 너무 이른　　　　　④ 흔하지 않은

해설 빈칸이 있는 문장을 통해 빈칸에 새로운 노력의 시작에서 당신이 당신 스스로에게 초조하게 며칠마다 열정을 찾았는지 물어보는 것이 어떠한지에 대한 내용이 나와야 적절하다는 것을 알 수 있다. 빈칸 앞 문장에서 지루함의 감정은 당신이 그것을 느낄 때 알기 때문에 늘 의식적이지만, 당신의 관심이 새로운 행동이나 경험에 이끌릴 때는 일어나고 있는 것에 대한 사색적인 감상을 거의 갖지 못할 수도 있다고 설명하고 있다. 따라서 당신 스스로에게 초조하게 며칠마다 당신의 열정을 찾았는지 물어보는 것은 '너무 이른' 것을 의미한다고 한 ③번이 정답이다.

어휘 **paradoxically** 역설적이지만, 역설적으로　**unnoticed** 간과되는
boredom 지루함, 따분함　**self-conscious** 의식적인
attract (주의·흥미 따위)를 끌다　**reflective** 사색적인
appreciation 감상, 이해　**endeavor** 노력　**nervously** 초조하게
passion 열정　**premature** 너무 이른

25　문법　병치·도치·강조 구문　난이도 ★★☆

해석 많은 시행착오 끝에, Richard는 마침내 태양 전지판에 의해 충전된 오래된 자동차 배터리로 작동되는 번쩍이는 LED 조명 장치를 만들어 냈다. Richard는 울타리를 따라 조명들을 쭉 세웠다. 밤에 그 조명들은 마구간 바깥에서 보일 수 있었는데, 그것은 마치 사람들이 손전등을 들고 이리저리 움직이고 있는 것처럼 교대로 번쩍거렸다. 사자들은 Richard의 울타리를 두 번 다시 넘어오지 않았다. Richard는 그의 장치를 Lion Lights라고 불렀다. 이 간단하고 실용적인 장치는 사자들에게 아무런 해를 끼치지 않았고, 인간들, 소들, 그리고 사자들은 마침내 서로 평화를 이룰 수 있었다.

해설 ③ **도치 구문: 부사구 도치 1** 부정을 나타내는 부사구(Never again)가 강조되어 문장 맨 앞에 나오면 주어와 조동사가 도치되어 '조동사 + 주어(lions) + 동사'의 어순이 되어야 하므로 lions crossed를 did lions cross로 고쳐야 한다.

오답 분석 ① **현재분사 vs. 과거분사** 수식받는 명사(LED lights)와 분사가 'LED 조명 장치가 작동되다'라는 의미의 수동 관계이므로 과거분사 powered가 올바르게 쓰였다.
② **관계절의 용법** 관계절이 콤마(,) 뒤에서 계속적 용법으로 쓰여 앞에 나온 선행사(the lights)에 대한 부가 설명을 하고, 선행

사가 관계절 내에서 동사(appeared)의 주어 역할을 하고 있으므로 계속적 용법으로 쓰일 수 있는 주격 관계대명사 which가 올바르게 쓰였다.
④ **부정대명사: one·another·other** 문맥상 '인간들, 소들, 그리고 사자들은 마침내 서로 평화를 이룰 수 있었다'라는 의미가 되어야 자연스러운데, '서로'는 부정대명사 one another로 나타낼 수 있으므로 one another가 올바르게 쓰였다.

어휘 **trial and error** 시행착오　**flash** 번쩍이다
power 작동시키다, 동력을 공급하다　**charge** 충전하다
solar panel 태양 전지판　**set up** ~를 세우다　**fence** 울타리
stable 마구간　**take turns** 교대하다　**torch** 손전등
cattle (집합적으로) 소　**one another** 서로

👍 이것도 알면 **합격!**

제한을 나타내는 부사(구)가 강조되어 문장의 맨 앞에 나올 때도 주어와 조동사가 도치되어 '조동사 + 주어 + 동사'의 어순이 된다는 것을 알아두자.

(ex) Not only do they deal with domestic products, (but) they
　　　　　　조동사 주어　　동사
also carry imports.
그들은 국내 상품 뿐만 아니라 수입품도 취급한다.

정답

p.81

01	④ 독해 – 논리적 흐름 파악	11	② 독해 – 논리적 흐름 파악	21	④ 독해 – 세부내용 파악
02	① 독해 – 추론	12	③ 독해 – 논리적 흐름 파악	22	④ 독해 – 전체내용 파악
03	③ 독해 – 논리적 흐름 파악	13	④ 독해 – 추론	23	③ 독해 – 논리적 흐름 파악
04	③ 독해 – 논리적 흐름 파악	14	④ 독해 – 추론	24	③ 문법 – 조동사
05	③ 문법 – 주어·동사/목적어·보어/수식어&명사절	15	② 독해 – 전체내용 파악	25	③ 독해 – 추론
06	③ 독해 – 논리적 흐름 파악	16	③ 독해 – 전체내용 파악		
07	① 독해 – 추론	17	② 독해 – 논리적 흐름 파악		
08	① 독해 – 전체내용 파악	18	② 독해 – 전체내용 파악		
09	② 문법 – 관계절	19	② 독해 – 세부내용 파악		
10	③ 독해 – 논리적 흐름 파악	20	③ 독해 – 추론		

취약영역 분석표

영역	세부 유형	문항 수	소계
어휘	어휘&표현	0	/0
	생활영어	0	
문법	주어·동사/목적어·보어/수식어&명사절	1	/3
	관계절	1	
	조동사	1	
독해	전체내용 파악	5	/22
	세부내용 파악	2	
	추론	6	
	논리적 흐름 파악	9	
	총계		/25

· 자신이 취약한 영역은 '법원직 9급 영어, 이렇게 출제된다!'(p.8)를 통해 다시 한 번 확인하고 학습하시기 바랍니다.

---

01 독해 논리적 흐름 파악 (문맥상 부적절한 어휘) 난이도 ★☆☆

끊어읽기 해석

All living things share / basic characteristics.
모든 생물은 공유한다 / 기본적인 특징을

These common threads / can be explained / by descent from a common ancestor.
이러한 공통된 특징은 / 설명될 수 있다 / 공통 조상의 혈통이라는 것으로

Many kinds of evidence suggest / that life began with ① single cells / and that the present rainbow of organisms / evolved from this common origin / over hundreds of millions of years.
많은 종류의 증거들은 암시한다 / 생명체가 ① 단일 세포로 시작되었다는 것을 / 그리고 현재의 가지각색의 유기체들은 / 이 공통 근원으로부터 진화했다는 것을 / 수억 년 동안

In other words, / the process of ② evolution explains / the unity / we observe in living things.
다시 말해서 / ② 진화의 과정은 설명해 준다 / 통일성을 / 우리가 생물에서 관찰하는

The other striking thing / about life on earth / is its diversity.
또 다른 놀라운 점은 / 지구상의 생명체에 대한 / 그것의 다양성이다

The same coral reef contains / a multitude of animal species.
동일한 산호초는 품고 있다 / 수많은 동물의 종들을

Yet, / each body type suits / a ③ particular lifestyle.
그러나 / 각각의 동체의 형태는 적합하다 / ③ 특정한 생활 방식에

The process of evolution, / which involves changes in the genetic material / and then physical modifications / suited to different environments, / explains the ④ unity / we observe in living things.
진화의 과정은 / 유전적인 물질의 변화를 수반하는 / 그리고 그 후에 신체적 변형을 (수반하는) / 다른 환경에 적합한 / ④ 통일성을 설명해준다 / 우리가 생물에서 관찰하는

해석 모든 생물은 기본적인 특징을 공유한다. 이러한 공통된 특징은 공통 조상의 혈통이라는 것으로 설명될 수 있다. 많은 종류의 증거들은 생명체가 ① 단일 세포로 시작되었으며, 현재의 가지각색의 유기체들은 이 공통 근원으로부터 수억 년 동안 진화했다는 것을 암시한다. 다시 말해서, ② 진화의 과정은 우리가 생물에서 관찰하는 통일성을 설명해 준다. 지구상의 생명체에 대한 또 다른 놀라운 점은 그것의 다양성이다. 동일한 산호초는 수많은 동물의 종들을 품고 있다. 그러나 각각의 동체의 형태는 ③ 특정한 생활 방식에 적합하다. 유전적인 물질의 변화와 그 후에 다른 환경에 적합한 신체적 변형을 수반하는 진화의 과정은 우리가 생물에서 관찰하는 ④ 통일성을 설명해준다.

해설 지문 중간에서 또 다른 놀라운 점은 지구상의 생명체에 대한 다양성이라고 했으므로, 유전적인 물질의 변화와 그 후에 다른 환경에 적합한 신체적 변형을 수반하는 진화의 과정이 우리가 생물에서 관찰하는 '통일성'(unity)을 설명해준다는 것은 문맥상 적절하지 않다. 따라서 ④ unity가 정답이다. 참고로, 주어진 unity를 대신할 수 있는 어휘로는 '다양성'이라는 의미의 diversity가 있다.

어휘 thread 특징, 요소 descent 혈통 ancestor 조상
rainbow 가지각색의; 무지개 unity 통일성 striking 놀라운
diversity 다양성 genetic 유전적인 modification 변형

---

02 독해 추론 (빈칸 완성 - 구) 난이도 ★★☆

끊어읽기 해석

A biology teacher cannot teach / proteins, carbohydrates, fats, and vitamins, / without having understood / the basics of organic chemistry.
생물학 선생님은 가르칠 수 없다 / 단백질, 탄수화물, 지방, 그리고 비타민을 / 이해하지 않고는 / 유기 화학의 기초를

The teacher / while teaching the use of a thermometer / can discuss various scales / of measuring temperature.

선생님은 / 온도계 사용을 가르치는 동안 / 다양한 척도에 대해 논의할 수 있다 / 온도를 측정하는

If he or she says / that the body temperature of a healthy human being is 37°C / and a student wants to know the temperature / in Kelvin or Fahrenheit, / then the teacher can satisfy the student / only if he or she knows the process / of converting one scale of temperature to another.
만약 그 혹은 그녀가 말한다면 / 건강한 사람의 체온은 37°C라고 / 그리고 어떤 학생이 그 온도를 알고 싶어 한다면 / 켈빈이나 화씨로 / 그 선생님은 그 학생을 만족시킬 수 있다 / 그나 그녀가 과정을 아는 경우에만 / 하나의 온도의 척도를 다른 것으로 바꾸는

In the same way, / a chemistry teacher / when teaching proteins, enzymes, carbohydrates, and fats, etc. / should have some understanding / of the human digestive system / to be able to explain these concepts effectively / by relating the topic / to the life experiences of the learners.
마찬가지로 / 화학 선생님은 / 단백질, 효소, 탄수화물, 그리고 지방 등을 가르칠 때 / 어느 정도 지식을 가지고 있어야 한다 / 인간의 소화 체계에 대해 / 이러한 개념들을 효과적으로 설명할 수 있기 위해 / 그 주제를 관련시킴으로써 / 학생들의 삶의 경험과

Thus, / all branches of science / cannot be taught and learned / in isolation.
따라서 / 과학의 모든 분야들은 / 가르치고 배울 수 없다 / 별개로

해석　생물학 선생님은 유기 화학의 기초를 이해하지 않고는 단백질, 탄수화물, 지방, 그리고 비타민을 가르칠 수 없다. 온도계 사용을 가르치는 동안 선생님은 온도를 측정하는 다양한 척도에 대해 논의할 수 있다. 만약 그 혹은 그녀가 건강한 사람의 체온은 37°C라고 말하고, 어떤 학생이 켈빈이나 화씨로 그 온도를 알고 싶어 한다면, 그 선생님은 하나의 온도의 척도를 다른 것으로 바꾸는 과정을 아는 경우에만 그 학생을 만족시킬 수 있다. 마찬가지로, 화학 선생님은 단백질, 효소, 탄수화물, 그리고 지방 등을 가르칠 때 그 주제를 학생들의 삶의 경험과 관련시킴으로써 이러한 개념들을 효과적으로 설명할 수 있기 위해 인간의 소화 체계에 대해 어느 정도 지식을 가지고 있어야 한다. 따라서, 과학의 모든 분야들은 별개로 가르치고 배울 수 없다.
① 별개로 가르치고 배울 수 없다
② 유기 화학에 대한 지식으로 수렴한다
③ 각각의 학생의 경험과 밀접한 연관을 가지고 있다
④ 화학의 기초와 함께 습득되어야 한다

해설　빈칸이 있는 문장을 통해 빈칸에 과학의 모든 분야들이 어떠한지에 대한 내용이 들어가야 한다는 것을 알 수 있다. 지문 처음에 생물학 선생님은 유기 화학의 기초를 이해해야 단백질, 탄수화물, 지방, 그리고 비타민을 가르칠 수 있다는 내용이 있고, 빈칸 앞 문장에 화학 선생님은 인간의 소화 체계에 대해 어느 정도 지식을 가지고 있어야 단백질, 효소, 탄수화물, 지방 등의 개념을 효과적으로 설명할 수 있다는 내용이 있으므로, 과학의 모든 분야들은 '별개로 가르치고 배울 수 없다'라고 한 ①번이 정답이다.

어휘　biology 생물학　carbohydrate 탄수화물
organic chemistry 유기 화학　thermometer 온도계　scale 척도
Kelvin 켈빈(절대 온도의 단위)　Fahrenheit 화씨
convert 바꾸다, 전환하다　enzyme 효소
understanding 지식, 이해　digestive 소화의　branch 분야
isolation 별개, 분리, 고립　converge 수렴하다, 모이다
interrelate 밀접한 연관을 가지다

03 독해 논리적 흐름 파악 (문맥상 부적절한 어휘) 난이도 ★☆☆

끊어읽기 해석

Left alone, / Dodge quickly ① lay down / on the burnt soil.
혼자 남겨져서 / Dodge는 재빨리 ① 누웠다 / 타버린 땅 위에

As the flames approached him, / he covered his mouth / with a wet handkerchief / in order not to ② breathe in the smoke.
불길이 그에게 다가왔을 때 / 그는 그의 입을 가렸다 / 젖은 손수건으로 / 연기를 ② 들이마시지 않기 위해

As the fire surrounded him, / Dodge closed his eyes / and tried to breathe / from the ③ thick layer of oxygen / that remained near the ground.
불이 그를 둘러싸자 / Dodge는 그의 눈을 감았다 / 그리고 들이마시려고 노력했다 / ③ 두꺼운 산소층을 / 땅 주변에 남아 있는

Several painful minutes passed, / and Dodge survived the fire, / unharmed.
고통스러운 몇 분이 지났다 / 그리고 Dodge는 화재에서 살아남았다 / 다치지 않은 채로

Sadly, / with the ④ exception of two men / who found shelter in a small crack in a rock, / all of the other men died / in the awful fire.
슬프게도 / 두 사람을 ④ 제외하고 / 바위 속의 작은 틈에서 피신처를 찾은 / 다른 모든 사람들은 사망했다 / 끔찍한 화재 속에서

해석　혼자 남겨져서, Dodge는 재빨리 타버린 땅 위에 ① 누웠다. 불길이 그에게 다가왔을 때, 그는 연기를 ② 들이마시지 않기 위해 젖은 손수건으로 그의 입을 가렸다. 불이 그를 둘러싸자, Dodge는 그의 눈을 감고 땅 주변에 남아 있는 ③ 두꺼운 산소층을 들이마시려고 노력했다. 고통스러운 몇 분이 지나고, Dodge는 다치지 않은 채로 화재에서 살아남았다. 슬프게도, 바위 속의 작은 틈에서 피신처를 찾은 두 사람을 ④ 제외하고, 다른 모든 사람들은 끔찍한 화재 속에서 사망했다.

해설　지문 앞부분에서 Dodge는 연기를 들이마시지 않기 위해 젖은 손수건으로 그의 입을 가렸고, 불이 그를 둘러싼 후, 고통스러운 몇 분이 지났다고 했으므로, 그가 땅 주변에 남아 있는 '두꺼운'(thick) 산소층을 들이마시려고 노력했다는 것은 문맥상 적절하지 않다. 따라서 ③ thick이 정답이다. 참고로, 주어진 thick을 대신할 수 있는 어휘로는 '얇은'이라는 의미의 thin이 있다.

어휘　lie down 눕다　burnt 탄　flame 불길　handkerchief 손수건
breathe in ~을 들이마시다　painful 고통스러운
unharmed 다치지 않은　with the exception of ~은 제외하고
shelter 피신처, 대피처　crack (갈라진) 틈　awful 끔찍한

04 독해 논리적 흐름 파악 (문장 삽입) 난이도 ★★☆

끊어읽기 해석

One population of Berwick's swans / wintering in England / put on fat more rapidly than usual, / making them ready / to begin their Siberian migration early.
Berwick 백조의 한 집단은 / 영국에서 겨울을 보내는 / 평소보다 더 빨리 살이 찐다 / 그것들이 준비되게 만든다 / 시베리아로의 이주를 일찍 시작하도록

Wherever human light spills / into the natural world, / some aspect of life / —breeding, feeding, migration— / is affected.
인간의 조명이 쏟아져 들어가는 곳이라면 어디서든지 / 자연 세계로 / 삶의 일부 측면이 / 번식, 섭식, 이동과 같은 / 영향을 받는다.

Some birds / —blackbirds and nightingales, among others— /

sing at unnatural hours / in the presence of artificial light.
일부 새들 / 그중에서도 찌르레기와 나이팅게일과 같은 / 자연 법칙에 어긋나는 시간에 노래를 한다 / 인공적인 불빛이 있으면

(①) Scientists have determined / that long artificial days / —and artificially short nights— / induce early breeding / in a wide range of birds.
과학자들은 결론을 내렸다 / 긴 인공적인 낮이 / 그리고 인공적으로 짧은 밤이 / 조기 번식을 유도한다고 / 다양한 새들의

(②) And because a longer day allows / for longer feeding, / it can also affect migration schedules.
그리고 더 길어진 낮을 가능하게 하기 때문에 / 더 오랜 섭식을 / 그것은 이주 일정에도 영향을 미칠 수 있다

(③) The problem with them is / that migration, / like most other aspects of bird behavior, / is a precisely timed biological behavior.
그것들의 문제는 ~이다 / 이주가 / 조류 행동의 대부분의 다른 측면들과 마찬가지로 / 정확하게 시간이 정해져 있는 생물학적인 행동이라는 것이다

(④) Leaving early may mean / arriving too soon / for nesting conditions to be right.
일찍 떠나는 것은 의미할 수도 있다 / 너무 일찌감치 도착해서 / 둥지를 틀 조건이 적절하지 않다는 것을

해석 인간의 조명이 자연 세계로 쏟아져 들어가는 곳이라면 어디서든지, 번식, 섭식, 이동과 같은 삶의 일부 측면이 영향을 받는다. 일부 새들, 그중에서도 찌르레기와 나이팅게일과 같은 새들은 인공적인 불빛이 있으면 자연법칙에 어긋나는 시간에 노래를 한다. 과학자들은 긴 인공적인 낮과 인공적으로 짧은 밤이 다양한 새들의 조기 번식을 유도한다고 결론을 내렸다. 그리고 더 길어진 낮은 더 오랜 섭식을 가능하게 하기 때문에, 그것은 이주 일정에도 영향을 미칠 수 있다. ③ 영국에서 겨울을 보내는 Berwick 백조의 한 집단은 평소보다 더 빨리 살이 찌고, 이는 그것들이 시베리아로의 이주를 일찍 시작하도록 준비되게 만든다. 그것들의 문제는 이주가 조류 행동의 대부분의 다른 측면들과 마찬가지로, 정확하게 시간이 정해져 있는 생물학적인 행동이라는 것이다. 일찍 떠나는 것은 너무 일찌감치 도착해서 둥지를 틀 조건이 적절하지 않다는 것을 의미할 수도 있다.

해설 ③번 앞 문장에 더 길어진 낮이 새들의 이주 일정에도 영향을 미칠 수 있다는 내용이 있고, ③번 뒤 문장에 그것들의 문제는 이주가 정확하게 시간이 정해져 있는 생물학적인 행동이라는 내용이 있으므로, ③번 자리에 영국에서 겨울을 보내는 Berwick 백조 집단은 평소보다 더 빨리 살이 찌고, 이는 그것들이 시베리아로의 이주를 일찍 시작하도록 준비되게 만든다는 주어진 문장이 나와야 지문이 자연스럽게 연결된다. 따라서 ③번이 정답이다.

어휘 population 집단, 개체군 winter 겨울을 보내다
put on fat 살이 찌다 migration 이주, 이동
spill into ~로 쏟아져 들어가다 breeding 번식
feeding 섭식, 음식 섭취 blackbird 찌르레기
nightingale 나이팅게일 unnatural 자연 법칙에 어긋나는
artificial 인공적인 precisely 정확하게 timed 시간이 정해진
nest 둥지를 틀다

05 문법 주어·동사/목적어·보어/수식어&명사절 난이도 ★★★

해석 일단 우리가 아동기에서 벗어나면, 눈 맞춤은 사실 속임수에 대해 매우 신뢰할 수 없는 단서가 된다. 왜일까? 정답은 눈 맞춤이 매우 통제하기가 쉽다는 것이다. 손에 땀이 나거나 입이 마르는 것과 같이 우리가 긴장할 때 우리에게 일어나는 일의 많은 부분은 통제가 불가능하다. 하지만 우리 대부분은 우리가 보고 있는 것에 대해서는 상당히 잘 통제할 수 있다. 따라서 많은 성인들은 다른 사람들에

게 거짓말을 하는 동안 그들의 눈을 바라보는 데 문제가 거의 없다. 게다가, 능숙한 소통가들은 사람들이 눈 맞춤의 부족함과 속임수를 동일시한다는 것을 알고 있기 때문에, 그들은 상대방이 의심하지 않도록 그들이 거짓말을 할 때 의도적으로 정상적인 눈 맞춤을 유지한다. 속담에서 말하듯 눈이 영혼의 창일 수는 있지만, 눈 맞춤이 정직함의 창은 아니다!

해설 (A) 동사 자리 주어(Much of ~ in the mouth)와 주격 보어 (uncontrollable) 사이에 올 수 있는 것은 동사이므로 동명사 being이 아닌 동사 is를 써야 한다.
(B) 명사절 접속사 3: 의문사 목적어가 없는 불완전한 절(we're looking at)을 이끌며 전치사(over)의 목적어 자리에 올 수 있는 것은 명사절 접속사 what이므로 관계대명사 which가 아닌 what을 써야 한다.
(C) 명사절 자리와 쓰임 동사 know 뒤의 목적어 자리에 that절이 왔고, that절은 '명사절 접속사(that) + 주어(people) + 동사'의 형태가 되어야 하므로 동사 자리에 동명사 equating이 아닌 동사 equate를 써야 한다.
따라서 ③ (A) is – (B) what – (C) equate가 정답이다.

어휘 emerge from ~에서 벗어나다 unreliable 신뢰할 수 없는
deception 속임수, 기만 sweaty 땀이 나는 equate 동일시하다
deliberately 의도적으로 suspicious 의심하는 saying 속담, 격언
honesty 정직함

👍 이것도 알면 **합격!**

명사절을 이끌 수 있는 의문대명사 what과 which는 둘 다 '무엇'을 의미하지만, 가리키는 대상의 범위가 특정하게 정해져 있을 때만 which를 쓴다는 것을 기억하자.

(ex) No one could tell which is better between the two drawings.
두 그림 중에 무엇이 더 나은지 아무도 알 수 없었다.

No one could tell what I wanted.
내가 원하는 것이 무엇인지 아무도 알 수 없었다.

06 독해 논리적 흐름 파악 (문맥상 부적절한 문장) 난이도 ★★☆

끊어읽기 해석

Tips for Conflict Resolution
갈등 해결을 위한 조언

(A) Make / the relationship / your priority.
(A) 만들어라 / 관계를 / 당신의 우선순위로

Maintaining and strengthening the relationship, / rather than "winning" the argument, / should always be your first priority.
관계를 유지하고 강화시키는 것이 / 논쟁에서 '이기는 것'보다는 / 항상 당신의 첫 번째 우선순위여야 한다

Be respectful / of the other person / and his or her viewpoint.
존중해라 / 다른 사람을 / 그리고 그 사람의 관점을

(B) Focus on the present.
(B) 현재에 집중해라.

If you're holding on / to old hurts and resentments, / your ability / to see the reality of the current situation / will be impaired.
만약 당신이 매달리고 있다면 / 오래된 상처와 분노에 / 당신의 능력이 / 현재 상황의 현실을 바라보는 / 손상될 것이다

Rather than looking to the past and assigning blame, / focus on what you can do / right now / to solve the problem.
과거를 생각하며 책임을 돌리기보다는 / 당신이 무엇을 할 수 있는지에 집중해라 / 지금 바로 / 문제를 해결하기 위해

(C) Weigh your words / before speaking.
(C) 말을 신중하게 골라 써라 / 말하기 전에

Conflicts can be draining, / so it's important to consider / whether the issue is really worthy / of your time and energy.
갈등은 지치게 할 수 있다 / 그러므로 고려해보는 것이 중요하다 / 그 문제가 정말로 가치가 있는지를 / 당신의 시간과 에너지를 쏟아 부을

Maybe you don't want to yield / a parking space / if you've been circling / for 15 minutes.
어쩌면 당신은 양보하고 싶지 않을지도 모른다 / 주차 공간을 / 만약 당신이 (주차 공간을) 빙빙 돌고 있었다면 / 15분 동안

But if there are dozens of spots, / arguing over a single space / isn't worth it.
하지만 수십 개의 주차 공간이 있다면 / 하나의 공간을 두고 싸우는 것은 / 그만한 가치가 없다

(D) Know / when / to let something go.
(D) 알아라 / 때를 / 무언가를 놓아줄

If you can't come / to an agreement, / agree / to disagree.
만약 당신이 도달할 수 없다면 / 합의에 / 동의하라 / 동의하지 않는 것에

It takes two people / to keep an argument going.
두 사람이 필요하다 / 논쟁이 계속되기 위해서는

If a conflict is going nowhere, / you can choose / to move on.
만약 갈등이 아무런 진전을 보이지 않으면 / 당신은 선택할 수 있다 / 그냥 넘어가는 것을

해석 갈등 해결을 위한 조언
(A) 관계를 당신의 우선순위로 만들어라.
논쟁에서 '이기는 것'보다는 관계를 유지하고 강화시키는 것이 항상 당신의 첫 번째 우선순위여야 한다. 다른 사람과 그 사람의 관점을 존중해라.
(B) 현재에 집중하라.
만약 당신이 오래된 상처와 분노에 매달리고 있다면, 현재 상황의 현실을 바라보는 당신의 능력이 손상될 것이다. 과거를 생각하며 책임을 돌리기보다는, 문제를 해결하기 위해 당신이 지금 바로 무엇을 할 수 있는지에 집중해라.
(C) 말하기 전에 말을 신중하게 골라 써라.
갈등은 지치게 할 수 있으므로, 그 문제가 정말로 당신의 시간과 에너지를 쏟아부을 가치가 있는지를 고려해보는 것이 중요하다. 만약 당신이 15분 동안 (주차 공간을) 빙빙 돌고 있었다면, 어쩌면 당신은 주차 공간을 양보하고 싶지 않을지도 모른다. 하지만 수십 개의 주차 공간이 있다면, 하나의 공간을 두고 싸우는 것은 그만한 가치가 없다.
(D) 무언가를 놓아줄 때를 알아라.
만약 당신이 합의에 도달할 수 없다면, 동의하지 않는 것에 동의하라. 논쟁이 계속되기 위해서는 두 사람이 필요하다. 만약 갈등이 아무런 진전을 보이지 않으면, 당신은 그냥 넘어가는 것을 선택할 수 있다.
① (A) 관계를 당신의 우선순위로 만들어라.
② (B) 현재에 집중해라.
③ (C) 말하기 전에 말을 신중하게 골라 써라.
④ (D) 무언가를 놓아줄 때를 알아라.

해설 (C) 뒤 문장에 갈등은 지치게 할 수 있으므로 그 문제가 정말로 시간과 에너지를 쏟아부을 가치가 있는지를 고려해보는 것이 중요하다고 했으므로, '말하기 전에 말을 신중하게 골라 써라'라는 것은 문맥상 적절하지 않다. 따라서 ③번이 정답이다. 참고로, 주어진 Weigh your words before speaking을 대신할 수 있는 문장으로는 '논쟁을 신중하게 선택해라'라는 의미의 'Choose your arguments carefully' 등이 있다.

어휘 conflict 갈등, 논쟁 priority 우선순위 strengthen 강화시키다

argument 논쟁 viewpoint 관점 hold on to ~에 매달리다
resentment 분노 impair 손상시키다 blame 책임, 비난
weigh one's words 말을 신중하게 골라 쓰다, 말을 신중하게 하다
draining 지치게 하는 let go 놓아주다, 그만두다
go nowhere 아무런 진전을 못보다, 아무런 성과가 없다

07 독해 추론 (빈칸완성 - 구)   난이도 ★★★

끊어읽기 해석

By "scarcity," / most of us mean / that goods are in short supply: / there isn't enough / of something to go around.
'희소성'을 / 우리 대부분은 ~라는 뜻으로 말한다 / 물품의 공급이 부족하다는 / 즉 충분하지 않다는 것이다 / 사람들에게 돌아갈 몫이

While there often is no clear-cut understanding / of what constitutes "enough," / the simple fact / is that there is more than sufficient food / to sustain everyone / on the planet.
보통 분명한 이해가 없지만 / 무엇이 '충분한 것'으로 여겨지는지에 대해서는 / 단순한 사실은 / 충분한 것 이상의 식량이 있다는 것이다 / 모든 사람들을 먹여 살리기에 / 지구상에는

The same is true of / land and renewable energy.
~에서도 마찬가지이다 / 땅과 재생 가능 에너지

The important question, / then, / is why the staples of life / are so unequally distributed / —why, / for example, / the United States, / with a little more than 5 percent / of the world's population, / uses approximately 40 percent / of the world's resources.
중요한 질문은 / 그렇다면 / 왜 삶의 주요 상품들이 / 그렇게 불평등하게 분배되는가 하는 것이다 / 왜 / 예를 들어 / 미국이 / 5퍼센트가 조금 넘는 / 세계 인구의 / 약 40퍼센트를 사용하는가 / 전 세계 자원의

What appears to be a problem of scarcity / usually turns out, / on closer inspection, / to be a problem of distribution.
부족의 문제로 보이는 것은 / 대개 드러난다 / 자세히 조사해보면 / 분배의 문제인 것으로

But / mainstream economists / avert their eyes from this problem: / they talk / only about whether a given system is productive or efficient, / and it is up to us / to ask, / "For whom?"
그러나 / 주류 경제학자들은 / 이 문제로부터 그들의 시선을 회피한다 / 그들은 이야기한다 / 단지 주어진 시스템이 생산적인지 혹은 효율적인지에 대해서만 / 그리고 우리에게 달려 있다 / ~라고 묻는 것은 / '누구를 위해서인가?'

해석 우리 대부분은 '희소성'을 물품의 공급이 부족하다는 뜻으로 말한다. 즉 사람들에게 돌아갈 몫이 충분하지 않다는 것이다. 보통 무엇이 '충분한 것'으로 여겨지는지에 대해서는 분명한 이해가 없지만, 단순한 사실은 지구상에는 모든 사람들을 먹여 살리기에 충분한 것 이상의 식량이 있다는 것이다. 땅과 재생 가능 에너지도 마찬가지이다. 그렇다면 중요한 질문은 왜 삶의 주요 상품들이 그렇게 불평등하게 분배되는가 하는 것이다. 예를 들어, 왜 세계 인구의 5퍼센트가 조금 넘는 미국이 전 세계 자원의 약 40퍼센트를 사용하는가. 부족의 문제로 보이는 것은 자세히 조사해보면 대개 분배의 문제인 것으로 드러난다. 그러나, 주류 경제학자들은 이 문제로부터 그들의 시선을 회피한다. 그들은 단지 주어진 시스템이 생산적인지 혹은 효율적인지에 대해서만 이야기하며, '누구를 위해서인가?'라고 묻는 것은 우리에게 달려 있다.
① 이 문제로부터 그들의 시선을 회피한다
② 불평등을 줄이는 데 집중한다
③ 분배의 문제를 해결하는 데 매달린다
④ 효율성을 개선하는 데 관심이 없다

해설 빈칸이 있는 문장을 통해 빈칸에 주류 경제학자들이 어떻게 하고

있는지에 대한 내용이 와야 하는 것을 알 수 있다. 빈칸 뒤에서 그들은 단지 주어진 시스템이 생산적인지 혹은 효율적인지에 대해서만 이야기하며, '누구를 위해서인가?'라고 묻는 것은 우리에게 달려 있다고 했으므로, 주류 경제학자들은 '이 문제로부터 그들의 시선을 회피한다'라고 한 ①번이 정답이다.

어휘 scarcity 희소성 mean 뜻으로 말하다, 의미하다 in short 부족한
go around (사람들에게 많이) 돌아가다 clear-cut 분명한
constitute ~이 되는 것으로 여겨지다, ~을 구성하다
renewable 재생 가능한 staple 주요 상품 unequally 불평등하게
inspection 조사 distribution 분배 mainstream 주류의
be up to ~에 달려 있다 avert 회피하다 inequality 불평등
cling to ~에 매달리다, 집착하다

08 독해 전체내용 파악 (문단 요약) 난이도 ★★☆

끊어읽기 해석

Injuries sometimes occur / when people do not take adequate carefulness / with everyday activities.
부상은 종종 발생한다 / 사람들이 충분히 조심하지 않을 때 / 일상적인 활동에서

Although some such injuries occur / because of pure carelessness or misfortune, / others happen / because the person did not want / others to perceive him or her as too careful.
비록 그런 몇몇 부상들은 일어나지만 / 순전한 부주의나 불운 때문에 / 다른 것들은 발생한다 / 그 사람이 원하지 않기 때문에 / 다른 사람들이 그 사람을 지나치게 조심한다고 여기는 것을

For example, / many people seem to avoid / wearing seat belts in automobiles, / helmets on bicycles and motorcycles, / and life preservers in boats / because such devices convey an impression / of excessive carefulness.
예를 들어 / 많은 사람들은 ~을 피하는 것처럼 보인다 / 차 안에서 안전벨트를 매는 것 / 자전거와 오토바이를 탈 때 헬멧(을 착용하는 것) / 그리고 배에서 구명조끼(를 입는 것) / 이러한 장치들이 인상을 전하기 때문이다 / 지나치게 조심하는

In addition, / many people seem reluctant / to wear protective gear (e.g., safety goggles, gloves, and helmets) / when operating power tools or dangerous machinery / because they will be viewed as nervous or extremely careful.
게다가 / 많은 사람들은 꺼리는 것처럼 보인다 / 보호 장비(예를 들어, 보호 안경, 장갑, 그리고 헬멧)를 착용하는 것을 / 전동 공구나 위험한 기계를 가동할 때 / 그들이 불안해 하거나 지나치게 조심하는 것처럼 보일 것이기 때문에

This concern emerges / at a young age; / anecdotally, / children as young as 6 or 7 years old / are sometimes unwilling to wear / knee pads and helmets / when rollerskating / because of what other children will think of them.
이런 우려는 나타난다 / 어린 나이에 / 일화로 / 6세 또는 7세 정도의 아이들은 / 때때로 착용하는 것을 꺼린다 / 무릎 보호대와 헬멧을 / 롤러스케이트를 탈 때 / 다른 아이들이 그들에 대해 어떻게 생각할지 때문에

해석 부상은 사람들이 일상적인 활동에서 충분히 조심하지 않을 때 종종 발생한다. 비록 그런 몇몇 부상들은 순전한 부주의나 불운 때문에 일어나지만, 다른 것들은 그 사람이 다른 사람들이 그 사람을 지나치게 조심한다고 여기는 것을 원하지 않기 때문에 발생한다. 예를 들어, 많은 사람들은 차 안에서 안전벨트를 매는 것, 자전거와 오토바이를 탈 때 헬멧을 착용하는 것, 그리고 배에서 구명조끼를 입는 것을 피하는 것처럼 보이는데, 이러한 장치들이 지나치게 조심하는 인상을 전하기 때문이다. 게다가, 많은 사람들은 그들이 불안해하거나 지나치게 조심하는 것처럼 보일 것이기 때문에 전동 공구나 위험한 기계를 가동할 때 보호 장비(예를 들어, 보호

안경, 장갑, 그리고 헬멧)를 착용하는 것을 꺼리는 것처럼 보인다. 이런 우려는 어린 나이에 나타난다. 일화로, 6세 또는 7세 정도의 아이들은 때때로 다른 아이들이 그들에 대해 어떻게 생각할지 때문에 롤러스케이트를 탈 때 무릎 보호대와 헬멧을 착용하는 것을 꺼린다.

> 사람들은 왜 부상을 당하는가?
> 1. 사람들은 (A) 조심이 부족하다.
> 2. 사람들은 (B) 지나치게 조심하는 것으로 여겨지기보다는 위험을 감수하는 경향이 있다.

	(A)	(B)
①	조심	지나치게 조심하는
②	부주의	겁을 내는
③	신중	대담한
④	부주의함	취약한

해설 지문 처음에서 부상은 일상적인 활동에서 충분히 조심하지 않을 때 종종 발생하며, 부주의나 불운으로 발생한 것 외의 부상은 사람들이 다른 사람들에게 지나치게 조심한다고 여겨지는 것을 원하지 않기 때문에 발생한다고 했으므로, (A)와 (B)에는 사람들이 부상을 당하는 이유가 사람들은 '조심'이 부족하고, '지나치게 조심하는' 것으로 여겨지기보다는 위험을 감수하는 경향이 있기 때문이라는 내용이 와야 적절하다.
따라서 ① (A) vigilance(조심) – (B) overcautious(지나치게 조심하는)가 정답이다.

어휘 adequate 충분한, 적당한 carelessness 부주의, 경솔
misfortune 불운 life preserver 구명조끼
excessive 지나친, 과도한 reluctant 꺼리는, 주저하는
anecdotally 일화로 vigilance 조심, 경계
overcautious 지나치게 조심하는 inattention 부주의
intimidated 겁을 내는 prudence 신중, 조심 audacious 대담한
heedlessness 부주의함, 경솔함 vulnerable 취약한

09 문법 관계절 난이도 ★★☆

해석 외워서 연주하는 것은 대개 음악성과 음악적 소통을 신장시키는 효과가 있는 것처럼 보인다. 암기하는 바로 그 행위가 음악에 대한 더욱더 완전한 지식과 음악과의 밀접한 관계를 보장할 수 있다는 것이 일반적으로 주장된다. 게다가, 암기는 악보를 참고하는 것보다 더 설득력 있는, 관객들과의 직접적인 눈 맞춤을 이용할 수 있게 한다. 이런 방식으로 음악을 '소유하는' 사람들은 보통 그들이 마음으로부터 자연스럽게 그리고 진심으로 소통하고 있다는 인상을 주며, 실제로, 최신 증거는 이를 달성하는 음악가들은 그들의 관객들이 더 호응한다는 것을 깨달을 가능성이 있다는 것을 보여준다. 게다가, 연주자들이 관객들로부터 시각적인 반응을 받고 반응할 때, 공연은 진정으로 상호적이게 될 수 있으며, 관련된 모든 사람들 사이의 진정한 소통을 수반할 수 있다.

해설 ② 관계대명사 선행사 use of direct eye contact가 사물이고 관계절 내에서 동사 is의 주어 역할을 하므로 사람을 가리키는 주격 관계대명사 who를 사물을 가리키는 주격 관계대명사 which로 고쳐야 한다. 참고로, 선행사와 관계절 사이의 수식어 거품 (with an audience)은 관계사의 선택에 영향을 주지 않는다.

오답 분석
① 5형식 동사의 수동태 동사원형을 목적격 보어로 취하는 5형식 동사 see가 수동태가 되면 목적격 보어는 to 부정사가 되어 수동태 동사 뒤에 그대로 남으므로 수동태 is often seen 뒤에 to 부정사 to have가 올바르게 쓰였다.
③ 주어와 동사의 수 일치 that절의 주어 자리에 복수 명사 musicians가 왔으므로 복수 동사 are가 올바르게 쓰였다. 참

고로, 동사 suggest가 해야 할 것에 대한 제안과 주장의 의미가 아닌 '암시하다'라는 의미를 나타낼 때는 종속절에 '(should + 동사원형)'을 쓸 수 없다.

④ 분사구문의 형태 주절의 주어(a performance)와 분사구문이 '공연이 수반하다'라는 의미의 능동 관계이므로 현재분사 involving이 올바르게 쓰였다.

어휘   from memory 외워서, 기억을 더듬어   boost 신장시키다, 북돋우다
musicality 음악성   memorize 암기하다   guarantee 보장하다
thorough 완전한, 빈틈없는   intimate 밀접한
memorization 암기, 기억   convincing 설득력이 있는
reference 참고, 참조   score 악보, 모음 악보
impression 인상, 느낌   spontaneously 자연스럽게
sincerely 진심으로   contemporary 최신의, 현대의
responsive 호응하는, 열의를 보이는
interactive 상호적인, 서로 영향을 미치는

👍 이것도 알면 합격!

목적격 관계대명사와 '주격 관계대명사 + be 동사'는 생략할 수 있다는 것을 알아두자.

(ex) The monument (that is) located in the town square was erected a few years ago.
마을 광장에 있는 그 기념비는 몇 전 전에 세워졌다.

---

10 독해 논리적 흐름 파악 (문맥상 부적절한 어휘)   난이도 ★★★

끊어읽기 해석

Even though people seek / both social status and affluence, / their primary goal / is to attain social status.
비록 사람들이 추구하지만 / 사회적 지위와 부를 모두 / 그들의 첫째 목표는 / 사회적 지위를 얻는 것이다

A case can be made, / in particular, / that their pursuit of affluence / is instrumental: / they pursue it / not for its own sake / but because ① increased affluence will enhance / their social standing.
주장이 나올 수 있다 / 특히 / 그들의 부에 대한 추구가 / 수단이라는 / 즉 그들은 그것을 추구한다 / 그 자체를 위해서가 아니라 / ① 증가한 부가 높여줄 것이기 때문에 / 그들의 사회적 지위를

Why, / after all, / do they want the clothes, the car, and the house / they long for?
왜 / 결국 / 그들은 옷, 차, 그리고 집을 원하는 걸까 / 그들이 열망하는?

In large part / because ② attaining these things will impress / other people.
대부분은 / 이런 것들을 ② 얻는 것이 깊은 인상을 줄 것이기 때문이다 / 다른 사람들에게

Indeed, / if there were no one around to impress, / few would feel driven / to live a life of ③ frugality, / even if they could gain that / without having to work for it.
실제로 / 주변에 깊은 인상을 줄 사람이 없다면 / 충동에 사로잡힐 사람은 거의 없을 것이다 / ③ 검소한 삶을 살려는 / 그들이 그것을 얻을 수 있더라도 / 그것을 얻기 위해 노력할 필요 없이

Likewise, / if wealthy individuals found themselves living / in a culture in which people ④ despised / rather than admired / those who live in luxury, / one imagines / that they would abandon / their mansion and late-model car / in favor of a modest home / with an old car parked in the driveway.
마찬가지로 / 만일 부유한 사람들이 자신들이 살고 있다는 것을 깨닫는다면 / 사람들이 ④ 경멸하는 문화에서 / 동경하는 것이 아니라 / 사치스럽게 사는 사람들을 / 사람들은 생각한다 / 그들(부유한 사람들)이 버릴 것이라고 / 그들의 대저택과 신형 자동차를 / 검소한 집을 선호하여 / 진입로에 오래된 차가 주차되어 있는

해석   비록 사람들이 사회적 지위와 부를 모두 추구하지만, 그들의 첫째 목표는 사회적 지위를 얻는 것이다. 특히, 그들의 부에 대한 추구가 수단이라는 주장이 나올 수 있다. 즉, 그들은 (부) 그 자체를 위해서가 아니라 ① 증가한 부가 그들의 사회적 지위를 높여줄 것이기 때문에 그것을 추구한다는 것이다. 결국, 그들은 왜 그들이 열망하는 옷, 차, 그리고 집을 원하는 걸까? 대부분은 이런 것들을 ② 얻는 것이 다른 사람들에게 깊은 인상을 줄 것이기 때문이다. 실제로, 주변에 깊은 인상을 줄 사람이 없다면, 그들이 그것을 얻기 위해 노력할 필요 없이 그것을 얻을 수 있더라도 ③ 검소한 삶을 살려는 충동에 사로잡힐 사람은 거의 없을 것이다. 마찬가지로, 만일 부유한 사람들이 자신들이 사치스럽게 사는 사람들을 동경하는 것이 아니라 ④ 경멸하는 문화에서 살고 있다는 것을 깨닫는다면, 사람들은 그들(부유한 사람들)이 진입로에 오래된 차가 주차되어 있는 검소한 집을 선호하여 그들의 대저택과 신형 자동차를 버릴 것이라고 생각한다.

해설   지문 중간에서 대부분의 사람들은 다른 사람들에게 깊은 인상을 주기 위해 부를 추구한다고 했으므로, 주변에 깊은 인상을 줄 사람이 없는 상황에서는 노력할 필요 없이 부를 얻을 수 있더라도 '검소한'(frugality) 삶을 살려는 충동에 사로잡힐 사람은 거의 없다는 것은 문맥상 적절하지 않다. 따라서 ③ frugality가 정답이다. 참고로, 주어진 frugality를 대신할 수 있는 어휘로는 '풍부함'이라는 의미의 abundance 등이 있다.

어휘   seek 추구하다   status 지위   affluence 부, 부유
primary 첫째의, 주된   attain 얻다, 차지하다   pursuit 추구
instrumental 수단이 되는, 도움이 되는
for its own sake 그 자체를 위한   enhance 높이다
standing 지위   long for 열망하다   impress 깊은 인상을 주다
driven (충동에) 사로잡힌   frugality 검소, 절약   despise 경멸하다
admire 동경하다   in luxury 사치스럽게   in favor of ~을 선호하여
modest 검소한, 별로 크지 않은

---

11 독해 논리적 흐름 파악 (무관한 문장 삭제)   난이도 ★☆☆

끊어읽기 해석

It is generally believed / that primates first appeared on Earth / approximately 80 million years ago.
일반적으로 여겨진다 / 영장류는 지구에 처음으로 등장했다고 / 대략 8천만 년 전에

Unlike reptiles, / they were very sociable animals, / creating a large community.
파충류와 달리 / 그들은 매우 사교적인 동물이었다 / 큰 공동체를 형성하는

① One of the many ways / in which the primates built / a network of social support / was grooming.
많은 방법 중 하나는 / 영장류가 형성했던 / 사회적 지지 관계를 / 털 손질이었다

② In most cases, / primates have visible folds / that they would not have / if they had, even lightly, / groomed the area.
대부분의 경우 / 영장류는 눈에 띄는 주름을 가지고 있다 / 그들이 가지지 않았을 / 만일 그들이 가볍게라도 ~라면 / 그 부위를 손질했

③ For instance, / apes spent a large amount of time / grooming each other.
예를 들어 / 유인원은 많은 시간을 보냈다 / 서로 털을 손질해주며

④ Interestingly, / in the case of Barbary macaques, / the giving of grooming / resulted in / more stress relief / than the receiving of grooming.
흥미롭게도 / 바바리마카크의 경우 / 털 손질을 해주는 것이 / 가져왔다 / 더 큰 스트레스의 해소를 / 털 손질을 받는 것보다

해석   일반적으로 영장류는 대략 8천만 년 전에 지구에 처음으로 등장했

다고 여겨진다. 파충류와 달리, 그들은 큰 공동체를 형성하는 매우 사교적인 동물이었다. ① 영장류가 사회적 지지 관계를 형성했던 많은 방법 중 하나는 털 손질이었다. ② 대부분의 경우, 영장류는 만일 그들이 그 부위를 가볍게라도 손질했더라면 가지지 않았을 눈에 띄는 주름을 가지고 있다. ③ 예를 들어, 유인원은 서로 털을 손질해주며 많은 시간을 보냈다. ④ 흥미롭게도, 바바리마카크의 경우, 털 손질을 해주는 것이 털 손질을 받는 것보다 더 큰 스트레스의 해소를 가져왔다.

해설 지문 앞부분에서 '영장류의 사교성과 공동체 형성'에 대해 언급하고, ①번은 털 손질이 영장류가 사회적 지지 관계를 형성하는 방법이었다는 내용, ③, ④번은 유인원들에게서 보이는 털 손질 행태와 그것의 긍정적인 영향에 대해 설명하고 있으므로 첫 문장과 관련이 있다. 그러나 ②번은 '영장류의 눈에 띄는 주름'에 대한 내용으로, 지문 앞부분의 내용과 관련이 없으므로 ②번이 정답이다.

어휘 primate 영장류 approximately 대략 reptile 파충류
sociable 사교적인 grooming 털 손질 visible 눈에 띄는, 두드러진
fold 주름 groom (털을) 손질하다 ape 유인원 relief 해소, 제거

---

12 독해 논리적 흐름 파악 (무관한 문장 삭제) 난이도 ★★★

끊어읽기 해석

Most people agree / that Plato was a pretty good teacher.
대부분의 사람들은 동의한다 / 플라톤이 꽤 좋은 선생님이었다는 것에

He frequently used stories / to teach people / how to think.
그는 이야기를 자주 사용했다 / 사람들에게 가르쳐 주기 위해 / 생각하는 법을

One story Plato used / to teach about the limitations of democracy / was about a ship / in the middle of the ocean.
플라톤이 사용했던 한 가지 이야기는 / 민주주의의 한계에 대해 가르치기 위해 / 한 배에 관한 것이었다 / 바다 한가운데 있는

On this ship / was a captain / who was rather shortsighted / and slightly deaf.
이 배에는 / 선장이 있었다 / 다소 근시인 / 그리고 약간 귀가 먹은

① He and his crew / followed the principles of majority rule / on decisions / about navigational direction.
그와 그의 선원들은 / 다수결 원칙을 따랐다 / 결정 과정에서 / 항해의 방향에 대한

② They had a very skilled navigator / who knew how to read the stars on voyages, / but the navigator was not very popular / and was rather introverted.
그들에게는 노련한 항해사가 있었다 / 항해 중에 별을 읽는 법을 아는 / 하지만 그 항해사는 별로 인기가 없었다 / 그리고 다소 내성적이었다

③ As you know, / it's not easy to communicate / with introverted people, / in particular, / on the ship.
당신이 알다시피 / 소통을 하는 것은 쉽지 않다 / 내성적인 사람들과 / 특히 / 배에서

④ In the panic / of being lost, / the captain and crew made a decision / by voting to follow / the most charismatic and persuasive / of the crew members.
두려움 상태에서 / 길을 잃은 것에 대한 / 선장과 선원들은 결정을 내렸다 / 따르는 것에 투표함으로써 / 가장 카리스마 있고 설득력 있는 사람을 / 선원들 중

They ignored and ridiculed / the navigator's suggestions, / remained lost, / and ultimately starved to death / at sea.
그들은 무시하고 비웃었다 / 항해사의 제안을 / 길을 잃은 채 남겨졌다 / 그리고 결국 굶어 죽었다 / 바다에서

해설 대부분의 사람들은 플라톤이 꽤 좋은 선생님이었다는 것에 동의한다. 그는 사람들에게 생각하는 법을 가르쳐 주기 위해 이야기를 자

주 사용했다. 플라톤이 민주주의의 한계에 대해 가르치기 위해 사용했던 한 가지 이야기는 바다 한가운데 있는 한 배에 관한 것이었다. 이 배에는 다소 근시이고 약간 귀가 먹은 선장이 있었다. ① 그와 그의 선원들은 항해의 방향에 대한 결정 과정에서 다수결 원칙을 따랐다. ② 그들에게는 항해 중에 별을 읽는 법을 아는 노련한 항해사가 있었지만, 그 항해사는 별로 인기가 없었고 다소 내성적이었다. ③ 당신이 알다시피, 특히 배에서 내성적인 사람들과 소통을 하는 것은 쉽지 않다. ④ 길을 잃은 것에 대한 두려움 상태에서, 선장과 선원들은 선원들 중 가장 카리스마 있고 설득력 있는 사람을 따르는 것에 투표함으로써 결정을 내렸다. 그들은 항해사의 제안을 무시하고 비웃었으며, 길을 잃은 채 남겨졌고, 결국 바다에서 굶어 죽었다.

해설 지문 앞부분에서 '민주주의의 한계에 대해 가르치기 위해 바다 한가운데 있는 배의 일화를 사용한 플라톤'에 대해 언급하고, ①, ②, ④번은 다수결의 원칙에 따라 별을 읽는 법을 알고 노련하지만 내성적인 항해사 대신에 카리스마 있고 설득력 있는 선원을 따르는 것에 투표하여 결국 굶어 죽은 선장과 선원들의 일화에 대해 설명하고 있으므로, 지문 앞부분과 관련이 있다. 그러나 ③번은 '배 위에서 특히 소통하기 쉽지 않은 내성적인 사람들'이라는 내용으로, 지문의 앞부분과 관련이 없으므로 ③번이 정답이다.

어휘 limitation 한계, 제한 democracy 민주주의
shortsighted 근시의, 근시안적인 deaf 귀가 먹은, 청각 장애가 있는
crew 선원 majority rule 다수결 원칙 navigational 항해의
navigator 항해사 voyage 항해 introverted 내성적인
panic 두려움, 공포 persuasive 설득력 있는 ridicule 비웃다
starve to death 굶어 죽다

---

13 독해 추론 (빈칸 완성 - 연결어) 난이도 ★★☆

끊어읽기 해석

Before the creation of money, / people used to exchange / something they had / for something they needed.
화폐의 발생 이전에 / 사람들은 교환하곤 했다 / 그들이 가진 무언가를 / 그들에게 필요한 무언가와

This system of exchange / is called bartering.
이런 교환 제도는 / 물물교환이라고 불린다

People traded / things like animal furs, shells, beads / for necklaces, and cloth.
사람들은 교환했다 / 동물의 털, 조개껍데기, 구슬 같은 것들을 / 목걸이와 옷으로

Later, / people realized / that some items were easier to trade than others, / and those items became more common / in bartering.
나중에 / 사람들은 깨달았다 / 어떤 물품은 다른 것들보다 교환하기가 더 쉽다는 것을 / 그리고 그러한 물품들은 더욱 흔해졌다 / 물물교환에서

(A) For example, / people could trade gold / for almost any other item / because most people knew / that it was valuable / and that they could easily trade it again / if they needed to.
(A) 예를 들어 / 사람들은 금을 교환할 수 있었다 / 거의 모든 다른 물품과 / 대부분의 사람들이 알고 있었기 때문이다 / 이것(금)이 가치 있다는 것을 / 그리고 이것을 다시 쉽게 거래할 수 있다는 것을 / 그들이 필요하면

After some time, / certain goods became / the standard goods of exchange, / and everyone began to trade / with the same items.
얼마 후 / 특정 물건들은 ~이 되었다 / 교환의 표준이 되는 상품이 / 그리고 모두가 거래하기 시작했다 / 똑같은 물건으로

Eventually, / the standard goods became money / —one common unit of trade / most people accepted and used / in business and for their daily lives.

결국 / 표준이 되는 상품은 화폐가 되었다 / 하나의 공통된 거래 단위인 / 대부분의 사람들이 받아들이고 사용했던 / 거래와 그들의 일상생활을 위해

(B) Nevertheless, / some people still use the barter system today, / especially in developing countries, / where people exchange different kinds of food / in order to survive.
(B) 그럼에도 불구하고 / 일부 사람들은 오늘날에도 여전히 물물교환 제도를 이용한다 / 특히 개발도상국에서 / 사람들이 다양한 종류의 음식을 교환하는 / 생존하기 위해

해석 화폐의 발생 이전에, 사람들은 그들이 가진 무언가를 그들에게 필요한 무언가와 교환하곤 했다. 이런 교환 제도는 물물교환이라고 불린다. 사람들은 동물의 털, 조개껍데기, 구슬 같은 것들을 목걸이와 옷으로 교환했다. 나중에, 사람들은 어떤 물품은 다른 것들보다 교환하기가 더 쉽다는 것을 깨달았고, 그러한 물품들은 물물교환에서 더욱 흔해졌다. (A) 예를 들어, 사람들은 금을 거의 모든 다른 물품과 교환할 수 있었는데, 대부분의 사람들이 이것(금)이 가치 있으며 그들이 필요하면 이것을 다시 쉽게 거래할 수 있다는 것을 알고 있었기 때문이다. 얼마 후, 특정 물건들은 교환의 표준이 되는 상품이 되었고, 모두가 똑같은 물건으로 거래하기 시작했다. 결국, 표준이 되는 상품은 대부분의 사람들이 거래와 그들의 일상생활을 위해 받아들이고 사용했던 하나의 공통된 거래 단위인 화폐가 되었다. (B) 그럼에도 불구하고, 일부 사람들은 오늘날에도 여전히 물물교환 제도를 이용하는데, 특히 사람들이 생존하기 위해 다양한 종류의 음식을 교환하는 개발도상국에서 그렇다.

	(A)	(B)
①	게다가	– 예를 들어
②	다시 말해서	– 게다가
③	대조적으로	– 하지만
④	예를 들어	– 그럼에도 불구하고

해설 (A) 빈칸 앞 문장은 다른 것들보다 교환하기 쉬운 물품들이 물물교환에서 흔해졌다는 내용이고, (A) 빈칸 뒤 문장은 사람들은 금을 거의 모든 다른 물품과 교환할 수 있었다는 예를 드는 내용이다. 따라서, 예시를 나타내는 연결어인 For example(예를 들어)이 나와야 적절하다. (B) 빈칸 앞 문장은 교환의 표준이 되는 상품이 하나의 공통된 거래 단위인 화폐가 되었다는 내용이고, (B) 빈칸 뒤 문장은 오늘날에도 여전히 물물교환 제도를 이용하는 사람들이 있다는 대조적인 내용이다. 따라서 대조를 나타내는 연결어인 Nevertheless(그럼에도 불구하고)가 나와야 적절하다.

따라서 ④ (A) For example(예를 들어) – (B) Nevertheless(그럼에도 불구하고)가 정답이다.

어휘 creation 발생, 창조 exchange 교환하다; 교환
barter 물물교환하다, 교역하다 trade 교환하다, 거래하다
bead 구슬 valuable 가치 있는
standard 표준이 되는, 기준이 되는

14 독해 추론 (빈칸 완성 – 연결어) 난이도 ★☆☆

끊어읽기 해석

Many people find it difficult / to relate to someone / who has a physical disability, / often because they have not had any personal interaction / with anyone with a disability.
많은 사람들은 어려워한다 / 사람을 이해하는 것을 / 신체장애가 있는 / 보통 그들은 그 어떠한 개인적인 관계를 맺어본 적이 없기 때문에 / 장애가 있는 사람과

(A) For example, / they might be unsure / what to expect from a person / who has a mobility impairment / and uses a wheelchair / because they have never spent any time / with wheelchair users.
(A) 예를 들어, / 그들은 확신이 없을 수도 있다 / 사람으로부터 무엇을 예상해야 할지 / 이동성 장애를 가지고 있는 / 그리고 휠체어를 사용하는 / 그들은 한번도 시간을 보내본 적이 없기 때문에 / 휠체어를 사용하는 사람들과

This lack of understanding / can create additional challenges / for people with disabilities.
이러한 이해의 부족은 / 추가적인 어려움을 줄 수 있다 / 장애를 가진 사람들에게

If society responded more adequately / to people who have impairments, / they would not experience / nearly as many challenges and limitations.
만약 사회가 더 적절하게 대응한다면 / 장애를 가진 사람들에게 / 그들은 경험하지 않을 것이다 / 그렇게 많은 어려움과 한계를

Consider / office workers / who happen to use wheelchairs.
생각해보자 / 직장인들을 / 휠체어를 사용하게 된

Provided that there is only one level / or there are ramps or elevators between levels, / they may need no assistance whatsoever / in the workplace.
오직 1층만 있다면 / 또는 층들 사이에 경사로나 엘리베이터가 있다면 / 그들은 도움이 전혀 필요하지 않을 것이다 / 직장에서

(B) In other words, / in an adapted work environment, / they do not have a disability.
(B) 다시 말해서 / 적합한 근로 환경에서 / 그들은 장애를 가지지 않는다

해석 많은 사람들은 보통 장애가 있는 사람과 그 어떠한 개인적인 관계를 맺어본 적이 없기 때문에 신체장애가 있는 사람을 이해하는 것을 어려워한다. (A) 예를 들어, 그들은 휠체어를 사용하는 사람들과 한번도 시간을 보내본 적이 없기 때문에 이동성 장애를 가지고 있고 휠체어를 사용하는 사람으로부터 무엇을 예상해야 할지 확신이 없을 수도 있다. 이러한 이해의 부족은 장애를 가진 사람들에게 추가적인 어려움을 줄 수 있다. 만약 사회가 장애를 가진 사람들에게 더 적절하게 대응한다면, 그들은 그렇게 많은 어려움과 한계를 경험하지 않을 것이다. 휠체어를 사용하게 된 직장인들을 생각해보자. 오직 1층만 있거나 층들 사이에 경사로나 엘리베이터가 있다면 그들은 직장에서 도움이 전혀 필요하지 않을 것이다. (B) 다시 말해서, 적합한 근로 환경에서, 그들은 장애를 가지지 않는다.

	(A)	(B)
①	하지만	– 그러므로
②	반면에	– 이와 같이
③	게다가	– 게다가
④	예를 들어	– 다시 말해서

해설 (A) 빈칸 앞 문장은 많은 사람들은 장애가 있는 사람과 그 어떠한 개인적인 관계를 맺어본 적이 없기 때문에 신체장애가 있는 사람을 이해하는 것을 어려워한다는 내용이고, 빈칸 뒤 문장은 사람들이 휠체어를 사용하는 사람들과 한번도 시간을 보내본 적이 없기 때문에 이동성 장애를 가지고 있고 휠체어를 사용하는 사람으로부터 무엇을 예상해야 할지 확신이 없다는 예를 드는 내용이다. 따라서 예시를 나타내는 연결어인 For example(예를 들어)이 나와야 적절하다. (B) 빈칸 앞 문장은 직장에 1층만 있거나 층들 사이에 경사로나 엘리베이터가 있다면 휠체어를 사용하는 직장인은 직장에서 도움이 전혀 필요하지 않을 것이라는 내용이고, 빈칸 뒤 문장은 적합한 근로 환경에서 휠체어를 사용하는 사람들은 장애를 가지지 않는다는 앞의 문장을 요약하는 내용이다. 따라서 요약을 나타내는 연결어인 In other words(다시 말해서)가 나와야 적절하다.

따라서 ④ (A) For example(예를 들어) – (B) In other words(다시 말해서)가 정답이다.

어휘 relate to ~을 이해하다, ~와 관련되다 disability 장애
interaction 관계 unsure 확신하지 못하는 mobility 이동성
impairment 장애 ramp 경사로

끊어읽기 해석

I was always mad / at Charles / even though I couldn't ever put my finger on exactly / what he was doing / to make me angry.
나는 항상 화가 나 있었다 / Charles에게 / 비록 나는 정확히 지적할 수는 없었지만 / 그가 무엇을 하고 있는지 / 나를 화나게 하기 위해

Charles was just one / of those people / who rubbed me the wrong way.
Charles는 그저 하나였다 / 그런 사람들 중에 / 나를 불쾌하게 만들었던

Yet, / I was constantly upset.
그러나 / 나는 끊임없이 화가 나 있었다

When we began looking at anger / in this class, / I thought, / "What's my primary feeling / about Charles?"
우리가 분노를 보기 시작했을 때 / 이 수업에서 / 나는 ~라고 생각했다 / '나의 주된 감정은 무엇일까 / Charles에 대한?'

I almost hate to admit / what I found out / because it makes me look / like I'm a lot more insecure / than I feel I really am, / but my primary feeling was fear.
나는 거의 인정하기 싫었다 / 내가 발견한 것을 / 그것이 내가 보이게 만들기 때문에 / 훨씬 더 불안한 것처럼 / 내가 실제로 그렇다고 느끼는 것보다 / 하지만 나의 주된 감정은 두려움이었다

I was afraid / that Charles / with his brilliance and sharp tongue / was going to make me look stupid / in front of the other students.
나는 두려웠다 / Charles가 / 그의 뛰어난 두뇌와 독설로 / 나를 멍청해 보이게 만들까 봐 / 다른 학생들 앞에서

Last week / I asked him / to stay after class / and I just told him / how threatened I get / when he pins me down / on some minor point.
지난주에 / 나는 그에게 부탁했다 / 수업이 끝나고 남아달라고 / 그리고 나는 그에게 말했다 / 내가 얼마나 위협을 느끼게 되는지 / 그가 나를 꼼짝 못 하게 할 때 / 사소한 문제로

He was kind of stunned, / and said / he wasn't trying to make me look bad, / that he was really trying to score brownie points / with me.
그는 약간 놀랐다 / 그리고 말했다 / 그는 나를 나빠 보이게 만들려고 했던 것이 아니라 / 사실은 점수를 따려고 했었다고 / 나에게

We ended up laughing / about it / and I'm not threatened / by him / anymore.
우리는 결국 웃게 되었다 / 그것에 대해 / 그리고 나는 위협을 느끼지 않는다 / 그에게서 / 더 이상

When he forgets / and pins me down / now, / I just laugh and say, / "Hey, / that's another brownie point for you."
그가 잊어버릴 때 / 그리고 나를 꼼짝 못 하게 할 때 / 이제는 / 나는 그냥 웃으면서 ~라고 말한다 / "이봐, / 그건 너한테 또 다른 점수야"

해석 나는 비록 Charles가 나를 화나게 하기 위해 무엇을 하고 있는지 정확히 지적할 수는 없었지만, 나는 항상 Charles에게 화가 나 있었다. Charles는 그저 나를 불쾌하게 만들었던 그런 사람들 중에 하나였다. 그러나 나는 끊임없이 화가 나 있었다. 우리가 이 수업에서 분노를 보기 시작했을 때 나는 'Charles에 대한 나의 주된 감정은 무엇일까?'라고 생각했다. 나는 그것이 내가 실제로 그렇다고 느끼는 것보다 내가 훨씬 더 불안한 것처럼 보이게 만들기 때문에 내가 발견한 것을 거의 인정하기 싫었지만, 나의 주된 감정은 두려움이었다. 나는 Charles가 그의 뛰어난 두뇌와 독설로 나를 다른 학생들 앞에서 멍청해 보이게 만들까 봐 두려웠다. 지난주에 나는 그에게 수업이 끝나고 남아달라고 부탁했고, 나는 그에게 그가 사소한 문제로 나를 꼼짝 못 하게 할 때 내가 얼마나 위협을 느끼게 되는지를 말했다. 그는 약간 놀랐고, 그는 나를 나빠 보이게 만들려고 했던 것이 아니라, 사실은 나에게 점수를 따려고 했었다고 말

했다. 우리는 결국 그것에 대해 웃게 되었고, 나는 그에게서 더 이상 위협을 느끼지 않는다. 이제는 그가 잊어버리고 나를 꼼짝 못하게 할 때, 나는 그냥 웃으면서 "이봐, 그건 너한테 또 다른 점수야."라고 말한다.

① 안심한 → 짜증 난
② 불편한 → 안심한
③ 평화로운 → 부러워하는
④ 무서운 → 무관심한

해설 지문 전반에 걸쳐 필자는 Charles가 자신을 불쾌하게 만들었으며, 그가 다른 학생들 앞에서 자신을 멍청해 보이게 만들까 봐 두려워했다고 설명한 뒤, Charles가 단지 자신에게 점수를 따려고 했었다는 것을 알게 되자 더 이상 그에게 위협을 느끼지 않게 되었다는 일화를 소개하고 있다. 따라서 지문에서 I(나)가 느꼈을 심경 변화를 '불편한 → 안심한'이라고 표현한 ②번이 정답이다.

어휘 put one's finger on ~을 정확히 지적하다
rub ~ the wrong way ~를 불쾌하게 만들다
primary 주된, 기본적인   sharp tongue 독설
pin down ~을 꼼짝 못 하게 하다   score 점수를 따다
brownie point (아첨하여 얻은) 점수

끊어읽기 해석

Amid the confusion and clutter of the natural environment, / redators concentrate their search / on telltale signs, / ignoring everything else.
자연환경의 혼란과 어수선함 속에서 / 포식자들은 그들의 수색을 집중시킨다 / 숨길 수 없는 흔적에 / 그 외의 다른 것은 무시한다

There is a great benefit to this: / When you specialize / in searching for specific details, / even cryptically colored prey / can seem obvious.
이것에는 아주 큰 장점이 있다 / 당신이 전문으로 하면 / 구체적인 세부 사항을 수색하는 것을 / 애매한 색의 사냥감조차도 / 분명하게 보일 수 있다

But there is also a cost / to paying too close attention, / since you can become blind / to the alternatives.
하지만 대가도 있다 / 너무 세심한 주의를 기울이는 것에는 / 당신이 보지 못하게 될 수 있기 때문에 / 선택 가능한 것들을

When a bird searches intently / for caterpillars that look like twigs, / it misses nearby moths / that look like bark.
새가 집중하여 수색할 때 / 작은 가지처럼 생긴 애벌레를 / 그것은 근처의 나방을 놓친다 / 나무껍질처럼 생긴

The benefit of concealing coloration / is not that it provides a solid guarantee of survival, / but that it consistently yields a small advantage / in the chance of living / through each successive threatening encounter.
천연색을 숨기는 것의 장점은 / 그것이 확실한 생존의 보장을 제공하는 것이 아니라 / 항상 약간의 이점을 준다는 것이다 / 생존 가능성에 있어서 / 각각의 연속적이고 위협적인 마주침 동안

At a minimum, / even a tiny delay / between the approach of a predator and its subsequent attack / can help / a prey animal / escape.
최소한 / 약간의 지연조차도 / 포식자의 접근과 그것의 뒤이은 공격 사이의 / 도움이 될 수 있다 / 사냥감인 동물이 / 도망치는 데

And at best, / the prey will be completely overlooked.
그리고 잘하면 / 그 사냥감은 완전히 간과될 것이다

해석 자연환경의 혼란과 어수선함 속에서, 포식자들은 그들의 수색을 숨길 수 없는 흔적에 집중시키고, 그 외의 다른 것은 무시한다. 이것에는 아주 큰 장점이 있다. 당신이 구체적인 세부 사항을 수색하

는 것을 전문으로 하면, 애매한 색의 사냥감조차도 분명하게 보일 수 있다. 하지만 너무 세심한 주의를 기울이는 것에는 대가도 있는데, 선택 가능한 것들을 보지 못하게 될 수 있기 때문이다. 새가 작은 가지처럼 생긴 애벌레를 집중하여 수색할 때, 그것은 근처의 나무껍질처럼 생긴 나방을 놓친다. 천연색을 숨기는 것의 장점은 그것이 확실한 생존의 보장을 제공하는 것이 아니라, 각각의 연속적이고 위협적인 마주침 동안 생존 가능성에 있어서 항상 약간의 이점을 준다는 것이다. 최소한, 포식자의 접근과 그것의 뒤이은 공격 사이의 약간의 지연조차도 사냥감인 동물이 도망치는 데 도움이 될 수 있다. 그리고 잘하면, 그 사냥감은 완전히 간과될 것이다.

① 위장한 포식자
② 집중의 장점
③ 위장: 약간의 유리함
④ 전문화된 수색의 장점

해설 지문 중간에서 새가 작은 가지처럼 생긴 애벌레를 집중하여 수색할 때, 나무껍질처럼 생긴 나방을 놓친다는 것을 예로 들며 사냥감들이 천연색을 숨기는 것의 장점은 생존 가능성에 있어서 약간의 이점을 주는 것이라고 설명하고 있다. 따라서 이 지문의 제목을 '위장: 약간의 유리함'이라고 표현한 ③번이 정답이다.

어휘 confusion 혼란 clutter 어수선함 predator 포식자
telltale 숨길 수 없는 cryptically 애매하게, 아리송하게
prey 사냥감, 먹이 obvious 분명한
blind to ~을 못 보는, 깨닫지 못하는 alternative 선택 가능한 것, 대안
intently 집중하여, 열심히 caterpillar 애벌레 twig 작은 가지
bark 나무껍질 coloration 천연색 solid 확실한, 믿을 수 있는
yield 주다, 가져오다 successive 연속적인
encounter 마주침, 접촉; 맞닥뜨리다 disguise 위장, 변장
camouflage 위장 edge 유리함

---

17 독해 논리적 흐름 파악 (문장 삽입) 난이도 ★☆☆

끊어읽기 해석

But / let us say / that the ranger / who painted the sign / meant to say / just the opposite.
하지만 / 가정해보자 / 관리인이 / 그 표지판을 그린 / 의미하려고 했었다고 / 정반대를

An ambiguous term is one / which has more than a single meaning / and whose context does not clearly indicate / which meaning is intended.
모호한 용어는 용어이다 / 한 가지 이상의 의미를 지니는 / 그리고 그것의 문맥이 명확히 나타내지 않는 / 어떤 의미로 의도되었는지를

For instance, / a sign / posted at a fork in a trail / which reads "Bear To The Right" / can be understood / in two ways.
예를 들어 / 표지판은 / 산길의 갈라진 곳에 게시된 / 'Bear To The Right'라고 적혀 있는 / 이해될 수 있다 / 두 가지 방식으로

(①) The more probable meaning / is that it is instructing hikers / to take the right trail, / not the left.
좀 더 그럴듯한 의미는 / 그것이 등산객들에게 지시한다는 것이다 / 오른쪽 산길로 가라고 / 왼쪽이 아니라

(②) He was trying to warn / hikers / against taking the right trail / because there is a bear in the area / through which it passes.
그는 경고하려고 했었다 / 등산객들에게 / 오른쪽 산길로 가지 말 것을 / 지역에 곰이 있기 때문에 / 그것이 지나가는

(③) The ranger's language was therefore careless, / and open to misinterpretation / which could have serious consequences.
따라서 그 관리인의 표현은 부정확했다 / 그리고 오역의 여지가 있었다 / 심각한 결과를 초래할 수도 있는

(④) The only way / to avoid ambiguity / is to spell things out / as explicitly as possible: / "Keep left. / Do not use trail / to the right. / Bears in the area."
유일한 방법은 / 모호함을 피하는 / 자세히 설명하는 것이다 / 가능한 한 명확하게 / "계속 왼쪽으로 가시오 / 산길을 사용하지 마시오 / 오른쪽으로 가는 / 그 지역에는 곰이 있습니다"

해석 모호한 용어는 한 가지 이상의 의미를 지니며, 그것의 문맥이 어떤 의미로 의도되었는지를 명확히 나타내지 않는 용어이다. 예를 들어, 산길의 갈라진 곳에 게시된 'Bear To The Right'라고 적혀 있는 표지판은 두 가지 방식으로 이해될 수 있다. 좀 더 그럴듯한 의미는 그것이 등산객들에게 왼쪽이 아니라, 오른쪽 산길로 가라고 지시한다는 것이다. ② 하지만 그 표지판을 그린 관리인이 정반대를 의미하려고 했었다고 가정해보자. 그는 그것이 지나가는 지역에 곰이 있기 때문에, 등산객들에게 오른쪽 산길로 가지 말 것을 경고하려고 했었다. 따라서 그 관리인의 표현은 부정확했고, 심각한 결과를 초래할 수도 있는 오역의 여지가 있었다. 모호함을 피하는 유일한 방법은 가능한 한 명확하게 자세히 설명하는 것이다. "계속 왼쪽으로 가시오. 오른쪽으로 가는 산길을 사용하지 마시오. 그 지역에 곰이 있습니다."

해설 주어진 문장의 just the opposite(정반대)를 통해 주어진 문장 앞에 표지판이 가지는 정반대의 의미에 대한 내용이 나올 것임을 알 수 있다. ②번 앞 문장에서 'Bear To The Right'가 가진 하나의 의미인 '왼쪽이 아니라 오른쪽 산길로 가라(오른쪽으로 향하라)'는 의미에 대해서 언급하고, ②번 뒤 문장에서 '곰이 있으므로 오른쪽 산길로 가지 말라(오른쪽에 곰이 있다)'고 경고하려고 했었다는 그 반대의 의미에 대해서 설명하므로, ②번 자리에 주어진 문장이 들어가야 글의 흐름이 자연스럽게 연결된다. 따라서 ②번이 정답이다.

어휘 ranger 관리원 ambiguous 모호한 term 용어 context 문맥
fork 갈라진 곳, 분기점 bear 향하다, 나아가다; 곰
careless 부정확한, 부주의한 be open to ~의 여지가 있다
misinterpretation 오역, 오해 ambiguity 모호함
spell out 자세히 설명하다 explicitly 명확하게

---

18 독해 전체내용 파악 (제목 파악) 난이도 ★★★

끊어읽기 해석

River otters have / webbed toes, short legs, and tapered tails.
강에 사는 수달은 가지고 있다 / 물갈퀴가 있는 발가락, 짧은 다리, 그리고 점점 가늘어지는 꼬리를

For this reason, / the river otter has / a streamlined body, / which helps / it to move through the water / very easily.
이런 이유로 / 강에 사는 수달은 가지고 있다 / 유선형의 몸을 / 이는 도와준다 / 그것이 물에서 움직일 수 있도록 / 매우 쉽게

Sea otters are near-sighted / largely because aquatic life is much more important / to them / than terrestrial life.
해달(바다에 사는 수달)은 근시이다 / 그 주된 이유는 물에서의 생활이 훨씬 더 중요하기 때문이다 / 그들에게 / 육지에서의 생활보다

As a result, / the sea otter is not as well-equipped / for terrestrial life / as for aquatic life.
결과적으로 / 해달은 그렇게 잘 준비되어 있지 않다 / 육지에서의 생활에는 / 물에서의 생활에 그런 만큼

해석 강에 사는 수달은 물갈퀴가 있는 발가락, 짧은 다리, 그리고 점점 가늘어지는 꼬리를 가지고 있다. 이런 이유로, 강에 사는 수달은 유선형의 몸을 가지고 있는데, 이는 그것이 물에서 매우 쉽게 움직일 수 있도록 도와준다. 해달(바다에 사는 수달)은 근시인데, 그 주된 이유는 그들에게 물에서의 생활이 육지에서의 생활보다 훨씬 더

중요하기 때문이다. 결과적으로, 해달은 물에서의 생활에 그런 만큼 육지에서의 생활에는 그렇게 잘 준비되어 있지 않다.

① 수중에서와 육지에서의 생활의 차이는 무엇인가?
② 수달은 수중 동물인가, 육상 동물인가?
③ 해달의 신체적 특성
④ 수달: 완벽한 육상 생명체

해설 지문 전반에 걸쳐 강에 사는 수달은 유선형의 몸을 가지고 있어서 물에서 매우 쉽게 움직일 수 있다고 했고, 해달(바다에 사는 수달)은 물에서의 생활에 준비되어 있는 만큼 육지에서의 생활에 그렇게 잘 준비되어 있지 않다는 것을 설명하고 있다. 따라서 지문의 제목을 '수달은 수중 동물인가, 육상 동물인가?'라고 표현한 ②번이 정답이다.

어휘 otter 수달 webbed 물갈퀴가 있는 taper 점점 가늘어지다
streamlined 유선형의, 날씬한 near-sighted 근시의
terrestrial 육지의, 육상의 equipped for ~을 위해 준비된

19 독해 세부내용 파악 (지칭 대상 파악) 난이도 ★☆☆

끊어읽기 해석

Black pepper is one / of the most widely used spices / in the world.
후추는 하나이다 / 가장 널리 사용되는 향신료 중 / 세상에서

At first, / it was cultivated / in India / as a simple ingredient / for cooking.
처음에 / 그것은 재배되었다 / 인도에서 / 단순한 재료로 / 요리를 위한

However, / ① it became a lot more important / to some Europeans / who also used it / for keeping meat from going bad.
하지만 / ① 그것은 훨씬 더 중요하게 되었다 / 일부 유럽인들에게 / 또한 그것을 사용한 / 고기가 상하는 것을 막기 위해

Until the 15th century, / some cities in Italy / were the center / for trading black pepper.
15세기까지 / 이탈리아의 몇몇 도시들은 / 중심지였다 / 후추 무역의

As the Ottoman Empire / in the Middle East / grew stronger / in the 16th century, / however, / ② it forced / the European traders to pay them / a high tax.
오스만 제국이 / 중동에 있는 / 점점 더 강해지면서 / 16세기에 / 하지만 / ② 그것은 강요했다 / 유럽의 상인들이 그들에게 지급하도록 / 더 높은 세금을

This made black pepper so expensive / that only a few rich people / could afford ③ it.
이는 후추를 너무 비싸게 만들었다 / 그래서 소수의 부자들만이 / ③ 그것을 살 여유가 되었다

In some parts of Europe, / black pepper was even considered / as valuable as gold.
유럽의 어떤 지역에서는 / 후추가 심지어 여겨졌다 / 금만큼 가치 있는 것으로

The great demand / for ④ it / caused Europeans to search / for new sea routes / to India.
엄청난 수요는 / ④ 그것에 대한 / 유럽인들로 하여금 찾게 했다 / 새로운 항로를 / 인도로 가는

해석 후추는 세상에서 가장 널리 사용되는 향신료 중 하나이다. 처음에 그것은 인도에서 요리를 위한 단순한 재료로 재배되었다. 하지만, ① 그것은 또한 고기가 상하는 것을 막기 위해 그것을 사용한 일부 유럽인들에게 훨씬 더 중요하게 되었다. 15세기까지, 이탈리아의 몇몇 도시들은 후추 무역의 중심지였다. 하지만, 중동에 있는 오스만 제국이 16세기에 점점 더 강해지면서 ② 그것은 유럽의 상인들이 그들에게 더 높은 세금을 지급하도록 강요했다. 이는 후추를 너

무 비싸게 만들어서 소수의 부자들만이 ③ 그것을 살 여유가 되었다. 유럽의 어떤 지역에서는, 후추가 심지어 금만큼 가치 있는 것으로 여겨졌다. ④ 그것에 대한 엄청난 수요는 유럽인들로 하여금 인도로 가는 새로운 항로를 찾게 했다.

해설 ①, ③, ④번 모두 후추를 지칭하지만, ②번은 오스만 제국을 지칭하므로 ②번이 정답이다.

어휘 spice 향신료 cultivate 재배하다 ingredient 재료
go bad 상하다 valuable 가치 있는 sea route 항로

20 독해 추론 (빈칸 완성 - 단어) 난이도 ★★☆

끊어읽기 해석

In addition to the problems / of individual resources, / there are increasing links / among energy, food, and water.
문제 이외에도 / 개별 자원의 / 관련성이 증가하고 있다 / 에너지, 식량 그리고 물 사이의

As a result, / problems in one area / can spread to another, / creating a (A) destructive circle.
그 결과 / 한 영역에서의 문제가 / 다른 영역으로 퍼질 수 있다 / (A) 파괴적인 순환을 만들어낸다

For instance, / Uganda experienced a prolonged drought / in 2004 and 2005, / threatening the food supply.
예를 들어 / 우간다는 장기간의 가뭄을 겪었다 / 2004년과 2005년에 / 식량 공급을 위협했다

The country was using so much water / from massive Lake Victoria / that the water level fell / by a full meter, / and Uganda cut back / on hydroelectric power generation at the lake.
그 나라는 너무 많은 물을 사용하고 있었다 / 광활한 빅토리아 호수로부터 / 그래서 수위가 떨어졌다 / 무려 1미터나 / 그리고 우간다는 축소시켰다 / 호수에서의 수력 발전을

Electricity prices nearly doubled, / so Ugandans began / to use more wood / for fuel.
전기 값은 거의 두 배가 되었다 / 그래서 우간다 사람들은 시작했다 / 더 많은 목재를 사용하기 / 연료로

People cut heavily into forests, / which (B) degraded / the soil.
사람들은 숲을 대량으로 베어냈다 / 이는 (B) 저하시켰다 / 토질을

The drought / that began / as a threat to food sources / became an electricity problem / and, / eventually, / an even more profound food problem.
가뭄은 / 시작된 / 식량 공급원에 대한 위협으로 / 전기 문제가 되었다 / 그리고 / 결국에는 / 훨씬 더 심각한 식량 문제가 되었다

Cycles like these / can end in political unrest and disasters / for whole populations.
이러한 순환은 / 정치적 불안과 재앙으로 끝날 수도 있다 / 전 인구에 대한

해석 개별 자원의 문제 이외에도 에너지, 식량 그리고 물 사이의 관련성이 증가하고 있다. 그 결과, 한 영역에서의 문제가 다른 영역으로 퍼질 수 있으며, 이는 (A) 파괴적인 순환을 만들어낸다. 예를 들어, 우간다는 2004년과 2005년에 장기간의 가뭄을 겪었으며, 이는 식량 공급을 위협했다. 그 나라는 광활한 빅토리아 호수로부터 너무 많은 물을 사용하고 있어서 수위가 무려 1미터나 떨어졌으며, 우간다는 호수에서의 수력 발전을 축소시켰다. 전기 값은 거의 두 배가 되어서, 우간다 사람들은 연료로 더 많은 목재를 사용하기 시작했다. 사람들은 숲을 대량으로 베어냈고, 이는 토질을 (B) 저하시켰다. 식량 공급원에 대한 위협으로 시작된 가뭄은 전기 문제가 되었고, 결국에는 훨씬 더 심각한 식량 문제가 되었다. 이러한 순환은 전 인구에 대한 정치적 불안과 재앙으로 끝날 수도 있다.

	(A)	(B)
①	악한	비옥하게 했다
②	선한	악화시켰다
③	파괴적인	저하시켰다
④	건설적인	악화시켰다

해설 (A) 빈칸이 있는 문장에 한 영역에서의 문제가 다른 영역으로 퍼질 수 있다는 내용이 있으므로, 빈칸에 '악한'(vicious) 순환 또는 '파괴적인'(destructive) 순환이라는 내용이 들어가는 것이 적절하다. (B) 빈칸이 있는 문장에 우간다 사람들이 숲을 대량으로 베어냈다는 내용이 있으므로, 빈칸에는 토질을 '저하시켰다'(degraded)는 내용이 들어가는 것이 적절하다.

따라서 ③ (A) destructive(파괴적인) – (B) degraded(저하시켰다)가 정답이다.

어휘 circle 순환 prolonged 장기간의, 오래 계속되는 full 무려
cut back on 축소하다, 줄이다 hydroelectric 수력의
power generation 발전 fuel 연료 profound 심각한
unrest 불안 vicious 악한 fertilize 비옥하게 하다 virtuous 선한
deteriorate 악화시키다 destructive 파괴적인
degrade 저하시키다 constructive 건설적인
undermine 악화시키다

21 독해 세부내용 파악 (내용 일치 파악) 난이도 ★★☆

끊어읽기 해석

This graph compares / the percentages of male and female students / in OECD countries / who achieved various levels of reading proficiency / at age 15.
이 그래프는 비교한다 / 남녀 학생 비율을 / OECD 국가의 / 다양한 수준의 읽기 능력을 달성한 / 15세에

① The percentage of girls / is more than three times / the percentage of boys / at Below Level 1b.
여자 아이들의 비율은 / 3배 이상이다 / 남자 아이들의 비율의 / 1b단계 이하에서

② The percentage of girls / is more than twice / the percentage of boys / at Level 5.
여자 아이들의 비율은 / 2배 이상이다 / 남자 아이들의 비율의 / 5단계에서

③ The difference / between the percentages of boys and girls / is smallest / at Level 4 / and greatest / at Level 6.
차이는 / 남자 아이들과 여자 아이들 비율 간의 / 가장 작다 / 4단계에서 / 그리고 가장 크다 / 6단계에서

④ The percentage of girls / is always higher / than that of boys / at Level 3 and above, / whereas / the percentage of boys / is higher / than that of girls / at Level 2 and below.
여자 아이들의 비율은 / 항상 더 높다 / 남자 아이들의 그것(비율)보다 / 3단계 이상에서 / 반면 / 남자 아이들의 비율이 / 더 높다 / 여자 아이들의 그것(비율)보다 / 2단계 이하에서는

해석 이 그래프는 15세에 다양한 수준의 읽기 능력을 달성한 OECD 국가의 남녀 학생 비율을 비교한다. ① 1b단계 이하에서 여자 아이들의 비율은 남자 아이들의 비율의 3배 이상이다. ② 5단계에서 여자 아이들의 비율은 남자 아이들의 비율의 2배 이상이다. ③ 남자 아이들과 여자 아이들 비율 간의 차이는 4단계에서 가장 작고, 6단계에서 가장 크다. ④ 3단계 이상에서 여자 아이들의 비율은 항상 남자 아이들의 그것(비율)보다 더 높은 반면, 2단계 이하에서는 남자 아이들의 비율이 여자 아이들의 그것(비율)보다 더 높다.

해설 제시된 도표를 보면, 3단계 이상에서는 여자 아이들의 비율이 항상 남자 아이들의 비율보다 더 높은 반면, 2단계 이하에서는 남자 아이들의 비율이 여자 아이들의 비율보다 더 높으므로, ④번이 정답이다.

오답분석 ① 1b단계 이하에서는 남자 아이들의 비율이 1.8%이고 여자 아이들의 비율이 0.5%로 남자 아이들의 비율이 여자 아이들의 비율의 3배 이상이므로, 1b단계 이하에서 여자 아이들의 비율이 남자 아이들의 비율의 3배 이상이라는 것은 도표의 내용과 반대이다.
② 5단계에서는 여자 아이들의 비율이 8.8%이고 남자 아이들의 비율이 4.8%이므로, 5단계에서 여자 아이들의 비율이 남자 아이들의 비율의 2배 이상이라는 것은 도표의 내용과 다르다.
③ 4단계에서 남자 아이들과 여자 아이들의 비율의 차이(7.9%)가 가장 크고, 6단계에서 차이(0.7%)가 가장 작으므로, 4단계에서 남자 아이들과 여자 아이들의 비율의 차이가 가장 작고, 6단계에서 가장 크다는 것은 도표의 내용과 반대이다.

어휘 achieve 달성하다, 성취하다 reading proficiency 읽기 능력

22 독해 전체내용 파악 (주제 파악) 난이도 ★★☆

끊어읽기 해석

Béla Bartók's *Duos for Two Violins* / is characterized / by dissonance.
벨라 바르톡의 '두 개의 바이올린을 위한 듀오'는 / 특징지어진다 / 불협화음으로

By employing dissonance / in this work, / Bartók tries to reveal / the rich diversity of sounds.
불협화음을 사용함으로써 / 이 작품에서 / 바르톡은 드러내려고 한다 / 소리의 풍부한 다양성을

However, / dissonance is a relative concept, / and it needs to be understood / in relation to consonance.
하지만 / 불협화음은 상대적인 개념이다 / 그리고 그것은 이해되어야 한다 / 화음과 비교하여

Further, / the dissonance / prevalent in this work / does not express disorder.
게다가 / 불협화음은 / 이 작품에서 널리 퍼져있는 / 무질서를 나타내지 않는다

Rather, / it tries to evoke / subtle harmony / among individual sounds.
오히려 / 그것은 자아내려고 한다 / 미묘한 조화를 / 개별적인 소리들 간의

This is mainly because / dissonance can be perceived / as an expression of harmonious individuality.
이는 주로 ~ 때문이다 / 불협화음이 인식될 수 있기 (때문이다) / 조화로운 개성의 표출로

해석 벨라 바르톡의 '두 개의 바이올린을 위한 듀오'는 불협화음으로 특징지어진다. 이 작품에서 불협화음을 사용함으로써, 바르톡은 소리의 풍부한 다양성을 드러내려고 한다. 하지만 불협화음은 상대적인 개념이며, 그것은 화음과 비교하여 이해되어야 한다. 게다가, 이 작품에서 널리 퍼져있는 불협화음은 무질서를 나타내지 않는다. 오히려, 그것은 개별적인 소리들 간의 미묘한 조화를 자아내려고 한다. 이는 주로 불협화음이 조화로운 개성의 표출로 인식될 수 있기 때문이다.
① 소리의 다양성을 드러내는 방법
② 바이올린 연주에서 화음의 역할
③ '두 개의 바이올린을 위한 듀오'에서 화음의 중요성
④ 벨라 바르톡의 작품에서 불협화음의 진정한 의미

해설 지문 전반에 걸쳐 벨라 바르톡의 '두 개의 바이올린을 위한 듀오'는 불협화음으로 특징지어지며, 이 작품에서 불협화음은 무질서를 나타내는 것이 아니라, 오히려 개별적인 소리들 간의 미묘한 조화를 자아내려고 한다고 설명하고 있다. 따라서 이 지문의 주제를 '벨라 바르톡의 작품에서 불협화음의 진정한 의미'라고 표현한

④번이 정답이다.

어휘　characterize 특징짓다　dissonance 불협화음, 부조화
employ 사용하다, 고용하다　reveal 드러내다, 밝히다
diversity 다양성　relative 상대적인　in relation to ~와 비교하여
consonance 화음, 조화　prevalent 널리 퍼져있는
disorder 무질서, 혼란　evoke 자아내다, 불러일으키다
harmony 조화, 화음　harmonious 조화로운

23 　독해　논리적 흐름 파악 (문장 삽입)　난이도 ★☆☆

끊어읽기 해석

> Nevertheless, / Schulz believed in his work / and did not change Peanuts.
> 그럼에도 불구하고 / 슐츠는 자신의 작품을 믿었다 / 그리고 피너츠를 바꾸지 않았다
>
> ---
>
> These dull characters / created by Charles Schulz / attracted neither cartoon critics / nor the people at Walt Disney, / who didn't want to buy Peanuts.
> 이러한 활기 없는 등장인물들은 / 찰스 슐츠에 의해 만들어진 / 만화 평론가의 관심도 끌지 못했다 / 그리고 월트 디즈니 사람들의 관심도 끌지 못했다 / 이들은 피너츠를 사고 싶어하지 않았다
>
> They said / the characters did not inspire people to dream / or encourage them to hope.
> 그들은 말했다 / 그 등장인물들이 사람들이 꿈꾸도록 격려하지 않는다고 / 또는 그들이 희망을 가지도록 용기를 북돋지 (않는다고)
>
> (①) Even after it became popular / in many newspapers, / critics still thought / the comic strip would fail, / criticizing it for having uninteresting characters.
> 심지어는 그것이 인기를 얻게 된 후에도 / 많은 신문에서 / 평론가들은 여전히 생각했다 / 그 연재만화가 실패할 것이라고 / 재미없는 등장인물들을 가졌다고 그것을 비판하며
>
> (②) Some people said / that Snoopy, the dog, / should be taken out.
> 어떤 사람들은 말했다 / 강아지인 스누피가 / 빠져야 한다고
>
> (③) He even kept Snoopy, / who is now one of the most loved cartoon characters / of all time.
> 그는 오히려 스누피를 계속 유지했다 / 그는 이제 가장 사랑받는 만화 등장인물 중 하나이다 / 역사상
>
> (④)

해석　찰스 슐츠에 의해 만들어진 이러한 활기 없는 등장인물들은 만화 평론가의 관심도 끌지 못했고 월트 디즈니 사람들의 관심도 끌지 못했는데, 이들은 피너츠를 사고 싶어하지 않았다. 그들은 그 등장인물들이 사람들이 꿈꾸도록 격려하거나 희망을 가지도록 용기를 북돋지 않는다고 말했다. 심지어 그것이 많은 신문에서 인기를 얻게 된 후에도, 평론가들은 그것이 재미없는 등장인물들을 가졌다고 비판하며, 그 연재만화가 실패할 것이라고 여전히 생각했다. 어떤 사람들은 강아지인 스누피가 빠져야 한다고 말했다. ③ 그럼에도 불구하고, 슐츠는 자신의 작품을 믿었고 피너츠를 바꾸지 않았다. 그는 오히려 스누피를 계속 유지했고, 그는 이제 역사상 가장 사랑받는 만화 등장인물 중 하나이다.

해설　주어진 문장의 Nevertheless(그럼에도 불구하고)를 통해 주어진 문장 앞에 피너츠를 바꿔야 한다는 의견에 관한 내용이 나올 것임을 알 수 있다. ③번 앞 문장에서 어떤 사람들은 피너츠에서 스누피가 빠져야 한다고 말했다고 했으므로, ③번 자리에 주어진 문장이 들어가야 글의 흐름이 자연스럽게 연결된다. 따라서 ③번이 정답이다.

어휘　dull 활기 없는　critic 평론가　comic strip 연재만화

---

uninteresting 재미없는, 흥미롭지 못한　take out 빼다, 제거하다

24 　문법　조동사　난이도 ★★☆

해석　대부분의 경우 언론은 몹시 급하게 수집된 사건의 순간적인 기록만을 제공할 수밖에 없다. 사실상, 많은 뉴스 기사들은 발생한 일에 대한 가설이다. 물론 과학은 가설들에 의해 작동하며, 오류가 발견되었을 때는 그것들을 버리고 심지어는 실수가 목숨을 희생시킬 때조차도 비난받지 않고 대체로 그렇게 한다. 과학적인 정확성에 대한 권리를 주장하지 않는 언론은 그것의 오류를 쉽게 용서받지 못한다. 명백히, 언론은 종종 불충분한 정보를 가지고 급하게 인쇄하여, 이따금 뉴스에 대한 아무 생각 없는 갈망에 응답한다. 이상적인 사회는 언론이 절대적인 확실성에 이르고 나서야 어떤 것을 인쇄하도록 요구할 수도 있다. 하지만 그러한 사회는 사건에 대한 최종적인 설명을 기다리는 동안 소문, 불안 그리고 거짓말로 너무 가득 차서 우리 언론의 실수는 그에 비해 진실의 본보기로 보일 것이다.

해설　③ 조동사 should의 생략 요청을 나타내는 동사 demand가 주절에 나오면 종속절에는 '(should +) 동사원형'이 와야 하므로 동사원형 print가 올바르게 쓰였다.

오답분석　① 현재분사 vs. 과거분사 수식받는 명사(a fleeting records of events)와 분사가 '사건의 순간적인 기록이 수집되다'라는 의미의 수동 관계이므로 현재분사 compiling을 과거분사 compiled로 고쳐야 한다.
② 관계절의 용법 관계절이 콤마(,) 뒤에서 계속적 용법으로 쓰여 앞에 나온 선행사(The press)에 대한 부가 설명을 하고, 관계절 내에서 동사 lays의 주어 역할을 하고 있으므로 관계대명사 that을 계속적 용법으로 쓰일 수 있는 주격 관계대명사 which로 고쳐야 한다.
④ 부사절 접속사 2: 기타 문맥상 '거짓말로 너무 가득 차서 ~하다'라는 의미가 되어야 자연스러우므로 부사절 접속사 so ~ that(너무 ~해서 -하다)이 와야 한다. 따라서 관계대명사 which를 부사절 접속사 that으로 고쳐야 한다.

어휘　journalism 언론　fleeting 순간적인　compile 수집하다, 편집하다
at bottom 사실상　hypothesis 가설　discard 버리다
on the whole 대체로　the press 언론
lay claim to ~에 대한 권리를 주장하다　accuracy 정확성
admittedly 명백히　rush into 급하게 ~하다　insufficient 불충분한
mindless 아무 생각 없는, 부주의한　certainty 확실성
version 설명, 형태　rife with ~로 가득 찬
by comparison 그에 비해, 비교해 보면

👍 **이것도 알면 합격!**

주절에 아래와 같은 제안·의무·요청·주장을 나타내는 동사 또는 형용사가 나오면, 종속절에는 주어가 3인칭 단수이거나 문맥상 시제가 과거여도 3인칭 단수 동사나 과거 동사가 아닌 '(should +) 동사원형'이 와야 한다는 것을 기억하자. 참고로 부정형이 쓰일 경우 'not + 동사원형'의 형태가 된다는 것에 주의하자.

동사	require 요구하다 request 요청하다 suggest 제안하다 recommend 추천하다	ask 요청하다 insist 주장하다 demand 요구하다 command 명령하다
형용사	necessary 필수적인 imperative 필수적인	essential 필수적인 important 중요한

끊어읽기 해석

Children often invent / novel ways / to express desired meanings.
어린이들은 종종 생각해낸다 / 참신한 방법을 / 원하는 의미를 표현하는

In her 1995 article, / linguist Clark cited / such examples as / a 24-month-old saying, / "There comes the rat-man" / and a 25-month-old saying, / "Mommy just fixed this spear-page."
그녀의 1995년 논설에서 / 언어학자 Clark는 인용했다 / ~와 같은 예를 / 24개월 된 아이의 말인 / "저기 쥐사람이 와" / 그리고 25개월 된 아이의 말인 / "엄마가 방금 이 창페이지를 붙였어"

The "rat-man" was a colleague of her father's / who worked with rats / in a psychology laboratory; / the "spear-page" was a torn picture / of a jungle tribe holding spears / that her mother had taped together.
'쥐 사람'은 그녀의 아빠의 동료였다 / 쥐를 연구 대상으로 하는 / 심리학 연구소에서 / '창 페이지'는 찢어진 사진이었다 / 창을 들고 있는 정글 부족의 / 그녀의 엄마가 테이프로 함께 붙여놓은

Clark also cited / the example of a 28-month-old saying, / "You're the sworder and I'm the gunner."
Clark는 또한 인용했다 / 28개월 된 아이의 말의 예시를 / "너는 검 하는 사람이고 나는 총 하는 사람이야"라는

As these examples suggest, / children's innovative uses / of language / are far from random.
이런 예들이 제시하듯 / 어린이들의 독창적인 사용은 / 언어의 / 결코 마구잡이가 아니다

They reflect rules / for forming new words, / such as combining words or other components / that are meaningful in their own right / and that, when put together, have an unambiguous meaning.
그것들은 규칙을 반영한다 / 새로운 단어를 만드는 / 단어나 다른 요소들을 결합하는 것과 같은 / 그 자체로 의미가 있는 / 그리고 함께 쓰였을 때 명확한 의미를 갖는

Such linguistic creativity / allows children to express meanings / that are well beyond / what their limited vocabularies / would otherwise allow.
이러한 언어적 창의성은 / 아이들이 의미를 표현할 수 있게 한다 / 훨씬 넘어서는 / 그들의 제한된 어휘가 / 다른 식으로 허용하는 것을

해석　어린이들은 종종 원하는 의미를 표현하는 참신한 방법을 생각해낸다. 언어학자 Clark는 그녀의 1995년 논설에서 24개월 된 아이의 말인 "저기 쥐 사람이 와"와 25개월 된 아이의 말인 "엄마가 방금 이 창페이지를 붙였어."와 같은 예를 인용했다. '쥐 사람'은 심리학 연구소에서 쥐를 연구 대상으로 하는 그녀의 아빠의 동료였고, '창 페이지'는 그녀의 엄마가 테이프로 함께 붙여놓은 창을 들고 있는 정글 부족의 찢어진 사진이었다. Clark는 또한 "너는 검 하는 사람이고 나는 총 하는 사람이야."라는 28개월 된 아이의 말의 예시를 인용했다. 이런 예들이 제시하듯이, 어린이들의 독창적인 언어의 사용은 결코 마구잡이가 아니다. 그것들은 그 자체로 의미가 있으면서 함께 쓰였을 때 명확한 의미를 갖는 단어나 다른 요소들을 결합하는 것과 같은 새로운 단어를 만드는 규칙을 반영한다. 이러한 언어적 창의성은 아이들이 그들의 제한된 어휘가 다른 식으로 허용하는 것을 훨씬 넘어서는 의미를 표현할 수 있게 한다.

① 즉흥적인
② 상당히 임의적인
③ 결코 마구잡이가 아닌
④ 끝없는 반복 연습의 결과인

해설　빈칸이 있는 문장을 통해 빈칸에 어린이들의 독창적인 언어 사용이 어떠한지에 대한 내용이 나와야 적절하다는 것을 알 수 있다. 지문 뒷부분에서 아이들의 독창적인 언어 사용은 그 자체로 의미

가 있고, 함께 쓰였을 때 명확한 의미를 갖는 단어나 다른 요소들을 결합하는 것과 같은 새로운 단어를 만드는 규칙을 반영한다고 했으므로, '결코 마구잡이가 아닌'이라고 한 ③번이 정답이다.

어휘　novel 참신한, 신기한, 새로운　linguist 언어학자
cite 인용하다, 예로 들다　fix 붙이다　spear 창
work with ~을 연구 대상으로 하다　psychology 심리학
tear 찢다　innovative 독창적인, 획기적인
reflect 반영하다, 나타내다　unambiguous 명확한, 모호하지 않은
impromptu 즉흥적인　arbitrary 임의적인, 제멋대로인
endless 끝없는　drill 반복 연습

7회 | 2016년 법원직 9급

정답

p.90

01	② 독해 – 추론	11	② 독해 – 논리적 흐름 파악	21	① 독해 – 추론
02	③ 독해 – 논리적 흐름 파악	12	③ 독해 – 논리적 흐름 파악	22	① 독해 – 추론
03	④ 문법 – 능동태·수동태	13	② 독해 – 전체내용 파악	23	④ 독해 – 전체내용 파악
04	③ 독해 – 논리적 흐름 파악	14	② 독해 – 추론	24	③ 독해 – 전체내용 파악
05	④ 독해 – 세부내용 파악	15	④ 문법 – 수 일치&분사 &능동태·수동태	25	③ 독해 – 논리적 흐름 파악
06	③ 독해 – 논리적 흐름 파악	16	④ 독해 – 논리적 흐름 파악		
07	④ 독해 – 전체내용 파악	17	② 독해 – 추론		
08	③ 독해 – 논리적 흐름 파악	18	④ 독해 – 논리적 흐름 파악		
09	④ 독해 – 추론	19	③ 독해 – 논리적 흐름 파악		
10	③ 독해 – 논리적 흐름 파악	20	④ 독해 – 추론		

취약영역 분석표

영역	세부 유형	문항 수	소계
어휘	어휘&표현	0	/0
	생활영어	0	
문법	능동태·수동태	1	/2
	수 일치&분사&능동태·수동태	1	
독해	전체내용 파악	4	/23
	세부내용 파악	1	
	추론	7	
	논리적 흐름 파악	11	
총계			/25

· 자신이 취약한 영역은 '법원직 9급 영어, 이렇게 출제된다!'(p.8)를 통해 다시 한 번 확인하고 학습하시기 바랍니다.

---

01 독해 추론 (빈칸 완성 - 단어)   난이도 ★☆☆

끊어읽기 해석

Anthropologists believe / wisdom teeth, or the third set of molars, / were the evolutionary answer / to our ancestor's early diet / of coarse, rough food / —like leaves, roots, nuts and meats— / which required more chewing power / and resulted in excessive wear of the teeth.
인류학자들은 여긴다 / 사랑니, 즉 세 번째 어금니가 / 진화적인 해결책이었다고 / 우리 조상들의 초기 식단에 대한 / 거칠고 다듬지 않은 음식으로 된 / 나뭇잎, 뿌리, 견과류 그리고 고기와 같이 / 더 큰 씹는 힘을 필요로 했던 / 그래서 치아의 지나친 마모를 초래했던

The modern diet with its softer foods, / along with marvels of modern technologies / such as forks, spoons and knives, / has made / the need for wisdom teeth / nonexistent.
더 부드러운 음식을 포함하는 현대 식단은 / 현대 기술의 경이로움과 더불어 / 포크, 숟가락, 그리고 칼과 같은 / 만들었다 / 사랑니의 필요성을 / 존재하지 않게

As a result, / evolutionary biologists now classify / wisdom teeth / as vestigial organs, / or body parts / that have become functionless / due to evolution.
그 결과 / 진화 생물학자들은 이제 분류한다 / 사랑니를 / 흔적 기관으로 / 혹은 신체 부분으로 / 기능이 없어진 / 진화로 인해

해석 인류학자들은 사랑니, 즉 세 번째 어금니가 더 큰 씹는 힘을 필요로 했고 치아의 지나친 마모를 초래했던 나뭇잎, 뿌리, 견과류 그리고 고기와 같이 거칠고 다듬지 않은 음식으로 된 우리 조상들의 초기 식단에 대한 진화적인 해결책이었다고 여긴다. 포크, 숟가락, 그리고 칼과 같은 현대 기술의 경이로움과 더불어, 더 부드러운 음식을 포함하는 현대 식단은 사랑니의 필요성을 존재하지 않게 만들었다. 그 결과, 진화 생물학자들은 이제 사랑니를 흔적 기관, 혹은 진화로 인해 기능이 없어진 신체 부분으로 분류한다.

① 충치
② 진화
③ 단단함
④ 그것들의 모양

해설 빈칸이 있는 문장을 통해 빈칸에 진화 생물학자들이 사랑니를 무엇으로 인해 기능이 없어진 신체 부분으로 분류하는지에 대한 내용이 나와야 적절하다는 것을 알 수 있다. 빈칸 앞 문장에서 식사 도구와 부드러운 음식을 포함하는 현대 식단이 사랑니의 필요성을 존재하지 않게 만들었다고 했으므로, 진화 생물학자들은 사랑니를 '진화'로 인해 기능이 없어진 신체 부분으로 분류한다고 한 ②번이 정답이다.

어휘 anthropologist 인류학자 wisdom teeth 사랑니 molar 어금니
evolutionary 진화적인, 진화의 ancestor 조상
coarse 거친, 조잡한 rough 다듬지 않은, 가공하지 않은
excessive 지나친 wear 마모, 소모 marvel 경이로움, 놀라움
nonexistent 존재하지 않는 vestigial organ 흔적 기관
functionless 기능이 없는 dental decay 충치 hardness 단단함

---

02 독해 논리적 흐름 파악 (문단 순서 배열)   난이도 ★☆☆

끊어읽기 해석

In today's technology-driven world, / almost everyone, / at some point in their lives, / has either used or had some sort of contact / with a microwave oven.
오늘날 기술 중심의 세계에서 / 거의 모든 사람들이 / 삶의 어느 시점에서는 / 사용해 보았거나 어느 정도 접해본 적이 있다 / 전자레인지를

Like many of the great inventions of our past, / the idea behind the microwave oven / was accidentally stumbled upon / in 1946.
과거의 많은 위대한 발명품들처럼 / 전자레인지 이면의 아이디어는 / 우연히 발견되었다 / 1946년에

(A) Shortly after the accidental discovery, / engineers at Raytheon / went to work on Spencer's new idea, / developing and refining it / to be of practical use.
그 우연한 발견 직후에 / 레이시언의 기술자들은 / 스펜서의 새로운 아이디

해커스법원직 15개년 기출문제집 영어

어에 착수하기 시작했으며 / 그것을 발전시키고 개선시켰다 / 실용적이기 위해

(B) Dr. Percy Spencer was working / as an engineer with the Raytheon Corporation / at the time, / when he discovered / something very unusual / one day / while working on a radar-related research project.
퍼시 스펜서 박사는 일하고 있었다 / 레이시언사의 기술자로 / 그 당시에 / 그가 발견했을 때 / 매우 특이한 무언가를 / 어느 날 / 레이더 관련 연구 프로젝트 작업을 하는 동안

While testing a new vacuum tube / known as a magnetron, / he discovered / that a candy bar in his pocket had melted.
새로운 진공관을 시험하던 중에 / 마그네트론으로 알려진 / 그는 발견했다 / 그의 주머니 안에 있던 초코바가 녹았다는 것을

(C) Intrigued as he was, / Spencer decided upon further experimentation.
강한 흥미를 느껴서 / 스펜서는 추가 실험을 결정했다

Later on, / having pointed the tube / at such objects as a bag of popcorn kernels and an egg, / with similar results in both experiments / (the popcorn popped and the egg exploded), / he correctly concluded that / the observed effects in each case / were all attributed to exposure / to low-density microwave energy.
이후에 / 그 관을 향하도록 하여 / 팝콘 알맹이 한 봉지와 계란과 같은 그러한 물체로 / 두 실험 모두에서 비슷한 결과를 얻은 후 / (팝콘은 펑하고 튀었고 계란은 터졌다) / 그는 ~라고 정확하게 결론을 내렸다 / 각각의 경우에서 관찰된 결과가 / 모두 노출에 기인한 것이었다 / 저밀도의 마이크로파 에너지에의

해석
오늘날 기술 중심의 세계에서, 거의 모든 사람들이 삶의 어느 시점에서는 전자레인지를 사용해 보았거나 어느 정도 전자레인지를 접해본 적이 있다. 과거의 많은 위대한 발명품들처럼, 전자레인지 이면의 아이디어는 1946년에 우연히 발견되었다.

(B) 어느 날 레이더 관련 연구 프로젝트 작업을 하는 동안 그가 매우 특이한 무언가를 발견했을 때, 퍼시 스펜서 박사는 그 당시에 레이시언사의 기술자로 일하고 있었다. 마그네트론으로 알려진 새로운 진공관을 시험하던 중에, 그는 그의 주머니 안에 있던 초코바가 녹았다는 것을 발견했다.

(C) 강한 흥미를 느껴서, 스펜서는 추가 실험을 결정했다. 이후에, 그 관을 팝콘 알맹이 한 봉지와 계란과 같은 그러한 물체로 향하도록 하여 두 실험 모두에서 비슷한 결과를 얻은 후(팝콘은 펑하고 튀었고 계란은 터졌다), 그는 각각의 경우에서 관찰된 결과가 모두 저밀도의 마이크로파 에너지에의 노출에 기인한 것이었다고 정확하게 결론을 내렸다.

(A) 그 우연한 발견 직후에, 레이시언의 기술자들은 스펜서의 새로운 아이디어에 착수하기 시작했으며, 실용적이기 위해 그것을 발전시키고 개선시켰다.

해설
주어진 문단에서 전자레인지 이면의 아이디어는 1946년에 우연히 발견되었다고 한 후, (B)에서 레이시언사에서 기술자로 일하고 있던 스펜서 박사가 마그네트론으로 알려진 새로운 진공관을 시험하던 중에, 그의 주머니 안에 있던 초코바가 녹은 것을 발견했다고 한 뒤, (C)에서 흥미를 느낀 스펜서 박사는 팝콘과 계란으로도 실험을 해 보고, 각각의 경우에서 관찰된 결과가 모두 저밀도의 마이크로파 에너지에의 노출에 기인한 것이었다고 정확하게 결론을 내렸다고 설명하고 있다. 이어서 (A)에서 그 우연한 발견 직후에, 레이시언의 기술자들이 스펜서의 새로운 아이디어를 발전시키고 개선시켰다는 것을 알려주고 있다. 따라서 ③ (B) – (C) – (A)가 정답이다.

어휘
technology-driven 기술 중심의 microwave oven 전자레인지 stumble 우연히 발견하다 work on 착수하다, 공들이다

refine 개선시키다 be of practical use 실용적이다
vacuum tube 진공관 intrigue 강한 흥미를 불러일으키다
kernel 알맹이 attribute 기인하다, (~의 결과로) 보다

---

03 문법 능동태·수동태 난이도 ★☆☆

해석 '쉽게 승리하다' 또는 '거의 노력하지 않고 또는 아무 노력 없이 승리하다'를 의미하는 'win hands down(쉽게 이기다)'은 그것의 기원이 경마에 있다. 접전의 사진 판정 경주에서, 기수는 보통 속도를 유지하거나 높이기 위해서 말을 채찍이나 고삐로 때린다. 말이 몇 마신 정도 앞서 승리가 확실시 될 때, 기수는 보통 말을 때리는 것을 중단하거나, 고삐가 느슨해지도록 둔다. 사실상, 그는 그의 '손을 내려' 놓는다. 그 표현은 19세기 중반에 등장했다. 그 세기말에는 이것이 '전혀 어려움이 없다'라는 뜻을 의미하기 위해 경마 이외에서 사용되었다.

해설 ④ 수동태로 쓸 수 없는 동사 동사 appear는 목적어를 갖지 않는 자동사이고 수동태로 쓸 수 없으므로 수동태 was appeared를 능동태 appeared로 고쳐야 한다.

오답 분석
① 인칭대명사 대명사가 지시하는 것이 단수 취급하는 to 부정사 구(To "win hands down")이므로 단수 소유대명사 its가 올바르게 쓰였다.
② 부사 자리 동사를 앞에서 수식하는 것은 부사이므로 동사 strikes 앞에 부사 typically가 올바르게 쓰였다.
③ 원형 부정사를 목적격 보어로 취하는 동사 사역동사 let은 목적격 보어로 동사원형을 취하는 5형식 동사이므로 목적격 보어 자리에 동사원형 go가 올바르게 쓰였다.

어휘 win hands down 쉽게 이기다 origin 기원 close 접전의
photo-finish 사진 판정의 jockey 기수 bat 채찍 rein 고삐
length (경마의) 1마신(馬身) cease 중단하다

👍 이것도 알면 **합격!**

1형식 동사 appear, occur, fly, work, belong, happen, last, exist 등은 목적어나 보어 없이 '주어 + 동사'만으로도 완전한 문장을 만들 수 있는 완전 자동사라는 것을 알아두자.

---

04 독해 논리적 흐름 파악 (문맥상 적절한 어휘) 난이도 ★★☆

끊어읽기 해석

In many ways, / the differences between pairs of training shoe / are marginal.
많은 면에서 / 운동화들 간의 차이점은 / 미미하다

Mr. Twitchell calls them fungible, / "essentially interchangeable."
Mr. Twitchell은 그것들을 대체 가능한 것이라고 부른다 / '본질적으로 서로 바꿀 수 있는'

But successive savvy advertising strategies / turned a little Oregon sports outfitter / into the globally (A) dominant sports giant Nike.
하지만 연이은 영리한 광고 전략은 / 오레곤에 있는 작은 스포츠용품점을 바꿔 놓았다 / 세계적으로 (A) 우세한 스포츠 거대 기업인 나이키로

Their swoosh logo / is now one of the most recognizable images / on the planet, / rendering the actual name unnecessary.
그들의 부메랑 모양의 로고는 / 이제 가장 잘 알아볼 수 있는 이미지 중 하나이다 / 전 세계적으로 / (그리고) 실제 이름을 불필요하게 만들었다

And while Nike may not have been the first company / to

seek (B) celebrity plugs, / its relationship with Michael Jordan is arguably the most successful endorsement / in history.
그리고 나이키가 최초의 회사는 아니었을지 모른다 / (B) 유명인 광고를 추구하는 / 그 회사와 마이클 조던의 관계는 거의 틀림없이 가장 성공적인 홍보이다 / 역사상

The release of the Just Do It motto in 1988 / was a (C) transformative moment for the company, / weaving their brand, / seemingly forever, / with the inspiring and dramatic physicality of sport.
1988년에 표어 Just Do It의 발표는 / 그 회사를 (C) 변화시키는 순간이었다 / 그들의 브랜드에 엮어 넣었다 / 겉보기에는 영원히 / 스포츠의 고무적이며 극적인 운동 능력을

해석 많은 면에서, 운동화들 간의 차이점은 미미하다. Mr. Twitchell은 그것들을 대체 가능한, 즉 '본질적으로 서로 바꿀 수 있는' 것이라고 부른다. 하지만, 연이은 영리한 광고 전략은 오레곤에 있는 작은 스포츠용품점을 세계적으로 (A) 우세한 스포츠 거대 기업인 나이키로 바꿔 놓았다. 그들의 부메랑 모양의 로고는 이제 전 세계적으로 가장 잘 알아볼 수 있는 이미지 중 하나이며, 실제 이름을 불필요하게 만들었다. 그리고 나이키가 (B) 유명인 광고를 추구하는 최초의 회사는 아니었을지 모르지만, 그 회사와 마이클 조던의 관계는 거의 틀림없이 역사상 가장 성공적인 홍보이다. 1988년에 표어 Just Do It의 발표는 그 회사를 (C) 변화시키는 순간이었으며, 그들의 브랜드에 스포츠의 고무적이며 극적인 운동 능력을 겉보기에는 영원히 엮어 넣었다.

(A)	(B)	(C)
① 우세한	– 축하자	– 투명한
② 휴면기의	– 축하자	– 변화시키는
③ 우세한	– 유명인	– 변화시키는
④ 휴면기의	– 유명인	– 투명한

해설 (A) 빈칸 뒤 문장에서 그들의 부메랑 모양의 로고는 전 세계적으로 가장 잘 알아볼 수 있는 이미지 중 하나라고 했으므로, 빈칸에는 세계적으로 '우세한'(dominant)이라는 내용이 들어가야 적절하다. (B) 빈칸 뒤 문장에서 나이키와 마이클 조던의 관계는 역사상 가장 성공적인 홍보라고 했으므로, 빈칸에는 '유명인'(celebrity) 광고라는 내용이 들어가야 적절하다. (C) 빈칸이 있는 문장에서 표어 Just Do It의 발표가 그들의 브랜드에 스포츠의 고무적이며 극적인 운동 능력을 엮어 넣었다고 했으므로, 빈칸에는 '변화시키는'(transformative) 순간이라는 내용이 들어가야 적절하다.
따라서 ③ (A) dominant(우세한) – (B) celebrity(유명인) – (C) transformative(변화시키는)가 정답이다.

어휘 marginal 미미한, 중요하지 않은 fungible 대체 가능의
essentially 본질적으로 interchangeable 서로 바꿀 수 있는
successive 연이은, 연속적인 savvy 영리한 outfitter 용품점
dominant 우세한, 지배적인 dormant 휴면기의, 활동을 중단한
giant 거대 기업 recognizable 알아볼 수 있는
render (어떤 상태가 되게) 만들다 celebrity 유명인 plug 광고, 선전
arguably 거의 틀림없이 endorsement 홍보, 지지
transparent 투명한 transformative 변화시키는
weave 엮어 넣다, 만들어내다 physicality 운동 능력, 신체적 특징

05 독해 세부내용 파악 (지칭 대상 파악) 난이도 ★☆☆

끊어읽기 해석

"There may be a devilish Indian / behind every tree." / said Goodman Brown to himself; / and ① he glanced fearfully / behind him / as he added, / "What if the devil himself should be / at my very elbow!"

"사악한 인디언이 있을지도 몰라 / 모든 나무 뒤에" / Goodman Brown은 혼잣말을 했다 / 그리고 ① 그는 두려운 듯이 흘끗 보았다 / 그의 뒤를 / 그는 덧붙이면서 / "악마가 있으면 어떡하지 / 아주 가까이에!"

His head being turned back, / ② he passed / a crook of the road, / and, looking forward again, / beheld the figure of a man, / in grave and decent attire / seated at the foot of an old tree.
다시 고개를 돌리며 / ② 그는 지났다 / 길의 구부러진 곳을 / 그리고 다시 앞을 보았을 때 / 한 남자의 형상을 보았다 / 근엄하고 품위 있는 복장을 한 / 고목의 기슭에 앉아있는

He arose / at Goodman Brown's approach / and walked onward side by side with ③ him.
그는 일어났다 / Goodman Brown이 다가가자 / 그리고 ③ 그와 나란히 앞으로 걸었다

"You are late, Goodman Brown," / said the man.
"Goodman Brown씨, 늦으셨군요" / 남자가 말했다

"My wife kept me back / a while," / he replied, / with a tremor in his voice, / caused by the sudden appearance of ④ him, / though not wholly unexpected.
"제 아내가 저를 지체시켰어요 / 잠시" / 그는 대답했다 / 떨림이 있는 목소리로 / ④ 그의 갑작스러운 등장으로 인해 / 비록 완전히 예상하지 못했던 것은 아니었지만

해석 "모든 나무 뒤에 사악한 인디언이 있을지도 몰라." Goodman Brown은 혼잣말을 했다. 그리고 ① 그는 "악마가 아주 가까이에 있으면 어떡하지!"라고 덧붙이면서 두려운 듯이 그의 뒤를 흘끗 보았다. 다시 고개를 돌리며 ② 그는 길의 구부러진 곳을 지났고, 다시 앞을 보았을 때 그는 고목의 기슭에 앉아있는 근엄하고 품위 있는 복장을 한 한 남자의 형상을 보았다. 그는 Goodman Brown이 다가가자 일어났고 ③ 그와 나란히 앞으로 걸었다. "Goodman Brown씨, 늦으셨군요."라고 남자가 말했다. 비록 완전히 예상하지 못했던 것은 아니었지만, ④ 그의 갑작스러운 등장으로 인해 떨림이 있는 목소리로 "제 아내가 저를 잠시 지체시켰어요"라고 그는 대답했다.

해설 ①, ②, ③번 모두 Goodman Brown을 지칭하지만, ④번은 Goodman Brown 앞에 나타난 근엄하고 품위 있는 복장의 남자를 지칭하므로 ④번이 정답이다.

어휘 devilish 사악한, 악마 같은 glance 흘끗 보다
fearfully 두려운 듯이, 무서워하며 at one's elbow 가까이에
crook 구부러진 곳, 굽이 behold 보다 grave 근엄한, 엄숙한
decent 품위 있는, 괜찮은 attire 복장, 의복
onward 앞으로, 전방으로 side by side 나란히 tremor 떨림, 미진

06 독해 논리적 흐름 파악 (문맥상 부적절한 어휘) 난이도 ★☆☆

끊어읽기 해석

Our "ego" or self-conception could be pictured / as a leaking balloon, / forever requiring / the helium of external love / to remain ① inflated, / and ever vulnerable to the smallest pinpricks / of neglect.
우리의 '자아' 즉 자아개념은 묘사될 수 있다 / (바람이) 새는 풍선으로 / 이것은 끝없이 필요로 하며 / 외부의 사랑이라는 헬륨을 / 계속 ① 부푼 상태를 유지하기 위해 / 그리고 가장 작은 구멍에 언제나 취약하다 / 무시라는

There is something / at once sobering and absurd / in the extent to / which we are lifted / by the attentions of others / and sunk by their ② disregard.
무엇인가가 있다 / 진지해지게 하기도 하고 터무니없기도 한 / 정도까지 / 우리가 기분이 좋아진다 / 다른 사람들의 관심으로 인해 / 그리고 그들의 ② 무시로 인해 풀이 죽는다

해커스법원직 15개년 기출문제집 영어

Our mood may ③ brighten / because a colleague greets us distractedly / or our telephone calls go unreturned.
우리의 감정은 ③ 밝아질 수 있다 / 동료가 주의가 산만하게 인사하기 때문에 / 또는 우리의 전화가 응답 받지 못하기 때문에

And we are capable of thinking / life ④ worthy of living / because someone remembers our name / or sends us a fruit basket.
그리고 우리는 생각할 수 있다 / 인생이 살만한 ④ 가치가 있다고 / 누군가가 우리의 이름을 기억하기 때문에 / 또는 우리에게 과일바구니를 보내기 때문에

해석 우리의 '자아' 즉 자아개념은 (바람이) 새는 풍선으로 묘사될 수 있는데, 이것은 계속 ① 부푼 상태를 유지하기 위해 외부의 사랑이라는 헬륨을 끊임없이 필요로 하며, 무시라는 가장 작은 구멍에 언제나 취약하다. 우리가 다른 사람들의 관심으로 인해 기분이 좋아지고, 그들의 ② 무시로 인해 풀이 죽는 정도까지 진지해지게 하기도 하고 터무니없기도 한 무엇인가가 있다. 동료가 주의가 산만하게 인사하거나 우리의 전화가 응답 받지 못하기 때문에 우리의 감정은 ③ 밝아질 수 있다. 그리고 우리는 누군가가 우리의 이름을 기억하거나, 우리에게 과일바구니를 보내기 때문에 인생이 살만한 ④ 가치가 있다고 생각할 수 있다.

해설 지문 앞부분에서 우리는 다른 사람들의 관심으로 인해 기분이 좋아지고, 그들의 무시로 인해 풀이 죽는다고 했으므로, 동료가 주의 산만하게 인사하거나 우리의 전화에 응답하지 않는 것으로 인해 우리의 감정이 '밝아질'(brighten) 수 있다는 것은 문맥상 적절하지 않다. 따라서 ③번이 정답이다. 참고로, 주어진 brighten을 대신할 수 있는 어휘로는 '약해지다'라는 의미의 dampen 등이 있다.

어휘 ego 자아 self-conception 자아개념 picture 묘사하다
leak 새다 external 외부의, 밖의 inflated 부푼, 팽창한
vulnerable to ~에 취약한 pinprick 아주 작은 구멍
neglect 무시, 방치 sobering 진지해지게 하는
absurd 터무니없는, 어이없는 extent 정도
lift 기분이 좋아지게 하다 sink 풀이 죽다 disregard 무시, 묵살
brighten 밝아지다 colleague 동료 greet 인사하다
distractedly 주의가 산만하게

---

07 독해 전체내용 파악 (제목 파악)   난이도 ★☆☆

끊어읽기 해석

If a black hole has a non-zero temperature / —no matter how small— / the most basic and well-established physical principles / would require it to emit radiation, / much like a glowing poker.
만약 블랙홀이 절대 영도가 아닌 온도를 지닌다면 / 아무리 낮더라도 / 가장 근본적이고도 확고부동한 물리학 법칙은 / 그것이 방사선을 방출하도록 할 것이다 / 타오르는 부지깽이처럼

But black holes, / as everyone knows, / are black; / they supposedly do not emit anything.
하지만 블랙홀은 / 모든 사람이 알고 있듯이 / 암흑이다 / 아마 어떤 것도 방출하지 않을 것이다

This was the case / until Hawking, in 1974, discovered / something truly amazing.
그것은 사실이었다 / 호킹이 1974년에 발견했을 때까지 / 정말 놀라운 무언가를

Black holes, / Hawking announced, / are not completely black.
블랙홀이 / 호킹은 발표했다 / 완전히 암흑은 아니다

If one ignores quantum mechanics / and invokes only the

---

laws of classical general relativity, / then as originally found some six decades previously, / black holes certainly do not allow anything / —not even light— / to escape their gravitational grip.
만약 누군가가 양자역학을 무시한다면 / 그리고 단지 종래의 일반 상대론의 법칙만을 적용한다면 / 그렇다면 약 60년 전에 처음 밝혀진 것처럼 / 블랙홀은 분명히 아무 것도 ~하게 하지 않는다 / 심지어 빛조차도 / 중력의 붙드는 힘에서 벗어나도록

But the inclusion of quantum mechanics modifies this conclusion / in a profound way, / and Hawking found / that black holes do emit radiation, / quantum mechanically.
하지만 양자역학의 도입은 이 결론을 바꾸었다 / 엄청난 방식으로 / 그리고 호킹은 알아냈다 / 블랙홀이 정말 방사선을 방출한다는 것을 / 양자역학적으로

해석 만약 블랙홀이 아무리 낮더라도 절대 영도가 아닌 온도를 지닌다면, 가장 근본적이고도 확고부동한 물리학 법칙은 그것이 타오르는 부지깽이처럼 방사선을 방출하도록 할 것이다. 하지만 모든 사람이 알고 있듯이 블랙홀은 암흑이며, 아마 어떤 것도 방출하지 않을 것이다. 1974년에 호킹이 정말 놀라운 무언가를 발견했을 때까지 그것은 사실이었다. 호킹은 블랙홀이 완전히 암흑은 아니라고 발표했다. 만약 누군가가 양자역학을 무시하고 단지 종래의 일반 상대론 법칙만을 적용한다면, 약 60년 전에 처음 밝혀진 것처럼, 블랙홀은 분명히 아무 것도, 심지어 빛조차도, 중력의 붙드는 힘에서 벗어나게 하지 않는다. 하지만 양자역학의 도입은 엄청난 방식으로 이 결론을 바꾸었고, 호킹은 블랙홀이 양자역학적으로 정말 방사선을 방출한다는 것을 알아냈다.

① 블랙홀 내부에서는 무슨 일이 생기는가?
② 양자 세계의 미스터리
③ 일반 상대론의 탄생
④ 블랙홀은 정말 암흑일까?

해설 지문 전반에 걸쳐 일반 상대론 법칙에 따르면 블랙홀은 암흑이며 어떤 것도 방출하지 않지만, 호킹은 블랙홀이 완전히 암흑은 아니라고 발표했으며 양자역학을 통해 블랙홀이 방사선을 방출한다는 것을 알아냈다고 설명하고 있다. 따라서 이 지문의 제목을 '블랙홀은 정말 암흑일까?'라고 표현한 ④번이 정답이다.

어휘 physical 물리학의 principle 법칙, 원리 emit 방출하다, 발산하다
radiation 방사선 glow 타오르다, 빛나다
poker 부지깽이, 찌르는 물건 case 사실, 진상
quantum mechanics 양자역학 invoke 적용하다, 들먹이다
classical 종래의, 전통적인 general relativity 일반 상대론
gravitational 중력의 grip 붙드는 힘, 통제 modify 바꾸다
profound 엄청난, 심오한

---

08 독해 논리적 흐름 파악 (무관한 문장 삭제)   난이도 ★☆☆

끊어읽기 해석

For the New World as a whole, / the Indian population decline / in the century or two following Columbus's arrival / is estimated / to have been as large as 95 percent.
전체적으로 신세계에서 / 아메리칸 인디언 인구의 감소는 / 콜럼버스가 도착한 그 세기 또는 그 다음의 2세기의 / 추정된다 / 95퍼센트에 달했던 것으로

The main killers were Old World germs / to which Indians had never been exposed, / and against which they therefore had neither immune / nor genetic resistance.
주범은 구세계의 세균이었다 / 아메리칸 인디언들이 한 번도 노출된 적이 없었던 / 그리고 따라서 그들은 그것에 대한 면역도 가지고 있지 않았다 / 유전적인 저항력도 (가지고 있지 않았다)

① Smallpox, measles, influenza, and typhus / competed for top rank / among the killers.
천연두, 홍역, 유행성 감기, 그리고 발진티푸스는 / 상위를 다투었다 / 사망 원인들 중에서

② For example, / in 1837 / the Mandan Indian tribe, / with one of the most elaborate cultures / in our Great Plains, / contracted smallpox / from a steamboat / traveling up the Missouri River from St. Louis.
예를 들어 / 1837년에 / 맨던 인디언 부족은 / 가장 정교한 문명을 가진 부족 중 하나였던 / 대평원에서 / 천연두에 걸렸다 / 증기선으로 인해 / 세인트루이스에서 미주리강을 거슬러 올라오던

③ The Mandan survived / mainly by hunting, farming and gathering wild plants, / though some food came from trade.
맨던 족은 생존했다 / 주로 사냥, 농업, 야생식물 채집으로 / 비록 일부 식량은 무역으로 얻었지만

④ The population of one Mandan village plummeted / from 2,000 to fewer than 40 / within a few weeks.
맨던 족 마을의 인구는 급락했다 / 2천 명에서 40명 이하로 / 몇 주 내에

해석　전체적으로 신세계에서, 콜럼버스가 도착한 그 세기 또는 그 다음의 2세기의 아메리칸 인디언 인구의 감소는 95퍼센트에 달했던 것으로 추정된다. 주범은 아메리칸 인디언들이 한 번도 노출된 적이 없었던 구세계의 세균이었고, 따라서 그들은 그것에 대한 면역도 유전적 저항력도 가지고 있지 않았다. ① 천연두, 홍역, 유행성 감기, 그리고 발진티푸스는 사망 원인들 중에서 상위를 다투었다. ② 예를 들어, 대평원에서 가장 정교한 문명을 가진 부족 중 하나였던 맨던 인디언 부족은 1837년에 세인트루이스에서 미주리강을 거슬러 올라오던 증기선으로 인해 천연두에 걸렸다. ③ 맨던 족은 비록 일부 식량은 무역으로 얻었지만, 주로 사냥, 농업, 야생식물 채집으로 생존했다. ④ 맨던 족 마을의 인구는 몇 주 내에 2천 명에서 40명 이하로 급락했다.

해석　지문 처음에서 콜럼버스의 도착 후 아메리칸 인디언 인구는 95퍼센트가 감소했으며, 이것의 주범은 구세계의 세균이었다고 한 뒤, ①, ②, ④번에서 천연두, 홍역, 독감, 그리고 발진티푸스가 주요 사망 원인이었으며, 한 예로 맨던 인디언 부족의 인구가 천연두로 인해 급락했다는 것을 설명하고 있으므로 모두 첫 문장과 관련이 있다. 그러나 ③번은 '맨던 족의 생존 수단'에 대한 내용으로, 첫 문장의 내용과 관련이 없다. 따라서 ③번이 정답이다.

어휘　Indian 아메리칸 인디언의　population 인구
Old World 구세계(유럽·아시아·아프리카)　germ 세균
immune 면역의　genetic 유전의　resistance 저항력, 내성
smallpox 천연두　measles 홍역　influenza 유행성 감기
typhus 발진티푸스　elaborate 정교한　contract (병에) 걸리다
steamboat 증기선　plummet 급락하다, 곤두박질치다

09　독해　추론 (빈칸 완성 - 구)　난이도 ★★☆

끊어읽기 해석

Most of the world's great cities have grown randomly, / little by little, / in response to the needs of the moment; / very rarely is a city planned / for the remote future.
세상의 위대한 도시들 대부분은 임의로 성장해왔다 / 조금씩 / 그 당시의 필요성에 대한 응답으로 / 도시가 계획되는 것은 매우 드물다 / 먼 미래를 위해

The evolution of a city is like the evolution of the brain: / it develops from a small center / and slowly grows and changes, / leaving many old parts still functioning.
한 도시의 발전은 두뇌의 진화와 비슷하다 / 그것은 작은 중심부에서 발전한다 / 그리고 천천히 성장하고 변화한다 / 그리고 많은 오래된 부분들을

여전히 기능하는 채로 둔다

There is no way / for evolution to remove the ancient interior of the brain / and replace it / with something of more modern manufacture.
일은 없다 / 진화가 두뇌의 오래된 내부를 제거하는 / 그리고 그것을 교체하는 / 더 최신 제품으로

The brain must function / during the renovation.
두뇌는 기능해야 한다 / 수리하는 동안에

That is why / our brain stem is surrounded / by the R-complex, / then the limbic system / and finally the cerebral cortex.
그것이 이유이다 / 우리의 뇌간이 둘러싸여 있는 / R 영역으로 / 그다음에 대뇌변연계로 / 그리고 마지막으로 대뇌피질로

The old parts are in charge of / too many fundamental functions / for them to be replaced altogether.
오래된 부분들은 담당하고 있다 / 너무 많은 기본적인 기능을 / 그들이 전부 교체되기에는

So they wheeze along, / out-of-date and sometimes counterproductive, / but a necessary consequence of our evolution.
그래서 그들은 숨을 헐떡이며 함께 있다 / 구식이면서 가끔은 역효과를 낳는 채로 / 그러나 우리의 진화의 필연적인 결과이다

해석　세상의 위대한 도시들 대부분은 그 당시의 필요성에 대한 응답으로 임의로 조금씩 성장해왔고, 먼 미래를 위해 도시가 계획되는 것은 매우 드물다. 한 도시의 발전은 두뇌의 진화와 비슷하다. 그것은 작은 중심부에서 발전하며 천천히 성장하고 변화하며, 많은 오래된 부분들을 여전히 기능하는 채로 둔다. 진화가 두뇌의 오래된 내부를 제거하고 그것을 더 최신 제품으로 교체하는 일은 없다. 두뇌는 수리하는 동안에 기능해야 한다. 그것이 바로 우리의 뇌간이 R 영역으로, 그다음에 대뇌변연계로, 마지막으로 대뇌피질로 둘러싸여 있는 이유이다. 오래된 부분들은 그들이 전부 교체되기에는 너무 많은 기본적인 기능을 담당하고 있다. 그래서 그들은 구식이면서 가끔은 역효과를 낳는 채로 숨을 헐떡이며 함께 있지만, 우리의 진화의 필연적인 결과이다.

① 신도시의 도로 배치
② 외부 물질의 침입
③ 자연 선택의 이점
④ 두뇌의 오래된 내부

해석　빈칸이 있는 문장을 통해 빈칸에 진화가 무엇을 제거하고 그것을 더 최신 제품으로 교체하지 않는지에 대한 내용이 나와야 적절하다는 것을 알 수 있다. 빈칸 앞 문장에서 두뇌는 천천히 성장하고 변화하며, 많은 오래된 부분들을 여전히 기능하는 채 둔다고 한 뒤, 지문 뒷부분에서 오래된 부분들은 전부 교체되기에는 너무 많은 기본적인 기능을 담당하고 있다고 했으므로, 진화가 '두뇌의 오래된 내부'를 제거하고 그것을 더 최신 제품으로 교체하는 일은 없다고 한 ④번이 정답이다.

어휘　randomly 임의로　remote 먼　evolution 발전, 진화
manufacture 제품　renovation 수리, 혁신　surround 둘러싸다
fundamental 기본적인　wheeze 숨을 헐떡이다, 색색거리다
out-of-date 구식의　counterproductive 역효과를 낳는
necessary 필연적인　consequence 결과　invasion 침입, 침략
alien 외부의, 외래의

끊어읽기 해석

> The "denotation" of a word / is what the word literally means.
> 한 단어의 '명시적 의미'는 / 그 단어가 문자 그대로 의미하는 것이다
>
> *Blue*, for instance, means / "the color of the sky on a sunny day."
> 예를 들어 Blue는 의미한다 / '화창한 날의 하늘의 색깔'을
>
> (A) Likewise, / we would like to have friends / who are "true *blue*," / to win a "*blue* ribbon", / and to own "*blue*-chip stocks".
> 마찬가지로 / 우리는 친구를 가지고 싶어 한다 / '충실한(true blue)' / '최고의 상(blue ribbon)'을 차지하고 (싶어 한다) / 그리고 '우량주(blue-chip stocks)'를 보유하고 (싶어 한다)
>
> But we might not like / being called a "*bluenose*".
> 그러나 우리는 좋아하지 않을 수도 있다 / '청교도적인 사람(bluenose)'이라고 불리는 것을
>
> (B) As you see above, / even a simple word / naming a color / can have / a wide range of possible meanings, / depending on how it's used.
> 위에서 보다시피 / 간단한 단어조차 / 색깔을 일컫는 / 가질 수 있다 / 광범위한 가능한 의미를 / 그것이 어떻게 사용되는지에 따라
>
> This is / what is meant by connotation, / the implied (suggested) meaning of a word.
> 이것은 ~이다 / 함축에 의해 의미를 가지는 것 / 단어의 함축된(암시된) 뜻인
>
> (C) Beyond the denotation of the word, / however, / we also can find / many other meanings / in the name of the color.
> 그 단어의 명시적 의미 너머로 / 그러나 / 우리는 또한 찾을 수 있다 / 많은 다른 의미들을 / 그 색깔의 이름에서
>
> We usually do not like / feeling *blue*, / but we may enjoy / hearing a great *blues* singer.
> 우리는 보통 좋아하지 않는다 / 기분이 '울적한 것(feeling blue)'을 / 그러나 우리는 즐길지도 모른다 / 멋진 '블루스(blues)' 가수의 노래를 듣는 것을

해석

> 한 단어의 '명시적 의미'는 그 단어가 문자 그대로 의미하는 것이다. 예를 들어, Blue는 '화창한 날의 하늘의 색깔'을 의미한다.
>
> (C) 그러나, 그 단어의 명시적 의미 너머로, 우리는 또한 그 색깔의 이름에서 많은 다른 의미들을 찾을 수 있다. 우리는 보통 기분이 '울적한' 것(feeling blue)을 좋아하지 않지만, 멋진 '블루스(blues)' 가수의 노래를 듣는 것을 즐길지도 모른다.
>
> (A) 마찬가지로, 우리는 '충실한(true blue)' 친구를 가지고 싶어 하고, '최고의 상(blue ribbon)'을 차지하고 싶어 하며, '우량주(blue-chip stocks)'를 보유하고 싶어 한다. 그러나 우리는 '청교도적인 사람(bluenose)'이라고 불리는 것을 좋아하지 않을 수도 있다.
>
> (B) 위에서 보다시피, 색깔을 일컫는 간단한 단어조차, 그것이 어떻게 사용되는지에 따라 광범위한 가능한 의미를 가질 수 있다. 이것은 단어의 함축된(암시된) 뜻인 함축에 의해 의미를 가지는 것이다.

해설 주어진 글에서 한 단어의 '명시적 의미'는 그 단어가 문자 그대로 의미하는 것이라고 하며 Blue를 예로 든 후, (C)에서 우리는 또한 그 단어의 명시적 의미 너머로 그 색깔의 이름에서 많은 다른 의미들을 찾을 수 있다고 했다. 이어서 (A)에서 'blue'가 포함된 다양한 의미를 지닌 단어의 다른 예시들을 추가적으로 언급한 뒤, (B)에서 위에서 보다시피 색깔을 일컫는 간단한 단어조차, 어떻게 사

용되는지에 따라 광범위한 가능한 의미를 가질 수 있다고 설명하고 있다. 따라서 ③ (C) − (A) − (B)가 정답이다.

어휘 **denotation** 명시적 의미 **literally** 문자 그대로 **likewise** 마찬가지로 **true blue** 충실한 **blue ribbon** 최고의 상, 최고의 명예 **blue-chip stock** 우량주 **bluenose** 청교도적인 사람, 도덕군자 **a wide range of** 광범위한 **connotation** 함축 **imply** 함축하다 **suggest** 암시하다 **feel blue** 기분이 울적하다 **blues** (재즈 음악의) 블루스

끊어읽기 해석

> "Begin with the End in Mind" is based on the principle / that all things are created twice.
> '목적을 염두에 두고 시작하라'는 원칙에 근거한다 / 모든 것이 두 번 만들어진다는
>
> There's a mental or first creation, / and a physical or second creation / to all things.
> 정신적인 또는 첫 번째 창조가 있다 / 그리고 물리적인 또는 두 번째 창조가 / 모든 것에는
>
> (A) If you want a family-centered home, / you plan a family room / where it would be a natural gathering place.
> 만약 당신이 가족 중심의 집을 원한다면 / 당신은 거실을 계획한다 / 자연스러운 모임의 장소가 될
>
> You plan sliding doors and a patio / for children to play outside.
> 당신은 미닫이문과 테라스를 계획한다 / 아이들이 밖에서 놀 수 있도록
>
> You work with ideas.
> 당신은 아이디어를 생각해낸다.
>
> You work with your mind / until you get a clear image / of what you want to build.
> 당신은 생각을 갖고 일한다 / 당신이 확실한 이미지를 얻을 때까지 / 당신이 짓고 싶어 하는 것의
>
> (B) Take the construction of a home, / for example.
> 집의 건설을 생각해 보자 / 예를 들어
>
> You design it in every detail / before you ever hammer the first nail into place.
> 당신은 그것을 상세하게 계획한다 / 당신이 언제나 집에 첫 번째 못을 박기 전에
>
> You try to get a very clear sense / of what kind of house you want.
> 당신은 분명한 이해를 얻기 위해 노력한다 / 당신이 어떤 종류의 집을 원하는지에 대한
>
> (C) Then you reduce it to blueprint / and develop construction plans.
> 그 이후에 당신은 그것을 청사진으로 바꾼다 / 그리고 설계도로 발전시킨다
>
> All of this is done / before the earth is touched.
> 이 모든 것이 이루어진다 / 땅에 손을 대기 전에
>
> If not, / then in the second creation, the physical creation, / you will have to make expensive changes / that may double the cost of your home.
> 그렇지 않다면 / 두 번째 창조인 물리적 창조에서 / 당신은 비싼 변경을 해야 할 것이다 / 당신 집의 비용을 두 배로 만들지도 모르는

해석

> '목적을 염두에 두고 시작하라'는 모든 것이 두 번 만들어진다는 원칙에 근거한다. 모든 것에는 정신적인 또는 첫 번째 창조와, 물리적인 또는 두 번째 창조가 있다.

(B) 예를 들어, 집의 건설을 생각해 보자. 당신은 언제나 집에 첫 번째 못을 박기 전에 그것을 상세하게 계획한다. 당신은 어떤 종류의 집을 원하는지에 대한 분명한 이해를 얻기 위해 노력한다.

(A) 만약 당신이 가족 중심의 집을 원한다면, 당신은 자연스러운 모임의 장소가 될 거실을 계획한다. 당신은 아이들이 밖에서 놀 수 있도록 미닫이문과 테라스를 계획한다. 당신은 아이디어를 생각해낸다. 당신은 당신이 짓고 싶어 하는 것의 확실한 이미지를 얻을 때까지 생각을 갖고 일한다.

(C) 그 이후에 당신은 그것을 청사진으로 바꾸고 설계도로 발전시킨다. 이 모든 것이 땅에 손을 대기 전에 이루어진다. 그렇지 않다면, 두 번째 창조인 물리적 창조에서 당신은 당신 집의 비용을 두 배로 만들지도 모르는 비싼 변경을 해야 할 것이다.

해설 주어진 문단에서 모든 것에는 정신적인 첫 번째 창조와 물리적인 두 번째 창조가 있다고 한 뒤, (B)에서 집의 건설을 예로 들며 당신은 첫 번째 못을 박기 전에 그것을 상세하게 계획한다고 한다. 이어서 (A)에서 당신은 아이디어를 생각해내며 짓고 싶어 하는 것의 확실한 이미지를 얻을 때까지 생각을 갖고 일한다고 설명한 뒤, (C)에서 그 이후에 그것(생각)을 청사진으로 바꾸고 설계도를 발전시킨다고 설명하고 있다. 따라서 ② (B) – (A) – (C)가 정답이다.

어휘 principle 원칙, 원리 physical 물리적인 gathering 모임
sliding door 미닫이문 patio 테라스 take 생각하다, (예를) 들다
hammer 박다, 못질하다 reduce (~으로) 바꾸다, 변형시키다
blueprint 청사진

---

12 **독해** **논리적 흐름 파악 (문단 순서 배열)** 난이도 ★★☆

끊어읽기 해석

> Observations are not always undertaken / with a clear sense / of what data may be relevant.
> 관찰이 항상 시작되는 것은 아니다 / 분명한 통찰로 / 어떤 자료가 관련이 있을 수 있는지에 대한
>
> On a long and rough sea voyage in 1882, / many of the ship's passengers / were afflicted with seasickness.
> 1882년의 길고 거친 바다 항해에서 / 그 배의 많은 승객들이 / 뱃멀미에 시달렸다
>
> ---
>
> (A) James speculated / that seasickness must be due to / some temporary disturbance of the inner ear, / a problem / to which the deaf mutes were not sensitive at all.
> James는 추측했다 / 뱃멀미가 ~으로 인한 것임이 틀림없다고 / 내이의 일시적인 이상 / 문제인 / 농아들은 전혀 민감하지 않은
>
> Later experimentation, / some carried out by James, / confirmed this suspicion.
> 이후의 실험에서 / James에 의해 시행된 몇몇 (실험은) / 이러한 생각이 사실임을 보여주었다
>
> (B) This crucial clue about the causes of seasickness / came thanks to James' ability / to see the importance of something interesting / that others had overlooked.
> 뱃멀미의 원인에 대한 이러한 결정적인 단서는 / James의 능력 덕분이었다 / 흥미로운 무언가의 중요성을 보는 / 다른 사람들이 간과했던
>
> (C) One / who was not / was the American philosopher and psychologist, William James.
> 한 사람은 / 그렇지 않았던 / 미국의 철학자이자 심리학자인 William James였다.
>
> James had the great good fortune to notice / that 15 of the passengers, / all of whom were deaf and mute, / were completely unaffected.

James는 대단히 운이 좋게도 알아차렸다 / 15명의 승객들은 / 그들 모두 농아였던 / 전혀 영향을 받지 않았다는 것을

해설
> 관찰이 항상 어떤 자료가 관련이 있을 수 있는지에 대한 분명한 통찰로 시작되는 것은 아니다. 1882년의 길고 거친 바다 항해에서 그 배의 많은 승객들이 뱃멀미에 시달렸다.

(C) 그렇지 (뱃멀미에 시달리지) 않았던 한 사람은 미국의 철학자이자 심리학자인 William James였다. James는 대단히 운이 좋게도 모두 농아였던 15명의 승객들은 전혀 영향을 받지 않았다는 것을 알아차렸다.

(A) James는 뱃멀미가 농아들은 전혀 민감하지 않은 문제인 내이의 일시적인 이상으로 인한 것임이 틀림없다고 추측했다. 이후의 실험에서, James에 의해 시행된 몇몇 실험은 이러한 생각이 사실임을 보여주었다.

(B) 뱃멀미의 원인에 대한 이러한 결정적인 단서는 다른 사람들이 간과했던 흥미로운 무언가의 중요성을 보는 James의 능력 덕분이었다.

해설 주어진 문단에서 관찰이 항상 분명한 통찰로 시작되는 것은 아니라고 하며 많은 승객들이 뱃멀미에 시달렸던 1882년의 한 항해를 언급한 뒤, (C)에서 뱃멀미에 시달리지 않았던 미국의 철학자이자 심리학자인 William James는 승객들 중 농아였던 15명이 전혀 영향을 받지 않았다는 것을 알아차렸다고 했다. 이어서 (A)에서 James가 농아들은 민감하지 않은 내이의 일시적 이상이 뱃멀미의 원인이라고 추측하여 몇몇 실험을 통해 이것이 사실임이 밝혀졌다고 하고, (B)에서 뱃멀미의 원인에 대한 이러한 결정적인 단서는 다른 사람들이 간과하는 것의 중요성을 보는 James의 능력 덕분에 발견될 수 있었다고 설명하고 있다. 따라서 ③ (C) – (A) – (B)가 정답이다.

어휘 observation 관찰, 관측 undertake 시작하다, 착수하다
relevant 관련 있는, 적절한 voyage 항해, 여행
afflict 시달리게 하다, 괴롭히다 seasickness 뱃멀미
speculate 추측하다 temporary 일시적인
disturbance 이상, 장애 inner ear 내이 deaf mute 농아
confirm 사실임을 보여주다 suspicion (의심쩍은) 생각, 의혹
crucial 결정적인, 중대한 overlook 간과하다
unaffected 영향을 받지 않은

---

13 **독해** **전체내용 파악 (문단 요약)** 난이도 ★★☆

끊어읽기 해석

> Umpires and other sports officials / are the decision-makers and rulebook enforcers / whose word is law on the field of play.
> 심판이나 다른 운동 경기 임원들은 / 의사 결정자이자 규정 집행자이다 / 자신들의 말이 경기에서 곧 법인
>
> Such authority comes with / heavy responsibility / to match.
> 이러한 권한에는 ~이 함께 딸려 온다 / 무거운 책임감이 / 상응하는
>
> Sports officials must be / unbiased masters of the rules / and have thick skins.
> 운동 경기 임원들은 ~이어야 한다 / 규정에 정통한 공정한 사람 / 그리고 쉽게 동요하지 않아야 (한다)
>
> They must keep control of / the conduct of games / at all times, / be good communicators, / and stay cool in situations / that can quickly grow heated / —both on the field and in the stands.
> 그들은 통제해야 한다 / 경기의 운영을 / 언제나 / 좋은 의사전달자여야 한다 / 그리고 상황에서 침착해야 한다 / 빠르게 가열될 수 있는 / 경기장과 관람석 양쪽에서

For every winner in sports there is a loser, / of course, / and the outcome may ride / on a few crucial calls.
운동 경기에서 모든 승자에게는 패자가 있다 / 물론 / 그리고 결과는 달려 있을 수 있다 / 몇 번의 중요한 판정에

Was that three-and-two pitch a ball / or a strike?
쓰리 볼 투 스트라이크에서 투구가 볼이었는가 / 아니면 스트라이크?

Was that last-second basket a buzzer-beater / or not?
마지막 순간의 골이 버저비터였는가 / 아니면 아니었는가?

While instant replay provides a fallback / in professional and big-time college sports, / officials at other levels / are on their own.
비디오의 즉시 재생이 대비책을 제공하기는 하지만 / 프로나 일류 대학의 경기에서 / 다른 규모의 경기 임원들은 / 혼자 힘으로 한다

The stakes can be higher / than just one game.
더 큰 이해관계가 있을 수 있다 / 단지 한 경기를 넘어서는

High school athletes may hope / for college scholarships, / and key calls against them / could hurt their chances / when scouts are on hand.
고등학교 운동선수들은 바랄 수도 있다 / 대학교 장학금을 / 그리고 그들에게 불리한 중요한 판정은 / 그들의 기회를 망칠 수 있다 / 스카우터들이 참가할 때

As one veteran high school official / put it, / "You never know / who's in the stands."
한 노련한 고등학교 경기 임원은 / 말한다 / "아무도 모르는 일이다 / 관중석에 누가 와 있는지는"

해석 심판이나 다른 운동 경기 임원들은 자신들의 말이 경기에서 곧 법인 의사 결정자이자 규정 집행자이다. 이러한 권한에는 상응하는 무거운 책임감이 함께 딸려 온다. 운동 경기 임원들은 규정에 정통한 공정한 사람이어야 하고 쉽게 동요하지 않아야 한다. 그들은 언제나 경기의 운영을 통제해야 하고, 좋은 의사전달자여야 하며 경기장과 관람석 양쪽에서 빠르게 가열될 수 있는 상황에서 침착해야 한다. 운동 경기에서 모든 승자에게는 물론 패자가 있고, 결과는 몇 번의 중요한 판정에 달려있을 수 있다. 쓰리 볼 투 스트라이크에서 투구가 볼이었는가 아니면 스트라이크였는가? 마지막 순간의 골이 버저비터였는가 아니었는가? 비디오의 즉시 재생이 프로나 일류 대학의 경기에서 대비책을 제공하기는 하지만, 다른 규모의 경기 임원들은 혼자 힘으로 한다. 단지 한 경기를 넘어서는 더 큰 이해관계가 있을 수 있다. 고등학교 운동선수들은 대학교 장학금을 바랄 수도 있고, 스카우터들이 참가할 때 그들에게 불리한 중요한 판정은 그들의 기회를 망칠 수 있다. 한 노련한 고등학교 경기 임원은 "관중석에 누가 와 있는지는 아무도 모르는 일이다."라고 말한다.

> 심판의 역할은 너무 (A) 광범위해서 그들은 경기장에서의 움직임뿐만 아니라 선수들 각각의 미래 계획에도 (B) 중대한 영향을 미칠 수 있다.

	(A)	(B)
①	전문적인	약간의
②	광범위한	중대한
③	모호한	소중한
④	포괄적인	결정적인

해설 지문 전반에 걸쳐 경기 중에 심판과 경기 임원의 말은 곧 법이며, 경기의 결과는 몇 번의 중요한 판정에 달려 있을 수 있고, 스카우터들이 참가할 때 고등학교 운동선수들에게 내려진 불리한 판정은 그들의 기회를 망칠 수 있다고 했으므로 심판의 역할이 너무 '광범위해서' 선수들 각각의 미래 계획에도 '중대한' 영향을 미칠 수 있다고 한 ②번이 정답이다.

어휘 umpire 심판 official 경기 임원 unbiased 공정한, 편견이 없는

---

ride on ~에 달려 있다 call 판정 pitch 투구
buzzer-beater 버저비터(경기에서 신호음과 동시에 득점하는 것)
fallback 대비책 stake 이해관계 be on hand 참가하다
comprehensive 포괄적인

14 독해 추론 (빈칸 완성 - 단어)   난이도 ★★☆

끊어읽기 해석

Why would anyone be foolish / enough to argue / about the money supply?
왜 누군가는 어리석을까 / 논쟁할 정도로 / 통화 공급에 대해?

The more money, the merrier, right? // Wrong.
돈이 많으면 많을수록 더욱 즐겁다, 그렇지 않은가? // 틀렸다.

In slapstick movie, / bumbling gangsters drop suitcases / filled with bills, / and bystanders dive past one another / hoping to grab a few.
슬랩스틱 영화에서 / 실수를 잘하는 갱단들이 가방을 떨어뜨린다 / 지폐로 가득 찬 / 그리고 행인들은 서로를 지나 뛰어든다 / 몇 장이라도 집기를 희망하며

The passer-bys always smile, / but the bad guys wail / and so do economists.
행인들은 항상 미소를 짓는다 / 하지만 나쁜 갱단들은 울부짖는다 / 그리고 경제학자들 또한 그렇다

Why do economists cry / with the gangsters?
왜 경제학자들이 울까 / 갱단들 때문에?

A problem does not arise / when just a few suitcases burst open.
문제가 발생하지 않는다 / 단지 몇 개의 가방이 벌컥 열렸을 때에는

But if lots of luggage / were to suddenly flood a town / with bills, / inflation might follow.
하지만 만약 많은 가방이 / 갑자기 한 도시를 넘쳐나게 한다면 / 지폐로 / 통화 팽창이 뒤따를 수도 있다

If the amount of money / overwhelms the capacity to produce goods, / consumers, with more money to spend, / bid up prices.
만약 돈의 양이 / 재화를 생산하는 능력을 압도한다면 / 소비할 더 많은 돈을 가진 소비자들은 / 경합하여 값을 끌어올린다

The town is no wealthier than before; / more bills do not bring / a higher standard of living / any more than if everyone added two zeroes to his or her salary.
그 도시는 전보다 더 부유하지 않다 / 더 많은 돈은 가져다 주지 않는다 / 더 높은 생활수준을 / 모든 사람들이 그들의 월급에 두 개의 0을 더하는 것이 (더 높은 생활 수준을 가져다 주지) 않는 것처럼

해석 왜 누군가는 통화 공급에 대해 논쟁할 정도로 어리석을까? 돈이 많으면 많을수록 더욱 즐겁다, 그렇지 않은가? 틀렸다. 슬랩스틱 영화에서, 실수를 잘하는 갱단들이 지폐로 가득 찬 가방을 떨어뜨리고, 행인들은 몇 장이라도 집기를 희망하며 서로를 지나 뛰어든다. 행인들은 항상 미소를 짓지만, 나쁜 갱단들은 울부짖으며 경제학자들 또한 그렇다. 왜 경제학자들이 갱단들 때문에 울까? 단지 몇 개의 가방이 벌컥 열렸을 때에는 문제가 발생하지 않는다. 하지만 만약 많은 가방이 갑자기 한 도시를 지폐로 넘쳐나게 한다면, 통화 팽창이 뒤따를 수도 있다. 만약 돈의 양이 재화를 생산하는 능력을 압도한다면, 소비할 더 많은 돈을 가진 소비자들은 경합하여 값을 끌어올린다. 그 도시는 전보다 더 부유하지 않다. 모든 사람들이 그들의 월급에 두 개의 0을 더하는 것이 더 높은 생활수준을 가져다 주지 않는 것처럼 더 많은 돈은 더 높은 생활수준을 가져다 주지 않는다.

① 불경기	② 통화 팽창
③ 파산	④ 실업

해설 빈칸이 있는 문장을 통해 빈칸에 많은 가방이 갑자기 한 도시를 지폐로 넘쳐나게 한다면 무엇이 뒤따를 수도 있는지에 대한 내용이 나와야 적절하다는 것을 알 수 있다. 빈칸 뒤 문장에서 만약 돈의 양이 재화를 생산하는 능력을 압도한다면, 소비할 더 많은 돈을 가진 소비자들이 경합하여 값을 끌어올린다고 했으므로, 만약 많은 가방이 갑자기 한 도시를 지폐로 넘쳐나게 한다면, '통화 팽창'이 뒤따를 수도 있다고 한 ②번이 정답이다.

어휘 merry 즐거운 slapstick 슬랩스틱, 저속한 익살극
bumbling 실수를 잘하는 gangster 갱단, 폭력배
bystander 행인, 구경꾼 passer-by 행인 wail 울부짖다, 통곡하다
burst open 벌컥 열리다 overwhelm 압도하다, 제압하다
bid up 경합하여 값을 끌어올리다 recession 불경기, 불황
inflation 통화 팽창, 인플레이션 bankruptcy 파산
unemployment 실업

15 문법 수 일치 & 분사 & 능동태·수동태 난이도 ★★☆

해석 정확히 어떻게, 언제, 왜, 그리고 어디에서 최초의 지도가 만들어지게 되었는지를 알아내기는 어렵다. 선사시대와 초기 역사 시대에 그려진 많은 것들은 잔존하지 않아서, 오늘날 우리가 발견하는 것은 한때 그곳에 존재했었던 것을 전적으로 대표하지 않을 수 있다. 현대 관찰자에게는 다른 문제들도 있다. 선사시대에 만들어진 지도는 그림의 의미를 설명하거나 그것의 내용을 묘사하는 제목이 덧붙여져 있지 않다. 하지만, 우리는 오늘날과 마찬가지로, 옛날에 지도가 다양한 목적을 위해 만들어졌으며 여러 형태를 가지고 있었다고 확신할 수 있다. 일반적인 생각과는 반대로, 지도가 오랜 세월 동안 사용되어 온 모든 목적들 중에, 가장 덜 중요한 하나의 목적이 길을 찾는 것이었다는 점 또한 분명할 수도 있다. 해도는 유럽의 중세시대가 되어서야 생겨났고, 지형도는 18세기가 되어서야 육지 여행자들에 의해 평소에 지니고 다녀졌다.

해설 (A) 수량 표현의 수 일치 주어 자리에 단수 취급하는 수량 표현 'Much of + 명사절(what ~ historical times)'이 왔으므로 복수 동사 have가 아닌 단수 동사 has를 써야 한다.
(B) 분사의 역할 주어(Maps)와 동사(cannot be accompanied)를 모두 갖춘 완전한 절에 또 다른 동사가 올 수 없으므로 동사 make가 아닌 수식어 거품 자리에 올 수 있는 과거분사 made를 써야 한다. 참고로, 수식받는 명사(Maps)와 분사가 '지도가 만들어지다'라는 의미의 수동 관계이므로 과거분사 made가 쓰였다.
(C) 병치 구문 접속사(and)로 연결된 병치 구문에서는 같은 구조끼리 연결되어야 하는데, and 앞에 과거 동사(were created)가 왔으므로 and 뒤에도 과거 동사 took을 써야 한다. 참고로, 주어 maps와 동사가 '지도가 여러 형태를 가지고 있다'라는 의미의 능동 관계로 해석되는 것이 자연스러우므로 과거분사 created와 taken은 병렬 관계로 볼 수 없다.
따라서 ④ (A) has – (B) made – (C) took이 정답이다.

어휘 prehistoric 선사시대의 wholly 전적으로, 완전히
representative of ~을 대표하는 observer 관찰자
accompany 덧붙이다, 수반하다 sea chart 해도
topographical 지형의

👉 이것도 알면 합격!

times(시대)와 같이 가산·불가산일 때 의미가 다른 명사들을 알아두자.
· a light (가산) 조명 / light (불가산) 빛
· times (가산) 시대 / time (불가산) 시간, 시기
· a room (가산) 방 / room (불가산) 여지, 공간
· a work (가산) 작품 / work (불가산) 일

16 독해 논리적 흐름 파악 (문장 삽입) 난이도 ★★☆

끊어읽기 해석

Recordings at theaters around the world show / that the pattern transcends / different cultural habits / and that different crowds all follow / one universal curve / showing how the sound rises / over several seconds.
전 세계 극장에서 녹음된 것들은 보여준다 / 그 패턴이 초월한다는 것을 / 다양한 문화적 습관을 / 그리고 다른 관중들 모두가 따른다는 것을 / 하나의 보편적인 곡선을 / 어떻게 그 소리가 상승하는지를 보여주는 / 몇 초 동안에

When the curtain closes / at any stage theater, / the audience bursts into applause.
막이 내리면 / 어떤 연극 무대에서든지 / 관중들은 박수갈채를 보낸다

㉠ It's usually a few clappers / who hesitantly start / on their own, / and then others join in.
그것은 대개 몇 명 안 되는 박수 치는 사람들이다 / 주저하며 시작하는 / 스스로 / 그리고 그 후에 다른 사람들이 참여한다

㉡ Applause is a funny thing / in which each person tries to give credit to the performers, / but also tries to blend into the crowd; / you don't want to clap / before everyone else, / or to go on / after others have stopped.
박수는 재미있는 것이다 / 각 사람이 배우들을 인정하려는 / 또한 관중들과 화합하려고 하는 / 당신은 박수를 치기를 원하지 않는다 / 다른 모든 사람들보다 먼저 / 또는 계속하기를 / 다른 사람들이 멈춘 이후에

㉢ In fact, / if you study it, / you'll discover / there is a pronounced pattern / in the way / an audience goes / from silence to full volume of applause.
실제로 / 당신이 그것을 살펴본다면 / 당신은 발견할 것이다 / 분명한 패턴이 있다는 것을 / 방식에 있어 / 관중들이 가는 / 침묵에서 박수의 최대 음량으로

㉣ Even more remarkably, / this curve is absolutely identical to a curve / known from physics / that describes / how a group of atoms or molecules collectively go / from one kind of behavior to another, / rapidly and abruptly, / because what one does / depends very strongly / on what others nearby do.
훨씬 더 놀랍게도 / 이 곡선은 한 곡선과 완전히 동일하다 / 물리학에서 알려진 / 설명하는 / 원자나 분자 집단이 공동으로 이동하는 방식을 / 한 가지 행동에서 다른 행동으로 / 빠르게 갑자기 / 누군가가 행동하는 것은 ~이기 때문이다 / 매우 강력하게 의존한다 / 주변의 다른 사람들이 행동하는 것에

해석 어떤 연극 무대에서든지 막이 내리면, 관중들은 박수갈채를 보낸다. 그것은 대개 스스로 주저하며 시작하는 몇 명 안 되는 박수 치는 사람들이며, 그 후에 다른 사람들이 참여한다. 박수는 각 사람이 배우들을 인정하려는 재미있는 것이지만, 또한 관중들과 화합하려고 하는 것이기도 하다. 당신은 다른 모든 사람들보다 먼저 박수를 치거나 다른 사람들이 멈춘 이후에 계속하기를 원하지 않는다. 실제로, 당신이 그것을 살펴본다면, 당신은 관중들이 침묵에서 박수의 최대 음량으로 가는 방식에 있어 분명한 패턴이 있다는 것을 발견할 것이다. ㉣ 전 세계 극장에서 녹음된 것들은 그 패턴이 다양한 문화적 습관을 초월하며 다른 관중들 모두가 몇 초 동안에 어떻게 그 소리가 상승하는지를 보여주는 하나의 보편적인 곡선을 따른다는 것을 보여준다. 훨씬 더 놀랍게도, 누군가가 행동하는 것은 주변의 다른 사람들이 행동하는 것에 매우 강력하게 의존하기 때문에, 이 곡선은 원자나 분자 집단이 공동으로 한 가지 행동에서 다른 행동으로 빠르게 갑자기 이동하는 방식을 설명하는 물리학에서 알려진 한 곡선과 완전히 동일하다.

해설 ㉣ 앞 문장에 관중들이 침묵에서 박수의 최대 음량으로 가는 방식에 있어 분명한 패턴이 있다는 것을 발견할 것이라는 내용이 있고,

ⓔ 뒤 문장에 이 곡선(this curve)은 물리학에서 알려진 한 곡선과 완전히 동일하다는 내용이 있으므로, ⓔ 자리에 전 세계 극장에서 녹음된 것들은 그 패턴이 하나의 보편적인 곡선을 따른다는 것을 보여준다는 주어진 문장이 나와야 지문이 자연스럽게 연결된다. 따라서 ④번이 정답이다.

어휘 recording 녹음, 녹화 transcend 초월하다 universal 보편적인
curve 곡선 audience 관중
burst into applause 박수갈채를 보내다 clapper 박수 치는 사람
credit 인정, 칭찬 blend 화합하다, 뒤섞이다
pronounced 분명한, 뚜렷한 volume 음량
remarkably 놀랍게도, 현저하게 identical 동일한, 똑같은
physics 물리학 atom 원자 molecule 분자
collectively 공동으로, 집합으로 rapidly 빠르게 abruptly 갑자기

17 독해 추론 (빈칸 완성 - 연결어) 난이도 ★★☆

끊어읽기 해석

Fifty years ago, / bees lived healthy lives / in our cities and rural areas / because they had plenty of flowers / to feed on, / fewer insecticides / contaminating their floral food / and fewer exotic diseases and pests.
50년 전에 / 벌들은 건강한 삶을 살았다 / 우리 도시와 시골에서 / 그들이 많은 꽃들을 가졌기 때문에 / 먹고 살 / 더 적은 살충제를 / 그들의 꽃 먹이를 오염시키는 / 그리고 더 적은 외래성 질병과 해충을

Wild bees nested successfully / in undisturbed soil and twigs.
야생 벌들은 성공적으로 둥지를 틀었다 / 누구의 방해도 받지 않는 토양과 나뭇가지에

(A) However, / bees have trouble / finding pollen and nectar sources / because of the extensive use of herbicides / that kill off so many flowering plants / among crops / and in ditches, roadsides and lawns.
(A) 하지만 / 벌은 애를 먹는다 / 꽃가루와 밀원을 찾는 데 / 제초제의 광범위한 사용 때문에 / 너무나 많은 꽃식물들을 죽이는 / 작물 사이 / 그리고 배수로, 길가, 잔디에

Flowers can be contaminated / with insecticides / that can kill bees directly / or lead to chronic, debilitating effects / on their health.
꽃들은 오염될 수 있다 / 살충제에 / 벌을 직접적으로 죽일 수 있는 / 또는 만성적이며 쇠약하게 하는 영향을 초래할 수 있는 / 그들의 건강에

(B) In addition, / with the increase in global trade and transportation, / blood-sucking parasites, viruses and other bee pathogens / have been inadvertently transmitted / to bees throughout the world.
(B) 게다가 / 세계 무역 및 운송의 증가와 함께 / 피를 빨아먹는 기생충, 바이러스, 그리고 다른 벌의 병원균이 / 부주의하게 전염되었다 / 전 세계 도처에 있는 벌들에게

These parasites and pathogens weaken / bees' immune systems, / making them even more susceptible / to effects of poor nutrition / from lack of flowers, / particularly in countries / with high agricultural intensity and pesticide use.
이러한 기생충과 병원균은 약화시킨다 / 벌의 면역 체계를 / 그것들을 훨씬 더 민감하게 만들며 / 영양결핍의 영향에 / 꽃의 부족으로 인한 / 특히 국가에서 / 농업 집약도와 살충제 사용이 높은

해석 50년 전에, 벌들은 그들이 먹고 살 많은 꽃들, 그들의 꽃 먹이를 오염시키는 더 적은 살충제 그리고 더 적은 외래성 질병과 해충을 가졌었기 때문에 우리 도시와 시골에서 건강한 삶을 살았다. 야생 벌들은 누구의 방해도 받지 않는 토양과 나뭇가지에 성공적으로 둥지를 틀었다. (A) 하지만, 작물 사이와 배수로, 길가, 잔디에 있는 너무나 많은 꽃식물들을 죽이는 제초제의 광범위한 사용 때문에

벌은 꽃가루와 밀원을 찾는 데 애를 먹는다. 꽃들은 벌을 직접적으로 죽일 수 있거나, 그들의 건강에 만성적이며 쇠약하게 하는 영향을 초래할 수 있는 살충제에 오염될 수 있다. (B) 게다가, 세계 무역 및 운송의 증가와 함께, 피를 빨아먹는 기생충, 바이러스, 그리고 다른 벌의 병원균이 전 세계 도처에 있는 벌들에게 부주의하게 전염되었다. 이러한 기생충과 병원균은 벌의 면역 체계를 약화시켜서, 특히 농업 집약도와 살충제 사용이 높은 국가에서 꽃의 부족으로 인한 영양결핍의 영향에 훨씬 더 민감하게 만들었다.

        (A)   (B)
① 하지만 - 결과적으로
② 하지만 - 게다가
③ 따라서 - 대조적으로
④ 따라서 - 반면

해설 (A) 앞 문장은 야생 벌들이 누구의 방해도 받지 않는 토양과 나뭇가지에 성공적으로 둥지를 틀었다는 내용이고, (A) 뒤 문장은 제초제의 광범위한 사용 때문에 벌이 꽃가루와 밀원을 찾는 데 애를 먹는다는 대조적인 내용이므로, (A)에는 대조를 나타내는 연결어인 However(하지만)가 나와야 적절하다. (B) 앞 문장은 꽃들이 벌을 직접적으로 죽일 수 있거나 건강을 쇠약하게 하는 살충제에 오염될 수 있다는 내용이고, (B) 뒤 문장은 기생충, 바이러스, 그리고 다른 벌의 병원균이 부주의하게 전 세계 도처에 있는 벌들에게 전염되었다는 추가적인 내용이므로, (B)에는 추가를 나타내는 연결어인 In addition(게다가)이 나와야 적절하다.
따라서 ② (A) However(하지만) - (B) In addition(게다가)이 정답이다.

어휘 rural 시골의, 지방의 insecticide 살충제
contaminate 오염시키다 exotic 외래의, 이국적인
pest 해충, 유해 동물 undisturbed 누구의 방해도 받지 않는
twig 나뭇가지 pollen 꽃가루 nectar source 밀원(蜜源)
herbicide 제초제 ditch 배수로 chronic 만성적인
debilitate 쇠약하게 하다 blood-sucking 피를 빨아먹는
parasite 기생충 pathogen 병원균
inadvertently 부주의하게, 무심코 transmit 전염시키다, 옮기다
immune system 면역 체계
susceptible to ~에 민감한, 영향받기 쉬운 agricultural 농업의
pesticide 살충제, 농약

18 독해 논리적 흐름 파악 (문맥상 적절한 어휘) 난이도 ★★☆

끊어읽기 해석

Sea foam forms / when the ocean is agitated / by wind and waves.
바다 거품은 형성된다 / 바다가 흔들릴 때 / 바람과 파도에 의해

Each coastal region has / (A) differing conditions / governing the formation / of sea foams.
각각의 해안지대는 가지고 있다 / (A) 다른 조건들을 / 형성을 좌우하는 / 바다 거품의

Algal blooms are one common source / of thick sea foams.
조류 대증식은 한 일반적인 원인이다 / 두꺼운 바다 거품의

When large blooms of algae decay offshore, / great amounts of / decaying algal matter / often wash ashore.
대량 발생한 조류가 연안에서 부패하면 / 엄청난 양의 / 부패하는 조류 물질이 / 종종 해안으로 밀려온다

Foam forms / as this organic matter is churned up / by the (B) surf.
거품은 형성된다 / 이런 유기 물질이 마구 휘저어질 때 / (B) 파도에 의해

Most sea foam is not harmful to humans / and is often an indication / of a productive ocean ecosystem.

대부분의 바다 거품은 인간에게 해롭지 않다 / 그리고 보통 지표이다 / 생산적인 해양 생태계의

But / when large harmful algal blooms decay / near shore, / there are potential for impacts / to human health and the environment.
하지만 / 많은 유해한 조류 대증식이 부패하면 / 해안 근처에서 / 있을 수 있다 / 영향의 가능성이 / 인간의 건강과 자연에 대한

Along Gulf coast beaches / during blooms of Karenia brevis, / for example, / popping sea foam bubbles are one way / that algal toxins become airborne.
멕시코 연안 지역의 해안을 따라 / Karenia brevis 대증식 동안 / 예를 들어 / 튀어 오르는 바다 거품은 한 방법이다 / 조류의 독소가 공기로 운반되는

The resulting aerosol can (C) irritate / the eyes of beach goers / and poses a health risk / for those with asthma or other respiratory conditions.
그 결과로 초래된 에어로졸은 (C) 자극할 수 있다 / 해수욕하는 사람들의 눈을 / 그리고 건강상의 위험을 제기할 수 있다 / 천식이나 다른 호흡기 질환이 있는 사람들에게

해석 바다 거품은 바다가 바람과 파도에 의해 흔들릴 때 형성된다. 각각의 해안지대는 바다 거품의 형성을 좌우하는 (A) 다른 조건들을 가지고 있다. 조류 대증식은 두꺼운 바다 거품의 한 일반적인 원인이다. 대량 발생한 조류가 연안에서 부패하면, 엄청난 양의 부패하는 조류 물질이 종종 해안으로 밀려온다. 거품은 이런 유기 물질이 (B) 파도에 의해 마구 휘저어질 때 형성된다. 대부분의 바다 거품은 인간에게 해롭지 않으며 보통 생산적인 해양 생태계의 지표이다. 하지만 많은 유해한 조류 대증식이 해안 근처에서 부패하면, 인간의 건강과 자연에 대한 영향의 가능성이 있을 수 있다. 예를 들어, Karenia brevis 대증식 동안 멕시코 연안 지역의 해안을 따라 튀어 오르는 바다 거품은 조류의 독소가 공기로 운반되는 한 방법이다. 그 결과로 초래된 에어로졸은 해수욕하는 사람들의 눈을 (C) 자극할 수 있으며, 천식이나 다른 호흡기 질환이 있는 사람들에게 건강상의 위험을 제기할 수 있다.

	(A)	(B)	(C)
①	다른	표면	물을 대다
②	퍼지는	표면	자극하다
③	퍼지는	파도	물을 대다
④	다른	파도	자극하다

해설 (A) 빈칸이 있는 문장에서 각각의 해안지대가 바다 거품의 형성을 좌우하는 조건들을 가지고 있다고 했으므로, 빈칸에는 '다른'(differing) 조건들을 가지고 있다는 내용이 들어가야 적절하다. (B) 지문 처음에서 바다 거품은 바다가 바람과 파도에 의해 흔들릴 때 형성된다고 했으므로, 거품은 이런 유기 물질이 '파도'(surf)에 의해 마구 휘저어질 때 형성된다는 내용이 들어가야 적절하다. (C) 빈칸이 있는 문장에서 조류 대증식 동안 튀어 오르는 바다 거품의 결과로 초래된 에어로졸이 천식이나 다른 호흡기 질환이 있는 사람들에게 건강상의 위험을 제기할 수 있다고 했으므로, 해수욕하는 사람들의 눈을 '자극할'(irritate) 수 있다는 내용이 들어가야 적절하다.
따라서 ④ (A) differing(다른) – (B) surf(파도) – (C) irritate(자극하다)가 정답이다.

어휘 agitate 흔들다, 휘젓다 differ 다르다 diffuse 퍼지다, 발산하다 govern 좌우하다, 지배하다 algal bloom 조류 대증식, 녹조 bloom 대량 발생, 개화 algae 조류 decay 부패하다 offshore 연안의, 앞바다의 ashore 해안으로 churn 마구 휘젓다 toxin 독소 airborne 공기로 운반되는 aerosol 에어로졸, 연무제 irrigate 물을 대다, 세척하다 irritate 자극하다 pose 제기하다 asthma 천식 respiratory 호흡기의 condition 질환, 상태

---

19 독해 논리적 흐름 파악 (문장 삽입)   난이도 ★★☆

끊어읽기 해석

However, / elevated levels and/or long term exposure to air pollution / can lead / to more serious symptoms and conditions / affecting human health.
하지만 / 높은 수치와 장기적인 공기 오염 또는 그중 어느 쪽에의 노출은 / 이어질 수 있다 / 더 심각한 증상과 병으로 / 인간의 건강에 영향을 미치는

A variety of air pollutants / have known or suspected / harmful effects / on human health and the environment.
다양한 공기 오염 물질은 / 알려져 있거나 의심을 받아 왔다 / 해로운 영향으로 / 인간의 건강과 환경에 대한

In most areas of Europe, / these pollutants are principally the products of combustion / from space heating, power generation / or from motor vehicle traffic.
유럽 대부분의 지역에서 / 이러한 오염 물질은 주로 연소의 산물이다 / 실내 난방과 발전으로부터 나오는 / 또는 자동차 운행으로부터 나오는

㉠ Pollutants from these sources / may not only prove a problem / in the immediate vicinity of these sources / but can travel long distances.
이러한 원천에서 나오는 오염 물질은 / 문제가 될 뿐만 아닐 수 있다 / 이러한 원천 바로 가까이에서 / 그러나 먼 거리로 퍼질 수 있다

㉡ Generally / if you are young / and in a good state of health, / moderate air pollution levels are unlikely to have / any serious short term effects.
일반적으로 / 만약 당신이 젊다면 / 그리고 건강 상태가 좋다면 / 적당한 공기 오염 수치는 주지 않을 것이다 / 어떤 심각한 단기적인 영향을

㉢ This mainly affects / the respiratory and inflammatory systems, / but can also lead to / more serious conditions / such as heart disease and cancer.
이것은 주로 영향을 미친다 / 호흡 기관과 염증을 일으키는 기관에 / 그러나 또한 이어질 수 있다 / 더 심각한 병으로 / 심장병과 암과 같은

㉣ People with lung or heart conditions / may be more susceptible / to the effects of air pollution.
폐 질환이나 심장 질환이 있는 사람들은 / 더욱 민감할 수 있다 / 공기 오염의 영향에

해석 다양한 공기 오염 물질은 인간의 건강과 환경에 대한 해로운 영향으로 알려져 있거나 의심을 받아 왔다. 유럽 대부분의 지역에서, 이러한 오염 물질은 주로 실내 난방과 발전으로부터 나오거나 자동차 운행으로부터 나오는 연소의 산물이다. 이러한 원천에서 나오는 오염 물질은 이러한 원천 바로 가까이에서 문제가 될 뿐만 아니라 먼 거리로 퍼질 수 있다. 일반적으로 만약 당신이 젊고 건강 상태가 좋다면, 적당한 공기 오염 수치는 어떤 심각한 단기적인 영향을 주지 않을 것이다. ㉢ 하지만, 높은 수치와 장기적인 공기 오염 또는 그중 어느 쪽에의 노출은 인간의 건강에 영향을 미치는 더 심각한 증상과 병으로 이어질 수 있다. 이것은 주로 호흡 기관과 염증을 일으키는 기관에 영향을 미치지만, 또한 심장병과 암과 같은 더 심각한 병으로도 이어질 수 있다. 폐 질환이나 심장 질환이 있는 사람들은 공기 오염의 영향에 더욱 민감할 수 있다.

해설 ㉢ 앞 문장에서 만약 당신이 젊고 건강 상태가 좋다면 적당한 공기 오염 수치는 어떤 심각한 단기적인 영향도 주지 않을 것이라고 했고, ㉢ 뒤 문장에서 이것은 주로 호흡 기관과 염증을 일으키는 기관에 영향을 미치지만 심장병과 암과 같이 더 심각한 병으로도 이어질 수 있다고 했으므로, ㉢ 자리에 높은 수치와 장기적인 공기 오염 또는 그중 어느 쪽에의 노출은 인간의 건강에 영향을 미치는 더 심각한 증상과 병으로 이어질 수 있다는 주어진 문장이 들어가야 글의 흐름이 자연스럽게 연결된다. 따라서 ③번이 정답이다.

어휘 elevated 높은 condition 병, 질환 pollutant 오염 물질 principally 주로 combustion 연소 power generation 발전

motor vehicle 자동차 prove ~이 되다 vicinity 가까이 있음, 부근
travel 퍼지다, 이동하다 moderate 적당한
respiratory 호흡 기관의, 호흡의
inflammatory 염증을 일으키는, 염증의 lung 폐
susceptible to ~에 민감한

20 독해 추론 (빈칸 완성 - 연결어)
난이도 ★★☆

끊어읽기 해석

Sea snakes are some of the most venomous creatures / on Earth.
바다뱀은 가장 독이 강한 생물 중 일부이다 / 지구 상에서

Their venom is far deadlier / than the venom of coral snakes, rattlesnakes, or even king cobras.
그들의 독은 훨씬 더 치명적이다 / 산호뱀, 방울뱀, 또는 심지어 킹코브라의 독보다도

Sea snakes use their venom / to kill the fish / they eat / and to defend themselves / against predators.
바다뱀은 그들의 독을 사용한다 / 물고기를 죽이기 위해 / 그들이 먹는 / 그리고 스스로를 방어하기 위해 / 포식자로부터

It's not necessarily a good thing, / however, / for a sea snake / to use its venom / to defend itself.
반드시 좋은 것만은 아니다 / 하지만 / 바다뱀이 / 그것의 독을 사용하는 것은 / 스스로를 방어하기 위해

Venom can take a lot of energy to make / —energy that could be used for growing or hunting.
독은 만드는 데 많은 에너지가 들 수 있다 / 그 에너지는 성장이나 사냥을 위해 사용될 수도 있던 것이다

(A) Also, / the more often a sea snake or other venomous animal is attacked, / the more likely it is to get hurt / —even if it can defend itself.
(A) 또한 / 바다뱀이나 독이 있는 다른 동물들은 더 자주 공격받을수록 / 다칠 위험이 더 커진다 / 비록 그것이 스스로를 방어할 수 있다고 하더라도

Like coral snakes, / many sea snakes solve this problem / by warning predators / up front.
산호뱀처럼 / 많은 바다뱀은 이 문제를 해결한다 / 포식자에게 경고함으로써 / 미리

(B) For example, / the yellow-bellied sea snake has bright, splashy colors / that tell predators not to try anything.
(B) 예를 들어 / 배가 노란 바다뱀은 밝고 눈에 확 띄는 색깔을 가지고 있다 / 포식자에게 아무 것도 시도하지 말라고 알리는

Over millions of years, / predators have evolved to pay attention / to this warning.
수백만 년 동안 / 포식자는 주의를 기울이도록 진화해 왔다 / 이 경고에

Only a few kinds of sharks and sea eagles / dare attack sea snakes.
단지 몇몇 종류의 상어와 흰꼬리수리만이 / 감히 바다뱀을 공격한다

This keeps sea snakes from constantly having to defend themselves / and increases their chances of survival.
이것은 바다뱀이 끊임없이 스스로를 방어할 필요가 없도록 한다 / 그리고 그들의 생존 가능성을 증가시킨다

해석 바다뱀은 지구 상에서 가장 독이 강한 생물 중 일부이다. 그들의 독은 산호뱀, 방울뱀, 또는 심지어 킹코브라의 독보다도 훨씬 더 치명적이다. 바다뱀은 그들의 독을 그들이 먹는 물고기를 죽이고 포식자로부터 스스로를 방어하기 위해 사용한다. 하지만, 바다뱀이 스스로를 방어하기 위해 그것의 독을 사용하는 것은 반드시 좋은 것만은 아니다. 독은 만드는 데 많은 에너지가 들 수 있는데, 그 에너지는 성장이나 사냥을 위해 사용될 수도 있던 것이다. (A) 또한, 바다뱀이나 독이 있는 다른 동물들은 더 자주 공격받을수록, 비록

그것이 스스로를 방어할 수 있다고 하더라도, 다칠 위험이 더 커진다. 산호뱀처럼, 많은 바다뱀은 포식자에게 미리 경고함으로써 이 문제를 해결한다. (B) 예를 들어, 배가 노란 바다뱀은 포식자에게 아무 것도 시도하지 말라고 알리는 밝고 눈에 확 띄는 색깔을 가지고 있다. 수백만 년 동안, 포식자는 이 경고에 주의를 기울이도록 진화해 왔다. 단지 몇몇 종류의 상어와 흰꼬리수리만이 감히 바다뱀을 공격한다. 이것은 바다뱀이 끊임없이 스스로를 방어할 필요가 없도록 하며, 그들의 생존 가능성을 증가시킨다.

	(A)	(B)
①	하지만	다시 말해서
②	또한	그에 반해
③	하지만	게다가
④	또한	예를 들어

해설 (A) 앞 문장은 독을 만드는 데 성장이나 사냥에 쓰일 수도 있었던 많은 에너지를 사용한다는 바다뱀의 불리한 상황에 대한 내용이고, (A) 뒤 문장은 바다뱀이나 독이 있는 다른 동물들은 더 자주 공격받을수록 다칠 위험이 더 커진다는 바다뱀의 불리한 상황에 대한 추가적인 내용이므로, (A)에는 추가를 나타내는 연결어인 Also(또한)가 나와야 적절하다. (B) 앞 문장은 많은 바다뱀이 포식자에게 미리 경고함으로써 문제를 해결한다는 내용이고, (B) 뒤 문장은 배가 노란 바다뱀은 포식자에게 아무 것도 시도하지 말라고 알리는 밝고 눈에 확 띄는 색깔을 가지고 있다고 하며 예시를 드는 내용이므로, (B)에는 예시를 나타내는 연결어인 For example(예를 들어)이 나와야 적절하다.
따라서 ④ (A) Also(또한) – (B) For example(예를 들어)이 정답이다.

어휘 sea snake 바다뱀 venomous 독이 있는 venom 독
deadly 치명적인 coral snake 산호뱀 rattlesnake 방울뱀
defend 방어하다, 지키다 predator 포식자 up front 미리, 솔직히
yellow-bellied 배가 노란, 겁이 많은 splashy 눈에 확 띄는
evolve 진화하다 sea eagle 흰꼬리수리
dare 감히 ~하다, ~할 엄두를 내다

21 독해 추론 (빈칸 완성 - 절)
난이도 ★☆☆

끊어읽기 해석

Despite what you might think, / luck isn't matter of fate or destiny, / according to research by psychologist Richard Wiseman.
당신이 생각하는 것에도 불구하고 / 행운은 숙명이나 운명의 문제가 아니다 / 심리학자 리처드 와이즈먼에 의한 연구에 따르면

Instead, / it's a result of the way / lucky people think and act / —which means that / anyone can learn to be lucky!
대신 / 그것은 방식의 결과이다 / 운이 좋은 사람들이 생각하고 행동하는 / 이것은 의미한다 / 누구든지 운이 좋아지는 것을 배울 수 있다는 것을!

For instance, / Wiseman found / that lucky people always take notice of / what's going on around them / and stay open / to new experiences and opportunities.
예를 들어 / 와이즈먼은 알아냈다 / 운이 좋은 사람들은 항상 주목한다는 것을 / 그들 주변에서 무엇이 일어나고 있는지 / 그리고 열려 있다 / 새로운 경험과 기회에

Meanwhile, / unlucky people tend to be tenser / and too focused on certain tasks, / which stops them from noticing opportunities / they aren't explicitly looking for.
한편 / 운이 나쁜 사람들은 신경이 더 날카로운 경향이 있다 / 그리고 특정 일에 지나치게 초점을 맞추는 / 이는 그들에 기회들을 알아차리는 것을 막는다 / 그들이 명백하게는 찾고 있지 않은

So, / next time you're heading to a party, / don't go in with

a goal in mind / (no matter how much you want / to attract someone).
그러므로 / 다음에 당신이 파티에 갈 때는 / 마음 속에 목표를 가지고 가지 마라 / (당신이 아무리 원하더라도 / 누군가를 매혹하는 것을)

Instead, / take things / as they come / and you never know / what might happen.
대신 / 일을 받아들여라 / 그것들이 다가오는 대로 / 그러면 당신은 결코 모른다 / 어떤 일이 일어날지

You could even make / some awesome new friends.
당신은 심지어 만들 수도 있을 것이다 / 아주 멋진 새로운 친구들을

해석 심리학자 리처드 와이즈먼에 의한 연구에 따르면 당신이 생각하는 것에도 불구하고, 행운은 숙명이나 운명의 문제가 아니다. 대신, 그것은 운이 좋은 사람들이 생각하고 행동하는 방식의 결과이며, 이것은 누구든지 운이 좋아지는 것을 배울 수 있다는 것을 의미한다! 예를 들어, 와이즈먼은 운이 좋은 사람들은 항상 그들 주변에서 무엇이 일어나고 있는지 주목하며, 새로운 경험과 기회에 열려 있다는 것을 알아냈다. 한편, 운이 나쁜 사람들은 신경이 더 날카롭고 특정 일에 지나치게 초점을 맞추는 경향이 있는데, 이는 그들이 명백하게는 찾고 있지 않는 기회들을 알아차리는 것을 막는다. 그러므로, 다음에 당신이 파티에 갈 때는, 마음 속에 목표를 가지고 가지 마라(당신이 누군가를 매혹하는 것을 아무리 원하더라도). 대신 그것들이 다가오는 대로 일을 받아들이면 당신은 어떤 일이 일어날지 결코 모른다. 당신은 심지어 아주 멋진 새로운 친구들을 만들 수도 있을 것이다.

① 행운은 숙명이나 운명의 문제가 아니다
② 행운은 당신에게 더 가까운 관계를 가져다 준다
③ 행운은 무슨 일이 있어도 얻어질 수 없다
④ 행운은 사람에게 가장 소중한 자산이다

해설 빈칸이 있는 문장을 통해 빈칸에 우리가 생각하는 것과는 다른 한 심리학자의 연구에 대한 내용이 나와야 한다는 것을 알 수 있다. 빈칸 뒤 문장에서 대신에 행운은 운이 좋은 사람들이 생각하고 행동하는 방식의 결과이며, 이것은 누구든지 운이 좋아지는 것을 배울 수 있다는 것을 의미한다고 했으므로, 심리학자 리처드 와이즈먼에 의한 연구에 따르면 '행운은 숙명이나 운명의 문제가 아니다'라고 한 ①번이 정답이다.

어휘 take notice of ~을 주목하다, 알아차리다
tense 신경이 날카로운, 긴장한 explicitly 명백하게
attract 매혹하다, 유인하다 awesome 아주 멋진
at any cost 무슨 일이 있어도 asset 자산

22 독해 추론 (빈칸 완성 - 구) 난이도 ★★☆

끊어읽기 해석

Coral reefs are some / of the most diverse and valuable ecosystems / on Earth.
산호초는 일부이다 / 가장 다양하고 가치 있는 생태계의 / 지구 상에서

Coral reefs support more species / per unit area / than any other marine environment, / including about 4,000 species of fish, 800 species of hard corals and hundreds of other species.
산호초는 더 많은 종들을 부양한다 / 단위면적 당 / 다른 어떤 해양 환경보다 / 약 4천 종의 물고기들, 8백 종의 단단한 산호, 그리고 수백 개의 다른 종들을 포함하여

Scientists estimate / that there may be another 1 to 8 million undiscovered species of organisms / living in and around reefs.
과학자들은 추정한다 / 백만에서 팔백만 개의 발견되지 않은 다른 생물 종

이 있을 것이라고 / 산호초 내부와 주변에 사는

This biodiversity is considered key / to finding new medicines / for the 21st century.
이러한 생물의 다양성은 핵심으로 여겨진다 / 신약을 찾아내는 데에 있어 / 21세기에

Many drugs are now being developed / from coral reef animals and plants / as possible cures / for cancer, arthritis, human bacterial infections, viruses, and other diseases.
많은 약들이 현재 개발되고 있다 / 산호초 동식물에서 / 가능한 치료제로써 / 암, 관절염, 인간의 박테리아 감염, 바이러스 그리고 다른 질병의

Storehouses of immense biological wealth, / reefs also provide economic and environmental services / to millions of people.
엄청난 생물학적 자원의 저장소인 / 산호초는 또한 경제적 및 환경적 서비스도 제공한다 / 수백 만 명의 사람들에게

Coral reefs may provide goods and services / worth $375 billion / each year.
산호초는 상품과 서비스를 제공할 수 있다 / 3천 7백 5십억 달러 가치의 / 매년

This is an amazing figure / for an environment / that covers less than 1 percent of the Earth's surface.
이것은 놀라운 수치이다 / 환경치고는 / 지구의 표면의 1퍼센트 미만을 덮고 있는

해석 산호초는 지구 상에서 가장 다양하고 가치 있는 생태계의 일부이다. 산호초는 약 4천 종의 물고기들, 8백 종의 단단한 산호, 그리고 수백 개의 다른 종들을 포함하여 다른 어떤 해양 환경보다 단위면적 당 더 많은 종들을 부양한다. 과학자들은 산호초 내부와 주변에 사는 백만에서 팔백만 개의 발견되지 않은 다른 생물 종이 있을 것이라고 추정한다. 이러한 생물의 다양성은 21세기에 신약을 찾아내는 데에 있어 핵심으로 여겨진다. 암, 관절염, 인간의 박테리아 감염, 바이러스 그리고 다른 질병의 가능한 치료제로써 많은 약들이 현재 산호초 동식물에서 개발되고 있다. 엄청난 생물학적 자원의 저장소인 산호초는 또한 수백 만 명의 사람들에게 경제적 및 환경적 서비스도 제공한다. 산호초는 매년 3천 7백 5십억 달러 가치의 상품과 서비스를 제공할 수 있다. 이것은 지구의 표면의 1퍼센트 미만을 덮고 있는 환경 치고는 놀라운 수치이다.

① 이러한 생물의 다양성
② 그들의 아름다움
③ 산호초의 생존 기술
④ 먹이사슬

해설 빈칸이 있는 문장을 통해 빈칸에 21세기에 신약을 찾아내는 데 핵심으로 여겨지는 것이 무엇인지에 대한 내용이 나와야 적절하다는 것을 알 수 있다. 빈칸 앞에서 산호초는 약 4천 종의 물고기들, 8백 종의 단단한 산호, 그리고 수백 개의 다른 종들을 포함하여 다른 어떤 해양 환경보다 단위면적 당 더 많은 종들을 부양한다고 한 뒤, 산호초 내부와 주변에 사는 다른 생물 종이 있을 것으로 추정한다고 했으므로 '이러한 생물의 다양성'은 21세기에 신약을 찾아내는 것의 핵심으로 여겨진다고 한 ①번이 정답이다.

어휘 coral reef 산호초 diverse 다양한
marine environment 해양 환경 organism 생물, 유기체
cure 치료제, 치료 arthritis 관절염 infection 감염
storehouse 저장소, (지식 등의) 보고 immense 엄청난
wealth 자원, 귀중한 산물 figure 수치 biodiversity 생물의 다양성
food chain 먹이사슬

끊어읽기 해석

Dear Charles,
친애하는 Charles씨에게,

It was a pleasure / having lunch with you / yesterday.
즐거웠습니다 / 당신과의 점심 식사는 / 어제

I am very interested / in the new household product / you mentioned / and how I might work with you develop it.
저는 많은 관심이 있습니다 / 새 가정용품에 / 당신이 언급했던 / 그리고 어떻게 당신과 함께 작업하여 그것을 개발시킬지에

I have seen / nothing like it / advertised in any of the trade journals, / so it may be an original, one-of-a-kind product.
저는 본 적이 없습니다 / 그것과 같은 것이 / 어떤 업계 잡지에서도 광고된 것을 / 그래서 그것은 독창적이고 특별한 제품일 것입니다

If so, / you will want to move fast / to register it / to protect your intellectual property rights / in it.
만약 그렇다면 / 당신은 빨리 조치를 취하길 원할 것입니다 / 그것을 등록하고자 / 당신의 지적 재산권을 보호하기 위해 / 그것에 있는

Let me know / if you want to pursue this / and I will have our patent associate contact you / with a proposal.
저에게 알려주십시오 / 이것을 실행할 의향이 있다면 / 그러면 제가 우리의 특허 담당 동료가 당신에게 연락을 드리도록 하겠습니다 / 제안서를 가지고

Let's get together again soon.
곧 다시 만납시다.

Until then,
그때까지,

Frank
Frank 드림

해석 친애하는 Charles씨에게,

어제 당신과의 점심 식사는 즐거웠습니다. 저는 당신이 언급했던 새 가정용품과 어떻게 당신과 함께 작업하여 그것을 개발시킬지에 많은 관심이 있습니다. 저는 어떤 업계 잡지에서도 그것과 같은 것이 광고된 것을 본 적이 없기 때문에, 그것은 독창적이고 특별한 제품일 것입니다. 만약 그렇다면, 당신은 그것에 있는 당신의 지적 재산권을 보호하기 위해 그것을 등록하고자 빨리 조치를 취하길 원할 것입니다. 이것을 실행할 의향이 있다면 저에게 알려주시고, 그러면 제가 우리의 특허 담당 동료가 제안서를 가지고 당신에게 연락을 드리도록 하겠습니다.
곧 다시 만납시다.
그때까지,
Frank 드림

해설 지문 중간에서 Charles는 새 가정용품의 지적 재산권을 보호하기 위해 빨리 조치를 취하길 원할 것이라고 한 뒤, 이것을 실행할 의향이 있다면 자신에게 알려달라고 이야기하고 있다. 따라서 지문의 목적을 '새로 개발한 가정용품의 특허 등록을 제안하려고'라고 한 ④번이 정답이다.

어휘 **household product** 가정용품 **trade** 업계 **journal** 잡지, 신문
original 독창적인 **one-of-a-kind** 특별한, 독특한
register 등록하다 **intellectual property right** 지적 재산권
pursue 실행하다 **patent** 특허, 특허권
associate 동료, 공동 경영자

끊어읽기 해석

I have always taught my children / that politeness, learning, and order are good things, / and that something good is to be desired and developed / for its own sake.
나는 아이들에게 항상 가르쳐 왔다 / 공손함, 배움, 그리고 질서가 좋은 것이라고 / 그리고 좋은 것은 추구되고 계발되어야 한다고 / 그 자체를 위해

But at school they learned, and very quickly, / that children earn Nature Trail tickets / for running the quarter-mile track / during lunch recess.
하지만 그들은 학교에서 매우 빨리 배웠다 / 아이들이 자연 산책로 티켓을 얻는다는 것을 / 4분의 1마일 트랙을 달리는 것으로 / 점심 휴식 동안

Or Lincoln Dollars / for picking up trash on the playground / or for helping a young child find the bathroom / —deeds that used to be called 'good citizenship.'
또는 링컨 달러를 (얻는다는 것을) / 운동장에 있는 쓰레기를 줍는 것으로 / 또는 어린이가 화장실을 찾는 것을 도와주는 것으로 / 행동인 / 과거에는 '좋은 시민 정신'이라고 불렸던

Why is it necessary / to buy the minimal cooperation of children / with rewards or treats?
왜 필요가 있는가 / 아이들의 최소의 협동을 살 / 보상이나 특별한 선물로?

What disturbs me / is the idea / that good behavior must be reinforced / with incentives.
나를 걱정시키는 것은 / 생각이다 / 선행이 강화되어야 한다는 / 보상으로

Children must be taught / to perform good deeds / for their own sake, / not in order to receive stickers, stars, and candy bars.
아이들은 배워야 한다 / 선행을 하도록 / 그 자체를 위해 / 스티커, 별 그리고 초코바를 받기 위해서가 아니라

해석 나는 아이들에게 공손함, 배움, 그리고 질서가 좋은 것이며, 좋은 것은 그 자체를 위해 추구되고 계발되어야 한다고 항상 가르쳐 왔다. 하지만 아이들은 학교에서 그들이 점심 휴식 동안 4분의 1마일 트랙을 달리는 것으로 자연 산책로 티켓을 얻는다는 것을 매우 빨리 배웠다. 또는 과거에는 '좋은 시민 정신'이라고 불렸던 행동인 운동장에 있는 쓰레기를 줍거나 어린이가 화장실을 찾는 것을 도와주는 것으로 링컨 달러를 (얻는다는 것을). 아이들의 최소의 협동을 왜 보상이나 특별한 선물로 살 필요가 있는가? 나를 걱정시키는 것은 선행이 보상으로 강화되어야 한다는 생각이다. 아이들은 스티커, 별 그리고 초코바를 받기 위해서가 아니라, 그 자체를 위해 선행을 하도록 배워야 한다.

해설 지문 뒷부분에서 필자는 아이들이 스티커, 별 그리고 초코바를 받기 위해서가 아니라, 그 자체를 위해 선행을 하도록 배워야 한다고 주장하고 있다. 따라서 필자가 주장하는 바를 '아이들이 보상 없이도 선행하도록 교육시켜야 한다'라고 표현한 ③번이 정답이다.

어휘 **politeness** 공손함, 정중함 **order** 질서, 정돈
recess 휴식, 휴회 시간 **deed** 행동, 행위
citizenship 시민 정신, 시민성 **minimal** 최소의 **cooperation** 협동
reward 보상, 보상금 **treat** 특별한 선물, 대접
disturb 걱정시키다, 혼란시키다 **reinforce** 강화하다
incentive 보상

끊어읽기 해석

Lead is a naturally occurring toxic metal / found in the Earth's crust.
납은 자연적으로 발생하는 독성 금속이다 / 지구 표면에서 발견되는

Its widespread use has resulted / ① in extensive environmental contamination, human exposure and significant public health problems / in many parts of the world.
그것의 광범위한 사용은 야기했다 / 대규모의 환경 오염, 인체로의 노출, 그리고 상당한 공중 보건 문제①를 / 세계의 많은 지역들에서

Young children are particularly vulnerable / to the toxic effects of lead / and can suffer / profound and permanent ② adverse health effects, / particularly affecting the development of the brain and nervous system.
어린이들은 특히 취약하다 / 납의 독성의 영향에 / 그리고 겪을 수 있다 / 엄청나고 영구적인 건강에 ② 해로운 영향을 / 이는 특히 뇌의 발달과 신경계에 영향을 미친다

Lead also causes / long-term harm / in adults, / including ③ decreased risk / of high blood pressure and kidney damage.
납은 또한 초래할 수 있다 / 장기적인 손상을 / 성인들에게 / ③ 감소된 위험을 포함한 / 고혈압과 신장 손상의

④ Exposure of pregnant women / to high levels of lead / can cause miscarriage, stillbirth, premature birth and low birth weight, / as well as minor malformations.
임신한 여성의 ④ 노출은 / 높은 수준의 납에 대한 / 유산, 사산, 조산, 그리고 저체중아를 야기할 수 있다 / 소기형뿐만 아니라

해석 납은 지구 표면에서 발견되는 자연적으로 발생하는 독성 금속이다. 그것의 광범위한 사용은 세계의 많은 지역들에서 대규모의 환경 오염, 인체로의 노출, 그리고 상당한 공중 보건 문제①를 야기했다. 어린이들은 특히 납의 독성의 영향에 취약하고, 엄청나고 영구적인 건강에 ② 해로운 영향을 겪을 수 있으며, 이는 특히 뇌의 발달과 신경계에 영향을 미친다. 납은 또한 성인들에게도 고혈압과 신장 손상의 ③ 감소된 위험을 포함하여 장기적인 손상을 초래할 수 있다. 임신한 여성의 높은 수준의 납에 대한 ④ 노출은 소기형뿐만 아니라 유산, 사산, 조산, 그리고 저체중아를 야기할 수 있다.

해설 지문 앞부분에 납의 널리 퍼진 사용이 세계의 많은 지역들에서 광범위한 환경 오염, 인체로의 노출, 그리고 상당한 공중 보건 문제를 야기했다는 내용이 있으므로, 납이 성인들에게도 고혈압과 신장 손상에 대한 '감소된'(decreased) 위험을 포함한 장기적인 손상을 초래할 수 있다는 것은 문맥상 적절하지 않다. 따라서 ③ decreased가 정답이다. 참고로, 주어진 decreased를 대신할 수 있는 어휘로는 '증가한'이라는 의미의 increased가 있다.

어휘 lead 납 toxic 독성의 crust 표면, 껍질
widespread 광범위한, 널리 퍼진 extensive 대규모의, 광범위한
contamination 오염 exposure 노출 significant 상당한
vulnerable 취약한, 연약한 profound 엄청난, 깊은
permanent 영구적인 adverse 해로운 nervous system 신경계
long-term 장기적인 blood pressure 혈압 kidney 신장
miscarriage 유산 stillbirth 사산 premature birth 조산
minor malformation 소기형(가벼운 국소적인 기형)

정답

01	① 독해 – 세부내용 파악	**11**	③ 문법 – 부사절 & 전치사	**21**	③ 독해 – 세부내용 파악
02	③ 독해 – 전체내용 파악	**12**	④ 독해 – 전체내용 파악	**22**	③ 독해 – 전체내용 파악
03	④ 독해 – 논리적 흐름 파악	**13**	③ 독해 – 세부내용 파악	**23**	③ 독해 – 논리적 흐름 파악
04	③ 독해 – 세부내용 파악	**14**	④ 독해 – 전체내용 파악	**24**	③ 독해 – 세부내용 파악
05	② 독해 – 논리적 흐름 파악	**15**	① 독해 – 논리적 흐름 파악	**25**	② 독해 – 전체내용 파악
06	③ 독해 – 추론	**16**	② 독해 – 논리적 흐름 파악		
07	④ 독해 – 논리적 흐름 파악	**17**	④ 독해 – 논리적 흐름 파악		
08	④ 독해 – 논리적 흐름 파악	**18**	① 독해 – 전체내용 파악		
09	③ 독해 – 논리적 흐름 파악	**19**	① 독해 – 논리적 흐름 파악		
10	① 독해 – 전체내용 파악	**20**	④ 독해 – 전체내용 파악		

취약영역 분석표

영역	세부 유형	문항 수	소계
어휘	어휘 & 표현	0	/0
	생활영어	0	
문법	부사절 & 전치사	1	/1
독해	전체내용 파악	8	/24
	세부내용 파악	5	
	추론	1	
	논리적 흐름 파악	10	
총계			**/25**

· 자신이 취약한 영역은 '법원직 9급 영어, 이렇게 출제된다!'(p.8)를 통해 다시 한 번 확인하고 학습하시기 바랍니다.

01 　독해　세부내용 파악 (지칭 대상 파악)

난이도 ★★☆

끊어읽기 해석

> The idea / of ① <u>using a product once</u> or for a brief period and then replacing it / runs counter / to the grain of societies or individuals / steeped in a heritage of poverty.
> 사고방식은 / ① 물건을 한 번만 사용하거나 짧은 기간만 사용한 후에 교체하는 / 상반된다 / 사회나 개인의 기질과 / 부모로부터 물려받은 가난이 깊이 배어들어 있는
>
> Not long ago / Uriel Rone, / a market researcher for the French advertising agency Publicis, / told me: / "The French housewife / ② is not used to disposable products.
> 얼마 전에 / Uriel Rone은 / 프랑스 광고 회사 Publicis의 시장 조사원인 / 나에게 말했다 / "프랑스의 주부는 / ② 일회용품에 익숙하지 않습니다
>
> She likes / ③ <u>to keep things</u>, / even old things, / rather than throw them away.
> 그녀(프랑스의 주부)는 좋아합니다 / ③ 물건을 보관하는 것을 / 오래된 물건이라 하더라도 / 그것들을 버리기보다는
>
> We represented / one company / that wanted to introduce / a kind of plastic throw-away curtain.
> 우리는 대변했었습니다 / 한 회사를 / 내놓고 싶어했던 / 일종의 일회용 플라스틱 커튼을
>
> We did a marketing study / for them / and found ④ <u>the resistance too strong</u>."
> 우리는 시장 조사를 했습니다 / 그들을 위해 / 그리고 ④ 저항이 너무 거세다는 것을 알게 되었습니다"
>
> This resistance, / however, / is dying / all over the developed world.
> 이 저항은 / 하지만 / 사라지고 있다 / 전 세계의 선진국에서

해석 ① 물건을 한 번만 사용하거나 짧은 기간만 사용한 후에 교체하는 사고방식은 부모로부터 물려받은 가난이 깊이 배어들어 있는 사회나 개인의 기질과 상반된다. 얼마 전에, 프랑스 광고 회사 Publicis의 시장 조사원인 Uriel Rone은 나에게 "프랑스의 주부는 ② 일회

용품에 익숙하지 않습니다. 그녀(프랑스의 주부)는 오래된 물건이라 하더라도 그것들을 버리기보다는 ③ 물건을 보관하는 것을 좋아합니다. 우리는 일종의 일회용 플라스틱 커튼을 내놓고 싶어했던 한 회사를 대변했었습니다. 우리는 그들을 위해 시장 조사를 했고 ④ 저항이 너무 거세다는 것을 알게 되었습니다."라고 말했다. 하지만 이 저항은 전 세계의 선진국에서 사라지고 있다.

해설 ②, ③, ④번은 모두 일회용품에 대한 반대를 나타내지만, ①번의 '물건을 한 번 사용하는 것'은 일회용품의 사용을 의미하므로 나머지 보기와 의미하는 바가 아주 다르다. 따라서 ①번이 정답이다.

어휘 brief 짧은, 잠시 동안의　replace 교체하다, 바꾸다
run counter 상반되다　grain 기질, 성질　steep 깊이 배어들게 하다
heritage 부모로부터 물려받은 것, 유산　disposable 일회용의
throw-away 일회용의, 쓰고 버리는　resistance 저항, 반대

02 　독해　전체내용 파악 (요지 파악)

난이도 ★★☆

끊어읽기 해석

> Parents have to be optimists.
> 부모들은 낙천주의자가 되어야 한다
>
> They have faith / in the world and its future, / or they can't expect / their children to have it.
> 그들은 믿음을 갖고 있다 / 세상과 그것의 미래에 대해 / 그렇지 않으면 그들은 기대할 수 없다 / 자신의 아이들이 그것(믿음)을 갖기를
>
> Without faith, / it's like an Army captain muttering, / "We'll never take that hill," / before the battle begins.
> 믿음이 없다면 / 그것은 마치 육군 대위가 투덜거리는 것과 같다 / "우리는 절대 저 언덕을 점령할 수 없을 거야"라고 / 전쟁이 시작되기도 전에
>
> If you really feel / that the world is in a hopeless mess, / hide it.
> 만약 당신이 정말로 느낀다면 / 이 세상이 가망 없는 엉망인 상태에 있다고 / 그것을 드러내지 마라

Whatever you say / should be honest, / but don't confuse / honesty with total confession; / not everything must be said.
당신이 말하는 것은 모두 / 솔직해야 한다 / 하지만 혼동하지 마라 / 솔직함과 완전한 고백을 / 모든 것을 말할 필요는 없다

Don't share / your uncertainties about the future / with your adolescent.
공유하지 마라 / 미래에 대한 당신의 불확실성을 / 당신의 사춘기 아이와

Allow him to explore the future / on his own, / with your support.
그(아이)가 미래를 탐험할 수 있도록 하라 / 스스로 / 당신의 지지를 받고

해석　부모들은 낙천주의자가 되어야 한다. 그들이 세상과 그것의 미래에 대해 믿음을 갖고 있지 않으면, 그들은 자신의 아이들이 그것(믿음)을 갖기를 기대할 수 없다. 믿음이 없다면, 이것은 마치 육군 대위가 전쟁이 시작되기도 전에 "우리는 절대 저 언덕을 점령할 수 없을 거야,"라고 투덜거리는 것과 같다. 만약 당신이 정말로 이 세상이 가망 없는 엉망인 상태에 있다고 느낀다면, 그것을 드러내지 마라. 당신이 말하는 것은 모두 솔직해야 하지만, 솔직함과 완전한 고백을 혼동하지 마라. 모든 것을 말할 필요는 없다. 미래에 대한 당신의 불확실성을 당신의 사춘기 아이와 공유하지 마라. 그(아이)가 당신의 지지를 받고 스스로 미래를 탐험할 수 있도록 하라.

해설　지문 처음에서 부모가 세상과 그것의 미래에 대해 믿음을 갖고 있지 않으면 아이들도 믿음을 가질 수 없다고 하고, 지문 중간에서 그렇기 때문에 부모들은 세상이 정말로 엉망인 상태에 있다고 느끼더라도 이를 아이들에게 드러내지 않아야 하며, 아이들이 부모의 지지를 받고 스스로 미래를 탐험할 수 있도록 해야 한다는 것을 설명하고 있다. 따라서 필자가 주장하는 바를 '부모는 자녀들이 자신의 미래를 스스로 개척하도록 도와주어야 한다'라고 표현한 ③번이 정답이다.

어휘　faith 믿음　mutter 투덜거리다, 중얼거리다　mess 엉망인 상태, 곤경　honest 솔직한　confession 고백, 자백　uncertainty 불확실성　adolescent 사춘기 아이; 청춘의　explore 탐험하다　support 지지

03　독해　논리적 흐름 파악 (문맥상 부적절한 어휘)　난이도 ★★☆

끊어읽기 해석

In 2009, / *New York Times* reporter Matt Richtel / earned a Pulitzer Prize for National Reporting / with a series of articles ("Driven to Distraction") / on the ① <u>dangers</u> of driving while texting or using cell phones.
2009년에 / 『뉴욕 타임즈』의 기자 Matt Richtel은 / 국내 보도 부문에서 퓰리처 상을 받았다 / 연재 기사('방심 운전')로 / 운전 중에 문자를 하거나 휴대전화를 사용하는 것의 ① 위험성에 대한

He found / that distracted driving is ② <u>responsible</u> / for 16 percent of all traffic fatalities / and nearly half a million injuries / annually.
그는 알아냈다 / 주의가 산만한 운전이 ② 원인이 된다는 것을 / 모든 교통사고 사망자의 16퍼센트 / 그리고 대략 50만 건의 부상의 / 매년

Even an idle phone conversation / when driving / takes a 40 percent bite out of your ③ <u>focus</u> / and, surprisingly, / can have the same effect / as being drunk.
쓸데없는 한 번의 전화 통화도 / 운전 중에는 / ③ 집중력의 40퍼센트를 삭감한다 / 그리고 놀랍게도 / 같은 영향을 미칠 수 있다 / 술에 취해 있는 것과

The evidence is so ④ <u>elusive</u> / that many states and municipalities / have outlawed cell phone use / while driving.
그 증거는 너무 ④ 찾기 힘들어서 / 많은 주와 지방 자치 단체는 / 휴대전화 사용을 금지했다 / 운전 중

해석　2009년에 『뉴욕 타임즈』의 기자 Matt Richtel은 운전 중에 문자를 하거나 휴대전화를 사용하는 것의 ① 위험성에 대한 연재 기사('방심 운전')로 국내 보도 부문에서 퓰리처 상을 받았다. 그는 주의가 산만한 운전이 매년 모든 교통사고 사망자의 16퍼센트와 대략 50만 건의 부상의 ② 원인이 된다는 것을 알아냈다. 운전 중에는 쓸데없는 한 번의 전화 통화도 ③ 집중력의 40퍼센트를 삭감하고, 놀랍게도 술에 취해 있는 것과 같은 영향을 미칠 수 있다. 그 증거는 너무 ④ 찾기 힘들어서 많은 주와 지방 자치 단체는 운전 중 휴대전화 사용을 금지했다.

해설　지문 앞부분에 『뉴욕 타임즈』의 기자 Matt Richtel이 주의가 산만한 운전이 교통사고로 인한 사망과 부상의 원인이 된다는 것을 알아냈다는 내용이 있으므로, 방심 운전이 위험하다는 증거가 너무 '찾기 힘들'(elusive)어서 많은 주와 지방 자치 단체가 운전 중 휴대전화 사용을 금지했다는 것은 문맥상 적절하지 않다. 따라서 ④ elusive가 정답이다. 참고로, 주어진 elusive를 대신할 수 있는 어휘로는 '분명한'이라는 의미의 evident, manifest, obvious 등이 있다.

어휘　earn 받다, 얻다　distraction 방심, 주의 산만　fatality 사망자　idle 쓸데없는, 한가한　take a bite out of ~을 삭감하다　elusive 찾기 힘든　municipality 지방 자치 단체　outlaw 금지하다

04　독해　세부내용 파악 (지칭 대상 파악)　난이도 ★☆☆

끊어읽기 해석

Once upon a time, / there was a snake / that lived on a path / leading from a village to a temple.
옛날에 / 뱀이 한 마리 있었다 / 길에 사는 / 마을에서 사원으로 이어지는

The villagers were scared of it, / so they threw stones at it / and stepped on its home.
마을 사람들은 이것을 무서워했다 / 그래서 그들은 이것에게 돌을 던졌다 / 그리고 이것의 집을 짓밟았다

Then the snake / started to bite the villagers, / and they stopped / going to the temple.
그러자 뱀은 / 마을 사람들을 물기 시작했다 / 그리고 그들은 그만두었다 / 사원에 가는 것을

A monk / who lived in the temple / was unhappy about this, / so he went to the snake and told it / that it was wrong to bite people.
한 수도승은 / 사원에 사는 / 이것이 못마땅했다 / 그래서 그는 뱀에게 가서 말했다 / 사람들을 무는 것은 잘못된 것이라고

The snake agreed and promised / never to do it again.
뱀은 동의하며 약속했다 / 다시는 그러지 않겠다고

However, / when the villagers realized / that the snake was no longer dangerous, / they started / throwing stones at it and stepping on its home again.
하지만 / 마을 사람들이 깨닫자 / 뱀이 더 이상 위험하지 않다는 것을 / 그들은 시작했다 / 다시 이것에게 돌을 던지고 이것의 집을 짓밟기

A few days later, / the snake, / hurt and bleeding, / came to the temple / to see the monk.
며칠 후 / 뱀은 / 다치고 피를 흘리는 채로 / 사원으로 왔다 / 수도승을 만나기 위해

'What happened?' / asked the monk. // The snake said, / 'No one is afraid of me now / and the villagers / treat me / very badly!'
"무슨 일이니?" / 수도승은 물었다 // 뱀은 말했다 / "이제 아무도 저를 두려워하지 않습니다 / 그리고 마을 사람들은 / 저를 대합니다 / 몹시 나쁘게!"

The monk sighed. // 'I told you not to bite,' / he said. // 'I didn't tell you not to hiss.'
수도승은 한숨을 쉬었다 // "나는 물지 말라고 했지" / 그는 말했다 // "위협하지 말라고는 안 했단다"

해석 옛날에, 마을에서 사원으로 이어지는 길에 사는 뱀이 한 마리 있었다. 마을 사람들은 이것을 무서워해서 이것에게 돌을 던지고 이것의 집을 짓밟았다. 그러자 뱀은 마을 사람들을 물기 시작했고 그들은 사원에 가는 것을 그만두었다. 사원에 사는 한 수도승은 이것이 못마땅해서 뱀에게 가서 사람들을 무는 것은 잘못된 것이라고 말했다. 뱀은 동의하며 다시는 그러지 않겠다고 약속했다. 하지만 마을 사람들이 뱀이 더 이상 위험하지 않다는 것을 깨닫자 그들은 다시 이것에게 돌을 던지고 이것의 집을 짓밟기 시작했다. 며칠 후, 뱀은 다치고 피를 흘리는 채로 수도승을 만나기 위해 사원으로 왔다. 수도승은 "무슨 일이니?"라고 물었다. 뱀은 "이제 아무도 저를 두려워하지 않고 마을 사람들은 저를 몹시 나쁘게 대합니다!"라고 말했다. 수도승은 한숨을 쉬었다. 그는 "나는 물지 말라고 했지, 위협하지 말라고는 안 했단다."라고 말했다.
① 곤경에 빠졌을 때에는 언제든지 폭력을 사용해도 괜찮다.
② 당신이 화났다는 것을 사람들에게 알리는 것은 당신을 보호하는 데 도움이 되지 않으며 심지어 상황을 더 나쁘게 만든다.
③ 폭력적으로 행동하고 다른 사람들을 다치게 하는 것은 잘못된 것이지만, 누군가가 당신을 부당하게 대할 때 분노를 나타내는 것은 잘못된 것이 아니다.
④ 뱀이 사람들을 무는 것을 그만두기로 동의했다고 해서 이것이 사원으로 이어지는 길에 있는 것이 허용된다는 것을 의미하지는 않았다.

해설 밑줄 친 'I told you not to bite,' he said. 'I didn't tell you not to hiss.'를 통해 수도승이 뱀에게 무엇을 알려 주려고 했는지를 지문에서 추론해야 한다는 것을 알 수 있다. 지문 전반에 걸쳐 마을 사람들에게 괴롭힘을 당하던 뱀이 사람들을 물자 한 수도승은 뱀에게 사람들을 무는 것은 잘못된 것이라고 말했는데, 이 말을 들은 뱀은 사람들에게 위협조차 하지 않아 결국 상처를 입었다는 내용이 있다. 따라서 'I told you not to bite,' he said. 'I didn't tell you not to hiss.'의 의미를 '폭력적으로 행동하고 다른 사람들을 다치게 하는 것은 잘못된 것이지만, 누군가가 당신을 부당하게 대할 때 분노를 나타내는 것은 잘못된 것이 아니다'라고 한 ③번이 정답이다.

어휘 temple 사원, 신전 step on ~을 짓밟다 bite 물다 monk 수도승 sigh 한숨을 쉬다 violence 폭력 unfairly 부당하게

에서 / 목숨을 빼앗는 원인이 되는 / 전 세계적으로 성인 열 명 중 한 명의

(②) Developing countries are the most susceptible / because eighty-four percent of all smokers currently live / in middle to low income countries, / where tobacco use has been increasing / since 1970.
개발 도상국들이 가장 영향을 받기 쉽다 / 현재 전체 흡연자의 84퍼센트가 살고 있기 때문에 / 중간 소득에서 저소득 국가들에 / 담배 소비가 증가해온 / 1970년 이후로

(③) Though many governments have taken measures / to ban public smoking / and educate young potential smokers of health hazards, / until tobacco products are entirely prohibited, / it will ultimately be up to the individual / to choose to take the risk or not. (④)
비록 많은 정부들은 여러 조치들을 취해왔지만 / 공공 흡연을 금지하기 위해 / 그리고 흡연자가 될 가능성이 있는 젊은 사람들에게 건강상의 위험을 교육한다 / 담배 제품들이 전면적으로 금지되기 전까지는 / 결국 개인에게 달려 있을 것이다 / 그 위험을 감수할지 말지를 선택하는 것은

해석 세계 보건 기구(WHO)에 따르면, 2030년에 세계에서 가장 큰 사망 요인은 예방할 수는 있으나 자유 의지에 의한 무언가가 될 것이다. 오늘날, WHO는 담배가 전 세계적으로 성인 열 명 중 한 명의 목숨을 빼앗는 원인이 되는 세계에서 두 번째로 주된 사망 요인이라고 말한다. ② 이 수치가 같은 속도로 계속해서 증가한다면, 담배와 많은 흡연 관련 질병들은 단 15년 안에 세계에서 가장 큰 사망 요인이 될 것이다. 현재 전체 흡연자의 84퍼센트가 1970년 이후로 담배 소비가 증가해온 중간 소득에서 저소득 국가들에 살고 있기 때문에 개발 도상국들이 가장 영향을 받기 쉽다. 비록 많은 정부들은 공공 흡연을 금지하고 흡연자가 될 가능성이 있는 젊은 사람들에게 건강상의 위험을 교육하기 위해 여러 조치들을 취해왔지만, 담배 제품들이 전면적으로 금지되기 전까지는 그 위험을 감수할지 말지를 선택하는 것은 결국 개인에게 달려 있을 것이다.

해설 ②번 앞 문장에 담배가 성인 열 명 중 한 명(one in ten adults)의 목숨을 빼앗는 세계에서 두 번째로 주된 사망 요인이라는 내용이 있으므로, ②번 자리에 그 수치(the numbers)가 같은 속도로 계속해서 증가한다면, 담배와 많은 흡연 관련 질병들은 단 15년 안에 세계에서 가장 큰 사망 요인이 될 것이라고 예측하는 주어진 문장이 나와야 지문이 자연스럽게 연결된다. 따라서 ②번이 정답이다.

어휘 tobacco 담배 preventable 예방할 수 있는
voluntary 자유 의지에 의한, 자발적인 susceptible 영향을 받기 쉬운
hazard 위험, 모험 prohibit 금지하다 ultimately 결국, 궁극적으로
be up to ~에 달려 있다

05 독해 논리적 흐름 파악 (문장 삽입)   난이도 ★★☆

끊어읽기 해석

If the numbers continue to rise / at the same rates, / tobacco and a number of smoking-related diseases / will be the world's biggest killer / in just 15 years.
이 수치가 계속해서 증가한다면 / 같은 속도로 / 담배와 많은 흡연 관련 질병들은 / 세계에서 가장 큰 사망 요인이 될 것이다 / 단 15년 안에

According to the World Health Organization (WHO), / the world's biggest killer / in 2030 / will be something / that is preventable, but voluntary.
세계 보건 기구(WHO)에 따르면 / 세계에서 가장 큰 사망 요인은 / 2030년에 / 무언가가 될 것이다 / 예방할 수는 있으나 자유 의지에 의한

(①) Today, / the WHO says / that tobacco is the second major cause of death / in the world, / responsible for killing / one in ten adults worldwide.
오늘날 / WHO는 말한다 / 담배가 두 번째로 주된 사망 요인이라고 / 세계

06 독해 추론 (빈칸 완성 - 구)   난이도 ★★☆

끊어읽기 해석

The way in which we phrase our words / has an enormous psychological impact / on our reasoning.
우리가 단어들을 표현하는 방식은 / 엄청난 심리적인 영향을 미친다 / 우리의 추론에

The most famous idiom / to illustrate this point / is to say / that a glass is "half full" / instead of "half empty."
가장 유명한 관용구는 / 이러한 주장을 설명하는 / 말하는 것이다 / 유리잔이 '절반이 차 있다'라고 / '절반이 비어 있다' 대신에

The positive connotations of a half-full glass allow / for a more content and susceptible frame of mind, / as opposed to / the negative distancing effect / of considering a glass half-empty.
절반이 차 있는 유리잔의 긍정적인 함축은 허용한다 / 더 만족스럽고 여지가

있는 사고방식을 / 대조적으로 / 부정적인 거리 효과와는 / 유리잔의 절반이 비어 있다고 생각하는 것의

For instance, / more people are likely to buy / a box of cookies / that are advertised / as being 75% fat free / than a box / that was simply 25% fat.
예를 들어 / 더 많은 사람들이 살 가능성이 있다 / 과자 상자를 / 광고되는 / 무지방 75퍼센트라고 / (과자) 상자 보다는 / 단순히 지방 25퍼센트인

The subtle effects / of carefully choosing our words / are far-reaching and extraordinarily common.
미묘한 효과는 / 단어들을 신중하게 선택하는 것의 / 지대한 영향을 가져오며 몹시 흔히 일어난다

해석 우리가 단어들을 표현하는 방식은 우리의 추론에 엄청난 심리적인 영향을 미친다. 이러한 주장을 설명하는 가장 유명한 관용구는 유리잔이 '절반이 비어 있다' 대신에 '절반이 차 있다'라고 말하는 것이다. 유리잔의 절반이 비어 있다고 생각하는 것의 부정적인 거리 효과와는 대조적으로, 절반이 차 있는 유리잔의 긍정적인 함축은 더 만족스럽고 여지가 있는 사고방식을 허용한다. 예를 들어, 더 많은 사람들이 단순히 지방 25퍼센트인 과자 상자보다는 무지방 75퍼센트라고 광고되는 과자 상자를 살 가능성이 있다. 단어들을 신중하게 선택하는 것의 미묘한 효과는 지대한 영향을 가져오며 몹시 흔히 일어난다.

① 선택적으로 영향력이 있으며 한정된
② 사적이고 개인적인 경험에서 오는
③ 지대한 영향을 가져오며 몹시 흔히 일어나는
④ 대인 관계와 직접적으로 관련이 있는

해설 빈칸이 있는 문장을 통해 빈칸에 단어들을 신중하게 선택하는 것의 미묘한 효과가 어떠한지에 대한 내용이 나와야 적절하다는 것을 알 수 있다. 지문 처음에서 우리가 단어들을 표현하는 방식은 우리의 추론에 엄청난 심리적인 영향을 미친다고 설명한 뒤, 이어서 그 예시로 절반이 비어 있는 유리잔 대신 절반이 차 있는 유리잔, 지방 25퍼센트인 과자 대신 무지방 75퍼센트인 과자라고 하는 것의 긍정적인 함축에 대해 설명하고 있으므로, 단어들을 신중하게 선택하는 것의 미묘한 효과는 '지대한 영향을 가져오며 몹시 흔히 일어난다'라고 한 ③번이 정답이다.

어휘 phrase 표현하다, 말하다 enormous 엄청난, 막대한 psychological 심리적인, 정신적인 reasoning 추론, 추리 idiom 관용구 illustrate 설명하다 connotation 함축, 내포 susceptible 여지가 있는 subtle 미묘한 far-reaching 지대한 영향을 가져올 extraordinarily 몹시 interpersonal relationship 대인 관계

07 독해 논리적 흐름 파악 (문장 삽입) 난이도 ★★☆

끊어읽기 해석

On the other hand, / a marine mammal trainer / may study and utilize knowledge / from marine biology / like anatomy, physiology or behavior.
반면에 / 해양 포유동물 조련사는 / 지식을 연구하고 활용할 수 있다 / 해양 생물학의 /해부학, 생리학 또는 습성과 같은

We often hear / people say, / "I want to be a marine biologist / so I can train dolphins."
우리는 흔히 듣는다 / 사람들이 말하는 것을 / "나는 해양 생물학자가 되고 싶어 / 돌고래를 조련할 수 있도록"

① While it is true / that some marine biologists do train dolphins, / the descriptions for a marine biologist and a marine mammal trainer / are really quite different.
이것은 사실이지만 / 일부 해양 생물학자들이 돌고래를 조련하는 것은 / 해

양 생물학자와 해양 포유동물 조련사에 대한 묘사는 / 사실 상당히 다르다

② A marine biologist is someone / who studies, observes, or protects marine organisms.
해양 생물학자는 사람이다 / 해양 생물들을 연구하거나, 관찰하거나, 또는 보호하는

③ Generally, / very few of these scientists train / living marine mammal species / themselves.
일반적으로 / 이 과학자들 중 극히 소수가 조련한다 / 살아 있는 해양 포유동물 종들을 / 직접

④ A marine mammal trainer / is actually taught / to specialize in each of these fields.
해양 포유동물 조련사는 / 실제로 교육을 받는다 / 이러한 각각의 분야를 전문적으로 다루도록

해석 우리는 흔히 사람들이 "나는 돌고래를 조련할 수 있도록 해양 생물학자가 되고 싶어"라고 말하는 것을 듣는다. 일부 해양 생물학자들이 돌고래를 조련하는 것은 사실이지만, 해양 생물학자와 해양 포유동물 조련사에 대한 묘사는 사실 상당히 다르다. 해양 생물학자는 해양 생물들을 연구하거나, 관찰하거나, 또는 보호하는 사람이다. 일반적으로, 이 과학자들 중 극히 소수가 살아 있는 해양 포유동물 종들을 직접 조련한다. ④ 반면에, 해양 포유동물 조련사는 해부학, 생리학 또는 습성과 같은 해양 생물학의 지식을 연구하고 활용할 수 있다. 해양 포유동물 조련사는 실제로 이러한 각각의 분야를 전문적으로 다루도록 교육을 받는다.

해설 ④번 앞 문장에 이 과학자들(해양 생물학자) 중 극히 소수가 살아 있는 해양 포유동물 종들을 직접 조련한다는 내용이 있고, ④번 뒤 문장에 해양 포유동물 조련사는 실제로 이러한 각각의 분야(each of these field)를 전문적으로 다루도록 교육을 받는다는 내용이 있으므로, ④번 자리에 반면에(On the other hand), 해양 포유동물 조련사는 해부학, 생리학 등과 같은 해양 생물학의 지식을 연구하고 활용할 수 있다고 하며 해양 포유동물 조련사가 해양 생물학자와 다른 점에 대해 설명하는 주어진 문장이 나와야 지문이 자연스럽게 연결된다. 따라서 ④번이 정답이다.

어휘 mammal 포유동물 utilize 활용하다 biology 생물학 anatomy 해부학 physiology 생리학 organism 생물, 유기체 specialize 전문적으로 다루다

08 독해 논리적 흐름 파악 (문장 삽입) 난이도 ★★☆

끊어읽기 해석

These students may be confused / after reading / when their classmates can answer questions and they can't / because they're not comprehending.
이러한 학생들은 혼란스러워할 수 있다 / 독서 후 / 그들의 반 친구들은 질문에 답할 수 있지만 자신은 답할 수 없을 때 / 이해하고 있지 못해서

As they read through / a short passage in a text, / proficient readers / accomplish many tasks; / make predictions, infer information, visualize a scene, and generate questions.
그들이 꼼꼼히 읽는 동안에 / 본문의 짧은 구절을 / 능숙한 독서가들은 / 많은 일들을 해낸다 / 예측을 하고, 정보를 추론하며, 장면을 상상하고, 또 의문을 만들어 내는

(①) They usually do these tasks / without even realizing / they are doing them.
그들은 보통 이 일들을 한다 / 인지하지도 못한 채 / 자신이 이것들을 하고 있다고

(②) But / beginning readers often don't realize / that they are supposed to do this, / in part because they are focusing / on decoding words.

하지만 / 초보 독서가들은 흔히 인지하지 못한다 / 그들이 이것을 해야 한다는 것을 / 이는 부분적으로 그들이 집중하고 있기 때문이다 / 단어들의 의미를 이해하는 데

(③) Teachers tell the struggling readers / to re-read, / but they often do so / with the same results. (④)
교사들은 분투하는 독서가들에게 말한다 / 다시 읽으라고 / 하지만 보통 그들은 그렇게 하고도 / 같은 결과를 낸다

해석 그들이 본문의 짧은 구절을 꼼꼼히 읽는 동안에, 능숙한 독서가들은 많은 일들을 해낸다. 예측을 하고, 정보를 추론하며, 장면을 상상하고, 또 의문을 만들어 낸다. 그들은 보통 자신이 이것들을 하고 있다고 인지하지도 못한 채 이 일들을 한다. 하지만 초보 독서가들은 흔히 그들이 이것을 해야 한다는 것을 인지하지 못하는데, 이는 부분적으로 그들이 단어들의 의미를 이해하는 데 집중하고 있기 때문이다. ③ 이러한 학생들은 독서 후 그들의 반 친구들은 질문에 답할 수 있지만 자신은 이해하고 있지 못해서 답할 수 없을 때 혼란스러워할 수 있다. 교사들은 분투하는 독서가들에게 다시 읽으라고 말하지만, 보통 그들은 그렇게 하고도 같은 결과를 낸다.

해설 ③번 앞 문장에 초보 독서가들(beginning readers)은 단어들의 의미를 이해하는 데 집중하느라 글을 읽을 때 해야 하는 것들을 인지하지 못한다는 내용이 있으므로, ③번 자리에 이러한 학생들(These students)은 독서 후 그들의 반 친구들은 질문에 답할 수 있는 반면 자신은 이해하지 못해서 답할 수 없을 때 혼란스러워할 수 있다는 초보 독서가들이 겪는 어려움에 대해 설명하는 주어진 문장이 나와야 지문이 자연스럽게 연결된다. 따라서 ③번이 정답이다.

어휘 comprehend 이해하다, 파악하다 proficient 능숙한
accomplish 해내다 prediction 예측 infer 추론하다
visualize 상상하다, 구체화하다 generate 만들어 내다
decode ~의 의미를 이해하다 struggling 분투하는

09 독해 논리적 흐름 파악 (문단 순서 배열) 난이도 ★★☆

끊어읽기 해석

Most of us / who have ever cleaned a house / would be much happier / if there was less dust.
우리 대부분은 / 집을 청소해 본 적 있는 / 훨씬 더 행복할 것이다 / 먼지가 더 적다면

However, / without dust / there would be less rainfall / and sunsets would be less beautiful.
하지만 / 먼지가 없다면 / 강수량은 줄어들 것이다 / 그리고 석양은 덜 아름다워질 것이다

(A) At the sunrise and sunset, / the dust and water vapour molecules reflect / the longer, red rays of light / in such a way / that we can see them for more time.
일출과 일몰 시에, / 먼지와 수증기 분자는 반사한다 / 더 길고 붉은 파장을 / 방식으로 / 우리가 그것들을 더 많이 볼 수 있는

The more dust particles / in the air, / the more colorful the sunrise or sunset.
먼지 입자가 더 많을수록 / 공기 중에 / 일출이나 일몰은 더 다채롭다

(B) Thus / water vapour would be much less likely to turn to rain / without the dust particles.
그러므로 / 수증기가 비로 변할 가능성이 훨씬 더 적어질 것이다 / 먼지 입자가 없다면

The water vapour and dust particles / also reflect / the rays of the sun.
수증기와 먼지 입자는 / 또한 반사한다 / 태양의 직사광선을

(C) Rain is formed / when water molecules in the air / collect around particles of dust.
비는 형성된다 / 공기 중의 물 분자가 ~할 때 / 먼지 입자 주위에 모인다

When the collected water becomes heavy enough, / the water droplets fall / to the earth / as rain.
모여진 물이 충분히 무거워지면 / 물방울들은 떨어진다 / 땅으로 / 비가 되어

해석
집을 청소해 본 적 있는 우리 대부분은 먼지가 더 적다면 훨씬 더 행복해할 것이다. 하지만, 먼지가 없다면 강수량은 줄어들 것이고 석양은 덜 아름다워질 것이다.

(C) 비는 공기 중의 물 분자가 먼지 입자 주위에 모일 때 형성된다. 모여진 물이 충분히 무거워지면, 물방울들은 비가 되어 땅으로 떨어진다.

(B) 그러므로 먼지 입자가 없다면 수증기가 비로 변할 가능성이 훨씬 더 적어질 것이다. 또한 수증기와 먼지 입자는 태양의 직사광선을 반사한다.

(A) 일출과 일몰 시에, 먼지와 수증기 분자는 우리가 그것들을 더 많이 볼 수 있는 방식으로 더 길고 붉은 파장을 반사한다. 공기 중에 먼지 입자가 더 많을수록, 일출이나 일몰은 더 다채롭다.

해설 주어진 글에서 먼지가 없다면 강수량(rainfall)은 줄어들 것이고 석양(sunsets)은 덜 아름다워질 것이라고 언급한 후, (C)에서 비(Rain)는 공기 중의 물 분자가 먼지 입자 주위에 모일 때 형성된다고 하며 먼지가 강수량에 영향을 미치는 방식을 설명하고 있다. 이어서 (B)에서 그러므로(Thus) 먼지가 없다면 수증기가 비로 변할 가능성이 훨씬 더 적어질 것이고, 먼지는 태양의 직사광선(the rays of the sun)을 반사한다고 하며 먼지가 석양에 미치는 영향을 설명한 뒤, (A)에서 먼지와 수증기 분자는 빛의 파장(rays of light)을 반사하여 더 다채로운 일출과 일몰을 만든다고 설명하고 있다. 따라서 ③ (C) – (B) – (A)가 정답이다.

어휘 water vapour 수증기 molecule 분자 particle 입자, 작은 조각
collect around 주위에 모이다 water droplet 물방울

10 독해 전체내용 파악 (문단 요약) 난이도 ★★☆

끊어읽기 해석

Perhaps / the biggest problem for men / who want to do more with their children / is that employers rarely make it easy for them.
아마도 / 남성들에게 가장 큰 문제는 / 아이들과 더 많은 것을 하고 싶은 / 고용주들이 좀처럼 그들에게 이것이 쉽도록 해 주지 않는다는 점일 것이다

According to a recent study / of 1,300 major corporations made by Catalyst, / a career think tank for women, / few companies pay more than lip service / to the idea of paternal participation.
최근 연구에 따르면 / Catalyst가 1,300개의 주요 기업을 대상으로 실시한 / 여성을 위한 직장 생활 두뇌 집단인 / 몇 안 되는 회사들만이 입에 발린 말 이상을 한다 / 아버지의 참여라는 의견에 대해

More than 80 percent / of the executives surveyed / acknowledged / that men now feel more need / to share child-raising responsibilities / —but nearly 40 percent also agreed / that "realistically, certain positions in my firm cannot be attained by a man / who combines career and parenting."
80퍼센트 이상이 / 조사받은 경영진의 / 인정했다 / 남성이 이제는 더 많은 필요성을 느낀다고 / 육아의 책임을 분담해야 할 / 하지만 또한 거의 40퍼센트는 동의했다 / "현실적으로, 우리 회사의 특정 직위는 남성에 의해 얻어질 수 없다"는 것에 / 직장 생활과 육아를 병행하는

While a quarter of the companies said / they favored the idea

of paternity leaves, / fewer than one in ten / actually offered them.
회사들의 4분의 1이 말했지만 / 아버지의 육아 휴가라는 의견에 찬성한다고 / 10분의 1보다 더 적은 회사가 / 실제로 이를 제공했다

해석 아마도 아이들과 더 많은 것을 하고 싶은 남성들에게 가장 큰 문제는 고용주들이 좀처럼 그들에게 이것이 쉽도록 해 주지 않는다는 점일 것이다. 여성을 위한 직장 생활 두뇌 집단인 Catalyst가 1,300개의 주요 기업을 대상으로 실시한 최근 연구에 따르면, 아버지의 참여라는 의견에 대해 몇 안 되는 회사들만이 입에 발린 말 이상을 한다. 조사받은 경영진의 80퍼센트 이상이 남성이 이제는 육아의 책임을 분담해야 할 더 많은 필요성을 느낀다고 인정했지만, 또한 거의 40퍼센트는 "현실적으로, 우리 회사의 특정 직위는 직장 생활과 육아를 병행하는 남성에 의해 얻어질 수 없다."는 것에 동의했다. 회사들의 4분의 1이 아버지의 육아 휴가라는 의견에 찬성한다고 말했지만, 10분의 1보다 더 적은 회사가 실제로 이를 제공했다.

최근 연구는 육아에 대한 (B) 아버지의 참여를 좀처럼 지원하지 않는 회사들 때문에 남성이 (A) 육아를 함께 하는 것이 현실적으로 어렵다는 것을 보여 준다.

```
     (A)        (B)
① 육아    –  아버지의
② 육아    –  경영의
③ 직업    –  아버지의
④ 직업    –  경영의
```

해설 지문 중간에서 몇 안 되는 회사들만이 아버지가 육아에 참여하도록 한다고 하고, 지문 뒷부분에서 조사받은 경영진의 40퍼센트는 현실적으로 회사의 특정 직위가 직장 생활과 육아를 병행하는 남성에 의해 얻어질 수 없다는 것에 동의했다고 했으므로, (A)에는 최근 연구는 남성이 '육아'(parenting)를 함께 하는 것이 현실적으로 어렵다는 것을 보여 준다는 내용이, (B)에는 육아에 대한 '아버지의'(paternal) 참여를 좀처럼 지원하지 않는 회사라는 내용이 나와야 적절하다.
따라서 ① (A) parenting(육아) – (B) paternal(아버지의)이 정답이다.

어휘 think tank 두뇌 집단 paternal 아버지의
executive 경영진; 경영의 attain 얻다, 달성하다
combine 병행하다 parenting 육아 favor 찬성하다
paternity leave 아버지의 육아 휴가 child rearing 육아

11 문법 부사절 & 전치사 난이도 ★★★

해석 당신이 어떤 경로를 선택하든 간에, 킬리만자로를 등반하는 것은 만만치 않은 일이라는 것을 명심하라. 수백 명의 등반가들이 큰 어려움 없이 Uhuru Peak에 도달하지만, 더 많은 등반가들은 너무 빠르게 올라가서 고산병을 앓기 때문에 성공하지 못한다. 그리고 매년 몇 명의 등반가들은 산 위에서 목숨을 잃는다. 적절한 신발과 옷을 입고 준비된 상태로 오고, 무엇보다도 스스로에게 충분한 시간을 주어라. 만약 당신이 정상에 도달할 의향이 있다면, 당신이 어떤 경로로 가는지에 상관없이 '표준' 등반 일정에 적어도 하루의 추가일을 더하는 것을 진지하게 고려해라. 비록 여행을 계획할 때 추가되는 하루에 미화 150달러 정도를 더 지불하는 것이 많아 보일 수도 있지만, 추후에 만일 당신이 등반을 시작하기 위해 비용과 노력을 들였는데도 정상에 도달하지 못하고 내려와야 한다면 이것은 상대적으로 약소한 절약으로 보일 것이다.

해설 ③ 부사절 자리와 쓰임 완전한 절(paying an additional ~ planning your trip)을 이끄는 부사절 접속사 자리에 전치사는 올 수 없으므로 전치사 Despite를 '비록 ~이지만'이라는 의미의 부사절 접속사 Although 또는 Though로 고쳐야 한다.

오답 분석
① 재귀대명사 문맥상 '스스로에게 충분한 시간을 주어라'라는 의미가 되어야 자연스럽고, 동사 allow의 목적어가 지칭하는 대상이 생략된 의미상 주어(you)와 동일하므로 재귀대명사 yourself(스스로에게)가 목적어 자리에 올바르게 쓰였다. 참고로, 명령문은 주어를 생략하고 동사원형(Come)으로 문장을 시작한다.
② 동명사를 목적어로 취하는 동사 동사 consider는 동명사를 목적어로 취하는 동사이므로 동명사 adding이 올바르게 쓰였다.
④ 동명사의 형태 전치사(without) 뒤에는 명사 역할을 하는 것이 와야 하고, 당신이 '정상에 도달하지 못하는' 것이 '(산에서) 내려오는' 시점보다 이전이므로 동명사의 완료형 having reached가 올바르게 쓰였다.

어휘 serious 만만치 않은, 심각한 undertaking 일, 프로젝트
ascend 올라가다 altitude sickness 고산병 itinerary 일정, 여정
relatively 상대적으로 insignificant 약소한, 대수롭지 않은

👍 이것도 알면 합격!
'~에도 불구하고'라는 의미의 양보를 나타내는 전치사와 접속사를 구분하여 알아두자.

전치사	despite, in spite of + 명사
접속사	although, though, even if, even though + 주어 + 동사

12 독해 전체내용 파악 (글의 감상) 난이도 ★☆☆

끊어읽기 해석

On a mid-September day, / British climbers Rachel Kelsey and Jeremy Colenso / were climbing / in the Swiss Alps.
9월 중순의 어느 날 / 영국인 등반가 Rachel Kelsey와 Jeremy Colenso는 / 오르고 있었다 / 스위스 알프스 산맥을

They were both experienced climbers / and when they left their base, / the weather was good.
그들은 모두 노련한 등반가였다 / 그리고 그들이 기지를 떠날 때는 / 날씨가 좋았다

They reached the summit, / but as they started / the climb down, / an electric storm / struck the mountain.
그들은 정상에 도달했다 / 하지만 그들이 시작하자마자 / 하산을 / 뇌우가 / 산을 덮쳤다

Snow began to fall, / making it difficult to see / where they could put / their hands and feet / on the rock.
눈이 내리기 시작했다 / 이는 살피기 어렵게 만들었다 / 그들이 어느 곳에 놓을 수 있을지를 / 그들의 손과 발을 / 바위 위

After several frightening minutes, / they found a narrow ledge / and climbed on to it, / hoping the snow would stop and they could continue their descent.
무서운 몇 분이 지나고 / 그들은 좁은 바위 턱을 발견했다 / 그리고는 그 위로 기어올랐다 / 눈이 멈춰서 그들이 하산을 계속할 수 있기를 바라면서

The snow did not stop / and the temperature dropped / to -10°C.
눈은 멈추지 않았다 / 그리고 온도는 떨어졌다 / 섭씨 영하 10도까지

해석 9월 중순의 어느 날, 영국인 등반가 Rachel Kelsey와 Jeremy Colenso는 스위스 알프스 산맥을 오르고 있었다. 그들은 모두 노련한 등반가였고 그들이 기지를 떠날 때는 날씨가 좋았다. 그들은 정상에 도달했지만, 그들이 하산을 시작하자마자 뇌우가 산을 덮

쳤다. 눈이 내리기 시작했고 이는 그들이 바위 위 어느 곳에 그들의 손과 발을 놓을 수 있을지를 살피기 어렵게 만들었다. 무서운 몇 분이 지나고, 그들은 좁은 바위 턱을 발견하고는 눈이 멈춰서 그들이 하산을 계속할 수 있기를 바라면서 그 위로 기어올랐다. 눈은 멈추지 않았고 온도는 섭씨 영하 10도까지 떨어졌다.

① 축하하는   ② 불가사의한
③ 단조로운   ④ 걱정스러운

해설   지문 전반에 걸쳐 두 명의 등반가가 알프스 산맥에서 하산하던 중에 갑작스럽게 뇌우를 만나 어려움을 겪는 상황에 대해 묘사하고 있다. 따라서 지문의 분위기를 '걱정스러운'이라고 표현한 ④번이 정답이다.

어휘   **experienced** 노련한, 경험이 많은   **summit** 정상
electric storm 뇌우   **strike** 덮치다, 발생하다
ledge 바위 턱, 튀어나온 바위   **descent** 하산, 강하
festive 축하하는   **monotonous** 단조로운   **worrisome** 걱정스러운

---

13   독해   세부내용 파악 (지칭 대상 파악)   난이도 ★☆☆

끊어읽기 해석

One day, / I looked out our dining room window / to see our strawberry patch / spreading its leaves and getting started with some new vines.
어느 날 / 나는 우리 식당 창밖을 내다보았다 / 우리 딸기밭을 보게 되었다 / 잎사귀를 펼치고 새로운 줄기를 내기 시작한

Towards one edge of the area / was one of those really spiky, thorny weeds.
그 장소의 한쪽 귀퉁이 쪽에는 / 끝이 매우 뾰족하고 가시가 많은 잡초 하나가 있었다

Figuring I'd grab ① it out of there / when I had my yard-work gloves on, / I got back to my housework / and promptly forgot all about ② it.
① 그것을 거기에서 뽑아내야겠다고 생각하고 / 내가 정원용 장갑을 끼고 있을 때 / 나는 집안일로 되돌아갔다 / 그리고 곧바로 ② 그것에 대해 까맣게 잊어버렸다

Time passed, / and I glanced out of the window again / to find a really spiky, thorny bush flourishing next to my strawberries, / choking them out a bit.
시간이 지났다 / 그리고 나는 창밖을 다시 힐끗 보았다 / (그리고는) 끝이 매우 뾰족하고 가시가 많은 덤불이 내 딸기 옆에서 무성하게 자라고 있는 것을 발견했다 / 그것을 조금 시들게 하며

③ It took a shovel / to get that thing out! // Why didn't I take care of it / when I first saw ④ it?
③ 삽이 필요했다 / 그것을 뽑아내기 위해서는! // 나는 왜 그것을 처리하지 않았을까 / 처음에 ④ 그것을 보았을 때?

I guess I thought / it wasn't going to get worse.
나는 생각했던 것 같다 / 이것이 더 악화되지는 않을 것이라고

It may seem silly / to go after a little thing like a weed, / but there is never just one little weed.
어리석어 보일지도 모른다 / 잡초 같은 하찮은 것을 쫓아다니는 것이 / 하지만 그저 하찮은 잡초라는 것은 없다

해석   어느 날 나는 우리 식당 창밖을 내다보았는데 잎사귀를 펼치고 새로운 줄기를 내기 시작한 우리 딸기밭을 보게 되었다. 그 장소의 한쪽 귀퉁이 쪽에는 끝이 매우 뾰족하고 가시가 많은 잡초 하나가 있었다. 내가 정원용 장갑을 끼고 있을 때 ① 그것을 거기에서 뽑아내야겠다고 생각하고, 나는 집안일로 되돌아갔고 곧바로 ② 그것에 대해 까맣게 잊어버렸다. 시간이 지났고, 나는 창밖을 다시 힐끗 보고는 끝이 매우 뾰족하고 가시가 많은 덤불이 내 딸기를 조금 시들게 하며 그것 옆에서 무성하게 자라고 있는 것을 발견했다.

그것을 뽑아내기 위해서는 삽이 필요했다! 나는 왜 처음에 ④ 그것을 보았을 때 처리하지 않았을까? 나는 이것이 더 악화되지는 않을 것이라고 생각했던 것 같다. 잡초 같은 하찮은 것을 쫓아다니다니는 것이 어리석어 보일지도 모르지만, 그저 하찮은 잡초라는 것은 없다.

해설   ①, ②, ④번 모두 딸기 옆에서 자란 끝이 매우 뾰족하고 가시가 많은 잡초를 지칭하지만, ③번은 진짜 주어 to get that thing out(그것을 뽑아내는 것)을 대신해서 쓰인 가주어이므로 ③번이 정답이다.

어휘   **patch** 밭, 작은 땅   **vine** 줄기   **spiky** 끝이 뾰족한
thorny 가시가 많은   **weed** 잡초   **promptly** 곧바로, 지체 없이
bush 덤불   **flourish** 무성하게 자라다   **choke** 시들게 하다
shovel 삽

---

14   독해   전체내용 파악 (제목 파악)   난이도 ★★★

끊어읽기 해석

The origins of contemporary Western thought / can be traced back / to the golden age of ancient Greece / in the sixth and fifth centuries BC, / when Greek thinkers laid the foundations / for modern Western politics, philosophy, science, and law.
현대 서양 사상의 기원은 / 거슬러 올라갈 수 있다 / 고대 그리스 황금기까지 / 기원전 5, 6세기의 / 그리스 사상가들이 기반을 다지던 / 현대 서양의 정치, 철학, 과학, 그리고 법의

Their novel approach was to pursue rational inquiry / through adversarial discussion: / The best way / to evaluate one set of ideas, they decided, / was by testing it / against another set of ideas.
그들의 새로운 접근법은 합리적인 탐구를 추구하는 것이었다 / 대립적인 토론을 통해 / 최상의 방법은 / 그들이 결정한 일련의 사상을 평가하는 / 이것을 시험하는 것이었다 / 일련의 다른 사상과 비교하여

In the political sphere, / the result was democracy, / in which supporters of rival policies / vied for rhetorical supremacy; / in philosophy, / it led to reasoned arguments and dialogues / about the nature of the world; / in science, / it prompted / the construction of competing theories / to try to explain natural phenomena; / in the field of law / the result was the adversarial legal system.
정치 영역에서 / 그 결과는 민주주의였다 / 경쟁하는 정책의 지지자들이 / 수사적 우위를 겨루던 / 철학에서 / 이것은 이성적인 논쟁과 대화로 이어졌다 / 세계의 본질에 대한 / 과학에서 / 이것은 유도했다 / 대립되는 이론의 구성을 / 자연 현상을 설명하려고 시도하는 / 법 분야에서 / 그 결과는 대립적인 법률 제도였다

This approach underpins / the modern Western way of life, / in which politics, commerce, science, and law are all rooted / in orderly competition.
이 접근법은 뒷받침한다 / 현대 서양의 삶의 방식을 / 모든 정치, 상업, 과학, 그리고 법이 기반을 둔 / 질서 있는 경쟁에

해석   현대 서양 사상의 기원은 그리스 사상가들이 현대 서양의 정치, 철학, 과학, 그리고 법의 기반을 다지던 기원전 5, 6세기의 고대 그리스 황금기까지 거슬러 올라갈 수 있다. 그들의 새로운 접근법은 대립적인 토론을 통해 합리적인 탐구를 추구하는 것이었다. 그들이 결정한 일련의 사상을 평가하는 최상의 방법은 이것을 일련의 다른 사상과 비교하여 시험하는 것이었다. 정치 영역에서, 그 결과는 경쟁하는 정책의 지지자들이 수사적 우위를 겨루던 민주주의였다. 철학에서, 이것은 세계의 본질에 대한 이성적인 논쟁과 대화로 이어졌다. 과학에서, 이것은 자연 현상을 설명하려고 시도하는 대립되는 이론의 구성을 유도했다. 법 분야에서, 그 결과는 대립적인 법

률 제도였다. 이 접근법은 모든 정치, 상업, 과학, 그리고 법이 질서 있는 경쟁에 기반을 둔 현대 서양의 삶의 방식을 뒷받침한다.

① 현대 사회의 공통 관심사
② 대립적인 관계의 중요성
③ 현대 서양 사회와 고대 그리스
④ 경쟁에 기반을 둔 서양 사상의 발상지

해설 지문 처음에서 현대 서양 사상의 기원은 고대 그리스 황금기까지 거슬러 올라갈 수 있다고 언급하고, 이어서 고대 그리스 사상가들의 대립적인 토론을 통한 접근법이 정치, 철학, 과학, 법의 영역에서 어떤 체계를 마련했는지를 나열한 후, 지문 마지막에서 이 접근법은 질서 있는 경쟁에 기반을 둔 현대 서양의 삶의 방식을 뒷받침한다고 설명하고 있다. 따라서 이 지문의 제목을 '경쟁에 기반을 둔 서양 사상의 발상지'라고 표현한 ④번이 정답이다.

어휘 origin 기원 contemporary 현대의, 당대의
foundation 기반, 기초 novel 새로운, 참신한 pursue 추구하다
rational 합리적인 inquiry 탐구, 연구 adversarial 대립적인
evaluate 평가하다 sphere 영역 vie 겨루다 rhetorical 수사적인
supremacy 우위, 패권 prompt 유도하다, 촉발하다
underpin 뒷받침하다 orderly 질서 있는 cradle 발상지, 요람

---

15 독해 논리적 흐름 파악 (문단 순서 배열) 난이도 ★★☆

끊어읽기 해석

The first brands were invented / as a 'guarantee of quality'.
첫 번째 브랜드는 발명되었다 / '품질 보증'으로써

Customers could feel safe / that if they bought Sunlight soap, / they were buying a safe and reliable product.
소비자들은 안전한 느낌을 받을 수 있었다 / 만약 그들이 Sunlight 비누를 구매한다면 / 그들이 안전하고 믿을 수 있는 제품을 구매하고 있다는

(A) Your preferred brand is an indication / of your status. // Talk to any user of an Apple computer.
당신이 선호하는 브랜드는 암시이다 / 당신의 신분에 대한 // 아무 애플 컴퓨터의 사용자와 대화를 해 보아라.

(B) Today, / brands have a similar function / as a guarantee of quality.
오늘날 / 브랜드는 유사한 기능을 가지고 있다 / 품질 보증과

But brands have become / more than just a simple guarantee. // The brands you buy define / who you are.
하지만 브랜드는 되어왔다 / 단순한 보증 이상의 것이 // 당신이 구매하는 브랜드는 명백히 보여 준다 / 당신이 누구인지를

(C) Secretly or openly, / they believe / that they are different / and slightly superior / to Windows users.
남몰래 혹은 공개적으로 / 그들은 생각한다 / 자신이 특별하다고 / 그리고 조금 더 우월하다고 / 윈도우 사용자들보다

Apple, / in their advertising, / has reinforced this distinctive image.
애플은 / 그들의 광고에서 / 이러한 차이를 나타내는 이미지를 강화해왔다

해석 첫 번째 브랜드는 '품질 보증'으로써 발명되었다. 소비자들은 만약 그들이 Sunlight 비누를 구매한다면 그들이 안전하고 믿을 수 있는 제품을 구매하고 있다는 안전한 느낌을 받을 수 있었다.

(B) 오늘날, 브랜드는 품질 보증과 유사한 기능을 가지고 있다. 하지만 브랜드는 단순한 보증 이상의 것이 되어왔다. 당신이 구매하는 브랜드는 당신이 누구인지를 명백히 보여 준다.

(A) 당신이 선호하는 브랜드는 당신의 신분에 대한 암시이다. 아무 애플 컴퓨터의 사용자와 대화를 해 보아라.

(C) 남몰래 혹은 공개적으로, 그들은 자신이 특별하고 윈도우 사용자들보다 조금 더 우월하다고 생각한다. 애플은 그들의 광고에서 이러한 차이를 나타내는 이미지를 강화해왔다.

해설 주어진 문장에서 브랜드는 '품질 보증'(guarantee of quality)으로서 처음 발명되었다고 언급한 후, (B)에서 오늘날 브랜드는 품질 보증과 유사한 기능을 가지고 있지만 이제는 소비자가 누구인지(who you are)를 명백히 보여 주기까지 한다고 설명하고 있다. 이어서 (A)에서 당신이 선호하는 브랜드는 당신의 신분에 대한 암시라고 하며 애플 컴퓨터의 사용자(user of an Apple computer)를 예시로 언급하고, (C)에서 그들(they)은 자신이 특별하고 윈도우 사용자들보다 조금 더 우월하다고 생각하며 애플이 광고에서 이러한 이미지를 강화해왔다는 것을 설명하고 있다. 따라서 ① (B) – (A) – (C)가 정답이다.

어휘 invent 발명하다 guarantee 보증 reliable 믿을 수 있는
indication 암시, 지시 define 명백히 보여 주다 reinforce 강화하다
distinctive 차이를 나타내는, 변별적인

---

16 독해 논리적 흐름 파악 (문단 순서 배열) 난이도 ★★☆

끊어읽기 해석

Dinosaurs dominated the world / 65 million years ago, / until a comet / 6 miles in diameter streaking 20 miles per second / slammed into the Earth.
공룡은 지구를 지배했다 / 6,500만 년 전에 / 혜성이 ~하기 전까지 / 지름 6마일에 초속 20마일로 질주하는 / 지구에 충돌했다

The catastrophic collision / instantaneously plunged the world / into a very dark and cold nuclear winter / that lasted for 12 months.
이 파멸적인 충돌은 / 순간적으로 지구를 몰아넣었다 / 몹시 어둡고 추운 핵겨울로 / 12개월 동안 지속된

(A) Their flexibility allowed them to survive / the Armageddon caused by the comet, / and when the dust finally settled, / the early mammals crawled out of their burrows, / squinted at the warm sun, / and evolved to become the dominant creatures of the Earth.
그들의 적응성은 그들이 살아남게 했다 / 혜성으로 인한 대충돌에서 / 그리고 마침내 먼지가 가라앉자 / 초기 포유동물들은 굴에서 기어 나왔다 / 눈을 가늘게 뜨고 따스한 태양을 보았다 / 그리고 진화하여 지구의 지배적인 동물이 되었다

(B) They, / though large and powerful, / were cold-blooded and hairless, / and proved incapable of adjusting / to the radical climate changes / including a sudden and sharp drop in temperature, / and thus quickly died off in a mass extinction.
그들은 / 거대하고 강했지만 / 냉혈이고 털이 없었다 / 그래서 적응하지 못한 것으로 드러났다 / 급진적인 기후 변화에 / 갑작스럽고 급격한 기온의 하락을 포함하는 / 그리고 그로 인해 급속히 차례차례 죽어 대량 멸종하게 되었다

(C) In contrast, / a group of small, furry, warm-blooded creatures (early mammals and our distant ancestors) / proved to be superbly adjustable / to the drastic changes.
대조적으로 / 작고, 털이 많으며, 온혈인 동물군(초기 포유동물과 우리의 먼 조상)은 / 훌륭하게 적응할 수 있는 것으로 드러났다 / 극단적인 변화에

해석 공룡은 6,500만 년 전에 지름 6마일에 초속 20마일로 질주하는 혜성이 지구에 충돌하기 전까지 지구를 지배했다. 이 파멸적인 충돌은 순간적으로 지구를 12개월 동안 지속된 몹시 어둡고 추운 핵겨울로 몰아넣었다.

(B) 그들은 거대하고 강했지만 냉혈이고 털이 없어서, 갑작스럽고 급격한 기온의 하락을 포함하는 급진적인 기후 변화에 적응하지 못한 것으로 드러났고, 그로 인해 급속히 차례차례 죽어 대량 멸종하게 되었다.

(C) 대조적으로, 작고, 털이 많으며, 온혈인 동물군(초기 포유동물과 우리의 먼 조상)은 극단적인 변화에 훌륭하게 적응할 수 있는 것으로 드러났다.

(A) 그들의 적응성은 그들이 혜성으로 인한 대충돌에서 살아남게 했고, 마침내 먼지가 가라앉자 초기 포유동물들은 굴에서 기어 나와, 눈을 가늘게 뜨고 따스한 태양을 보았으며, 진화하여 지구의 지배적인 동물이 되었다.

해설 주어진 문장에서 지구에 혜성이 지구에 충돌하여 핵겨울이 오기 전까지는 공룡(Dinosaurs)이 지구를 지배했다고 하고, (B)에서 그들(They)은 거대하고 강했지만 냉혈이고 털이 없어서 급진적인 기후 변화에 적응하지 못하고 대량 멸종하게 되었다고 설명하고 있다. 이어서 (C)에서 이와 대조적으로(In contrast) 작고 털이 많으며 온혈인 동물은 변화에 적응할 수 있었다고 한 뒤, (A)에서 그들의 적응성(Their flexibility)은 그들이 살아남아서 지구의 지배적인 동물이 되게 했다는 것을 설명하고 있다. 따라서 ② (B) - (C) - (A)가 정답이다.

어휘 dominate 지배하다 comet 혜성 streak 질주하다
slam into ~에 충돌하다 catastrophic 파멸적인, 대재앙의
collision 충돌 instantaneously 순간적으로
plunge 몰아넣다, 내던지다 nuclear winter 핵겨울
flexibility 적응성, 유연성 Armageddon 대충돌, 대전쟁
crawl out of ~에서 기어 나오다 burrow 굴
squint 눈을 가늘게 뜨고 보다 adjust 적응하다 radical 급진적인
die off 차례차례 죽다 extinction 멸종 superbly 훌륭하게
drastic 극단적인

17 독해 논리적 흐름 파악 (무관한 문장 삭제) 난이도 ★★☆

끊어읽기 해석

It's easy to lose objectivity / or to overlook errors, inconsistencies, or problems / when you have focused too intensely or for too long / on a particular task.
객관성을 잃기 쉽다 / 혹은 오류, 모순, 또는 문제를 간과하기 / 당신이 지나치게 열심히 혹은 지나치게 오랫동안 집중했을 때는 / 특정한 일에

You may have revised your essay / so many times / that you have forgotten / what the question is, / and your essay / no longer adequately responds to it.
당신은 과제물을 수정했을 수도 있다 / 너무 여러 번 / 그리하여 잊었을 (수도 있다) / 질문이 무엇인지를 / 그래서 당신의 과제물은 / 더 이상 그것에 적절하게 답하지 않을 (수도 있다)

① Or you may have crafted / what you think is a witty and clever remark, or an eloquent statement, / while in reality you have just written / something inappropriate.
아니면 당신은 정성 들여 만들었을 수도 있다 / 스스로 생각하기에 재치 있고 기발한 말이나 유창한 표현을 / 하지만 사실 당신은 그저 써놓은 것이다 / 부적절한 무언가를

② Also, / even the best writers make grammatical and typographical errors, / and spell-checking and grammar-checking software / won't reveal every problem.
또한 / 최고의 작가들조차 문법 및 인쇄상 실수를 한다 / 그리고 철자 검토와 문법 검토 소프트웨어가 / 모든 문제를 알려 주지는 않을 것이다

③ There is little possibility / to misspell anything / nowadays when there are computer programs available / to help check grammar, spelling, punctuation and content.
가능성은 거의 없다 / 어떤 것의 철자를 잘못 쓸 / 이용 가능한 컴퓨터 프로그램이 있는 오늘날에 / 문법, 철자, 구두법 그리고 내용을 검토하는 것을 도와 주는

④ Before typing that final version, / by all means show your essays / to a few other people / —perhaps your peers or faculty advisor— / to get their feedback.
최종판을 인쇄하기 전에 / 반드시 당신의 과제물을 보여 주어라 / 다른 몇몇 사람들에게 / 가능하다면 당신의 친구들이나 학부 지도 교수인 / 피드백을 받기 위해

해석 당신이 특정한 일에 지나치게 열심히 혹은 지나치게 오랫동안 집중했을 때는 객관성을 잃거나 오류, 모순, 또는 문제를 간과하기 쉽다. 당신은 과제물을 너무 여러 번 수정하여 질문이 무엇인지를 잊었을 수도 있고, 그래서 당신의 과제물은 더 이상 그것에 적절하게 답하지 않을 수도 있다. ① 아니면 당신은 스스로 생각하기에 재치 있고 기발한 말이나 유창한 표현을 정성 들여 만들었을 수도 있지만, 사실 당신은 그저 부적절한 무언가를 써놓은 것이다. ② 또한, 최고의 작가들조차 문법 및 인쇄상 실수를 하고, 철자 검토와 문법 검토 소프트웨어가 모든 문제를 알려 주지는 않을 것이다. ③ 문법, 철자, 구두법 그리고 내용을 검토하는 것을 도와 주는 이용 가능한 컴퓨터 프로그램이 있는 오늘날에 어떤 것의 철자를 잘못 쓸 가능성은 거의 없다. ④ 최종판을 인쇄하기 전에, 반드시 당신의 과제물을 피드백을 받기 위해 가능하다면 당신의 친구들이나 학부 지도 교수인 다른 몇몇 사람들에게 보여 주어라.

해설 지문 처음에서 특정한 일에 지나치게 집중했을 때는 객관성을 잃거나 오류, 모순, 또는 문제를 간과하기 쉽다고 언급한 후, 그 예로 과제물을 너무 여러 번 수정하여 질문에 적절하게 답하지 못하는 경우를 제시하고 있다. 뒤이어 ①, ②, ④번에서 스스로 생각하기에 기발하지만 사실 부적절한 말이나 표현을 쓰는 경우와 작가들도 문법 및 인쇄상 실수를 한다는 것을 언급한 뒤, 과제물을 인쇄하기 전에 피드백을 받을 것을 제안하며 이 문제에 대한 예시와 해결책을 설명하고 있다. 그러나 ③번은 '오늘날 컴퓨터 프로그램의 이용으로 인해 줄어든 오류'에 대한 내용으로, 특정한 일에 지나치게 집중하여 일어나는 문제와는 관련이 없다. 따라서 ③번이 정답이다.

어휘 objectivity 객관성 overlook 간과하다, 못보고 넘어가다
inconsistency 모순 intensely 열심히, 열렬하게
craft 정성 들여 만들다 eloquent 유창한 typographical 인쇄상의
misspell 철자를 잘못 쓰다 punctuation 구두법
by all means 반드시 faculty 학부

18 독해 전체내용 파악 (요지 파악) 난이도 ★★☆

끊어읽기 해석

When you ask for what you want, / you're basically placing an order, / just like an Amazon.com.
당신이 원하는 것을 구할 때 / 당신은 기본적으로 주문을 하는 것이다 / Amazon.com과 같은 방식으로

But you have to be clear / in your mind / what you want. // To get clear on what you want, / make a list.
하지만 당신은 분명히 해야 한다 / 마음속에서 / 당신이 무엇을 원하는지를 // 원하는 것을 분명히 하기 위해서는 / 목록을 작성해라

Take out a notepad / and scribble down / whatever it is you want to have, do or be.
메모장을 꺼내라 / 그리고 아무렇게나 써 보아라 / 당신이 가지고 싶은 것, 하고 싶은 것, 또는 되고 싶은 것이 무엇이든

Whether that's perfect health, great relationships, and awesome career, travel, / or peace on Earth and goodwill / to all men.

그것이 완벽한 건강, 훌륭한 관계, 최고의 직업, 여행 / 또는 지구의 평화와 선의이든 간에 말이다 / 전 인류를 향한

Whatever you're hanging out / waiting for. // Just be clear / in your mind / what it is you want, / because a confused mind creates a confusing order.
당신이 참고 있는 것이라면 무엇이든지 말이다 / 기다리며 // 단지 분명히 해라 / 마음속에서 / 당신이 원하는 것이 무엇인지를 / 혼란스러운 마음은 혼란스러운 주문을 만들기 때문에

And a confusing order could see / Amazon.com accidentally sending you / Timbaland instead of Timberlake.
그리고 혼란스러운 주문은 발생시킬 수 있다 / Amazon.com이 잘못하여 당신에게 보내는 것을 / Timberlake 대신에 Timbaland를

해석 당신이 원하는 것을 구할 때, 당신은 기본적으로 Amazon.com 과 같은 방식으로 주문을 하는 것이다. 하지만 당신은 당신이 무엇을 원하는지를 마음속에서 분명히 해야 한다. 원하는 것을 분명히 하기 위해서는, 목록을 작성해라. 메모장을 꺼내고 당신이 가지고 싶은 것, 하고 싶은 것, 또는 되고 싶은 것이 무엇이든 아무렇게나 써 보아라. 그것이 완벽한 건강, 훌륭한 관계, 최고의 직업, 여행, 또는 지구의 평화와 전 인류를 향한 선의이든 간에 말이다. 당신이 기다리며 참고 있는 것이라면 무엇이든지 말이다. 혼란스러운 마음은 혼란스러운 주문을 만들기 때문에 단지 당신이 원하는 것이 무엇인지를 마음속에서 분명히 해라. 그리고 혼란스러운 주문은 Amazon.com이 잘못하여 당신에게 Timberlake 대신에 Timbaland를 보내는 것을 발생시킬 수 있다.

해설 지문 앞부분에서 주문을 할 때는 원하는 것이 무엇인지를 마음속에서 분명히 해야 한다고 언급한 뒤, 그 방법으로 목록을 작성하라는 조언을 하고 있다. 지문 뒷부분에서 혼란스러운 마음은 혼란스러운 주문을 만들기 때문에 원하는 것이 무엇인지를 마음속에서 분명히 해야 한다고 다시 한 번 강조하여 설명하고 있다. 따라서 필자가 주장하는 바를 '원하는 것이 무엇인지 분명히 해라'라고 표현한 ①번이 정답이다.

어휘 place an order 주문하다 scribble 아무렇게나 쓰다
awesome 최고의, 아주 멋진 goodwill 선의, 호의
hang out 참다, 노력하다 accidentally 잘못하여

19 독해 논리적 흐름 파악 (문맥상 적절한 어휘) 난이도 ★★☆

끊어읽기 해석

The custom of sending greeting cards / to friends and relatives / for special occasions / originated in England, / where the practice was limited to people / who could (A) afford to pay private messengers / to carry their greetings / across great distances.
인사장을 발송하는 풍습은 / 친구들과 친척들에게 / 특별한 행사에 / 영국에서 유래했다 / 이 관행은 사람들에게 한정되었다 / 개인 배달원에게 돈을 지불할 (A) 여유가 있는 / 그들의 인사장을 전달하는 / 꽤 먼 거리를 가로질러

With the (B) advent of a British law / that established inexpensive mail delivery, / a market for sending greeting cards / for birthdays, anniversaries / —almost any occasion imaginable— / opened up overnight.
영국 법률의 (B) 도래로 / 저가 편지 배달을 실시한 / 인사장 발송 시장은 / 생일과 기념일을 위한 / 상상할 수 있는 거의 모든 행사 / 하룻밤 사이에 생겨났다

In America / the card market was (C) expanded / by the founder of Hallmark Cards, / whose company led the way / in other products of social expression / such as gift wrap, stationery, and calendars.
미국에서는 / 인사장 시장이 (C) 확장되었다 / Hallmark Cards사의 창립자에 의해 / 그의 회사가 앞장선 / 다른 인사장 제품에 / 선물 포장지, 편지지, 그리고 달력과 같은

해석 특별한 행사에 친구들과 친척들에게 인사장을 발송하는 풍습은 영국에서 유래했는데, 이 관행은 꽤 먼 거리를 가로질러 그들의 인사장을 전달하는 개인 배달원에게 돈을 지불할 (A) 여유가 있는 사람들에게 한정되었다. 저가 편지 배달을 실시한 영국 법률의 (B) 도래로 생일과 기념일, 상상할 수 있는 거의 모든 행사를 위한 인사장 발송 시장은 하룻밤 사이에 생겨났다. 미국에서는 선물 포장지, 편지지, 그리고 달력과 같은 다른 인사장 제품에 앞장선 Hallmark Cards사의 창립자에 의해 인사장 시장이 (C) 확장되었다.

	(A)	(B)	(C)
①	여유가 있다	도래	확장된
②	여유가 있다	폐지	소비된
③	시도하다	폐지	확장된
④	시도하다	도래	소비된

해설 (A) 빈칸이 있는 문장에서 특별한 행사에 발송하는 인사장은 개인 배달원이 꽤 먼 거리를 가로질러 전달한다고 했으므로, 빈칸에는 개인 배달원에게 돈을 지불할 '여유가 있는'(afford) 사람들이라는 내용이 들어가야 적절하다. (B) 지문 중간에서 행사를 위한 인사장 발송 시장은 하룻밤 사이에 생겨났다고 했으므로, 빈칸에는 저가 편지 배달을 실시한 영국 법률의 '도래'(advent)라는 내용이 들어가야 적절하다. (C) 빈칸이 있는 문장에서 Hallmark Cards사의 창립자는 다른 인사장 제품에 앞장 섰다고 했으므로, 빈칸에는 인사장 시장이 '확장되었다'(expanded)라는 내용이 들어가야 적절하다.
따라서 ① (A) afford(여유가 있다) – (B) advent(도래) – (C) expanded(확장된)가 정답이다.

어휘 custom 풍습, 관습 advent 도래 open up 생겨나다, 만들어지다
overnight 하룻밤 사이에 founder 창립자
lead the way 앞장서다 stationery 편지지, 문방구
abolition 폐지

20 독해 전체내용 파악 (요지 파악) 난이도 ★★☆

끊어읽기 해석

Recently / I was consulting / with a manufacturing company / in direct competitive bid warfare / with a lower-price opponent.
최근에 / 나는 상담하고 있었다 / 한 제조 회사와 / 직접적인 경쟁입찰 싸움 중인 / 저가 경쟁사와

My client was losing / bid after bid.
나의 고객은 지고 있었다 / 계속해서 입찰에서

I said, "Something has to change here." // They said, / "It can't. // We can't cut our prices any lower."
나는 말했다 / "지금 무언가가 바뀌어야 합니다" / 그들은 말했다 / "그럴 수 없습니다 // 우리는 가격을 더 이상 낮출 수 없어요."

I said, / "If we can't come in / with the lower bid, / we might as well come in / with an even higher bid / —but let's change / the rules of the game / when we do it."
나는 말했다 / "우리가 참여할 수 없다면 / 더 낮은 입찰가격으로 / 우리는 참여하는 편이 낫습니다 / 훨씬 더 높은 입찰가격으로 / 하지만 바꿔 봅시다 / 게임의 규칙을 / 우리가 입찰할 때"

They began / changing the specifications for the bids, / adding value, / bundling goods and services together, / extending warranties, / and including delivery and completion guarantees.

그들은 시작했다 / 입찰을 위한 사양을 바꾸고 / 가치를 더하고 / 상품과 서비스를 함께 일괄된 가격에 제공하고 / 보증기간을 연장하고 / 또한 배송 및 책임준공을 포함하기

Then / we built / a "How to Compare Our Bid with Others Checklist."
그러고 나서 / 우리는 만들어냈다 / '점검표로 자사의 입찰을 타사와 비교하는 방법'을

When it was all said and done, / my client started getting projects / the company had been losing / to low bidders before.
모든 것이 고려되었을 때 / 나의 고객은 사업을 낙찰받기 시작했다 / 회사가 빼앗겨졌던 / 이전에 낮은 가격의 입찰자들에게

해석 최근에 나는 저가 경쟁사와 직접적인 경쟁입찰 싸움 중인 한 제조 회사와 상담하고 있었다. 나의 고객은 계속해서 입찰에서 지고 있었다. 나는 "지금 무언가가 바뀌어야 합니다."라고 말했다. 그들은 "그럴 수 없습니다. 우리는 가격을 더 이상 낮출 수 없어요."라고 말했다. 나는 "우리가 더 낮은 입찰가격으로 참여할 수 없다면, 우리는 훨씬 더 높은 입찰가격으로 참여하는 편이 낫습니다. 하지만 우리가 입찰할 때 게임의 규칙을 바꿔 봅시다."라고 말했다. 그들은 입찰을 위한 사양을 바꾸고, 가치를 더하고, 상품과 서비스를 함께 일괄된 가격에 제공하고, 보증기간을 연장하고, 또한 배송 및 책임준공을 포함하기 시작했다. 그러고 나서 우리는 '점검표로 자사의 입찰을 타사와 비교하는 방법'을 만들어냈다. 모든 것이 고려되었을 때, 나의 고객은 회사가 이전에 낮은 가격의 입찰자들에게 빼앗겨왔던 사업을 낙찰받기 시작했다.

해설 지문 전반에 걸쳐 저가 경쟁사와 경쟁입찰 싸움 중인 한 제조 회사를 상담했던 저자가 고객에게 더 낮은 입찰가격으로 참여하는 대신에 입찰 조건을 개선하여 훨씬 더 높은 입찰가격으로 참여하라는 조언을 해서 결국 고객의 회사가 빼앗겨왔던 사업을 낙찰받기 시작했다는 것을 설명하고 있다. 따라서 저자가 주장하는 바를 '입찰가격을 못 내리면 다른 부분의 질을 높여야 한다'라고 표현한 ④번이 정답이다.

어휘 direct 직접적인 bid 입찰, 입찰가격 warfare 싸움
specification 사양, 명세서 bundle 일괄된 가격에 제공하다
extend 연장하다

21 독해 세부내용 파악 (내용 일치 파악) 난이도 ★★☆

끊어읽기 해석

① By 1993 / more than 56 million American households / owned dogs, / and consumers spent $15 billion / on veterinary care, dog food, toys, accessories, and funeral arrangements.
1933년까지 / 5천6백만이 넘는 미국 가구가 / 개를 키웠다 / 그리고 소비자들은 150억 달러를 소비했다 / 수의학적 관리, 개의 먹이, 장난감, 액세서리, 그리고 장례 절차에

② Not only do more Americans own dogs, / but an unprecedented number of animals / are enjoying elevated status / as true members of the family.
더 많은 미국인들이 개를 키울 뿐만 아니라 / 전례 없는 수의 동물들이 / 높아진 지위를 누리고 있다 / 진정한 가족 구성원으로서의

In a recent survey / of ten thousand households, / almost 70 percent of respondents said / they would risk their own lives / to save their dogs.
최근 설문 조사에서 / 만 가구에 대한 / 응답자 중 거의 70퍼센트가 말했다 / 그들은 목숨을 걸 것이라고 / 자신의 개를 구하기 위해

③ A nearly equal number of people also said / they would seek emergency medical care / for their pets / before

obtaining it / for themselves.
또한 거의 동일한 수의 사람들은 말했다 / 응급 치료를 요구할 것이라고 / 애완동물을 위해 / 이것을 받기 전에 / 자신을 위해

④ Three-quarters of the respondents said / they routinely give / wrapped Christmas and birthday presents / to their dogs.
응답자 중 4분의 3은 말했다 / 그들이 일상적으로 준다 / 포장된 성탄절 선물과 생일 선물을 / 자신들의 개에게

해석 1933년까지 5천6백만이 넘는 미국 가구가 개를 키웠고, 소비자들은 150억 달러를 수의학적 관리, 개의 먹이, 장난감, 액세서리, 그리고 장례 절차에 소비했다. 더 많은 미국인들이 개를 키울 뿐만 아니라, 전례 없는 수의 동물들이 진정한 가족 구성원으로서의 높아진 지위를 누리고 있다. 최근 만 가구에 대한 설문 조사에서 응답자 중 거의 70퍼센트가 그들은 자신의 개를 구하기 위해 목숨을 걸 것이라고 말했다. 또한 거의 동일한 수의 사람들은 자신을 위해 응급 치료를 받기 전에 애완동물을 위해 이것을 요구할 것이라고 말했다. 응답자 중 4분의 3은 그들이 일상적으로 자신들의 개에게 포장된 성탄절 선물과 생일 선물을 준다고 말했다.

해설 지문 중간에 만 가구에 대한 설문 조사에서 응답자 중 거의 70퍼센트가 자신을 위해 응급 치료를 받기 전에 애완동물을 위해 이것을 요구할 것이라고 말했다는 내용이 있으므로, 최근 만 가구에 대한 설문 조사에서 응답자 중 약 70퍼센트가 자신보다 애완동물에게 먼저 응급 치료를 받도록 할 것이라고 말했다는 것을 알 수 있다. 따라서 ③번이 정답이다.

오답 분석
① 1933년까지 소비자들은 150억 달러를 수의학적 관리, 개의 먹이, 장난감 등에 소비했다고 했으므로, 1993년까지 5천6백만이 넘는 미국 가구가 개를 키우고 15억 달러의 돈을 개를 돌보는데 소비했다는 것은 지문의 내용과 다르다.
② 전례 없는 수의 동물들이 가족 구성원으로서의 높아진 지위를 누리고 있다고는 했지만, 미국에서 많은 반려 동물들이 가족들보다 더 높은 지위를 즐기고 있는지는 알 수 없다.
④ 설문 조사 응답자 중 4분의 3이 일상적으로 자신들의 개에게 포장된 성탄절 선물과 생일 선물을 준다고 했으므로, 전체 미국인들의 약 75퍼센트가 그렇게 한다고 말했다는 것은 지문의 내용과 다르다.

어휘 veterinary 수의학의 funeral arrangement 장례 절차
unprecedented 전례 없는 elevated 높아진
respondent 응답자 seek 요구하다 emergency 응급, 비상
routinely 일상적으로

22 독해 전체내용 파악 (제목 파악) 난이도 ★★☆

끊어읽기 해석

Web ads very frequently instruct / users to *click here*. // In online advertising, / the imperative is an indicator / of direct user addressing.
인터넷 광고는 매우 자주 지시한다 / 사용자들에게 '이곳을 클릭하라'고 // 온라인 광고에서 / 명령문은 하나의 장치이다 / 사용자에게 직접적으로 말을 거는

As a matter of language use, / these directive speech acts / are not strict commands, / which would be too offensive an addressing / in the advertising context.
언어 사용에서 / 이러한 지시적인 발화 행위는 / 엄격한 명령이 아니다 / 지나치게 공격적인 말하기일 수 있는 / 광고의 맥락에서

Instead, / they function / as a kind of polite request / with a reduced impact / on interactants.
대신에 / 이것은 기능한다 / 일종의 정중한 요청으로서 / 줄어든 영향을 미치는 / 상호작용하는 사람들에게

The illocutionary force of the advertising message / gives the users / some space to act.
광고 메시지의 발화 수반력은 / 사용자들에게 준다 / 행동을 취할 시간을

In their implicit communication, / it is initially the advertiser / who wants something from the user, / and not vice versa.
그들의 암시적인 의사소통에서 / 애당초 광고주이다 / 사용자에게 무언가를 원하는 사람은 / 그 반대가 아니다

Nevertheless, / the use of imperatives / is still far more forceful, more striking, and often shorter / than a politely worded request or an indirect speech act / that avoids imposing on the other.
그럼에도 불구하고 / 명령문의 사용은 / 여전히 훨씬 더 설득력 있고, 더 눈에 띄며, 흔히 더 짧게 느껴진다 / 정중하게 쓰인 요청이나 간접적인 발화 행위보다 / 다른 사람에게 강요하는 것을 피하는

Online advertising / needs to initiate an action, / and for this reason, / imperatives are employed.
온라인 광고는 / 행위를 일으켜야 한다 / 그리고 이러한 이유로 / 명령문이 사용된다

According to DoubleClick.com, / the instruction *click here* tends to increase / click rates / by 15 percent.
DoubleClick.com에 따르면 / '이곳을 클릭하라'는 지시는 증가시키는 경향이 있다 / 클릭률을 / 15퍼센트까지

해석 인터넷 광고는 사용자들에게 '이곳을 클릭하라'고 매우 자주 지시한다. 온라인 광고에서 명령문은 사용자에게 직접적으로 말을 거는 하나의 장치이다. 언어 사용에서, 이러한 지시적인 발화 행위는 광고의 맥락에서 지나치게 공격적인 말하기일 수 있는 엄격한 명령이 아니다. 대신에, 이것은 상호작용하는 사람들에게 줄어든 영향을 미치는 일종의 정중한 요청으로서 기능한다. 광고 메시지의 발화 수반력은 사용자들에게 행동을 취할 시간을 준다. 그들의 암시적인 의사소통에서, 애당초 사용자에게 무언가를 원하는 사람은 광고주이지 그 반대가 아니다. 그럼에도 불구하고, 명령문의 사용은 정중하게 쓰인 요청이나 다른 사람에게 강요하는 것을 피하는 간접적인 발화 행위보다 여전히 훨씬 더 설득력 있고, 더 눈에 띄며, 흔히 더 짧게 느껴진다. 온라인 광고는 행위를 일으켜야 하고, 이러한 이유로 명령문이 사용된다. DoubleClick.com에 따르면, '이곳을 클릭하라'는 지시는 클릭률을 15퍼센트까지 증가시키는 경향이 있다.

① 사람들은 인터넷 광고에 어떻게 반응하는가?
② 더 많은 판매를 위해 DoubleClick.com을 광고하는 것
③ 인터넷 광고는 왜 명령문을 사용하는가?
④ 인터넷 광고의 기능

해설 지문 처음에서 인터넷 광고는 명령문을 사용한다고 한 뒤, 지문 중간에서 이러한 지시적인 발화 행위는 엄격한 명령이 아니라 일종의 정중한 요청으로서 기능하며 사용자들에게 행동을 취할 시간을 준다고 설명하고 있다. 또한 지문 마지막에서 명령문은 정중하게 쓰인 요청이나 간접적인 발화 행위보다 훨씬 더 설득력 있고 더 눈에 띌 뿐만 아니라 더 짧게 느껴진다고 하며 광고에서 명령문을 사용하는 이유를 설명하고 있다. 따라서 이 지문의 제목을 '인터넷 광고는 왜 명령문을 사용하는가?'라고 표현한 ③번이 정답이다.

어휘 instruct 지시하다, 명령하다 imperative 명령문
indicator 장치, 지시하는 것 address 말을 걸다
directive 지시적인 offensive 공격적인
interactant 상호작용하는 사람 illocutionary force 발화 수반력
implicit 암시적인 vice versa 반대로, 거꾸로 forceful 설득력 있는
striking 눈에 띄는 impose 강요하다, 간섭하다
initiate 일으키다, 시작하다

23 독해 논리적 흐름 파악 (문맥상 부적절한 어휘)   난이도 ★★☆

끊어읽기 해석

Statistical studies / in a broad spectrum / of developing countries / have provided strong support / for the economic theory of fertility.
통계학적 연구들은 / 폭넓은 범위의 / 개발 도상국에 관한 / 강력한 증거를 제공해왔다 / 출산율에 대한 경제 이론에

For example, / it has been found / that high female employment opportunities / outside the home / and greater female school attendance, / especially at the primary and secondary levels, / are associated with significantly ① lower levels of fertility.
예를 들어 / 밝혀졌다 / 높은 여성 취업 기회는 / 가정 외부에서의 / 그리고 더 높은 여성 학교 출석률은 / 특히 초등 및 중등 교육 수준에서의 / 현저하게 ① 더 낮은 수준의 출산율과 관련이 있는 것으로

As women become better educated, / they tend to earn / a larger share of household income / and to produce fewer children.
여성이 더 좋은 교육을 받게 되면서 / 그들은 버는 경향이 있다 / 가계 소득의 더 큰 부분을 / 그리고 더 적은 수의 아이들을 낳는 (경향이 있다)

Moreover, / these studies have confirmed / the ② strong association / between declines in child mortality and the subsequent decline in fertility.
게다가 / 이러한 연구들은 확인했다 / ② 강력한 연관성을 / 아동 사망률의 감소와 그로 인한 출산율의 감소 사이의

Assuming / that households desire a target number of surviving children, / increased female education and higher levels of income / can decrease child mortality / and therefore ③ decrease the chances / that the firstborn will survive.
가정하면 / 가정이 목표로 하는 수의 살아남은 아이들을 바란다고 / 증가한 여성 교육과 더 높은 소득 수준은 / 아동 사망률을 줄일 수 있다 / 그리고 따라서 가능성을 ③ 감소시킬 (수 있다) / 첫째 아이가 살아남을

As a result, / fewer births may be necessary / to attain the same number of surviving children.
결과적으로 / 더 적은 출산이 불가피할 수도 있다 / 같은 수의 살아남은 아이들을 얻기 위해서는

This fact alone / ④ underscores the importance / of educating women and improving public health and child nutrition programs / in reducing fertility levels
이 사실 하나만으로도 / 중요성을 ④ 분명히 보여 준다 / 여성을 교육하는 것과 공공 보건 그리고 어린이 영양 프로그램을 개선하는 것의 / 출산율을 감소시키는 데 있어

해석 개발 도상국에 관한 폭넓은 범위의 통계학적 연구들은 출산율에 대한 경제 이론에 강력한 증거를 제공해왔다. 예를 들어, 가정 외부에서의 높은 여성 취업 기회와 특히 초등 및 중등 교육 수준에서의 더 높은 여성 학교 출석률은 현저하게 ① 더 낮은 수준의 출산율과 관련이 있는 것으로 밝혀졌다. 여성이 더 좋은 교육을 받게 되면서, 그들은 가계 소득의 더 큰 부분을 벌고 더 적은 수의 아이들을 낳는 경향이 있다. 게다가, 이러한 연구들은 아동 사망률의 감소와 그로 인한 출산율의 감소 사이의 ② 강력한 연관성을 확인했다. 가정이 목표로 하는 수의 살아남은 아이들을 바란다고 가정하면, 증가한 여성 교육과 더 높은 소득 수준은 아동 사망률을 줄일 수 있고 따라서 첫째 아이가 살아남을 가능성을 ③ 감소시킬 수 있다. 결과적으로, 같은 수의 살아남은 아이들을 얻기 위해서는 더 적은 출산이 불가피할 수도 있다. 이 사실 하나만으로도 출산율을 감소시키는 데 있어 여성을 교육하는 것과 공공 보건 그리고 어린이 영양 프로그램을 개선하는 것의 중요성을 ④ 분명히 보여 준다.

해설 지문 중간에서 증가한 여성 교육과 더 높은 소득 수준은 아동 사망률을 줄일 수 있다고 했으므로, 첫째 아이가 살아남을 가능성을 '감소시킨다'(decrease)는 것은 문맥상 적절하지 않다. 따라서 ③ decrease가 정답이다. 참고로, 주어진 decrease를 대신할 수 있는 어휘로는 '증가시키다'라는 의미의 increase, augment 등이 있다.

어휘 broad 폭넓은 spectrum 범위 fertility 출산율
secondary 중등 교육의 mortality 사망률 attain 얻다
underscore 분명히 보여 주다, 강조하다 nutrition 영양

24 독해 세부내용 파악 (내용 불일치 파악) 난이도 ★★★

끊어읽기 해석

If there's anyone / in this assembly, / any dear friend of Caesar's, / I say to him / that my love for Caesar / was no less than his.
만일 한 명이라도 있다면 / 이 의회에 / 카이사르의 친애하는 벗이 / 저는 그에게 말씀드리고자 합니다 / 카이사르를 향한 저의 사랑이 / 그의 것(사랑)에 못지않다고

If, then, / that friend demands to know / why I rose against Caesar, / this is my answer: / it's not that I loved Caesar less, but that I loved Rome more.
그리고 나서 만약 / 그 벗이 알고 싶어 하신다면 / 제가 왜 카이사르에 맞서 반란을 일으켰는지를 / 이것이 저의 대답입니다 / 제가 카이사르를 덜 사랑해서가 아니라 제가 로마를 더 사랑했기 때문입니다

Would you prefer to die / in slavery / with Caesar living / or would you be free / with Caesar dead?
여러분은 죽기를 원하십니까 / 노예로 / 카이사르가 살고 / 아니면 여러분이 자유롭게 되길 원하십니까 / 카이사르가 죽고?

As Caesar loved me, / I wept for him. // As he was fortunate, / I rejoiced.
카이사르가 저를 사랑했기에 / 저는 그를 위해 눈물을 흘렸습니다 // 그에게 행운이 따랐기에 / 저는 크게 기뻤습니다

As he was brave, / I honored him. // But as he was ambitious, / I killed him.
그가 용맹했기에 / 저는 그를 존경했습니다 // 그러나 그가 야심을 품었기에 / 저는 그를 죽였습니다

There are / tears for his love, joy for his fortune, honor for his bravery, and death for his ambition.
(~가) 있습니다 / 그의 사랑에 대한 눈물이, 그의 행운에 대한 기쁨이, 그의 용맹에 대한 존경이, 그리고 그의 야심에 대한 죽음이

Who here is so base a man / that he would want to be a slave? // If any, speak, / for I have offended him.
여기 있는 사람 중에 누가 너무도 비겁하여 / 노예가 되고자 하십니까? // 만약 있다면 말씀하십시오 / 제가 그를 불쾌하게 했으니

Who here is so barbarous / that he wouldn't want to be a Roman? // If any, speak, / for I have offended him.
여기 있는 사람 중에 누가 너무도 야만스러워서 / 로마인이기를 원하지 않으십니까? // 만약 있다면 말씀하십시오 / 제가 그를 불쾌하게 했으니

Who here is so wicked / that he does not love his country? / If any, speak, / for I have offended him.
여기 있는 사람 중에 누가 너무도 사악하여 / 자신의 조국을 사랑하지 않으십니까? / 만약 있다면 말씀하십시오 / 제가 그를 불쾌하게 했으니

I pause / for a reply.
저는 잠시 멈추겠습니다 / 대답을 위해

해석 만일 이 의회에 카이사르의 친애하는 벗이 한 명이라도 있다면, 저는 그에게 카이사르를 향한 저의 사랑이 그의 것(사랑)에 못지않다고 말씀드리고자 합니다. 그리고 나서 만약 그 벗이 제가 왜 카이사르에 맞서 반란을 일으켰는지를 알고 싶어 하신다면, 이것이

저의 대답입니다. 제가 카이사르를 덜 사랑해서가 아니라, 제가 로마를 더 사랑했기 때문입니다. 여러분은 카이사르가 살고 노예로 죽기를 원하십니까 아니면 카이사르가 죽고 여러분이 자유롭게 되길 원하십니까? 카이사르가 저를 사랑했기에, 저는 그를 위해 눈물을 흘렸습니다. 그에게 행운이 따랐기에, 저는 크게 기뻐했습니다. 그가 용맹했기에, 저는 그를 존경했습니다. 그러나 그가 야심을 품었기에, 저는 그를 죽였습니다. 그의 사랑에 대한 눈물이, 그의 행운에 대한 기쁨이, 그의 용맹에 대한 존경이, 그리고 그의 야심에 대한 죽음이 있습니다. 여기 있는 사람 중에 누가 너무도 비겁하여 노예가 되고자 하십니까? 만약 있다면, 제가 그를 불쾌하게 했으니 말씀하십시오. 여기 있는 사람 중에 누가 너무도 야만스러워서 로마인이기를 원하지 않으십니까? 만약 있다면 제가 그를 불쾌하게 했으니 말씀하십시오. 여기 있는 사람 중에 누가 너무도 사악하여 자신의 조국을 사랑하지 않으십니까? 만약 있다면 제가 그를 불쾌하게 했으니 말씀하십시오. 저는 대답을 위해 잠시 멈추겠습니다.

해설 지문 중간에 사람들에게 카이사르가 살고 노예로 죽기를 바라는지 아니면 카이사르가 죽고 자유롭게 되길 원하는지를 질문하며 카이사르의 죽음이 노예제도의 폐지와 자유로 이어짐을 암시하는 내용이 있으므로, Caesar(카이사르)가 죽게 되면 로마시민들은 노예의 처지에서 살게 된다는 것은 지문의 내용과 반대이다. 따라서 ③번이 정답이다.

어휘 assembly 의회 rise 반란을 일으키다 slavery 노예
weep 눈물을 흘리다 rejoice 크게 기뻐하다 ambitious 야심을 품은
base 비겁한, 비도덕적인 offend 불쾌하게 하다
barbarous 야만스러운 wicked 사악한

25 독해 전체내용 파악 (주제 파악) 난이도 ★★☆

끊어읽기 해석

There is a widely held notion / that does plenty of damage, / the notion of 'scientifically proved.'
널리 신봉되는 개념이 있다 / 많은 해를 끼치는 / '과학적으로 증명된'이라는 개념이다

It is nearly an oxymoron. // The very foundation of science / is to keep the door open to doubt.
이것은 거의 모순 어법이다. // 과학의 참된 기초는 / 의심의 문을 항상 열어두는 것이다

Precisely because we keep questioning everything, / especially our own premises, / we are always ready / to improve our knowledge.
바로 우리가 계속해서 모든 것에 의문을 제기하기 때문에 / 특히 우리가 가진 전제에 관해 / 우리는 언제나 준비가 되어 있다 / 우리의 지식을 향상시킬

Therefore / a good scientist is never 'certain.'
그러므로 / 훌륭한 과학자는 절대로 '확신하지' 않는다

Lack of certainty is precisely / what makes conclusions more reliable / than the conclusions / of those who are certain, / because the good scientist will be ready / to shift to a different point of view / if better evidence or novel arguments emerge.
확신의 부족이야말로 바로 / 결론을 더 신뢰할 수 있게 만드는 것이다 / 결론보다 / 확신하는 사람의 / 훌륭한 과학자는 준비가 되어 있을 것이기 때문에 / 다른 관점으로 바꿀 / 더 알맞은 증거나 새로운 주장이 생겨나면

Therefore / certainty is not only something useless / but is also in fact damaging, / if we value reliability.
그러므로 / 확신은 쓸모없는 것일 뿐만 아니라 / 사실 해를 끼치기도 하는 것이다 / 만약 우리가 신뢰성을 가치 있게 생각한다면

해석 널리 신봉되는 개념이 있는데, 이는 많은 해를 끼치는 '과학적으로 증명된'이라는 개념이다. 이것은 거의 모순 어법이다. 과학의 참된 기초는 의심의 문을 항상 열어두는 것이다. 바로 우리가 계속해서 모든 것에, 특히 우리가 가진 전제에 관해 의문을 제기하기 때문에, 우리는 언제나 우리의 지식을 향상시킬 준비가 되어 있다. 그러므로 훌륭한 과학자는 절대로 '확신하지' 않는다. 훌륭한 과학자는 더 알맞은 증거나 새로운 주장이 생겨나면 다른 관점으로 바꿀 준비가 되어 있을 것이기 때문에 확신의 부족이야말로 바로 결론을 확신하는 사람의 결론보다 더 신뢰할 수 있게 만드는 것이다. 그러므로 확신은 쓸모없는 것일 뿐만 아니라 만약 우리가 신뢰성을 가치 있게 생각한다면 사실 해를 끼치기도 하는 것이다.

① 신뢰성은 지식을 가치 있게 생각한다
② 과학적 확신은 쓸모없다
③ 변할 수 있는 결론들은 무한하다
④ 의문을 제기하는 것은 이론의 유효성을 약화시킨다

해설 지문 전반에 걸쳐 과학의 참된 기초는 의심의 문을 항상 열어두는 것이고 훌륭한 과학자는 절대 확신하지 않기 때문에, 확신은 쓸모없는 것일 뿐만 아니라 만약 우리가 신뢰성을 가치 있게 생각한다면 확신이 해를 끼치기도 한다고 설명하고 있다. 따라서 이 지문의 주제를 '과학적 확신은 쓸모없다'라고 표현한 ②번이 정답이다.

어휘 oxymoron 모순 어법 foundation 기초, 토대 doubt 의심, 의혹
precisely 바로, 정확히 premise 전제 certain 확신하는
reliable 신뢰할 수 있는 novel 새로운, 신기한
emerge 생겨나다, 나오다 confidence 확신 infinite 무한한
theoretical 이론의 validity 유효성

정답

p.110

01	② 독해 – 전체내용 파악	11	④ 독해 – 추론	21	① 독해 – 전체내용 파악
02	④ 독해 – 세부내용 파악	12	① 독해 – 전체내용 파악	22	④ 독해 – 논리적 흐름 파악
03	③ 독해 – 전체내용 파악	13	② 독해 – 논리적 흐름 파악	23	④ 독해 – 논리적 흐름 파악
04	④ 독해 – 전체내용 파악	14	④ 독해 – 전체내용 파악	24	③ 독해 – 논리적 흐름 파악
05	④ 문법 – 전치사	15	③ 독해 – 세부내용 파악	25	③ 독해 – 전체내용 파악
06	① 독해 – 전체내용 파악	16	① 독해 – 세부내용 파악		
07	② 독해 – 전체내용 파악	17	③ 독해 – 추론		
08	① 독해 – 추론	18	① 문법 – 명사절		
09	③ 독해 – 논리적 흐름 파악	19	④ 독해 – 논리적 흐름 파악		
10	③ 독해 – 논리적 흐름 파악	20	③ 독해 – 논리적 흐름 파악		

취약영역 분석표

영역	세부 유형	문항 수	소계
어휘	어휘 & 표현	0	/0
	생활영어	0	
문법	전치사	1	/2
	명사절	1	
독해	전체내용 파악	9	/23
	세부내용 파악	3	
	추론	3	
	논리적 흐름 파악	8	
총계			/25

· 자신이 취약한 영역은 '법원직 9급 영어, 이렇게 출제된다!'(p.8)를 통해 다시 한 번 확인하고 학습하시기 바랍니다.

---

01 독해 전체내용 파악 (제목 파악)

난이도 ★★☆

끊어읽기 해석

Subject: Annual Photography Contest of Liz Claiborne
제목: Liz Claiborne의 연례 사진 대회

Inspired by the Special Olympics, / this year's theme highlights / competitive and charitable sports situations / among Liz Claiborne, Inc., employees, their families, their friends.
스페셜 올림픽에 감명을 받아서 / 올해의 주제는 강조합니다 / 경쟁을 하고 자선을 베푸는 스포츠 환경을 / 주식회사 Liz Claiborne의 직원들, 그들의 가족들, 친구들 간의

You might snap / a shot of a friend or employee / participating in / a walkathon to raise funds, a five-mile run, or a company volleyball or soccer game.
당신은 찍을 수 있습니다 / 친구나 직원의 사진을 / 참가하는 / 기금을 모으기 위한 걷기 대회, 5마일 달리기, 또는 단체 배구나 축구 경기에

All Liz Claiborne, Inc., employees worldwide / are encouraged to submit photos.
전 세계의 주식회사 Liz Claiborne의 모든 직원들은 / 사진을 제출하도록 권장됩니다

The first, second, and third prizes / will again be $500, $250, and $100.
1등, 2등, 그리고 3등 상금은 / 다시 500달러, 250달러, 그리고 100달러가 될 것입니다

Now's the time for you to start / taking pictures focused on the spirit of competition / for Liz Claiborne people and friends!
이제는 당신이 시작할 때입니다 / 경쟁의 정신에 중점을 둔 사진을 찍는 것을 / Liz Claiborne 사람들과 친구들의!

Because of the overwhelming number of entries / last year, / we're making one contest change / this year.
엄청난 수의 참가자들 때문에 / 지난해의 / 우리는 대회에 한 가지 변화를 만들었습니다 / 이번 해에

For further information / call Rosemary at Extension 7645.
더 많은 정보를 위해서는 / 내선 7645번 Rosemary에게 전화하세요

해석 제목: Liz Claiborne의 연례 사진 대회
스페셜 올림픽에 감명을 받아서, 올해의 주제는 주식회사 Liz Claiborne의 직원들, 그들의 가족들, 친구들 간의 경쟁을 하고 자선을 베푸는 스포츠 환경을 강조합니다. 당신은 기금을 모으기 위한 걷기 대회, 5마일 달리기, 또는 단체 배구나 축구 경기에 참가하는 친구나 직원의 사진을 찍을 수 있습니다. 전 세계의 주식회사 Liz Claiborne의 모든 직원들은 사진을 제출하도록 권장됩니다. 1등, 2등, 그리고 3등 상금은 다시 500달러, 250달러, 그리고 100달러가 될 것입니다. 이제는 당신이 Liz Claiborne 사람들과 친구들의 경쟁의 정신에 중점을 둔 사진을 찍는 것을 시작할 때입니다! 지난해의 엄청난 수의 참가자들 때문에, 이번 해에 우리는 대회에 한 가지 변화를 만들었습니다. 더 많은 정보를 위해서는 내선 7645번 Rosemary에게 전화하세요.

① 스페셜 올림픽: 시간과 장소
② Liz Claiborne의 연례 사진 대회
③ Liz Claiborne의 진보된 서비스 품질
④ 크리스마스의 기조 연설

해설 지문 중간에서 주식회사 Liz Claiborne의 모든 직원들이 사진을 찍어 제출하는 것이 권장된다고 했고, 이어서 대회의 상금에 대해 알려 주며 경쟁의 정신에 중점을 둔 사진을 찍을 것을 권하고 있다. 따라서 이 이메일의 제목을 'Liz Claiborne의 연례 사진 대회'라고 표현한 ②번이 정답이다.

어휘 inspire 감명을 주다 theme 주제 charitable 자선을 베푸는
walkathon 걷기 대회, 장거리 경보 entry 참가자
annual 연례의 keynote speech 기조 연설

끊어읽기 해석

> Anger makes problems for relationships / when there is too much of ① it, / and when people are unable to control / the way they express it, / and become, for instance, argumentative, aggressive, or violent.
> 분노는 관계에서 문제를 일으킨다 / ① 그것이 너무 많을 때 / 그리고 사람들이 제어하지 못할 때 / 그들이 이를 표현하는 방식을 / 그래서 예를 들어 (그것이) 논쟁적이고, 공격적이거나, 폭력적이 될 때
>
> It also causes problems / when people cannot express their anger / and try to keep ② it hidden.
> 그것은 또한 문제를 일으킨다 / 사람들이 그들의 분노를 표현하지 못할 때 / 그리고 ② 그것을 숨겨 두려 할 때
>
> It is normal, however, / to feel angry at times, / and it can also have useful effects.
> 하지만 정상적이다 / 때때로 분노를 느끼는 것은 / 그리고 그것은 또한 유용한 효과가 있을 수 있다
>
> Anger can mobilize you to take action, / for example, / to set limits / to the demands others make of you, / to think about / why something matters to you / or to defend yourself / if attacked.
> 분노는 당신이 행동을 취하도록 할 수 있다 / 예를 들어 / 제한하기 위해 / 다른 사람들이 당신에게 하는 요구를 / 생각하기 위해 / 어떤 것이 왜 당신에게 문제가 되는지 / 또는 스스로를 방어하기 위해 / 공격받았을 때
>
> ③ It can be constructively expressed, / and prompt you to explain / what ④ it is that is distressing or alarming you, / and to ask for / what you need.
> ③ 그것은 건설적으로 표현될 수 있다 / 그리고 당신이 설명하도록 할 수 있다 / 당신을 괴롭히거나 불안하게 하는 ④ 것이 무엇인지 / 그리고 요청하도록 (할 수 있다) / 당신이 필요한 것을

해석　분노는 ① 그것이 너무 많을 때, 그리고 사람들이 이를 표현하는 방식을 제어하지 못해서 예를 들어 (그것이) 논쟁적이고, 공격적이거나, 폭력적이 될 때 관계에서 문제를 일으킨다. 그것은 또한 사람들이 그들의 분노를 표현하지 못하고 ② 그것을 숨겨 두려 할 때 문제를 일으킨다. 하지만 때때로 분노를 느끼는 것은 정상적이고, 그것은 또한 유용한 효과가 있을 수 있다. 예를 들어, 분노는 다른 사람들이 당신에게 하는 요구를 제한하거나, 어떤 것이 왜 당신에게 문제가 되는지 생각하거나, 또는 공격받았을 때 스스로를 방어하기 위해 당신이 행동을 취하도록 할 수 있다. ③ 그것은 건설적으로 표현될 수 있고, 당신을 괴롭히거나 불안하게 하는 ④ 것이 무엇인지 설명하도록 할 수 있고, 당신이 필요한 것을 요청하도록 할 수 있다.

해설　①, ②, ③번의 대명사 it은 모두 anger(분노)를 지칭하지만 ④번은 that is distressing or alarming you(당신을 괴롭히거나 불안하게 하는 것)를 지칭하므로 ④번이 정답이다.

어휘　argumentative 논쟁적인, 시비를 거는　set limits to ~을 제한하다
constructively 건설적으로　prompt (~하도록) 하다, 촉발하다
distress 괴롭히다　alarm 불안하게 하다

---

03 **독해** 전체내용 파악 (글의 감상)　난이도 ★☆☆

끊어읽기 해석

> Are you embarrassed / by excessive body hair / or body hair in the most awkward areas?
> 당신은 난처합니까 / 지나친 체모로 인해 / 또는 가장 곤란한 곳에 있는 체모로 (인해)?
>
> Well, you can remove / unsightly, unwanted hair / with laser

---

hair removal treatment.
자, 당신은 제거할 수 있습니다 / 보기 흉하고 원하지 않는 털을 / 레이저 제모 치료로

> Laser hair removal is / a safe and effective medical procedure / that uses laser light / to remove unwanted hair painlessly / within a few minutes.
> 레이저 제모는 / 안전하고 효과적인 의학적 시술입니다 / 레이저 광선을 사용하는 / 원치 않는 털을 고통 없이 제거하기 위해 / 몇 분 내로
>
> During the procedure, / the laser passes through the skin / and hits the hair follicle / where hair growth originates.
> 그 시술 동안 / 레이저는 피부를 통과합니다 / 그리고 모낭에 도달합니다 / 털의 성장이 시작되는
>
> Thereafter, / the intense heat destroys / the hair follicle instantly, / clearing the skin of any hair.
> 그 후에 / 강한 열이 파괴합니다 / 모낭을 즉시 / 피부에서 모든 털을 제거하면서
>
> Treat / your legs, armpits, upper lip, chin, bikini line, and any other area.
> 치료하세요 / 당신의 다리, 겨드랑이, 윗입술, 턱, 비키니 라인, 그리고 다른 어떤 부위든
>
> You can finally be free / of unwanted body hair, / so call our clinic today / for more information.
> 당신은 마침내 자유로워질 수 있습니다 / 원치 않는 체모로부터 / 그러니 오늘 저희 진료소로 전화하세요 / 더 많은 정보를 위해

해석　당신은 지나친 체모나 가장 곤란한 곳에 있는 체모로 인해 난처합니까? 자, 당신은 보기 흉하고 원하지 않는 털을 레이저 제모 치료로 제거할 수 있습니다. 레이저 제모는 원치 않는 털을 몇 분 내로 고통 없이 제거하기 위해 레이저 광선을 사용하는 안전하고 효과적인 의학적 시술입니다. 그 시술 동안, 레이저는 피부를 통과하고 털의 성장이 시작되는 모낭에 도달합니다. 그 후에, 강한 열이 모낭을 즉시 파괴하고, 피부에서 모든 털을 제거합니다. 당신의 다리, 겨드랑이, 윗입술, 턱, 비키니 라인, 그리고 다른 어떤 부위든 치료하세요. 당신은 마침내 원치 않는 체모로부터 자유로워질 수 있으니, 더 많은 정보를 위해 오늘 저희 진료소로 전화하세요.

① 수필　　　　　　② 소설
③ 광고　　　　　　④ 기사

해설　지문 전반에 걸쳐 필자는 레이저 제모 치료에 대해 설명하며 그것의 안전성과 효과를 홍보하고 있다. 또한 지문 마지막에서 더 많은 정보를 위해서는 진료소로 전화하라고 안내하고 있다. 따라서 이 글의 종류를 '광고'라고 표현한 ③번이 정답이다.

어휘　excessive 지나친　awkward (처리하기) 곤란한, 어색한
unsightly 보기 흉한　painlessly 고통 없이　follicle 모낭
originate 시작되다　clear 제거하다, 치우다　armpit 겨드랑이

---

04 **독해** 전체내용 파악 (요지 파악)　난이도 ★☆☆

끊어읽기 해석

> 'Zero tolerance' is a phrase / that first came to light / as a description of the crackdown / on trivial crime.
> '무관용 원칙'은 문구이다 / 처음 알려진 / 엄중 단속의 묘사로서 / 사소한 범죄에 대한
>
> The aim of zero tolerance is to prevent / petty criminals graduating to serious crime / by imposing immediate and harsh sentences / for trivial offences / such as under-age drinking, small-scale drug use and dealing, shoplifting or vandalism.
> 무관용 원칙의 목적은 방지하는 것이다 / 사소한 범죄자가 심각한 범죄로 옮겨 가는 것을 / 즉각적이고 혹독한 형을 부과함으로써 / 경범죄에 / 미성

년자 음주, 소규모의 마약 사용 및 거래, 들치기 또는 공공기물 파손과 같은

I think / 'Zero tolerance' is an innovative and effective weapon / to fight against crime.
나는 생각한다 / '무관용 원칙'이 혁신적이고 효과적인 무기라고 / 범죄에 맞서기 위한

It sends a clear, tough message / that the state will condemn and punish / rather than be soft and 'understanding.'
그것은 명확하고 냉정한 메시지를 전달한다 / 국가가 규탄하고 벌을 줄 것이라는 / 관대하고 '이해심 있기'보다는

This stance functions / as an effective deterrent / to potential offenders, / especially potential young offenders, / and also raises public confidence / in the police and judiciary.
이러한 입장은 작용한다 / 효과적인 제지물로써 / 잠재적인 범죄자들에 대한 / 특히 어린 잠재적 범죄자들(에 대한) / 그리고 또한 공신력을 높인다 / 경찰과 사법부에 대한

해석 '무관용 원칙'은 사소한 범죄에 대한 엄중 단속의 묘사로서 처음 알려진 문구이다. 무관용 원칙의 목적은 미성년자 음주, 소규모의 마약 사용 및 거래, 들치기 또는 공공기물 파손과 같은 경범죄에 즉각적이고 혹독한 형을 부과함으로써 사소한 범죄자가 심각한 범죄로 옮겨 가는 것을 방지하는 것이다. 나는 '무관용 원칙'이 범죄에 맞서기 위한 혁신적이고 효과적인 무기라고 생각한다. 그것은 국가가 관대하고 '이해심 있기'보다는 규탄하고 벌을 줄 것이라는 명확하고 냉정한 메시지를 전달한다. 이러한 입장은 잠재적인 범죄자들, 특히 어린 잠재적 범죄자들에 대한 효과적인 제지물로써 작용하고 또한 경찰과 사법부에 대한 공신력을 높인다.

해설 지문 전반에 걸쳐 필자는 경범죄에 즉각적이고 혹독한 형을 부과하는 '무관용 원칙'에 대해 설명하며 이것이 범죄에 맞서기 위한 혁신적이고 효과적인 무기라고 생각한다고 말하고 있다. 따라서 필자가 주장하는 바를 '정부는 소소한 범죄 행위에도 강력하게 대처하여야 한다'라고 표현한 ④번이 정답이다.

어휘 **zero tolerance** 무관용 원칙, 엄중 처벌 원칙 **crackdown** 엄중 단속
trivial 사소한 **petty** 사소한 **impose** 부과하다, 강요하다
harsh 혹독한, 가혹한 **sentence** 형, 형벌
shoplifting 들치기(상점에서 물건을 훔치는 것)
vandalism 공공기물 파손 **condemn** 규탄하다 **deterrent** 제지물
judiciary 사법부

---

05 문법 전치사   난이도 ★☆☆

해석 나라 전역에서, 동티모르는 인도네시아로부터의 독립을 얻기 위해 30년 이상 분쟁에 휘말려왔다. 전쟁으로 피폐해진 나라에서, 지적장애가 있는 사람들은 종종 잊혀지고 버려진다. 동티모르 출신의 지적장애가 있고 말을 할 수 없는 고아인 Alcino Pereira는 의료 서비스를 이용해 본 적이 한 번도 없었다. 그는 그의 한쪽 팔을 사용할 수 있지만 매우 제한된 정도로만이며, 절뚝거리며 걷는다. 이러한 지적, 신체적 장애에도 불구하고, 그는 달리는 것을 좋아한다. 그의 닳아 해진 신발을 신고, Pereira는 그의 고향 딜리에서 매일 달린다. 그래서 그는 '달리는 남자'라는 별명을 얻었다.

해설 ④ <u>전치사 자리</u> 명사구(these intellectual and physical challenges) 앞에 올 수 있는 것은 전치사이므로 부사절 접속사 Although를 양보를 나타내는 전치사 Despite(~에도 불구하고) 또는 In spite of(~에도 불구하고)로 고쳐야 한다.

오답 분석 ① <u>시제 일치 | 능동태·수동태 구별</u> 현재완료 시제와 자주 함께 쓰이는 시간 표현 'for + 시간 표현'(for more than 30 years)이 왔고, 주어(East Timor)와 동사가 '동티모르가 휘말려왔다'라는 의미의 수동 관계이므로 현재완료 수동태 has been

---

involved가 올바르게 쓰였다.

② <u>형용사 자리</u> 명사(country)를 앞에서 수식하는 형용사 war-torn이 올바르게 쓰였다. 참고로, war-torn과 같이 분사가 다른 품사와 하이픈(-)으로 연결된 경우, 명사를 앞에서 수식할 수 있다.

③ <u>관계대명사</u> 선행사 Alcino Pereira가 사람이고 관계절 내에서 동사 is의 주어 역할을 하므로 사람을 가리키는 주격 관계대명사 who가 올바르게 쓰였다. 참고로, 'an intellectually ~ East Timor'는 선행사 Alcino Pereira와 관계대명사 who 사이에 삽입된 명사구로 관계대명사의 격 선택에 영향을 미치지 않는다.

어휘 **independence** 독립 **war-torn** 전쟁으로 피폐해진
abandon 버리다 **intellectually challenged** 지적장애가 있는
orphan 고아 **limp** 절뚝거리기; 절뚝거리다
worn-out 닳아 해진

👍 **이것도 알면 합격!**

현재완료 시제와 자주 쓰이는 표현을 알아두자.

| · yet 아직 | · since + 과거 시간 표현 ~ 이래로 |
| · so far 지금까지 | · over/for + 시간 표현 ~ 동안 |

---

06 독해 전체내용 파악 (글의 감상)   난이도 ★☆☆

끊어읽기 해석

I still remember the incident / that happened last summer.
나는 아직도 그 사건을 기억한다 / 지난 여름에 일어났던

We were staying at a country inn / that had a small movie theater.
우리는 시골 여관에 묵고 있었다 / 작은 영화관이 있는

Before every evening's presentation, / my husband and I / instructed our three-year-old son / to sit quietly.
매일 저녁의 상연 전에 / 내 남편과 나는 / 세 살짜리 아들에게 지시했다 / 조용히 앉아 있을 것을

Except for an occasional whispered question, / he concentrated on the movie quietly.
이따금 속삭이는 질문을 제외하고 / 그는 조용히 영화에 집중했다

The soundtrack, / however, / was impossible to hear.
영화 음악은 / 하지만 / 듣는 것이 불가능했다

That's because / two children bounced on their seats, / talked loudly / and raced up and down the aisles. // Never once did I see / their parents.
그것은 왜냐하면 / 두 아이들이 그들의 좌석에서 뛰어오르고 / 크게 말하고 / 통로를 달리며 오르내렸기 때문이다 // 나는 한 번도 보지 못했다 / 그들의 부모를

After several evenings of this, / I followed the children / to the dining room. // There sat their parents / enjoying a relaxed meal.
이런 저녁을 몇 번 보낸 이후 / 나는 그 아이들을 따라갔다 / 식당으로 // 그곳에는 그들의 부모가 앉아 있었다 / 편안한 식사를 즐기며

해석 나는 지난 여름에 일어났던 그 사건을 아직도 기억한다. 우리는 작은 영화관이 있는 시골 여관에 묵고 있었다. 매일 저녁의 상연 전에, 내 남편과 나는 세 살짜리 아들에게 조용히 앉아 있을 것을 지시했다. 이따금 속삭이는 질문을 제외하고, 그는 조용히 영화에 집중했다. 하지만 영화 음악은 듣는 것이 불가능했다. 그것은 왜냐하면 두 아이들이 그들의 좌석에서 뛰어오르고, 크게 말하고 통로를 달리며 오르내렸기 때문이다. 나는 그들의 부모를 한 번도 보지 못

했다. 이런 저녁을 몇 번 보낸 이후, 나는 그 아이들을 따라 식당으로 갔다. 그곳에는 그들의 부모가 편안한 식사를 즐기며 앉아 있었다.

① 짜증나고 화가 난　　② 유감스럽고 미안한
③ 차갑고 무관심한　　④ 겁먹고 무서운

해설　지문에서 필자는 자신이 묵었던 여관에 있는 영화관에서 매우 시끄러운 두 아이들 때문에 영화에 집중할 수 없었는데, 이런 일이 몇 번 있은 뒤에 그 아이들을 따라 식당으로 갔더니 그들의 부모가 편안한 식사를 즐기며 앉아 있는 모습을 보았다는 일화를 소개하고 있다. 따라서 지문에서 필자가 느꼈을 심경을 '짜증나고 화가 난'이라고 표현한 ①번이 정답이다.

어휘　incident 사건　occasional 이따금의　aisle 통로

07　독해　전체내용 파악 (제목 파악)　난이도 ★☆☆

끊어읽기 해석

A common but seriously hindering medical condition, / stuttering is something / that everyone wants to avoid / if possible.
흔하지만 심각하게 방해가 되는 질환인 / 말더듬은 어떤 것이다 / 모든 이들이 피하고 싶어 하는 / 가능하다면

Some people simply have / a genetic predisposition / towards stuttering, / but there are other factors / that contribute to it, / though only a few are well understood.
어떤 사람들은 단순히 가진다 / 유전적 소인을 / 말더듬에 대한 / 하지만 다른 요인들이 있다 / 그것의 원인이 되는 / 비록 몇 안 되는 것들만이 잘 알려져 있더라도

Learning a new language is often the cause / for stuttering in children, / but this is a rather benign form of stuttering.
새로운 언어를 배우는 것은 종종 원인이다 / 아이들의 말더듬의 / 하지만 이것은 꽤 양호한 형태의 말더듬이다

Some people have neurological problems / that inhibit the proper brain functions / regarding speech, / and these problems are often the result / of a stroke, accident, or some other trauma.
어떤 사람들은 신경학적인 문제들을 가진다 / 제대로 된 두뇌 기능을 방해하는 / 언어 능력과 관련된 / 그리고 이러한 문제들은 종종 결과이다 / 뇌졸중, 사고, 혹은 몇몇 다른 정신적 외상의

However, / the problem might be psychological, too, / such as a severe lack of self-confidence / or the presence of disproportionate stress.
하지만 / 그 문제는 심리적인 것일 수도 있다 / 심각한 자신감 결여와 같은 / 또는 불균형적인 스트레스의 존재(와 같은)

Also, / behavioral disorders / like autism and attention deficit disorder / can lead to the speech disorder.
또한 / 행동 장애들이 / 자폐증이나 주의력 결핍 장애와 같은 / 언어 장애로 이어질 수 있다

해석　흔하지만 심각하게 방해가 되는 질환인 말더듬은 모든 이들이 가능하다면 피하고 싶어 하는 것이다. 어떤 사람들은 단순히 말더듬에 대한 유전적 소인을 가지지만, 비록 몇 안 되는 것들만이 잘 알려져 있더라도 그것의 원인이 되는 다른 요인들이 있다. 새로운 언어를 배우는 것은 종종 아이들의 말더듬의 원인이지만, 이것은 꽤 양호한 형태의 말더듬이다. 어떤 사람들은 언어 능력과 관련된 제대로 된 두뇌 기능을 방해하는 신경학적인 문제들을 가지고, 이러한 문제들은 종종 뇌졸중, 사고, 혹은 몇몇 다른 정신적 외상의 결과이다. 하지만 그 문제는 심각한 자신감 결여 또는 불균형적인 스트레스의 존재와 같은 심리적인 것일 수도 있다. 또한, 자폐증이나 주의력 결핍 장애와 같은 행동 장애들이 언어 장애로 이어질 수 있다.

---

① 말더듬의 흔한 증상
② 말더듬 질환의 다양한 원인들
③ 말더듬을 악화시키는 요인들
④ 말더듬의 해로운 영향들

해설　지문 앞부분에서 어떤 사람들은 단순히 말더듬에 대한 유전적 소인을 가지지만 그것(말더듬)의 원인이 되는 다른 요인들이 있다고 한 뒤, 새로운 언어를 배우는 것, 신경학적인 문제, 심리적인 문제, 자폐증이나 주의력 결핍 장애와 같은 행동 장애들을 언급하며 말더듬의 여러 다른 원인들에 대해 설명하고 있다. 따라서 이 지문의 제목을 '말더듬 질환의 다양한 원인들'이라고 표현한 ②번이 정답이다.

어휘　hinder 방해가 되다　medical condition 질환　stuttering 말더듬
predisposition 소인　benign 양호한, 유순한
neurological 신경학적인　inhibit 방해하다　stroke 뇌졸중
trauma 정신적 외상, 트라우마　disproportionate 불균형적인
autism 자폐증

08　독해　추론 (빈칸 완성 - 단어)　난이도 ★☆☆

끊어읽기 해석

Have you ever stopped and spent some time / thinking about the two amazing machines / located at the ends of your arms?
당신은 잠시 멈추어 시간을 보낸 적이 있는가 / 두 개의 놀라운 기계에 대해 생각하는 데 / 당신의 팔 끝에 위치한?

Your hands are really incredible: / they work all day, / hardly ever taking a break, / but they rarely get tired.
당신의 손은 정말 놀랍다 / 그것들은 온종일 일한다 / 거의 휴식을 취하지 않고 / 하지만 좀처럼 피로해지지 않는다

And not only are your hands strong, / they are also versatile.
그리고 당신의 손은 튼튼할 뿐 아니라 / 그것들은 또한 다재다능하다

Think about / all the different things they do!
생각해 보라 / 그것들이 하는 그 모든 각양각색의 것들에 대해!

They knock on doors / and turn doorknobs.
그것들은 문을 두드린다 / 그리고 손잡이를 돌린다

If you're hungry, / they'll take the lid off a cookie jar / and then put the cookies to your mouth!
만약 당신이 배가 고프면 / 그것들은 과자 단지의 뚜껑을 열 것이다 / 그러고는 과자를 당신의 입에 넣을 것이다!

And if you are good at computer games, / you can thank your hands / for that, too.
그리고 만약 당신이 컴퓨터 게임을 잘한다면 / 당신은 당신의 손에게 감사할 수 있다 / 그것에 대해서도

Whatever you are doing, / your hands can help you.
당신이 무엇을 하든지 간에 / 당신의 손이 당신을 도울 수 있다

해석　당신은 잠시 멈추어 당신의 팔 끝에 위치한 두 개의 놀라운 기계에 대해 생각하는 데 시간을 보낸 적이 있는가? 당신의 손은 정말 놀라운데, 그것들은 거의 휴식을 취하지 않고 온종일 일하지만 좀처럼 피로해지지 않는다. 그리고 당신의 손은 튼튼할 뿐 아니라 또한 다재다능하다. 그것들이 하는 그 모든 각양각색의 것들에 대해 생각해 보라! 그것들은 문을 두드리고 손잡이를 돌린다. 만약 당신이 배가 고프면, 그것들은 과자 단지의 뚜껑을 열고는 과자를 당신의 입에 넣을 것이다! 그리고 만약 당신이 컴퓨터 게임을 잘한다면, 당신은 그것에 대해서도 당신의 손에게 감사할 수 있다. 당신이 무엇을 하든지 간에, 당신의 손이 당신을 도울 수 있다.

① 다재다능한　　② 명확한
③ 자격이 있는　　④ 진짜의

해설 빈칸이 있는 문장을 통해 손이 튼튼할 뿐 아니라 어떠한지에 대한 내용이 나와야 적절하다는 것을 알 수 있다. 빈칸 뒤에서 문을 두드리거나 손잡이를 돌리고, 과자 단지의 뚜껑을 열거나 컴퓨터 게임을 하는 등 손이 할 수 있는 각양각색의 것들에 대해 언급하고 있으므로, 손은 또한 '다재다능하다'라고 한 ①번이 정답이다.

어휘 locate 위치시키다 incredible 놀랍다 rarely 좀처럼 ~하지 않는
doorknob (문의) 손잡이 lid 뚜껑 versatile 다재다능한, 다용도의
tangible 명확한, 만질 수 있는 eligible 자격이 있는
genuine 진짜의

09 독해 논리적 흐름 파악 (문맥상 부적절한 어휘) 난이도 ★★☆

끊어읽기 해석

Euphemisms are also problematic / for English learners / because they often contain / more difficult words / than their more direct ① counterparts.
완곡 어구는 또한 문제가 된다 / 영어 학습자들에게 / 왜냐하면 그것들이 종종 포함하기 때문이다 / 더 어려운 단어들을 / 좀 더 직접적인 ① 대응 관계에 있는 것들보다

Learners of English, / for instance, / have to memorize / that an old person can be referred to / as "a senior citizen," / while a police officer can be described / as "a law-enforcement officer."
영어 학습자들은 / 예를 들어 / 암기해야 한다 / 노인이 불릴 수 있다는 것을 / '고령자'라고 / 경찰이 묘사될 수 있는 한편 / '법 집행관'으로

They also have to learn to use euphemisms / like "② vertically challenged" / when they can get by with "short."
그들은 또한 완곡 어구를 사용하는 것을 배워야 한다 / '② 수직으로 문제가 있는'과 같은 / 그들이 '키가 작은'이라고 할 수 있을 때도

Despite the burden / that euphemisms pose on learners of English, / it is clear / that euphemisms are tools / which allow us to talk / about all kinds of things / in ③ impolite ways.
부담에도 불구하고 / 완곡 어구가 영어 학습자들에게 가하는 / 분명하다 / 완곡 어구가 도구라는 것은 / 우리가 말할 수 있도록 허락하는 / 모든 종류의 것들에 대해 / ③ 무례한 방법으로

As old euphemisms fall out of use / and new ones come into use, / English is ever ④ evolving / to handle every situation, / pleasant or unpleasant.
오래된 완곡 어구들이 쓰이지 않게 되고 / 새로운 것들이 사용되면서 / 영어는 계속 ④ 발전하고 있다 / 모든 상황을 다룰 수 있도록 / 유쾌하거나 불쾌한

해석 완곡 어구는 영어 학습자들에게도 문제가 되는데, 왜냐하면 그것들이 종종 좀 더 직접적인 ① 대응 관계에 있는 것들보다 더 어려운 단어들을 포함하기 때문이다. 예를 들어, 영어 학습자들은 경찰이 '법 집행관'으로 묘사될 수 있는 한편, 노인이 '고령자'라고 불릴 수 있다는 것을 암기해야 한다. 그들은 또한 그들이 '키가 작은'이라고 할 수 있을 때도 '② 수직으로 문제가 있는'과 같은 완곡 어구를 사용하는 것을 배워야 한다. 완곡 어구가 영어 학습자들에게 가하는 부담에도 불구하고, 완곡 어구가 우리가 모든 종류의 것들에 대해 ③ 무례한 방법으로 말할 수 있도록 허락하는 도구라는 것은 분명하다. 오래된 완곡 어구들이 쓰이지 않게 되고 새로운 것들이 사용되면서, 영어는 유쾌하거나 불쾌한 모든 상황을 다룰 수 있도록 계속 ④ 발전하고 있다.

해설 지문 앞부분에서 직설적인 표현 대신에 완곡 어구를 사용하여 노인들을 '고령자'라고 돌려 말하고, 키가 작다는 말을 '수직적으로 문제가 있는'이라고 돌려 말한다는 내용이 있으므로, 완곡 어구가 우리로 하여금 모든 종류의 것들에 대해 '무례한'(impolite) 방

법으로 말할 수 있도록 허락하는 도구라는 것은 문맥상 적절하지 않다. 따라서 ③ impolite가 정답이다. 참고로, 주어진 impolite를 대신할 수 있는 어휘로는 '정중한'이라는 의미의 polite, courteous 등이 있다.

어휘 euphemism 완곡 어구 counterpart 대응 관계에 있는 것
law-enforcement 법 집행 vertically 수직으로
fall out of use 쓰이지 않게 되다 evolve 발전하다, 진화하다

10 독해 논리적 흐름 파악 (문장 삽입) 난이도 ★★☆

끊어읽기 해석

She recommended / better meal planning, / more protein and fresh vegetables, / and supplements / containing B vitamins, magnesium, and F-theanine.
그녀는 추천했다 / 더 나은 식단을 / 더 많은 단백질과 신선한 채소들을 / 그리고 보충제를 / 비타민 B, 마그네슘, F-테아닌을 함유한

Angie was always anxious and impatient.
Angie는 항상 불안하고 참을성이 없었다.

She regularly skipped meals / and ended up driving through fast-food restaurants / to eat / just as her blood sugar was crashing.
그녀는 자주 끼니를 걸렀다 / 그리고 결국 패스트푸드 식당으로 가게 되었다 / 식사를 하기 위해 / 막 그녀의 혈당이 급속히 감소하고 있을 때

(①) Then she usually felt / fuzzy brained / and wanted to take a nap.
그러고 나서 그녀는 보통 느꼈다 / 머리가 멍해지는 것을 / 그리고 낮잠을 자고 싶어했다

(②) She eventually sought / the advice of a nutritionally oriented physician / for her bouts of fatigue.
그녀는 결국 구했다 / 영양적인 면에 중점을 둔 의사의 조언을 / 수차례의 피로 때문에

(③) Her response / to eating more protein / —a rotisserie chicken and steamed vegetables / on the first day— / was nothing short of dramatic.
그녀의 반응은 / 더 많은 단백질을 먹은 것에 대한 / 전기구이 닭고기와 찐 채소들 같은 / 첫째 날에 / 아주 인상적이었다

(④) Several months later, / Angie's sister described her / as a new person / —she slept more soundly / and woke up feeling alert and energetic.
몇 달 후 / Angie의 언니는 그녀를 묘사했다 / 새로운 사람으로 / 그녀는 더 깊이 잤다 / 그리고 일어났다 / 정신이 초롱초롱하고 힘이 넘치는 것을 느끼며

해석 Angie는 항상 불안하고 참을성이 없었다. 그녀는 자주 끼니를 걸렀고 막 그녀의 혈당이 급속히 감소하고 있을 때 식사를 하기 위해 결국 패스트푸드 식당으로 가게 되었다. 그러고 나서, 그녀는 보통 머리가 멍해지는 것을 느꼈고, 낮잠을 자고 싶어 했다. 그녀는 결국 수차례의 피로 때문에 영양적인 면에 중점을 둔 의사의 조언을 구했다. ③ 그녀(의사)는 더 나은 식단, 더 많은 단백질과 신선한 채소들, 그리고 비타민 B, 마그네슘, F-테아닌을 함유한 보충제를 추천했다. 첫째 날에 전기구이 닭고기와 찐 채소들 같은 더 많은 단백질을 먹은 것에 대한 그녀의 반응은 아주 인상적이었다. 몇 달 후, Angie의 언니는 그녀를 새로운 사람으로 묘사했는데, 그녀는 더 깊이 잤고 정신이 초롱초롱하고 힘이 넘치는 것을 느끼며 일어났다.

해설 ③번 앞 문장에서 Angie가 수차례의 피로 때문에 결국 영양적인 면에 중점을 둔 의사의 조언을 구했다고 했으므로, ③번 자리에 그녀(의사)가 더 나은 식단을 추천했다는 내용의 주어진 문장이 나와야 글의 흐름이 자연스럽게 연결된다. 따라서 ③번이 정답이다.

어휘 supplement 보충제 impatient 참을성이 없는 fuzzy 멍한
oriented ~에 중점을 둔, ~를 지향하는 bout 한차례
soundly 깊이, 곤히 alert 정신이 초롱초롱한, 기민한

11 독해 추론 (빈칸 완성 - 구) 난이도 ★★☆

끊어읽기 해석

In a new study, / it was found / that species that live in restrictive environments / such as the tropics / cannot adapt to a changing climate / as well as species in more diverse environments.
새로운 연구에서 / 발견되었다 / 제한된 환경에 살고 있는 종이 / 열대 지방과 같은 / 변화하는 기후에 적응할 수 없다는 것이 / 더 다양한 환경에 살고 있는 종만큼 잘

The reason is the lack of variation in their genes.
그 이유는 그들의 유전자 내 변이의 결여 때문이다

A species adapts to its environment / and becomes better at surviving / by undergoing physical and behavioral changes.
한 종은 그것의 환경에 적응한다 / 그리고 더 잘 생존할 수 있게 된다 / 신체적 및 행동적 변화를 겪음으로써

These usually occur / due to a gene mutation.
이러한 것들은 주로 발생한다 / 유전자 돌연변이로 인해

If a species already has / a more varied set of genes, / it is more likely to undergo / the necessary changes.
만약 한 종이 이미 가지고 있다면 / 더 다양한 유전자 집합을 / 겪을 가능성이 더 높다 / 필요한 변화들을

However, / species in the tropics have / less varied sets of genes.
하지만 / 열대 지방의 종은 가지고 있다 / 덜 다양한 유전자 집합을

해석 새로운 연구에서, 열대 지방과 같은 제한된 환경에 살고 있는 종이 더 다양한 환경에 살고 있는 종만큼 변화하는 기후에 잘 적응할 수 없다는 것이 발견되었다. 그 이유는 그들의 유전자 내 변이의 결여 때문이다. 한 종은 그것의 환경에 적응하고 신체적 및 행동적 변화를 겪음으로써 더 잘 생존할 수 있게 된다. 이러한 것들은 주로 유전자 돌연변이로 인해 발생한다. 만약 한 종이 더 다양한 유전자 집합을 이미 가지고 있다면, 필요한 변화들을 겪을 가능성이 더 높다. 하지만, 열대 지방의 종은 덜 다양한 유전자 집합을 가지고 있다.

① 파괴된 환경
② 그들의 서식지로부터의 고립
③ 그들의 포식자로부터의 공격
④ 그들의 유전자 내 변이의 결여

해설 빈칸 앞 문장을 통해 제한된 환경에 살고 있는 종이 더 다양한 환경에 살고 있는 종만큼 변화하는 기후에 잘 적응할 수 없는 이유가 빈칸에 나와야 적절하다는 것을 알 수 있다. 빈칸 뒤에서 어떤 종이 환경에 적응하고 더 잘 생존할 수 있게 되는 것은 유전자 돌연변이로 인한 신체적 및 행동적 변화를 겪는 것에 의한 것이라고 했으므로, 제한된 환경에 살고 있는 종이 변화하는 기후에 잘 적응할 수 없는 이유가 '그들의 유전자 내 변이의 결여' 때문이라고 한 ④번이 정답이다.

어휘 restrictive 제한된 the tropics 열대 지방 adapt to ~에 적응하다
diverse 다양한 undergo 겪다, 경험하다
gene mutation 유전자 돌연변이 isolation 고립 habitat 서식지
predator 포식자 variation 변이, 변형

12 독해 전체내용 파악 (주제 파악) 난이도 ★★☆

끊어읽기 해석

Scientists are currently studying / the navigational systems and locomotive strategies of insects / to help design / the next generation of autonomous robots and vehicles.
과학자들은 현재 연구하고 있다 / 곤충들의 비행 체계와 이동 방법을 / 설계하는 것을 돕기 위해 / 다음 세대의 자율 로봇과 운송수단을

Also, / researchers have recently found / that the flipper of the humpback whale / is a more efficient wing design / than the current model / used by the aeronautics industry / on airplanes.
또한 / 연구원들은 최근에 발견했다 / 혹등고래의 지느러미발이 / 더 효율적인 날개 설계라는 것을 / 현재의 모델보다 / 항공 산업에서 사용되는 / 비행기에

They are working / to apply their findings / to future airplane and automotive design.
그들은 노력하고 있다 / 그들의 발견을 적용하기 위해 / 미래 비행기와 자동차 설계에

Similarly, / engineers have used / the rough skin of the shark / as inspiration / in developing a ridged foil coating / for the wings of aircraft, / a design / which has resulted in six percent less friction / and improved fuel efficiency.
마찬가지로 / 기술자들은 사용해왔다 / 상어의 거친 피부를 / 영감으로 / 능선 모양의 금속 도금을 개발하는 데 / 항공기 날개를 위한 / 설계인 / 6퍼센트 더 적은 마찰로 이어진 / 그리고 향상된 연료 효율성으로 (이어진)

해석 과학자들은 현재 다음 세대의 자율 로봇과 운송수단을 설계하는 것을 돕기 위해 곤충들의 비행 체계와 이동 방법을 연구하고 있다. 또한, 연구원들은 혹등고래의 지느러미발이 항공 산업에서 비행기에 사용되는 현재의 모델보다 더 효율적인 날개 설계라는 것을 최근에 발견했다. 그들은 미래 비행기와 자동차 설계에 그들의 발견을 적용하기 위해 노력하고 있다. 마찬가지로, 기술자들은 상어의 거친 피부를 항공기 날개를 위한 능선 모양의 금속 도금을 개발하는 데 영감으로 사용해왔는데, 이것은 6퍼센트 더 적은 마찰과 향상된 연료 효율성으로 이어진 설계였다.

① 자연으로부터의 차용
② 자연의 신비
③ 항공우주 산업의 미래
④ 우리가 야생동물을 보호해야 하는 이유

해설 지문 중간에서 과학자들이 미래 비행기와 자동차 설계에 그들의 발견을 적용하기 위해 노력하고 있다고 했고, 여기서 '그들의 발견'은 지문 전반에 걸쳐 언급하고 있는 곤충들의 비행 체계와 이동 방법, 혹등고래의 지느러미, 상어의 거친 피부 등을 의미하는 것이므로, 이 지문의 주제를 '자연으로부터의 차용'이라고 표현한 ①번이 정답이다.

어휘 navigational 비행의, 항해의 locomotive 이동의
strategy 방법, 전략 autonomous 자율의 flipper 지느러미발
humpback whale 혹등고래 aeronautic 항공의 friction 마찰
borrow 차용하다, 빌리다 aerospace 항공우주 산업
preserve 보호하다, 지키다

13 독해 논리적 흐름 파악 (문단 순서 배열) 난이도 ★★☆

끊어읽기 해석

President Roosevelt openly blamed / the greed of many Americans / for the Depression / and acted to rectify the problem.

루즈벨트 대통령은 공개적으로 비난했다 / 많은 미국인들의 탐욕을 / 대공황에 대한 (책임으로) / 그리고 그 문제를 바로잡기 위해 행동했다

At that time, / people with a lot of currency or gold / hoarded them / and did not put them into banks / because of the fear of losing their money.
그 시기에 / 많은 현금이나 금을 가진 사람들은 / 그것들을 비축했다 / 그리고 그것들을 은행에 넣지 않았다 / 그들의 돈을 잃을 것에 대한 두려움 때문에

(A) It also allowed the government to seize / the gold of private citizens / in exchange for paper money.
그것은 또한 정부가 점유케 하는 것을 허용했다 / 시민 개인의 금을 / 지폐와 교환하여

(B) This made the Depression worse / because banks had no money / and were forced to close.
이것은 대공황을 더 악화시켰다 / 은행에 돈이 없었기 때문에 / 그래서 문을 닫을 수밖에 없었기 때문에

(C) In response, / Roosevelt enacted the "Emergency Banking Act" / which worked to shut down insolvent banks / so that they could be reconstructed.
이에 대응하여 / 루즈벨트는 '긴급은행법'을 제정했다 / 파산한 은행을 일시적으로 폐쇄하는 / 그래서 그들이 재건될 수 있도록 한

해석

> 루즈벨트 대통령은 대공황에 대한 (책임으로) 많은 미국인들의 탐욕을 공개적으로 비난했고, 그 문제를 바로잡기 위해 행동했다. 그 시기에, 많은 현금이나 금을 가진 사람들은 그들의 돈을 잃을 것에 대한 두려움 때문에 그것들을 비축했고 은행에 넣지 않았다.

(B) 은행에 돈이 없어서 문을 닫을 수밖에 없었기 때문에, 이것은 대공황을 더 악화시켰다.

(C) 이에 대응하여, 루즈벨트는 파산한 은행을 일시적으로 폐쇄해서 그들이 재건될 수 있도록 한 '긴급은행법'을 제정했다.

(A) 그것은 또한 정부가 시민 개인의 금을 지폐와 교환하여 점유케 하는 것을 허용했다.

해설 주어진 지문의 뒷부분에서 대공황 시기에 미국인들이 돈을 잃을 것에 대한 두려움 때문에 은행에 돈을 넣지 않았다고 한 뒤, (B)에서 이것(This)은 은행이 문을 닫도록 만들었기 때문에 대공황을 더 악화시켰다고 했다. 그 후, (C)에서 이에 대응하여(In response) 루즈벨트 대통령이 '긴급은행법'을 제정했다고 설명한 뒤, (A)에서 긴급은행법의 또 다른 결과를 언급하고 있다. 따라서 ② (B) – (C) – (A)가 정답이다.

어휘 greed 탐욕 rectify 바로잡다 currency 현금, 통화
hoard 비축하다, 사장하다 seize 점유케 하다, 빼앗다
enact 제정하다 insolvent 파산한
shut down (일시적으로) 폐쇄하다 reconstruct 재건하다

---

14 **독해** **전체내용 파악 (목적 파악)** 난이도 ★☆☆

끊어읽기 해석

Feel like a cup of tea, / but don't have the time to brew one up? // Take a "tea pill" instead.
차 한 잔을 마시고 싶지만 / 그것을 끓일 시간이 없는가? // 대신에 '차 알약'을 섭취하라.

Indian tea scientists have produced / a tea-flavored pill / that can be chewed / or quickly dissolved / in hot or cold water.
인도의 차 과학자들은 만들었다 / 차 향이 나는 알약을 / 씹을 수 있는 / 또는 빨리 녹을 수 있는 / 뜨겁거나 차가운 물에서

The brownish tablet weighs 0.3 grams / and is composed of / 80 percent tea and 20 percent their flavors.
이 갈색을 띄는 약은 무게가 0.3그램이 나간다 / 그리고 구성되어 있다 / 80퍼센트의 차와 20퍼센트의 차 향료로

The inventors at the research center say / that it peps you up / just like a traditional tea.
연구소의 발명가들은 말한다 / 그것이 당신에게 생기를 불어넣어 준다고 / 전통 차와 같이

"You can suck it, chew it, or dissolve it in water / the way you like to have it, / and still feel the taste of a real cup of tea," / they said.
"당신은 그것을 빨아 먹거나, 씹거나, 물에 녹일 수 있습니다 / 당신이 섭취하기를 원하는 방법으로 / 그리고 여전히 진짜 차 한 잔의 맛을 느낄 수 있습니다" / 그들은 말했다

"As the liquid tea refreshes, / this tea pill will also refresh people / because it contains / pure tea ingredients."
"액체 형태의 차가 생기를 되찾게 하는 것처럼 / 이 차 알약 또한 사람들이 생기를 되찾게 할 것입니다 / 왜냐하면 그것이 포함하고 있기 때문입니다 / 순수한 차 성분들을"

They said / the center had applied for a patent, / and that the pill should hit the market / in six months.
그들은 말했다 / 연구소가 특허를 신청했다고 / 그리고 그 알약이 시중에 출시될 것이라고 / 6개월 후에

해석 차 한 잔을 마시고 싶지만 그것을 끓일 시간이 없는가? 대신에 '차 알약'을 섭취하라. 인도의 차 과학자들은 씹을 수 있고 또는 뜨겁거나 차가운 물에서 빨리 녹을 수 있는 차 향이 나는 알약을 만들었다. 이 갈색을 띄는 약은 무게가 0.3그램이 나가고 80퍼센트의 차와 20퍼센트의 차 향료로 구성되어 있다. 연구소의 발명가들은 그것이 전통 차와 같이 당신에게 생기를 불어넣어 준다고 말한다. "당신은 당신이 섭취하기를 원하는 방법으로 그것을 빨아 먹거나, 씹거나, 물에 녹일 수 있고, 여전히 진짜 차 한 잔의 맛을 느낄 수 있습니다."라고 그들은 말했다. "액체 형태의 차가 생기를 되찾게 하는 것처럼, 이 차 알약 또한 사람들이 생기를 되찾게 할 것인데, 왜냐하면 그것이 순수한 차 성분들을 포함하고 있기 때문입니다." 그들은 연구소가 특허를 신청했고, 6개월 후에 그 알약이 시중에 출시될 것이라고 말했다.

해설 지문 앞부분에서 인도의 차 과학자들이 새로 개발한 차 알약을 소개하며, 그것의 구성 요소, 효능, 섭취 방법 등을 설명한 뒤, 지문 마지막에서 이 차 알약의 출시 시기를 언급하고 있다. 따라서 이 지문의 목적을 '새로 시판될 알약 형태의 차를 소개하려고'라고 표현한 ④번이 정답이다.

어휘 brew up (차 등을) 끓이다 dissolve 녹이다, 녹다
pep up 생기를 불어넣다 suck 빨아 먹다
refresh 생기를 되찾게 하다 patent 특허 ingredient 성분, 재료
hit 출시되다

---

15 **독해** **세부내용 파악 (내용 불일치 파악)** 난이도 ★★☆

끊어읽기 해석

Heart attacks, / which take about 550,000 lives each year, / occur / when the coronary arteries / that supply blood to the heart muscle / become obstructed.
심장마비는 / 매년 대략 55만 명의 생명을 앗아가는 / 발생한다 / 심장의 관상동맥들이 / 혈액을 심장 근육으로 공급하는 / 막힐 때

Without oxygen and other nutrients / carried in the blood, / heart tissue dies or is damaged.
산소와 다른 영양소들 없이는 / 혈액으로 전달되는 / 심장 조직은 죽거나 손상된다

If too much tissue is affected, / the heart is so weakened / that it cannot pump.
만약 너무 많은 조직이 영향을 받는다면 / 심장은 너무 약해져서 / 심하게 고동칠 수 없다

But / even mild damage can kill / by disrupting the electrical impulses / that govern the heart's rhythmic beating.
하지만 / 가벼운 손상조차도 생명을 앗아갈 수 있다 / 전기 자극을 방해함으로써 / 심장의 주기적인 박동을 통제하는

Each year, / stroke claims another 170,000 lives, / and is also caused / by impeded blood flow, / this time to the brain.
매년 / 뇌졸중이 또 다른 17만 명의 생명을 앗아간다 / 그리고 (그것은) 또한 야기된다 / 지연된 혈류로 인해 / 이번에는 뇌 쪽으로의

해석 매년 대략 55만 명의 생명을 앗아가는 심장마비는 혈액을 심장 근육으로 공급하는 심장의 관상동맥들이 막힐 때 발생한다. 혈액으로 전달되는 산소와 다른 영양소들 없이는 심장 조직은 죽거나 손상된다. 만약 너무 많은 조직이 영향을 받는다면, 심장은 너무 약해져서 심하게 고동칠 수 없다. 하지만 가벼운 손상조차도 심장의 주기적인 박동을 통제하는 전기 자극을 방해함으로써 생명을 앗아갈 수 있다. 매년 뇌졸중이 또 다른 17만 명의 생명을 앗아가고 (그것은) 또한 이번에는 뇌 쪽으로의 지연된 혈류로 인해 야기된다.

해설 지문 뒷부분에서 심장 조직의 가벼운 손상조차도 심장의 주기적인 박동을 통제하는 전기 자극을 방해함으로써 생명을 앗아갈 수 있다고 했으므로, 심장 조직이 약간 손상되는 경우에는 큰 위험이 없다는 것은 지문의 내용과 일치하지 않는다. 따라서 ③번이 정답이다.

어휘 coronary artery 심장의 관상동맥 obstruct 막다, 방해하다 tissue 조직 disrupt 방해하다 impulse 자극, 충격 stroke 뇌졸중 claim 앗아가다, 주장하다 impede 지연시키다, 방해하다

16 독해 세부내용 파악 (지칭 대상 파악)   난이도 ★★☆

끊어읽기 해석

It's my Aunt Grace's practice / to travel by bus and to notice / what ① most people miss.
나의 숙모 Grace의 습관이다 / 버스로 다니면서 알아채는 것은 / ① 대부분의 사람들이 놓치는 것을

One Saturday morning / the 144 bus passed a busy intersection.
어느 토요일 아침 / 144번 버스가 붐비는 교차로를 지나갔다

She saw two young girls / outfitted for camping. // They looked nervous.
그녀는 두 젊은 여자들을 보았다 / 캠핑을 떠날 채비를 한 // 그들은 초조해 보였다.

When her bus arrived at the next intersection, / she saw two young men / outfitted in the same manner / standing by a car.
그녀의 버스가 다음 교차로에 도착했을 때 / 그녀는 두 젊은 남자들을 보았다 / 같은 방식으로 채비를 한 / 차 옆에 서 있는

They were waiting for an appointment. // Grace got off the bus / and approached the young men.
그들은 약속을 기다리고 있었다. // Grace는 버스에서 내렸다 / 그리고 그 젊은 남자들에게 다가갔다

They spoke to her / in a foreign accent. // Grace described the girls / she had seen, / and the young men left.
그들은 그녀에게 말했다 / 외국인의 억양으로 // Grace는 여자들을 묘사했다 / 그녀가 보았던 / 그리고 젊은 남자들은 떠났다

When ② the small happy band returned / to thank her, / what she had supposed / was confirmed.

② 그 작은 행복한 무리가 돌아왔을 때 / 그녀에게 감사하기 위해 / 그녀가 생각했었던 것이 / 사실임이 확인되었다

There had, indeed, been a mix-up!
정말로 혼동이 있었던 것이다!

Anxious to return good for good, / ③ the chattering little group insisted / they be allowed / to take her home. // Grace refused.
선의를 선의로 보답하고 싶어서 / ③ 그 재잘거리는 작은 무리는 주장했다 / 그들이 허락되어야 한다고 / 그녀를 집에 데려다 주도록 // Grace는 거절했다.

Instead, / the young people crossed the avenue / to gift shop / and returned / with a little cotton elephant.
대신에 / 그 젊은 사람들은 길을 건넜다 / 선물 가게를 향해 / 그리고 돌아왔다 / 작은 코끼리 솜인형을 가지고

Now there is a remembrance / in Grace's apartment, / but there are also ④ four young people / who are bound to remember a friendly lady.
지금 기념품이 있다 / Grace의 아파트에는 / 하지만 또한 ④ 네 명의 젊은 이들도 있다 / 한 친절한 여성을 반드시 기억할

해석 버스로 다니면서 ① 대부분의 사람들이 놓치는 것을 알아채는 것은 나의 숙모 Grace의 습관이다. 어느 토요일 아침, 144번 버스가 붐비는 교차로를 지나갔다. 그녀는 캠핑을 떠날 채비를 한 두 젊은 여자들을 보았다. 그들은 초조해 보였다. 그녀의 버스가 다음 교차로에 도착했을 때, 그녀는 차 옆에 서 있는 같은 방식으로 채비를 한 두 젊은 남자들을 보았다. 그들은 약속을 기다리고 있었다. Grace는 버스에서 내렸고 그 젊은 남자들에게 다가갔다. 그들은 그녀에게 외국인의 억양으로 말했다. Grace는 그녀가 보았던 여자들을 묘사했고, 젊은 남자들은 떠났다. ② 그 작은 행복한 무리가 그녀에게 감사하기 위해 돌아왔을 때, 그녀가 생각했었던 것이 사실임이 확인되었다. 정말로 혼동이 있었던 것이다! 선의를 선의로 보답하고 싶어서, ③ 그 재잘거리는 작은 무리는 그들이 그녀를 집에 데려다 주도록 허락되어야 한다고 주장했다. Grace는 거절했다. 대신에 그 젊은 사람들은 선물 가게를 향해 길을 건넜고, 작은 코끼리 솜인형을 가지고 돌아왔다. 지금 Grace의 아파트에는 기념품이 있지만, 또한 한 친절한 여성을 반드시 기억할 ④ 네 명의 젊은이들도 있다.

해설 ②, ③, ④번 모두 Grace에게 도움을 받은 네 명의 남녀를 지칭하지만, ①번은 불특정한 사람들을 지칭하므로 ①번이 정답이다.

어휘 practice 습관, 연습 intersection 교차로 outfit 채비하다; 복장 suppose 생각하다, 가정하다 confirm 사실임을 확인해 주다 mix-up 혼동 chatter 재잘거리다, 수다스럽게 지껄이다 remembrance 기념품 be bound to 반드시 ~하다

17 독해 추론 (빈칸 완성 - 구)   난이도 ★★☆

끊어읽기 해석

Despite progress / in the field of child and adolescent mental health, / millions of young people every year / do not get proper help.
발전에도 불구하고 / 어린이와 청소년 정신 건강 분야에서의 / 매년 수백만 명의 청소년들이 / 적절한 도움을 받지 못한다

Only one in five children / with a serious emotional disturbance / actually uses / specialized mental health services.
다섯 명의 아이들 중 한 명만이 / 심각한 정서적 장애를 가진 / 실제로 이용한다 / 전문적인 정신 건강 서비스를

Although today, / child welfare services, the juvenile justice system, and our schools / often provide care / to children in

need, / none of these institutions has as its first priority / the delivery of mental health care.
비록 오늘날 / 아동 복지 서비스, 청소년 사법제도, 그리고 우리의 학교들이 / 종종 치료를 제공하지만 / 어려움에 처한 아이들에게 / 이 기관들 중 어떤 곳도 우선 사항으로 두지 않는다 / 정신 건강 치료의 전달을

In addition, / the complexity of promoting collaboration / across agency lines of all professionals / serving the same child / is daunting.
게다가 / 협력을 촉진하는 것의 복잡성은 / 모든 전문가 기관 간의 / 같은 아이를 돕는 / 벅차다

All too often / there is no cooperation, not enough money, / and limited access / to trained mental health professionals / —and children and their families / suffer the tragic consequences.
너무나도 자주 / 협력이 없고, 충분한 돈이 없다 / 그리고 접근이 제한되어 있다 / 훈련된 정신 건강 전문가들에 대한 / 그래서 아이들과 그들의 가족들은 / 비극적인 결과에 시달린다

해석 어린이와 청소년 정신 건강 분야에서의 발전에도 불구하고, 매년 수백만 명의 청소년들이 적절한 도움을 받지 못한다. 심각한 정서적 장애를 가진 다섯 명의 아이들 중 한 명만이 전문적인 정신 건강 서비스를 실제로 이용한다. 비록 오늘날 아동 복지 서비스, 청소년 사법제도, 그리고 우리의 학교들이 어려움에 처한 아이들에게 종종 치료를 제공하지만, 이 기관들 중 어떤 곳도 정신 건강 치료의 전달을 우선 사항으로 두지 않는다. 게다가, 같은 아이를 돕는 모든 전문가 기관 간의 협력을 촉진하는 것의 복잡성은 벅차다. 너무나도 자주 협력이 없고, 충분한 돈이 없으며, 그리고 훈련된 정신 건강 전문가들에 대한 접근이 제한되어 있어서, 아이들과 그들의 가족들은 비극적인 결과에 시달린다.

① 그들의 권리를 요구한다
② 좋은 의료 서비스를 받는다
③ 비극적인 결과에 시달린다
④ 병원에 가는 것을 꺼린다

해설 빈칸 앞에서 정신 건강 서비스와 관련하여 너무나도 자주 협력이 없고, 충분한 돈이 없으며, 훈련된 정신 건강 전문가들에 대한 접근이 제한되어 있다고 했으므로, 심각한 정서적 장애를 가진 아이들과 그들의 가족들이 결국 '비극적인 결과에 시달린다'라고 한 ③번이 정답이다.

어휘 adolescent 청소년 disturbance 장애, 방해 welfare 복지
juvenile 청소년의 justice system 사법제도 priority 우선 사항
complexity 복잡성 promote 촉진하다 collaboration 협력
daunting 벅찬 consequence 결과, 중요성 reluctant 꺼리는

18 문법 명사절   난이도 ★★☆

해석 만족하는 사람들은 그들이 삶에서 가진 것에 감사하고 그것이 다른 사람들이 가진 것과 얼마나 비교가 되는지에 대해 걱정하지 않는다. 당신이 가진 것을 당신이 가지고 있지 않거나 가질 수 없는 것보다 더 가치 있게 생각하는 것은 더 큰 행복으로 이어진다. 4살인 Alice는 크리스마스 트리로 달려가서 그 아래에 있는 멋진 선물들을 본다. 어쩌면 그녀는 그녀의 몇몇 친구들보다 더 적은 선물을 받았을 것이고, 아마 그녀가 가장 원했던 것들 중 일부는 받지 못했을 것이다. 하지만 그 순간 그녀는 왜 더 많은 선물들이 없는지 생각하거나 그녀가 요구했을지도 모르는데 받지 못한 것이 무엇인지 궁금해하기 위해 멈추지 않는다. 대신에 그녀는 그녀 앞에 놓인 보물들에 경탄한다.

해설 ① 명사절 접속사 3: 의문사 목적어가 없는 불완전한 절(others have)을 이끌며 전치사(over)의 목적어 자리에 올 수 있는 것은

명사절 접속사 what이므로 관계대명사 which를 명사절 접속사 what으로 고쳐야 한다.

오답분석
② 주어와 동사의 수 일치 동명사 주어(Valuing ~ cannot have)는 단수 취급하므로 단수 동사 leads가 올바르게 쓰였다.
③ 비교급 문맥상 '친구들보다 더 적은 선물을 받았을 것이다'라는 의미가 되어야 자연스러운데, '~보다 더 적은'은 비교급 표현 'fewer + 명사 + than'(fewer presents than)의 형태로 나타낼 수 있으므로 than이 올바르게 쓰였다.
④ 동명사와 to 부정사 둘 다 목적어로 취하는 동사 문맥상 '~라고 생각하기 위해 멈추다'라는 의미가 되어야 자연스러운데, 동사 stop이 '~하기 위해 (하던 일을) 멈추다'라는 의미를 나타낼 때 to 부정사가 부사적 용법으로 쓰이므로 stop to think가 올바르게 쓰였다.

어휘 appreciate 감사하다 value 가치 있게 생각하다
wonder 궁금해하다, 생각하다 marvel 경탄하다, 경이로워하다

👍 이것도 알면 합격!

stop 뒤의 동명사는 목적어로 '~하는 것을 멈추다'라는 의미이고, to 부정사는 부사적 용법으로 '~하기 위해 (하던 일을) 멈추다'라는 의미라는 것을 알아두자.
(ex) They stopped eating. 그들은 식사하는 것을 멈췄다.
They stopped to eat. 그들은 식사하기 위해 멈췄다.

19 독해 논리적 흐름 파악 (문단 순서 배열)   난이도 ★★★

끊어읽기 해석

It would be hard / to find anything more controversial / than the subject of cloning.
어려울 것이다 / 더 논란이 많은 것을 찾아내기는 / 복제에 관한 주제보다

People find / it either totally fantastic / or totally frightening.
사람들은 생각한다 / 그것이 완전히 환상적이거나 / 혹은 완전히 섬뜩하다고

(A) But / for most people, / the cloning of humans is different.
하지만 / 대부분의 사람들에게 / 인간 복제는 다르다

The idea of duplicating human beings / the same way / we make copies of book pages / on a copy machine / is terrible.
인간을 복제하겠다는 생각은 / 같은 방식으로 / 우리가 책 페이지의 사본을 만드는 것과 / 복사기로 / 끔찍하다

(B) In addition, / it could be useful / in increasing the world's food supply / by the cloning of animals. // Bigger and healthier animals / could be produced.
게다가 / 그것은 유용할 수도 있다 / 세계의 식량 공급을 증가시키는 데에 / 동물 복제로 / 더 크고 더 건강한 동물들이 / 만들어질 수 있다

(C) Cloning holds the promise of cures / for what are now incurable diseases, sight for the blind, hearing for the deaf, new organs to replace old worn-out ones.
복제는 치료의 가능성을 가진다 / 현재 불치병인 것, 시각 장애인을 위한 시력, 청각 장애인을 위한 청력, 낡아서 못 쓰게 된 것을 대체할 새로운 장기에 대한

해석
복제에 관한 주제보다 더 논란이 많은 것을 찾아내기는 어려울 것이다. 사람들은 그것이 완전히 환상적이거나 완전히 섬뜩하다고 생각한다.

(C) 복제는 현재 불치병인 것, 시각 장애인을 위한 시력, 청각 장애인을 위한 청력, 낡아서 못쓰게 된 것을 대체할 새로운 장기에

대한 치료의 가능성을 가진다.

(B) 게다가 그것은 동물 복제로 세계의 식량 공급을 증가시키는 데에 유용할 수도 있다. 더 크고 더 건강한 동물들이 만들어질 수 있다.

(A) 하지만 대부분의 사람들에게 인간 복제는 다르다. 우리가 복사기로 책 페이지의 사본을 만드는 것과 같은 방식으로 인간을 복제하겠다는 생각은 끔찍하다.

해설 주어진 문단에서 사람들은 복제가 완전히 환상적이거나 섬뜩하다고 생각한다고 언급한 뒤, (C)에서 복제의 장점 중 하나로 치료에 대한 가능성(the promise of cures)에 대해 언급하고, (B)에서 게다가(In addition) 복제는 유용할 수 있다고 하며 복제의 또다른 장점인 식량 공급 증가를 설명했다. 이어서 (A)에서 하지만(But) 대부분의 사람들에게 인간 복제는 끔찍하게 여겨진다고 말하며 마무리하고 있다. 따라서 ④ (C) – (B) – (A)가 정답이다.

어휘 clone 복제하다   controversial 논란이 많은
frightening 섬뜩한, 무서운   duplicate 복제하다
incurable disease 불치병   organ 장기, 기관
worn-out 낡아서 못 쓰게 된, 닳아 해진

20   독해   논리적 흐름 파악 (문맥상 부적절한 어휘)   난이도 ★★☆

끊어읽기 해석

Britain caused hardship / in the Indian cloth industry / by putting a 30 percent import tax / on Indian cloth.
영국은 고난을 야기했다 / 인도의 섬유 산업에 / 30퍼센트의 수입세를 붙임으로써 / 인도산 직물에

This made Indian cloth / too ① expensive to sell in Britain.
이것은 인도산 직물을 만들었다 / 영국에서 팔기에 너무 ① 비싸게

When the Indian lost / their British customers, / their cloth industry was ruined.
인도가 잃었을 때 / 그들의 영국 고객들을 / 그들의 섬유 산업은 파산했다

Then / British cloth factories profited / by selling British cloth / to the Indians. // The Indian people were ② discontent / under British rule.
그리고 나서 / 영국 섬유 공장들은 수익을 얻었다 / 영국산 직물을 판매함으로써 / 인도 사람들에게 // 인도 사람들은 ② 불만스러웠다 / 영국의 지배 아래에서

In 1930 / Mohandas Gandhi took up / the cause of Indian independence.
1930년에 / 모한다스 간디는 시작했다 / 인도 독립 운동을

He encouraged Indians / to protest in nonviolent ways.
그는 인도 사람들을 격려했다 / 비폭력적인 방법으로 항의하도록

He encouraged them / not to pay taxes / to the British, / and he ③ resisted / a boycott of British-made product.
그는 그들을 장려했다 / 세금을 내지 않도록 / 영국에 / 그리고 그는 ③ 저항했다 / 영국산 제품에 대한 구매 거부 운동에

After great struggle, / both nonviolent and violent, / the British ④ withdrew, / and in 1947 India / became a self-governing, independent country.
큰 투쟁 이후에 / 비폭력적인 그리고 폭력적인 / 영국은 ④ 철수했다 / 그리고 1947년에 인도는 / 자치 행정의 독립 국가가 되었다

해석 영국은 인도산 직물에 30퍼센트의 수입세를 붙임으로써 인도의 섬유 산업에 고난을 야기했다. 이것은 인도산 직물을 영국에서 팔기에 너무 ① 비싸게 만들었다. 인도가 그들의 영국 고객들을 잃었을 때, 그들의 섬유 산업은 파산했다. 그리고 나서, 영국 섬유 공장들은 인도 사람들에게 영국산 직물을 판매함으로써 수익을 얻었다. 인도 사람들은 영국의 지배 아래에서 ② 불만스러웠다. 1930년에 모한다스 간디는 인도 독립 운동을 시작했다. 그는 인도 사람들을 비

폭력적인 방법으로 항의하도록 격려했다. 그는 영국에 세금을 내지 않도록 그들을 장려했고, 그는 영국산 제품에 대한 구매 거부 운동에 ③ 저항했다. 비폭력적인 그리고 폭력적인 큰 투쟁 이후에 영국은 ④ 철수했고 1947년에 인도는 자치 행정의 독립 국가가 되었다.

해설 지문 앞부분에서 영국이 부당한 방법으로 인도의 섬유 산업을 파산시켜서 인도에 영국산 직물을 팔아서 수익을 얻었다고 설명하고 있다. 이후 인도 사람들이 영국의 지배에 불만스러워 했고, 간디가 독립 운동을 시작하여 비폭력적인 방법으로 저항하도록 격려했다는 내용이 있으므로, 그가 영국산 제품에 대한 구매 거부 운동에 '저항했다'는 것은 문맥상 적절하지 않다. 따라서 ③번이 정답이다. 참고로 주어진 resisted를 대신할 수 있는 어휘로는 '장려했다, 지지했다'라는 의미의 promoted, supported 등이 있다.

어휘 import 수입   ruin 파산시키다, 망치다   discontent 불만스러운
take up 시작하다   cause 운동, 주장   boycott 구매 거부 운동
nonviolent 비폭력적인   withdraw 철수하다
self-governing 자치 행정의

21   독해   전체내용 파악 (제목 파악)   난이도 ★☆☆

끊어읽기 해석

A study by the USA's Northwestern University / provides biological evidence / that people who are bilingual / have a more powerful brain.
미국의 노스웨스턴 대학에서의 한 연구는 / 생물학적 증거를 제시한다 / 2개 국어를 하는 사람들이 / 더 강력한 두뇌를 가지고 있다는

Drs Viorica Marian and Nina Kraus investigated / how bilingualism affects the brain.
Drs Viorica Marian과 Nina Kraus는 조사했다 / 2개 국어를 말하는 능력이 뇌에 어떻게 영향을 미치는지를

They found / that studying another language / "fine-tunes" people's attention span / and enhances their memory.
그들은 발견했다 / 다른 언어를 공부하는 것이 / 사람들의 주의 지속 기간을 '미세 조정'한다는 것을 / 그리고 그들의 기억력을 향상시킨다는 것을

In particular / they discovered / that when language learners attempt to understand / speech in another language, / it activates and energizes the brainstem / —an ancient part of the brain.
특히 / 그들은 발견했다 / 언어 학습자들이 이해하려고 시도할 때 / 다른 언어의 말을 / 그것이 뇌간을 활성화시키고 활기차게 한다는 것을 / 뇌의 아주 오래된 부분인

Professor Kraus stated: / "Bilingualism / serves as enrichment for the brain / and has real consequences / when it comes to attention and working memory."
Kraus 교수는 말했다 / "2개 국어를 말하는 능력은 / 뇌를 강화하는 역할을 한다 / 그리고 실질적인 영향력을 가진다 / 주의력과 작동 기억에 있어서"

해석 미국의 노스웨스턴 대학에서의 한 연구는 2개 국어를 하는 사람들이 더 강력한 두뇌를 가지고 있다는 생물학적 증거를 제시한다. Drs Viorica Marian과 Nina Kraus는 2개 국어를 말하는 능력이 뇌에 어떻게 영향을 미치는지를 조사했다. 그들은 다른 언어를 공부하는 것이 사람들의 주의 지속 기간을 '미세 조정'하고 그들의 기억력을 향상시킨다는 것을 발견했다. 특히, 그들은 언어 학습자들이 다른 언어의 말을 이해하려고 시도할 때, 그것이 뇌의 아주 오래된 부분인 뇌간을 활성화시키고 활기차게 한다는 것을 발견했다. "2개 국어를 말하는 능력은 뇌를 강화하는 역할을 하고, 주의력과 작동 기억에 있어서 실질적인 영향력을 가진다."라고 Kraus 교수는 말했다.

① 2개 국어를 말하는 능력이 뇌에 미치는 영향

② 외국어 학습을 위한 조언
③ 2개 국어를 말하는 능력의 부정적인 영향
④ 외국어 학습의 필요성

해설 지문 전반에 걸쳐 2개 국어를 말하는 능력이 뇌에 어떤 영향을 미치는지에 대한 조사 결과를 설명하고 있고, 지문 뒷부분에서 다른 언어를 이해하려고 시도하는 것은 뇌간을 활성화시키고 활기차게 할 뿐만 아니라 2개 국어를 말하는 능력은 뇌를 강화하는 역할을 한다고 설명하고 있다. 따라서 이 지문의 제목을 '2개 국어를 말하는 능력이 뇌에 미치는 영향'이라고 표현한 ①번이 정답이다.

어휘 bilingual 2개 국어를 하는 attention span 주의 지속 기간
enhance 향상시키다 activate 활성화시키다
energize 활기차게 하다 brainstem 뇌간 enrichment 강화, 농축
consequence 영향력, 결과

22 독해 논리적 흐름 파악 (문장 삽입) 난이도 ★★☆

끊어읽기 해석

However, / poor people began / making their own boxes / and asking employers and customers for money / in recognition of their service.
하지만 / 가난한 사람들은 시작했다 / 그들 자신의 상자를 만드는 것을 / 그리고 고용주들과 손님들에게 돈을 요청하는 것을 / 그들의 봉사에 대한 답례로

Have you ever heard of Boxing Day?
박싱 데이에 대해 들어본 적이 있는가?

It's a holiday celebrated / in the United Kingdom and British Commonwealth countries / on December 26 every year.
이것은 기념되는 공휴일이다 / 영국과 영연방 국가들에서 / 매년 12월 26일에

(①) Some people say / that the ancient Roman tradition of gift giving / during the winter festival / inspired Boxing Day, / but no one knows for certain.
몇몇 사람들은 말한다 / 고대 로마의 선물 주기 전통이 / 겨울 축제 동안에 / 박싱 데이에 영감을 주었다고 / 하지만 아무도 확실히 알지 못한다

(②) This gift giving eventually took the form / of placing alms boxes in churches / on Christmas Day / so that people could drop coins into them / for later distribution to poor people.
이 선물 주기는 마침내 형태를 띠게 되었다 / 교회 안에 자선함을 설치하는 / 크리스마스에 / 그래서 사람들이 그 안에 동전을 넣을 수 있도록 / 후에 가난한 사람들에게 분배하기 위해

These early "Christmas Boxes" / were made of clay / and had holes cut in their tops / but no 'stoppers' at the bottoms.
이러한 초기 '크리스마스 상자들'은 / 진흙으로 만들어졌다 / 그리고 윗부분에 절개된 구멍이 있었다 / 하지만 바닥에 '마개'가 없었다

It was "smashing fun" / opening them!
'기막히게 좋은(깨부수는) 재미'였다 / 그것들을 개봉하는 것은!

(③) During the seventeenth century, / the alms-box of giving stopped.
17세기 동안 / 이 기부 자선함은 중단되었다

(④) From that time on, / it became a tradition / to give money / to delivery people and other service workers / on Boxing Day.
그때 이후로 / 전통이 되었다 / 돈을 주는 것이 / 배달부나 다른 종업원들에게 / 박싱 데이에

해석 박싱 데이에 대해 들어 본 적이 있는가? 이것은 영국과 영연방 국가들에서 매년 12월 26일에 기념되는 공휴일이다. 몇몇 사람들은 고대 로마의 겨울 축제 동안의 선물 주기 전통이 박싱 데이

에 영감을 주었다고 말하지만, 아무도 확실히 알지 못한다. 이 선물 주기는 마침내 후에 가난한 사람들에게 분배하기 위해 크리스마스에 사람들이 그 안에 동전을 넣을 수 있도록 교회 안에 자선함을 설치하는 형태를 띠게 되었다. 이러한 초기 '크리스마스 상자들'은 진흙으로 만들어졌고, 윗부분에 절개된 구멍이 있었지만 바닥에 '마개'가 없었다. 그것들을 개봉하는 것은 '기막히게 좋은 (깨부수는) 재미'였다! 17세기 동안 이 기부 자선함은 중단되었다. ④ 하지만 가난한 사람들은 그들 자신의 상자를 만들고, 고용주들과 손님들에게 그들의 봉사에 대한 답례로 돈을 요청하는 것을 시작했다. 그때 이후로, 박싱 데이에 배달부나 다른 종업원들에게 돈을 주는 것이 전통이 되었다.

해설 ④번 앞 문장에서 17세기 동안 이 기부 자선함이 중단되었다고 했고, ④번 뒤 문장에서 그때 이후로 박싱 데이에 배달부나 다른 종업원들에게 돈을 주는 것이 전통이 되었다고 했으므로 ④번 자리에 자선함 풍습이 중단되었으나, 하지만(However) 가난한 사람들이 그들 자신의 상자를 만들어 고용주들과 손님들에게 돈을 요청하기 시작했다는 주어진 문장이 들어가야 글의 흐름이 자연스럽게 연결된다. 따라서 ④번이 정답이다.

어휘 British Commonwealth 영연방 inspire 영감을 주다
take the form of ~의 형태를 띠다 alms box 자선함
distribution 분배 stopper 마개
smashing 기막히게 좋은, 깨부수는

23 독해 논리적 흐름 파악 (문맥상 적절한 어휘) 난이도 ★★☆

끊어읽기 해석

Companies often seek the services / of well-known sports or entertainment personalities / to promote their products.
회사들은 종종 도움을 구한다 / 잘 알려진 스포츠나 연예계의 유명 인사들의 / 그들의 상품을 홍보하기 위해

Although this is a good practice / when the person embodies wholesome qualities, / it can backfire / when the person engages in / scandalous or (A) immoral behavior.
비록 이것은 좋은 수완이지만 / 그 사람이 건전한 자질을 체현할 때는 / 그것은 역효과를 낳을 수 있다 / 그 사람이 관여할 때 / 불명예스럽거나 (A) 비도덕적인 행동에

In such cases, / the public comes to associate antisocial behavior / with the product, / and will avoid buying it.
그러한 경우에 / 대중은 반사회적인 행동을 결부시키게 된다 / 그 상품과 / 그리고 그것을 구매하기를 피할 것이다

It is advisable / that before deciding / whom to star, / a complete background check be made.
현명하다 / 결정하기 전에 / 누구에게 주연을 맡길지를 / 완벽한 신원 조사가 행해지는 것이

If a person has exhibited / (B) undesirable behavior / in the past, / he will probably exhibit / undesirable behavior / in the future.
만약 어떤 사람이 보였다면 / (B) 바람직하지 않은 행동을 / 과거에 / 그는 아마 보일 것이다 / 바람직하지 않은 행동을 / 미래에도

Also, / the contract should cancel automatically, / should the personality bring (C) discredit / to the product advertised.
또한 / 계약은 자동적으로 취소되어야 한다 / 그 유명 인사가 (C) 불명예를 가져온다면 / 광고된 상품에

해석 회사들은 종종 그들의 상품을 홍보하기 위해 잘 알려진 스포츠나 연예계의 유명 인사들의 도움을 구한다. 비록 이것은 그 사람이 건전한 자질을 체현할 때는 좋은 수완이지만, 그 사람이 불명예스럽거나 (A) 비도덕적인 행동에 관여할 때, 그것은 역효과를 낳을 수 있다. 그러한 경우에, 대중은 반사회적인 행동을 그 상품과 결부

시키게 되고, 그것을 구매하기를 피할 것이다. 누구에게 주연을 맡길지를 결정하기 전에 완벽한 신원 조사가 행해지는 것이 현명하다. 만약 어떤 사람이 과거에 (B) 바람직하지 않은 행동을 보였다면, 그는 아마 미래에도 바람직하지 않은 행동을 보일 것이다. 또한, 그 유명 인사가 광고된 상품에 (C) 불명예를 가져온다면, 계약은 자동적으로 취소되어야 한다.

	(A)	(B)	(C)
①	도덕적인	바람직한	명예
②	도덕적인	바람직한	불명예
③	비도덕적인	바람직하지 않은	명예
④	비도덕적인	바람직하지 않은	불명예

해설 (A) 유명 인사가 건전한 자질을 체현할 때 상품 홍보의 목적으로 그의 도움을 구하는 것은 좋은 수완이지만 '그 사람이 불명예스럽거나 _____ 한 행동에 관여할 때, 그것은 역효과를 낳을 수 있다'라는 문맥에서 빈칸에는 '비도덕적인'(immoral)이라는 의미가 들어가야 적절하다. (B) 누구에게 주연을 맡길지를 결정하기 전에, 완벽한 신원 조사가 행해지는 것이 현명하다고 했으므로, '만약 어떤 사람이 과거에 _____ 한 행동을 보였다면, 그는 아마 미래에도 바람직하지 않은 행동을 보일 것이다'라는 문맥에서 빈칸에는 '바람직하지 않은'(undesirable)이라는 의미가 들어가야 적절하다. (C) '그 유명 인사가 광고된 상품에 _____ 을/를 가져온다면 계약은 자동적으로 취소되어야 한다'라는 문맥에서 빈칸에는 '불명예'(discredit)라는 의미가 들어가야 적절하다. 따라서 ④ (A) immoral(비도덕적인) – (B) undesirable(바람직하지 않은) – (C) discredit(불명예)이 정답이다.

어휘 embody 체현하다, 포함하다 wholesome 건전한 backfire 역효과를 낳다 scandalous 불명예스러운 moral 도덕적인 associate 결부 짓다, 연상하다 antisocial behavior 반사회적 행동 star 주연을 맡다 exhibit 보이다 background check 신원 조사 desirable 바람직한 automatically 자동적으로 credit 명예, 신용

---

24 독해 논리적 흐름 파악 (문단 순서 배열) 난이도 ★★☆

끊어읽기 해석

The only way / for different marine animals / to survive in their harsh aquatic environment / is to help each other.
유일한 방법은 / 각양각색의 해양 동물들이 / 가혹한 수생 환경에서 살아남기 위한 / 서로를 돕는 것이다

This is especially true / in the case of the clownfish and the poisonous sea anemone.
이것은 특히 사실이다 / 클라운피시와 독이 있는 말미잘의 경우에

(A) Other fish, / fearing the anemone's poison, / won't attack the clownfish there.
다른 물고기들은 / 말미잘의 독을 두려워하는 / 그곳의 클라운피시를 공격하지 않을 것이다

(B) On the other hand, / the anemone benefits / by eating leftover food / provided by the clownfish.
한편 / 말미잘은 이득을 본다 / 남은 음식을 먹음으로써 / 클라운피시에 의해 제공된

(C) In return for cleaning the anemone, / the clownfish, / which is not affected by the anemone's poison, / lives safely / among the animal's tentacles.
말미잘을 청소해 주는 보답으로 / 클라운피시는 / 말미잘의 독에 영향을 받지 않는 / 안전하게 산다 / 그 동물의 촉수들 사이에서

해석 각양각색의 해양 동물들이 가혹한 수생 환경에서 살아남기 위한 유일한 방법은 서로를 돕는 것이다. 이것은 특히 클라운피시와 독이 있는 말미잘의 경우에 사실이다.

(C) 말미잘의 독에 영향을 받지 않는 클라운피시는 말미잘을 청소해 주는 보답으로 그 동물의 촉수들 사이에서 안전하게 산다.
(A) 말미잘의 독을 두려워하는 다른 물고기들은 그곳의 클라운피시를 공격하지 않을 것이다.
(B) 한편, 말미잘은 클라운피시에 의해 제공된 남은 음식을 먹음으로써 이득을 본다.

해설 주어진 문장에서 해양 동물들이 가혹한 수생 환경에서 살아남는 유일한 방법은 서로를 돕는 것이라고 하며 그 예로 클라운피시와 말미잘을 언급한 후, (C)에서 클라운피시가 말미잘을 청소해 주는 보답으로 말미잘의 촉수들 사이에서 안전하게 산다(lives safely)고 했다. 그리고 (A)에서 말미잘의 독을 두려워하는 다른 물고기들은 촉수 사이에 있는 클라운피시를 공격하지 않을 것(Other fish ~ won't attack)이라고 한 후, (B)에서 한편(On the other hand) 말미잘이 클라운피시로부터 어떤 혜택을 얻는지 설명하고 있다. 따라서 ③ (C) – (A) – (B)가 정답이다.

어휘 harsh 가혹한 aquatic 수생의 poisonous 독이 있는 sea anemone 말미잘 leftover 남은 음식 tentacle 촉수

---

25 독해 전체내용 파악 (요지 파악) 난이도 ★☆☆

끊어읽기 해석

ABC Airlines uses / the same scent everywhere, / for instance, / in the perfume worn by its flight attendants, in its hot towels, and in other elements of its service.
ABC 항공은 사용한다 / 모든 곳에 같은 향기를 / 예를 들어 / 승무원이 뿌리는 향수에, 더운 물수건에, 그리고 서비스의 다른 요소들에

Among the sensory elements, / using a scent is / a relatively recent marketing strategy / adopted by many retailers.
감각 요소 중에서 / 향기를 사용하는 것은 / 상대적으로 최근의 마케팅 전략이다 / 많은 소매상들에 의해 쓰이는

More and more research shows / that smell affects consumer behavior, / which stimulates / the demand for scent marketing / by stores, hotels, and even museums.
점점 더 많은 연구들이 보여 준다 / 냄새가 소비자의 행동에 영향을 미친다는 것을 / 그것은 자극한다 / 향기 마케팅에 대한 수요를 / 가게, 호텔, 그리고 심지어는 박물관의

Advertising studies / in Martin Lindstrom's book Brand Sense / suggest / that although most contemporary commercial messages / are aimed at our eyes, / many of the emotional moments / people remember on a given day / are actually prompted by smell.
광고 연구 / Martin Lindstrom의 책 『Brand Sense』에서의 / 나타낸다 / 비록 대부분의 현대 상업적 메시지가 / 우리의 시각을 겨냥하지만 / 감동적인 순간의 많은 경우는 / 사람들이 특정한 날에 기억하는 / 사실 냄새에 의해 상기된다는 것을

해석 ABC 항공은 모든 곳, 예를 들어 승무원이 뿌리는 향수에, 더운 물수건에, 그리고 서비스의 다른 요소들에 같은 향기를 사용한다. 감각 요소 중에서 향기를 사용하는 것은 많은 소매상들에 의해 쓰이는 상대적으로 최근의 마케팅 전략이다. 점점 더 많은 연구들이 냄새가 소비자의 행동에 영향을 미친다는 것을 보여 주는데, 그것은 가게, 호텔, 그리고 심지어는 박물관의 향기 마케팅에 대한 수요를 자극한다. Martin Lindstrom의 책 『Brand Sense』에서의 광고 연구는 비록 대부분의 현대 상업적 메시지가 우리의 시각을 겨냥하지만, 사람들이 특정한 날에 기억하는 감동적인 순간의 많은 경우

는 사실 냄새에 의해 상기된다는 것을 나타낸다.

① 특정한 향기들은 우리가 일하도록 힘을 준다.
② 시각은 후각보다 강하다.
③ 향기 마케팅에 대한 수요는 증가하고 있다.
④ 우리의 후각은 세월이 흐르면서 둔해진다.

해설 지문 중간에서 점점 더 많은 연구들이 냄새가 소비자의 행동에 영
    향을 미친다는 것을 보여준다고 했고, 그것이 가게, 호텔 심지어
    는 박물관에 의한 향기 마케팅의 수요를 자극한다고 설명하고 있
    다. 따라서 이 지문의 요지를 '향기 마케팅에 대한 수요는 증가하
    고 있다'라고 표현한 ③번이 정답이다.

어휘 scent 향기 sensory 감각의 strategy 전략 retailer 소매상
    stimulate 자극하다 demand 수요 contemporary 현대의
    commercial 상업적인 aim at ~을 겨냥하다
    prompt 상기시키다, 유도하다 mighty 강한, 강력한
    dull 둔한, 따분한

정답   p.117

01 ② 독해 - 전체내용 파악	**11** ② 독해 - 전체내용 파악	**21** ② 문법 - to 부정사 & 명사절
02 ③ 독해 - 논리적 흐름 파악	**12** ② 독해 - 추론	**22** ④ 독해 - 세부내용 파악
03 ② 독해 - 전체내용 파악	**13** ① 독해 - 전체내용 파악	**23** ① 독해 - 전체내용 파악
04 ③ 독해 - 논리적 흐름 파악	**14** ② 독해 - 전체내용 파악	**24** ③ 독해 - 전체내용 파악
05 ① 독해 - 전체내용 파악	**15** ④ 독해 - 논리적 흐름 파악	**25** ④ 독해 - 논리적 흐름 파악
06 ③ 독해 - 논리적 흐름 파악	**16** ④ 독해 - 전체내용 파악	
07 ③ 문법 - 수 일치	**17** ③ 독해 - 추론	
08 ① 독해 - 세부내용 파악	**18** ③ 독해 - 논리적 흐름 파악	
09 ④ 독해 - 논리적 흐름 파악	**19** ④ 독해 - 세부내용 파악	
10 ③ 독해 - 추론	**20** ② 독해 - 세부내용 파악	

취약영역 분석표

영역	세부 유형	문항 수	소계
어휘	어휘 & 표현	0	/0
	생활영어	0	
문법	수 일치	1	/2
	to 부정사 & 명사절	1	
독해	전체내용 파악	9	/23
	세부내용 파악	4	
	추론	3	
	논리적 흐름 파악	7	
총계			**/25**

· 자신이 취약한 영역은 '법원직 9급 영어, 이렇게 출제된다!'(p.8)를 통해 다시 한 번 확인하고 학습하시기 바랍니다.

---

01 독해 전체내용 파악 (글의 감상)   난이도 ★★☆

끊어읽기 해석

It was weird / being back at Foothills Hospital, / in the same room / where she rested / after going through many hours of labor / and finally giving birth to me.
이상했다 / Foothill 병원에 다시 돌아온 것이 / 같은 방에 / 그녀가 쉬었던 / 오랜 시간의 진통을 겪고 나서 / 그리고 마침내 나를 낳고 (나서)

There were beautiful hand-painted pictures / on the wall / and a clock / that ticked so loud / that it sounded like a timer / on an explosive.
손으로 칠한 아름다운 그림들이 있었다 / 벽에 / 그리고 시계가 (있었다) / 너무 크게 똑딱거려서 / 타이머처럼 들리는 / 폭발물에 설치된

In the corner / was a vase of flowers / surrounded by gifts, get-well cards and stuffed animals.
모퉁이에는 / 꽃을 꽂아 놓은 꽃병이 있었다 / 선물, 병문안 카드와 동물 인형들에 둘러싸인

I sat on the left side of the bed / holding her hand.
나는 침대 왼편에 앉았다 / 그녀의 손을 잡으면서

"Mom," / I said. // "Today I bought a new watch. / It has a video game built into it!"
"엄마" / 나는 말했다 // "오늘 새 시계를 샀어요 / 이것은 비디오 게임이 내장되어 있어요!"

Usually, / stuff like that would get me / into lots of trouble, / because she didn't want / me to waste money / on stupid things.
보통 / 이런 일은 나를 처하게 했을 것이다 / 매우 곤란한 상황에 / 그녀는 원하지 않았기 때문이다 / 내가 돈을 낭비하는 것을 / 하찮은 것들에

Today was an exception, though; / today, she didn't say a word.
하지만 오늘은 예외였다 / 오늘 그녀는 한마디도 하지 않았다

It was the only time / I ever wished / that I would get yelled at, / but she just lay there asleep.

이는 유일한 순간이었다 / 이제까지 내가 바랐던 / 호통을 듣기를 / 하지만 그녀는 그저 잠이 든 채 거기에 누워 있었다

해석 오랜 시간의 진통을 겪고 마침내 나를 낳고 나서 그녀가 쉬었던 Foothill 병원의 같은 방에 다시 돌아온 것이 이상했다. 벽에 손으로 칠한 아름다운 그림들이 있었고 너무 크게 똑딱거려서 폭발물에 설치된 타이머처럼 들리는 시계가 있었다. 모퉁이에는 선물, 병문안 카드와 동물 인형들에 둘러싸인 꽃병이 있었다. 나는 그녀의 손을 잡으면서 침대 왼편에 앉았다. "엄마," 나는 말했다. "오늘 새 시계를 샀어요. 이것은 비디오 게임이 내장되어 있어요!" 보통, 그녀는 내가 하찮은 것들에 돈을 낭비하는 것을 원하지 않았기 때문에, 이런 일은 나를 매우 곤란한 상황에 처하게 했을 것이다. 하지만 오늘은 예외였는데, 오늘 그녀는 한마디도 하지 않았다. 이는 이제까지 내가 호통을 듣기를 바랐던 유일한 순간이었지만, 그녀는 그저 잠이 든 채 거기에 누워 있었다.

① 유쾌한   ② 우울한
③ 재미있는   ④ 편안한

해설 지문 처음에서 엄마가 예전에 자신을 낳고 쉬었던 병원에 다시 돌아왔다고 했고, 지문 마지막에서 보통 때는 많은 호통을 들었을 상황에서 엄마는 아무 말도 하지 않았고 그저 잠이 든 채 누워 있다는 것을 통해 저자의 엄마가 현재 아프다는 것을 짐작할 수 있다. 따라서 지문의 분위기를 '우울한'이라고 표현한 ②번이 정답이다.

어휘 weird 이상한, 기이한   labor 진통, 노동
give birth to ~을 낳다, 출산하다   tick 똑딱거리다
explosive 폭발물; 폭발성의   built into ~에 내장된
get into 처하게 하다   exception 예외, 제외
lie 누워 있다, 거짓말하다

끊어읽기 해석

> 'Pride,' / observed Mary, / who piqued herself upon / the solidity of her reflections, / is a very ① common failing / I believe.
> '자부심'이란 / Mary는 말했다 / 자랑했던 / 자신의 생각의 확실함을 / 아주 ① 흔한 결점이라고 / 내가 생각하는
>
> By all that I have ever read, / I am convinced / that it is very common indeed, / that human nature is particularly prone to it, / and that there are very few of us / who do not ② cherish / a feeling of self-complacency / on the score of some quality or other, / real or imaginary.
> 내가 읽어왔던 모든 것을 토대로 / 나는 확신한다 / 정말 흔하다고 / 인간 본성이 특히 이것을 하기 쉽다는 것이 / 그리고 우리 중 매우 극소수라는 것이 / ② 소중히 여기지 않는 사람이 / 자기 만족의 감정을 / 그 어떤 자질을 이유로 한 / 현실이든 상상이든
>
> Vanity and pride are ③ similar things, / though the words are often used synonymously.
> 자만심과 자부심은 ③ 비슷한 것이다 / 하지만 그 단어들은 자주 같은 뜻으로 쓰인다
>
> A person may be proud / without being vain. // Pride ④ relates more / to our opinion of ourselves, / vanity / to what we would have others think of us.
> 사람은 자랑스러워할 수 있다 / 자만하지 않고 // 자부심은 더 ④ 관련이 있다 / 우리 자신에 대한 우리의 생각에 / 자만심은 (더 관련이 있다) / 다른 사람들이 우리를 어떻게 생각하게 할지에

해석 자신의 생각의 확실함을 자랑했던 Mary는 '자부심'이란 내가 생각하는 아주 ① 흔한 결점이라고 말했다. 내가 읽어왔던 모든 것을 토대로, 나는 인간 본성이 특히 이것을 하기 쉽다는 것, 그리고 현실이든 상상이든 그 어떤 자질을 이유로 한 자기 만족의 감정을 ② 소중히 여기지 않는 사람이 우리 중 매우 극소수라는 것이 정말 흔하다고 확신한다. 자만심과 자부심은 ③ 비슷한 것이지만, 그 단어들은 자주 같은 뜻으로 쓰인다. 사람은 자만하지 않고 자랑스러워할 수 있다. 자부심은 우리 자신에 대한 우리의 생각에 더 ④ 관련이 있고, 자만심은 다른 사람들이 우리를 어떻게 생각하게 할지에 더 관련이 있다.

해설 ③번 밑줄이 있는 문장 뒤에 하지만(though) 자만심과 자부심이 자주 같은 뜻으로 쓰인다고 했고, 지문 마지막에서 자부심은 우리 자신에 대한 우리의 생각에, 자만심은 다른 이들의 생각에 더 관련이 있다는 둘의 차이점에 대한 내용이 있으므로, 자만심과 자부심을 '비슷한'(Similar) 것이라고 한 내용은 문맥상 적절하지 않다. 따라서 ③ similar가 정답이다. 주어진 similar를 대신할 수 있는 어휘로는 '다른'이라는 의미의 dissimilar, different, distinct 등이 있다.

어휘 pique 자랑하다 solidity 확실함, 견고함 reflection 생각
prone to ~하기 쉬운, ~의 경향이 있는
cherish 소중히 여기다, 간직하다
self-complacency 자기 만족, 자아 도취
on the score of ~의 이유로 vanity 자만심, 허영심
synonymously 같은 뜻으로, 동의어로 vain 자만하는

---

03 독해 전체내용 파악 (글의 감상) 난이도 ★☆☆

끊어읽기 해석

> When my eighth-grade teacher announced / a graduation trip to Washington, D.C., / it never crossed my mind / that I would be left behind.

> 나의 8학년 선생님이 발표했을 때 / 워싱턴으로의 졸업여행을 / 나는 생각도 못했다 / 내가 남겨질 것이라고는
>
> We would visit Glen Echo Amusement Park / in Maryland.
> 우리는 Glen Echo 놀이공원을 방문할 것이었다 / 메릴랜드에 있는
>
> My heart beating wildly, / I raced home / to deliver the news.
> 내 심장이 거칠게 뛰면서 / 나는 집으로 달려갔다 / 그 소식을 전하러
>
> But / when my mother found out / how much the trip cost, / she just shook her head. // We couldn't afford it.
> 하지만 / 엄마가 알았을 때 / 여행이 얼마나 드는지 / 그녀는 그저 고개를 저었다 // 우리는 비용을 댈 형편이 되지 않았다.
>
> After feeling sad for 10 seconds, / I decided / to try to earn money for myself.
> 10초 동안 슬픔을 느낀 후 / 나는 결심했다 / 스스로 돈을 벌어 보기로
>
> For the next eight weeks, / I sold candy bars, delivered newspapers and mowed lawns.
> 그 이후 8주 동안 / 나는 초코바를 팔고, 신문 배달을 했으며 잔디를 깎았다
>
> Three days before the deadline, / I'd made just barely enough. // I was going!
> 최종 기한 3일 전에 / 나는 겨우 간신히 돈을 모았다 // 나도 가는 것이었다!

해석 나의 8학년 선생님이 워싱턴으로의 졸업여행을 발표했을 때, 나는 내가 남겨질 것이라고는 생각도 못했다. 우리는 메릴랜드에 있는 Glen Echo 놀이공원을 방문할 것이었다. 내 심장이 거칠게 뛰면서, 그 소식을 전하러 집으로 달려갔다. 하지만 엄마가 여행이 얼마나 드는지를 알았을 때, 그녀는 그저 고개를 저었다. 우리는 비용을 댈 형편이 되지 않았다. 10초 동안 슬픔을 느낀 후, 나는 스스로 돈을 벌어 보기로 결심했다. 그 이후 8주 동안, 나는 초코바를 팔고, 신문 배달을 했으며 잔디를 깎았다. 최종 기한 3일 전에, 나는 겨우 간신히 돈을 모았다. 나도 가는 것이었다!

① 걱정하는 → 화난 → 슬픈
② 신이 난 → 실망한 → 희망에 찬
③ 희망에 찬 → 분한 → 불안한
④ 흥분한 → 슬픈 → 걱정하는

해설 지문 앞부분에서 주인공은 졸업여행 소식을 듣고 심장이 거칠게 뛸 만큼 신이 났지만 이어서 엄마로부터 여행 비용을 댈 형편이 되지 않음을 듣고 실망했다가, 마지막에 스스로 돈을 벌어서 모은 돈으로 졸업여행을 간다는 희망에 찬 심경의 변화를 보여주고 있다. 따라서 '신이 난 → 실망한 → 희망에 찬'이라고 표현한 ②번이 정답이다.

어휘 announce 발표하다, 알리다 cross one's mind 생각이 나다
afford (~을 할) 형편이 되다 mow 깎다 lawn 잔디 barely 간신히
resentful 분한 thrilled 흥분한, 황홀한

---

04 독해 논리적 흐름 파악 (문맥상 적절한 어휘) 난이도 ★★☆

끊어읽기 해석

> It seems odd / that a sound can sometimes be heard / at its source / and (A) vanish at a distance, / only to be heard again / still farther away.
> 이상하게 여겨진다 / 소리가 때때로 들릴 수 있는 것은 / 그것의 근원에서 / 그리고 멀리서는 (A) 사라지다가도 / 결국 다시 들릴 수 있다는 것은 / 훨씬 더 멀리서
>
> For a long time / this "zone of silence" defeated / all attempts at its explanation.
> 오랫동안 / 이 '무성역'은 좌절시켰다 / 이를 설명하려는 모든 시도를
>
> At length / a meteorologist discovered / that layers of air of different temperature / interfere with sound.

마침내 / 어느 기상학자가 발견했다 / 서로 다른 온도의 공기층들이 / 소리를 방해한다는 것을

Since the air immediately above the ground / is usually warmer / than that in higher layers / the sound waves are deflected / diagonally upwards.
지면 바로 위 공기는 / 대개 더 따뜻하기 때문에 / 높은 층에 있는 공기보다 / 음파는 방향이 바뀐다 / 비스듬하게 위로

The consequences are easily deduced. // A certain distance from the source / a sound becomes (B) inaudible / because it passes over our heads.
그 결과는 쉽게 추론된다. // 근원에서 떨어진 특정한 거리에서 / 소리는 (B) 들리지 않는다 / 그것이 우리의 머리 위로 지나가기 때문에

At a height of about twenty-five miles, / however, / there is usually another layer of warm air / and this deflects the sound back / towards the earth.
약 25마일의 높이에서는 / 하지만 / 보통 따뜻한 공기층이 하나 더 있다 / 그리고 이것은 소리가 다시 방향을 바꾸게 한다 / 지면을 향해서

This explains / why there is a region of audibility / (C) beyond the zone of silence.
이것은 설명한다 / 왜 가청 지역이 있는지를 / 무성역 (C) 너머에

해석 소리가 때때로 그것의 근원에서 들리고, 멀리서는 (A) 사라지다가도 결국 훨씬 더 멀리서 다시 들릴 수 있다는 것은 이상하게 여겨진다. 오랫동안 이 '무성역'은 이를 설명하려는 모든 시도를 좌절시켰다. 마침내 어느 기상학자가 서로 다른 온도의 공기층들이 소리를 방해한다는 것을 발견했다. 지면 바로 위 공기는 높은 층에 있는 공기보다 대개 더 따뜻하기 때문에 음파는 비스듬하게 위로 방향이 바뀐다. 그 결과는 쉽게 추론된다. 근원에서 떨어진 특정한 거리에서 소리는 우리의 머리 위로 지나가기 때문에 (B) 들리지 않는다. 하지만 약 25마일의 높이에서는 보통 따뜻한 공기층이 하나 더 있는데, 이것은 소리가 지면을 향해서 다시 방향을 바꾸게 한다. 이것은 왜 무성역 (C) 너머에 가청 지역이 있는지를 설명한다.

	(A)	(B)	(C)
①	나타나다	들리지 않는	이내에
②	나타나다	들리는	너머에
③	사라지다	들리지 않는	너머에
④	사라지다	들리는	너머에

해설 (A) 빈칸이 있는 문장에서 소리가 때때로 그것의 근원에서 들리고 결국 훨씬 더 멀리서 다시 들릴 수 있다는 내용이 있으므로, 빈칸에는 멀리서는 소리가 '사라지다'(vanish)가도 다시 들린다는 내용이 들어가야 적절하다. (B) 지문 중간에서 한 기상학자가 서로 다른 온도의 공기층들이 소리를 방해한다는 것을 발견했다고 했으며 빈칸 앞에서 그 결과가 쉽게 추론된다는 내용이 있으므로, 빈칸에는 근원에서 떨어진 특정한 거리에서 소리가 '들리지 않는다'(inaudible)는 내용이 들어가야 적절하다. (C) 빈칸 앞에서 (무성역보다 높은) 약 25마일의 높이에 있는 따뜻한 공기층이 소리가 다시 지면을 향해서 방향을 바꾸게 한다는 내용이 있으므로, 빈칸에는 무성역 '너머에'(beyond) 가청 지역이 있다는 내용이 들어가야 적절하다.

따라서 ③ (A) vanish(사라지다) – (B) inaudible(들리지 않는) – (C) beyond(너머에)가 정답이다.

어휘 meteorologist 기상학자 interfere with ~을 방해하다
deflect 방향을 바꾸다, 방향을 바꾸게 하다
diagonally 비스듬하게, 대각선으로 deduce 추론하다, 유래를 찾다
inaudible 들리지 않는

끊어읽기 해석

Take high cholesterol. // Anyone can have it.
고 콜레스테롤을 섭취하세요. // 누구나 먹을 수 있습니다.

Here's something else / that you might not know.
여기에 또 다른 것이 있습니다 / 당신이 알지 못할 수도 있는

About one-fifth of your cholesterol / comes from what you eat.
당신의 콜레스테롤의 5분의 1 정도가 / 당신이 먹는 것으로부터 옵니다

That's because high cholesterol / often has as much to do / with family genes / as food.
이것은 고 콜레스테롤이 / 종종 밀접한 관련이 있기 때문입니다 / 가족 유전자와 / 음식만큼이나

So, / even if you diet and exercise / you may need some help / to lower it.
그래서 / 당신이 다이어트를 하고 운동을 해도 / 당신은 도움이 필요할 수도 있습니다 / 그 수치를 낮추기 위해서는

The good news is / that having Zelous can help.
좋은 소식은 / Zelous를 먹는 것이 도움이 될 수 있다는 것입니다

It can lower your total cholesterol / 29% to 45%.
이것은 당신의 총 콜레스테롤을 낮출 수 있습니다 / 29퍼센트에서 45퍼센트까지

Ask your doctor / if it's right for you. // Of all the cholesterol medicines, / doctors prescribe Zelous the most.
의사에게 물어보십시오 / 이것이 당신에게 맞는지 // 모든 콜레스테롤 약 중에 / 의사들은 Zelous를 가장 많이 처방합니다

Learn more. // Call us at 1-888-Zelous / or find us on the web at www.zelous.com.
더 많이 알아보세요. // 1-888-Zelous로 전화 주세요 / 또는 웹 www.zelous.com에서 저희를 찾아 주세요

해석 고 콜레스테롤을 섭취하세요. 누구나 먹을 수 있습니다. 여기에 당신이 알지 못할 수도 있는 또 다른 것이 있습니다. 당신의 콜레스테롤의 5분의 1 정도가 당신이 먹는 것으로부터 옵니다. 이것은 고 콜레스테롤이 음식만큼이나 가족 유전자와 자주 밀접한 관련이 있기 때문입니다. 그래서 당신이 다이어트를 하고 운동을 해도 그 수치를 낮추기 위해서는 도움이 필요할 수도 있습니다. 좋은 소식은 Zelous를 먹는 것이 도움이 될 수 있다는 것입니다. 이것은 당신의 총 콜레스테롤을 29퍼센트에서 45퍼센트까지 낮출 수 있습니다. 이것이 당신에게 맞는지 의사에게 물어보십시오. 모든 콜레스테롤 약 중에, 의사들은 Zelous를 가장 많이 처방합니다. 더 많이 알아보세요. 1-888-Zelous로 전화 주시거나 웹 www.zelous.com에서 저희를 찾아 주세요.

① 광고하기 위해서　　　　② 칭찬하기 위해서
③ 거절하기 위해서　　　　④ 감사하기 위해서

해설 지문 중간에서 콜레스테롤은 음식만큼이나 가족 유전자와도 관련이 있기 때문에, 콜레스테롤 수치를 낮추기 위해서는 다이어트나 운동을 하더라도 도움이 필요할 수 있으며 Zelous가 도움이 될 수 있다고 말하고 있다. 또한 지문 마지막에서 전화 또는 사이트 방문을 통해 Zelous에 대해 더 알아보라고 말하고 있다. 따라서 이 지문의 목적을 '광고하기 위해서'라고 표현한 ①번이 정답이다.

어휘 come from ~로부터 오다, 비롯되다 gene 유전자
prescribe 처방하다 reject 거절하다

06 독해 논리적 흐름 파악 (무관한 문장 삭제) 난이도 ★★☆

끊어읽기 해석

There are subtle signals / you can send / to the other person / that will bring the conversation to its close / without hurting anyone's feelings.
미묘한 신호들이 있다 / 당신이 보낼 수 있는 / 다른 사람에게 / 대화를 끝낼 / 누구의 기분도 나쁘게 하지 않으면서

① Breaking eye contact is a good way / of signaling to the other person / that you are ready / to end the conversation.
시선을 피하는 것은 좋은 방법이다 / 다른 사람에게 신호를 보내는 / 당신이 이제 준비가 되었다고 / 대화를 끝낼

② Another way to signal / that a conversation is coming to an end / is to use transition words / like "Well" or "At any rate," / or even statements / like "It was really nice talking to you."
신호를 보내는 또 하나의 방법은 / 대화가 이제 끝나간다는 / 전환어를 쓰는 것이다 / '자' 혹은 '어쨌든'과 같은 / 또는 심지어 표현을 / '당신과 이야기하게 되어 정말 즐거웠습니다'와 같은

③ The ability to converse / with those you encounter / without effort / is a very important element / of all your personal and business relationships.
대화하는 능력은 / 당신이 만나는 사람들과 / 문제없이 / 매우 중요한 요소이다 / 모든 개인적 그리고 비즈니스 관계에서

④ When you leave, / it's essential / to leave a positive final impression / as the initial impression you made.
당신이 떠날 때에는 / 매우 중요하다 / 긍정적인 마지막 인상을 남기는 것이 / 당신이 준 첫인상과 더불어

해석 누구의 기분도 나쁘게 하지 않으면서 당신이 다른 사람에게 보낼 수 있는, 대화를 끝낼 미묘한 신호들이 있다. ① 시선을 피하는 것은 당신이 이제 대화를 끝낼 준비가 되었다고 다른 사람에게 신호를 보내는 좋은 방법이다. ② 대화가 이제 끝나간다는 신호를 보내는 또 하나의 방법은 '자' 혹은 '어쨌든'과 같은 전환어나 심지어는 '당신과 이야기하게 되어 정말 즐거웠습니다.'와 같은 표현을 쓰는 것이다. ③ 당신이 만나는 사람들과 문제없이 대화하는 능력은 모든 개인적 그리고 비즈니스 관계에서 매우 중요한 요소이다. ④ 당신이 떠날 때에는, 당신이 준 첫인상과 더불어 긍정적인 마지막 인상을 남기는 것이 매우 중요하다.

해설 지문 처음에서 누구의 기분도 나쁘게 하지 않으면서 대화를 끝내는 미묘한 신호들이 있다고 언급한 후, 그 신호의 예로 ①번에서는 시선을 피하는 방법, ②번에서는 대화가 끝나간다는 신호를 보내는 말과 표현을 쓰는 것을 제시하고, 이러한 신호들이 필요한 이유로 ④번에서 긍정적인 마지막 인상을 남기는 것의 중요성을 설명하였다. 그러나 ③번은 '문제없이 대화할 수 있는 능력의 중요성'에 대한 내용으로, 기분을 상하지 않게 대화를 끝내는 방법에 대한 내용과 관련이 없다. 따라서 ③번이 정답이다.

어휘 subtle 미묘한, 교묘한 signal 신호; 신호를 보내다
transition word 전환어 at any rate 어쨌든
statement 표현, 진술 encounter 만나다, 마주치다
without effort 문제없이, 거뜬히 converse 대화하다, 이야기하다
essential 매우 중요한, 필수적인 initial impression 첫인상

07 문법 수 일치 난이도 ★★☆

해석 책임감 있는 관광객은 환경을 보호하는 것이 그것을 복원하는 것보다 훨씬 더 쉽다는 것을 안다. 당신이 여행하는 동안 자연을 보호하기 위해 할 수 있는 많은 간단한 것들이 있다. 산호나 상아와 같이 멸종 위기에 처한 식물이나 동물로 만들어진 기념품들을 사지 말아라. 만약에 아무도 그것들을 사지 않는다면, 사람들은 멸종 위기에 처한 그 동물들을 죽이는 것을 멈출 것이다. 책임감 있는 관광은 지역 자원도 고려한다. 인도 서부 해안에 위치한 Goa의 한 5성급 호텔은 다섯 개의 현지 마을이 쓰는 양만큼 물을 쓰고, 거기서 묵는 한 사람은 지역 주민보다 28배 더 많은 전기를 쓴다. 책임감 있는 관광객은 자신이 써야 하는 것보다 더 많이 쓰면 안 된다. 책임감 있는 관광은 지구온난화를 감소시키기 위해 탄소 배출을 줄이는 것 또한 목표로 한다. 가능하다면, 비행기 대신 기차나 버스를 타라. 근거리에서는, 자전거를 타거나 걸어라. 걷기는 자연에 가장 좋고, 당신이 방문하고 있는 곳을 더 자세히 알게 해 준다.

해설 ③ 주어와 동사의 수 일치 주어 자리에 단수 명사 one person이 왔으므로 복수 동사 use를 단수 동사 uses로 고쳐야 한다. 참고로, 주어와 동사 사이에 온 수식어 거품(staying there)은 동사의 수 결정에 영향을 주지 않는다.

오답분석 ① to 부정사의 역할 '자연을 보호하기 위해'라는 의미를 표현하기 위해 부사처럼 목적을 나타낼 수 있는 to 부정사 to protect가 올바르게 쓰였다.
② 동명사와 to 부정사 둘 다 목적어로 취하는 동사 동사 stop 뒤에는 동명사와 to 부정사가 둘 다 올 수 있는데, '~하는 것을 멈추다'라는 의미를 나타낼 때는 동명사를 목적어로 취하므로 동명사 killing이 올바르게 쓰였다.
④ 5형식 동사 사역동사 let은 목적격 보어로 동사원형을 취하므로 동사원형 get이 목적격 보어 자리에 올바르게 쓰였다.

어휘 restore 복원하다 souvenir 기념품, 선물
endangered 멸종 위기에 처한 coral 산호 ivory 상아
resource 자원 resident 주민, 거주자 carbon 탄소
emission 배출(물), 발산

👍 **이것도 알면 합격!**

동사 stop 뒤에는 동명사와 to 부정사가 둘 다 올 수 있는데, stop 뒤에 동명사가 목적어로 오면 '~하는 것을 멈추다'라는 의미를 나타내고, to 부정사가 오면 목적어가 아닌 to 부정사의 부사적 용법으로 쓰여 '~하기 위해 (하던 일을) 멈추다'라는 의미를 나타낸다는 것을 알아두자.

08 독해 세부내용 파악 (지칭 대상 파악) 난이도 ★☆☆

끊어읽기 해석

Imagine / that opportunities fall / in the form of rain, / and you are standing / in that rain / holding an umbrella.
상상해 보라 / 기회가 내린다고 / 비의 형태로 / 그리고 당신은 서 있다고 / 그 빗속에 / 우산을 들고

Even though / the raindrops are abundant, / you aren't catching / any of them.
비록 / 빗방울이 넘칠 정도로 많더라도 / 당신은 받고 있지 않다 / 그 중 한 방울도

But / suppose / that underneath the edges of the umbrella / is a circle of buckets.
그러나 / 생각해 보라 / 우산의 가장자리 아래에 / 둥글게 놓여진 양동이들이 있다고

As you stand / holding the umbrella perfectly straight, / most of the raindrops fall off the edges / down into the empty buckets, / with some falling in between.
당신이 서 있을 때 / 우산을 완벽하게 똑바로 들고 / 대부분의 빗방울은 가장자리에서 떨어진다 / 아래의 빈 양동이들로 / 몇몇은 그 사이로 떨어지면서

If these buckets have no purpose, / they will have no meaning for you, / and the raindrops will be wasted.

만약에 이 양동이들에 목적이 없다면 / 그것들은 당신에게 아무런 의미도 없을 것이다 / 그리고 빗방울들은 낭비될 것이다

해석 기회가 비의 형태로 내리고 당신은 그 빗속에 우산을 들고 서 있다고 상상해 보라. 비록 빗방울이 넘칠 정도로 많더라도, 당신은 그중 한 방울도 받고 있지 않다. 그러나 우산의 가장자리 아래에 둥글게 놓여진 양동이들이 있다고 생각해 보라. 당신이 우산을 완벽하게 똑바로 들고 서 있을 때, 몇몇은 그 사이로 떨어지면서 대부분의 빗방울은 가장자리에서 아래의 빈 양동이들로 떨어진다. 만약에 이 양동이들에 목적이 없다면, 그것들은 당신에게 아무런 의미도 없을 것이고, 빗방울들은 낭비될 것이다.

① 기회　　　　　　② 노력
③ 결과　　　　　　④ 목적

해설 밑줄 친 raindrops가 있는 문장의 앞에서 기회가 비의 형태로 내린다고 상상해 보라고 하며 지문 전반에 걸쳐 기회를 빗방울에 빗대어 설명하고 있으므로, raindrops는 '기회'를 의미한다. 따라서 ① opportunities가 정답이다.

어휘 abundant 넘칠 정도로 많은, 풍부한　underneath ~의 아래에
edge 가장자리　bucket 양동이

끊어읽기 해석

(A) The concept of laissez faire / is often paired with capitalism, / an economic system / that is based on private ownership / of the factors of production.
자유방임주의라는 개념은 / 흔히 자본주의와 짝지어진다 / 경제 체제인 / 개인 소유에 기반을 둔 / 생산 요소들의

Capitalism, / the foundation of market economies, / operates on the belief / that, on their own, producers will create / the goods and services / that consumers demand.
자본주의는 / 시장 경제의 기반인 / 믿음에 의해 작동한다 / 생산자가 자기 스스로 만들 것이라는 / 상품과 서비스를 / 고객들이 요구하는

(B) Therefore, / according to laissez faire capitalism, / there is no need for government involvement / in the marketplace.
그러므로 / 자유방임주의적 자본주의에 따르면 / 정부의 개입이 필요하지 않다 / 시장에는

This laissez faire capitalism is / a market economy / in its pure form.
이 자유방임주의적 자본주의는 / 시장 경제이다 / 순수한 형태의

However, / there are no pure market economies / —all real-world market economies have / some degree of government involvement.
하지만 / 완전한 시장 경제는 없다 / 모든 현실 사회의 시장 경제는 가지고 있다 / 어느 정도의 정부의 개입을

(C) Sometimes the government's economic role / is to stay out of the marketplace.
때때로 정부의 경제적 역할은 / 시장에 관여하지 않는 것이다

The principle / that the government should not interfere / in the economy / is called laissez faire, / a French phrase meaning "leave things alone."
그 원칙은 / 정부가 개입해서는 안 된다는 / 경제에 / 자유방임주의라고 불린다 / '내버려두다'를 의미하는 불어 표현인

해석 (C) 때때로 정부의 경제적 역할은 시장에 관여하지 않는 것이다. 정부가 경제에 개입해서는 안 된다는 그 원칙은 '내버려두다'를 의미하는 불어 표현인 자유방임주의라고 불린다.
(A) 자유방임주의라는 개념은 생산 요소들의 개인 소유에 기반을 둔 경제 체제인 자본주의와 흔히 짝지어진다. 시장 경제의 기

반인 자본주의는 생산자가 고객들이 요구하는 상품과 서비스를 자기 스스로 만들 것이라는 믿음에 의해 작동한다.
(B) 그러므로 자유방임주의적 자본주의에 따르면, 시장에는 정부의 개입이 필요하지 않다. 이 자유방임주의적 자본주의는 순수한 형태의 시장 경제이다. 하지만 완전한 시장 경제는 없으며, 모든 현실 사회의 시장 경제는 어느 정도의 정부의 개입을 가지고 있다.

해설 (C)에서 정부가 경제에 개입해서는 안 된다는 원칙이 자유방임주의라는 것을 언급하고, (A)에서 이 자유방임주의가 흔히 자본주의와 짝지어진다고 설명한 뒤, 이어서 (B)에서 그러므로(Therefore) 자유방임주의적 자본주의에 따르면 시장에는 정부의 개입이 필요하지 않지만, 현실 사회의 시장 경제에서는 어느 정도 정부의 개입이 있다고 설명하고 있다. 따라서 ④ (C) – (A) – (B)가 정답이다.

어휘 laissez faire 자유방임주의　capitalism 자본주의
foundation 기반, 기초　involvement 개입, 관여
stay out of ~에 관여하지 않다　interfere 개입하다

끊어읽기 해석

Most people think / the world is (random) to them.
대부분의 사람들은 생각한다 / 세상이 그들에게 (임의적)이라고

They allow events to pass / without connecting them to other events.
그들은 사건을 지나가게 한다 / 다른 사건들과 연결 짓지 않은 채

Whatever happens, / and there's nothing else to it.
무슨 일이 일어나든 / 그것에 그 밖에 다른 것은 없다

Unlike most people, / scientists see the world / in a very orderly way. // They look for / what goes with what.
대부분의 사람들과는 다르게 / 과학자들은 세상을 바라본다 / 매우 질서정연한 방식으로 // 그들은 찾는다 / 무엇이 무엇에 동반되는지

Events and conditions are not (random); / they have cause and effect.
사건과 환경은 (임의적)이지 않다 / 그것들에는 원인과 결과가 있다

Scientists everywhere, all the time, see connections / because they are looking for connections.
과학자들은 모든 곳에서 언제나 연관성을 살핀다 / 그들은 연관성을 찾고 있기 때문에

What happens / when you throw a rock / up in the air?
어떤 일이 벌어질까 / 돌을 던지면 / 하늘 높이?

It comes back down every time. // That is the pattern, / the essence of science.
그것은 매번 다시 아래로 떨어진다. // 그것은 패턴이다 / 과학의 본질인

해석 대부분의 사람들은 세상이 그들에게 (임의적)이라고 생각한다. 그들은 다른 사건들과 연결 짓지 않은 채 사건을 지나가게 한다. 무슨 일이 일어나든, 그것에 그 밖에 다른 것은 없다. 대부분의 사람들과는 다르게, 과학자들은 매우 질서정연한 방식으로 세상을 바라본다. 그들은 무엇이 무엇에 동반되는지 찾는다. 사건과 환경은 (임의적)이지 않고, 그것들에는 원인과 결과가 있다. 과학자들은 연관성을 찾고 있기 때문에, 모든 곳에서 언제나 연관성을 살핀다. 돌을 하늘 높이 던지면 어떤 일이 벌어질까? 그것은 매번 다시 아래로 떨어진다. 그것은 과학의 본질인 패턴이다.

① 일관된　　　　　② 창조적인
③ 임의적인　　　　④ 잔인한

해설 지문 앞부분에 대부분의 사람들은 사건을 다른 사건들과 연결 짓

어휘 **orderly** 질서정연한, 정돈된 **essence** 본질 **consistent** 일관된
creative 창조적인 **random** 임의적인 **cruel** 잔인한

11 독해 전체내용 파악 (목적 파악) 난이도 ★☆☆

끊어읽기 해석

Dear Amy,
Amy에게,

Don't give up! // I know / you can do this assignment.
포기하지 말게나! // 나는 알고 있어 / 자네가 이 과제를 할 수 있다는 것을

I think / you need to start / by changing the way / you look at yourself and your metaphor.
나는 생각하네 / 자네가 시작할 필요가 있다고 / 방식을 바꿈으로써 / 자네 스스로와 자네의 비유를 바라보는

You have already come up with many things / that are half one thing / and half another thing.
자네는 벌써 많은 것들을 찾아냈어 / 한 가지의 절반인 / 그리고 다른 하나의 절반인

I want you to make a list / of things that are good combinations of two parts.
나는 자네가 목록을 만들어 보았으면 하네 / 두 부분의 조합이 좋은 것들의

There are lots of things / that are better / when they're combined / with something else.
많은 것들이 있네 / 더 나은 / 조합되었을 때 / 다른 무엇과

Here, / I'll start your list: / peanut butter and jelly are better together / than they are apart.
여기 / 자네의 목록을 시작하겠네 / 땅콩버터와 잼은 함께일 때 더 맛있지 / 따로일 때보다

And think / about all those exciting varieties / of hybrid roses.
그리고 생각해 보게 / 그 모든 흥미로운 품종들에 대해 / 교배종 장미의

If you keep on going with this list, / I think / you can finish the assignment / by Friday.
이 목록을 계속 작성해나가면 / 나는 생각하네 / 자네가 이 과제를 끝낼 수 있을 거라고 / 금요일까지

If you're still stuck, / come and talk to me before then.
만약 여전히 막히면 / 그 전에 나한테 다시 와서 이야기하게

Mrs. Thomas
Mrs. Thomas로부터

해석 Amy에게,
포기하지 말게나! 나는 자네가 이 과제를 할 수 있다는 것을 알고 있어. 나는 자네가 자네 스스로와 자네의 비유를 바라보는 방식을 바꿈으로써 시작할 필요가 있다고 생각하네. 자네는 벌써 한 가지의 절반 그리고 다른 하나의 절반인 많은 것들을 찾아냈어.
나는 자네가 두 부분의 조합이 좋은 것들의 목록을 만들어 보았으면 하네. 다른 무엇과 조합되었을 때 더 나은 많은 것들이 있네. 여기, 자네의 목록을 시작하겠네. 땅콩버터와 잼은 따로일 때보다 함께일 때 더 맛있지. 그리고 교배종 장미의 그 모든 흥미로운 품종들에 대해 생각해 보게.
이 목록을 계속 작성해나가면, 나는 자네가 금요일까지 이 과제를 끝낼 수 있을 거라고 생각하네. 만약 여전히 막히면, 그 전에 나한테 다시 와서 이야기하게.

Mrs. Thomas로부터

① 알리기 위해서   ② 격려하기 위해서
③ 경고하기 위해서   ④ 불평하기 위해서

해설 지문 앞부분에서 화자는 Amy에게 포기하지 말라고 했고, Amy가 과제를 할 수 있다는 것을 알고 있다고 하며 용기를 주고 있다. 따라서 이 지문의 목적을 '격려하기 위해서'라고 표현한 ②번이 정답이다.

어휘 **metaphor** 비유, 은유 **come up with** ~을 찾아내다, 제안하다
variety 품종, 다양성 **hybrid** 교배종의, 잡종의 **stuck** 막힌

12 독해 추론 (빈칸 완성 - 구) 난이도 ★★☆

끊어읽기 해석

In sudden infant death syndrome (SIDS), / a sleeping baby stops breathing / and dies.
유아 돌연사 증후군(SIDS)에서 / 잠자는 아기는 호흡이 멈춘다 / 그래서 죽는다

In the United States, / SIDS strikes / about two of every thousand infants, / usually when they are two to four months old.
미국에서 / SIDS는 발생한다 / 유아 천 명 가운데 두 명꼴로 / 보통 그들이 생후 2개월에서 4개월일 때

SIDS is less common / in cultures / where infants and parents sleep / in the same bed, / suggesting that sleeping position may be important.
SIDS는 덜 흔하다 / 문화에서는 / 유아와 부모가 자는 / 같은 침대에서 / (이는) 수면 자세가 중요할 수도 있다는 것을 시사한다

Indeed, / about half of apparent SIDS cases / maybe accidental suffocations / caused / when infants lie face down / on soft surfaces.
실제로 / SIDS인 것처럼 여겨지는 경우의 절반 가량은 / 우연한 질식일 수도 있다 / 일어난 / 유아가 엎드렸을 때 / 푹신한 지면에

Other SIDS cases may stem / from problems with brain systems / regulating breathing / or from exposure to cigarette smoke.
다른 SIDS의 경우는 기인할 수도 있다 / 두뇌 체계의 문제에서 / 호흡을 조절하는 / 또는 담배 연기에의 노출에서

해설 유아 돌연사 증후군(SIDS)에서, 잠자는 아기는 호흡이 멈춰서 죽는다. 미국에서 SIDS는 보통 그들이 생후 2개월에서 4개월일 때, 유아 천 명 가운데 두 명꼴로 발생한다. SIDS는 유아와 부모가 같은 침대에서 자는 문화에서는 덜 흔한데, 이는 수면 자세가 중요할 수도 있다는 것을 시사한다. 실제로, SIDS인 것처럼 여겨지는 경우의 절반 가량은 유아가 푹신한 지면에 엎드렸을 때 일어난 우연한 질식일 수도 있다. 다른 SIDS의 경우는 호흡을 조절하는 두뇌 체계의 문제 또는 담배 연기에의 노출에서 기인할 수도 있다.

① 식습관   ② 수면 자세
③ 가정 폭력   ④ 유아의 나이

해설 빈칸 앞에 유아와 부모가 함께 자는 문화에서는 SIDS가 덜 흔하다는 내용이 있고, 빈칸 뒤에 실제로 SIDS인 것처럼 여겨지는 경우의 절반은 유아가 푹신한 지면에 엎드렸을 때 우연히 일어난 질식일 수 있다는 내용이 있으므로, 이것이 '수면 자세'가 중요할 수도 있다는 것을 시사한다고 한 ②번이 정답이다.

어휘 **infant** 유아; 유아용의 **strike** 발생하다, 때리다
apparent ~인 것처럼 여겨지는, 분명한
accidental 우연한, 돌발적인 **suffocation** 질식
lie face down 엎드리다 **stem from** ~에서 기인하다
regulate 조절하다 **exposure** 노출
domestic violence 가정 폭력

13 독해 전체내용 파악 (제목 파악)   난이도 ★★☆

끊어읽기 해석

We humans are not bad / at smelling. // We can distinguish / about 10,000 different smells, / and we do it / in just a few milliseconds.
우리 인간은 못하는 것이 아니다 / 냄새 맡는 것을 // 우리는 구별할 수 있다 / 대략 만 개의 다른 냄새를 / 그리고 우리는 이것을 한다 / 단지 천 분의 몇 초 내에

But / we use our brains / for all kinds of other things, / like interpreting images from our eyes / and engaging in a variety of mental activities.
하지만 / 우리는 뇌를 사용한다 / 다른 모든 종류의 것들을 위해 / 눈으로 이미지를 해석하는 것과 같은 / 그리고 여러 가지 정신적 활동에 참여하는 것(과 같은)

Other animals don't have / this kind of distraction, / so their sense of smell / is much better / than ours.
다른 동물들은 갖지 않는다 / 이러한 종류의 집중을 방해하는 것들을 / 그래서 그들의 후각은 / 훨씬 더 낫다 / 우리의 것보다

Sharks, / for example, / can smell 10,000 times better / than we do.
상어는 / 예를 들어 / 만 배나 더 냄새를 잘 맡을 수 있다 / 우리가 맡는 것보다

Salmon are even better. // It is known / that they can smell 30,000 times better / than us.
연어는 훨씬 더 잘한다 // 알려져 있다 / 그들은 삼만 배나 더 냄새를 잘 맡을 수 있다고 / 우리보다

Many scientists believe / that's how they smell their way back home / when they are ready to give birth.
많은 과학자들은 믿는다 / 그것이 그들이 고향으로 돌아가는 경로의 냄새를 맡는 방법이라고 / 그들이 산란할 준비가 되었을 때

For fish like these, / the whole world must be full / of patterns of scents.
이러한 물고기들에게는 / 온 세상이 분명 가득 차 있을 것이다 / 냄새의 패턴들로

By contrast, / for us, / the world is full / of patterns of sights.
그에 반해 / 우리에게 / 세상은 가득 차 있다 / 장면의 패턴들로

해석 우리 인간은 냄새 맡는 것을 못하는 것이 아니다. 우리는 대략 만 개의 다른 냄새를 구별할 수 있고, 우리는 이것을 단지 천 분의 몇 초 내에 한다. 하지만 우리는 눈으로 이미지를 해석하고 여러 가지 정신적 활동에 참여하는 것과 같은 다른 모든 종류의 것들을 위해 뇌를 사용한다. 다른 동물들은 이러한 종류의 집중을 방해하는 것들을 갖지 않아서, 그들의 후각은 우리의 것보다 훨씬 더 낫다. 예를 들어, 상어는 우리가 맡는 것보다 만 배나 더 냄새를 잘 맡을 수 있다. 연어는 훨씬 더 잘한다. 그들은 우리보다 삼만 배나 더 냄새를 잘 맡을 수 있다고 알려져 있다. 많은 과학자들은 그것이 그들이 산란할 준비가 되었을 때 고향으로 돌아가는 경로의 냄새를 맡는 방법이라고 믿는다. 이러한 물고기들에게는 온 세상이 분명 냄새의 패턴들로 가득 차 있을 것이다. 그에 반해, 우리에게 세상은 장면의 패턴들로 가득 차 있다.

① 누가 가장 냄새를 잘 맡는가?
② 냄새와 고향
③ 냄새가 동물들에게 의미하는 것
④ 인간의 정신적 활동

해설 지문 처음에서 인간이 냄새 맡는 것을 못하는 게 아니라고 언급하고, 이어서 동물들의 후각이 우리보다 훨씬 낫다고 하며 상어와 연어의 후각을 예로 들어 인간과 비교하고 있다. 따라서 이 지문의 제목을 '누가 가장 냄새를 잘 맡는가?'라고 표현한 ①번이 정답이다.

어휘 distinguish 구별하다   interpret 해석하다, 설명하다
engage in ~에 참여하다, 종사하다
distraction 집중을 방해하는 것들, 정신 착란   scent 냄새, 자취

14 독해 전체내용 파악 (주제 파악)   난이도 ★☆☆

끊어읽기 해석

Some societies have a custom / called the couvade.
어떤 사회에는 관습이 있다 / 쿠바드라고 불리는

The couvade is a ceremony / in which the husband acts / as if he is suffering from labor pains / at the same time that his wife actually gives birth.
쿠바드는 의식이다 / 남편이 행동을 취하는 / 마치 그가 분만통을 겪고 있는 것처럼 / 그의 아내가 실제로 출산하는 동시에

Although no one seems able to explain fully / the meaning of the couvade, / there are several theories.
아무도 충분히 설명할 수 있는 것 같지 않지만 / 쿠바드의 의미를 / 몇몇 이론들이 있다

According to one, / the couvade is a way / of warding off evil spirits.
한 가지에 따르면 / 쿠바드는 방식이다 / 악령을 물리치는

In effect, / the husband directs attention away / from his wife and toward himself.
실제로 / 남편은 관심을 돌린다 / 그의 아내에게서 자신에게로

Another theory speculates / that the couvade is a way / of publicly identifying the father / so that his paternity will not be in doubt.
또 다른 이론은 추측한다 / 쿠바드가 방법이라고 / 공개적으로 아버지를 확인하는 / 그래서 그가 아버지임을 의심받지 않도록

해석 어떤 사회에는 쿠바드라고 불리는 관습이 있다. 쿠바드는 그의 아내가 실제로 출산하는 동시에 남편이 마치 그가 분만통을 겪고 있는 것처럼 행동을 취하는 의식이다. 아무도 쿠바드의 의미를 충분히 설명할 수 있는 것 같지 않지만, 몇몇 이론들이 있다. 한 가지에 따르면, 쿠바드는 악령을 물리치는 방식이다. 실제로, 남편은 그의 아내에게서 자신에게로 관심을 돌린다. 또 다른 이론은 쿠바드가 그가 아버지임을 의심받지 않도록 공개적으로 아버지를 확인하는 방법이라고 추측한다.

① 일부 사회에서 출산의 의미
② 쿠바드의 의미를 설명하는 이론들
③ 출산에 대해 일부 사람들이 갖고 있는 미신
④ 남편이 출산의 고통을 함께하는 것의 중요성

해설 지문 처음에서 쿠바드라고 불리는 관습을 소개한 후, 이어서 쿠바드의 의미를 추측하는 두 가지 이론을 설명하고 있다. 따라서 이 지문의 주제를 '쿠바드의 의미를 설명하는 이론들'이라고 표현한 ②번이 정답이다.

어휘 couvade 쿠바드, 의만   labor pain 분만통, 산통
ward off ~을 물리치다, 피하다   speculate 추측하다, 투기하다
paternity 아버지임   superstition 미신

15 독해 논리적 흐름 파악 (문단 순서 배열)   난이도 ★☆☆

끊어읽기 해석

The Taj Mahal was designated / a UNESCO World Heritage Site / in 1983 / because of its architectural splendor.
타지마할은 지정되었다 / 유네스코 세계 문화유산 보호지역으로 / 1983년에 / 그것의 건축학적 화려함 때문에

(A) Since the Taj Mahal is not only a famous tourist attraction / but also a masterpiece in the history of architecture, / the efforts to preserve it / should be continued.
타지마할은 유명한 관광 명소일 뿐만 아니라 / 건축 역사의 걸작이기 때문에 / 이것을 보존하려는 노력은 / 지속되어야 한다

(B) Therefore, / recently, / industries have moved / farther away from the site / in an attempt to retain / the quality of its facade.
그 결과 / 최근에 / 산업들은 이전했다 / 이 부지로부터 멀리 / 유지하기 위해 / 그 건물 외관의 품질을

(C) But / its brilliance has faded / over the years, / mainly due to air pollution of the Agra area.
하지만 / 이것의 화려함은 점점 희미해졌다 / 수년에 걸쳐 / 주로 아그라 지역의 대기 오염 때문에

해석 | 타지마할은 그것의 건축학적 화려함 때문에 1983년에 유네스코 세계 문화유산 보호지역으로 지정되었다.

(C) 하지만 주로 아그라 지역의 대기 오염 때문에 이것의 화려함은 수년에 걸쳐 점점 희미해졌다.

(B) 그 결과, 최근에 산업들은 그 건물 외관의 품질을 유지하기 위해 이 부지로부터 멀리 이전했다.

(A) 타지마할은 유명한 관광 명소일 뿐만 아니라 건축 역사의 걸작이기 때문에, 이것을 보존하려는 노력은 지속되어야 한다.

해설 | 주어진 문장에서 건축학적 화려함 때문에 타지마할이 유네스코 세계 문화유산 보호지역으로 지정됐다고 한 뒤, (C)에서 하지만(But) 대기 오염으로 인해 그 화려함이 점점 사라졌다고 했다. (B)에서 그 결과(Therefore) 그 건물 외관의 품질을 유지하기 위한 노력으로 최근 산업들이 다른 곳으로 이전하게 되었음을 설명하고 있고, 뒤이어 (A)에서 타지마할을 보존하려는 노력이 필요한 이유를 강조하고 있다. 따라서 ④ (C) – (B) – (A)가 정답이다.

어휘 | **designate** 지정하다, 지명하다 **splendor** 화려함, 훌륭함
masterpiece 걸작 **preserve** 보존하다
in an attempt to ~하기 위해, ~하려는 시도로 **retain** 유지하다
facade (건물의) 외관 **brilliance** 화려함, 광명
fade 점점 희미해지다

16 독해 전체내용 파악 (글의 감상) 난이도 ★★☆

끊어읽기 해석

Habitat for humanity is a program / aimed at eliminating / substandard housing homelessness / around the world.
'해비타트 운동'은 프로그램이다 / 없애는 것을 목표로 한 / 열악한 주택 노숙을 / 전 세계의

Habitat employees and dedicated volunteers / work together / to build new homes / and renovate old ones / that are then sold / at no profit / to families in need.
해비타트 직원들과 헌신적인 자원봉사자들은 / 함께 일한다 / 새 집을 짓기 위해 / 그리고 헌 집을 보수하기 (위해) / 이후에 팔리는 / 이윤 없이 / 필요로 하는 가족들에게

The *Habitat* volunteers are rewarded / with a keen sense of accomplishment / and strong bonds of friendship.
'해비타트' 자원봉사자들에게는 주어진다 / 강한 성취감이 / 그리고 단단한 우호의 결속력이

New volunteers are needed / throughout the country / to continue / the work of this wonderful organization.
새로운 자원봉사자들이 필요하다 / 전국적으로 / 지속하기 위해서는 / 이 멋진 단체의 일을

No special building skills are required. // Wouldn't you like to join the thousands / who have enabled / more than 300,000 people around the world / to live in sturdy, decent housing?
전문 건설 기술이 요구되는 건 아니다. // 수천 명에 합류하고 싶지 않은가 / 가능하게 한 / 전 세계 삼십만 명 이상의 사람들이 / 튼튼하고 제대로 된 집에서 사는 것을?

해석 | '해비타트 운동'은 전 세계의 열악한 주택 노숙을 없애는 것을 목표로 한 프로그램이다. 해비타트 직원들과 헌신적인 자원봉사자들은 필요로 하는 가족들에게 이후에 이윤 없이 팔리는 새 집을 짓고 헌 집을 보수하기 위해 함께 일한다. '해비타트' 자원봉사자들에게는 강한 성취감과 단단한 우호의 결속력이 주어진다. 이 멋진 단체의 일을 지속하기 위해서는 전국적으로 새로운 자원봉사자들이 필요하다. 전문 건설 기술이 요구되는 건 아니다. 전 세계 삼십만 명 이상의 사람들이 튼튼하고 제대로 된 집에서 사는 것을 가능하게 한 수천 명에 합류하고 싶지 않은가?

① 연민 어린 ② 감탄하는
③ 비판하는 ④ 명랑한

해설 | 지문 전반에 걸쳐 '해비타트 운동'이라는 프로그램을 소개하며, 지문 마지막에서 자원봉사에 전문 건설 기술이 요구되지 않으니, 삼십만 명 이상의 사람들을 튼튼하고 제대로 된 집에서 살 수 있도록 해 준 이 단체에 합류하지 않겠느냐고 하며 자원봉사에 참여할 것을 권유하고 있다. 따라서 필자의 태도를 '명랑한'이라고 표현한 ④번이 정답이다.

어휘 | **eliminate** 없애다, 제거하다 **substandard** 열악한, 수준 이하의
dedicated 헌신적인 **renovate** 보수하다 **keen** 강한
accomplishment 성취 **sturdy** 튼튼한 **decent** 제대로 된, 괜찮은
compassionate 연민 어린, 동정하는 **admiring** 감탄하는
lighthearted 명랑한, 마음 편한

17 독해 추론 (빈칸 완성 - 구) 난이도 ★★☆

끊어읽기 해석

Conjoined twins are usually classified / into three basic categories / depending on the point where they are joined.
샴쌍둥이는 일반적으로 분류된다 / 세 가지 기본적인 범주로 / 그들이 붙어 있는 지점에 따라서

Twins of the first type / are conjoined / in a way / that never involves the heart or the midline of the body.
첫 번째 유형의 쌍둥이는 / 연결되어 있다 / 방식으로 / 심장이나 몸의 정중선을 절대 포함하지 않는

For example, / about 2 percent of all conjoined twins / are attached at the head only, / and about 19 percent / are joined at the buttocks.
예를 들어 / 전체 샴쌍둥이 중 약 2퍼센트는 / 머리만 붙어 있다 / 그리고 약 19퍼센트는 / 엉덩이가 붙어 있다

Twins of the second type / are always joined / in a way / that involves the midline of the body.
두 번째 유형의 쌍둥이는 / 항상 붙어 있다 / 방식으로 / 몸의 정중선을 포함하는

Many twins joined at the midline / share a heart.
정중선이 붙어 있는 많은 쌍둥이는 / 심장을 공유한다

Around 35 percent are fused together / at the upper half of the trunk.
약 35퍼센트는 함께 결합되어 있다 / 몸통의 위쪽 절반이

Another 30 percent are joined / at the lower half of their bodies.
또 다른 30퍼센트는 붙어 있다 / 그들 몸의 아래쪽 절반이

Finally, / the third major type of conjoined twins / includes the very rare forms.
마지막으로 / 세 번째 주요 유형의 샴쌍둥이는 / 매우 드문 형태를 포함한다

In this category are those / in which one twin is smaller, less formed, / and dependent on the other, / as well as the cases / involving one twin born completely / within the body of his or her sibling.
이 범주에는 그것(경우)들이 있다 / 쌍둥이 한 명이 더 작고, 덜 형성되고 / 다른 쌍둥이에게 의존적인 / 경우들뿐만 아니라 / 완전히 태어난 쌍둥이 한 명을 포함한 / 자신의 형제자매의 몸 안에서

해석 샴쌍둥이는 그들이 붙어 있는 지점에 따라서 일반적으로 세 가지 기본적인 범주로 분류된다. 첫 번째 유형의 쌍둥이는 심장이나 몸의 정중선을 절대 포함하지 않는 방식으로 연결되어 있다. 예를 들어, 전체 샴쌍둥이 중 약 2퍼센트는 머리만 붙어 있고, 약 19퍼센트는 엉덩이가 붙어 있다. 두 번째 유형의 쌍둥이는 몸의 정중선을 포함하는 방식으로 항상 붙어 있다. 정중선이 붙어 있는 많은 쌍둥이는 심장을 공유한다. 약 35퍼센트는 몸통의 위쪽 절반이 함께 결합되어 있다. 또 다른 30퍼센트는 그들 몸의 아래쪽 절반이 붙어 있다. 마지막으로, 세 번째 주요 유형의 샴쌍둥이는 매우 드문 형태를 포함한다. 이 범주에는 자신의 형제자매의 몸 안에서 온전히 태어난 쌍둥이 한 명을 포함한 경우들뿐만 아니라, 쌍둥이 한 명이 더 작고, 덜 형성되고, 다른 쌍둥이에게 의존적인 경우들이 있다.

① 그들이 붙어 있는 시간
② 그들이 붙어 있는 원인
③ 그들이 붙어 있는 지점
④ 그들이 머리에 붙어 있는지

해설 빈칸 뒤에서 첫 번째 유형의 샴쌍둥이는 심장이나 몸의 정중선을 절대 포함하지 않는 방식으로 연결되어 있다고 했고, 두 번째 유형의 샴쌍둥이는 몸의 정중선을 포함하는 방식으로 항상 붙어 있다고 했다. 또한, 지문 뒷부분에서 세 번째 유형의 샴쌍둥이는 매우 드문 형태를 포함하는데, 이는 한 명의 쌍둥이가 다른 쌍둥이에게 의존하거나 다른 쌍둥이의 몸 안에서 태어나는 경우라고 했다. 따라서 샴쌍둥이는 '그들이 붙어 있는 지점'에 따라서 일반적으로 세 가지 기본적인 범주로 분류된다고 한 ③번이 정답이다.

어휘 conjoined twins 샴쌍둥이(접착 쌍둥이) classify 분류하다
buttocks 엉덩이 fuse 결합시키다, 융해시키다
trunk (사람의) 몸통, (코끼리) 코 rare 드문, 보기 힘든
dependent 의존적인 sibling 형제자매

18 독해 논리적 흐름 파악 (문맥상 부적절한 어휘) 난이도 ★★☆

끊어읽기 해석

We should endeavor / to give our children / a wholesome variety of mental food, / and to cultivate their tastes / and ① stimulate their interests, / rather than to fill their minds / with dry facts.
우리는 노력해야 한다 / 아이들에게 주기 위해 / 건전한 갖가지 정신적 양식을 / 그리고 그들의 취향을 기르고 / 그들의 흥미를 ① 자극하기 위해 / 그들의 마음을 채우는 대신 / 메마른 사실로

The important thing / is not so much that every child should be taught, / as that every child should be given / the wish to ② learn.
중요한 것은 / 모든 아이들이 가르침을 받아야 한다는 것이라기보다 / 모든 아이들이 받아야 한다는 것이다 / ② 배우고 싶은 희망을

What does it matter / if the pupil knows / a little more or a little less?
무슨 상관인가 / 학생이 아는지가 / 조금 더 혹은 조금 덜?

A boy who leaves school / knowing ③ less, but hating his lessons, / will soon have forgotten / almost all he ever learnt; / while another who has acquired a thirst for ④ knowledge, / even if he had learnt little, / will soon teach himself / more than the first ever knew.
학교를 떠난 남자아이는 / ③ 덜 알지만 수업을 싫어한 상태로 / 금방 잊어버릴 것이다 / 자신이 배운 거의 모든 것을 / 반면 ④ 지식에 대한 목마름을 얻은 다른 아이는 / 배운 것이 거의 없었을지라도 / 곧 스스로 배울 것이다 / 전자가 알았던 것보다 더 많은 것을

해석 우리는 메마른 사실로 아이들의 마음을 채우는 대신 그들에게 건전한 갖가지 정신적 양식을 주고, 그들의 취향을 기르고, 그들의 흥미를 ① 자극하기 위해 노력해야 한다. 중요한 것은 모든 아이들이 가르침을 받아야 한다는 것이라기보다 모든 아이들이 ② 배우고 싶은 희망을 받아야 한다는 것이다. 학생이 조금 더 혹은 조금 덜 아는지가 무슨 상관인가? ③ 덜 알지만 수업을 싫어한 상태로 학교를 떠난 남자아이는 자신이 배운 거의 모든 것을 금방 잊어버릴 것이지만, 반면 ④ 지식에 대한 목마름을 얻은 다른 아이는 배운 것이 거의 없었을지라도 곧 전자가 알았던 것보다 더 많은 것을 스스로 배울 것이다.

① 자극하다   ② 배우다
③ 덜   ④ 지식

해설 지문 앞부분에서 중요한 것은 모든 아이들에게 배우고 싶은 희망을 주는 것이라는 내용이 있고, 지문 마지막에는 지식에 대한 목마름을 얻은 아이는 배운 것이 거의 없었을지라도 더 많은 것을 스스로 배울 것이라는 내용이 있으므로, '덜'(less) 알지만 수업을 싫어한 상태로 학교를 떠난 남자아이가 자신이 배운 모든 것을 금방 잊어버릴 것이라고 한 내용은 문맥상 적절하지 않다. 따라서 ③ less가 정답이다. 참고로 주어진 less를 대신할 수 있는 어휘로는 '더'라는 의미의 more가 있다.

어휘 endeavor 노력하다, 시도하다 wholesome 건전한, 건강에 좋은
cultivate 기르다, 재배하다 stimulate 자극하다 pupil 학생, 제자
thirst 목마름

19 독해 세부내용 파악 (지칭 대상 파악) 난이도 ★★☆

끊어읽기 해석

I am honored and deeply humbled / to take the oath of office / as your governor / for the next four years.
저는 영광스럽고 매우 겸허한 마음이 듭니다 / 이 취임 선서를 하게 되어 / 여러분의 주지사로서 / 앞으로 4년간

My priorities are clear. // We will focus / on creating jobs / by keeping taxes low / and building an advanced transportation system.
저의 우선 사항은 분명합니다. // 우리는 초점을 맞출 것입니다 / 일자리를 창출하는 데 / 세금을 낮게 유지하고 / 선진 교통 체계를 세움으로써

We will improve / access to health-care / by allowing doctors to spend more time / examining patients.
우리는 향상시킬 것입니다 / 의료 서비스에 대한 접근성을 / 의사들이 더 많은 시간을 쓰는 것을 허락함으로써 / 환자들을 진찰하는 데

We will continue to invest / in the education of our children, / all of our children.
우리는 계속해서 투자할 것입니다 / 우리 아이들의 교육에 / 모든 아이들의 (교육에)

There are other challenges / before us / that did not arise yesterday / and that will not be solved tomorrow.
다른 과제들이 있습니다 / 우리 앞에 / 어제는 일어나지 않았던 / 그리고 내일에 해결되지 않을

All the answers may not be found this session, / but we will work / until they are found.
모든 해답을 이 기간에 찾을 수는 없습니다 / 하지만 우리는 노력할 것입니다 / 그것들을 찾아낼 때까지

해석 저는 앞으로 4년간 여러분의 주지사로서 이 취임 선서를 하게 되어 영광스럽고 매우 겸허한 마음이 듭니다. 저의 우선 사항은 분명합니다. 우리는 세금을 낮게 유지하고 선진 교통 체계를 세움으로써 일자리를 창출하는 데 초점을 맞출 것입니다. 우리는 의사들이 환자들을 진찰하는 데 더 많은 시간을 쓰는 것을 허락함으로써 의료 서비스에 대한 접근성을 향상시킬 것입니다. 우리는 우리 아이들, 모든 아이들의 교육에 계속해서 투자할 것입니다. 어제는 일어나지 않았고 내일에 해결되지 않을 다른 과제들이 우리 앞에 있습니다. 모든 해답을 이 기간에 찾을 수는 없겠지만, 우리는 그것들을 찾아낼 때까지 노력할 것입니다.

① 더 나은 교통 체계
② 감세
③ 교육에의 투자
④ 의료 서비스의 비용

해설 지문 앞부분에서 주지사는 일자리 창출을 위해 낮은 세금을 유지하는 것과 선진 교통 체계를 갖추는 것에 초점을 둘 것이고, 지문 뒷부분에서 아이들 교육에 계속해서 투자할 것이라고 했다. 또한 지문 중간에서 의료 서비스에 대한 접근성을 향상시킬 것이라고 했지만, 의료 서비스의 비용적인 측면에 대한 언급은 하지 않았으므로 priorities(우선 사항)에 해당하지 않는 것을 '의료 서비스의 비용'이라고 한 ④번이 정답이다.

어휘 humble 겸허하게 만들다 oath of office 취임 선서
priority 우선 사항 advanced 선진의 transportation 교통
improve 향상시키다 examine 진찰하다, 조사하다
invest 투자하다

---

20 독해 세부내용 파악 (내용 불일치 파악)   난이도 ★★☆

끊어읽기 해석

What can you expect / when you arrive in San Francisco? // High rent!
당신은 무엇을 예상할 수 있는가 / 샌프란시스코에 도착했을 때? // 높은 집세이다!

Rents have been rising / for the last few years, / and it doesn't seem / as if they will come down.
집세는 오르고 있다 / 지난 몇 년간 / 그리고 그것은 보이지 않는다 / 내려올 것처럼

Everybody complains / about the high cost of living / in San Francisco, / but few complain / about the quality of life here.
모든 이가 불평한다 / 높은 생활비에 대해 / 샌프란시스코에서의 / 하지만 불평하는 사람은 거의 없다 / 이곳의 삶의 질에 대해

San Francisco is a most active city, / and also many people say / that it is the "most European city" / in the United States.
샌프란시스코는 가장 활동적인 도시이다 / 그리고 또한 많은 사람들은 말한다 / 이곳이 '가장 유럽 같은 도시'라고 / 미국에서

I've never seen any European city / like San Francisco / that can take so many different cultures / so comfortably.
나는 유럽 도시를 본 적이 없다 / 샌프란시스코 같이 / 매우 다양한 문화를 포용하는 / 아무 문제없이

해석 샌프란시스코에 도착했을 때 당신은 무엇을 예상할 수 있는가? 높은 집세이다! 집세는 지난 몇 년간 오르고 있고 그것은 내려올 것처럼 보이지 않는다. 모든 이가 샌프란시스코에서의 높은 생활비

에 대해 불평하지만, 이곳의 삶의 질에 대해 불평하는 사람은 거의 없다. 샌프란시스코는 가장 활동적인 도시이고, 또한 많은 사람들은 이곳이 미국에서 '가장 유럽 같은 도시'라고 말한다. 나는 샌프란시스코 같이 아무 문제없이 매우 다양한 문화를 포용하는 유럽 도시를 본 적이 없다.

① 사람들은 집을 임대할 때 많은 돈을 내야 한다.
② 많은 사람들은 삶의 질이 좋지 않다고 생각한다.
③ 그 도시는 활기 넘친다고 말해진다.
④ 많은 다양한 문화들이 조화롭게 섞여 있다.

해설 ②번의 키워드인 the quality of life(삶의 질)가 그대로 언급된 지문 주변의 내용을 살펴보면, 그곳의 삶의 질에 대해 불평하는 사람은 거의 없다고 했으므로, 많은 사람들이 삶의 질이 좋지 않다고 생각한다는 것은 지문의 내용과 다르다. 따라서 ②번이 정답이다.

어휘 rent 집세; 임대하다 complain 불평하다 cost of living 생활비
active 활동적인 comfortably 아무 문제없이, 편안하게
lively 활기 넘치는 harmoniously 조화롭게

---

21 문법 to 부정사 & 명사절   난이도 ★★☆

해석 외국 문화를 이해하려고 시도할 때, 우리는 의식과 관례에 초점을 맞추는 경향이 있지만, 사람들이 하지 않는 것을 관찰하는 것에서도 학습할/학습될 많은 것들이 있다. 이런 의미에서, 사람들이 먹지 않는 것을 아는 것은 그들의 사회에 대한 균형 잡힌 이해를 위해 필수적인 부분이다. 음식물 금기 이면에 있는 동기를 조사하는 것은 그렇게 하지 않으면 우리가 이상하다고 생각할 수도 있는 사람들의 생각이나 신념의 이해를 돕는 관점을 우리에게 제공한다. 우리가 누구/무엇인지는 우리가 무엇을 먹을 것인지를 비롯해 무엇을 먹지 않을 것인지에도 반영된다.

해설 (A) to 부정사의 형태 '~할 많은 것들이 있다'는 to 부정사를 사용하여 나타낼 수 있는데, to 부정사의 능동형(learn)이 쓰이면 '학습할 많은 것들'이라는 의미이고, 수동형(be learned)이 쓰이면 '학습될 많은 것들'이라는 의미가 되므로 learn과 be learned 둘 다 쓸 수 있다.
(B) 명사절 접속사 3: 의문사 '우리가 누구인지'라는 의미로 사람의 인격 등을 나타내기 위해 '명사절 접속사 who + 주어 + be동사'(Who we are)의 형태가 쓰일 수 있고, '우리가 무엇인지(우리가 누구인지)'라는 의미로 사람이나 사물의 특성을 나타내기 위해 '명사절 접속사 what + 주어 + be 동사'(What we are)의 형태가 쓰일 수 있으므로 명사절 접속사 Who와 What 둘 다 쓸 수 있다.
*본 문제는 정답이 ② (A) be learned – (B) Who인 것으로 고지되었으나, 실제로 모든 선택지가 어법상으로 가능합니다.

어휘 ritual 의식 practice 관례 integral 필수적인
comprehension 이해 motivation 동기, 유인 taboo 금기
illuminating 이해를 돕는 perspective 관점
reflect 반영하다

👍 이것도 알면 **합격!**
명사와 to 부정사가 '명사가 ~되다'라는 의미의 수동 관계이면 to 부정사의 수동형 'to be p.p.'의 형태를 쓴다는 것을 기억하자.
ex There are many **items** to be sold at the weekend market.
주말 시장에는 팔리는 많은 상품들이 있다. (상품들이 팔리게 되다)

22 독해 세부내용 파악 (내용 불일치 파악)   난이도 ★★☆

끊어읽기 해석

> While European artists had developed / a tradition of working / in a realistic style, / other cultures had / a long tradition of abstract art form.
> 유럽의 예술가들이 발전시킬 동안 / 작업하는 전통을 / 사실주의 형식으로 / 다른 문화들은 갖고 있었다 / 추상미술 형태의 오랜 전통을
>
> Some native American artists also work / in an abstract style.
> 일부 북아메리카 원주민 예술가들도 작업한다 / 추상적인 형식으로
>
> Navajo Indian artists make / abstract paintings / that do not use / oil paints, watercolors, or any kind of wet materials.
> 나바호 인디언 예술가들은 그린다 / 추상화를 / 쓰지 않는 / 유화 물감, 수채화 물감, 혹은 어떠한 종류의 젖은 재료도
>
> Their artworks are called / sand paintings / because the artist's materials are crushed charcoal, cornmeal, crushed rocks, and sand.
> 그들의 예술 작품은 불린다 / 모래그림이라고 / 예술가들의 재료가 석탄 부순 것, 옥수수 가루, 바위 부순 것, 그리고 모래이기 때문에
>
> The artist makes a sand painting / by pouring these materials / onto the ground / according to one of hundreds of traditional designs.
> 예술가는 모래그림을 만든다 / 이 재료들을 쏟음으로써 / 땅에 / 수백 가지의 전통 문양 중 하나를 따라
>
> It is a delicate task / to make this kind of artwork / because, as you can imagine, / once the materials are poured / it is very hard / to correct mistakes.
> 섬세한 작업이다 / 이러한 종류의 예술 작품을 만드는 것은 / 당신이 생각할 수 있는 것처럼 ~ 때문에 / 재료들이 일단 쏟아지면 / 매우 어렵기 때문이다 / 실수를 바로잡는 것이

해석   유럽의 예술가들이 사실주의 형식으로 작업하는 전통을 발전시킬 동안, 다른 문화들은 추상미술 형태의 오랜 전통을 갖고 있었다. 일부 북아메리카 원주민 예술가들도 추상적인 형식으로 작업한다. 나바호 인디언 예술가들은 유화 물감, 수채화 물감, 혹은 어떠한 종류의 젖은 재료도 쓰지 않는 추상화를 그린다. 예술가들의 재료가 석탄 부순 것, 옥수수 가루, 바위 부순 것, 그리고 모래이기 때문에 그들의 예술 작품은 모래그림이라고 불린다. 예술가는 수백 가지의 전통 문양 중 하나를 따라 이 재료들을 땅에 쏟음으로써 모래그림을 만든다. 당신이 생각할 수 있는 것처럼, 재료들이 일단 쏟아지면 실수를 바로잡는 것이 매우 어렵기 때문에, 이러한 종류의 예술 작품을 만드는 것은 섬세한 작업이다.

해설   지문 마지막에서 모래그림의 재료들이 일단 쏟아지면 실수를 바로잡는 것이 매우 어렵다고 했으므로, 재료를 땅에 쏟은 후 잘못된 부분의 수정이 섬세하게 이루어진다는 것은 지문의 내용과 다르다. 따라서 ④번이 정답이다.

어휘   realistic 사실주의의, 사실적인   abstract 추상적인
    oil paint 유화 물감   watercolor 수채화 물감
    sand painting 모래그림   cornmeal 옥수수 가루
    delicate 섬세한

23 독해 전체내용 파악 (제목 파악)   난이도 ★★☆

끊어읽기 해석

> Thousands of discarded computers / from Western Europe and the U.S.A. / arrive / in the ports of West Africa / every day, / ending up in massive toxic dumps, / where children burn and pull them apart / to extract metals for cash.
> 수천 대의 폐기된 컴퓨터들은 / 서유럽과 미국에서 온 / 도착한다 / 서아프리카의 항구들에 / 매일 / 결국 거대한 유독성 폐기장이 되면서 / 아이들이 그것들을 태우고 뜯어내는 / 돈을 벌기 위한 금속을 얻기 위해
>
> The exportation / of the developed world's electronic trash, or e-waste, / is in direct violation of international legislation / and is causing serious health problems / for the inhabitants of the area.
> 수출은 / 선진국의 전자폐기물, 또는 e폐기물의 / 직접적인 국제 입법 위반이다 / 그리고 심각한 건강상의 문제를 일으키고 있다 / 그 지역 주민들에게
>
> Apparently, / dishonest waste merchants unload / millions of tons of dangerous waste / in the developing world / by claiming / that it will be used / in schools and hospitals.
> 분명히 / 정직하지 못한 폐기물 상인들은 떠넘긴다 / 수백만 톤의 위험한 폐기물들을 / 개발도상국에 / 주장함으로써 / 그것이 이용될 것이라고 / 학교와 병원에서
>
> Campaigners are calling for / better policing / of the ban on exports of e-waste, / which can release / lead, mercury, and other dangerous chemicals.
> 운동가들은 요청하고 있다 / 더 나은 감시 활동을 / e폐기물의 수출 금지에 대한 / 이것들은 방출할 수 있다 / 납, 수은, 그리고 다른 위험한 화학 물질을

해석   서유럽과 미국에서 온 수천 대의 폐기된 컴퓨터들은 매일 서아프리카의 항구들에 도착하는데, 이곳은 결국 아이들이 돈을 벌기 위한 금속을 얻기 위해 그것들을 태우고 뜯어내는 거대한 유독성 폐기장이 된다. 선진국의 전자폐기물, 또는 e폐기물의 수출은 직접적인 국제 입법 위반이고 그 지역 주민들에게 심각한 건강상의 문제를 일으키고 있다. 분명히, 정직하지 못한 폐기물 상인들은 그것이 학교와 병원에서 이용될 것이라고 주장함으로써 개발도상국에 수백만 톤의 위험한 폐기물들을 떠넘긴다. 운동가들은 e폐기물의 수출 금지에 대한 더 나은 감시 활동을 요청하고 있는데, 이것들은 납, 수은, 그리고 다른 위험한 화학 물질을 방출할 수 있다.

① 전자폐기물의 불법적인 처리
② 컴퓨터 재활용 운동
③ 아프리카의 유독성 폐기장에 대한 금지
④ 전자폐기물을 폐기하는 것의 이득

해설   지문 중간에서 선진국에서 전자폐기물을 수출하는 것은 직접적인 국제 입법 위반이라고 했고, 정직하지 못한 폐기물 상인들은 수백만 톤의 위험한 폐기물들을 개발도상국에 떠넘긴다고 설명하고 있다. 따라서 이 지문의 제목을 '전자폐기물의 불법적인 처리'라고 표현한 ①번이 정답이다.

어휘   discard 폐기하다, 버리다   toxic 유독성의   dump 폐기장
    extract 얻다, 추출하다   exportation 수출   violation 위반
    legislation 입법   inhabitant 주민   merchant 상인
    unload 떠넘기다, 내리다   campaigner 운동가   release 방출하다
    lead 납   mercury 수은

24 독해 전체내용 파악 (글의 감상)   난이도 ★☆☆

끊어읽기 해석

> Driving home through the quiet lane / early one morning, / my headlights picked out a shape / in the middle of the road.
> 조용한 도로를 거쳐 집으로 운전하는 동안 / 어느 이른 아침에 / 나의 전조등이 한 형체를 비추었다 / 도로 한가운데의
>
> Only at the last moment / did the shape turn its head / and look straight at me.
> 마지막 순간에서야 / 그 형체는 고개를 돌렸다 / 그리고 나를 똑바로 쳐다봤다
>
> The owl apparently / neither heard nor saw / my car coming.
> 그 부엉이는 분명히 / 듣지도 보지도 못했다 / 내 차가 오는 것을

It was too late. // There was nothing / I could do.
너무 늦은 것이었다. // 아무것도 없었다 / 내가 할 수 있는 것은

There was a horrible sound / as I hit the bird head-on.
끔찍한 소리가 났다 / 그 새와 정면으로 부딪히는 순간

I thought about stopping / to see / if it was lying injured yet alive / by the side of the road, / but decided / that it wouldn't have stood a chance.
나는 멈춰 서는 것을 생각했다 / 확인하기 위해 / 그 새가 다쳤지만 아직 살아서 누워 있는지 / 도로 한쪽에 / 하지만 판단했다 / 그럴 가능성이 없으리라

I tried / to put the incident out of my mind / as I drove home, / only to be confronted a new horror / when I got out of the car.
나는 노력했다 / 그 사건을 잊어버리려고 / 집으로 운전하면서 / 결국 새로운 공포에 직면했을 뿐이었다 / 차에서 내리는 순간

The evening / had taken a distinctively dreadful turn.
그날 저녁은 / 명백히 끔찍하게 바뀌었다

I discovered / that the owl had gotten stuck / in my radiator grill.
나는 발견했다 / 그 부엉이가 박힌 것을 / 내 라디에이터 그릴에

해석 어느 이른 아침에 조용한 도로를 거쳐 집으로 운전하는 동안, 나의 전조등이 도로 한가운데의 한 형체를 비추었다. 마지막 순간에서야 그 형체는 고개를 돌렸고 나를 똑바로 쳐다봤다. 그 부엉이는 분명히 내 차가 오는 것을 듣지도 보지도 못했다. 너무 늦은 것이었다. 내가 할 수 있는 것은 아무것도 없었다. 그 새와 정면으로 부딪히는 순간 끔찍한 소리가 났다. 나는 그 새가 다쳤지만 아직 살아서 도로 한쪽에 누워 있는지 확인하기 위해 멈춰 서는 것을 생각했지만, 그럴 가능성이 없으리라 판단했다. 나는 집으로 운전하면서 그 사건을 잊어버리려고 노력했지만, 차에서 내리는 순간 결국 새로운 공포에 직면했을 뿐이었다. 그날 저녁은 명백히 끔찍하게 바뀌었다. 나는 그 부엉이가 내 라디에이터 그릴에 박힌 것을 발견했다.

① 따분하고 무관심한
② 호기심 많고 기대하는
③ 충격을 받고 혐오감을 느끼는
④ 안도하고 격려하는

해설 지문 중간에서 필자의 차가 부엉이와 정면으로 부딪혔다고 했고, 집에 도착한 후 부엉이가 차의 라디에이터 그릴에 박혀 있는 것을 보고 그날 저녁이 끔찍하게 바뀌었다는 것을 설명하고 있다. 따라서 지문에서 필자의 심경을 '충격을 받고 혐오감을 느끼는'이라고 표현한 ③번이 정답이다.

어휘 lane 도로, 길 head-on 정면으로 stand a chance 가능성이 있다 put out of one's mind 잊어버리다 incident 사건 confront 직면하다, 맞서다 distinctively 명백히, 두드러지게 dreadful 끔찍한 get stuck 박히다

25 독해 논리적 흐름 파악 (문단 순서 배열) 난이도 ★★☆

끊어읽기 해석

Avalanches / are among the world's most dangerous natural disasters.
눈사태는 / 세계의 가장 위험한 자연재해에 속한다

Fortunately, / they usually occur / in remote mountain areas, / where they threaten neither human life nor property.
다행스럽게도 / 그것들은 보통 발생한다 / 외진 산지에서 / 그들이 사람의 목숨이나 재산에 위협을 가하지 않는

(A) Suddenly they were overtaken / by an avalanche / that left only a few survivors.
갑자기 그들은 만났다 / 눈사태를 / 소수의 생존자만을 남긴

Three members of the party / were buried / in the snow.
그 무리의 세 명의 일원은 / 파묻혔다 / 눈 속에

When, after almost half a century, / the bodies were found, / they were perfectly preserved.
거의 반세기 이후 / 시체들이 발견되었을 때 / 그들은 완벽하게 보존되어 있었다

(B) They were so well preserved, / in fact, / that a surviving member of the original party, / by then an old man, / was able to recognize them.
그들이 너무 잘 보존되어 있어서 / 사실상 / 원래 무리에서 생존한 일원은 / 그 당시에는 노인이 된 / 그들을 알아볼 수 있었다

(C) Occasionally, however, / an avalanche can strike / without warning, / taking hikers and skiers / by surprise.
하지만 가끔 / 눈사태는 엄습할 수 있다 / 경고 없이 / 등산객과 스키 타는 사람을 덮치며 / 불시에

This is precisely what happened / more than a century ago / when a small group of mountain climbers tried to scale / the huge alpine peak Mont Blanc.
이것은 정확히 일어난 일이다 / 한 세기도 더 전에 / 한 작은 무리의 등산가들이 오르려고 시도했던 때에 / 거대한 알프스 산맥의 몽블랑 산 정상을

해석 눈사태는 세계의 가장 위험한 자연재해에 속한다. 그것들은 다행스럽게도 보통 사람의 목숨이나 재산에 위협을 가하지 않는 외진 산지에서 발생한다.

(C) 하지만 가끔 눈사태는 등산객과 스키 타는 사람들을 불시에 덮치며 경고 없이 엄습할 수 있다. 이것은 정확히 한 세기도 더 전에, 한 작은 무리의 등산가들이 거대한 알프스 산맥의 몽블랑 산 정상을 오르려고 시도했던 때에 일어난 일이다.

(A) 갑자기 그들은 소수의 생존자만을 남긴 눈사태를 만났다. 그 무리의 세 명의 일원은 눈 속에 파묻혔다. 거의 반세기 이후 시체들이 발견되었을 때, 그들은 완벽하게 보존되어 있었다.

(B) 사실상, 그들이 너무 잘 보존되어 있어서, 그 당시에는 노인이 된 원래 무리에서 생존한 일원은 그들을 알아볼 수 있었다.

해설 주어진 문장에서 눈사태는 보통 사람의 목숨이나 재산에 위협을 가하지 않는 외진 산지에서 발생한다고 한 후, (C)에서 하지만 (however) 눈사태는 가끔 경고 없이 엄습하여 등산객과 스키 타는 사람을 불시에 덮칠 수 있다고 하며 그와 관련된 일화로 몽블랑 산 정상을 오르려 했던 등산가 무리를 소개하고 있다. 이어서 (A)에서 그들(they)이 갑자기 눈사태를 만나 눈 속에 파묻혔고, 반세기 뒤에 시체들이 발견되었을 때 완벽하게 보존되어 있었다고 한 뒤, (B)에서 그들이 사실상 너무 잘 보존되어 있어서 살아남은 일원들이 그들을 알아봤다는 내용을 설명하고 있다. 따라서 ④ (C) - (A) - (B)가 정답이다.

어휘 be among ~에 속하다 avalanche 눈사태, 산사태 natural disaster 자연재해 remote 외진, 먼 bury 파묻다 preserve 보존하다 strike 엄습하다 by surprise 불시에 precisely 정확히 alpine 알프스 산맥의 peak 정상, 봉우리

정답

p.124

01	④ 독해 – 전체내용 파악	11	④ 독해 – 추론	21	① 독해 – 전체내용 파악
02	② 문법 – 동사의 종류&명사절&관계절	12	① 독해 – 논리적 흐름 파악	22	③ 독해 – 추론
03	③ 독해 – 추론	13	② 독해 – 추론	23	③ 독해 – 추론
04	④ 독해 – 전체내용 파악	14	④ 독해 – 전체내용 파악	24	④ 독해 – 논리적 흐름 파악
05	④ 독해 – 논리적 흐름 파악	15	④ 독해 – 전체내용 파악	25	③ 독해 – 논리적 흐름 파악
06	③ 독해 – 논리적 흐름 파악	16	④ 독해 – 논리적 흐름 파악		
07	④ 독해 – 전체내용 파악	17	④ 독해 – 전체내용 파악		
08	③ 독해 – 전체내용 파악	18	② 독해 – 전체내용 파악		
09	② 독해 – 추론	19	① 독해 – 전체내용 파악		
10	② 독해 – 추론	20	③ 독해 – 전체내용 파악		

취약영역 분석표

영역	세부 유형	문항 수	소계
어휘	어휘 & 표현	0	/0
	생활영어	0	
문법	동사의 종류 & 명사절 & 관계절	1	/1
독해	전체내용 파악	11	/24
	세부내용 파악	0	
	추론	7	
	논리적 흐름 파악	6	
총계			/25

· 자신이 취약한 영역은 '법원직 9급 영어, 이렇게 출제된다!'(p.8)를 통해 다시 한 번 확인하고 학습하시기 바랍니다.

---

01 독해 전체내용 파악 (문단 요약)

난이도 ★★☆

끊어읽기 해석

The idea of public works projects / as a device to prevent or control depression / was designed / as a means of creating job opportunities / for unemployed workers / and as a "pump-priming" device / to aid business to revive.
공공 사업 프로젝트에 대한 아이디어는 / 불경기를 예방하거나 제어하기 위한 장치로서의 / 고안되었다 / 직업 기회 창출의 한 수단으로서 / 실업자들을 위한 / 그리고 '경기 부양 정책'의 장치로서 / 사업이 활기를 되찾도록 돕는

By 1933, / the number of unemployed worker / had reached about 13 million.
1933년까지 / 실업자의 수는 / 약 천삼백만 명에 도달했다

This meant / that about 59 million people / —about one-third of the nation— / were without means of support.
이는 의미했다 / 약 오천구백만 명의 사람들이 / 국민의 약 1/3에 해당하는 수인 / 소득이 없었다는 것을

At first, / direct relief in the form of cash or food / was provided / to these people.
처음에는 / 현금이나 음식 형태의 직접적인 원조가 / 제공되었다 / 이러한 사람들에게

This made them / recipients of government charity.
이것은 그들을 만들었다 / 정부 구호품의 수혜자로

In order to remove this stigma / and restore to the unemployed / some measure of respectability and human dignity, / a plan was devised / to create governmentally sponsored work projects / that private industry would not or could not provide.
이러한 오명을 벗기 위해 / 그리고 실업자들이 되찾게 하기 위해 / 어느 정도의 체면과 인간 존엄성을 / 계획이 고안되었다 / 정부가 후원하는 공공 사업 프로젝트를 만들기 위한 / 민간 기업은 제공하지 않았을 것이고 제공할 수도 없었던

This would also stimulate production / and revive business activity.
이는 또한 생산을 자극할 것이었다 / 그리고 사업 활동을 되살아나게 만들 것이었다

해석 불경기를 예방하거나 제어하기 위한 장치로서의 공공 사업 프로젝트에 대한 아이디어는 실업자들을 위한 직업 기회 창출의 한 수단이자 사업이 활기를 되찾도록 돕는 '경기 부양 정책'의 장치로서 고안되었다. 1933년까지 실업자의 수는 약 천삼백만 명에 도달했다. 이는 국민의 약 1/3에 해당하는 수인 약 오천구백만 명의 사람들이 소득이 없었다는 것을 의미했다. 처음에는 현금이나 음식 형태의 직접적인 원조가 이러한 사람들에게 제공되었다. 이것은 그들을 정부 구호품의 수혜자로 만들었다. 이러한 오명을 벗고 실업자들이 어느 정도의 체면과 인간 존엄성을 되찾게 하기 위해, 민간 기업은 제공하지 않았을 것이고 제공할 수도 없었던 정부가 후원하는 공공 사업을 만들기 위한 계획이 고안되었다. 이는 또한 생산을 자극할 것이었고, 사업 활동을 되살아 나게 만들 것이었다.

'경기 부양 정책'이라는 표현을 공공 사업 프로젝트의 묘사로 사용함으로써, 저자는 그것이 사업에 초반 추진력을 제공했다는 것을 시사한다.

① 쓸모없었다
② 인간 존엄성을 낮췄다
③ 돈을 물쓰듯 썼다
④ 사업에 초반 추진력을 제공했다

해설 지문 중간에서 실업자 수가 천삼백만 명에 도달하여 국민의 1/3이 소득이 없게 되자, 처음에는 정부가 현금이나 음식 형태의 직접적인 원조를 제공했다고 했다. 하지만 그 후 실업자들의 체면과 존엄성을 회복하기 위해 정부가 후원하는 공공 사업을 만드는 계획이 고안되었는데, 이것이 바로 '경기 부양 정책'이며, 이는 생산을 자극하고 사업 활동을 되살아나게 할 것이라는 내용이 있다. 따라서 작가가 '경기 부양 정책'이라는 표현을 사용함으로써 공공 사업 프로젝트가 '사업에 초반 추진력을 제공했다'는 것을 시사한다고 한 ④번이 정답이다.

어휘 depression 불경기 pump-priming 경기 부양 정책
revive 활기를 되찾게 하다 means of support 소득 relief 원조
recipient 수혜자 charity 구호품, 자선 stigma 오명
restore 되찾게 하다 respectability 체면, 훌륭함
human dignity 인간 존엄성
pour money down the drain 돈을 물쓰듯 쓰다
initial 초반의, 최초의 impetus 추진력, 자극

02 문법 동사의 종류&명사절&관계절 난이도 ★★☆

해석 다른 사람들처럼 과학자들도 그들의 생각이 사실로 입증되는 것에 항상 기뻐한다. 그래서 나는 『영국 천문학 협회 저널』의 1963년 8월 발행본에 실린 보고서로 인해 기뻤다. 이 보고서는 달의 몇몇 분화구들이 현재 활화산이 있는 장소라는 믿음을 지지하기 위해 몇 년 전 망원경 사진들에서 증거를 발견한 유명한 소련 천문학자 Dr. Nikolai Kozyrev에 의해 쓰여졌다. Dr. Kozyrev가 처음으로 그가 달에서 보았다고 생각한 것을 게재했을 때, 그의 설명은 다른 나라의 많은 천문학자들에 의해 의심을 받았다. 하지만 결과적으로, 이곳의 천문학자들도 이전에 달의 죽은 부분으로 생각되었던 곳에서, 그들 역시 계속되는 화산 활동의 흔적이라고 생각하는 색의 변화를 보았다.

해설 (A) 5형식 동사 사역동사 have는 목적어와 목적격 보어가 수동 관계일 때 과거분사를 목적격 보어로 취하는 5형식 동사인데, 목적어(their own ideas)와 목적격 보어가 '생각이 사실로 입증되다'라는 의미의 수동 관계이므로 목적격 보어 자리에 과거분사 confirmed를 써야 한다.
(B) what vs. that 동사 published 뒤 목적어 자리에 목적어가 없는 불완전한 절(he had seen ~ moon)이 왔으므로 불완전한 절을 이끌 수 있는 명사절 접속사 what을 써야 한다. 참고로, 명사절 접속사 뒤 'he thought'는 삽입절이다.
(C) 관계부사와 관계대명사 비교 선행사 color changes가 사물이고 관계사 뒤에 주어가 없는 불완전한 절(are signs ~ moon)이 왔으므로 사물을 나타내는 주격 관계대명사 which를 써야 한다. 참고로, 주어와 동사 사이에 온 'they, too, believe'는 삽입절로 관계대명사의 격 선택에 아무런 영향을 미치지 않는다.
따라서 ② (A) confirmed – (B) what – (C) which가 정답이다.

어휘 confirm 사실로 입증하다, 확인하다 gratified 기쁜
astronomical 천문학의 astronomer 천문학자
telescopic photograph 망원경 사진 crater 분화구
active volcano 활화산 subsequently 결과적으로

👍 이것도 알면 합격!

관계대명사 바로 뒤에 '주어 + know/say/think/feel/hope/believe' 등의 어구가 삽입될 수 있는데, 이는 관계대명사의 격 선택에 아무런 영향을 미치지 않는다는 것을 알아두자.
ex She is the runner (who, ~~whom~~) I hope wins the race.
그녀는 내가 경주에서 우승하길 바라는 선수이다.

03 독해 추론 (빈칸 완성 - 절) 난이도 ★★☆

끊어읽기 해석

A scorpion wanted to pass the pond / but it could not swim.
전갈은 연못을 건너고 싶었다 / 하지만 그것(전갈)은 수영을 할 수 없었다

Thus, / it climbed on a frog's back, / and asked the frog / to take it to the other side of the pond.
그래서 / 전갈은 개구리의 등에 올라갔다 / 그리고 개구리에게 요청했다 / 연못 반대편으로 데려다 달라고

The frog refused / because the scorpion might sting him / when he swims.
개구리는 거절했다 / 전갈이 그를 찌를 수도 있기 때문에 / 그가 헤엄칠 때

The scorpion promised / not to do so. // Though the frog knew / how vicious the scorpion was, / it felt that its words were correct.
전갈은 약속했다 / 그러지 않겠다고 // 비록 개구리는 알았지만 / 전갈이 얼마나 공격적인지 / 그것의 말이 사실이라고 생각했다

When they swam / in the middle of the pond, / the scorpion suddenly stung the frog.
그들이 헤엄치고 있을 때 / 연못 한가운데를 / 전갈이 갑자기 개구리를 찔렀다

The heavily wounded frog yelled out, / "Why did you sting me? / Stinging me is not useful for you totally."
크게 부상을 입은 개구리가 소리쳤다 / "왜 나를 찌른 거야? / 나를 찌르는 것은 너에게도 전혀 도움이 되지 않아"

"I know." / the scorpion said, / while sinking down.
"나도 알아" / 전갈이 말했다 / 가라앉으면서

"But I'm a scorpion. / I must sting you / because this is my instinct."
"하지만 나는 전갈이야 / 나는 너를 찌를 수밖에 없어 / 왜냐하면 이것이 나의 본능이기 때문이야"

As the saying goes: / the leopard cannot change its spots, / everyone has / their own advantages and disadvantages.
속담에서 말하듯이 / 표범은 제 반점을 바꿀 수 없다(세 살 버릇 여든까지 간다) / 모든 사람들은 가진다 / 각자의 장점과 단점을

Therefore, / we should be aware of / that changing one person is limited.
그러므로 / 우리는 알아야 한다 / 어떤 사람을 바꾸는 것은 제한적이라는 것을

What we need to do is / try not to eliminate these drawbacks, / but to reasonably use their advantages.
우리가 해야 하는 것은 / 이러한 결점을 없애려고 노력하는 것이 아니라 / 그들의 장점을 합리적으로 이용하는 것이다.

해석 전갈은 연못을 건너고 싶었지만 수영을 할 수 없었다. 그래서 전갈은 개구리의 등에 올라가서 개구리에게 연못 반대편으로 데려다 달라고 요청했다. 개구리는 그가 헤엄칠 때 전갈이 그를 찌를 수도 있기 때문에 거절했다. 전갈은 그러지 않겠다고 약속했다. 비록 개구리는 전갈이 얼마나 공격적인지 알았지만, 그것의 말이 사실이라고 생각했다. 그들이 연못 한가운데를 헤엄치고 있을 때, 전갈이 갑자기 개구리를 찔렀다. 크게 부상을 입은 개구리가 "왜 나를 찌른 거야? 나를 찌르는 것은 너에게도 전혀 도움이 되지 않아."라고 소리쳤다. "나도 알아." 전갈이 가라앉으면서 말했다. "하지만 나는 전갈이야. 이것이 나의 본능이기 때문에 나는 너를 찌를 수밖에 없어." 표범은 제 반점을 바꿀 수 없다(세 살 버릇 여든까지 간다)는 속담에서 말하듯이, 모든 사람들은 각자의 장점과 단점을 가진다. 그러므로 우리는 어떤 사람을 바꾸는 것이 제한적이라는 것을 알아야 한다. 우리가 해야 하는 것은 이러한 결점을 없애려고 노력하는 것이 아니라 그들의 장점을 합리적으로 이용하는 것이다.

① 도움을 받았으면 갚아야 한다(가는 정이 있으면 오는 정이 있다)
② 친구와 포도주는 오래될수록 좋다
③ 표범은 제 반점을 바꿀 수 없다(세 살 버릇 여든까지 간다)
④ 물에 빠진 사람은 지푸라기라도 잡는다

해설 빈칸 앞에서 전갈은 개구리에게 그를 찌르지 않는 조건으로 연못 반대편으로 자신을 데려다 줄 것을 부탁했지만, 결국 전갈이 자신의 본능 때문에 개구리를 찔렀다는 일화를 소개하고 있고, 빈칸 뒤에서는 모든 사람들이 각자의 장점과 단점이 있으므로 어떤 사

람을 바꾸는 것이 제한적이라는 것을 알아야 한다는 내용이 있다. 따라서 지문과 관련된 속담을 '표범은 제 반점을 바꿀 수 없다(세 살 버릇 여든까지 간다)'라고 한 ③번이 정답이다.

어휘 scorpion 전갈 sting 찌르다, 쏘다 vicious 공격적인, 사나운 heavily 크게, 심하게 wounded 부상을 입은, 상처 입은 yell out 소리치다 instinct 본능 eliminate 없애다, 제거하다 reasonably 합리적으로, 상당히 leopard 표범 spot 반점, 얼룩 drown 물에 빠지다, 익사하다 straw 지푸라기

04 독해 전체내용 파악 (글의 감상) 난이도 ★☆☆

끊어읽기 해석

My clothes were drenched. // Sweat flowed in torrents from my forehead, / requiring constant mopping with a bandanna / to keep my glasses from steaming up / to the point where I couldn't see anything.
내 옷이 흠뻑 젖었다. // 땀이 내 이마에서 억수같이 흘렀다 / 스카프로 끊임없이 닦는 것이 필요할 정도로 / 안경에 김이 서리는 것을 막기 위해 / 내가 아무것도 보지 못할 정도로

Keeping my eyes riveted to the ground / wasn't enough / because there was plenty to watch out / for overhead too.
땅에 눈을 고정시키는 것으로는 / 충분하지 않았다 / 조심할 것이 너무 많았기 때문에 / 머리 위에도

Vines yanked my hat off. // Thorns ripped at my sleeves.
덩굴들이 내 모자를 잡아당겼다. // 가시들이 내 소매를 찢었다.

Trees with trunks and limbs / encased in three-inch spikes / threatened to impale an eyeball / in a moment of carelessness.
몸통과 나뭇가지가 있는 나무들이 / 3인치의 뾰족한 것으로 둘러싸인 / 눈알을 찌르려고 위협했다 / 부주의한 순간을 틈타

Deadly pit vipers also lurked / in the trees, / camouflaged bright green.
치명적인 살모사 또한 숨어 있었다 / 나무들 속에 / 밝은 녹색으로 위장하여

해석 내 옷이 흠뻑 젖었다. 내가 아무것도 보지 못할 정도로 안경에 김이 서리는 것을 막기 위해 스카프로 끊임없이 닦는 것이 필요할 정도로, 땀이 내 이마에서 억수같이 흘렀다. 머리 위에도 조심할 것이 너무 많았기 때문에 땅에 눈을 고정시키는 것으로는 충분하지 않았다. 덩굴들이 내 모자를 잡아당겼다. 가시들이 내 소매를 찢었다. 3인치의 뾰족한 것으로 둘러싸인 몸통과 나뭇가지가 있는 나무들이 부주의한 순간을 틈타 눈알을 찌르려고 위협했다. 치명적인 살모사 또한 밝은 녹색으로 위장하여 나무들 속에 숨어 있었다.

① 흥분되는　　　　　② 안도한
③ 지루한　　　　　　④ 겁먹은

해설 지문 전반에 걸쳐 필자는 가시들로 둘러싸인 나무와 살모사가 숨어 있는 위협적인 환경 속에서 옷이 흠뻑 젖고 땀을 억수같이 흘린 상황을 묘사하고 있다. 따라서 지문에서 필자가 느꼈을 심정을 '겁먹은'이라고 표현한 ④번이 정답이다.

어휘 drenched 흠뻑 젖은 in torrents 억수같이, 폭포처럼 mop 닦다 rivet 고정시키다 vine 덩굴(식물) yank 잡아당기다 thorn 가시 rip 찢다 trunk (나무의) 몸통 limb 나뭇가지 encase 둘러싸다 spike 뾰족한 것, 못 impale 찌르다 eyeball 눈알 pit vipers 살모사 lurk 숨어 있다 camouflage 위장하다

05 독해 논리적 흐름 파악 (문맥상 부적절한 어휘) 난이도 ★★☆

끊어읽기 해석

Political power in Rome / had traditionally rested with the aristocrats; / now, / it lay increasingly with / the families of the new commercial class.
로마의 정권은 / 전통적으로 귀족의 책임이었다 / 이제 / 그것은 점점 더 ~의 책임이 되고 있다 / 새로운 상인 계층 가문들의

The ① attainment of high political office / became the main goal of these families / because it meant / prestige, power, and more wealth.
고위 행정 관직에 대한 ① 성취는 / 이러한 가문들의 주요 목표가 되었다 / 왜냐하면 그것이 의미했기 때문이다 / 위신, 권력, 그리고 더 많은 부를

Individuals ② captured office / not so much on the strength of their political philosophy and policy / but on the appeal of their personalities, charisma, and conquests.
개인들은 공직을 ② 얻었다 / 그들의 정치적 철학과 정책에 힘입어서가 아니라 / 그들의 인격, 카리스마, 그리고 승리에 대한 호소로

Rome began to be ③ dominated / by men who were self-seeking, larger-than-life figures / who won the support of the masses / through the distribution of free food, olive oil, and wine, / and the sponsoring of public entertainment.
로마는 ③ 지배되기 시작했다 / 이기적이고 실제보다 과장된 인물들에 의해 / 대중의 지지를 얻은 / 무료 음식, 올리브 오일, 와인의 배급을 통해서 / 그리고 공공 오락을 후원하는 것을 통해서

④ Shortages / that flowed to Rome / from the fertile fields of its provinces overseas / —Carthage, Sicily, Sardinia, and Numidia— / allowed free distributions / to the restless and unemployed urban proletariat.
④ 부족함은 / 로마로 흘러 들어오는 / 그것의 바다 건너 지방들의 기름진 땅으로부터 / 카르타고, 시칠리아, 사르디니아, 누미디아와 같은 / 무료 배급을 가능하게 했다 / 불안하고 직업이 없는 도시의 노동자 계급에게로의

해석 로마의 정권은 전통적으로 귀족의 책임이었는데, 이제 그것은 점점 더 새로운 상인 계층 가문들의 책임이 되고 있다. 고위 행정 관직에 대한 ① 성취는 이러한 가문들의 주요 목표가 되었는데, 왜냐하면 그것이 위신, 권력, 그리고 더 많은 부를 의미했기 때문이다. 개인들은 그들의 정치적 철학과 정책에 힘입어서가 아니라 그들의 인격, 카리스마, 승리에 대한 호소로 공직을 ② 얻었다. 로마는 무료 음식, 올리브 오일, 와인의 배급과 공공 오락을 후원하는 것을 통해서 대중의 지지를 얻은 이기적이고 실제보다 과장된 인물들에 의해 ③ 지배되기 시작했다. 카르타고, 시칠리아, 사르디니아, 누미디아와 같은 그것(로마)의 바다 건너 지방들의 기름진 땅으로부터 로마로 흘러 들어오는 ④ 부족함은 불안하고 직업이 없는 도시의 노동자 계급에게로의 무료 배급을 가능하게 했다.

해설 ④의 앞 문장에 로마의 지배자들이 무료 음식, 올리브 오일, 와인의 배급 등을 통해서 대중의 지지를 얻었다는 내용이 있고, ④의 뒤 문장에는 바다 건너 지방들의 기름진 땅에서 로마로 흘러 들어오는 것이 도시의 노동자 계급에게 이러한 무료 배급을 가능하게 했다는 내용이 있으므로, 로마로 흘러 들어오는 '부족함'(shortages)이 무료 배급을 가능하게 했다는 것은 문맥상 적절하지 않다. 따라서 ④ Shortages가 정답이다. 참고로, 주어진 Shortages를 대신할 수 있는 어휘로는 '풍부함'이라는 의미의 Abundance 등이 있다.

어휘 rest with ~의 책임이다 aristocrat 귀족 lie with ~의 책임이다 attainment 성취 prestige 위신 on the strength of ~에 힘입어 philosophy 철학, 원리 charisma 카리스마 conquest 승리, 정복 self-seeking 이기적인 larger-than-life 실제보다 과장된 distribution 배급, 분배 province 지방 restless 불안한, 가만히 못 있는 proletariat 노동자 (계급)

끊어읽기 해석

A group of British psychologists have recently shown / that the youngest children in class / are more (A) sensitive to stress at school / than their older classmates.
한 영국의 심리학자 집단은 최근에 증명했다 / 학급에서 가장 어린 아이들이 / 학교에서의 스트레스에 더 (A) 예민하다는 것을 / 나이가 더 많은 그들의 급우들보다

The study examined / over 20,000 school children / between the ages of five and twelve / in England, / and symptoms were evaluated / by psychopathology questionnaires / (B) completed by parents, teachers, and 10–12 year old study participants.
이 연구는 조사했다 / 2만 명 이상의 학생들을 / 5살에서 12살 사이의 / 영국의 / 그리고 증상들은 평가되었다 / 정신병리학 설문지에 의해서 / 부모, 선생님, 10살에서 12살 사이의 실험 참가자들에 의해 (B) 작성된

According to the study, / the youngest in each group experienced / more emotional and behavioral problems at school, / and this effect was (C) observed / throughout all the age groups in the study.
그 연구에 따르면 / 각 집단의 가장 어린 아이들은 경험했다 / 학교에서 더 많은 정서적, 행동적 문제들을 / 그리고 이 결과는 (C) 관찰되었다 / 그 연구의 모든 연령대의 집단에 걸쳐

해석 한 영국의 심리학자 집단은 최근에 학급에서 가장 어린 아이들이 나이가 더 많은 그들의 급우들보다 학교에서의 스트레스에 더 (A) 예민하다는 것을 증명했다. 이 연구는 영국의 5살에서 12살 사이의 2만 명 이상의 학생들을 조사했고, 증상들은 부모, 선생님, 10살에서 12살 사이의 실험 참가자들에 의해 (B) 작성된 정신병리학 설문지에 의해서 평가되었다. 그 연구에 따르면, 각 집단의 가장 어린 아이들은 학교에서 더 많은 정서적, 행동적 문제들을 경험했고, 이 결과는 그 연구의 모든 연령대 집단에 걸쳐 (C) 관찰되었다.

	(A)	(B)	(C)
①	합리적인	경쟁된	관찰되었다
②	합리적인	작성된	보존되었다
③	예민한	작성된	관찰되었다
④	예민한	경쟁된	보존되었다

해설 (A) 지문 마지막에서 각 집단의 가장 어린 아이들이 학교에서 더 많은 정서적, 행동적 문제들을 경험했다고 했으므로, 그들이 스트레스에 더 '예민하다'(sensitive)는 내용이 들어가야 적절하다. (B) 빈칸 앞에서 증상들이 설문지에 의해 평가되었다고 했으므로, 부모, 선생님, 실험 참가자들에 의해 '작성된'(completed) 설문지라는 내용이 들어가야 적절하다. (C) 빈칸에는 문맥상 이 결과가 연구의 모든 연령대의 집단에 걸쳐 '관찰되었다'(observed)라는 내용이 들어가야 적절하다.
따라서 ③ (A) sensitive(예민한) – (B) completed(작성된) – (C) observed (관찰되었다)가 정답이다.

어휘 sensible 합리적인 sensitive 예민한 symptom 증상 questionnaire 설문지 participant 참가자

---

07 독해 전체내용 파악 (주제 파악) 난이도 ★★☆

끊어읽기 해석

The railroad was the first institution / to impose regularity on society, / or to draw attention / to the importance of precise timekeeping.
철도는 최초의 시설이었다 / 사회에 규칙성을 부여한 / 혹은 주의를 환기시킨 / 정확한 시간 엄수의 중요성에

For as long as merchants have set out their wares / at daybreak / and religious services have begun / on the hour, / people have been in rough agreement / with their neighbors / as to the time of day.
상인들이 그들의 상품을 진열하는 한 / 동틀 녘에 / 그리고 종교 의식이 시작되는 한 / 정시에 / 사람들은 대략적으로 동의해왔다 / 그들의 이웃들과 / 하루의 시간에 대해

The value of this tradition / is today more apparent than ever.
이 전통의 가치는 / 오늘날 그 어느 때보다 더 명확하다

Were it not for public acceptance / of a single yardstick of time, / social life would be unbearably chaotic: / the massive daily transfers of goods, services, and information / would proceed in fits and starts; / the very fabric of modern society / would begin to unravel.
공공의 동의가 없다면 / 단일한 시간 기준에 관한 / 사회생활은 견딜 수 없을 정도로 혼란스러울 것이다 / 매일 이루어지는 상품, 서비스 그리고 정보의 대량 이동은 / 간헐적으로 진행될 것이다 / 현대사회의 바로 그 기본 구조가 / 흐트러지기 시작할 것이다

해석 철도는 사회에 규칙성을 부여하거나 정확한 시간 엄수의 중요성에 주의를 환기시킨 최초의 시설이었다. 상인들이 동틀 녘에 그들의 상품을 진열하고 종교 의식이 정시에 시작하는 한, 사람들은 하루의 시간에 대해 그들의 이웃들과 대략적으로 동의해왔다. 이 전통의 가치는 오늘날 그 어느 때보다 더 명확하다. 단일한 시간 기준에 관한 공공의 동의가 없다면, 사회생활은 견딜 수 없을 정도로 혼란스러울 것인데, 매일 이루어지는 상품, 서비스 그리고 정보의 대량 이동은 간헐적으로 진행될 것이고, 현대사회의 바로 그 기본 구조가 흐트러지기 시작할 것이다.

① 사회의 전통은 영원하다.
② 특정한 활동들은 제시간에 수행되어야 한다.
③ 현대 사회는 사람들이 특정 활동을 하는 횟수로 그들을 평가한다.
④ 시간 측정법에 대한 사람들의 합의는 사회의 기능을 위해 필수적이다.

해설 지문 뒷부분에서 단일한 시간 기준에 관한 공공의 동의가 없다면, 사회생활은 견딜 수 없을 정도로 혼란스러울 것이고, 현대사회의 바로 그 기본 구조는 흐트러지기 시작할 것이라고 했다. 따라서 이 지문의 주제를 '시간 측정법에 대한 사람들의 합의는 사회의 기능을 위해 필수적이다'라고 표현한 ④번이 정답이다.

어휘 institution 시설, 기관 impose 부여하다 regularity 규칙성 precise 정확한, 정밀한 timekeeping 시간 엄수 merchant 상인 ware 상품 daybreak 동틀 녘, 새벽 yardstick 기준, 척도 unbearably 견딜 수 없을 정도로 chaotic 혼란스러운 in fits and starts 간헐적으로, 하다가 말다가 fabric 기본 구조 unravel 흐트러지기 시작하다 measurement 측정법, 치수

---

08 독해 전체내용 파악 (글의 감상) 난이도 ★☆☆

끊어읽기 해석

Having just moved / into his new office, / a pompous colonel was sitting / at his desk / when a private knocked on the door.
막 이사를 온 후 / 그의 새로운 사무실로 / 거만한 대령은 앉아있었다 / 그의 책상에 / 이등병이 문을 두드렸을 때

Conscious of his new position, / the colonel told the private to enter, / then quickly picked up the phone / and said, / "Yes, General, I'll pass along your message. // In the meantime, / thank you for your good wishes, sir."
그의 새로운 지위를 의식해서, / 대령은 이등병에게 들어오라고 말했다 / 그러고는 빠르게 수화기를 들었다 / 그리고 말했다 / "예, 장군님 / 메시지

를 전달하겠습니다 // 더불어 / 장군님의 호의에 감사드립니다"

Feeling as though he had sufficiently impressed / the young enlisted man, / he asked, / "What do you want?"
마치 그가 충분히 감명을 준 것처럼 느끼며 / 젊은 입대자에게 / 그는 물었다 / "무슨 일로 왔는가?"

"Nothing important, sir," / the private replied. // "Just here to hook up your telephone, sir."
"별로 중요한 일은 아닙니다" / 그 이등병이 말했다 // "전화선을 연결하러 왔을 뿐입니다."

해석 그의 새로운 사무실로 막 이사를 온 후, 거만한 대령은 이등병이 문을 두드렸을 때 그의 책상에 앉아있었다. 그의 새로운 지위를 의식해서, 대령은 이등병에게 들어오라고 말하고는 빠르게 수화기를 들고 말했다. "예, 장군님, 메시지를 전달하겠습니다. 더불어 장군님의 호의에 감사드립니다." 마치 그가 젊은 입대자에게 충분히 감명을 준 것처럼 느끼며 그는 "무슨 일로 왔는가?"라고 물었다. "별로 중요한 일은 아닙니다."라고 그 이등병이 말했다. "전화선을 연결하러 왔을 뿐입니다."

① 자랑스러운　　　　② 만족하는
③ 부끄러운　　　　　④ 무관심한

해설 지문 전반에 걸쳐 이등병에게 감명을 주려고 장군과 통화를 하는 척 하다가 거짓말인 것을 들킨 거만한 대령의 이야기를 소개하고 있다. 따라서 글 맨 뒤에 the colonel(대령)이 느꼈을 심경을 '부끄러운'이라고 표현한 ③번이 정답이다.

어휘 pompous 거만한, 전체하는　colonel 대령
private 이등병; 개인적인　conscious 의식하는
sufficiently 충분히　enlist 입대하다　hook up 연결하다

09　독해　추론 (빈칸 완성 - 연결어)　난이도 ★☆☆

끊어읽기 해석

Fast food is everywhere. // It's available / on the main corners of a busy street / and in the luxury of your own home.
패스트푸드는 어디에나 있다. // 그것은 구해질 수 있다 / 바쁜 거리의 큰 모퉁이에서 / 그리고 당신의 집에서 호사스럽게

Effects of fast food / are quickly catching up with us.
패스트푸드의 영향은 / 결국 빠르게 우리의 발목을 잡고 있다

The nation has become a culture / of fast food eating and on-the-go living, / ultimately creating "fat" America.
이 나라는 문화가 되었다 / 패스트푸드를 먹고 바쁘게 돌아가는 삶을 사는 / 결국 '뚱뚱한' 미국을 만들면서

(A) However, / fast food has some advantages / in the short term: / people appreciate / the fact that it's fast and convenient.
(A) 하지만 / 패스트푸드는 몇 가지 이점이 있다 / 단기적인 관점에서 / 사람들은 감사한다 / 이것이 빠르고 간편하다는 사실에

There is no other food / that you can pick up / and have ready at a moment's notice.
다른 음식은 없다 / 당신이 살 수 있는 / 그리고 즉석에서 준비될 수 있는

It involves no cooking, shopping, or dishwashing. // In the end, / you are saving / an immense amount of time.
그것은 요리, 장보기, 설거지가 필요 없다 // 결국 / 당신은 절약하고 있다 / 엄청난 양의 시간을

(B) Nevertheless, / there seems to be a direct link / in America / between obesity and fast food.
(B) 그럼에도 불구하고 / 직접적인 관계가 있는 것처럼 보인다 / 미국에서는 / 비만과 패스트푸드 사이에

A typical meal from a fast-food restaurant, / say a serving of

fries and cheeseburger, / adds up to over 1,000 calories / per serving.
패스트푸드 식당에서의 일반적인 식사는 / 예를 들어 감자튀김과 치즈버거 1인분은 / 총 천 칼로리 이상이 된다 / 1인분당

This is about half / the recommended dietary allowance / for an individual per day.
이는 약 절반이다 / 권장 식사 허용량의 / 하루 한 사람의

해석 패스트푸드는 어디에나 있다. 그것은 바쁜 거리의 큰 모퉁이에서 그리고 당신의 집에서 호사스럽게 구해질 수 있다. 패스트푸드의 영향은 결국 빠르게 우리의 발목을 잡고 있다. 이 나라는 결국 '뚱뚱한' 미국을 만들면서 패스트푸드를 먹고 바쁘게 돌아가는 삶을 사는 문화가 되었다. (A) 하지만, 패스트푸드는 단기적인 관점에서 몇 가지 이점이 있는데, 사람들은 이것이 빠르고 간편하다는 사실에 감사한다. 당신이 사서 즉석에서 준비될 수 있는 다른 음식은 없다. 그것은 요리, 장보기, 설거지가 필요 없다. 결국, 당신은 엄청난 양의 시간을 절약하고 있다. (B) 그럼에도 불구하고, 미국에서는 비만과 패스트푸드 사이에 직접적인 관계가 있는 것처럼 보인다. 예를 들어 감자튀김과 치즈버거 1인분인 패스트푸드 식당에서의 일반적인 식사는 1인분당 총 천 칼로리 이상이 된다. 이는 하루 한 사람의 권장 식사 허용량의 약 절반이다.

　　(A)　　　(B)
① 하지만 – 그 결과
② 하지만 – 그럼에도 불구하고
③ 게다가 – 그 결과
④ 게다가 – 그럼에도 불구하고

해설 (A) 빈칸 앞 문장은 패스트푸드가 이 나라를 결국 '뚱뚱한' 미국으로 만들었다는 부정적인 내용이고, 빈칸 뒤 문장은 단기적인 관점에서 패스트푸드는 몇 가지 이점이 있다는 대조적인 내용이다. 따라서 대조를 나타내는 연결어인 However(하지만)가 나와야 적절하다. (B) 빈칸 앞 문장은 패스트푸드의 경우 요리, 장보기, 설거지가 필요 없으므로 결국 많은 시간을 절약할 수 있다는 긍정적인 내용이고, 빈칸 뒤 문장은 미국에서는 비만과 패스트푸드의 사이에 직접적인 관계가 있는 것처럼 보인다는 부정적인 내용이다. 따라서 양보를 나타내는 연결어인 Nevertheless(그럼에도 불구하고)가 나와야 적절하다.
따라서 ② (A) However(하지만) – (B) Nevertheless(그럼에도 불구하고)가 정답이다.

어휘 catch up with (문제가) 결국 ~의 발목을 잡다
on-the-go 바쁘게 돌아가는, 끊임없이 일하는
at a moment's notice 즉석에서, 당장　immense 엄청난
obesity 비만　serving (음식의) 1인분
recommended dietary allowance 권장 식사 허용량

10　독해　추론 (빈칸 완성 - 구)　난이도 ★★☆

끊어읽기 해석

Here is one scene from the drama / of the differences / in men's and women's ways of talking.
여기 드라마의 한 장면이 있다 / 차이에 대한 / 남자와 여자의 말하는 방식의

A woman and a man / return home from work.
한 여자와 남자가 / 일을 마치고 집으로 돌아온다

She tells / everything that happened / during the day: / what she did, / whom she met, / what they said, / what that made her think.
그녀는 얘기한다 / 일어났던 모든 일들을 / 그날 하루 동안 / 그녀가 무엇을 했고 / 그녀가 누구를 만났고 / 그들이 무슨 말을 했고 / 그것이 그녀가 무슨 생각을 하게 했는지를

Then she turns to him / and asks, / "How was your day?"
그러고 나서 그녀는 그를 돌아본다 / 그리고 묻는다 / "당신은 오늘 하루 어땠어?"

He says, / "Same fierce struggle for existence!"
그는 말한다 / "어느 때와 같이 살기 위한 격렬한 투쟁이지!"

She feels locked out: / "You don't tell me anything."
그녀는 닫혀버린 기분을 느낀다 / "당신은 나에게 아무것도 얘기하지 않아"

He protests, / "Nothing happened at work."
그는 항변한다 / "직장에서 아무 일도 일어나지 않았어"

They have different assumptions / about what is anything to tell.
그들은 다른 전제를 갖고 있다 / 말할 것이 무엇인지에 대한

To her, / telling life's daily events and impressions means / she's not alone in the world.
그녀에게 / 매일의 사건들과 감정을 말하는 것은 의미한다 / 그녀가 이 세상에 혼자가 아니라는 것을

Such talk is / the essence of intimacy / —evidence / that she and her partner are best friends.
이러한 대화는 / 친밀함의 본질이다 / 증거인 / 그녀와 그녀의 파트너가 최고의 친구라는

Since he never spent time / talking in this way / with his friends, / best or otherwise, / he doesn't expect it, / doesn't know how to do it, / and doesn't miss it / when it isn't there.
그는 시간을 보낸 적이 없기 때문에 / 이런 방식으로 이야기하는 데 / 그의 친구들과 / 가장 친하든 그렇지 않든 / 그는 그것을 기대하지 않고 / 어떻게 해야 하는지도 모르며 / 그것을 아쉬워하지 않는다 / 그것이 없을 때

해석 여기 남자와 여자의 말하는 방식의 차이에 대한 드라마의 한 장면이 있다. 한 여자와 남자가 일을 마치고 집으로 돌아온다. 그녀는 그녀가 무엇을 했고, 그녀가 누구를 만났고, 그들이 무슨 말을 했고, 그것이 그녀가 무슨 생각을 하게 했는지와 같은 그날 하루 동안 일어났던 모든 일들을 얘기한다. 그러고 나서 그녀는 그를 돌아보고 "당신은 오늘 하루 이땼어?"라고 묻는다. "어느 때와 같이 살기 위한 격렬한 투쟁이지!"라고 그는 말한다. 그녀는 닫혀버린 기분을 느끼며 "당신은 나에게 아무 것도 얘기하지 않아."라고 말한다. 그는 "직장에서 아무 일도 일어나지 않았어."라고 항변한다. 그들은 말할 것이 무엇인지에 대한 다른 전제를 갖고 있다. 그녀에게 매일의 사건들과 감정을 말하는 것은 그녀가 이 세상에 혼자가 아니라는 것을 의미한다. 이러한 대화는 그녀와 그녀의 파트너가 최고의 친구라는 증거인 친밀함의 본질이다. 그는 가장 친하든 그렇지 않든 그의 친구들과 이런 방식으로 이야기하는 데 시간을 보낸 적이 없기 때문에, 그것을 기대하지 않고, 어떻게 해야 하는지도 모르며, 그것이 없을 때 그것을 아쉬워하지도 않는다.

① 어떤 것들이 비슷한지
② 말할 것이 무엇인지
③ 그 드라마가 사실인지 아닌지
④ 그들에게 어떤 말이 더 좋은지

해설 빈칸이 있는 문장을 통해 남자와 여자가 무엇에 대한 다른 전제를 갖고 있는지에 대한 내용이 나와야 적절하다는 것을 알 수 있다. 지문 앞부분에서 남자와 여자의 말하는 방식의 차이에 대한 드라마의 한 장면을 언급한 뒤, 지문 뒷부분에서 매일의 사건들과 감정을 말하는 것은 여자에게는 친밀함의 본질이지만, 남자는 친구들과 이런 방식으로 이야기하는 데 시간을 보내지 않으며, 그것을 기대하거나 잘 하지 못한다는 내용이 있다. 따라서 그들이 '말할 것이 무엇인지'에 대한 다른 전제를 갖고 있다고 한 ②번이 정답이다.

어휘 fierce 격렬한 struggle 투쟁; 투쟁하다 protest 항변하다, 항의하다
assumptions 전제, 가정 essence 본질 intimacy 친밀함

끊어읽기 해석

Given how little we know / about our inner ecology, / carpet-bombing it / might not always be the best idea.
우리가 얼마나 거의 모르고 있는지를 생각하면 / 우리의 내부 생태학에 대해 / 그것을 대대적으로 광고하는 것이 / 항상 가장 좋은 생각은 아닐지도 모른다

"I would put it very bluntly," / Margulis told me.
"저는 그것을 매우 노골적으로 표현할 것입니다" / Margulis가 내게 말했다

"When you advocate your soaps / that say they kill all harmful bacteria, / you are committing suicide."
"당신이 당신의 비누를 지지할 때 / 모든 해로운 박테리아를 죽인다고 말하는 / 당신은 자살을 하고 있는 것입니다"

The bacteria in the intestines / can take up to four years / to recover from a round of antibiotics, / recent studies have found, / and the steady attack / of detergents, preservatives, and chemicals / are also harmful.
장 속의 박테리아는 / 4년까지 걸릴 수 있다 / 한 차례의 항생물질로부터 회복하는 데 / 최근의 연구는 알아냈다 / 그리고 지속적인 공격은 / 세제, 방부제, 그리고 화학제품들의 / 또한 해로울 수 있다는 것을

The immune system builds up fewer antibodies / in a clean environment; / the deadliest pathogens can grow / more resistant to antibiotics.
면역 체계는 더 적은 항체를 만든다 / 깨끗한 환경에서 / 가장 치명적인 병원균은 성장할 수 있다 / 항생물질에 더 저항력 있게

All of which may explain / why a number of studies have found / that children raised on farms / are less likely to be influenced / by allergies, asthma, and autoimmune diseases.
이 모든 것은 설명할 수 있다 / 왜 많은 연구들이 발견했는지를 / 농장에서 자란 아이들이 / 영향을 받을 가능성이 덜하다는 것을 / 알레르기, 천식, 자기면역 질환으로부터

It sometimes seems / as we are cleaner, we get sicker.
가끔은 ~인 것처럼 보인다 / 우리가 더 깨끗해질수록 더 아파지는

해석 우리가 우리의 내부 생태학에 대해 얼마나 거의 모르고 있는지를 생각하면, 그것을 대대적으로 광고하는 것이 항상 가장 좋은 생각은 아닐지도 모른다. "저는 그것을 매우 노골적으로 표현할 것입니다."라고 Margulis가 내게 말했다. "당신이 모든 해로운 박테리아를 죽인다고 말하는 당신의 비누를 지지할 때 당신은 자살을 하고 있는 것입니다." 장 속의 박테리아는 한 차례의 항생물질로부터 회복하는 데 4년까지 걸릴 수 있고, 세제, 방부제, 그리고 화학제품들의 지속적인 공격 또한 해로울 수 있다고 최근의 연구는 알아냈다. 면역 체계는 깨끗한 환경에서 더 적은 항체를 만드는데, 가장 치명적인 병원균은 항생물질에 더 저항력 있게 성장할 수 있다. 이 모든 것은 왜 많은 연구들이 농장에서 자란 아이들이 알레르기, 천식, 자기면역 질환으로부터 영향을 받을 가능성이 덜하다는 것을 발견했는지를 설명할 수 있다. 가끔은 우리가 더 깨끗해질수록 더 아파지는 것처럼 보인다.

① 사람들은 건강한 생활방식을 피한다
② 전원 생활을 하는 것은 면역력을 신장시킨다
③ 오염물질이 알레르기 반응을 촉발시킬 수 있다
④ 우리가 더 깨끗해질수록 더 아파진다

해설 지문 중간에서 면역 체계는 깨끗한 환경에서 더 적은 항체를 만들고, 치명적인 병원균은 항생물질에 더 저항력 있게 성장할 수 있다고 하며, 이것이 농장에서 자란 아이들이 알레르기, 천식, 자기면역 질환으로부터 영향을 받을 가능성이 덜한 것을 설명할 수 있다는 내용이 있다. 따라서 '우리가 더 깨끗할수록 더 아파지는' 것처럼 보인다고 한 ④번이 정답이다.

어휘 ecology 생태학 carpet-bomb 대대적인 광고를 하다
bluntly 노골적으로 advocate 지지하다, 옹호하다
commit suicide 자살하다 intestine 장 antibiotics 항생물질
detergent 세제 preservative 방부제
immune system 면역 체계 pathogen 병원균
resistant 저항력 있는 antibiotic 항생물질, 항체
asthma 천식 autoimmune 자기면역의

따라서 ① (A) extend(확장되다) – (B) condenses(응결되다) –
(C) feed(공급하다)가 정답이다.

어휘 funnel 깔때기 churning 휘도는 width 너비, 폭 track 진로, 자취
extend 확장되다, 연장하다 contract 수축하다
condense 응결되다 condescend 거들먹거리다, 자신을 낮추다
thundercloud 뇌운 feed 공급하다, 먹이를 주다
thwart 좌절시키다 updraft 상승 기류

12 독해 논리적 흐름 파악 (문맥상 적절한 어휘) 난이도 ★★☆

끊어읽기 해석

A tornado is a dark, funnel-shaped cloud / made up of violently churning winds.
토네이도는 어두운 깔때기 모양의 구름이다 / 격렬하게 휘도는 바람으로 이루어진

A tornado's width can measure / from a few feet to a mile, / and its track can (A) extend / from less than a mile to several hundred miles.
토네이도의 너비는 측정될 수 있다 / 몇 피트에서 1마일까지 / 그리고 그 진로는 (A) 확장될 수 있다 / 1마일 이하에서 수백 마일까지

Tornados are most often caused / by giant thunderstorms.
토네이도는 가장 빈번하게 발생한다 / 거대한 뇌우에 의해

These highly powerful storms form / when warm, moist air / along the ground / rushes upward, / meeting cooler, drier air.
이러한 매우 강력한 폭풍은 형성된다 / 따뜻하고 습한 공기가 / 땅 부근의 / 위쪽으로 돌진할 때 / 더 차갑고 건조한 공기를 만나면서

As the rising warm air cools, / the moisture it carries (B) condenses, / forming a massive thundercloud.
상승하는 따뜻한 공기가 차가워지면서 / 그것이 운반하는 습기는 (B) 응결된다 / 거대한 뇌운을 형성하며

Winds at different levels of the atmosphere / (C) feed the updraft / and cause the formation / of the tornado's characteristic funnel shape.
각기 다른 대기층의 바람은 / 상승 기류를 (C) 공급한다 / 그리고 형성을 야기한다 / 토네이도의 특징적인 깔때기 모양의

해석 토네이도는 격렬하게 휘도는 바람으로 이루어진 어두운 깔때기 모양의 구름이다. 토네이도의 너비는 몇 피트에서 1마일까지 측정될 수 있으며, 그 진로는 1마일 이하에서 수백 마일까지 (A) 확장될 수 있다. 토네이도는 거대한 뇌우에 의해 가장 빈번하게 발생한다. 이러한 매우 강력한 폭풍은 땅 부근의 따뜻하고 습한 공기가 위쪽으로 돌진할 때, 더 차갑고 건조한 공기를 만나면서 형성된다. 상승하는 따뜻한 공기가 차가워지면서, 그것이 운반하는 습기는 거대한 뇌운을 형성하며 (B) 응결된다. 각기 다른 대기층의 바람은 상승 기류를 (C) 공급하고, 토네이도의 특징적인 깔때기 모양의 형성을 야기한다.

    (A)   (B)   (C)
① 확장되다 – 응결되다   – 공급하다
② 확장되다 – 거들먹거리다 – 좌절시키다
③ 수축하다 – 응결되다   – 공급하다
④ 수축하다 – 거들먹거리다 – 좌절시키다

해설 (A) 그 진로가 1마일 이하에서 몇 백 마일까지 '확장될'(extend) 수 있다는 내용이 들어가야 적절하다. (B) 주변에서 따뜻한 공기가 차가워지면서 그것이 운반하는 습기가 거대한 뇌운을 형성한다고 했으므로, 습기가 '응결된다'(condenses)는 내용이 들어가야 적절하다. (C) 뒤에서 토네이도의 특징적인 깔때기 모양의 형성에 대해 언급하고 있으므로 문맥상 바람이 상승 기류(위쪽으로 돌진하는 공기)를 '공급한다'(feed)라는 내용이 들어가야 적절하다.

13 독해 추론 (빈칸 완성 - 절) 난이도 ★★☆

끊어읽기 해석

It is crucial / for parents to teach children / that their intelligence is under their control.
중요하다 / 부모들이 아이들에게 가르치는 것은 / 그들의 지능은 그들의 통제하에 있다는 것을

Asians are particularly likely to believe / that ability or intelligence / is something you have to work for.
아시아 사람들은 특히 생각할 가능성이 있다 / 능력이나 지능은 / 누구든 얻기 위해 노력해야 하는 것이라고

Not surprisingly, / Asian Americans work harder / to achieve academic goals / than European Americans.
놀랄 것 없이 / 아시아계 미국인들은 더 열심히 노력한다 / 학문적인 목표를 성취하기 위해 / 유럽계의 미국인들보다

And Asians work harder / after failure than after success / —unlike North Americans of European descent / who work harder / after success than after failure.
그리고 아시아 사람들은 더 열심히 일한다 / 성공 이후보다 실패 이후에 / 유럽인 혈통의 북아메리카 사람들과는 다르게 / 더 열심히 일하는 / 실패보다는 성공 이후에

It is important to teach children / that if at first you don't succeed / try again harder.
아이들에게 가르치는 것은 중요하다 / 만약 처음에 성공하지 못했다면 / 다시 더 열심히 해볼 것을

해석 부모들이 아이들에게 그들의 지능은 그들의 통제하에 있다는 것을 가르치는 것은 중요하다. 아시아 사람들은 특히 능력이나 지능은 누구든 얻기 위해 노력해야 하는 것이라고 생각할 가능성이 있다. 놀랄 것 없이, 아시아계 미국인들은 유럽계의 미국인들보다 학문적인 목표를 성취하기 위해 더 열심히 노력한다. 그리고 실패보다는 성공 후에 더 열심히 일하는 유럽인 혈통의 북아메리카 사람들과는 다르게 아시아 사람들은 성공 이후보다 실패 이후에 더 열심히 일한다. 아이들에게 만약 처음에 성공하지 못했다면 다시 더 열심히 해볼 것을 가르치는 것은 중요하다.

① 지능은 매우 유전적이다
② 그들의 지능은 그들의 통제하에 있다
③ 똑똑한 사람들이 항상 성공하는 것은 아니다
④ 인생에서의 성공이 항상 행복을 보장하는 것은 아니다

해설 지문 앞부분에서 아시아 사람들은 능력이나 지능은 우리가 얻기 위해 노력해야 하는 것이라고 생각하여 학문적인 목표를 성취하기 위해 더 열심히 노력한다는 내용이 있고, 지문 마지막에 부모들이 아이들에게 만약 처음에 성공하지 못했다면 다시 더 열심히 해볼 것을 가르치는 것이 중요하다는 내용이 있다. 따라서 부모들이 아이들에게 '그들의 지능은 그들의 통제하에 있다'는 것을 가르치는 것이 중요하다고 한 ②번이 정답이다.

어휘 crucial 중요한, 결정적인 descent 혈통 hereditary 유전적인
guarantee 보장하다

끊어읽기 해석

The magnetic field is oddly prevalent / in all kinds of animal orientation.
자기장은 특이하게도 널리 퍼져있다 / 온갖 종류의 동물의 방향 설정에

Termites line up / along its cardinal axes. // Yellow eels also use / the magnetic field.
흰개미들은 줄을 선다 / 그들의 기본 축을 따라서 // 노란 뱀장어 또한 이용한다 / 자기장을

Homing pigeons, / however, / are more of a mystery.
전서구(통신에 이용하기 위해 훈련된 비둘기)들은 / 하지만 / 오히려 수수께끼이다

It was long thought / that they, too, relied / solely upon the magnetic field / to find their way.
오랫동안 생각되었다 / 그들(비둘기들)도 의지한다고 / 오직 자기장에만 / 그들의 길을 찾기 위해

In studies / that disrupt the field, / the pigeons' path was thrown off.
연구들에서 / 자기장을 방해하는 / 비둘기의 경로는 벗어났다

But / after tracking pigeons / with GPS satellites / for ten years, / researchers announced their findings: / rather than using sun for directional bearings, / it turns out that the pigeons use / roads they've traveled in the past / as a guide.
하지만/ 비둘기들을 추적한 후에 / GPS 위성으로 / 10년 동안 / 연구원들은 그들의 발견을 발표했다 / 방향 파악을 위해서 태양을 이용하기보다 / 비둘기들은 이용하는 것으로 드러났다 / 과거에 그들이 여행했던 길들을 / 가이드로써

Then, / three years after this study, / different scientists found / that iron-containing structures / within the birds' beaks / apparently also aid in their sense of direction.
그리고 / 이 연구가 있은지 3년 뒤에 / 다른 과학자들은 알아냈다 / 철을 함유한 구조가 / 새들의 부리 속에 있는 / 또한 명백하게 그들의 방향 감각을 돕는다는 것을

They might even have / the ability to use atmospheric odors.
그들은 심지어 가졌을지도 모른다 / 대기의 냄새를 사용하는 능력을

해석 자기장은 특이하게도 온갖 종류의 동물의 방향 설정에 널리 퍼져 있다. 흰개미들은 그들의 기본 축을 따라서 줄을 선다. 노란 뱀장어 또한 자기장을 이용한다. 하지만 전서구(통신에 이용하기 위해 훈련된 비둘기)들은 오히려 수수께끼이다. 그들(비둘기들)도 그들의 길을 찾기 위해 오직 자기장에만 의지한다고 오랫동안 생각되어졌다. 자기장을 방해하는 연구들에서 비둘기의 경로는 벗어났다. 하지만 GPS 위성으로 10년 동안 비둘기들을 추적한 후에, 연구원들은 그들의 발견을 발표했는데, 비둘기들은 방향 파악을 위해서 태양을 이용하기보다 과거에 그들이 여행했던 길들을 가이드로써 이용하는 것으로 드러났다. 그리고 이 연구가 있은지 3년 뒤에, 다른 과학자들은 새들의 부리 속에 있는 철을 함유한 구조 또한 명백하게 그들의 방향 감각을 돕는다는 것을 알아냈다. 그들은 심지어 대기의 냄새를 사용하는 능력을 가졌을지도 모른다.

① 전서구들은 그들의 본능을 따른다
② 왜 새들은 철마다 이동할까?
③ 새들이 이동 중에 마주치는 제약
④ 전서구들의 신비한 방향 감각

해설 지문 중간에서 전서구들은 오직 자기장을 이용해서 길을 찾는다고 오랫동안 생각되었지만, 연구 결과 이 비둘기들이 과거에 여행했던 길을 가이드로 이용해 방향을 파악하고, 부리 속에 있는 철을 함유한 구조가 방향 감각을 도우며, 심지어 대기의 냄새를 사용하는 능력을 가졌을지도 모른다고 추측하고 있다. 따라서 이 지

문의 제목을 '전서구들의 신비한 방향 감각'이라고 표현한 ④번이 정답이다.

어휘 **magnetic field** 자기장 **oddly** 특이하게도, 이상하게
prevalent 널리 퍼진 **orientation** 방향 설정, 귀소본능
termite 흰개미 **cardinal axes** 기본 축 **eel** 뱀장어
solely 오직, 단지 **disrupt** 방해하다 **directional** 방향의, 지향성의
bearing (방향 등의) 파악, 방위
atmospheric 대기의, 분위기 있는 **odor** 냄새
constraint 제약, 제한 **migration** 이동, 이주

끊어읽기 해석

Most native English speakers / don't actually talk / in correct English.
영어가 모국어인 사람 대부분은 / 실제로 말하지 않는다 / 올바른 영어로

What we usually consider correct English / is a set of guidelines / developed over time / to help standardize written expression.
우리가 보통 올바른 영어라고 여기는 것은 / 일련의 지침들이다 / 시간이 흐름에 따라 개발된 / 문자로 된 표현을 표준화하는 것을 돕기 위해서

This standardization is / a matter of use and convenience.
이러한 표준화는 / 사용과 편리함의 문제이다

Suppose / you went to a vegetable stand / and asked for a pound of peppers / and the storekeeper gave you a half pound / but charged you for a full one.
가정하자 / 당신이 채소 가판대에 가서 / 후추 1파운드를 요청했다고 / 그리고 가게 주인이 당신에게 0.5파운드를 주었다고 / 하지만 당신에게 1파운드의 값을 요구했다고

When you complained, / he said, / "But that's what I call a pound."
당신이 불만을 세기했을 때 / 그는 밀했다 / "하지만 이것이 내가 1파운드라고 부르는 것이오"

Life would be very frustrating / if everyone had / a different set of standards: / Imagine what would happen / if some states used / a red light to signal "go" / and a green one for "stop."
삶은 매우 불만스러울 것이다 / 만약 모두가 가지고 있다면 / 다른 일련의 기준을 / 무슨 일이 일어날지 상상해보라 / 만약 일부 주들이 사용한다면 / 빨간불을 '운행'을 표시하는 데 / 그리고 파란불을 '정지'로

Languages are not that different. // In all cultures, / languages have gradually developed / certain general rules and principles / to make communication / as clear and efficient as possible.
언어들은 그렇게 다르지 않다. // 모든 문화에서 / 언어는 점진적으로 발달시켜 왔다 / 어떤 보편적인 규칙과 원리를 / 의사소통을 하기 위해서 / 가능한 한 명확하고 효율적으로

해석 영어가 모국어인 사람 대부분은 실제로 올바른 영어로 말하지 않는다. 우리가 보통 올바른 영어라고 여기는 것은 문자로 된 표현을 표준화하는 것을 돕기 위해서 시간이 흐름에 따라 개발된 일련의 지침들이다. 이러한 표준화는 사용과 편리함의 문제이다. 당신이 채소 가판대에 가서 후추 1파운드를 요청했는데, 가게 주인이 당신에게 0.5파운드를 주었지만 1파운드의 값을 요구했다고 가정하자. 당신이 불만을 제기했을 때, 그는 "하지만 이것이 내가 1파운드라고 부르는 것이오."라고 말했다. 만약 모두가 다른 기준을 가지고 있다면 삶은 매우 불만스러울 것이다. 만약 일부 주들이 빨간불을 '운행'을 표시하는 데, 그리고 파란불을 '정지'로 사용한다면 무슨 일이 일어날지 상상해보라. 언어들은 그렇게 다르지 않다. 언어는 모든 문화에서 의사소통을 가능한 한 명확하고 효율적으로

하기 위해서 어떤 보편적인 규칙과 원리를 점진적으로 발달시켜 왔다.

해설 지문 앞부분에서 우리가 보통 올바른 영어라고 여기는 것은 문자로 된 표현을 표준화하는 것을 돕기 위해 개발된 일련의 지침들이라고 했고, 지문 마지막에서 언어는 모든 문화에서 의사소통을 가능한 한 명확하고 효율적으로 하기 위해서 보편적인 규칙과 원리를 발달시켜 왔다고 설명하고 있다. 따라서 이 지문의 요지를 '언어는 명확한 의사소통을 위해 표준화되어 왔다'라고 표현한 ③번이 정답이다.

어휘 guideline 지침 standardize 표준화하다
charge (지불을) 요구하다, 청구하다 suppose 가정하다

16 독해 논리적 흐름 파악 (문맥상 부적절한 어휘) 난이도 ★★☆

끊어읽기 해석

> The intangibles / we attach to tangible property / are still rapidly multiplying.
> 무형 자산들이 / 우리가 유형 자산과 연관짓는 / 여전히 빠르게 증가하고 있다
>
> Every day / there are more legal precedents, more real-estate records, more transactional data and the like.
> 매일 / 더 많은 법적 판례, 더 많은 부동산 기록, 더 많은 상거래 자료와 같은 것들이 있다
>
> Each piece of tangible property, / therefore, / contains ① higher component of untouchability.
> 유형 자산의 각 부분은 / 그러므로 / 손댈 수 없는 ① 더 중요한 부분을 포함한다
>
> In advanced economies / the degree of intangibility / in society's property base / is spiraling ② upward.
> 발전된 경제에서 / 무형의 정도는 / 사회적 재산의 토대에서의 / ② 위로 급증하고 있다
>
> What's more, / even industrial-age manufacturing giants now depend / on ③ ever-growing inputs of skill, R&D findings, smart management, market intelligence, etc.
> 게다가 / 산업 시대의 거대 제조 기업조차도 현재 의존한다 / ③ 계속 늘어나는 기술의 투입, 연구 개발 결과, 스마트 관리, 시장 정보 등에
>
> All this changes the tangibility ratio / in the economy's property base, / further ④ increasing / the role of touchables.
> 이러한 모든 것은 유형의 비율을 변화시킨다 / 경제적 재산의 토대에서 / 나아가 ④ 증가시키면서 / 만질 수 있는 것들(유형)의 역할을

해석 우리가 유형 자산과 연관짓는 무형 자산들이 여전히 빠르게 증가하고 있다. 매일 더 많은 법적 판례, 더 많은 부동산 기록, 더 많은 상거래 자료와 같은 것들이 있다. 그러므로 유형 자산의 각 부분은 손댈 수 없는 ① 더 중요한 부분을 포함한다. 발전된 경제에서 사회적 재산의 토대에서의 무형의 정도는 ② 위로 급증하고 있다. 게다가 산업 시대의 거대 제조 기업조차도 현재 ③ 계속 늘어나는 기술의 투입, 연구 개발 결과, 스마트 관리, 시장 정보 등에 의존한다. 이러한 모든 것은 나아가 만질 수 있는 것들(유형)의 역할을 ④ 증가시키면서 경제적 재산의 토대에서 유형의 비율을 변화시킨다.

해설 지문 처음에 무형 자산들이 빠르게 증가하고 있다는 내용이 있고, 지문 중간에 발전된 경제에서 사회적 재산의 토대에서의 무형의 정도가 급증하고 있다는 내용이 있으므로, 이러한 모든 것들이 만질 수 있는 것들(유형)의 역할을 '증가시키면서'(increasing) 유형의 비율을 변화시킨다는 내용은 문맥상 적절하지 않다. 따라서 ④ increasing이 정답이다. 참고로, 주어진 increasing을 대신할 수 있는 어휘로는 '감소시키다'라는 의미의 동사 decrease의 현재분사형 decreasing 등이 있다.

어휘 intangibles 무형 자산 tangible 유형의 property 자산, 재산
multiply 증가하다, 곱하다 precedent 판례, 전례
real-estate 부동산의 transactional 상거래의
higher 더 중요한, 고등의 untouchability 손댈 수 없음
spiral 급증하다; 나선형 ever-growing 계속 늘어나는

17 독해 전체내용 파악 (글의 감상) 난이도 ★☆☆

끊어읽기 해석

> I cannot believe / what I am seeing: / plants, and trees everywhere.
> 나는 믿을 수 없다 / 내가 보고 있는 것을 / 곳곳에 있는 식물들과 나무들을
>
> The scents are sweet / and the air is pure and clean.
> 그 향기는 달콤하다 / 그리고 공기는 맑고 깨끗하다
>
> I like the silence / that greets me / as I arrive at hotel.
> 나는 고요함이 좋다 / 나를 반기는 / 내가 호텔에 도착할 때
>
> Upstairs, / my heart is all aflutter / at finding I have a good room, / with a good-enough balcony view / of the distant water.
> 위층에서 / 내 심장은 매우 들떴다 / 내가 좋은 방을 가졌다는 것을 발견하고 / 충분히 좋은 발코니 경관을 가진 / 멀리 떨어져 있는 호수의
>
> I take out clean clothes, / shower, / and, camera in hand, / head downstairs / to ask the attendant / where I can find Moreno gardens.
> 나는 깨끗한 옷을 꺼내 / 샤워를 하고 / 그리고 카메라를 손에 든 채 / 밑으로 내려갔다 / 종업원에게 묻기 위해서 / 내가 모레노 정원을 어디서 찾을 수 있는지
>
> The man at the desk looks puzzled / and says / he's never heard of the Moreno gardens.
> 데스크의 남자는 어리둥절해 보인다 / 그리고 말한다 / 모레노 정원을 들어본 적이 없다고
>
> He steps into the back office / and comes out / accompanied by a woman.
> 그는 뒤의 사무실로 들어간다 / 그리고 나온다 / 여자와 동행해서
>
> She has never heard of / the Moreno gardens, / either.
> 그녀는 들어본 적이 없었다 / 모레노 정원을 / 마찬가지로
>
> My second question, / regarding the house painted by Monet, / brings me no closer to the truth.
> 나의 두 번째 질문은 / 모네에 의해 칠해진 한 집에 관한 / 나를 보다 진실에 가깝게 해주지 않았다
>
> Neither has heard / of such a house. // It makes my shoulders droop.
> 그 둘 중 누구도 들어본 적이 없었다 / 그러한 집에 대해 // 이는 내 어깨를 쳐지게 만들었다.

해석 나는 내가 보고 있는 곳곳에 있는 식물들과 나무들을 믿을 수 없다. 그 향기는 달콤하고 공기는 맑고 깨끗하다. 나는 내가 호텔에 도착할 때 나를 반기는 고요함이 좋다. 위층에서, 내가 멀리 떨어져 있는 호수의 충분히 좋은 발코니 경관을 가진 좋은 방을 가졌다는 것을 발견하고 내 심장은 매우 들떴다. 나는 깨끗한 옷을 꺼내 샤워를 하고, 카메라를 손에 든 채 내가 모레노 정원을 어디서 찾을 수 있는지 종업원에게 묻기 위해서 밑으로 내려갔다. 데스크의 남자는 어리둥절해 보였고, 모레노 정원을 들어본 적이 없다고 말한다. 그는 뒤의 사무실로 들어가 여자와 동행해서 나온다. 그녀도 마찬가지로 모레노 정원을 들어본 적이 없었다. 모네에 의해 칠해진 한 집에 관한 나의 두 번째 질문은 나를 보다 진실에 가깝게 해주지 않았다. 그 둘 중 누구도 그러한 집에 대해 들어본 적이 없었다. 이는 내 어깨를 쳐지게 만들었다.

① 지루한 → 기대하는　　② 걱정하는 → 기쁜
③ 슬픈 → 안도하는　　④ 흥분한 → 실망한

④ 신중하게 써라, 하지만 그 순간을 즐겨라

해설 지문 처음에서 작문에서 당신의 의도는 글쓰기의 목표 혹은 목적이라고 한 뒤, 지문 뒷부분에서 명쾌하게 구술된 의도는 독자들이 당신의 주장이나 관점을 이해하도록 돕는다는 내용이 있다. 따라서 이 지문의 제목을 '당신의 수필의 의도를 명확히 표현하라'라고 표현한 ②번이 정답이다.

어휘 composition 작문, 작품 endorse 지지하다
rally support 지지를 모으다 explicitly 명쾌하게
anchor 닻을 내리다 aimlessly 목적 없이 float 떠다니다, 부유하다

18 독해 전체내용 파악 (제목 파악) 난이도 ★☆☆

끊어읽기 해석

In composition, / your purpose is / your overall goal or aim / in writing.
작문에서 / 당신의 의도는 / 당신의 종합적인 목표 혹은 목적이다 / 글에서의

It is basically / what you hope to accomplish / by writing / —whether it is to promote / or endorse a certain point of view, / rally support for a cause, / criticize a film or a book, / or examine the effects of a social trend.
이는 기본적으로 / 당신이 성취하기를 바라는 그 무엇이다 / 글을 씀으로써 / 그것이 홍보하는 것이든 / 특정 견해를 지지하는 것이든 / 어떤 조직을 위해 지지를 모으는 것이든 / 영화나 책을 비평하는 것이든 / 사회적 경향의 효과를 조사하는 것이든 간에

Your purpose / may or may not be expressed explicitly / (in creative writing, for example, / it rarely is), / but in essays it is usually important / that your reader understand / the purpose behind your writing.
당신의 의도는 / 명쾌하게 표현될 수도 있고 그렇지 않을 수도 있다 / (예를 들어서 독창적인 글쓰기에서는 / 거의 그렇지 않다) / 하지만 수필에서는 보통 중요하다 / 당신의 독자가 이해하는 것이 / 당신의 글 뒤에 있는 의도를

An explicitly stated purpose / not only helps / the reader follow your argument or perspective / but also helps ensure / that everything you write / reflects that purpose.
명쾌하게 구술된 의도는 / 도울 뿐만 아니라 / 독자들이 당신의 주장이나 관점을 이해하도록 / 확실히 하도록 돕는다 / 당신이 쓴 모든 것들이 / 그 의도를 반영하는 것을

A carefully expressed purpose will help / anchor your essay / and keep it from aimlessly floating all over.
신중하게 표현된 의도는 도울 것이다 / 당신의 글이 닻을 내리도록 / 그리고 그것이 목적 없이 사방을 떠다니지 않도록 하는 것을

해석 작문에서 당신의 의도는 글에서의 당신의 종합적인 목표 혹은 목적이다. 이는 그것이 홍보하는 것이든, 특정 견해를 지지하는 것이든, 어떤 조직을 위해 지지를 모으는 것이든, 영화나 책을 비평하는 것이든, 사회적 경향의 효과를 조사하는 것이든 간에 기본적으로 당신이 글을 씀으로써 성취하기를 바라는 그 무엇이다. 당신의 의도는 명쾌하게 표현될 수도 있고 그렇지 않을 수도 있지만 (예를 들어, 독창적인 글쓰기에서는 거의 그렇지 않다), 수필에서는 보통 독자가 당신의 글 뒤에 있는 의도를 이해하는 것이 중요하다. 명쾌하게 구술된 의도는 독자들이 당신의 주장이나 관점을 이해하도록 도울 뿐만 아니라, 당신이 쓴 모든 것들이 그 의도를 반영하는 것을 확실히 하도록 돕는다. 신중하게 표현된 의도는 당신의 글이 닻을 내리고, 목적 없이 사방을 떠다니지 않도록 도울 것이다.

① 비판: 수필을 쓰는 것의 목표
② 당신의 수필의 의도를 명확히 표현하라
③ 간결성: 글쓰기의 기초

19 독해 전체내용 파악 (목적 파악) 난이도 ★☆☆

끊어읽기 해석

The U.S. is shrinking physically. // It has lost / nearly 20 meters of beach / from its East Coast / during the 20th century.
미국은 물리적으로 가라앉고 있다. // 그것은 잃었다 / 거의 20미터의 해변을 / 동쪽 해안부터 / 20세기 동안에

The oceans have risen / by roughly 17 centimeters / since 1900 / through expansion / (warmer water taking up more space) / and the ongoing melt down of polar ice.
바다는 상승했다 / 대략 17센티미터만큼 / 1900년 이후로 / 확장에 의해 / (따뜻한 물이 더 많은 공간을 차지하며 생긴) / 그리고 계속 진행 중인 북극 얼음의 용해(에 의해)

That increase, / however, / is a small fraction / compared with what's to come.
그러한 증가는 / 하지만 / 작은 부분이다 / 앞으로 닥칠 일에 비교해보면

In fact, / unless greenhouse gas emissions are tamed, / the seas will keep rising / as the ice sheets covering mountain ranges / melt away.
사실상 / 온실 가스 배출이 다스려지지 않는 이상 / 바다는 계속해서 높아질 것이다 / 산맥을 덮고 있는 빙상이 / 녹아버림에 따라

Just how humans will adapt / to a more watery world / is still not known.
다만 인간이 어떻게 적응할지는 / 물이 더 많은 세상에 / 아직 알려지지 않았다

Of today's trend, / Robert Bindschadler, / an emeritus scientist at NASA, / notes, / "We're not going to avoid this one."
오늘날 이러한 추세에 대해 / Robert Bindschadler는 / 나사의 명예직 과학자 / 말한다 / "우리는 이것을 피할 수 없을 것이다"

해석 미국은 물리적으로 가라앉고 있다. 그것은 20세기 동안에 동쪽 해안부터 거의 20미터의 해변을 잃었다. 바다는 1900년 이후로 확장(따뜻한 물이 더 많은 공간을 차지하며 생긴)과 계속 진행 중인 북극 얼음의 용해에 의해 대략 17센티미터만큼 상승했다. 하지만 그러한 증가는 앞으로 닥칠 일에 비교해보면 작은 부분이다. 사실상 온실 가스 배출이 다스려지지 않는 이상, 산맥을 덮고 있는 빙상이 녹아버림에 따라 바다는 계속해서 높아질 것이다. 다만 인간이 어떻게 물이 더 많은 세상에 적응할지는 아직 알려지지 않았다. 오늘날 이러한 추세에 대해 나사의 명예직 과학자 Robert Bindschadler는 "우리는 이것을 피할 수 없을 것이다"라고 말한다.

해설 지문 처음에서 미국이 물리적으로 가라앉고 있다고 했고, 지문 뒷부분에서 온실 가스 배출이 다스려지지 않는 이상 빙상이 녹아 바다는 계속 높아질 것이라고 경고하고 있다. 따라서 이 지문의 목적을 '온실가스 배출로 인한 해수면 상승을 경고하려고'라고 표현한 ①번이 정답이다.

어휘 shrink 가라앉다, 줄어들다 roughly 대략, 거의
ongoing 계속 진행 중인 fraction 부분
greenhouse gas 온실 가스 emission 배출, 방출
tame 다스리다 ice sheet 빙상, 대륙 빙하 mountain range 산맥
adapt 적응하다, 맞추다 watery 물이 많은, 물기가 많은
emeritus 명예직의

20 독해 전체내용 파악 (문단 요약) 난이도 ★☆☆

끊어읽기 해석

In dealing with the inevitable behavior problems / in their classrooms, / teachers may sometimes go too far.
불가피한 행동 문제들을 다룸에 있어서 / 교실 안에서의 / 교사들은 가끔 도를 넘을 수도 있다

Often, / teachers will humiliate / a misbehaving student / in front of the entire class.
종종 / 교사들은 굴욕감을 줄 것이다 / 품행이 좋지 못한 학생들에게 / 학급 전체 앞에서

Despite bringing about an immediate, temporary end / to the problematic behavior, / taking such action can cause / long-term educational repercussions.
즉각적이고 일시적인 종료를 가져옴에도 불구하고 / 문제되는 행동들의 / 이러한 행동을 취하는 것은 야기할 수 있다 / 장기적으로는 교육적으로 좋지 못한 영향을

Prominent psychologists have noted / that humiliating experiences in school are correlated / with a drop-off in academic performance.
저명한 심리학자들은 주목해왔다 / 학교에서의 굴욕적인 경험이 연관성이 있다고 / 학문적인 성과의 하락과

The students lose self-confidence / and begin to believe / that positive grades are out of their reach.
학생들은 자신감을 잃는다 / 그리고 생각하기 시작한다 / 바람직한 성적이 그들의 힘이 미치지 않는 곳에 있다고

해석 교실 안에서의 불가피한 행동 문제들을 다룸에 있어서, 교사들은 가끔 도를 넘을 수도 있다. 종종 교사들은 학급 전체 앞에서 품행이 좋지 못한 학생들에게 굴욕감을 줄 것이다. 문제되는 행동들의 즉각적이고 일시적인 종료를 가져옴에도 불구하고, 이러한 행동을 취하는 것은 장기적으로는 교육적으로 좋지 못한 영향을 야기할 수 있다. 저명한 심리학자들은 학교에서의 굴욕적인 경험이 학문적인 성과의 하락과 연관성이 있다고 주목해왔다. 학생들은 자신감을 잃고, 바람직한 성적이 그들의 힘이 미치지 않는 곳에 있다고 생각하기 시작한다.

> 학생들을 부끄럽게 하는 것은 그들의 교육적인 발전에 (A) 해를 끼칠 수 있기 때문에 교사들은 학문적인 성과를 위해 그들의 (B) 심리적인 요소들을 고려해야만 한다.

　　　　(A)　　　　　(B)
① 해를 끼치다 – 육체의
② 향상시키다 – 육체의
③ 해를 끼치다 – 심리적인
④ 향상시키다 – 심리적인

해설 지문 뒷부분에서 학교에서의 굴욕적인 경험이 학문적인 성과의 하락과 연관성이 있다고 했고, 지문 마지막에서 이러한 굴욕적인 경험은 학생들이 자신감을 잃게 한다고 했으므로 (A)에는 학생들을 부끄럽게 하는 것은 그들의 교육적인 발전에 '해를 끼친다'(harm)는 내용이, (B)에는 교사들은 학문적인 성과를 위해 그들의 '심리적인'(psychological) 요소들을 고려해야 한다는 내용이 나와야 적절하다.

따라서 ③ (A) harm(해를 끼치다) – (B) psychological(심리적인)이 정답이다.

어휘 inevitable 불가피한, 필연적인 humiliate 굴욕감을 주다
misbehave 품행이 좋지 못하다, 못된 짓을 하다
repercussion (보통 좋지 못한) 영향 prominent 저명한
correlated with ~과 연관성이 있다 drop-off 하락, 쇠퇴
out of reach 힘이 미치지 않는 곳에, 손이 닿지 않는 곳에

21 독해 전체내용 파악 (문단 요약) 난이도 ★★★

끊어읽기 해석

Soccer is the man-on-the-street's game / in Europe, / and the politicians, academics, and high-end journalists / who would normally shun exhibitionist patriotism / support their national teams / as a means of proving / they are really men-in-the-street themselves.
축구는 일반인들의 게임이다 / 유럽에서 / 그리고 정치인들, 교수들, 최상위의 저널리스트들은 / 일반적으로 과시적인 애국심을 꺼리는 / 그들의 국가 대표팀을 응원한다 / 증명하는 수단으로 / 그들 스스로가 실제로 일반인이라는 것을

But / it may also be / that high national emotions are permissible / when a soccer team is playing precisely / because they are impermissible / at most other times.
하지만 / 이것은 또한 ~일 수도 있다 / 숭고한 국민 정서가 허용되는 것인 / 꼭 축구팀이 경기를 하고 있을 때 / 그것들이 허용되지 않기 때문에 / 대부분의 다른 경우에는

There aren't, simply, many other places / where you can sing your national anthem / until you lose your voice / without causing a riot.
정말로 다른 장소들은 많지 않다 / 당신이 국가를 부를 수 있는 / 목소리가 나오지 않을 때까지 / 폭동을 일으키지 않고

해석 유럽에서 축구는 일반인들의 게임이고, 일반적으로 과시적인 애국심을 꺼리는 정치인들, 교수들, 최상위의 저널리스트들은 그들 스스로가 실제로 일반인이라는 것을 증명하는 수단으로 그들의 국가 대표팀을 응원한다. 하지만 이것은 또한 그것들이 대부분의 다른 경우에는 허용되지 않기 때문에 꼭 축구팀이 경기를 하고 있을 때 숭고한 국민 정서가 허용되는 것일 수도 있다. 당신이 폭동을 일으키지 않고 목소리가 나오지 않을 때까지 국가를 부를 수 있는 다른 장소들은 정말로 많지 않다.

> 위의 문단에서, 축구는 애국심의 허용되는 형태라는 것을 추론할 수 있다.

① 애국심의 허용되는 형태
② 스트레스를 해소하기 위한 최고의 스포츠
③ 이제껏 만들어진 것 중 가장 대중적인 스포츠
④ 사람들을 조화롭게 결속하는 독특한 스포츠

해설 지문 중간에서 유럽에서의 축구는 숭고한 국민 정서가 허용되는 곳이라고 하며 목소리가 나오지 않을 때까지 국가를 부를 수 있는 다른 장소가 축구 경기에서를 제외하고 정말로 많지 않다고 설명하고 있다. 따라서 축구는 '애국심의 허용되는 형태'라는 것을 추론할 수 있다고 한 ①번이 정답이다.

어휘 man-on-the-street 일반인의 high-end 최상위의, 고급의, 세련된
shun 꺼리다, 피하다 exhibitionist 과시적인, 과시욕이 강한
patriotism 애국심 permissible 허용되는 precisely 꼭, 바로
impermissible 허용되지 않는 national anthem 국가 riot 폭동

11회 2012년 법원직 9급 **329**

끊어읽기 해석

Etiquette / —the sets of rules / that give expression to manners— / can vary / from culture to culture.
에티켓은 / 일련의 규칙들인 / 예절을 표현하는 / 달라질 수 있다 / 문화에 따라

In Japan, / you would remove your shoes / before entering someone's house.
일본에서 / 당신은 신발을 벗을 것이다 / 누군가의 집에 들어가기 전에

If you did this in America, / people would give you strange looks / and hold their noses.
만약 당신이 미국에서 이렇게 한다면 / 사람들은 당신을 이상한 시선으로 쳐다볼 것이다 / 그리고 그들의 코를 막을 것이다

In some Asian and Middle Eastern countries, / belching and smacking your lips / is a way to compliment the chef. // In the United States, / it's a way / to get sent to your room.
몇몇 아시아와 중동 국가에서는 / 트림을 하고 입맛을 쩝쩝 다시는 것이 / 요리사를 칭찬하는 방법이다 // 미국에서 / 이것은 방법이다 / (당신을) 당신의 방으로 억지로 보내지게 하는

It's important to know / the manners of the culture / in which you're operating.
아는 것은 중요하다 / 그 문화의 예절을 / 당신이 활동하고 있는

Otherwise, / an innocent, friendly gesture / could <u>cause offense or embarrassment</u>.
그렇지 않으면 / 악의 없고 친근한 행동이 / <u>불쾌함과 당황스러움을 유발할</u> 수 있다

해석 예절을 표현하는 일련의 규칙들인 에티켓은 문화에 따라 달라질 수 있다. 일본에서, 당신은 누군가의 집에 들어가기 전에 신발을 벗을 것이다. 만약 당신이 미국에서 이렇게 한다면, 사람들은 당신을 이상한 시선으로 쳐다보고 코를 막을 것이다. 몇몇 아시아와 중동 국가에서는, 트림을 하고 입맛을 쩝쩝 디시는 것이 요리사를 칭찬하는 방법이다. 미국에서 이것은 (당신을) 당신의 방으로 억지로 보내지게 하는 방법이다. 당신이 활동하고 있는 문화의 예절을 아는 것은 중요하다. 그렇지 않으면, 악의 없고 친근한 행동이 <u>불쾌함과 당황스러움을 유발할</u> 수 있다.

① 새로운 친구를 만드는 것을 돕다
② 옳게 해석되다
③ 불쾌함과 당황스러움을 유발하다
④ 다른 사람들이 당신을 높이 평가하게 만들다

해설 지문 처음에서 에티켓은 문화에 따라 달라질 수 있다고 언급한 후, 이어서 문화에 따라 다른 에티켓들을 예로 들며 어떤 국가에서는 당연하게 받아들여지는 행위가 다른 국가에서는 불쾌함을 주는 행위가 될 수 있음을 설명하고 있다. 따라서 특정 문화의 에티켓을 알지 못한 채 행한 악의 없고 친근한 행동이 '불쾌함과 당황스러움을 유발할' 수 있다고 한 ③번이 정답이다.

어휘 belch 트림하다; 트림 smack one's lips 입맛을 쩝쩝 다시다
compliment 칭찬하다, 찬사하다 innocent 악의 없는, 아무 잘못 없는
gesture 행동, 표현

끊어읽기 해석

An economist Gary Becker has applied / Marshallian economics / to family law and to criminal law.
경제학자 Gary Becker는 적용했다 / 마샬의 경제학을 / 가족법과 형법에

Becker's crime model posits / criminals who apparently weigh / the costs and benefits of committing offences.
Becker의 범죄 모델은 가정한다 / 명백하게 저울질하는 범죄자들을 / 범죄를 저지르는 것의 대가와 이득을

If we have a crime problem, / Becker implies, / it's because crime does pay.
만약 우리가 범죄 문제를 가지고 있다면 / Becker는 주장한다 / 그것은 범죄가 이득이 되기 때문이다

Economists have tried to calculate / what deters criminals.
경제학자들은 계산하려고 시도했다 / 무엇이 범죄자들을 단념시키는지

Two variables seem most important: / apprehension rates and severity of punishment.
두 개의 변수가 가장 중요해 보였는데 / 체포율과 벌의 엄격함이다

The deterrent effect differs / for different types of crimes.
억제 효과는 다르다 / 범죄의 다양한 종류들에 따라

For some crimes, / police should concentrate / on catching the criminals.
어떤 범죄들은 / 경찰들이 집중해야 한다 / 범죄자를 잡는 것에

For other crimes, / apprehension rates do not scare / offenders.
다른 범죄들은 / 체포율이 두려움을 주지 않는다 / 범죄자들에게

Instead / they are deterred / by <u>severe punishments</u>.
대신에 / 그들은 단념하게 된다 / <u>엄격한 처벌</u>로 인해

해석 경제학자 Gary Becker는 가족법과 형법에 마샬의 경제학을 적용했다. Becker의 범죄 모델은 범죄를 저지르는 것의 대가와 이득을 명백하게 저울질하는 범죄자들을 가정한다. 만약 우리가 범죄 문제를 가지고 있다면 그것은 범죄가 이득이 되기 때문이라고 Becker는 주장한다. 경제학자들은 무엇이 범죄자들을 단념시키는지 계산하려고 시도했다. 체포율과 벌의 엄격함이라는 두 개의 변수가 가장 중요해 보였다. 억제 효과는 범죄의 다양한 종류들에 따라 다르다. 어떤 범죄들은, 경찰들이 범죄자를 잡는 것에 집중해야 한다. 다른 범죄들은 체포율이 범죄자들에게 두려움을 주지 않는다. 대신에 그들은 <u>엄격한 처벌</u>로 인해 단념하게 된다.

① 경찰 심문   ② 높은 체포율
③ 엄격한 처벌   ④ 회유 정책

해설 빈칸이 있는 문장을 통해 체포율에 두려움을 느끼지 않는 범죄자들이 무엇을 통해 단념하게 되는지에 대한 내용이 나와야 적절하다는 것을 알 수 있다. 지문 중간에서 범죄자들을 단념시키는 가장 중요한 두 개의 변수로 체포율과 벌의 엄격함을 제시하고 있으므로 체포율이 두려움을 주지 않는 대신 그들이 '엄격한 처벌'로 인해 단념하게 된다고 한 ③번이 정답이다.

어휘 family law 가족법 criminal law 형법 posit 가정하다, 단정하다
weigh 저울질하다, 무게를 재다 offence 범죄, 위법 행위
deter 단념시키다, 그만두게 하다 variable 변수
apprehension 체포 severity 엄격함
deterrent effect 억제 효과 offender 범죄자 questioning 심문
arrest 체포; 체포하다 appeasement 회유, 달램

끊어읽기 해석

> But / not all arguments attempt to persuade, / and many attempts to persuade / do not involve arguments.
> 하지만 / 모든 논쟁이 설득하기를 시도하는 것은 아니다 / 그리고 설득하기 위한 많은 시도들은 / 논쟁을 포함하지 않는다.
>
> ──────────
>
> Some writers define an argument / as an attempt to persuade somebody of something. // This is not correct.
> 일부 작가들은 논쟁을 정의한다 / 누군가에게 무엇을 설득하려는 시도로 // 이것은 옳지 않다.
>
> (①) An argument attempts / to prove or support a conclusion.
> 논쟁은 시도한다 / 결과를 증명하거나 지지하는 것을
>
> (②) When you attempt to persuade someone, / you attempt to win him or her / to your point of view; / trying to persuade and trying to argue / are logically distinct projects.
> 당신이 누군가를 설득하려고 시도할 때 / 당신은 그 사람에게 설득하려고 시도한다 / 당신의 견해를 / 설득하려는 것과 논쟁하려는 것은 / 논리적으로 별개의 목표이다
>
> (③) True, / when you want to persuade somebody of something, / you might use an argument.
> 실제로 / 당신이 누군가에게 무엇을 설득하려고 할 때 / 당신은 아마도 논쟁을 이용할 것이다
>
> (④) In fact, / giving an argument / is often one of the least effective methods / of persuading people / —which, of course, / is why so few advertisers bother with arguments.
> 사실 / 논쟁을 하는 것은 / 대개 가장 효과가 없는 방법 중의 하나이다 / 사람들을 설득하는 데 있어서 / 물론 이것은 / 논쟁에 신경을 쓰는 광고주들이 거의 없는 이유이다

해석 일부 작가들은 논쟁을 누군가에게 무엇을 설득하려는 시도로 정의한다. 이것은 옳지 않다. 논쟁은 결과를 증명하거나 지지하는 것을 시도한다. 누군가를 설득하려고 시도할 때, 당신은 그 사람에게 당신의 견해를 설득하려고 시도한다. 설득하려는 것과 논쟁하려는 것은 논리적으로 별개의 목표이다. 실제로 당신이 누군가에게 무엇을 설득하려고 할 때, 당신은 아마도 논쟁을 이용할 것이다. ④ 하지만 모든 논쟁이 설득하기를 시도하는 것은 아니며, 설득하기 위한 많은 시도들은 논쟁을 포함하지 않는다. 사실, 논쟁을 하는 것은 대개 사람들을 설득하는 데 있어서 가장 효과가 없는 방법 중의 하나인데, 물론 이것은 논쟁에 신경을 쓰는 광고주들이 거의 없는 이유이다.

해설 ④번 앞 문장에서 당신은 누군가를 설득하려고 할 때 아마도 논쟁을 이용할 것이라고 했고, ④번 뒤 문장에서 사실 논쟁을 하는 것은 사람들을 설득하는 데 있어서 가장 효과가 없는 방법 중 하나라고 했으므로, ④번에 하지만(But) 모든 논쟁이 설득하기를 시도하는 것은 아니며, 설득하기 위한 많은 시도들은 논쟁을 포함하지 않는다는 내용의 앞 문장과 상반되는 주어진 문장이 나와야 지문이 자연스럽게 연결된다. 따라서 ④번이 정답이다.

어휘 define as ~으로 정의하다
win somebody to something ~에게 ~을 설득하다
point of view 견해, 관점   distinct 별개의
bother 신경을 쓰다, 괴롭히다

끊어읽기 해석

> They weren't quite green, / however.
> 그것들이 전적으로 환경 친화적인 것은 아니었다 / 하지만
>
> ──────────
>
> Green buildings are not new. // For thousands of years, / humans have built structures / with local natural materials.
> 친환경 건축물들은 새로운 것이 아니다. // 수천 년 동안 / 사람들은 건물을 세워왔다 / 지역의 천연 재료로
>
> These structures did not use energy / or damage the planet.
> 이러한 건축물들은 에너지원을 사용하지 않는다 / 혹은 지구에 해를 입히지 않는다
>
> (①) When the people who lived in them moved on, / the structures usually collapsed, / and their materials returned / to the earth.
> 그것에 살던 사람들이 이사를 갔을 때 / 그 건물들은 보통 무너졌다 / 그리고 그 재료들은 다시 돌아갔다 / 흙으로
>
> (②) Before the 1930s, / most buildings used far less energy / than today's buildings.
> 1930년대 이전에 / 대부분의 건물들은 훨씬 적은 에너지원을 사용했다 / 오늘날의 건물들에 비해
>
> Instead of air-conditioning, / they had windows / that opened to let in breezes.
> 에어컨 대신에 / 창문이 있었다 / 미풍이 들어오도록 열었던
>
> (③) Coal-burning furnaces were used / for heating. // As a result, / many buildings spewed dirty smoke / into the air.
> 석탄 연소 난로가 사용되었다 / 난방을 위해 // 그 결과 / 많은 건물들이 더러운 연기를 분출했다 / 공기 중으로
>
> (④) Beginning in the 1970s, / in the United States and much of the world, / air-pollution laws were passed / to reduce or eliminate pollution / given off by buildings.
> 1970년대 초반부터 / 미국과 세계의 많은 곳에서 / 대기오염법이 통과되었다 / 오염을 줄이거나 없애기 위해서 / 건물들로부터 발산된

해석 친환경 건축물들은 새로운 것이 아니다. 수천 년 동안, 사람들은 지역의 천연 재료로 건물을 세워왔다. 이러한 건축물들은 에너지원을 사용하거나 지구에 해를 입히지 않는다. 그것에 살던 사람들이 이사를 갔을 때, 그 건물들은 보통 무너졌고 그 재료들은 다시 흙으로 돌아갔다. 1930년대 이전에, 대부분의 건물들은 오늘날의 건물들에 비해 훨씬 적은 에너지원을 사용했다. 에어컨 대신에 미풍이 들어오도록 열었던 창문이 있었다. ③ 하지만, 그것들이 전적으로 환경 친화적인 것은 아니었다. 석탄 연소 난로가 난방을 위해 사용되었다. 그 결과, 많은 건물들이 공기 중으로 더러운 연기를 분출했다. 1970년대 초반부터, 미국과 세계의 많은 곳에서 건물들로부터 발산된 오염을 줄이거나 없애기 위해 대기오염법이 통과되었다.

해설 ③번 뒤 문장에서 난방을 위해 사용된 석탄 난로가 공기 중으로 더러운 연기를 분출했다는 내용이 있으므로, ③번에 하지만(however) 그것들(1930년대 이전의 건물들)이 전적으로 환경 친화적인 것은 않았다고 언급하며, 환경 친화적이지 않은 석탄 난로를 예로 들어 부연설명할 수 있는 주어진 문장이 나와야 지문이 자연스럽게 연결된다. 따라서 ③번이 정답이다.

어휘 green 환경 친화적인   collapse 무너지다, 붕괴되다
energy (석유, 전기, 태양열 등의) 에너지원   breeze 미풍, 산들바람
coal-burning 석탄 연소   furnace 난로, 용광로
spew 분출하다   eliminate 없애다, 제거하다   give off 발산하다

정답

p.133

01	① 독해 - 전체내용 파악	**11**	② 독해 - 논리적 흐름 파악	**21**	① 문법 - 동사의 종류
02	② 독해 - 전체내용 파악	**12**	④ 독해 - 전체내용 파악	**22**	③ 문법 - 형용사와 부사
03	④ 독해 - 논리적 흐름 파악	**13**	① 독해 - 추론	**23**	④ 문법 - 병치·도치·강조 구문
04	③ 독해 - 추론	**14**	④ 문법 - 수 일치	**24**	③ 독해 - 추론
05	③ 독해 - 논리적 흐름 파악	**15**	③ 문법 - 능동태·수동태	**25**	② 독해 - 추론
06	① 독해 - 추론	**16**	④ 독해 - 전체내용 파악		
07	② 독해 - 전체내용 파악	**17**	④ 독해 - 전체내용 파악		
08	② 문법 - 관계절	**18**	③ 독해 - 논리적 흐름 파악		
09	③ 독해 - 전체내용 파악	**19**	① 어휘 - 어휘 & 표현		
10	④ 문법 - to 부정사&분사&병치·도치·강조 구문	**20**	③ 독해 - 논리적 흐름 파악		

취약영역 분석표

영역	세부 유형	문항 수	소계
어휘	어휘 & 표현	1	/1
	생활영어	0	
문법	관계절	1	/7
	to 부정사 & 분사 & 병치·도치·강조 구문	1	
	수 일치	1	
	능동태·수동태	1	
	동사의 종류	1	
	형용사와 부사	1	
	병치·도치·강조 구문	1	
독해	전체내용 파악	7	/17
	세부내용 파악	0	
	추론	5	
	논리적 흐름 파악	5	
	총계		**/25**

· 자신이 취약한 영역은 '법원직 9급 영어, 이렇게 출제된다!'(p.8)를 통해 다시 한 번 확인하시고 학습하시기 바랍니다.

---

01 독해 전체내용 파악 (문단 요약)

난이도 ★★☆

끊어읽기 해석

Problems, problems! // Some would-be problem solvers / are so overwhelmed / by the problem / that they usually fail.
문제들, 문제들! // 문제 해결자가 되고자 하는 일부 사람들은 / 너무나 압도되어서 / 문제에 / 그들은 주로 실패한다

There are others / who approach the problem calmly and practically, / and usually solve it.
다른 사람들이 있다 / 문제에 차분하고 실질적으로 접근하는 / 그리고 주로 그것을 해결하는

Still others / —only the truly inventive— / find a unique solution / to the problem / in order to prove a point.
그런데도 다른 이들 / 진실로 독창적인 (이들만이) / 독특한 해결법을 찾는다 / 문제에 대한 / 주장을 증명하기 위해

For example, / Alexander the Great, an ancient Greek ruler, / was said to have been challenged / to untie the Gordian knot.
예를 들어 / 고대 그리스 통치자인 알렉산더 대왕은 / 요구받은 것으로 전해졌다 / 고르디우스의 매듭을 풀도록

In mythology, / this knot was fastened / to a wagon / and was thought / to be impossible to undo.
신화에서 / 이 매듭은 매여있었다 / 마차에 / 그리고 생각되었다 / 푸는 것이 불가능하다고

The great ruler / was able to accomplish the task easily, / however.
그 훌륭한 통치자는 / 그 일을 쉽게 달성할 수 있었다 / 하지만

He simply cut the knot / with his sword!
그는 간단히 매듭을 잘랐다 / 그의 검으로!

Tradition has it / that Christopher Columbus was once given a challenge, too.
전설에 의하면 / 크리스토퍼 콜럼버스도 한때 도전을 받았다고 한다

In 1493, / he attended a banquet / in his honor, / where he was questioned / about how he had coped with / the difficulties of his voyage to the New World.
1493년에 / 그는 연회에 참석했는데 / 그를 위한 / 그곳에서 그는 질문을 받았다 / 그가 어떻게 대처했는지에 대해 / 신세계로의 항해에서의 고난을

Columbus replied / by challenging his questioners / to balance an egg.
콜럼버스는 대답했다 / 질문자에게 요구함으로써 / 계란 하나를 넘어지지 않게 세워보라고

When they couldn't, / he did. // How? // He cracked the shell / to create a flat bottom!
그들이 할 수 없을 때 / 그는 해냈다 // 어떻게? // 그는 껍질을 깨뜨렸다 / 납작한 바닥을 만들기 위해!

해석 문제들, 문제들! 문제 해결자가 되고자 하는 일부 사람들은 문제에 너무나 압도되어서 주로 실패한다. 문제에 차분하고 실질적으로 접근하여 주로 그것을 해결하는 다른 사람들이 있다. 그런데도 진실로 독창적인 다른 이들만이 주장을 증명하기 위해 문제에 대한 독특한 해결법을 찾는다. 예를 들어, 고대 그리스 통치자인 알렉산더 대왕은 고르디우스의 매듭을 풀도록 요구받은 것으로 전해졌다. 신화에서, 이 매듭은 마차에 매여있었고 푸는 것이 불가능하다고 생각되었다. 하지만 그 훌륭한 통치자는 그 일을 쉽게 달성할 수 있었다. 그는 그의 검으로 간단히 매듭을 잘랐다! 전설에 의하면 크리스토퍼 콜럼버스도 한때 도전을 받았다고 한다. 1493년에, 그는 그를 위한 연회에 참석했는데, 그곳에서 그는 그가 신세계로의 항해에서의 고난을 어떻게 대처했는지에 대해 질문을 받았다. 콜럼버스는 질문자에게 계란 하나를 넘어지지 않게 세워보라고 요구함으로써 대답했다. 그들이 할 수 없을 때, 그는 해냈다. 어떻게? 그는 납작한 바닥을 만들기 위해 껍질을 깨뜨렸다!

> 위 지문에 따르면, 우리는 어떤 어려운 문제들은 쉽게 풀릴 수 있었다는 것을 추론할 수 있다.

① 쉽게 풀릴 수 있었다

② 우리에게 질문들을 주었다
③ 우리에게 도전들을 주었다
④ 과학에 의해 풀릴 수 있었다

해설 　지문 앞부분에서 진실로 독창적인 이들만이 문제에 대한 독특한 해결법을 찾는다고 한 뒤, 이에 대한 예로 지문 중간에서 알렉산더 대왕이 그의 검으로 매듭을 잘라 쉽게 고르디우스의 매듭을 푼 일화와 콜럼버스가 계란 껍질을 깨뜨려서 계란을 넘어지지 않게 세웠던 일화에 대해 설명하고 있다. 따라서 어려운 문제들은 '쉽게 풀릴 수 있었다'는 것을 추론할 수 있다고 한 ①번이 정답이다.

어휘 　would-be ~이 되고자 하는　overwhelm 압도하다
practically 실질적으로　inventive 독창적인　untie 풀다
knot 매듭　fasten 매다, 채우다　undo 풀다　banquet 연회
cope with 대처하다

02 　독해 　전체내용 파악 (문단 요약)　난이도 ★★☆

끊어읽기 해석

The discovery / that the seeds of the coffee fruit tasted good / when roasted / was undoubtedly the key moment / in coffee history.
그 발견은 / 커피 열매의 씨앗이 맛이 좋다는 / 볶았을 때 / 의심할 여지 없는 중대한 순간이었다 / 커피 역사에서

It marked the beginning / of the transformation of coffee / from an obscure medicinal herb / known only / in the Horn of Africa and southern Arabia / to the most popular beverage / in the world.
그것은 기점이 되었다 / 커피의 변신의 / 무명의 약초에서 / 오직 알려진 / 아프리카 대륙의 북동부와 남아라비아에서만 / 가장 인기 있는 음료로의 / 세계에서

A skeptic might counter / that it is caffeine, not flavor / that made coffee / into one of the world's most important commodities.
의심이 많은 사람은 아마 반박할 것이다 / 풍미가 아니라 카페인이라고 / 커피를 만든 것이 / 세계의 가장 중요한 상품 중 하나로

This argument is difficult to sustain, however. // Tea, yerba mate, cocoa and other less famous plants also / contain substances / that wake us up / and make us feel good.
그러나 이 논쟁은 지속하기가 어렵다. // 차, 마테차, 코코아 그리고 다른 덜 유명한 식물들 또한 / 물질들을 포함하고 있다 / 우리를 정신이 들게 하고 / 우리를 기분 좋게 만드는

Yet / none has achieved / quite the same universal success / as coffee.
하지만 / 아무것도 달성하지 못했다 / 똑같은 전 세계적인 성공을 / 커피와 같은

Furthermore / coffee figures as important flavoring / in countless candies, cookies, cakes and confections.
게다가 / 커피는 중요한 향료의 역할을 한다 / 무수히 많은 사탕, 과자, 케이크 그리고 당과 제품들에서

해석 　커피 열매의 씨앗이 볶았을 때 맛이 좋다는 발견은 커피 역사에서 의심할 여지 없는 중대한 순간이었다. 그것은 커피가 아프리카 대륙의 북동부와 남아라비아에서만 알려진 무명의 약초에서, 세계에서 가장 인기 있는 음료로 변신한 기점이 되었다. 의심이 많은 사람은 아마 커피를 세계의 가장 중요한 상품 중 하나로 만든 것이 풍미가 아니라 카페인이라고 반박할 것이다. 그러나 이 논쟁은 지속하기가 어렵다. 차, 마테차, 코코아 그리고 다른 덜 유명한 식물들 또한 우리를 정신이 들게 하고 기분 좋게 만드는 물질들을 포함하고 있다. 하지만 아무것도 커피와 같은 전 세계적인 성공을 달성

하지 못했다. 게다가 커피는 무수히 많은 사탕, 과자, 케이크 그리고 당과 제품들에서 중요한 향료의 역할을 한다.

> (A) 볶은 커피의 풍미가 세계에서 (B) 가장 인기 있는 음료로서의 그것의 성공과 커다란 관계가 있다는 것은 명확하다.

　　　　　　(A)　　　　　　　　　　(B)
① 볶은 커피의 풍미 　– 가장 인기 있는 인공 향료
② 볶은 커피의 풍미 　– 가장 인기 있는 음료
③ 볶은 커피의 카페인 – 가장 인기 있는 인공 향료
④ 볶은 커피의 카페인 – 가장 인기 있는 음료

해설 　지문 처음에서 커피 열매의 씨앗이 볶았을 때 맛이 좋다는 발견에 대해 언급한 후, 지문 중간에서 의심이 많은 사람은 커피를 세계의 가장 중요한 상품 중 하나로 만든 것이 풍미가 아니라 카페인이라고 반박할 것이지만, 카페인을 포함한 다른 식물들은 커피와 같은 세계적인 성공을 달성하지 못했다는 내용이 있으므로, (A)에는 '볶은 커피의 풍미'라는 의미의 aromatics of roasted coffee가, (B)에는 세계에서 '가장 인기 있는 음료'로서의 그것의 성공과 커다란 관계가 있다고 한 most favored beverage가 나와야 적절하다. 따라서 ② (A) aromatics of roasted coffee(볶은 커피의 풍미)-(B) most favored beverage(가장 인기 있는 음료)가 정답이다.

어휘 　undoubtedly 의심할 여지 없이　transformation 변신, 전환
obscure 무명의, 잘 알려져 있지 않은　medicinal herb 약초
Horn of Africa 아프리카 대륙의 북동부 (소말리아 공화국과 그 인근 지역)
skeptic 의심이 많은 사람, 회의론자　counter 반박하다
commodity 상품　sustain 지속하다　substance 물질
figure as ~의 역할을 하다　countless 무수히 많은
confection 당과 제품　artificial flavor 인공 향료

03 　독해 　논리적 흐름 파악 (문맥상 부적절한 어휘)　난이도 ★★★

끊어읽기 해석

In 1953 / Eisenhower appointed Earl Warren / as chief justice of the Supreme Court, / an appointment that began a new era / in ① judicial history.
1953년에 / 아이젠하워는 얼 워런을 임명했다 / 대법원장으로 / 새로운 시대를 연 임명인 / ① 사법 역사에

The Warren Court transformed / the American legal system / by expanding civil rights and civil liberties.
워런 법정은 바꿨다 / 미국의 법률 제도를 / 시민권과 시민의 자유를 확대함으로써

In Brown v. Board of Education of Topeka(1954), / the Warren Court declared / state laws establishing separate public schools / for black and white students / ② unconstitutional.
브라운 대 토피카 교육위원회 사건(1954)에서 / 워런 법정은 선언했다 / 분리된 공립 학교를 설립한다는 주법이 / 흑인과 백인 학생들을 위한 / ② 위헌이라고

In 1955 / the Court ordered the states / to desegregate schools / "with all deliberate speed."
1955년에 / 그 법원은 주에 명령했다 / 학교의 인종 차별 정책을 철폐할 것을 / "최대한 신중한 속도로"

However, / many people resisted school ③ integration. // In 1957 / the governor of Arkansas, Orval Faubus, / tried to ④ expedite / the enrollment of nine black students / into Little Rock High School.
하지만 / 많은 사람들은 학교 ③ 통합에 반대했다 // 1957년에 / 아칸소 주의 주지사인 오르발 포버스는 / ④ 더 신속히 처리하는 것을 시도했다 / 아홉 명의 흑인 학생들의 입학을 / 리틀 락 고등학교로의

In response, / Eisenhower sent federal troops / to desegregate the school. // The Brown decision / began a new era / in civil rights.
그에 대응하여 / 아이젠하워는 연방 부대를 보냈다 / 그 학교의 인종 차별 정책을 철폐하기 위해 // 브라운 판결은 / 새로운 시대를 시작했다 / 시민권의

해석 1953년에 아이젠하워는 얼 워런을 대법원장으로 임명했는데, 그것은 ① 사법 역사에 새로운 시대를 연 임명이었다. 워런 법정은 시민권과 시민의 자유를 확대함으로써 미국의 법률 제도를 바꿨다. 브라운 대 토피카 교육위원회 사건(1954)에서 워런 법정은 흑인과 백인 학생들을 위한 분리된 공립 학교를 설립한다는 주법이 ② 위헌이라고 선언했다. 1955년에 법원은 주에 '최대한 신중한 속도로' 학교의 인종 차별 정책을 철폐할 것을 명령했다. 하지만 많은 사람들은 학교 ③ 통합에 반대했다. 1957년에 아칸소 주의 주지사인 오르발 포버스는 아홉 명의 흑인 학생들의 리틀 락 고등학교로의 입학을 ④ 더 신속히 처리하는 것을 시도했다. 그에 대응하여 아이젠하워는 그 학교의 인종 차별 정책을 철폐하기 위해 연방 부대를 보냈다. 브라운 판결은 시민권의 새로운 시대를 시작했다.

해설 ④ expedite(더 신속히 처리하다)가 있는 문장 앞에 법원은 주에 학교의 인종 차별 정책을 철폐할 것을 명령했지만 많은 이들이 학교의 통합에 반대했다는 내용이 있고, 마지막 문장에 아이젠하위가 리틀 락 고등학교의 인종 차별 정책을 철폐하기 위해 연방 부대를 보냈다는 내용이 있으므로, 흑인 학생들의 입학을 '더 신속히 처리하는'(expedite) 것을 시도했다는 내용은 문맥상 적절하지 않다. 따라서 ④ expedite가 정답이다. 참고로 주어진 expedite를 대신할 수 있는 어휘로는 '막다, 못하게 하다'라는 의미의 stop, halt, block, hinder 등이 있다.

어휘 appoint 임명하다 era 시대 judicial 사법의 transform 바꾸다
legal system 법률 제도 civil right 시민권 liberty 자유
unconstitutional 위헌의 desegregate 인종 차별 정책을 철폐하다
deliberate 신중한 integration 통합
expedite 더 신속히 처리하다 enrollment 입학, 등록

04 독해 추론 (빈칸 완성 - 구) 난이도 ★☆☆

끊어읽기 해석

Governments become more vulnerable / when economies falter; / in fact, / the credibility of government is often thought / to be linked very closely / to effective economic performance.
정부들은 더 취약해진다 / 경제가 불안정해질 때 / 사실 / 정부의 신뢰도는 종종 생각된다 / 매우 밀접하게 관련되어 있다고 / 효과적인 경제적 성과와

In the early stages of the 2008 crisis, / the governments of Belgium, Iceland, and Latvia fell.
2008년 위기의 초기 단계에 / 벨기에, 아이슬란드 그리고 라트비아의 정부들은 무너졌다

In 2009, / the government of Kuwait dismissed the parliament / after a dispute / over the handling of the financial crisis.
2009년에 / 쿠웨이트 정부는 의회를 해산시켰다 / 논쟁 후에 / 경제적 위기의 처리에 관한

The Hungarian government collapsed / in 2009 / for similar reasons.
헝가리 정부는 붕괴했다 / 2009년에 / 비슷한 이유로

So did that of the Czech Republic, / leaving the rotating presidency of the European Union / in chaos.
체코 공화국도 마찬가지였다 / 유럽 연합의 순회 의장직을 떠나며 / 혼란 속에서

There are many historic examples / of government collapse / in the wake of financial disaster.
많은 역사적인 예시들이 있다 / 정부의 붕괴에 대한 / 경제적 재앙에 뒤이은

해석 경제가 불안정해질 때 정부들은 더 취약해지는데, 사실 정부의 신뢰도는 종종 효과적인 경제적 성과와 매우 밀접하게 관련되어 있다고 생각된다. 2008년 위기의 초기 단계에, 벨기에, 아이슬란드 그리고 라트비아의 정부들은 무너졌다. 2009년에, 쿠웨이트 정부는 경제적 위기의 처리에 관한 논쟁 후에 의회를 해산시켰다. 헝가리 정부는 비슷한 이유로 2009년에 붕괴했다. 혼란 속에서 유럽 연합의 순회 의장직을 떠나며, 체코 공화국도 마찬가지였다. 경제적 재앙에 뒤이은 정부의 붕괴에 대한 많은 역사적인 예시들이 있다.

① 문화적 갈등 관리
② 과거에 대한 역사적인 분석
③ 효과적인 경제적 성과
④ 정부의 민주적인 체계

해설 빈칸이 있는 문장을 통해 정부의 신뢰도가 무엇과 밀접하게 관련되어 있다고 생각되는지에 대한 내용이 나와야 적절하다는 것을 알 수 있다. 지문 처음에서 정부들은 경제가 불안정해질 때 더 취약해진다고 했고, 이어서 경제적 위기 이후에 무너진 정부들을 예로 든 후에, 지문 마지막에서 다시 경제적 재앙에 뒤이은 정부의 붕괴에 대한 많은 역사적인 예시들이 있다고 했으므로, 정부의 신뢰도가 종종 '효과적인 경제적 성과'와 밀접하게 관련되어 있다고 생각된다고 한 ③번이 정답이다.

어휘 vulnerable 취약한 falter 불안정해지다 credibility 신뢰도
link to ~과 관련시키다 dismiss 해산시키다, 해고하다
parliament 의회, 국회 dispute 논쟁 collapse 붕괴하다
rotating presidency 순회 의장직 chaos 혼란
in the wake of ~에 뒤이어 conflict 갈등

05 독해 논리적 흐름 파악 (문장 삽입) 난이도 ★☆☆

끊어읽기 해석

They believe / that executing a criminal / is the only way / to protect society / from further crime.
그들은 믿는다 / 범죄자를 처형하는 것이 / 유일한 방법이라고 / 사회를 보호하는 / 추가적인 범죄로부터

Capital punishment is / the legal infliction of death / as the penalty / for violating capital laws.
사형 제도는 / 죽음을 합법적으로 가하는 것이다 / 처벌로서 / 극형에 처해질 수 있는 법을 위반하는 것에 대한

It is also known / as the death penalty, / and it is one of the most controversial practices / in the modern world.
그것은 또한 알려져 있다 / 극형으로도 / 그리고 이것은 가장 논란이 많은 관행 중 하나이다 / 현대 세계에서

(①) Arguments both for and against the practice / are often based / on religion and emotions.
그 관행에 찬성하고 반대하는 주장들 모두 / 종종 기반을 둔다 / 종교와 감정에

(②) Those in favor of capital punishment believe / that it deters crime / and offers closure or a sense of justice / for the family of the victim.
사형 제도에 찬성하는 사람들은 믿는다 / 그것이 범죄를 막는다고 / 그리고 종결이나 정의감을 제공한다고 / 희생자의 가족에게

(③) On the other hand, / those opposed believe / that it is barbaric / and allows government to sink / to the level of the criminal.

반면에 / 반대하는 사람들은 믿는다 / 그것이 야만적이라고 / 그리고 정부를 타락하게 한다고 / 범죄자 수준으로

(④) There is also the possibility / that the person being executed / is really innocent, / even with extensive background checks, and investigations.
가능성 또한 있다 / 처형되는 사람이 / 사실상 결백할 / 대규모의 신원 조사와 수사에도 불구하고

해석 사형 제도는 극형에 처해질 수 있는 법을 위반하는 것에 대한 처벌로서 죽음을 합법적으로 가하는 것이다. 그것은 또한 극형으로도 알려져 있고, 이것은 현대 세계에서 가장 논란이 많은 관행 중 하나이다. 그 관행에 찬성하고 반대하는 주장들 모두 종종 종교와 감정에 기반을 둔다. 사형 제도에 찬성하는 사람들은 그것이 범죄를 막고 희생자의 가족에게 종결이나 정의감을 제공한다고 믿는다. ③ 그들은 범죄자를 처형하는 것이 사회를 추가적인 범죄로부터 보호하는 유일한 방법이라고 믿는다. 반면에, 반대하는 사람들은 그것이 야만적이고 정부를 범죄자의 수준으로 타락하게 한다고 믿는다. 대규모의 신원 조사와 수사에도 불구하고, 처형되는 사람이 사실상 결백할 가능성 또한 있다.

해설 ③번 앞 문장에 사형 제도에 찬성하는 사람들은 그것이 범죄를 막고 희생자의 가족에게 종결이나 정의감을 제공한다고 믿는다는 내용이 있고, 뒤 문장에는 사형 제도에 반대하는 사람들의 믿음에 대한 내용이 있으므로, ③번 자리에 그들(찬성하는 사람들)은 범죄자를 처형하는 것이 사회를 추가적인 범죄로부터 보호하는 유일한 방법이라고 믿는다는 내용의 사형 제도를 찬성하는 추가적인 의견에 대한 주어진 문장이 들어가야 글의 흐름이 자연스럽게 연결된다. 따라서 ③번이 정답이다.

어휘 execute 처형하다 capital punishment 사형 (제도)
infliction 가함, 형벌 penalty 처벌 controversial 논란이 많은
deter 막다 closure (힘든 일의) 종결 victim 희생자
barbaric 야만적인 criminal 범죄자 extensive 대규모의
background check 신원 조사 investigation 수사

06 독해 추론 (빈칸 완성 - 단어) 난이도 ★★☆

끊어읽기 해석

On 26 April 2003, / the civil courts of the English legal system / are to undergo a huge change.
2003년 4월 26일 / 영국 법률 제도의 민사 법원은 / 커다란 변화를 겪을 예정이다

A new set of rules / is being brought in / to simplify and streamline procedures, / in an attempt to make litigation / quicker, cheaper and simpler.
새로운 규칙들이 / 도입되고 있다 / 절차를 간단하게 만들고 간소화하기 위해 / 소송을 만들려는 시도로 / 더 빠르고 저렴하고 간단하게

An 800-page document / published by the Lord Chancellor's Department / abandons traditions / in favor of new procedures / that give judges an active role / in managing cases / and dictating the pace of litigation.
800장에 달하는 문서는 / 대법관 부서에서 발행된 / 기존의 것들을 버린다 / 새로운 절차들을 지지하면서 / 판사에게 적극적인 역할을 주는 / 사건을 다루는 데 있어 / 그리고 소송의 속도를 지시하는 (데 있어)

One of the more significant changes is / that of (A) language. // For the first time, / people outside the legal system / have been involved / in the process of drawing up the rules.
더 큰 변화들 중 하나는 / (A) 언어에 관한 것이다 // 처음으로 / 법률 제도 밖의 사람들이 / 포함되었다 / 규칙들을 작성하는 과정에

As a result, / many common but (B) obscure legal terms / have been discarded, / to be replaced by simple English, /

or at least English / that is as simple to understand as possible / in such a complex field.
그 결과 / 수많은 흔하지만 (B) 이해하기 힘든 법률 용어들이 / 폐기되었다 / 간단한 영어로 대체되기 위해 / 또는 적어도 영어로 (대체되기 위해) / 가능한 한 이해될 수 있을 정도로 간단한 / 그러한 복잡한 분야에서

The Plain English Campaign, / which has been fighting for 20 years / to change legal language, / is delighted: / "This may be our greatest victory yet," / its founder, Chrissie Maher, is quoted as saying.
쉬운 영어 운동은 / 20년간 싸워온 / 법률 용어를 바꾸기 위해 / 기뻐했다 / "이것은 아마 지금까지 우리의 가장 큰 성공일 것입니다." / 그것의 창시자인 Chrissie Maher는 이렇게 말한 것으로 알려진다

해석 2003년 4월 26일, 영국 법률 제도의 민사 법원은 커다란 변화를 겪을 예정이다. 소송을 더 빠르고 저렴하고 간단하게 만들려는 시도로, 절차를 간단하게 만들고 간소화하기 위해 새로운 규칙들이 도입되고 있다. 대법관 부서에서 발행된 800장에 달하는 문서는 사건을 다루고 소송의 속도를 지시하는 데 있어 판사에게 적극적인 역할을 주는 새로운 절차들을 지지하면서 기존의 것들을 버린다. 더 큰 변화들 중 하나는 (A) 언어에 관한 것이다. 처음으로, 법률 제도 밖의 사람들이 규칙들을 작성하는 과정에 포함되었다. 그 결과, 수많은 흔하지만 (B) 이해하기 힘든 법률 용어들이 간단한 영어로, 또는 적어도 그러한 복잡한 분야에서 가능한 한 이해될 수 있을 정도로 간단한 영어로 대체되기 위해 폐기되었다. 20년간 법률 용어를 바꾸기 위해 싸워온 쉬운 영어 운동은 기뻐했다. 그것의 창시자인 Chrissie Maher는 "이것은 아마 지금까지 우리의 가장 큰 성공일 것입니다."라고 말한 것으로 알려진다.

    (A)   (B)
① 언어 – 이해하기 힘든
② 언어 – 명백한
③ 행동 – 이해하기 힘든
④ 행동 – 명백한

해설 (A) 빈칸에 많은 법률 용어들이 간단한 영어로 대체되기 위해 폐기되었다는 내용이 있고, 지문 마지막에서 20년간 법률 용어를 바꾸기 위해 싸워온 영어 운동의 성공을 언급하고 있으므로, 빈칸에는 더 큰 변화들 중 하나가 '언어'(language)에 관한 것이라는 내용이 들어가야 적절하다. (B) 빈칸 뒤 문장에 법률 용어들이 간단한 혹은 적어도 이해할 수 있을 정도의 영어로 대체되었다는 내용이 있으므로, 빈칸에는 '이해하기 힘든'(obscure) 법률 용어들이 폐기되었다는 내용이 들어가야 적절하다. 따라서 ① (A) language(언어) – (B) obscure(이해하기 힘든)이 정답이다.

어휘 undergo 겪다 simplify 간단하게 만들다 streamline 간소화하다
litigation 소송 abandon 버리다 in favor of ~을 지지하여
pace 속도 discard 폐기하다 delighted (아주) 기뻐하는
obscure 이해하기 힘든

07 독해 전체내용 파악 (주제 파악) 난이도 ★☆☆

끊어읽기 해석

There is a small amount of scientific evidence / for an increase / in certain types of rare tumors(cancer) / in long-time, heavy mobile phone users.
적은 양의 과학적 증거가 있다 / 증가에 대한 / 특정한 종류의 희귀 종양(암)의 / 장시간 휴대전화를 많이 사용한 사람들에서의

More recently / a pan-European study provided / significant evidence of genetic damage / under certain conditions.
더 최근에 / 한 범유럽적인 연구는 제공했다 / 유전적 손상에 대한 중요한 증거를 / 특정 조건에서의

Some researchers also report / the mobile phone industry has interfered / with further research on health risks.
어떤 연구원들은 또한 발표한다 / 휴대전화 산업이 저해해왔다고 / 건강상의 위험에 관한 추가 연구를

So far, however, / the World Health Organization Task Force on EMF effects on health / has no definitive conclusion / on the veracity of these allegations.
하지만 지금까지 / EMF(전자계)가 건강에 미치는 영향에 대한 세계보건기구의 대책위원회는 / 확정적인 결론을 내리지 않았다 / 이러한 주장들의 진실성에 대한

It is generally thought, however, / that RF is incapable of producing / any more than heating effects, / as it is considered Non-ionizing Radiation; / in other words, / it lacks the energy / to disrupt molecular bonds / such as occurs in genetic mutations.
하지만 일반적으로 생각된다 / RF(무선 주파수)는 만들어낼 수 없다고 / 발열 효과 외의 것은 / 그것이 비이온 방사선으로 간주되기 때문에 / 다시 말해서 / 그것은 에너지가 부족하다 / 분자 결합을 방해할 만큼의 / 유전적 변이에서 발생하는 것과 같은

해석 장시간 휴대전화를 많이 사용한 사람들에서의 특정한 종류의 희귀 종양(암)의 증가에 대한 적은 양의 과학적 증거가 있다. 더 최근에, 한 범유럽적인 연구는 특정 조건에서의 유전적 손상에 대한 중요한 증거를 제공했다. 어떤 연구원들은 또한 휴대전화 산업이 건강상의 위험에 관한 추가 연구를 저해해왔다고 발표한다. 하지만 EMF(전자계)가 건강에 미치는 영향에 대한 세계보건기구의 대책위원회는 지금까지 이러한 주장들의 진실성에 대한 확정적인 결론을 내리지 않았다. 하지만 일반적으로 RF(무선 주파수)는 그것이 비이온 방사선으로 간주되기 때문에, 발열 효과 외의 것은 만들어낼 수 없다고 생각되는데, 다시 말해서, 그것은 유전적 변이에서 발생하는 것과 같은 분자 결합을 방해할 만큼의 에너지가 부족하다.

① 휴대전화를 사용하는 것의 이점
② 휴대전화를 사용하는 것의 건강상의 영향
③ 휴대전화의 방사선 특징
④ 휴대전화 사용에 대한 예방책의 필요성

해설 지문 처음에서 휴대전화를 장시간 많이 사용한 사람들에서 특정 종양이 증가했다는 적은 양의 과학적 증거가 있다고 한 뒤, 이어서 한 범유럽적인 연구와 세계보건기구의 대책위원회를 언급하며 휴대폰과 건강의 관계에 대한 논란에 대해 설명하고 있다. 따라서 이 지문의 주제를 '휴대폰을 사용하는 것의 건강상의 영향'이라고 표현한 ②번이 정답이다.

어휘 tumor 종양 pan-European 범유럽적인
definitive 확정적인, 결정적인 veracity 진실성
allegation 주장, 혐의 RF(= radio frequency) 무선 주파수
non-ionizing 비이온 radiation 방사선 disrupt 방해하다
molecular 분자의 genetic mutation 유전적 변이
precaution 예방책

08 　문법　관계절　　난이도 ★☆☆

해석 코드 토커(암호통신병)는 암호화된 언어를 사용하여 말하는 사람들을 묘사하는 데 사용되는 용어이다. 그것은 그들의 주된 임무가 기밀 전략 메시지의 전송이었던 미 해병대에서 근무한 미국 원주민들을 묘사하는 데 흔히 쓰인다. 코드 토커들은 이러한 메시지들을 군 전화기 혹은 라디오 통신망을 통해 공식적인 또는 그들의 모국어에 기반해 비공식적으로 개발된 암호를 사용하면서 전송했다. 그것이 제2차 세계대전 동안 극히 중대한 최전방 작전에 대한 의사소통의 보안을 강화했기 때문에 그들의 업무는 매우 가치 있었다.

해설 ② 관계대명사 선행사 Native Americans(미국 원주민들)가 사람이고 관계절 내에서 primary job(주된 임무)이 누구의 것인지 나타내므로 사물을 가리키는 주격 또는 목적격 관계대명사 which를 사람을 가리키는 소유격 관계대명사 whose로 고쳐야 한다.

오답 분석 ① 주격 관계대명사 선행사 people이 사람이고 관계절 내에서 동사(talk)의 주어 역할을 하므로 사람을 가리키는 주격 관계대명사 who가 올바르게 쓰였다.
③ 현재분사 vs. 과거분사 주어(Code talkers)와 분사가 '코드 토커들이 사용하다'라는 의미의 능동 관계이므로 현재분사 using이 올바르게 쓰였다.
④ 전치사 2: 기간 명사(World War II) 앞에 와서 '기간'을 나타내는 전치사 during(~ 동안)이 올바르게 쓰였다.

어휘 coded 암호화된, 부호로 적힌 transmission 전송, 송신
tactical 전략의 transmit 전송하다 enhance 강화하다
vital 극히 중대한, 필수적인 front line 최전방

👆 이것도 알면 합격!

관계대명사는 선행사의 종류와 그것이 관계절 내에서 하는 역할에 따라서 선택해야 한다는 것을 알아두자.

	주격	목적격	소유격
사람	who	whom	whose
사물, 동물	which	which	of which/whose
사람, 사물, 동물	that	that	-

09 　독해　전체내용 파악 (목적 파악)　　난이도 ★☆☆

끊어읽기 해석

Every hour of every day, / one thousand children, women and men die / from preventable illness.
매일 매시간 / 천 명의 아이들, 여성들, 남성들이 죽는다 / 예방 가능한 병으로 인해

While life expectancy has continued to climb / in the world's most affluent countries, / it is decreasing / in many of the poorest countries.
기대 수명이 계속해서 올라가고 있지만 / 세계의 가장 부유한 나라들에서는 / 그것은 줄어들고 있다 / 가장 가난한 많은 나라들에서는

That is simply not right. // And the world has means / to address this injustice.
그것은 그야말로 옳지 않다. // 그리고 세계는 수단들을 가지고 있다 / 이 불평등을 다룰

For more than 30 years, / we have worked / to see / that these means are put into action.
30년이 넘도록 / 우리는 일해왔다 / 보기 위해 / 이러한 수단들이 행동으로 옮겨지는 것을

Tremendous strides have been made / but much is left to accomplish.
엄청난 진전이 있었다 / 하지만 성취되어야 할 많은 것들이 남아 있다.

You can help us / as we work with governments and multilateral agencies / to ensure / that adequate resources and sound policies / are applied to global health.
당신은 우리를 도울 수 있다 / 우리가 정부들과 국제 기구들과 함께 일할 때 / 확실히 하기 위해 / 적절한 자원과 건전한 정책들이 / 세계 건강에 쓰이는 것을

Your support also enables us / to make sure / that effective, low-cost health-care practices / are recognized and promoted.

당신의 지원은 또한 우리가 할 수 있게 한다 / 확실히 하도록 / 효과적이면서 비용이 낮은 건강 관리 실행이 / 인지되고 촉진되는 것을

Your financial support / helps us save lives. // Not dozens or even hundreds of lives, / but millions.
당신의 경제적 지원은 / 우리가 생명을 구하도록 돕는다 // 수십 또는 심지어 수백의 생명이 아닌 / 수백만의

해석　매일 매시간, 천 명의 아이들, 여성들, 남성들이 예방 가능한 병으로 인해 죽는다. 세계의 가장 부유한 나라들에서는 기대 수명이 계속해서 올라가고 있지만, 가장 가난한 많은 나라들에서는 그것은 줄어들고 있다. 그것은 그야말로 옳지 않다. 그리고 세계는 이 불평등을 다룰 수단들을 가지고 있다. 우리는 이러한 수단들이 행동으로 옮겨지는 것을 보기 위해 30년이 넘도록 일해왔다. 엄청난 진전이 있었지만 성취되어야 할 많은 것들이 남아 있다. 당신은 우리가 적절한 자원과 건전한 정책들이 세계 건강에 쓰이는 것을 확실히 하기 위해 정부들과 국제 기구들과 함께 일할 때, 우리를 도울 수 있다. 당신의 지원은 또한 우리가 효과적이면서 비용이 낮은 건강 관리 실행이 인지되고 촉진되는 것을 확실히 하도록 할 수 있게 한다. 당신의 경제적 지원은 우리가 생명을 구하도록 돕는다. 수십 또는 심지어 수백의 생명이 아닌 수백만의 생명을.

해설　지문 뒷부분에서 당신의 지원을 통해 적절한 자원과 건전한 정책들이 세계 건강에 쓰이는 것을 확실히 할 수 있고, 효과적이면서 비용이 낮은 건강 관리 실행이 인지되고 촉진되도록 할 수 있으며, 당신의 경제적 지원은 수백만의 생명을 구하도록 도울 수 있다고 설명하고 있다. 따라서 이 지문의 목적을 '세계적 보건문제 해결을 위한 기금을 모으려고'라고 표현한 ③번이 정답이다.

어휘　**preventable** 예방 가능한　**life expectancy** 기대 수명
affluent 부유한　**injustice** 불평등　**means** 수단, 방법
tremendous 엄청난, 무수한　**stride** 진전
multilateral 국제의, 다자간의　**adequate** 적절한
sound 건전한, 건강한

10　문법　to 부정사&분사&병치·도치·강조 구문　난이도 ★★★

해석　자연 서식지는 자연적인 이유들 또는 비자연적인 이유들로 변화할 수 있다. 전자와 관련하여, 기후 변화는 주요한 가능성이다. 자연 초지는 일련의 특정한 기후적 특징들의 결과이다. 그래서 만약 그러한 기후 요소들이 변화한다면, 당신은 마찬가지로 초지가 변화할 것을 예상할 것이다. 지금 아프리카 기후 변화의 충분한 증거들이 존재한다. 하지만 그것의 유형과 규모는 지도에 표시된 넓은 범위에 걸친 초지의 대량 소실을 설명하기에는 불충분하다. 그래서 기후는 장본인이 아니다. 대신에, 책임은 어느 곳에나 놓여 있고, 주로 인간의 모습으로 나타난다.

해설　**(A)** to 부정사를 취하는 동사 동사 expect는 to 부정사를 목적어로 취하는 동사이므로 to 부정사 to change를 써야 한다.
(B) 현재분사 vs. 과거분사 수식받는 명사(the wide area)와 분사가 '(지도에) 넓은 범위의 지역이 표시되다'라는 의미의 수동 관계이므로 과거분사 indicated를 써야 한다.
(C) 병치 구문 접속사(and)로 연결된 병치 구문에서는 같은 구조끼리 연결되어야 하는데, and 앞에 단수 주어 the fault의 동사로 단수 동사 lies가 왔으므로 and 뒤에도 단수 동사 takes를 써야 한다.
따라서 ④ (A) to change – (B) indicated – (C) takes가 정답이다.

어휘　**habitat** 서식지, 거주지　**former** (둘 중) 전자; 이전의
grassland 초지, 풀밭　**ample** 충분한　**extent** 규모, 정도
insufficient 불충분한　**wholesale** 대량의

---

disappearance 소실, 사라짐　**culprit** 장본인
take the form of ~의 모습으로 나타나다, ~의 모습을 취하다

👍 이것도 알면 **합격!**

to 부정사를 목적격 보어로 취하는 동사들을 알아두자.

- **want** ~이 -하는 것을 원하다
- **cause** ~이 -하게 하다
- **allow** ~이 -하게 허락하다
- **ask** ~이 -할 것을 요청하다
- **lead** ~이 -하게 이끌다
- **get** ~이 -하게 시키다

11　독해　논리적 흐름 파악 (문장 삽입)　난이도 ★★☆

끊어읽기 해석

But / what are the causes / of this trend?
그러나 / 원인들은 무엇인가 / 이런 추세의?

Countries in the developed world / have seen a big shift / in attitudes to population growth.
선진 세계의 나라들은 / 큰 변화를 겪어왔다 / 인구 증가에 대한 태도에 있어서

Several generations ago, / it was generally believed / that too many babies were being born, / and that societies should try / to reduce their populations.
몇 세대 전에는 / 일반적으로 생각되어졌다 / 너무 많은 아기들이 태어나고 있다고 / 그리고 사회가 노력해야 한다고 / 그들의 인구를 줄이기 위해

(①) Nowadays, however, / the concern is the reverse / —that birthrates are falling too low / and that urgent action is needed / to encourage people / to have more children.
하지만 요즘 / 걱정은 반대이다 / 출산률이 너무 낮게 떨어지고 있다 / 그리고 시급한 조치가 필요하다 / 사람들에게 장려하기 위해서 / 더 많은 아이들을 갖도록

(②) And how much are the attitudes and lifestyles / of young people to blame?
그리고 태도와 삶의 방식은 어느 정도인가 / 책임이 있는 젊은이들의?

(③) This essay will consider / a number of explanations / for the so-called "baby crash."
이 글은 숙고할 것이다 / 많은 이유들을 / 소위 '베이비 크래쉬'에 대한

(④) My argument will be / that to hold young people responsible / is neither valid nor helpful.
나의 주장은 / 젊은이들에게 책임을 묻는 것이 / 타당하지도 않고 도움이 되지도 않는다는 것이다

The best explanation, / I believe, / is to be found / in the condition of increased economic insecurity / faced by the young.
최고의 이유는 / 내가 믿는 / 찾아진다 / 증가한 경제적 불안정의 상황에서 / 젊은이들이 마주한

해석　선진 세계의 나라들은 인구 증가에 대한 태도에 있어서 큰 변화를 겪어왔다. 몇 세대 전에는 너무 많은 아기들이 태어나고 있고, 사회가 그들의 인구를 줄이기 위해 노력해야 한다고 일반적으로 생각되어졌다. 하지만 요즘 걱정은 반대인데, 출산률이 너무 낮게 떨어지고 있고 사람들에게 더 많은 아이들을 갖도록 장려하기 위해서 시급한 조치가 필요하다. ② 그러나 이런 추세의 원인들은 무엇인가? 그리고 책임이 있는 젊은이들의 태도와 삶의 방식은 어느 정도인가? 이 글은 소위 '베이비 크래쉬'에 대한 많은 이유들을 숙고할 것이다. 나의 주장은 젊은이들에게 책임을 묻는 것이 타당하지도 않고 도움이 되지도 않는다는 것이다. 내가 믿는 최고의 이유는 젊은이들이 마주한, 증가한 경제적 불안정의 상황에서 찾아진다.

해설 　②번 앞에 출산률이 너무 낮게 떨어지고 있다는 요즘의 추세에 대한 내용이 있고, ②번 뒤에서 여기에 책임이 있는 젊은이들의 태도와 삶의 방식에 대해 질문하는 내용이 있으므로, ②번 자리에 그러한 추세들의 원인을 묻는 주어진 문장이 들어가야 글의 흐름이 자연스럽게 연결된다. 따라서 ②번이 정답이다.

어휘 　trend 추세, 경향 shift 변화 reverse 반대; 뒤바꾸다
　　　urgent 시급한 so-called 소위, 이른바
　　　hold somebody responsible ~에게 책임을 묻다
　　　valid 타당한 insecurity 불안정

해설 　지문 전반에 걸쳐 대기에 의한 태양 광선의 굴절로 인해 수평선에 가까울수록 태양의 수직 폭이 작게 보여 결과적으로 타원형으로 보이는, 즉 편평률(회전 타원체의 편평도를 나타내는 양)의 원리를 설명하고 있다. 따라서 이 지문의 주제를 '태양 편평률의 원인'이라고 표현한 ④번이 정답이다.

어휘 　ray 광선 refract 굴절시키다 horizon 수평선 vertical 수직의
　　　ellipse 타원 swelling 팽창
　　　flattening 편평률(회전 타원체의 편평도를 나타내는 양), 타원율

---

12 독해 전체내용 파악 (주제 파악) 난이도 ★★★

끊어읽기 해석

The light rays from the sun / are refracted / by the atmosphere.
태양으로부터 발하는 광선은 / 굴절된다 / 대기에 의해

The closer the sun is to the horizon, / the more this refraction is.
태양이 수평선과 더 가까울수록 / 굴절은 더 많이 일어난다

Consider the sun / when its lower edge appears / to be on the horizon.
태양을 생각해보아라 / 그것의 아랫변이 보일 때의 / 수평선 위에 있는 것처럼

Were it not for the refraction, / the sun would just then actually have / its lower edge a little more than half a degree / below the horizon.
굴절이 아니라면 / 태양은 바로 그때 실제로 가질 것이다 / 0.5도보다 조금 더 되는 아랫변을 / 수평선 아래로

The upper edge, / in the meantime, / appears to be slightly less than half a degree / from where it would be / if there were no refraction.
윗변은 / 한편 / 0.5도보다 조금 더 작게 보일 것이다 / 그것이 보였을 것(각도)으로부터 / 만약 굴절이 없다면

As a result, / the vertical width of the sun appears / to be somewhat less / than it would be with the sun overhead.
결과적으로 / 태양의 수직 폭은 보일 것이다 / 다소 더 작게 / 태양이 하늘 높이 있을 때보다

The horizontal width suffers very little shortening / due to refraction.
수평 폭은 단축을 거의 겪지 않는다 / 굴절로 인해

Thus, / when the sun is on the horizon, / it appears to be an ellipse.
그러므로 / 태양이 수평선 위에 있을 때 / 그것은 타원인 것처럼 보인다

해설 　태양으로부터 발하는 광선은 대기에 의해 굴절된다. 태양이 수평선과 더 가까울수록 굴절은 더 많이 일어난다. 그것의 아랫변이 수평선 위에 있는 것처럼 보일 때의 태양을 생각해보아라. 굴절이 아니라면, 태양은 바로 그때 실제로 수평선 아래로 0.5도보다 조금 더 되는 아랫변을 가질 것이다. 한편, 윗변은 만약 굴절이 없다면 그것이 보였을 것(각도)으로부터 0.5도보다 조금 더 작게 보일 것이다. 결과적으로, 태양의 수직 폭은 태양이 하늘 높이 있을 때보다 다소 더 작게 보일 것이다. 수평 폭은 굴절로 인해 단축을 거의 겪지 않는다. 그러므로 태양이 수평선 위에 있을 때, 그것은 타원인 것처럼 보인다.
　　　① 왜 굴절이 일어나는가
　　　② 빛의 굴절 법칙
　　　③ 무엇이 태양의 팽창을 만드는가
　　　④ 태양 편평률의 원인

---

13 독해 추론 (빈칸 완성 - 구) 난이도 ★★☆

끊어읽기 해석

In Bootle, England, / a city of 55,000, / people were bombed nightly / for a week / during World War II / with only 10 percent of the houses / escaping serious damage.
잉글랜드의 Bootle에서 / 5만 5천 명이 사는 도시인 / 사람들은 밤마다 폭격을 당했다 / 일주일 동안 / 제2차 세계 대전 중에 / 오직 10퍼센트의 집들만이 / 심각한 피해를 면하면서

Yet / one-fourth of the population / remained asleep / in their homes / during the raids.
하지만 / 인구의 4분의 1은 / 잠들어 있었다 / 그들의 집에서 / 습격 중에

Only 37 percent of the London mothers and children / who were eligible for evacuation / left the city / during the war crisis.
오직 37퍼센트의 런던 어머니들과 아이들만이 / 피난할 수 있었던 / 도시를 떠났다 / 전쟁의 위기 동안

Furthermore, / even during periods of heavy bombing / in London, / evacuees drifted back / nearly as rapidly as / they were being evacuated.
게다가 / 심지어 심각한 폭격 기간 동안에도 / 런던의 / 피난민들은 되돌아왔다 / 거의 같은 빠른 속도로 / 그들이 피난을 떠났었던 것만큼이나

Similar findings are on record / for Germany and Japan / during World War II.
비슷한 발견은 기록에도 있다 / 독일과 일본의 / 제2차 세계 대전 동안의

This should not be surprising. // Human beings have / a very strong tendency / to continue with their established behavior patterns.
이것은 놀랍지 않을 것이다. // 인간은 가진다 / 매우 강한 성향을 / 그들의 확립된 행동 양식을 계속하는

해설 　5만 5천 명이 사는 도시인 잉글랜드의 Bootle에서 제2차 세계 대전 중에 사람들은 오직 10퍼센트의 집들만이 심각한 피해를 면하면서 일주일 동안 밤마다 폭격을 당했다. 하지만 습격 중에 인구의 4분의 1은 그들의 집에서 잠들어 있었다. 피난할 수 있었던 오직 37퍼센트의 런던 어머니들과 아이들만이 전쟁의 위기 동안 도시를 떠났다. 게다가, 심지어 런던의 심각한 폭격 기간 동안에도 피난민들은 그들이 피난을 떠났었던 것만큼이나 거의 같은 빠른 속도로 되돌아왔다. 비슷한 발견은 제2차 세계 대전 동안의 독일과 일본의 기록에도 있다. 이것은 놀랍지 않을 것이다. 인간은 그들의 확립된 행동 양식을 계속하는 매우 강한 성향을 가진다.
　　　① 그들의 확립된 행동 양식을 계속한다
　　　② 그들의 집단 내에서 분명한 역할을 한다
　　　③ 긴급 상황 동안 당황하여 도망친다
　　　④ 새로운 행동 방침을 착수시킨다

해설 　지문 뒷부분에서 피난민들은 피난을 떠났던 것만큼이나 빠른 속도로 다시 돌아왔고, 이는 독일과 일본에서도 비슷하게 기록되었다고 했으므로, 인간은 '그들의 확립된 행동 양식을 계속하는' 강한 성향이 있다고 한 ①번이 정답이다.

어휘 bomb 폭격하다; 폭탄 nightly 밤마다 raid 습격, 급습
eligible ~할 수 있는 crisis 위기, 고비 evacuation 피난
evacuee 피난민 findings 발견, 조사 결과 tendency 성향, 경향
established 확립된

14 문법 수 일치   난이도 ★☆☆

해석 요즘에 건강하고 균형 잡힌 식사를 하는 것은 흔하다. 이것은 당신
이 먹는 것을 주의하는 것을 의미한다. 여러 가지 음식들은 건강한
몸을 유지하는 데에 좋다. 물론 당신의 몸이 더 건강할수록, 당신
은 병을 덜 마주할 가능성이 있다. 과체중이 되거나 심장마비를 얻
는 대부분의 사람들은 그들이 나쁜 종류의 지방을 포함하는 너무
많은 음식들을 먹기 때문에 건강하지 않다. 그러므로, 문제들을 피
하는 최고의 방법은 고기, 생선, 채소 그리고 유제품을 균형을 맞추
어 먹는 것이다.

해설 ④ 주어와 동사의 수 일치 주어(the best way)가 단수 명사이므
로 복수 동사 are를 단수 동사 is로 고쳐야 한다. 참고로, 주어와
동사 사이의 수식어 거품(to avoid problems)은 동사의 수 결정
에 영향을 주지 않는다.

오답
분석
① 명사절 접속사 3: 의문사 동명사(watching)의 목적어 자리에
서 불완전한 절(you eat)을 이끌 수 있는 명사절 접속사 what
이 올바르게 쓰였다.
② 비교급 문맥상 '더 건강할수록, 덜 마주할 가능성이 있다'라는
의미가 되어야 자연스럽고, '더 ~할수록, 더 -하다'는 비교급
표현 'the + 비교급(healthier) + 주어(your body) + 동사 ~,
the + 비교급(less likely) + 주어(you) + 동사(are)'의 형태
로 나타낼 수 있으므로 the less가 올바르게 쓰였다. 참고로,
해당 문장은 주어 your body 뒤에 be동사 is가 생략된 형태
이다.
③ 부사절 자리와 쓰임 | 부사절 접속사 2: 이유 절(Most people
~ unhealthy)과 절(they eat ~ fat)을 연결하면서 이유를 나
타내는 부사절 접속사 because(~기 때문에)가 올바르게 쓰였
다.

어휘 a variety of 여러 가지의 maintain 유지하다
encounter 마주하다 overweight 과체중인
heart attack 심장마비 dairy product 유제품

👍 이것도 알면 **합격!**

다음의 비교급 표현의 형태를 확실하게 알아두도록 하자.

'the + 비교급 + 주어 + 동사 ~, the + 비교급 + 주어 + 동사 -'
더 ~할수록, 더 -하다

(ex) The healthier you are, the longer you will live.
네가 더 건강할수록, 더 오래 살 것이다.

15 문법 능동태·수동태   난이도 ★★☆

해석 우리는 매일 문제를 해결한다. 컴퓨터가 문제를 해결하기 위해 그
해결책은 매우 상세해야 할 뿐 아니라, 그것은 컴퓨터가 이해할 수
있는 형태로 쓰여져야 한다. 알고리즘은 문제를 해결하기 위한 과
정이다. 그것은 실행된다면 문제를 정확하게 해결하는 명령들의
단계적인 집합이다. 컴퓨터가 명령들을 매우 빨리 따르는 반면에,
그것은 명령된 것만 정확하게 시행한다. 알고리즘은 이러한 매우
구체적인 명령들을 설계하기 위해 사용된다.

해설 ③ 능동태·수동태 구별 명사절 접속사 what이 이끄는 명사절 내
의 주어 it(a computer)과 동사가 '그것이 명령되다(명령을 받
다)'라는 의미의 수동 관계이므로 능동태 tells를 수동태 is told로
고쳐야 한다.

오답
분석
① 도치 구문: 부사구 도치 1 제한을 나타내는 부사구(not only)
가 강조되어 절의 맨 앞에 나오면 주어와 조동사가 도치되어
'조동사(must) + 주어(the solution) + 동사'의 어순이 되어
야 하므로 must the solution 뒤에 동사원형 be가 올바르게
쓰였다.
② 분사구문의 형태 분사구문의 생략된 주어(a step-by-step
set of instructions)와 동사가 '명령들의 단계적인 집합이 실
행되다'라는 의미의 수동 관계이므로 과거분사 carried out이
올바르게 쓰였다.
④ 동명사 관련 표현 문맥상 '설계하기 위해 사용되다'라는 의미
가 되어야 자연스러운데, '~하기 위해 사용되다'는 'be used
to + 동사원형'를 사용하여 나타낼 수 있으므로 be used to
뒤에 동사원형 design이 올바르게 쓰였다.

어휘 procedure 과정, 절차 instruction 명령, 지시 carry out 실행하다

👍 이것도 알면 **합격!**

비슷한 형태를 가진 아래 표현들의 의미 차이를 알아두자.

· be used to + 동사원형 -하는 데 사용되다
· be used to -ing -하는 데 익숙하다
· used to + 동사원형 (과거에) -하곤 했다

16 독해 전체내용 파악 (요지 파악)   난이도 ★★☆

끊어읽기 해석

The saying goes: / you can bring the horse to water, / but you
cannot make him drink.
속담이 있다 / 말을 물가로 데려갈 수는 있어도 / 물을 마시도록 할 수는 없
다.

In language teaching, / teachers can provide / all the
necessary circumstances and input, / but learning can only
happen / if learners are willing to contribute.
언어를 가르칠 때 / 교사들은 제공할 수 있다 / 모든 필요한 상황과 조언들
을 / 하지만 학습은 오직 일어날 수 있다 / 학습자들이 기꺼이 참여할 때만

Their passive presence / will not suffice. // In order for
learners to be actively involved / in the learning process, /
they first need to realize and accept / that success in learning
depends / as much on the student / as on the teacher.
그들의 소극적인 참석은 / 충분하지 않을 것이다 // 학습자들이 적극적으로
참여하도록 하기 위해서 / 학습 과정에 / 그들은 먼저 깨닫고 받아들일 필
요가 있다 / 학습의 성공은 달려있다는 것을 / 학생들에게 / 선생님들만큼
이나

That is, / they share responsibility / for the outcome. // In
other words, / success in learning very much depends / on
learners having a responsible attitude.
즉 / 그들은 책임을 공유하는 것이다 / 결과에 대해서 // 다시 말해서 / 학
습의 성공은 매우 많이 달려 있다 / 책임감 있는 태도를 가지는 학습자들에

해석 말을 물가로 데려갈 수는 있어도, 물을 마시도록 할 수는 없다는
속담이 있다. 언어를 가르칠 때, 교사들은 모든 필요한 상황과 조
언들을 제공할 수 있지만, 학습은 오직 학습자들이 기꺼이 참여할
때만 일어날 수 있다. 그들의 소극적인 참석은 충분하지 않을 것이
다. 학습자들이 학습 과정에 적극적으로 참여하도록 하기 위해서,
그들은 먼저 학습의 성공은 선생님들만큼이나 학생들에게 달려있

다는 것을 깨닫고 받아들일 필요가 있다. 즉, 그들은 결과에 대해서 책임을 공유하는 것이다. 다시 말해서, 학습의 성공은 책임감 있는 태도를 가지는 학습자들에게 매우 많이 달려 있다.

① 뛰기 전에 걷는 법을 배워라(모든 일엔 순서가 있다)
② 쥐를 놀라게 하기 위해 집을 태우지 말아라(빈대 잡으려다 초가삼간 다 태운다)
③ 대부분의 사람들이 하는 대로 행하면 대부분의 사람들이 당신을 좋게 말할 것이다
④ 말을 물가로 데려갈 수는 있어도 물을 마시도록 할 수는 없다

해설 지문 앞부분에서 언어를 가르칠 때, 교사가 모든 필요한 상황과 조언을 제공할 수는 있어도, 학습은 오직 학습자가 기꺼이 참여할 때만 일어난다고 했고, 지문 마지막에서 학습의 성공은 학습자들의 책임감 있는 태도에 달려 있다는 내용이 있으므로, 이를 표현한 속담을 '말을 물가로 데려갈 수는 있어도 물을 마시도록 할 수는 없다'라고 한 ④번이 정답이다.

어휘 input 조언 contribute 참여하다, 공헌하다
passive 소극적인, 수동적인 presence 참석, 존재
suffice 충분하다 fright 놀라게 하다

---

17 독해 전체내용 파악 (글의 감상) 난이도 ★☆☆

끊어읽기 해석

When Marjorie and Bernice reached home / at half past midnight, / they said good night / at the top of the stairs.
Marjorie와 Bernice가 집에 도착했을 때 / 자정을 30분 넘겨 / 그들은 잘 자라는 인사를 했다 / 계단 위에서

Although they were cousins, / they were not close friends. // In fact, / Marjorie had no female friends / —she considered girls stupid.
비록 그들이 사촌이긴 했지만 / 가까운 친구는 아니었다 // 사실 / Marjorie는 여자 친구들이 없었다 / 그녀는 여자애들이 멍청하다고 생각했다

Bernice, on the other hand, / had hoped / that she and Marjorie would share their secrets.
반면 Bernice는 / 소망했다 / 그녀와 Marjorie가 그들의 비밀을 공유하는 것을

She had looked forward to long talks / full of girlish laughter and tears.
그녀는 긴 대화를 기대했다 / 소녀다운 웃음과 눈물로 가득 찬

For her / these were an important part / of all feminine conversation. // However, / she found Marjorie rather cold.
그녀에게 / 이러한 것들은 중요한 부분이었다 / 모든 여성스러운 대화의 // 하지만 / 그녀는 Marjorie가 꽤 냉담하다고 생각했다

For Bernice / it was as difficult / to talk to Marjorie / as it was to talk to men.
Bernice에게 / 어려웠다 / Marjorie에게 말을 거는 것은 / 남자들에게 말을 거는 것만큼

해석 Marjorie와 Bernice가 자정을 30분 넘겨 집에 도착했을 때, 그들은 계단 위에서 잘 자라는 인사를 했다. 비록 그들이 사촌이긴 했지만, 가까운 친구는 아니었다. 사실, Marjorie는 여자 친구들이 없었는데, 그녀는 여자애들이 멍청하다고 생각했다. 반면 Bernice는 그녀와 Marjorie가 그들의 비밀을 공유하는 것을 소망했다. 그녀는 소녀다운 웃음과 눈물로 가득 찬 긴 대화를 기대했다. 그녀에게 이러한 것들은 모든 여성스러운 대화의 중요한 부분이었다. 하지만 그녀는 Marjorie가 꽤 냉담하다고 생각했다. Bernice에게, Marjorie에게 말을 거는 것은 남자들에게 말을 거는 것만큼 어려웠다.

---

① 만족하고 행복한
② 안도하고 피로가 풀린
③ 겁이 나고 공황상태에 빠진
④ 불편하고 어색한

해설 지문 중간에서 Bernice는 Marjorie와 서로의 비밀을 공유하는 친구가 되기를 바라고 긴 대화를 기대했지만, 그와 다르게 Marjorie는 냉담한 태도를 보여 그녀에게 말을 거는 것은 남자들에게 말을 거는 것만큼 어려웠다는 일화를 소개하고 있다. 따라서 지문에서 Bernice가 느꼈을 심경을 '불편하고 어색한'이라고 표현한 ④번이 정답이다.

어휘 look forward to ~을 기대하다 laughter 웃음
feminine 여성스러운 relieved 안도한 rested 피로가 풀린
terrified 겁이 난 panicked 공황상태에 빠진 awkward 어색한

---

18 독해 논리적 흐름 파악 (무관한 문장 삭제) 난이도 ★★☆

끊어읽기 해석

Friendship is a long conversation. // I suppose / I could imagine / a nonverbal friendship / revolving around shared physical work or sport, / but for me, / good talk is the point of the thing.
우정은 긴 대화이다. // 나는 생각한다 / 내가 상상할 수 있다고 / 비언어적인 우정을 / 함께하는 신체 활동 또는 운동을 중심으로 삼은 / 하지만 나에게는 / 좋은 대화가 그것의 요점이다

(A) Indeed, / the ability to generate conversation / by the hour / is the most promising indication, / during the uncertain early stages, / that a possible friendship will take hold.
사실 / 대화를 만들어내는 능력은 / 시간 단위로 / 가장 조짐이 좋은 암시이다 / 불확실한 초기 단계에서 / 가능성 있는 우정이 강해질 것이라는

(B) In the first few conversations / there may be an exaggeration of agreement, / as both parties angle for / adhesive surfaces.
처음 몇 번의 대화에서는 / 동의에 대한 과장이 있을 것이다 / 양쪽 모두 노림에 따라 / 붙임성 있는 첫인상을

(C) Friendship based on utility and pleasure / are founded on circumstances / that could easily change.
유용성과 기쁨에 기반을 둔 우정은 / 상황에서 만들어진다 / 쉽게 변할 수 있는

(D) But later on, / trust builds / through the courage to assert disagreement, / through the tactful acceptance / that differences of opinion will have to remain.
하지만 나중에 / 신뢰가 쌓인다 / 반대를 주장하는 용기를 통해 / 능숙한 수용을 통해 / 의견의 차이가 여전히 남아 있을 수밖에 없다는

해석 우정은 긴 대화이다. 나는 내가 함께하는 신체 활동 또는 운동을 중심으로 삼은 비언어적인 우정을 상상할 수 있다고 생각하지만, 나에게는 좋은 대화가 우정의 요점이다. (A) 사실, 시간 단위로 대화를 만들어내는 능력은 불확실한 초기 단계 동안 가능성 있는 우정이 강해질 것이라는 가장 조짐이 좋은 암시이다. (B) 처음 몇 번의 대화에서는, 양쪽 모두 붙임성 있는 첫인상을 노림에 따라 동의에 대한 과장이 있을 것이다. (C) 유용성과 기쁨에 기반을 둔 우정은 쉽게 변할 수 있는 상황에서 만들어진다. (D) 하지만 나중에, 반대를 주장하는 용기를 통해 의견의 차이가 여전히 남아 있을 수밖에 없다는 능숙한 수용을 통해 신뢰가 쌓인다.

해설 지문 처음에서 필자는 우정은 긴 대화이며, 좋은 대화가 그것의 요점이라고 생각한다고 언급한 뒤, (A)에서 대화를 하는 능력이 우정이 강해질 것이라는 좋은 암시라고 설명하고, (B)에서 처음 몇 번의 대화에서는 붙임성 있는 첫인상을 주기 위한 과장된 동의가 있을 것이지만, (D)에서 나중에 반대를 주장하는 용기와 능숙

한 수용을 통해 신뢰가 쌓인다고 설명하고 있다. 그러나 (C)는 '쉽게 변할 수 있는 상황에서 만들어지는 우정'에 관한 내용으로, 대화를 통해 우정과 신뢰가 형성되는 과정을 설명하는 지문의 내용과 관련이 없으므로 ③ (C)가 정답이다.

어휘 nonverbal 비언어적인 revolve around ~을 중심으로 삼다
generate 만들어내다 promising 조짐이 좋은 indication 암시
exaggeration 과장 angle for ~을 노리다
adhesive 붙임성 있는, 접착성의 assert 주장하다 tactful 능숙한
acceptance 수용

19 어휘 어휘&표현 bluff = deceive 난이도 ★★☆

해석 빅터는 무엇을 말할지 몰랐다. 선생님은 그의 입술을 축였고 불어로 다른 무언가를 물었다. 교실은 고요해졌다. 빅터는 모든 눈들이 그를 응시하고 있는 것을 느꼈다. 그는 불어처럼 들리는 소리를 만들어냄으로써 속여서 (그 상황을) 벗어나기를 시도했다.

① 속임수를 쓰다 ② 애도하다
③ 피하다 ④ 조사하다

어휘 stare 응시하다 bluff 속이다, 허세를 부리다 deceive 속임수를 쓰다
lament 애도하다, 한탄하다 investigate 조사하다

👍 이것도 알면 **합격!**
bluff(속이다)의 유의어
= trick, pretend, cheat, mislead

20 독해 논리적 흐름 파악 (무관한 문장 삭제) 난이도 ★☆☆

끊어읽기 해석

A child born into society / must be fed and looked after. // In many societies, / the parents of the child are responsible / for his welfare / and therefore perform a function / for society / by looking after the next generation.
사회에 태어난 아이는 / 먹여지고 돌봐져야 한다 // 많은 사회에서 / 아이의 부모들은 책임이 있다 / 그의 안녕에 / 그렇기 때문에 기능을 수행한다 / 사회를 위한 / 다음 세대를 돌봄으로써

① As the child grows up, / surrounded by brothers and sisters, his parents / and sometimes by a member of the extended family group, / he gradually learns / things about the society / in which he lives.
아이가 자람에 따라 / 형제 자매, 그의 부모에 둘러싸여 / 그리고 때로는 확대 가족 구성원에 (둘러싸여) / 그는 점점 배운다 / 사회에 대하여 / 그가 살고 있는

② For example, / he will learn / its language, / its idea about right and wrong, / its ideas about what is funny and what is serious and so on.
예를 들어 / 그는 배울 것이다 / 언어 / 옳고 그름에 대한 생각 / 무엇이 재미있고 무엇이 심각한지에 대한 생각 등을

③ Census estimates / the number of unmarried heterosexual couples / who cohabit / has reached a startling 6.4 million couples / in 2007.
인구 조사는 추정한다 / 결혼하지 않은 이성애자 커플들의 수가 / 동거하는 / 아주 놀랍게도 640만 명에 다다랐다고 / 2007년에

④ In other words, / the child will learn / the culture of his society / through his contact / with, at first, the members of his family.
다시 말해서 / 그 아이는 배울 것이다 / 그 사회의 문화를 / 접촉을 통하여 / 처음으로, 그의 가족 구성원들과의

해석 사회에 태어난 아이는 먹여지고 돌봐져야 한다. 많은 사회에서, 아이의 부모들은 그의 안녕에 책임이 있기 때문에 다음 세대를 돌봄으로써 사회를 위한 기능을 수행한다. ① 아이가 자람에 따라, 형제 자매, 그의 부모 그리고 때로는 확대 가족 구성원에 둘러싸여 그는 그가 살고 있는 사회에 대하여 점점 배운다. ② 예를 들어, 그는 언어, 옳고 그름에 대한 생각, 무엇이 재미있고 무엇이 심각한지에 대한 생각 등을 배울 것이다. ③ 인구 조사는 결혼하지 않은 동거하는 이성애자 커플들의 수가 2007년에 아주 놀랍게도 640만 명에 다다랐다고 추정한다. ④ 다시 말해서, 그 아이는 처음으로, 그의 가족 구성원들과의 접촉을 통하여 그 사회의 문화를 배울 것이다.

해설 지문 처음에서 아이의 부모들은 아이의 안녕에 책임이 있고, 다음 세대를 돌봄으로써 사회를 위한 기능을 수행한다고 설명한 뒤, ①, ②, ④번에서 아이가 가족 구성원들을 통하여 자신이 사는 사회에 대해 배우는 과정을 설명하고 있다. 그러나 ③번은 '결혼하지 않고 동거하는 이성 커플들의 수'에 관한 내용으로, 아이가 사회에 대해 배우는 과정에 대한 내용과는 관련이 없으므로 ③번이 정답이다.

어휘 census 인구 조사 estimate 추정하다 heterosexual 이성애자의
cohabit 동거하다 startling 아주 놀라운

21 문법 동사의 종류 난이도 ★★☆

해석 세계를 식량 전쟁으로 밀어넣을 것처럼 위협하면서 세계 식량 가격이 급등하고 있다. 이달 초, UN 식량 농업 기구는 세계 식량 가격이 1월에 사상 최고 수치에 다다랐고 다가올 달들에도 계속 오르도록 예정되어 있었다는 것을 말했다. 그것은 심각한 세계 식량 위기가 임박하거나 진행 중이라는 강한 신호이다.

해설 ① 혼동하기 쉬운 자동사와 타동사 | 숙어 표현 빈칸은 명사절 (world food prices ~ to come) 내에서 동사 hit과 접속사 and로 연결된 동사 자리이다. 문맥상 '다가올 달들에도 가격이 계속 오르다'라는 의미가 되어야 자연스럽고, '~이 오르다'는 자동사 rise를 사용하여 나타낼 수 있으므로 동명사를 목적어로 취하는 동사 keep 뒤에 rising이 쓰인 ①, ③번이 정답 후보이다. 또한 문맥상 '계속 오르도록 예정되어 있다'는 숙어 표현 be set to(~하도록 예정되어 있다)를 사용하여 나타낼 수 있으므로 빈칸에는 were set to keep rising이 들어가야 한다.

어휘 go through the roof 급등하다, 치솟다 agricultural 농업의
crisis 위기 imminent 임박한 under way 진행 중인

👍 이것도 알면 **합격!**
형태가 비슷해서 혼동하기 쉬운 자동사와 타동사를 알아두자.

자동사	타동사
lie-lay-lain 놓여있다, 눕다 lie-lied-lied 거짓말하다	lay-laid-laid ~을 놓다, ~을 두다, (알을) 낳다
sit-sat-sat 앉다	seat-seated-seated ~을 앉히다
rise-rose-risen 오르다	raise-raised-raised ~을 모으다, 올리다

22 문법 형용사와 부사 난이도 ★☆☆

해석 모든 세대의 발견의 업적들은 글을 읽고 쓸 줄 아는 공동체 전체의 생각을 형성하고 일깨운다. 그리고 이 영향은 민주주의와 글을 읽고 쓰는 능력의 증가와 함께 증대된다. 물론, 친숙한 예는 코페르

니쿠스와 그의 동료들의 업적이 지구가 더 이상 중심이 아니라는 깨달음으로 서양 문화를 혼란시킨 방식이다. 더 최근의 예들은 다윈 생물학과 프로이트 심리학의 영향이다. 요즘은, 비록 우주 과학이 신비로워지고 전문화되었지만, 그것(우주 과학)은 계속해서 전체 공동체의 생각에 심오하고 광범위한 영향을 준다.

해설 ③ 형용사 자리 명사(examples)를 앞에서 수식할 수 있는 것은 형용사이므로 부사 recently(최근에)를 형용사 recent(최근의)로 고쳐야 한다.

오답 분석
① 주어와 동사의 수 일치 주어 자리에 복수 명사 The works가 왔으므로 복수 동사 shape가 올바르게 쓰였다. 참고로, 주어와 동사 사이의 수식어 거품(of discovery in every age)은 동사의 수 결정에 영향을 주지 않는다.
② 명사절 접속사 3: 의문사 완전한 절(the works of ~ the center)을 이끌면서 be 동사(is)의 보어 자리에 올 수 있는 의문부사 how가 올바르게 쓰였다.
④ 부사절 접속사 2: 양보 문맥상 '비록 신비로워지고 전문화되었지만'이라는 의미가 되어야 자연스러우므로 양보를 나타내는 부사절 접속사 though(비록 ~이지만)가 올바르게 쓰였다.

어휘 discovery 발견 shake up ~을 일깨우다, 개혁하다
literate 글을 읽고 쓸 줄 아는 multiply 증대시키다
democracy 민주주의 literacy 글을 읽고 쓰는 능력
arcane 신비로운, 불가사의한 profound 심오한

👍 이것도 알면 합격!
의문부사 when, where, how, why가 이끄는 명사절은 뒤에 완전한 절이 오지만, 의문대명사 who, whose, what, which가 이끄는 명사절은 뒤에 주어나 목적어, 보어가 없는 불완전한 절이 온다는 것을 알아두자.
(ex) **What** caused the accident is unclear.
　　　주어가 없는 불완전한 절
　무엇이 사고를 일으켰는지는 불확실하다.

---

23 문법 병치·도치·강조 구문 난이도 ★★☆

해석 당신의 가장 위대한 정신력 중 하나는 상상력이다. 당신은 원하는 어떤 것이든 마음속에 그려볼 수 있고 당신의 상상을 원하는 만큼 많이 꾸미고 과장할 수 있다. 예를 들어, 당신은 유리지방산이 에너지를 위해 '세포 발전소', 즉 미토콘드리아에서 연소되는 것을 상상할 수 있고 그 미토콘드리아를 불타는 용광로로 상상할 수 있다 ... 그 지방을 '소각하는 것'! 나는 당신의 지방 세포들이 줄어드는 것을 '보는' 것과 당신의 몸을 '지방을 태우는 용광로'로 상상하는 것이 꽤 멋진 아이디어라고 생각한다.

해설 ④ 병치 구문 접속사(and)로 연결된 병치 구문에서는 같은 구조끼리 연결되어야 하는데, and 앞에 to 부정사구(to "see" ~ shrinking)가 왔으므로 and 뒤에도 to 부정사구가 와야 한다. 병치 구문에서 두 번째 나온 to는 생략될 수 있으므로 현재분사 visualizing을 (to) visualize로 고쳐야 한다.

오답 분석
① 수량 표현의 수 일치 주어 자리에 단수 취급하는 수량 표현(One of)이 왔으므로 단수 동사 is가 올바르게 쓰였다.
② 원급 원급 표현 'as + 형용사/부사의 원급 + as'(~만큼 -한/하게)에서 as ~ as 사이가 형용사 자리인지 부사 자리인지는 as, as를 지우고 구별할 수 있는데, 동사(embellish, exaggerate)를 수식하는 것은 부사이므로 부사 much가 올바르게 쓰였다.
③ 동명사의 형태 동사 imagine은 동명사를 목적어로 취하는 동사인데, 동명사의 의미상의 주어 the free fatty acids와 동명

사가 '유리지방산이 연소되다'라는 의미의 수동 관계이므로 동명사의 수동형 being burned가 올바르게 쓰였다.

어휘 imagination 상상력 visualize 마음속에 그리다, 상상하다
embellish 꾸미다 exaggerate 과장하다
free fatty acid 유리지방산 cellular 세포의 powerhouse 발전소
fiery 불타는 furnace 용광로 incinerate 소각하다

👍 이것도 알면 합격!
보통 동명사의 의미상 주어는 '명사의 소유격' 또는 '소유격 대명사'를 동명사 앞에 쓰지만, 보기 ③번의 문장처럼 동명사가 수동형(being burned)일 경우, 일반 명사(the free fatty acids)를 그대로 의미상 주어로 쓸 수 있다는 것을 알아두자.

---

24 독해 추론 (빈칸 완성 - 단어) 난이도 ★★☆

끊어읽기 해석

With the publication in 1789 / of the *Elements of Chemistry* by Lavoisier, / the science of chemistry served / its remaining connections / with the alchemical past / and assumed a modern form.
1789년의 출판과 함께 / 라부아지에의 『화학 요론』의 / 화학은 다했다 / 남아있는 연관성을 / 지난날 연금술과의 / 그리고 현대적 형태를 띠었다

Lavoisier stressed / the importance of quantitative methods / of investigation in chemistry, / and in this connection / he introduced / the principle of the <u>conservation</u> of matter / which stated that nothing was lost or gained / during the course of a chemical reaction, / the weight of the products equalling / the weight of the starting materials.
라부아지에는 강조했다 / 양적인 방법들의 중요성을 / 화학 조사의 / 그리고 이와 관련하여 / 그는 소개했다 / 질량 보존의 법칙을 / 아무것도 없어지거나 더해지지 않는다고 말하는 / 화학적 반응 동안에 / 사물의 무게가 동일하다고 / 최초 물질의 무게와

해석 1789년 라부아지에의 『화학 요론』의 출판과 함께, 화학은 지난날 연금술과의 남아있는 연관성을 다했고 현대적 형태를 띠었다. 라부아지에는 화학 조사의 양적인 방법들의 중요성을 강조했으며, 이와 관련하여 그는 화학적 반응 동안에 아무것도 없어지거나 더해지지 않아 사물의 무게가 최초 물질의 무게와 동일하다고 말하는 질량 보존의 법칙을 소개했다.

① 축소　　　　　　② 박탈
③ 보존　　　　　　④ 축적

해설 빈칸 뒤에서 화학적 반응 동안에 아무것도 없어지거나 더해지지 않고 사물의 무게가 최초 물질의 무게와 동일하다는 내용이 있으므로, 질량 '보존'의 법칙이라고 한 ③번이 정답이다.

어휘 publication 출판 alchemical 연금술의 assume 띠다, 추정하다
stress 강조하다 quantitative 양적인 principle 법칙
reduction 축소 deprivation 박탈 conservation 보존
accumulation 축적

---

25 독해 추론 (빈칸 완성 - 단어) 난이도 ★★☆

끊어읽기 해석

Ideas are created / by integrating previous ideas and sensory input.
발상은 만들어진다 / 이전의 발상과 감각 입력을 통합함으로써

Due to this dependency of ideas / on previous ideas or

sensory input, / we know / that knowledge is hierarchical.
발상의 의존성 때문에 / 이전의 발상 혹은 감각 입력에 대한 / 우리는 안다 / 지식이 계층적이라는 것을

Every higher level concept is based / on a lower level information. // At the root of all of this, / of course, / is perception.
모든 높은 수준의 개념은 기반을 둔다 / 낮은 수준의 정보에 // 이 모든 것들의 뿌리에는 / 물론 / 지각이 있다

The very first concepts are derived directly / from perceptions, / via reason.
바로 그 최초의 개념들은 직접적으로 얻어진다 / 지각으로부터 / 이성을 통해서

Future concepts can then use / the first concepts / as part of their base, / but the foundation is always there.
그러고 나서 향후의 개념들은 사용할 수 있다 / 최초의 개념들을 / 그들의 기반의 일부로서 / 하지만 토대는 항상 그곳에 있다

해석 발상은 이전의 발상과 감각 입력을 통합함으로써 만들어진다. 이전의 발상 혹은 감각 입력에 대한 발상의 의존성 때문에, 우리는 지식이 계층적이라는 것을 안다. 모든 높은 수준의 개념은 낮은 수준의 정보에 기반을 둔다. 이 모든 것들의 뿌리에는 물론 지각이 있다. 바로 그 최초의 개념들은 이성을 통해서 지각으로부터 직접적으로 얻어진다. 그러고 나서 향후의 개념들은 그들의 기반의 일부로서 최초의 개념들을 사용할 수 있지만, 토대는 항상 그곳에 있다.

① 수평의   ② 계층적인
③ 목표 지향적인   ④ 다방면의

해설 빈칸 뒤 문장에서 모든 높은 수준의 개념은 낮은 수준의 정보에 기반을 두고, 모든 것들의 뿌리에는 지각이 있다고 했으므로, 지식이 '계층적'이라고 한 ②번이 정답이다.

어휘 integrate 통합하다 previous 이전의 sensory 감각의
input 입력 derive from ~으로부터 얻다 perception 지각
reason 이성, 근거 horizontal 수평의 hierarchical 계층적인
goal-oriented 목표 지향적인 multidirectional 다방면의

정답

p.141

01	① 독해 – 세부내용 파악	11	④ 독해 – 추론	21	① 독해 – 전체내용 파악
02	② 독해 – 세부내용 파악	12	① 독해 – 추론	22	② 독해 – 논리적 흐름 파악
03	① 독해 – 추론	13	④ 문법 – 관계절	23	④ 독해 – 논리적 흐름 파악
04	③ 독해 – 세부내용 파악	14	② 독해 – 추론	24	④ 독해 – 전체내용 파악
05	② 문법 – 부사절	15	④ 독해 – 논리적 흐름 파악	25	② 문법 – 명사와 관사
06	③ 독해 – 추론	16	② 독해 – 논리적 흐름 파악		
07	④ 독해 – 논리적 흐름 파악	17	① 독해 – 논리적 흐름 파악		
08	② 독해 – 논리적 흐름 파악	18	③ 독해 – 논리적 흐름 파악		
09	④ 독해 – 추론	19	② 독해 – 전체내용 파악		
10	② 독해 – 세부내용 파악	20	③ 독해 – 논리적 흐름 파악		

취약영역 분석표

영역	세부 유형	문항 수	소계
어휘	어휘 & 표현	0	/0
	생활영어	0	
문법	부사절	1	/3
	관계절	1	
	명사와 관사	1	
독해	전체내용 파악	3	/22
	세부내용 파악	4	
	추론	6	
	논리적 흐름 파악	9	
총계			/25

· 자신이 취약한 영역은 '법원직 9급 영어, 이렇게 출제된다!'(p.8)를 통해 다시 한 번 확인하고 학습하시기 바랍니다.

---

01 독해 세부내용 파악 (특정 정보 파악)

난이도 ★☆☆

끊어읽기 해석

> Jetway's New Bike Hits the Mark!
> Jetway의 새로운 자전거가 출시되었습니다!
>
> Jetway's new 2010 Jetway MX200 / is the fastest motorbike available / and can be ridden by the widest range of riders, / including those with a little experience.
> Jetway의 새로운 2010 Jetway MX200은 / 구할 수 있는 가장 빠른 오토바이입니다 / 그리고 가장 광범위한 운전자들이 탈 수 있습니다 / 경험이 거의 없는 사람들을 포함해서
>
> The new 2010 Jetway MX200 is available / in four different color schemes.
> 새로운 2010 Jetway MX200은 구입이 가능합니다 / 4가지의 다른 색채 배합으로
>
> It also looks better / than previous motorcycles from this company / and appears to have / a sleeker and more curvaceous look.
> 그것은 또한 더 좋아 보입니다 / 이 회사의 이전 오토바이들보다 / 그리고 가지고 있는 것처럼 보입니다 / 더 매끈하고 곡선미가 있는 외관을
>
> Thanks to new fully adjustable suspension technology, / the handling of each motorcycle can be individually adjusted / to a rider's weight or the street environment.
> 완전히 조절 가능한 새로운 완충 기술 덕분에 / 각 오토바이의 조작은 개별적으로 조절될 수 있습니다 / 운전자의 체중 또는 도로 환경에 맞춰
>
> This can greatly improve / a rider's ability to drive it. // The onboard computer fan also automatically adjusts / speed, acceleration and braking forces / in order to keep the bike's handling optimal.
> 이것은 크게 향상시킬 수 있습니다 / 운전자의 운전 능력을 // 내장된 컴퓨터 팬 또한 자동적으로 조절합니다 / 속도, 가속 그리고 제동력을 / 오토바이의 최적의 조작을 유지하기 위해서
>
> The tires designed for this bike / are capable of performing well / in all types of road conditions / and prevent slipping better / than any other bike available on the market.
> 이 오토바이를 위해 설계된 타이어들은 / 잘 움직일 수 있습니다 / 모든 유형의 도로 조건에서 / 그리고 미끄럼을 더 잘 방지합니다 / 시중에서 구할 수 있는 어떤 오토바이보다도

해석 Jetway의 새로운 자전거가 출시되었습니다!
Jetway의 새로운 2010 Jetway MX200은 구할 수 있는 가장 빠른 오토바이이고, 경험이 거의 없는 사람들을 포함해서 가장 광범위한 운전자들이 탈 수 있습니다. 새로운 2010 Jetway MX200은 4가지의 다른 색채 배합으로 구입이 가능합니다. 그것은 또한 이 회사의 이전 오토바이들보다 더 좋아 보이고 더 매끈하고 곡선미가 있는 외관을 가지고 있는 것처럼 보입니다. 완전히 조절 가능한 새로운 완충 기술 덕분에 각 오토바이의 조작은 운전자의 체중 또는 도로 환경에 맞춰 개별적으로 조절될 수 있습니다. 이것은 운전자의 운전 능력을 크게 향상시킬 수 있습니다. 내장된 컴퓨터 팬 또한 오토바이의 최적의 조작을 유지하기 위해서 속도, 가속 그리고 제동력을 자동적으로 조절합니다. 이 오토바이를 위해 설계된 타이어들은 모든 유형의 도로 조건에서 잘 움직일 수 있고 시중에서 구할 수 있는 어떤 오토바이보다도 미끄럼을 더 잘 방지합니다.

① 이것은 다른 모델들보다 연비가 좋다.
② 이것은 모든 조건의 도로에서 잘 조작된다.
③ 이것은 다른 모델들보다 운전자들에게 더 매력적이다.
④ 이것은 운전자들 각각의 선호에 따라 주문 제작될 수 있다.

해설 지문 앞부분에서 이 새로운 오토바이는 운전자의 기호에 따라 4가지의 다른 색채 배합으로 구입이 가능하다고 했고(④), 지문 중간에서 이 오토바이는 외관을 포함한 여러 가지 측면에서 다른 모델들보다 더 좋아 보인다고 했으며(③), 지문 마지막에서 이 오토바이는 모든 유형의 도로 조건에서 잘 움직일 수 있다고 했다(②). 하지만, 새로운 오토바이의 연비에 대해서는 언급되지 않았으므로 ①번이 정답이다.

어휘 hit the mark(= market) (시장에) 출시되다
color scheme 색채 배합 sleek 매끈한

curveaceous 곡선미가 있는 **adjustable** 조절 가능한
suspension 완충 (장치), 정직 **onboard** 내장된, 탑재된
acceleration 가속 **braking force** 제동력
optimal 최적의 **slip** 미끄러지다 **fuel-efficient** 연비가 좋은
customize 주문 제작하다 **preference** 선호, 기호

aim for ~을 목표로 하다 **strive for** ~을 얻기 위해 노력하다

---

02 독해 세부내용 파악 (지칭 대상 파악) 난이도 ★★☆

끊어읽기 해석

> When I was a boy, / my father decided to build a basketball court / for my brother and me.
> 내가 소년이었을 때 / 나의 아버지는 농구 코트를 만들기로 결심했다 / 형과 나를 위해
>
> He made a cement driveway, / put a backboard on the garage / and was just getting ready to put up ① the basket / when he was called away / on an emergency.
> 그는 시멘트 진입로를 만들었다 / 차고에 백보드를 붙였다 / 그리고 막 ① 바스켓을 올릴 준비를 하고 있던 참이었다 / 그가 불려 나갔을 때는 / 급한 일로
>
> He promised to put up the hoop / as soon as he returned.
> 그는 링을 올려주겠다고 약속했다 / 그가 돌아오자마자
>
> "No problem," / I thought. // "I have a brand-new basketball / and ② a new cement driveway / on which to dribble it."
> "괜찮아요" / 나는 생각했다 // "나는 새 농구공을 가지고 있어요 / 그리고 ② 새로운 시멘트 진입로도 (가지고 있어요) / 그것을 드리블할"
>
> For a few minutes / I bounced the ball on the cement. // Soon that became boring, / so I threw the ball up / against the backboard / —once.
> 몇 분 동안 / 나는 시멘트 위에서 공을 튀겼다 // 곧 그것이 지루해졌다 / 그래서 나는 공을 던졌다 / 백보드에 / 딱 한 번
>
> I let the ball run off the court / and didn't pick it up again / until Dad returned to put up the rim.
> 나는 공이 코트 밖으로 나가도록 두었다 / 그리고 그것을 다시 줍지 않았다 / 아버지가 와서 링을 달아줄 때까지
>
> Why? // It's no fun / playing basketball without ③ a goal. // How true that is to life!
> 왜일까? // 재미가 없다 / ③ 골대 없이 농구를 하는 것은 // 삶에서도 그것은 얼마나 진실인가!
>
> The joy is in having / ④ something to aim for and strive for.
> 기쁨은 가지는 데 있다 / 얻기 위해 노력하고 ④ 목표로 하는 무언가를

해석 내가 소년이었을 때, 나의 아버지는 형과 나를 위해 농구 코트를 만들기로 결심했다. 그는 시멘트 진입로를 만든 뒤 차고에 백보드를 붙였고, 그가 급한 일로 불려 나갔을 때는 막 ① 바스켓을 올릴 준비를 하고 있던 참이었다. 그는 그가 돌아오자마자 링을 올려주겠다고 약속했다. "괜찮아요"라고 나는 생각했다. "나는 새 농구공과 그것을 드리블할 ② 새로운 시멘트 진입로도 가지고 있어요." 몇 분 동안 나는 시멘트 위에서 공을 튀겼다. 곧 그것이 지루해져서 나는 백보드에 공을 딱 한 번 던졌다. 나는 공이 코트 밖으로 나가도록 두었고, 아버지가 와서 링을 달아줄 때까지 그것을 다시 줍지 않았다. 왜일까? ③ 골대 없이 농구를 하는 것은 재미가 없다. 삶에서도 그것은 얼마나 진실인가! 기쁨은 얻기 위해 노력하고 ④ 목표로 하는 무언가를 가지는 데 있다.

해설 ①, ③, ④번은 모두 농구를 할 때나 인생에서의 '목표'를 의미하지만 ②번의 '새로운 시멘트 진입로'는 그것(새 농구공)을 드리블한다는 내용이 있으므로 단순히 소년의 아버지가 만든 농구 코트를 의미한다. 따라서 ②번이 정답이다.

어휘 backboard (농구대의) 백보드 **hoop** 링, 테 **brand-new** 새로운 **dribble** (공 따위를) 드리블하다, 질질 흘리다 **bounce** 튀기다, 튀다

---

03 독해 추론 (빈칸 완성 – 단어) 난이도 ★☆☆

끊어읽기 해석

> If an expectant mother knew / that dangerous creatures lurked / around her, / and knew also / that she wouldn't be around / to take care of her young, / she might be stressed.
> 만약 임산부가 알고 있다면 / 위험한 존재가 숨어있다는 것을 / 그녀의 근처에 / 그리고 또한 알고 있다면 / 그녀가 근처에 있지 않을 것이라는 것을 / 그녀의 자식을 돌보기 위해 / 그녀는 아마도 스트레스를 받을 것이다
>
> And if she had / a way to warn her young / before they were born, / surely she would.
> 그리고 만약 그녀가 가진다면 / 그녀의 자식들에게 주의를 줄 방법을 / 그들이 태어나기 전에 / 분명히 그녀는 그렇게 할 것이다
>
> Human mothers cannot do this, / to the best of our knowledge.
> 인간 어머니들은 이것을 할 수 없다 / 우리가 알고 있는 한에서는
>
> But pregnant crickets, / it appears, / do have / the ability to forewarn.
> 하지만 알을 밴 귀뚜라미들은 / 보인다 / 정말 가진 것처럼 / 미리 경고하는 능력을
>
> This is especially useful / since crickets abandon their young / after birth.
> 이것은 특히 유용하다 / 귀뚜라미가 그들의 새끼들을 버리고 떠나기 때문에 / 산란 후에

해석 만약 임산부가 그녀의 근처에 위험한 존재가 숨어있다는 것을 알고 있다면, 그리고 또한 그녀가 그녀의 자식을 돌보기 위해 근처에 있지 않을 것이라는 것을 알고 있다면, 그녀는 아마도 스트레스를 받을 것이다. 그리고 만약 그녀가 자식이 태어나기 전에 그들에게 주의를 줄 방법을 가진다면, 분명히 그녀는 그렇게 할 것이다. 인간 어머니들은 우리가 알고 있는 한에서는 이것을 할 수 없다. 하지만 알을 밴 귀뚜라미들은 정말 미리 경고하는 능력을 가진 것처럼 보인다. 이것은 귀뚜라미가 산란 후에 그들의 새끼들을 버리고 떠나기 때문에 특히 유용하다.

① 스트레스를 받는 – 미리 경고하다
② 아주 기쁜 – 미리 경고하다
③ 스트레스를 받는 – 참다
④ 아주 기쁜 – 참다

해설 첫 번째 빈칸이 있는 문장에서 임산부가 그녀 주위에 위험한 존재가 있고 그녀가 자식을 돌보기 위해 근처에 있지 않을 것이라는 것을 아는 상황을 가정하고 있으므로, 첫 번째 빈칸에는 그녀가 아마 그런 상황에서 '스트레스를 받을'(stressed) 것이라는 내용이 들어가는 것이 적절하다. 지문 중간에서 인간에게는 자식이 태어나기 전에 그들에게 주의를 줄 수 있는 능력이 없다는 내용이 있고, 두 번째 빈칸 뒤 문장에서 이 능력은 귀뚜라미들이 산란 후 새끼들을 버리고 떠나기 때문에 특히 유용하다는 내용이 있으므로, 두 번째 빈칸에는 사람과는 달리 알을 밴 귀뚜라미들은 '미리 경고하는'(forewarn) 능력이 있는 것처럼 보인다는 내용이 들어가는 것이 적절하다. 따라서 ① stressed(스트레스를 받는) – forewarn(미리 경고하다)이 정답이다.

어휘 expectant mother 임산부 **lurk** 숨어있다, 도사리다
to the best of ~하는 한 **cricket** 귀뚜라미 **abandon** 버리다
forewarn 미리 경고하다 **delighted** 아주 기쁜 **bear** 참다

끊어읽기 해석

Scientists working in Central America / have discovered ruins / of one of the largest and most important palaces / built by the ancient Mayan people / at Cancun, Guatemala.
중앙 아메리카에서 근무하는 과학자들은 / 잔해를 발견했다 / 가장 크고 중요한 궁전들 중 하나의 / 고대 마야인에 의해 지어진 / 과테말라의 칸쿤에서

It was built / about 1,300 years ago.
그것은 지어졌다 / 약 1,300년 전에

Jungle plants have covered the ruins / for hundreds of years, / and the area looks / like a huge hill / covered by jungle.
정글 식물들은 그 잔해들을 뒤덮었다 / 수백 년 동안 / 그리고 그 지역은 보인다 / 큰 언덕처럼 / 정글에 의해 뒤덮인

The palace has 170 rooms / built around 11 open areas.
그 궁전은 170개의 방들을 가지고 있다 / 11개의 공지 주위에 지어진

The discovery of the ruins will certainly increase / historians' understanding / of the political life of the Mayan people, / who were at the height of power / in Central America and Mexico / more than one thousand years ago.
그 잔해의 발견은 확실히 증가시킬 것이다 / 역사가들의 이해를 / 마야인들의 정치적 삶에 대한 / 그들(마야인들)은 권력의 절정에 있었다 / 중앙 아메리카와 멕시코에서 / 천 년도 더 이전에

Writings on the newly found palace walls say / it was built by King Tah ak Chaan, / who ruled Cancun / for about fifty years / beginning in the year 740 A.D.
새로 발견된 궁전 벽들에 쓰여진 문구는 말한다 / 그것이 Tah ak Chaan 왕에 의해 지어졌음을 / 그는 칸쿤을 지배했었다 / 약 50년간 / 서기 740년부터 시작해

해석 중앙 아메리카에서 근무하는 과학자들은 과테말라의 칸쿤에서 고대 마야인에 의해 지어진 가장 크고 중요한 궁전들 중 하나의 잔해를 발견했다. 그것은 약 1,300년 전에 지어졌다. 정글 식물들은 수백 년 동안 그 잔해들을 뒤덮었고, 그 지역은 정글에 의해 뒤덮인 큰 언덕처럼 보인다. 그 궁전은 11개의 공지 주위에 지어진 170개의 방들을 가지고 있다. 그 잔해의 발견은 마야인들의 정치적 삶에 대한 역사가들의 이해를 확실히 증가시킬 것인데, 그들(마야인들)은 천 년도 더 이전에 중앙 아메리카와 멕시코에서 권력의 절정에 있었다. 새로 발견된 궁전 벽들에 쓰여진 문구는 그것이 Tah ak Chaan 왕에 의해 지어졌음을 말하는데, 그는 서기 740년부터 시작해 약 50년간 칸쿤을 지배했었다.

① 가장 크고 중요한 궁전들 중의 하나는 약 1,300년 전에 지어졌다.
② 그 지역은 정글로 뒤덮인 큰 언덕처럼 보인다.
③ 그 궁전은 7세기에 마야 왕에 의해 지어졌다.
④ 마야 민족은 중앙 아메리카와 멕시코에서 권력의 절정에 있었다.

해설 지문 마지막에서 그 궁전이 서기 740년부터 대략 50년간 (740~790 A.D.) 칸쿤을 지배한 마야 왕인 Tah ak Chaan에 의해 지어졌다고 했는데, 서기 700년대는 8세기이므로 그 궁전이 7세기에 마야 왕에 의해 지어졌다는 것은 지문의 내용과 다르다. 따라서 ③번이 정답이다.

어휘 ruin 잔해, 유적 palace 궁전 ancient 고대의, 아주 오래된
hill 언덕 open area 공지(空地)
at the height of ~의 절정에 있는 rule 지배하다

해석 수돗물을 규제하는 35년 된 연방법은 너무 시대에 뒤떨어져서, 미국인들이 마시는 물이 과학자들이 말하는 심각한 건강상의 위험을 지닐 수 있음에도 여전히 합법적이다. 91가지의 오염 물질들만이 안전한 식수 법안에 의해 규제되고, 환경 보호 단체의 추정에 따르면 아직 60,000가지 이상의 화학 물질들이 미국에서 소비된다. 뉴욕 타임즈의 정부 기록에 대한 분석에 따르면, 정부와 독자적인 과학자들은 최근 수십 년간 수천 가지의 그러한 화학 물질들을 면밀히 조사했고, 암과 다른 질병들의 위험성과 관련된 수백 가지를 식수에서 적은 농도로 확인했다.

해설 ② 부사절 접속사 문맥상 '연방법이 너무 시대에 뒤떨어져서 건강상의 위험을 지닐 수 있다'라는 의미가 되어야 자연스러운데, '너무 ~해서 -하다'는 부사절 접속사 'so ~ that'을 써서 나타낼 수 있으므로 관계대명사 which를 부사절 접속사 that으로 고쳐야 한다.

오답
분석 ① 수량 표현 '수사(35) + 하이픈(-) + 단위 표현(year-old)'이 명사(federal law)를 수식하는 경우, 단위 표현은 반드시 단수형이 되어야 하므로 35-year-old가 올바르게 쓰였다.
③ 능동태·수동태 구별 동사 are used 뒤에 목적어가 없고, 주어(chemicals)와 동사가 '화학 물질들이 소비되다'라는 의미의 수동 관계이므로 수동태 are used가 올바르게 쓰였다.
④ 지시대명사 지시형용사 those는 복수 명사 앞에 쓰이므로 복수 명사 chemicals 앞에 지시형용사 those가 올바르게 쓰였다.

어휘 federal law 연방법 regulate 규제하다 tap water 수돗물
pose 지니다, 제기하다 legal 합법적인 contaminant 오염 물질
Act 법안, 조례 estimate 추정; 추정하다
scrutinize 면밀히 조사하다 associated with ~과 관련된
concentration 농도

👍 이것도 알면 **합격!**

지시형용사 this/that은 가산 단수 명사와 불가산 명사 앞에, these/those는 가산 복수 명사 앞에 쓰여 '이 ~', '저 ~'의 의미를 갖는다는 것을 알아두자.
(ex) This bag is mine. 이 가방은 내 것이다.
Those bags are mine. 저 가방들은 내 것이다.

끊어읽기 해석

If solar energy can be produced cheaply, / it will benefit / both the environment and the world's economies.
만약 태양 에너지가 저렴하게 생산될 수 있다면 / 그것은 이로울 것이다 / 환경과 세계 경제 모두에

At this time / a major economic obstacle for poorer nations / is the cost of electricity.
이 시기에 / 가난한 나라들의 주된 경제적 방해물은 / 전기료이다

It is impossible / to run factories and communications systems / without electric power.
불가능하다 / 공장들과 통신 시스템을 운영하는 것은 / 전력 없이

So when poor nations try / to build up their economies, / they are forced to use / the cheapest fossil fuels available, / and this can cause / environmental and health problems.
그래서 가난한 나라들이 노력할 때 / 그들의 경제를 개발하려고 / 그들은 사용하도록 강요된다 / 이용 가능한 가장 저렴한 화석 연료를 / 그리고 이것은 야기할 수 있다 / 환경적, 건강적 문제를

The prospect of cheap and clean solar electricity means / that economic development around the world / will not <u>create environmental disasters</u>.
저렴하고 깨끗한 태양 전기에 대한 전망은 의미한다 / 세계 전반의 경제 개발이 / 환경적 재앙을 만들어내지 않을 것임을

Some people think / large-scale use of solar energy / is a kind of fantasy, / but / many great inventions in history, / including the airplane, / seemed impossible initially.
어떤 사람들은 생각한다 / 태양 에너지의 광범위한 사용이 / 환상같은 것이라고 / 하지만 / 역사 속의 많은 훌륭한 발명들은 / 비행기를 포함한 / 처음에 불가능하게 보였다

해석 만약 태양 에너지가 저렴하게 생산될 수 있다면, 그것은 환경과 세계 경제 모두에 이로울 것이다. 이 시기에 가난한 나라들의 주된 경제적 방해물은 전기료이다. 전력 없이 공장들과 통신 시스템을 운영하는 것은 불가능하다. 그래서 가난한 나라들이 그들의 경제를 개발하려고 노력할 때, 그들은 이용 가능한 가장 저렴한 화석 연료를 사용하도록 강요되는데, 이것은 환경적, 건강적 문제를 야기할 수 있다. 저렴하고 깨끗한 태양 전기에 대한 전망은 세계 전반의 경제 개발이 환경적 재앙을 만들어내지 않을 것임을 의미한다. 어떤 사람들은 태양 에너지의 광범위한 사용이 환상 같은 것이라고 생각하지만, 비행기를 포함한 역사 속의 많은 훌륭한 발명들은 처음에 불가능하게 보였다.

① 어떠한 장애물 없이 계속된다
② 환경 친화적인 정책을 보장한다
③ 환경적 재앙을 만들어낸다
④ 냉난방 시스템에 영향을 미친다

해설 지문 처음에 태양 에너지가 저렴하게 생산될 수 있다면 환경과 세계 경제 모두에 도움이 될 것이라는 내용이 있고, 지문 중간에 가난한 나라들은 경제 개발에 가장 저렴한 화석 연료를 사용하도록 강요되는데, 이것이 환경 문제를 유발할 수 있다는 내용이 있다. 따라서 저렴하고 깨끗한 태양 전기에 대한 전망은 세계 전반의 경제 개발이 '환경적 재앙을 만들어내지' 않을 것임을 의미한다고 한 ③번이 정답이다.

어휘 **solar energy** 태양 에너지 **obstacle** 방해물, 장애물 **build up** 개발하다 **fossil fuel** 화석 연료 **prospect** 전망 **large-scale** 광범위한 **initially** 처음에 **barrier** 장애물, 장벽 **eco-friendly** 환경 친화적인

07 독해 논리적 흐름 파악 (문단 순서 배열) 난이도 ★★☆

끊어읽기 해석

Defying the Odds at Craig's Records
Craig's Records 사(社)가 예상을 꺾다

Craig's Records has experienced remarkable growth / over the last few years, / having opened an additional ten stores / across the country / in the last five years.
Craig's Records 사는 놀라운 성장을 경험했다 / 지난 몇 년간 / 추가적인 10곳의 가게들을 열면서 / 전국에 / 지난 5년간

When Craig Milligan, the owner of the chain was asked / what the secret of his success was,
그 체인의 소유주인 Craig Milligan이 질문을 받았을 때 / 그의 성공의 비밀이 무엇인지

(A) From the beginning, / he wanted to restore / the feeling of a neighborhood record store / where people could enjoy / spending countless hours.
처음부터 / 그는 되찾기를 원했다 / 이웃 음반가게의 느낌을 / 사람들이 즐길 수 있었던 / 수많은 시간을 보내며

(B) he responded / that it was probably the atmosphere of the store.
그는 대답했다 / 그것은 아마 그 가게의 분위기였을 거라고

(C) That was why / when he expanded nationwide / he kept the same design / at every new location.
그것은 이유였다 / 그가 전국적으로 (체인점들을) 확장했을 때 / 같은 디자인을 유지했던 / 모든 새로운 장소에서

A tiny store / where the staff could get to know / all the customers and their music preferences.
작은 가게 / 직원이 알게 될 수 있는 / 모든 손님들과 그들의 음악 선호도를

The formula seems to have paid off for him / as profits have increased 45% / this year alone.
그에게 그 공식은 성공한 것처럼 보인다 / 이윤이 45퍼센트 증가하면서 / 올해에만

해석
Craig's Records 사(社)가 예상을 꺾다
Craig's Records 사는 지난 5년간 전국에 추가적인 10곳의 가게들을 열면서, 지난 몇 년간 놀라운 성장을 경험했다. 그 체인의 소유주인 Craig Milligan이 그의 성공의 비밀이 무엇인지 질문을 받았을 때,

(B) 그는 그것은 아마 그 가게의 분위기였을 거라고 대답했다.
(A) 처음부터, 그는 사람들이 수많은 시간을 보내며 즐길 수 있었던 이웃 음반가게의 느낌을 되찾기를 원했다.
(C) 그것은 그가 전국적으로 (체인점들을) 확장했을 때, 모든 새로운 장소에서 같은 디자인을 유지했던 이유였다. 직원이 모든 손님들과 그들의 음악 선호도를 알게 될 수 있는 작은 가게. 이윤이 올해에만 45퍼센트 증가하면서 그에게 그 공식은 성공한 것처럼 보인다.

해설 주어진 문장에서 Craig's Records가 지난 몇 년간 놀라운 성장을 경험했다고 했고, 그 체인점의 주인인 Craig Milligan이 그의 성공의 비밀에 대해 질문 받았다고 하며 문장이 완료되지 않았음을 알 수 있다. 따라서, 주어진 문장 뒤에는 콤마(,) 뒤에 연결될 수 있도록 소문자(he)로 시작하며 그 성공의 비결이 가게의 분위기라고 대답했다는 내용의 (B)가 와야 한다. 이어서 (A)에서 처음부터 그가 이웃 음반가게의 느낌을 되찾기를 원했었다고 하며 창업 배경을 언급한 뒤, (C)에서 그것(That)이 그가 모든 가게에서 같은 디자인을 유지했던 이유라고 설명하고 있다. 따라서 ④ (B) – (A) – (C)가 정답이다.

어휘 **defy** 꺾다, 저항하다 **odds** 예상, 가능성 **remarkable** 놀라운 **restore** 되찾다 **countless** 수많은 **atmosphere** 분위기, 공기 **preference** 선호도, 애호 **pay off** 성공하다, 성과를 올리다

08 독해 논리적 흐름 파악 (문맥상 적절한 어휘) 난이도 ★★☆

끊어읽기 해석

The tsunami of December 2004 / resulted in a severe loss of life and property / along coastal Tamil Nadu / in southern India.
2004년 12월의 쓰나미는 / 심각한 생명과 재산의 손실을 초래했다 / Tamil Nadu 해안을 따라 / 인도 남부의

For 15 years now, / residents of that district have been trying / to persuade coastal communities / not to destroy / the mangrove forests along the coast.
15년째 / 그 지역의 거주자들은 애써왔다 / 해안 공동체를 설득하기 위해 / 파괴하지 않도록 / 해안을 따라 있는 맹그로브 숲을

But / the coastal people's preoccupation / with their livelihood / did not allow them to (A) <u>heed</u> that request.

하지만 / 해안 사람들의 집착은 / 그들의 생계에 대한 / 그들이 그 요구에 (A) <u>주의를 기울이도록</u> 하지 않았다

The tsunami miraculously changed / their outlook.
쓰나미는 기적적으로 바꾸었다 / 그들의 견해를

Villages (B) <u>adjoining</u> thick mangrove forests / were saved / from the fury of the tsunami / because of the wave breaking role / played by the mangroves.
울창한 맹그로브 숲에 (B) 인접한 마을들은 / 구해졌다 / 쓰나미의 격렬함으로부터 / 방파 역할 때문에 / 맹그로브에 의해 수행된

But / in nearby villages, / where mangroves had been (C) <u>destroyed</u> / either for fuel wood or to create fish ponds, / several hundred fishermen died.
하지만 / 인근의 마을들에서는 / 맹그로브가 (C) 파괴되었던 / 장작 또는 양어장을 만들기 위한 목적으로 / 수백 명의 어부들이 죽었다

해석 2004년 12월의 쓰나미는 인도 남부의 Tamil Nadu 해안을 따라 심각한 생명과 재산의 손실을 초래했다. 15년째, 그 지역의 거주자들은 해안을 따라 있는 맹그로브 숲을 파괴하지 않도록 해안 공동체를 설득하기 위해 애써왔다. 하지만, 그들의 생계에 대한 해안 사람들의 집착은 그들이 그 요구에 (A) 주의를 기울이도록 하지 않았다. 쓰나미는 기적적으로 그들의 견해를 바꾸었다. 울창한 맹그로브 숲에 (B) 인접한 마을들은 맹그로브에 의해 수행된 방파 역할 때문에 쓰나미의 격렬함으로부터 구해졌다. 하지만 장작 또는 양어장을 만들기 위한 목적으로 맹그로브가 (C) 파괴되었던 인근의 마을들에서는 수백 명의 어부들이 죽었다.

	(A)	(B)	(C)
①	무시하다	인접한	보존되었던
②	주의를 기울이다	인접한	파괴되었던
③	주의를 기울이다	결합한	보존되었던
④	무시하다	결합한	파괴되었던

해설 (A) 지문 앞부분에 지역 거주자들이 맹그로브 숲을 파괴하지 않도록 해안 공동체를 설득하는 데 애써왔다는 내용이 있고, 빈칸이 있는 문장에 연결어 But(하지만)이 왔으므로 '하지만 그들의 생계에 대한 해안 사람들의 집착은 그들이 그 요구에 주의를 기울이게(heed) 하지 않았다'는 내용이 들어가야 적절하다. (B) 빈칸이 있는 문장에서 맹그로브의 방파 역할 때문에 쓰나미의 격렬함으로부터 구해졌다고 했으므로 '울창한 맹그로브 숲에 인접한(adjoining) 마을들'이라는 내용이 들어가야 적절하다. (C) 빈칸 앞에서 울창한 맹그로브 숲에 인접한 마을들은 쓰나미로부터 구해졌다고 했고, 빈칸이 있는 문장에서는 하지만(But) 인근 마을들에서는 수백 명의 어부들이 죽었다고 했으므로 '맹그로브가 장작 또는 양어장을 만들기 위한 목적으로 파괴되었던(destroyed) 인근의 마을들'이라는 내용이 들어가야 적절하다.
따라서 ② (A) heed(주의를 기울이다) – (B) adjoining(인접한) – (C) destroyed(파괴되었던)가 정답이다.

어휘 property 재산, 소유물 coastal 해안의, 연안의
resident 거주자, 주민 district 지역, 구역
preoccupation with ~에 대한 집착, 몰두 livelihood 생계
miraculously 기적적으로 outlook 견해, 전망
wave breaking 방파, 쇄파 fuel wood 장작, 땔나무
fish pond 양어장 heed 주의를 기울이다 adjoin 인접하다
conserve 보존하다, 아끼다 conjoin 결합하다

09 독해 추론 (빈칸 완성 - 단어) 난이도 ★★☆

끊어읽기 해석

In fluid dynamics, / Bernoulli's principle states / that for an inviscid flow, / an increase in the speed of the fluid / occurs simultaneously / with a decrease in pressure / or a decrease in the fluid's potential energy.
유체 역학에서 / 베르누이의 법칙은 명시한다 / 비점성의 흐름에서 / 유체 속도의 증가는 / 동시에 일어난다고 / 압력의 감소와 함께 / 또는 유체의 위치 에너지의 감소와 함께

Bernouilli's principle also tells us / why windows tend to explode, / rather than implode / in hurricanes: / the very high speed of the air / just outside the window / causes the pressure just outside to be much less / than the pressure inside, / where the air is still.
베르누이의 법칙은 또한 우리에게 알려준다 / 왜 창문이 바깥쪽으로 폭발하는 경향이 있는지 / 안쪽으로 폭발하기보다 / 허리케인이 올 때 / 매우 빠른 공기의 속도는 / 창문 바로 밖의 / 바로 밖의 압력을 훨씬 더 낮게 만든다 / 안쪽의 압력보다 / 공기가 움직이지 않는

The difference in force / pushes the windows <u>outward</u>, / and hence explode.
압력의 차이가 / 창문을 <u>바깥쪽으로</u> 민다 / 그리고 이런 이유로 폭발한다

If you know / that a hurricane is coming / it is therefore better to open / as many windows as possible, / to equalize the pressure inside and out.
만약 당신이 안다면 / 허리케인이 오고 있다는 것을 / 그러므로 여는 것이 낫다 / 가능한 한 많은 창문을 / 안과 밖의 압력을 같게 하기 위하여

해석 유체 역학에서 베르누이의 법칙은 비점성의 흐름에서 유체 속도의 증가는 압력의 감소 또는 유체의 위치 에너지의 감소와 함께 동시에 일어난다고 명시한다. 베르누이의 법칙은 또한 왜 허리케인이 올 때 창문이 안쪽으로 폭발하기보다 바깥쪽으로 폭발하는 경향이 있는지 우리에게 알려주는데, 창문 바로 밖의 매우 빠른 공기의 속도는 공기가 움직이지 않는 안쪽의 압력보다 바로 밖의 압력을 훨씬 더 낮게 만든다. 압력의 차이가 창문을 바깥쪽으로 밀고, 이런 이유로 바깥쪽으로 폭발한다. 만약 당신이 허리케인이 오고 있다는 것을 안다면, 그러므로 안과 밖의 압력을 같게 하기 위하여 가능한 한 많은 창문을 여는 것이 낫다.

① 스스로 ② 아래쪽
③ 안쪽으로 ④ 바깥쪽으로

해설 지문 중간에서 허리케인이 올 때 창문은 바깥쪽으로 폭발하는 경향이 있는데, 이것은 창문 안쪽과 바깥쪽의 압력이 다르기 때문이며 창문 안쪽보다 바깥쪽의 압력이 훨씬 더 낮다는 내용이 있으므로, 압력의 차이가 창문을 '바깥쪽으로' 민다고 한 ④번이 정답이다.

어휘 fluid dynamics 유체 역학 state 명시하다, 진술하다
inviscid 비점성의 fluid 유체, 유동체
simultaneously 동시에, 일제히 potential energy 위치 에너지
explode (바깥쪽으로) 폭파하다 implode (안쪽으로) 폭파하다
hurricane 허리케인 still 움직이지 않는, 고요한
hence 이런 이유로 equalize 같게 하다, 동등하게 하다

10 독해 세부내용 파악 (특정 정보 파악) 난이도 ★★☆

끊어읽기 해석

CLOSED BY COURT ORDER
법원 명령으로 인해 폐쇄되다

This building has been closed and sealed / by the Sheriff pursuant to an Order / issued by Judge B. R. O'Reilly, / 3rd

District Magistrate's Court, / and may not be entered into, / demolished, or materially altered / in any manner.
이 건물은 폐쇄되고 봉쇄되었다 / 명령에 따른 보안관에 의해 / 판사 B. R. O'Reilly에 의해 내려진 / 제3지구 치안 판사 법원의 / 따라서 출입이 안 되고 / 철거되거나 실질적으로 변경되어서도 안 된다 / 어떤 식으로든

Violation may result in severe criminal penalties / including fine and imprisonment.
위반은 심각한 형사 처벌을 낳을 것이다 / 벌금과 구속을 포함한

This order shall stand and be effective / until removed / by Order of the same Court.
이 명령은 지속되고 유효할 것이다 / 해제될 때까지 / 같은 법정의 명령에 의해

Such a removal Order will be issued / only upon presentation to the Court / of Proof of Payment / of the amount of Seven Thousand Three Hundred and Twenty Four Dollars ($7,324) in property tax arrears / by the deeded owner of the property, / Peter Paltram Holdings Inc., / or its representative.
그러한 해제 명령이 내려질 수 있다 / 법원에 제출될 시에만 / 납세 증명이 / 재산세 체납금 7,324달러에 대한 / 그 부동산의 소유권이 증명된 소유주에 의해 / Peter Paltram Holdings 주식회사인 / 혹은 그 대리인들에 의해

In the event that such payment is not made / within Ninety (90) days of the posting of this Order, / the property may be seized / by the City of Hamston / and sold at auction / with any proceeds in excess of the stated tax arrears / (plus any costs of sale) / being remitted to the deeded owner.
그러한 납세가 이루어지지 않을 경우 / 이 명령을 게재한 후 90일 이내에 / 그 부동산은 압류될 수도 있다 / Hamston시에 의해 / 그리고 경매에서 팔릴 수도 있다 / 명시된 세금 체납금을 초과한 수익금이 / (어떤 매각 비용도 포함해서) / 양도된 주인에게 송금되며

해석 법원 명령은 언제 해제될 것인가?

법원 명령으로 인해 폐쇄되다
이 건물은 제3지구 치안 판사 법원의 판사 B. R. O'Reilly에 의해 내려진 명령에 따른 보안관에 의해 폐쇄되고 봉쇄되었으며, 따라서 출입이 안 되고, 철거되거나 어떤 식으로든 실질적으로 변경되어서도 안 된다. 위반은 벌금과 구속을 포함한 심각한 형사 처벌을 낳을 것이다. 이 명령은 같은 법정의 명령에 의해 해제될 때까지 지속되고 유효할 것이다. Peter Paltram Holdings 주식회사인 그 부동산의 소유권이 증명된 소유주 혹은 그 대리인들에 의해 재산세 체납금 7,324달러에 대한 납세 증명이 법원에 제출될 시에만 그러한 해제 명령이 내려질 수 있다. 그러한 납세가 이루어지지 않을 경우 이 명령을 게재한 후 90일 이내에 그 부동산은 Hamston시에 의해 압류될 수도 있고, 명시된 세금 체납액을 초과한 수익금이(어떤 매각 비용도 포함해서) 양도된 주인에게 송금되며 경매에서 팔릴 수도 있다.

① 90일 이내에
② 세금이 지불될 때
③ 판매 비용이 지불된 후에
④ 건물 소유주가 벌금에 처해진 후에

해설 지문 중간에서 부동산 소유주 혹은 대리인이 재산세 체납금 지불 증명을 법원에 제출했을 시에만 법적 처벌에 대한 해제 명령이 내려질 수 있다는 내용이 있다. 따라서 법원 명령이 '세금이 지불될 때' 해제된다고 표현한 ②번이 정답이다.

어휘 court order 법원 명령 seal 봉쇄하다 sheriff 보안관
pursuant to ~에 따른 judge 판사 demolish 철거하다
materially 실질적으로 alter 변경하다 violation 위반
penalty 처벌, 형벌 fine 벌금 imprisonment 구속
arrear 체납금 representative 대리인, 대표 seize 압류하다

---

auction 경매; 경매로 팔다 proceeds 수익금
cost of sale 매각 비용 remit 송금하다

11 독해 추론 (빈칸 완성 - 구) 난이도 ★☆☆

끊어읽기 해석

Everyday life in the British colonies of North America / may now seem to have been glamorous, / especially as reflected in antique shops.
북아메리카 영국 식민지의 일상은 / 지금은 아마 화려했던 것으로 보일지도 모른다 / 특히 골동품 상점들에서 비춰지는 것처럼

But judged by modern standards, / it was quite a(n) miserable existence.
하지만 현대의 기준에 의해 판단하면 / 그것은 꽤 비참한 생활이었다

For most people, / the labor was heavy / and constant from daybreak to nightfall. // Basic comforts / now taken for granted / were lacking.
대부분의 사람들에게 / 노동은 가혹했다 / 그리고 새벽부터 해질녘까지 계속되었다 // 기본적인 편의 시설이 / 지금은 당연하게 여겨지는 / 부족했다

Public buildings were often / not heated at all. // Drafty homes were heated / only by inefficient fireplaces.
공공건물은 흔히 / 난방이 전혀 되지 않았다 // 외풍이 있는 집들은 난방되었다 / 비효율적인 벽난로에 의해서만

There was no running water or indoor plumbing. // The flickering light of candles and whale oil lamps / provided inadequate illumination.
수돗물이나 실내 배관이 없었다 // 초와 경유 램프의 깜박거리는 빛만이 / 불충분한 빛을 제공했다

There was no sanitation service / to dispose of garbage; / instead, / long-snouted hogs were allowed / to roam the streets, consuming refuse.
위생 관리 서비스도 없었다 / 쓰레기를 처리할 / 대신 / 긴 주둥이가 달린 돼지가 허용되었다 / 쓰레기를 먹으며 거리를 돌아다니도록

해석 북아메리카 영국 식민지의 일상은 특히 골동품 상점들에서 비춰지는 것처럼 지금은 아마 화려했던 것으로 보일지도 모른다. 하지만 현대의 기준에 의해 판단하면, 그것은 꽤 비참한 생활이었다. 대부분의 사람들에게 노동은 가혹했고 새벽부터 해질녘까지 계속되었다. 지금은 당연하게 여겨지는 기본적인 편의 시설이 부족했다. 공공건물은 흔히 난방이 전혀 되지 않았다. 외풍이 있는 집들은 비효율적인 벽난로에 의해서만 난방되었다. 수돗물이나 실내 배관이 없었다. 초와 경유 램프의 깜박거리는 빛만이 불충분한 빛을 제공했다. 쓰레기를 처리할 위생 관리 서비스도 없었으며, 대신, 긴 주둥이가 달린 돼지가 쓰레기를 먹으며 거리를 돌아다니도록 허용되었다

① 구식의 스타일   ② 기발한 생활
③ 완벽한 삶의 방식   ④ 비참한 생활

해설 빈칸이 있는 문장을 통해 빈칸에 북아메리카 영국 식민지의 일상 생활이 현대의 기준에 의해 어떻게 보이는지에 대한 내용이 나와야 적절하다는 것을 알 수 있다. 빈칸 뒤에서 대부분의 사람들에게 가혹했던 노동과 기본적인 편의 시설의 부족 등을 예로 들어 북아메리카 영국 식민지의 일상 생활이 열악했음을 보여주는 내용이 있으므로, 현대의 기준에 의해 판단하면 그것은 꽤 '비참한 생활'이었다고 한 ④번이 정답이다.

어휘 glamorous 화려한 reflect 비추다 antique 골동품; 고풍스런
judge 판단하다 standard 기준 heavy 가혹한
constant 계속되는, 지속되는 daybreak 새벽 nightfall 해질녘
take for granted ~을 당연하게 여기다 drafty 외풍이 있는

fireplace 벽난로 running water 수돗물 plumbing 배관
flickering 깜박거리는 whale oil 경유
inadequate 불충분한, 부족한 illumination 빛, 조명
sanitation 위생 관리 dispose of ~을 처리하다, 처분하다
long-snouted 긴 주둥이가 달린 hog 돼지
roam 돌아다니다, 배회하다 consume 먹다, 소비하다
refuse 쓰레기 outdated 구식의 ingenious 기발한, 독창적인
miserable 비참한, 우울한 existence 생활, 현존

---

12 독해 추론 (빈칸 완성 - 단어) 난이도 ★★★

끊어읽기 해석

> Mount Everest is legendary. // Massive snow and ice avalanches / are a constant threat / to all expeditions, / sometimes burying / valleys, glaciers, and climbing routes.
> 에베레스트 산은 전설적이다. // 거대한 눈과 얼음 사태들은 / 끊임없는 위협이다 / 모든 탐험대들에게 / 때때로 뒤덮으며 / 계곡, 빙하 그리고 등산로를
>
> Hurricane-force winds are / a well-known hazard on Everest, / and many people have been killed / when their tents were ripped to shreds / by the gales.
> 허리케인급의 바람들은 / 에베레스트에서 잘 알려진 위험 요소이다 / 그리고 많은 사람들이 사망했다 / 그들의 텐트가 갈기갈기 찢겨서 조각났을 때 / 강풍에 의해
>
> Hypothermia, / the dramatic loss of body heat, / is also a major and debilitating problem / in this region of high winds and low temperatures.
> 저체온증은 / 체온의 급격한 손실인 / 주요하고 쇠약하게 하는 문제이다 / 이 강풍과 저온의 지역에서

해석 에베레스트 산은 전설적이다. 거대한 눈과 얼음 사태들은 때때로 계곡, 빙하 그리고 등산로를 뒤덮으며 모든 탐험대들에게 끊임없는 위협이다. 허리케인급의 바람들은 에베레스트에서 살 알려진 위험 요소이고, 그들의 텐트가 강풍에 의해 갈기갈기 찢겨서 조각났을 때 많은 사람들이 사망했다. 체온의 급격한 손실인 저체온증은 이 강풍과 저온의 지역에서 주요하고 쇠약하게 하는 문제이다.

① 저체온증   ② 고체온증
③ 비대증   ④ 신경 쇠약

해설 빈칸이 있는 문장을 통해 빈칸에 체온의 급격한 손실을 지칭하는 단어가 나와야 적절하다는 것을 알 수 있다. 따라서 이를 '저체온증'이라고 한 ①번이 정답이다.

어휘 legendary 전설적인 ice avalanche 얼음 사태
expedition 탐험(대) gale 강풍 debilitating 쇠약하게 하는
hypothermia 저체온증 hyperthermia 고체온증
hypertrophy 비대(증)

---

13 문법 관계절 난이도 ★★☆

해석 아사히 맥주 회사는 환경 단체들의 반대에 따라 플라스틱 병에 든 맥주를 팔겠다는 그것의 계획을 취소했다. 아사히는 편리함과 스타일에 가치를 두는 젊은 소비자들을 위한 음료를 홍보하겠다는 그들의 전략의 일부로서 일본의 첫 번째 플라스틱 맥주 용기를 출시하는 것을 계획했었다. 하지만 일본 그린피스는 플라스틱 병의 도입이 폐기물 처리 문제를 만들 것이라고 주장하면서 그 계획에 반대하는 캠페인을 이끌었다. 그린피스는 맥주 산업이 현재 사용되는 유리병을 고수해야 한다고 말했는데, 그것을 위해 재활용 시스템은 존재한다.

해설 (A) 관계대명사 선행사 younger consumers가 사람이고 관계절 내에서 동사 value의 주어 역할을 하므로 사람을 가리키는 주격 관계대명사 who를 써야 한다.
(B) 전치사 + 관계대명사 '전치사 + 관계대명사'에서 전치사는 선행사 또는 관계절의 동사에 따라 결정되는데, 관계절의 동사 exist는 전치사 for와 짝을 이루어 '~을 위해 존재하다'라는 의미를 나타내므로 for which를 써야 한다.
따라서 ④ (A) who – (B) for which가 정답이다.

어휘 brewery 맥주 회사[공장] objection 반대, 이의 launch 출시하다
Greenpeace 그린피스(국제 환경 보호 단체) claim 주장하다
waste disposal 폐기물 처리 stick to ~을 고수하다
recycling 재활용

👍 이것도 알면 **합격!**

'전치사 + 관계대명사'에서 전치사는 선행사 또는 관계절의 동사에 따라 결정되며, 그 뒤에는 완전한 절이 온다는 것을 알아두자.

(ex) The staff brought the items **for which** the customer was looking.
직원은 손님이 찾고 있었던 물품들을 가져왔다.

---

14 독해 추론 (빈칸 완성 - 단어) 난이도 ★★☆

끊어읽기 해석

> As more women gain / the work experience and education / necessary to qualify for leadership positions, / the supply of capable women leaders grows.
> 더 많은 여성들이 얻을수록 / 직업 경험과 교육을 / 지도자 지위의 자격을 얻는 데 필요한 / 능력 있는 여성 지도자의 공급이 늘어난다
>
> Organizations are subsequently called on / to reestablish and expand their notions / of what constitutes effective leadership / as it relates / to gender stereotype, and role expectations.
> 그 뒤에 조직들은 할 필요가 있다 / 그들의 개념을 재정립하고 확장하는 것을 / 효과적인 리더십을 구성하는 것이 무엇인가에 관한 / 그것이 관련 있기 때문이다 / 성 고정관념과 역할 기대와
>
> If traditional perspectives of leadership / center on masculine-oriented concepts / of authoritarian and task-oriented behavior, / then these same perspectives may contribute / to a 'glass ceiling' / prohibiting relationship-oriented (i.e. feminine) leadership behaviors / from being integrated into organization management structures.
> 만약 전통적인 리더십에 대한 관점이 / 남성 중심적 개념들에 초점을 맞춘다면 / 권위주의적이고 과업지향적인 행동의 / 그러면 이같은 관점들은 기여할지도 모른다 / '유리 천장'에 / 관계 중심적인(즉 여성적인) 리더십 행동들이 하지 못하게 하는 / 조직 관리 구조로 통합되는 것을

해석 더 많은 여성들이 지도자 지위의 자격을 얻는 데 필요한 직업 경험과 교육을 얻을수록 능력 있는 여성 지도자의 공급이 늘어난다. 그것이 성 고정관념과 역할 기대와 관련 있기 때문에, 그 뒤에 조직들은 효과적인 리더십을 구성하는 것이 무엇인가에 관한 그들의 개념을 재정립하고 확장하는 것을 할 필요가 있다. 만약 전통적인 리더십에 대한 관점이 권위주의적이고 과업지향적인 행동의 남성 중심적 개념들에 초점을 맞춘다면, 이 똑같은 관점들은 관계 중심적인(즉 여성적인) 리더십 행동들이 조직 관리 구조로 통합되는 것을 하지 못하게 하는 '유리 천장'에 기여할지도 모른다.

① 과업지향적인 리더십
② 유리 천장
③ 고속 성장
④ 여성적 행동

해설 빈칸이 있는 문장을 통해 빈칸에 남성 중심적 개념들에 초점을 맞춘 전통적인 리더십이 무엇에 기여하는지에 대한 내용이 나와야 한다는 것을 알 수 있다. 빈칸 뒤에서 이것이 관계 중심적인(즉 여성적인) 리더십 행동들이 조직 관리 구조로 통합되지 못하게 한다는 내용이 있으므로, 전통적인 리더십에 대한 관점이 '유리 천장'(여성의 승진을 막는 눈에 보이지 않는 장벽)에 기여한다고 한 ②번이 정답이다.

어휘 **gain** 얻다　**subsequently** 그 뒤에, 이어서
be called on to do ~할 필요가 있다　**reestablish** 재정립하다
notion 개념　**constitute** 구성하다　**stereotype** 고정관념
perspective 관점, 시각　**center on** ~에 초점을 맞추다
masculine 남성의　**authoritarian** 권위주의적인
task-oriented 과업지향적인
prohibit A from B A가 B하지 못하게 하다
feminine 여성적인　**integrate** 통합하다
glass ceiling 유리 천장(여성의 승진을 막는 눈에 보이지 않는 장벽)

---

15 독해 논리적 흐름 파악 (문맥상 부적절한 어휘)　난이도 ★★☆

끊어읽기 해석

The pressure is almost as heavy / on students / who just want to graduate and get a job.
압박감은 역시 무겁다 / 학생들에게 / 단지 졸업을 하고 직장을 구하기를 원하는

Long gone are the days of the "gentleman's C," / when students ① journeyed through college / with a certain relaxation, / ② sampling a wide variety of courses / that would send them out / as liberally ③ educated men and women.
'gentleman's C'의 시대는 오래 전에 없어졌다 / 학생들이 대학을 ① 여행했던 때인 / 어느 정도의 여유를 가지고 / 다양한 종류의 강의들을 ② 맛보며 / 그들을 내보내는 / 자유로이 ③ 교육받은 남성과 여성으로

If I were an employer / I would rather employ / graduates who have this range and curiosity / than those who narrowly pursued / safe subjects and high grades.
만약 내가 고용주라면 / 나는 고용하겠다 / 이러한 다양성과 호기심을 가진 졸업생들을 / 편협하게 추구한 사람들보다 / 안전한 과목들과 높은 성적만을

I know countless students / whose inquiring minds ④ exhaust me.
나는 무수히 많은 학생들을 안다 / 그들의 탐구심이 나를 ④ 진이 빠지게 하는

I like to hear / the play of their ideas. // I don't know / if they are getting As or Cs, / and I don't care.
나는 듣기를 좋아한다 / 그들 생각의 반짝임을 // 나는 모른다 / 그들이 A 혹은 C를 받는지 / 그리고 신경 쓰지 않는다

해석 단지 졸업을 하고 직장을 구하기를 원하는 학생들에게 압박감은 역시 무겁다. 학생들이 그들을 자유로이 ③ 교육받은 남성과 여성으로 내보내는 다양한 종류의 강의들을 ② 맛보며 어느 정도의 여유를 가지고 대학을 ① 여행했던 때인 'gentlemen's C'의 시대는 오래 전에 없어졌다. 만약 내가 고용주라면, 나는 편협하게 안전한 과목들과 높은 성적만을 추구한 사람들보다 이러한 다양성과 호기심을 가진 졸업생들을 고용하겠다. 나는 탐구심이 나를 ④ 진이 빠지게 하는 무수히 많은 학생들을 안다. 나는 그들 생각의 반짝임을 듣기를 좋아한다. 나는 그들이 A 혹은 C를 받는지 모르고, 신경 쓰지 않는다.

① 여행하다　② 맛보다
③ 교육받다　④ 진이 빠지게 하다

해설 ④번 앞 문장에 내(I)가 고용주라면 편협하게 안전한 과목과 높은 성적만을 추구한 사람들보다 다양성과 호기심을 가진 사람들을 고용할 것이라고 말하는 내용이 있으므로, 그들의 탐구심이 나를 '진이 빠지게 한다'(exhaust)는 것은 문맥상 적절하지 않다. 따라서 ④ exhaust가 정답이다. 참고로, 주어진 exhaust를 대신할 수 있는 어휘로는 '지지하다'라는 의미의 support, endorse, assist 등이 있다.

어휘 **pressure** 압박감　**journey** 여행하다　**relaxation** 여유, 휴식
sample 맛보다　**liberally** 자유로이, 개방적으로　**range** 다양성
curiosity 호기심　**narrowly** 편협하게, 간신히　**pursue** 추구하다
countless 무수히 많은　**inquiring mind** 탐구심
exhaust 진이 빠지게 하다　**play** 반짝임, 놀이

---

16 독해 논리적 흐름 파악 (문장 삽입)　난이도 ★☆☆

끊어읽기 해석

But nothing seems to work.
하지만 아무것도 효과가 있는 것 같지 않다.

Korean police have a very hard time / trying to control the situation.
한국 경찰은 매우 힘든 시간을 보낸다 / 그 상황을 제어하려고 노력하며

(　①　) They've tried everything / from policemen dummies / to hidden cameras to crackdowns.
그들은 모든 것을 시도했다 / 경찰 마네킹부터 / 몰래 카메라와 엄중 단속까지

(　②　) Drivers soon figure out / where the dummies are / and then just ignore them.
운전자들은 곧 알아낸다 / 어디에 마네킹이 있는지 / 그래서 그것들을 그저 무시한다

(　③　) They memorize / where the cameras are hidden, / so they slow down / before they get to them / and speed up again / as soon as they pass.
그들은 기억한다 / 어디에 카메라가 숨겨져 있는지 / 그래서 그들은 속도를 늦춘다 / 그들이 그것들에 도착하기 전에 / 그리곤 다시 속도를 높인다 / 그들이 (카메라를) 지나치자마자

(　④　)

해석 한국 경찰은 그 상황을 제어하려고 노력하며 매우 힘든 시간을 보낸다. 그들은 경찰 마네킹부터 몰래 카메라와 엄중 단속까지 모든 것을 시도했다. ② 하지만 아무것도 효과가 있는 것 같지 않다. 운전자들은 곧 어디에 마네킹이 있는지 알아서 그것들을 그저 무시한다. 그들은 어디에 카메라가 숨겨져 있는지 기억해서 그들이 그것들에 도착하기 전에 속도를 늦추곤, (카메라를) 지나치자마자 다시 속도를 높인다.

해설 ②번 앞 문장에서 경찰들이 경찰 마네킹부터 몰래 카메라와 엄중 단속까지 모든 것을 시도했다고 했고, ②번 뒤 문장에서 그럼에도 불구하고 운전자들은 곧 어디에 마네킹이 있는지 알아내 무시한다고 했으므로, ②번 자리에 하지만(But) 앞서 언급된 시도들이 효과가 있는 것 같지 않다는 내용의 주어진 문장이 들어가야 글의 흐름이 자연스럽게 연결된다. 따라서 ②번이 정답이다.

어휘 **dummy** 마네킹, 모조품　**crackdown** 엄중 단속
figure out ~을 알아내다　**ignore** 무시하다

끊어읽기 해석

> Government authorities in the United States / have no control over / what is published.
> 미국의 정부 당국은 / 통제권을 가지고 있지 않다 / 무엇이 출판되는지에 대한
>
> The freedom has allowed the development / of a fiercely independent and diverse communications industry.
> 자유는 발전을 허락했다 / 치열하게 독립적이고 다양한 통신 산업의
>
> One result is / the press exerts more influence / in the United States / than any other country.
> 한 가지 결과는 / 언론이 더 많은 영향력을 행사한다는 것이다 / 미국에서 / 다른 어떤 나라보다
>
> Often this influence is / a force for reform, / uncovering shortcomings in society / and providing information / that people in powerful positions / are sometimes reluctant to divulge.
> 종종 이 영향은 / 개혁에 대한 힘이다 / 사회의 단점을 밝히는 / 그리고 정보를 제공하는 / 영향력 있는 지위의 사람들이 / 때때로 밝히기를 주저하는
>
> Anyone who does not want / his article to get censored / must then start / his or her own newspaper.
> 원하지 않는 사람은 누구나 / 그의 기사가 검열되는 것을 / 그러면 시작해야 한다 / 그 자신의 신문을
>
> ① Many people argue / that censoring is unconstitutional / and an infringement / on the right of press.
> 많은 사람들은 주장한다 / 검열이 헌법에 위배된다고 / 그리고 침해라고 / 언론의 자유에 대한
>
> ② Another result, / however, / is a tendency to ignore, / as much as possible, / the occasional errors, excesses and lapses in fairness / by the press itself.
> 다른 결과는 / 하지만 / 무시하는 경향이다 / 되도록 / 공정함에 있어서의 가끔의 오류들, 과잉, 과실들을 / 언론 스스로에 의한
>
> ③ For many decades / attacks on specific flaws were regarded / as undermining the basic freedom of the press / —particularly when the attacks came from outside.
> 수십 년간 / 특정한 결함에 대한 공격들은 간주되었다 / 언론의 기본적 자유를 약화시키는 것으로 / 특히 그 공격이 외부에서 올 때
>
> ④ Inside, / the general practice was silence.
> 내부에서 / 일반적인 관행은 침묵이었다

해석 미국의 정부 당국은 무엇이 출판되는지에 대한 통제권을 가지고 있지 않다. 자유는 치열하게 독립적이고 다양한 통신 산업의 발전을 허락했다. 한 가지 결과는 다른 어떤 나라보다 미국에서 언론이 더 많은 영향력을 행사한다는 것이다. 종종 이 영향은 사회의 단점을 밝히고, 영향력 있는 지위의 사람들이 때때로 밝히기를 주저하는 정보를 제공하는 개혁에 대한 힘이다. 그의 기사가 검열되는 것을 원하지 않는 사람은 누구나 그 자신의 신문을 시작해야 한다. ① 많은 사람들은 검열이 헌법에 위배되고 언론의 자유에 대한 침해라고 주장한다. ② 하지만 다른 결과는 언론 스스로에 의한 공정함에 있어서의 가끔의 오류들, 과잉, 과실들을 되도록 무시하는 경향이다. ③ 수십 년간 특정한 결함에 대한 공격들은 특히 그 공격이 외부에서 올 때 언론의 기본적 자유를 약화시키는 것으로 간주되었다. ④ 내부에서, 일반적인 관행은 침묵이었다.

해설 지문 앞부분에서 미국에서의 언론의 자유와 그 힘에 대해서 언급하고, ②, ③, ④ 번에서 하지만(however) 언론이 자유를 보장하기 위해 외부의 공격을 차단하고 내부에서 침묵을 유지하는 등의 방법으로 스스로의 과실을 무시한다고 설명했다. 그러나 ①번은 검열이 언론의 자유에 대한 침해라고 주장한다는 내용으로, 언론이 내부의 과실에 대해 무시하는 것에 관한 내용과 관련이 없

다. 따라서 ①번이 정답이다.

어휘 authority 당국 publish 출판하다 fiercely 치열하게
press 언론, 신문 exert 행사하다 reform 개혁; 개혁하다
uncover 밝히다, 덮개를 벗기다 shortcoming 단점
reluctant to ~하기를 주저하다 divulge 밝히다
censor 검열하다 unconstitutional 헌법에 위배되는
infringement 침해 tendency 경향 occasional 가끔의
excess 과잉, 지나침 lapse 과실, 실수 flaw 결함, 흠
undermine 약화시키다 practice 관행, 실행

끊어읽기 해석

> Many birds pursue prey / by swimming under water, / but / none is so superbly adapted to the task / as the penguins.
> 많은 새들은 먹이를 쫓는다 / 물속에서 헤엄침으로써 / 하지만 / 그 일에 훌륭하게 적응된 것(새)은 없다 / 펭귄만큼
>
> **(A)** The entire anatomy of the penguin wing / has been modified / so that it is a stiff, oar-like flipper / like that of a dolphin.
> 펭귄 날개의 전체 구조는 / 바뀌어왔다 / 뻣뻣하고 노 같은 지느러미가 되기 위하여 / 돌고래의 것과 같은
>
> **(B)** Awkward on land, / penguins use their wings / for underwater propulsion / as efficiently / as other birds use wings for flying.
> 땅에선 불편하지만 / 펭귄은 그들의 날개를 사용한다 / 물속에서의 추진력을 위해서 / 효과적으로 / 다른 새들이 날기 위해서 날개를 사용하는 것만큼
>
> **(C)** Although all birds share / a generally similar body plan, / they vary greatly / in size and proportions, / being adapted to so many ways of life.
> 비록 모든 새들이 공유하지만 / 일반적으로 비슷한 체제를 / 그들은 매우 다양하다 / 크기와 비율이 / 매우 많은 삶의 방식에 맞게 적응하며
>
> **(D)** Most other underwater swimmers— / such as loons, cormorants and some ducks— / are propelled by their powerful feet, / although some use their wings / for balance.
> 대부분의 다른 물속의 수영부들은 / 아비새, 가마우지, 그리고 일부 오리와 같은 / 그들의 힘 있는 양발에 의해 나아간다 / 비록 몇몇은 그들의 날개를 사용하지만 / 균형을 위해

해석 많은 새들은 물속에서 헤엄침으로써 먹이를 쫓지만 펭귄만큼 그 일에 훌륭하게 적응된 것(새)은 없다. (A) 펭귄 날개의 전체 구조는 돌고래의 것과 같은 뻣뻣하고 노 같은 지느러미가 되기 위하여 바뀌어왔다. (B) 땅에선 불편하지만 펭귄은 다른 새들이 날기 위해서 날개를 사용하는 것만큼 효과적으로 물속에서의 추진력을 위해서 그들의 날개를 사용한다. (C) 비록 모든 새들이 일반적으로 비슷한 체제를 공유하지만, 그들은 매우 많은 삶의 방식에 맞게 적응하며 크기와 비율이 매우 다양하다. (D) 비록 몇몇은 균형을 위해 그들의 날개를 사용하지만, 아비새, 가마우지, 그리고 일부 오리와 같은 대부분의 다른 물속 수영부들은 그들의 힘 있는 양발에 의해 나아간다.

해설 지문 첫 문장에서 물속에서 먹이를 쫓는 데 훌륭하게 적응된 펭귄에 대해서 언급한 후, (A), (B)에서는 펭귄의 날개 구조와 수영법에 대해 설명하고, (D)에서는 다른 새들의 수영법에 대해 설명했다. 그러나 (C)는 매우 많은 삶의 방식에 맞게 적응하며 그 크기와 비율면에서 매우 다양해진 새들에 대한 내용으로 첫 문장과 관련이 없다. 따라서 ③ (C)가 정답이다.

어휘 pursue 쫓다, 추구하다 prey 먹이, 희생자 superbly 훌륭하게
adapt 적응하다, 맞추다 anatomy 구조 modify 바꾸다, 수정하다

stiff 뻣뻣한　oar 노　flipper 지느러미　awkward 불편한, 어색한
propulsion 추진력　body plan 체제(동물 몸의 기본 형식)
proportion 비율　loon 아비새　cormorant 가마우지
propel 나아가게 하다

19　독해　전체내용 파악 (주제 파악)　난이도 ★★☆

끊어읽기 해석

> We are now beginning to realize / that the great age of expansion of man / over the face of this planet / is rapidly drawing to a close.
> 우리는 이제 깨닫기 시작하고 있다 / 인류 팽창의 위대한 시대가 / 이 행성의 표면 위에서의 / 빠르게 가까워지고 있다는 사실을
>
> There are no great open spaces any more / and we are forced to recognize / the very limited nature of the earth's resources.
> 넓고 개방된 공간이 더는 없다 / 그리고 우리는 인지하도록 강요받는다 / 지구 자원의 매우 제한된 본질을
>
> The geological capital / in the shape of fuel and minerals / which has made our present achievements possible / will have been exhausted / and is unlikely to be renewed.
> 지질학적 자원은 / 연료와 광물 형태의 / 우리의 현재의 성취를 가능하게 한 / 고갈될 것이다 / 그리고 회복될 것 같지 않다
>
> Man's voyages to the moon, / and later no doubt to other planets, / are not likely to open up any new resources, / simply because of the enormous energy requirement for transportation.
> 달을 향한 인류의 항해 / 그리고 후에는 분명 다른 행성으로 향할 (항해는) / 어떠한 새로운 자원도 이용할 수 있게 할 것 같지 않다 / 단순히 운송을 위한 막대한 에너지의 필요 때문에
>
> The whole space enterprise / is more likely to be resource using / than resource-finding.
> 전체 우주 사업은 / 자원 소비에 더 가까울 것이다 / 자원 탐색보다는
>
> It will eventually bring us face to face / with the realization / that the earth is all we have, / and that this precious beautiful, blue-green planet / must be cherished and preserved / if we are to continue to inhabit it.
> 그것은 결국 우리를 대면하게 할 것이다 / 깨달음에 / 지구는 우리가 가진 전부라는 / 그리고 이 귀중하고 아름다운 푸른 행성은 / 소중히 여겨져야 하고 보존되어야 한다는 / 만약 우리가 계속해서 그곳에 거주할 것이라면

해석　우리는 이제 이 행성의 표면 위에서의 인류 팽창의 위대한 시대가 빠르게 가까워지고 있다는 사실을 깨닫기 시작하고 있다. 넓고 개방된 공간이 더는 없고, 우리는 지구 자원의 매우 제한된 본질을 인지하도록 강요받는다. 우리의 현재의 성취를 가능하게 한 연료와 광물 형태의 지질학적 자원은 고갈될 것이고 회복될 것 같지 않다. 달을 향한 인류의 항해, 그리고 후에는 분명 다른 행성으로 향할 항해는 단순히 운송을 위한 막대한 에너지의 필요 때문에 어떠한 새로운 자원도 이용할 수 있게 할 것 같지 않다. 전체 우주 사업은 자원 탐색보다는 자원 소비에 더 가까울 것이다. 그것은 결국 지구는 우리가 가진 전부라는, 그리고 만약 우리가 계속해서 그곳에 거주할 것이라면 이 귀중하고 아름다운 푸른 행성은 소중히 여겨져야 하고 보존되어야 한다는 깨달음에 우리를 대면하게 할 것이다.

① 우주 개발의 필요성
② 지구 보존의 필요성
③ 인류 역사의 제한
④ 문명 발전의 에너지

해설　지문 마지막에서 결국 우리는 지구가 우리가 가진 전부이며, 만약 우리가 계속해서 지구에 거주할 것이라면 이 귀중하고 아름다운 푸른 행성이 소중히 여겨져야 하고 보존되어야 한다는 인식에 대

면하게 될 것이라고 설명하고 있다. 따라서 이 지문의 주제를 '지구 보존의 필요성'이라고 표현한 ②번이 정답이다.

어휘　expansion 팽창, 확장　geological 지질학적인　capital 자원, 자본
exhaust 고갈시키다, 진이 빠지게 하다　renew 회복하다, 재개하다
voyage 항해　transportation 운송, 교통　enterprise 사업
face to face with ~에 대면한　cherish 소중히 여기다
preserve 보존하다　inhabit 거주하다　limitation 제한
civilization 문명

20　독해　논리적 흐름 파악 (문단 순서 배열)　난이도 ★☆☆

끊어읽기 해석

> Exhausted from studying for final exams, / he returned one December day / to his rented, off-campus room / and fell into a deep sleep.
> 기말고사 공부로 인해 진이 빠진 채 / 그는 12월 어느 날 돌아갔다 / 그가 세 들어 사는 캠퍼스 밖의 방으로 / 그리고 깊은 잠에 빠졌다
>
> **(A)** An incredibly heavy weight / compressed his rib cage.
> 놀랄 정도로 무거운 무게가 / 그의 흉곽을 압박했다
>
> Breathing became difficult, / and he felt / a pair of hands encircle his neck / and start to squeeze.
> 숨쉬기가 어려워졌다 / 그리고 그는 느꼈다 / 한 쌍의 손이 그의 목을 둘러싸는 것을 / 그리고 조르기 시작하는 것을
>
> **(B)** An hour later, / he awoke with a start / to the sound of the bedroom door creaking open / —the same door he had locked / before going to bed.
> 한 시간 후에 / 그는 깜짝 놀라서 일어났다 / 침실 문이 삐걱거리며 열리는 소리에 / 그가 잠근 것과 같은 문인 / 자러 가기 전에
>
> He then heard footsteps / moving toward his bed / and felt an evil presence.
> 그리고 나서 그는 발소리를 들었다 / 그의 침대로 다가오는 / 그리고 사악한 존재를 느꼈다
>
> **(C)** It gripped the young man, / who couldn't move a muscle, / his eyes wide open.
> 그것은 그 젊은 남자를 꽉 붙잡았다 / 근육도 움직이지 못하는 / 눈이 크게 떠진 채로
>
> Without warning, / the evil entity, / whatever it was, / jumped onto his chest.
> 경고도 없이 / 그 사악한 존재는 / 그것이 무엇이든 간에 / 그의 가슴 위로 뛰어 올랐다

해석

> 기말고사 공부로 인해 진이 빠진 채, 그는 12월 어느 날 그가 세 들어 사는 캠퍼스 밖의 방으로 돌아갔고, 깊은 잠에 빠졌다.

(B) 한 시간 후에, 그는 그가 자러 가기 전에 잠근 것과 같은 문인 침실 문이 삐걱거리며 열리는 소리에 깜짝 놀라서 일어났다. 그리고 나서 그는 그의 침대로 다가오는 발소리를 들었고 사악한 존재를 느꼈다.

(C) 그것은 눈이 크게 떠진 채로 근육도 움직이지 못하는 그 젊은 남자를 꽉 붙잡았다. 경고도 없이 그것이 무엇이든 간에 그 사악한 존재는 그의 가슴 위로 뛰어 올랐다.

(A) 놀랄 정도로 무거운 무게가 그의 흉곽을 압박했다. 숨쉬기가 어려워졌고, 그는 한 쌍의 손이 그의 목을 둘러싸고 조르기 시작하는 것을 느꼈다.

해설　주어진 문장에서 그가 방으로 돌아가 깊은 잠에 빠졌다고 한 후, (B)에서 한 시간 후에 그가 문이 열리는 소리에 잠이 깼고, 발소리와 사악한 존재(evil presence)를 느꼈다고 말하고 있다. 이어서 (C)에서 그것(It)이 그를 붙잡고 그의 가슴 위로 뛰어 올랐다고

한 뒤, (A)에서 그것이 그의 흉곽을 압박하며 목을 조르기 시작했다고 말하고 있다. 따라서 주어진 문장 다음에 이어질 순서는 ③ (B) – (C) – (A)이다.

어휘 compress 압박하다 rib cage 흉곽 encircle 둘러싸다
squeeze 조르다 creaking 삐걱거리는 evil 사악한
presence 존재 entity 존재, 독립체

의 증가를 낳아 체질량 지수의 상승으로 이어졌다고 설명하고 있다. 따라서 이 지문의 주제를 '최근 비만의 빠른 증가의 이유들'이라고 표현한 ①번이 정답이다.

어휘 obesity 비만 genetic 유전적인, 유전학의 component 요소
given 특정한 obese 비만인 genetic characteristic 유전적 특성
seek to ~하기를 시도하다 take the lead ~에 앞장서다
agriculture 농업 contribute to ~에 기여하다 surge 급등
intake 섭취 account for ~의 원인이 되다, ~을 설명하다
body mass index 체질량 지수 culprit 장본인, 범인

21 독해 전체내용 파악 (주제 파악) 난이도 ★★☆

끊어읽기 해석

Obesity has a strong genetic component, / and this plays an important role / in explaining / why a given individual is obese.
비만은 강한 유전적 요소를 가지고 있다 / 그리고 이것은 중요한 역할을 한다 / 설명하는 데에 / 왜 특정한 개인이 비만인지를

But / genetic characteristics in the population / change very slowly, / and so they clearly cannot explain / why obesity has increased so rapidly / in recent decades.
하지만 / 인구의 유전적 특성은 / 매우 느리게 변한다 / 그래서 그것들은 명확히 설명하지 못한다 / 왜 비만이 그렇게 빠르게 증가했는지 / 최근 수십 년간

Researchers have instead sought / to explain obesity / by looking at / technological changes, changes in consumer habits, and changes in the social environment.
대신에 연구원들은 시도한다 / 비만을 설명하기를 / 고려함으로써 / 기술적 변화, 소비자 습관의 변화, 그리고 사회 환경의 변화를

Economists have taken the lead / in these efforts.
경제학자들은 앞장섰다 / 이러한 노력들에

According to them, / technological advances in agriculture have caused / grocery prices to fall, / and these declines have caused / consumers to demand more groceries.
그들에 따르면 / 농업에서의 기술적 신보는 야기했다 / 식료품의 가격이 하락하는 것을 / 그리고 이러한 하락은 야기했다 / 소비자들이 더 많은 식료품들을 요구하는 것을

The increase of food consumption has contributed / to a surge in caloric intake / that can account for / as much as 40 percent of the increase / in the body mass index of adults / since 1980.
식품 소비의 증가는 기여했다 / 열량 섭취의 급등에 / 원인이 될 수 있는 / 40퍼센트나 되는 높은 증가의 / 성인 체질량 지수의 / 1980년 이후

해석 비만은 강한 유전적 요소를 가지고 있고, 이것은 왜 특정한 개인이 비만인지를 설명하는 데에 중요한 역할을 한다. 하지만 인구의 유전적 특성은 매우 느리게 변해서, 그것들은 왜 비만이 최근 수십 년간 그렇게 빠르게 증가했는지 명확히 설명하지 못한다. 대신에 연구원들은 기술적 변화, 소비자 습관의 변화, 그리고 사회 환경의 변화를 고려함으로써 비만을 설명하기를 시도한다. 경제학자들은 이러한 노력들에 앞장섰다. 그들에 따르면 농업에서의 기술적 진보는 식료품의 가격이 하락하는 것을 야기했고, 이러한 하락은 소비자들이 더 많은 식료품들을 요구하는 것을 야기했다. 식품 소비의 증가는 1980년 이후 성인 체질량 지수의 40퍼센트나 되는 높은 증가의 원인이 될 수 있는 열량 섭취의 급등에 기여했다.

① 최근 비만의 빠른 증가의 이유들
② 열량 섭취를 줄이기 위한 세계적인 노력
③ 과체중인 사람들이 겪을지도 모르는 위험들
④ 증가한 식품 소비의 주된 장본인

해설 지문 중간에서 연구원들이 기술적 변화, 소비자 습관의 변화 등을 고려함으로써 비만이 최근 수십 년간 빠르게 증가한 이유를 설명하기를 시도한다고 했고, 이어서 식료품 가격의 하락이 식품 소비

22 독해 논리적 흐름 파악 (문장 삽입) 난이도 ★★☆

끊어읽기 해석

However, / people growing up in different cultures / have very different ideas / about what is natural / and very different assumptions / about human nature.
하지만 / 다른 문화에서 성장하는 사람들은 / 매우 다른 생각을 가진다 / 무엇이 자연스러운지에 관한 / 그리고 매우 다른 가정을 가진다 / 인간의 본성에 대한

We tend to feel / that the way we do things, say things, and think about things / is only logical.
우리는 느끼는 경향이 있다 / 우리가 행동하고, 말하고, 생각하는 방식이 / 유일하게 논리적이라고

(①) The level of aggression / that seems appropriate, / and ways of expressing agreement or disagreement, / come to seem natural.
공격성의 정도와 / 적절해 보이는 / 그리고 동의나 의견 차이를 표현하는 방법은 / 자연스럽게 보인다

(②) Observing / how people in other cultures / deal with conflict, disagreement, and aggression / can give new perspectives / in our attempts / to manage conflict / and use opposition / in positive rather than negative ways.
관찰하는 것은 / 어떻게 다른 문화의 사람들이 / 갈등과 의견 차이와 공격성에 대처하는지를 / 새로운 시각을 줄 수 있다 / 우리의 시도에 / 갈등을 다루려는 / 그리고 반대를 이용하려는 / 부정적이기보다는 긍정적인 방법으로

(③) Such a newly-acquired view / suggests possibilities / —for example, / of how similar ends can be achieved / with different means.
그러한 새롭게 습득된 관점은 / 가능성을 제시한다 / 예를 들어 / 어떻게 비슷한 결론이 얻어질 수 있는가에 대한 / 다른 수단을 이용하여

(④)

해석 우리는 우리가 행동하고, 말하고, 생각하는 방식만이 유일하게 논리적이라고 느끼는 경향이 있다. 적절해 보이는 공격성의 정도와 그리고 동의나 의견 차이를 표현하는 방법은 자연스럽게 보인다. ② 하지만 다른 문화에서 성장하는 사람들은 무엇이 자연스러운지에 관한 매우 다른 생각을 가지고 인간의 본성에 대한 매우 다른 가정을 가진다. 다른 문화의 사람들이 어떻게 갈등과 의견 차이와 공격성에 대처하는지를 관찰하는 것은 갈등을 다루고 반대를 부정적이기보다는 긍정적인 방법으로 이용하려는 우리의 시도에 새로운 시각을 줄 수 있다. 그러한 새롭게 습득된 관점은 예를 들어, 어떻게 다른 수단을 이용하여 비슷한 결론이 얻어질 수 있는가에 대한 가능성을 제시한다.

해설 주어진 문장의 However(하지만)를 통해 주어진 문장과 상반되는 내용이 앞에 나와야 함을 예상한다. ②번 앞 문장에서 적절해 보이는 공격성의 정도와 동의나 의견 차이를 표현하는 방법은 자연스럽게 보인다고 했고, ②번 뒤 문장에서 다른 문화의 사람들이 갈등과 의견 차이 등에 어떻게 대처하는지 관찰하는 것이 갈등을

다루는 것에 대한 새로운 시각을 줄 수 있다고 했으므로, ②번 자리에 하지만(However) 다른 문화에서 자라는 사람들은 무엇이 자연스러운 것인지에 대해 매우 다른 생각을 가지고 있다는 내용의 주어진 문장이 들어가야 글의 흐름이 자연스럽게 연결된다. 따라서 ②번이 정답이다.

어휘 assumption 가정, 추정 tend to ~하는 경향이 있다
aggression 공격성 appropriate 적절한, 자연스러운
deal with ~에 대처하다, ~을 다루다 perspective 시각
opposition 반대, 항의 acquired 습득된, 획득한

23 독해 논리적 흐름 파악 (문장 삽입) 난이도 ★★★

끊어읽기 해석

Yet / even the most superficial look / into history / shakes such an opinion.
하지만 / 가장 표면적인 관찰조차 / 역사에 대한 / 그러한 의견을 흔들리게 한다

The price of art attracts / more public attention / than any other commodity / —except perhaps oil.
예술품의 가격은 끈다 / 더 많은 대중의 관심을 / 다른 어떤 상품보다 / 아마도 석유를 제외하고는

(①) The ups and downs of the price / are debated / by those both inside and outside the business.
가격의 기복은 / 논의된다 / 그 사업의 내부와 외부에 있는 이들 모두에 의해

(②) An exceptionally high price attracts / wide media coverage / together with a public response / that ranges from outrage and ridicule to admiration.
예외적으로 높은 가격은 불러일으킨다 / 여러 매체의 보도를 / 대중들의 반응과 함께 / 격분과 비웃음부터 감탄에까지 이르는

(③) The orthodox view is / that this situation is not only new but bad / and that art is not subject to / financial speculators.
전통적인 시각은 / 이 상황이 새로울 뿐만 아니라 나쁘다는 것이다 / 그리고 예술은 지배를 받지 않는다는 것이다 / 재정적 투기꾼들의

(④) Holland, a rich and powerful imperial nation / in the seventeenth century, / traded and speculated in art.
네덜란드는 / 부유하고 강한 제국이었던 / 17세기의 / (예술 작품을) 거래하고 예술에 투기했다

A historian records / that it was quite usual / to find Dutch farmers paying / the equivalent of up to £3,000 / for painting / and then reselling them / at 'very great gains.'
한 역사가는 기록한다 / 상당히 일반적이었다고 / 네덜란드 농부들이 지불하는 것을 발견하는 것이 / 3,000파운드까지에 상당하는 값을 / 그림을 위해 / 그리고 그것들을 되파는 것을 / '굉장한 이익을 남기며'

해석 예술품의 가격은 아마도 석유를 제외하고 다른 어떤 상품보다 더 많은 대중의 관심을 끈다. 가격의 기복은 그 사업의 내부와 외부에 있는 이들 모두에 의해 논의된다. 예외적으로 높은 가격은 격분과 비웃음부터 감탄에까지 이르는 대중들의 반응과 함께 여러 매체의 보도를 불러일으킨다. 전통적인 시각은 이 상황이 새로울 뿐만 아니라 나쁘다는 것이고, 예술은 재정적 투기꾼들의 지배를 받지 않는다는 것이다. ④ 하지만 역사에 대한 가장 표면적인 관찰조차 그러한 의견을 흔들리게 한다. 17세기의 부유하고 강한 제국이었던 네덜란드는 (예술 작품을) 거래하고 예술에 투기했다. 한 역사가는 네덜란드 농부들이 3,000파운드까지에 상당하는 값을 그림을 위해 지불하고 그것들을 '굉장한 이익을 남기며' 되파는 것을 발견하는 것이 상당히 일반적이었다고 기록한다.

해설 ④번 앞 문장에서 예술품의 가격에 대한 전통적인 시각은 예술이

재정적 투기꾼들의 지배를 받지 않는다는 것이라고 했고, ④번 뒤 문장에서 네덜란드를 예로 들며 과거에도 예술 작품에 대한 거래와 투기가 일반적이었다고 했으므로, ④번 자리에 하지만(Yet) 역사에 대한 가장 표면적인 관찰조차 그러한 의견을 흔들리게 한다는 내용의 주어진 문장이 들어가야 글의 흐름이 자연스럽게 연결된다. 따라서 ④번이 정답이다.

어휘 superficial 표면적인 commodity 상품
the ups and downs 기복 coverage 보도 outrage 격분
ridicule 비웃음, 조롱 admiration 감탄 orthodox 전통적인
speculator 투기꾼 Holland 네덜란드 imperial 제국의
Dutch 네덜란드의 equivalent 상당하는 resell 되팔다

24 독해 전체내용 파악 (목적 파악) 난이도 ★★☆

끊어읽기 해석

In the past few decades, / biochemistry has come a long way / towards explaining / how the cell produces / all its various proteins.
과거 수십 년 동안 / 생화학은 먼 길을 왔다 / 설명하기 위해 / 세포가 어떻게 생성해내는지 / 그것의 모든 다양한 단백질을

But as to the breaking down of proteins, / not so many researchers were interested.
하지만 단백질을 분해하는 것에 관해서는 / 많은 연구원들이 흥미를 가지지 않았다

Aaron Ciechanover, Avram Hershko and Irwin Rose / went against the stream / and at the beginning of the 1980s / discovered / one of the cell's most important cyclical processes / —regulated protein degradation.
Aaron Ciechanover와 Avram Hershko 그리고 Irwin Rose는 / 그 흐름을 거슬러 갔다 / 그리고 1980년대 초반에 / 발견했다 / 세포의 가장 중요한 순환 과정들 중 하나를 / 통제된 단백질 분해

For going against the tide / with their bold research, / they were rewarded / with this year's Nobel Prize in Chemistry.
시류를 거스른 것으로 / 그들의 대담한 연구와 함께 / 그들은 수여받았다 / 올해의 노벨 화학상을

The work of the three laureates / has brought us to realize / that the cell functions / as a highly-efficient checking station / where proteins are built up and broken down / at a furious rate.
세 수상자들의 연구는 / 우리가 깨닫게 했다 / 세포가 기능한다는 것을 / 매우 효율적인 점검 기관으로서 / 단백질이 쌓이고 분해되는 / 맹렬한 속도로

해석 과거 수십 년 동안 생화학은 세포가 어떻게 그것의 모든 다양한 단백질을 생성해내는지 설명하기 위해 먼 길을 왔다. 하지만 단백질을 분해하는 것에 관해서는 많은 연구원들이 흥미를 가지지 않았다. Aaron Ciechanover와 Avram Hershko 그리고 Irwin Rose는 그 흐름을 거슬러 갔고, 1980년대 초반에 세포의 가장 중요한 순환 과정들 중 하나인 통제된 단백질 분해를 발견했다. 그들의 대담한 연구와 함께 시류를 거스른 것으로 그들은 올해의 노벨 화학상을 수여받았다. 세 수상자들의 연구는 세포가 단백질이 맹렬한 속도로 쌓이고 분해되는 매우 효율적인 점검 기관으로서 기능한다는 것을 우리가 깨닫게 했다.

해설 지문 앞부분에서 많은 연구원들이 단백질을 분해하는 것에 관해서는 흥미를 가지지 않았지만, Aaron Ciechanover를 포함한 세 명의 연구원들이 1980년대에 시류를 거스르며 단백질 분해를 발견했고, 이에 대해 노벨 화학상을 받았다고 설명하고 있다. 따라서 이 지문의 목적을 '생화학에서 시류를 따르지 않았던 비주류 연구자들의 업적을 설명하기 위해'라고 표현한 ③번이 정답이다.

어휘 biochemistry 생화학 protein 단백질 break down 분해하다
cyclical 순환의, 주기적인 degradation 분해 tide 시류, 추세, 조류
laureate 수상자 furious 맹렬한

25 문법 명사와 관사

해석 1941년 12월 7일 아침, 일본 잠수함들과 군 수송기들이 진주만의
미 태평양 함대를 공격하기 시작했다. 200대의 미국 항공기들이
파괴되었고, 여덟 대의 전함들이 침몰했으며, 대략 8,000명의 해
군 그리고 육군 장병들이 죽거나 부상당했다. 이 무지막지한 공격
과 그것의 섬뜩한 결과는 미국을 제2차 세계대전으로 몰고 갔다.

해설 ② 가산 명사 가산 명사 aircraft는 단수형과 복수형이 모두
aircraft로 같으므로 aircrafts를 aircraft로 고쳐야 한다.

오답 ① 시제 일치 특정 과거 시점을 나타내는 시간 표현(December
분석   7, 1941)이 왔으므로 이미 끝난 과거의 일을 나타내는 과거 동
사 launched가 올바르게 쓰였다.

③ 수량 표현 가산 명사 battleship 앞에 복수 명사 앞에 오는 수
량 표현(eight)이 왔으므로 가산 명사의 복수형 battleships
가 올바르게 쓰였다.

④ 인칭대명사 대명사가 지시하는 명사(This savage attack)
가 단수이므로 단수 소유격 대명사 its가 올바르게 쓰였다.

어휘 submarine 잠수함 carrier plane 군 수송기
launch 시작하다, 착수하다 fleet 함대 Pearl Harbor 진주만
battleship 전함 sink 침몰하다, 가라앉다 approximately 대략
naval 해군의 personnel 장병, 인사 wound 부상을 입히다
savage 무지막지한, 흉포한 horrifying 섬뜩한, 몸서리처지는
propel 몰고 가다, 나아가게 하다

👍 이것도 알면 합격!

보기 ②번의 aircraft와 같이 단수형과 복수형이 같은 다음의 가산 명
사들을 알아두자.

· deer 사슴	· buffalo 물소
· salmon 연어	· offspring 자식, 새끼
· series 시리즈, 연속	· means 수단, 방법

정답
p.148

01	③ 독해 - 논리적 흐름 파악	**11**	③ 독해 - 논리적 흐름 파악	**21**	② 독해 - 세부내용 파악		
02	③ 어휘 - 어휘 & 표현	**12**	② 독해 - 추론	**22**	③ 독해 - 전체내용 파악		
03	② 어휘 - 어휘 & 표현	**13**	② 독해 - 전체내용 파악	**23**	④ 독해 - 전체내용 파악		
04	① 독해 - 논리적 흐름 파악	**14**	③ 문법 - 대명사	**24**	② 독해 - 전체내용 파악		
05	② 문법 - 분사	**15**	③ 문법 - 대명사	**25**	③ 독해 - 전체내용 파악		
06	④ 독해 - 추론	**16**	② 독해 - 전체내용 파악				
07	④ 독해 - 전체내용 파악	**17**	② 독해 - 논리적 흐름 파악				
08	① 독해 - 전체내용 파악	**18**	③ 독해 - 논리적 흐름 파악				
09	② 독해 - 추론	**19**	③ 독해 - 추론				
10	② 독해 - 세부내용 파악	**20**	④ 독해 - 추론				

취약영역 분석표

영역	세부 유형	문항 수	소계
어휘	어휘 & 표현	2	/2
	생활영어	0	
문법	분사	1	/3
	대명사	2	
독해	전체내용 파악	8	/20
	세부내용 파악	2	
	추론	5	
	논리적 흐름 파악	5	
총계			/25

· 자신이 취약한 영역은 '법원직 9급 영어, 이렇게 출제된다!'(p.8)를 통해 다시 한 번 확인하고 학습하시기 바랍니다.

---

01 독해 논리적 흐름 파악 (문단 순서 배열)
난이도 ★★☆

끊어읽기 해석

"Cloud seeding" is a process / used by several western state governments and private businesses, / such as ski resorts, / to increase the amount of rainfall or snow / over a certain area.
'구름 모립살포'는 방법이다 / 서부의 몇몇 주 정부들과 민간 기업에 의해 사용되는 / 스키장 같은 / 강우량이나 강설량을 증가시키기 위해 / 특정 지역에 걸쳐

(A) Then / they measure / a storm's clouds for temperature, wind, and composition.
그 후 / 그들은 측정한다 / 폭풍 구름의 온도, 바람 그리고 구성 요소를

When the meteorologists determine / that conditions are right, / pilots are sent / to "seed" the clouds / with dry ice (frozen carbon dioxide).
기후학자들이 판단하면 / 그 조건이 적절하다고 / 비행사들이 보내진다 / 구름을 '씨 뿌리기' 위해 / 드라이아이스(얼린 이산화탄소)로

An aircraft flies / above the clouds / and dry ice pellets are dropped / directly into them.
비행기는 난다 / 구름 위를 / 그리고 드라이아이스 알갱이들은 떨어진다 / 바로 그 안으로

Almost immediately, / the dry ice begins / attracting the clouds' moisture, / which freezes / to the dry ice's crystalline structure.
거의 즉각적으로 / 드라이아이스는 시작하는데 / 구름의 습기를 끌어당기는 것을 / 이것은 언다 / 드라이아이스의 수정 같은 구조로

(B) Meteorologists use / radar, satellites, and weather stations / to track storm fronts.
기후학자들은 사용한다 / 전파 탐지기, 위성, 기상관측소를 / 폭풍 전선을 추적하기 위해

(C) Precipitation drops / from the clouds / to the earth / in the form of rain or snow.
강수는 떨어진다 / 구름에서 / 땅으로 / 비나 눈의 형태로

해석
> '구름 모립살포'는 특정 지역에 걸쳐 강우량이나 강설량을 증가시키기 위해 서부의 몇몇 주 정부들과 스키장 같은 민간 기업에 의해 사용되는 방법이다.

(B) 기후학자들은 폭풍 전선을 추적하기 위해 전파 탐지기, 위성, 기상관측소를 사용한다.
(A) 그 후, 그들은 폭풍 구름의 온도, 바람 그리고 구성 요소를 측정한다. 기후학자들이 그 조건이 적절하다고 판단하면, 드라이아이스(얼린 이산화탄소)로 구름을 '씨 뿌리기' 위해 비행사들이 보내진다. 비행기는 구름 위를 날고 드라이아이스 알갱이들은 바로 그 안으로 떨어진다. 거의 즉각적으로, 드라이아이스는 구름의 습기를 끌어당기는 것을 시작하는데, 이것은 드라이아이스의 수정 구조로 언다.
(C) 강수는 비나 눈의 형태로 구름에서 땅으로 떨어진다.

해설 주어진 문장에서 강우량이나 강설량의 증가를 위해 사용되는 '구름 모립살포'에 대해서 언급한 뒤, (B)에서 기후학자 (meteorologists)들은 폭풍 전선을 추적하기 위해 전파 탐지기, 위성 등을 사용한다고 설명하고 있다. 이어서 (A)에서 그들 (They)이 폭풍의 온도, 바람 등을 측정한 뒤 조건이 적절하다고 판단하면 구름을 '씨 뿌리기' 위해 비행사들이 보내진다고 하며 구름 모립살포의 과정을 설명한 뒤, (C)에서 그 결과 강수가 구름에서 땅으로 떨어진다는 것을 알려주고 있다. 따라서 ③ (B) – (A) – (C)가 정답이다.

어휘 cloud seeding 구름 모립살포, 구름 씨 뿌리기
private business 민간 기업, 사기업 amount of rainfall 강우량
measure 측정하다 composition 구성 요소
meteorologist 기후학자 carbon dioxide 이산화탄소
pellet 알갱이 crystalline 수정 같은 front 전선
precipitation 강수

02 어휘 어휘&표현 tension ↔ calmness 난이도 ★☆☆

끊어읽기 해석

> Any headache can make you miserable, / but a migraine can be excruciating.
> 어떤 두통도 당신을 괴롭게 만들 수 있다 / 하지만 편두통은 몹시 고통스러울 수 있다
>
> More than 28 million Americans / suffer from migraine headaches.
> 2천8백만 명 이상의 미국인들이 / 편두통으로부터 고통받는다
>
> Their frequency and severity varies / from person to person, / but they strike women / three times more often / than men.
> 그것의 빈도와 고통은 다양하다 / 사람마다 / 하지만 그것들은 여성에게 발생한다 / 3배 더 자주 / 남성보다
>
> And / if there is a history of migraine / in your family, / there is an 80 percent chance / you will have them as well.
> 그리고 / 만약 편두통 내력이 있다면 / 당신의 가족에 / 80퍼센트의 가능성이 있다 / 당신 또한 그것을 가질
>
> It's important / for migraine sufferers / to avoid certain triggers, smoking, or certain foods / that may have triggered their headaches / in the past.
> 중요하다 / 편두통으로 고통받는 사람들에게 / 특정한 자극, 흡연 또는 특정한 음식을 피하는 것은 / 그들의 두통을 촉발시켰을 수도 있는 / 과거에
>
> Regular aerobic exercise is highly recommended / to reduce (A) tension / and to help prevent migraines.
> 규칙적인 유산소 운동은 매우 권장된다 / (A) 긴장을 줄이기 위해 / 그리고 편두통을 예방하는 것을 돕기 위해

해석 어떤 두통도 당신을 괴롭게 만들 수 있지만, 편두통은 몹시 고통스러울 수 있다. 2천8백만 명 이상의 미국인들이 편두통으로부터 고통받는다. 그것의 빈도와 고통은 사람마다 다양하지만, 그것들은 남성보다 여성에게 3배 더 자주 발생한다. 그리고 만약 당신의 가족에 편두통 내력이 있다면, 당신 또한 그것을 가질 80퍼센트의 가능성이 있다. 편두통으로 고통받는 사람들에게 과거에 그들의 두통을 촉발시켰을 수도 있는 특정한 자극, 흡연 또는 특정한 음식을 피하는 것은 중요하다. 규칙적인 유산소 운동은 (A) 긴장을 줄이고 편두통을 예방하는 것을 돕기 위해 매우 권장된다.

① 압박　　　　　　　　② 불안
③ 평온　　　　　　　　④ 신경과민

어휘 miserable 괴로운, 비참한 migraine 편두통
excruciating 몹시 고통스러운 suffer from ~으로부터 고통받다
frequency 빈도 severity 고통, 심각성 trigger 자극; 촉발시키다
tension 긴장 strain 압박 anxiety 불안 calmness 평온
nervousness 신경과민

👍 **이것도 알면 합격!**

tension(긴장)의 유의어
= stress, anxiety, pressure

03 어휘 어휘&표현 a wide range[array] of 난이도 ★★☆

해설 ② 한 문장에 두 개의 동사(offer, arrange)는 올 수 없고, 제시된 문장의 '다양한 종류의'는 'a wide range of'(다양한) 또는 'a wide array of'(다수의)로 나타낼 수 있으므로 동사 arrange를 명사 range나 array로 고쳐야 한다.

어휘 at the same time 동시에 arrange 정리하다, 배열하다
bother 귀찮게 하다 make sure 꼭[반드시] ~하다

👍 **이것도 알면 합격!**

a wide range[array] of(다양한)와 유사한 의미의 표현
= a variety of, a lot of, various, diverse, multiple

04 독해 논리적 흐름 파악 (문단 순서 배열) 난이도 ★★☆

끊어읽기 해석

> ⓐ It is caused by factories / that burn coal, oil or gas.
> 그것은 공장들에 의해 일어난다 / 석탄, 기름 또는 가스를 연소시키는
>
> ⓑ The wind often carries the smoke / far from these factories.
> 바람은 종종 그 연기를 나른다 / 이러한 공장들로부터 멀리
>
> ⓒ Acid rain / is a kind of air pollution.
> 산성비는 / 대기 오염의 한 종류이다
>
> ⓓ These factories send smoke / high into the air.
> 이러한 공장들은 연기를 보낸다 / 대기 높은 곳으로

해석 ⓒ 산성비는 대기 오염의 한 종류이다.
ⓐ 그것은 석탄, 기름 또는 가스를 연소시키는 공장들에 의해 일어난다.
ⓓ 이러한 공장들은 대기 높은 곳으로 연기를 보낸다.
ⓑ 바람은 종종 이러한 공장들로부터 멀리 그 연기를 나른다.

해설 ⓒ에서 대기 오염의 한 종류인 산성비(Acid rain)에 대해 언급하고, ⓐ에서 그것(It)의 원인이 공장들이라고 설명하고 있다. 이어서 ⓓ에서 이러한 공장들(These factories)이 연기를 대기 높은 곳으로 보낸다고 한 뒤, ⓑ에서 바람이 그 연기(the smoke)를 멀리 이동시킨다는 것을 설명하고 있다. 따라서 ① ⓒ → ⓐ → ⓓ → ⓑ가 정답이다.

어휘 coal 석탄 acid rain 산성비 air pollution 대기 오염

05 문법 분사 난이도 ★★☆

해석 가장 비극적인 사고들 중에는 총기를 포함한 것들이 있다. 매년, 대략 5천 명의 20세 이하의 사람들이 총기로 인해 죽는다. 이러한 죽음의 10분의 1은 우발적이라고 알려지는데, 그들 중 많은 수는 집에서 장전된 총을 발견한 아이들에 의해 발생한다. 모든 미국 가정의 대략 절반 정도가 총을 소지하고 있고, 종종 안전한 곳에 넣어져 있는 대신에 그것들은 단지 숨겨져 있거나 심지어 서랍에 탄약이 가득 채워진 채로 놓여진다. 우발적인 총기 피해들은 너무 만연해져서 미국 의학 협회는 의사들이 총기 소유자인 부모들에게 그들의 총기에 안전 장치를 사용하는 것과 탄약을 따로 보관하는 것에 대해 반드시 이야기하도록 권고한다.

해설 ② 현재분사 vs. 과거분사 수식받는 명사 guns와 분사가 '총이 장전되다(장전된 총)'라는 의미의 수동 관계이므로 현재분사 loading을 과거분사 loaded로 고쳐야 한다.

오답분석 ① 지시대명사 | 현재분사 vs. 과거분사 지시대명사가 가리키는 명사 the most tragic accidents가 복수이므로 복수 지시대명사 those가 올바르게 쓰였고, 수식받는 대명사 those와 분사가 '그것들이 포함하다'라는 의미의 능동 관계이므로 현재분사 involving이 쓰인 those involving이 올바르게 쓰였다.
③ 보어 자리 동사 become은 주격 보어를 취하는 동사인데, 보어 자리에는 명사나 형용사 역할을 하는 것이 올 수 있으므로 동사 become 뒤에 형용사 prevalent가 올바르게 쓰였다.
④ 부사 자리 동명사(storing)를 뒤에서 수식할 수 있는 것은 부

사이므로 부사 separately가 동명사 storing 뒤에 올바르게 쓰였다.

어휘　tragic 비극적인　firearm 총기　accidental 우발적인, 돌발적인
　　　load 장전하다　household 가정　lock up ~을 안전한 곳에 넣어두다
　　　ammunition 탄약　prevalent 만연한
　　　make a point of something 반드시 ~하다　separately 따로

👍 이것도 알면 **합격!**

주격 보어를 취하는 2형식 동사들을 알아두자.

- be ~이다, ~이 되다
- smell ~한 냄새가 나다
- taste ~한 맛이 나다
- remain 여전히 ~이다
- sound ~하게 들리다
- feel ~처럼 느끼다

06 독해 추론 (빈칸 완성 - 절)　난이도 ★☆☆

끊어읽기 해석

You're aware of the health benefits / of eating fresh vegetables, / you have the space / for a small garden, / but just don't know / where to start?
당신은 건강상의 이점을 알고 있다 / 신선한 채소를 먹는 것의 / 당신은 공간을 가지고 있다 / 작은 정원을 위한 / 다만 모르는가 / 어디에서부터 시작할지를?

Look no further. // Here's all / you need to know / to put fresh, crisp vegetables / on your dinner table.
더 멀리서 찾지 말라. // 여기에 모든 것이 있다 / 당신이 알아야 할 / 신선하고 아삭한 채소를 올려놓기 위해 / 당신의 저녁 식탁에

First, / think small. // Don't bite off more / than you can chew.
첫 번째로 / 작게 생각하라 // 더 베어 물지 말라 / 당신이 씹을 수 있는 것보다(너무 무리하지 말라)

It's like starting out / an exercise program / by running five miles / the first day.
그것은 시작하는 것과 같다 / 운동 프로그램을 / 5마일을 달리면서 / 첫날에

You get tired, sore / and you quit.
당신은 피로해지고, 아프게 된다 / 그래서 그만둔다

Likewise, / if you plant a huge garden / the first year, / you'll curse, cuss / and turn your sore back / on gardening / for good.
마찬가지로 / 만약 당신이 큰 정원을 가꾼다면 / 첫해에 / 당신은 악담을 퍼붓고 욕을 할 것이다 / 그리고 당신의 아픈 등을 돌릴 것이다 / 원예로부터 / 영원히

So, / if you're new to gardening, / start off with a garden / no larger than 8' X 10'.
그래서 / 만약 당신이 원예에 경험이 없다면 / 정원으로 시작하라 / 8피트 X 10피트보다 크지 않은

You can always expand later / if you can't get enough / of those fresh, crispy vegetables.
당신은 나중에 언제든지 확장할 수 있다 / 만약 당신이 충분히 얻을 수 없다면 / 신선하고 아삭한 채소들을

Choose a location / that receives as much sun as possible / throughout the day.
장소를 선택해라 / 가능한 한 햇빛을 많이 받는 / 낮 동안에

Northern gardeners should insist / on full sun. // Now / you're ready / to work up the soil.
북쪽 지방의 채소 재배자들은 고집해야 한다 / 충분한 햇빛을 // 이제 / 당신은 준비가 되어 있다 / 흙을 일굴

You can rent / a rear tine tiller / or borrow one / from a friend

or neighbor / for this task.
당신은 대여할 수 있다 / 뒤쪽에 갈래가 있는 경작 도구를 / 혹은 빌릴 수 있다 / 친구 또는 이웃으로부터 / 이 일을 위해

해석　당신은 신선한 채소를 먹는 것의 건강상의 이점을 알고, 작은 정원을 위한 공간을 가지고 있지만, 어디에서부터 시작할지를 모르는가? 더 멀리서 찾지 말라. 여기에 신선하고 아삭한 채소를 당신의 저녁 식탁에 올려놓기 위해 당신이 알아야 할 모든 것이 있다.
　　　첫 번째로, 작게 생각하라. 당신이 씹을 수 있는 것보다 더 베어 물지 말라. 그것은 첫날에 5마일을 달리면서 운동 프로그램을 시작하는 것과 같다. 당신은 피로해지고, 아프게 되서 그만둔다. 마찬가지로, 만약 당신이 첫해에 큰 정원을 가꾼다면, 당신은 악담을 퍼붓고 욕을 할 것이고 당신의 아픈 등을 원예로부터 영원히 돌릴 것이다. 그래서 만약 당신이 원예에 경험이 없다면, 8피트 X 10피트보다 크지 않은 정원으로 시작하라. 만약 당신이 신선하고 아삭한 채소들을 충분히 얻을 수 없다면, 당신은 나중에 언제든지 확장할 수 있다.
　　　낮 동안에 가능한 한 햇빛을 많이 받는 장소를 선택하라. 북쪽 지방의 채소 재배자들은 충분한 햇빛을 고집해야 한다. 이제 당신은 흙을 일굴 준비가 되어 있다. 당신은 이 일을 위해 뒤쪽에 갈래가 있는 경작 도구를 대여하거나 혹은 친구 또는 이웃으로부터 빌릴 수 있다.

　　　① 언제나 울타리 너머의 잔디가 더 푸르게 보인다(남의 떡이 더 커 보인다).
　　　② 내 등을 긁어주면 네 등을 긁어주겠다(오는 정이 있어야 가는 정이 있다).
　　　③ 당신이 뿌린 것을 거둔다(뿌린 대로 거둔다).
　　　④ 당신이 씹을 수 있는 것보다 더 베어 물지 말라(너무 무리하지 말라).

해설　빈칸이 있는 문장에 어디서 시작해야 할지를 모른다면 작게 생각하라는 내용이 있고, 지문 중간에서 원예를 시작하는 첫해에는 큰 정원을 가꾸기보다 작은 면적의 정원으로 시작하라는 내용이 있으므로, '당신이 씹을 수 있는 것보다 더 베어 물지 말라(너무 무리하지 말라)'라고 한 ④번이 정답이다.

어휘　further 더 멀리　crisp 아삭한　start out ~을 시작하다
　　　sore 아픈, 화가 난　curse 악담을 퍼붓다　cuss 욕하다
　　　turn someone's back on ~으로부터 등을 돌리다
　　　start off ~을 시작하다　insist on ~을 고집하다　rear 뒤쪽의; 뒤쪽
　　　tine 갈래, (빗의) 살　tiller 경작 도구　reap 거두다, 수확하다
　　　sow 뿌리다　bite off ~을 베어 물다

07 독해 전체내용 파악 (글의 감상)　난이도 ★☆☆

끊어읽기 해석

Rainforests are home / to more than half / of the world's plants and animals.
우림은 서식지이다 / 반 이상의 / 전 세계 동식물들의

Rainforests used to cover / as much as 14% of the Earth's land. // Now they cover / less than 6%.
우림은 뒤덮곤 했다 / 지구 육지의 14퍼센트만큼을 // 지금 그것들은 뒤덮는다 / 6퍼센트보다 적게

The problem is / that the rainforests are being destroyed.
문제는 / 우림이 파괴되고 있다는 것이다

The amount being destroyed each minute / would fill 20 football fields.
매분 파괴되는 양은 / 20개의 축구장을 채울 것이다

And / about 50,000 species of rainforest animals and plants / are disappearing every year.

해석 우림은 전 세계 동식물들의 반 이상의 서식지이다. 우림은 지구 육지의 14퍼센트만큼을 뒤덮기도 했다. 지금 그것들은 6퍼센트보다 적게 뒤덮는다. 문제는 우림이 파괴되고 있다는 것이다. 매분 파괴되는 양은 20개의 축구장을 채울 것이다. 그리고 대략 5만 종의 우림 동식물이 매년 사라지고 있다. 이것은 우리가 당신의 도움으로 그들을 구하지 않는다면 당신이 자랄 때쯤엔 그들이 모두 사라질 것이라는 것을 의미한다!

① 흥분한   ② 기쁜
③ 안도한   ④ 염려하는

해설 지문 중간에서 우림이 파괴되고 있다는 것이 문제라고 하며 대략 5만 종의 동식물이 매년 사라지고 있다고 했고, 지문 마지막에서 우리가 구하지 않으면 그들(5만 종의 우림 동식물)이 모두 사라질 것이라고 말하며 도움을 촉구하고 있다. 따라서 글쓴이의 심정을 '염려하는'이라고 표현한 ④번이 정답이다.

어휘 **rainforest** 우림   **species** 종   **pleasant** 기쁜

---

08 독해 전체내용 파악 (글의 감상)   난이도 ★★☆

끊어읽기 해석

With the arrival of twentieth-century technology, / medical professions were able to think seriously / about creating artificial replacements / for damaged human hearts / that no longer functioned effectively.
20세기 기술의 도래로 / 의료계는 진지하게 생각할 수 있었다 / 인공 대체물을 만드는 것에 대해 / 손상된 인간의 심장을 위한 / 더 이상 효과적으로 기능할 수 없는

In 1957, / Dr. Willem Kolff created / the first artificial heart / and implanted it / in a dog, / who promptly died from the experiment.
1957년에 / Dr. Willem Kolff는 만들었다 / 첫 번째 인공 심장을 / 그리고 그것을 이식했는데 / 개에게 / 그 실험에서 곧바로 죽었다

Still, / animal research continued, / and, in 1969, / Dr. Denton Cooley implanted / the first artificial heart / into the body of a human.
여전히 / 동물 연구는 계속되었다 / 그리고 1969년에 / Dr. Denton Cooley는 이식했다 / 첫 번째 인공 심장을 / 인간의 몸에

The device, / made largely of plastic, / only had to function for a brief period of time, / while the patient awaited / a transplanted human heart.
그 장치는 / 주로 플라스틱으로 만들어진 / 짧은 시간 동안 기능하기만 하면 됐다 / 환자가 기다리는 동안 / 이식된 인간의 심장을

In 1979, / Dr. Robert Jarvik patented / the first artificial heart.
1979년에 / Dr. Robert Jarvik은 특허를 받았다 / 첫 번째 인공 심장의

Three years later, / the Jarvik heart, as it came to be called, / was implanted / in the body of Barney Clark, / a retired dentist / dying of heart disease.
삼 년 후에 / Jarvik 심장이라고 불리게 된 것은 / 이식되었다 / Barney Clark의 몸에 / 은퇴한 치과 의사인 / 심장병으로 죽어가는

Clark lived for 112 days / after the surgery, / and his survival raised hopes / for the future success of artificial hearts.
Clark는 112일간 살았다 / 수술 후 / 그리고 그의 생존은 희망을 드높였다 / 인공 심장의 미래의 성공에 대한

해석 20세기 기술의 도래로, 의료계는 더 이상 효과적으로 기능할 수 없는 손상된 인간의 심장을 위한 인공 대체물을 만드는 것에 대해 진지하게 생각할 수 있었다. 1957년에 Dr. Willem Kolff는 첫 번째 인공 심장을 만들었고 그것을 개에게 이식했는데, 그것은 그 실험에서 곧바로 죽었다. 여전히 동물 연구는 계속되었고, 1969년에 Dr. Denton Cooley는 첫 번째 인공 심장을 인간의 몸에 이식했다. 주로 플라스틱으로 만들어진 그 장치는 환자가 이식된 인간의 심장을 기다리는 짧은 시간 동안 기능하기만 하면 됐다. 1979년에, Dr. Robert Jarvik은 첫 번째 인공 심장의 특허를 받았다. 삼 년 후에, Jarvik 심장이라고 불리게 된 것은 심장병으로 죽어가는 은퇴한 치과 의사인 Barney Clark의 몸에 이식되었다. Clark는 수술 후 112일간 살았고, 그의 생존은 인공 심장의 미래의 성공에 대한 희망을 드높였다.

① 시간적 순서   ② 원인과 결과
③ 분류   ④ 정의

해설 지문 앞부분에서 1957년에 Dr. Willem Kolff가 첫 번째 인공 심장을 개에게 이식한 것을 시작으로, 이후 1969년 처음으로 인간의 몸에 인공 심장을 이식하고, 1979년 인공 심장의 특허를 받은 후 삼 년 뒤 성공적인 이식을 하기까지의 과정을 시간의 흐름에 따라 설명하고 있다. 따라서 이 지문의 전개 방식을 '시간적 순서'라고 표현한 ①번이 정답이다.

어휘 **medical profession** 의료계   **artificial** 인공의
replacement 대체물   **function** 기능하다   **implant** 이식하다, 심다
promptly 곧바로, 즉시   **transplant** 이식하다   **patent** 특허를 받다
retired 은퇴한   **heart disease** 심장병   **survival** 생존
classification 분류

---

09 독해 추론 (빈칸 완성 - 단어)   난이도 ★☆☆

끊어읽기 해석

Q: When praised, / Koreans often insist / they did nothing / deserving of praise.
칭찬 받았을 때 / 한국인들은 종종 주장한다 / 그들이 아무것도 한 게 없다고 / 칭찬받을 만한 일을

Why do you do this / instead of accepting the praise / and saying Thank you?
당신은 왜 이렇게 행동하는가 / 대신에 칭찬을 받아들이고 / 감사하다고 말하는?

A: This is done out of modesty; / in other words, / we feel like / we are not deserving / of so much praise.
이것은 겸손으로 인한 것이다 / 다시 말해서 / 우리는 느낀다 / 우리가 받을 자격이 없다고 / 그렇게 많은 칭찬을

However, / don't think / that Koreans really dislike / being praised.
하지만 / 생각하지 말라 / 한국인들이 정말로 싫어한다고 / 칭찬받는 것을

Even though we react this way, / we very much appreciate / the compliment.
비록 우리가 이런 식으로 반응하지만 / 우리는 매우 고마워한다 / 칭찬을

해석 Q: 칭찬 받았을 때, 한국인들은 종종 그들이 칭찬받을 만한 일을 아무것도 한 게 없다고 주장한다. 당신은 왜 칭찬을 받아들이고 감사하다고 말하는 대신에 이렇게 행동하는가?
A: 이것은 겸손으로 인한 것인데, 다시 말해서 우리는 우리가 그렇게 많은 칭찬을 받을 자격이 없다고 느낀다. 하지만, 한국인들이 정말로 칭찬받는 것을 싫어한다고 생각하지 말라. 비록 우리가 이런 식으로 반응하지만, 우리는 칭찬을 매우 고마워한다.

① 책임감   ② 겸손
③ 비난   ④ 자신감

해설 칭찬을 받았을 때 한국인들은 왜 칭찬을 받아들이는 대신 스스로 칭찬받을 만한 일을 한 게 없다고 말하느냐는 질문에 대해, 우리는 스스로가 그렇게 많은 칭찬을 받을 자격이 없다고 느끼기 때문이라고 답변하는 내용이 있으므로, 이것이 '겸손'으로 인한 것이라고 한 ②번이 정답이다.

어휘 praise 칭찬하다; 칭찬 deserve of ~할 만하다, ~할 자격이 있다 react 반응하다 appreciate 고마워하다 compliment 칭찬 modesty 겸손 condemnation 비난

10 독해 세부내용 파악 (지칭 대상 파악) 난이도 ★★☆

끊어읽기 해석

This is a gift / given by physical or legal persons, / typically for charitable purposes / and / or to benefit a cause.
이것은 선물이다 / 사람이나 법인으로부터 주어진 / 전형적으로 자선의 목적으로 / 그리고 / 또는 단체에 이득을 주기 위해

This may take various forms, / including cash, services, new or used goods / including but not limited to clothing, toys, food, vehicles, / it also may consist of / emergency, relief or humanitarian aid items, development aid support, / and can also relate / to medical care needs / as i.e. blood or organs for transplant.
이것은 다양한 형태를 취할 수도 있다 / 현금, 서비스, 새것이거나 중고의 물품들을 포함하여 / 옷, 장난감, 음식, 탈것을 포함하지만 그것들에만 제한되어 있지 않는 / 그것은 또한 구성되어 있을 수도 있다 / 긴급, 구호 혹은 인도주의적인 원조 물품들, 개발 원조 지원으로 / 그리고 또한 관련 있을 수도 있다 / 의료의 필요 / 즉, 혈액과 이식을 위한 장기와 같은 것에

Charitable gifts of goods or services / are also called gifts in kind.
상품 또는 서비스의 자선품들은 / 또한 현물로의 선물이라고 불린다

해설 이것은 전형적으로 자선의 목적으로 그리고/또는 단체에 이득을 주기 위해 사람이나 법인으로부터 주어진 선물이다. 이것은 현금, 서비스, 옷, 장난감, 음식, 탈것을 포함하지만 그것들에만 제한되어 있지 않는 새것이거나 중고의 물품들을 포함하여 다양한 형태를 취할 수도 있고, 그것은 또한 긴급, 구호 혹은 인도주의적인 원조 물품들, 개발 원조 지원으로 구성되어 있거나 의료의 필요, 즉, 혈액과 이식을 위한 장기와 같은 것에 관련 있을 수도 있다. 상품 또는 서비스의 자선품들은 현물로의 선물이라고도 불린다.

① 기업 　　　　　② 기부
③ 기금 　　　　　④ 자원봉사

해설 지문 처음에서 이것(This)은 자선의 목적 혹은 단체에 이득을 주기 위해 사람이나 법인으로부터 주어진 선물이라고 하며 이것이 현금, 서비스, 물품들을 포함한 다양한 형태를 취할 수도 있다고 했으므로 이를 '기부'라고 한 ②번이 정답이다.

어휘 legal person 법인 typically 전형적으로, 주로 charitable 자선의 cause 단체, 대의명분 humanitarian 인도주의적인 aid 원조 organ 장기 transplant 이식 operation 기업 donation 기부 fund 기금 volunteering 자원봉사

11 독해 논리적 흐름 파악 (문장 삽입) 난이도 ★☆☆

끊어읽기 해석

This is the keystone.
이것이 쐐기돌입니다

The Romans have just invented / a new building technique: / the arch.
로마 사람들은 발명했다 / 새로운 건축 기술을 / 그것은 아치다

It is the strongest way / to support walls and bridges. // A master builder explains / the process.
그것은 가장 튼튼한 방법이다 / 벽과 다리를 지지하는 // 건축 기사는 설명한다 / 그 과정을

㉮ "First, / take some stone blocks / and shape them / as wedges.
"먼저, / 돌덩어리를 몇 개 가지고 와서 / 그것들을 만듭니다 / 쐐기 형태로

㉯ Take another stone / and shape it / to fit perfectly / in the middle of the arch.
다른 돌을 가져와서 / 그것의 모양을 만듭니다 / 딱 맞도록 / 아치의 중간에

㉰ Use wood / to hold the wedges together / until the keystone can be placed / in the middle.
목재를 사용합니다 / 쐐기들을 뭉치게 만들기 위해 / 쐐기돌이 자리잡을 수 있을 때까지 / 중간에

㉱ Finally, / put stones / on top of the wedges / and build up the entire wall."
마지막으로 / 돌을 올려서 / 쐐기 꼭대기에 / 그리고 전체 벽을 쌓아 올립니다"

해설 로마 사람들은 새로운 건축 기술을 발명했는데 그것은 아치다. 그것은 벽과 다리를 지지하는 가장 튼튼한 방법이다. 건축 기사는 그 과정을 설명한다. "먼저, 돌덩어리를 몇 개 가지고 와서 그것들을 쐐기 형태로 만듭니다. 다른 돌을 가져와서 아치의 중간에 딱 맞도록 그것의 모양을 만듭니다. ㉰ 이것이 쐐기돌입니다. 쐐기돌이 중간에 자리잡을 수 있을 때까지 쐐기들을 뭉치게 만들기 위해 목재를 사용합니다. 마지막으로, 쐐기 꼭대기에 돌을 올리고 전체 벽을 쌓아 올립니다."

해설 ㉯ 앞에서 다른 돌(another stone)을 가져와서 아치의 중간에 딱 맞도록 모양을 만들라고 했고, ㉰ 뒤에서 그 쐐기돌(the keystone)이 자리잡을 수 있을 때까지 그것들을 뭉치게 만들기 위해 목재를 사용하라고 했으므로, ㉰의 앞에서 언급된 다른 돌(another stone)이 바로 쐐기돌(the keystone)이라는 것을 알려주는 주어진 문장이 나와야 지문이 자연스럽게 연결된다. 따라서 ③번이 정답이다.

어휘 keystone 쐐기돌 support 지지하다 shape 모양을 만들다 wedge 쐐기 hold together 뭉치게 만들다 build up ~을 쌓아 올리다 entire 전체의

12 독해 추론 (빈칸 완성 - 단어) 난이도 ★★☆

끊어읽기 해석

Increasing numbers of Americans / are turning to hypnosis / to stop smoking / or to lose weight.
점점 더 많은 수의 미국인들이 / 최면에 의지하고 있다 / 금연을 하기 위해 / 또는 살을 빼기 위해

Similarly, / arthritis sufferers are using acupuncture, / an ancient method of Chinese healing, / to gain some relief / from their pain.
비슷하게 / 관절염 환자들은 침술을 이용하고 있다 / 고대 중국의 치료 방

법인 / 약간의 경감을 얻기 위해 / 그들의 고통으로부터

Cancer patients have also been using / nontraditional treatments / like creative visualization / to fight their disease.
암 환자들은 또한 사용해왔다 / 비전통적인 치료법을 / 창의적 시각화와 같은 / 그들의 병과 맞서 싸우기 위해

Some cancer sufferers, / for example, / imagine themselves / as huge and powerful sharks.
어떤 암 환자들은 / 예를 들어 / 그들 스스로를 상상한다 / 거대하고 강한 상어라고

They imagine their cancer cells / as much smaller fish / that easily fall prey / to the larger and more dangerous sharks.
그들은 그들의 암세포를 상상한다 / 훨씬 작은 물고기라고 / 쉽사리 먹이가 되는 / 더 크고 위험한 상어의

Even some businesses are supporting / nontraditional medical treatments / and encouraging employees / to use <u>meditation</u> / to ward off migraine headaches and high blood pressure.
심지어 어떤 회사들은 지지한다 / 비전통적인 치료법들을 / 그리고 직원들에게 권장한다 / 명상을 사용할 것을 / 편두통과 고혈압을 피하도록 하기 위해

해석 점점 더 많은 수의 미국인들이 금연을 하거나 살을 빼기 위해 최면에 의지하고 있다. 비슷하게, 관절염 환자들은 그들의 고통으로부터 약간의 경감을 얻기 위해 고대 중국의 치료 방법인 침술을 이용하고 있다. 암 환자들은 또한 그들의 병과 맞서 싸우기 위해 창의적 시각화와 같은 비전통적인 치료법을 사용해왔다. 예를 들어, 어떤 암 환자들은 그들 스스로를 거대하고 강한 상어라고 상상한다. 그들은 그들의 암세포를 쉽사리 더 크고 위험한 상어의 먹이가 되는 훨씬 작은 물고기라고 상상한다. 심지어 어떤 회사들은 편두통과 고혈압을 피하도록 하기 위해 비전통적인 치료법들을 지지하고 직원들에게 명상을 사용할 것을 권장한다.

① 중재   ② 명상
③ 절단   ④ 약물

해설 지문 처음에서 금연이나 체중 감량을 위한 최면에 대해 언급한 뒤, 지문 중간에서 암 환자들의 창의적 시각화와 같은 비전통적인 치료법을 소개하고 있다. 빈칸이 있는 문장에서 어떤 회사들은 비전통적인 치료법을 지지한다고 했으므로, 빈칸에는 그들이 비전통적인 치료법 중 하나인 '명상'을 사용할 것을 권장한다고 한 ②번이 정답이다.

어휘 turn to ~에 의지하다   hypnosis 최면   arthritis 관절염
acupuncture 침술   nontraditional 비전통적인
treatment 치료법   creative 창의적인   visualization 시각화
fall prey to ~의 먹이가 되다   ward off ~을 피하다
migraine 편두통   high blood pressure 고혈압   mediation 중재
meditation 명상   mutilation 절단   medication 약물

---

13   독해   전체내용 파악 (주제 파악)   난이도 ★☆☆

끊어읽기 해석

Infants spend / most of their days / fast asleep.
유아들은 보낸다 / 그들의 하루 대부분을 / 깊이 잠들어서

In the period immediately after birth, / newborns sleep / an average of sixteen hours / per day.
출생 직후의 기간에 / 신생아들은 잠을 잔다 / 평균 16시간 / 하루에

But / the amount they sleep / decreases steadily / with each passing month.
하지만 / 그들이 자는 양은 / 꾸준히 줄어든다 / 매달이 지나면서

By the age of six months, / babies average about thirteen to

fourteen hours of sleep / per day.
6개월이 되면 / 아기들은 평균 13시간에서 14시간을 잔다 / 하루에

By twenty-four months, / they average only eleven or twelve hours / per day.
24개월이 되면 / 그들은 평균 11시간 혹은 12시간만 잔다 / 하루에

In short, / babies sleep a lot, / but the amount of sleep they need / decreases over time.
요약하자면 / 아기들은 잠을 많이 잔다 / 하지만 그들이 필요로 하는 잠의 양은 / 시간이 지나면서 줄어든다

해석 유아들은 그들의 하루 대부분을 깊이 잠들어 보낸다. 출생 직후의 기간에, 신생아들은 하루에 평균 16시간 정도 잠을 잔다. 하지만 매달이 지나면서 그들이 자는 양이 꾸준히 줄어든다. 6개월이 되면, 아기들은 하루에 평균 13시간에서 14시간을 잔다. 24개월이 되면, 그들은 평균 하루에 11시간 혹은 12시간만 잔다. 요약하자면, 아기들은 잠을 많이 자지만 그들이 필요로 하는 잠의 양은 시간이 지나면서 줄어든다.

① 적당한 잠의 양
② 유아들의 수면 패턴
③ 신생아들의 습관
④ 유아들의 성장

해설 지문 처음에서 출생 직후 신생아들은 하루 대부분을 잠든 채로 보내지만, 시간이 지날수록 그들이 자는 양은 꾸준히 줄어든다고 하며 출생 직후부터 24개월이 될 때까지 유아들의 수면 시간이 줄어드는 것에 대해 설명하고 있다. 따라서 이 지문의 주제를 '유아들의 수면 패턴'이라고 표현한 ②번이 정답이다.

어휘 infant 유아   fast asleep 깊이 잠들어서   newborn 신생아
steadily 꾸준히, 지속적으로   average 평균 ~이 되다
in short 요약하자면   decrease 줄어들다
over time 시간이 지나면서   reasonable 적당한

---

14   문법   대명사   난이도 ★☆☆

해석 예를 들어, 미국의 대학생들은 더 오래 살고, 더 오래 결혼한 채로 있으며, 평균보다 유럽을 더 자주 여행하기를 기대한다. 그들은 자신들이 재능이 있는 아이를 갖고, 자기 집을 소유하고, 신문에 나올 가능성이 좀 더 높고 심장마비, 성병, 알코올 의존증, 자동차 사고, 골절, 잇몸 질환을 가질 가능성은 좀 더 낮다고 믿는다. 모든 연령의 미국인들은 그들의 미래가 그들의 현재보다 개선되리라 기대하고, 비록 다른 나라의 국민들은 미국인들만큼 꽤 낙관적이지 않지만 그들 또한 그들의 미래가 또래들보다 더 밝을 것이라고 상상한다. 이러한 우리의 개인적인 미래에 대한 지나치게 낙관적인 기대는 쉽게 파괴되지 않는다. 지진을 경험하는 것은 사람들이 일시적으로 미래의 재앙으로 인한 그들의 죽음의 위험성에 현실적이게 하지만, 몇 주 내에 지진 생존자들 조차도 그들의 원래 수준의 근거 없는 낙관으로 돌아간다.

해설 ③ 지시대명사 지시대명사가 가리키는 명사 their futures가 복수이므로 단수 지시대명사 that을 복수 지시대명사 those로 고쳐야 한다.

오답 분석 ① 보어 자리 동사 stay는 주격 보어를 취하는 동사인데, 보어 자리에는 명사나 형용사 역할을 하는 것이 올 수 있으므로 동사 stay 뒤에 형용사 married가 올바르게 쓰였다.
② 병치 구문 접속사(and)로 연결된 병치 구문에서는 같은 구조끼리 연결되어야 하는데, 접속사 and 앞뒤로 to 부정사(to have, to appear)가 나열되고 있으므로 to 부정사 to own이 올바르게 쓰였다.
④ 능동태·수동태 구별 주어(These overly optimistic

expectations)와 동사가 '이러한 지나치게 낙관적인 기대가 파괴되지 않다'라는 의미의 수동 관계이므로 be동사(are)와 함께 쓰여 수동태를 완성하는 과거분사 undone이 올바르게 쓰였다.

어휘 **likely to** ~할 가능성이 있는 **gifted** 재능이 있는
heart attack 심장마비 **venereal disease** 성병 **gum** 잇몸
improvement 개선, 향상 **optimistic** 낙관적인 **peer** 또래
undo 파괴하다, 망치다 **earthquake** 지진
temporarily 일시적으로 **risk** 위험성 **unfounded** 근거 없는

👍 이것도 알면 **합격!**

지시대명사(that/those)는 앞에 나온 명사를 대신하여 쓰이므로 반드시 대신하는 명사와 수 일치해야 한다.

ex His car is faster than that of his brother. (that = a car)
그의 자동차는 그의 형제의 것보다 빠르다.

others/ other	others는 '이미 언급한 것 이외의 것들 중 몇몇'이란 뜻의 대명사로 쓰이고, other는 형용사로 복수 명사 앞에 쓰인다. ex Your son gets along well with others. 당신의 아들은 다른 이들과 잘 지낸다. Other students were in uniform. 다른 학생들은 교복을 입고 있다.
the other(s)	'정해진 것 중 남은 것 하나/전부'란 뜻의 대명사로 쓰이고, the other는 형용사로도 쓰인다. ex I bought two skirts. One is pink and the other is blue. 나는 두 개의 치마를 가지고 왔다. 하나는 분홍색이고 다른 하나는 파란색이다.

15 문법 대명사   난이도 ★☆☆

해석 미식축구 경기를 보고 있는 두 사람을 예로 들어보자. 미식축구를 거의 이해하지 못하는 한 사람은, 그저 다수의 성인 남자들이 뚜렷한 이유 없이 서로 부딪치는 것을 본다. 미식축구를 좋아하는 다른 한 사람은, 복잡한 경기 양상, 대담한 지도 전략, 효과적인 블로킹과 태클 기술들, 그리고 리시버들이 '가르는' 것을 시도하는 '갈라진 틈'이 있는 구역 방어를 본다. 두 사람 모두 같은 경기에 시선이 고정되어 있지만, 그들은 두 가지의 완전히 다른 상황을 인지하고 있다. 그 인지는 각각의 사람이 이용 가능한 자극을 다른 방식으로 능동적으로 선택하고, 정리하고, 이해하기 때문에 다르다.

해설 ③ **부정대명사: one·another·other** 지문 처음에서 미식축구 경기를 보고 있는 두 사람을 예시로 든 뒤, 빈칸 앞 문장에 미식축구를 거의 이해하지 못하는 한 사람(One person)에 대해 언급했으므로 빈칸이 있는 문장은 문맥상 '미식축구 경기를 보고 있는 (둘 중) 다른 한 사람'이라는 의미가 되어야 자연스럽다. 따라서 '정해진 것 중 남은 것(상대방)의'라는 의미의 부정형용사 The other를 써야 한다. 참고로, 부정형용사 Other는 복수 명사 앞에 쓰이므로 ①번은 정답이 될 수 없다.

어휘 **merely** 그저, 단지 **a bunch of** 다수의 **apparent** 뚜렷한
complex 복잡한 **pattern** 양상 **daring** 대담한 **strategy** 전략
defense 방어 **seam** 갈라진 틈, 경계선 **receiver** 리시버, 포수
glue 고정하다, 주의를 집중하다 **perceive** 인지하다
perception 인지 **interpret** 이해하다 **stimuli** 자극

👍 이것도 알면 **합격!**

다음의 부정대명사/부정형용사를 구분하여 알아두자.

one(ones)	정해지지 않은 가산 명사를 대신한다. ex The new worker seems brighter than the previous one. 그 새로운 근로자는 이전의 사람보다 더 밝아 보인다.
another	'이미 언급한 것 이외의 또 다른 하나'란 뜻의 대명사, 형용사로 쓰인다. ex These apples are so good that I would like another. 이 사과들은 너무 맛있어서 나는 또 다른 하나를 원한다.

16 독해 전체내용 파악 (요지 파악)   난이도 ★★☆

끊어읽기 해석

Among life's cruelest truths is this one: / Wonderful things are especially wonderful / the first time they happen, / but their wonderfulness wanes / with repetition.
삶의 가장 잔혹한 진실 중 하나는 이것이다 / 훌륭한 일들은 특히 훌륭하다 / 그것들이 처음으로 일어날 때 / 하지만 그것들의 훌륭함은 약해진다 / 반복되면서

Just compare the first and last time / your child said "Mama" / or your partner said "I love you" / and you'll know exactly / what I mean.
처음과 마지막을 비교해보라 / 당신의 아이가 '엄마'라고 말했을 때의 / 혹은 당신의 배우자가 '사랑해'라고 말했을 때의 / 그러면 당신은 정확히 알 것이다 / 내가 무엇을 의미하는지

When you have an experience / —hearing a particular sonata, / making love with a particular person, / watching the sun set / from a particular window of a particular room— / on successive occasions, / we quickly begin to adapt to it, / and the experience yields / less pleasure / each time.
당신이 경험이 있을 때 / 특정한 소나타를 듣는 것, / 특정한 사람과 사랑을 하는 것, / 일몰을 보는 것과 같은 / 특정한 방의 특정한 창문에서 / 연속적인 경우로 / 우리는 빠르게 그것에 적응하기 시작한다 / 그리고 그 경험은 가져온다 / 더 적은 기쁨을 / 매번

Psychologists call this / habituation, / economists call it / declining marginal utility, / and the rest of us call it / marriage.
심리학자들은 이것을 부른다 / 습관화라고 / 경제학자들은 그것을 부른다 / 감소하는 한계 효용이라고 / 그리고 나머지 우리들은 그것을 부른다 / 결혼이라고

해석 삶의 가장 잔혹한 진실 중 하나는 훌륭한 일들은 그것들이 처음으로 일어날 때 특히 훌륭하지만, 그것들의 훌륭함은 반복되면서 약해진다는 것이다. 당신의 아이가 '엄마'라고 말했을 때의, 혹은 당신의 배우자가 '사랑해'라고 말했을 때의 처음과 마지막을 비교해보면, 당신은 내가 무엇을 의미하는지 정확히 알 것이다. 당신이 특정한 소나타를 듣는 것, 특정한 사람과 사랑을 하는 것, 특정한 방의 특정한 창문에서 일몰을 보는 것과 같은 경험이 연속적인 경우로 있을 때, 우리는 빠르게 그것에 적응하기 시작하고, 그 경험은 매번 더 적은 기쁨을 가져온다. 심리학자들은 이것을 습관화라고 부르고, 경제학자들은 그것을 감소하는 한계 효용이라고 부르며, 나머지 우리들은 그것을 결혼이라고 부른다.

해설 지문 처음에서 훌륭함은 그것이 반복되면서 약해진다는 것이 삶의 가장 잔혹한 진실 중 하나라고 언급한 뒤, 아이가 엄마라고 말할 때나 특정한 소나타를 듣는 등의 경험을 예로 들며 그 경험들이 연속적으로 일어나는 경우 우리는 빠르게 그것에 적응하기 시

작하여 처음보다 더 적은 기쁨을 느끼게 된다고 설명하고 있다. 따라서 필자가 주장하는 바를 '아무리 좋은 일도 반복되면 식상해진다'라고 표현한 ②번이 정답이다.

어휘 cruel 잔혹한 wane 약해지다, 시들해지다 successive 연속적인
adapt 적응하다 yield 가져오다, 산출하다 habituation 습관화
decline 감소하다 marginal utility 한계 효용

---

17 독해 논리적 흐름 파악 (문맥상 적절한 어휘)   난이도 ★★☆

끊어읽기 해석

Clouds darken / from a pleasant soft white / just before rain begins to fall / because they absorb more light.
구름은 어두워진다 / 쾌적하고 은은한 흰색에서 / 비가 오기 시작하기 바로 전에 / 왜냐하면 그것들이 더 많은 빛을 흡수하기 때문이다

Clouds normally appear white / when the light that strikes them / is (A) scattered / by the small ice or water particles / from which they are composed.
구름은 일반적으로 하얗게 보인다 / 그것들에 부딪치는 빛이 / (A) 분산될 때 / 작은 얼음이나 물 입자들에 의해서 / 그것들을 구성하고 있는

However, / when the size of these ice and water particles (B) increases / —as it does just before clouds begin to deposit rain— / this scattering of light is increasingly (C) replaced / by absorption.
하지만 / 이러한 얼음과 물 입자들의 크기가 (B) 증가할 때 / 구름이 비를 내리기 시작하기 바로 전에 하는 것처럼 / 이 빛의 분산은 점점 더 (C) 대체된다 / 흡수로

As a result, / much less light reaches / the observer on the ground below / and the clouds look darker.
결과적으로 / 훨씬 적은 빛이 전달된다 / 아래 지면에 있는 관찰자들에게 / 그리고 구름은 더 어두워 보인다

해석 구름은 그것들이 더 많은 빛을 흡수하기 때문에, 비가 오기 시작하기 바로 전에 쾌적하고 은은한 흰색에서 어두워진다. 구름은 일반적으로 그것들에 부딪치는 빛이 그것들을 구성하고 있는 작은 얼음이나 물 입자들에 의해서 (A) 분산될 때 하얗게 보인다. 하지만, 구름이 비를 내리기 시작하기 바로 전에 하는 것처럼 이러한 얼음과 물 입자들의 크기가 (B) 증가할 때, 이 빛의 분산은 점점 더 흡수로 (C) 대체된다. 결과적으로, 훨씬 적은 빛이 아래 지면에 있는 관찰자들에게 전달되고 구름은 더 어두워 보인다.

         (A)   (B)   (C)
① 집중되다 – 줄어들다 – 발달되다
② 분산되다 – 증가하다 – 대체되다
③ 집중되다 – 증가하다 – 발달되다
④ 분산되다 – 줄어들다 – 대체되다

해설 (A) 빈칸 앞 문장에서 구름은 더 많은 빛을 흡수하면 어두워진다는 내용이 있으므로, 빈칸에는 구름은 빛이 '분산될'(scattered) 때 하얗게 보인다는 내용이 들어가야 적절하다. (B) 빈칸 뒤에서 구름이 비를 내리기 시작하기 바로 전의 상황을 언급하고 있으므로, 빈칸에는 이러한 얼음과 물 입자들의 크기가 '증가할'(increases) 때라는 내용이 들어가야 적절하다. (C) 빈칸 뒤 문장에서 결과적으로 훨씬 적은 빛이 지면에 있는 관찰자들에게 전달되어 구름이 더 어두워 보인다고 했으므로, 빈칸에는 이 빛의 분산이 흡수로 '대체된다'(replaced)는 내용이 들어가야 적절하다. 따라서 ② (A) scattered(분산되다) – (B) increases(증가하다) – (C) replaced(대체되다)가 정답이다.

어휘 pleasant 쾌적한, 기분 좋은 absorb 흡수하다 strike 부딪치다
scatter 분산시키다 particle 입자, 분자 compose 구성하다

---

18 독해 논리적 흐름 파악 (문맥상 부적절한 어휘)   난이도 ★★☆

끊어읽기 해석

For everywhere we look, / there is work to be done.
우리가 어디를 보더라도 / 해야 할 일이 있다

The state of the economy ① calls for action, / bold and swift, / and we will act / not only to create new jobs, / but to lay a new foundation / for growth.
경제의 상태는 행동을 ① 필요로 한다 / 대담하고 신속한 / 그리고 우리는 행동할 것이다 / 새로운 일자리를 만들기 위해서 뿐만 아니라 / 새로운 토대를 놓기 위해서도 / 성장을 위한

We will build / the roads and bridges, / the electric grids and digital lines / that ② bolster our commerce / and bind us together.
우리는 만들 것이다 / 도로와 다리와 / 배전관과 디지털 회선을 / 우리의 상업을 ② 강화하고 / 우리를 결속시키는

We will restore science / to its rightful place, / and wield technology's wonders / to ③ erode health care's quality / and lower its cost.
우리는 과학을 회복시킬 것이다 / 그것의 정당한 자리로 / 그리고 기술의 경이를 사용할 것이다 / 의료 서비스의 질을 ③ 약화시키고 / 그 비용을 낮추는 데

We will harness / the sun and the winds and the soil / to fuel our cars / and ④ run our factories.
우리는 이용할 것이다 / 태양과 바람과 토양을 / 차에 연료를 넣고 / 공장을 ④ 가동하기 위해

And / we will transform / our schools and colleges and universities / to meet / the demands of a new age.
그리고 / 우리는 개혁할 것이다 / 학교와 단과 대학과 종합 대학들을 / 충족시키기 위해 / 새 시대의 요구를

All this we can do. // And all this we will do.
이 모든 것을 우리는 할 수 있다. // 그리고 이 모든 것을 우리는 할 것이다.

해석 우리가 어디를 보더라도 해야 할 일이 있다. 경제의 상태는 대담하고 신속한 행동을 ① 필요로 하고, 우리는 새로운 일자리를 만들기 위해서 뿐만 아니라 성장을 위한 새로운 토대를 놓기 위해서도 행동할 것이다. 우리는 우리의 상업을 ② 강화하고 우리를 결속시키는 도로와 다리, 배전관과 디지털 회선을 만들 것이다. 우리는 과학을 그것의 정당한 자리로 회복시키고, 기술의 경이를 의료 서비스의 질을 ③ 약화시키고 그 비용을 낮추는 데 사용할 것이다. 우리는 차에 연료를 넣고 공장을 ④ 가동하기 위해 태양과 바람과 토양을 이용할 것이다. 그리고 우리는 새 시대의 요구를 충족시키기 위해 학교와 단과 대학과 종합 대학들을 개혁할 것이다. 이 모든 것을 우리는 할 수 있다. 그리고 이 모든 것을 우리는 할 것이다.

해설 지문 처음에 새로운 일자리 창출과 성장을 위한 토대를 놓기 위해 행동할 것이라는 내용이 있고, ③번 밑줄이 있는 문장에 과학을 정당한 자리로 회복시킬 것이라는 내용이 있으므로, 기술의 경이를 의료 서비스의 질을 '약화시키는'(erode) 데 사용한다는 것은 문맥상 적절하지 않다. 따라서 ③번이 정답이다. 참고로, 주어진 erode를 대신할 수 있는 어휘로는 '향상시키다'라는 의미의 raise, increase, boost 등이 있다.

어휘 state 상태 call for ~을 필요로 하다 swift 신속한
foundation 토대 electric grid 배전관 bolster 강화하다
commerce 상업 bind 결속시키다 restore 회복시키다
rightful 정당한 wield 사용하다, 휘두르다 wonder 경이
erode 약화시키다, 침식시키다 harness 이용하다
transform 개혁하다, 변형하다

끊어읽기 해석

In order to live well / after you stop working, / you should begin / saving for retirement / early.
잘 살기 위해서 / 당신이 일을 그만둔 후에 / 당신은 시작해야 한다 / 은퇴를 위한 저축을 / 일찍

Experts suggest / that after you retire, / you will need / 75 percent to 80 percent of your salary / to live on every month.
전문가들은 말한다 / 당신이 은퇴한 후에 / 당신은 필요로 할 것이라고 / 급여의 75퍼센트에서 80퍼센트를 / 매달 생활하기 위해

In other words, / if you make $3,000 per month / while working, / you will need / between $2,250 and $2,400 / per month / to live on during retirement.
다시 말해서 / 만약 당신이 한 달에 3천 달러를 번다면 / 일하는 동안 / 당신은 필요로 할 것이다 / 2,250달러에서 2,400달러 사이를 / 매달 / 은퇴 생활 동안 살아가는 데

This calculation assumes / that you have no mortgage on a house / to continue paying, / or any other major expenses.
이 계산은 가정한다 / 당신이 주택 담보 대출이 없다고 / 계속해서 지불해야 하는 / 혹은 다른 어떤 주요 지출이 없다고

However, / many retired people now rent / their housing, / and so they will pay more money / in housing costs / over time.
하지만 / 많은 은퇴한 사람들은 지금 임대한다 / 그들의 집을 / 그래서 그들은 더 많은 돈을 내야 할 것이다 / 집세로 / 시간이 지날수록

Older people now also have to spend more / on health care / because they live longer; / many people in developed countries / now live / into their eighties or nineties.
지금의 나이든 사람들은 또한 더 많은 돈을 써야 한다 / 의료 서비스에 / 왜냐하면 그들은 더 오래 살기 때문이다 / 선진국의 많은 사람들은 / 현재 산다 / 80대 또는 90대까지

해석   당신이 일을 그만둔 후에 잘 살기 위해서, 당신은 은퇴를 위한 저축을 일찍 시작해야 한다. 당신이 은퇴한 후에 매달 생활하기 위해 당신은 급여의 75퍼센트에서 80퍼센트를 필요로 할 것이라고 전문가들은 말한다. 다시 말해서, 만약 당신이 일하는 동안 한 달에 3천 달러를 번다면, 당신은 은퇴 생활 동안 살아가는 데 2,250달러에서 2,400달러 사이를 필요로 할 것이다. 이 계산은 당신이 계속해서 지불해야 하는 주택 담보 대출 혹은 다른 어떤 주요 지출이 없다고 가정한다. 하지만 많은 은퇴한 사람들은 지금 그들의 집을 임대해서, 그들은 시간이 지날수록 더 많은 돈을 집세로 내야 할 것이다. 지금의 나이든 사람들은 또한 더 오래 살기 때문에 더 많은 돈을 의료 서비스에 써야 하는데, 선진국의 많은 사람들은 현재 80대 또는 90대까지 산다.

① 대조적으로
② 마찬가지로
③ 다시 말해서
④ 게다가

해설   빈칸 앞 문장에 전문가들에 따르면 은퇴한 후에 매달 생활하기 위해서는 월급의 75~80퍼센트가 필요할 것이라는 내용이 있고, 빈칸 뒤 문장에 만약 일하는 동안 한 달에 3천 달러를 번다면 은퇴 동안 살아가는 데 2,250달러에서 2,400달러 사이를 필요로 할 것이라고 하며 앞에 언급된 내용을 더 자세히 설명하는 내용이 있다. 따라서 ③ In other words(다시 말해서)가 정답이다.

어휘   retirement 은퇴   expert 전문가   salary 급여, 월급
calculation 계산   assume 가정하다   mortgage 담보 대출
expense 지출   rent 임대하다, 임차하다
developed country 선진국   conversely 대조적으로
likewise 마찬가지로

끊어읽기 해석

We normally think / of the expressions on our face / as the reflection of an inner state.
우리는 보통 생각한다 / 우리의 얼굴 표정을 / 내면 상태의 반영이라고

I feel happy, / so I smile. // I feel sad, / so I frown. // Emotion goes inside-out.
나는 행복함을 느낀다 / 그래서 나는 웃는다 // 나는 슬픔을 느낀다 / 그래서 나는 찌푸린다 // 감정은 안에서 바깥으로 간다

Emotional contagion, though, suggests / that the opposite is also true.
그럼에도 불구하고, 감정적 전염은 나타낸다 / 그 반대 또한 사실이라는 것을

If I can make you smile, / I can make you happy. // If I can make you frown, / I can make you sad. // Emotion, in this sense, / goes outside-in.
만약 내가 당신을 웃게 만들 수 있다면 / 나는 당신을 행복하게 할 수 있다 // 만약 내가 당신을 찌푸리게 할 수 있다면 / 나는 당신을 슬프게 할 수 있다 // 감정은 / 이런 의미에서 / 바깥에서 안으로 간다

If we think about emotion / this way / —as outside-in, not inside-out— / it is possible to understand / how some people can have / an enormous amount of influence / over others.
만약 우리가 감정에 대해서 생각한다면 / 이런 방식으로 / 안에서 바깥으로가 아니라 바깥에서 안으로 간다는 / 이해하는 것이 가능하다 / 어떻게 몇몇 사람들이 가질 수 있는지를 / 엄청난 양의 영향력을 / 다른 사람들에게

Some of us, / after all, / are very good / at expressing emotions and feelings, / which means / that we are far more emotionally contagious / than the rest of us.
우리 중 일부는 / 결국 / 매우 능숙한데 / 감정과 기분을 표현하는 데 / 그것은 의미한다 / 우리가 훨씬 더 감정적으로 전염된다는 것을 / 우리 중 나머지보다

해석   우리는 보통 우리의 얼굴 표정을 내면 상태의 반영이라고 생각한다. 나는 행복함을 느껴서 웃는다. 나는 슬픔을 느껴서 찌푸린다. 감정은 안에서 바깥으로 간다. 그럼에도 불구하고, 감정적 전염은 그 반대 또한 사실이라는 것을 나타낸다. 만약 내가 당신을 웃게 만들 수 있다면, 나는 당신을 행복하게 할 수 있다. 만약 내가 당신을 찌푸리게 할 수 있다면, 나는 당신을 슬프게 할 수 있다. 이런 의미에서, 감정은 바깥에서 안으로 간다. 만약 우리가 감정에 대해서 안에서 바깥으로가 아니라 바깥에서 안으로 간다는 이런 방식으로 생각한다면, 어떻게 몇몇 사람들이 다른 사람들에게 엄청난 양의 영향력을 가질 수 있는지를 이해하는 것이 가능하다. 결국, 우리 중 일부는 감정과 기분을 표현하는 데 매우 능숙한데, 그것은 우리 중 나머지보다 훨씬 더 감정적으로 전염성이 강하다는 것을 의미한다.

① 기분
② 행동
③ 유창성
④ 영향력

해설   빈칸이 있는 문장에서 우리가 감정이 안에서 바깥으로가 아니라 바깥에서 안으로 간다는 방식으로 생각한다는 내용이 있으므로, 몇몇 사람들이 다른 사람들에게 엄청난 양의 '영향력'을 가질 수 있다는 내용이 들어가는 것이 적절하다. 따라서 ④번이 정답이다.

어휘   expression 표정   reflection 반영   inner 내면의   frown 찌푸리다
contagion 전염   enormous 엄청난   fluency 유창성
influence 영향(력)

끊어읽기 해석

In discussing / the relative difficulties of analysis / which the exact and inexact sciences face, / let me begin with an analogy.
논의하는 데 있어서 / 분석의 상대적인 어려움을 / 정밀 과학과 비정밀 과학이 마주하는 / 하나의 비유로 시작하겠다

Would you agree / that (A) swimmers are less skillful athletes / than runners / because swimmers do not move / as fast as runners?
당신은 동의하는가 / (A) 수영선수가 덜 능숙한 운동선수라는 데 / 육상선수보다 / 수영선수가 움직이지 않기 때문에 / 육상선수만큼 빨리?

You probably would not. // You would quickly point out / that water offers greater resistance / to swimmers / than the air and ground do / to runners.
당신은 아마 그러지 않을 것이다. // 당신은 곧 지적할 것이다 / 물이 더 큰 저항을 준다는 것을 / 수영선수에게 / 공기와 땅이 주는 것보다 / 육상선수에게

Agreed, / that is just the point. // In seeking to solve their problems, / the social scientists encounter / greater resistance / than the physical scientists.
그렇다 / 그것이 바로 요점이다 // 그들의 문제를 해결하는 것을 시도하는 데 있어 / 사회과학자들은 마주한다 / 더 큰 저항을 / 물리과학자들보다

By that I do not mean to belittle / the great accomplishments of physical scientists / who have been able, for example, to determine / the structure of atom / without seeing it.
그렇다고 과소평가하는 것은 아니다 / 물리과학자들의 훌륭한 업적들을 / 예를 들어, 밝힐 수 있었던 / 원자의 구조를 / 그것을 보지 않고

That is a tremendous achievement; / yet in many ways / it is not so difficult / as what the social scientists are expected to do.
그것은 대단한 성취이다 / 하지만 여러모로 / 그것은 그렇게 어렵지는 않다 / 사회과학자들이 하도록 기대되는 것만큼

해석 정밀 과학과 비정밀 과학이 마주하는 분석의 상대적인 어려움을 논의하는 데 있어서, 하나의 비유로 시작하겠다. 당신은 (A) 수영선수가 육상선수만큼 빨리 움직이지 않기 때문에 육상선수보다 수영선수가 덜 능숙한 운동선수라는 데 동의하는가? 당신은 아마 그러지 않을 것이다. 당신은 곧 공기와 땅이 육상선수에게 주는 저항보다 물이 수영선수에게 더 큰 저항을 준다는 것을 지적할 것이다. 그렇다, 그것이 바로 요점이다. 그들의 문제를 해결하는 것을 시도하는 데 있어, 사회과학자들은 물리과학자들보다 더 큰 저항을 마주한다. 그렇다고, 예를 들어, 그것을 보지 않고 원자의 구조를 밝힐 수 있었던 물리과학자들의 훌륭한 업적들을 과소평가하는 것은 아니다. 그것은 대단한 성취이지만, 여러모로 그것은 사회과학자들이 하도록 기대되는 것만큼 그렇게 어렵지는 않다.

① 육상선수들   ② 사회과학자들
③ 물리과학자들   ④ 운동선수들

해설 지문 중간에서 수영선수는 육상선수보다 더 큰 저항을 받고 사회과학자들은 문제를 해결하는 데 있어 물리과학자들보다 더 큰 저항을 마주한다고 하며 수영선수를 사회과학자에 비유하는 내용이 있으므로, swimmers(수영선수)는 '사회과학자들'을 의미한다는 것을 알 수 있다. 따라서 ②번이 정답이다.

어휘 relative 상대적인   inexact 비정밀한, 부정확한   analogy 비유
point out ~을 지적하다, 언급하다   resistance 저항
encounter 마주하다   belittle 과소평가하다   tremendous 대단한

끊어읽기 해석

To my mother, / it was a big occasion / to give me a ride / to the college / for my freshman year.
나의 어머니에게 / 큰 일이었다 / 나를 태워다 주는 것은 / 대학까지 / 내가 신입생일 때

She wore one of her "outfits" / —a purple pantsuit, a scarf, high heels, and sunglasses, / and she insisted / that I wear / a white shirt and a necktie.
그녀는 그녀의 '의상' 중 하나를 입었다 / 보라색 바지 정장, 스카프, 하이힐 그리고 선글라스를 / 그리고 그녀는 고집했다 / 내가 입을 것을 / 흰 셔츠와 넥타이를

"You're starting college, / not going fishing," / she said.
"너는 대학에 가는 거지 / 낚시를 가는 게 아니야" / 그녀가 말했다

Together / we would have stood out badly enough / in Pepperville Beach, / but remember, / this was college / in the mid-60s, / where the less correctly you were dressed, / the more you were dressed correctly.
함께 / 우리는 몹시 눈에 띄었을 것이다 / 페퍼빌 해변가에서도 / 하지만 기억해라 / 이것은 대학이었다는 것을 / 60년대 중반의 / 당신이 덜 올바르게 입을수록 / 더 올바르게 입은 것이던

So / when we finally got to campus / and stepped out of our Chevy station wagon, / we were surrounded / by young women / in sandals and peasant skirts, / and young men / in tank tops and shorts, / their hair worn long / over their ears.
그래서 / 우리가 마침내 교내에 도착해서 / 쉐보레 스테이션왜건에서 내렸을 때 / 우리는 둘러싸였다 / 젊은 여성들에게 / 샌들과 페전트 스커트를 입은 / 그리고 젊은 남성들에게 / 민소매 티셔츠와 반바지를 입고 / 그들의 머리를 기른 / 귀 밑으로

And / there we were, / a necktie and a purple pantsuit, / and I felt, once more, / that my mother was shining ridiculous light / on me.
그리고 / 그곳에 우리가 있었다 / 넥타이를 매고 보라색 바지 정장을 입은 / 그리고 나는 다시 한 번 느꼈다 / 나의 어머니가 우스꽝스러운 빛을 비춘다고 / 나에게

해석 나의 어머니에게, 내가 신입생일 때 나를 대학까지 태워다 주는 것은 큰 일이었다. 그녀는 그녀의 '의상' 중 하나인, 보라색 바지 정장, 스카프, 하이힐 그리고 선글라스를 썼고, 내가 흰 셔츠와 넥타이를 입을 것을 고집했다. "너는 대학에 가는 거지, 낚시를 가는 게 아니야"라고 그녀가 말했다. 우리는 함께 페퍼빌 해변가에서도 몹시 눈에 띄었을 것이지만, 이것은 당신이 덜 올바르게 입을수록 더 올바르게 입은 것이던 60년대 중반의 대학이었다는 것을 기억해라. 그래서 우리가 마침내 교내에 도착해서 쉐보레 스테이션왜건에서 내렸을 때, 우리는 샌들과 페전트 스커트를 입은 젊은 여성들과 민소매 티셔츠와 반바지를 입고 그들의 머리를 귀 밑으로 기른 젊은 남성들에게 둘러싸였다. 그리고 그곳에 넥타이를 매고 보라색 바지 정장을 입은 우리가 있었고, 나는 다시 한 번 나의 어머니가 나에게 우스꽝스러운 빛을 비춘다고 느꼈다.

① 매료된   ② 기쁜
③ 당황스러운   ④ 무심한

해설 지문에서 I(나)는 신입생일 때 어머니가 자신을 대학까지 태워다 준 일화를 소개하고 있는데, 보라색 바지 정장에서 선글라스까지 갖춰 입은 어머니의 의상과 그녀가 I(나)에게 입으라고 고집한 흰 셔츠와 넥타이가 교내에 도착해보니 다른 학생들의 옷차림과 너무 달라 몹시 눈에 띄었다고 말하고 있다. 따라서 이 지문에서 I(나)가 느꼈을 심경을 '당황스러운'이라고 표현한 ③번이 정답이다.

어휘 outfit 의상, 옷   surround 둘러싸다   ridiculous 우스꽝스러운

끊어읽기 해석

> Will you get more sick / if you exercise / while you have a cold?
> 당신은 더 아파질까 / 만약 운동한다면 / 당신이 감기에 걸렸을 때?
>
> In one experiment, / a team of researchers injected / a group of fifty students / with rhinovirus, / and then had part of the group / run, climb stairs, or cycle / at moderate intensity / for forty minutes / every other day, / while the second group remained relatively sedentary.
> 한 실험에서 / 한 팀의 연구원들이 주입했다 / 50명의 학생 그룹에게 / 코감기 바이러스를 / 그리고 그 다음에 그룹의 일부는 하게 했다 / 달리거나 계단을 오르거나 또는 자전거를 타는 것을 / 적당한 강도로 / 40분간 / 이틀에 한 번씩 / 반면 두 번째 집단은 상대적으로 주로 앉아 있게 했다
>
> They found / that the exercise regimen / neither eased nor worsened / symptoms of the common cold.
> 그들은 발견했다 / 운동 요법이 / 완화시키거나 악화시키지 않는다는 것을 / 일반적인 감기의 증상을
>
> Several similar studies conducted elsewhere / have found the same thing.
> 다른 곳에서 수행된 몇몇 비슷한 연구들도 / 같은 것을 발견했다
>
> Doctors refer to / a good rule of thumb / as the neck check.
> 의사들은 언급한다 / 어림 감정법에 대해 / 경부(목) 점검과 같은
>
> It's safe to exercise / if you have / only "above the neck" symptoms, / like a runny nose or sneezing.
> 운동하는 것은 안전하다 / 만약 당신이 가지고 있다면 / '경부(목) 위'에 나타나는 증상만을 / 콧물 또는 재채기 같은
>
> If your symptoms are "below the neck" / —a fever or diarrhea— / you're better off sitting it out / for a few days.
> 만약 당신의 증상이 '경부(목) 아래'에 나타난다면 / 열 혹은 설사와 같이 / 당신은 그것이 끝나기를 기다리는 것이 낫다 / 며칠 동안

해석   만약 당신이 감기에 걸렸을 때 운동한다면 당신은 더 아파질까? 한 실험에서, 한 팀의 연구원들이 50명의 학생 그룹에게 코감기 바이러스를 주입했고, 그 다음에 그룹의 일부는 이틀에 한 번씩 적당한 강도로 40분간 달리거나, 계단을 오르거나 또는 자전거를 타는 것을 하게 한 반면, 두 번째 집단은 상대적으로 주로 앉아 있게 했다. 그들은 운동 요법이 일반적인 감기의 증상을 완화시키거나 악화시키지 않는다는 것을 발견했다. 다른 곳에서 수행된 몇몇 비슷한 연구들도 같은 것을 발견했다. 의사들은 경부(목) 점검과 같은 어림 감정법에 대해 언급한다. 만약 당신이 콧물 또는 재채기 같은 '경부(목) 위'에 나타나는 증상만을 가지고 있다면 운동하는 것은 안전하다. 만약 당신의 증상이 열 혹은 설사와 같이 '경부(목) 아래'에 나타난다면, 당신은 며칠 동안 그것이 끝나기를 기다리는 것이 낫다.

    ① 익살스러운   ② 감정을 자극하는
    ③ 설득력 있는   ④ 유익한 정보를 주는

해설   지문 앞부분에서 코감기 바이러스와 운동 간의 연관성을 실험한 연구를 언급한 뒤, 운동이 감기의 증상을 완화하거나 악화시키지 않는다는 실험의 결과를 설명하며 의사들이 언급한 경부(목) 점검과 같은 어림 감정법(실제에 근거한 방법)에 관한 정보를 제공하고 있다. 따라서 글의 어조를 '유익한 정보를 주는'이라고 표현한 ④번이 정답이다.

어휘   inject 주입하다   rhinovirus 코감기 바이러스(감기의 주된 바이러스) moderate 적당한   intensity 강도   sedentary 주로 앉아 있는 regimen 요법   ease 완화하다   conduct 수행하다 refer to ~에 대해 언급하다   rule of thumb 어림 감정법, 경험 법칙 sneezing 재채기   fever 열, 발열   diarrhea 설사 sit out ~이 끝나기를 기다리다   persuasive 설득력 있는

끊어읽기 해석

> I was not aware / that the quality of university education in England / is in decline / until I read your article.
> 나는 알지 못했다 / 영국의 대학 교육의 질이 / 쇠퇴하고 있다는 것을 / 내가 당신의 기사를 읽기 전까지는
>
> The situation appears similar / in Japan, / where I lecture in English.
> 이런 상황은 비슷하게 나타난다 / 일본에서도 / 내가 영어로 강의하는 곳인
>
> I find / many students ill-prepared / for university education.
> 나는 생각한다 / 많은 학생들이 준비가 되지 않았다고 / 대학 교육에
>
> Many lack / the necessary intellectual abilities, / while many more have very little interest / in actually learning anything.
> 많은 이들은 부족하고 / 필수적인 지적 능력이 / 동시에 더 많은 이들이 흥미가 거의 없다 / 정말로 어떤 것을 배우는 데
>
> Why do parents pay so much money / for an education / when their children are too lazy / to study?
> 왜 부모들은 그렇게 많은 돈을 지불하는가 / 교육을 위해 / 그들의 자녀들이 너무 게으른데 / 공부하기에?
>
> Parents often force their children / into university / not to challenge them academically / but simply for the social prestige and reputation / associated with certain universities.
> 부모들은 종종 그들의 자녀들에게 강요한다 / 대학에 가도록 / 학문적으로 도전 의식을 갖게 하기 위해서가 아니라 / 단순히 사회적 위신과 명성을 위해서 / 특정 대학들과 관련된

해석   나는 내가 당신의 기사를 읽기 전까지는 영국의 대학 교육의 질이 쇠퇴하고 있다는 것을 알지 못했다. 이런 상황은 내가 영어로 강의하는 곳인 일본에서도 비슷하게 나타난다. 나는 많은 학생들이 대학 교육에 준비가 되지 않았다고 생각한다. 많은 이들은 필수적인 지적 능력이 부족하고, 동시에 더 많은 이들은 정말로 어떤 것을 배우는 데 흥미가 거의 없다. 왜 부모들은 그들의 자녀들이 공부하기에 너무 게으른데 교육을 위해 그렇게 많은 돈을 지불하는가? 부모들은 종종 학문적으로 도전 의식을 갖게 하기 위해서가 아니라 단순히 특정 대학들과 관련된 사회적 위신과 명성을 위해서 그들의 자녀들에게 대학에 가도록 강요한다.

해설   지문 처음에서 영국의 대학 교육의 질이 쇠퇴하고 있다는 것을 언급한 뒤, 일본 학생들의 상황과 교육의 문제점에 대해 설명하고, 지문 마지막에서 부모들은 자녀들이 학문적으로 도전 의식을 갖게 하기 위해서가 아니라 사회적 위신과 명성을 위해서 대학에 가도록 강요한다고 지적하고 있다. 따라서 이 지문의 목적을 '자녀교육에 대한 부모의 잘못된 가치관을 지적하려고'라고 표현한 ②번이 정답이다.

어휘   in decline 쇠퇴하여, 기울어   appear 나타나다   similar 비슷한 lecture 강의하다   ill-prepared 준비가 안된   lack 부족하다 necessary 필수적인   intellectual 지적인   force 강요하다 prestige 위신   reputation 명성   associated with ~과 관련된

끊어읽기 해석

> Are you keen to discover / new music, / but put off / by most of the stuff / you hear?
> 당신은 발견하고 싶은가요 / 새로운 음악을 / 하지만 미뤄지나요 / 대부분의 것들에 의해 / 당신이 듣는?

Then visit MusicAll. // It's a cunning website / that allows users / to recommend music / to one another / based on shared tastes.
그렇다면 MusicAll을 방문하세요. // 그것은 정교한 웹사이트입니다 / 사용자들에게 허용하는 / 음악을 추천하도록 / 서로에게 / 공유하는 취향에 기반하여

As a member / you upload / a playlist of your own favorite tunes: / the site then makes recommendations / based on the music / enjoyed by other people / who also like those tracks.
회원으로서 / 당신은 업로드합니다 / 당신이 가장 좋아하는 곡들의 재생 목록을 / 그러면 그 사이트는 추천합니다 / 음악에 기반하여 / 다른 사람들에 의해 즐겨진 / 또한 그 곡들을 좋아하는

It will also make suggestions / based on what you're listening to / at the time; / you can listen / to clips of the recommendations / to see whether they appeal.
그것은 또한 제안합니다 / 당신이 듣고 있는 것에 기반하여 / 그 시간에 / 당신은 들을 수 있습니다 / 추천된 것들의 클립을 / 그것들이 관심을 끄는지 보기 위하여

If so, / you can download them / for free. // The more you put into the site, / the more useful it becomes.
만약 그렇다면 / 당신은 그것들을 다운받을 수 있습니다 / 무료로 // 당신이 그 사이트에 더 많이 들어갈수록 / 그것은 더 유용해질 것입니다

해석 당신은 새로운 음악을 발견하고 싶지만, 당신이 듣는 대부분의 것들에 의해 미뤄지나요? 그렇다면 MusicAll을 방문하세요. 그것은 사용자들에게 공유하는 취향에 기반하여 서로에게 음악을 추천하도록 허용하는 정교한 웹사이트입니다. 회원으로서 당신이 가장 좋아하는 곡들의 재생 목록을 업로드하면, 그 사이트는 그 곡들을 좋아하는 또 다른 사람들에 의해 즐겨진 음악에 기반하여 추천합니다. 그것은 또한 당신이 그 시간에 듣고 있는 것에 기반하여 제안하는데, 당신은 그것들이 관심을 끄는지 보기 위하여 추천된 것들의 클립을 들을 수 있습니다. 만약 그렇다면, 당신은 그것들을 무료로 다운받을 수 있습니다. 당신이 그 사이트에 더 많이 들어갈수록, 그것은 더 유용해질 것입니다.

① 음악은 당신의 삶에 기여할 수 있다
② 변화를 위해 당신이 추천하고 싶은 것
③ 웹사이트에서 음악에 대한 의견들을 공유하라
④ 매력적인 웹사이트를 만드는 방법

해설 지문 앞부분에 사용자들이 공유하는 취향에 기반하여 음악을 추천하는 웹사이트인 MusicAll을 소개하는 내용이 있고, 이어서 사이트에 자신이 좋아하는 곡들의 재생 목록을 업로드하면 그것에 기반하여 사이트가 음악을 추천해준다는 이용 방식을 설명하고 있다. 따라서 이 지문의 제목을 '웹사이트에서 음악에 대한 의견들을 공유하라'라고 표현한 ③번이 정답이다.

어휘 keen 하고 싶어하는, 열망하는 put off 미루다
cunning 정교한, 교묘한 tune 곡 appeal 관심을 끌다, 매력적이다
put into ~에 들어가다 contribute 기여하다, 기부하다

정답

p.155

01	② 독해 – 세부내용 파악	**11**	④ 독해 – 논리적 흐름 파악	**21**	② 독해 – 추론	
02	④ 독해 – 논리적 흐름 파악	**12**	④ 독해 – 전체내용 파악	**22**	① 문법 – 비교 구문 & 병치·도치·강조 구문	
03	④ 독해 – 세부내용 파악	**13**	① 독해 – 추론	**23**	② 문법 – 전치사 & 시제 & 병치·도치·강조 구문	
04	④ 독해 – 세부내용 파악	**14**	② 독해 – 세부내용 파악	**24**	③ 독해 – 전체내용 파악	
05	③ 독해 – 논리적 흐름 파악	**15**	① 독해 – 추론	**25**	① 독해 – 추론	
06	④ 어휘 – 어휘 & 표현	**16**	③ 어휘 – 어휘 & 표현			
07	③ 문법 – 부사절 & 능동태·수동태	**17**	② 독해 – 전체내용 파악			
08	③ 문법 – 등위접속사와 상관접속사	**18**	① 어휘 – 어휘 & 표현			
09	② 독해 – 전체내용 파악	**19**	④ 독해 – 전체내용 파악			
10	① 독해 – 전체내용 파악	**20**	④ 독해 – 전체내용 파악			

취약영역 분석표

영역	세부 유형	문항 수	소계
어휘	어휘 & 표현	3	/3
	생활영어	0	
문법	부사절 & 능동태·수동태	1	/4
	등위접속사와 상관접속사	1	
	비교 구문 & 병치·도치·강조 구문	1	
	전치사 & 시제 & 병치·도치·강조 구문	1	
독해	전체내용 파악	7	/18
	세부내용 파악	4	
	추론	4	
	논리적 흐름 파악	3	
총계			**/25**

· 자신이 취약한 영역은 '법원직 9급 영어, 이렇게 출제된다!'(문제집 p.8)를 통해 다시 한번 확인하고 학습하시기 바랍니다.

---

01 독해 세부내용 파악 (지칭 대상 파악) 난이도 ★☆☆

끊어읽기 해석

It was in the spring / of his thirty-fifth year / that father married my mother, / then a country school teacher, / and in the following spring / I came crying into the world.
봄이었다 / 그가 서른다섯이던 해의 / 아버지가 나의 어머니와 결혼했던 / 당시 시골 학교 선생님이었던 / 그리고 이듬해 봄에 / 나는 울면서 세상에 나왔다

Something happened to the two people. // They became ambitious.
두 사람에게 무슨 일이 일어났다. // 그들은 야망이 생겼다.

The American passion / for getting up in the world / took possession of them.
미국인의 열정이 / 출세하려는 / 그들을 장악했다

It may have been / that mother was responsible.
그건 ~이었을지도 모른다 / 어머니 때문이었다

Being a school teacher, / she had no doubt read books and magazines.
학교 선생님이었기 때문에 / 그녀는 분명 책과 잡지를 읽었을 것이다

She had, I suppose, read / of Garfield, Lincoln, and other Americans / rose from poverty to fame and greatness / and as I lay beside / she may have dreamed / that I would some day rule men and cities.
그녀는 읽었을 것이다 / 가필드, 링컨과 다른 미국인들에 대해 / 가난에서부터 명성과 위대함으로 출세한 / 그리고 내가 옆에 누워 있을 때 / 그녀는 꿈을 꿨을지도 모른다 / 내가 언젠가 인류와 도시를 다스릴 것이라는

해석 아버지가 당시 시골 학교 선생님이었던 나의 어머니와 결혼한 것은 그가 서른다섯이던 해의 봄이었고, 이듬해 봄에 나는 울면서 세상에 나왔다(태어났다). 두 사람에게 무슨 일이 일어났다. 그들은 야망이 생겼다. 출세하려는 미국인의 열정이 그들을 장악했다. 그건 어머니 때문이었을지도 모른다. 학교 선생님이었기 때문에, 그

녀는 분명 책과 잡지를 읽었을 것이다. 그녀는 가필드, 링컨과 가난에서부터 명성과 위대함으로 출세한 다른 미국인들에 대해 읽었을 것이고 내가 옆에 누워 있었을 때 그녀는 내가 언젠가 인류와 도시를 다스릴 것이라는 꿈을 꿨을지도 모른다.

해설 지문 중간에서 화자의 부모님이 야망이 생겨 출세하려는 열정이 있었다고 했고, 밑줄이 있는 문장에서 화자의 어머니가 가난에서부터 명성과 위대함으로 출세한 사람들에 대한 책을 읽었을 것이라고 했으므로, '② 나의 출세에 대한 어머니의 야심'이 밑줄 친 부분의 의미로 가장 적절하다.

어휘 ambitious 야망이 있는 get[go] up in the world 출세하다 take possession of ~를 장악하다, 손에 넣다 poverty 가난 fame 명성 rule 다스리다, 통치하다

---

02 독해 논리적 흐름 파악 (문장 삽입) 난이도 ★☆☆

끊어읽기 해석

But nature has solved this problem / for the flounder.
하지만 자연은 이 문제를 해결해주었다 / 가자미에게

The flounder is a kind of flatfish.
가자미는 넙치의 일종이다.

The odd thing about this fish is / that both its eyes are on the same side / of its head.
이 물고기에 관한 특이한 점은 / 그것의 두 눈이 같은 면에 있다는 것이다 / 그것의 머리의

(①) Flounder are not born that way, though.
하지만 가자미는 그런 상태로 태어나지 않는다.

When a flounder hatched, / it looks like any other fish.
가자미가 부화되었을 때 / 그것은 다른 여느 물고기들처럼 보인다

As it grows, however, / its body becomes flattened.
그러나, 그것이 자라면서 / 그것의 몸통은 납작해진다

해커스법원직 15개년 기출문제집 영어

(②) One side of the fish is white / and the other is a sandy color.
그 물고기의 한 면은 흰색이다 / 그리고 다른 한 면은 모래색이다

The flounder lies on its white side / on the ocean floor.
가자미는 그것의 흰 면을 댄 상태로 있다 / 바다 밑바닥에

Its sandy-colored side faces up.
그것의 모래색 면이 위로 오게 한다.

(③) This makes the flounder blend in / with the sand, / so it can't be easily seen.
이것은 가자미가 섞여 들게 만든다 / 모래에 / 그래서 그것이 잘 보이지 않도록

For any other fish, / this would cause a problem.
다른 물고기들에게 / 이것은 문제를 일으킬 것이다

One eye would be looking right / into the sand.
한쪽 눈이 곧바로 들여다보고 있을 것이다 / 모래를

(④) As the fish grows, / the eye on the bottom moves / to the upper side.
그 물고기는 자라면서 / 바닥에 있는 눈이 이동한다 / 위쪽으로

해석 가자미는 넙치의 일종이다. 이 물고기에 관한 특이한 점은 그것의 두 눈이 머리의 같은 면에 있다는 것이다. 하지만 가자미는 그런 상태로 태어나지 않는다. 가자미는 부화되었을 때, 다른 여느 물고기들처럼 보인다. 그러나, 그것은 자라면서 몸통이 납작해진다. 그 물고기의 한 면은 흰색이고 다른 한 면은 모래색이다. 가자미는 바다 밑바닥에 그것의 흰 면을 댄 상태로 있다. 그것의 모래색 면이 위로 오게 한다. 이것은 가자미가 모래에 섞여 들어 잘 보이지 않게 만든다. 다른 물고기들에게, 이것(몸통의 한 면을 바닥에 댄 상태로 있는 것)은 문제를 일으킬 것이다. 한쪽 눈이 모래를 곧바로 들여다보고 있을 것이다. ④ 하지만 자연은 가자미에게 이 문제를 해결해주었다. 그 물고기는 자라면서 바닥에 있는 눈이 위쪽으로 이동한다.

해설 ④번 앞부분에 가자미처럼 몸통의 양면 중 흰 면을 바닥에 댄 상태로 있는 것은 한쪽 눈이 바로 모래를 바라보기 때문에 다른 물고기들에게 문제를 일으킬 것이라는 내용이 있고, ④번 뒤 문장에 가자미는 자라면서 바닥에 있는 눈이 위쪽으로 이동한다는 내용이 있으므로, ④번에 하지만(But) 가자미의 한쪽 눈이 모래를 곧바로 바라보는 이 문제(this problem)를 자연이 해결해 주었다는 내용의 주어진 문장이 들어가야 지문이 자연스럽게 연결된다.

어휘 flounder 가자미; 몸부림치다   flatfish 넙치·가자미류의 물고기
odd 특이한, 이상한   hatch 부화되다   flatten 납작하게 만들다
blend in ~에 섞여 들다

03   독해   세부내용 파악 (특정 정보 파악)   난이도 ★★☆

끊어읽기 해석

The common plant starch / —found in flour, cereal grains and potatoes / —is built of glucose.
일반적인 식물 전분은 / 밀가루, 곡물과 감자에서 발견되는 / 포도당으로 만들어진다

Starch can be split / in several ways / and eventually yields glucose.
전분은 분열될 수 있다 / 여러 가지 방법으로 / 그리고 궁극적으로는 포도당을 생산한다

Digestion is one such way. // After digestion takes place / the glucose goes into the blood / and is burned.
소화도 그런 방법 중 하나이다. // 소화가 일어난 후 / 포도당은 혈액으로 들어간다 / 그리고 연소된다

Some glucose may not be burned. // The liver takes it / and

converts it / to glycogen.
일부 포도당은 연소되지 않을 수도 있다. // 간은 그것(포도당)을 가져간다 / 그리고 그것을 전환시킨다 / 글리코겐으로

The body then stores this glycogen / until the body is hungry, / at which time it is digested again.
그 후 신체는 이 글리코겐을 저장한다 / 신체가 배가 고파질 때까지 / 그리고 이때 그것(포도당)은 다시 소화된다

해석 밀가루, 곡물과 감자에서 발견되는 일반적인 식물 전분은 포도당으로 만들어진다. 전분은 여러 가지 방법으로 분열될 수 있으며, 궁극적으로는 포도당을 생산한다. 소화도 그런 방법 중 하나이다. 소화가 일어난 후 포도당은 혈액으로 들어가서 연소된다. 일부 포도당은 연소되지 않을 수도 있다. 간은 그것(연소되지 않은 포도당)을 가져다가 글리코겐으로 전환시킨다. 그 후 신체는 배가 고파질 때까지 이 글리코겐을 저장하는데, 이때(배고플 때) 그것(포도당)은 다시 소화된다.

* 글리코겐은 신체에 의해 언제 사용되는가?
① 그것이 분열된 다음이다.
② 연소된 지 얼마 안 되었을 때이다.
③ 그것이 체내에 저장되자마자이다.
④ 신체가 에너지를 필요로 할 때이다.

해설 지문 뒷부분에서 연소되지 않은 포도당이 간에서 글리코겐으로 전환되어 신체에 저장되어 있다가 배가 고플 때 다시 소화된다고 했으므로, '④ 신체가 에너지를 필요로 할 때이다'가 질문에 대한 답변으로 적절하다.

어휘 common 일반적인, 흔한   starch 전분, 녹말   flour 밀가루
cereal grain 곡물   glucose 포도당   split 분열시키다, 분리하다
yield 생산하다, 항복하다   digestion 소화   take place 일어나다
liver 간   convert 전환시키다   glycogen 글리코겐, 당원
store 저장하다

04   독해   세부내용 파악 (내용 일치 파악)   난이도 ★☆☆

끊어읽기 해석

Hibernation of bears presents / several wonders to us.
곰의 겨울잠은 보여준다 / 우리에게 몇 가지 경이로운 것을

Although they are mammals, / their life is a repetition / of winter sleep and a preparation period / unlike humans.
그것들은 포유동물이지만 / 그것들의 삶은 반복이다 / 겨울잠과 준비 기간의 / 인간과 달리

Basically, / the bear stocks up energy / before winter / and expends it / during hibernation.
기본적으로 / 곰은 에너지를 비축한다 / 겨울 전에 / 그리고 그것을 쓴다 / 겨울잠을 자는 동안

In the process, / the bear's body goes through drastic change.
이 과정에서 / 곰의 몸은 급격한 변화를 겪는다

④The preparation for hibernation starts / as early as summer.
겨울잠을 위한 준비는 시작된다 / 빠르면 여름에

Bears gain weight / up to 15kg to 20kg per week / by eating everything available.
곰은 체중이 늘어난다 / 일주일에 15킬로그램에서 20킬로그램까지 / 구할 수 있는 모든 것을 먹음으로써

The energy is stored / in the form of fat / under the skin, / which grows inches thick / at its peak.
그 에너지는 저장된다 / 지방의 형태로 / 가죽 아래에 / 그리고 이것은 인치 두께로 커진다 / 그것(겨울잠)이 절정일 때는

As winter approaches, / the bear slows down its activity / and eventually goes into a winter sleep / in its cave.
겨울이 다가옴에 따라 / 곰은 활동 속도를 늦춘다 / 그리고 마침내 겨울잠을 자기 시작한다 / 그것의 동굴 속에서

③The bear sleeps / until winter is over / unless it gets disturbed.
곰은 잔다 / 겨울이 끝날 때까지 / 그것이 방해받지 않는 한

①During the winter, / the bear does not eat or drink / for almost 100 days, / and it loses between 15% to 40% / of its weight / just by sleeping.
겨울 동안 / 곰은 먹거나 마시지 않는다 / 거의 100일 동안 / 그래서 그것은 15에서 40퍼센트가 줄어든다 / 그것의 체중이 / 잠자는 것만으로도

②Despite the tremendous change / in the body, / virtually every single bear survives / this long starvation period.
엄청난 변화에도 불구하고 / 몸의 / 사실상 모든 곰은 살아남는다 / 이 긴 단식 기간 동안

In late spring, / when the food is in great supply again, / the bear walks out from the cave / and resumes its life.
늦봄에 / 먹이가 다시 넉넉해지면 / 곰은 동굴에서 나온다 / 그리고 다시 그것의 생활을 시작한다

해석 곰의 겨울잠은 우리에게 몇 가지 경이로운 것을 보여준다. 그것들은 포유동물이지만, 인간과 달리 그것들의 삶은 겨울잠과 준비 기간의 반복이다. 기본적으로, 곰은 겨울 전에 에너지를 비축하고 겨울잠을 자는 동안 그것을 쓴다. 이 과정에서, 곰의 몸은 급격한 변화를 겪는다. 겨울잠을 위한 준비는 빠르면 여름에 시작된다. 곰은 구할 수 있는 모든 것을 먹음으로써 일주일에 15킬로그램에서 20킬로그램까지 체중이 늘어난다. 그 에너지는 가죽 아래에 지방의 형태로 저장되며, 이것은 그것(겨울잠)이 절정일 때는 인치 두께로 커진다. 겨울이 다가옴에 따라, 곰은 활동 속도를 늦추고 마침내 동굴 속에서 겨울잠을 자기 시작한다. 곰은 방해받지 않는 한 겨울이 끝날 때까지 잔다. 겨울 동안, 곰은 거의 100일 동안 먹거나 마시지 않아서 잠자는 것만으로도 체중의 15에서 40퍼센트가 줄어든다. 몸의 엄청난 변화에도 불구하고, 사실상 모든 곰이 이 긴 단식 기간 동안 살아남는다. 늦봄에, 먹이가 다시 넉넉해지면, 곰은 동굴에서 나와 다시 생활을 시작한다.

해설 지문 중간에서 겨울잠을 위한 준비가 빠르면 여름에 시작된다고 했으므로, '④ 곰의 겨울잠 준비는 여름부터 시작된다'는 것은 지문의 내용과 일치한다.

오답
분석
① 열 번째 문장에서 겨울 동안 곰은 거의 100일 동안 먹거나 마시지 않는다고 했으므로 지문의 내용과 반대이다.
② 열한 번째 문장에서 몸의 엄청난 변화에도 불구하고 사실상 모든 곰이 긴 단식 기간 동안 살아남는다고 했으므로 지문의 내용과 반대이다.
③ 아홉 번째 문장에서 곰은 방해받지 않는 한 겨울이 끝날 때까지 잔다고 했으므로 지문의 내용과 다르다.

어휘 hibernation 겨울잠, 동면 wonder 경이로운 것; 궁금해 하다
mammal 포유동물 stock up ~을 비축하다
expend 쓰다, 소비하다 go through ~을 겪다 drastic 급격한
thick 두껍게; 두꺼운 peak 절정, 정상 disturb 방해하다
virtually 사실상 starvation 단식, 기아 resume 다시 시작하다

05 독해 논리적 흐름 파악 (무관한 문장 삭제) 난이도 ★★☆

끊어읽기 해석

Many experts think / that the artists in prehistoric times believed / they captured the animal's soul / when they painted it.
많은 전문가들은 생각한다 / 선사시대의 예술가들이 믿었다고 / 그들이 동물의 영혼을 담아낸다고 / 그들이 그것(동물)을 그리면

① This could be / why the images are so lifelike.
이것은 ~일 수도 있다 / 그 이미지들이 실물과 매우 똑같은 이유

② According to their belief, / if the artists captured an animal's true likeness, / they would be sure / to capture the real thing / during the hunt.
그들의 생각에 따르면 / 만약 예술가들이 동물의 실물과 꼭 닮은 모습을 담아낸다면 / 그들은 반드시 ~할 것이다 / 실제 동물을 포획할 / 사냥하는 동안

③ Prehistoric men hunted / bulls, bison and mammoths for their survival.
선사시대 사람들은 사냥했다 / 황소, 들소와 매머드를 / 생존을 위해

④ Whatever the paintings meant, / surely no one would have crawled / so deep / into these caves / to paint / had the pictures not had a special meaning.
그 그림들이 무엇을 의미하든 간에 / 확실히 아무도 기어들어 가지 않았을 것이다 / 그렇게 깊이 / 이러한 동굴로 / 그림을 그리려고 / 그 그림들이 특별한 의미를 지니지 않았다면

The dark caves were sacred places / for prehistoric people, / and this art was part / of their beliefs.
어두운 동굴은 신성한 장소였다 / 선사시대 사람들을 위한 / 그리고 이 예술은 일부였다 / 그들 생각의

해석 많은 전문가들은 선사시대의 예술가들이 그것(동물)을 그릴 때 동물의 영혼을 담아낸다고 믿었다고 생각한다. ① 이것이 그 이미지들이 실물과 매우 똑같은 이유일 수 있다. ② 그들의 생각에 따르면, 만약 예술가들이 동물의 실물과 꼭 닮은 모습을 담아낸다면, 그들은 사냥하는 동안 반드시 실제 동물을 포획할 것이다. ③ 선사시대 사람들은 생존을 위해 황소, 들소와 매머드를 사냥했다. ④ 그 그림들이 무엇을 의미하든 간에, 그 그림들이 특별한 의미를 지니지 않았다면, 확실히 아무도 그림을 그리려고 이러한 동굴로 그렇게 깊이 기어들어 가지 않았을 것이다. 어두운 동굴은 선사시대 사람들을 위한 신성한 장소였고, 이 예술은 그들 생각의 일부였다.

해설 지문 처음에서 동물을 그리면 동물의 영혼을 담아낸다고 믿었던 선사시대 예술가들에 대해 언급한 뒤, ①번에서 이것(This)이 그 동물 이미지들이 실물과 매우 똑같은 이유일 수 있다고 설명하고 있다. 이어서 ②번에서 동물의 실물과 꼭 닮은 모습을 담아내면 반드시 사냥 중 실제 동물을 포획하게 된다는 그들(선사시대 예술가들)의 생각(their belief)에 대해 언급하고, ④번에서 동굴 속 그 그림들이 특별한 의미를 지니고 있기 때문에 사람들이 깊은 동굴 속에까지 들어가 그렸을 것이라고 설명하고 있다. 그러나 ③번은 선사시대 사람들이 생존을 위해 사냥했다는 내용으로, 선사시대 예술가들이 동물을 그렸던 이유에 대해 설명하는 지문 전반의 내용과 관련이 없다.

어휘 prehistoric 선사시대의 capture 담아내다, 포획하다
lifelike 실물과 매우 똑같은 true likeness 실물과 꼭 닮음
bull 황소 bison 들소
mammoth 매머드(멸종한 코끼리과의 포유동물) crawl 기어들어 가다
sacred 신성한

06 어휘 어휘&표현 provide 난이도 ★☆☆

해석 그 후보는 맹세코 공립학교에 새 교과서와 세금 삭감을 제공하겠다고 말했지만 그는 당선되자마자 어느 공약도 따르지 않았다.

① 구매하다 ② 팔다
③ 고심하다 ④ 제공하다

어휘 **vow** 맹세코 ~을 하겠다고 말하다, 서약하다 **cutback** 삭감
act on ~을 따르다, ~에 따라 행동하다 **elect** 당선시키다, 선출하다
address (문제·상황 등에 대해) 고심하다, 연설하다

👍 이것도 알면 **합격!**

provide(제공하다)의 유의어
= supply, support, afford, arrange

---

07 문법 부사절 & 능동태·수동태 난이도 ★★☆

해석 비록 랠프 엘리슨의 첫 소설인 『보이지 않는 인간』은 1952년에 순
식간에 비평가들의 찬사를 받았지만, 그는 두 번째 소설을 결코 완
성하지 못했고, 대신 많은 짧은 작품들을 출판했다.

해설 ③ 부사절 자리와 쓰임 │ 능동태·수동태 구별 빈칸은 필수 성분을
모두 갖춘 완전한 절(he never ~ novel) 앞에 온 부사절의 자리
이다. 부사절은 '부사절 접속사(Although) + 주어 + 동사'의 형
태가 되어야 하고, 문맥상 '랠프 엘리슨의 첫 소설인 『보이지 않는
인간』이 찬사를 받다'라는 의미가 되어야 자연스러우므로 주어 자
리에 Ralph Ellison's first novel, *Invisible Man*(랠프 엘리슨의
첫 소설인 『보이지 않는 인간』)이 쓰인 ③, ④번이 정답의 후보이
다. 동사 receive 뒤에 목적어(instant critical acclaim)가 있고,
주어(Ralph Ellison's first novel, *Invisible Man*)와 동사가 '랠
프 엘리슨의 첫 소설인 『보이지 않는 인간』이 찬사를 받다'라는
의미의 능동 관계이므로 능동태 received를 써야 한다.

어휘 **instant** 순식간의, 즉각적인 **acclaim** 찬사 **invisible** 보이지 않는

👍 이것도 알면 **합격!**

부사절 접속사는 절 앞에 오는 것이 원칙이지만, 분사구문 앞에 오기
도 한다는 것을 알아두자.

(ex) Cellphones can jam the airplane's radio signals **when**
switched on.
휴대 전화는 켜져 있을 때 비행기의 전파 신호를 방해할 수도 있다.

---

08 문법 등위접속사와 상관접속사 난이도 ★★☆

해석 당신의 십 대 자녀에게 가정용 전화기는 온 가족을 위한 것이라고
가르쳐라. 만약 당신의 자녀가 가정의 전화기로 통화를 과도하게
한다면, 15분 동안 통화를 할 수 있지만, 그 후에는 적어도 같은 시
간 동안 통화를 삼가야 한다고 그(자녀)에게 말하라. 이것은 다른
가족 구성원들이 전화를 걸고 받을 수 있도록 전화가 사용중이 아
니게 할 뿐만 아니라, 당신의 십 대 자녀에게 절제와 규율도 가르
친다. 아니면 만약 당신이 그 생각에 찬성하지 않는다면, 당신의
수다스러운 십 대 자녀가 그의 용돈이나 아르바이트로 돈을 지불
하는 그 자신만의 전화기를 가지도록 허락하라.

해설 ③ 상관접속사 문맥상 '전화가 사용중이 아니게 할 뿐만 아니라
절제와 규율도 가르친다'라는 의미가 되어야 자연스러운데, 'A뿐
만 아니라 B도'는 상관접속사 not only A but also B를 사용하
여 나타낼 수 있고, but 앞에 3인칭 단수 동사 frees가 왔으므로
but 뒤의 동명사 teaching을 3인칭 단수 동사 teaches로 고쳐
야 한다.

오답
분석 ① 보어 자리 be동사(is)는 주격 보어를 취하는 동사인데, 보어
자리에는 명사나 형용사 역할을 하는 것이 올 수 있으므로 명
사 역할을 하는 전치사구 for the whole family가 올바르게
쓰였다.

---

② 혼동하기 쉬운 어순 '동사(must stay) + 부사(off)'로 이루어
진 구동사는 목적어가 명사(the phone)이면 '동사 + 부사 +
명사' 혹은 '동사 + 명사 + 부사'의 어순으로 모두 쓰이므로
he must stay off the phone이 올바르게 쓰였다.

④ 관계대명사 that 선행사 his own phone이 사물이고 관계절
내에서 전치사 for의 목적어 역할을 하므로 목적격 관계대명사
that이 올바르게 쓰였다.

어휘 **excessively** 과도하게 **stay off** ~을 삼가다, 멀리하다
moderation 절제 **discipline** 규율 **talkative** 수다스러운
allowance 용돈

👍 이것도 알면 **합격!**

여러 가지 상관접속사를 알아두자.

• either A or B A 또는 B 중 하나	• not A but A A가 아니라 B
• neither A nor B A도 B도 아닌	• A as well as B B뿐만 아니라 A도

---

09 독해 전체내용 파악 (요지 파악) 난이도 ★★☆

끊어읽기 해석

Mr. Jones, the owner of a small company, wanted / to bring
his nephew Carl, into the business.
작은 회사의 주인인 Jones 씨는 원했다 / 그의 조카 Carl을 그 사업에 끌
어들이기를

At first / he sent Carl out / on the road selling, / but he
didn't make many sales.
처음에 / 그는 Carl을 보냈다 / 거리에서 물건을 팔도록 / 하지만 그는 많
은 물건을 팔지 못했다

Then he tried Carl / in the manufacturing department, / but
Carl was too thorough / and took too much time.
그러고 나서 그(Jones)는 Carl을 시험해 보았다 / 제조 부서에서 / 하지
만 Carl은 지나치게 꼼꼼했다 / 그래서 시간이 너무 많이 걸렸다

Then he tried Carl / in human resources, / but Carl was too
kind / and the other employees took advantage of him.
그러고 나서 그는 Carl을 시험해 보았다 / 인사과에서 / 하지만 Carl은 지
나치게 친절했다 / 그래서 다른 직원들은 그를 이용했다

Finally, / Mr. Jones put Carl / in customer relations, / and he
was wonderful!
결국 / Jones 씨는 Carl을 배치했다 / 고객 상담실에 / 그리고 그는 훌륭
했다!

He was kind / to all who called, / and made everyone happy.
그는 친절했다 / 전화를 걸어오는 모든 사람들에게 / 그리고 모두를 만족하
게 했다

The customers were pleased / and spread the word / to all
their friends / about Mr. Jones' great company.
고객들은 만족해했다 / 그리고 입소문을 냈다 / 모든 동료들에게 / Jones
씨의 훌륭한 회사에 대해

해석 작은 회사의 주인인 Jones 씨는 그의 조카 Carl을 그 사업에 끌어
들이기를 원했다. 처음에 그는 Carl이 거리에서 물건을 팔도록 보
냈지만, 그는 많은 물건을 팔지 못했다. 그러고 나서 그(Jones 씨)
는 제조 부서에서 Carl을 시험해 보았지만, Carl은 지나치게 꼼꼼
해서 시간이 너무 많이 걸렸다. 그러고 나서 그는 인사과에서 Carl
을 시험해 보았지만, Carl이 지나치게 친절해서 다른 직원들은 그
를 이용했다. 결국, Jones 씨는 Carl을 고객 상담실에 배치했고, 그
는 훌륭했다! 그는 전화를 걸어오는 모든 사람들에게 친절했고, 모
두를 만족하게 했다. 고객들은 만족해하며 Jones 씨의 훌륭한 회
사에 대해 모든 동료들에게 입소문을 냈다.

① 뜻이 있는 곳에 길이 있다(어떤 일을 이루고자 하는 의지가 있다면 그 일을 이룰 방법을 찾을 수 있다).

② 사람은 누구나 자기 직업이 있다(굼벵이도 구르는 재주가 있다).

③ 한 사람에게는 음악이지만 다른 사람에게는 소음이다(같은 것이라고 모두에게 좋은 것은 아니다).

④ 모두의 일은 결국 그 누구의 일도 아니다(공동이 책임지는 일은 무책임하게 되기 쉽다).

해설 지문 전반에 걸쳐 작은 회사를 운영하는 Jones 씨의 조카 Carl이 초반에 투입되었던 부서와는 잘 맞지 않았지만, 고객 상담실에 배치되자 일을 훌륭하게 해내서 고객들이 만족하며 Jones 씨 회사의 훌륭함에 대해 입소문을 냈다고 설명하고 있으므로, '② 사람은 누구나 자기 직업이 있다(굼벵이도 구르는 재주가 있다)'가 이 글의 내용을 가장 잘 표현한 속담이다.

어휘 nephew 조카 manufacturing 제조 thorough 꼼꼼한, 철저한
take advantage of ~를 이용하다
customer relations 고객 상담실
spread the word 입소문을 내다

10 독해 전체내용 파악 (문단 요약) 난이도 ★☆☆

끊어읽기 해석

In 1960, / presidential candidates Richard M. Nixon and John F. Kennedy agreed / to a series of debates, / which were broadcast simultaneously / on television and radio.
1960년에 / 대통령 후보 리처드 M. 닉슨과 존 F. 케네디는 동의했다 / 일련의 토론을 하는 것에 / 그리고 이것은 동시에 방영되었다 / 텔레비전과 라디오에서

According to surveys, / most radio listeners felt / that Nixon had won the debates, / while television viewers picked / the younger, more photogenic Kennedy.
조사에 따르면 / 대부분의 라디오 청취자들은 느꼈다 / 닉슨이 토론에서 이겼다고 / 반면에 텔레비전 시청자들은 선택했다 / 더 젊고, 사진이 더 잘 나왔던 케네디를

Kennedy went on to win / the general election that fall.
이어서 케네디는 승리하였다 / 그해 가을 총선거에서

Television coverage was also influential / during the Vietnam War.
텔레비전 보도는 또한 영향력이 있었다 / 베트남 전쟁 동안에도

By the mid-1960s, / major networks were broadcasting daily images of the war / into virtually every home / in the United States.
1960년대 중반까지 / 주요 방송사들은 매일 전쟁의 모습을 방영하고 있었다 / 거의 모든 가정에 / 미국의

For many viewers, / the horrors they saw on television were more significant / than the optimistic reports of impending victory / issued by government officials / and repeated in print accounts.
많은 시청자들에게 / 그들이 텔레비전에서 본 참상은 더 중요했다 / 임박한 승리에 대한 낙관적인 보도보다 / 정부 관리들에 의해 발포된 / 그리고 서면 기사로 전해졌던

해석 1960년에, 대통령 후보 리처드 M. 닉슨과 존 F. 케네디는 일련의 토론을 하는 것에 동의했고, 이것은 텔레비전과 라디오에서 동시에 방영되었다. 조사에 따르면, 대부분의 라디오 청취자들은 닉슨이 토론에서 이겼다고 느낀 반면, 텔레비전 시청자들은 더 젊고, 사진이 더 잘 나왔던 케네디를 선택했다. 이어서 케네디는 그해 가을 총선거에서 승리하였다. 텔레비전 보도는 베트남 전쟁 동안에도 영향력이 있었다. 1960년대 중반까지, 주요 방송사들은 미국의

거의 모든 가정에 매일 전쟁의 모습을 방영하고 있었다. 많은 시청자들에게, 그들이 텔레비전에서 본 참상은 정부 관리들에 의해 발포되어 서면 기사로 전해졌던 임박한 승리에 대한 낙관적인 보도보다 더 중요했다.

> 1960년대 미국에서는, (A) 텔레비전이 다른 어떤 미디어보다 일부 (B) 정치적 이슈에 더 엄청난 영향을 미쳤다.

	(A)	(B)
①	텔레비전	정치적인
②	라디오	경제상의
③	신문	정치적인
④	텔레비전	경제상의

해설 지문 중간에서 토론에 참여한 닉슨과 케네디 중에서 텔레비전 시청자들은 더 젊고 사진이 잘 나왔던 케네디를 선택했는데, 실제로 그해 가을 총선거에서 케네디가 이겼다고 설명하고 있다. 이어서 텔레비전 보도가 베트남 전쟁 동안에도 영향력이 있었다고 하며 많은 시청자들에게는 텔레비전에서 본 전쟁의 참상이 서면 기사로 전해진 임박한 승리에 대한 낙관적인 보도보다 더 중요했다고 설명하고 있으므로, 빈칸 (A)와 (B)에 텔레비전(television)이 다른 어떤 미디어보다 일부 정치적(political) 이슈에 더 엄청난 영향을 미쳤다는 내용이 와야 적절하다. 따라서 ①번이 정답이다.

어휘 presidential 대통령의 broadcast 방영하다, 방송하다
simultaneously 동시에 photogenic 사진이 잘 나오는
general election 총선거 coverage 보도, 방송
influential 영향력 있는 virtually 거의, 사실상 optimistic 낙관적인
impending 임박한, 곧 닥칠 repeat 전하다, 반복하다
account 기사, 보고 profound 엄청난, 깊은
economical 경제상의, 알뜰한

11 독해 논리적 흐름 파악 (문맥상 적절한 어휘) 난이도 ★★☆

끊어읽기 해석

School uniforms are becoming more and more popular.
교복은 점점 더 인기가 많아지고 있다.

That's no surprise, / because they offer many benefits.
그것은 놀라운 일도 아니다 / 그것들은(교복은) 많은 혜택을 제공하기 때문에

They instantly end / the powerful social sorting and labeling / that come from clothing.
그것들은 즉시 끝낸다 / 강력한 사회적 구분과 꼬리표를 붙이는 행위를 / 옷에서 오는

If all students are dressed / in the same way, / they will not be (A) distracted by fashion competition.
만약 모든 학생이 옷을 입는다면 / 같은 방식으로 / 그들은 (A) 산만해지지 않을 것이다 / 패션 경쟁에 의해

Some students will also not be excluded / or laughed at / because they wear the "wrong" clothes.
일부 학생들 또한 배제되지 않을 것이다 / 혹은 웃음거리가 / 그들이 '잘못된' 옷을 입어서

Some people (B) object / to the "regimentation" of school uniforms, / but they do not realize / that students already accept a kind of regimentation / —wanting to look just like their friends.
일부 사람들은 (B) 반대한다 / 교복의 '규격화'에 / 하지만 그들은 깨닫지 못하고 있다 / 학생들이 일종의 규격화를 이미 받아들이고 있다는 것을 / 그들의 친구들과 똑같이 보이고 싶어 하는

The difference is that / the clothing students choose for themselves / creates social barrier; / school uniform (C) tear those barriers down.

차이점은 ~라는 점이다 / 학생들이 그들 스스로를 위해 선택하는 옷이 / 사회적 장벽을 만든다는 / 교복은 그러한 장벽을 (C) 허물어 버린다

해석 교복은 점점 더 인기가 많아지고 있다. 그것들은(교복) 많은 혜택을 제공하기 때문에 놀라운 일도 아니다. 그것들은 옷에서 오는 강력한 사회적 구분과 꼬리표를 붙이는 행위를 즉시 끝낸다. 만약 모든 학생이 같은 방식으로 옷을 입는다면, 그들은 패션 경쟁에 의해 (A) 산만해지지 않을 것이다. 일부 학생들 또한 '잘못된' 옷을 입어서 배제되거나 웃음거리가 되지 않을 것이다. 일부 사람들은 교복의 '규격화'에 (B) 반대하지만, 그들은 학생들이 그들의 친구들과 똑같이 보이고 싶어 하는 일종의 규격화를 이미 받아들이고 있다는 것을 깨닫지 못하고 있다. 차이점은 학생들이 그들 스스로를 위해 선택하는 옷은 사회적 장벽을 만들고 교복은 그러한 장벽을 (C) 허물어 버린다는 것이다.

     (A)   (B)   (C)
① 습관이 들다 – 반대하다 – 허물다
② 습관이 들다 – 제시하다 – 약화시키다
③ 산만해지다 – 제시하다 – 약화시키다
④ 산만해지다 – 반대하다 – 허물다

해설 (A) 빈칸 앞부분에 교복이 옷에서 오는 강력한 사회적 구분과 꼬리표를 붙이는 행위를 즉시 끝낸다는 내용이 있고, (A) 빈칸 뒤 문장에 일부 학생들이 '잘못된' 옷을 입어서 배제되거나 웃음거리가 되지 않을 것이라는 내용이 있으므로, (A)에는 모든 학생이 같은 방식으로 옷을 입게 되면 학생들이 패션 경쟁에 의해 산만해지지 (distracted) 않을 것이라는 내용이 와야 적절하다. (B) 빈칸 앞부분에 교복을 입음으로써 모두가 같은 방식으로 입는 것의 장점에 대한 내용이 있고, (B) 빈칸이 있는 문장에 학생들이 친구들과 똑같이 보이고 싶어 하는 일종의 규격화를 이미 받아들였다는 것을 깨닫지 못하는 사람들에 대한 내용이 있으므로, (B)에는 일부 사람들이 교복의 '규격화'에 반대한다(object)는 내용이 와야 적절하다. (C) 빈칸 앞부분에 사회적 구분과 꼬리표를 붙이는 행위를 끝내는 교복의 장점에 대한 내용이 있으므로, (C)에는 교복이 사회적 장벽을 허물어(tear) 버린다는 내용이 와야 적절하다. 따라서 ④번이 정답이다.

어휘 benefit 혜택 sort 구분하다; 종류 distract 산만하게 하다
contract 습관이 들다, 병에 걸리다 exclude 배제하다, 제외하다
be laughed at 웃음거리가 되다 object 반대하다
subject 제시하다, 복종시키다 regimentation 규격화, 통제
barrier 장벽, 장애물 wear 약화시키다, 마모시키다
tear down ~을 허물다

12 독해 전체내용 파악 (문단 요약) 난이도 ★☆☆

끊어읽기 해석

For the normal emotional and physical development of infants, / sensory and perceptual stimulation is necessary.
유아의 정상적인 정서 및 신체적 발달을 위해서는 / 감각과 지각의 자극이 필요하다

Healthy babies experience this stimulation / while in contact with the mother or other adults / who feed, diaper, or wash the infant.
건강한 아기들은 이 자극을 경험한다 / 엄마나 다른 어른들과 접촉하는 동안 / 그 젖먹이에게 젖을 먹이고, 기저귀를 채우거나 씻기는

However, / infants who are born prematurely / or are sick / miss these experiences / during the early weeks of their lives / when they live in incubators, / an artificial environment / devoid of normal stimuli.
그러나 / 미숙아로 태어난 유아들은 / 혹은 아픈 / 이러한 경험들을 놓친다 /

그들 삶의 초기 몇 주 동안 / 그들이 인큐베이터에서 살 때 / 인공적인 환경인 / 정상적인 자극이 없는

These babies tend to become listless / and seem uninterested / in their surroundings.
이 아기들은 무기력해지는 경향이 있다 / 그리고 관심이 없어 보인다 / 그들의 주변 환경에

However, / when they are stimulated / by being handled and spoken to / and by being provided with bright objects / such as hanging mobiles or pictures, / they began to respond by smiling, / becoming more active physically, / and gaining weight more rapidly.
그러나 / 그들이 자극을 받을 때 / 손으로 만져지고 (그들에게) 말을 검으로써 / 그리고 밝은 물체가 주어짐으로써 / 걸려 있는 모빌이나 사진 같은 / 그들은 웃으면서 반응하기 시작한다 / 신체적으로 더 활발해진다 / 그리고 더 빠르게 살이 찌게 된다

해석 유아의 정상적인 정서 및 신체적 발달을 위해서는 감각과 지각의 자극이 필요하다. 건강한 아기들은 그 젖먹이에게 젖을 먹이고, 기저귀를 채우거나 씻기는 엄마나 다른 어른들과 접촉하는 동안 이 자극을 경험한다. 그러나, 미숙아로 태어났거나 아픈 유아들은 정상적인 자극이 없는 인공적인 환경인 인큐베이터에서 살 때 그들 삶의 초기 몇 주 동안 이러한 경험들을 놓친다. 이 아기들은 무기력해지고 그들의 주변 환경에 관심이 없어 보이는 경향이 있다. 그러나, 그들을 손으로 만지거나 말을 걸고 걸려 있는 모빌이나 사진 같은 밝은 물체를 그들에게 줌으로써 자극을 받을 때, 그들은 웃으면서 반응하기 시작하고, 신체적으로 더 활발해지며, 더 빠르게 살이 찌게 된다.

이 지문에 따르면, 인큐베이터에서 보살핌을 받는 미숙아들은 열 달을 다 채우고 태어난 영아에 비해 신체적으로 덜 활동적이기 쉽다.

① 체중이 더 빨리 늘어난다
② 자연적인 자극을 더 많이 받는다
③ 밝은 물체에 더 빨리 반응한다
④ 신체적으로 덜 활동적이다

해설 지문 중간에 미숙아로 태어난 아이들은 인큐베이터에서 살 때 무기력해지는 경향이 있다는 내용이 있으므로, 빈칸에는 인큐베이터에서 보살핌을 받는 미숙아들이 열 달을 다 채우고 태어난 영아보다 '④ 신체적으로 덜 활동적이기' 쉽다는 내용이 와야 적절하다.

어휘 infant 유아, 젖먹이 sensory 감각의 perceptual 지각의
stimulation 자극 feed 젖을 먹이다, 밥을 먹이다
diaper 기저귀를 채우다 incubator 인큐베이터, 부화기
artificial 인공적인 devoid of ~이 없는 premature 미숙아의
full-term 열 달을 다 채우고 태어난

13 독해 추론 (내용 추론) 난이도 ★★☆

끊어읽기 해석

You can see this / in the way / Americans treat their children.
당신은 이것을 볼 수 있다 / 방식에서 / 미국인들이 그들의 아이들을 대하는

Even very young children are given opportunities / to make their own choices / and express their opinions.
심지어 아주 어린 아이들에게도 기회가 주어진다 / 스스로 선택할 수 있는 / 그리고 그들의 의견을 말할

A parent will ask a one-year-old child / what color balloon he or she wants, / which candy bar he or she would prefer, / or whether he or she wants to sit / next to mommy or daddy.

부모는 한 살짜리 아이에게 물어볼 것이다 / 어떤 색깔의 풍선을 원하는 지 / 어떤 초코바를 선호하는지 / 앉고 싶은지 / 엄마와 아빠 중 누구 옆에

The child's preference will normally be accepted.
아이의 선택은 대개 받아들여질 것이다.

Through this process, / Americans come to consider themselves / as equal beings / with the right / to have their own individual opinions and decisions respected.
이 과정을 통해 / 미국인들은 그들 스스로를 생각하게 된다 / 평등한 존재 라고 / 권리를 가진 / 자신의 개인적인 의견과 결정을 존중 받을

At the same time, / they are also taught / to respect the opinions and decisions of others.
동시에 / 그들(아이들)은 또한 배운다 / 타인의 의견과 결정을 존중하도록

해석 당신은 미국인들이 아이들을 대하는 방식에서 이것을 볼 수 있다. 심지어 아주 어린 아이들에게도 스스로 선택하고 그들의 의견을 말할 수 있는 기회가 주어진다. 부모는 한 살짜리 아이에게 어떤 색깔의 풍선을 원하는지, 어떤 초코바를 선호하는지, 엄마와 아빠 중 누구 옆에 앉고 싶은지 물어볼 것이다. 아이의 선택은 대개 받아들여질 것이다. 이 과정을 통해, 미국인들은 그들 스스로가 자신 의 개인적인 의견과 결정을 존중 받을 권리를 가진 평등한 존재라 고 생각하게 된다. 동시에, 그들(아이들)은 또한 타인의 의견과 결 정을 존중하도록 배운다.

해설 지문 첫 문장에서 미국인들이 아이를 대하는 방식에서 이것(this) 을 볼 수 있다고 한 뒤, 지문 전반에 걸쳐 아이들의 선택을 존중해 주고 아이들이 타인의 의견을 존중하도록 가르치는 미국인들의 태도에 대해 설명하고 있으므로, '① 개인의 의사가 존중되는 미 국 사회의 특성'이 이 글의 바로 앞에 올 내용으로 가장 적절하다.

어휘 **preference** 선택, 선호 **equal** 평등한, 동등한 **respect** 존중하다

---

14 독해 세부내용 파악 (특정 정보 파악) 난이도 ★☆☆

끊어읽기 해석

Dear Ms. Larson,
친애하는 Larson 씨,

Thank you / for inquiry of 12 September / asking for the latest edition / of our catalogue.
감사합니다 / 9월 12일 문의를 주셔서 / 최신판을 요청하는 / 당사 카탈로 그의

We are pleased / to enclose our latest brochure.
저희는 기쁩니다 / 저희의 최신 책자를 동봉해 드리게 되어

Purchases can be made online / by visiting our website / at mortmonbros.com.
구매는 온라인으로 할 수 있습니다 / 저희 웹사이트 방문하셔서 / mortmonbros.com를

We would also like to inform you / that we are having a special sale / on HP printers / all throughout the month / and have already included in this mailing / an order sheet.
저희는 또한 당신에게 알려드리고자 합니다 / 저희가 특별 할인 판매를 하 고 있다는 것을 / HP 프린터에 대해 / 이번 달 내내 / 그리고 이 메일에 이 미 포함해 두었다는 것을 / 주문서를

Orders can be filled out on paper / and sent by post / or filled in on our website / and submitted electrically.
주문서는 서면으로 작성될 수 있습니다 / 그리고 우편으로 보내질 수 있습 니다 / 혹은 저희 웹사이트에서 작성될 수 있습니다 / 그리고 메일로 제출 될 수 있습니다

The phone ordering method will take / three extra days / for shopping / but no additional costs will be attached.
휴대폰 주문 방식은 걸릴 것입니다 / 3일이 더 / 쇼핑에 / 하지만 추가 비용 이 붙지 않을 것입니다

Our company policy is / that all first time customers receive / free shipping and handling / for their first three months for business, / so the new printers would have no extra costs.
당사의 방침은 / 모든 첫 고객들이 받는다는 것입니다 / 무료 배송 및 취급 수수료를 / 처음 3개월 동안은 / 그래서 새 프린터는 추가 비용이 들지 않 을 것입니다

We look forward / to welcoming you as our customer.
저희는 고대하고 있습니다 / 당신을 저희 고객으로 맞이하기를

Your sincerely, John Mortmon // *Marketing Director of Mortmon Brothers*
John Mortmon 드림 // Mortmon Brothers의 마케팅 이사

해석 친애하는 Larson 씨,
9월 12일 당사 카탈로그의 최신판을 요청하는 문의를 주셔서 감 사합니다. 저희의 최신 책자를 동봉해 드리게 되어 기쁩니다. 구매 는 저희 웹사이트 mortmonbros.com를 방문하셔서 온라인으로 할 수 있습니다. 저희가 이번 달 내내 HP 프린터에 대한 특별 할인 판매를 하고 있으며, 이 메일에 주문서를 이미 포함해 두었다는 것 또한 알려드리고자 합니다. 주문서는 서면으로 작성해서 우편으로 보내시거나 저희 웹사이트에서 작성해서 메일로 제출하실 수 있습니다. 휴대폰을 통한 주문 방식은 쇼핑에 3일이 더 걸리지만 추가 비용이 붙지 않을 것입니다. 당사의 방침은 모든 첫 고객들이 처음 3개월 동안은 무료 배송 및 취급 수수료를 받을 수 있다는 것이기 때문에 새 프린터는 추가 비용이 들지 않을 것입니다. 당신을 저희 고객으로 맞이하기를 고대하고 있겠습니다.
John Mortman 드림
Mortmon Brothers의 마케팅 이사

* 첫 고객에게 제공되는 혜택은 무엇인가?

① 그들은 그 회사로부터 무료 프린터를 얻는다.
② 그들은 몇 달 동안 무료 배달을 받는다.
③ 그들은 인터넷을 통해 주문을 제출할 수 있다.
④ 그들은 새로운 품목의 목록을 기재하고 있는 책자를 받을 수 있다.

해설 지문 뒷부분에서 모든 첫 고객들이 처음 3개월 동안은 무료 배송 및 취급 수수료를 받는 방침 때문에 새 프린터에 추가 비용이 들 지 않는다고 했으므로, '② 그들은 몇 달 동안 무료 배달을 받는 다'는 것이 첫 고객에게 제공되는 혜택으로 적절하다.

어휘 **inquiry** 문의 **enclose** 동봉하다 **throughout** ~ 내내 **submit** 제출하다 **attach** 붙이다, 첨부하다 **look forward to** ~하기를 고대하다

---

15 독해 추론 (빈칸 완성 - 단어) 난이도 ★★☆

끊어읽기 해석

When you want to remind yourself / to do something, / link that activity / to another event / that you know / will take place.
당신이 스스로 상기시키고 싶을 때 / 무언가를 하는 것을 / 그 활동을 관련 지어라 / 또 다른 일에 / 당신이 알고 있는 / 일어날 거란 걸

Say you're walking to work / and suddenly you realize / that your books are (A) due / at the library tomorrow.
당신이 일하러 걸어가고 있다고 하자 / 그리고 갑자기 당신은 깨닫는다 / 당신의 책을 반납(A)하기로 되어 있다는 것을 / 내일 도서관에

Switch your watch / from your left to your right wrist.
당신의 손목시계를 바꿔라(옮겨라) / 당신의 왼쪽에서 오른쪽 손목으로

Every time you look / at your watch / it becomes a (B) reminder / that you were supposed to remember something.
당신이 볼 때마다 / 당신의 시계를 / 그것은 (B) 상기시키는 것이 된다 / 당 신이 무언가를 기억해야 한다는 것을

If you empty your pockets / every night, / put an unusual item / in your pocket / to remind yourself / to do something / before you go to bed.
만약 당신이 주머니를 비운다면 / 매일 밤 / 특이한 물건을 넣어라 / 당신의 주머니에 / 당신이 스스로 상기시키기 위해 / 무언가를 해야 하는 것을 / 당신이 잠자리에 들기 전에

To remember to call your sister / for her birthday, / pick an object / from the kitchen / —a fork, perhaps— /and put it in your pocket.
당신 여동생에게 전화하는 것을 잊지 않으려면 / 그녀의 생일에 / 물건을 골라라 / 부엌에서 / 포크 같은 / 그리고 그것을 당신의 주머니에 넣어라

해석 당신이 무언가를 하는 것을 스스로 상기시키고 싶을 때, 일어날 거란 걸 당신이 알고 있는 또 다른 일에 그 활동을 관련지어라. 당신이 일하러 걸어가고 있는데 갑자기 내일 도서관에 당신의 책을 반납(A)하기로 되어 있다는 것을 깨달았다고 하자. 당신의 손목시계를 왼쪽에서 오른쪽 손목으로 옮겨라. 당신이 시계를 볼 때마다 그것은 당신이 무언가를 기억해야 한다는 것을 (B) 상기시키는 것이 된다. 만약 당신이 매일 밤 주머니를 비운다면, 당신이 잠자리에 들기 전에 무언가를 해야 하는 것을 스스로 상기시키기 위해 특이한 물건을 주머니에 넣어라. 당신 여동생의 생일에 전화하는 것을 잊지 않으려면, 부엌에서 포크 같은 물건을 골라 당신의 주머니에 넣어라.

	(A)	(B)
①	~하기로 되어 있는	상기시키는 것
②	~하기로 되어 있는	안락의자
③	즉시 이용할 수 있는	상기시키는 것
④	즉시 이용할 수 있는	안락의자

해설 (A) 빈칸 앞 문장에 당신이 무언가를 하는 것을 스스로 상기시키기 위한 방법을 언급하는 내용이 있고, (A) 빈칸이 있는 문장에 일하러 걸어가는 도중 무언가를 깨닫는 상황을 예시로 드는 내용이 있으므로, (A)에는 당신의 책을 도서관에 반납하기로 되어 있다(due)는 것을 깨닫는다는 내용이 나와야 적절하다. (B) 빈칸 앞 문장에 책을 반납하는 것을 기억해내기 위해 손목시계를 다른 손목에 옮기는 것을 예시로 드는 내용이 있고, (B) 빈칸 뒤 문장에 해야 할 일을 상기시키기 위해 특이한 물건을 주머니에 넣는 것과 여동생의 생일에 전화하는 것을 잊지 않기 위해 포크를 주머니에 넣는 것을 예시로 드는 내용이 있으므로, (B)에는 손목시계가 당신이 무언가를 기억해야 한다는 것을 상기시키는 것(reminder)이 된다는 내용이 나와야 적절하다. 따라서 ①번이 정답이다.

어휘 remind 상기시키다, 생각나게 하다 take place 일어나다
switch 바꾸다 wrist 손목 unusual 특이한
due ~하기로 되어 있는 reminder 상기시키는 것 recliner 안락의자

16 어휘 어휘&표현 breed 난이도 ★☆☆

해석 * 무지는 편견을 낳는다.

> breed 동사.
> 1. 성관계를 맺고 새끼를 낳다: 많은 동물들이 일 년 중 특정 시기에만 번식한다.
> 2. 통제된 방식으로 계속 새끼를 낳게 하기 위해 동물이나 식물을 기르다: 토끼는 그것들의 긴 털 때문에 사육된다.
> 3. 어떤 것의 원인이 되다: 성공만큼 성공을 낳는 것은 없다.
> 4. 누군가를 그가 자라남에 따라 특정한 방식으로 가르치다: 실패에 대한 두려움이 어린 나이에 그에게서 자라났다.

해설 주어진 문장에서 breed(낳다)는 '~의 원인이 되다(야기하다)'라는 의미로 사용되었으므로 '③ 어떤 것의 원인이 되다'가 정답이다.

어휘 ignorance 무지
breed 번식하다, 사육하다, ~을 야기하다, ~을 가르치다
prejudice 편견 young 새끼, 자식

👍 이것도 알면 합격!

breed(~을 야기하다)와 유사한 의미의 표현
= cause, induce, generate, arouse, bring about, give rise to

17 독해 전체내용 파악 (제목 파악) 난이도 ★★☆

끊어읽기 해석

> Personal qualities generally have / either positive or negative connotations.
> 개인적 특성은 일반적으로 가지고 있다 / 긍정적이거나 부정적인 함축 의미를
>
> Our attitudes toward such personal qualities / are partly personal, partly social, / and partly cultural.
> 그러한 개인적 특성에 대한 우리의 태도는 / 부분적으로 개인적이고, 부분적으로 사회적이기도 하다 / 그리고 부분적으로 문화적이다
>
> Some people also feel / that gender plays a role, / with some qualities being more positively valued / by women than by men / and vice versa.
> 어떤 사람들은 또한 생각한다 / 성별이 역할을 한다고 / 일부 특성이 더 긍정적으로 평가되기 때문에 / 남성보다 여성에게서 / 그리고 그 반대도 마찬가지이다
>
> Such attitudes are not always static, / and they can change / with changing economic and social circumstances.
> 그러한 태도가 항상 고정적인 것은 아니다 / 그래서 그것들은 변할 수 있다 / 경제적 및 사회적 환경의 변화에 따라
>
> In some places, / during the 1970s, / ambition was seen to be bad, / and then, during the 1980s, / it was seen to be good.
> 어떤 곳에서는 / 1970년대에 / 야망이 나쁜 것으로 여겨졌다 / 그리고 그 후 1980년대에는 / 야망이 좋은 것으로 여겨졌다
>
> During the harsh economic times / of the 1990s, / a high value was placed / on generosity and compassion.
> 경제적으로 힘들었던 시기 동안 / 1990년대의 / 높은 가치가 두어졌다 / 관대함과 동정심에

해석 개인적 특성은 일반적으로 긍정적이거나 부정적인 함축 의미를 가지고 있다. 그러한 개인적 특성에 대한 우리의 태도는 부분적으로 개인적이고, 부분적으로 사회적이기도 하며, 부분적으로 문화적이기도 하다. 또한 어떤 사람들은 일부 특성이 남성보다 여성에게서 더 긍정적으로 평가되고 그 반대(일부 특성이 여성보다 남성에게 더 긍정적으로 평가되는 것)도 마찬가지이기 때문에 성별도 역할을 한다고 생각한다. 이러한 태도는 항상 고정적인 것이 아니어서, 경제적이고 사회적인 환경의 변화에 따라 변할 수 있다. 1970년대에 어떤 곳에서는 야망이 나쁜 것으로 여겨졌고, 그 후 1980년대에는 야망이 좋은 것으로 여겨졌다. 1990년대의 경제적으로 힘들었던 시기 동안에는, 관대함과 동정심에 높은 가치가 두어졌다.

① 개인적 특성이 형성되는 방법
② 개인적 특성에 대한 변하기 쉬운 가치 기준
③ 개인적 특성의 의미
④ 일부 개인적 특성이 긍정적인 함축 의미를 갖는 이유

해설 지문 전반에 걸쳐 개인적 특성은 일반적으로 긍정적이거나 부정적인 함축 의미를 가지고 있는데, 그러한 특성에 대한 우리의 태도가 부분적으로 다를 뿐만 아니라 항상 고정적인(static) 것이 아니라고 하며 일부 특성들이 성별과 시기에 따라 긍정적이거나 부정적으로 평가되었던 예시를 들어 설명하고 있다. 따라서 '② 개

인적 특성에 대한 변하기 쉬운 가치 기준'이 이 글의 제목이다.

어휘 quality 특성, 품질 connotation 함축(된 의미) gender 성별
and vice versa 그 반대도 마찬가지이다 static 고정적인, 정적인
ambition 야망 generosity 관대함 compassion 동정심

18 어휘 어휘&표현 proximity = closeness   난이도 ★★☆

해석 행성이 하나의 궤도를 도는 데 걸리는 시간은 태양에의 근접성과
관련이 있다.

① ~에 가까움   ② ~과의 연결
③ ~과의 차이   ④ ~으로부터의 반사

어휘 make an orbit 궤도를 돌다 proximity 근접성
attachment 연결, 애착 variance 차이, 변화 reflection 반사

👍 이것도 알면 합격!

proximity(근접성)와 유사한 의미의 표현
= nearness, adjacency, vicinity, propinquity

19 독해 전체내용 파악 (주제 파악)   난이도 ★☆☆

끊어읽기 해석

Recently, / scientists have discovered / that ancient
Egyptians mummified animals.
최근 / 과학자들은 발견했다 / 고대 이집트인들이 동물을 미라로 만들었다
는 것을

Some of the animals / found in tombs / were pets / such as
cats, dogs, and rabbits.
동물들 중 일부는 / 무덤에서 발견된 / 반려동물이었다 / 고양이, 개, 토끼
와 같은

Scientists believe / that animals were mummified / using the
same technique / as for humans.
과학자들은 믿는다 / 동물이 미라로 만들어졌다고 / 같은 기술을 사용하
여 / 인간을 위한

Apparently, / the early Egyptians had many household pets /
and were quite fond of them.
분명히 / 초기 이집트인들은 가정에서 많은 반려동물을 기르고 있었다 / 그
리고 그것들을 꽤 좋아했다

They believed / their pets would live on / into the afterlife /
to protect and comfort their masters.
그들은 믿었다 / 그들의 반려동물이 계속 살 것이라고 / 저승에서까지 / 그
것들의 주인을 보호하고 위로하기 위해

In addition, / other animals have also been discovered.
게다가 / 다른 동물들도 발견되었다

In other tombs, / mummified bulls and crocodiles were found.
다른 무덤에서는 / 미라로 만들어진 황소와 악어가 발견되었다

For the ancient Egyptians, / these animals were sacred /
and were the living spirits of gods.
고대 이집트인들에게 / 이 동물들은 신성했다 / 그리고 신의 살아있는 영
혼이었다

The Egyptians took good care of them / while they were
alive, / and when they died, / they buried them like kings.
이집트 사람들은 그것들을 잘 보살폈다 / 그것들이 살아 있는 동안 / 그리
고 그것들이 죽으면 / 그들은 그것들을 왕처럼 묻었다

해석 최근, 과학자들은 고대 이집트인들이 동물을 미라로 만들었다는
것을 발견했다. 무덤에서 발견된 동물들 중 일부는 고양이, 개, 토

끼와 같은 반려동물이었다. 과학자들은 동물이 인간을 위한 것과
같은 기술을 사용하여 미라로 만들어졌다고 믿는다. 분명히, 초기
이집트인들은 가정에서 많은 반려동물을 기르고 있었고 그것들을
꽤 좋아했다. 그들은 그들의 반려동물이 주인을 보호하고 위로하
기 위해 저승에서까지 살 것이라고 믿었다. 게다가, 다른 동물들도
발견되었다. 다른 무덤에서는, 미라로 만들어진 황소와 악어가 발
견되었다. 고대 이집트인들에게, 이 동물들은 신성했고 신의 살아
있는 영혼이었다. 이집트 사람들은 그것들이 살아 있는 동안 잘 보
살폈고, 그것들이 죽으면 왕처럼 묻었다.

① 고대 이집트의 신성한 동물 무덤
② 고대 이집트의 장례식에서의 동물 숭배
③ 인간과 동물 사이의 관계
④ 고대 이집트에서 동물을 미라로 만든 이유

해설 지문 전반에 걸쳐 고대 이집트인들이 동물을 미라로 만들었다는
사실이 발견되었다고 하며 이집트인들이 가정에서 기르는 반려동
물과 그들이 신성하게 여겼던 황소와 악어를 미라로 만든 이유를
설명하고 있으므로, '④ 고대 이집트에서 동물을 미라로 만든 이
유'가 이 글의 주제이다.

어휘 mummify 미라로 만들다 tomb 무덤 household 가정
fond of ~을 좋아하다 afterlife 저승, 사후세계 bull 황소
sacred 신성한 bury 묻다 worship 숭배

20 독해 전체내용 파악 (글의 감상)   난이도 ★☆☆

끊어읽기 해석

'I work at home / for my children's sake!'
'나는 집에서 일하는 거야 / 나의 아이들을 위해서!'

I repeat this to myself / until maybe I can believe it.
나는 이것을 나 자신에게 거듭 말한다 / 어쩌면 내가 그것이 사실이라고 믿
을 수 있을 때까지

Too often lately / I feel / like the worst parent on the planet.
요즘 들어서 너무나도 자주 / 나는 느낀다 / 지구상에서 가장 못난 부모라
고

As a freelance writer, / I make my own hours / and can work
at home / with my kids.
프리랜서 작가로서 / 나는 내가 근무 시간을 정한다 / 그래서 집에서 일할
수 있다 / 아이들을 곁에 두고

A good deal, right? // Not always.
꽤 괜찮다, 그렇지 않은가? // 항상 그런 것은 아니다.

Some days / I take four-year-old Hewson / to the park.
어떤 날엔 / 나는 네 살짜리 Hewson을 데려간다 / 공원에

The older kids are at school, / I'm staring at a deadline, /
but I'm eaten up / with guilt / because I'm not spending
time with him.
큰아이들은 학교에 있다 / 나는 마감일을 주시하고 있다 / 하지만 나는 사
로잡혀 있다 / 죄책감에 / 왜냐하면 나는 그(Hewson)와 시간을 보내고
있지 않기 때문이다

Then I think, / Hey, I'm my own boss!
그리고 나서 나는 생각한다 / '에이, 나는 독립했잖아!'

We can go to the park!
'우리는 공원에 갈 수 있어!'

I can work / while he plays / —the best of both worlds.
나는 일을 할 수 있다 / 그가 노는 동안 / 두 가지 장점을 누리는 것이다

I grab my cell phone and my laptop, / and pull into the park, /
thinking, Yes! You can have it all!
나는 내 휴대폰과 노트북을 움켜쥔다 / 그리고 공원에 도착한다 / '그래! 넌
모두 가질(해낼)수 있어!'라고 생각하면서

자질을 가지고 있다고 확신한다. 게다가, 그들은 이러한 자질들이 다른 사람들에게 과학을 가르침으로써 어느 정도 전해질 수 있다고 생각한다.

① 그러나   ② 게다가
③ 반대로   ④ 그럼에도 불구하고

해설 빈칸 앞 문장에 과학자들이 스스로 갖고 있다고 확신하는 매우 존경할 만한 인간의 자질(human qualities)에 대한 내용이 있고, 빈칸이 있는 문장에 과학자들은 다른 사람들에게 과학을 가르침으로써 이러한 자질들(these qualities)이 전해질 수 있다고 생각한다는 내용이 있으므로, 빈칸에는 추가를 나타내는 연결어인 '② Furthermore(게다가)'가 들어가야 적절하다.

어휘 convince 확신하다   possess 가지다   admirable 존경할 만한
accuracy 정확성   reasoning 추리, 추론   curiosity 호기심
tolerance 관용   humility 겸손   impart 전하다, 가르치다
to an extent 어느 정도

---

22   문법   비교 구문 & 병치·도치·강조 구문   난이도 ★★☆

해석 메모하는 것은, 불완전한 것(메모)조차도 (사람의) 기억력에 의존하는 것보다 보통 더 효율적이다.

① 대개 기억력에 의존하는 것보다 불완전한 메모를 하는 것이 더 효율적이다.
② 메모는 대개 불완전하기 때문에, 기억력에 의존하는 것이 더 효율적이다.
③ 불완전한 메모를 하는 것은 대개 기억력에 의존하는 것보다 덜 효율적이다.
④ 사람의 기억력은 대개 불완전한 메모보다 더 효율적이다.

해설 ① 비교급 | 병치 구문 제시된 문장의 '기억력에 의존하는 것보다 보통 더 효율적이다'는 비교급 표현 '형용사의 비교급 + than(~보다 더 -한)'을 사용하여 나타낼 수 있으므로 more efficient가 사용된 ①, ②, ④번이 정답의 후보이다. 제시된 문장에 메모하는 것과 기억력 사이의 인과 관계가 언급되지 않았으므로 부사절 접속사 Because(~ 때문에)가 쓰인 ②번은 정답이 될 수 없고, ④번의 경우 One's memory(사람의 기억력)가 더 효율적이라는 의미로 제시된 문장과 반대 의미로 쓰였으므로 정답이 될 수 없다. 따라서 진짜 주어인 긴 to 부정사구(to take incomplete notes)를 뒤로 보내고 가주어 It을 문장 맨 앞에 써서 It is usually more efficient to take ~ than to rely ~(대개 기억력에 의존하는 것보다 불완전한 메모를 하는 것이 더 효율적이다)라고 표현한 ①번이 정답이다.

어휘 take notes 메모하다   efficient 효율적인   rely on ~에 의존하다

👍 **이것도 알면 합격!**

'~보다 덜 -한'을 의미하는 경우 'less + 형용사/부사 + than'을 사용한다는 것을 알아두자.

ex The latest model is less heavy than the original one.
최신 모델은 기존 것보다 덜 무겁다.

The next thing I know, / I'm sitting on a park bench / with my laptop balanced on my knees / while other mothers keep an eye / on my son.
어느 틈엔가 / 나는 공원 벤치에 앉아 있다 / 무릎 위에 노트북을 반듯이 올려놓은 채 / 다른 엄마들이 지켜보고 있는 동안 / 내 아들을

해석 '나는 아이들을 위해서 집에서 일하는 거야!' 나는 어쩌면 그것이 사실이라고 내가 믿을 수 있을 때까지 이것을 나 자신에게 거듭 말한다. 나는 요즘 들어서 너무나도 자주 내가 지구상에서 가장 못난 부모라고 느낀다. 프리랜서 작가로서, 나는 내가 근무 시간을 정해서 아이들을 곁에 두고 집에서 일할 수 있다. 꽤 괜찮다, 그렇지 않은가? 항상 그런 것은 아니다. 나는 어떤 날엔 네 살짜리 Hewson을 공원에 데려간다. 큰아이들은 학교에 있고, 나는 마감일을 주시하고 있지만, 나는 그(Hewson)와 시간을 보내고(Hewson에게 집중하고) 있지 않기 때문에 죄책감에 사로잡혀 있다. 그리고 나서 나는 '에이, 나는 독립했잖아! 우리는 공원에 갈 수 있어!'라고 생각한다. 그가 노는 동안 나는 일을 할 수 있으니 두 가지 장점을 누리는 것이다. 나는 내 휴대폰과 노트북을 움켜쥐고 '그래! 넌 모두 가질(육아와 직장 모두 해낼) 수 있어!'라고 생각하며 공원에 도착했다. 어느 틈엔가, 다른 엄마들이 내 아들을 지켜보고 있는 동안 나는 무릎 위에 노트북을 반듯이 올려놓은 채 공원 벤치에 앉아 있다.

① 흥분한
② 따분한
③ 쓸쓸한
④ 죄책감을 느끼는

해설 지문 처음에 필자가 요즘 들어 자주 스스로를 못난 부모처럼 느끼고 있다는 내용이 있고 프리랜서 작가로 일하면서 아이를 공원에 데려가는 날에도 원고 마감일을 주시하고 있어 죄책감(guilt)에 사로잡혀 있다고 설명하고 있다. 이에 필자는 프리랜서로 독립해서 일하고 있기 때문에 아이와 공원에 가도 된다고 긍정적으로 생각해보지만, 결국에는 다른 엄마들이 놀고 있는 필자의 아들을 주시하는 동안 필자 자신은 노트북을 보고 있게 된다고 설명하고 있다. 따라서 '④ 죄책감을 느끼는'이 필자의 심경으로 적절하다.

어휘 for one's sake ~를 위해   stare 주시하다, 응시하다
eat up (감정이) ~를 사로잡다   guilt 죄책감
be one's own boss 독립해 있다, 누구의 지배도 안 받다
best of both worlds 두 가지 (상이한 것의) 장점, 일거양득
pull into ~에 도착하다   balance 반듯이 올려놓다
keep an eye on ~를 지켜보다

---

21   독해   추론 (빈칸 완성 - 연결어)   난이도 ★☆☆

끊어읽기 해석

The scientists are convinced / that they, as scientists, possess / a number of very admirable human qualities, / such as accuracy, observation, reasoning power, intellectual curiosity, tolerance and even humility.
과학자들은 확신한다 / 그들이 과학자로서 가지고 있다고 / 매우 존경할 만한 인간의 많은 자질을 / 정확성, 관찰력, 추리력, 지적 호기심, 관용과 심지어는 겸손과 같은

Furthermore, / they suppose / that these qualities can be imparted / to other people, / to a certain extent, / by teaching them science.
게다가 / 그들은 생각한다 / 이러한 자질들이 전해질 수 있다고 / 다른 사람들에게 / 어느 정도 / 그들에게 과학을 가르침으로써

해석 과학자들은 그들이 과학자로서 정확성, 관찰력, 추리력, 지적 호기심, 관용과 심지어는 겸손과 같은 매우 존경할 만한 인간의 많은

---

23   문법   전치사 & 시제 & 병치·도치·강조 구문   난이도 ★★☆

해석 일부 지역에서는, 학교와 미디어에서의 영어 사용이 것이 소수 언어 감소의 원인이 되었다. 1991년 스코틀랜드에서는, 그 해의 인구 조사에 따르면 약 6만 9천 명의 게일어 사용자가 있었다. 그 언어는 일부 학교에서 여전히 사용되고 있지만 사용자들은 제한된

법적 권리를 가지고 있다. 그것(게일어)은 법정에서 사용되지 않으며, 정부 기관에서 아무런 역할도 하지 않는다.

해설 (A) 기타 전치사 동사 contribute는 전치사 to와 함께 쓰여 '~의 원인이 되다'라는 의미를 나타내므로 to를 써야 한다.

(B) 시제 일치 특정 과거 시점을 나타내는 표현(in 1991)이 왔으므로 이미 끝난 과거의 일을 나타내는 과거 시제 were를 써야 한다.

(C) 병치 구문 접속사(and)로 연결된 병치 구문에서는 같은 구조끼리 연결되어야 하는데, and 앞에 현재 시제 is not used가 왔으므로 and 뒤에도 현재 시제 plays를 써야 한다.

따라서 ② (A) to – (B) were – (C) plays가 정답이다.

어휘 contribute to ~의 원인이 되다 decline 감소
Gaelic 게일어(스코틀랜드 지방의 켈트어) census 인구 조사

👍 이것도 알면 **합격!**

to 부정사구 병치 구문에서 두 번째 나온 to는 생략될 수 있다는 것을 알아두자.

(ex) The audience started to stand up and (to) sing along with the band.
청중은 일어서서 밴드와 함께 노래를 부르기 시작했다.

---

24 독해 전체내용 파악 (글의 감상) 난이도 ★★☆

끊어읽기 해석

People seem to forget / that nature has been "cloning" / since the beginning of time.
사람들은 잊어버리는 것 같다 / 자연이 '복제를 해왔다'는 것을 / 태초부터

Identical twins are exactly the same cell / —split into two.
일란성 쌍둥이는 정확히 같은 세포이다 / 둘로 분열된

Despite this, / they are different human beings / with different "souls".
이것에도 불구하고 / 그들은 서로 다른 인간이다 / 별개의 '영혼'을 가진

Similarly, / through technology / we may create a being / with identical attributes / but cannot clone a soul.
마찬가지로 / 기술을 통해 / 우리는 존재를 만들 수도 있다 / 동일한 속성을 가진 / 하지만 영혼을 복제할 수는 없다

If, through cloning, / we can eliminate many genetic disorders, / then surely this should be welcomed / as a wonderful opportunity.
만약 복제를 통해 / 우리가 많은 유전적 장애를 제거할 수 있다면 / 이것은 분명 환영받을 것이다 / 멋진 기회로

Though perfected, / there may still be risks, / as there are / in choosing to vaccinate your child.
비록 완벽하게 만들어졌다고 하더라도 / 여전히 위험이 있을 수 있다 / (위험이) 있는 것처럼 / 당신의 자녀에게 백신 주사를 맞기로 결정하는 것에

But the potential benefits / may far outweigh the risks.
하지만 잠재적 혜택은 / 위험보다 훨씬 클 수도 있다

How can we allow / ourselves and our children / to suffer / when there could be a solution?
어째서 우리는 내버려 두는 것인가 / 우리 자신과 아이들을 / 고통받도록 / 해결책이 있을 수도 있는데

해석 사람들은 자연이 태초부터 '복제를 해왔다'는 것을 잊어버리는 것 같다. 일란성 쌍둥이는 둘로 분열된 정확히 같은 세포이다. 이것에도 불구하고, 그들은 별개의 '영혼'을 가진 서로 다른 인간이다. 마찬가지로, 기술을 통해 우리는 동일한 속성을 가진 존재를 만들 수도 있지만 영혼을 복제할 수는 없다. 만약 복제를 통해 우리가 많

은 유전적 장애를 제거할 수 있다면, 이것(복제)은 분명 멋진 기회로 환영받을 것이다. 비록 완벽하게 만들어졌다고 하더라도, 당신의 자녀에게 백신 주사를 맞기로 결정하는 것이 그러하듯 (복제에는) 여전히 위험이 있을 수 있다. 하지만 잠재적 혜택이 위험보다 훨씬 클 수도 있다. 해결책이 있을 수도 있는데 우리는 어째서 우리 자신과 아이들이 고통받도록 내버려 두는 것인가?

① 중립적인   ② 비판적인
③ 지지하는   ④ 걱정하는

해설 지문 전반에 걸쳐 자연이 태초부터 복제를 해왔다고 하며 복제를 통해 유전적 장애를 제거하는 것은 환영받을 일일 뿐만 아니라 복제가 가진 잠재적 혜택이 위험보다 훨씬 더 클 수 있다고 설명하고 있다. 따라서 '③ 지지하는'이 필자의 태도로 적절하다.

어휘 clone 복제하다; 복제 identical 일란성의, 동일한
split 분열시키다, 쪼개다 attribute 속성 genetic 유전의
disorder 장애 perfect 완벽하게 하다, 끝마치다
vaccinate 백신 주사를 맞히다 outweigh ~보다 더 크다
neutral 중립적인 supportive 지지하는

---

25 독해 추론 (빈칸 완성 - 구) 난이도 ★☆☆

끊어읽기 해석

The second great force / behind immigration / has been political oppression.
두 번째로 큰 세력은 / 이민의 배후에 있는 / 정치적 억압이었다

America has always been a refuge / from tyranny.
미국은 항상 피난처였다 / 폭정으로부터의

As a nation conceived / in liberty, / it has held out to the world / the promise of respect for human rights.
착안한 국가로서 / 자유에 / 그것은 전 세계에 드러냈다 / 인권에 대한 존중의 약속을

Every time a revolution has failed / in Europe, / every time a nation has succumbed / to tyranny, / men and women / who love freedom / have assembled their families and their belongings / and set sail across the sea.
혁명이 실패할 때마다 / 유럽에서 / 한 국가가 굴복할 때마다 / 폭정에 / 남녀는 / 자유를 사랑하는 / 그들의 가족과 재산을 모았다 / 그리고 바다를 건너 항해했다

해석 이민의 배후에 있는 두 번째로 큰 세력은 정치적 억압이었다. 미국은 항상 폭정으로부터의 피난처였다. 자유에 착안한 국가로서, 그것은 인권을 존중하겠다는 약속을 전 세계에 드러냈다. 유럽에서 혁명이 실패하거나 한 국가가 폭정에 굴복할 때마다, 자유를 사랑하는 남녀는 그들의 가족과 재산을 모아 바다를 건너 항해했다.

① 정치적 억압
② 경제적 요인
③ 가난으로부터의 탈출
④ 예배의 자유에 대한 추구

해설 지문 전반에 걸쳐 미국이 폭정으로부터의 피난처이자 자유에 착안한 국가였다고 하며 유럽에서 혁명이 실패하거나 한 국가가 폭정에 굴복할 때마다 사람들이 자유를 찾아 바다를 건너 항해했다고 설명하고 있으므로, 빈칸에는 이민의 배후에 있는 두 번째로 큰 세력이 '① 정치적 억압'이었다는 내용이 들어가야 적절하다.

어휘 immigration 이민 refuge 피난처 tyranny 폭정
conceive 착안하다, 생각하다 hold out (가능성·희망을) 드러내다
succumb to ~에 굴복하다 assemble 모으다, 조립하다
belongings 재산 oppression 억압, 압박 flight 탈출, 도피
worship 예배; 숭배하다

MEMO

해커스법원직
15개년
기출문제집
영어

초판 1쇄 발행 2022년 10월 14일

지은이	해커스 공무원시험연구소
펴낸곳	해커스패스
펴낸이	해커스공무원 출판팀

주소	서울특별시 강남구 강남대로 428 해커스공무원
고객센터	1588-4055
교재 관련 문의	gosi@hackerspass.com
	해커스공무원 사이트(gosi.Hackers.com) 교재 Q&A 게시판
	카카오톡 플러스 친구 [해커스공무원강남역], [해커스공무원노량진]
학원 강의 및 동영상강의	gosi.Hackers.com

ISBN	979-11-6880-666-5 (13740)
Serial Number	01-01-01

최단기 합격 공무원학원 1위,
해커스공무원 gosi.Hackers.com

ⓘ 해커스공무원

· 해커스공무원 학원 및 인강(교재 내 인강 할인쿠폰 수록)
· 어휘 잡는 **핵심 기출 단어암기장** 및 다회독에 최적화된 **회독용 답안지**
· 내 점수와 석차를 확인하는 **모바일 자동 채점 및 성적 분석 서비스**
· '회독'의 방법과 공부 습관을 제시하는 **해커스 회독증강 콘텐츠**(교재 내 할인쿠폰 수록)
· 해커스 스타강사의 **공무원 영어 무료 동영상강의**

헤럴드미디어 2018 대학생 선호 브랜드 대상 '대학생이 선정한 최단기 합격 공무원학원' 부문 1위